Seventh Edition

FINANCIAL AND MANAGEMENT ACCOUNTING

Pauline Weetman

Professor of Accounting
University of Edinburgh

PEARSON

Harlow, England • London • New York • Boston • San Francisco • Toronto • Sydney • Auckland • Singapore • Hong Kong
Tokyo • Seoul • Taipei • New Delhi • Cape Town • São Paulo • Mexico City • Madrid • Amsterdam • Munich • Paris • Milan

PEARSON EDUCATION LIMITED
Edinburgh Gate
Harlow CM20 2JE
United Kingdom
Tel: +44 (0)1279 623623
Fax: +44 (0)1279 431059
Web: www.pearson.com/uk

First published under the Financial Times Pitman Publishing imprint 1996 (print)
Second edition published 1999 (print)
Third edition 2003 (print)
Fourth edition 2006 (print)
Fifth edition 2011 (print)
Sixth edition 2013 (print and electronic)
Seventh edition 2016 (print and electronic)

The Financial Times. With a worldwide network of highly respected journalists, *The Financial Times* provides global business news, insightful opinion and expert analysis of business, finance and politics. With over 500 journalists reporting from 50 countries worldwide, our in-depth coverage of international news is objectively reported and analysed from an independent, global perspective. To find out more, visit www.ft.com/pearsonoffer.

ISBN: 978-1-292-08659-0 (print)
       978-1-292-08666-8 (PDF)
       978-1-292-08660-6 (eText)

British Library Cataloguing-in-Publication Data
A catalogue record for the print edition is available from the British Library

Library of Congress Cataloging-in-Publication Data
A catalog record for the print edition is available from the Library of Congress

10 9 8 7 6 5 4 3 2
19 18 17 16 15

Front cover image © Getty Images
Print edition typeset in 9.5/12pt Palatino by 71
Printed and bound by L.E.G.O S.p.A., Italy

NOTE THAT ANY PAGE CROSS REFERENCES REFER TO THE PRINT EDITION

Contents in brief

Contents

FINANCIAL ACCOUNTING

Part 1 A conceptual framework: setting the scene

Part 2 Reporting the transactions of a business

Chapter 5 Accounting information for service businesses

Chapter 6 Accounting information for trading businesses

Part 3 Recognition in financial statements

Chapter 11   Provisions and non-current (long-term) liabilities

Chapter 12   Ownership interest

Part 4 Analysis and issues in reporting

MANAGEMENT ACCOUNTING

Part 5   Setting the scene and defining the basic tools of management accounting

Chapter 23 Performance evaluation and feedback reporting

Part 9 Capital investment appraisal and business strategy

Chapter 24 Capital investment appraisal

Chapter 25   Business strategy and management accounting   713

Preface to the seventh edition

Introduction

This book uses the international *Conceptual Framework* and International Financial Reporting Standards (IFRS) as its primary focus. It enables students in their early stages of study to understand and analyse the published annual reports and financial statements of our largest businesses and public sector institutions. IFRS are now applied in many aspects of government, local authority and other public sector accounting. Where relevant it also refers to the approach used in small and medium-sized businesses where the traditions of UK GAAP continue to be applied.

The book is written for the first level of undergraduate degree study in accounting and business studies, or equivalent introductory accounting courses for any professional training where an understanding of accounting is a basic requirement. While UK listed companies apply IFRS in their published financial statements, the remainder of the annual report is governed by UK-based regulations and codes. All UK companies operate under the Companies Act 2006. Their annual reports are influenced by the regulatory process applied to listed companies in the UK. This seventh edition is thoroughly revised to reflect these regulatory changes, particularly the restructuring of the Financial Reporting Council to take responsibility for the standards previously issued by the UK Accounting Standards Board, and the introduction of the strategic report.

All 'Real World' case studies at the start of each chapter have been updated to reflect current conditions, especially the changes that have resulted from the banking and credit crisis of 2008–09. The underlying pedagogy of previous editions has been retained in response to encouraging comments from reviewers and from users of the book.

As institutions come under increasing scrutiny for the quality of the teaching and learning experience offered, a textbook must do more than present the knowledge and skills of the chosen subject. It must make explicit to the students what targets are to be achieved and it must help them to assess realistically their own achievements of those targets. It must help the class lecturer prepare, deliver, explain and assess the knowledge and skills expected for the relevant level of study. This is achieved by stating learning outcomes at the start of each chapter and by ensuring that the chapter headings and the end-of-chapter questions address the stated outcomes.

The management accounting chapters continue the approach of previous editions in taking some of the newer costing techniques into mainstream discussion, reflecting their increasing acceptance in management accounting practice. Business strategy and competitive position are recurring themes.

An accompanying website at **www.pearsoned.co.uk/weetman** provides the lecturer with a complete resource pack for each chapter. Student handouts containing a skeleton outline of each chapter, leaving slots for students to complete; overhead-projector masters that match the lecture handouts; additional multiple-choice questions and further graded questions in application of knowledge and in problem solving; all are features for this seventh edition.

End-of-chapter questions are graded according to the skills being assessed. There are tests of retained knowledge, tests of application of knowledge in straightforward situations and tests of problem solving and evaluation using the acquired knowledge in less familiar situations.

Overall the aim of the seventh edition is to provide an introduction to financial accounting and management accounting which engages the interest of students and encourages a desire for further study. It also contributes to developing the generic skills of application, problem solving, evaluation and communication, all emphasised by employers.

Subject coverage

Financial reporting is an essential component in the process of communication between a business and its stakeholders. The importance of communication increases as organisations become larger and more complex. Reporting financial information to external stakeholders not involved in the day-to-day management of the business requires a carefully balanced process of extracting the key features while preserving the essential core of information. The participants in the communication process cover a wide range of expertise and educational background, so far as accounting is concerned. The range begins with those who prepare financial statements, who may have a special training in accounting techniques, but it ends with those who may be professional investors, private investors, investment advisers, bankers, employee representatives, customers, suppliers and journalists.

One very significant group of stakeholders in any business is the internal management of the organisation. Managers have access to a wealth of detailed financial information and a responsibility for the careful management of the assets and operations of the organisation. The way in which the managers of an organisation use financial information is very much contingent on the purpose for which the information is intended. Management accounting is a specialist area of study within accounting more generally. Ideally, management accounting and financial accounting would coalesce if the external users could be given access to all internal information, but that might damage the competitive position of the business and would probably swamp the external users in detail.

First-level degree courses in accounting are increasingly addressed to this broad base of potential interest and this book seeks to provide such a broad base of understanding while also supplying a sound technical base for those intending to pursue specialised study of the subject further. In particular it makes use of the *Conceptual Framework* which is used by the International Accounting Standards Board in developing and reviewing accounting standards. That *Conceptual Framework* is intended to help preparers, users and auditors of financial statements to understand better the general nature and function of information reported in financial statements. Fair value accounting principles are introduced.

Aim of the book

The seventh edition has been updated throughout. It aims to provide a full understanding of the key aspects of the annual report, concentrating in particular on companies in the private sector but presenting principles of wider application which are relevant also to organisations operating in the public sector.

In the management accounting section, the book aims to establish a firm understanding of the basic techniques, while recognising that more recent developments in management accounting are becoming widespread. A contingency approach is adopted which emphasises that the selection of management accounting techniques is conditional on management's purpose. To meet this purpose, the management accountant performs the roles of directing attention, keeping the score and solving problems. Strategic management accounting is emphasised from the outset so that students are aware that management accounting must take an outward-looking approach. These themes are reiterated throughout, concluding with an explanation of the role of management accounting in business strategy, particularly e-business in the new economy. A student who has completed this first-level study of management accounting will be aware of many of the day-to-day practices of management accounting in business and the relevance of those practices. It also provides a self-contained, broad introduction to management accounting for business students who do not need to develop specialist knowledge.

In particular

An international perspective reflects the convergence in accounting standards across the European Union for listed companies. *Features specific to the UK* are retained where these continue to be relevant to other enterprises.

Concepts of financial accounting are identified by applying the principles enunciated by the International Accounting Standards Board in its *Conceptual Framework*. The *Conceptual Framework* emphasises the desirability of meeting the needs of users of financial statements and it takes a balance sheet-oriented approach. That approach is applied consistently throughout the book, with some indication of the problems which may arise when it is clear that the established emphasis on the matching of revenues and costs may give a more rational explanation of existing practice.

User needs are explained in every chapter and illustrated by including first-person commentary from a professional fund manager, holding a conversation with an audit manager. The conversations are based on the author's research in the area of communication through the annual report.

The *accounting equation* is used throughout the financial accounting section for analysis and processing of transactions. It is possible for students who do not seek a technical specialism to complete the text without any reference to debit and credit bookkeeping. It is, however, recognised that particular groups of students may wish to understand the basic aspects of debit and credit bookkeeping and for this purpose the end-of-chapter supplements revisit, on a debit and credit recording basis, material already explored in the chapter. Debit and credit aspects of management accounting are not covered since these are regarded as best reserved for later specialist courses if the student so chooses.

Practical illustration is achieved by drawing on the financial information of a fictitious major listed company, taking an overview in early chapters and then developing the detailed disclosures as more specific matters are explored.

Interpretation of financial statements is a feature of all financial reporting chapters, formally brought together in Chapters 13 and 14. The importance of the wider range of corporate communication is reinforced in Chapter 14. This chapter also includes a discussion of some *current developments* that are under debate in the context of international convergence.

A *running case study example* of the fictitious company Safe and Sure plc provides illustration and interpretation throughout the chapters. Safe and Sure plc is in the service sector. The Instructor's Manual contains a parallel example, Craigielaw plc, in the manufacturing sector. In the Instructor's Manual there are questions on Craigielaw to accompany most of the chapters.

Self-evaluation is encouraged by setting learning outcomes at the start of each chapter and reviewing these in the chapter summaries. Activity questions are placed at various stages throughout each chapter. Self-testing questions at the end of the chapter may be answered by referring again to the text. Further end-of-chapter questions provide a range of practical applications. Group activities are suggested at the end of each chapter with the particular aim of encouraging participation and interaction. Answers are available to all computational questions, either at the end of the book or in the Instructor's Manual.

A *sense of achievement* is engendered in the reader of the financial accounting section by providing a general understanding of the entire annual report by the end of Chapter 7. Thereafter specific aspects of the annual report are explored in Chapters 8–12. Lecturers who wish to truncate a first-level course or leave specific aspects to a later level will find Chapters 8–12 may be used on a selective basis.

A *spreadsheet* approach to financial accounting transactions is used in the body of the relevant chapters to show processing of transactions using the accounting equation. The author is firmly convinced, after years of trying every conceivable approach, that the spreadsheet encourages students to apply the accounting equation analytically, rather than trying to memorise T-account entries. Furthermore students now use spreadsheets as a tool of analysis on a regular basis and will have little difficulty in applying suitable software in preparing spreadsheets. In the bookkeeping supplementary sections, the three-column ledger account has been adopted in the knowledge that school teaching is moving increasingly to adopt this approach which cuts out much of the bewilderment of balancing T-accounts. Computerised accounting systems also favour the three-column presentation with continuous updating of the balance.

Flexible course design

There was once a time when the academic year comprised three terms and we all knew the length of a typical course unit over those three terms. Now there are semesters, trimesters, modules and half-modules so that planning a course of study becomes an exercise in critical path analysis. This text is written for one academic year comprising two semesters of 12 weeks each but may need selective guidance to students for a module of lesser duration.

In financial accounting, Chapters 1–4 provide an essential conceptual framework which sets the scene. For a general appreciation course, Chapters 5 and 6 are practical so that one or both could be omitted, leading directly to Chapter 7 as a guide to published accounts. Chapters 8–12 are structured so that the explanation of principles is contained early in each chapter, but the practical implementation is later in each chapter. For a general appreciation course, it would be particularly important to refer to the section of each chapter which analyses users' needs for information and discusses information provided in the financial statements. However, the practical sections of these chapters could be omitted or used on a selective basis rather than attempting full coverage. Chapters 13 and 14 are important to all readers for a sense of interpretation and awareness of the range of material within corporate reports. Chapter 15 takes the reader through a cash flow statement item-by-item with the emphasis on understanding and interpretation.

In teaching and learning management accounting various combinations are possible, depending on course design and aims. Chapters 16, 17 and 18 provide an essential set of basic tools of analysis but thereafter some flexibility is feasible. For applications in job costing, Chapter 19 provides further material. For concentrating on decision making and awareness of business strategy, Chapters 20, 24 and 25 are recommended. For concentrating on planning and control, Chapters 21, 22 and 23 give students experience of the variety of techniques in use.

Approaches to teaching and learning

Learning outcomes

Targets for student achievement in relation to knowledge and understanding of the subject are specified in learning outcomes at the head of each chapter. The achievements represented by these learning outcomes are confirmed against graded questions at the end of each chapter. The achievement of some learning outcomes may be confirmed by Activities set out at the appropriate stage within the chapter.

Skills outcomes

The end-of-chapter questions test not only subject-specific knowledge and technical skills but also the broader general skills that are transferable to subsequent employment or further training.

Graded questions

End-of-chapter questions are graded and each is matched to one or more learning outcomes. Where a solution is provided to a question this is shown by an *[S]* after the question number.

A series questions: test your understanding

The A series questions confirm the application of technical skills. These are skills specific to the subject of accounting which add to the specialist expertise of the student. More generally they show the student's capacity to acquire and apply a technical skill of this type.

The answers to these questions can be found in relevant sections of the chapter, as indicated at the end of each question.

B series questions: application

The B series questions apply the knowledge gained from reading and practising the material of the chapter. They resemble closely in style and content the technical material of the chapter. Confidence is gained in applying knowledge in a situation that is very similar to that illustrated. Answers are given in Appendix II or in the Instructor's Manual. These questions test skills of problem solving and evaluation that are relevant to many subjects and many activities in life, especially in subsequent employment. Some initiative is required in deciding how to apply relevant knowledge and in solving problems.

C series questions: problem solving and evaluation

The C series questions apply the knowledge gained from reading the chapter, but in a varied style of question. Problem-solving skills are required in selecting relevant data or in using knowledge to work out what further effort is needed to solve the problem. Evaluation means giving an opinion or explanation of the results of the problem-solving exercise. Some answers are given in Appendix II but others are in the Instructor's Manual so that they can be used in tutorial preparation or class work.

Group and individual cases

Cases apply knowledge gained from the chapter but they also test communication skills. Communication may involve writing or speaking, or both. It may require, for example, explanation of a technical matter to a non-technical person, or discussion with other students to explore a controversial issue, or presentation of a report to a business audience.

S series questions in supplementary sections

The S series questions test knowledge of the accounting records system (bookkeeping entries) to confirm understanding by those who have chosen to study the supplementary bookkeeping sections.

Instructor's Manual

A website is available at **www.pearsoned.co.uk/weetman** by password access to lecturers adopting this book. The Instructor's Manual contains additional problem questions for each chapter, with full solutions to these additional questions as well as any solutions not provided in the book. The Instructor's Manual also includes basic tutorial instructions and overhead-projector masters to support each chapter.

Target readership

This book is targeted at a broad-ranging business studies type of first-level degree course. It is intended to support the equivalent of one semester of 12 teaching weeks. There is sufficient basic bookkeeping (ledger accounts) in the end-of-chapter supplements to make the book suitable for those intending to pursue a specialised study of accounting beyond the first level but the bookkeeping material is optional for those who do not have such special intentions. The book has been written with undergraduate students particularly in mind, but may also be suitable for professional and postgraduate business courses where financial reporting is taught at an introductory level.

Acknowledgements

I am grateful to academic colleagues and to reviewers of the text for helpful comments and suggestions. I am also grateful to undergraduate students of five universities who have taken my courses and thereby helped in developing an approach to teaching and learning the subject. Professor Graham Peirson and Mr Alan Ramsay of Monash University provided a first draft of their text based on the conceptual framework in Australia which gave valuable assistance in designing the structure of this book, which was also guided from the publishing side by Pat Bond and Ron Harper. Professor Ken Shackleton of the University of Glasgow helped plan the structure of the management accounting chapters. The Institute of Chartered Accountants of Scotland gave permission for use of some of the end-of-chapter questions.

Subsequently I have received valuable support in successive editions from the editorial staff at Pearson Education. For this latest edition I am grateful to colleagues and students who have used the book in their teaching and learning. I have also been helped by constructive comments from reviewers and by guidance from Rebecca Pedley, Acquisitions Editor, and Natasha Whelan, Senior Project Editor.

Publisher's acknowledgements

We are grateful to the following for permission to reproduce copyright material:

Figures

Figure 4.1 from https://www.frc.org.uk/About-the-FRC/FRC-structure.aspx, © Financial Reporting Council (FRC). All rights reserved. For further information, please visit www.frc .org.uk or call +44 (0)20 7492 2300. Figure on page 354 from *Annual Report and Accounts 2014* (National Express plc 2014) p. 15, http://nexgroup.blob.core.windows.net/media/2293/ ar2014-full.pdf, Reproduced with permission from National Express Group.

Tables

Table on page 27 from *Annual Report and Accounts 2013/14* (BBC 2014) p. 125, http:// downloads.bbc.co.uk/annualreport/pdf/2013-14/bbc_annualreport_201314.pdf; Table on page 354 from *Annual Report and Financial Statements 2014* (Stagecoach Group plc 2014) p. 14, http://www.stagecoach.com/investors/financial-analysis/reports/2014.aspx; Table on page 355 from *Annual Report and Accounts* January 2014 (Next plc 2014) p. 19, http://www.nextplc .co.uk/~/media/Files/N/Next-PLC/pdfs/reports-and-results/2014/Next%20AR2014%20web .pdf; Table on page 476 from HGCA, http://www.hgca.com/markets/survey-results.aspx, 2014

Text

Case Study on pages 4–5 from *Annual Report and Accounts 2013/14* (Oxfam 2014) pp. front cover, 6, 8, 38, reproduced with the permission of Oxfam GB, Oxfam House, John Smith Drive, Cowley, Oxford OX4 2JY, UK www.oxfam.org.uk. Oxfam GB does not necessarily endorse any text or activities that accompany the materials.; Extract on page 28 from *Annual Report and Accounts 2013/14* (BBC 2014) p. 2, http://downloads.bbc.co.uk/annualreport/pdf/2013-14/ bbc_annualreport_201314.pdf; Case Study on page 54 from *Annual Report and Form 20-F, 2014* (AstraZeneca 2014) pp. 11, 74, http://www.astrazeneca.com/Investors/Annual-reports; Case Study extract on page 77 from *The FRC and its regulatory approach, January* (2014) p. 1, https:// www.frc.org.uk/Our-Work/Publications/FRC-Board/The-FRC-and-its-Regulatory-Approach. pdf; Case Study extract on page 78 from *Corporate Reporting Review - Annual Reports 2013*, October 2013 (Financial Reporting Council 2014) p. 5, https://frc.org.uk/Our-Work/Publications/ Corporate-Reporting-Review/Coporate-Reporting-Review-Annual-Report-2013.pdf; Case Study extract on pages 77–8 from *Amendments to the Financial Reporting Standard for Small Enterprises (effective January 2015), FRC, April 2014, revision to section 2.40.* , https://www.frc.org.uk/ Our-Work/Publications/Accounting-and-Reporting-Policy/Amendments-to-the-FRSSE-Micro-entities.pdf, all Case Study extracts on pages 77–8 © Financial Reporting Council (FRC). All rights reserved. For further information, please visit www.frc.org.uk or call +44 (0)20 7492 2300; Case Study on pages 112–13 from *Annual Report and Accounts* January 2014 (Next plc) pp. 20 and 22, http://www.nextplc.co.uk/~/media/Files/N/Next-PLC/pdfs/reports-and-results/2014/ Next%20AR2014%20web.pdf; Case Study on page 142 from *Annual Report and Accounts 2014* (National Express plc 2014) p. 36, http://nexgroup.blob.core.windows.net/media/2293/ ar2014-full.pdf, Reproduced with permission from National Express Group; Case Study on pages 142–3 from *Annual Report and Financial Statements* (Stagecoach 2014) p. 15, http://www .stagecoach.com/investors/financial-analysis/reports/2014.aspx; Case Study on page 170–1 from *Annual Report 2013/14,* (Morrisons plc 2014) pp. 5–6, 44 http://www.morrisons-corporate .com/Documents/Corporate2014/Morrisons_AnnualReport13-14_Complete.pdf; Comment from Financial Times on page 171 from Strategy not shame should determine scaled of BarCap,

Financial Times, 13/03/2014 (Smith, Al and Guthrie, J.); Case Study on pages 211–12 from *Annual Report and Financial Statements 2014–15* (Royal Mail plc 2015) pp. 2, 28, 135, 121–2, http://www.royalmailgroup.com/sites/default/files/Annual%20Report%20and%20Accounts%202014–15.pdf; Case Study on pages 250–51 from *Annual Report and Accounts 2014* (Associated British Foods plc. 2014) pp. ii, 2, 38, 94, 113, http://www.abf.co.uk/documents/pdfs/2014/2014_abf_annual_report_and_accounts.pdf; Case Study on pages 281–2 from *Annual Report and Accounts 2014* (W H Smith plc 2014) pp. 1, 18, 20, 74, http://www.whsmithplc.co.uk/investors/company_reports/; Case Study on pages 301–2 from *Annual Report 2013* (Rio Tinto 2013) pp 1, 129–30, 154, http://www.riotinto.com/annualreport2013/_pdfs/rio-tinto-2013-annual-report.pdf; Case Study on pages 323–4 from Mothercare launches £100m rights issue, *Financial Times*, 23/09/2014 (Barrett, C.), © The Financial Times Limited. All Rights Reserved; Extract on page 355 from *Annual Report and Financial Statements 2013/14* (Wm Morrisons Supermarkets plc 2014) p. 5, http://www.morrisons-corporate.com/Documents/Corporate2014/Morrisons_AnnualReport13-14_Complete.pdf; Case Study on pages 379–80 from *Financial Times*, http://www.ft.com/cms/s/0/8588d422-b6ca-11e1-8c96-00144feabdc0.html#ixzz21tpdndrN, © The Financial Times Limited. All Rights Reserved; Case Study on pages 385–6 from *Annual Report and Accounts 2014* (Associated British Foods 2014) p. 9, http://www.abf.co.uk/documents/pdfs/2014/2014_abf_annual_report_and_accounts.pdf; Case Study on page 421 from ITV: no news, good news?, *Financial Times*, 08/10/2014 (Lex Team), http://www.ft.com/cms/s/3/64144f84-4e2a-11e4-bfda-00144feab7de.html#axzz3G6ZBpeuK, © The Financial Times Limited. All Rights Reserved; Case Study on pages 450–1 from Chartered Institute of Management Accountants (CIMA), http://www.cimaglobal.com/About-us/What-is-management-accounting/ CIMA Global website, October 2014; Case Study on pages 475–6 from HGCA, http://www.hgca.com/press/2014/may/09/grain-haulage-survey.aspx; Case Study on pages 534–5 from http://www.cakeboss.com/Cake-Stuff/Articles/How-Much-Should-I-Charge; Case Study on page 558 from Gemfields eyes Colombian emerald venture, *Financial Times*, 22/09/2014 (Wilson, J.), http://www.ft.com/cms/s/0/6977e036-4249-11e4-a9f4-00144feabdc0.html#ixzz3GCVPUa8X, © The Financial Times Limited. All Rights Reserved; Case Study on pages 588–9 from *Budget Booklet 2014/15* (Lancashire Fire and Rescue Service 2015) http://www.lancsfirerescue.org.uk/financial-summary/; Case Study on p. 626 'Summary of Industry Standards', information provided by RestaurantOwner.com. For more information, go to www.RestaurantOwner.com; Case Study on pages 656–8 from *Annual Report and Accounts 2013–14* (Natural England 2014) pp. 4, 67–70, 80, https://www.gov.uk/government/uploads/system/uploads/attachment_data/file/326495/ne-annual-report-accounts-2013-2014-print-ready.pdf, Contains public sector information licensed under the Open Government Licence (OGL) v3.0.http://www.nationalarchives.gov.uk/doc/open-government-licence.; Case Study on page 683 from Drax biomass conversion a first for Osborne infrastructure scheme, *Financial Times*, 24/04/2013 (Pickard, J.), http://www.ft.com/cms/s/0/26526d1c-acf4-11e2-b27f-00144feabdc0.html?siteedition=uk#axzz3G82tUShy, © The Financial Times Limited. All Rights Reserved; Case Study on pages 682–3 from *Annual Report 2013* (Drax Group plc 2013) p. 42, http://www.drax.com/media/32649/drax_ar13_final.pdf; Case Study on pages 713–14 from *The Evolution of Mobility: Bombardier Transportation Presents Solutions for the Future of Public Transportation at InnoTrans 2014* (Bombardier) Berlin Transportation, Press Release, http://uk.bombardier.com/en/media/newsList/details.bombardier-transportation20140917theevolutionofmobilitybombardie.bombardiercom.html?

Picture Credits

123RF.com: 558, 588; Alamy Images: Arterra Picture Library 656, lee avison 211, Kevin Britland 170, Robert Convery 250, 281, Jeff Gilbert 28, R Heyes Design 421, Carolyn Jenkins 385, Justin Kase z11z 142, Gary Moseley 354, Paul Robbins 112, studiomode 498, Urbanimages 323; picture courtesy of Bombardier Transportation UK Ltd: 713; Corbis: 475; Imagestate Media: John Foxx Collection 301; Oxfam: Pablo Tosco 4; Shutterstock.com: Konstantin Chagin 450, kentoh 534, krsmanovic 626t, Nomad_Soul 54, Pressmaster 77, TTstudio 682

All other images © Pearson Education

FINANCIAL ACCOUNTING

Part 1

A conceptual framework: setting the scene

Chapter 1

Who needs accounting?

Oxfam: meeting users' needs
Extracts from Annual Report and Accounts

Purpose and charitable objects

Oxfam's purpose is to help create lasting solutions to the injustice of poverty.

As stated in its Memorandum of Association, the objects for which Oxfam is established for the public benefit are:

Oxfam/Pablo Tosco

- to prevent and relieve poverty and to protect vulnerable people, including through humanitarian intervention;

- to advance sustainable development;

- to promote human rights, equality and diversity, in particular where to do so contributes to the prevention and relief of poverty; in all cases working anywhere in the world.

Highlights

11 million people reached directly in 52 countries, and millions more benefiting from changes in governments' policy and practice influenced by Oxfam

6.1 million people supported in 24 humanitarian emergencies

600,000 people globally who took online campaign actions

1,337 grants to 81 partner organisations

400,000 people in the UK made a regular donation

Being accountable for the impact of our work

Oxfam is committed to ensuring that, in all that we do, we are accountable to those with whom we work, from our programme partners, communities and donors to other stakeholder groups such as our staff, volunteers, or those who we campaign through and with. We use several tools to monitor, evaluate, assess and learn from our stakeholders. We:

- report data on the numbers of people and communities reached by our programmes

- complete review exercises to understand – and speak about – our outcome achievements as well as our challenges, and how we deal with them
- undertake evaluations to assess our overall strategies, test the core assumptions about how Oxfam contributes to social change, and assess our effectiveness in different contexts
- consult with key stakeholders to gather their insights and assessments about our overall efforts.

Our success in achieving this commitment to accountability is measured annually through our membership of, and compliance with, the International NGO Accountability Charter and International Aid Transparency Initiative. More detail on our accountability objectives and achievements are published on our website.

Accounting conventions

The financial statements are prepared on a going concern basis, under the historical cost convention, as modified by the inclusion of investments at market value, and on an accruals basis except where specified separately below. The Financial Statements are prepared in compliance with the Companies Act 2006, the Charities Act 2011, Accounting and Reporting by Charities: Statement of Recommended Practice 2005 (Revised 2008) ('the SORP'), the Charities Accounts (Scotland) regulations 2006 and Charities and Trustee Investment (Scotland) Act 2005, and applicable accounting standards in the United Kingdom.

Source: Oxfam Annual Report & Accounts 2013/14, pp. front cover, 6, 8, 38. http://www.oxfamannualreview.org.uk/wp-content/uploads/2014/09/6182_Oxfam_ARA_web_final.pdf

Discussion points

1 Who might be included in the stakeholders to whom Oxfam is accountable?
2 To what extent do the 'Highlights' meet the information needs of users of the annual report?
3 What is the role of accounting in achieving Oxfam's commitment to accountability?

Contents

Learning outcomes

After studying this chapter you should be able to:

- Define, and explain the definition of, accounting.
- Explain what is meant by a *conceptual framework.*
- Explain the distinguishing features of a sole trader, a partnership and a limited company.
- List the main users of financial information and their particular needs.
- Discuss the usefulness of financial statements to the main users.

Additionally, for those who choose to study the supplement:

- Define the basic terminology of business transactions.

1.1 Introduction

Activity 1.1

Before starting to read this section, write down one paragraph stating what you think the word 'accounting' means. Then read this section and compare it with your paragraph.

There is no single 'official' definition of accounting, but for the purposes of this text the following wording will be used:

Definition

Accounting is the process of identifying, measuring and communicating financial information about an entity to permit informed judgements and decisions by users of the information.[1]

This definition may appear short, but it has been widely quoted over a number of years and is sufficient to specify the entire contents of this introductory textbook.

Taking the definition word by word, it leads to the following questions:

1 What is the process?
2 How is financial information identified?
3 How is financial information measured?
4 How is financial information communicated?
5 What is an entity?
6 Who are the users of financial information about an entity?
7 What types of judgements and decisions do these users make?

Writing the questions in this order is slightly dangerous because it starts by emphasising the process and waits until the final question to ask about the use of the information. The danger is that accountants may design the process first and then hope to show that it is suitable to allow judgements and decisions by users. This is what has often happened over many years of developing the process by accountants.

In order to learn about, and understand, **accounting** by taking a critical approach to the usefulness of the current processes and seeing its limitations and the potential for improvement, it is preferable to reverse the order of the questions and start by specifying the users of **financial information** and the judgements and decisions they make. Once the users and their needs have been identified, the most effective forms of communication may be determined and only then may the technical details of measurement and identification be dealt with in a satisfactory manner.

Reversing the order of the questions arising from the definition of accounting is the approach used in this book, because it is the one which has been taken by those seeking to develop a **conceptual framework** of accounting.

This chapter outlines in particular the Conceptual Framework of the International Accounting Standards Board which has been developed for international use in accounting practice. The chapter explains the nature of three common types of business **entity** and concludes by drawing on various views relating to the users of accounting information and their information needs.

Because the understanding of users' needs is essential throughout the entire text, the chapter introduces David Wilson, a **fund manager** working for a large insurance company. In order to balance the demands of users with the restrictions and constraints on preparers of financial information, the chapter also introduces Leona Rees who is a member of the **accountancy profession** and who works as an **audit manager** with an **accountancy firm**. Both of them will offer comments and explanations as you progress through the text.

Activity 1.2	How does this section compare with your initial notions of what accounting means? If they are similar, then it is likely that the rest of this book will meet your expectations. If they are different, then it may be that you are hoping for more than this book can achieve. If that is the case, this may be a useful point at which to consult your lecturer, tutor or some other expert in the subject to be sure that you are satisfied that this book will meet your personal learning outcomes.

1.2 The development of a conceptual framework

A **conceptual framework** for accounting is a statement of principles which provides generally accepted guidance for the development of new reporting practices and for challenging and evaluating the existing practices. Conceptual frameworks have been developed in several countries around the world. The structure of most conceptual frameworks is along the following lines:

- Who are the users of **financial statements**?
- What are the information needs of users?
- What types of financial statements will best satisfy their needs?
- What are the characteristics of financial statements which meet these needs?
- What are the principles for defining and recognising items in financial statements?
- What are the principles for measuring items in financial statements?

The most widely applicable conceptual framework originated as the *Framework for the Preparation and Presentation of Financial Statements* issued by the International Accounting Standards Board (IASB) in 1989. In 2010 the *Framework* was partially updated, and completed in 2016, after some challenging accounting issues had been addressed. The thinking in those documents can be traced to two discussion papers of the 1970s in the UK and the USA. In the UK, *The Corporate Report*[2] was a slim but highly influential document setting out the needs of users and how these might be met. Two years earlier the *Trueblood Report*[3] in the USA had taken a similar approach of identifying the needs of users, although perhaps coming out more strongly in support of the needs of shareholders and creditors than of other user groups. In the UK, various documents on the needs of users have been prepared by individuals invited to help the process[4] or those who took it on themselves to propose radical new ideas.[5]

Since January 2005, all **listed companies** in member states of the European Union (EU) have been required by an accounting regulation called the IAS Regulation[6] to use a system of international financial reporting standards set by the International Accounting Standards Board. The UK standard-setter has been influential in the development of these international reporting standards and, over a period of years, has been moving UK accounting practice closely into line with the international standards. For **unlisted** companies and other organisations not covered by the IAS Regulation of the EU, the UK Financial Reporting Council (FRC) has a conceptual framework of its own, called the *Statement of Principles*.[7] This document has many similarities to the IASB's *Conceptual Framework*.

Activity 1.3	Most conceptual frameworks start with the question: Who are the users of financial statements? Write down a list of the persons or organisations you think would be interested in making use of financial statements, and their possible reasons for being interested. Have you included yourself in that list? Keep your list available for comparing with a later section of this chapter.

1.3 The *Conceptual Framework* for financial reporting

The *Conceptual Framework* has been in the process of gradual revision over several years, as a joint project of the IASB and the Financial Accounting Standards Board (FASB) of the USA. Progress was delayed by the financial crisis of 2007–08 and eventually the IASB decided to complete the project alone for 2016. The structure is as follows:

Chapters (revised 2016)
1 The objective of general purpose financial reporting.
2 Qualitative characteristics of useful financial information.
3 Financial statements and the reporting entity.
4 The elements of financial statements.
5 Recognition and derecognition.
6 Measurement.
7 Presentation and disclosure.
8 Concepts of capital and capital maintenance.

Chapters 1 and 2 of the *Conceptual Framework* are written at a general level and a reader would find no difficulty in reviewing these at an early stage of study, to gain a flavour of what is expected of financial statements. The remaining sections are a mixture of general principles, which are appropriate to first-level study of the subject, and some quite specific principles which deal with more advanced problems. Some of those problems need an understanding of accounting which is beyond a first level of study. This book will refer to aspects of the various sections of the *Conceptual Framework,* as appropriate, when particular issues are dealt with. You should be aware, however, that this book concentrates on the basic aspects of the *Conceptual Framework* and does not explore every complexity.

A conceptual framework is particularly important when practices are being developed for reporting to those who are not part of the day-to-day running of the business. This is called **external reporting** or **financial accounting** and is the focus of the *Financial Accounting* studied in this book. For those who are managing the business on a day-to-day basis, special techniques have been developed and are referred to generally as **internal reporting** or **management accounting**.

Before continuing with the theme of the conceptual framework, it is useful to pause and consider the types of business for which accounting information may be required.

Activity 1.4	*Visit the website of the International Accounting Standards Board at* **www.ifrs.org** *and find the link to the* Conceptual Framework. *What does the IASB say about the purpose of the* Conceptual Framework? *How has it been developed?* *Visit the UK website of the Financial Reporting Council at* **www.frc.org.uk** *and find the link to the Statement of Principles. What is the stated purpose of the Statement of Principles? How was it developed?*

1.4 Types of business entity

The word **entity** means 'something that exists independently'. A business entity is a business that exists independently of those who own the business. There are three main categories of business which will be found in all countries, although with different titles in different ones. This chapter uses the terminology common to the UK. The three main categories are: **sole trader**, **partnership** and **limited liability company**. This list is by no means exhaustive but provides sufficient variety to allow explanation of the usefulness of most accounting practices and their application.

Activity 1.5	*Before reading the next sections, take out a newspaper with business advertisements or a business telephone directory, or take a walk down your local high street or drive round the trading estate. Write down the names of five businesses, shops or other organisations. Then read the sections and attempt to match your list against the information provided in each.*

1.4.1 Sole trader

An individual may enter into business alone, either selling goods or providing a service. Such a person is described as a **sole trader**. The business may be started because the sole trader has a good idea which appears likely to make a profit, and has some cash to buy the equipment and other resources to start the business. If cash is not available, the sole trader may borrow from a bank to enable the business to start up. Although this is the form in which many businesses have started, it is one which is difficult to expand because the sole trader will find it difficult to arrange additional finance for expansion. If the business is not successful and the sole trader is unable to meet obligations to pay money to others, then those persons may ask a court of law to authorise the sale of the personal possessions, and even the family home, of the sole trader. Being a sole trader can be a risky matter and the cost of bank borrowing may be at a relatively unfavourable rate of interest because the bank fears losing its money.

From this description it will be seen that the sole trader's business is very much intertwined with the sole trader's personal life. However, for accounting purposes, the business is regarded as a separate economic entity, of which the sole trader is the owner who takes the risk of the bad times and the benefit of the good times. Take as an example the person who decides to start working as an electrician and advertises their services in a newspaper. The electrician travels to jobs from home and has no business premises. Tools are stored in the loft at home and the business records are in a cupboard in the kitchen. Telephone calls from customers are received on the domestic phone and there are no clearly defined working hours. The work is inextricably intertwined with family life.

For accounting purposes that person is seen as the owner of a business which provides electrical services and the business is seen as being separate from the person's other interests and private life. The owner may hardly feel any great need for accounting information because they know the business very closely, but accounting information will be needed by other persons or entities, mainly the government (in the form of **HM Revenue and Customs**) for tax collecting purposes. It may also be required by a bank for the purposes of lending money to the business or by another sole trader who is intending to buy the business when the existing owner retires.

1.4.2 Partnership

One method by which the business of a sole trader may expand is to enter into **partnership** with one or more people. This may permit a pooling of skills to allow more efficient working, or may allow one person with ideas to work with another who has the money to provide the resources needed to turn the ideas into a profit. There is thus more potential for being successful. If the business is unsuccessful, then the consequences are similar to those for the sole trader. Persons to whom money is owed by the business may ask a court of law to authorise the sale of the personal property of the partners in order to meet the obligation. Even more seriously, one partner may be required to meet all the obligations of the partnership if the other partner does not have sufficient personal property, possessions and cash. This is described in law as **joint and several liability** and the risks have to be considered very carefully by those entering into partnership.

Partnership may be established as a matter of fact by two persons starting to work together with the intention of making a profit and sharing it between them. More often there is a legal agreement, called a **partnership deed**, which sets out the rights and duties of each partner and specifies how they will share the profits. There is also **partnership law**, which governs the basic relationships between partners and which they may use to resolve their disputes in a court of law if there is no partnership deed, or if the partnership deed has not covered some aspect of the partnership.

For accounting purposes the partnership is seen as a separate economic entity, owned by the partners. The owners may have the same intimate knowledge of the business as does the sole trader and may therefore feel that accounting information is not very important for them. On the other hand, each partner may wish to be sure that they are receiving a fair share of the partnership profits. There will also be other persons requesting accounting information, such as HM Revenue and Customs, banks who provide finance and individuals who may be invited to join the partnership so that it can expand even further.

1.4.3   Limited liability company

The main risk attached to either a sole trader or a partnership is that of losing personal property and possessions, including the family home, if the business fails. That risk would inhibit many persons from starting or expanding a business. Historically, as the UK changed from a predominantly agricultural to a predominantly industrial economy in the nineteenth century, it became apparent that owners needed the protection of **limited liability**. This meant that if the business failed, the owners might lose all the money they had put into the business but their personal wealth would be safe.

There are two forms of limited liability company. The **private limited company** has the word 'Limited' (abbreviated to 'Ltd') in its title. The **public limited company** has the abbreviation 'plc' in its title. The private limited company is prohibited by law from offering its **shares** to the public, so it is a form of limited liability appropriate to a family-controlled business. The public limited company is permitted to offer its shares to the public. In return it has to satisfy more onerous regulations. Where the shares of a public limited company are bought and sold on a **stock exchange**, the public limited company is called a **listed company** because the shares of the company are on a list of share prices.

In either type of company, the owners are called **shareholders** because they share the ownership and share the profits of the good times and the losses of the bad times (to the defined limit of liability). Once they have paid in full for their shares, the owners face no further risk of being asked to contribute to meeting any obligations of the business. Hopefully, the business will prosper and the owners may be able to receive a share of that prosperity in the form of a cash **dividend**. A cash dividend returns to the owners, on a regular basis and in the form of cash, a part of the profit created by the business.

If the company is very small, the owners may run the business themselves. If it is larger, then they may prefer to pay someone else to run the business. In either case, the persons running the business on a day-to-day basis are called the **directors**.

Because limited liability is a great privilege for the owners, the company must meet regulations set out by Parliament in the form of a **Companies Act**. At present the relevant law is the Companies Act 2006.

For accounting purposes the company is an entity with an existence separate from the owners. In the very smallest companies the owners may not feel a great need for accounting information, but in medium- or large-sized companies, accounting information will be very important for the shareholders as it forms a report on how well the directors have run the company. As with other forms of business accounting information must be supplied to HM Revenue and Customs for tax-collecting purposes. The list of other users will expand considerably because there will be a greater variety of sources of finance, the company may be seeking to attract more **investors**, employees will be concerned about the well-being of the business and even the customers and suppliers may want to know more about the financial strength of the company.

Although the law provides the protection of limited liability, this has little practical meaning for many small family-controlled companies because a bank lending money to the business will ask for personal guarantees from the shareholder directors. Those personal guarantees could involve a mortgage over the family home, or an interest in life assurance policies. The potential consequences of such personal guarantees, when a company fails, are such that the owners may suffer as much as the sole trader whose business fails.

1.4.4   Limited liability partnership

A limited liability partnership (LLP) is a corporate body, which means it has a legal personality separate from that of its members. It is formed by being incorporated under the Limited Liability Partnerships Act 2000. Any new or existing partnership firm of two or more persons can incorporate as an LLP. There is no limit on the number of members. There must be at least two designated members who take responsibility for compliance with statutory requirements. The minimum capital requirement is only £2. An LLP structure may be used by any business seeking to make a profit. It has been used in particular by professional firms such as accountants, solicitors and architects.

The LLP may be managed like a normal partnership. All members may participate actively in the management of the business. However, the LLP is responsible for the debts of the business. The individual members do not have the unlimited liability that they would have in a normal partnership. Taxation procedures are those that apply to a partnership.

From an accounting perspective in the UK the disclosure requirements are similar to those of a company. LLPs are required to provide financial information equivalent to that of companies, including the filing of annual accounts with the Registrar of Companies.

1.4.5 Comparing partnership and limited liability company

Table 1.1 summarises the differences between a partnership and a limited liability company that are relevant for accounting purposes.

Table 1.2 identifies the differences between the public limited company and the private limited company that are relevant for accounting purposes.

Table 1.1
Differences between a partnership and a limited liability company

	Partnership	Limited liability company
Formation	Formed by two or more persons, usually with written agreement but not necessarily in writing.	Formed by a number of persons registering the company under the Companies Act, following legal formalities. In particular there must be a written **memorandum** and **articles of association** setting out the powers allowed to the company.
Running the business	All partners are entitled to share in the running of the business.	Shareholders must appoint **directors** to run the business (although shareholders may appoint themselves as directors).
Accounting information	Partnerships are not obliged to make accounting information available to the wider public.	Companies must make accounting information available to the public through the **Registrar of Companies**.
Meeting obligations	All members of a general partnership are jointly and severally liable for money owed by the firm.	The personal liability of the owners is limited to the amount they have agreed to pay for shares.
Powers to carry out activities	Partnerships may carry out any legal business activities agreed by the partners.	The company may only carry out the activities set out in its **memorandum** and **articles of association**.
Status in law	The partnership is not a separate legal entity (under English law), the partnership property being owned by the partners. (Under Scots law the partnership is a separate legal entity.)	The company is seen in law as a separate person, distinct from its members. This means that the company can own property, make contracts and take legal action or be the subject of legal action.

Table 1.2

Brief comparison of private and public companies

	Public company	Private company
Running the business	Minimum of two directors.	Minimum of one director.
	Must have a company secretary who holds a relevant qualification (responsible for ensuring the company complies with the requirements of company law).	The sole director may also act as the company secretary and is not required to have a formal qualification.
Ownership	Shares may be offered to the public, inviting subscription.	Shares must not be offered to the public. May only be sold by private arrangements.
	Minimum **share capital** £50,000.	No minimum share capital.
Accounting information	Extensive information required on transactions between directors and the company.	Less need for disclosure of transactions between directors and the company.
	Information must be made public through the Registrar of Companies.	
	Provision of financial information to the public is determined by size of company, more information being required of medium- and large-sized companies.	
	Accounting information must be sent to all shareholders.	

Activity 1.6

Look at the list of five organisations which you prepared before reading this section. Did the list match what you have just read? If not, there are several possible explanations. One is that you have written down organisations which are not covered by this book. That would apply if you have written down 'museum', 'town hall' or 'college'. These are examples of public sector bodies that require specialised financial statements not covered by this text. Another is that you did not discover the name of the business enterprise. Perhaps you wrote down 'Northern Hotel' but did not find the name of the company owning the hotel. If your list does not match the section, ask for help from your lecturer, tutor or other expert in the subject so that you are satisfied that this book will continue to meet your personal learning outcomes.

1.5 Users and their information needs

Who are the users of the information provided by these reporting entities? This section shows that there is one group, namely the **management** of an organisation, whose information needs are so specialised that a separate type of accounting has evolved called **management accounting**. However, there are other groups, each of which may believe it has a reasonable right to obtain information about an organisation, that do not enjoy unrestricted access to the business and so have to rely on management to supply suitable information. These groups include the owners, where the owners are not also the managers, but extend further to employees, lenders, suppliers, customers, government and its branches and the public interest. Those in the wider interest groups are sometimes referred to as **stakeholders**.

Definition

> **Stakeholder** A general term to indicate all those who might have a legitimate interest in receiving financial information about a business because they have a 'stake' in it.

1.5.1 Management

Many would argue that the foremost users of accounting information about an organisation must be those who manage the business on a day-to-day basis. This group is referred to in broad terms as **management**, which is a collective term for all those persons who have responsibilities for making judgements and decisions within an organisation. Because they have close involvement with the business, they have access to a wide range of information (much of which may be confidential within the organisation) and will seek those aspects of the information which are most relevant to their particular judgements and decisions. Because this group of users is so broad, and because of the vast amount of information potentially available, a specialist branch of accounting has developed, called management accounting, to serve the particular needs of management.

It is management's responsibility to employ the resources of the business in an efficient way and to meet the objectives of the business. The information needed by management to carry out this responsibility ought to be of high quality and in an understandable form so far as the management is concerned. If that is the case, it would not be unreasonable to think that a similar quality (although not necessarily quantity) of information should be made available more widely to those stakeholders who do not have the access available to management.[8] Such an idea would be regarded as somewhat revolutionary in nature by some of those who manage companies, but more and more are beginning to realise that sharing information with investors and other stakeholders adds to the general atmosphere of confidence in the enterprise.

1.5.2 Owners as investors

Where the owners are the managers, as is the case for a sole trader or a partnership, they have no problem in gaining access to information and will select information appropriate to their own needs. They may be asked to provide information for other users, such as HM Revenue and Customs or a bank which has been approached to provide finance, but that information will be designed to meet the needs of those particular users rather than the owners.

Where the ownership is separate from the management of the business, as is the case with a limited liability company, the owners are more appropriately viewed as investors who entrust their money to the company and expect something in return, usually a **dividend** and a growth in the value of their investment as the company prospers. Providing money to fund a business is a risky act and investors are concerned with the **risk** inherent in, and **return** provided by, their investments. They need information to help them decide whether they should buy, hold or sell.[9] They are also interested in information on the entity's financial performance and financial position that helps them to assess both its cash-generation abilities and how management discharges its responsibilities.[10]

Much of the investment in shares through the Stock Exchange in the UK is carried out by **institutional investors**, such as pension funds, insurance companies, unit trusts and investment trusts. The day-to-day business of buying and selling shares is carried out by a **fund manager** employed by the institutional investor. Private investors are in the minority as a group of investors in the UK. They will often take the advice of an **equities analyst** who investigates and reports on share investment. The fund managers and the equities analysts are also regarded as users of accounting information.

The kinds of judgements and decisions made by investors could include any or all of the following:

(a) Evaluating the performance of the entity.

(b) Assessing the effectiveness of the entity in achieving objectives (including compliance with **stewardship** obligations) established previously by its management, its members or owners.

(c) Evaluating managerial performance, efficiency and objectives, including investment and dividend distribution plans.

(d) Ascertaining the experience and background of company directors and officials including details of other directorships or official positions held.

(e) Ascertaining the economic stability and vulnerability of the reporting entity.

(f) Assessing the **liquidity** of the entity, its present or future requirements for additional **working capital**, and its ability to raise long-term and short-term finance.

(g) Assessing the capacity of the entity to make future reallocations of its resources for economic purposes.

(h) Estimating the future prospects of the entity, including its capacity to pay **dividends**, and predicting future levels of investment.

(i) Making economic comparisons, either for the given entity over a period of time or with other entities at one point in time.

(j) Estimating the value of present or prospective interests in or claims on the entity.

(k) Ascertaining the ownership and control of the entity.[11]

That list was prepared in 1975 and, while it is a valid representation of the needs of investors, carries an undertone which implies that the investors have to do quite a lot of the work themselves in making estimates of the prospects of the entity. Today there is a stronger view that the management of a business should share more of its thinking and planning with the investors. The list may therefore be expanded by suggesting that it would be helpful for investors (and all external users) to know:

(a) the entity's actual performance for the most recent accounting period and how this compares with its previous plan for that period;

(b) management's explanations of any significant variances between the two; and

(c) management's financial plan for the current and forward accounting periods, and explanations of the major assumptions used in preparing it.[12]

In the **annual reports** of all but small companies you will find a section called the **strategic report**. This is where companies will include forward-looking statements which stop short of making a forecast but give help in understanding which of the trends observed in the past are likely to continue into the future.

1.5.3   Lenders

Lenders are interested in information that enables them to determine whether their loans, and the related interest, will be paid when due.[13]

Loan **creditors** provide finance on a longer-term basis. They will wish to assess the economic stability and vulnerability of the borrower. They are particularly concerned with the risk of **default** and its consequences. They may impose conditions (called **loan covenants**) which require the business to keep its overall borrowing within acceptable limits. The financial statements may provide evidence that the loan covenant conditions are being met.

Some lenders will ask for special reports as well as the general financial statements. Banks in particular will ask for **cash flow projections** showing how the business plans to repay, with interest, the money borrowed.

1.5.4 Suppliers and other trade creditors

Suppliers of goods and services (also called trade creditors) are interested in information that enables them to decide whether to sell to the entity and to determine whether amounts owing to them will be paid when due. The IASB mentions 'other lenders' as users of financial statements.[14] Suppliers (trade creditors) are likely to be interested in an entity over a shorter period than lenders unless they are dependent upon the continuation of the entity as a major customer. The amount due to be paid to the supplier is called a trade payable or an account payable.

Trade creditors supply goods and services to an entity and have very little protection if the entity fails because there are insufficient assets to meet all **liabilities**. They are usually classed as **unsecured creditors**, which means they are a long way down the queue for payment. So they have to exercise caution in finding out whether the business is able to pay and how much risk of non-payment exists. This information need not necessarily come from accounting statements; it could be obtained by reading the local press and trade journals, joining the Chamber of Trade, and generally listening in to the stories and gossip circulating in the geographic area or the industry. However, the financial statements of an entity may confirm the stories gained from other sources.

In recent years there has been a move for companies to work more closely with their suppliers and to establish 'partnership' arrangements where the operational and financial plans of both may be dovetailed by specifying the amount and the timing of goods and services required. Such arrangements depend heavily on confidence, which in turn may be derived partly from the strength of financial statements.

1.5.5 Employees

Employees and their representatives are interested in information about the stability and profitability of their employers. They are also interested in information that helps them to assess the ability of the entity to provide remuneration, retirement benefits and employment opportunities. Employees continue to be interested in their employer after they have retired from work because in many cases the employer provides a pension fund.

The matters which are likely to be of interest to past, present and prospective employees include: the ability of the employer to meet wage agreements; management's intentions regarding employment levels, locations and working conditions; the pay, conditions and terms of employment of various groups of employees; job security; and the contribution made by employees in other divisions of the organisation. Much of this is quite specialised and detailed information. It may be preferable to supply this to employees by means of special purpose reports on a frequent basis rather than waiting for the annual report, which is slow to arrive and more general in nature. However, employees may look to financial statements to confirm information provided previously in other forms. The IASB regards employees as persons who might find the general purpose financial statements useful. However, the IASB says that such financial statements are not primarily directed to these groups.[15]

1.5.6 Customers

Customers have an interest in information about the continuance of an entity, especially when they have a long-term involvement with, or are dependent upon, its prosperity. In particular, customers need information concerning the current and future supply of goods and services offered, price and other product details, and conditions of sale. Much of this information may be obtained from sales literature or from sales staff of the enterprise, or from trade and consumer journals.

The financial statements provide useful confirmation of the reliability of the enterprise itself as a continuing source of supply, especially when the customer is making payments in advance. They also confirm the capacity of the entity in terms of **non-current assets** (also called **fixed assets**) and working **capital** and give some indication of the strength of the entity to meet any obligations under guarantees or warranties.

1.5.7 Governments and their agencies

Governments and their agencies are interested in the allocation of resources and, therefore, in the activities of entities. They also require information in order to regulate the activities of entities, assess taxation and provide a basis for national income and economic statistics.

Acting on behalf of the UK government's Treasury Department, HM Revenue and Customs collects taxes from businesses based on profit calculated according to commercial accounting practices (although there are some specific rules in the taxation legislation which modify the normal accounting practices). HM Revenue and Customs has the power to demand more information than appears in published financial statements, but will take these as a starting point.

Other agencies include the regulators of the various utility companies. Examples are Ofcom[16] (the Office of Communications) and Ofgem[17] (the Office of Gas and Electricity Markets). They use accounting information as part of the package by which they monitor the prices charged by these organisations to consumers of their services. They also demand additional information designed especially to meet their needs.

1.5.8 Public interest

Enterprises affect members of the public in a variety of ways. For example, enterprises may make a substantial contribution to the local economy by providing employment and using local suppliers. Financial statements may assist the public by providing information about the trends and recent developments in the prosperity of the entity and the range of its activities.

A strong element of public interest has been aroused in recent years by environmental issues and the impact of companies on the environment. There are costs imposed on others when a company pollutes a river or discharges harmful gases into the air. It may be perceived that a company is cutting corners to prune its own reported costs at the expense of other people. Furthermore, there are activities of companies today which will impose costs in the future. Where an oil company has installed a drilling rig in the North Sea, it will be expected one day to remove and destroy the rig safely. There is a question as to whether the company will be able to meet that cost. These costs and future liabilities may be difficult to identify and quantify, but that does not mean that companies should not attempt to do so. More companies are now including descriptions of environmental policy in their annual reports, but regular accounting procedures for including environmental costs and obligations in the financial statements have not yet been developed.

Activity 1.7	Look back to the list of users of financial statements which you prepared earlier in this chapter. How closely does your list compare with the users described in this section? Did you have any in your list which are not included here? Have you used names which differ from those used in the chapter? Are there users in the chapter which are not in your list? If your list does not match the section, ask for help from your lecturer, tutor or other expert in the subject so that you are satisfied that this book will continue to meet your personal learning outcomes.

1.6 General purpose or specific purpose financial statements?

Some experts who have analysed the needs of users in the manner set out in the previous section have come to the conclusion that no single set of **general purpose financial statements** could meet all these needs. It has been explained in the previous section that some users already turn to special reports to meet specific needs. Other experts hold that there could be a form of general purpose financial statements which would meet all the needs of some user groups and some of the needs of others.

This book is written on the assumption that it *is* possible to prepare a set of general purpose financial statements which will have some interest for all users. The existence of such reports is particularly important for those who cannot prescribe the information they would like to receive from an organisation. That is perhaps because they have no bargaining power, or because they are many in number but not significant in economic influence.

Preparers of general purpose financial statements tend to regard the owners and long-term lenders as the primary users of the information provided. There is an expectation or hope that the interests of these groups will overlap to some extent with the interests of a wider user group and that any improvements in financial statements will be sufficient that fewer needs will be left unmet.[18]

The primary focus of the *Conceptual Framework* is on general purpose financial statements.[19] It takes the view that many users have to rely on the financial statements as their major source of financial information. Financial statements should be prepared with their needs in mind. The *Conceptual Framework* assumes that if financial statements meet the needs of investors, they will also meet the needs of most other users.[20]

1.7 Stewards and agents

In an earlier section, the needs of investors as users were listed and the word 'stewardship' appeared. In the days before an industrial society existed, stewards were the people who looked after the manor house and lands while the lord of the manor enjoyed the profits earned. Traditionally, accounting has been regarded as having a particular role to play in confirming that those who manage a business on behalf of the owner take good care of the resources entrusted to them and earn a satisfactory profit for the owner by using those resources.

As the idea of a wider range of users emerged, this idea of the 'stewardship' objective of accounting was mentioned less often (although its influence remains strong in legislation governing accounting practice). In the academic literature it has been reborn under a new heading – that of **agency**. Theories have been developed about the relationship between the owner, as 'principal', and the manager, as 'agent'. A conscientious manager, acting as an agent, will carry out their duties in the best interest of the owners, and is required by the law of agency to do so. However, not all agents will be perfect in carrying out this role and some principals will not trust the agent entirely. The principal will incur costs in monitoring (enquiring into) the activities of the agent and may lose some wealth if the interests of the agent and the interests of the principal diverge. The view taken in **agency theory** is that there is an inherent conflict between the two parties and so they spend time agreeing contracts which will minimise that conflict. The contracts will include arrangements for the agent to supply information on a regular basis to the principal.

While the study of agency theory in all its aspects could occupy a book in itself, the idea of conflicts and the need for compromise in dealing with pressures of demand for, and supply of, accounting information may be helpful in later chapters in understanding why it takes so long to find answers to some accounting issues.

1.8 Who needs financial statements?

In order to keep the flavour of debate on accounting issues running through this text, two people will give their comments from time to time. The first of these is David Wilson, a fund manager of seven years' experience working for an insurance company. He manages a UK equity **portfolio** (a collection of company shares) and part of his work requires him to be an equities analyst. At university he took a degree in history and has subsequently passed examinations to qualify as a chartered financial analyst (CFA).[21]

The second is Leona Rees, an audit manager with a major accountancy firm. She has five years' experience as a qualified accountant and had previously spent three years in training with the same firm. Her university degree is in accounting and economics and she has passed the examinations to qualify for membership of one of the major accountancy bodies.

David and Leona had been at school together but then went to different universities. More recently they have met again at workout sessions at a health club, relaxing afterwards at a nearby bar. David is very enthusiastic about his work, which demands long hours and a flexible attitude. He has absorbed a little of the general scepticism of audit which is expressed by some of his fund manager colleagues.

Leona's main role at present is in company audit and she is now sufficiently experienced to be working on the audit of one listed company as well as several private companies of varying size. For two years she worked in the corporate recovery department of the accountancy firm, preparing information to help companies find sources of finance to overcome difficult times. She feels that a great deal of accounting work is carried out behind the scenes and the careful procedures are not always appreciated by those who concentrate only on the relatively few well-publicised problems.

We join them in the bar at the end of a hectic working week.

DAVID: *This week I've made three visits to companies, attended four presentations of preliminary announcements of results, received copies of the projector slides used for five others that I couldn't attend, and collected around 20 annual reports. I have a small mound of brokers' reports, all of which say much the same thing but in different ways. I've had to read all those while preparing my monthly report to the head of Equities Section on the performance of my fund and setting out my strategy for three months ahead consistent with in-house policy. I think I'm suffering from information overload and I have reservations about the reliability of any single item of information I receive about a company.*

LEONA: *If I had to give scores for reliability to the information crossing your desk, I would give top marks to the 20 annual reports. They have been through a very rigorous process and they have been audited by reputable audit firms using established standards of auditing practice.*

DAVID: *That's all very well, but it takes so long for annual reports to arrive after the financial year-end that they don't contain any new information. I need to get information at the first available opportunity if I'm to keep up the value of the share portfolio I manage. The meetings that present the preliminary announcements are held less than two months after the accounting year-end. It can take another six weeks before the printed annual report appears. If I don't manage to get to the meeting I take a careful look at what the company sends me in the way of copies of projector slides used.*

LEONA: *Where does accounting information fit in with the picture you want of a company?*

DAVID: *It has some importance, but accounting information is backward-looking and I invest in the future. We visit every company in the portfolio once a year and I'm looking for a confident management team, a cheerful-looking workforce and a general feeling that things are moving ahead. I'll also ask questions about prospects: how is the order book; which overseas markets are expanding; have prices been increased to match the increase in raw materials?*

LEONA: *Isn't that close to gaining insider information?*

DAVID: *No – I see it as clarification of information which is already published. Companies are very careful not to give an advantage to one investor over another – they would be in trouble with the Stock Exchange and perhaps with the Financial Services Authority if they did give price-sensitive information. There are times of the year (running up to the year-end and to the half-yearly results) when they declare a 'close season' and won't even speak to an investor.*

LEONA: *So are you telling me that I spend vast amounts of time auditing financial statements which no one bothers to read?*

DAVID: *Some people would say that, but I wouldn't. It's fairly clear that share prices are unmoved by the issue of the annual report, probably because investors already have that information from the preliminary announcement. Nevertheless, we like to know that there is a regulated document behind the information we receive – it allows us to check that we're not being led astray. Also, I find the annual report very useful when I want to find out about a company I don't know. For the companies I understand well, the annual report tells me little that I don't already know.*

LEONA: *I'll take that as a very small vote of confidence for now. If your offer to help me redecorate the flat still stands, I might try to persuade you over a few cans of emulsion that you rely on audited accounts more than you realise.*

Activity 1.8	As a final activity for this chapter, go back to the start of the chapter and make a note of every word you have encountered for the first time. Look at the glossary at the end of the book for the definition of each technical word. If the word is not in the glossary it is probably in sufficiently general use to be found in a standard dictionary.

1.9 Summary

This chapter has explained that accounting is intended to provide information that is useful to a wide range of interested parties (stakeholders).

Key points are:

- **Accounting** is the process of identifying, measuring and communicating financial information about an entity to permit informed judgements and decisions by users of the information.

- A **conceptual framework** for accounting is a statement of principles which provides generally accepted guidance for the development of new reporting practices and for challenging and evaluating the existing practices.

- The *Conceptual Framework* of the IASB provides broad principles that guide accounting practice in many countries.

- Since January 2005, all **listed companies** in member states of the EU have been required by an accounting regulation to use a system of international financial reporting standards (IFRS) set by the IASB.

- Business **entities** in the UK are either **sole traders**, **partnerships** or **limited liability** companies.

- **Users** of accounting information include management, owners, employees, lenders, suppliers, customers, governments and their agencies and the public interest.

- **Stakeholders** are all those who might have a legitimate interest in receiving financial information about a business because they have a 'stake' in it.

- General purpose **financial statements** aim to meet the needs of a wide range of users.

- The relationship between the owner, as 'principal', and the manager, as 'agent', is described in the theory of **agency** relationships. Accounting information helps to reduce the potential conflicts of interest between principal and agent.

Further reading

IASB (2016), *The Conceptual Framework for Financial Reporting*, International Accounting Standards Board.

ICAEW (2009), *Developments in new reporting models*. Information for better markets initiative. The Institute of Chartered Accountants in England and Wales. www.icaew.co.uk.

QUESTIONS

The Questions section of each chapter has three types of question. 'Test your understanding' questions to help you review your reading are in the 'A' series of questions. You will find the answers to these by reading and thinking about the material in the book. 'Application' questions to test your ability to apply technical skills are in the 'B' series of questions. Questions requiring you to show skills in problem solving and evaluation are in the 'C' series of questions. A letter [S] indicates that there is a solution at the end of the book. Some questions here have no solution because they are open ended for your thoughts. Further parallel questions are provided in the Instructor's Manual.

A Test your understanding

A1.1 Define 'accounting' and identify the separate questions raised by the definition. (Section 1.1)

A1.2 The following technical terms appear for the first time in this chapter. Check that you know the meaning of each. (If you can't find them again in the text, there is a glossary at the end of the book.)

- accountancy firm
- accountancy profession
- accounting
- agency
- agency theory
- annual report
- articles of association

- audit manager
- business entity
- capital
- cash flow projections
- Companies Act
- conceptual framework
- creditors

- default
- directors
- dividend
- entity
- equities analyst
- external reporting
- financial accounting
- financial information
- financial reporting standards
- financial statements
- fixed assets
- fund manager
- general purpose financial statements
- HM Revenue and Customs
- institutional investors
- internal reporting
- investors
- joint and several liability
- limited liability
- limited liability company
- liquidity
- listed companies
- loan covenants
- management

- management accounting
- memorandum
- non-current assets
- partnership
- partnership deed
- partnership law
- portfolio
- private limited company
- public limited company
- Registrar of Companies
- return
- risk
- share capital
- shareholders
- shares
- sole trader
- specific purpose financial statements
- stakeholders
- stewardship
- stock exchange
- strategic report
- unlisted companies
- unsecured creditors
- working capital

B   Application

B1.1

Brian and Jane are planning to work in partnership as software consultants. Write a note (100–200 words) to explain their responsibilities for running the business and producing accounting information about the financial position and performance of the business.

B1.2

Jennifer has inherited some shares in a public company which has a share listing on the Stock Exchange. She has asked you to explain how she can find out more about the financial position and performance of the company. Write a note (100–200 words) answering her question.

B1.3

Martin is planning to buy shares in the company that employs him. He knows that the directors of the company are his employers but he wonders what relationship exists between the directors and the shareholders of the company. Write a note (100–200 words) answering his question.

C   Problem solving and evaluation

C1.1

The following extracts are typical of the annual reports of large listed companies. Which of these extracts satisfy the definition of 'accounting'? What are the user needs that are most closely met by each extract?

(a) Suggestions for improvements were made by many employees, alone or in teams. Annual savings which have been achieved total £15m. The best suggestion for improvement will save around £0.3m per year for the next five years.

(b) As of 31 December, 3,000 young people were learning a trade or profession with the company. This represents a studentship rate of 3.9%. During the reporting period we hired 1,300 young people into training places. This is more than we need to satisfy our employment needs in the longer term and so we are contributing to improvement of the quality of labour supplied to the market generally.

(c) During the year to 31 December our turnover (sales) grew to £4,000 million compared to £2,800 million last year. Our new subsidiary contributed £1,000 million to this increase.

(d) It is our target to pay our suppliers within 30 days. During the year we achieved an average payment period of 33 days.

(e) The treasury focus during the year was on further refinancing of the group's borrowings to minimise interest payments and reduce risk.

(f) Our plants have emission rates that are 70% below the national average for sulphur dioxide and 20% below the average for oxides of nitrogen. We will tighten emissions significantly over the next ten years.

C1.2

Explain how you would class each of the following – as a sole trader, partnership or limited company. List any further questions you might ask for clarification about the nature of the business.

(a) Miss Jones works as an interior decorating adviser under the business name 'U-decide'. She rents an office and employs an administrative assistant to answer the phone, keep files and make appointments.

(b) George and Jim work together as painters and decorators under the business name 'Painting Partners Ltd'. They started the business ten years ago and work from a rented business unit on a trading estate.

(c) Jenny and Chris own a hotel jointly. They operate under the business name 'Antler Hotel Company' and both participate in the running of the business. They have agreed to share profits equally.

Activities for study groups (4 or 5 per group)

Obtain the annual report of a listed company. Each member of the group should choose a different company. Most large companies will provide a copy of the annual report at no charge in response to a polite request – or you may know someone who is a shareholder and receives a copy automatically. Many companies have websites with a section for 'Investor Relations' where you will find a document file containing the annual report.

1 Look at the contents page. What information does the company provide?

2 Find the financial highlights page. What are the items of accounting information which the company wants you to note? Which users might be interested in this highlighted information, and why?

3 Is there any information in the annual report which would be of interest to employees?

4 Is there any information in the annual report which would be of interest to customers?

5 Is there any information in the annual report which would be of interest to suppliers?

6 Find the auditors' report. To whom is it addressed? What does that tell you about the intended readership of the annual report?

7 Note the pages to which the auditors' report refers. These are the pages which are regulated by company law, accounting standards and Stock Exchange rules. Compare these pages with the other pages (those which are not regulated). Which do you find more interesting? Why?

8 Each member of the group should now make a five-minute presentation evaluating the usefulness of the annual report examined. When the presentations are complete the group should decide on five criteria for judging the reports and produce a score for each. Does the final score match the initial impressions of the person reviewing it?

9 Finally, as a group, write a short note of guidance on what makes an annual report useful to the reader.

Notes and references

1. AAA (1966), *A Statement of Basic Accounting Theory*, American Accounting Association, p. 1.
2. ASSC (1975), *The Corporate Report*, Accounting Standards Steering Committee.
3. AICPA (1973), *Report of a Study Group on the Objectives of Financial Statements* (The Trueblood Committee), American Institute of Certified Public Accountants.
4. Solomons, D. (1989), *Guidelines for Financial Reporting Standards*, Research Board of The Institute of Chartered Accountants in England and Wales.
5. ICAS (1988), *Making Corporate Reports Valuable*, Research Committee of The Institute of Chartered Accountants of Scotland.
6. The IAS Regulation (2002), see Chapter 4.
7. FRC (1999), *Statement of Principles for Financial Reporting*, Accounting Standards Board of the Financial Reporting Council.
8. ICAS (1988), para. 3.3.
9. IASB (2016) *Conceptual Framework*, para. OB 2.
10. IASB (2016) *Conceptual Framework*, para. OB 4.
11. ASSC (1975), para. 2.8.
12. ICAS (1988), para. 3.12.
13. IASB (2016) *Conceptual Framework*, para. OB 3.
14. *Ibid.*, para. OB 10.
15. *Ibid.*, para. OB 10.
16. www.ofcom.org.uk
17. www.ofgem.gov.uk
18. ICAS (1988), para. 3.7.
19. IASB (2016) *Conceptual Framework*, para. OB 1.
20. IASB (2016) *Conceptual Framework*, para. OB 10.
21. www.cfainstitute.org

Introduction to the terminology of business transactions

The following description explains the business terminology which will be encountered frequently in describing transactions in this textbook. The relevant words are highlighted in bold lettering. These technical accounting terms are explained in the Financial accounting terms defined *section at the end of the book.*

Most businesses are established with the intention of earning a **profit**. Some do so by selling goods at a price greater than that paid to buy or manufacture the goods. Others make a profit by providing a service and charging a price greater than the cost to them of providing the service. By selling the goods or services the business is said to earn *sales revenue.*

Profit arising from transactions relating to the operation of the business is measured by deducting from sales revenue the expenses of earning that revenue.

Revenue from sales (often abbreviated to 'sales' and sometimes referred to as 'turn-over') means the value of all goods or services provided to customers, whether for *cash* or for *credit*. In a *cash sale* the customer pays immediately on receipt of goods or services. In a *credit sale* the customer takes the goods or service and agrees to pay at a future date. By agreeing to pay in the future the customer becomes a **debtor** of the business. The amount due to be collected from the debtor is called a **trade receivable** or an **account receivable**. The business will send a document called a **sales invoice** to the credit customer, stating the goods or services provided by the business, the price charged for these and the amount owing to the business.

Eventually the credit customer will pay cash to settle the amount shown on the invoice. If they pay promptly the business may allow a deduction of discount for prompt payment. This deduction is called *discount allowed* by the business. As an example, if the customer owes £100 but is allowed a 5% discount by the business, he will pay £95. The business will record cash received of £95 and discount allowed of £5.

The business itself must buy goods in order to manufacture a product or provide a service. When the business buys goods it *purchases* them and holds them as an **inventory** of goods (also described as a 'stock' of goods) until they are used or sold. The goods will be purchased from a supplier, either for **cash** or for **credit**. In a **credit purchase** the business takes the goods and agrees to pay at a future date. By allowing the business time to pay, the supplier becomes a **creditor** of the business. The name creditor is given to anyone who is owed money by the business. The amount due to be paid to a creditor is called a **trade payable** or an **account payable**. The business will receive a purchase invoice from the supplier describing the goods supplied, stating the price of the goods and showing the amount owed by the business.

Eventually the business will pay cash to settle the amount shown on the purchase invoice. If the business pays promptly the supplier may permit the business to deduct a discount for prompt payment. This is called **discount received** by the business. As an example, if the business owes an amount of £200 as a **trade payable** but is permitted a 10% discount by the supplier, the business will pay £180 and record the remaining £20 as **discount received** from the supplier.

The purchase price of goods sold is one of the **expenses** of the business, to be deducted from sales revenue in calculating profit. Other expenses might include wages, salaries, rent, rates, insurance and cleaning. In each case there will be a document providing evidence of the expense, such as a wages or salaries slip, a landlord's bill for rent, a local authority's demand for rates, an insurance renewal note or a cleaner's time sheet. There will also be a record of the cash paid in each case.

Sometimes an expense is incurred but is not paid for until some time later. For example, electricity is consumed during a quarter but the electricity bill does not arrive until after the end of the quarter. An employee may have worked for a week but not yet have received a cash payment for that work. The unpaid expense of the business is called an *accrued expense* and must be recorded as part of the accounting information relevant to the period of time in which the expense was incurred.

On other occasions an expense may be paid for in advance of being used by the business. For example, a fire insurance premium covering the business premises is paid annually in advance. Such expenditure of cash will benefit a future time period and must be excluded from any profit calculation until that time. In the meantime it is recorded as a **prepaid expense** or a **prepayment**.

Dissatisfaction may be expressed by a customer with the quantity or quality of goods or service provided. If the business accepts that the complaint is justified it may replace goods or give a cash refund. If the customer is a credit customer who has not yet paid, then a cash refund is clearly inappropriate. Instead the customer would be sent a **credit note** for sales returned, cancelling the customer's debt to the business for the amount in dispute. The credit note would record the quantity of goods or type of service and the amount of the cancelled debt.

In a similar way the business would expect to receive a credit note from a supplier for *purchases returned* where goods have been bought on credit terms and later returned to the supplier because of some defect.

S   Test your understanding

S1.1 The following technical terms appear in this supplement. Check that you know the meaning of each.

- Profit
- Sales revenue
- Cash sale
- Credit sale
- Debtor
- Trade receivable
- Discount allowed
- Purchases
- Credit purchase
- Inventory
- Creditor

- Trade payable
- Discount received
- Expense
- Accrued expense
- Prepaid expense
- Credit note for sales returned
- Credit note for purchases returned
- Account receivable
- Sales invoice
- Account payable

Chapter 2

A systematic approach to financial reporting: the accounting equation

REAL WORLD CASE

The BBC: meaning and interpretation of a balance sheet

Extracts from Annual Report and Accounts

Summary consolidated balance sheet

Year ended 31 March 2014

Balance sheet classification	What is it?	2014 £m	Restated 2013 £m	What has happened this year?
Non-current assets	Mainly the BBC's property, plant, equipment and investments	1,702	1,783	Increased depreciation on new infrastructure offset by additions in the year
Current assets	Programme and other stocks and amounts to be received in the next 12 months	2,258	2,166	Increase in prepayments to acquire future programme-related rights
Current liabilities	Amounts to be paid in the next 12 months	(1,038)	(1,149)	Reduction in provisions through utilisation and releases
Non-current liabilities (excluding pension liabilities)	Amounts to be paid after the next 12 months	(1,098)	(1,144)	Reduced borrowings and long-term provisions
Net assets (excluding pension liabilities)		1,824	1,656	
Net pension liabilities	The net deficit of the BBC Pension Scheme	(1,516)	(1,616)	Decrease to reflect changes in assumptions and contributions paid during the year
Net assets		308	40	
Represented by:				
BBC reserves	The net resources available to the BBC for future use	308	40	

Alamy Images/Jeff Gilbert

Our role and purpose

The BBC exists to serve the public, and its mission is to inform, educate and entertain. Within the overall public purposes, the Trust sets the strategic framework for the BBC, and the Executive, led by the Director-General, delivers the BBC's services and creative output.

Source: BBC Annual Report and Accounts, 2013/14, pp. 2, 125. http://downloads.bbc.co.uk/annualreport/pdf/2013-14/bbc_annualreport_201314.pdf

Discussion points

1 How does the summary balance sheet (statement of financial position) reflect the accounting equation?

2 How does the style of presentation help the reader understand and interpret the balance sheet?

Contents

Learning outcomes

After studying this chapter you should be able to:

- Define and explain the accounting equation.
- Define assets.
- Apply the definition to examples of assets.
- Explain and apply the guidance for recognition of assets.
- Define liabilities.
- Apply the definition to examples of liabilities.
- Explain and apply the guidance for recognition of liabilities.
- Define ownership interest.
- Explain how the recognition of ownership interest depends on the recognition of assets and liabilities.
- Use the accounting equation to show the effect of changes in the ownership interest.
- Explain how users of financial statements can gain assurance about assets and liabilities.

Additionally, for those who choose to study the supplement:

- Explain how the rules of debit and credit recording are derived from the accounting equation.

2.1 Introduction

Chapter 1 considered the needs of a range of users of financial information and summarised by suggesting that they would all have an interest in the resources available to the business and the obligations of the business to those outside it. Many of these users will also want to be reassured that the business has an adequate flow of cash to support its continuation. The owners of the business have a claim to the resources of the business after all other obligations have been satisfied. This is called the **ownership interest** or the **equity interest**. They will be particularly interested in how that ownership interest grows from one year to the next and whether the resources of the business are being applied to the best advantage.

Accounting has traditionally applied the term **assets** to the resources available to the business and has applied the term **liabilities** to the obligations of the business to persons other than the owner. Assets and liabilities are reported in a financial statement called a **statement of financial position** (also called a **balance sheet**). The statement of the financial position of the entity represents a particular point in time. It may be described by a very simple equation.

2.2 The accounting equation

The **accounting equation** as a statement of financial position may be expressed as:

Assets	minus	**Liabilities**	equals	**Ownership interest**

The ownership interest is the residual claim after liabilities to third parties have been satisfied. The equation expressed in this form emphasises that residual aspect.

Another way of thinking about an equation is to imagine a balance with a bucket on each end. In one bucket are the assets (A) minus liabilities (L). In the other is the ownership interest (OI).

If anything happens to disturb the assets then the balance will tip unevenly unless some matching disturbance is applied to the ownership interest. If anything happens to disturb the liabilities then the balance will tip unevenly unless some matching disturbance is applied to the ownership interest. If a disturbance applied to an asset is applied equally to a liability, then the balance will remain level.

2.2.1 Form of the equation: international preferences

If you have studied simple equations in a maths course you will be aware that there are other ways of expressing this equation. Those other ways cannot change the magnitudes of each item in the equation but can reflect a different emphasis being placed on the various constituents. The form of the equation used in this chapter is the sequence which has, for many years, been applied in most statements of financial position (balance sheets) reported to external users of accounting information in the UK. The statements of financial position that have been reported to external users in some Continental European countries and in the USA are better represented by another form of the equation:

Assets	equals	Liabilities	plus	Ownership interest

The 'balance' analogy remains applicable here, but the contents of the buckets have been rearranged.

A disturbance on one side of the balance will require a corresponding disturbance on the other side if the balance is to be maintained.

2.2.2 Flexibility

The International Accounting Standards Board (IASB) has developed a set of accounting standards which together create an accounting system which in this book is described as the **IASB system**. The IASB offers no indication as to which of the above forms of the accounting equation is preferred. That is because of the different traditions in different countries. Consequently, for companies reporting under the IASB system, the form of the equation used in any particular situation is a matter of preference related to the choice of presentation of the statement of financial position (balance sheet). That is a communication issue which will be discussed later. This chapter will concentrate on the nature of the various elements of the equation, namely assets, liabilities and ownership interest. You should be prepared to find different variations of the accounting equation in different companies' financial statements.

Activity 2.1

Make a simple balance from a ruler balanced on a pencil and put coins on each side. Satisfy yourself that the ruler only remains in balance if any action on one side of the balance is matched by an equivalent action on the other side of the balance. Note also that rearranging the coins on one side will not disturb the balance. Some aspects of accounting are concerned with taking actions on each side of the balance. Other aspects are concerned with rearranging one side of the balance.

2.2.3 Measurement in the accounting equation

Measurements used in the accounting equation may use historical cost, or fair value, or a mixture of both.

Definition

Historical cost is the amount paid for an asset or agreed for a liability on the date that the transaction first occurred.

Traditionally accounting has been based on historical cost, with no regard for any effects of subsequent market prices or values. In historical cost accounting, assets have initially been measured at their cost on the date they were acquired. Liabilities have been measured at the amount agreed as owing on the date that the borrowing took place. Changes in historical cost caused by the passage of time, or use of resources, have been recognised through changes of the reported measurement of long-term assets and some long-term liabilities.

Definition

Fair value is defined as the price that would be received to sell an asset or paid to transfer a liability in an orderly transaction between market participants at the measurement date.

The measurement date for fair value is taken as the end date of the accounting period. This means that reported fair values of assets and liabilities change frequently. The market to be used in deciding on the fair value should be the principal market for the asset or liability. If there is no principal market then the fair value should be found in the most advantageous market for the asset or liability. Guidance on the use of fair value for specific assets and liabilities is found in accounting standards, explained in more detail in Chapter 4. The relationship to theories of value is explained in Chapter 14, section 14.9.

2.3 Defining assets

An **asset** is defined as 'a present economic resource controlled by the entity as a result of past events'. An **economic resource** is defined as 'a right that has the potential to produce economic benefits'.[1]

To understand this definition fully, each phrase must be considered separately.

2.3.1 Economic resource

Businesses use resources that have the potential to produce economic benefits. Eventually most resources generate an economic benefit in the form of cash. Some resources generate cash more quickly than others. If the business manufactures goods in order to sell them to customers, those goods have the potential to produce economic benefit through making a sale. That benefit comes to the entity relatively quickly. The business may own a warehouse in which it stores the goods before they are sold. The warehouse has the potential to produce economic benefits because it helps create the cash flow from sale of the goods (by keeping them safe from damage and theft) and also because at some time in the future the warehouse could itself be sold for cash.

The example of the warehouse is relatively easy to understand, but in other cases there may be some uncertainty about whether the resource has the potential to produce economic benefit. When goods are sold to a customer who is allowed time to pay, the customer becomes a **debtor** of the business (a person who owes money to the business) and the amount of the **trade receivable** is regarded as an asset. There may be some uncertainty as to whether the customer will eventually pay for the goods. That uncertainty does not prevent the trade receivable being regarded as an asset but may require some caution as to how the asset is measured in money terms.

The definition uses the word 'right' because sometimes the entity does not have legal ownership of the resource but does have the right to use the resource. Such a right could include an agreement to lease or rent a resource, and a licence allowing exclusive use of a resource.

2.3.2 Controlled by the entity

Control means the ability to obtain the economic benefits and to restrict the access of others. The items which everyone enjoys, such as the benefit of a good motorway giving access to the business or the presence of a highly skilled workforce in a nearby town, provide benefits to the business which are not reported in financial statements because there would be considerable problems in identifying the entity's share of the benefits. If there is no control, the item is omitted.

The condition of control is also included to prevent businesses from leaving out of the statement of financial position (balance sheet) some items which ought to be in there. In past years, practices emerged of omitting an asset and a corresponding liability from a statement of financial position on the grounds that there was no effective obligation remaining in respect of the liability. At the same time, the business carefully retained effective control of the asset by suitable legal agreements. This practice of omitting items from the statement of financial position was felt to be unhelpful to users because it was concealing some of the resources used by the business and concealing the related obligations.

The strongest form of control over an asset is the right of ownership. Section 2.3.1 explains that there are other forms of rights that give control, such as agreement to lease or rent a resource, and a licence allowing exclusive use of a resource.

2.3.3 Past events

Accounting depends on finding some reasonably objective way of confirming that the entity has gained control of the resource. The evidence provided by a past transaction is an objective starting point. A transaction is an agreement between two parties which usually involves exchanging goods or services for cash or a promise to pay cash. (The supplement to Chapter 1 explains basic business transactions in more detail.) Sometimes there is no transaction but there is an event which is sufficient to give this objective evidence. The event could be the performance of a service which, once completed, gives the right to demand payment.

Activity 2.2

Write down five items in your personal possession which you regard as assets. Use the definition given in this section to explain why each item is an asset from your point of view. Then read the next section and compare your list with the examples of business assets. If you are having difficulty in understanding why any item is, or is not, an asset you should consult your lecturer, tutor or other expert in the subject area for a discussion on how to apply the definition in identifying assets.

2.4 Examples of assets

The following items are commonly found in the assets section of the statement of financial position (balance sheet) of a company:

- land and buildings (property) owned by the company
- buildings leased by the company on a 50-year lease
- plant and equipment owned by the company
- equipment leased (rented) by the company under a finance lease
- vehicles
- raw materials
- goods for resale
- finished goods
- work in progress
- trade receivables (amounts due from customers who have promised to pay for goods sold on credit)
- prepaid insurance and rentals
- investments in shares of other companies
- cash held in a bank account.

Do all these items meet the definition of an asset? Tables 2.1 and 2.2 test each item against the aspects of the definition which have already been discussed. Two tables have been used because it is conventional practice to separate assets into current assets and non-current assets. **Current assets** are held with the intention of converting

Table 2.1
Analysis of some frequently occurring non-current assets (fixed assets)

	Economic benefits	Controlled by the entity by means of	Past event
Land and buildings owned by the company	Used in continuing operations of the business; potential for sale of the item.	Ownership.	Signing the contract as evidence of purchase of land and buildings.
Buildings leased (rented) by the company on a 50-year lease	Used in continuing operations of the business.	Contract for exclusive use as a tenant.	Signing a lease agreeing the rental terms.
Plant and equipment owned by the company	Used in continuing operations of the business.	Ownership.	Purchase of plant and equipment, evidenced by receiving the goods and a supplier's invoice.
Equipment used under a finance lease	Used in continuing operations of the business.	Contract for exclusive use.	Signing lease agreeing rental terms.
Vehicles owned by the company	Used in continuing operations of the business.	Ownership.	Purchase of vehicles, evidenced by taking delivery and receiving a supplier's invoice.

them into cash within the business cycle. **Non-current assets**, also called **fixed assets**, are held for continuing use in the business. The business cycle is the period (usually 12 months) during which the peaks and troughs of activity of a business form a pattern which is repeated on a regular basis. For a business selling swimwear, production will take place all winter in preparation for a rush of sales in the summer. Painters and decorators work indoors in the winter and carry out exterior work in the summer. Because many businesses are affected by the seasons of the year, the business cycle is normally 12 months. Some of the answers are fairly obvious but a few require a little further comment here.

First, there are the items of buildings and equipment which are rented under a lease agreement. The benefits of such leases are felt to be so similar to the benefits of ownership that the items are included in the statement of financial position (balance sheet) as assets. Suitable wording is used to describe the different nature of these items so that users, particularly **creditors**, are not misled into believing that the items belong to the business.

Second, it is useful to note at this stage that partly finished items of output may be recorded as assets. The term 'work in progress' is used to describe work of the business which is not yet completed. Examples of such work in progress might be: partly finished items in a manufacturing company; a partly completed motorway being built by a construction company; or a continuing legal case being undertaken by a firm of lawyers. Such items are included as assets because there has been an event in the partial completion of the work and it is capable of completion and eventual payment by a customer for the finished item.

Finally, it is clear that the economic benefits to be produced by these assets have a wide variation in potential risk. This risk is a matter of great interest to those who

Table 2.2
Analysis of some frequently occurring current assets

	Economic benefits	Controlled by the entity by means of	Past event
Raw materials	Used to manufacture goods for sale.	Ownership.	Receiving raw materials into the company's store, evidenced by goods received note.
Goods purchased from supplier for resale	Expectation of sale.	Ownership.	Receiving goods from supplier into the company's store, evidenced by the goods received note.
Finished goods (manufactured by the entity)	Expectation of sale.	Ownership.	Transfer from production line to finished goods store, evidenced by internal transfer form.
Work in progress (partly finished goods)	Expectation of completion and sale.	Ownership.	Evaluation of the state of completion of the work, evidenced by work records.
Trade receivables (amounts due from customers)	Expectation that the customer will pay cash.	Contract for payment.	Delivery of goods to the customer, obliging customer to pay for goods at a future date.
Prepaid insurance premiums	Expectation of continuing insurance cover.	Contract for continuing benefit of insurance cover.	Paying insurance premiums in advance, evidenced by cheque payment.
Investments in shares of other companies	Expectation of dividend income and growth in value of investment, for future sale.	Ownership.	Buying the shares, evidenced by broker's contract note.
Cash held in a bank account	Expectation of using the cash to buy resources which will create further cash.	Ownership.	Depositing cash with the bank, evidenced by bank statement or certificate.

use accounting information, but there are generally no accounting techniques for reporting this risk directly in financial statements. Consequently, it is very important to have adequate descriptions of assets. Accounting information is concerned with the words used to describe items in financial statements, as well as the numbers attributed to them. (The narrative description of business risks is explained in Chapter 14, section 14.10.)

Definition

An **asset** is 'a present economic resource controlled by the entity as a result of past events. An **economic resource** is a right that has the potential to produce economic benefits'.[2]

A **current asset** is an asset that satisfies any of the following criteria:

(a) it is expected to be realised in, or is intended for sale or consumption in, the entity's normal operating cycle;
(b) it is held primarily for the purpose of being traded;
(c) it is expected to be realised within 12 months after the reporting period;
(d) it is cash or a cash equivalent.[3]

A **non-current asset** is any asset that does not meet the definition of a current asset.[4] Non-current assets include tangible, intangible and financial assets of a long-term nature. These are also described as **fixed assets**.[5]

2.5 Recognition of assets

When an economic resource has passed the tests of definition of an asset, it has still not acquired the right to a place in the statement of financial position (balance sheet). To do so it must meet further guidance on recognition. **Recognition** means depicting an item by means of words and amounts within the main financial statements in such a way that the item is included in the arithmetic totals. An item which is reported in the notes to the accounts is said to be **disclosed** but *not* **recognised**.

2.5.1 Recognition criteria

The recognition criteria are expressed as in the following definition.

Definition

An **asset** is **recognised** in the statement of financial position (balance sheet) when:

- it meets the definition of an asset; and
- the resulting information is relevant and provides a faithful representation; and
- the benefits of the information exceed the costs of providing it.[6]

Information might not be relevant if, for example, it is uncertain whether the asset exists, if it is unlikely that future flows of economic benefits will occur or if there is very significant measurement uncertainty associated with the item.

The *Conceptual Framework* sets out broad guidance that provides a narrative discussion of the thought process to go through in making recognition decisions. The IASB then applies this thought process in developing specific accounting standards.

The following are indicators that recognition might *not* provide relevant information about an asset:

(a) The range of possible outcomes is extremely wide and the likelihood of each outcome is exceptionally difficult to estimate.
(b) An asset exists, but there is only a low probability that an inflow of economic benefits will result.
(c) Identifying the resource is unusually difficult.
(d) Measuring a resource requires unusually difficult or exceptionally subjective allocations of cash flows that do not relate solely to the item being measured.

2.5.2   Non-recognition

Consider some items which pass the definition test but do not appear in a statement of financial position (balance sheet):

- the workforce of a business (a human resource)
- the strength of the management team (another human resource)
- the reputation established for the quality of the product
- the quality of the regular customers
- a tax refund which will be claimable against profits in two years' time.

These items all meet the conditions of an economic resource, control and a past event. However, they all have associated with them a high level of uncertainty. The range of possible outcomes is extremely wide and the likelihood of each outcome is exceptionally difficult to estimate. This means that recognition would not meet the test of relevance.

The workforce as a whole may be reliable and predictable, but unexpected circumstances can come to all and the illness or death of a member of the management team in particular can have a serious impact on the perceived value of the business. A crucial member of the workforce might give notice and leave. In relation to the product, a reputation for quality may become well established and those who would like to include brand names in the statement of financial position (balance sheet) argue for the permanence of the reputation. Others illustrate the relative transience of such a reputation by bringing out a list of well-known biscuits or sweets of 30 years ago and asking who has heard of them today. Reliable customers of good quality are valuable to a business, but they are also fickle and may change their allegiance at a moment's notice. The tax refund may be measurable in amount, but will there be taxable profits in two years' time against which the refund may be claimed?

It could be argued that the assets which are not recognised in the financial statements should be reported by way of a general description in a note to the accounts. In practice, this rarely happens because accounting tries to avoid raising hopes which might subsequently be dashed. This cautious approach is part of what is referred to more generally as **prudence** in accounting practice.

2.6 Measurement of assets

Assets in the financial statements may be measured at **historical cost** or at **fair value**, depending on the nature of the asset and the requirements of accounting standards under which an entity is reporting.

2.6.1   Historical cost of assets

In historical cost accounting, assets have initially been measured at their cost on the date they were acquired. Liabilities have been measured at the amount agreed as owing on the date that the borrowing took place. In the historical cost system, the accounting treatment after the date of acquisition depends on the nature of the asset as described in Table 2.1.

- ***Non-current assets*** (usually those held for long-term use in the business) are valued at historical cost less **depreciation**. Depreciation is a measure of the use of the asset over its life. The calculation of depreciation is explained in more detail in Chapter 8.
- ***Current assets***, such as inventories, accounts receivable and cash, usually remain recorded at historical cost until they are used in the operations of the business or are sold. The methods of recording current assets are explained in more detail in Chapter 9.

2.6.2 Fair value of assets

Fair value is the price that would be received to sell an asset in an orderly transaction between market participants at the measurement date.

- *Non-current assets* are held for use in the business and so their fair value cannot be measured directly through selling them. Instead the reporting entity must estimate the fair value of an asset of similar type and condition. Methods of making this estimate are described in more detail in Chapter 8.
- *Current assets* are used or sold within the reporting period. Their value in a market can usually be reported relatively easily. Methods of reporting the fair value of current assets are described in more detail in Chapter 9.

2.7 Defining liabilities

A **liability** is defined as 'a present obligation of the entity to transfer an economic resource as a result of past events'. An **economic resource** is defined as 'a right that has the potential to produce economic benefits'.[7]

The most familiar types of liabilities arise in those situations where specific amounts of money are owed by an entity to specific persons called creditors. There is usually no doubt about the amount of money owed and the date on which payment is due. Such persons may be **trade creditors**, the general name for those suppliers who have provided goods or services in return for a promise of payment later. Amounts due to **trade creditors** are described as **trade payables**. Other types of creditors include bankers or other lenders who have lent money to the entity.

There are also situations where an obligation is known to exist but the amount due is uncertain. That might be the case where a court of law has found an entity negligent in failing to meet some duty of care to a customer. The company will have to pay compensation to the customer but the amount has yet to be determined.

Even more difficult is the case where an obligation might exist if some future event happens. Neither the existence nor the amount of the obligation is known with certainty at the date of the financial statements. An example would arise where one company has guaranteed the overdraft borrowing of another in the event of that other company defaulting on repayment. At the present time there is no reason to suppose a default will occur, but it remains a possibility for the future.

The definition of a liability tries to encompass all these degrees of variation and uncertainty. It has to be analysed for each separate word or phrase in order to understand the full implications.

2.7.1 Present obligation

A legal obligation is evidence that a liability exists because there is another person or entity having a legal claim to payment. Most liabilities arise because a legal obligation exists, either by contract or by statute law.

However, a legal obligation is not a necessary condition. There may be a commercial penalty faced by the business if it takes a certain action. For example, a decision to close a line of business will lead to the knowledge of likely redundancy costs long before the employees are actually made redundant and the legal obligation becomes due. There may be an obligation imposed by custom and practice, such as a condition of the trade that a penalty operates for those who pay bills late. There may be a future obligation caused by actions and events of the current period where, for example, a profit taken by a company now may lead to a taxation liability at a later date which does not arise at this time because of the wording of the tax laws.

The wording 'present obligation' is intended to indicate that the entity has no practical ability to avoid the transfer and the amount is determined by reference to past actions or benefits received. An entity would have no practical ability to avoid a transfer if, for example, avoiding the transfer would cause significant business disruption or have economic consequences significantly more adverse than the transfer itself. Another case would be that the transfer could be avoided only by liquidating the entity or ceasing trading.

2.7.2   Transfer of economic resource

The resource of cash is the economic benefit transferable in respect of most obligations. The transfer of property in settlement of an obligation would also constitute a transfer of economic benefits. More rarely, economic benefits could be transferred by offering a resource such as labour in settlement of an obligation.

Activity 2.3

Write down five items in your personal experience which you regard as liabilities. Use the definition given in this section to explain why each item is a liability from your point of view. Then read the next section and compare your list with the examples of business liabilities. If you are having difficulty in understanding why any item is, or is not, a liability you should consult your lecturer, tutor or other expert in the subject area for a discussion on how to apply the definition in identifying liabilities.

2.7.3   Past events

A decision to buy supplies or to acquire a new non-current asset is not sufficient to create a liability. It could be argued that the decision is an event creating an obligation, but it is such a difficult type of event to verify that accounting prefers not to rely too much on the point at which a decision is made.

Most liabilities are related to a transaction. Normally the transaction involves receiving goods or services, receiving delivery of new non-current assets such as vehicles and equipment, or borrowing money from a lender. In all these cases there is documentary evidence that the transaction has taken place.

Where the existence of a liability is somewhat in doubt, subsequent events may help to confirm its existence at the date of the financial statements. For example, when a company offers to repair goods under a warranty arrangement, the liability exists from the moment the warranty is offered. It may, however, be unclear as to the extent of the liability until a pattern of customer complaints is established. Until that time there will have to be an estimate of the liability. In accounting this estimate is called a **provision**. Amounts referred to as **provisions** are included under the general heading of liabilities.

2.8   Examples of liabilities

Here is a list of items commonly found in the liabilities section of the statements of financial position (balance sheets) of companies:

- bank loans and overdrafts
- trade payables (amounts due to suppliers of goods and services on credit terms)
- taxation payable
- accruals (amounts owing, such as unpaid expenses)
- provision for deferred taxation
- long-term loans.

The first two items in this list would be classified as **current liabilities** because they will become due for payment within one year of the date of the financial statements. The last two items would be classified as **non-current liabilities** because they will remain due by the business for longer than one year.

Definitions

> A **liability** is a present obligation of the entity to transfer an economic resource as a result of past events. An **economic resource** is a right that has the potential to produce economic benefits.[8]
>
> A **current liability** is a liability which satisfies any of the following criteria:
>
> (a) it is expected to be settled in the entity's normal operating cycle;
> (b) it is held primarily for the purpose of being traded;
> (c) it is due to be settled within 12 months after the reporting period.[9]
>
> A **non-current liability** is any liability that does not meet the definition of a current liability.[10] Non-current liabilities are also described as **long-term liabilities.**

An analysis of some common types of liability is given in Table 2.3.

Table 2.3
Analysis of some common types of liability

Type of liability	Obligation	Transfer of economic resource	Past event
Bank loans and overdrafts (repayable on demand or in the very short term)	The entity must repay the loans on the due date or on demand.	Cash, potentially within a short space of time.	Receiving the borrowed funds.
Trade payables (amounts due to suppliers of goods and services)	Suppliers must be paid for the goods and services supplied, usually about one month after the supplier's invoice is received.	Cash within a short space of time.	Taking delivery of the goods or service and receiving the supplier's invoice.
Taxation payable (tax due on company profits after the financial year-end date)	Cash payable to HMRC. Penalties are charged if tax is not paid on the due date.	Cash.	Making profits in the accounting year and submitting an assessment of tax payable.
Accruals (a term meaning 'other amounts owing', such as unpaid bills)	Any expense incurred must be reported as an accrued liability (e.g. electricity used, gas used, unpaid wages), if it has not been paid at the financial year-end date.	Cash.	Consuming electricity or gas, using employees' services, receiving bills from suppliers (note that it is not necessary to receive a gas bill in order to know that you owe money for gas used).
Provision for deferred taxation (tax due in respect of present profits but having a delayed payment date allowed by tax law)	Legislation allows companies to defer payment of tax in some cases. The date of future payment may not be known as yet.	Cash eventually, but could be in the longer term.	Making profits or incurring expenditure now which meets conditions of legislation allowing deferral.
Long-term loans (sometimes called debenture loans)	Statement of financial position will show repayment dates of long-term loans and any repayment conditions attached.	Cash.	Received borrowed funds.

2.9 Recognition of liabilities

As with an asset, when an item has passed the tests of definition of a liability it may still fail the guidance on recognition. In practice, because of the concern for prudence, it is much more difficult for a liability to escape the statement of financial position (balance sheet).

The recognition criteria for a liability uses wording which mirrors those used for recognition of the asset. The only difference is that the economic benefits now flow *from* the enterprise. The conditions for recognition are expressed in the following way:

Definition

> A **liability** is **recognised** in the statement of financial position (balance sheet) when:
>
> - it meets the definition of a liability; and
> - the resulting information is relevant and provides a faithful representation; and
> - the benefits of the information exceed the costs of providing it.[11]

Information might not be relevant if, for example, it is uncertain whether the liability exists, or it is unlikely that future transfers of economic benefits will occur or there is very significant measurement uncertainty associated with the item.

The following are indicators that recognition might *not* provide relevant information about a liability:

(a) The range of possible outcomes is extremely wide and the likelihood of each outcome is exceptionally difficult to estimate.

(b) A liability exists, but there is only a low probability that a transfer of economic benefits will result.

(c) Identifying the resource to be transferred is unusually difficult.

(d) Measuring the obligation requires unusually difficult or exceptionally subjective allocations of cash flows that do not relate solely to the item being measured.

Examples of liabilities which are not recognised in the statement of financial position (balance sheet) are:

- a commitment to purchase new machinery next year (but not a firm contract);
- a remote, but potential, liability for a defective product, where no court action has yet commenced;
- a guarantee given to support the bank overdraft of another company, where there is very little likelihood of being called upon to meet the guarantee.

Because of the prudent nature of accounting, the liabilities which are not recognised in the statement of financial position (balance sheet) may well be reported in note form under the heading **contingent liabilities**. This is referred to as **disclosure** by way of a note to the accounts.

Looking more closely at the list of liabilities which are not recognised, we see that the commitment to purchase is not legally binding and therefore the outflow of resources may not occur. The claim based on a product defect appears to be uncertain as to occurrence and as to amount. If there has been a court case or a settlement out of court then there should be a provision for further claims of a similar nature. In the case of the guarantee the facts as presented make it appear that an outflow of resources is unlikely. However, such appearances have in the past been deceiving to all concerned and there is often interesting reading in the note to the financial statements which describes the contingent liabilities.

2.10 Measurement of liabilities

Liabilities in the financial statements may be measured at **historical cost** or at **fair value**, depending on the nature of the liability and the requirements of accounting standards under which an entity is reporting.

2.10.1 Historical cost of liabilities

Under historical cost accounting, liabilities have been measured at the amount agreed as owing on the date that the borrowing took place. In the historical cost system the accounting treatment after the date of acquisition depends on the nature of the liability as described in Table 2.3.

- *Current liabilities*, such as accounts payable and accruals, usually remain recorded at historical cost until they are paid or settled. The methods of recording current liabilities are explained in more detail in Chapter 10.
- *Non-current liabilities*, extending over a period of years, are in some cases reported at historical cost throughout the period of their life. In other cases, the complexities of the interest charges and repayment conditions are used in calculating the spread of the historical cost obligation over the period of the loan. The methods of recording non-current liabilities are explained in more detail in Chapter 11.

2.10.2 Fair value

Fair value is the price that would be paid to transfer a liability in an orderly transaction between market participants at the measurement date. This idea is sometimes difficult intuitively because it can be hard to imagine why anyone would take on a liability. Let's suppose Chris owes Peter £100, due for payment in one year's time. Typical interest rates are 4% per annum. Chris says to Robin, 'I don't want to continue owing money to Peter. What can I pay you now to take on this liability?' The lowest payment Robin will accept is £96.15 because, if invested at 4%, that will grow to £100 in one year's time. Robin can then repay Peter. The fair value is the price at which Robin would be indifferent, which is £96.15.

2.11 Defining the ownership interest

The ownership interest is defined in the *Conceptual Framework* as equity. **Equity** is the residual interest in the assets of the entity after deducting all its liabilities.[12]

The term **net assets** is used as a shorter way of saying 'total assets less total liabilities'. Because the ownership interest is the residual item, it will be the owners of the business who benefit from any increase in assets after liabilities have been met. Conversely it will be the owners who bear the loss of any decrease in assets after liabilities have been met. The ownership interest applies to the entire net assets. It is sometimes described as the owners' wealth, although economists would take a view that the owners' wealth extends beyond the items recorded in a statement of financial position (balance sheet).

If there is only one owner, as in the sole trader's business, then there is no problem as to how the ownership interest is shared. In a partnership, the partnership agreement will usually state the profit-sharing ratio, which may also be applied to the net assets shown in the statement of financial position (balance sheet). If nothing is said in the partnership agreement, the profit sharing must be based on equal shares for each partner.

In a company the arrangements for sharing the net assets depend on the type of ownership chosen. The owners may hold **ordinary shares** in the company, which entitle them to a share of any dividend declared and a share in net assets on closing down the business. The ownership interest is in direct proportion to the number of shares held.

Some investors like to hold **preference shares**, which give them a preference (although not an automatic right) to receive a dividend before any ordinary share dividend is declared. The rights of preference shareholders are set out in the articles of association of the company. Some will have the right to share in a surplus of net assets on winding up, but others will only be entitled to the amount of capital originally contributed.

Definitions

> The **ownership interest** is called **equity** in the IASB *Conceptual Framework*.
>
> **Equity** is the residual interest in the assets of the entity after deducting all its liabilities.
>
> **Net assets** means the difference between the total assets and the total liabilities of the business: it represents the amount of the ownership interest in the entity.

2.12 Recognition of the ownership interest

There can be no separate recognition criteria for the ownership interest because it is the result of recognising assets and recognising liabilities. Having made those decisions on assets and liabilities the enterprise has used up its freedom of choice.

2.13 Changes in the ownership interest

It has already been explained that the owner will become better off where the net assets are increasing. The owner will become worse off where the net assets are decreasing. To measure the increase or decrease in net assets, two accounting equations are needed:

At time t = 0	**Assets$_{(t0)}$ – Liabilities$_{(t0)}$**	equals	**Ownership interest$_{(t0)}$**
At time t = 1	**Assets$_{(t1)}$ – Liabilities$_{(t1)}$**	equals	**Ownership interest$_{(t1)}$**

Taking one equation away from the other may be expressed in words as:

Change in (assets – liabilities)	equals	**Change in ownership interest**

or, using the term 'net assets' instead of 'assets – liabilities':

Change in net assets	equals	**Change in ownership interest**

The change in the ownership interest between these two points in time is a measure of how much better or worse off the owner has become, through the activities of the business. The owner is better off when the ownership interest at time t = 1 is higher than that at time t = 0. To calculate the ownership interest at each point in time requires knowledge of all assets and all liabilities at each point in time. It is particularly interesting to know about the changes in assets and liabilities which have arisen from the day-to-day operations of the business.

The term **revenue** is given to any increase in the ownership interest arising from the operations of the business and caused by an increase in an asset which is greater than any decrease in another asset (or increase in a liability). The term **expense** is given to any reduction in the ownership interest arising from the operations of the business and caused by a reduction in an asset to the extent that it is not replaced by a corresponding increase in another asset (or reduction in a liability).

The owner or owners of the business may also change the amount of the ownership interest by deciding to contribute more cash or other resources in order to finance the business, or deciding to withdraw some of the cash and other resources previously contributed or accumulated. The amount contributed to the business by the owner is usually referred to as **capital**. Decisions about the level of capital to invest in the business are financing decisions. These financing decisions are normally distinguished separately from the results of operations.

So another equation may now be derived as a subdivision of the basic accounting equation, showing analysis of the changes in the ownership interest.

Change in ownership interest	equals	Capital contributed/withdrawn by the ownership plus Revenue minus Expenses

The difference between revenue and expenses is more familiarly known as profit. So a further subdivision of the basic equation is:

Profit	equals	Revenue minus Expenses

2.13.1 Revenue and expense

Revenue is created by a transaction or event arising during the operations of the business which causes an increase in the ownership interest. It could be due to an increase in cash or trade receivables, received in exchange for goods or services. Depending on the nature of the business, revenue may be described as sales, turnover, fees, commission, royalties or rent.

An **expense** is caused by a transaction or event arising during the operations of the business which causes a decrease in the ownership interest. It could be due to an outflow or depletion of assets such as cash, inventory (stock) or non-current assets (fixed assets). It could be due to a liability being incurred without a matching asset being acquired.

Definitions

Revenue is income arising in the course of an entity's ordinary activities.[13]

Income is defined as 'increases in assets or decreases in liabilities that result in increases in equity, other than those relating to contributions from holders of equity claims'.[14]

Expenses are defined as 'decreases in assets or increases in liabilities that result in decreases in equity, other than those relating to distributions to holders of equity claims'.[15]

Contributions from equity participants means new share capital contributed. Distributions to equity participants means dividends paid or share capital returned. These topics are dealt with in Chapter 12.

2.13.2 Position after a change has occurred

At the end of the accounting period there will be a new level of assets and liabilities recorded. These assets and liabilities will have resulted from the activities of the business during the period, creating revenue and incurring expenses. The owner may also have made voluntary contributions or withdrawals of capital as a financing decision. The equation in the following form reflects that story:

Assets minus **Liabilities** at the end of the period	equals	**Ownership interest at the start of the period** plus **Capital contributed/ withdrawn in the period** plus **Revenue of the period** minus **Expenses of the period**

2.14 Assurance for users of financial statements

The definitions of assets and liabilities refer to expected flows into or out of the business. The recognition criteria refer to the evidence that the expected flows in or out will occur. The directors of a company are responsible for ensuring that the financial statements presented by them are a faithful representation of the assets and liabilities of the business and of the transactions and events relating to those assets and liabilities. Shareholders need reassurance that the directors, as their agents, have carried out this responsibility with sufficient care. To give themselves this reassurance, the shareholders appoint a firm of auditors to examine the records of the business and give an opinion as to whether the financial statements correspond to the accounting records and present a true and fair view. (Chapter 1 explained the position of directors as agents of the shareholders. Chapter 4 explains the regulations relating to company financial statements and the appointment of auditors.)

Meet David and Leona again as they continue their conversation on the work of the auditor and its value to the shareholder as a user of accounting information provided by a company.

DAVID: *I've now coated your ceiling with apple green emulsion. In return you promised to convince me that I rely on audited accounting information more than I realise. Here is your chance to do that. I was looking today at the annual report of a company which is a manufacturing business. There is a production centre in the UK but most of the production work is carried out in Spain where the operating costs are lower. The distribution operation is carried out from Swindon, selling to retail stores all over the UK. There is an export market, mainly in France, but the company has only scratched the surface of that market. Let's start with something easy – the inventories (stocks) of finished goods which are held at the factory in Spain and the distribution depot in Swindon.*

LEONA: *You've shown right away how limited your understanding is, by choosing the asset where you need the auditor's help the most. Everything can go wrong with inventories (stocks)! Think of the accounting equation:*

Assets – Liabilities = Ownership interest

If an asset is overstated, the ownership interest will be overstated. That means the profit for the period, as reported, is higher than it should be. But you won't know that because everything will appear to be in order from the accounts. You have told me repeatedly that you buy the future, not the past, but I know you look to the current profit and loss account as an indicator of future trends of profit. And so do all your friends.

DAVID: *How can the asset of finished goods inventories be overstated? It's quite a solid item.*

LEONA: *There are two types of potential error – the physical counting of the inventory and the valuation placed on it. There are two main causes of error, one being carelessness and the other an intention to deceive. I've seen situations where the stocktakers count the same stack of goods twice because they don't have a marker pen to put a cross on the items counted. I've also heard of situations where items are counted twice deliberately. We always attend the end-of-year counting of the inventory and observe the process carefully. I wish there weren't so many companies with December year-ends. Counting inventory on 2 January is never a good start to the new year.*

DAVID: *I suppose I can believe that people lose count but how does the valuation go wrong? All companies say that they value inventories at cost as the usual rule. How can the cost of an item be open to doubt?*

LEONA: *Answering that question needs a textbook in itself. The subject comes under the heading of 'management accounting'. Take the goods that you know are manufactured in Spain. There are costs of materials to make the goods, and labour to convert raw materials into finished goods. There are also the running costs of the production unit, which are called the overheads. There is an unbelievable variety of ways of bringing those costs together into one item of product. How much does the company tell you about all that? I know the answer – nothing.*

DAVID: *Well, I could always ask them at a briefing meeting. I usually ask about the profit margin on the goods sold, rather than the value of the goods unsold. But I can see that if the inventories figure is wrong then so is the profit margin. Do you have a systematic procedure for checking each kind of asset?*

LEONA: *Our magic word is **CEAVOP**. That stands for:*

Completeness of information presented.
Existence of the asset or liability at a given date.
Amount of the transaction is correctly recorded.
Valuation reported for assets and liabilities is appropriate.
Occurrence of the transaction or event took place in the period.
Presentation and disclosure is in accordance with regulations and accounting standards or other comparable regulations.

Every aspect of that list has to be checked for each of the assets and liabilities you see in the statement of financial position. We need good-quality evidence of each aspect before we sign off the audit report.

DAVID: *I probably believe that you do a great deal of work with your CEAVOP. But next time I come round to paint your kitchen I'll bring a list of the situations where the auditors don't appear to have asked all the questions in that list.*

2.15 Summary

This chapter has set out the accounting equation for a situation at any one point in time:

Assets	minus	**Liabilities**	equals	**Ownership interest**

Key points are:

- An **asset** is a present economic resource controlled by the entity as a result of past events. An **economic resource** is a right that has the potential to produce economic benefits.
- A **current asset** is an asset that satisfies any of the following criteria:
  (a) it is expected to be realised in, or is intended for sale or consumption in, the entity's normal operating cycle;

(b) it is held primarily for the purpose of being traded;

(c) it is expected to be realised within 12 months after the date of the financial year-end;

(d) it is cash or a cash equivalent.

- A **non-current asset** is any asset that does not meet the definition of a current asset. Non-current assets include tangible, intangible and financial assets of a long-term nature. These are also described as **fixed assets**.

- A **liability** is a present obligation of the entity to transfer an economic resource as a result of past events. An **economic resource** is a right that has the potential to produce economic benefits.

- A **current liability** is a liability which satisfies any of the following criteria:

  (a) it is expected to be settled in the entity's normal operating cycle;

  (b) it is held primarily for the purpose of being traded;

  (c) it is due to be settled within 12 months after the date of the financial year-end.

- A **non-current liability** is any liability that does not meet the definition of a current liability. Non-current liabilities are also described as **long-term liabilities**.

- The **ownership interest** is called **equity** in the *Conceptual Framework*.

- **Equity** is the residual interest in the assets of the entity after deducting all its liabilities.

- **Net assets** means the difference between the total assets and the total liabilities of the business: it represents the amount of the ownership interest in the entity.

- **Recognition** means reporting an economic resource in the financial statements, in words and in amount, so that the amount is included in the arithmetic totals of the financial statements. Any other form of reporting by way of note is called disclosure. The criteria for recognition of assets and liabilities are similar in wording.

- At the end of an accounting period the assets and liabilities are reported in a statement of financial position (balance sheet). Changes in the assets and liabilities during the period have caused changes in the ownership interest through revenue and expenses of operations. The owner may also have voluntarily added or withdrawn capital. The final position is explained on the left-hand side of the equation and the movement to that position is explained on the right-hand side:

Assets minus **Liabilities** at the end of the period	equals	**Ownership interest at the start of the period** plus **Capital contributed/withdrawn in the period** plus **Revenue of the period** minus **Expenses of the period**

- As with any equation, it is possible to make this version more complex by adding further details. That is not necessary for the purpose of explaining the basic processes, but the equation will be revisited later in the book when some of the problems of accounting are opened up. The helpful aspect of the accounting equation is that it can always be used as a basis for arguing a feasible answer. The limitation is that it cannot give an opinion on the most appropriate answer when more than one option is feasible.

In Chapter 3 there is an explanation of how the information represented by the accounting equation is displayed in a form which is useful to the user groups identified in Chapter 1.

Further reading

IASB (2016), *The Conceptual Framework for Financial Reporting*, 'The Elements of Financial Statements' and 'Recognition and derecognition', International Accounting Standards Board.

QUESTIONS

The Questions section of each chapter has three types of question. 'Test your understanding' questions to help you review your reading are in the 'A' series of questions. You will find the answers to these by reading and thinking about the material in the book. 'Application' questions to test your ability to apply technical skills are in the 'B' series of questions. Questions requiring you to show skills in problem solving and evaluation are in the 'C' series of questions. A letter [S] indicates that there is a solution at the end of the book. Other solutions are provided in the Instructor's Manual, where there are further questions parallel to those set out here.

A Test your understanding

A2.1 Write out the basic form of the accounting equation. (Section 2.2)

A2.2 Define an asset and explain each part of the definition. (Section 2.3)

A2.3 Give five examples of items which are assets. (Section 2.4)

A2.4 Use the definition to explain why each of the items in your answer to A2.3 is an asset. (Section 2.4)

A2.5 Explain what 'recognition' means in accounting. (Section 2.5)

A2.6 State the criteria for recognition of an asset. (Section 2.5)

A2.7 Explain why an item may pass the definition test but fail the recognition conditions for an asset. (Section 2.5)

A2.8 Give three examples of items which pass the definition test for an asset but fail the recognition criteria. (Section 2.5)

A2.9 Some football clubs include the players in the statement of financial position (balance sheet) as an asset. Others do not. Give the arguments to support each approach. (Section 2.5)

A2.10 Explain what is meant by the 'fair value of an asset'. (Section 2.6)

A2.11 Define a liability and explain each part of the definition. (Section 2.7)

A2.12 Give five examples of items which are liabilities. (Section 2.8)

A2.13 Use the definition to explain why each of the items in your answer to A2.11 is a liability. (Section 2.8)

A2.14 State the criteria for recognition of a liability. (Section 2.9)

A2.15 Explain why an item may pass the definition test but fail the recognition criteria for a liability. (Section 2.9)

A2.16 Explain what is meant by the 'fair value of a liability'. (Section 2.10)

A2.17 Define the term 'equity'. (Section 2.11)

A2.18 Explain what is meant by 'net assets'. (Section 2.11)

A2.19 Set out the accounting equation for a change in the ownership interest. (Section 2.13)

A2.20 Define 'revenue' and 'expenses'. (Section 2.13.1)

A2.21 Set out the accounting equation which represents the position after a change has occurred. (Section 2.13.2)

A2.22 Explain the auditor's approach to giving assurance about assets and liabilities. (Section 2.14)

B   Application

B2.1 [S]

Classify each of the items in the following list as: asset; liability; neither an asset nor a liability.

(a) cash at bank
(b) loan from the bank
(c) letter from the bank promising an overdraft facility at any time in the next three months
(d) trade receivable (an amount due from a customer who has promised to pay later)
(e) trade receivable (an amount due from a customer who has promised to pay later but has apparently disappeared without leaving a forwarding address)
(f) trade payable (an amount due to a supplier of goods who has not yet received payment from the business)
(g) inventory of finished goods (fashion clothing stored ahead of the spring sales)
(h) inventory of finished goods (fashion clothing left over after the spring sales)
(i) investment in shares of another company where the share price is rising
(j) investment in shares of another company where the share price is falling
(k) lender of five-year loan to the business
(l) customer to whom the business has offered a 12-month warranty to repair goods free of charge
(m) a motor vehicle owned by the business
(n) a motor vehicle rented by the business for one year
(o) an office building owned by the business
(p) an office building rented by the business on a 99-year lease, with 60 years' lease period remaining.

B2.2 [S]

Explain whether each of the items from question B2.1 above which you have identified as assets and liabilities would also meet the criteria for recognition of the item in the statement of financial position (balance sheet).

B2.3 [S]

Explain why each of the following items would not meet either the definition or the recognition criteria of an asset of the business:

(a) a letter from the owner of the business, addressed to the bank manager, promising to guarantee the bank overdraft of the business
(b) a list of the customers of the business
(c) an order received from a customer
(d) the benefit of employing a development engineer with a high level of 'know-how' specifically relevant to the business
(e) money spent on an advertising campaign to boost sales
(f) structural repairs to a building.

C   Problem solving and evaluation

C2.1

The following information has been gathered from the accounting records of Pets Parlour:

Assets and liabilities at 31 December Year 4

	£
Cash at bank	500
Borrowings	6,000
Trade receivables (debtors)	5,000
Property, plant and equipment	29,000

Revenue and expenses for the year ended 31 December Year 4

	£
Fees charged for work done	20,000
Interest paid on borrowings	1,000
Administration costs incurred	1,500
Salaries paid to employees	14,000

Required

Using the accounting equation, calculate:

(a) The amount of ownership interest at 31 December Year 4.
(b) The amount of net profit for the year.
(c) The amount of the ownership interest at 1 January Year 4.

Activities for study groups

Obtain the annual report of a listed company. From the statement of financial position (balance sheet) list the items shown as assets and liabilities. (This will require you to look in detail at the notes to the accounts using the references on the face of the statement of financial position (balance sheet). Share out the list of assets and liabilities so that each person has four or five assets and four or five liability items.

1 Separately, using the definitions and recognition criteria, prepare a short statement explaining why each item on your list passes the tests of definition and recognition. State the evidence you would expect to see, as auditor, to confirm the expected future inflow of economic benefit from any asset and the expected future outflow of benefit from any liability.

2 Present your explanations to the group and together prepare a list of assets and a separate list of liabilities in order of the uncertainty which attaches to the expected future benefit.

3 Read the 'contingent liability' note, if there is one, to find examples of liabilities which have not been recognised but have been disclosed. Why will you not find a 'contingent asset' note?

Notes and references

1. IASB (2016), *Conceptual Framework.*
2. *Ibid.*
3. IAS 1 (2016), para. 66.
4. *Ibid.*
5. IAS 1 para. 67 permits the use of alternative descriptions for non-current assets provided the meaning is clear.
6. IASB (2016), *Conceptual Framework.*
7. *Ibid.*
8. *Ibid.*
9. IAS 1 (2016), para. 69.
10. *Ibid.*
11. IASB (2016), *Conceptual Framework.*
12. *Ibid.*
13. *Ibid.*
14. *Ibid.*
15. IASB (2016), *Conceptual Framework.*

Debit and credit bookkeeping

You do not have to read this supplement to be able to progress through the rest of the textbook. In the main body of each chapter the explanations are all given in terms of changes in elements of the accounting equation. However, for those who would like to know how debits and credits work, each chapter will have a supplement putting into debit and credit form the material contained in the chapter.

Recording in ledger accounts

The double-entry system of bookkeeping records business transactions in ledger accounts. It makes use of the fact that there are two aspects to every transaction when analysed in terms of the accounting equation.

A ledger account accumulates the increases and reductions either in a category of business activities such as sales or in dealings with individual customers and suppliers.

Ledger accounts may be subdivided. Sales could be subdivided into home sales and export sales. Separate ledger accounts might be kept for each type of non-current asset, e.g. buildings and machinery. The ledger account for machinery might be subdivided as office machinery and production machinery.

Ledger accounts for rent, business rates and property insurance might be kept separately or the business might instead choose to keep one ledger account to record transactions in all of these items, giving them the collective name administrative expenses. The decision would depend on the number of transactions in an accounting period and on whether it was useful to have separate records.

The managers of the business have discretion to combine or subdivide ledger accounts to suit the information requirements of the business concerned.

Using the accounting equation

Before entries are made in ledger accounts, the double entry system of bookkeeping assigns to each aspect of a business transaction a debit or a **credit** notation, based on the analysis of the transaction using the accounting equation.

In its simplest form the accounting equation is stated as:

Assets	minus	**Liabilities**	equals	**Ownership interest**

To derive the debit and credit rules it is preferable to rearrange the equation so that there is no minus sign.

Assets	equals	**Liabilities**	plus	**Ownership interest**

There are three elements to the equation and each one of these elements may either *increase* or *decrease* as a result of a transaction or event. The six possibilities are set out in Table 2.4.

Table 2.4
Combinations of increases and decreases of the main elements of transactions

Left-hand side of the equation

Assets	Increase	Decrease

Right-hand side of the equation

Liabilities	Decrease	Increase
Ownership interest	Decrease	Increase

The double-entry bookkeeping system uses this classification (which preserves the symmetry of the equation) to distinguish debit and credit entries as shown in Table 2.5.

Table 2.5
Rules of debit and credit for ledger entries, basic accounting equation

	Debit entries in a ledger account	*Credit entries in a ledger account*
Left-hand side of the equation		
Asset	Increase	Decrease
Right-hand side of the equation		
Liability	Decrease	Increase
Ownership interest	Decrease	Increase

It was shown in the main body of the chapter that the ownership interest may be increased by:

- earning revenue; and
- new capital contributed by the owner;

and that the ownership interest may be decreased by:

- incurring expenses; and
- capital withdrawn by the owner.

So the 'ownership interest' section of Table 2.5 may be expanded as shown in Table 2.6.

That is all you ever have to know about the rules of bookkeeping. All the rest can be reasoned from this table. For any transaction there will be two aspects. (If you find there are more than two, the transaction needs breaking down into simpler steps.) For each aspect there will be a ledger account. Taking each aspect in turn you ask yourself: *Is this an asset, a liability, or an aspect of the ownership interest?* Then you ask yourself: *Is it an increase or a decrease?* From Table 2.6 you then know immediately whether to make a debit or a credit entry.

Examples of the application of the rules of debit and credit recording are given in the supplement to Chapter 5 for a service business and in the supplement to Chapter 6 for a manufacturing business. They will also be used in later chapters to explain how particular transactions are reported.

Table 2.6
Rules of debit and credit for ledger entries, distinguishing different aspects of ownership interest

	Debit entries in a ledger account	Credit entries in a ledger account
Left-hand side of the equation		
Asset	Increase	Decrease
Right-hand side of the equation		
Liability	Decrease	Increase
Ownership interest	Expense	Revenue
	Capital withdrawn	Capital contributed

S Test your understanding

(The answer to each of the following questions is either **debit** or **credit**)

S2.1   What is the bookkeeping entry for an increase in an asset?

S2.2   What is the bookkeeping entry for a decrease in a liability?

S2.3   What is the bookkeeping entry for an increase in an expense?

S2.4   What is the bookkeeping entry for a withdrawal of owner's capital?

S2.5   What is the bookkeeping entry for an increase in revenue?

Chapter 3

Financial statements from the accounting equation

REAL WORLD CASE

AstraZeneca plc: cash flow

Extracts from Annual Report

We are a global, science-led biopharmaceutical business.

Return to shareholders

Revenue from the sale of our medicines generates cash flow, which helps us fund business investment. It also enables us to follow our progressive dividend policy and meet our debt service obligations. This involves balancing the interests of our business, financial creditors and shareholders. See the Financial Review from page 70 for more information.

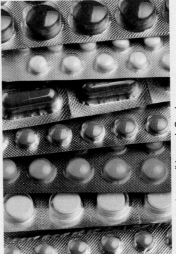

Cash flow and liquidity – 2014

Net cash generated from operating activities was $7,058 million in the year ended 31 December 2014, compared with $7,400 million in 2013. Reductions in working capital partially offset the lower operating profit and higher tax payments. Working capital movements were principally driven by general increases in trade payables and accruals as a result of our increased R&D and SG&A spend, an increase in the US rebate and chargeback liabilities as described on page 82, an additional year's Branded Pharmaceutical Fee and a reduction in trade receivables principally in Japan and the US. Non-cash and other movements include $512 million relating to fair value adjustments on contingent consideration arising from business combinations. Investment cash outflows of $7,125 million (2013: $3,112 million) included $3,804 million (2013: $1,158 million) on completion of business acquisitions, inclusive of BMS's share of the global diabetes alliance ($2,703 million), the rights to Almirall's respiratory franchise ($876 million) and the acquisition of Definiens ($150 million). The comparative period of 2013 included payments on the completion of the acquisitions of Pearl Therapeutics, Omthera, Amplimmune and Spirogen . . . Net cash distributions to shareholders were $3,242 million (2013: $2,979 million), through dividends of $3,521 million (2013: $3,461 million) partially offset by proceeds from the issue of shares of $279 million (2013: $482 million) due to the exercise of share options.

Source: AstraZeneca Annual Report and Form 20-F, 2014 http://www.astrazeneca.com/Investors/Annual-reports

Discussion points

1 What do we learn about cash flow from the information provided by AstraZeneca?
2 Which stakeholders received cash from the company in 2014?

Contents

Learning outcomes

After studying this chapter you should be able to:

- Explain the benefits and problems of producing annual financial statements.
- Explain the purpose and structure of the statement of financial position (balance sheet).
- Explain the purpose and structure of the income statement (profit and loss account).
- Explain the purpose and structure of the statement of cash flows.
- Comment on the usefulness to users of the financial statements prepared.

Additionally for those who choose to study the supplement:

- Apply the debit and credit form of analysis to the transactions of a short period of time, summarising them in a list which may be used for preparation of simple financial statements.

3.1 Introduction

In the previous chapter the accounting equation was developed as a representation of the relationships among key items of accounting information: assets, liabilities and the ownership interest. An understanding of the accounting equation and the various elements of the equation provides a systematic approach to analysing transactions and events, but it gives no guidance as to how the results should be communicated in a manner which will be helpful and meaningful to users. The accounting equation is used in this chapter as a basis for explaining the structure of financial statements. Ideas beyond the accounting equation are required as to what qualities are expected of financial statements.

The various financial statements produced by enterprises for the owners and other external users are derived from the accounting equation. The *Conceptual Framework* identifies the purposes of financial reporting as producing information about the financial position, performance and financial adaptability of the enterprise. The three most familiar **primary financial statements**, and their respective purposes, are:

Primary financial statement	Purpose is to report
Statement of financial position (balance sheet)	Financial position
Income statement (profit and loss account)	Financial performance
Statement of cash flows	Financial adaptability

This chapter explains the general shape and content of each of these financial statements.

3.2 Who is in charge of the accounting system?

Since 2005 two different accounting systems have existed for companies in the UK, depending on the type of company. When you look at the name of a company listed on the Stock Exchange, such as Vodaphone, BskyB, Burberry and Marks and Spencer, you are really looking at a family group of companies all owned by one parent company. One set of financial statements represents all the companies in the group. Under the law of the European Union (EU), these group financial statements for listed companies must apply the International Financial Reporting Standards (IFRS) accounting system set out by the International Accounting Standards Board (**IASB system**). Other companies in the UK may choose to follow the IASB system of standards but there is no requirement to do so. All companies in the UK that do not apply the IASB system must apply the accounting system set out by the UK Financial Reporting Council (FRC). Many public bodies in the UK, including central government and local authorities, now use the IASB system of IFRS.

Fortunately for those studying the subject, the FRC and the IASB have been working closely together for many years and there are relatively few differences between the two systems. However, there is a potential difference in the appearance and the wording of financial statements. Companies applying the UK FRC's accounting system must use specifications of the sequence and content of items (called **formats** of financial statements) set out in UK company law which is based on EU directives. Companies applying the IASB's system to their listed group reporting have a choice in how they present their financial statements. As a consequence we are now seeing variety in the content and sequence of financial statements published in the annual reports of groups listed on the Stock Exchange. This chapter gives you a flavour of the formats that you might see in financial statements. Where there are differences in words used, this chapter gives the wording of the IASB system first, followed by the wording of UK company law in brackets. As an example, the description:

income statement (profit and loss account)

means that the IASB system uses **income statement** in its illustrations of a profit statement, while UK company law uses **profit and loss account** in its specification of a profit statement.

3.3 The accounting period

In the far-away days of traders sailing out of Italian ports on three-year voyages, the **accounting period** was determined by the date of return of the ship, when the accounts could be prepared for the whole voyage. That rather leisurely view of the scale of time would not be tolerated in an industrial and commercial society where there is always someone demanding information. The convention is that businesses should prepare financial statements at least once in every calendar year. That convention is a requirement of law expressed in the Companies Act 2006 in the case of limited liability companies. Where companies have a Stock Exchange listing they are required to produce an interim report six months into the accounting year. Some companies voluntarily produce quarterly reports to shareholders, reflecting the practice of listed companies in the USA. For internal management accounting purposes, a business may produce reports more frequently (e.g. on a monthly or a weekly basis).

Businesses may choose their accounting date as a time convenient to their activities. Many companies choose 31 December for the year-end, but others (including many of the utility companies which were formerly owned by the government) use 31 March. Some prefer a September or October date after the peak of the summer sales has passed. Whatever the choice, companies are expected to keep the same date from one year to the next unless there is a strong reason for changing.

The use of a 12-month accounting period should not be too much of a problem where the trading cycle fits neatly into a year. If the business is seasonal, there will be a peak of production to match the seasonal peak of sales and the pattern will be repeated every year. There could be a few technical problems of deciding exactly how to close the door on 31 December and whether transactions towards the end of the year are to be included in that year or carried to the next period. These problems can be dealt with by having systematic 'cut-off' rules. There is a bigger problem for those companies whose trading cycle is much longer. It could take two years to build a section of a motorway or three years to build a bridge over a wide river estuary. Such a company will have to subdivide the work on the main contract so that some can be reported each year.

The use of the 12-month accounting period also causes problems for recognition of assets and liabilities. Waiting for the ship to arrive was much safer evidence for the Venetian traders than hoping it was still afloat or relying on reported sightings. For today's business the equivalent situation would be waiting for a property to be sold or for a large customer to pay the amount due as a debt. However, in practice the statement of financial position (balance sheet) cannot wait. Notes to the accounts give additional explanations to help users of financial statements evaluate the risk, but it is all quite tentative. Narrative descriptions of risk are explained further in Chapter 14, section 14.10.

3.4 The statement of financial position (balance sheet)

The **statement of financial position (balance sheet)** reflects the accounting equation. Both descriptions are used in this textbook because you will find both in use. The International Accounting Standards Board prefers the term 'statement of financial position' while company law in the UK uses the term 'balance sheet'. You saw in Chapter 2 that there is more than one way to write the accounting equation. That means there is more than one way to present a statement of financial position (balance sheet). You will find throughout your study of accounting that there is often more than one approach to dealing with an activity or solving a problem. This is the first time but there will be more. It means that you need to be flexible in your approach to reading and using financial statements.

3.4.1   Focus on the ownership interest

One form of the accounting equation focuses on the ownership interest as the result of subtracting liabilities from assets. The equation is as follows:

Assets	minus	Liabilities	equals	Ownership interest

UK companies who apply this form of the equation will present the statement of financial position (balance sheet) in a narrative form, reading down the page, as follows:

Assets
minus
Liabilities
equals
Ownership interest

The assets are subdivided into current assets and non-current assets (defined in Chapter 2), while the liabilities are subdivided into current liabilities and non-current liabilities (also defined in Chapter 2). The ownership interest may also be subdivided to show separately the capital contributed or withdrawn and the profit of the period. Because current assets and current liabilities are closely intertwined in the day-to-day operations of the business, they are often grouped close to each other in the statement of financial position (balance sheet) (Table 3.1).

Table 3.1
Structure of a statement of financial position (balance sheet)

Non-current assets
plus
Current assets
minus
Current liabilities
minus
Non-current liabilities
equals
Capital at start of year
plus/minus
Capital contributed or withdrawn
plus
Profit of the period

Table 3.1 represents a typical sequence used by UK public companies. Most companies will try to confine the statement of financial position (balance sheet) to a single side of A4 paper but there is not much space on one sheet of A4 paper to fit in all the assets and liabilities of a company. Consequently a great deal of use is made of notes to the accounts which explain the detail. The statement of financial position (balance sheet) shows only the main categories of assets and liabilities.

3.4.2 Balancing assets and claims on assets

Another form of the accounting equation focuses on balancing the assets against the claims on assets. The claims on assets come from the ownership interest and from liabilities of all types. The equation is:

Assets	equals	Liabilities	plus	Ownership interest

UK companies who apply this form of the equation will present the statement of financial position (balance sheet) vertically on one sheet of paper but the sequence will be different:

Assets
equals
Liabilities
plus
Ownership interest

In some countries there is a preference for lining up the statement of financial position (balance sheet) horizontally to match the accounting equation even more closely.

	Liabilities
Assets	plus
	Ownership interest

Activity 3.1

Before reading further, make sure that you can explain why each item in the accounting records is an asset or a liability, as shown in the foregoing list. If you have any doubts, read Chapter 2 again before proceeding with this chapter.

3.4.3 Example of presentation

The following list of assets and liabilities of P. Mason's legal practice was prepared from the accounting records of transactions summarised at 30 September Year 5:

	£
Land and buildings	250,000
Office furniture	30,000
Receivables (debtors) for fees	1,200
Prepayment of insurance premium	540
Cash at bank	15,280
Total assets (A)	**297,020**
Trade payables (creditors)	2,800
Long-term loan	150,000
Total liabilities (L)	**152,800**
Ownership interest (A – L)	**144,220**

Table 3.2 shows how this would appear in a statement of financial position (balance sheet) based on the 'ownership interest' form of the equation. Table 3.3 shows how the same information would appear in a statement of financial position (balance sheet) based on the 'claims on assets' form of the equation.

The statement of financial position (balance sheet) in Table 3.2 is more informative than the list of assets and liabilities from which it was prepared because it has been arranged in a helpful format. The first helpful feature is the use of headings (shown in Table 3.2 in bold) for similar items grouped together, such as non-current assets, current assets, current liabilities and non-current liabilities. The second helpful feature is the use of **subtotals** (identified in Table 3.2 by descriptions in italics and shaded) for similar items grouped together. The subtotals used in this example are those for: total non-current assets; total current assets; total assets; and total liabilities. There are no standard rules on use of subtotals. They should be chosen in a manner most appropriate to the situation. Brackets round figures show the 'minus' in the accounting equation.

A person using this statement of financial position (balance sheet) can see at a glance that there is no problem for the business in meeting its current liabilities from its resources of current assets. The financing of the business is split almost equally between the non-current liabilities and the ownership interest, a split which would not be regarded as excessively risky by those who lend to businesses. The non-current assets used as a basis for generating profits from one year to the next are collected together as a group, although the statement of financial position (balance sheet) alone cannot show how effectively those assets are being used. For that, an income statement (profit and loss account) is needed.

The statement of financial position (balance sheet) in Table 3.3 is again more informative than the list of assets and liabilities from which it was prepared because it has been arranged in a helpful format. It offers a helpful feature in the use of headings (in bold) for similar items grouped together. It is also helpful in providing subtotals

Table 3.2
Statement of financial position (balance sheet): Assets minus liabilities equals ownership interest

P. Mason's legal practice Statement of financial position (balance sheet) at 30 September Year 5	£
Non-current assets	
Land and buildings	250,000
Office furniture	30,000
Total non-current assets	280,000
Current assets	
Receivables (debtors) for fees	1,200
Prepayment of insurance premium	540
Cash at bank	15,280
Total current assets	17,020
Total assets	297,020
Current liabilities	
Trade payables (creditors)	(2,800)
Non-current liabilities	
Long-term loan	(150,000)
Total liabilities	(152,800)
Net assets	144,220
Ownership interest	144,220

Table 3.3

Statement of financial position (balance sheet): Assets equal liabilities plus ownership interest

P. Mason's legal practice Statement of financial position (balance sheet) at 30 September Year 5	
	£
Non-current assets	
Land and buildings	250,000
Office furniture	30,000
Total non-current assets	280,000
Current assets	
Receivables for fees	1,200
Prepayment of insurance premium	540
Cash at bank	15,280
Total current assets	17,020
Total assets	297,020
Current liabilities	
Trade payables	2,800
Non-current liabilities	
Long-term loan	150,000
Total liabilities	**152,800**
Ownership interest	144,220
Total liabilities plus ownership interest	297,020

(identified by descriptions in italics and shaded) for similar items grouped together. The subtotals used in this example are those for: total non-current assets and total current assets. Some financial statements include a subtotal for the current assets less current liabilities (not current assets). There are no standard rules on use of subtotals. They should be chosen in a manner most appropriate to the situation.

A person using this statement of financial position (balance sheet) can again see at a glance that there is no problem for the business in meeting its current liabilities from its resources of current assets. The financing of the business is split almost equally between the non-current liabilities and the ownership interest, a split which would not be regarded as excessively risky by those who lend to businesses. The non-current assets used as a basis for generating profits from one year to the next are collected together as a group, although the statement of financial position (balance sheet) alone cannot show how effectively those assets are being used.

3.5 The income statement (profit and loss account)

For many years in the UK, **profit and loss account** was the only title used for the financial statement reporting profit of the period. From 2005 many of those listed groups following the IASB's system have chosen to follow an example given by the IASB which uses the heading **income statement**, found more commonly in US company reports. It is not compulsory for listed group companies to use 'income statement' and some retain the 'profit and loss account' heading. The income statement (profit and loss account) reflects that part of the accounting equation which defines profit:

Profit	equals	Revenue minus Expenses

The expenses of a period are matched against the revenue earned in that period. This is described as the application of the **matching** concept in accounting.

As with the statement of financial position (balance sheet), it is presented in a vertical form so that it can be read down the page as a narrative (Table 3.4).

Table 3.4
Structure of an income statement (profit and loss account)

Revenue
minus
Expenses
equals
Profit

3.5.1   Example of presentation

The accounting records of P. Mason's legal practice at 30 September Year 5 showed that the ownership interest could be explained as follows (using brackets to show negative items):

	£
Increases in ownership interest	
Capital contributed at start of month	140,000
Fees	8,820
Decreases in ownership interest	
Computer rental and online searches	(1,500)
Gas	(100)
Electricity	(200)
Telephone/fax	(1,000)
Salary of assistant	(1,800)
Ownership interest at end of month	144,220

The statement of profit is quite simple, as shown in Table 3.5.

Table 3.5
Financial statement of profit, in a useful format

P. Mason's legal practice Income statement (profit and loss account) for the month of September		
	£	£
Revenues		
Fees		8,820
Expenses		
Computer rental and online searches	(1,500)	
Gas	(100)	
Electricity	(200)	
Telephone/fax	(1,000)	
Salary of assistant	(1,800)	
Total expenses		(4,600)
Net profit of the month		4,220

3.5.2 Comment

The income statement (profit and loss account) improves on the mere list of constituent items by providing headings (shown in bold) for each main category. As this is a very simple example, only two headings and one subtotal are required. Headings and subtotals are most useful where there are groups of items of a similar nature. The resulting net profit shows how the revenues and expenses have contributed overall to increasing the ownership interest during the month.

Activity 3.2	*Taking each item of the income statement (profit and loss account) in turn, explain to an imaginary friend why each item of revenue and expense is regarded as increasing or decreasing the ownership interest. If necessary, look back to the definitions of revenue and expense in Chapter 2. Make sure that you feel confident about the income statement (profit and loss account) before you move on.*

3.6 The statement of cash flows

It was shown in Chapter 1 that liquidity is of interest to more than one user group, but of particular interest to creditors of the business.

Liquidity is measured by the cash and near-cash assets and the change in those assets, so a financial statement which explains cash flows should be of general interest to user groups:

Cash flow	equals	**Cash inflows to the enterprise** minus **Cash outflows from the enterprise**

The **statement of cash flows** will appear in a vertical form:

Cash inflows
minus
Cash outflows
equals
Change in cash assets

In a business there will be different factors causing the inflows and outflows of cash. The enterprise will try to make clear what the different causes are. Subdivisions are commonly used for operating activities, investing activities and financing activities:

- *Operating activities* are the actions of buying and selling goods, or manufacturing goods for resale, or providing a service to customers.
- *Investing activities* are the actions of buying and selling non-current assets for long-term purposes.
- *Financing activities* are the actions of raising and repaying the long-term finance of the business.

Table 3.6 sets out the basic structure of a basic statement of cash flows.

Table 3.6
Structure of a statement of cash flows

Operating activities
Cash inflows
minus
Cash outflows
plus
Investing activities
Cash inflows
minus
Cash outflows
plus
Financing activities
Cash inflows
minus
Cash outflows
equals
Change in cash assets

3.6.1   Example of presentation

The cash transactions of P. Mason's legal practice for the month of September were recorded as follows:

Accounting records

Year 5		£
Cash received		
Sept. 1	Capital contributed by P. Mason	140,000
Sept. 1	Loan from bank	150,000
Sept. 19	Fees received from clients	7,620
	Total cash received	297,620
Cash paid		
Sept. 1	Land and buildings	250,000
Sept. 5	Prepayment of insurance premium	540
Sept. 26	Supplier for office furniture	30,000
Sept. 30	Salaries	1,800
	Total cash paid	282,340
	Cash remaining at 30 September	15,280

The statement of cash flows would be presented as shown in Table 3.7.

3.6.2   Comment

The cash flows, listed at the start of Section 3.6.1 in the accounting records for the legal practice, relate to three different types of activity which are brought out more clearly in the statement of cash flows by the use of headings and subtotals. The headings are shown in bold and the subtotals are highlighted by italics and shading. The story emerging from the statement of cash flows is that the owner put in £140,000 and the bank lent £150,000, providing a total of £290,000 in start-up finance. Of this amount, £280,000 was used during the month to pay for non-current assets. That left £10,000 which, when added to the positive cash flow from operations, explains why the cash resources increased by £15,280 over the month.

Table 3.7
Financial statement showing cash flows of an enterprise

P. Mason's legal practice Statement of cash flows for the month of September Year 5	£
Operating activities	
Inflow from fees	7,620
Outflow to insurance premium	(540)
Outflows to salaries	(1,800)
Net inflow from operations	5,280
Investing activities	
Payment for land and building	(250,000)
Payment for office furniture	(30,000)
Net outflow for investing activities	(280,000)
Financing activities	
Capital contributed by owner	140,000
Five-year loan from bank	150,000
Net inflow from financing activities	290,000
Increase in cash at bank over period	15,280

Table 3.8
Comparison of profit and operating cash flow for the month of September

P. Mason's legal practice	Profit	Operating cash flow
	£	£
Revenues		
Fees/cash received	8,820	7,620
Expenses		
Computer rental and online searches	(1,500)	nil
Gas	(100)	nil
Electricity	(200)	nil
Telephone/fax	(1,000)	nil
Salary of assistant	(1,800)	(1,800)
Payment for insurance premium	nil	(540)
Total expenses/total cash paid	4,600	(2,340)
Net profit of the month	4,220	
Increase in cash in the month		5,280

It is quite common to compare the increase in ownership claim caused by making a profit with the increase in the cash resources of a business caused by operations. In this case the profit is £4,220 (Table 3.5) but the operations have added £15,280 to the cash assets of the business.

To make the comparison, Table 3.8 takes the income statement (profit and loss account) of Table 3.5 and sets alongside it the cash flows relating to operations.

Table 3.8 shows that the cash flow from fees was £1,200 less than the fee revenue earned because some customers had not paid at the month end. This is the amount shown in the statement of financial position (balance sheet) (Table 3.2) as receivables for fees. Table 3.8 also shows that expenses of rental, gas, electricity and telephone amounting to £2,800 in total had not been paid at the month end. These are shown as **trade payables** in the statement of financial position (balance sheet). The cash flow from operations is reduced by the payment for the insurance premium which does not affect the income statement (profit and loss account) for the month.

Users of financial statements regard both the profit and the cash flow as interesting items of information. The profit shows the overall increase in ownership claim which contributes to the overall wealth of the business. The cash flow shows the ability of the business to survive financially through planning the timing and amount of inflows and outflows of cash.

3.7 Usefulness of financial statements

Here are Leona and David, still working on Leona's flat, discussing the usefulness of financial statements.

LEONA: *Which financial statement is the most important for you?*

DAVID: *It has to be the income statement (profit and loss account). Profit creates wealth. Future profit creates future wealth. I have to make a forecast of each company's profit as part of my planning to meet our overall investment strategy. Maybe I should qualify that by adding that cash flow is also important, especially where there is high uncertainty about future prospects. We talk about 'quality of profits' and regard some types of profit as of higher quality than others. Cash flow support is one aspect of that quality. We have doubts about some accounting amounts which don't have a close relationship to cash. A business cannot survive if it can't pay its way.*

LEONA: *Where does that leave the statement of financial position?*

DAVID: *I'm not sure. It is a list of resources and claims on those resources. We are shareholders and so we have a claim on those resources but we don't think about it to any great extent because we are concentrating on the going concern aspects of the business, rather than closing down and selling the assets. The numbers in the statement of financial position don't mean very much because they are out of date.*

LEONA: *We studied research at university which suggested that cash flow is the answer and income statements (profit and loss accounts) are too difficult to understand. It was suggested that the statement of financial position (balance sheet) should show what the assets could be sold for. I see those ideas on value are gradually appearing in practice where fair values are applied.*

DAVID: *I like to know the dynamics of the business. I like to see the movements of different aspects and the interactions. I think I would feel that cash flow alone is concentrating on only one aspect of the wealth of the business. I suppose the statement of financial position is a useful check on the position which has been reached as a result of making profits for the period. One thing we do look at in the statement of financial position is how much has been borrowed for use in the business. We don't like to see that become too high in comparison with the ownership interest.*

LEONA: *At least you are admitting to seeing something in the financial statements. I still have to persuade you that the auditors are important in giving you the reassurance you obviously obtain.*

Activity 3.3	*Analyse your own view of wealth and changes in wealth. Which items would you include in your personal statement of financial position (balance sheet) today? Which items would you include in your personal 'profit or loss' calculation for the past year? Which items would you include in your personal statement of cash flows? Has your view of 'wealth' been modified as a result of reading these first three chapters? If so, how have your views changed?*

3.8 Summary

This chapter has explained the structure of the main financial statements produced by business and non-business entities.

Key points are:

- An **accounting period** of 12 months is common for financial reporting.
- The **primary financial statements** produced by a wide range of entities are the statement of financial position (balance sheet), the income statement (profit and loss account) and the statement of cash flows.
- A **statement of financial position (balance sheet)** presents financial position at a point in time. The **format** of the statement of financial position (balance sheet) will vary depending on which version of the accounting equation is preferred by the entity preparing the statement.
- An **income statement** (profit and loss account) presents the performance over a period of time. The income statement (profit and loss account) presents financial performance by **matching** revenue and expenses to arrive at a profit of the period.
- A **statement of cash flows** presents the financial adaptability over a period of time. It explains changes in the cash position over a period caused by operating cash flows, investing cash flows and financing cash flows.
- Since 2005 two different accounting systems (consisting of **accounting standards** and legislation) have existed for companies in the UK, depending on the type of company. The **IASB system** applies to the group financial statements of listed companies. Other companies may choose voluntarily to follow the IASB system. The **UK system**, based on UK law and the standards of the UK FRC, applies to all companies that do not follow the IASB system.
- The **accounting standards** of the UK FRC are very similar to those of the IASB. The main UK standards are combined in one document, FRS 102, *The Financial Reporting Standard.*

QUESTIONS

The Questions section of each chapter has three types of question. 'Test your understanding' questions to help you review your reading are in the 'A' series of questions. You will find the answers to these by reading and thinking about the material in the book. 'Application' questions to test your ability to apply technical skills are in the 'B' series of questions. Questions requiring you to show skills in problem solving and evaluation are in the 'C' series of questions. A letter [S] indicates that there is a solution at the end of the book. Other solutions are provided in the Instructor's Manual, where there are further questions parallel to those set out here.

A   Test your understanding

A3.1   Explain why an accounting period of 12 months is used as the basis for reporting to external users of financial statements. (Section 3.3)

A3.2   Explain how the structure of the statement of financial position (balance sheet) corresponds to the accounting equation. (Section 3.4)

A3.3   Explain how the structure of the income statement (profit and loss account) represents a subsection of the accounting equation. (Section 3.5)

A3.4   Explain how the structure of the statement of cash flows represents another subsection of the accounting equation. (Section 3.6)

A3.5 List three features of a statement of financial position (balance sheet) which are particularly useful in making the format helpful to readers. (Section 3.4.3)

A3.6 List three features of an income statement (profit and loss account) format which are particularly useful in making the format helpful to readers. (Section 3.5.1)

A3.7 List three features of a statement of cash flows which are particularly useful in making the format helpful to readers. (Section 3.6.1)

B Application

B3.1 [S]

John Timms is the sole owner of Sunshine Wholesale Traders, a company which buys fruit from farmers and sells it to supermarkets. All goods are collected from farms and delivered to supermarkets on the same day, so no inventories (stocks) of fruit are held. The accounting records of Sunshine Traders at 30 June Year 2, relating to the year then ended, have been summarised by John Timms as follows:

	£
Fleet of delivery vehicles, after deducting depreciation	35,880
Furniture and fittings, after deducting depreciation	18,800
Trade receivables	34,000
Bank deposit	19,000
Trade payables (creditors)	8,300
Sales	294,500
Cost of goods sold	188,520
Wages and salaries	46,000
Transport costs	14,200
Administration costs	1,300
Depreciation of vehicles, furniture and fittings	1,100

Required
(a) Identify each item in the accounting records as either an asset, a liability, or ownership interest (identifying separately the expenses and revenues which contribute to the change in the ownership interest).
(b) Prepare a statement of financial position (balance sheet) at 30 June Year 2.
(c) Prepare an income statement (profit and loss statement) for the year ended 30 June Year 2.

B3.2 [S]

Prepare a statement of financial position (balance sheet) from the following list of assets and liabilities, regarding the ownership interest as the missing item.

	£
Trade payables (creditors)	43,000
Cash at bank	9,000
Inventories (stocks) of goods for resale	35,000
Land and buildings	95,000
Wages due to employees but not paid	2,000
Vehicles	8,000
Five-year loan from a bank	20,000

Explain how the statement of financial position (balance sheet) will change for each of the following transactions:

(a) The wages due to the employees are paid at £2,000.
(b) One-quarter of the inventory (stock) of goods held for resale is destroyed by fire and there is no insurance to cover the loss.
(c) Goods for resale are bought on credit at a cost of £5,000.

There are no questions in the C series for this chapter.

Activities for study groups

Return to the annual reports your group obtained for the exercise in Chapter 1. Find the statement of financial position (balance sheet), income statement (profit and loss account) and statement of cash flows. Use the outline formats contained in this chapter to identify the main areas of each of the published statements. Work together in preparing a list of features which make the formats useful to the reader. Note also any aspects of the presentation which you find unhelpful at this stage. (It may be useful to look back on this note at the end of the course as a collective check on whether your understanding and awareness of annual report items has improved.)

Using the accounting equation to analyse transactions

In the main body of the chapter the transactions of P. Mason's legal practice are set out in summary form and are then presented in financial statements. This supplement goes back one stage and looks at the transactions and events for the month of September which resulted in the summary and financial statements shown in the chapter.

The list of transactions and events is as follows:

Sept. 1	P. Mason deposits £140,000 in a bank account to commence the business under the name *P. Mason's legal practice.*
Sept. 1	P. Mason's legal practice borrows £150,000 from a finance business to help with the intended purchase of a property for use as an office. The loan is to be repaid in five years' time.
Sept. 1	A property is purchased at a cost of £75,000 for the land and £175,000 for the buildings. The full price is paid from the bank account.
Sept. 3	Office furniture is purchased from Stylecraft at a cost of £30,000. The full price is to be paid within 90 days.
Sept. 5	An insurance premium of £540 is paid in advance. The insurance cover will commence on 1 October.
Sept. 8	An applicant is interviewed for a post of legal assistant. She agrees to start work on 10 September for a salary of £24,000 per annum.
Sept. 11	Invoices are sent to some clients for work done in preparing contracts for them. The total of the invoiced amounts is £8,820. Clients are allowed up to 30 days to pay.
Sept. 19	Cheques received from clients in payment of invoices amount to £7,620.
Sept. 26	Payment is made to Stylecraft for the amount due for office furniture, £30,000.
Sept. 28	Bills are received as follows: for computer rental and online searches, £1,500; gas, £100; electricity, £200; and telephone/fax, £1,000.
Sept. 30	Legal assistant is paid salary of £1,800 for period to end of month.

In the supplement to Chapter 2 a table was prepared, based on the accounting equation, showing the classification used for debit and credit bookkeeping entries. As a reminder, the form of the equation used to derive the debit and credit rules is:

Assets	equals	Liabilities	plus	Ownership interest

As a further reminder, the rules are set out again in Table 3.9. Each of the transactions of P. Mason's legal practice for the month of September is now analysed in terms of the effect on the accounting equation and the resulting debit and credit entries which would be made in the accounting records.

Table 3.9
Rules for debit and credit recording

	Debit entries in a ledger account	Credit entries in a ledger account
Left-hand side of the equation		
Asset	Increase	Decrease
Right-hand side of the equation		
Liability	Decrease	Increase
Ownership interest	Expense	Revenue
	Capital withdrawn	Capital contributed

Analysis of each transaction

Sept. 1   P. Mason deposits £140,000 in a bank account to commence the business under the name *P. Mason's legal practice.*

The business acquires an asset (cash in the bank) and an ownership interest is created through contribution of capital.

Transaction number: 1	Debit	Credit
Asset	Bank £140,000	
Ownership interest		Capital contributed £140,000

Sept. 1   P. Mason's legal practice borrows £150,000 from a finance business to help with the intended purchase of a property for use as an office. The loan is to be repaid in five years' time.

The business acquires an asset of cash and a long-term liability is created.

Transaction number: 2	Debit	Credit
Asset	Bank £150,000	
Liability		Long-term loan £150,000

Sept. 1   A property is purchased at a cost of £75,000 for the land and £175,000 for the buildings. The full price is paid from the bank account.

The business acquires an asset of land and buildings (£250,000 in total) and the asset of cash in the bank is reduced.

Transaction number: 3	Debit	Credit
Asset	Land and buildings £250,000	Bank £250,000

Sept. 3   Office furniture is purchased from Stylecraft at a cost of £30,000. The full price is to be paid within 90 days.

The business acquires an asset of furniture and also acquires a liability to pay the supplier, Stylecraft. The liability is called a trade payable (creditor).

Transaction number: 4	Debit	Credit
Asset	Furniture £30,000	
Liability		Trade payable (Stylecraft) £30,000

Sept. 5   An insurance premium of £540 is paid in advance. The insurance cover will commence on 1 October.

The business acquires an asset of prepaid insurance (the benefit of cover exists in the future) and the asset of cash at bank is reduced.

Transaction number: 5	Debit	Credit
Asset	Prepayment £540	Bank £540

Sept. 8   An applicant is interviewed for a post of legal assistant. She agrees to start work on 10 September for a salary of £24,000 per annum.

The successful outcome of the interview is an *event* and there is an expected future benefit from employing the new legal assistant. The employee will be controlled by the organisation through a contract of employment. The organisation has a commitment to pay her the agreed salary. It could be argued that the offer of employment, and acceptance of that offer, create an asset of the human resource and a liability equal to the future salary. That does not happen because the *recognition* criteria are applied and it is felt too risky to recognise an asset when there is insufficient evidence of the future benefit. Commercial prudence dictates that it is preferable to wait until the employee has done some work and pay her at the end of the month for work done during the month. The accounting process is similarly prudent and no accounting recognition takes place until the payment has occurred. Even then it is the expense of the past which is recognised, rather than the asset of benefit for the future.

Sept. 11   Invoices are sent to some clients showing fees due for work done in preparing contracts for them. The total of the invoiced amounts is £8,820. Clients are allowed up to 30 days to pay.

Earning fees is the main activity of the legal practice. Earning fees makes the owner better off and is an example of the more general activity *of increasing the ownership interest* by creating revenue. The clients have not yet paid and therefore the business has an asset called a **trade receivable (debtor)**.

Transaction number: 6	Debit	Credit
Asset	Trade receivables £8,820	
Ownership interest (revenue)		Fees for work done £8,820

Sept. 19   Cheques received from clients in payment of invoices amount to £7,620.

When the customers pay, the amount due to the business from debtors will be decreased. So the asset of trade receivables decreases and the asset of cash in the bank increases.

Transaction number: 7	Debit	Credit
Asset	Bank £7,620	Trade receivables £7,620

Sept. 26   Payment is made to Stylecraft for the amount due for office furniture, £30,000.

The asset of cash in the bank decreases and the liability to Stylecraft decreases to nil.

Transaction number: 8	Debit	Credit
Asset		Bank £30,000
Liability	Trade payable (Stylecraft) £30,000	

Sept. 28   Bills are received as follows: for computer rental and online searches, £1,500; gas, £100; electricity, £200; and telephone/fax £1,000 (total £2,800).

The computer rental, online searches, gas, electricity and telephone have been used up during the period and are all expenses which reduce the ownership interest. They are unpaid and, therefore, a liability is recorded.

Transaction number: 9	Debit	Credit
Liability		Trade payables £2,800
Ownership interest	Expenses £2,800	

Sept. 30   Legal assistant is paid salary of £1,800 for period to end of month.

The asset of cash at bank decreases and the salary paid to the legal assistant is an expense of the month.

Transaction number: 10	Debit	Credit
Asset		Bank £1,800
Ownership interest	Expense £1,800	

Summarising the debit and credit entries

The formal system of bringing together debit and credit entries is based on ledger accounts. These are explained in the supplement to Chapter 5. For the present it will be sufficient to use a spreadsheet (Table 3.10) to show how the separate debit and credit entries analysed in this supplement lead to the list of items used in the main part of the chapter as the basis for the financial statements presented there.

In the spreadsheet there are dates which correspond to the dates of the foregoing ten separate analyses of transactions. The debit and credit entries are shown with Dr or Cr alongside to distinguish them. For each column all the debit entries are totalled and all

Table 3.10
Spreadsheet of transactions for P. Mason's legal practice, during the month of September

Date	Assets					Liabilities		Ownership interest		
	Land and buildings £	Office furniture £	Trade receivables £	Pre-payments £	Cash at bank £	Trade payables £	Bank loan £	Revenue £	Expenses £	Owner's capital contributed £
1 Sept.					140,000 Dr					140,000 Cr
1 Sept.					150,000 Dr		150,000 Cr			
1 Sept.	250,000 Dr				250,000 Cr					
3 Sept.		30,000 Dr				30,000 Cr				
5 Sept.				540 Dr	540 Cr					
11 Sept.			8,820 Dr					8,820 Cr		
19 Sept.			7,620 Cr		7,620 Dr					
26 Sept.					30,000 Cr	30,000 Dr				
28 Sept.						2,800 Cr			2,800 Dr	
30 Sept.					1,800 Cr				1,800 Dr	
Total debit entries in each column										
	250,000 Dr	30,000 Dr	8,820 Dr	540 Dr	297,620 Dr	30,000 Dr	nil	nil	4,600 Dr	nil
Total credit entries in each column										
	nil	nil	7,620 Cr	nil	282,340 Cr	32,800 Cr	150,000 Cr	8,820 Cr	nil	140,000 Cr
Surplus of debits over credits (or credits over debits)										
	250,000 Dr	30,000 Dr	1,200 Dr	540 Dr	15,280 Dr	2,800 Cr	150,000 Cr	8,820 Cr	4,600 Dr	140,000 Cr

the credit entries are totalled separately. The surplus of debits over credits (or credits over debits) is calculated and shown in the final line. This allows a summarised list to be prepared as shown in Table 3.11.

A spreadsheet is useful where there are not too many entries, but ledger accounts become essential when the volume of information increases.

Table 3.11

Summary of debit and credit entries for each category of asset, liability and ownership interest

	Debit	Credit
	£	£
Assets		
Land and buildings	250,000	
Office furniture	30,000	
Trade receivables (debtors)	1,200	
Prepayment	540	
Cash at bank	15,280	
Liabilities		
Trade payables (creditors)		2,800
Long-term loan		150,000
Ownership interest		
Revenue		8,820
Expenses	4,600	
Capital contributed		140,000
Totals	301,620	301,620

Note: The totals of each column have no particular meaning, but they should always be equal because of the symmetry of the debit and credit records, and so are useful as an arithmetic check that no item has been omitted or recorded incorrectly.

Turning the spreadsheet back to a vertical listing, using the debit column for items where the debits exceed the credits, and using the credit column for items where the credits exceed the debits, the list becomes as in Table 3.11. You will see that this list is the basis of the information provided about P. Mason's legal practice in the main body of the chapter, except that the debit and credit notation was not used there.

Activity 3.4

The most serious problem faced by most students, once they have understood the basic approach, is that of making errors. Look back through this Supplement and think about the errors which might have been made. What type of error would be detected by finding totals in Table 3.11 which were not in agreement? What type of error would not be detected in this way because the totals would be in agreement despite the error? Types of error will be dealt with in the supplement to Chapter 5.

S Test your understanding

S3.1 [S] Analyse the debit and credit aspect of each transaction listed at (a), (b) and (c) of question B3.2.

S3.2 Prepare a spreadsheet similar to that presented in Table 3.10, setting out on the first line the items contained in the list of assets and liabilities of question B3.2 and then on lines 2, 3 and 4 adding in the transactions (a), (b) and (c). Calculate the totals of each column of the spreadsheet and show that the accounting equation remains equal on both sides.

Chapter 4

Ensuring the quality of financial statements

Financial Reporting Council: regulating and developing accounting information

Extracts from FRC documents

Our mission and supporting strategies

The FRC's mission is to promote high quality corporate governance and reporting to foster investment.

Why have we landed on this mission? The capital markets are important to the health and growth of the economy. Our functions contribute to the effective functioning of the capital markets. We help ensure that investors have what they need to place their money with reasonable confidence that any risk is taken on an informed basis and managed as well as it can be. In turn, the entities in receipt of that investment can have the confidence to invest in their own strategies and work forces.

We believe that this confidence should be based on

- Effective boards who communicate well
- Robust and effective accounting, reporting, auditing and actuarial standards
- Useful and reliable annual reports and accounts, assurance reports and other information produced by accountants and actuaries
- Well regulated accountancy and actuarial professions

Source: The FRC and its Regulatory Approach, January 2014, p. 1. https://www.frc.org.uk/Our-Work/Publications/FRC-Board/The-FRC-and-its-Regulatory-Approach.pdf

New regime for very small companies

A micro-entity preparing its financial statements in accordance with section 393(1A) of the Act shall prepare a balance sheet in which only those items listed in the following formats must be shown, where applicable:

BALANCE SHEET FORMAT 1
A CALLED UP SHARE CAPITAL NOT PAID
B FIXED ASSETS
C CURRENT ASSETS

D Prepayments and accrued income

E Creditors: amounts falling due within one year

F Net current assets (liabilities)

G Total assets less current liabilities

H Creditors: amounts falling due after more than one year

I Provisions for liabilities

J Accruals and deferred income

K Capital and reserves

Source: *Amendments to the Financial Reporting Standard for Smaller Enterprises (effective January 2015)*, FRC, April 2014, revision to section 2.40. https://www.frc.org.uk/Our-Work/Publications/Accounting-and-Reporting-Policy/Amendments-to-the-FRSSE-Micro-entities.pdf

From 2016 the FRC will simplify the accounting framework for micro-entities in a new Financial Reporting Standard for Micro-Entities (FRSME).

Source: https://www.frc.org.uk/Our-Work/Publications/Accounting-and-Reporting-Policy/Consultation-Document-Accounting-standards-for-sma-File.pdf

Corporate Reporting Review

Smaller listed and AIM quoted companies

- Our reviews of accounts produced by smaller listed and other entities often give rise to issues that are the result of the company not having sufficient or appropriate resource to recognise or address accounting questions. We tend to see straightforward areas of non-compliance, rather than management misjudgement of complex matters.

- We encourage the boards of the smaller listed and AIM quoted companies, in particular, to consider whether they have access to the level of technical resource and expertise needed to prepare corporate reports and accounts to an acceptable standard.

Source: FRC, *Corporate Reporting Review – Annual Report 2013*, October 2013, p. 5. https://frc.org.uk/Our-Work/Publications/Corporate-Reporting-Review/Coporate-Reporting-Review-Annual-Report-2013.pdf

Discussion points

1 The FRC explains its mission in terms of the functioning of the capital markets. Is that mission sufficient to ensure high quality in corporate financial statements?

2 The EU has directed member states to relax the accounting requirements for very small (micro) companies. Is the balance sheet format set out in the second extract consistent with the mission and strategies of the FRC as set out in the first extract, and its findings on small companies as indicated in the third extract?

Contents

Learning outcomes

After studying this chapter you should be able to:

- List and explain the qualitative characteristics desirable in financial statements.
- Explain the approach to measurement used in financial statements.
- Explain why there is more than one view on the role of prudence in accounting.
- Understand and explain how and why financial reporting is regulated or influenced by external authorities.
- Be aware of the process by which financial statements are reviewed by an investor.

4.1 Introduction

The previous chapter used the accounting equation as a basis for explaining the structure of financial statements. It showed that design of formats for financial statements is an important first step in creating an understandable story from a list of accounting data.

The IASB's stated objective of general purpose financial reporting is to provide financial information about the reporting entity that is useful to existing and potential investors, lenders and other creditors in making decisions about providing resources to the entity. Those decisions involve buying, selling or holding equity and debt instruments, and providing or settling loans and other forms of credit. Critics of this objective argue for information being useful to a wide range of users in making economic decisions. The IASB's response is that meeting the needs of investors and lenders is likely to meet the needs of other users also.[1]

Information about financial position is provided in a **statement of financial position (balance sheet)**. Information about performance is provided in an **income statement** (profit and loss account).[2] Information about changes in the cash position is provided in a **statement of cash flows**. These three statements were explained in outline in Chapter 3. Information about changes in equity is also provided in a separate statement, described in Chapter 12. Notes to the financial statements provide additional information relevant to the needs of users. These notes may include information about risks and uncertainties relating to assets, liabilities, revenue and expenses.[3]

4.2 Qualitative characteristics of financial statements

The IASB *Conceptual Framework* sets out qualitative characteristics that make the information provided in financial statements useful to users. The two fundamental qualitative characteristics are:

- relevance
- faithful representation.[4]

The fundamental qualitative characteristics of relevance and faithful representation have further component characteristics:

- relevance
  - predictive value
  - confirmatory value

- faithful representation
  - neutrality
  - freedom from error
  - completeness.

A general quality of materiality applies across these fundamental characteristics.

There are four further characteristics which are described as 'enhancing qualitative characteristics'. These are:

- comparability
- verifiability
- timeliness
- understandability.

Each of these characteristics is now described.

4.2.1 Relevance[5]

Financial information is **relevant** if it is capable of making a difference in the decisions made by users. Even when users already know the information, or they receive the information but choose not to use it, it is still *capable* of making a difference. Preparers do not have to show that the information actually did make a difference. The information is capable of making a difference if it has predictive value, or confirmatory value, or both.

If the level of uncertainty associated with an estimate is sufficiently large, that estimate might not provide relevant information and consequently the estimated item might not be recognised (see Chapter 2, sections on Recognition).

It may be argued that fair value is more relevant than historical cost value when assets and liabilities are reported (see Chapter 2, section 2.2.3). This is because fair values are up-to-date when the financial statements are prepared, whereas historical cost was measured at some time in the past.

Predictive value[6]

Financial information has predictive value if it can be used as an input to processes employed by users to predict future outcomes. The information could be a forecast provided by the user. Alternatively it could be information that others, such as investors or financial analysts, use as input data for their own predictions.

Confirmatory value[7]

Financial information has confirmatory value if it provides feedback about (confirms or changes) previous evaluations.

Example

A company provides information about revenue (sales) in its income statement. Investors use this information to predict future trends of revenue for that company. Based on these predictions the investors buy shares in the company. In subsequent years the company provides further information about revenue. The investors are able to confirm the predictions they made previously. Information about revenue (sales) is therefore **relevant** information.

4.2.2 Faithful representation[8]

To be useful, financial information must faithfully represent the economic phenomena that it purports to represent. The use of the words 'economic phenomena' sounds scary – a single phenomenon is worrying enough but several pheonomena together sound worse. The easiest way to think of this is to substitute for 'economic phenomena' the wording 'economic events that can be observed'. An economic event could be a transaction, such as where an asset is purchased for cash. An economic event could be a change in value, such as where a plot of land falls in value through contamination being discovered. Financial information can be used to report both of those economic events.

Faithful representation ideally requires the financial information to have three characteristics. It will be complete, neutral and free from error. The IASB acknowledges that perfection is seldom, if ever, achievable.

Complete[9]

A complete depiction includes all information necessary for a user to understand what is being reported. This includes the words used to describe the item, and any notes of explanation that help the reader to understand. We will see in later chapters that words and numbers in financial statements are often supported by explanations and notes.

Neutral[10]

Financial information that is neutral has no bias in the selection or presentation of that information. The *Conceptual Framework* says that a neutral depiction of financial information is not slanted, weighted, emphasised, de-emphasised or otherwise manipulated to increase the probability that such formation will be received favourably or unfavourably by users. It uses the word 'depiction' to cover words as well as numbers and also the location and prominence of information. Preparers who want to give a favourable information might consistently choose the upper end of range of estimated values. Even if there was no bias in the valuation, preparers might use confusing words, or different sized fonts, or different colours, to distract users away from bad news information. Actions of these kinds could lead to bias and non-neutral depiction.

Free from error[11]

'Free from error' means there are no errors or omissions in the description of the phenomenon, and the process used to produce the reported information has been selected and applied with no errors in the process. It does not mean the financial statements are totally accurate. Preparers should make their best efforts but they will not have certainty about all economic events. There may be a list of accounts receivable (customers given credit who have not yet paid). It is likely that some of the accounts receivable will not be received but all the preparer can do is make an estimate for non-recovery. Equipment depreciates in value but the preparer can only estimate depreciation. It cannot be measured with total accuracy.

4.2.3 Materiality[12]

Information is material if omitting it or misstating it could influence decisions that users make on the basis of financial formation about a specific reporting entity. The measure of materiality is specific to the entity and is linked to **relevance**. The IASB does not specify a quantitative threshold for materiality and does not provide any specific guidance. It is for preparers of financial information to decide what is material when they prepare that information.

For example, it might be the case that in the statement of financial position (balance sheet) a company gives separate headings for inventory of raw materials and inventory of work-in-progress. This is because the company knows that investors and lenders are interested in the materially different types of risk attached to these two types of inventory. However, the inventory of finished goods is given as a single item with no separation into the types of finished goods. That is because the company knows that investors see no material differences of risk in the types of finished goods; it is the overall amount that is of material interest.

4.2.4 Enhancing qualitative characteristics

The enhancing qualitative characteristics are: comparability; verifiability; timeliness; and understandability.

Comparability[13]

Comparability enables users to identify and understand similarities in, and differences among, items. Consistency refers to the use of the same methods for the same items, either from period to period within a reporting entity or in a single period across entities. Comparability is the goal; consistency helps to achieve that goal. Does this mean that everything has to be treated in exactly the same way? The *Conceptual Framework* notes that comparability is not uniformity. For information to be comparable, like things must look alike and different things must look different. Comparability is not enhanced by making unlike things look alike any more than it is enhanced by making like things look different.

To test this idea, find statements of financial position for two companies. Compare the way in which non-current assets are reported. Can you see similarities? Can you see differences? Do you think the financial statements meet the test of comparability?

It may be argued that fair value provides more comparability than historical cost value when assets and liabilities are reported (see Chapter 2, section 2.2.3). This is because fair values are all measured at the same date when the financial statements are prepared, whereas historical cost was measured at varying times in the past.

Verifiability[14]

Verifiability means that different knowledgeable and independent observers could reach consensus (broad agreement), although not necessarily complete agreement, that a particular depiction is a faithful representation. Direct verification is usually carried out by auditors on behalf of investors. Auditors have access to information underlying the financial statements. Other users might verify information by reference to other external sources or by comparisons. Preparers can help users by disclosing the assumptions on which financial information is based.

It may be argued that fair value is more difficult to verify than historical cost value when assets and liabilities are reported (see Chapter 2, section 2.2.3). This is because fair values are based on market values which may, in some cases, fluctuate frequently or be difficult to determine. Historical cost is measured using a transaction for which there is evidence in the documentation of the transaction.

Timeliness[15]

Timeliness means having information available to decision-makers in time to be capable of influencing their decisions. Generally, the older the information is the less useful it is. However, some information may continue to be timely long after the end of a reporting period because, for example, some users may need to identify and assess trends. You will see in company annual reports that there are tables of 5-year trends as well as the most recent financial information. National regulators know that timeliness is important and often impose time deadlines for reporting, particularly where companies have a stock market listing.

Understandability[16]

Financial information is understandable if it is presented clearly and concisely, using recognisable classification and descriptions. That seems obvious but the *Conceptual Framework* makes it explicit. There is also a warning that complex transactions may be difficult to understand because they are complex. Financial information cannot take away that type of complexity. All it can do is try to make the complexity understandable by clear descriptions. One very significant assumption in the *Conceptual Framework* is that users have a reasonable knowledge of business and economic activities and will review and analyse the information diligently. Even then such persons may sometimes need to take advice on complex matters.

4.2.5 Cost constraint on useful financial reporting[17]

Reporting financial information imposes costs, and it is important that those costs are justified by the benefits of reporting that information. The cost to preparers is eventually born by investors in reduced profits. The benefits are seen in more efficient operation of the capital markets. The standard-setter has to balance such costs and benefits in developing accounting standards.

4.2.6 Other characteristics of financial information

When the IASB revised its *Conceptual Framework* in 2010 it omitted some characteristics that appeared in the original 1989 version. However, these terms remain widely used in discussion of accounting. In particular you may hear about **prudence**, **reliability** and **substance over form**. Strong objections to the omission led to the reinstatement of *prudence* and *substance over form* in the 2016 version.

Prudence

The preparers of financial statements have to contend with uncertainty surrounding many events and circumstances. The existence of uncertainties is recognised by the disclosure of their nature and extent and by the exercise of prudence in the preparation of the financial statements. Prudence is the inclusion of a degree of caution in the exercise of the judgements needed in making the estimates required under conditions of uncertainty, such that gains and assets are not overstated and losses and liabilities are not understated.

This guidance was provided in the 1989 version of the IASB *Framework*.[18] It was removed from the 2010 version because the standard-setters concluded that describing *prudence* or *conservatism* as a qualitative characteristic or a desirable response to uncertainty would conflict with the quality of *neutrality*. They felt that encouraging preparers to be prudent was likely to lead to a bias in the reported financial position and financial performance. Introducing biased understatement of assets (or overstatement of liabilities) in one period frequently leads to overstating financial performance in later periods – a result that cannot be described as prudent. The 2016 version reinstates the definition of *prudence*.

Definition	**Prudence** is the exercise of caution when making judgements under conditions of uncertainty. The exercise of prudence is consistent with neutrality and should not allow the overstatement or understatement of assets, liabilities, income or expenses.[19]

Reliability[20]

In the IASB *Framework* (1989) reliability was defined as:

Information has the quality of reliability when it is free from material error and bias and can be depended upon by users to represent faithfully that which it either purports to represent or could reasonably be expected to represent.

This characteristic sat alongside relevance as a principal characteristic. It was replaced in the 2010 version by 'faithful representation'. The standard-setters explained that when they consulted on the changes they found different respondents had different interpretations of 'reliability'. Some thought it meant freedom from error, others thought it meant verifiability. The standard-setters tried to clarify the meaning of reliability but eventually concluded that 'faithful representation' gave the clearest understanding of what reliability is intended to mean.[21]

Substance over form

The IASB *Framework* (1989) made clear that if information is to meet the test of faithful representation, then the method of accounting must reflect the **substance** of the economic reality of the transaction and not merely its **legal form**.[22]

For example, a company has sold its buildings to a bank to raise cash and then pays rent for the same buildings for the purpose of continued occupation. The company carries all the risks and problems (such as repairs and insurance) that an owner would carry. One view is that the commercial substance of that sequence of transactions is comparable to retaining ownership. Another view is that the legal form of the transaction is a sale. The characteristic of substance over form requires that the information in the financial statements should show the commercial substance of the situation.

This characteristic was omitted from the 2010 *Conceptual Framework* because the standard -setters thought that any attempt to represent legal form in a way that differed from the economic substance of the underlying economic phenomenon could not result in a faithful representation. Accordingly, it was not necessary to be explicit. In response to objections, the explicit statement is made in the 2016 version, within faithful representation.

Definition	When the legal form of an item is different from its underlying economic substance, reporting that item in accordance with its legal form would not result in a **faithful representation**.[23]

4.3 Accounting principles

The accounting principles that are most widely known in the UK are found within the Companies Act 2006:[24]

- going concern
- accruals

- consistency
- prudence.

The IASB *Conceptual Framework* refers to the accrual basis as a means of reflecting financial performance and to going concern as an 'underlying assumption' in the preparation of financial statements. Consistency is an aspect of comparability. Prudence is a 'qualitative characteristic'.

4.3.1   Going concern

Definition

> The financial statements are normally prepared on the assumption that an entity is a **going concern** and will continue in operation for the foreseeable future. Hence, it is assumed that the entity has neither the intention nor the need to liquidate or curtail materially the scale of its operations; if such an intention or need exists the financial statements may have to be prepared on a different basis and, if so, the basis used is disclosed.[25]

The UK Companies Act statement on **going concern** is rather like a crossword clue, in being short and enigmatic. It states: 'The company shall be presumed to be carrying on business as a going concern.'

The Financial Reporting Council (FRC) provides practical guidance for directors on going concern assessment and disclosure. As a consequence of the financial crisis of 2007–08, the FRC asked Lord Sharman to chair a Panel of Inquiry to consider going concern and liquidity risks. The inquiry report, published in 2012, raised questions about the quality of information provided on companies' financial health and their ability to withstand economic and financial stresses in the short, medium and longer term.

Among the Sharman recommendations were the following:

1 The FRC should consider a requirement for integrating the going concern assessment with the directors' disclosures of business planning and risk management, focusing on both liquidity and solvency risks.
2 The FRC should move away from a position where disclosures are only highlighted where there are significant doubts about an entity's survival, to an approach integrated with the discussion of strategy and principal risks and the audit committee's discussion of the process adopted and issues considered.
3 The FRC should consider requiring auditors to report whether they have anything to add to or emphasise in relation to the directors' going concern disclosures.

Following consultation, the FRC published *Guidance on Risk Management, Internal Control and Related Financial and Business Reporting* in 2014. Boards of those companies applying the UK Corporate Governance Code must provide two statements as follows:

1 In annual and half-yearly financial statements, the directors should state whether they considered it appropriate to adopt the going concern basis of accounting in preparing them, and identify any material uncertainties to the company's ability to continue to do so over a period of at least 12 months from the date of approval of the financial statements; and
2 The directors should state whether, taking account of the company's current position and principal risks, they have a reasonable expectation that the company will be able to continue in operation and meet its liabilities as they fall due over the period of their assessment, drawing attention to any qualifications or assumptions as necessary.

The FRC explains that its *Guidance* refers to the 'going concern basis of accounting' for the preparation of financial statements, as defined in accounting standards. This is different from the ordinary English usage of the term 'going concern' to describe an entity that has a viable longer-term future. The international standard IAS 1 requires that the minimum period considered for the going concern basis of accounting be at least, but not limited to, 12 months from the reporting date. The UK standard FRS 102 is similar. In practice most companies refer to a 12-month period.

Companies that have a Premium listing in the UK are required by the Listing Rules to include in their annual financial report a statement that the business is a going concern, together with supporting assumptions or qualifications as necessary, that has been prepared in accordance with the FRC *Guidance*.

The auditor is required to consider the disclosures about going concern and liquidity risk made in the financial statements. If the auditor concludes that the disclosures are not adequate to meet the requirements of accounting standards and CA 2006, including the need for financial statements to give a true and fair view, the auditor is required to qualify its opinion and to provide its reasons for doing so.

4.3.2 Accruals (also called 'matching')

Definition

Accrual accounting depicts the effects of transactions and other events and circumstances on a reporting entity's economic resources and claims in the periods in which those effects occur, even if the resulting cash receipts and payments occur in a different period. This is important because information about a reporting entity's economic resources and claims and changes in its economic resources and claims during a period provides a better basis for assessing the entity's past and future performance than information solely about cash receipts and payments during that period.[26]

Financial statements prepared on the accruals basis are useful for stewardship purposes because they report past transactions and events but are also helpful to users for forward-looking information because they show obligations to pay cash in the future and resources that represent cash to be received in the future.

The UK Companies Act explains the accruals concept as a requirement that all income and charges (i.e. expenses) relating to the financial year shall be taken into account, without regard to the date of receipt or payment.

The word 'accrue' means 'to fall due' or 'to come as a natural result'. If, during a year, a company sells £100m of goods but collects only £80m from customers, it records sales as £100m in the profit and loss account. The cash yet to be collected from customers is reported as an asset called 'debtor' in the statement of financial position (balance sheet). If, during the year, it uses electricity costing £50m but has only paid £40m so far, it records the expense of £50m in the profit and loss account. The unpaid electricity bill is reported as a liability called 'accruals' in the statement of financial position (balance sheet).

The idea of matching is also used in applying the idea of accruals. Matching has two forms, matching losses or gains against time and matching expenses against revenue. Time matching occurs when a gain or loss is spread over the relevant period of time, such as receiving interest on a loan or paying rent on a property. Matching of revenues and expenses occurs when costs such as labour are matched against the revenue earned from providing goods or services.

4.3.3 Consistency

Consistency is described in the IASB *Conceptual Framework* as an aspect of comparability (see Section 4.2.4). The UK Companies Act requires that accounting policies shall be applied consistently within the same accounts and from one period to the next.

4.3.4   Prudence

The Companies Act does not define prudence but uses the word prudent in relation to measurement. It requires that the amount of any item shall be determined on a prudent basis, and in particular:

(a) only profits realised at the date of the financial year-end shall be included in the profit and loss account; and

(b) all liabilities and losses which have arisen or are likely to arise in respect of the financial year shall be taken into account, including those which only become apparent between the date of the financial year-end and the date on which it is signed by the board of directors.[27]

The IASB's definition of prudence is in section 4.2.6.

4.3.5   Realisation

There is no clear statement of the conditions that will make a profit **realised**. If you turn to a dictionary, you will find 'realise' equated to 'covert into cash'. The Companies Act 2006 refers to realised profit, in setting conditions for dividend payments, but does not define the term. It is not defined in the IASB system. For UK companies there is professional guidance in a Technical Release issued in 2010. The Technical Release states:

It is generally accepted that profits shall be treated as realised for the purpose of applying the definition of realised profits in companies legislation only when realised in the form of cash or other assets the ultimate cash realisation of which can be assessed with reasonable certainty. In this context, 'realised' may encompass profits relating to assets that are readily realisable. This would embrace profits and losses resulting from the recognition of changes in fair values, in accordance with relevant accounting standards, to the extent that they are readily convertible to cash.[28]

This guidance leaves scope for professional judgement on what is meant by 'reasonable certainty' when something other than ready access to cash is involved. The ultimate decision will rest with a court of law when a dividend payment is challenged.

Activity 4.1	*Take a piece of paper having two wide columns. Head the left-hand column 'My thoughts on measurement in accounting' and head the right-hand column 'What the book tells me about measurement'. Fill in both columns and then exchange your paper with a fellow student. Discuss with each other any similarities and differences in the left-hand column and relate these to your personal views and prior experience. Discuss with each other any similarities and differences in the right-hand column and evaluate the extent to which different people see books differently. Finally, discuss with each other the extent to which reading this section has changed your views on measurement as a subject in accounting.*

4.4   Applying prudence

Section 4.3.4 shows that the Companies Act 2006 makes an explicit link between prudence and realisation. Traditional conservatism of accounting practice tends towards understatement on grounds of caution.

The IASB encourages a neutral approach:

the exercise of prudence is consistent with neutrality and should not allow the overstatement or understatement of assets, liabilities, income or expenses.[29]

Why are there different views on understatement and overstatement, depending on the item being reported? Here is your first chance to use the accounting equation to solve a problem:

Assets	minus	Liabilities	equals	Capital contributed/withdrawn plus Profit

Profit		equals	Revenue minus Expenses

Activity 4.2	*Ask yourself what will happen to profit in the accounting equation if the amount of an asset is increased while the liabilities and the capital contributed remain the same. Then ask yourself what will happen to profit in the accounting equation if the amount of a liability is decreased while the assets and the capital contributed remain the same. Next ask yourself what will happen to profit if revenue is overstated. Finally ask yourself what will happen to profit if expenses are understated.*

Assuming that capital contributed/withdrawn remains constant, overstating assets will overstate profit. Understating liabilities will overstate profit. Overstating revenue will overstate profit. Understating expenses will overstate profit.

Examples

A market trader buys £100 of stock on credit, promising to pay the supplier at the end of the day. The trader sells three-quarters of the stock at a price of £90 and takes the rest home to keep for next week's market. At the end of the day the trader has £90 in cash, one-quarter of the stock which cost £25, and owes £100 to the supplier. How much profit has the trader made? The answer is that the profit is £15 (£90 received for the sale of stock less the cost of the items sold, £75, being three-quarters of the stock purchased). The accounting equation is:

Assets minus Liabilities at the end of the period	equals	Ownership interest at the start of the period plus Capital contributed/ withdrawn plus Revenue of the period minus Expenses of the period
stock £25 + cash £90 − liability £100	equals	nil + nil + revenue £90 − expenses £75
£15	equals	£15

1 Supposing the trader 'forgets' part of the liability and thinks it is only £84 owing, rather than £100. The assets remain at stock £25 + cash £90, which equals £115. The liability is now thought to be £84 and therefore the equation becomes:

£25 + £90 − £84	equals	nil + nil + revenue £90 − expenses £75 + [?] £16 [?]
£31	equals	£31

For the equation to be satisfied there must be a total of £31 on both sides. The total of £31 is therefore written in. The recorded profit is still only £15, calculated as revenue £90 minus expenses £75, so there is a 'hole' amounting to £16 on the right-hand side of the equation. The accounting equation has to balance so the extra £16 is written in, surrounded by question marks, on the right-hand side. It is assumed on the right-hand side that the trader has either forgotten to record revenue of £16 or has recorded too much expense, so that the amount appears to represent an unexplained profit. Thus *understating a liability will overstate profit.* That favourable news might mislead a competitor or investor. It might be bad news when HMRC demands tax on profit of £31. Also there is the unpaid supplier who may not be entirely patient when offered £84 rather than £100.

2 Supposing instead that the trader 'forgets' there is some unsold inventory left. The only recorded asset would be the cash at £90 and there would be a liability of £100. This gives negative net assets of (£10) and, because the accounting equation has to balance, suggests that there is a 'forgotten' expense of £25 on the right-hand side. The equation then becomes:

£90 − £100	equals	nil + nil + £90 − £75 − [?] £25 [?]
(£10)	equals	(£10)

This would cause the tax authority, HMRC, to ask a lot of questions as to why there was no record of stock remaining, because they know that omitting inventory from the record is a well-tried means of fraudulently reducing profits and therefore reducing tax bills. *Understating an asset will understate profit.*

These two examples have illustrated the meaning of the warning that deliberate understatement or overstatement is not acceptable. The general message of prudence is: *avoid overstating profit.* In down-to-earth terms, don't raise the readers' hopes too high, only to have to tell them later that it was all in the imagination.

4.5 Regulation of financial reporting

Because the external users of accounting information do not have day-to-day access to the records of the business, they rely on the integrity and judgement of management to provide suitable information of a high quality. But will the management be honest, conscientious and careful in providing information? In an ideal world there should be no problem for investors in a company because, as shareholders, they appoint the directors and may dismiss them if dissatisfied with the service provided. However, the world is not ideal. Some companies are very large and they have many shareholders whose identity changes as shares are bought and sold. Over the years it has been found that regulation is needed, particularly for financial reporting by companies. The general regulation of companies in the UK is provided by parliamentary legislation, through the Companies Act 2006.

However, since 2005 the regulation of financial reporting by UK companies has taken two separate routes depending on the type of company.[30]

The group financial statements of listed companies must comply with the IAS Regulation set by the European Commission. The IAS Regulation takes precedence over the relevant sections of the Companies Act. The IAS Regulation was issued in 2002, requiring listed group financial statements from 2005 to apply approved International Financial Reporting Standards (IFRS) (previously called International Accounting Standards, IAS). The UK government subsequently permitted individual companies and non-listed groups to choose to apply IFRS. Any companies not taking up this choice must continue to apply the relevant sections of the Companies Act and follow the accounting standards set by the UK Financial Reporting Council (previously set by the Accounting Standards Board (ASB)). Other organisations that are not companies (such as sole traders, partnership, public sector bodies) have to look to the regulations that govern their operations to decide which accounting guidance to follow.

So how can we tell which accounting system has been applied in any situation? Look first for the audit report, if there is one. That will include a paragraph starting 'In our opinion'. In that paragraph the auditors will specify the accounting system on which their opinion is based. If there is no auditors' report, look for the Note on Accounting Policies. There will usually be a paragraph stating the accounting system that has been applied.

4.5.1 The IAS Regulation

In 2002 the European Commission issued the *IAS Regulation* which took effect from 1 January 2005. Its purpose is to harmonise the financial information presented by public listed companies in order to ensure a high degree of transparency and comparability of financial statements. The Regulation is relatively short but has been extended and clarified by a trail of subsequent documents. The European Commission publishes all documents on its website[31] in the languages of all member states but that is more detail than is necessary for a first-year course.

A Regulation is directly applicable in member states. It has a higher status than a Directive, which is an instruction to member states on the content of their national laws. Before the Regulation was issued, the company law of member states was harmonised by following the Fourth and Seventh Directives on company law. Companies in member states did not need to know the Directives because the national company law applied the Directives. Now that the IAS Regulation is directly applicable, member states must ensure that they do not seek to apply to a company any additional elements of national law that are contrary to, conflict with or restrict a company's compliance with IASs.

The Commission decides on the applicability of IFRS within the Community. It is assisted by an Accounting Regulatory Committee and is advised by a technical group called the European Financial Reporting and Accounting Group (EFRAG).[32] The tests for adoption of IFRS are that the standards:

(a) do not contradict the true and fair view principles of the Fourth and Seventh Directive (now combined in the Accounting Directive 2013),
(b) are conducive to the European public good, and
(c) meet the criteria of understandability, relevance, reliability and comparability required of financial information needed for making economic decisions and assessing the stewardship of management.

A standard that is adopted is said to be **endorsed**. If a standard is awaiting endorsement, or is rejected, it may be used as guidance if it is not inconsistent with endorsed standards. If a rejected standard is in conflict with adopted standards, it may not be used. When the European Commission first announced the endorsement process there were fears expressed that this would be used to create 'European IFRS' by selecting some IFRS and rejecting others. The Commission's reply was that the EU cannot give its powers to a body (the IASB) that is not subject to EU jurisdiction, and it is necessary for the EU to endorse standards as part of its duty in setting laws for member states.

4.5.2 UK company law

Companies Act 2006

The Companies Act 2006 sets many rules to protect those investing in companies and to guide those operating companies. Parts of the Act cover the information presented in financial statements. For companies and other organisations that do not follow the IAS Regulation, the Companies Act 2006, by means of Statutory Instruments, prescribes formats of presentation of the statement of financial position (balance sheet) and profit and loss account. Companies must select one of the permitted formats. It also prescribes methods of valuation of the assets and liabilities contained in the statement of financial position (balance sheet), broadly expecting that normally these items will be recorded at their cost at the date of acquisition, subject to diminutions in value since that date. Some other approaches to valuation are permitted, but these are carefully regulated and are subject to requirements for prudence, consistency and an expectation that the business is a going concern (i.e. will continue for some time into the future). The UK legislation places strong emphasis on the requirement to present a **true and fair view** in financial statements.

Since the early 1980s company law on financial reporting has been harmonised with that of other Member States in the EU through the Fourth and Seventh Directives of the EU, now the Accounting Directive 2013 (see Chapter 7).

The directors are responsible for the preparation of company accounts. Exhibit 4.1 (see p. 94) sets out the statement made by directors of one major public company regarding their responsibilities in these matters. This type of statement will be found in the annual reports of most of the large listed companies. It is regarded as an important aspect of giving reassurance to investors and others that there is a strong system of corporate governance within the company. It is also intended to clarify any misunderstandings the shareholders may have about the work of directors as distinct from the work of the auditors (see below).

The Companies (Audit, Investigations and Community Enterprise) Act, 2004 made changes intended to improve the reliability of financial reporting, the independence of auditors and disclosure to auditors. In particular it required a statement to be inserted in the directors' report confirming that there is no relevant information that has not been disclosed to the auditors.

4.5.3   The Financial Reporting Council[33]

The Financial Reporting Council (FRC) describes itself as the UK's independent regulator responsible for promoting high quality corporate governance and reporting to foster investment. It is recognised in its regulatory role by the UK government's Department for Business, Innovation and Skills. The government effectively delegates responsibility to an independent body but maintains close interest in the strategy and operations of the FRC.

There was a major restructuring of the FRC in July 2012. This section describes the current structure but also refers to the previous structure to explain terms that you may still encounter.

The FRC carries out a range of roles. Most relevant to this textbook is that it monitors and enforces accounting and auditing standards. It promotes high standards of corporate governance through the UK Corporate Governance Code. It sets standards for corporate reporting and actuarial practice. It also oversees the regulatory activities of the professional accountancy bodies and the actuarial profession and operates independent disciplinary arrangements for public interest cases involving accountants and actuaries.

The FRC is an independent body governed by a Board whose members are drawn from a wide range of business expertise.

The structure is summarised in Figure 4.1. Aspects of the FRC's work relevant to financial reporting are then described in this section.

Accounting role

One role of the FRC is to issue UK accounting standards. UK accounting standards apply to all companies, and other entities that prepare accounts that are intended to provide a true and fair view, unless International Financial Reporting Standards apply. IFRS apply to companies listed on a Stock Exchange.

The FRC took over this standard-setting role in July 2012. Until then it was carried out by the Accounting Standards Board (ASB) as a subsidiary of the FRC. The ASB had

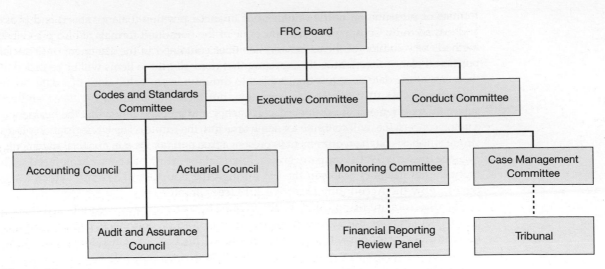

Figure 4.1
Structure of the Financial Reporting Council

previously taken over the task of setting accounting standards from the Accounting Standards Committee (ASC) in 1990. Accounting standards are now combined in one document, FRS 102 *The Financial Reporting Standard.*

The FRC also collaborates with accounting standard-setters from other countries and with the International Accounting Standards Board (IASB). In this way the FRC seeks to influence the development of international standards and to ensure that its own standards are developed with due regard to international developments.

Codes and Standards Committee

The Codes and Standards Committee is responsible for advising the FRC Board on maintaining an effective framework of UK codes and standards for Corporate Governance, Stewardship, Accounting, Auditing and Assurance, and Actuarial technical standards. For this textbook the most important functions of this committee relate to accounting standards and auditing and assurance standards.

Accounting Council

The detailed remit uses 'consider and advise' to describe the activities of the Accounting Council. The FRC receives the advice in its role of setting accounting standards. A Council which provides strategic input and thought leadership, within widespread consultation and research, is valuable in maintaining UK influence on the international standard-setting process.

The Council consists of up to twelve members, at least half of which are practising members of the relevant profession and the remainder will be other stakeholders. Members of the Councils are appointed through an open process overseen by the Chair of the Codes and Standards Committee (CSC) subject to the overall guidance of the Nominations Committee of the FRC.

Audit and Assurance Council

The Audit and Assurance Council has remit of similar type to that of the Accounting Council. The words are 'considers and comments' or 'considers and advises'. The FRC's Codes and Standards Committee advises the FRC on developing and maintaining standards and guidance for Audit and Assurance engagements that are performed in the public interest within the United Kingdom and Republic of Ireland. It also seeks to influence the development of international auditing and assurance standards and policy, issues that are relevant to its remit.

Conduct Committee

The Conduct Committee oversees the Conduct Division which encompasses the FRC's monitoring, oversight, investigative and disciplinary functions. It covers audit quality review, corporate reporting review, professional discipline and professional oversight, and supervisory enquiries.

Of particular relevance to this chapter, the work of the Conduct Division includes direct monitoring of financial reports and audits of public interest entities.

Under the Companies Act 2006 ('the Act') the Conduct Committee has been authorised and appointed by the Secretary of State for the Department of Business, Innovation and Skills (BIS) to exercise functions with a view to ensuring that accounts and financial and other reports, including annual reports, and directors' reports (Reports) of companies and other entities comply with the law and relevant reporting requirements.

The Conduct Committee's policy is to select Reports for review (a) by methods which take into account the Conduct Committee's assessment of the risk of non-compliance and the consequence of non-compliance, and (b) as a result of complaints.

The Conduct Committee maintains a Financial Reporting Review Panel (FRRP) comprising individuals who have the appropriate qualifications and experience to sit on a Review Group including the Chairman and Deputy Chairman or Chairmen who are also members of the Conduct Committee and the Monitoring Committee. Review Groups will be appointed from the FRRP by the Monitoring Committee.

The legal powers and duties described above for the Conduct Committee were, prior to July 2011, allocated to the FRRP. Consequently this type of monitoring work has been in place for many years and previous reports will be found under the authorship of the Financial Reporting Review Panel.

The Conduct Committee can ask directors to explain apparent departures from the requirements. If it is not satisfied by the directors' explanations it aims to persuade them to adopt a more appropriate accounting treatment. The directors may then voluntarily withdraw their accounts and replace them with revised accounts that correct the matters in error. Depending on the circumstances, the Conduct Committee may accept another form of remedial action – for example, correction of the comparative figures in the next set of annual financial statements. Failing voluntary correction, the Conduct Committee can exercise its powers to secure the necessary revision of the original accounts through a court order. The FRC maintains a legal costs fund of £2m for this purpose. The Conduct Committee's predecessor, the FRRP, enjoyed a long and successful record in resolving all cases brought to its attention without having to apply for a court order. The Conduct Committee does not offer advice on the application of accounting standards or on the accounting requirements of the Companies Act 2006.

4.5.4   Corporate governance[34]

UK listed companies are required by the Stock Exchange to apply the Corporate Governance Code. Institutional investors are encouraged to recognise their responsibilities by adhering to the Stewardship Code. Both are explained in this section.

Corporate governance code

Corporate governance is a term applied to the way in which a company is managed by its directors to show a high level of responsibility to shareholders and the wider capital market. The UK has a tradition of codes of corporate governance dating

Exhibit 4.1
Statement of directors' responsibilities as expressed in the annual report of a public limited company

Financial Statements and accounting records

The Directors are responsible for preparing the Annual Report and Accounts including the Directors' Remuneration Report and the Financial Statements in accordance with applicable law and regulations.

Company law requires the Directors to prepare financial statements for each financial year. The Directors are required by the International Accounting Standards Regulation (the 'IAS Regulation') to prepare the Group Financial Statements under International Financial Reporting Standards as adopted by the European Union ('IFRS') and have also elected to prepare the Parent Company Financial Statements in accordance with IFRS. The Financial Statements are also required by law to be properly prepared in accordance with the Companies Act 2006 and Article 4 of the IAS Regulation. Under the Disclosure and Transparency Rules, the Directors must not approve the Accounts unless they are satisfied that they give a true and fair view of the state of affairs of the Company and of the profit or loss of the Company for that period.

International Accounting Standard 1 requires that Financial Statements present fairly for each financial year the Company's financial position, financial performance and cash flows. This requires the faithful representation of the effects of transactions, other events and conditions in accordance with the definitions and recognition criteria for assets, liabilities, income and expenses set out in the International Accounting Standards Board's 'Framework for the preparation and presentation of financial statements'. In virtually all circumstances, a fair presentation will be achieved by compliance with all applicable IFRS. Directors are also required to:

- properly select and apply accounting policies;
- present information, including accounting policies, in a manner that provides relevant, reliable, comparable and understandable information;
- provide additional disclosures when compliance with the specific requirements in IFRS are insufficient to enable users to understand the impact of particular transactions, other events and conditions on the entity's financial position and financial performance; and
- make an assessment of the Company's ability to continue as a going concern.

The Directors are responsible for keeping adequate accounting records that are sufficient to show and explain the Company's transactions and disclose with reasonable accuracy at any time the financial position of the Company and enable them to ensure that the Financial Statements comply with the Companies Act 2006. They are also responsible for safeguarding the assets of the Company and hence for taking reasonable steps for the prevention and detection of fraud and other irregularities.

The Directors are responsible for the maintenance and integrity of the corporate and financial information included on the Company's website. Legislation in the United Kingdom governing the preparation and dissemination of financial statements may differ from legislation in other jurisdictions.

Fair, balanced and understandable

The Board considers, on the advice of the Audit Committee, that the Annual Report and Accounts, taken as a whole, is fair, balanced and understandable and provides the information necessary for shareholders to assess the Company's performance, business model and strategy.

Disclosure and Transparency Rules

The Directors confirm that, to the best of each person's knowledge:

(a) the Group and Parent Company Financial Statements in this Annual Report and Accounts, which have been prepared in accordance with IFRS, Standing Interpretation Committee interpretations as adopted and endorsed by the European Union, International Financial Reporting Interpretations Committee interpretations and those parts of the Companies Act 2006 applicable to companies reporting under IFRS, give a true and fair view of the assets, liabilities, financial position and profit or loss of the Company and of the Group taken as a whole; and

(b) the Annual Report and Accounts includes a fair review of the development and performance of the business and the position of the Company and the Group taken as a whole, together with a description of the principal risks and uncertainties they face.

Directors' statement under the UK Corporate Governance Code

Having taken advice from the Audit Committee, the Board considers that the Annual Report taken as a whole is fair, balanced and understandable and that it provides the information necessary for shareholders to assess the Company's performance, business model and strategy.

Exhibit 4.1 continued

Disclosure of information to Auditor

The Directors who held office as at the date of approval of this report confirm that they have taken steps to make themselves aware of relevant audit information (as defined by section 418(3) of the Companies Act 2006). None of the Directors are aware of any relevant audit information which has not been disclosed to the Company's Auditor.

By order of the Board

(signed) .... Group Chief Executive, ... Group Finance Director
(Date)

from 1992. Initially the codes were written by committees and given the names of the chairs of the committees. Thus during the 1990s we saw in succession the Cadbury Code, the Greenbury Code and the Hampel Code (explained further in Chapter 14, section 14.7.1). These were consolidated as the *UK Corporate Governance Code*. Responsibility for maintaining the *UK Corporate Governance Code* now rests with the Financial Reporting Council.

The Code sets out good practice covering issues such as board composition and effectiveness, the role of board committees, risk management, remuneration and relations with shareholders. It operates on the principle of 'comply or explain'. If companies comply with the recommendations of the Code they do not need to describe compliance at great length. If they do not comply with any specific aspect, they must provide an explanation in the annual report.

The main recommendations of the Code include:

- separate Chairman and Chief Executive;
- a balance of executive and independent non-executive directors;
- strong, independent audit and remuneration committees;
- annual evaluation by the board of its performance;
- transparency on appointments and remuneration;
- effective rights for shareholders, who are encouraged to engage with the companies in which they invest.

Stewardship code

Experience with the Corporate Governance Code, particularly in the period of financial crisis around 2007 and 2008, indicated that something more was needed to enhance the quality of engagement between institutional investors and companies. The Stewardship Code was introduced to meet this need and to complement the Corporate Governance Code. It is written with the aim of helping to improve long-term returns to shareholders and the efficient exercise of governance responsibilities.

The word 'engagement' is used to emphasise the idea of all parties meeting and talking to each other. It expects purposeful dialogue on strategy, performance and the management of risk, as well as on issues that are the immediate subject of votes at general meetings.

Institutional shareholders are free to choose whether or not to engage as recommended by the Code but once the institution has agreed, their employees and agents are expected to follow the agreed procedures.

The main principles are that institutional investors should:

- publicly disclose their policy on how they will discharge their stewardship responsibilities;
- have a robust policy on managing conflicts of interest in relation to stewardship and this policy should be publicly disclosed;
- monitor their investee companies;

- establish clear guidelines on when and how they will escalate their activities as a method of protecting and enhancing shareholder value;
- be willing to act collectively with other investors where appropriate;
- have a clear policy on voting and disclosure of voting activity;
- report periodically on their stewardship and voting activities.

4.5.5 Stock Exchange regulation

The Financial Conduct Authority (FCA) is a single regulator with responsibility across a wide range of financial market activity. In particular it regulates listing of companies' shares on the UK Stock Exchange. The FCA has a department called the UK Listing Authority (UKLA). When a company first has its shares listed, it must produce a prospectus, which is normally much more detailed than the annual report. The regulations covering the content of a prospectus have been set by the UKLA. Once a company has achieved a listing, it must keep up with ongoing obligations under the Listing Rules and the Disclosure and Transparency Rules. This ongoing obligation includes providing accounting information to the market in the annual report and making press releases. Details of the Listing Rules are not necessary for first-level study but you should be aware that these have an influence on the content of a company's annual report. The Disclosure and Transparency Rules affect the content and timing of annual reports published by companies.

There are three kinds of listing on the UK Stock Exchange: Premium (previously called Primary); Standard (previously called Secondary); and AIM (the Alternative Investment Market). Different levels of regulation and disclosure apply to each. A Premium Listing means the company is expected to meet the UK's highest standards of regulation and corporate governance – and as a consequence may enjoy a lower cost of capital through greater transparency and through building investor confidence. Issuers with a Premium Listing are required to meet the UK's 'super-equivalent' rules which are higher than the EU minimum requirement. Such companies are eligible for inclusion in the FTSE indices. A Standard Listing is more commonly used by overseas companies, as it allows issuers to access the main market by meeting EU harmonised standards only rather than the UK 'super-equivalent' requirements. AIM companies are usually newer and smaller companies making their initial entry to market trading for their shares. AIM listed companies are regulated but not as strongly as the Premium listed companies. Consequently the annual reports of AIM listed companies are less detailed.

4.5.6 Auditors

The shareholders of companies do not have a right of access to the records of the day-to-day running of the business, and so they need someone to act on their behalf to ensure that the directors are presenting a true and fair view of the company's position at a point in time and of the profits generated during a period of time. To achieve this reassurance, the shareholders appoint a firm of auditors to investigate the company's financial records and give an opinion on the truth and fairness of the financial information presented. Exhibit 4.2 sets out the wording of a typical audit report to the shareholders of a public company. You will see that there are separate opinions on the financial statements and on other aspects of the accounting information recorded or provided by the company.

You will note that the auditors do not look at all the pages of the annual report. The earlier part of the annual report is important to the companies in setting the scene and explaining their businesses. These earlier pages are reviewed by the auditors to ensure that anything said there is consistent with the information presented in the

Exhibit 4.2
Sample audit report

Independent Auditors' Report to the Members of XYZ plc

We have audited the Group financial statements of XYZ plc for the year ended 31 December 2015 which comprise the Consolidated Income Statement, the Consolidated Statement of Comprehensive Income, the Consolidated Balance Sheet, the Consolidated Statement of Changes in Equity, the Consolidated Cash Flow Statement and the related notes 1 to 35. The financial reporting framework that has been applied in their preparation is applicable law and International Financial Reporting Standards (IFRSs) as adopted by the European Union.

This report is made solely to the Company's members, as a body, in accordance with Chapter 3 of Part 16 of the Companies Act 2006. Our audit work has been undertaken so that we might state to the Company's members those matters we are required to state to them in an auditor's report and for no other purpose. To the fullest extent permitted by law, we do not accept or assume responsibility to anyone other than the Company and the Company's members as a body, for our audit work, for this report, or for the opinions we have formed.

Respective responsibilities of directors and auditor

As explained more fully in the Directors' Responsibilities Statement set out on page nn, the directors are responsible for the preparation of the Group financial statements and for being satisfied that they give a true and fair view. Our responsibility is to audit and express an opinion on the Group financial statements in accordance with applicable law and International Standards on Auditing (ISAs) (UK and Ireland). Those standards require us to comply with the Auditing Practices Board's Ethical Standards for Auditors.

Scope of the audit of the financial statements

An audit involves obtaining evidence about the amounts and disclosures in the financial statements sufficient to give reasonable assurance that the financial statements are free from material misstatement, whether caused by fraud or error. This includes an assessment of: whether the accounting policies are appropriate to the Group's circumstances and have been consistently applied and adequately disclosed; the reasonableness of significant accounting estimates made by the directors; and the overall presentation of the financial statements. In addition, we read all the financial and non-financial information in the Annual Report and Accounts to identify material inconsistencies with the audited financial statements and to identify any information that is apparently materially incorrect based on, or materially inconsistent with, the knowledge acquired by us in the course of performing the audit. If we become aware of any apparent material misstatements or inconsistencies we consider the implications for our report.

Our assessment of risks of material misstatement

We consider that the following areas present the greatest risk of material misstatement in the financial statements and consequently have had the greatest impact on our audit strategy, the allocation of resources and the efforts of the engagement team, including the more senior members of the team:

- The assessment of the online sales debt provision;
- The assessment of inventory provisions;
- The assessment of underlying risk and valuation of, financial instruments; and
- The risk of misstatement arising from management override of internal controls with regard to estimates and other provisions relevant to the retail environment.

Our application of materiality

We apply the concept of materiality both in planning and performing our audit, and in evaluating the effect of misstatements on our audit and on the financial statements. For the purposes of determining whether the financial statements are free from material misstatement, we define materiality as the magnitude of misstatement that makes it probable that the economic decisions of a reasonably knowledgeable person, relying on the financial statements, would be changed or influenced.

We also determine a lower level of performance materiality which we use to determine the extent of testing needed to reduce to an appropriately low level the probability that the aggregate of uncorrected and undetected misstatements exceeds materiality for the financial statements as a whole.

When establishing our overall audit strategy, we determined a magnitude of uncorrected misstatements that we judged would be material for the financial statements as a whole. We determined materiality for the Group to be £35 million, which is approximately 5% of pre-exceptional pre-tax profit.

Exhibit 4.2 continued

On the basis of our risk assessments, together with our assessment of the Group's overall control environment, our judgement is that performance materiality for the Group should be 50% of materiality, namely £17.5 million. Our approach is designed to have a reasonable probability of ensuring that the total of uncorrected and undetected audit differences does not exceed our materiality for the financial statements as a whole.

We agreed with the Audit Committee that we would report to the Committee all audit differences in excess of £1.7 million, as well as differences below that threshold that, in our view, warranted reporting on qualitative grounds.

An overview of the scope of our audit

The Retail and Online Sales business operations accounting for 95% of the Group's revenue and 93% of total segment profit were subject to a full scope audit. The overseas Group purchasing division and the property management division contribute 5% of total segment profit and were subject to specific scope audits in areas where we assessed there was a risk of material misstatement. For the remaining components of the Group, we performed other procedures to confirm there were no significant risks of material misstatement in the Group financial statements.

In view of the nature of the main risk areas noted above, the Group audit team is supported by experts in auditing the financial instruments and their valuation.

The principal way in which we scoped our response to the risks noted above was as follows:

We checked management's categorisation of the debtor book based on payment in accordance with agreed terms. We challenged the reasonableness of the key assumptions in determining management's provision for future default, being the Group's assumed default rates (which represent the likelihood of eventual default for debt within each category), and expected recovery rates on such debts, in combination with evidence of historical default and recovery rates, current performance, and any observed changes in debtor profile in the current period. We checked the arithmetical accuracy of the provision based on management's assumptions and compared the underlying debtor book categorisation to the financial accounting system and the mapping of external affordability data.

The adequacy of the inventory provision depends on the level of stock on hand which is expected to be sold below cost plus attributable selling costs. We examined the Group's historical trading patterns of stock sold at full price, stock marked down below full price in a sale period, and the element of inventory that is passed to clearance; along with the related margins achieved for each of these sales channels. We then challenged the reasonableness of the inventory provision, taking into account a combination of the evidence of these historical trading patterns and any observed changes to the current year buying cycle.

We determined the different types of financial instruments held by the Group and the level of risk inherent in each of the transaction types. We analysed the features of a selected sample of financial instruments by comparison to the originating contractual agreements. With our experts, we challenged the reasonableness of the valuation of the selected sample where the Group's valuation was outside a reasonable tolerance of our own expectations.

We performed analytical procedures and journal entry testing in order to identify and test the risk of misstatement arising from management override of controls, which in addition to the risks disclosed above, focused on accruals and provisions of a judgemental nature capable of being manipulated by management. These comprised accruals for sales returns, gift card exposure, share based payments and long-term incentive plan (LTIP) arrangements; along with provisions for dilapidations, onerous leases and vacant leasehold properties.

Opinion on financial statements

In our opinion the Group financial statements:

- give a true and fair view of the state of the Group's affairs as at 31 December 2015 and of its profit for the year then ended;
- have been properly prepared in accordance with IFRSs as adopted by the European Union; and
- have been prepared in accordance with the requirements of the Companies Act 2006 and Article 4 of the IAS Regulation.

Opinion on other matters prescribed by the Companies Act 2006

In our opinion:

- the information given in the Strategic Report and the Directors' Report for the financial year for which the Group financial statements are prepared is consistent with the Group financial statements.

Exhibit 4.2 continued

Matters on which we are required to report by exception

We have nothing to report in respect of the following:

- Under the ISAs (UK and Ireland), we are required to report to you if, in our opinion, information in the annual report is:
  - materially inconsistent with the information in the audited financial statements; or
  - apparently materially incorrect based on, or materially inconsistent with, our knowledge of the Group acquired in the course of performing our audit; or
  - is otherwise misleading.

In particular, we are required to consider whether we have identified any inconsistencies between our knowledge acquired during the audit and the directors' statement that they consider the annual report is fair, balanced and understandable and whether the annual report appropriately discloses those matters that we communicated to the Audit Committee which we consider should have been disclosed.

- Under the Companies Act 2006 we are required to report to you if, in our opinion:
  - certain disclosures of directors' remuneration specified by law are not made; or
  - we have not received all the information and explanations we require for our audit.

- Under the Listing Rules we are required to review:
  - the directors' statement, set out on page nn, in relation to going concern; and
  - the part of the Corporate Governance Statement relating to the Company's compliance with the provisions of the UK Corporate Governance Code specified for our review.

Other matter

We have reported separately on the parent company financial statements of XYZ plc for the year ended 31 December 2015 and on the information in the Directors' Remuneration Report that is described as having been audited.

A B Name (Senior Statutory Auditor)
for and on behalf of DEF LLP
Statutory Auditor
London
Date

audited financial statements. You will also note that the auditors have their own code of practice, referred to as International Standards for Auditing (ISAs). The ISAs are prepared by the International Auditing and Assurance Standards Board (IAASB) which operates under a body called the International Financial Accounting Committee (IFAC). The standards are then adopted by national standard-setters. In the UK the national standard-setter is the Financial Reporting Council.

What surprises some readers is the phrase 'reasonable assurance that the financial statements are free from material misstatement'. The auditors are not expected to be totally certain in their opinion and they are only looking for errors or fraud which is material. Auditors are required to explain how they have applied 'materiality'.

A definition of materiality is provided in an auditing standard on the subject:

Definition   Misstatements, including omissions, are considered to be **material** if they, individually or in the aggregate, could reasonably be expected to influence the economic decisions of users taken on the basis of the financial statements.[35]

4.5.7 The tax system

Businesses pay tax to HM Revenue and Customs (HMRC) (as the tax-collecting agent of the government) based on the profits they make. Sole traders and partnerships pay income tax on their profits while companies pay corporation tax. There are differences in detail of the law governing these two types of taxes but broadly they both require as a starting point a calculation of profit using commercial accounting practices. The law governing taxation is quite separate from the law and regulations governing financial reporting, so in principle the preparation of financial statements is not affected by tax matters. That is very different from some other countries in the EU where the tax law stipulates that an item must be in the financial accounting statements if it is to be considered for tax purposes. Those countries have an approach to financial reporting which is more closely driven by taxation matters.

In the UK the distinction may be blurred in practice in the case of sole traders because HMRC is the main user of the financial statements of the sole trader. Similarly, tax factors may influence partnership accounts, although here the fairness of sharing among the partners is also important. The very smallest companies, where the owners also run the business, may in practice have the same attitude to tax matters as does the sole trader or partnership. For larger companies with a wider spread of ownership, the needs of shareholders will take priority.

4.5.8 Is regulation necessary?

There are those who would argue that all this regulatory mechanism is unnecessary. They take the view that in a market-based economy, competitive forces will ensure that those providing information will meet the needs of users. It is argued that investors will not entrust their funds to a business which provides inadequate information. Banks will not lend money unless they are provided with sufficient information to answer their questions about the likelihood of receiving interest and eventual repayment of the loan. Employee morale may be lowered if a business appears non-communicative regarding its present position and past record of performance. Suppliers may not wish to give credit to a business which appears secretive or has a reputation for producing poor-quality information. Customers may be similarly doubtful.

Against that quite attractive argument for the abolition of all regulations stand some well-documented financial scandals where businesses have failed. Employees have lost their jobs, with little prospect of finding comparable employment elsewhere; suppliers have not been paid and have found themselves in financial difficulties as a result. Customers have lost a source of supply and have been unable to meet the requirements of their own customers until a new source is found. Those who have provided long-term finance for the business, as lenders and investors, have lost their investment. Investigation shows that the signs and warnings had existed for those who were sufficiently experienced to see them, but these signs and warnings did not emerge in the published accounting information for external use.

Such financial scandals may be few in number but the large-scale examples cause widespread misery and lead to calls for action. Governments experience pressure from the electorate and lobby groups; professional bodies and business interest groups decide they ought to be seen to react; and new regulations are developed which ensure that the particular problem cannot recur. All parties are then reasonably satisfied that they have done their best to protect those who need protection against the imbalance of business life, and the new practices are used until the next scandal occurs and the process starts over again.

There is no clear answer to the question 'Is regulation necessary?' Researchers have not found any strong evidence that the forces of supply and demand in the market fail to work and have suggested that the need for regulation must be justified by showing that the benefits exceed the costs. That is quite a difficult challenge but is worth keeping in mind as you explore some of the more intricate aspects of accounting regulation.

Activity 4.3	*Look back through this section and, for each subheading, make a note of whether you were previously aware that such regulation existed. In each case, irrespective of your previous state of knowledge, do you now feel a greater or a lesser sense of confidence in accounting information? How strong is your confidence in published accounting information? If not 100%, what further reassurance would you require?*

4.6 Reviewing published financial statements

If you look at the annual report of any large listed company you will find that it has two main sections. The first part contains a variety of diagrams and photographs, a statement by the chairman, and a **strategic report** which may extend to a considerable number of pages. A directors' report will cover corporate governance. Other aspects of the business, such as the environmental policy, may also be explained. This first part is a mixture of regulated and unregulated material. There are many sources of influence on its contents, some of which will be explained in later chapters of this book.

The second part contains the financial statements, which are heavily regulated. As if to emphasise this change of status, the second part of the annual report will often have a different appearance, perhaps being printed on a different colour or grade of paper, or possibly having a smaller print size. Appendix I to this book contains extracts from the financial statements of a fictitious company, Safe and Sure plc, which will be used for illustration in this and subsequent chapters.

Relaxing after a hard workout at the health club, David Wilson took the opportunity to buy Leona a drink and tell her something about Safe and Sure prior to a visit to the company's headquarters to meet the finance director.

 DAVID: *This is a major listed company, registered in the UK but operating around the world selling its services in disposal and recycling, cleaning and security. Its name is well known and its services command high prices because of the company's reputation gained over many years. Basically it is a very simple business to understand. It sells services by making contracts with customers and collects cash when the service is performed.*

In preparation for my visit I looked first at the performance of the period. This company promises to deliver growth of at least 20% in revenue and in profit before tax so first of all I checked that the promise had been delivered. Sure enough, at the front of the annual report under 'Highlights of the year' there was a table showing revenue had increased by 22.4% and profit before tax had increased by 20.4%. I knew I would need to look through the profit and loss account in more detail to find out how the increases had come about, but first of all I read the operating review (written by the chief executive) and the financial review (written by the finance director). The chief executive gave more details on which areas had the greatest increase in revenue and operating profit and which areas had been disappointing. That all helps me in making my forecast of profit for next year.

The chief executive made reference to acquisitions during the year, so I knew I would also need to think whether the increase in revenue and profits was due to an improvement in sales and marketing as compared with last year or whether it reflected the inclusion of new business for the first time.

In the strategic report, the finance director explained that the business tries to use as little working capital as possible (that means they try to keep down the current assets and match them as far as possible with current liabilities). I guessed I would need to look at the statement of financial position to confirm that, so I headed next for the financial statements at the back of the annual report, pausing to glance at the auditors' report to make sure there was nothing highlighted by them as being amiss.

The financial statements are quite detailed and I wanted a broad picture so I noted down the main items from each in a summary format which leaves out some of the detail but which I find quite useful.

4.6.1 Income statement (profit and loss account)

Safe and Sure plc
Summarised income statement (profit and loss account) with comparative figures

	Notes	Year 7 £m	Year 6 £m
Continuing operations			
Revenue		7,146	5,893
Cost of sales		(4,910)	(4,063)
Gross profit		2,236	1,830
Expenses and interest		(261)	(260)
Profit before tax		1,975	1,570
Tax on profit		(622)	(524)
Profit for the period from continuing operations		1,353	1,046
Discontinued operations			
Loss for the period from discontinued operations		(205)	(100)
Profit for the period attributable to ordinary shareholders		1,148	946

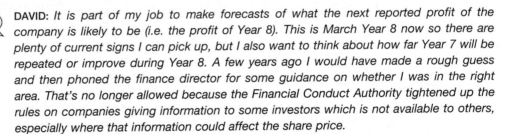

DAVID: *It is part of my job to make forecasts of what the next reported profit of the company is likely to be (i.e. the profit of Year 8). This is March Year 8 now so there are plenty of current signs I can pick up, but I also want to think about how far Year 7 will be repeated or improve during Year 8. A few years ago I would have made a rough guess and then phoned the finance director for some guidance on whether I was in the right area. That's no longer allowed because the Financial Conduct Authority tightened up the rules on companies giving information to some investors which is not available to others, especially where that information could affect the share price.*

One easy way out is for me to collect the reports which come in from our stockbrokers. Their analysts have specialist knowledge of the industry and can sometimes work out what is happening in a business faster than some of the management. However, I like to form my own opinion using other sources, such as trade journals, and I read the annual report to give me the background structure for my forecast. The company has helpfully separated out the effect of continuing and discontinued operations, which helps me in making a forecast.

When I meet the finance director next week I'll have with me a spreadsheet analysing revenue and profit before tax – so far as I can find the data – by product line and for each of the countries in which the company trades. I'll also ask the following questions:

1 *Although the revenue has increased, the ratio of gross profit to revenue on continuing operations has increased only very slightly, from 31.1% in Year 6 to 31.3% in Year 7. That suggests that the company has increased revenue by holding price rises at a level matching the increase in operating costs. I would like to see the company pushing ahead with price rises but does the company expect to see a fall in demand when its prices eventually rise?*

2 *The tax charge on continuing operations has decreased from approximately 33% to 31.5%, slightly higher than the rate which would be expected of UK companies.*

I know that this company is trading overseas. You say in your strategic report that the tax charge is 20% in the UK and rates on overseas profits will reduce, so am I safe in assuming that 20% is a good working guide for the future in respect of this company?

3 *With all this overseas business there must be an element of foreign exchange risk. You say in your strategic report that all material foreign currency transactions are matched back into the currency of the group company undertaking the transaction. You don't hedge the translation of overseas profits back into sterling. You also say that using Year 6 exchange rates the Year 7 profit from continuing operations would have been £1,389m rather than the £1,353m reported. That seems a fairly minimal effect but are these amounts hiding any swings in major currencies where large downward movements are offset by correspondingly large upward movements?*

4 *Your increase in revenue, comparing £7,146m to £5,893m, is 21.3% which is meeting the 20% target you set yourself. However, elsewhere in the financial statements I see that the acquisitions in Year 7 contributed £135m to revenue. If I strip that amount out of the total revenue I'm left with an increase in respect of activities continuing from Year 6 which is only 19%. When the scope for acquisitions is exhausted, will you be able to sustain the 20% target by organic growth alone?*

4.6.2 Statement of financial position (balance sheet)

DAVID: *Looking at the statement of financial position, this is a fairly simple type of business. It is financed almost entirely by equity capital (shareholders' funds), so there are none of the risks associated with high levels of borrowings which might be found in other companies.*
Again, I have summarised and left out some of the details which aren't significant in financial terms.

Safe and Sure plc
Summarised statement of financial position (balance sheet)
(with comparative amounts)

	Notes	Year 7 £m	Year 6 £m
Non-current assets			
Property, plant and equipment		1,375	1,219
Intangible assets		2,603	2,376
Investments		28	20
Taxation recoverable		59	49
Total non-current assets		4,065	3,664
Current assets			
Inventories (stocks)		266	243
Amounts receivable (debtors)		1,469	1,347
Six-month deposits		20	–
Cash and cash equivalents		1,053	905
Total current assets		2,808	2,495
Total assets		6,873	6,159
Current liabilities			
Amounts payable (creditors)		(1,598)	(1,575)
Bank overdraft		(401)	(626)
Total current liabilities		(1,999)	(2,201) ▶

Safe and Sure plc
Summarised statement of financial position (balance sheet)
(with comparative amounts) *continued*

	Notes	Year 7 £m	Year 6 £m
Non-current liabilities			
Amounts payable (creditors)	9	(27)	(26)
Bank and other borrowings	10	(2)	(6)
Provisions	11	(202)	(222)
Total non-current liabilities		(231)	(254)
Total liabilities		(2,230)	(2,455)
Net assets		4,643	3,704
Capital and reserves			
Shareholders' funds		4,643	3,704

DAVID: By far the largest non-current (fixed) asset is the intangible asset of goodwill arising on acquisition. It reflects the fact that the group has had to pay a price for the future prospects of companies it has acquired. Although the company reports this in the group's statement of financial position, and I like to see whether the asset is holding its value from the group's point of view, I have some reservations about the quality of the asset because I know it would vanish overnight if the group found itself in difficulties.

The other non-current assets are mainly equipment for carrying out the cleaning operations and vehicles in which to transport the equipment. I've checked in the notes to the accounts that vehicles are being depreciated over four to five years and plant and equipment over five to ten years, all of which sounds about right. Also, they haven't changed the depreciation period, or the method of calculation, since last year so the amounts are comparable. Estimated useful lives for depreciation are something I watch closely. There is a great temptation for companies which have underperformed to cut back on the depreciation by deciding the useful life has extended. (Depreciation is explained more fully in Chapter 8.)

I think I might ask a few questions about working capital (the current assets minus the current liabilities of the business). Normally I like to see current assets somewhat greater than current liabilities – a ratio of 1.5 to 1 could be about right – as a cushion to ensure the liabilities are met as they fall due. However, in this company the finance director makes a point of saying that they like to utilise as little working capital as possible, so I'm wondering why it increased from £294m in Year 6 to more than £800m in Year 7. There appear to be two effects working together: current assets went up and current liabilities went down. Amounts receivable (trade debtors) increased in Year 7 in absolute terms but that isn't as bad as it looks when allowance is made for the increase in revenue. Amounts receivable in Year 7 are 20.6% of continuing revenue, which shows some control has been achieved when it is compared with the Year 6 amount at 22.8% of revenue. My questions will be:

1 Mostly, the increase in the working capital (net current assets) appears to be due to the decrease in bank borrowing. Was this a voluntary action by the company or did the bank insist?

2 The second major cause of the increase in the working capital is the increase in the balance held in the bank account. Is that being held for a planned purpose and, if so, what?

3 The ratio of current assets to current liabilities has increased from last year. What target ratio are you aiming for?

I always shudder when I see 'provisions' in a statement of financial position. The notes to the financial statements show that these are broadly:

	£m
For treating a contaminated site	120
For restructuring part of the business	42
For tax payable some way into the future	40
Total	202

I shall want to ask whether the estimated liability in relation to the contaminated site is adequate in the light of any changes in legislation. I know the auditors will have asked this question in relation to existing legislation but I want to think also about forthcoming legislation.

I am always wary of provisions for restructuring. I shall be asking more about why the restructuring is necessary and when it will take place. I want to know that the provision is sufficient to cover the problem, but not excessive.

The provision for tax payable some way into the future is an aspect of prudence in accounting. I don't pay much attention unless the amount is very large or suddenly changes dramatically. (An explanation of deferred taxation is contained in Chapter 10.)

4.6.3   Statement of cash flows

DAVID: *Cash is an important factor for any business. It is only one of the resources available but it is the key to survival. I've summarised the totals of the various main sections of the cash flow statement. 'Net cash' means the cash less the bank borrowings.*

Safe and Sure plc
Summary statement of cash flows (with comparative amounts)
Consolidated statement of cash flows for the years ended 31 December

	Notes	Year 7	Year 6
		£m	£m
Net cash from operating activities		1,430	*1,163*
Net cash used in investing activities		(983)	*(853)*
Net cash used in financing activities		(102)	*(464)*
Net increase/(decrease) in cash and cash equivalents		345	*(154)*

What I'm basically looking for in the cash flow statement is how well the company is balancing various sources of finance. It generated £1,430m from operating activities and that was more than sufficient to cover its investing activities in new fixed assets and acquisitions. There was also enough to cover the dividend of £295m, which is a financing activity but that was partly covered by raising new loan finance. This is why the cash used in financing activities is only £102m. I come back to my earlier question of why they are holding so much cash.

Activity 4.4

Read David's explanation again and compare it carefully with the financial statements. It is quite likely that you will not understand everything immediately because the purpose of this book as a whole is to help you understand published financial statements and we are, as yet, only at the end of Chapter 4. Make a note of the items you don't fully understand and keep that note safe in a file. As you progress through the rest of the book, look back to that note and tick off the points which subsequently become clear. The aim is to have a page full of ticks by the end of the book.

4.7 Summary

The IASB's stated objective of general purpose financial reporting is to provide financial information about the reporting entity that is useful to existing and potential investors, lenders and other creditors in making decisions about providing resources to the entity. Those decisions involve buying, selling or holding equity and debt instruments, and providing or settling loans and other forms of credit.

The two fundamental qualitative characteristics are:

● relevance
● faithful representation.

Each of these has further contributing characteristics. Relevance consists of either predictive value or confirmatory value, or both. Faithful representation consists of neutrality, freedom from error, and completeness. There are four further enhancing qualitative characteristics. These are:

● comparability
● verifiability
● timeliness
● understandability.

The accounting principles that are most widely known in the UK are found within the Companies Act 2006:

● going concern
● accruals
● consistency
● prudence.

Regulation of financial reporting in the UK comes from several sources:

● The IAS Regulation requires all listed groups of companies to prepare financial statements using the system of the International Accounting Standards Board (IASB system). Other companies may choose to follow the IASB system.

● Companies that do not follow the IASB system must comply with UK company law.

● The Financial Reporting Council regulates accounting and auditing matters under the authority of UK company law. It sets UK accounting standards and auditing standards. It also takes action against companies whose annual reports do not comply with the relevant accounting system (IASB or UK company law).

● There are Stock Exchange Listing Rules which influence annual reports of listed companies.

● The UK tax system charges corporation tax on company profits. Her Majesty's Revenue and Customs (HMRC) starts with the accounting profit in calculating the amount of tax payable but there are some special rules of accounting for tax purposes.

● Auditors give an opinion on whether financial statements present a true and fair view of the profit or loss of the period and the state of affairs at the end of the period. They are professionally qualified accountants with auditing experience who are members of a recognised professional body.

Further reading

FRC (2012), *The UK Stewardship Code,* Financial Reporting Council.

FRC (2013), *The Impact and Implementation of the UK Corporate Governance and Stewardship Codes,* Annual report, Financial Reporting Council.

FRC (2014), *The UK Corporate Governance Code,* Financial Reporting Council.

IASB (2016), *The Conceptual Framework for Financial Reporting,* International Accounting Standards Board.

ICAEW (2010), *Rejected Accounts: Common reasons for accounts being rejected by Companies House & how to avoid them,* Financial Reporting Faculty, Institute of Chartered Accountants in England and Wales.

Sharman (2012), *The Sharman Inquiry. Going concern and liquidity risks: lessons for companies and auditors,* Final report, Financial Reporting Council.

QUESTIONS

The Questions section of each chapter has three types of question. 'Test your understanding' questions to help you review your reading are in the 'A' series of questions. You will find the answers to these by reading and thinking about the material in the book. 'Application' questions to test your ability to apply technical skills are in the 'B' series of questions. Questions requiring you to show skills in problem solving and evaluation are in the 'C' series of questions. A letter [S] indicates that there is a solution at the end of the book. Other solutions are provided in the Instructor's Manual where there are further questions parallel to those set out here.

A   Test your understanding

A4.1   Explain what is meant by each of the following: (Section 4.2)

(a) relevance;
(b) faithful representation;
(c) freedom from error
(d) neutrality;
(e) predictive value;
(f) completeness;
(g) comparability;
(h) understandability; and
(i) materiality.

A4.2   Explain the accounting principles of each of the following: (Section 4.3)

(a) going concern;
(b) accruals;
(c) consistency;
(d) the concept of prudence.

A4.3   Explain why companies should avoid overstatement of assets or understatement of liabilities. (Section 4.4)

A4.4   Explain the responsibilities of directors of a company towards shareholders in relation to the financial statements of a company. (Section 4.5.2)

A4.5 Explain the impact on financial statements of each of the following: (Section 4.5)

(a) company law;
(b) the International Accounting Standards Board; and
(c) the UK tax law.

A4.6 Explain how the monitoring of financial statements is carried out by each of the following: (Section 4.5)

(a) the auditors; and
(b) the Conduct Committee of the FRC (previously FRRP).

B Application

B4.1 [S]
Explain each of the following:

(a) The IAS Regulation
(b) The Financial Reporting Council
(c) Stock Exchange Listing Rules

B4.2 [S]
Explain any two accounting principles, explaining how each affects current accounting practice.

B4.3 [S]
Discuss the extent to which the regulatory bodies explained in this chapter have, or ought to have, a particular concern for the needs of the following groups of users of financial statements:

(a) shareholders;
(b) employees;
(c) customers; and
(d) suppliers.

C Problem solving and evaluation

C4.1
Choose one or more characteristics from the following list that you could use to discuss the accounting aspects of each of the statements 1 to 5 and explain your ideas:

- relevance
- verifiability
- comparability
- understandability
- materiality
- neutrality
- completeness
- predictive value
- faithful representation

1 Director: 'We do not need to tell shareholders about a loss of £2,000 on damaged stock when our operating profit for the year is £60m.'
2 Shareholder: 'I would prefer the statement of financial position (balance sheet) to tell me the current market value of land is £20m than to tell me that the historical cost is £5m, although I know that market values fluctuate.'
3 Analyst: 'If the company changes its stock valuation from average cost to FIFO, I want to hear a good reason and I want to know what last year's profit would have been on the same basis.'
4 Regulator: 'If the company reports that it has paid "*commission on overseas sales*", I don't expect to discover later that it really meant bribes to local officials.'
5 Director: 'We have made a profit on our drinks sales but a loss on food sales. In the Notes to the Accounts on segmental results I suggest we combine them as "food and drink". It will mean the annual report is less detailed for our shareholders but it will keep competitors in the dark for a while.'

C4.2

Choose one or more accounting principles from the following list that you could use to discuss the accounting aspects of each of the problems 1–5 and explain your ideas.

- going concern
- accruals
- consistency
- prudence.

1 Director: 'The fixed assets of the business are reported at depreciated historical cost because we expect the company to continue in existence for the foreseeable future. The market value is much higher but that is not relevant because we don't intend to sell them.'

2 Auditor: 'We are insisting that the company raises the provision for doubtful debts from 2% to 2.5% of debtor amount. There has been recession among the customer base and the financial statements should reflect that.'

3 Analyst: 'I have great problems in tracking the depreciation policy of this company. It owns several airports. Over the past three years the expected useful life of runways has risen from 30 years to 50 years and now it is 100 years. I find it hard to believe that the technology of tarmacadam has improved so much in three years.'

4 Auditor: 'We have serious doubts about the ability of this company to renew its bank overdraft at next month's review meeting with the bank. The company ought to put shareholders on warning about the implications for the financial statements.'

5 Shareholder: 'I don't understand why the company gives a profit and loss account and a cash flow statement in the annual report. Is there any difference between profit and cash flow?'

Activities for study groups

Continuing to use the annual reports of a company that you obtained for Chapter 1, look for the evidence in each report of the existence of the directors, the auditors and the various regulatory bodies.

In your group, draw up a list of the evidence presented by companies to show that the annual report has been the subject of regulation. Discuss whether the annual report gives sufficient reassurance of its relevance and faithful representation to the non-expert reader.

Notes and references

1. IASB (2016), *Conceptual Framework*, para. OB 2.
2. IAS 1 (2016), para. 10.
3. IAS 1 (2016), paras 10–12.
4. IASB (2016), *Conceptual Framework*, para. QC 5.
5. *Ibid.*, para. QC 6.
6. *Ibid.*, para. QC 8.
7. *Ibid.*, para. QC 9.
8. *Ibid.*, para. QC 12.
9. *Ibid.*, para. QC 13.
10. *Ibid.*, para. QC 14.
11. *Ibid.*, para. QC 15.
12. *Ibid.*, para. QC 11.
13. *Ibid.*, paras QC 20–25.
14. *Ibid.*, paras QC 26–28.
15. *Ibid.*, para. QC 29.
16. *Ibid.*, paras QC 30–32.
17. *Ibid.*, paras QC 35–39.
18. IASB *Framework* (1989), para. 37.
19. IASB (2016), *Conceptual Framework*.
20. IASB *Framework* (1989), para. 31.
21. IASB (2008), Exposure Draft on Conceptual Framework, para. BC 2.15.
22. IASB *Framework* (1989), para. 35.
23. IASB (2016), *Conceptual Framework*.

24. Under the Companies Act 2006, detailed accounting requirements are contained in Statutory Instruments. The accounting principles are specified in paras 11–15 of Schedule 1 of SI 2008/410 *The Large and Medium-sized Companies and Groups (Accounts and Reports) Regulations 2008*. Listed groups in the UK follow the International Financial Reporting Standards, where the same accounting principles apply. www.legislation.gov.uk/uksi/2008/410/contents/made.

25. IASB (2016), *Conceptual Framework*.

26. *Ibid.*, para. OB 17.

27. Companies Act 2006.

28. Para 3.3 Tech 2/10. *Guidance on the determination of realised profits and losses in the context of distributions under the Companies Act 2006*, issued by The Institute of Chartered Accountants in England and Wales and The Institute of Chartered Accountants of Scotland in October 2010.

29. IASB (2016) *Conceptual Framework*.

30. FRC (2012) FRS 100, *Application of Financial Reporting Requirements*.

31. http://europa.eu.int/comm/internal_market/accounting/index_en.htm.

32. www.efrag.org/.

33. www.frc.org.uk/.

34. FRC (2010), *The UK Approach to corporate governance*.

35. ISA320 (2010), International Standard on Auditing (UK and Ireland) 320: *Materiality in Planning and Performing an Audit*. www.frc.org.uk.

Part 2

Reporting the transactions of a business

Chapter 5

Accounting information for service businesses

NEXT plc: annual report of a service business

Extracts from Annual Report and Accounts

Next is a UK - based multi-channel retailer offering exciting, beautifully designed, excellent quality clothing, footwear, accessories and home products

Management team

The success of NEXT relies on the continued service of its senior management and technical personnel and on its ability to continue to attract, motivate and retain highly qualified employees. The retail sector is very competitive and NEXT staff are frequently targeted by other companies. The Remuneration Committee identifies senior personnel, reviews remuneration at least annually and formulates packages to retain and motivate these employees. In addition, the Board considers the development of senior managers to ensure adequate career development opportunities for key personnel, with orderly succession and promotion to important management positions.

Employees

NEXT's employees are key to achieving business objectives. NEXT has established policies for recruitment, training and development of personnel and is committed to achieving excellence in the areas of health, safety, welfare and protection of employees and their working environment.

Equal opportunities and diversity

NEXT is an equal opportunities employer and will continue to ensure it offers career opportunities without discrimination. Full consideration is given to applications for employment from disabled persons, having regard to their particular aptitudes and abilities. The Group has continued the employment wherever possible of any person who becomes disabled during their employment. Opportunities for training, career development and promotion do not operate to the detriment of disabled employees. The following table shows the gender mix of the Group's employees at the end of the financial year:

	2014		2013	
	Males	**Females**	**Males**	**Females**
Directors of NEXT plc	8	3	8	2
Subsidiary directors and other senior managers	29	13	27	17
Total employees	15,929	34,138	16,856	36,369

Training and development

NEXT aims to realise the potential of its employees by supporting their career progression and promotion wherever possible. It makes significant investment in the training and development of staff and in training and education programmes which contribute to the promotion prospects of employees.

Employee communication

NEXT has a policy of providing employees with financial and other information about the business and ensures that the suggestions and views of employees are taken into account. NEXT has an employee forum made up of elected representatives from throughout the business who attend meetings at least twice a year with directors and senior managers. This forum enables and encourages open discussion on key business issues, policies and the working environment.

Employee share ownership

Approximately 9,800 employees held options over 7.4 million shares in NEXT at January 2014, being 4.8% of the total shares in issue. Its employee share ownership trust ('ESOT') purchases shares for issue to employees when their options are exercised. At the year end the ESOT held 6.2 million shares, the voting rights of which are exercisable by the Trustee.

Pension provision

NEXT offers valuable pension benefits to participating employees, details of which are set out in the Remuneration Report and in Note 21 to the financial statements. At January 2014, there were 1,169 (2013: 1,242) active members in the Defined Benefit Section of the Next Group Pension Plan and 2,775 (2013: 2,375) UK employees with Defined Contribution arrangements.

Source: NEXT plc Annual Report and Accounts January 2014, pp. 20, 22. http://www.nextplc.co.uk/~/media/Files/N/Next-PLC/pdfs/reports-and-results/2014/Next%20AR2014%20web.pdf

Discussion points

1 The 'people' asset does not appear in the balance sheet of a company. What are the costs to the company of maintaining the 'people' asset?

2 What are the risks to a service business of strong reliance on the 'people' asset?

Contents

Learning outcomes

After studying this chapter you should be able to:

- Explain how the accounting equation is applied to transactions of a service business.
- Analyse the transactions of a service business during a specific period of time, using the accounting equation.
- Prepare a spreadsheet analysing the transactions and show that the results of the spreadsheet are consistent with the financial statements provided by the organisation.
- Explain the main aspects of the statement of cash flows, income statement (profit and loss account) and statement of financial position (balance sheet) of a service business.

Additionally, for those who read the supplement:

- Analyse the transactions of a service business using the rules of debit and credit bookkeeping.
- Prepare, from a list of transactions of an organisation, ledger accounts and a trial balance which could be used to prepare the financial statements provided by the organisation.

5.1 Introduction

A person who starts a service business intends to offer a service based on personal skills for which other people will be willing to pay a fee. The most important asset of the service business is the person or people providing the service. Despite that, the workforce as an asset never appears in an accounting statement of financial position (balance sheet). That is because, although it satisfies all the conditions of the definition, it is too difficult to measure objectively and so does not meet the criteria for recognition. (See Chapter 2 for the definition of an asset and the criteria for recognition of an asset.)

The service business will have other assets which accounting is able to record: for example, the taxi driver may own a taxi; the electrician will have electrical tools; the joiner will have a workbench and joinery tools; the car mechanic will have a repair garage and equipment; the lawyer will have an office and a word-processor. The service business will also buy materials for use in any particular job and the customer will be asked to pay for these materials as well as for the labour time involved. Moreover, it will have liabilities to suppliers of goods and services used by the business itself.

There will be an owner or owners having an ownership interest in the business. The service business will make profits for the owner (and thus increase the ownership interest) by charging a price for services which is greater than the cost of labour and materials used in providing the service.

All these aspects of the service business may be analysed and recorded on the basis of the accounting equation as specified in Chapter 2. This chapter will discuss the analysis of transactions using the accounting equation and will then apply that analysis to the transactions of a doctor providing a service of medical health screening for managerial and secretarial staff.

Activity 5.1	Choose a service business and write down the main activity of that business. Then write down the types of expense you would expect to find in the income statement (profit and loss account) of such a business. Write down the types of asset you would expect to find in the statement of financial position (balance sheet). Exchange your list with a fellow student. What are the similarities and what are the differences? Keep your list safe and when you have finished the chapter compare your list with the example in the chapter. Ask yourself, at that point, whether you would be able to apply what you have learned to the business you have chosen.

5.2 Analysing transactions using the accounting equation

Three main categories of accounting elements in the accounting equation have been defined in Chapter 2: **asset**, **liability** and **ownership interest**. Any one of these elements may increase or decrease during a period of time but the ownership interest may conveniently be subdivided. There will be increases and decreases caused by the decision of the owner(s) to make further contributions of capital or to withdraw capital. There will be increases and decreases due to the activity of the business, with **revenues** increasing the ownership claim and **expenses** decreasing it.

Decrease in ownership interest	Increase in ownership interest
Withdrawals of capital by the owner	Contributions of capital by the owner
Expenses	Revenues

Consequently there are several aspects to consider when transactions are analysed according to the accounting equation.

The accounting equation will be used in this chapter in the form:

Assets	minus	**Liabilities**	equals	**Ownership interest**

When one item in the equation increases, an upward arrow will be used and when one item decreases a downward arrow will be used:

| Assets ↓ | denotes a decrease in an asset.

| Liabilities ↑ | denotes an increase in a liability.

For further emphasis, **bold** highlighting will be used for the elements of the equation which are changed as a result of the transaction or event.

Each business transaction has two aspects in terms of the accounting equation. These aspects must be considered from the viewpoint of the *business*. Table 5.1 sets out a list of some common types of transaction encountered in a service business. Each transaction is then analysed using the accounting equation.

Table 5.1
List of transactions for a service business

	Transaction
1	Receive cash from the owner.
2	Buy a vehicle for cash.
3	Receive a bill for gas consumed.
4	Pay the gas bill in cash.
5	Buy materials for cash.
6	Buy materials on credit terms.
7	Sell services for cash.
8	Sell services on credit terms.
9	Pay wages to an employee.
10	Pay cash to the owner for personal use.

Transaction 1: receive cash from the owner

In this transaction the business *acquires* an **asset** (cash) and must note the **ownership interest** *created* by this contribution of capital from the owner:

Assets ↑ – Liabilities	equals	**Ownership interest ↑**

The equation remains in balance because an increase to the left-hand side is exactly matched by an increase to the right-hand side.

Transaction 2: buy a vehicle for cash

In this transaction the business *acquires* a new **asset** (the vehicle) but gives up another **asset** (cash):

Assets ↑↓ – Liabilities	equals	Ownership interest

Transaction 3: receive a bill for gas consumed

The business becomes aware that it has a **liability** to pay for gas consumed and also knows that the **ownership interest** has been *reduced* by the expense of using up gas in earning revenue for the business:

Assets – **Liabilities ↑**	equals	**Ownership interest ↓ (expense)**

Transaction 4: pay the gas bill in cash

The **asset** of cash is *reduced* and the **liability** to the gas supplier is *reduced*:

Assets ↓ – Liabilities ↓	equals	Ownership interest

Transaction 5: buy materials for cash

When the materials are acquired they will create an asset of inventory (stock), for future use. The **asset** of inventory (stock) will therefore *increase* and the **asset** of cash will *decrease*:

Assets ↓ ↑ – Liabilities	equals	Ownership interest

Transaction 6: buy materials on credit terms

Again, materials are acquired which cause an *increase* in the **asset** of inventory (stock). Obtaining goods on credit means that there is a **liability** *created* for amounts owing to the supplier:

Assets ↑ – Liabilities ↑	equals	Ownership interest

Transaction 7: sell services for cash

The cash received from the customer causes an *increase* in the **asset** of cash, while the act of selling services *increases* the **ownership interest** through earning revenue:

Assets ↑ – Liabilities	equals	**Ownership interest ↑ (revenue)**

Transaction 8: sell services on credit terms

The sale of services creates an *increase* in the **ownership interest** through earning revenue, but also creates an *increase* in the **asset** of trade receivables (debtors):

Assets ↑ – Liabilities	equals	**Ownership interest ↑ (revenue)**

Transaction 9: pay wages to an employee

The **asset** of cash *decreases* when the wage is paid and there is a *decrease* in the **ownership interest** because the business has used up the service provided by the employee (an expense has been incurred):

Assets ↓ – Liabilities	equals	**Ownership interest ↓ (expense)**

This is a transaction which often causes problems to those new to accounting. They would like to argue that paying wages creates an asset, rather than an expense, because there is an expected future benefit to be gained from the services of the employee. The answer to that argument is that, while there is no disputing the expected future benefit from the services of most employees, the wages paid are for work *already done* and so there can be no future expectations about that particular week's or month's work. The question of whether the workforce as a whole should be recognised as an asset of the business is one of the unresolved problems of accounting.

Transaction 10: pay cash to the owner for personal use

The **asset** of cash *decreases* and the **ownership interest** *decreases* because the owner has made a voluntary withdrawal of capital:

Assets ↓ – Liabilities	equals	**Ownership interest ↓ (voluntary withdrawal)**

Activity 5.2	Write down the transactions of Table 5.1 in a different order and put the piece of paper away for two days. Then take it out and practise the analysis of each transaction without looking at the answers in the book. If your answers are all correct, is it the result of memory or of genuine understanding? If your answers are not entirely correct, can you decide where the problem lies? It is very important that you can analyse transactions correctly using the accounting equation. It is also important that you use your powers of reasoning and not your powers of memory. You cannot possibly memorise the accounting treatment of every transaction you will meet.

5.3 Illustration of accounting for a service business

We now move on to an example which considers the private medical practice of Dr Lee. At the start of October Dr Lee commenced a new medical practice offering a general health screening service to managerial and secretarial staff at a standard fee of £500 per examination. Where patients make personal arrangements they will be asked to pay cash on the day of the examination. If the patient's employer has agreed to pay for the screening, Dr Lee will send an invoice to the employer, requiring payment within 30 days.

In Table 5.2 there is a list of transactions for Dr Lee's medical practice during the month of October. Try to work out the effect on the accounting equation of each transaction listed. Do this before you read the rest of this section. Then compare your answers and your reasoning with that in the rest of this section. Being able to reason correctly at this stage will reduce the likelihood of error later.

Oct. 1   When Dr Lee provides the practice with cash in a bank account to allow the business to start, the business *acquires* an **asset** of cash at bank and the transaction *creates* an **ownership interest** by Dr Lee in the assets of the business. This means that the business now has the use of £50,000, but, if the business ceases immediately, that £50,000 must be returned to Dr Lee. The accounting equation is satisfied because an increase in an asset is matched by an increase in the ownership interest:

Assets ↑ – Liabilities	equals	**Ownership interest** ↑

Oct. 2   The medical practice now becomes the business entity so far as accounting is concerned (although it is fairly clear that Dr Lee is making all the decisions as the manager of the business as well as being the owner). The entity *acquires* an **asset** of medical equipment in exchange for an equal *decrease* in the amount of an **asset** of cash. The accounting equation is satisfied because the increase in one asset is exactly equal to the decrease in another.

Assets ↑↓ – Liabilities	equals	Ownership interest

Oct. 2   The medical practice pays one month's rent in advance. At the moment of paying the rent, an asset is acquired representing the benefit to be gained from the use of the consulting rooms for the month ahead. However, this benefit only lasts for a short time and will have expired at the end of the accounting period (which has been chosen as one month for the purpose of this example). Once the benefit of an asset has expired, the business becomes

worse off and the ownership interest decreases. That decrease is called an expense of the business. To save the time and trouble of recording such transactions as assets and then re-naming them as expenses at the end of the accounting period, the short-cut is taken of calling them expenses from the outset. There needs to be a check on such items at the end of the accounting period to ensure that there is no part of the benefit remaining which could still be an asset.

Table 5.2

Transactions of Dr Lee's medical practice for the month of October

Date	Business transactions of the entity (nature of the entity: medical practice)	Amount
		£
Oct. 1	Dr Lee provides the practice with cash to allow business to start.	50,000
Oct. 2	The entity acquires medical equipment for cash.	30,000
Oct. 2	One month's rent is paid in advance for consulting rooms.	1,900
Oct. 2	Office furniture Is purchased on two months' credit from Office Supplies Company.	6,500
Oct. 7	The practice purchases medical supplies on credit from P. Jones and receives an invoice.	1,200
Oct. 8	Dr Lee pays the medical receptionist for one week's work, 2 to 8 October.	300
Oct. 10	Four patients are examined, each paying £500 cash.	2,000
Oct. 11	The business pays P. Jones in cash for the goods it acquired on credit.	1,200
Oct. 14	The business pays an electricity bill in cash.	100
Oct. 15	Dr Lee pays the medical receptionist for one week's work, 9 to 15 October.	300
Oct. 17	Three patients are examined, their employer (Mrs West) being sent an invoice requesting payment of £500 for each.	1,500
Oct. 22	Dr Lee pays the medical receptionist for one week's work, 16 to 22 October.	300
Oct. 23	The employer (Mrs West) pays in cash for the examination of three patients.	1,500
Oct. 24	Four patients are examined, their employer (Mr East) being sent an invoice requesting payment of £500 for each.	2,000
Oct. 28	Dr Lee draws cash from the business for personal use.	1,000
Oct. 29	Dr Lee pays the medical receptionist for one week's work, 23 to 29 October.	300
Oct. 31	The medical equipment and office furniture is estimated by Dr Lee to have fallen in value over the month.	250
Oct. 31	Dr Lee checks the inventory (stock) of medical supplies and finds that items costing £350 have been used during the month.	350

In terms of the accounting equation there is a *decrease* in the **ownership interest** due to an expense of the business. There is a corresponding *decrease* in the **asset** of cash.

Assets ↑ – Liabilities	equals	Ownership interest ↓ (expense)

Oct. 2   The entity acquires an asset of office furniture. It does not pay cash on this occasion, having been given two months to pay. Looking over the rest of the transactions for October it is clear that there has been no payment by the end of the month. At the moment of taking delivery of the asset, the business incurs a liability to the supplier, Office Supplies Company. The accounting equation is satisfied because the *increase* in an **asset** is exactly equal to the *increase* in a **liability**.

Assets ↑ – Liabilities ↑	equals	Ownership interest

Oct. 7   The practice purchases medical supplies on credit from P. Jones and receives an invoice. This is very similar to the previous transaction. An **asset** *is acquired* and a **liability** to a supplier is *created*. The liability is recognised when the practice accepts delivery of the goods because that is the moment of accepting legal liability. For convenience, accounting procedures normally use the arrival of the invoice as the occasion for recording the liability but, even if the invoice failed to arrive, the liability must be recognised in relation to accepting the goods.

Assets ↑ – Liabilities ↑	equals	Ownership interest

Oct. 8   The medical receptionist has worked for one week and is paid for the work done. The amount paid in wages is an expense of the business which *decreases* the **ownership interest** because the benefit of that work has been used up in providing support for the medical practice. There is a *decrease* in the **asset** of cash.

Assets ↓ – Liabilities	equals	Ownership interest ↓ (expense)

Oct. 10   The medical practice now begins to carry out the activities which increase the wealth of the owner by earning revenue. The patients pay cash, so there is an *increase* in the **asset** of cash, and the owner becomes better off so there is an *increase* in the **ownership interest**.

Assets ↑ – Liabilities	equals	Ownership interest ↑ (revenue)

Oct. 11   The business pays P. Jones in cash for the goods it acquired on credit. Payment of cash *decreases* the **asset** of cash and *decreases* the **liability** to the supplier. Because the supplier is paid in full, the liability is extinguished.

Assets ↓ – Liabilities ↓	equals	Ownership interest

Oct. 14   The business pays an electricity bill in full. The business has enjoyed the use of the electricity but there is no benefit remaining. This is an **expense** of the business which causes a *decrease* in the **ownership interest**. There is a *decrease* in the **asset** of cash.

Assets ↓ – Liabilities	equals	**Ownership interest ↓ (expense)**

Oct. 15   The payment to the medical receptionist is similar in effect to the payment made on 8 October, causing a further **expense** which *decreases* the **ownership interest** and causes a *decrease* in the **asset** of cash.

Assets ↓ – Liabilities	equals	**Ownership interest ↓ (expense)**

Oct. 17   There is an increase in the **ownership interest** which arises from the operations of the business and so is termed **revenue**. On this occasion the business *acquires* an **asset** of a trade receivable (debtor), showing that an amount of money is owed by the employer of these patients.

Assets ↑ – Liabilities	equals	**Ownership interest ↑ (revenue)**

Oct. 22   The payment to the medical receptionist causes a further **expense** and a *decrease* in the **asset** of cash.

Assets ↓ – Liabilities	equals	**Ownership interest ↓ (expense)**

Oct. 23   The cash received from the employer of the three patients examined on 17 October causes an *increase* in the **asset** of cash and a *decrease* in the **asset** of the trade receivable (debtor). Because the amount is paid in full, the asset of the trade receivable (debtor) is reduced to nil.

Assets ↑ ↓ – Liabilities	equals	Ownership interest

Oct. 24   Again the business carries out the activities intended to make the owner better off. The accounting effect is similar to that of 17 October, with an *increase* in the **ownership interest** and an *increase* in the **asset** of cash.

Assets ↑ – Liabilities	equals	**Ownership interest ↑ (revenue)**

Oct. 28   The owner of a sole trader business does not take a salary or wage as an employee would, but nevertheless needs cash for personal purposes. Taking cash for personal use is called taking 'drawings' and is recorded in terms of the accounting equation as a *decrease* in the **ownership interest** and a *decrease* in the **asset** of cash.

Assets ↓ – Liabilities	equals	**Ownership interest ↓ (drawings)**

Oct. 29   Paying wages causes an **expense** and a *decrease* in the **asset** of cash.

Assets ↓ – Liabilities	equals	**Ownership interest ↓ (expense)**

Oct. 31 The medical equipment and the office furniture are non-current (fixed) assets of the business. They are expected to have some years' useful life in the business but they will eventually be used up. In accounting, the term 'depreciation' is applied to this gradual using up and there are various ways of deciding how much of the fixed asset has been 'used up' in any period. (Chapter 8 gives more information on depreciation.) For this example the owner's estimate of depreciation is sufficient. There is a *decrease* in the non-current (fixed) **assets** which is not matched by an increase in any other asset and so there is a *decrease* in the **ownership interest** due to the operations of the business. **Depreciation** is an **expense** of the business.

Assets ↓ – Liabilities	equals	Ownership interest ↓ (expense)

Oct. 31 Dr Lee checks the inventory (stock) of medical supplies and finds that items costing £350 have been used during the month. When these medical supplies were received on 7 October, they were all treated as an asset of the business. It appears now that the asset has been reduced from £1,200 to £850 and that the items used up have caused a decrease of £350 in the ownership interest. This decrease is the expense of medical supplies which will appear in the income statement (profit and loss account) of the month. The two aspects of this event are therefore a *decrease* in the **ownership interest** and a *decrease* in the **asset** of inventory (stock) of medical supplies.

Assets ↓ – Liabilities	equals	Ownership interest ↓ (expense)

This analysis has been set out in some detail to show that each transaction must first of all be considered, in order to establish the nature of the two aspects of the transaction, before any attempt is made to deal with the monetary amounts. The next section uses the analysis based on the accounting equation to produce a spreadsheet which can be totalled to give a summary picture of the transactions of the month in terms of the accounting equation.

5.4 A process for summarising the transactions: a spreadsheet

In Table 5.3 the transactions are repeated in the left-hand column but the relevant money amounts are shown in columns which correspond to the assets, liabilities and ownership interest, using brackets to show a negative amount. (It would be equally acceptable to use a minus sign but minus signs tend to disappear or be confused with unintentional blobs on the paper, so brackets are frequently used in accounting in order to ensure clarity.)

Taking the first line as an example, the analysis of the transaction showed that there was an increase in the asset of cash and an increase in the ownership interest. Thus the amount of £50,000 is written in the spreadsheet column for cash and again in the spreadsheet column for ownership interest. In the second line, the asset of cash decreases by £30,000 and the asset of medical equipment increases by £30,000. A similar pattern follows down the spreadsheet for each transaction.

It may be seen that where there are more than a few transactions during the month, a spreadsheet of the type shown in Table 5.3 would need to be much larger and use more columns.

Table 5.3
Spreadsheet analysing transactions into the elements of the accounting equation

Date	Business transactions of the entity (nature of the entity: medical practice)	Assets				Liabilities	Ownership interest		
		Cash and bank	Trade rec'ble (debtor)	Inventory (stock)	Non-current assets	Trade payable (creditor)	Capital contributed or withdrawn	Revenue +	Expenses −
		£	£	£	£	£	£	£	£
Oct. 1	Dr Lee provides the practice with cash to allow business to start	50,000					50,000		
Oct. 2	The entity acquires medical equipment for cash	(30,000)			30,000				
Oct. 2	One month's rent is paid in advance for consulting rooms	(1,900)							1,900
Oct. 2	Office furniture is purchased on two months' credit from Office Supplies Company				6,500	6,500			
Oct. 7	The practice purchases medical supplies on credit from P. Jones and receives an invoice			1,200		1,200			
Oct. 8	Dr Lee pays the medical receptionist for one week's work, 2 to 8 October	(300)							300
Oct. 10	Four patients are examined, each paying £500 cash	2,000						2,000	
Oct. 11	The business pays P. Jones in cash for the goods it acquired on credit	(1,200)				(1,200)			
Oct. 14	The business pays an electricity bill in cash	(100)							100
Oct. 15	Dr Lee pays the medical receptionist for one week's work, 9 to 15 October	(300)							300
Oct. 17	Three patients are examined, their employer (Mrs West) being sent an invoice requesting payment of £500 for each		1,500					1,500	
Oct. 22	Dr Lee pays the medical receptionist for one week's work, 16 to 22 October	(300)							300
Oct. 23	The employer (Mrs West) pays in cash for the examination of three patients	1,500	(1,500)						
Oct. 24	Four patients are examined, their employer (Mr East) being sent an invoice requesting payment of £500 for each		2,000					2,000	
Oct. 28	Dr Lee draws cash from the business for personal use	(1,000)					(1,000)		
Oct. 29	Dr Lee pays the medical receptionist for one week's work, 23 to 29 October	(300)							300
Oct. 31	The medical equipment and office furniture is estimated by Dr Lee to have fallen in value over the month				(250)				250
Oct. 31	Dr Lee checks the inventory (stock) of medical supplies and finds that items costing £350 have been used during the month			(350)					350
	Totals	18,100	2,000	850	36,250	6,500	49,000	5,500	3,800

Assets total: 57,200

Liabilities + Ownership interest total: 50,700

At the foot of the spreadsheet in Table 5.3 there is a total for each column. Those totals from Table 5.3 are used in Table 5.4, which represents the accounting equation, to show the state of the accounting equation at the end of the month. It may be used to explain to Dr Lee how the ownership interest has changed over the month. The owner contributed £50,000 at the start of the month and has a claim of £50,700 at the end of the month. The ownership interest was increased by earning revenue of £5,500 but reduced by incurring expenses of £3,800 and withdrawing £1,000 for personal use.

Table 5.4
Summary of transactions analysed into the elements of the accounting equation

Assets	minus	Liabilities	=	Ownership interest at start of period	plus	Capital contributed/ withdrawn	plus	Revenue	minus	Expenses
£57,200	–	£6,500		nil	+	£49,000	+	£5,500	–	£3,800
└── £50,700 ──┘				└──────────── £50,700 ────────────┘						

5.5 Financial statements as a means of communication

This chapter has established the approach taken in accounting towards analysing and classifying transactions in such a way that Dr Lee as the owner of a business knows how much better or worse off she has become during a period. There is sufficient information contained in Table 5.3 and it is possible to write an interpretation based on Table 5.4. However, this presentation is not particularly informative or easy on the eye.

The process of communication requires some attention to a clear style of presentation. Accounting practice has evolved the statement of cash flows, the income statement (profit and loss account) and the statement of financial position (balance sheet) to give the owner a more informative presentation of the information contained in Tables 5.3 and 5.4.

Chapter 3 set out the structure of the financial statements of a business. These ideas are now applied to Dr Lee's medical practice. Don't worry too much about how the information is transferred from Table 5.3 to these financial statements, but look back to the table and satisfy yourself that you can find the corresponding pieces of information.

5.5.1 Statement of cash flows

Medical Practice of Dr Lee
Statement of cash flows for the month of October Year 20xx

	£
Operating activities	
Inflow from fees	3,500
Outflow: rent paid	(1,900)
payment to supplier (P. Jones)	(1,200)
wages	(1,200)
electricity	(100)
Net outflow from operations	(900)
Investing activities	
Payment for equipment	(30,000)
Net outflow for investing activities	(30,000)
Financing activities	£
Capital contributed by owner	50,000
Capital withdrawn as drawings	(1,000)
Net inflow from financing activities	49,000
Increase in cash at bank over period	18,100

Comment. All the amounts for this statement are taken from the 'Cash at bank' column of Table 5.3 but are regrouped for the three headings of operating activities, investing activities and financing activities. The statement shows that the business had a net outflow of cash of £900 due to operations and an outflow of cash amounting to £30,000 due to purchase of medical equipment. The owner contributed £50,000 at the start of the month but took drawings of £1,000 at the end, resulting in a net inflow of £49,000 from financing. The overall effect was an increase in cash over the period amounting to £18,100.

5.5.2 Income statement (profit and loss account)

Medical Practice of Dr Lee
Income statement (profit and loss account)
for the month of October Year 20xx

	£	£
Fees charged		5,500
Medical supplies used	(350)	
Wages	(1,200)	
Rent	(1,900)	
Electricity	(100)	
Depreciation	(250)	
Total expenses		(3,800)
Profit		1,700

Comment. The total fees charged constitute the total revenue of the period as may be seen in the column in Table 5.3 headed 'revenue'. The expenses of the period amount to £3,800 and are taken from the final column of Table 5.3. The difference between revenue and expenses is the profit of £1,700. This is the amount by which the ownership interest has increased to make the owner of the business better off.

Some students ask at this point why the owner's drawings are not included in the income statement (profit and loss account). The answer is that making drawings of cash has nothing to do with the operations of the business. It is a voluntary action taken by the owner, who is also the manager, balancing the owner's personal need for cash against the needs of the business for cash to ensure continued smooth running. Where the owner is the only person working in the business, the owner may regard the drawings as being closer to wages. The amount taken may represent wages in economic terms. However, accounting ignores this economic reality and reports all amounts withdrawn by the owner as drawings.

Activity 5.3

The medical practice of Dr Lee has made a profit of £1,700 over the month but the cash flow caused by operations is an outflow of £900. How can a business make a profit and yet see an outflow of cash caused by operations? This question is asked all too often in reality. You can provide the answer by comparing the cash flow due to operating activities and the calculation of net profit. If you are not sure how to make the comparison, look back to Chapter 3 where the financial statements of P. Mason's legal practice were analysed (Table 3.7).

5.5.3 Statement of financial position (balance sheet)

Medical Practice of Dr Lee
Statement of financial position (balance sheet)
at 31 October Year 20xx

	£
Non-current (fixed) assets	
Medical equipment at cost	30,000
Office furniture	6,500
	36,500
Depreciation	(250)
Depreciated cost of fixed assets	36,250
Current assets	
Inventory	850
Trade receivables (debtors)	2,000
Cash at bank	18,100
Total current assets	20,950
Total assets	57,200
Current liabilities	
Trade payables (creditors)	(6,500)
Net assets	50,700
Capital at start	50,000
Add: profit	1,700
Less: drawings	(1,000)
Total ownership interest	50,700

Comment. The statement of financial position (balance sheet) follows the pattern of the accounting equation. The non-current (fixed assets) are presented first of all, showing the resources available to the business over a longer period of time. The depreciation is deducted to leave an amount remaining which is probably best described as the 'depreciated cost' but is often labelled 'net book value' or 'written down value'. Chapter 8 contains more information on the procedures for measuring and recording depreciation and the limitations of using the word 'value' in relation to those procedures.

The next section contains the **current assets** which are expected to be converted into cash within a 12-month period. The medical supplies shown are those which have not yet been used and therefore remain as a benefit for the next month. Trade receivables (debtors) are those customers who are expected to pay in the near future. The other current asset is the cash held at the bank, which is very accessible in the short term.

The only liability is the amount of £6,500 owing to the Office Supplies Company, due for payment at the start of December. This is a **current liability** because it is due for payment within 12 months.

It is felt to be helpful in the statement of financial position (balance sheet) to set out subtotals which may guide the reader. These have been shaded in the statement of financial position (balance sheet). The total of non-current (fixed) assets is interesting as the long-term asset base used to generate profits. The difference between the **current assets** and the **current liabilities** is sometimes identified separately as the **working capital**. At the moment the current assets look rather high in relation to the need to cover current liabilities. This is because the amount of cash held is quite high in relation to the apparent needs of the business. It is possible that Dr Lee has plans to use the cash for business purposes quite soon but, in the absence of such plans, Dr Lee ought to consider investing it to earn interest or else withdrawing it for other uses.

The amount for total assets less total liabilities (A – L) is usually called the **net assets** of the business. (The word 'net' means 'after taking something away' – in this case, after taking away the liabilities.) There is not much to say here except to note that it equals the ownership interest as would be expected from the accounting equation. The ownership interest has increased over the period through making a profit of £1,700 but decreased by £1,000 through making drawings, so that the resulting increase is £700 overall.

Activity 5.4	*Compare the financial statements of Dr Lee's medical practice with the information collected in the spreadsheet of Table 5.3. Take a pencil and, very lightly, place a tick against each amount in the financial statements and a tick against each amount in the spreadsheet, as you match them together. If you are able to work backwards in this way from the financial statements to the spreadsheet then you will be well on the way to understanding how the financial statements are related to the original list of transactions.*

5.6 Summary

The first stage in recording a transaction is to think about its effect on the accounting equation.

Assets minus **Liabilities**	equals	**Ownership interest**

A transaction must have at least two effects on the accounting equation. For example, when cash is contributed by the owner there is an *increase* in the **asset** of cash and an *increase* in the **ownership interest**:

Assets ↑ – Liabilities	equals	**Ownership interest** ↑

Accounting transactions may be recorded in a spreadsheet where the columns record the assets and liabilities and the rows record each transaction. The totals at the foot of all columns contain the information for the statement of financial position (balance sheet) at the end of the period. The columns for revenue and expenditure allow the profit or loss to be calculated. The bank or cash column provides information for the statement of cash flows.

QUESTIONS

The Questions section of each chapter has three types of question. 'Test your understanding' questions to help you review your reading are in the 'A' series of questions. You will find the answers to these by reading and thinking about the material in the book. 'Application' questions to test your ability to apply technical skills are in the 'B' series of questions. Questions requiring you to show skills in problem solving and evaluation are in the 'C' series of questions. A letter [S] indicates that there is a solution at the end of the book. Other solutions are provided in the Instructor's Manual, when there are further questions parallel to those set out here.

A Test your understanding

A5.1 [S] The following list of transactions relates to a television repair business during the first month of business. Explain how each transaction affects the accounting equation: (Section 5.2)

(a) Owner puts cash into the business.
(b) Buy a vehicle for cash.

(c) Receive a bill for electricity consumed.

(d) Purchase stationery for office use, paying cash.

(e) Pay the electricity bill in cash.

(f) Pay rental for a computer, used to keep customer records.

(g) Buy spare parts for cash, to use in repairs.

(h) Buy spare parts on credit terms.

(i) Pay garage service bills for van, using cash.

(j) Fill van with petrol, using credit account at local garage, to be paid at the start of next month.

(k) Carry out repairs for cash.

(l) Carry out repairs on credit terms.

(m) Pay wages to an employee.

(n) Owner takes cash for personal use.

A5.2 [S] Which of the items in the list of transactions in question A5.1 will have an effect on an income statement (profit and loss account)?

A5.3 [S] Which of the items in the list of transactions in question A5.1 will have an effect on a statement of cash flows?

A5.4 [S] Which of the items in the list of transactions in question A5.1 will have an effect on a statement of financial position (balance sheet)?

A5.5 [S] Analyse each of the following transactions to show the two aspects of the transaction: (Section 5.3)

Apr. 1   Jane Gate commenced her dental practice on 1 April by depositing £60,000 in a business bank account.

Apr. 1   Rent for a surgery was paid, £800, for the month of April.

Apr. 2   Dental equipment was purchased for £35,000, paying in cash.

Apr. 3   Dental supplies were purchased for £5,000, taking 30 days' credit from a supplier.

Apr. 4   Fees of £1,200 were collected in cash from patients and paid into the bank account.

Apr. 15   Dental assistant was paid wages for two weeks, £700.

Apr. 20   Jane Gate withdrew £500 cash for personal use.

Apr. 21   Fees of £2,400 were collected in cash from patients and paid into the bank.

Apr. 29   Dental assistant was paid wages for two weeks, £700.

Apr. 29   Invoices were sent to patients who are allowed 20 days' credit, for work done during April amounting to £1,900.

Apr. 30   Telephone bill for April was paid, £80.

Apr. 30   Dental supplies unused were counted and found to be worth £3,500, measured at cost price.

B   Application

B5.1 [S]

(a) Using the list of transactions at question A5.5 prepare a spreadsheet similar to that presented in Table 5.3.

(b) Show that the spreadsheet totals satisfy the accounting equation.

B5.2 [S]

Using the totals from the columns of the spreadsheet of question B5.1, prepare for the dental practice in the month of April:

(a) a statement of cash flows;

(b) a statement of financial position (balance sheet); and

(c) an income statement (profit and loss account).

There are no questions in the C series for this chapter.

Recording transactions in ledger accounts: a service business

In the supplement to Chapter 2 it was shown that the rules for debit and credit bookkeeping may be summarised in terms of the elements of the accounting equation as shown in Table 5.5.

Table 5.5
Rules for debit and credit entries in ledger accounts

	Debit entries in a ledger account	Credit entries in a ledger account
Left-hand side of the equation		
Asset	Increase	Decrease
Right-hand side of the equation		
Liability	Decrease	Increase
Ownership interest	Expense	Revenue
	Capital withdrawn	Capital contributed

In the supplement to Chapter 3 a spreadsheet was used to show that a series of transactions could be analysed and summarised in tabular form. That spreadsheet format is becoming increasingly used as the basis for computer-based recording of transactions but the more conventional approach to analysing transactions is to collect them together in ledger accounts. This supplement takes the transactions of Chapter 5 and analyses them in debit and credit form in order to produce a trial balance as a basis for the preparation of financial statements.

In Table 5.1 some common transactions of a service business were listed and then analysed using the accounting equation. They will now be analysed in terms of where the debit and credit entries would be made in a ledger account. Test yourself by trying out the answer before you look at the answer in Table 5.6 below. Once you are satisfied that you could produce the correct answer for the transactions in Table 5.1, you are ready to deal with Dr Lee's medical practice.

Illustration: Dr Lee's medical practice

The first transaction in Table 5.2 reads:

> Oct. 1 Dr Lee provides the practice with cash, £50,000.

The two aspects of this transaction were identified as:

1 Acquisition of an asset (cash).
2 Increasing the ownership interest (voluntary contribution).

The bookkeeping system requires two ledger accounts in which to record this transaction. One ledger account is called Cash and the other is called Ownership

Table 5.6
Analysis of service business transactions (from Table 5.1) to identify two aspects of each

Transaction	Aspects of the transaction	Debit entry in	Credit entry in
Receive cash from the owner	Acquisition of an asset (cash)	Cash	
	Acceptance of ownership interest		Ownership interest
Buy a vehicle for cash	Acquisition of an asset (vehicle)	Vehicle	
	Reduction in an asset (cash)		Cash
Receive a bill for gas consumed	Incur an expense (gas consumed)	Gas expense	
	Incur a liability (to the gas supplier)		Supplier
Pay the gas bill in cash	Decrease a liability (to the gas supplier)	Supplier	
	Reduction in an asset (cash)		Cash
Buy materials for cash	Increase in an asset (inventory of materials)	Inventory (stock)	
	Decrease in an asset (cash)		Cash
Buy materials on credit	Acquisition of an asset (inventory of materials)	Inventory (stock)	
	Incur a liability (to the supplier)		Supplier
Sell services for cash	Acquisition of an asset (cash)	Cash	
	Earn revenue		Sales
Sell services on credit	Acquisition of an asset (trade receivables)	Trade receivables (debtors)	
	Earn revenue		Sales
Pay wages to an employee	Incur an expense (cost of wages)	Wages expense	
	Decrease in asset (cash)		Cash
Pay cash to the owner for personal use	Reduction in the ownership interest	Ownership interest	
	Reduction in an asset (cash)		Cash

interest. There will be a *debit* entry of £50,000 in the Cash ledger account showing that the business has acquired an asset of £50,000 cash. There will be a *credit* entry of £50,000 in the Ownership interest ledger account showing that the business acknowledges the claim of the owner for eventual return of the amount contributed.

The second transaction in Table 5.2 reads:

Oct. 2   The entity acquires medical equipment for cash, £30,000.

The two aspects of this transaction were identified as:

1 Acquisition of an asset (medical equipment).
2 Decrease of an asset (cash).

Table 5.7
Analysis of debit and credit aspect of each transaction of the medical practice

Date	Business transactions of medical practice	Amount	Debit	Credit
		£		
Oct. 1	Dr Lee provides the practice with cash to allow business to start.	50,000	Cash	Owner
Oct. 2	The entity acquires medical equipment for cash.	30,000	Equipment	Cash
Oct. 2	One month's rent is paid in advance for consulting rooms.	1,900	Rent	Cash
Oct. 2	Office furniture is purchased on two months' credit from Office Supplies Company.	6,500	Furniture	Office Supplies Company
Oct. 7	The practice purchases medical supplies on credit from P. Jones and receives an invoice.	1,200	Inventory (stock)	P. Jones
Oct. 8	Dr Lee pays the medical receptionist for one week's work, 2 to 8 October.	300	Wages	Cash
Oct. 10	Four patients are examined, each paying £500 cash.	2,000	Cash	Patients' fees
Oct. 11	The business pays P. Jones in cash for the goods it acquired on credit.	1,200	P. Jones	Cash
Oct. 14	The business pays an electricity bill in cash.	100	Electricity	Cash
Oct. 15	Dr Lee pays the medical receptionist for one week's work, 9 to 15 October.	300	Wages	Cash
Oct. 17	Three patients are examined, their employer (Mrs West) being sent an invoice requesting payment of £500 for each.	1,500	Mrs West	Fees
Oct. 22	Dr Lee pays the medical receptionist for one week's work, 16 to 22 October.	300	Wages	Cash
Oct. 23	The employer (Mrs West) pays in cash an invoice requesting payment of £500 for each.	1,500	Cash	Mrs West
Oct. 24	Four patients are examined, their employer (Mr East) being sent an invoice requesting payment of £500 for each.	2,000	Mr East	Fees
Oct. 28	Dr Lee draws cash from the business for personal use.	1,000	Owner	Cash
Oct. 29	Dr Lee pays the medical receptionist for one week's work, 23 to 29 October.	300	Wages	Cash
Oct. 31	The medical equipment and office furniture is estimated by Dr Lee to have fallen in value over the month.	250	Depreciation	Equipment and furniture
Oct. 31	Dr Lee checks the inventory (stock) of medical supplies and finds that items costing £350 have been used during the month.	350	Medical supplies expense	Inventory (stock)

The bookkeeping system requires two ledger accounts in which to record this transaction. One ledger account is called Medical equipment and the other is called Cash.

There will be a *debit* entry of £30,000 in the Medical equipment ledger account showing that the business has acquired an asset of £30,000 medical equipment.

There will be a *credit* entry of £30,000 in the Cash ledger account showing that the business has reduced its asset of cash by £30,000 to pay for the medical equipment.

Analysing the debit and credit entries for each transaction

Table 5.7 takes the information contained in Table 5.2 and analyses it under debit and credit headings showing the ledger accounts in which each entry will be made.

Ledger accounts required to record these transactions are:

L1 Cash	L8 Inventory (stock) of medical supplies
L2 Ownership interest	L9 P. Jones
L3 Medical equipment and office furniture	L10 Electricity
L4 Office Supplies Company	L11 Mrs West
L5 Rent	L12 Mr East
L6 Wages	L13 Depreciation
L7 Patients' fees	L14 Expense of medical supplies

Form of ledger accounts

There is no single standard form of ledger account rulings in which to record debit and credit transactions. Historically, ledger accounts were recorded in what were called 'T' accounts where all the debit entries were on the left-hand side and all the credit entries on the right-hand side. This was designed to minimise arithmetic errors by avoiding subtractions in systems which were dealt with manually.

Form of a 'T' ledger account

Page number and name of the account

Debit entries				**Credit entries**			
Date	Particulars	Page	£ p	Date	Particulars	Page	£ p

This type of layout requires a wide page if it is to be read clearly. In recent years ledger accounts have more frequently been prepared in a 'three-column' ruling which keeps a running total. This book will use the three-column ruling throughout. You will see by comparison of the column headings that the different types of rulings use the same information. If you have an opportunity to look at business ledgers you will probably come across yet more varieties, but they will all require the inclusion of this basic set of information.

Three-column ruling

Date	Particulars	Page	Debit	Credit	Balance
			£ p	£ p	£ p

Features are:

- The left-hand column will show the date of the transaction.
- The 'particulars' column will show essential narrative, usually confined to the name of the ledger account which records the other aspect of the transaction.
- The 'page' column will show the ledger account page number of the ledger account where the other aspect of the transaction is recorded.
- The amount of the transaction will be entered in the debit or credit column as appropriate.
- The 'balance' column will keep a running total by treating all debit entries as positive and all credit entries as negative. A credit balance will be shown in brackets as a reminder that it is negative. Some ledger systems print the letters 'dr' or 'cr' against the balance.

Illustration

The first transaction of Table 5.7 may now be shown in the appropriate ledger accounts. It will require a *debit* entry in a cash account to indicate an increase in the asset of cash and a *credit* entry in the ownership interest account to indicate an increase in the owner's claim.

L1 Cash

Date	Particulars	Page	Debit	Credit	Balance
			£	£	£
Oct. 1	Ownership interest	L2	50,000		50,000

L2 Ownership interest

Date	Particulars	Page	Debit	Credit	Balance
			£	£	£
Oct. 1	Cash	L1		50,000	(50,000)

Ledger accounts for Dr Lee's medical practice

The full ledger account record for the transactions in Table 5.7 is now set out. Leona Rees comments on each ledger account, showing how she interprets ledger accounts in her work of auditing and accounting.

L1 Cash

Date	Particulars	Page	Debit	Credit	Balance
			£	£	£
Oct. 1	Ownership interest	L2	50,000		50,000
Oct. 2	Medical equipment	L3		30,000	20,000
Oct. 2	Rent	L5		1,900	18,100
Oct. 8	Wages	L6		300	17,800
Oct. 10	Patients' fees	L7	2,000		19,800
Oct. 11	P. Jones	L9		1,200	18,600
Oct. 14	Electricity	L10		100	18,500
Oct. 15	Wages	L6		300	18,200
Oct. 22	Wages	L6		300	17,900
Oct. 23	Mrs West	L11	1,500		19,400
Oct. 28	Ownership interest taken as	L2		1,000	18,400
Oct. 29	Wages	L6		300	18,100

LEONA's comment: *The amount of £50,000 put into the business at the start is quickly eaten into by spending cash on medical equipment and paying rent in advance. Further items such as paying a supplier, paying the electricity account and the assistant's wages took the cash balance down further but it remained quite high throughout the month. With the benefit of hindsight the owner might not have needed to put so much cash into the business at the outset. Up to £18,000 could have been invested on a short-term basis to earn interest, either for the business or for Dr Lee.*

L2 Ownership interest

Date	Particulars	Page	Debit	Credit	Balance
			£	£	£
Oct. 1	Cash contributed	L1		50,000	(50,000)
Oct. 28	Cash drawn	L1	1,000		(49,000)

LEONA's comment: *The ownership interest is created when the owner contributes cash or resources to the business. In this case it was cash. The sole trader in business may withdraw cash for personal use at any time – it is called owner's drawings – but the desirability of that action depends on how useful cash is to the owner when compared to how useful it might have been if left in the business. The owner of this business has a claim remaining equal to £49,000 after making the drawing.*

L3 Medical equipment and office furniture

Date	Particulars	Page	Debit	Credit	Balance
			£	£	£
Oct. 2	Cash	L1	30,000		30,000
Oct. 2	Office Supplies Company	L4	6,500		36,500
Oct. 31	Depreciation	L13		250	36,250

LEONA's comment: *This ledger account is particularly useful as a reminder that some very valuable assets are owned by the business. Having a record in the ledger account encourages the owner to think about continuing care for the medical equipment and office furniture and also to review their value against the amount recorded. If Dr Lee intended to have a large number of fixed asset items it is possible to have a separate ledger account for each, but that seems a long-distant prospect at the moment.*

Depreciation is a way of showing that the original cost of the asset has to be spread over its useful life. If the estimate of depreciation is correct, this ledger account should reduce to nil on the day the equipment and furniture ceases to be of use. In reality, things usually are not quite so straightforward. (Depreciation of non-current (fixed) assets is dealt with in more detail in Chapter 8.)

L4 Office Supplies Company

Date	Particulars	Page	Debit	Credit	Balance
			£	£	£
Oct. 2	Office furniture	L3		6,500	(6,500)

LEONA's comment: *When the office furniture was purchased from the Office Supplies Company, an invoice was received from that company showing the amount due. That invoice was used to make the credit entry on 2 October showing that the business had a liability. The liability remained owing at 31 October, but that is acceptable because the supplier allowed two months' credit.*

L5 Rent

Date	Particulars	Page	Debit	Credit	Balance
			£	£	£
Oct. 2	Cash	L1	1,900		1,900

LEONA's comment: *This payment in advance starts by being an asset and gradually turns into an expense as the benefit is used up. For bookkeeping purposes, a debit entry records both an asset and an expense so it is only at the end of the month that some care is needed in thinking about the nature of the debit balance. In this case it is clear that the benefit is used up but there could be a situation where part of the benefit remained to be reported as an asset.*

L6 Wages

Date	Particulars	Page	Debit	Credit	Balance
			£	£	£
Oct. 8	Cash	L1	300		300
Oct. 15	Cash	L1	300		600
Oct. 22	Cash	L1	300		900
Oct. 29	Cash	L1	300		1,200

LEONA's comment: *This is a straightforward account in which to accumulate all wages expenses. A very enthusiastic accountant would estimate the liability for the final two days of the month and add these on, but there is a very useful idea in accounting called 'materiality' which, broadly interpreted, means the extra information provided would not justify the extra amount of work involved.*

L7 Patients' fees

Date	Particulars	Page	Debit	Credit	Balance
			£	£	£
Oct. 10	Cash	L1		2,000	(2,000)
Oct. 17	Credit: Mrs West (as employer)	L11		1,500	(3,500)
Oct. 24	Credit: Mr East (as employer)	L12		2,000	(5,500)

LEONA's comment: *This is a revenue account so credit entries are expected. The balance column shows the total patients' fees earned in the month were £5,500. This could be described as 'turnover' or 'sales' but both of those words sound rather out of place when a professional service is being described.*

L8 Inventory (stock) of medical supplies

Date	Particulars	Page	Debit	Credit	Balance
			£	£	£
Oct. 7	P. Jones	L9	1,200		1,200
Oct. 31	Expense of medical supplies	L14		350	850

LEONA's comment: *This is an asset account so when the medical supplies were acquired on credit from P. Jones the entire amount was recorded as an asset. These medical supplies will be quite small items and it would not be appropriate for Dr Lee to have to count every cotton wool swab, hypodermic needle or sample bottle used in each examination. It is sufficient for accounting purposes to count up what is left at the end of the period (we call it 'taking stock') and assume that the difference represents the amount used during the period. As an auditor, I might start to ask questions about possible errors, fraud or theft if the amounts of supplies used did not look sensible when compared with the number of examinations carried out on patients.*

L9 P. Jones

Date	Particulars	Page	Debit	Credit	Balance
			£	£	£
Oct. 7	Inventory (stock) of medical supplies	L8		1,200	(1,200)
Oct. 11	Cash	L1	1,200		nil

LEONA's comment: *When the medical supplies were delivered to Dr Lee, the business took on a liability to pay P. Jones. That liability was recorded by a credit entry in the ledger account for P. Jones and was extinguished on 11 October when the medical practice paid £1,200 to P. Jones.*

L10 Electricity

Date	Particulars	Page	Debit	Credit	Balance
			£	£	£
Oct. 14	Cash	L1	100		100

LEONA's comment: *This is a very straightforward expense account. The balance on this account will show the total expense of electricity consumed during the period.*

L11 Mrs West

Date	Particulars	Page	Debit	Credit	Balance
			£	£	£
Oct. 17	Patients' fees	L7	1,500		1,500
Oct. 23	Cash	L1		1,500	nil

L12 Mr East

Date	Particulars	Page	Debit	Credit	Balance
			£	£	£
Oct. 24	Patients' fees	L7	2,000		2,000

LEONA's comment: *The credit sale to the employees of Mrs West and Mr East made them trade receivables (debtors) of the business and so there is a debit entry. By the end of October Mr East had not paid, so remains a debtor, denoted by a debit balance. Mrs West has paid during October and a nil balance is the result.*

L13 Depreciation

Date	Particulars	Page	Debit	Credit	Balance
			£	£	£
Oct. 31	Medical equipment and office furniture	L3	250		250

LEONA's comment: *This is another expense account showing an item which has decreased the ownership interest through a decrease in the recorded amount of some assets. This is where accounting begins to look slightly complicated because no cash has changed hands. Recording depreciation is the accounting way of expressing caution as to the expected future benefits from an asset. These will be eroded as the asset is used up. Depreciation is a way of acknowledging that erosion.*

L14 Expense of medical supplies

Date	Particulars	Page	Debit	Credit	Balance
			£	£	£
Oct. 31	Inventory (stock) of medical supplies	L8	350		350

LEONA's comment: *This account continues the story from L8 where the inventory (stock) of medical supplies was found to have dwindled through use in examining patients. It is assumed that the difference between the amount purchased and the amount held at the end of the month represents the expense of using the asset during the month.*

Checking the accuracy of double-entry records

At periodic intervals it may be considered necessary for a number of reasons to check the accuracy of the entries made in ledger accounts. For instance, the omission of an entry on the debit side of a customer's ledger account for goods sold on credit terms could result in a failure to issue reminders for payment of an amount owed to the business.

There are methods in double-entry bookkeeping of discovering these and other errors. One such method is the use of the *trial balance.*

If a debit entry and a credit entry have been made in the appropriate ledger accounts for each business transaction, then the total money amount of all the debit entries will equal the total money amount of all the credit entries. If a debit entry has been made without a corresponding credit entry (or vice versa), then the totals will not agree.

In the ledger accounts shown in this example, the balances have been kept as running totals. It would be possible to add up all the debit and all the credit entries in each ledger account but the same arithmetic proof will be obtained by listing all the debit balances and all the credit balances. It was explained earlier in this supplement that brackets are used in the ledger accounts to show credit balances. The list of balances on all the ledger accounts for Dr Lee's medical practice is set out in Table 5.8.

Error detection using the trial balance

The calculation of the totals of each column of the trial balance is a useful precaution which will reveal some, but not all, of the errors it is possible to make in a debit and credit recording system. Think first about the errors you might make and then check against the following list:

Table 5.8
Trial balance at 31 October for Dr Lee's medical practice

Ledger account title		Debit	Credit
		£	£
L1	Cash	18,100	
L2	Ownership interest		49,000
L3	Medical equipment and office furniture	36,250	
L4	Office Supplies Company (trade payable)		6,500
L5	Rent	1,900	
L6	Wages	1,200	
L7	Patients' fees		5,500
L8	Inventory (stock) of medical supplies	850	
L9	P. Jones		nil
L10	Electricity	100	
L11	Mrs West	nil	
L12	Mr East (trade receivable)	2,000	
L13	Depreciation	250	
L14	Expense of medical supplies	350	
Totals		61,000	61,000

Errors which will be detected by unequal totals in the trial balance

- Omitting one aspect of a transaction (e.g. a debit entry but no credit entry).
- Writing incorrect amounts in one entry (e.g. debit £290 but credit £209).
- Writing both entries in one column (e.g. two debits, no credit).
- Incorrect calculation of ledger account balance.

Errors which will leave the trial balance totals equal

- Total omission of a transaction.
- Errors in both debit and credit entry of the same magnitude.
- Entering the correct amount in the wrong ledger account (e.g. debit for wages entered as debit for heat and light).

Preparing the financial statements

The main part of this chapter set out the statement of financial position (balance sheet) and income statement (profit and loss account) of Dr Lee's medical practice for the month of October. If you compare the amounts in the trial balance with the amounts in the financial statements you will see they are the same. The normal practice in accounting is to use the trial balance to prepare the statement of financial position (balance sheet) and income statement (profit and loss account).

In this case it would be a little easier to use the trial balance for this purpose if it were arranged so that all the statement of financial position (balance sheet) items are

Table 5.9
Rearranging the trial balance into statement of financial position (balance sheet) items and income statement (profit and loss account) items

Ledger account title		£	£
L3	Medical equipment and office furniture	36,250	
L8	Inventory (stock) of medical supplies	850	
L12	Mr East (trade receivable)	2,000	
L11	Mrs West	nil	
L1	Cash at bank	18,100	
L4	Office Supplies Company (trade payable)		6,500
L9	P. Jones		nil
L2	Ownership interest		49,000
Subtotal X		57,200	55,500
Difference: profit of the month (57,200 – 55,000)			1,700
L7	Patients' fees		5,500
L14	Expense of medical supplies	350	
L6	Wages	1,200	
L5	Rent	1,900	
L10	Electricity	100	
L13	Depreciation	250	
Subtotal Y		3,800	5,500
Difference: profit of the month (5,500 – 3,800)		1,700	
Total of ledger balances in each column X + Y		61,000	61,000

together and all the income statement (profit and loss account) items are together. This is done in Table 5.9.

This form of trial balance will be used in later chapters as the starting point for the preparation of financial statements.

By way of providing further help in preparing the income statement (profit and loss account) and statement of financial position (balance sheet), subtotals are calculated for each part of the trial balance in Table 5.9. The difference between the subtotals in each section gives the profit amount. That is because the exhibit has been subdivided according to two equations, each of which leads to profit:

Assets	*minus*	Liabilities	*minus*	Capital contributed/withdrawn	*equals*	Profit

Revenue	*minus*	Expenses	*equals*	Profit

S   Test your understanding

S5.1 Prepare ledger accounts for the transactions of Jane Gate's dental practice, listed in question A5.5.

S5.2 Which of the following errors would be detected at the point of listing a trial balance?

(a) The bookkeeper enters a cash sale as a debit of £49 in the cash book and as a credit of £94 in the sales account.

(b) The bookkeeper omits a cash sale of £23 from the cash book and from the sales accounts.

(c) The bookkeeper enters cash received of £50 from Peter Jones as a debit in the cashbook but enters the credit of £50 in the ledger account of Roger Jones.

(d) The bookkeeper enters a cash sale as a credit of £40 in the cash book and as a debit of £40 in the sales account.

Chapter 6

Accounting information for trading businesses

REAL WORLD CASE

National Express and Stagecoach: performance reporting – revenue and profit

National Express and Stagecoach are both major providers of transport services in the UK. Here we compare their accounts of financial performance in their UK Bus divisions.

Alamy Images/Justin Kase

National Express plc

UK Bus division – overview of 2014

UK Bus delivered a strong performance with revenue growth driven by a combination of increased passenger volume and price inflation. Passenger growth has reflected our continued investment in fleet, service and technology. Total revenue grew by 3% to £281.0 million (2013: £273.4m) with like-for-like commercial revenue growth of 3%. In the West Midlands commercial passenger journeys rose by nearly 1% in the year, whilst concession and other income increased by 3%.

	Growth %
Like-for-like commercial revenue	3
Mileage	–
Underlying commercial revenue	3
Concession and other revenue	3
Total revenue	3

Normalised operating profit was strong, with growth of 9% to £34.0 million (2013: £31.2m), reflecting both revenue growth and cost efficiencies. The operating margin has now risen to 12.1% (2013: 11.4%), and we believe this level of margin is sustainable supported by our strong partnership relationships.

Source: National Express plc, Annual Report and Accounts 2014, p. 36. http://nexgroup.blob.core.windows.net/media/2293/ar2014-full .pdf

Stagecoach Group

UK Bus division – financial performance

The financial performance of the UK Bus (regional operations) division for the year ended 30 April 2014 is summarised below:

Operating margin **14.6%** 14.8% (20)bp

Year to 30 April	2014 £m	2013 (restated) £m	Change
Revenue	**1,012.8**	966.7	4.8%
Like-for-like revenue	**982.7**	939.8	4.6%
Operating profit	**147.4**	143.2	2.9%
Operating margin	**14.6%**	14.8%	(20)bp

Our bus businesses are built on a successful commercial formula of low fares, investment and high customer service which has delivered continued passenger volume growth nearly every year for more than ten years. The Division's results reflect a continuation of our successful strategy to grow revenue and passenger volumes organically, as well as pursuing targeted small bolt-on acquisitions. The previous year's financial results to 30 April 2013 included revenue of £18.8m and operating profit of around £4m arising from the successful delivery of contracts to provide transport for the media and athletes at the London 2012 Olympic and Paralympic Games. Excluding that £4m operating profit, the division has increased operating profit by £8.2m or 5.9% in the year ended 30 April 2014.

Source: Stagecoach Group, Annual Report and Financial Statements 2014, p. 15. http://www.stagecoach.com/investors/financial-analysis/reports/2014.aspx

Discussion points

1 How does each company describe the trading performance of its UK Bus division?

2 What further information would you require to allow you to compare these two accounts of financial performance?

Contents

After studying this chapter you should be able to:

- Explain the application of the accounting equation to transactions involving the buying and selling of inventory (trading stock).
- Explain the application of the accounting equation to transactions involving the manufacture and sale of products.
- Analyse transactions of a trading or manufacturing business during a specific period of time, using the accounting equation.
- Prepare a spreadsheet analysing the transactions, and show that the results of the spreadsheet analysis are consistent with financial statements provided by the organisation.
- Explain the main aspects of the statement of cash flows, profit and loss account and statement of financial position (balance sheet) of a trading or a manufacturing business.

Additionally, for those who choose to study the supplement:

- Analyse the transactions of a trading or a manufacturing business using the rules of debit and credit bookkeeping.
- Prepare, from a list of transactions of an organisation, ledger accounts and a trial balance which could be used to confirm the financial statements provided by the organisation.

6.1 Introduction

Chapter 5 has shown in detail the application of the accounting equation to the analysis of transactions in service businesses. The same approach applies in the case of trading businesses, but with one significant addition. Businesses which engage in trading have either purchased or manufactured a product with the intention of selling that product to customers. It is the purchase or manufacture of a product and the act of selling the product which must be analysed carefully in terms of the accounting equation. This chapter first analyses the transactions and events occurring when goods are purchased for resale and sold to a customer. Secondly, it analyses the transactions and events occurring when goods are manufactured and then sold to a customer. Finally, there is a worked example which takes one month's transactions of a trading business and shows the resulting financial statements.

6.2 Goods purchased for resale

A trading business which buys goods for resale (e.g. a wholesaler buying goods from a manufacturer for distribution to retailers) makes a profit by selling the goods at a price which is higher than the price paid. The difference between the selling price and the purchase price is called the **gross profit** of the business. The gross profit must be sufficient to cover all the costs of running the business (e.g. administration, marketing and distribution costs) and leave a net profit which will increase the ownership interest in the business.

6.2.1 Analysis of transactions

Consider the transactions of a trading company set out in Table 6.1, relating to buying and selling goods.

Table 6.1
Transactions of a trading company

		£
Apr. 1	Purchase goods from manufacturer, 100 items at £2 each, paying in cash, and store in warehouse.	200
Apr. 4	Remove 70 items from warehouse to meet a customer's request. Those 70 items cost £2 each on 1 April. They are delivered to the customer, who accepts the delivery.	140
Apr. 4	The customer pays in cash. Selling price is £2.50 per item.	175

What is the profit on the sale of 70 items? Each one cost £2.00 and is sold for £2.50, so there is a profit of 50 pence per item or £35 for 70 items. In accounting, that calculation might be set out as follows:

	£
Sale of goods (70 items)	175
Cost of goods sold (70 items)	(140)
Gross profit	35

There is an asset of unsold goods (30 items) which cost £2 each or £60 in total. Since that item is an asset, it will appear in the statement of financial position (balance sheet).

That is a statement of the gross profit and of the monetary amount of the asset of unsold goods, using common sense and intuition to arrive at an answer. Now look at how a systematic analysis is undertaken in accounting.

6.2.2 Analysis of transactions and events

Apr. 1	Purchase goods from manufacturer, 100 items at £2 each, paying in cash, and store in warehouse	£200

This transaction has two aspects in terms of the accounting equation. It *increases* the **asset** of inventory (stock of goods) and it *decreases* the **asset** of cash. One asset increases, another decreases by an equal amount and there is no effect on the ownership interest.

Assets ↑↓ – Liabilities	equals	Ownership interest

Apr. 4	Remove 70 items from warehouse to meet customer's request. Those 70 items cost £2 each on 1 April. They are delivered to the customer, who accepts the delivery.	£140

This is an event which is not a transaction. The goods which are in the store are removed to a more convenient place for sale to the customer. In this case they are removed to a delivery van and transported to the customer. The moment of delivery to, and acceptance by, the customer is the event which transforms the goods from an asset to an expense. By that event, ownership is transferred to the customer, who either pays cash immediately or agrees to pay in the future. The expense is called **cost of goods sold**.

It should be noted at this point that the acts of physical removal and transport are events which financial accounting does not record, because at that point there is not sufficient evidence for recognition that a sale has taken place. In management accounting you will find that quite a different attitude is taken to events which involve moving goods from one location to another. In management accounting, such movements are recorded in order to help the managerial process of control.

In terms of the accounting equation there is a *decrease* in the **asset** of inventory (stock) because it is no longer owned by the business and there can be no future benefit from the item. The benefit has occurred on this day, creating a sale by the act of delivery and acceptance.

If an asset has decreased then the **ownership interest** must also have *decreased* through an expense. The expense is called cost of goods sold.

Assets ↓ – Liabilities	equals	**Ownership interest ↓** (expense: cost of goods sold)

Apr. 4	The customer pays in cash. Selling price is £2.50 per item.	£175

The final transaction is the payment of cash by the customer. In timing, it will occur almost simultaneously with the delivery and acceptance of the goods. In accounting it is nevertheless analysed separately. The business receives an *increase* in the **asset** of cash and the **ownership interest** *is increased* by an act which has earned **revenue** for the business.

Assets ↑ – Liabilities	equals	**Ownership interest ↑ (revenue)**

Activity 6.1

Return to Table 6.1 and change the cost price to £3 and the selling price to £3.50. Calculate the profit if the customer receives (a) 70 items, (b) 80 items, (c) 90 items and (d) 100 items. How many items remain in inventory (stock) in each of these four cases? What can you say about the pattern of profit which appears from the four calculations you have carried out? Now write down the effect on the accounting equation for each of these four separate situations. Doing this will help you to test your own understanding before you proceed further.

6.2.3 Spreadsheet summarising the transactions

It is possible to bring the analysis together in a spreadsheet similar to that used in Chapter 5, but containing column headings which are appropriate to the assets involved in these transactions. Table 6.2 shows the spreadsheet. Table 6.3 summarises the impact of the accounting equation, showing that the assets remaining at the end of the period, £35 in total, equal the sum of the opening capital at the start (nil in this case) plus revenue, £175, minus expenses, £140.

Table 6.2
Spreadsheet analysing transactions and events into elements of the accounting equation

Date	Transaction or event	Assets		Ownership interest	
		Cash	Inventory (stock)	Revenue +	Expense −
		£	£	£	£
Apr. 1	Purchase goods from manufacturer, paying in cash, 100 items at £2 each, and place in warehouse.	(200)	200		
Apr. 4	Remove 70 items from warehouse to meet customer's request. Those 70 items cost £2 each on Apr. 1. They are delivered to the customer, who accepts the delivery.		(140)		140
Apr. 4	The customer pays in cash. Selling price is £2.50 per item.	175		175	
	Totals at end of period	(25)	60	175	140

└──── 35 ────┘

Table 6.3
Summary of transactions analysed into the elements of the accounting equation

Assets	minus	Liabilities	=	Ownership interest at start of period	plus	Capital contributed/ withdrawn	plus	Revenue	minus	Expenses
£35	−	nil	=	nil	+	nil	+	£175	−	£140

6.3 Manufacturing goods for resale

The manufacture of goods for resale requires the purchase of raw materials which are used in production of the finished goods. There are several stages here where the business may hold an asset of one type or another. Any unused raw materials will represent a benefit for the future and therefore be treated as an asset. Any finished goods which are not sold will also represent a benefit for the future and therefore be treated as an asset. Less obvious than these two items is the expected future benefit of partly completed goods that may be in the production process at the accounting date. That is also regarded as an asset, called work in progress. If the manufacturing process is rapid, then at any date there will be relatively little work in progress. If the manufacturing process is slow, there could be significant amounts of work in progress at an accounting date.

6.3.1   Analysis of transactions

Consider the transactions of a manufacturing company which are set out in Table 6.4. The company buys breakfast trays and customises them to designs requested by catering outlets.

Table 6.4
Transactions of a manufacturing company

		£
July 1	Purchase raw materials from supplier, 100 trays at £2 each, paying in cash, and place in raw materials store.	200
July 3	Remove 80 trays from raw materials store to meet production department's request (cost £2 each).	160
July 4	Carry out labour work and use production facilities to convert raw materials into finished goods. Additional costs incurred for labour and use of facilities were £1.50 per tray processed.	120
July 5	Finished goods are transferred to finished goods store. The job has cost £3.50 per tray in total (80 trays × £3.50 = £280).	280
July 10	60 trays, which cost £3.50 each to manufacture, are delivered to a customer.	210
July 10	The customer pays a price of £5 cash per tray immediately on delivery.	300

What is the profit on the sale of 60 trays? Each one cost £3.50 to manufacture and is sold for £5.00 so there is a profit of £1.50 per item or £90 for 60 items.

The business retains an inventory (stock) of 20 unsold finished trays which cost £3.50 each to manufacture (a cost of £70 in total) and an inventory (stock) of unused raw materials (20 basic trays costing £2 each which is a total cost of £40).

That is a statement of the position using common sense and intuition to arrive at an answer. Now look at how a systematic analysis is undertaken in accounting.

6.3.2 Analysis of transactions and events

July 1	Purchase raw materials from supplier, 100 trays at £2 each, paying in cash, and place in raw materials store.	£200

The business experiences an *increase* in the **asset** of inventory (stock) of raw materials and a *decrease* in the **asset** of cash. In terms of the accounting equation there is an increase in one asset matched by a decrease in another and there is no effect on the ownership interest.

Assets ↑↓ – Liabilities	equals	Ownership interest

July 3	Remove 80 trays from raw materials store to meet production department's request (cost £2 each).	£160

Next, some of the raw materials are removed for use in production. This is an event, rather than a transaction, but is recorded because it creates a possible asset of work in progress. The **asset** of work in progress *increases* and the **asset** of raw materials *decreases*. There is no effect on the ownership claim.

Assets ↑↓ – Liabilities	equals	Ownership interest

July 4	Carry out labour work and use production facilities to convert raw materials into finished goods. Additional costs incurred for labour and use of facilities were £1.50 per tray processed.	£120

The next stage is that some work is done to convert the raw materials into the product desired by customers. The work involves labour cost and other costs of using the production facilities. (You will find in management accounting that the other costs of using production facilities are usually described as **production overheads**.) This payment for labour and use of production facilities is adding to the value of the basic tray and so is adding to the value of the asset of work in progress (which will eventually become the asset of finished goods). So there is an *increase* in the **asset** of work in progress and a *decrease* in the **asset** of cash. There is no effect on the ownership interest.

Assets ↑↓ – Liabilities	equals	Ownership interest

July 5	Finished goods are transferred to finished goods store. The job has cost £3.50 per tray in total (80 trays × £3.50 = £280).	£280

When the work in progress is complete, it becomes finished goods and is transferred to the store. The **asset** of work in progress *decreases* and the **asset** of finished goods *increases*. A measure of the value of the asset is the cost of making it which, in this case, is £3.50 per item or £280 for 80 items. Again, there is no effect on the ownership interest.

Assets ↑↓ – Liabilities	equals	Ownership interest

July 10	60 trays, which cost £3.50 each to manufacture, are delivered to a customer.	£210

The customer now requests 60 trays and these are delivered from the store to the customer. At the moment of acceptance by the customer, the 60 trays cease to be an asset of the business. There is a *decrease* in an **asset** and a *decrease* in the **ownership interest** which is recorded as an **expense** of cost of goods sold.

Assets ↓ – Liabilities	equals	**Ownership interest ↓** **(expense: cost of goods sold)**

The owner's disappointment is momentary because the act of acceptance by the customer results in immediate payment being received from the customer (or in some cases a promise of future payment).

July 10	The customer pays a price of £5 cash per tray immediately on delivery.	£300

When the customer pays immediately for the goods, there is an *increase* in the **asset** of cash and a corresponding *increase* in the **ownership interest**, recorded as **revenue** of the business.

Assets ↑ – Liabilities	equals	Ownership interest ↑ (revenue)

Activity 6.2

Return to Table 6.4. Without looking to the rest of the section, write down the effect of each transaction on the accounting equation. At what point in the sequence of events in Table 6.4 is the ownership interest affected? Why is it not affected before that point in the sequence? How would the ownership interest have been affected if, on 5 July, there had been a fire as the goods were being transferred to the finished goods store and one-quarter of the finished trays were destroyed?

6.3.3 Spreadsheet summarising the transactions

Table 6.5 brings the analysis together in a spreadsheet similar to that used in Table 6.2, showing the effect of each transaction separately and also the overall effect on the accounting equation. Table 6.6 sets out the accounting equation at the end of the period and shows that the assets remaining at the end of the period are equal to the ownership interest at the start (which is taken as nil in this example) plus the profit of the period.

Once you have understood the analysis up to this point, you are ready to embark on the financial statements of a trading business.

6.4 Illustration of accounting for a trading business

This example considers the business of M. Carter, wholesale trader. At the start of May, M. Carter commenced a trading business as a wholesaler, buying goods from manufacturers and storing them in a warehouse from which customers could be supplied. All the customers are small shopkeepers who need the services of the wholesaler because they are not sufficiently powerful in purchasing power to negotiate terms directly with the manufacturers.

In Table 6.7 there is a list of transactions for M. Carter's wholesaling business during the month of May. In Section 6.4.1 each transaction is analysed using the accounting equation.

Activity 6.3

Before reading Section 6.4.1, analyse each transaction in Table 6.7 using the accounting equation. (If necessary look back to Chapter 5 for a similar pattern of analysis.) Then compare your answer against the detail of Section 6.4.1. If there is any item where you have a different answer, consult your lecturer, tutor or other expert before proceeding with the rest of the chapter.

Table 6.5
Spreadsheet analysing transactions and events into elements of the accounting equation

Date	Transaction or event	Assets				Ownership interest	
		Cash at bank	Raw materials inventory (stock)	Work in progress	Finished goods	Revenue +	Expenses −
		£	£	£	£	£	£
July 1	Purchase raw materials from supplier, paying in cash, trays at £2 each, and place 100 in raw materials store.	(200)	200				
July 3	Remove 80 trays from raw materials store to meet production department's request (cost £2 each).		(160)	160			
July 4	Carry out labour work and use production facilities to convert raw materials into finished goods. Additional costs incurred for labour and use of facilities were £1.50 per tray processed.	(120)		120			
July 5	Finished goods are transferred to finished goods store. The job has cost £3.50 per tray in total (80 trays × £3.50 = £280).			(280)	280		
July 10	60 trays, which cost £3.50 each to manufacture, are delivered to a customer.				(210)		210
July 10	The customer pays a price of £5 cash per tray immediately on delivery.	300				300	
	Totals at the end of the period.	(20)	40	nil	70	300	210

└──────── 90 ────────┘

Table 6.6
Summary of transactions analysed into the elements of the accounting equation

Assets	minus	Liabilities	=	Ownership interest at start of period	plus	Capital contributed/ withdrawn	plus	Revenue	minus	Expenses
£90	−	nil	=	nil	+	nil	+	£300	−	£210

Table 6.7
Transactions of the business of M. Carter, wholesaler, for the month of May

Date	Business transactions and events (nature of the entity: wholesale trader)	Amount £
May 1	The owner pays cash into a bank account for the business.	50,000
May 2	The business acquires buildings for cash.	30,000
May 4	The business acquires equipment for cash.	6,000
May 6	The business purchases an inventory (stock) of goods for cash.	6,500
May 7	The business purchases an inventory (stock) of goods on credit from R. Busby and receives an invoice.	5,000
May 11	The business pays R. Busby in cash for the goods it acquired on credit.	5,000
May 14	The business pays an electricity bill in cash.	100
May 17	Items costing £3,500 are removed from the store because sales have been agreed with customers for this date.	3,500
May 17	The business sells items costing £2,000 to customers for a cash price of £4,000.	4,000
May 17	The business sells items costing £1,500 on credit to R. Welsby and sends an invoice for the price of £3,000.	3,000
May 24	R. Welsby pays in cash for the goods obtained on credit.	3,000
May 28	The owner draws cash from the business for personal use.	1,000
May 30	The business pays wages to an employee for the month, in cash.	2,000
May 31	The business discovers that its equipment has fallen in value over the month.	250

6.4.1 Explanation of the analysis of each transaction

May 1   When M. Carter provides the business with cash in a bank account to allow the company to proceed, the business *acquires* an **asset** of cash and the transaction *creates* an **ownership interest** for M. Carter on the assets of the business. Using the symbols of the accounting equation:

Assets ↑ – Liabilities	equals	**Ownership interest** ↑ **(contribution of capital)**

May 2   The wholesale business now becomes the business entity so far as accounting is concerned (although M. Carter may still be making the decisions as an owner/manager of the business). The entity acquires an asset of buildings in exchange for an asset of cash. There is an *increase* in one **asset** and a *decrease* in another **asset**. There is no impact on the ownership interest.

Assets ↑↓ – Liabilities	equals	Ownership interest

May 4 The entity acquires an asset of equipment in exchange for an asset of cash. There is an *increase* in the **asset** of equipment and a *decrease* in the **asset** of cash. There is no impact on the ownership interest.

Assets ↑↓ – Liabilities	equals	Ownership interest

May 6 The entity acquires an asset of inventory (stock) of goods in exchange for an asset of cash. There is an *increase* in the **asset** of inventory (stock) and a *decrease* in the **asset** of cash. There is no impact on the ownership interest.

Assets ↑↓ – Liabilities	equals	Ownership interest

May 7 The entity again acquires an asset of inventory (stock) of goods but this time it is related to the acquisition of a liability to R. Busby. There is an *increase* in the **asset** of inventory (stock) and an *increase* in the **liability** of receivables (creditors). There is no impact on the ownership interest.

Assets ↑ – **Liabilities** ↑	equals	Ownership interest

May 11 When payment is made to R. Busby there is a *decrease* in the **asset** of cash and a *decrease* in the **liability** to R. Busby.

Assets ↓ – **Liabilities** ↓	equals	Ownership interest

May 14 When the electricity bill is paid, the benefit of using the electricity has been consumed. There is a *decrease* in the **asset** of cash and a *decrease* in the **ownership interest**, reported as an expense.

Assets ↓ – Liabilities	equals	**Ownership interest** ↓ **(expense)**

May 17 At the moment of acceptance by the customer, the goods cease to be an asset of the business. There is a *decrease* in the **ownership interest** (recorded as an **expense** of cost of goods sold) and a *decrease* in the **asset** of inventory (stock).

Assets ↓ – Liabilities	equals	**Ownership interest** ↓ **(cost of goods sold)**

May 17 The owner's wealth is then immediately restored or enhanced because some customers pay cash for the goods. There is an *increase* in the **asset** of cash and a corresponding *increase* in the **ownership interest**, recorded as revenue of the business. The information about cost of goods sold has been dealt with in the previous equation.

Assets ↑ – Liabilities	equals	**Ownership interest** ↑ **(revenue)**

May 17 The owner's wealth is similarly restored by a promise from the customer to pay at a future date. This creates the asset of a trade receivable (debtor) which, in accounting, is regarded as acceptable in the overall measure of shareholder wealth. There is an *increase* in the **asset** of trade receivable (debtor) and a corresponding *increase* in the **ownership interest**, recorded as

revenue of the business. The information about cost of goods sold has been dealt with in the earlier equation.

Assets ↑ – Liabilities	equals	**Ownership interest** ↑ **(revenue)**

May 24   R. Welsby is a credit customer of the business, called a 'trade receivable' or a 'debtor'. When a credit customer makes payment to the business there is an *increase* in the **asset** of cash and a *decrease* in the **asset** of trade receivable (debtor). There is no effect on the ownership interest.

Assets ↑↓ – Liabilities	equals	Ownership interest

May 28   As was explained in Chapter 5, the owner of a sole trader business does not take a salary or wage as an employee would, but needs cash for personal purposes. Taking cash for personal use is called **drawings** and is recorded in terms of the accounting equation as a *decrease* in the **ownership interest** and a *decrease* in the **asset** of cash.

Assets ↓ – Liabilities	equals	**Ownership interest** ↓ **(withdrawal of capital)**

May 30   Paying wages is similar in effect to paying the electricity bill. The benefit of the employee's work has been consumed. There is a *decrease* in the **asset** of cash and a *decrease* in the **ownership interest**, reported as an **expense**.

Assets ↓ – Liabilities	equals	**Ownership interest** ↓ **(expense)**

May 31   All non-current (fixed) assets will eventually be used up by the business, after several years of useful life. Depreciation is a recognition of the *decrease* in the **asset** and the *decrease* in the **ownership interest**, reported as an **expense**. (There is more on **depreciation** in Chapter 8.)

Assets ↓ – Liabilities	equals	**Ownership interest** ↓ **(expense)**

6.5 A process for summarising the transactions: a spreadsheet

In Table 6.8 the transactions of Table 6.7 are repeated at the left-hand side and are analysed into columns headed for assets, liabilities and ownership interest using brackets to show a negative amount. It would be equally acceptable to use a minus sign but minus signs tend to disappear or be confused with unintentional blobs on the paper, so brackets are frequently used in accounting in order to ensure clarity.

At the foot of the spreadsheet in Table 6.8 there is a total for each column. Those totals are used in Table 6.9 to show the state of the accounting equation at the end of the month. It may be used to explain to M. Carter how the ownership interest has changed over the month. The owner contributed £50,000 at the start of the month and has a claim of £50,150 at the end of the month. The ownership interest was increased by earning revenue of £7,000 but reduced by incurring expenses of £5,850 and withdrawing £1,000 for personal use.

Spreadsheet analysing transactions into the elements of the accounting equation

Date	Business transactions	Assets			Liabilities	Ownership interest		
		Cash at bank	Inventory (stock) of goods	Non-current (fixed) assets and trade receivables (debtors)	Trade payables (creditors)	Capital contributed/ withdrawn	Revenue +	Expenses −
		£	£	£	£	£	£	£
May 1	The owner provides the business with cash.	50,000				50,000		
May 2	The business acquires buildings for cash.	(30,000)		30,000				
May 4	The business acquires equipment for cash.	(6,000)		6,000				
May 6	The business purchases an inventory (stock) of goods for cash.	(6,500)	6,500					
May 7	The business purchases an inventory (stock) of goods on credit from R. Busby and receives an invoice.		5,000		5,000			
May 11	The business pays R. Busby in cash for the goods it acquired on credit.	(5,000)			(5,000)			
May 14	The business pays an electricity bill in cash.	(100)						100
May 17	Some of the goods purchased for resale (items costing £3,500) are removed from the store because sales have been agreed with customers for this date.		(3,500)					3,500
May 17	The business sells some of the purchased goods for cash.	4,000					4,000	
May 17	The business sells the remaining purchased goods on credit to R. Welsby and sends an invoice.			3,000			3,000	
May 24	R. Welsby pays in cash for the goods obtained on credit.	3,000		(3,000)				
May 28	The owner draws cash from the business for personal use.	(1,000)				(1,000)		
May 30	The business pays wages to an employee for the past month, in cash.	(2,000)						2,000
May 31	The business discovers that its equipment has fallen in value over the month.			(250)				250
	Totals at the end of the period	6,400	8,000	35,750	nil	49,000	7,000	5,850

50,150

Table 6.9
Summary of transactions analysed into the elements of the accounting equation

Assets	minus	Liabilities	=	Capital contributed/ withdrawn	plus	Revenue	minus	Expenses
£50,150	–	nil	=	£49,000	+	£7,000	–	£5,850

| | £50,150 | | | £50,150 | | | | |

How has the ownership interest changed over the month? The owner contributed £50,000 at the start of the month and has a claim of £50,150 at the end of the month. The ownership interest was increased by earning revenue of £7,000 but reduced by incurring expenses of £5,850 and withdrawing £1,000 for personal use.

6.6 Financial statements of M. Carter, wholesaler

The transactions in Table 6.8 may be summarised in financial statements for use by interested parties. The first user will be the owner, M. Carter, but others such as the Inland Revenue may ask for a copy. If the owner seeks to raise additional finance by borrowing from a bank, the bank manager may ask for a copy of the financial statements.

There are no regulations regarding the format of financial statements for a sole trader, but it is good practice to try to match, as far as possible, the more onerous requirements imposed on limited liability companies. The financial statements presented in this section follow the general formats set out in Chapter 3.

6.6.1   Statement of cash flows

M. Carter, wholesaler
Statement of cash flows for the month of May Year 20xx

	£
Operating activities	
Cash from customers	7,000
Outflow: payment for goods	(6,500)
payment to supplier (R. Busby)	(5,000)
wages	(2,000)
electricity	(100)
Net outflow from operations	(6,600)
Investing activities	
Payment for buildings	(30,000)
Payment for equipment	(6,000)
Net outflow for investing activities	(36,000)
Financing activities	
Capital contributed by owner	50,000
Capital withdrawn as drawings	(1,000)
Net inflow from financing activities	49,000
Increase in cash at bank over period	6,400

Comment. The operating activities caused a drain on cash with a net effect that £6,600 flowed out of the business. A further £36,000 cash flow was used for investing activities. The owner contributed £50,000 at the start of the month but withdrew £1,000 at the end of the month. Cash in the bank increased by £6,400 over the month.

6.6.2 Income statement (profit and loss account)

M. Carter, wholesaler
Income statement (profit and loss account) for the month of
May Year 20xx

	£	£
Sales		7,000
Cost of goods sold		(3,500)
Gross profit		3,500
Other expenses		
Wages	(2,000)	
Electricity	(100)	
Depreciation	(250)	
		(2,350)
Net profit		1,150

Comment. This profit and loss account differs slightly from that presented for the service business in Chapter 5. It has a subtotal for gross profit. The difference between sales and the cost of purchasing or manufacturing the goods sold is regarded as an important indicator of the success of the business in its particular product line. The gross profit is sometimes referred to as the **margin** or **gross margin** and is a piece of information which is much explored by professional investors and analysts.

Making a subtotal for **gross profit** means that the final line needs a different label and so is called **net profit**. The word 'net' means 'after taking everything away', so in this case the net profit is equal to sales minus all expenses of the operations of the business.

Activity 6.4

The business of M. Carter, wholesaler, has made a profit of £1,150 from operations during the month but the cash flow due to operating activities has been negative to the extent of £6,600. Make a comparison of the cash flow from operating activities and the profit from operations. From your comparison, explain how a business can make a profit and yet see its cash drain away. Then make some recommendations about reducing the outflow of cash without affecting profit.

6.6.3 Statement of financial position (balance sheet)

M. Carter, wholesaler
Statement of financial position (balance sheet)
at 31 May Year 20xx

	£
Non-current (fixed) assets	
Buildings	30,000
Equipment	6,000
	36,000
Depreciation	(250)
Total non-current (fixed) assets	35,750
Current assets	
Inventory (stocks)	8,000
Cash at bank	6,400
Total current assets	14,400
Total assets	50,150
Ownership interest	
Capital at start	50,000
add: profit	1,150
less: drawings	(1,000)
Total ownership interest	50,150

Comment. There are no liabilities at the end of the month and so the net assets are the same as the total of fixed assets and current assets. That somewhat artificial situation arises from keeping the example fairly simple and manageable. The depreciation has been recorded for the equipment but many businesses would also depreciate buildings. The useful life of a building is much longer than that of equipment and so the depreciation for any single month would be a negligible amount in relation to other information for the period. The amount of £35,750 has been described here as depreciated cost but could also be called the **net book value** or the **written down value**.

The statement of financial position (balance sheet) is a statement of position and, on its own, is of limited usefulness. Companies which publish accounting information will present the previous year's amounts alongside the current year's data so that comparisons may be made. Some companies provide, in addition, five- or ten-year summaries which allow comparison over a longer period.

6.7 Summary

The following sequence summarises the effect on the accounting equation of buying goods and then selling them to customers.

1 Inventory (stock) is acquired for cash.

Assets ↑↓ − Liabilities	equals	Ownership interest

2 When the inventory is sold an expense of cost of goods sold is recorded.

Assets ↓ − Liabilities	equals	**Ownership interest** ↓ **(expense: cost of goods sold)**

3 At the same time the sale of the inventory increases an asset of cash or trade receivable (debtor) and creates revenue.

Assets ↑ − Liabilities	equals	**Ownership interest** ↑ **(revenue)**

The following sequence summarises the effect on the accounting equation of buying raw materials, converting them to finished products and then selling these to customers.

1 The asset of raw materials is converted to an asset of work in progress.

Assets ↑↓ − Liabilities	equals	Ownership interest

2 The asset of work in progress becomes an asset of finished goods.

Assets ↑↓ − Liabilities	equals	Ownership interest

3 When the finished goods are sold an expense of cost of goods sold is created.

Assets ↓ − Liabilities	equals	**Ownership interest** ↓ **(expense: cost of goods sold)**

4 At the same time the sale of the inventory increases an asset of cash or trade receivable (debtor) and creates revenue.

Assets ↑ – Liabilities	equals	**Ownership interest ↑ (revenue)**

QUESTIONS

The Questions section of each chapter has three types of question. 'Test your understanding' questions to help you review your reading are in the 'A' series of questions. You will find the answers to these by reading and thinking about the material in the book. 'Application' questions to test your ability to apply technical skills are in the 'B' series of questions. Questions requiring you to show skills in problem solving and evaluation are in the 'C' series of questions. A letter [S] indicates that there is a solution at the end of the book. Other solutions are provided in the Instructor's Manual, where there are further questions parallel to those set out here.

A   Test your understanding

A6.1   [S] On 1 May the Sea Traders Company purchased 200 spare parts for fishing boats, costing £20 each. On 5 May, 60 of these spare parts were sold to a customer at a price of £25 each. The customer paid in cash immediately.

(a) Calculate the profit made on this transaction.
(b) Explain the impact of each transaction on the accounting equation.

A6.2   [S] Summarise the transactions of question A6.1 in a spreadsheet and show that the totals of the spreadsheet satisfy the accounting equation.

A6.3   [S] The following transactions relate to Toy Manufacturers Company during the month of June.

Date	Business transactions	£
June 1	Purchase toy components from supplier, 100 items at £3 each, paying in cash, and place in raw materials store.	300
June 3	Remove 70 components from raw materials store to meet production department's request (cost £3 each).	210
June 5	Carry out labour work and use production facilities to convert components into finished goods. Additional costs incurred for labour and use of facilities were £2.50 per toy processed.	175
June 6	Finished goods are transferred to finished goods store. Each toy has cost £5.50 in total (70 toys × £5.50 = £385).	385
June 11	50 toys, which cost £5.50 each to manufacture, are delivered to a customer.	275
June 14	The customer pays a price of £8 cash per toy immediately on delivery.	400

(a) Calculate the profit on sale.
(b) Explain the effect of each transaction on the accounting equation.
(c) Prepare a spreadsheet summarising the transactions.

A6.4   [S] The following list of transactions relates to the business of Peter Gold, furniture supplier, during the month of April. Analyse each transaction to show the two aspects of the transaction.

Date	Business transactions and events (nature of the entity: wholesale trader)	Amount £
Apr. 1	The owner pays cash into a bank account for the business.	60,000
Apr. 2	The business acquires buildings for cash.	20,000
Apr. 4	The business acquires equipment for cash.	12,000
Apr. 6	The business purchases an inventory (stock) of goods for cash.	8,500
Apr. 7	The business purchases an inventory (stock) of goods on credit from R. Green and receives an invoice.	7,000
Apr. 11	The business pays R. Green in cash for the goods it acquired on credit.	7,000
Apr. 14	The business pays a gas bill in cash.	400
Apr. 17	Items costing £5,500 are removed from the store because sales have been agreed with customers for this date.	5,500
Apr. 17	The business sells some of the goods removed from store for cash of £6,000.	6,000
Apr. 17	The business sells the remainder of the goods removed from store on credit to P. Weatherall and sends an invoice.	4,200
Apr. 24	P. Weatherall pays in cash for the goods obtained on credit.	4,200
Apr. 28	The owner draws cash from the business for personal use.	2,700
Apr. 29	The business pays wages to employees for the past month, in cash.	2,800
Apr. 30	The business discovers that its equipment has fallen in value over the month.	550

B   Application

B6.1 [S]
(a) Using the list of transactions at question A6.4 above, prepare a spreadsheet similar to that presented in Table 6.8.
(b) Show the resulting impact on the accounting equation and demonstrate that it remains in balance.

B6.2 [S]
Using the total from the columns of the spreadsheet of question B6.1(a), prepare for the business in the month of April:

(a) a statement of cash flows;
(b) a statement of financial position (balance sheet); and
(c) a profit and loss account.

There are no questions in the C series for this chapter. These skills are tested in specific situations in Chapters 8 to 12.

Recording transactions in ledger accounts: a trading business

The supplement starts with a reminder of the rules of debit and credit bookkeeping, set out in Table 6.10.

Table 6.10
Rules of debit and credit

	Debit entries in a ledger account	Credit entries in a ledger account
Left-hand side of the equation		
Asset	Increase	Decrease
Right-hand side of the equation		
Liability	Decrease	Increase
Ownership interest	Expense	Revenue
	Capital withdrawn	Capital contributed

Activity 6.5	*It might be a useful test of your understanding of the chapter if you try to write down the debit and credit entries before looking at Table 6.11. If you find your answers don't agree with that table then you should go back to the analysis contained in the chapter and think about the various aspects of the accounting equation. Debit and credit entries do nothing more than follow the analysis based on the accounting equation so you should not have a problem if you have followed the analysis.*

Table 6.1 presented a short list of transactions for a trading company, relating to the purchase and sale of goods. That list of transactions is repeated in Table 6.11 but showing in the final two columns the ledger accounts in which debit and credit entries would be made. Compare Table 6.11 with Table 6.2 to see that the analysis of transactions and the analysis of debit and credit entries follow similar patterns.

Table 6.4 presented a short list of transactions for a manufacturing company. These are repeated in Table 6.12 with the ledger accounts for debit and credit entries being shown in the final two columns. Again, you should try this first and then check your answer against Table 6.12.

Table 6.11

Transactions of a trading company: debit and credit entries

		£	Debit	Credit
Apr. 1	Purchase goods from manufacturer, 100 items at £2 each, paying in cash, and store in warehouse.	200	Inventory (stock)	Cash
Apr. 4	Remove 70 items from warehouse to meet a customer's request. Those 70 items cost £2 each on 1 April. They are delivered to the customer who accepts the delivery.	140	Cost of goods sold	Inventory (stock)
Apr. 4	The customer pays in cash. Selling price is £2.50 per item.	175	Cash	Revenue

Table 6.12

Transactions of a manufacturing company: debit and credit entries

		£	Debit	Credit
July 1	Purchase raw materials from supplier, 100 trays at £2 each, paying in cash, and place in raw materials store.	200	Raw materials inventory (stock)	Cash
July 3	Remove 80 trays from raw materials store to meet production department's request (cost £2 each).	160	Work in progress	Raw materials inventory (stock)
July 4	Carry out labour work and use production facilities to convert raw materials into finished goods. Additional costs incurred for labour and use of facilities were £1.50 per tray processed.	120	Work in progress	Cash
July 5	Finished goods are transferred to finished goods store. The job has cost £3.50 per tray in total (80 trays × £3.50 = £280).	280	Finished goods	Work in progress
July 10	60 trays, which cost £3.50 each to manufacture, are delivered to a customer.	210	Cost of goods sold	Finished goods
July 10	The customer pays a price of £5 cash per tray immediately on delivery.	300	Cash	Revenue

M. Carter, wholesaler: analysing the debit and credit entries

Table 6.13 takes the information contained in Table 6.8 and analyses it under debit and credit headings showing the ledger accounts in which each entry will be made. Ledger accounts required to record these transactions are:

L1 Cash	L2 Owner	L3 Buildings	L4 Equipment
L5 Inventory (stock) of goods	L6 R. Busby	L7 Electricity	L8 Wages
L9 Cost of goods sold	L10 Sales	L11 R. Welsby	L12 Depreciation

The full ledger account records for the transactions in Table 6.13 are set out. Leona Rees has commented on each one, to show how she interprets them when she is carrying out work of audit or investigation.

L1 Cash

Date	Particulars	Page	Debit	Credit	Balance
			£	£	£
May 1	Owner's capital	L2	50,000		50,000
May 2	Buildings	L3		30,000	20,000
May 4	Equipment	L4		6,000	14,000
May 6	Inventory (stock) of goods	L5		6,500	7,500
May 11	R. Busby	L6		5,000	2,500
May 14	Electricity	L7		100	2,400
May 17	Sales	L10	4,000		6,400
May 24	R. Welsby	L11	3,000		9,400
May 28	Ownership interest drawn out	L2		1,000	8,400
May 30	Wages	L8		2,000	6,400

LEONA's comment: *The amount of £50,000 put into the business at the start is quickly swallowed up by spending cash on buildings, equipment, buying an inventory (stock) of goods and paying the supplier who gave credit. Paying the electricity account £100 took the cash balance down to £2,400 and it was only the sale of some goods which allowed the business to continue. If the sale of goods had not taken place, the owner might have needed to put more cash into the business at that point, or else ask the bank manager to make a loan to the business. With the benefit of hindsight, the owner might have waited a few days before paying R. Busby for goods supplied. It's not a good idea to delay paying the electricity bill in case there is a disconnection, and failing to pay wages usually means the employee does not return. It might have helped cash flow to have bought the buildings and equipment using a loan, but borrowing money has a cost in interest payments and perhaps the owner prefers not to start with a high level of borrowing.*

L2 Ownership interest

Date	Particulars	Page	Debit	Credit	Balance
			£	£	£
May 1	Cash contributed	L1		50,000	(50,000)
May 28	Cash drawn	L1	1,000		(49,000)

Table 6.13
Analysis of transactions for M. Carter, wholesaler

Date	Business transactions	Amount	Debit	Credit
		£		
May 1	The owner provides the business with cash.	50,000	Cash	Owner
May 2	The business acquires buildings for cash.	30,000	Buildings	Cash
May 4	The business acquires equipment for cash.	6,000	Equipment	Cash
May 6	The business purchases an inventory (stock) of goods for cash.	6,500	Inventory (stock)	Cash
May 7	The business purchases an inventory (stock) of goods on credit from R. Busby and receives an invoice.	5,000	Inventory (stock)	R. Busby
May 11	The business pays R. Busby in cash for the goods it acquired on credit.	5,000	R. Busby	Cash
May 14	The business pays an electricity bill in cash.	100	Electricity	Cash
May 17	Items costing £3,500 are removed from the store because sales have been agreed with customers for this date.	3,500	Cost of goods sold	Inventory (stock)
May 17	The business sells goods for cash.	4,000	Cash	Sales
May 17	The business sells goods on credit to R. Welsby and sends an invoice.	3,000	R. Welsby	Sales
May 24	R. Welsby pays in cash for the goods obtained on credit.	3,000	Cash	R. Welsby
May 28	The owner draws cash from the business for personal use.	1,000	Owner	Cash
May 30	The business pays wages to an employee for the past month, in cash.	2,000	Wages	Cash
May 31	The business discovers that its equipment has fallen in value over the month.	250	Depreciation	Equipment

LEONA's comment: *The ownership interest is created when the owner contributes cash or resources to the business. In this case, it was cash. The sole trader in business may withdraw cash for personal use at any time – it is called owner's drawings – but the desirability of that action depends on how useful it is to the owner when compared to how useful it might have been if left in the business. The owner of this business has a claim remaining equal to £49,000 after making the drawing.*

L3 Buildings

Date	Particulars	Page	Debit	Credit	Balance
			£	£	£
May 2	Cash	L1	30,000		30,000

LEONA's comment: *This ledger account is particularly useful as a reminder that a very valuable asset is owned by the business. Having a record in the ledger account encourages the owner to think about continuing care for the buildings and also to review their value against the amount recorded.*

L4 Equipment

Date	Particulars	Page	Debit	Credit	Balance
			£	£	£
May 4	Cash	L1	6,000		6,000
May 31	Depreciation	L12		250	5,750

LEONA's comment: *The equipment cost £6,000 but is being gradually used up over its life in the business. Depreciation is a way of showing that the original cost of the asset has to be spread over its useful life. If the estimate of depreciation is correct, this ledger account should reduce to nil on the day the equipment ceases to be of use. In reality things usually are not quite so straightforward. (Depreciation of fixed assets is dealt with in more detail in Chapter 8.)*

L5 Inventory (stock) of goods

Date	Particulars	Page	Debit	Credit	Balance
			£	£	£
May 6	Cash	L1	6,500		6,500
May 7	R. Busby	L6	5,000		11,500
May 17	Cost of goods sold	L9		3,500	8,000

LEONA's comment: *The balance on this ledger account at any point in time should equal the cost price of the goods held in the warehouse. So at the end of May, if the owner goes to the warehouse and carries out an inventory count (stock count), there should be goods to a total cost of £8,000. Checking the presence of an inventory (stock) of unsold goods which agrees with the ledger account is an important part of my work as an auditor. If they don't agree, I start to ask a lot of questions.*

L6 R. Busby

Date	Particulars	Page	Debit	Credit	Balance
			£	£	£
May 7	Inventory (stock) of goods	L5		5,000	(5,000)
May 11	Cash	L1	5,000		nil

LEONA's comment: *When the goods were purchased from R. Busby, the supplier, an invoice was received from that supplier showing the amount due. That invoice was used to make the credit entry on May 7 showing that the business had a liability. The liability was extinguished on May 11 by a payment to R. Busby, so at the end of May the business owes that supplier nothing.*

L7 Electricity

Date	Particulars	Page	Debit	Credit	Balance
			£	£	£
May 14	Cash	L1	100		100

LEONA's comment: *This is a very straightforward expense account. The balance on this account will show the total expense of electricity consumed during the period.*

L8 Wages

Date	Particulars	Page	Debit	Credit	Balance
			£	£	£
May 30	Cash	L1	2,000		2,000

LEONA's comment: *Another very straightforward account in which to accumulate all wages expenses.*

L9 Cost of goods sold

Date	Particulars	Page	Debit	Credit	Balance
			£	£	£
May 17	Inventory (stock) of goods	L5	3,500		3,500

LEONA's comment: *This is an expense account showing the cost of the goods sold during the month. The total sales are shown in ledger account L10 as £7,000 and the cost of goods sold is shown here as £3,500, so there is a profit ('margin') of 50% on sales before taking into account the expenses of electricity, wages and depreciation. As an auditor I have considerable interest in the profit margin on sales. It tells me a great deal about the business.*

L10 Sales

Date	Particulars	Page	Debit	Credit	Balance
			£	£	£
May 17	Cash	L1		4,000	(4,000)
May 17	R. Welsby	L11		3,000	(7,000)

LEONA's comment: *This is a revenue account, so credit entries are expected. The balance column shows the total sales of the month were £7,000.*

L11 R. Welsby

Date	Particulars	Page	Debit	Credit	Balance
			£	£	£
May 17	Sales	L10	3,000		3,000
May 24	Cash	L1		3,000	nil

LEONA's comment: *The credit sale to R. Welsby made him a trade receivable (debtor) of the business and so the first entry is a debit entry. When R. Welsby paid this extinguished the debt, by the end of the month R. Welsby owed nothing to the business.*

L12 Depreciation

Date	Particulars	Page	Debit	Credit	Balance
			£	£	£
May 31	Equipment	L4	250		250

LEONA's comment: *This is another expense account showing an item which has decreased the ownership interest through a decrease in the recorded amount of an asset. This is where accounting begins to look slightly complicated because no cash has changed hands. Recording depreciation is the accounting way of expressing caution as to the expected future benefits from the asset. These will be eroded as the asset is used up. Depreciation is a way of acknowledging that erosion.*

Checking the accuracy of double-entry records

In Chapter 5, the process of listing all ledger account balances in a trial balance was explained.

The trial balance for the accounting records of M. Carter, wholesaler, at 31 May year 1, is as shown in Table 6.14. This is a basic list summarising the transactions of the month. If you compare it with the financial statements in the main part of the chapter you will see that all the amounts correspond.

Table 6.14
Trial balance at 31 May for M. Carter, wholesaler

Ledger account title	£	£
L1 Cash	6,400	
L2 Ownership interest		49,000
L3 Buildings	30,000	
L4 Equipment	5,750	
L5 Inventory (stock) of goods	8,000	
L6 R. Busby		nil
L7 Electricity	100	
L8 Wages	2,000	
L9 Cost of goods sold	3,500	
L10 Sales		7,000
L11 R. Welsby	nil	
L12 Depreciation	250	
Totals	56,000	56,000

As was the case in the supplement to Chapter 5, it is rather easier to use the trial balance if it is arranged so that all the statement of financial position (balance sheet) items are together and all the profit and loss account items are together. This is done in Table 6.15. The unshaded lines are not part of the trial balance but take advantage of the various forms of the accounting equation to calculate profit in two different ways. In the first part of the table:

Profit	equals	Assets – Liabilities – Owner's capital at the start and any changes during the period

In the second part of the table:

Profit	equals	Revenue – Expenses

Table 6.15
Rearranging the trial balance into statement of financial position (balance sheet) items and profit and loss account items

Ledger account title	£	£
L3 Buildings	30,000	
L4 Equipment	5,750	
L5 Inventory (stock) of goods	8,000	
L11 R. Welsby	nil	
L1 Cash	6,400	
L6 R. Busby		nil
L2 Ownership interest		49,000
Subtotal X	50,150	49,000
Difference: profit of the month 50,150 – 49,000		1,150
L10 Sales		7,000
L9 Cost of goods sold	3,500	
L7 Electricity	100	
L8 Wages	2,000	
L12 Depreciation	250	
Subtotal Y	5,850	7,000
Difference: profit of the month 7,000 – 5,850	1,150	
Total of ledger balances in each column X + Y	56,000	56,000

The form of trial balance shown in Table 6.15 will be used in later chapters as the starting point for the preparation of financial statements.

S   Test your understanding

S6.1   Prepare ledger accounts for the transactions of Peter Gold, furniture supplier, listed in question A6.4.

Part 3

Recognition in financial statements

Chapter 7

Published financial statements

Morrisons plc: reporting annual performance

Extracts from Annual Report and Financial Statements

Chairman's review: Results

In the year, total turnover of £17.7bn was down 2% (2012/13: £18.1bn). When compared to the prior year the underlying operating margin of 4.9% fell by 40bps. This increased to 50bps after adjusting for the impact of a lower proportion of fuel sales in the mix this year.

Alamy Images_Kevin Britland

Net finance costs of £82m increased by £12m over the prior period as a result of a planned increase in net debt to accommodate our peak investment of capital expenditure. Underlying profit is calculated after removing property disposals, new business development costs, non-recurring exceptional costs and IAS19 pension interest.

Underlying operating profit of £865m fell by 11% when compared to the prior year, with underlying profit before tax of £785m, down by 13%.

Exceptional non-recurring costs of £903m were charged in the year including £163m in relation to Kiddicare, a business which is no longer strategic. We will look to sell this business in 2014. £319m relates to elements of our store pipeline. Following a reassessment of their potential to meet our required investment criteria we have impaired £90m of costs to date and provided for £229m of further costs. A charge of £379m has been incurred in relation to trading stores, comprising of £330m of impairment and £49m of onerous lease provisions.

A further cut in the rate of corporation tax and the positive impact of the Group's equity retirement programme partly helped to offset the impact of the reduction in underlying earnings on earnings per share (EPS). Underlying basic EPS decreased by 8% to 25.2p (2012/13: 27.3p) with statutory basic earnings per share of (10.2)p (2012/13: 26.7p).

Financial review: Operating profit

Productivity initiatives focusing on store payroll, unlocking efficiencies from new technology and savings in goods not for resale delivered £138m. Operating costs continued to be managed tightly despite inflationary pressures and the increase in space.

Underlying operating profit was £865m, 11% below prior year.

	2013/14 £m	2012/13 £m
Operating (loss)/profit	(95)	949
Underlying adjustments:		
– Non-recurring exceptional costs	903	–
– Multi-channel investment	66	17
– Property (profits)/losses	(9)	1
Underlying operating profit	865	967

Source: Morrisons plc Annual Report and Financial Statements 2013/14, pp. 5,44. http://www.morrisons-corporate.com/Documents/Corporate2014/Morrisons_AnnualReport13-14_Complete.pdf

Comment from *Financial Times*

Write-offs of £163m on Kiddicare, a retailer of strollers and other tot-wrangling kit, reflect the dither that left Wm Morrison with a £176m pre-tax loss in 2013–14. Chief executive Dalton Philips spent £70m on the acquisition in 2011 and ill-advisedly bought into dreams of a Mothercare rival hatched by Kiddicare boss Scott Weavers-Wright.

Instead, Mr Philips should have focused on the threat to Morrison from discounters such as Aldi. Thursday's strategy overhaul represents a belated Big Bang response.

Morrison will spend more than £300m a year for three years on price cuts. Underlying profits will drop to about £350m next year from £785m in 2013–14. Yet, surprisingly, the group, which is 60 per cent geared, expects to raise scantily covered dividends.

Mr Philips plans to release £1bn over three years in cash flow partly thanks to lower capex, and another £1bn from real estate sales. Ocado is supplying the online groceries platform Kiddicare failed to.

Why has it taken activist pressure and rumours of a bid from the Morrison family to prompt actions that should have been on Mr Philips' agenda for years? And are the planned price cuts enough in the context of a £170bn UK groceries market to tilt customer behaviour back in Morrison's favour?

The new strategy looks like a large, if unavoidable, gamble.

 Source: Alison Smith and Jonathan Guthrie, Financial Times Lombard, 13 March 2014. http://www.ft.com/cms/s/0/577f7e26-aaa4-11e3-9fd6-00144feab7de.html#ixzz3FXicWf00

Discussion points

1 The 'statutory' basic earnings per share is calculated on the basis recommended by the relevant accounting standard. Why does the company also report an 'underlying basic' earnings per share?

2 Why does the company report operating profit (or loss) and underlying operating profit?

3 How does the newspaper comment put a forward-looking interpretation on the reported results?

Contents

Learning outcomes

After reading this chapter you should be able to:

- Explain the key international influences that affect accounting practice in the UK.

- Explain the structure of company reporting as set out in the *Conceptual Framework* and in UK guidance.

- Explain the main contents of (a) the balance sheet, (b) the income statement (profit and loss account) and (c) the statement of cash flows as presented by larger companies.

- Define 'parent company' and 'subsidiary company' and explain how a group is structured.

- Explain the main features of group financial statements.

- Explain the nature of, and reason for, other forms of communication beyond the annual report.

7.1 Introduction

It is explained in Chapters 1 and 4 that in the case of sole traders and partnerships the groups of persons who have an interest in the financial statements are limited to the owners themselves, HM Revenue and Customs and organisations such as banks which are asked to provide finance for the company. For limited liability companies the list of potential users widens and the access to internal information becomes restricted. Even the owners of a limited liability company, called the equity holders (shareholders) are not permitted access to the day-to-day records of the company and are treated as being outsiders of (external to) the company they own. The quality and amount of information communicated to these users who are external to the company becomes a matter which is too important to be left entirely to the discretion of the directors running the company.

Chapter 4 outlined the various regulatory authorities which exist to establish the quality and quantity of information to be published by limited liability companies. There are over one million limited liability companies in the UK, although only a few thousand are listed on the Stock Exchange and of these only around 500 have their shares bought and sold regularly. The number of major listed companies, and their importance to the economy in terms of the funds invested in them, means it is appropriate to take them as the benchmark for current practice in external reporting. The practices applied by larger limited liability companies set a good example as a starting point for smaller ones and for organisations that are not limited liability companies, such as charitable trusts or public sector bodies.

In this chapter, and in Chapters 8 to 12, there is mention only of **limited liability companies** because the aim of this book is to provide an understanding of the accounting information published by companies. The more general word **enterprise** (meaning a business activity or commercial project) could be substituted throughout for limited liability company. Most of what is said in these chapters applies to all enterprises because the principles and practice described here have a wider application beyond companies, although modifications may be necessary when the needs of the users and the purposes of the enterprise are different from those relevant to a limited liability company.

7.2 International influences

Chapter 3 explained that, since January 2005, two different accounting systems have existed for companies in the UK, depending on the type of company. For the group financial statements of a listed company the accounting system set out by the International Accounting Standards Board (IASB) must be applied. All other companies, and the separate companies in the group, may choose to follow IASB standards but there is no requirement to do so. Companies that do not choose to follow the international accounting standards must continue to follow the rules of UK company law and the UK FRC's accounting standards.

For many years there has been a strong international influence on and from UK accounting practice so the change to international accounting standards in 2005 did not bring many surprises. The UK accounting standard-setting body was a founder member of the International Accounting Standards Committee (IASC), set up in 1973, and has been closely involved in its work since that date. In 2001, with an organisational change, the IASC became the IASB but the close similarity between international accounting standards and UK accounting standards continued. The UK FRC has worked continuously towards matching UK standards to IFRS.

Since 1980 the law regulating financial reporting in the UK (now contained in the Companies Act 2006 and related legislation) has reflected its membership of the European Union (EU) and the work of regulators across the EU to harmonise aspects of financial reporting. From 2005 the law governing financial reporting in the UK has been split into two routes. One route is the rule of UK company law influenced by the EU. The other route is the IASB system of accounting as endorsed by the EU.

7.2.1 The European Union

The UK is a member state of the EU and is required to develop its laws so as to harmonise with those of other member states of the EU. There are two procedures by which the EU influences the accounting practices of UK-based companies.

1 The European Commission, which is the permanent secretariat and staff of the EU, issues a Regulation which overrides national laws and applies to all companies specified in the Regulation.
2 The European Commission issues Directives which are incorporated in national laws of member states.

The IAS Regulation

In 2002 the European Commission issued the first IAS Regulation. The IAS Regulation is a direct instruction to companies in all member states. It required that, by 2005, all **listed companies** in the European Union would use IASB standards in preparing their **group** financial statements. This was intended to cause convergence ('bringing together') of accounting practices, and so improve the movement of capital across the stock markets of the EU. The Commission, which prepares and implements the legislation of the European Parliament, has established procedures for giving European approval to each of the IASB Standards. It takes advice from the European Financial Reporting Advisory Group (EFRAG), a team of experts that includes a UK member. The final recommendation to the Commission is made by the Accounting Regulatory Committee, which includes representatives of all member states. The process of approving IASB standards for use in the EU is called **endorsement**.

Harmonisation through Directives

For many aspects of regulation within the EU, the process of harmonisation starts when a **Directive** is issued by the European Commission, setting out the basic rules which should be followed in each member state's national laws. For limited liability companies in the UK, two such Directives have been particularly important. These are the Fourth Directive and the Seventh Directive. Together they specify the content of the Companies Act 2006. In 2013 both were combined in a single Accounting Directive. One important aspect of Directives is that they specify **formats** for the financial statements (see section 7.3.2) which ensure that all companies produce documents that are similar in appearance and present items in a systematic order. The idea of having standard formats was not a familiar concept in the UK before the Directives became effective in the 1980s, but became accepted during the 1980s and 1990. Having standard formats makes it easier for the reader to find the starting point in reading the financial statements. In later chapters we will see that having standard formats does not solve all the problems of comparability and understandability. For companies that do not apply IFRS these formats continue to apply. For companies using the IFRS there is potentially more flexibility of presentation.

Activity 7.1	From your general interest reading, or perhaps from your study of law, make a list of other areas of activity in which the UK law is harmonised with that of other countries in the EU.

7.2.2 IASB

The International Accounting Standards Board (IASB) is an independent body that sets International Financial Reporting Standards (IFRS). It was formed in 2000 as the successor to the International Accounting Standard Committee (IASC) which had been setting International Accounting Standards (IAS) since 1973. These IAS have been adopted by the IASB and will gradually be revised as IFRS. In the meantime the description 'IFRS' is used as a collective name for all forms of international accounting standard, whatever the precise title of the standard.

The IASB's objective is to bring about convergence of national accounting standards and international accounting standards to high-quality solutions. This will help participants in the world's capital markets and other users to make economic decisions.

There are many similarities between the UK accounting standards and the IASB Standards. There are also some differences where the UK standard-setter believes a particular approach is justified, or where historical developments have a strong influence. The UK Financial Reporting Council works on projects with the IASB, as do other countries' standard-setting bodies, all seeking to develop international convergence.

7.3 Accounting framework

Chapter 1, section 1.3 has explained that the IASB has developed a *Conceptual Framework* of principles and definitions that are used in setting accounting standards. The explanations in this chapter draw mainly on the IASB *Conceptual Framework*, adding more information where this is needed to understand the separate ideas of the UK FRC and UK Company Law.

7.3.1 The primary financial statements

The IASB system requires a complete set of financial statements to comprise:[1]

- a statement of financial position (balance sheet) at the end of the period
- an income statement (showing the profit or loss for the period), as part of a larger statement of comprehensive income (see Chapter 12)
- a statement of changes in equity for the period
- a statement of cash flows, and
- notes that summarise the accounting policies and give other explanations.

The IASB also gives general guidance on how to prepare and present the financial statements but stops short of giving precise rules on presentation. There is discretion for companies to present information in a way that best suits the company and those who are likely to use the information.

The UK system requires the same four primary statements in FRS 102. The Companies Act 2006 sets out formats of financial statements (see section 7.3.2) which give detailed rules on the sequence of information. These formats apply to companies that do *not* follow the IFRS.

The IASB's *Conceptual Framework* states that the objective of general purpose financial reporting is to provide financial information about the reporting entity that is useful to existing and potential investors, lenders and other creditors in making decisions about providing resources to the entity. Those decisions involve buying, selling or holding equity and debt instruments, and providing or settling loans and other forms of credit.[2]

Financial position

Information about financial position is reported primarily in a statement of financial position (balance sheet). It reports economic resources controlled by the company, its financial structure, its liquidity and its solvency. Information about economic resources held by the entity allows users of the information to estimate future cash flows from those resources. Information about financial structure is useful in predicting future needs for borrowing or for raising new equity finance. Liquidity refers to the availability of cash in the near future after taking account of commitments in the same period. Solvency refers to the availability of cash to meet financial commitments as they fall due. The balance sheet is not a statement of the value of the company because there are limitations in the measurement process and also because not all items which are of value to the company are included in the balance sheet.

Performance

Information about the performance of an entity is primarily provided in an income statement (profit and loss account). Performance is indicated by profitability and changes in profitability. Information about performance is useful in evaluating how well the resources of the entity have been used to generate profit. Statements of financial performance are seen as providing an account of the stewardship of management and also as helping readers to check the accuracy of previous estimates they may have made about the expected outcome of the period.

Changes in financial position

Information about changes in financial position of an entity is useful to help assess the operating, investing and financing activities of the period. It is usually found in a statement of cash flows.

7.3.2 Formats for financial statements

The word **format** means 'shape'. A format for a financial statement sets out the shape of the document. It sets out the items to be reported and the sequence in which they are reported. Section 7.2.1 explains that EU Directives have guided the formats used by UK companies for many years, as set out in company law and UK accounting standards. Since 2005 the group financial statements of listed companies have followed the IASB system of reporting. The IASB system does not specify formats. It does provide some lists of items to be included in financial statements but there is no requirement to present these items in any particular sequence. This means that companies have choices in the shape of their financial statements. This book describes the shapes of financial statements that you are likely to see in company reports but you will need to be flexible in understanding that companies do have choices.

7.3.3 Categories of financial information

The primary financial statements are the core of a much wider range of sources of financial information which users may obtain about a company. The relative position of the primary financial statements is shown in Figure 7.1.

Activity 7.2

Write down three items of narrative information about a company which you feel would be useful in the annual report of a company. Exchange lists with other members of the group and establish the similarities and differences across the group. To what extent would one general set of financial statements with notes and narrative information meet your collective expectations?

7.3.4 Notes and narrative reports

The annual report contains the primary financial statements, notes to the financial statements and narrative reports.

Notes to the financial statements

For listed companies, notes to the financial statements are based on required disclosures specified in the IFRS. For companies that do not follow the IFRS, many of the notes are required by regulations such as the Companies Act 2006 or the UK accounting standard FRS 102. Where the annual report is audited, the full audit covers the notes to the financial statements.

The notes are essential in amplifying and explaining the primary financial statements. The notes and the primary financial statements form an integrated whole. The wording of the notes is as important as the numbers if ambiguity is to be avoided. Notes provide narrative descriptions or disaggregations of items presented in those

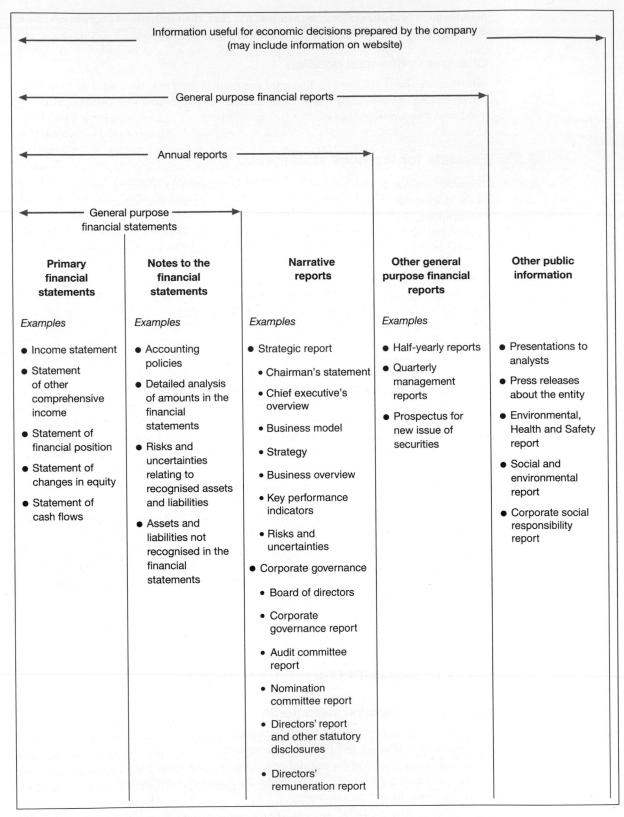

Figure 7.1
Categories of financial information

statements and information about items that do not qualify for recognition in those statements. An entity cannot rectify the use of an inappropriate accounting policy merely by describing the accounting policy or by providing explanatory material.

Narrative reports

Narrative reports are any other information additional to the primary financial statements and notes. It could be information which is highly relevant but is not required by regulation in the financial statements and notes. It could be information which will only interest a particular group of users. Such narrative reports may not be subject to the full audit process which is compulsory for the primary financial statements and notes. The IASB mandatory financial reporting standards relate only to the financial statements and the notes to the financial statements. There is non-mandatory guidance on the management commentary (see Chapter 14). Narrative reports are more commonly regulated at national level or is encouraged as voluntary by organisations that encourage good practice. The range of narrative reports found in the annual report of a UK listed company is explained later (see Chapter 14).

Many annual reports include highlights pages showing amounts, ratios and other calculations that distil a great deal of information into a few key items. There is a risk that companies are selective in how they choose the items for specific attention. You cannot read about financial statements for long without meeting the phrase 'the bottom line'. That refers to the line in the income statement (profit and loss account) which reports the profit attributable to the equity holders (ordinary shareholders). It may be described as **earnings** for equity holders (ordinary shareholders). When this amount is divided by the number of shares which have been issued by the company it becomes the **earnings per share**. Investors, financial journalists and brokers' analysts have traditionally paid great attention to the earnings per share. The standard-setters would prefer to discourage this narrow focus and encourage instead a 'building block' approach where the company produces information in such a way that the user of the annual statement can create useful arrangements and combinations of information.

Companies also produce narrative reports for specialised needs. Regulated industries (such as gas, electricity, telecommunications and water) provide supplementary information about their regulated activities. Some companies give non-financial performance indicators (such as speed of answering customer enquiries, or level of customer satisfaction). Graphs, charts, diagrams and even photographs are all ways of providing information which adds to users' understanding of a document.

7.4 Statement of financial position (balance sheet)

7.4.1 What items must be reported?

Companies that follow the IASB system of accounting in presenting a statement of financial position (balance sheet) have choices in the way they present their balance sheet. There is no particular **format** required[3] but some items are listed in the relevant standard as a minimum set of disclosures (see Supplement 7.1 to this chapter). Companies choose the form of layout for items in the balance sheet.

Companies that do not follow the IASB system of accounting must comply with the Companies Act 2006 and the UK accounting standards. The Companies Act 2006 contains more detail of the format that must be used. The details are set out in Supplement 7.2 to this chapter.

7.4.2 What formats are used?

Companies applying the IASB system do not have to follow any particular format but it is likely that any balance sheet you see will resemble one of the three formats described in this section because they will retain some of the traditions of the UK system that has existed for more than 20 years.

Companies that do not apply the IASB system of accounting must follow the requirements of the Companies Act 2006 and the standards of the UK FRC. The Companies Act 2006 permits two different formats of statement of financial position (balance sheet), each conforming to the accounting equation but permitting different layouts on the page. The word format means 'shape' so it covers the items to be reported and the sequence in which they are reported. The most commonly used format in the UK is Format 1, which uses the accounting equation to create a vertical format as shown in Exhibit 7.1.

Exhibit 7.1
Vertical format of statement of financial position (balance sheet)

Assets
minus
Liabilities
equals
Ownership interest

Format 2 uses the accounting equation to create a horizontal format as shown in Exhibit 7.2.

Exhibit 7.2
Horizontal form of statement of financial position (balance sheet)

		Liabilities
Assets	equal	plus
		Ownership interest

Format 2 is observed more commonly in the financial statements of continental European countries where the horizontal format is preferred.

Some companies use a variation on Format 2 which stacks the assets on top and the ownership interest and liabilities underneath (see Exhibit 7.3).

Exhibit 7.3
Assets above, ownership interest plus liabilities below

Assets
equals
Liabilities
plus
Ownership interest

When you read a statement of financial position (balance sheet) you should first of all look at the overall structure to see where the main sections of **assets, liabilities** and **ownership interest** are placed. Then you can begin to look at each section in more detail. The process is something like seeing a landscape painting for the first time. You stand back to look at the overall impression of the landscape and the main features first. Then you step forward to look at some of the details in different parts of the painting. Finally, if you are very enthusiastic you move in closer and start to examine the details of the texture, brush strokes and shading.

7.4.3 Descriptions in the statement of financial position (balance sheet)

You will see from the Supplement that the statement of financial position (balance sheet) formats contain some words you will recognise but also many new words. Non-current assets (fixed assets) are separated from current assets. Current liabilities (due in less than one year) are separated from non-current liabilities (due in more than one year). Some of the items under the Companies Act headings A to J may look rather strange at this stage (particularly A, D, I and J). Do not worry about that at present. If they are appropriate to first-level study they will be explained at some point in this text. If they are not explained, then they are relatively rare in occurrence and the time taken to explain them will outweigh the benefits you would gain from understanding.

The ownership interest is shown at heading K as **capital** and **reserves**. The word **capital** here means the claim which owners have because of the number of shares they own, and the word **reserves** means the claim which owners have because the company has created new wealth for them over the years. Various labels are used to describe the nature of that new wealth and how it is created. Some of the new wealth is created because new investors pay more than a specified amount for the shares. Paying more is referred to as paying a **premium**, so this kind of ownership interest is labelled the **share premium**. Some of the new wealth is created because the fixed assets held by the company increase in value and that new valuation is recorded. This kind of ownership interest is labelled the **revaluation reserve**. Some of the new wealth is created by making profits through operating activities. This kind of ownership interest is labelled the **retained earnings** reserve.

7.4.4 Subtotals

Subtotals in financial statements help to group information within financial statements into useful sections. There are no rules about the placing of subtotals in either the IASB lists or the Companies Acts formats. Companies have to decide for themselves where to place subtotals and totals in presentation of the list of items in the format. You will need to be flexible in reading statements of financial position (balance sheets) and using the subtotals provided.

Activity 7.3

Read again the format for the balance sheet. How many of the items there came as no surprise to you? How many looked unfamiliar? Make a note of these and check that you find out about them in later chapters.

7.4.5 Illustration

The remainder of this chapter explores the published financial statements of a hypothetical listed company, Safe and Sure plc, which operates in a service industry. There is a parent company called Safe and Sure plc and it owns some subsidiary companies that together make up a 'group'. The Safe and Sure Group sells recycling and cleaning services to customers based on the high reputation of the company's products and name. The Safe and Sure Group follows the IASB system of accounting and has chosen a format that is similar to Format 1 (see Supplement 7.2 to this chapter).

The following illustration sets out the balance sheet of the Safe and Sure Group plc for Year 7 with comparative amounts alongside for the previous year. The balance sheet is followed by a comment on matters of particular interest.

Safe and Sure Group plc
Group statement of financial position (balance sheet) at 31 December

	Notes	Year 7 £m	Year 6 £m
Non-current assets			
Property, plant and equipment	1	1,375	1,219
Intangible assets	2	2,603	2,376
Investments	3	28	20
Taxation recoverable	4	59	49
Total fixed assets		4,065	3,664
Current assets			
Inventories (stocks)	5	266	243
Amounts receivable (debtors)	6	1,469	1,347
Six-month deposits		20	–
Cash and cash equivalents		1,053	905
Total current assets		2,808	2,495
Total assets		6,873	6,159
Current liabilities			
Amounts payable (creditors)	7	(1,598)	(1,575)
Bank overdraft	8	(401)	(626)
Total current liabilities		(1,999)	(2,201)
Non-current liabilities			
Amounts payable (creditors)	9	(27)	(26)
Bank and other borrowings	10	(2)	(6)
Provisions	11	(202)	(222)
Total non-current liabilities		(231)	(254)
Total liabilities		(2,230)	(2,455)
Net assets		4,643	3,704
Capital and reserves (ownership interest)			
Called-up share capital	12	196	195
Share premium account	13	85	55
Revaluation reserve	14	46	46
Retained earnings	15	4,316	3,408
Equity holders' funds		4,643	3,704

7.4.6 Discussion

The first feature to note is the title, *Group statement of financial position (balance sheet)*. Companies listed on the Stock Exchange are generally using one name as an umbrella for a group of several companies linked together under one parent. It is thought to be more useful to the shareholders of the parent company to see all the assets controlled by that company within the single financial statement. The word **control** is important here. The parent company owns the other companies. They each own their separate assets. The parent company controls the use of those assets indirectly by controlling the companies it owns. The statement of financial position (balance sheet) as presented here represents a group where the parent company owns 100% of all the other companies in the group (called its subsidiary undertakings). A similar consolidated statement of financial position would be produced if the parent owned less than 100%, provided it had the same element of control. The only additional item would be a **non-controlling interest** in the ownership claim to indicate the proportion of the equity interest in subsidiaries held by shareholders outside the group. The non-controlling interest has previously been called the **minority interest**.

The second feature to note in the statement of financial position (balance sheet) as presented is that there are two columns of figures. Companies are required to present the figures for the previous year, in order to provide a basis for comparison.

The statement of financial position (balance sheet) follows the accounting equation and this company has helpfully set out in the left-hand margin the main elements of the equation. There are some phrases in the statement of financial position (balance sheet) which you are meeting for the first time but you should not feel intimidated by new titles when you can work out what they mean if you think about the ordinary meanings of words.

Intangible assets means assets which may not be touched – they have no physical existence. Examples are the goodwill of a business or the reputation of a branded product.

Property, plant and equipment is another phrase which you are seeing here for the first time, but again you can work out the meaning. It is also called tangible non-current assets. You know from Chapter 2 what **non-current assets** are and you know that tangible means 'something that may be touched'.

Investments here means shares in other companies which are not subsidiary undertakings within the group.

The *taxation recoverable* is an amount of tax which has been paid already but may be reclaimed in 18 months' time because of events that have occurred to reduce the tax due, after the tax was paid.

Current assets comprise inventories (stocks), receivables (debtors) and cash. They are set out in order of increasing liquidity. Inventories (stocks) are the least readily convertible into cash while amounts receivable (debtors) are closer to collection of cash. Cash itself is the most liquid asset. The notes to the accounts contain more detailed information. Take as an example note 5, relating to inventories (stocks). It appears as follows:

Note 5	Year 7	Year 6
Inventories (stocks)	£m	£m
Raw materials	62	54
Work in progress	19	10
Finished products	185	179
	266	243

The notes are shown in full in Appendix I at the end of this book. There is a note relating to amounts receivable (debtors), mainly relating to trade receivables (trade debtors). Amounts payable (creditors) has a similar type of note to the balance sheet.

The *non-current liabilities* include long-term borrowings, which are quite low in amount compared with those of many other companies of this size. The provisions relate to future obligations caused by: treating a contaminated site; reorganisation of part of the business; and future tax payable.

That stage of the statement of financial position (balance sheet) concludes with the net assets, defined as all assets minus all liabilities. Drawing a total at this point is not a requirement of any format, but is used by many companies as the point which creates a pause in the balance sheet before moving on to the ownership interest.

For a company the *ownership interest* is described as *capital and reserves.* The ownership interest in a company is specified in company law as comprising the claim created through the shares owned by the various equity holders (shareholders) and the claim representing additional reserves of wealth accumulated since the company began. That wealth is accumulated by making profits year after year. The claim is reduced when the owners take dividends from the company. (Further information on the reporting of share capital, reserves and dividends is contained in Chapter 12.)

The ownership interest is the part of the statement of financial position (balance sheet) which causes greatest confusion to most readers. It is purely a statement of a legal claim on the assets after all liabilities have been satisfied. The word *reserves* has no other significance. There is nothing to see, touch, count or hold. To add to the potential confusion, company law delights in finding names for various different kinds of ownership interest. If you are the kind of person who takes a broad-brush view of life you will not worry too much about share premium account, revaluation reserve and retained earnings. They are all part of accounting terminology which becomes important to a company lawyer when there is a dispute over how much dividend may be declared, but are less important to the investor who says 'How much is my total claim?'

7.5 Income statement (profit and loss account)

7.5.1 What items must be reported?

Companies that follow the IASB system of accounting in presenting an income statement must report the profit or loss for the period. There is no particular format required[4] but some items are listed in the relevant standard as a minimum set of disclosures (see Supplement 7.4 to this chapter). Companies choose the form of layout of the items in the income statement.

Companies that do not follow the IASB system of accounting must comply with the Companies Act 2006 and the UK accounting standards. The Companies Act 2006 contains more detail of the items to be reported and the format that must be used. The details are set out in Supplement 7.3 to this chapter.

7.5.2 What formats are used?

Companies applying the IASB system do not have to follow any particular format but it is likely that any income statement (profit and loss account) you see will resemble one of the formats described in this section because they will retain some of the traditions of the UK system that has existed for more than 20 years.

Companies that do not apply the IASB system of accounting must follow the requirements of the Companies Act 2006 and the standards of the UK FRC. The Companies Act 2006 permits four different formats of profit and loss account but the version most frequently observed in the UK is format 1 (see Supplement 7.4).

7.5.3 Illustration

The published income statements (profit and loss accounts) of most major companies are very similar to the illustration set out here for Safe and Sure plc.

Safe and Sure Group plc
Group income statement (profit and loss account)
for the years ended 31 December

	Notes	Year 7 £m	Year 6 £m
Continuing operations			
Revenue	16	7,146	5,893
Cost of sales	16	(4,910)	(4,063)
Gross profit		2,236	1,830
Distribution costs		(22)	(25)
Administrative expenses	17	(262)	(265)
Profit from operations		1,952	1,540
Interest receivable (net)	18	23	30
Profit before tax	19	1,975	1,570
Tax	20	(622)	(524)
Profit for the period from continuing operations		1,353	1,046
Discontinued operations			
Loss for the period from discontinued operations	21	(205)	(100)
Profit for the period attributable to equity holders		1,148	946
Earnings per share	22	11.74	9.71

7.5.4 Discussion

The first point to note is the heading. This is a consolidated group income statement (profit and loss account) bringing together the results of the activities of all the companies in the group during the year. The individual companies will also produce their own separate profit and loss accounts and these are added together to produce the consolidated picture. Where one company in the group sells items to another in the group, the sale and purchase are matched against each other on consolidation so that the results reported reflect only sales to persons outside the group.

The second point to note is that the income statement (profit and loss account) as presented by the company is more informative than the lists contained in Supplements 7.3 or 7.4 might suggest. That is partly because the company has used subtotals to break up the flow and make it digestible for the reader. One very common subtotal is the **gross profit** calculated as revenue minus the cost of the goods or services sold as revenue.

Starting at the top of the income statement we see that the word *revenue* is used to describe the sales of goods or services. **Revenue** is sometimes described as **turnover** or **sales**. Revenue (turnover) represents sales to third parties outside the group of companies. The **cost of sales** is the total of the costs of materials, labour and overheads which relate closely to earning the sales. The gross profit is sometimes referred to as the **gross margin** and is monitored closely by those who use the financial statements to make a judgement on the operations of the company. Within any industry the gross profit as a percentage of revenue (or turnover, or sales) is expected to be within known limits. If that percentage is low then the company is either underpricing its goods or else taking the market price but failing to control costs. If the percentage is high, then the company is perhaps a market leader which can command higher prices for its output because of its high reputation. However, it might also be seen by customers and competitors as charging too much for its goods or services.

The next item in the income statement (profit and loss account) is *distribution costs*, which would include the costs of delivering goods to customers. For this company the distribution costs are low because it provides services by contract and does not carry out much distribution work. For many users the trends in an amount are more interesting than the actual amount. They might ask why the amount has decreased. On the other hand, it is not a particularly significant component of the overall picture and the users might show little interest. They would pay more attention to the *administrative expenses,* a collective term for all those costs which have to be incurred in order to keep the business running but which are less closely related to the direct activity of creating revenue (making sales). The directors' salaries, head office costs and general maintenance of buildings and facilities are the kinds of details brought together under this heading. Directors' salaries are always a matter of some fascination and companies are expected to give considerable detail in the notes to the accounts about how much each director is paid and what other benefits are provided.

The *profit from operations* is the end of the first stage of the income statement (profit and loss account), where the story of the business operations is complete. The rest of the profit and loss account is concerned with the cost of financing the company.

As an example of finance costs, *interest* is paid on loans and received on investments, usually brought together in one net amount which shows, in this case, an excess of interest receivable over interest payable. That suggests a fairly cash-rich company with relatively low levels of borrowing. Next comes the *corporation tax,* which all companies must pay as a percentage of the profit before tax. The percentage is a standard percentage applied to the profit calculated according to the tax rules. Because the tax rules are not identical to the accounting rules, the percentage appears to vary when the reader looks at the income statement. Helpful companies will explain the tax charge in the strategic report, as well as providing more detailed notes to the accounts on the tax charge.

That information ends with the profit for the period from continuing operations. Investors or analysts who want to make a forecast of future profits may decide to use this figure as a starting point because the activities will continue. Separately below this line the group shows the results in this period of operations that have been discontinued. Usually operations are discontinued because they are performing poorly so it is no great surprise to see a loss here. The loss is part of the performance of the period but investors can see that the bad news of this operation will not continue in future. Finally the equity holders (ordinary shareholders) see the profit for the period attributable to them.

They do not see here any mention of a reward in the form of a dividend which returns to them some of the wealth created by the company during the period. That information will appear in a statement of changes in equity which is explained in Chapter 12.

7.6 Statement of cash flows

The presentation of cash flow statements by companies is guided by IAS 7, *Statement of Cash Flows.*[5]

The benefits of cash flow information are explained in IAS 7.[6] A statement of cash flows, when used in conjunction with the rest of the financial statements, provides users with information on solvency and liquidity. It shows how cash is generated in the business and helps users to understand how much flexibility is available to adapt to changing circumstances and opportunities.

7.6.1   What items must be reported?

The statement of cash flows presents three classifications of cash flows.[7] These are:

- operating activities
- investing activities
- financing activities.

Definitions
> **Operating activities** are the principal revenue-producing activities of the entity and other activities that are not investing or financing activities.
>
> **Investing activities** are the acquisition and disposal of long-term assets and other investments not included in cash equivalents.
>
> **Financing activities** are activities that result in changes in the size and composition of the contributed equity and borrowings of the entity.

Safe and Sure uses these classifications, as shown in the next section. We need two more definitions of terms in the cash flow statement. These are **cash** and **cash equivalents**.

Definitions
> **Cash** comprises cash on hand and demand deposits.
>
> **Cash equivalents** are short-term, highly liquid investments that are readily convertible to known amounts of cash and which are subject to an insignificant risk of changes in value.[8]

7.6.2   Illustration

Safe and Sure Group plc
Group statement of cash flows for the years ended 31 December

	Notes	Year 7 £m	Year 6 £m
Cash flows from operating activities			
Cash generated from operations	23	1,967	1,635
Interest paid		(31)	(24)
UK corporation tax paid		(201)	(183)
Overseas tax paid		(305)	(265)
Net cash from operating activities		1,430	1,163
Cash flows from investing activities			
Purchase of tangible non-current assets		(600)	(475)
Sale of tangible non-current assets		120	101
Purchase of companies and businesses		(277)	(901)
Sale of a company		31	–
Movement in short-term deposits		(307)	363
Interest received		50	59
Net cash used in investing activities		(983)	(853)

Safe and Sure Group plc
Group statement of cash flows for the years ended 31 December

	Notes	Year 7 £m	Year 6 £m
Cash flows from financing activities			
Issue of ordinary share capital		31	20
Dividends paid to equity holders		(295)	(244)
Net loan movement (excluding overdraft)		162	(240)
Net cash used in financing activities		(102)	(464)
Net increase/(decrease) in cash and cash equivalents*		345	(154)
Cash and cash equivalents at the beginning of the year		279	453
Exchange adjustments		28	(20)
Cash and cash equivalents at the end of the year	28	652	279

* Cash on demand and deposits of maturity less than three months, net of overdrafts.

Note 23 Cash flow from operating activities
Reconciliation of operating profit to net cash flow from operating activities

	Year 7 £m	Year 6 £m
Profit before tax from continuing operations	1,952	1,540
Loss from discontinued operations	(205)	(100)
Profit from operations	1,747	1,440
Depreciation charge	332	301
Increase in inventories (stocks)*	(19)	(11)
Increase in trade receivables (debtors)*	(74)	(53)
Decrease in trade payables (creditors)*	(4)	(36)
Net cash inflow from continuing activities	1,982	1,641
Cash outflow in respect of discontinued item	(15)	(6)
Net cash inflow from operating activities	1,967	1,635

* Note: It is not possible to reconcile these figures with the information in the statement of financial position because of the effect of acquisitions during the year.

7.6.3 Discussion

The first line of the statement of cash flows is *cash flows from operating activities*, highlighted by the company as an important feature. Note 23 to the accounts explains why this is not the same as operating profit. When a company makes a profit it earns revenue which is greater than the expenses. Some of the revenue is collected as cash but some will be collected later when the credit customers pay. When expenses are incurred, some are paid for immediately but others relate to goods and services taken from suppliers. Note 23 to the accounts is set out above and shows that cash is generated by profits but is used when inventory (stock) levels increase and when trade receivables (debtors) increase. Allowing inventories (stocks) to increase will use up cash because more has to be paid for them. Allowing trade receivables (debtors) to increase means that credit customers are not paying the cash so fast and therefore the cash is not coming in. That will diminish cash flow. Allowing trade payables (creditors) to decrease is a further way of diminishing cash flow because it means that suppliers are being paid faster.

There is one other line in note 23 which gives pause for thought. That is the fourth line, *depreciation charge.* **Depreciation** is a measure of how much a non-current (fixed) asset has been used up. It is an amount which is deducted from profits as a measure of using up the cost of the non-current (fixed) asset in the accounting period. It does not of itself generate cash, but it stops the owners removing so much cash from the company that they are unable to replace a non-current (fixed asset) at the end of its useful life. Since it is not a cash item it has to be added back to the reported profit. By way of illustration, suppose a company pays £100 for goods and sells them for £150. It has generated £50 cash. In the income statement £10 is deducted for depreciation, so the reported profit becomes £40. The reconciliation of profit to cash flow from operations will be written as:

	£
Operating profit	40
add Depreciation	10
Cash inflow from operating activities	50

(There is more about depreciation in Chapter 8 and more about cash flow in Chapter 14.)

The cash generated from operations is used first of all to pay interest on loans, as a reward to lenders, and to pay taxation to the government. Deducting these items leaves the net cash from operating activities. This is the amount left over for long-term investment.

In the next section we find the cash flows from investing activities. The purchase of tangible non-current (fixed) assets is also called **capital expenditure**. Cash is paid to purchase new businesses and cash is received from selling companies or businesses no longer required. Safe and Sure has put some of its cash into short-term deposits to earn interest. In Year 6, Safe and Sure reduced the amount on short-term deposit, converting it back to cash that was available for spending, but in Year 7 it increased the amount on deposit, reducing the amount of cash available to spend in other ways. The final item in this investment section is interest received which is the reward for investment.

The third section shows the cash flows from financing activities. For some companies the cash inflow from operating activities may be insufficient to cover all the investment requirements for capital expenditure and acquisitions, so more finance has to be raised from external sources. Safe and Sure is not in such a difficult position because the cash generated from operations is greater than the cash paid out for investing activities. However, there is one further important outflow in the dividends paid to equity holders (shareholders). Dividend is the reward to equity holders (shareholders) for investing in the company. For the particular cash flow statement presented here, the broad story is that the company generated sufficient cash from its operations to cover loan interest, to pay the tax due, meet its investment needs and pay dividends. Despite that positive amount, the company has increased its loans by £162m and marginally increased its share capital by £31m, so that a total of £345m has been added to cash and deposits repayable on demand.

The company explained its cash flow management as follows in the strategic report: 'The group's businesses are structured to use as little fixed and working capital as is consistent with the profit and earnings growth objective in order to produce a high cash flow.'

DAVID WILSON *comments on cash flow in the company.*

Cash is an important factor for any business. It is only one of the resources available but it is the key to survival.

What I'm basically looking for in the statement of cash flows is how well the company is balancing various sources of finance. It generated £1,967m from operating activities. The servicing of investment cost £31m in loan interest and the company paid taxes of £506m. That left net cash from operations amounting to £1,430m. That was used to cover its investing activities in new non-current (fixed) assets costing £480m (£600m less £120m) and acquisitions costing £246m after allowing for the sale of a company. Cash was used to increase short-term deposits by £307m. Interest received was £50m. The net cash used for investing activities amounted to £983m. If I deduct this from the £1,430m cash flow generated there is an increase in cash of £447m. The company had to pay a dividend of £295m, leaving £152m surplus cash. There was no immediate need for any long-term financing flows with a healthy cash flow like that. Nevertheless the company raised £31m in cash through an issue of shares to the employees' share option scheme and, perhaps surprisingly, there was an increase of £162m in short-term loans. Add the £152m to the £31m and £162m and you arrive at £345m which is the increase in cash and cash equivalents of the period. That brings me back to my earlier question of why they are holding so much cash and short-term deposits.

The company in this example has told me that it carries out its financial management by recognising that the tax bill has to be paid first of all. Then it plans its investment in non-current (fixed) assets and its programme of disposals. Once the investment has been decided the company aims to pay a dividend which will satisfy the expectations of investors. Surplus cash after that is available for acquisition of other companies and, because this company is always looking for good opportunities to expand, it will borrow ahead of time so that it is in a position to move quickly when a target presents itself. The company does not agree with IAS 7's requirement to separate out the bank deposits which had more than three months to run when they were made. The deposits are placed largely for six months, so that many have less than six months to run at the balance sheet date. It is all very accessible cash and the company sees it all as one pool.

In the strategic report the finance director explains the company's view of cash flow as follows:

The Group's businesses are structured to utilise as little fixed and working capital as is consistent with the profit and earnings growth objective in order to produce a high cash flow. The impact of working capital on cash flow was held to an increase in Year 7 of £97m (Year 6: £100m).

A net cash flow of £1,967m was generated from operating activities. That was boosted by other amounts of cash from interest received. After paying interest and tax, the Group had £1,430m remaining. Non-current assets required £480m after allowing for the proceeds of selling some of our vehicle fleet in the routine replacement programme. That left £950m from which £246m was required to pay for acquisitions. The remaining £704m covered dividends of £295m leaving £409m. We received £50m interest on investments and raised £31m in ordinary share capital to give a net inflow of liquid funds in the year of £490m. Out of that amount, short-term deposits have increased by £145m, leaving an increase in cash of £345m.

You can see there are lots of different ways of interpreting the information in the cash flow statement. What is important is that the information is available.

7.7 Group structure of companies

Most major companies in the UK operate using a group structure. Within a group there is a **parent company** which controls **subsidiary companies** undertaking various different aspects of the operations of the business. It would in theory be possible to have all the operations located within one company but in practice, because company law draws very tight boundaries around a single company, there is some safety for the organisation in having different parts of the business packaged separately. If something goes seriously wrong with one subsidiary company, that company may be allowed to fail without irreparable damage to the total group. This approach has not always worked out in practice because very often the banks which lend money to a subsidiary will request guarantees from other companies in the group. So if one subsidiary fails in a spectacular way, it may drag the rest of the group with it.

Other reasons for retaining separate subsidiaries include: employee loyalty, product reputation, taxation legislation and overseas operations. When a new company is taken into the group, a sense of pride in the formerly independent company may be retained by continuing to use the traditional company name. The company name may be linked to a reputation for a high-quality product so that it is desirable to perpetuate the benefit of that reputation. Tax legislation applies to individual companies and not to the group as a whole. Efficient use of the tax laws may require different types of business to operate in different companies. Operations located in other countries will come under the legal systems of those countries and may be required to have a separate legal identity.

For accounting purposes the group as a whole is the economic entity for which financial statements are prepared. An entity should prepare and publish financial statements if financial information about the economic activities of that entity has the potential to be useful in making decisions about providing resources to the entity and in assessing whether the management and the governing board have made efficient and effective use of the resources provided.[9] The process of combining all the financial statements of the companies within a group is called **consolidation**. This chapter will explain sufficient aspects of the preparation of consolidated financial statements to allow an understanding of annual reports of groups of companies. The full complexities of consolidation and the wider aspects of group accounting may be found in advanced textbooks.

Definition

> **Consolidated** financial statements are the financial statements of a **group** in which the assets, liabilities, equity, income, expenses and cash flows of the **parent** and its **subsidiaries** are presented as those of a single economic entity.[10]

Consolidated financial statements recognise the parent's control of its subsidiaries. Consolidation is a process that aggregates the total assets, liabilities and results of all companies in the group. The consolidated balance sheet brings together all the assets controlled by the parent and shows all the liabilities to be satisfied from those assets. The consolidated income statement (profit and loss account) brings together all the revenues and costs of the companies in the group.

7.7.1 Defining a group

The smallest group consists of two companies. A group is created when one company (the **parent**) has **control** of another company (the **subsidiary**). There is no upper limit to the number of companies which may form a group.

The IASB has defined a group as a parent and all its subsidiaries.[11] A parent is an entity that controls one or more other entities.[12] A subsidiary is an entity, including an unincorporated entity such as a partnership, that is controlled by another entity (known as the **parent**).[13] **Consolidated** financial statements must include all **subsidiaries** of the parent, apart from some limited exemptions.[14]

Control is defined by the IASB. An investor controls an investee when it is exposed, or has rights, to variable returns from its involvement with the investee and has the ability to affect those returns through its power over the investee.[15] There are three elements to this definition of control. The investor must have all of the following:[16]

(a) power over the investee;

(b) exposure, or rights, to variable returns from its involvement with the investee; and

(c) the ability to use its power over the investee to affect the amount of the investor's returns.

7.7.2 The nature of control

The IASB has explained the reason for the definition of control used in IFRS 10. The need arose from the global financial crisis that started in 2007. Subsequent to the crisis it was found that some of the banks and other financial entities affected by the crisis had exposed investors to risk through using 'off balance sheet vehicles'. Political leaders of major economies across the world (the G20 leaders) asked the IASB to review the accounting and disclosure requirements for such 'off balance sheet vehicles'. The IASB found that the conditions applied were not always clear and consistent. IFRS 10 is the attempt to create that clarity and consistency.

Take each of the components of control in turn. Power over the investee is established by having rights that are capable of being exercised in practice. The most obvious right is a majority voting right as a shareholder in the investee. If the investor does not have a clear majority, there could nevertheless be control if other investors are passive. The investor might have control through agreements with other investors. The investor might have the right to appoint or remove the majority of the board of directors. It is important to consider the facts of the case in deciding whether there is control.

The second component is a variable return. Such a return could be a dividend, share repurchase, or a surplus on winding up. It could be a fee, tax benefit, or cost saving. The standard does not give an exhaustive list. Again all the facts must be considered.

Finally the investor must be able to exercise the power to influence the return. As examples: the investor might be able to vote for the amount of dividend payable; or the investor might be able to instruct the directors on the amount of dividend to be paid.

7.7.3 The parent company's statement of financial position

In some annual reports the parent company may choose to continue to produce its own statement of financial position (balance sheet), showing as an asset the cost of the investment in the subsidiary, but this information is not regarded as being particularly useful. The investment in the subsidiary is reported by the parent company as a single-line item but the consolidated statement of financial position shows all the assets and all the liabilities of the group under each separate heading. The group statement of financial position is more useful to readers. In previous chapters, where the financial statements of Safe and Sure plc have been discussed, the group accounts have been used.

7.7.4 Acquisition

The general term **business combination** may be applied to any transaction whereby one company becomes a subsidiary of another. The most common form of business combination is an **acquisition** where one party (the **acquirer**) is clearly the dominant entity and the other (the **acquiree**) is seen to be under new control. The method of accounting used to produce consolidated financial statements in an acquisition is called the **acquisition method**[17] (sometimes described as the **purchase method**). In this introductory text you do not need to worry about the details of the method of producing consolidated financial statements. All you need to do is recognise the descriptions used and be aware that when you see these words you are reading information about a group of companies combined.

Activity 7.4	Check your understanding of the terms: parent, subsidiary, control, acquisition. Write down a definition of each and then look back through this section to test your definition against that in the text.

7.8 Group financial statements

This section explains how the acquisition of a subsidiary affects the balance sheet of the parent company. It shows how the group's balance sheet and income statement (profit and loss account) are created. It also explains the nature of goodwill arising on acquisition and it outlines the nature and treatment of associated companies.

7.8.1 The parent company's balance sheet

When an acquisition takes place, the parent company acquires shares in the subsidiary in exchange for cash or for shares in the parent. The parent company will offer cash if it has adequate cash resources to make the offer and it appears that those selling the shares would prefer to take cash for investment elsewhere. The parent company will offer its own shares in exchange where it may not have sufficient cash resources available or where it thinks it can persuade those selling their shares in the target company of the desirability of acquiring shares in the new parent. Many deals offer a mixture of shares and cash.

For a cash purchase the effect on the parent company's balance sheet, in terms of the accounting equation, is:

For a share exchange, the effect on the parent company's balance sheet is to increase the assets and increase the ownership interest. In terms of the accounting equation:

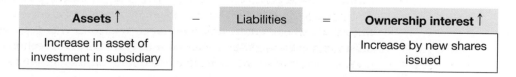

7.8.2 The group's consolidated statement of financial position

In the group's consolidated statement of financial position the parent company's assets and liabilities are added to the assets and liabilities of the subsidiary companies. The assets and liabilities of the subsidiary take the place of the parent company's

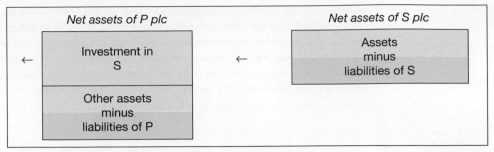

Figure 7.2
Separate net assets of parent and subsidiary

investment in the subsidiary. Figure 7.2 shows the net assets of P and S separately. The arrows indicate the net assets of S moving in to take the place of P's investment in S. Removing the investment in S from the statement of financial position of P and replacing it with the net assets of S leads to the group's consolidated statement of financial position. Figure 7.3(a) shows the resulting amalgamation. The assets and liabilities in Figure 7.3(a) are then rearranged under each asset and liability category to result in Figure 7.3(b).

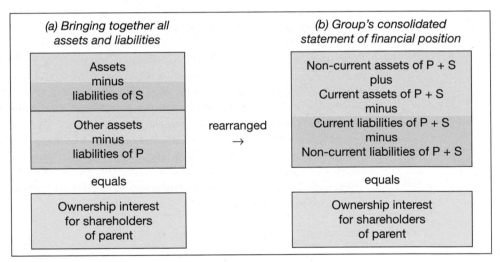

Figure 7.3
Completing the process of consolidation

7.8.3 The group income statement (profit and loss account)

Investors and their advisers may wish to use the income statement (profit and loss account) of the group to make predictions of the future profitability of the group. To be able to do this, they must know how much of the current year's profit relates to continuing operations and how much relates to changes during the year. The illustration of the income statement of Safe and Sure plc in Section 7.5.3 shows how the consolidated profit and loss is subdivided into continuing activities and discontinued activities.

One rule of acquisition accounting is that, where a subsidiary is acquired part-way through the year, only the profits earned after the date of acquisition may be included in the group income statement. The analyst seeking to make a forecast for the year ahead will be helped by a note to the accounts showing what the profit would have been from a full 12-month contribution.

Groups are not required to present separately the parent company's income statement (profit and loss account). It is not felt to be particularly interesting to users as, generally, the parent company's main income comprises the dividends received from its investments in subsidiaries. Usually it is the subsidiaries which carry out the operations generating profit. It is far more interesting to know about the underlying operating profits which allow those dividends to be paid to the parent.

Activity 7.5

P plc pays cash of £6m for an investment in net assets of S Ltd having a net book value (equal to fair value) of £6m. Explain how this transaction will affect the balance sheet of P plc as the parent company and explain how it will affect the group balance sheet of P Group plc, whose only subsidiary is S Ltd.

7.8.4 Goodwill on acquisition

In the illustration presented in Figure 7.2 and Figure 7.3 the net assets of the subsidiary were shown as being of the same magnitude as the amount of the investment in the subsidiary so that the substitution of the former for the latter was a neat replacement process. That situation is unlikely to apply in real life because the price paid for an investment will rarely depend solely on the net assets being acquired. The purchaser will be looking to the future expectations from the investment and the seller will be seeking a reward for all that has been built into the business which cannot readily be quantified in terms of tangible assets. The future expectations will rest upon the reputation of the product or service, the quality of the customers, the skills of the workforce and the state of the order book, amongst many other things. The price negotiated for the business will include some recognition of all these qualities under the global heading of **goodwill**.

In these circumstances the price paid for the investment in the subsidiary will be greater than the amount of the net assets of the subsidiary. When the consolidation into the group statement of financial position is attempted, a space will appear. Figure 7.4 shows the separate net assets of P plc and S plc. The amount of the cost of the investment in S is greater than the net assets of S plc.

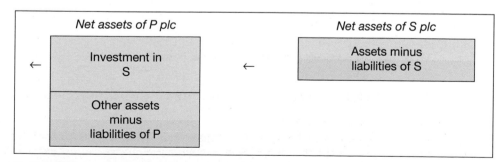

Figure 7.4
Net assets of the separate companies P plc and S plc

Figure 7.5 shows the resulting consolidation. The space shaded is equal to the difference between the amount of the investment in S and the net assets of S. This space is, in arithmetic terms, nothing more than a **difference on consolidation** but has traditionally been called **goodwill** because it is explained in terms of paying for something more than the underlying net assets.

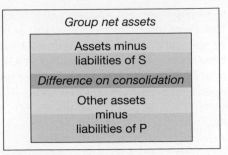

Figure 7.5
Group net assets of the P group

Definition

Goodwill is defined as 'an asset representing the future economic benefits arising from other assets acquired in a business combination that are not individually identified and separately recognised'.[18]

Goodwill is recognised in the statement of financial position as an asset and is measured as the excess of the cost of the business combination over the fair value of the net assets acquired.[19]

The existence of a difference on consolidation is an inescapable consequence of the process of combining the statements of financial position of parent and subsidiary. For many years it caused one of the most difficult problems facing the accounting standard-setters. The questions asked were: 'How should this consolidation difference be reported in the balance sheets of succeeding years?' and 'Is it an asset?'

After a great deal of international debate and disagreement, the IASB has taken the view that acquisition goodwill is an asset that should be tested regularly by means of an **impairment test** which asks, 'Can the business expect to recover the carrying value of the intangible asset, through either using it or selling it?' If the answer is 'no' then the asset is impaired and its value must be reduced. An expense of impairment will appear in the income statement (profit and loss account). If the answer is 'yes' then the asset value should remain in the balance sheet.

Definition

Impairment means 'damaged' or 'spoiled'. Where the carrying value of goodwill cannot be recovered through sale or use, it is said to be 'impaired'. The asset value in the balance sheet must be reduced.

Activity 7.6

P pays cash of £8m for an investment in net assets of S Ltd having a net book value (equal to fair value) of £6m. Explain how this transaction will affect the statement of financial position of P plc as the parent company and explain how it will affect the group statement of financial position of P Group plc, whose only subsidiary is S Ltd.

Where a UK group chooses to follow the UK standard FRS 102, it applies amortisation over the useful life of the goodwill, rather than use impairment testing. Amortisation is a less costly process than impairment testing and therefore reduces the burden for a smaller group.

7.8.5   Associated companies

Where company P holds less than a controlling interest in company A, it may nevertheless have a significant influence over company A. Such significant influence would involve the power to participate in the financial and operating policy decisions of company A. Significant influence is presumed to exist when one company or a group of companies holds 20% or more of the ordinary shareholders' voting rights of another company, unless the facts indicate that significant influence is not possible.[20]

Where significant influence over a company exists, that company is called an **associated company**. The group must show in its balance sheet the group's share of the net assets of the associated company as a single-line item, and must show in the income statement (profit and loss account) the group's share of the profits or losses of the associated company.

This treatment of an investment in an associated company is called **equity accounting** because it reports the parent's and the group's share of the investment in the ownership interest (also referred to as the equity).

For investments which do not meet the conditions of being reported as associated companies, the accounting treatment is to record the investment at cost in the balance sheet and to record in the income statement of the group only the dividend income received from the associate.

7.9 Small and medium-sized entities (SMEs)

7.9.1   Definitions

The amount of detail in the information presented by companies depends on their size. The Companies Act 2006 defines small and medium-sized companies. The definitions are based on turnover, balance sheet totals and average number of employees. Currently the limits for a small company are satisfying two or more of the conditions: turnover not more than £6.5m, balance sheet total not more than £3.26m and employees not more than 50 (section 382). The limits for a medium-sized company are satisfying two or more of the conditions: turnover not more than £25.9m, balance sheet total not more than £12.9m and employees not more than 250 (section 465). The amounts for turnover and balance sheet totals are altered from time to time by Statutory Instrument to keep pace with inflation, so it is perhaps easiest to take as a 'rule of thumb' the employee limits of 50 for a small company and 250 for a medium-sized company. For these companies there are substantial exemptions from requirements to publish information (although they must still provide details to shareholders if asked to do so). Generally they are not listed companies and so are not required to meet the obligations placed on listed companies. Most of these small and medium-sized companies are currently presenting financial statements based on UK FRC standards and company law.

During the 1980s, concerns were expressed about the 'burden' of regulation for small companies. This burden was seen as falling from all directions, including tax laws, employment laws, product protection laws, health and safety laws and accounting regulation. The government of the time committed itself to reducing this burden. One consequence was that the UK Accounting Standards Board (now FRC) introduced a Financial Reporting Standard for Smaller Entities (FRSSE). This condenses into one standard the essential aspects of all the separate accounting standards for larger companies. It reduces disclosure requirements but maintains standards for measurement. Small companies may choose either to apply the FRSSE in full or to comply with the full separate standards.

The Companies Act 2006 permits small and medium-sized companies to file 'abbreviated' financial statements with the Registrar of Companies. The word 'abbreviated' can be explained as 'cutting down the detail' but views have been expressed that this has gone too far and that abbreviated financial statements do not provide useful information about small companies. It allows them, for example, to maintain confidentiality of profit margins. During discussions on law reform leading to the Companies Act 2006, the White Paper of 2005[21] acknowledged this concern but noted that the option was popular with many companies. It said that the Government intended to retain the option for abbreviated financial statements but would require small and medium-sized companies to disclose revenue (turnover).

7.9.2 IFRS for SMEs and the future of UK GAAP

After many years of discussion the IASB issued a shortened form of accounting standards called *International Financial Reporting Standards for Small and Medium-sized Entities* (IFRS for SMEs).[22]

It maintains measurement principles that are consistent with the full IFRS but is a considerably shorter document. It achieves this in several ways. Firstly, topics not relevant to SMEs are omitted. Secondly, where the full IFRSs allow accounting policy choices, the IFRS for SMEs specifies one choice only and selects the least difficult one. Thirdly, while the measurement principles are consistent with full IFRS, the SME version simplifies the principles for recognising and measuring assets, liabilities, income and expenses. Fourthly, the required disclosures are significantly reduced in number. Finally, the standard has been written in clear language that can be translated relatively easily.

After 2005 there was a continuing need for UK GAAP for those companies that do not use the full IFRS. It was necessary for national regulators to decide whether their country would adopt the IFRS for SMEs.

Accordingly the UK FRC issued a discussion paper in 2009 asking whether, and how soon, UK SMEs could move to the IFRS for SMEs. The tentative target was 2012 but the proposals met some significant objections. This in turn led to a further consultation via an exposure draft, FRED 48, issued in January 2012 for comment, recommended:

(a) replacing all current financial reporting standards (Financial Reporting Standards and Statements of Standard Accounting Practice) in the UK and Republic of Ireland with a single FRS;

(b) introducing a reduced disclosure framework for the financial reporting of certain qualifying entities (see now FRS 101); and

(c) retaining the FRSSE with a further consultation on how to update it following the European Commission proposals for the future of financial reporting for small and micro companies.

These recommendations are implemented in FRS 100, 101 and 102, issued in November 2012 and in 2013.[23]

Following further consultation the FRC recommended that, from 2016, small companies should report using FRS 102, while micro-entities should report using a new Financial Reporting Standard for Micro-Entities (FRSME). The FRSSE is withdrawn from 2016.

7.10 Beyond the annual report

The annual report is a regulated base of information on which a reporting cycle is built. The cycle begins when the company makes its first announcement of the results of the financial year. This announcement is made in a manner dictated by the Disclosure and Transparency Rules of the FCA.

The cycle continues with reports being issued in the period between annual reports. These are called 'interim reports'. The FCA requires half-yearly reports. The regulators of the US stock exchanges require quarterly reports. All UK listed companies provide half-yearly reports and some voluntarily provide quarterly reports.

Other questions arising beyond the annual report are:

- How does the FCA ensure that companies announce the annual report in a way that is fair to all shareholders?
- How do larger companies avoid information overload for their shareholders?
- Can users have confidence in additional information provided beyond the annual report?
- What developments is the UK government currently implementing or planning?

This section outlines developments on these issues.

7.10.1 Announcing the annual report

For many years the **preliminary announcement** was the first external communication of the financial performance and position of a company in relation to the financial year most recently completed. When the year-end results and half-yearly results were ready for publication, a preliminary announcement of key information was made in a manner set out by the Stock Exchange, consistent with the aim of fair and equal access for all investors. The preliminary announcement was usually accompanied by a press release, giving the information to the media, and by meetings with professional investors and brokers' analysts at which key personnel in the company (usually the chairman, chief executive and finance director) would make speeches and answer questions.

This traditional route has been modified since 2007 by the Disclosure and Transparency Rules (DTR) of the Financial Services Authority. The DTR set out the methods by which a company may announce that its annual report is available. Companies must make public their annual report within four months of the financial year end. A company cannot make an announcement until the full text of the annual report is available on the company's website.

The Financial Conduct Authority (FCA) is obliged, by the EU Transparency Directive, to establish an official mechanism for storing all regulated information published by listed companies. Companies publish announcements (including annual reports) to the Stock Exchange through one of the Regulatory Information Services. The companies also send the announcement to the National Storage Mechanism (NSM), operated by a service provider called Morningstar. On Morningstar's webpage all users can access the regulated information provided by listed entities. The NSM allows end users to search all announcements and documents via company name, headline code, type of document or date and then to view and print the document for free. The website is located at http://www.morningstar.co.uk/uk/NSM.

The UKLA uses the title 'Annual Financial Report' to describe what might elsewhere be called 'Annual report' or 'Annual Report and Accounts'. The annual financial report produced by a listed company must include at least:

- audited financial statements prepared in accordance with the applicable accounting standards;
- a management report (i.e. the Strategic Report); and
- an appropriate statement of assurance from persons responsible in the issuer.

It should also provide an indication from which website the annual financial report is available. The headline 'Annual Financial Report' should be used when the following information is being released to the market:

- the unedited full text announcement;
- the indication of the website where the report can be found.

The Disclosure and Transparency Rules require issuers to publish regulated information in 'unedited full text'. While the Annual Financial Report is exempt from this requirement, certain key information contained in the report must be released in full text via a Regulatory Information Service. If you read a document in unedited full text you will find it has very little formatting but is easier to download for analysis of the wording in the text.

7.10.2 Periodic reporting within the financial year

The Transparency Directive of the European Union seeks to enhance transparency in EU capital markets through a common framework which includes periodic financial reports.

Half-yearly reports must be produced within two months of the end of the first six months of the financial year. Half-yearly reports have previously been called 'interim reports'. The international accounting standard IAS 34[24] provides guidance on interim reporting which is acceptable to the FCA for the purpose of half-yearly reporting.

One interesting accounting question is how to measure the results of half a year. One view is that the results of half a year should represent the actual events of that half-year. This is called the 'discrete' method. A different view is that the result for six months should represent half of the results of the full year. This is called the 'integral' method. Why does this make a difference? Imagine a company which manufactures and sells fireworks. The costs will fall evenly through the year but most of the sales will arise in the months leading to 5 November. Using the discrete method, the first six months of the calendar year will show low profits or perhaps losses. The second six months will show relatively high profits. Using the integral method each half-year will show the same profit at 50% of the total figure of the year.

IAS 34 requires the discrete method to be used as far as possible. Some expense items, such as taxation, may have to be spread evenly over the year.

In matters of disclosure the IASB recommends that the interim report should include a balance sheet, income statement, statement of changes in equity and cash flow, together with explanatory notes and comments.

Activity 7.7	Obtain the half-yearly report and the annual report of a major listed company. Compare the half-yearly report with the annual report. What are the information items in the half-yearly report? How do they compare with the full year in the annual report? What statements of accounting policy are made in the half-yearly report?

7.10.3 Prospectus

When a major company wants to raise significant amounts of finance through selling shares on the Stock Market, it issues a **prospectus**. The contents of the prospectus are regulated by the UK Listing Authority, backed up on some items by the Companies Act 2006. The document is often several hundred pages in length and quite formidable in appearance. It contains more detail than the annual report. The prospectus is a public document.

7.10.4 Avoiding information overload

Even the very largest companies may take advantage of the Companies Act rule which allows them to publish summary financial statements. These are usually very much shorter than the full annual report and are offered to shareholders as an alternative to the full report. There is a short form of the balance sheet, and profit and loss account and directors' remuneration, no notes to the accounts but usually an accompanying commentary by the company directors. Shareholders are reminded of the existence of the full report and invited to ask for a copy if desired.

7.10.5   Additional non-GAAP measures

A survey undertaken by the accountancy firm Deloitte[25] showed widespread use in 2013 and 2014 of additional non-GAAP measures of performance reported on the face of the income statement. Such additional measures are encouraged by IAS 1 when they are relevant to an understanding of the financial performance of the company. Deloitte found that companies define their non-GAAP measures so that readers can understand why they are being used. The most common adjustments observed are the exclusion of the costs of fundamental reorganisation from non-GAAP performance measures. Other exclusions covered impairment, amortisation of intangibles and asset disposal and items relating to changes in value of financial assets and liabilities. A common form of presentation observed was the use of the word 'exceptional' to describe such costs, locating them in a separate column on the income statement or in a separate box that can be removed from the performance measures. In the Real World case study at the start of this chapter you can see additional non-GAAP measures illustrated.

Two different views may be taken of this flexible approach. One is that it allows a company to provide a better understanding of its financial performance. The other is that it allows a company to confuse investors by presenting performance in a way that favours the company and distracts the reader from the overall picture.

7.10.6   'Pro forma' financial statements

'Pro forma' financial statements represent a recent development in company reporting that is causing some confusion among users of accounting information, and some concern among the regulators. According to the dictionary, the phrase 'pro forma' means 'as a matter of form'. The underlying accounting meaning is 'outside the normal reporting regulations'. It usually involves selective editing from a larger body of information that has been prepared under accounting rules, or the inclusion of some items that would not be permitted under the accounting standards applied. The risk is that the selective information may not, by itself, represent a true and fair view. This does not necessarily mean that the information is bad or misleading, but it does mean that the investor is deprived of the full protection of regulation. As an example, a company was formed by a demerger from a larger group, changing the capital structure and changing the accounting year-end. To preserve comparability the company adjusted the figures for earlier years to be presented on a basis consistent with more recent years. This company also defined its own 'benchmark' profit measures which are not specified in accounting standards. It claimed the pro forma and benchmark information helps readers better to understand the performance of the group.

7.10.7   Electronic publication of documents

One conclusion of the Company Law Review, leading to the Companies Act 2006, was that the law allows financial reporting to be a slow process that could be speeded up by use of electronic delivery. The Companies Act now confirms that a document supplied in electronic form will be validly delivered if that form has been agreed by the intended recipient (or the intended recipient had not replied when asked for a preference). However, shareholders and others having a right to receive information are able to ask for a paper copy of a document.

7.11 Summary

- Company law in the UK includes sections that implement EU Directives. This means that UK company accounting has for many years been harmonised with company accounting in other member states of the EU, but mainly in matters of disclosure. Member states have continued to require or permit different measurement practices.

- From 2005 listed groups of companies in EU member states have been required to follow the IASB system of reporting. Individual companies and unlisted groups have the choice of the IASB system or UK company law and UK FRC standards.

- The primary financial statements under both systems include a statement of financial position, income statement (profit and loss account), a statement of cash flows and a statement of changes in equity.

- Formats set out the content and layout of financial statements. Under UK company law there are detailed formats required for the balance sheet and profit and loss account. The IASB system is more flexible on layout but provides lists of essential items.

- A group of companies consists of a parent and subsidiaries. All must be included. A subsidiary is defined by the control exercised by the parent. Control is commonly evidenced by the parent holding more than half of the voting power in the subsidiary. Control may be evidenced in other kinds of agreements relating to shareholdings or to the board of directors.

- A consolidated statement of financial position contains the total assets and liabilities of the group of companies, after eliminating any amounts receivable and payable between group companies.

- A consolidated income statement (profit and loss account) contains the total revenues and expenses of the group of companies, after eliminating any transactions and profits made between group companies.

- A consolidated statement of cash flows contains the total cash flows of the group of companies, after eliminating any cash flows between group companies.

- Goodwill arising on acquisition is calculated by comparing the fair value of the payment for the subsidiary with the fair value of net assets acquired. It represents future economic benefits arising from assets that are not capable of being individually identified and separately recognised.

- Goodwill is recognised as an asset in the balance sheet and is tested annually for impairment.

- Beyond the annual report there is a range of corporate communications – often found most readily by visiting a company's website.

- For small companies special disclosure rules apply to reduce the burden of providing information.

Further reading

Deloitte LLP provide regular surveys of the content of annual report, published on the website www.deloitte.com in the Audit Section.

IAS 1 (2016), *Presentation of Financial Statements*. International Accounting Standards Board. This is a detailed standard, some of which is beyond a first-level course, but the examples of financial statements given in the Appendix show the types of presentation that companies might use or adapt.

IFRS 3 (2016), *Business Combinations.* International Accounting Standards Board. (This is a very detailed standard which is beyond a first-level course but the definitions in the Appendix may be useful in explaining terms encountered in financial statements.)

FRS 102 The Financial Reporting Standard applicable in the UK and Republic of Ireland issued by the Financial Reporting Council (2013).

The detailed accounting disclosures required by the Companies Act 2006 are in a separate Statutory Instrument:

Statutory Instrument 2008 No. 410, The Large and Medium-sized Companies and Groups (Accounts and Reports) Regulations 2008.

http://www.legislation.gov.uk/uksi/2008/410/pdfs/uksi_20080410_en.pdf

Useful websites

International Accounting Standards Board: www.ifrs.org

Financial Reporting Council: www.frc.org.uk

London Stock Exchange: www.londonstockexchange.com

Financial Conduct Authority: www.fca.gov.uk

QUESTIONS

The Questions section of each chapter has three types of question. 'Test your understanding' questions to help you review your reading are in the 'A' series of questions. You will find the answers to these by reading and thinking about the material in the book. 'Application' questions to test your ability to apply technical skills are in the 'B' series of questions. Questions requiring you to show skills in problem solving and evaluation are in the 'C' series of questions. A letter [S] indicates that there is a solution at the end of the book. Other solutions are provided in the Instructor's Manual, where there are further questions parallel to those set out here.

A   Test your understanding

A7.1   What is a Directive? (Section 7.2.1)

A7.2   What is the IAS Regulation? (Section 7.2.1)

A7.3   What is the role of the IASB? (Section 7.2.2)

A7.4   Name the primary financial statements and explain the purpose of each. (Section 7.3.1)

A7.5   The following technical terms appear in this chapter. Check that you know the meaning of each. (If you cannot find them again in the text, they are defined at the end of the book.)

    (a)   revenue
    (b)   capital
    (c)   non-current asset
    (d)   depreciation
    (e)   directors
    (f)   earnings for equity holders (ordinary shareholders)
    (g)   earnings per share
    (h)   external users (of financial statements)
    (i)   financial position
    (j)   gross
    (k)   gross margin
    (l)   gross profit
    (m) net

(n) net assets
(o) primary financial statements
(p) reserves
(q) revaluation reserve
(r) share premium
(s) property, plant and equipment
(t) revenue

A7.6 How do companies report: (Section 7.3.1)

(a) financial position;
(b) performance; and
(c) changes in financial position?

A7.7 What are the main headings to be found in most company statements of financial position? (Section 7.4)

A7.8 In the Companies Act formats, what is the reason for the order of items under heading C: current assets? (Section 7.4)

A7.9 What are the main headings to be found in most company income statements (profit and loss accounts)? (Section 7.5)

A7.10 What are the main sections of a statement of cash flows prepared according to IAS 7? (Section 7.6)

A7.11 Why does depreciation appear as a line item in the reconciliation of operating profit with cash flow? (Section 7.6.3)

A7.12 Explain why groups of companies are formed. (Section 7.7)

A7.13 Explain the purpose of consolidated financial statements. (Section 7.7)

A7.14 Define the terms: (Section 7.7.1)

(a) group;
(b) parent company; and
(c) subsidiary.

A7.15 Explain, using the accounting equation, the effect on the parent company's balance sheet of a cash payment for an investment in a subsidiary company. (Section 7.8.1)

A7.16 Explain, using the accounting equation, the effect on the parent company's balance sheet of a share issue in exchange for shares in the subsidiary company. (Section 7.8.1)

A7.17 Explain what is meant by goodwill on acquisition. (Section 7.8.4)

A7.18 What is an associated company? (Section 7.8.5)

A7.19 Apart from the annual report, what other documents do companies use to communicate financial statement information to investors, creditors and other users of financial statements? (Section 7.9)

B   Application

B7.1 [S]
Write a letter to the financial controller of a company advising on the factors which a company should take into consideration when deciding how to arrange information in financial statements.

B7.2 [S]
Write a note for financial analysts explaining how the published income statement (profit and loss account) provides a useful indication of the financial performance of a company.

B7.3 [S]
What features are likely to make a balance sheet helpful to users?

B7.4 [S]
Could a statement of cash flows be presented as the only financial statement reported by a company? Explain your view.

C   Problem solving and evaluation

C7.1 [S]

A listed company is of the view that shareholders might welcome a statement of highlights and supplementary information as a leaflet to be inserted in the annual report. Give advice on the principles to be followed in making such information useful to users.

Activities for study groups

Continuing to use the annual reports of companies which you obtained for Chapters 1 and 4, find the financial statements and the notes to the accounts.

1   Compare the financial statements with the formats and presentations shown in this chapter, and note any differences which you observe. Look at the notes to the accounts for items which are required by the regulations but are included in the notes rather than the main financial statements.

2   Find the strategic report and compare the cash flow discussion there with the FRS 1 presentation. Form a view on how readily the discussion may be related to the financial statement.

3   In your group, take the list of qualitative characteristics listed at section 4.2 and use the financial statements as a means of illustrating how the company has met those characteristics. If you have a set of different annual reports, each member of the group should take the role of a finance director pointing out the qualitative characteristics of their own company's financial statements. The group together should then decide on a ranking with a view to nominating one of the annual reports for an award of 'Communicator of the Year'.

Notes and references

1.   IAS 1 (2016), *Presentation of Financial Statements,* para. 10.
2.   IASB (2016) *Conceptual Framework.*
3.   The Appendix to IAS 1 (2016) gives an illustration which is not compulsory.
4.   The Appendix to IAS 1 (2016) gives an illustration which is not compulsory.
5.   IASB (2016), IAS 7 *Statement of Cash Flows*
6.   IASB (2016), IAS 7 *Statement of Cash Flows,* para. 4.
7.   IAS 7 (2016), para. 6.
8.   IAS 7 (2016), para. 6.
9.   IASB (2010), Exposure Draft: The Reporting Entity, para. RE 3.
10. IFRS 10 (2016), *Consolidated Financial Statements,* Appendix A.
11. IFRS 10 (2016), Appendix A.
12. IFRS 10 (2016), Appendix A.
13. IFRS 10 (2016), Appendix A.
14. IFRS 10 (2016), para. 4.
15. IFRS 10 (2016), para. 6.
16. IFRS 10 (2016), para. 7.
17. IFRS 3 (2016), para. 4.
18. IFRS 3 (2016), Appendix A.
19. IFRS 3 (2016), para. 32. In this section it is assumed in the explanations that fair value equals book value of net assets of subsidiary.
20. IAS 28 (2016), *Investments in Associates and Joint Venture,* para 5.
21. DTI Company Law Reform 2005, http://www.bis.gov.uk/files/file13958.pdf
22. IASB (2016), *International Financial Reporting Standard for Small and Medium-sized Entities.*
23. The Financial Reporting Council has issued the following:
     FRS 100 *Application of Financial Reporting Requirements* (Nov. 2012);
     FRS 101 *Reduced Disclosure Framework* (Nov. 2012);
     FRS 102 *The Financial Reporting Standard applicable in the UK and Republic of Ireland* (2013).
24. IASB (2012), IAS 34 *Interim Financial Reporting.*
25. *Annual report insights 2014.* Deloitte LLP (2014), www.deloitte.com.

Information to be presented on the face of the statement of financial position, as required by IAS 1

Note that this is a list of items, not a format, so a company could choose to present the items in a different sequence.

There must be separate headings for current and non-current assets, and current and non-current liabilities.[1]

As a minimum the face of the statement of financial position must include the following line items:[2]

(a) Property, plant and equipment
(b) Investment property
(c) Intangible assets
(d) Financial assets
(e) Investments accounted for using the equity method
(f) Biological assets
(g) Inventories
(h) Trade and other receivables
(i) Cash and cash equivalents
(j) The total of assets classified as 'held for sale'
(k) Trade and other payables
(l) Provisions
(m) Financial liabilities (excluding items shown under (k) and (l))
(n) Liabilities and assets for current tax
(o) Deferred tax assets and deferred tax liabilities
(p) Liabilities included in disposal groups classified as held for sale
(q) Non-controlling (minority) interests within equity (ownership interest)
(r) Issued capital and reserves attributable to equity holders of the parent.

An entity must disclose further subclassifications of these line items, classified in a manner appropriate to the entity's operations. These further subclassifications may be presented either on the face of the statement of financial position or in notes.[3]

1. IAS 1 (2016), para. 60.
2. IAS 1 (2016), para. 54.
3. IAS 1 (2016), para. 77.

Balance sheet format 1, as prescribed by the Companies Act 2006

The details of the Companies Act 2006 are implemented in regulations called Statutory Instruments (SI). SI 2008/410 *The Large and Medium-sized Companies and Groups (Accounts and Reports) Regulations 2008* sets out formats that should be used by UK companies that are not reporting under IFRS. The formats are specified as lists of headings. The list attaches letters A to K to the main headings and uses roman numerals for subheadings of items which are important but slightly less important than the main headings. The headings labelled by letters A to K and the subheadings labelled by roman numerals must be shown in the main body of the balance sheet. There are further lists of detailed items which must be reported but which may be contained in additional pages of notes to the balance sheet. These lists are given arabic numerals to identify them. There is a general rule that where an item under any heading is not relevant to the company, or is of zero amount, it need not be disclosed. So if a company does not mention one of the items in the format, it has to be presumed that the particular item is not relevant to that company.

A   **Called-up share capital not paid**

B   **Fixed assets**

    I   *Intangible assets*

        1 Development costs

        2 Concessions, patents, licences, trade marks and similar rights and assets

        3 Goodwill

        4 Payments on account

    II *Tangible assets*

        1 Land and buildings

        2 Plant and machinery

        3 Fixtures, fittings, tools and equipment

        4 Payments on account and assets in course of construction

    III *Investments*

        1 Shares in group undertakings

        2 Loans to group undertakings

        3 Participating interests (excluding group undertakings)

        4 Loans to undertakings in which the company has a participating interest

        5 Other investments other than loans

        6 Other loans

        7 Own shares

C   **Current assets**

    I   *Stocks*

        1 Raw materials and consumables

        2 Work in progress

        3 Finished goods and goods for resale

        4 Payments on account

    II *Debtors*

        1 Trade debtors

        2 Amounts owed by group undertakings

3 Amounts owed by undertakings in which the company has a participating interest
4 Other debtors
5 Called-up share capital not paid
6 Prepayments and accrued income

III *Investments*
1 Shares in group undertakings
2 Own shares
3 Other investments

IV *Cash at bank and in hand*

D Prepayments and accrued income

E Creditors: amounts falling due within one year
1 Debenture loans
2 Bank loans and overdrafts
3 Payments received on account
4 Trade creditors
5 Bills of exchange payable
6 Amounts owed to group undertakings
7 Amounts owed to undertakings in which the company has a participating interest
8 Other creditors including taxation and social security
9 Accruals and deferred income

F Net current assets (liabilities)

G Total assets less current liabilities

H Creditors: amounts falling due after more than one year
1 Debenture loans
2 Bank loans and overdrafts
3 Payments received on account
4 Trade creditors
5 Bills of exchange payable
6 Amounts owed to group undertakings
7 Amounts owed to undertakings in which the company has a participating interest
8 Other creditors including taxation and social security
9 Accruals and deferred income

I Provisions for liabilities and charges
1 Pensions and similar obligations
2 Taxation, including deferred taxation
3 Other provisions

J Accruals and deferred income

Minority interests*

K Capital and reserves
I *Called-up share capital*
II *Share premium account*
III *Revaluation reserve*
IV *Other reserves*
1 Capital redemption reserve
2 Reserve for own shares
3 Reserves provided by the articles of association
4 Other reserves
V *Profit and loss account*

Minority interests*

Note: Where minority interests are relevant, they are to be treated as having a letter attached. Companies may choose one of the two permitted locations.

Information to be presented on the face of the income statement, as required by IAS 1

The IASB sets out the contents of the full statement of comprehensive income and then explains how it may be separated into an income statement and a statement of other comprehensive income.

Information to be presented in the profit or loss section (income statement)[1]

In addition to items required by other IFRSs, the profit or loss section or the statement of profit or loss must include line items that present the following amounts for the period:

(a) revenue;

(b) gains and losses arising from the derecognition of financial assets measured at amortised cost;

(c) finance costs;

(d) share of the profit or loss of associates and joint ventures accounted for using the equity method;

(e) if a financial asset is reclassified so that it is measured at fair value, any gain or loss arising from a difference between the previous carrying amount and its fair value at the reclassification date (as defined in IFRS 9);

(f) tax expense;

(g) a single amount for the total of discontinued operations.

(h) profit or loss[2].

Information to be presented in the other comprehensive income section[3]

The other comprehensive income section must present line items for amounts of other comprehensive income in the period, classified by nature (including share of the other comprehensive income of associates and joint ventures accounted for using the equity method) and grouped into those that, in accordance with other IFRSs:

(a) will not be reclassified subsequently to profit or loss; and

(b) will be reclassified subsequently to profit or loss when specific conditions are met.

There must be a total of other comprehensive income and a total for the overall comprehensive income.[4]

An entity must allocate the profit or loss for the period, the other comprehensive income and the total comprehensive income for the period, attributable in each case to (1) non-controlling interests, and (2) owners of the parent.[5]

An entity must present additional line items, headings and subtotals in the statement(s) of profit or loss and other comprehensive income when such presentation is relevant to an understanding of the entity's financial performance.[6]

1. IAS 1 (2016), para. 82.
2. IAS 1 (2016), para. 81A.
3. IAS 1 (2016), para. 82A.
4. IAS 1 (2016), para. 81A.
5. IAS 1 (2016), para. 81B
6. IAS 1 (2016), para. 85.

UK Companies Act profit and loss account format 1 – list of contents

1 Turnover
2 Cost of sales
3 Gross profit or loss
4 Distribution costs
5 Administrative expenses
6 Other operating income
7 Income from shares in group undertakings
8 Income from participating interests (excluding group undertakings)
9 Income from other fixed asset investments
10 Other interest received and similar income
11 Amounts written off investments
12 Interest payable and similar charges
13 Tax on profit or loss of ordinary activities
14 Profit or loss on ordinary activities after taxation
15 Extraordinary income
16 Extraordinary charges
17 Extraordinary profit or loss
18 Tax on extraordinary profit or loss
19 Other taxes not shown under the above items
20 Profit or loss for the financial year

Chapter 8

Non-current (fixed) assets

Royal Mail plc: reporting property, plant and equipment

Extracts from Annual Report and Financial Statements

Who we are

Royal Mail is the UK's pre-eminent delivery company, connecting people, customers and businesses. As the UK's sole designated Universal Service Provider[1], we are proud to deliver a 'one-price-goes-anywhere' service on a range of letters and parcels to more than 29 million addresses, across the UK, six-days-a-week.

Alamy Images/Lee Avison

Financial Review: Property

On 14 October 2014, the Company announced that contracts had been exchanged for the sale of the former Paddington Mail Centre to Great Western Developments Limited for £111 million in cash. Total net cash proceeds of the sale of £108 million were received on completion on 8 December 2014 and a profit on disposal of £106 million has been recorded as a non-operating specific item. We continue to market the site at Nine Elms and to evaluate our options in relation to the site at Mount Pleasant. These larger sites will require further investment in order to optimise value, which will be mainly met by the proceeds from the sale of the Paddington site.

Accounting policies: Property, plant and equipment

Property, plant and equipment is recognised at cost, including directly attributable costs in bringing the asset into working condition for its intended use. Depreciation of property, plant and equipment is provided on a straight-line basis by reference to net book value and to the remaining useful economic lives of assets and their estimated residual values. The useful lives and residual values are reviewed annually and adjustments, where applicable, are made on a prospective basis. The lives assigned to major categories of property, plant and equipment are:

Land and buildings:

Freehold land	Not depreciated
Freehold buildings	Up to 50 years
Leasehold buildings	The shorter of the period of the lease, 50 years or the estimated remaining useful life
Plant and machinery	3–15 years
Motor vehicles and trailers	2–12 years
Fixtures and equipment	2–15 years

An item of property, plant and equipment is derecognised upon disposal or when no future economic benefits are expected from its use or disposal. Any gain or loss arising at derecognition of the asset (calculated as the difference between the net disposal proceeds and the carrying amount of the asset) is included in the income statement in the year that the asset is derecognised. Gains or losses from the disposal of assets are recognised in the income statement when all significant risks and rewards of ownership are transferred to the customer.

All subsequent expenditure on property, plant and equipment is capitalised if it meets the recognition criteria, and the carrying amount of those parts replaced is de-recognised. All other expenditure including repairs and maintenance expenditure is recognised in the income statement as incurred.

Impairment reviews

Unless otherwise disclosed in these accounting policies, assets and cash generating units are reviewed for impairment if events or changes in circumstances indicate that the carrying value may be impaired. The Group assesses at each reporting date whether such indications exist. Where appropriate, an impairment loss is recognised in the income statement for the amount by which the carrying value of the asset (or cash generating unit) exceeds its recoverable amount, which is the higher of an asset's net realisable value and its value in use.

Extract from Note 21 to the balance sheet

Net book values	29.3.2015	30.3.2014
Land and buildings:	£m	£m
Freehold	802	824
Long leasehold	93	98
Short leasehold	225	229
Plant and machinery	378	422
Motor vehicles	347	313
Fixtures and equipment	88	103
Total	1,933	1,989

Source: *Royal Mail plc Annual Report and Financial Statements 2014–15*, pp. 2, 28, 121–122, 135. http://www.royalmailgroup.com/sites/default/files/Annual%20Report%20and%20Accounts%202014-15.pdf

Discussion points

1 What information is provided in the accounting policies section that is not in the financial review or the Note to the balance sheet?

2 How does the combination of information from all parts of the Annual report help the user understand the relative significance of each type of asset to the company?

Contents

Learning outcomes

After studying this chapter you should be able to:

- Define a non-current (fixed) asset and apply the definition.
- Explain the recognition criteria that are applied to tangible non-current (fixed) assets, intangible non-current (fixed) assets and non-current (fixed) asset investments.
- Explain users' needs for information about non-current (fixed) assets.
- Describe and explain the non-current (fixed) asset information provided in annual reports of companies.
- Evaluate the usefulness of published information about non-current (fixed) assets.
- Explain the nature of depreciation.
- Calculate depreciation, record the effect on the accounting equation and report the result in financial statements.

Additionally, for those who choose to study the supplement:

- Record non-current (fixed) assets and depreciation in ledger accounts.

8.1 Introduction

If you have progressed through Chapters 1 to 7 you are now familiar with the accounting equation and the analysis of transactions or events using that equation. You know what is meant by the terms asset, liability, revenue, expense and ownership interest. You are aware of the structure of the primary financial statements and the way in which they seek to provide information which is relevant to decision making.

This chapter starts a new phase of the text which will help you to develop a critical awareness of some of the component items in the financial statements. Chapters 8 to 12 progress through the main sections of the statement of financial position (balance sheet). Inevitably, they also cover relevant aspects of the income statement (profit and loss account) and the statement of cash flows because transactions involving the statement of financial position (balance sheet) will sometimes have an effect in the other financial statements.

It is important at this stage not to become so enthusiastic for the intricacies of accounting procedures as to lose sight of the importance of user needs, which were set out in Chapter 1. That chapter set out, in section 1.2, the structure of most conceptual frameworks, which provides a sequence for each of Chapters 8 to 12, as follows:

- What are the principles for defining and recognising these items?
- What are the information needs of users in respect of the particular items?
- What information is currently provided by companies to meet these needs?
- Does the information show the desirable qualitative characteristics of financial statements?
- What are the principles for measuring, and processes for recording, these items?

That analysis is applied to non-current (fixed) assets in this chapter.

8.2 Definitions

The following definition of an asset was provided in Chapter 2.

Definition

An **asset** is a present economic resource controlled by the entity as a result of past events. An **economic resource** is a right that has the potential to produce economic benefits.[1]

The following definitions explain the nature of tangible and non-tangible non-current assets. The word 'tangible' means 'able to be touched'. So 'intangible' means 'not able to be touched'.

Definitions

A **non-current asset** is any asset that does not meet the definition of a current asset.[2] Non-current assets include tangible, intangible and financial assets of a long-term nature. These are also described as **fixed assets**.[3]

Tangible non-current (fixed) assets, such as property, plant and equipment, are assets that have physical substance and are held for use in the production or supply of goods or services, for rental to others, or for administrative purposes and an expected to be used during more than one period.[4]

An **intangible** asset is an identifiable non-monetary asset without physical substance.[5]

8.2.1   Examples of non-current (fixed) assets

The following is a sample of the non-current (fixed) assets found in a company's statement of financial position (balance sheet).

Tangible non-current (fixed) assets

Companies following the International Financial Reporting Standards (IFRS) will typically use a general heading of 'Property, plant and equipment'. This general heading might include:

- Land and buildings (property) owned by the entity
- Buildings leased by the entity
- Plant and equipment (owned or leased)
- Vehicles (owned or leased)
- Office equipment
- Assets under construction
- Telecommunications network
- Airport runways
- Water pipes and sewers
- Oil and mineral reserves.

Definition[6]

> Property, plant and equipment includes intangible items that:
>
> (a) are held for use in the production or supply of goods or services, for rental to others, or for administrative purposes; and
>
> (b) are expected to be used during more than one period.

Intangible non-current (fixed) assets

- Newspaper titles and publishing rights
- Patents
- Trade marks
- Goodwill purchased
- Brand names purchased.

Investments

- Long-term investments in subsidiary companies
- Long-term investments in other companies.

That sample was taken from only 10 annual reports of leading companies. Looking at more companies would soon extend the list considerably. The potential variety and the likelihood of encountering something new is one reason why definitions are essential.

8.2.2   Cost of a non-current (fixed) asset

There is one issue which is not as straightforward as it seems. That is the question of measuring the cost of a non-current (fixed) asset. When a toffee manufacturer buys a new toffee-shaping machine, the purchase price will be known from the supplier's invoice and the manufacturer's catalogue, but should the costs of delivery and installation be added to the amount recorded as the asset cost? When an insurance company buys a new head office, the purchase price will be shown in the contract, but should the legal costs be added to the amount recorded as the asset cost? When a new head office building is under development and interest is being paid on the funds borrowed to finance the development, should the interest paid on the borrowed funds be added to the cost of the development as part of the asset value?

The answer in all three cases is 'yes', although the third example causes greatest discussion and debate. The general principle is that the cost of a non-current (fixed) asset is the purchase price or the amount spent on its production together with any other expenditure incurred in bringing the non-current (fixed) asset to working condition for its intended use at its intended location.

Definition

> The **cost** of a non-current (fixed) asset is the purchase price or the amount spent on its production together with any costs directly attributable to bringing the non-current (fixed) asset to working condition for its intended use at its intended location.

8.2.3 Repairs and improvements

There are sometimes problems in deciding whether a payment for a repair to a non-current (fixed) asset should be treated as an expense of the business or an asset. The key lies in the words of the definition of an asset and the phrase *economic benefits*. If the payment relates to some act which merely preserves the existing life of the asset and the existing expectations of benefit from the asset, then the payment is treated as a repair and reported as an **expense**. The asset of cash decreases and there is a decrease in the ownership interest caused by the expense.

If the payment relates to some act which significantly extends the useful life of the asset, or increases the economic benefit expected from the asset, then the payment is treated as an **improvement** and reported as an asset. It may be reported as a separate asset but, more usually, the amount will be added to the cost or value recorded for the asset which has been improved. The asset of cash decreases and is replaced by an asset of improvements. There is no effect on the ownership interest.

The following are examples of improvements and repairs.

Improvements

- Extensions to a building which increase the operating capacity of the business.
- A new roof which gives a building an extra ten years of life.
- A new engine for a delivery van which is more powerful than the existing engine and allows faster delivery in hilly districts.
- Renewing the fittings and interior decoration of a hotel to attract international visitors instead of the traditional local customers.

Repairs

- A new roof, required because of storm damage, which will keep the building weatherproof for the remainder of its estimated life.
- A new engine for a delivery van which replaces an existing damaged engine.
- Redecorating inside a building to preserve the existing standards of cleanliness and appearance.

Activity 8.1

Imagine you are the owner of a big hotel in the centre of town. Make a list of the items you would expect to include in your business statement of financial position (balance sheet) as non-current (fixed) assets. Make a list of the types of repair which would be classed as 'improvements'. Use the definition of a non-current (fixed) asset to show that your list includes items which are correctly classified.

8.3 Recognition and measurement

This section outlines the recognition and measurement issues faced in reporting non-current assets in the separate categories of tangible assets, intangible assets and investment assets.

8.3.1 Tangible non-current (fixed) assets

Tangible non-current (fixed) assets are those items which can be touched, seen or heard and meet the conditions set out in the definition of a non-current (fixed) asset. **Recognition** by reporting in the statement of financial position (balance sheet) presents no problem where the economic benefit can be identified and the cost of the asset can be measured. (Look back to section 2.6 for an explanation of recognition.)

Historical cost measurement

The evidence of cost is usually a purchase invoice. As the list in the previous section indicates, there is considerable variety in tangible non-current (fixed) assets. The common feature is that they all have a limited life expectancy. They may wear out, be used up, go out of fashion, break down or be sold for scrap. Whatever the reason, the effect is the same and is called **depreciation**. Users have many questions to ask about tangible non-current (fixed) assets, such as:

- What kinds of tangible fixed assets are in use?
- How old are they?
- How has the company measured the depreciation?
- Where is the depreciation recorded?

Answering those questions will take up most of the remainder of this chapter.

Fair value measurement

The entity may choose to revalue tangible non-current assets at a time after the date of purchase. The revalued amount reported will be the fair value at the date of the revaluation less any subsequent accumulated depreciation. The frequency of revaluations depends upon the nature of changes in fair values. If there are significant and volatile changes in fair value, annual revaluation would be appropriate. In other cases where markets are relatively stable it may be sufficient to revalue the item only every three or five years. The evidence of fair value will be a record of market price at the date of valuation, with an explanation of the market that has been selected. Methods of reporting revaluations, using a revaluation reserve, are discussed in Chapter 12.

8.3.2 Intangible non-current (fixed) assets

An intangible non-current (fixed) asset is an item which meets the definition of a non-current (fixed) asset but has no physical substance. It cannot be touched, seen or heard. The evidence of its existence is the benefit flowing from it. For many years, items such as patents, trademarks and licences to manufacture products have been bought and sold between companies. The purchase has been recorded as a non-current (fixed) asset and depreciated over the estimated life of the patent, trademark or licence. The estimated life is decided by law (for patents and trademarks) or by legal contract (for licences). The depreciation of intangible non-current (fixed) assets is usually referred to as **amortisation** (in which you may recognise the French word *mort* meaning *death*).

The intangible non-current (fixed) asset which has attracted most accounting-related comment in recent years has been the brand name of a company's product. When a company works over many years to develop the reputation of its product, that reputation creates an expected future benefit for the company and meets the definition of an **asset** as set out in Chapter 2. However, the generally held view is that it should not be recognised in the statement of financial position (balance sheet) because it fails the **recognition** criteria of Chapter 2. The conventional argument is that there is no measurable **cost** of the reputation gained by the brand name and the value cannot be measured with reliability.

That is the generally held view which was challenged in the mid-1980s by a number of leading companies. Some had bought other companies which had developed brand names. The new owners argued that they were buying the other company purely because of the quality of the brand name and they wanted to show that brand name in the new statement of financial position (balance sheet). They had a reasonable argument because they had paid a price in the market and could show the cost of the brand name acquired. Other companies who had developed their own brand names did not want to be left behind and so paid expert valuers to calculate a value for their home-grown brands. A new professional specialism of brand valuation gained prominence and the experts claimed they could measure the value of a home-grown brand with reliability.

The companies which reported brand names in the statement of financial position (balance sheet) argued that the brand had a long life and did not require amortisation. This argument gave them the advantage of expanding the statement of financial position (balance sheet) without the disadvantage of amortisation appearing in the income statement (profit and loss account).

The IASB has issued a standard, IAS 38, covering accounting for intangible assets. Internally generated brand names must *not* be recognised as intangible assets. This rule applies to similar assets such as publishing titles, customer lists, or newspaper titles. Purchased brand names or trademarks or patents may be reported in a statement of financial position (balance sheet) if they meet the conditions for recognition. Recognition requires that an economic benefit will flow to the entity.

If the intangible asset has a finite life it must be amortised over its useful life. The method of amortisation must reflect the pattern of use of the asset.

An entity may choose whether to use historical cost or whether it prefers to apply fair value in periods after acquisition of the intangible asset. The procedure is similar to that applied for tangible non-current assets, as explained in section 8.3.1. If the intangible asset has a finite life it must be amortised over its useful life. The method of amortisation must reflect the pattern of use of the asset.

Activity 8.2	*A company which has manufactured a well-known brand of brown bread for many years has decided that the brand name is so well known that it should appear in the statement of financial position (balance sheet). Write down two arguments in favour of this, to be made by the company's finance director, and two arguments against, which will appear in a newspaper article.*

8.3.3 Investments

Investments exist in many different forms but the essential feature is an ability to generate economic benefits so that the wealth of the owner increases. This increase in wealth may arise because the value of the investment increases, or may arise because the investment creates income for the owner in the form of a distribution such as interest paid or dividends. Companies may hold investments for a variety of reasons. A non-current (fixed asset) investment is one which is held for long-term purposes, such as shares in another company which has close trading links with the investing company.

The number of shares held may be such as to give direct control of the investment or may be of a lesser amount which indicates a long-term relationship, without direct control, in a similar line of business.

Non-current (fixed) asset investments may be held so that resources are available to meet a long-term obligation, such as the payment of pensions. Such non-current (fixed) assets are normally found in the statements of financial position (balance sheets) of insurance companies or pension funds, rather than in the balance sheet of the company employing staff.

The features which make investments different as non-current (fixed) assets are the importance of the increase in value of the investment itself and the fact that they are not used in the production or service process. Both features require a different kind of accounting treatment from that given to other non-current (fixed) assets. The principle applied is that the investments are always valued at fair value in the statement of financial position (balance sheet). The increase or decrease in fair value is reported in the income statement (profit and loss account). The principle is straightforward but the application in practice becomes complex and will not be dealt with in any detail in this text. What you should look for in accounts is the existence of non-current (fixed) asset investments and the information provided about them. The questions users will ask are: 'How well is this investment keeping up its value?' and 'How important is the income from this investment to the overall profit of the company?'

8.4 Users' needs for information

Activity 8.3

Before you read this section, make a list of the information about non-current (fixed) assets which would be useful to you if you wished to learn more about a specific company. Then read the section and compare it with your list. How far-thinking are you in respect of accounting information?

Analysts who write reports for professional and private investors have a particular interest in the non-current (fixed) assets because these are the base from which profits are generated. They want to know what types of assets are held, how old they are and what plans the company has for future investment in non-current (fixed) assets.

The analysts also want to know about the impact of the depreciation charge on the profit of the year. They are aware that detailed aspects of calculations of depreciation may vary from one year to the next and this may affect the comparability of the profit amounts.

To estimate the remaining life of the assets, analysts compare the accumulated depreciation with the total cost (or value) of the non-current (fixed) assets. If the accumulated depreciation is relatively low, then the non-current (fixed) assets are relatively new. Other companies in the industry will be used for comparison. The analysts also compare the depreciation charge for the year with the total cost (or value) of the assets and expect to see a similar relationship from one year to the next. A sudden change will cause them to ask more questions about a change in the basis of calculation.

8.5 Information provided in the financial statements

In Chapter 7 the statement of financial position (balance sheet) of Safe and Sure plc was presented. The statement of financial position (balance sheet) showed a single line of information on property, plant and equipment. This section shows how that single line becomes understandable when read in conjunction with the notes to the accounts, the statement of accounting policy and the finance director's review.

8.5.1 Statement of financial position (balance sheet)

	Notes	Year 7 £m	Year 6 £m
Non-current assets			
Property, plant and equipment	1	1,375	1,219

8.5.2 Notes to the statement of financial position (balance sheet)

In the notes to the statement of financial position (balance sheet) there is considerably more information:

Note 1 Property, plant and equipment

	Land and buildings £m	Plant and equipment £m	Vehicles £m	Total £m
Cost or valuation				
At 1 January Year 7	283	964	1,048	2,295
Additions at cost	39	185	378	602
On acquisitions	3	10	7	20
Disposals	(6)	(31)	(247)	(284)
At 31 December Year 7	319	1,128	1,186	2,633
Aggregate depreciation				
At 1 January Year 7	22	588	466	1,076
Depreciation for the year	05	135	192	332
On acquisitions	1	7	6	14
Disposals	(2)	(28)	(134)	(164)
At 31 December Year 7	26	702	530	1,258
Net book value at 31 December Year 7	293	426	656	1,375
Net book value at 31 December Year 6	261	376	582	1,219

Analysis of land and buildings at cost or valuation

	Year 7 £m	Year 6 £m
At cost	104	71
At valuation	215	212
	319	283

The majority of the group's freehold and long-term leasehold properties were revalued during Year 5 by independent valuers. Valuations were made on the basis of the market value for existing use. The book values of the properties were adjusted to the revaluations and the resultant net surplus was credited to the revaluation reserve.

Analysis of net book value of land and buildings

	Year 7 £m	Year 6 £m
Freehold	245	210
Leasehold:		
Over 50 years unexpired	21	24
Under 50 years unexpired	27	27
	293	261

If the revalued assets were stated on the historical cost basis the amounts would be:

	Year 7 £m	Year 6 £m
Land and buildings at cost	157	145
Aggregate depreciation	(22)	(19)
	135	126

It is clear from the extensive nature of note 1 to the statement of financial position (balance sheet) that property, plant and equipment assets are regarded as important by those who regulate the information. All companies present a detailed note of this kind because the information is required by IAS 16, *Property, Plant and Equipment*.

8.5.3 Statement of accounting policy

In addition the company is required, by the accounting standard IAS 1, *Presentation of Financial Statements*, to disclose its significant accounting policies. For this company the wording of the accounting policy statement is as follows:

Freehold and leasehold property

Freehold and leasehold land and buildings are stated either at cost (Security and Cleaning) or at their revalued amounts less depreciation (Disposal and Recycling). Full revaluations are made at five-year intervals with interim valuations in the intervening years, the most recent full revaluation being in year 5.

Provision for depreciation of freehold land and buildings is made at the annual rate of 1% of cost or the revalued amounts. Leasehold land and buildings are amortised in equal annual instalments over the periods of the leases subject to a minimum annual provision of 1% of cost or the revalued amounts. When properties are sold the difference between sales proceeds and net book value is dealt with in the income statement (profit and loss account).

Plant and equipment

Plant and equipment are stated at cost less depreciation. Provision for depreciation is made mainly in equal annual instalments over the estimated useful lives of the assets as follows:

4 to 5 years	*vehicles*
5 to 10 years	*plant, machinery and equipment*

8.5.4 Strategic report

There is also a comment in the strategic report:

Capital expenditure

The major items of capital expenditure are vehicles, equipment used on customers' premises and office equipment, particularly computers. Disposals during the year were mainly of vehicles being replaced on a rolling programme.

Activity 8.4

Find the annual report of a company of your choice. This may be through access to the website, or by requesting a printed copy of the annual report through the website www.ft.com, or by using the free annual reports offer on the London Stock Exchange page of the Financial Times.

In the annual report find the information that corresponds to the extracts from Safe & Sure given in section 8.5. What are the similarities and differences? What do you learn about the non-current (fixed) asset base of your chosen company?

8.6 Usefulness of published information

Here is David Wilson to explain how useful he sees the information provided by companies about their tangible non-current (fixed) assets. If you look back to Chapter 4 you will see that he was about to visit the company and had made a preliminary list of questions. He has now made the visit and has a better understanding of what is reported in the statement of financial position (balance sheet). He talks to Leona in a break at a workout session.

DAVID: *I told you that in making my review before visiting the company I looked closely at the type of tangible non-current (fixed) assets held and the estimated useful life. I also checked that the depreciation period and method of calculation had not changed from previous years.*

As I was making a site visit I took the opportunity to look at the various non-current (fixed) assets. This is a group of companies, expanding by acquisition of other companies, and each acquisition brings in more land and buildings. Some of these assets are recorded at valuation rather than original cost. The company has to review the valuation on a regular basis. That is quite a common practice and I have confidence in the firm of valuers used.

Plant and equipment has an aggregate depreciation of £702m which is 62% of the cost of the assets at £1,128m. It seems to me that must be saying that the plant and equipment is more than halfway through its estimated life. The finance director wasn't too enthusiastic about this interpretation. He pointed out that when another company is acquired the non-current (fixed) assets may be quite old and have to be brought into the group statement of financial position, but once they are in group control there is a strict policy of evaluation and replacement. He views the depreciation policy as being at the prudent end of the spectrum, so the realistic life remaining might be marginally over half, but discretion and the fast-moving nature of the industry requires an element of caution. He called in the plant manager who showed me the replacement schedules for plant and equipment for the next three years. It certainly reassured me that risk of obsolescence is probably not a serious worry. I also met the vehicle fleet supervisor who showed me similar replacement schedules for the vehicles.

I saw how the vehicle fleet is managed so that every vehicle is idle for the minimum time. Each vehicle is assigned to a group of cleaning operatives, whose shifts are scheduled so that the vehicle's use is maximised. Plant and equipment are the responsibility of area managers who have to look after security, maintenance and efficiency of usage. I thought it was all really quite impressive.

The depreciation charge for the plant and equipment in Year 7 is £135m which is 12% of the cost of £1,128m and suggests an estimated life of just over eight years is being applied. That is within the range of five to ten years stated as the company's accounting policy. I think the wording 'five to ten years' is too vague. Using five years would double the depreciation charge compared with ten. I tried to pin down the finance director so that I can get a good figure for my forecast but all he would say was that there is no reason to suppose there are any unusual features in the amount in the accounts. The depreciation charge for vehicles is £192m which is 16% of the cost of £1,186m. That suggests an estimated life of just over six years is being applied. I asked the finance director how that squared with the accounting policy statement of estimated useful lives of four to five years for vehicles. He did seem to sigh a little at that point but was quite patient in explaining that there are some fully depreciated vehicles still in use (because they are quite prudent in their estimates of depreciation) and so the depreciation charge is not the 20% to 25% I was looking for. I'll need to think about that one but I might move my estimate for next year closer to 20%.

You asked me how this company's information measures up to the qualitative characteristics (set out in Chapter 4). Relevance I would rate highly, because there is plenty of information in the notes which I can use to ask questions about the effective use of non-current (fixed) assets and the impact on income statement (profit and loss account) through the depreciation charge. Faithful representation and neutrality are qualities I leave to the auditors. Prudence is something which seems to come out strongly in conversation with the finance director. The detailed schedule of assets which I saw suggests that completeness is not a problem. Comparability is fine because there are amounts for the previous year and the standard format allows me to make comparison with other companies in the industry. Understandability is perhaps more of a problem than I thought. Those fully depreciated assets caught me out.

LEONA: *Well, I have now heard you admit that there is some value in having auditors. Shall I tell you how much you have missed? You could have asked more searching questions about the way in which they measure the cost of plant and equipment. Does it include delivery charges and installation costs? You could have asked whether a technical expert inside the company estimates and reviews the asset lives used, or whether the finance director makes a guess. Did you ask whether they are perhaps verging on being over-prudent so that surprises come later when the depreciation charge is less than expected? You could have asked how the interim valuations are carried out. These are all questions we ask as auditors so that you may treat the information as being relevant and a faithful representation.*

Hopefully you now have a feeling for the information provided by companies on tangible non-current (fixed) assets and how it is used by the professional investor. The nature and recording of depreciation is now explained.

8.7 Depreciation: an explanation of its nature

Activity 8.5

Before you read this section, write down what you think 'depreciation' means. Then read the section and compare it with your initial views. Depreciation is a very subjective matter and there are different views of its purpose, so your answer may be interesting even if it does not match the text. You should consult your lecturer, tutor or other expert in the area to understand why your perceptions may be different.

Definitions[7]

Depreciation is the systematic allocation of the depreciable amount of an asset over its useful life.

The **depreciable amount** is the cost of an asset, or other amount substituted for cost, less its residual value.

Residual value is the estimated amount that an entity would currently obtain from disposal of the asset, after deducting the estimated cost of disposal, if the asset were already of the age and in the condition expected at the end of its useful life.

The asset may be an item of plant or equipment which is wearing out through being used. It may be a payment made by a company for the right to become a tenant of a property. That payment purchases a lease which reduces in value through the passage of time. The asset may be a computer system which becomes out of date in a very short space of time because of obsolescence. It may be a machine which produces goods for which demand falls because of changing market conditions.

The definition shows that depreciation is a device used in accounting to allocate (spread) the cost of a non-current (fixed) asset over its useful life. The process of spreading cost over more than one accounting period is called **allocation**.

In terms of the accounting equation, the useful life of the non-current (fixed) asset is being reduced and this will reduce the ownership interest.

	Assets		Liabilities		**Ownership** interest
Year		–		=	
1	↓				↓
2	↓				↓
3	↓				↓
etc.					

As the asset becomes older, the depreciation of one year is added to the depreciation of previous years. This is called the **accumulated depreciation** or **aggregate depreciation**. The accumulated depreciation at the end of any year is equal to the accumulated depreciation at the start of the year plus the depreciation charge for that year.

Deducting the accumulated depreciation from the original cost leaves the **net book value**. The net book value could also be described as the cost remaining as a benefit for future years.

Showing the effect of depreciation by use of arrows and the accounting equation is relatively easy. Deciding on the amount of depreciation each year is much more difficult because there are so many different views of how to calculate the amount of asset used up in each period.

8.7.1 Calculation of depreciation

Calculation of depreciation requires three pieces of information:

1 the cost of the asset;
2 the estimated useful life; and
3 the estimated residual value.

The total depreciation of the non-current (fixed) asset is equal to the cost of the non-current (fixed) asset minus the estimated residual value. The purpose of the depreciation calculation is to spread the total depreciation over the estimated useful life.

The first point at which differences of opinion arise is in the estimation of the useful life and residual value. These are matters of judgement which vary from one person to the next.

Unfortunately the differences do not stop at those estimates. There is also no agreement on the arithmetical approach to spreading the total depreciation over the useful life. Some people are of the opinion that a non-current (fixed) asset is used evenly over time and that the depreciation should reflect the benefit gained from its use. Others argue that the non-current (fixed) asset declines in value most in the early years and so the depreciation charge should be greater in earlier years.

8.7.2 Straight-line method

Those who are of the opinion that a non-current (fixed) asset is used evenly over time apply a method of calculation called straight-line depreciation. The formula is:

$$\frac{\text{Cost} - \text{Expected residual value}}{\text{Expected life}}$$

To illustrate the use of the formula, take a non-current (fixed) asset which has a cost of £1,000 and an estimated life of five years. The estimated residual value is nil. The calculation of the annual depreciation charge is:

$$\frac{£1,000 - \text{nil}}{5} = £200 \text{ per annum}$$

The depreciation rate is sometimes expressed as a percentage of the original cost. In this case the company would state its depreciation policy as follows:

Accounting policy:
Depreciation is charged on a straight-line basis at a rate of 20% of cost per annum.

Table 8.1
Pattern of depreciation and net book value over the life of an asset

End of year	Depreciation of the year (a) £	Total depreciation (b) £	Net book value of the asset (£1,000 − b) £
1	200	200	800
2	200	400	600
3	200	600	400
4	200	800	200
5	200	1,000	nil

The phrase 'straight-line' is used because a graph of the net book value of the asset at the end of each year produces a straight line. Table 8.1 sets out the five-year pattern of depreciation and net book value for the example used above.

Figure 8.1 shows a graph of the net book value at the end of each year. The graph starts at the cost figure of £1,000 when the asset is new (Year 0) and reduces by £200 each year until it is zero at the end of Year 5.

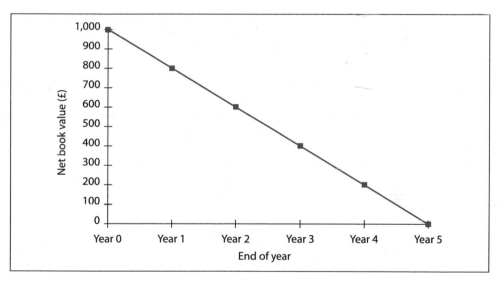

Figure 8.1
Graph of net book value over Years 1 to 5, for the straight-line method of depreciation

8.7.3 Reducing-balance method

Those who believe that the asset depreciates most in earlier years would calculate the depreciation using the formula:

Fixed percentage × Net book value at the start of the year

Take the example of the asset costing £1,000. The fixed percentage applied for the reducing-balance method might be as high as 50%. The calculations would be as shown in Table 8.2.

You will see from Table 8.2 that under the reducing-balance method there is always a small balance remaining. In this example, the rate of 50% is used to bring the net book value to a relatively small amount. The formula for calculating the exact rate requires a knowledge of compound interest and may be found at the end of the

Supplement to this chapter. For those whose main interest is in understanding and interpreting accounts it is not necessary to know the formula, but it is useful to be aware that a very much higher percentage rate is required on the reducing-balance method as compared with the straight-line method. As a useful guide, the reducing-balance rate must be at least twice the rate of the straight-line calculation if the major part of the asset is to be depreciated over its useful life.

Table 8.2
Calculation of reducing-balance depreciation

Year	Net book value at start of year (a) £	Annual depreciation (b) = 50% of (a) £	Net book value at end of year (a − b) £
1	1,000	500	500
2	500	250	250
3	250	125	125
4	125	63	62
5	62	31	31

A graph of the net book value at the end of each year under the reducing-balance method is shown in Figure 8.2. The steep slope at the start shows that the net book value declines rapidly in the early part of the asset's life and then less steeply towards the end when most of the benefit of the asset has been used up.

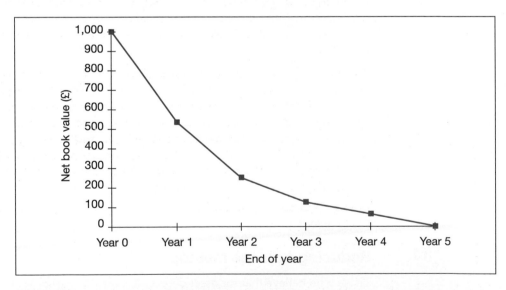

Figure 8.2
Graph of net book value over Years 1 to 5, for the reducing-balance method of depreciation

8.7.4 Which method to choose?

The separate recording of asset at cost and accumulated depreciation is accounting information provided in many countries. The UK practice at a general level is consistent with the IASB standard. Country-specific factors may lead to differences in matters of detail such as the choice of depreciation method or the estimated life of non-current (fixed) assets. In some countries, the depreciation expense in the accounting income statement (profit and loss account) must match that used for the purposes of calculating taxable profit. This may encourage the use of the reducing-balance method, giving a higher expense (and so a lower profit) in the early years of the asset's life. In the UK there are separate rules in tax law for calculating depreciation, and so this has no effect on accounting profit.

The choice of depreciation method should be based on the expected pattern of usage of the asset. If the usage is evenly spread then the straight-line method is appropriate. If the usage is heaviest in early years then the reducing-balance method is the best representation of the economic activity. In practice, it is found that most UK companies use straight-line depreciation. In some other countries, particularly those where tax rules and accounting laws are closely linked, the reducing-balance method is commonly observed. So it appears that there are different international practices that may reflect different conditions in the respective countries. David and Leona discuss the problem.

DAVID: *The choice of depreciation method may have a significant impact on reported profit. Companies that are actively investing in non-current (fixed) assets will do so in the expectation of increased profits. However, it may take some time for such profits to emerge. If, in the meantime, there is a relatively high charge to income statement (profit and loss account) through reducing-balance depreciation, profits may fall in the short term. In contrast the use of straight-line depreciation will have a less dramatic impact on reported profit immediately following the new investment, so the company avoids a dip in profits.*

LEONA: *I can't accept that as a valid argument to give to the auditor. I ask the company what the pattern of usage is. If the company tells me that the asset produces benefit evenly over its useful life, I can accept straight-line depreciation. If, on the other hand, I hear that the asset is more productive in its early years of life, I expect to see reducing-balance depreciation.*

DAVID: *Well let me try your social conscience. I came across a case of a UK company that had been taken over by a German parent company. The UK company had always used straight-line depreciation and was making small profits each year. The parent company had always used reducing-balance depreciation and so changed the accounting method of the UK subsidiary. Small profits turned into large losses and the parent company said that there would have to be a reduction in the workforce to cut costs. The employee representatives said that nothing had changed except that the accountants had redefined the game. They blamed the accountants for the resulting job losses and increased unemployment.*

LEONA: *My role is confined to giving an opinion on the accounting information. If a particular accounting process is detrimental to the public interest then it is the job of government to legislate.*

Activity 8.6

Consider the discussion between David and Leona. Do you share the concern of the employee representatives as described by David? Do you agree with Leona that the economic impact of accounting information is not a problem for the auditor? What is your view on the social responsibility attached to financial reporting?

8.7.5   Retaining cash in the business

Suppose that the policy of the owner is to take all the available profits as drawings for personal use. Take a company that has fee income of £120,000 and pays wages and other costs of £58,000. If the company did not recognise the expense of depreciation the owner's drawings could be as high as £62,000. Suppose now that depreciation of non-current (fixed) assets is calculated as £10,000. The net profit after depreciation becomes £52,000. The owner can still see £62,000 in the bank account but knows £10,000 of that amount represents using up non-current (fixed) assets. Leaving the £10,000 in the bank will allow the business to save cash for asset replacement. The owner should withdraw no more than £52,000.

It is often said that depreciation limits the amount of profits available for cash drawings by the owner and encourages saving for asset replacement. However, there is nothing to stop the business spending the £10,000 on some purpose other than replacement of non-current (fixed) assets. We can only say that cash withheld from shareholders *may* be used to replace assets at the end of the asset life.

8.8 Reporting non-current (fixed) assets and depreciation in financial statements

This section moves step by step through the recording process. First, it looks at a situation of straight-line depreciation with no residual value for the asset. Then it takes in the additional complication of an estimated residual value.

8.8.1 Straight-line depreciation, no residual value

When a retail company wants new premises, it must either buy a shop or rent one. Renting is referred to as **leasing**. When the rent agreement is signed, the tenant may pay an agreed price for the privilege of having the lease. This is called the initial payment for the lease. It is paid in addition to the annual rental payment. The initial payment to acquire the lease provides a benefit of occupation for the entire period of the lease and so is a non-current (fixed) asset. Because the lease has a known life, it must be depreciated.

On 1 January Year 2 Electrical Instruments purchased a three-year lease of a shop for a payment of £60,000. Using the straight-line method of depreciation the amount of depreciation each year will be calculated on a straight-line basis as £20,000 (one-third of the cost of the lease). The income statement (profit and loss account) will report this amount as an expense in each of the three years of the lease. The statement of financial position (balance sheet) will show on one line the original cost of £60,000 and, on a second line, the accumulated depreciation to be subtracted at the end of each year.

The financial statements over the period of three years will show the following information relating to this lease:

Income statement (profit and loss account) (extract)

Year ended 31 December	Year 2	Year 3	Year 4
	£000s	£000s	£000s
Depreciation expense	(20)	(20)	(20)

Statement of financial position (balance sheet) (extract)

At 31 December	Year 2	Year 3	Year 4
	£000s	£000s	£000s
Lease at cost	60	60	60
Less accumulated depreciation	20	40	60
Net book value	40	20	nil

8.8.2 Straight-line depreciation with a residual value

In the case of Electrical Instruments the lease had no residual value. Take now the example of The Removals Company which commences business on 1 January Year 2 by paying cash for a van costing £60,000. It is estimated to have a useful life of three years and is estimated to have a residual value of £6,000. On 31 December Year 2 the owner calculates annual depreciation of the van as £18,000, using the formula:

$$\frac{\text{Cost} - \text{Estimated residual value}}{\text{Estimated life}}$$

During each year of operating the van, the company collected £120,000 in cash from customers and paid £58,000 in cash for drivers' wages, fuel and other running costs.

These transactions and events may be summarised using the accounting equation and a spreadsheet similar to that used in Chapter 5 (Table 5.3). In Table 8.3 there is a spreadsheet for the first year of the use of the van by the company. The assets section of the spreadsheet has three columns, one of which is for cash but two of which are for the van. The two columns for the van keep a separate record of the original cost and the accumulated depreciation. The original cost is the positive part of the asset but the accumulated depreciation is the negative part of the asset. Taking the accumulated depreciation from the original cost leaves the net book value. That is the amount of cost not yet amortised which acts as a measure of the benefit remaining in the asset for the future. In Table 8.4 the information collected together by Table 8.3 is presented in the form of a statement of financial position (balance sheet) and an income statement (profit and loss account).

8.8.3 Continuing to use the non-current (fixed) asset

So far, the accounting entries have related to the first year of the business so that there was no need to ask any questions about the position at the start of the period. To show the full impact of the progressive depreciation of the asset, the spreadsheet and

Table 8.3

Spreadsheet analysing transactions and events of The Removals Company into the elements of the accounting equation

	Transaction or event	Assets			Ownership interest	
		Van at cost	Accumulated depreciation of van	Cash	Capital contributed or withdrawn	Profit = revenue minus (expenses)
Year 2		£	£	£	£	£
1 Jan.	Owner contributes cash			60,000	60,000	
1 Jan.	Purchase furniture van	60,000		(60,000)		
All year	Collected cash from customers			120,000		120,000
All year	Paid for wages, fuel, etc.			(58,000)		(58,000)
31 Dec.	Calculate annual depreciation		(18,000)			(18,000)
	Totals	60,000	(18,000)	62,000	60,000	44,000

└──── 104,000 ────┘   └── 104,000 ──┘

Table 8.4

The Removals Company: Statement of financial position (balance sheet) at end of Year 2 and Income statement (profit and loss account) for Year 2

The Removals Company
Statement of financial position (balance sheet) at 31 December Year 2

	£
Non-current (fixed) assets	
Furniture van at cost	60,000
Accumulated depreciation	(18,000)
Net book value	42,000
Current assets	
Cash	62,000
Total assets	104,000
Ownership interest	
Ownership interest at the start of the year	nil
Capital contributed during the year	60,000
Profit of the year	44,000
	104,000

The Removals Company
Income statement (profit and loss account)
for the year ended 31 December Year 2

	£	£
Revenue		
Fees for removal work		120,000
Expenses		
Wages, fuel and other running costs	(58,000)	
Depreciation	(18,000)	
		(76,000)
Net profit		44,000

Table 8.5

Spreadsheet analysis of transactions of The Removals Company, Year 3

	Transaction or event	Assets			Ownership interest		
		Van at cost	Accumulated depreciation of van	Cash	Ownership interest at start of year	Capital contributed or withdrawn	Profit = revenue minus (expenses)
Year 3		£	£	£	£	£	£
1 Jan.	Amounts brought forward at start of year	60,000	(18,000)	62,000	104,000		
All year	Collected cash from customers			120,000			120,000
All year	Paid for wages, fuel, etc.			(58,000)			(58,000)
31 Dec.	Calculate annual depreciation		(18,000)				(18,000)
	Totals	60,000	(36,000)	124,000	104,000		44,000
		└─── 148,000 ───┘			└─── 148,000 ───┘		

Table 8.6
The Removals Company statement of financial position (balance sheet) at end of Year 3 and Income statement (profit and loss account) for Year 3

<table>
<tr><td colspan="2" align="center">**The Removals Company**
Statement of financial position (balance sheet) at 31 December Year 3</td></tr>
<tr><td></td><td align="right">£</td></tr>
<tr><td>*Non-current (fixed) assets*</td><td></td></tr>
<tr><td>Furniture van at cost</td><td align="right">60,000</td></tr>
<tr><td>Accumulated depreciation</td><td align="right">(36,000)</td></tr>
<tr><td>Net book value</td><td align="right">24,000</td></tr>
<tr><td>*Current assets*</td><td></td></tr>
<tr><td>Cash</td><td align="right">124,000</td></tr>
<tr><td>Total assets</td><td align="right">148,000</td></tr>
<tr><td>*Ownership interest*</td><td></td></tr>
<tr><td>Ownership interest at the start of the year</td><td align="right">104,000</td></tr>
<tr><td>Profit of the year</td><td align="right">44,000</td></tr>
<tr><td></td><td align="right">148,000</td></tr>
</table>

<table>
<tr><td colspan="3" align="center">**The Removals Company**
Income statement (profit and loss account)
for the year ended 31 December Year 3</td></tr>
<tr><td></td><td align="right">£</td><td align="right">£</td></tr>
<tr><td>*Revenue*</td><td></td><td></td></tr>
<tr><td>Fees for removal work</td><td></td><td align="right">120,000</td></tr>
<tr><td>*Expenses*</td><td></td><td></td></tr>
<tr><td>Wages, fuel and other running costs</td><td align="right">(58,000)</td><td></td></tr>
<tr><td>Depreciation</td><td align="right">(18,000)</td><td></td></tr>
<tr><td></td><td></td><td align="right">(76,000)</td></tr>
<tr><td>Net profit</td><td></td><td align="right">44,000</td></tr>
</table>

financial statements are now presented for Year 3. Table 8.5 sets out the spreadsheet and Table 8.6 sets out the financial statements. It is assumed that for Year 3 the amounts of cash collected from customers and the amounts paid in cash for running costs are the same as for Year 2. No further capital is contributed by the owner and no new vans are acquired.

The first line of the spreadsheet in Table 8.5 shows the position at the start of the year. The asset columns show the amounts as they were at the end of the previous year. The ownership interest shows the amount resulting at the end of the previous year, as seen in the Year 2 statement of financial position (balance sheet). The columns for revenue and expenses are empty at the start of the year, awaiting the transactions and events of Year 3.

8.8.4 Disposing of the non-current (fixed) asset

During Year 4 the amounts of cash received from customers and cash paid for running costs are the same as they were in Year 3. Table 8.7 sets out the spreadsheet for the transactions and events.

Now suppose that the van is sold for £6,000 in cash on the final day of December Year 4. The spreadsheet contained in Table 8.7 requires further attention, the additional accounting impact of the sale being seen in Table 8.8.

The disposal of the van must be analysed in stages:

1 collecting cash;
2 transferring ownership of the vehicle;
3 removing the vehicle from the accounting records.

Table 8.7
Spreadsheet analysis of transactions of The Removals Company, Year 4

	Transaction or event	Assets			Ownership interest		
		Van at cost	Accumulated depreciation of van	Cash	Ownership interest at start of year	Capital contributed or withdrawn	Profit = revenue minus (expenses)
Year 4		£	£	£	£	£	£
1 Jan.	Amounts brought forward at start of year	60,000	(36,000)	124,000	148,000		
All year	Collected cash from customers			120,000			120,000
All year	Paid for wages, fuel, etc.			(58,000)			(58,000)
31 Dec.	Calculate annual depreciation		(18,000)				(18,000)
	Totals	60,000	(54,000)	186,000	148,000		44,000

└──── 192,000 ────┘   └──── 192,000 ────┘

Table 8.8
Spreadsheet analysis of transactions of The Removals Company, Year 4, including sale of non-current (fixed) asset

	Transaction or event	Assets			Ownership interest		
		Van at cost	Accumulated depreciation of van	Cash	Ownership interest at start of year	Capital contributed or withdrawn	Profit = revenue minus (expenses)
Year 4		£	£	£	£	£	£
1 Jan.	Amounts brought forward at start of year	60,000	(36,000)	124,000	148,000		
All year	Collected cash from customers			120,000			120,000
All year	Paid for wages, fuel, etc.			(58,000)			(58,000)
31 Dec.	Calculate annual depreciation		(18,000)				(18,000)
31 Dec.	Van disposal	(60,000)	54,000	6,000			
	Totals	nil	nil	192,000	148,000		44,000

└──── 192,000 ────┘   └──── 192,000 ────┘

When the vehicle is removed from the record, two columns must be reduced to zero. These are the *van at cost* column and the *accumulated depreciation* column. The van at cost column shows the original cost of £60,000 and the accumulated depreciation shows the amount of £54,000 which has to be deducted to show the amount of the net book value. The asset of cash increases by £6,000. In terms of the accounting equation:

Assets		−	Liabilities	=	Ownership interest
	£		no change		no change
Increase in cash	**6,000**				
Decrease van:					
At cost	60,000				
Accumulated depreciation	(54,000)				
	6,000				

The resulting statement of financial position (balance sheet) and income statement (profit and loss account) are shown in Table 8.9.

Table 8.9
The Removals Company: statement of financial position (balance sheet) at end of Year 4 and Income statement (profit and loss account) for Year 4

The Removals Company
Statement of financial position (balance sheet)
at 31 December Year 4

	£
Non-current (fixed) assets	Nil
Current assets	
Cash	192,000
Total assets	192,000
Ownership interest	
Ownership interest at the start of the year	148,000
Profit of the year	44,000
	192,000

The Removals Company
Income statement (profit and loss account)
for the year ended 31 December Year 4

	£	£
Revenue		
Fees for removal work		120,000
Expenses		
Wages, fuel and other running costs	(58,000)	
Depreciation	(18,000)	
		(76,000)
Net profit		44,000

8.8.5 Selling for a price which is not equal to the net book value

The previous illustration was based on selling the van for £6,000, an amount equal to the net book value. Suppose instead it was sold for £9,000. There is a gain on disposal of £3,000. This gain is reported in the income statement (profit and loss account).

Assets		–	Liabilities	=	Ownership interest
	£				
Increase cash	9,000				
Decrease van:			no change		Increase by £3,000
At cost	60,000				
Accumulated depreciation	(54,000)				
	6,000				

If the amount of the gain or loss on disposal is relatively small, it may be deducted from the depreciation charge. In that situation the income statement (profit and loss account) would appear as shown in Table 8.10 where bold printing highlights the difference when compared with the income statement (profit and loss account) in Table 8.9. If the gain or loss is **material** it will be reported separately.

Table 8.10
Income statement (profit and loss account) for Year 4 when proceeds of sale exceed net book value of non-current (fixed) asset

The Removals Company Income statement (profit and loss account) for the year ended 31 December Year 4		
	£	£
Revenue		
Fees for removal work		120,000
Expenses		
Wages, fuel and other running costs	(58,000)	
Depreciation (18,000 – 3,000)	**(15,000)**	
		(73,000)
Net profit		47,000

8.8.6 A table of depreciation expense

To test your understanding of the impact of depreciation you may wish to use a table of the type shown in Table 8.11. It shows that, whatever the proceeds of sale of the asset, the total expense in the income statement (profit and loss account) will always be the same but the amount of expense each year will vary.

If you compare the two tables (a) and (b) you will see that:

- total depreciation over the three years is the same in both cases;
- total net profit after depreciation over the three years is the same in both cases;
- annual depreciation in Years 1 and 2 is lower in table (b);
- net profit after depreciation in Years 1 and 2 is higher in table (b);
- net book value of the asset at the end of Years 1 and 2 is higher in table (b);
- the depreciation charge in Year 3 is higher in table (b);
- the net profit after depreciation in Year 3 is lower in table (b).

This is an example of what is referred to in accounting as an **allocation** problem (a 'sharing' problem). The expense is the same in total but is allocated (shared)

Table 8.11
Table of depreciation charge

(a) A van cost £60,000, was estimated to have a useful life of three years and a residual value of £6,000. It was sold for £9,000 on the last day of Year 3. Net profit before depreciation is £62,000.

Year	Net profit before depreciation	Depreciation expense of the year	Net profit after depreciation	Cost less accumulated depreciation	Net book value
	£	£	£	£	£
1	62,000	18,000	44,000	60,000 – 18,000	42,000
2	62,000	18,000	44,000	60,000 – 36,000	24,000
3	62,000	15,000	47,000	60,000 – 54,000	6,000
Total depreciation charge		51,000			
Total reported net profit			135,000		

Proceeds of sale exceed net book value by £3,000. This gain is deducted from the depreciation expense of £18,000 leaving £15,000 as the expense of the year.

(b) A van cost £60,000, was estimated to have a useful life of three years and a residual value of £9,000. The annual depreciation was calculated as £17,000. The van was sold for £9,000 on the last day of Year 3. Net profit before depreciation is £62,000.

Year	Net profit before depreciation	Depreciation expense of the year	Net profit after depreciation	Cost less accumulated depreciation	Net book value
	£	£	£	£	£
1	62,000	17,000	45,000	60,000 – 17,000	43,000
2	62,000	17,000	45,000	60,000 – 34,000	26,000
3	62,000	17,000	45,000	60,000 – 51,000	9,000
Total depreciation charge		51,000			
Total reported net profit			135,000		

Net book value equals proceeds of sale so the depreciation charge of Year 3 is the same as that of previous years.

differently across the years of the asset's life. As a result, there are different amounts in the income statement (profit and loss account) for each year but the total profit over the longer period is the same.

8.8.7 Impairment

An asset is impaired when the business will not be able to recover the amount shown in the statement of financial position (balance sheet), either through use or through sale. If the enterprise believes that impairment may have taken place, it must carry out an **impairment review**. This requires comparison of the net book value with the cash-generating ability of the asset. If the comparison indicates that the recorded net book value is too high, the value of the asset is reduced and there is an expense in the income statement (profit and loss account).[8]

The impairment test may be applied to intangible non-current (fixed) assets such as goodwill, in order to justify non-amortisation. If no impairment is detected it may be argued that the asset has maintained its value and so amortisation is not necessary. If there has been impairment of the historical cost net book value, then the loss in asset value becomes an expense for the income statement (profit and loss account).

8.9 Summary

- A **non-current asset** is any asset that does not meet the definition of a current asset.[9] Non-current assets include tangible, intangible and financial assets of a long-term nature. These are also described as **fixed assets**.

- **Tangible non-current (fixed) assets** such as property, plant and equipment are assets that have physical substance and are held for use in the production or supply of goods or services, for rental to others, or for administrative purposes on a continuing basis in the reporting entity's activities.

- An **intangible asset** is an identifiable non-monetary asset without physical substance.

- Users need information about the cost of an asset and the aggregate (accumulated) depreciation as the separate components of net book value. Having this detail allows users to estimate the proportion of asset life remaining to be used. This information will be reported in the notes to the statement of financial position (balance sheet).

- Users also need information about the accounting policy on depreciation and its impact on the reported asset values. This information will be found in the notes to the accounts on accounting policies and the notes. There may also be a description and discussion in the strategic report including a forward-looking description of intended capital expenditure.

- **Depreciation** is estimated for the total life of the asset and then allocated to the reporting periods involved, usually annual reporting. No particular method of depreciation is required by law. Preparers of financial statements have to exercise choices. Companies in the UK commonly use straight-line depreciation. An alternative is reducing-balance depreciation. This is found more commonly in some other countries. Choice of depreciation method affects the comparability of profit.

Further reading

The following standards are too detailed for a first level course but the definitions sections may be helpful:

IASB (2016), IAS 38, *Intangible Assets,* International Accounting Standards Board.

IASB (2016), IAS 16, *Property, Plant and Equipment,* International Accounting Standards Board.

QUESTIONS

The Questions section of each chapter has three types of question. 'Test your understanding' questions to help you review your reading are in the 'A' series of questions. You will find the answers to these by reading and thinking about the material in the book. 'Application' questions to test your ability to apply technical skills are in the 'B' series of questions. Questions requiring you to show skills in problem solving and evaluation are in the 'C' series of questions. A letter [S] indicates that there is a solution at the end of the book. Other solutions are provided in the Instructor's Manual, where there are further questions parallel to those set out here.

A   Test your understanding

A8.1   State the definition of a non-current (fixed) asset and explain why each condition is required. (Section 8.2)

A8.2   Explain the categories: (Section 8.2.1)

(a) tangible non-current (fixed) assets;
(b) intangible non-current (fixed) assets; and
(c) non-current (fixed) asset investments;

and give an example of each.

A8.3   What do users of financial statements particularly want to know about non-current (fixed) assets? (Section 8.4)

A8.4   What type of information would you expect to find about non-current (fixed) assets in the financial statements and notes of a major UK listed company? (Section 8.4)

A8.5   State the definition of depreciation. (Section 8.7)

A8.6   What is meant by accumulated depreciation (also called aggregate depreciation)? (Section 8.7)

A8.7   What information is needed to calculate annual depreciation? (Section 8.7.1)

A8.8   What is the formula for calculating straight-line depreciation? (Section 8.7.2)

A8.9   How is reducing-balance depreciation calculated? (Section 8.7.3)

A8.10   How does depreciation help to retain cash in a business for asset replacement? (Section 8.7.5)

A8.11   Why does the net book value of a non-current (fixed) asset not always equal the proceeds of sale? (Section 8.8.5)

A8.12   Why is depreciation said to cause an **allocation** problem in accounting? (Section 8.8.6)

A8.13   How should the cost of a non-current (fixed) asset be decided? (Section 8.2.2)

A8.14   [S] What are the matters of judgement relating to non-current (fixed) assets which users of financial statements should think about carefully when evaluating financial statements?

A8.15   What is meant by **impairment**? (Section 8.8.7)

B   Application

B8.1 [S]

On reviewing the financial statements of a company, the company's accountant discovers that expenditure of £8,000 on repair to factory equipment has been incorrectly recorded as a part of the cost of the machinery. What will be the effect on the income statement (profit and loss account) and statement of financial position (balance sheet) when the error is corrected?

B8.2

On 1 January Year 1, Angela's Employment Agency was formed. The owner contributed £300,000 in cash which was immediately used to purchase a building. It is estimated to have a 20-year life and a residual value of £200,000. During Year 1 the agency collects £80,000 in fee income and pays £60,000 in wages and other costs. Record the transactions and events of Year 1 in an accounting equation spreadsheet. (See Table 8.3 for an illustration.) Prepare the statement of financial position (balance sheet) at the end of Year 1 and the income statement (profit and loss account) for Year 1.

B8.3

Assume that fee income and costs are the same in Year 2 as in Year 1. Record the transactions and events of Year 2 in an accounting equation spreadsheet. Prepare the statement of financial position (balance sheet) at the end of Year 2 and the income statement (profit and loss account) for Year 2.

B8.4

Angela's Employment Agency sells the building for £285,000 on the final day of December Year 3. Record the transactions and events of Year 3 in an accounting equation spreadsheet. (See Table 8.7 for an illustration.) Assume depreciation is calculated in full for Year 3.

B8.5

Explain how the accounting equation spreadsheet of your answer to question B8.4 would alter if the building had been sold for £250,000.

B8.6

On 1 January Year 1, Company A purchased a bus costing £70,000. It was estimated to have a useful life of three years and a residual value of £4,000. It was sold for £8,000 on the last day of Year 3.

On 1 January Year 1, Company B purchased a bus also costing £70,000. It was estimated to have a useful life of three years and a residual value of £7,000. It was sold for £8,000 on the last day of Year 3.

Both companies have a net profit of £50,000 before depreciation. Calculate the depreciation charge and net profit of each company for each of the three years. Show that over the three years the total depreciation charge for each company is the same. (See Table 8.11 for an example.)

C   Problem solving and evaluation

C8.1 [S]

The Biscuit Manufacturing Company commenced business on 1 January Year 1 with capital of £22,000 contributed by the owner. It immediately paid cash for a biscuit machine costing £22,000. It was estimated to have a useful life of four years and at the end of that time was estimated to have a residual value of £2,000. During each year of operation of the machine, the company collected £40,000 in cash from sale of biscuits and paid £17,000 in cash for wages, ingredients and running costs.

Required
(a) Prepare spreadsheets for each of the four years analysing the transactions and events of the company.
(b) Prepare a statement of financial position (balance sheet) at the end of Year 3 and an income statement (profit and loss account) for that year.
(c) Explain to a non-accountant how to read and understand the statement of financial position (balance sheet) and income statement (profit and loss account) you have prepared.

C8.2 [S]

The biscuit machine in question C8.1 was sold at the end of Year 4 for a price of £3,000.

Required
(a) Prepare the spreadsheet for Year 4 analysing the transactions and events of the year.
(b) Prepare the statement of financial position (balance sheet) at the end of Year 4 and the income statement (profit and loss account) for Year 4.
(c) Explain to a non-accountant the accounting problems of finding that the asset was sold for £3,000 when the original expectation was £2,000.

C8.3 [S]

The Souvenir Company purchased, on 1 January Year 1, a machine producing embossed souvenir badges. The machine cost £16,000 and was estimated to have a five-year life with a residual value of £1,000.

Required

(a) Prepare a table of depreciation charges and net book value over the five-year life using straight-line depreciation.

(b) Make a guess at the percentage rate to be used in the reducing-balance calculation, and prepare a table of depreciation charges and net book value over the five years using reducing-balance depreciation.

(c) Using the straight-line method of depreciation, demonstrate the effect on the accounting equation of selling the asset at the end of Year 5 for a price of £2,500.

(d) Using the straight-line method of depreciation, demonstrate the effect on the accounting equation of disposing of the asset at the end of Year 5 for a zero scrap value.

Activities for study groups

Turn to the annual report of a listed company which you have used for activities in previous chapters. Find every item of information about non-current (fixed) assets. (Start with the financial statements and notes but look also at the strategic report, chief executive's review and other non-regulated information about the company.)

As a group, imagine you are the team of fund managers in a fund management company. You are holding a briefing meeting at which each person explains to the others some feature of the companies in which your fund invests. Today's subject is *non-current (fixed) assets.* Each person should make a short presentation to the rest of the team covering:

1 the nature and significance of non-current (fixed) assets in the company;

2 the asset lives stated in the accounting policies for depreciation purposes;

3 the asset lives estimated by you from calculations of annual depreciation as a percentage of asset cost;

4 the remaining useful life of assets as indicated by comparing accumulated depreciation with asset cost;

5 the company's plans for future investment in non-current (fixed) assets.

Notes and references

1. IASB (2016), *Conceptual Framework.*
2. IASB (2016), IAS 1 paras 66 and 67.
3. IASB (2016), IAS 1 para. 67 permits the use of alternative descriptions for non-current assets provided the meaning is clear.
4. IASB (2016), IAS 16, *Property, Plant and Equipment,* para. 6.
5. IASB (2016), IAS 38, *Intangible Assets,* para. 8.
6. IASB (2016), IAS 16, *Property, Plant and Equipment,* para. 6.
7. IASB (2016), IAS 16, *Property, Plant and Equipment,* para. 6.
8. There remain international differences on the precise method of estimating cash-generating ability. There are detailed rules in IAS 38 but these are beyond a first-level text.
9. IASB (2016), IAS 1 paras 66 and 67.

Recording non-current (fixed) assets and depreciation

The rules for debit and credit entries in a ledger account should by now be familiar but are set out again in Table 8.12 for convenience. If you still feel unsure about any aspect of Table 8.12 you should revisit the supplements of earlier chapters before attempting this one.

In this supplement you will concentrate primarily on the ledger accounts for the non-current (fixed) assets. It takes The Removals Company of the main chapter as the example for illustration.

Table 8.12
Rules for debit and credit entries in ledger accounts

	Debit entries in a ledger account	Credit entries in a ledger account
Left-hand side of the equation		
Asset	Increase	Decrease
Right-hand side of the equation		
Liability	Decrease	Increase
Ownership interest	Expense	Revenue
	Capital withdrawn	Capital contributed

Information to be recorded

The Removals Company commences business on 1 January Year 2 by paying cash for a van costing £60,000. The cash was contributed by the owner. The van is estimated to have a useful life of three years and is estimated to have a residual value of £6,000. On 31 December Year 2 the owner calculates annual depreciation of the van as £18,000, using the formula:

$$\frac{\text{Cost} - \text{Estimated residual value}}{\text{Estimated life}}$$

During each year of operating the van, the company collected £120,000 in cash from customers and paid £58,000 in cash for drivers' wages, fuel and other running costs.

The transactions of Year 2 have been analysed in Table 8.3 for their impact on the accounting equation. That same list may be used to set out the debit and credit bookkeeping entries, as shown in Table 8.13.

Table 8.13
Analysis of transactions for The Removals Company, Year 2

Date	Transaction or event	Amount	Dr	Cr
Year 2		£		
1 Jan.	Owner contributes cash	60,000	Cash	Ownership interest
1 Jan.	Purchase furniture van	60,000	Van at cost	Cash
All year	Collected cash from customers	120,000	Cash	Sales
All year	Paid for running costs	58,000	Running costs	Cash
31 Dec.	Calculate annual depreciation	18,000	Depreciation	Accumulated depreciation

Ledger accounts required to record transactions of Year 2 are as follows:

L1 Ownership interest	L4 Accumulated depreciation of van
L2 Cash	L5 Sales
L3 Van at cost	L6 Running costs
	L7 Depreciation of the year

L1 Ownership interest

Date	Particulars	Page	Debit	Credit	Balance
Year 2			£	£	£
Jan. 1	Cash	L2		60,000	(60,000)

LEONA's comment: *This ledger account shows the opening contribution to the start of the business which establishes the ownership interest.*

L2 Cash

Date	Particulars	Page	Debit	Credit	Balance
Year 2			£	£	£
Jan. 1	Ownership interest	L1	60,000		60,000
Jan. 1	Van	L3		60,000	nil
Jan.–Dec.	Sales	L5	120,000		120,000
Jan.–Dec.	Running costs	L6		58,000	62,000

LEONA's comment: *For convenience in this illustration all the sales and running costs have been brought together in one amount for the year. In reality there would be a large number of separate transactions recorded throughout the year. The balance at the end of the year shows that there is £62,000 remaining in the bank account.*

L3 Van at cost

Date	Particulars	Page	Debit	Credit	Balance
Year 2			£	£	£
Jan. 1	Cash	L2	60,000		60,000

LEONA's comment: *The van is recorded by a debit entry and this entry remains in the ledger account for as long as the van is in use by the company. A separate ledger account is maintained for the cost of the asset because it is regarded as a useful piece of information for purposes of financial statements.*

L4 Accumulated depreciation of van

Date	Particulars	Page	Debit	Credit	Balance
Year 2			£	£	£
Dec. 31	Depreciation of the year	L7		18,000	(18,000)

LEONA's comment: *The accumulated depreciation account completes the story about the van. It has an original cost of £60,000 and an accumulated depreciation at the end of Year 2 equal to £18,000. The accumulated depreciation account will always show a credit balance because it is the negative part of the asset. Deducting accumulated depreciation from cost gives a net book value of £42,000.*

L5 Sales

Date	Particulars	Page	Debit	Credit	Balance
Year 2			£	£	£
Jan.–Dec.	Cash	L2		120,000	(120,000)

LEONA's comment: *For convenience all the sales transactions of the year have been brought together in one single amount, but in reality there would be many pages of separate transactions.*

L6 Running costs

Date	Particulars	Page	Debit	Credit	Balance
Year 2			£	£	£
Jan.–Dec.	Cash	L2	58,000		58,000

LEONA's comment: *As with the sales transactions of the year, all running costs have been brought together in one single amount, but in reality there will be several pages of separate transactions recorded over the year.*

L7 Depreciation of the year

Date	Particulars	Page	Debit	Credit	Balance
Year 2			£	£	£
Dec. 31	Depreciation of Year 2	L4	18,000		18,000

LEONA's comment: *The depreciation of the year is a debit entry because it is an expense. The process of depreciation is continuous but that is not convenient for ledger account recording, so companies prefer a single calculation at the end of the year.*

At this point a trial balance may be prepared, as explained in the supplement to Chapter 5, and shown in Table 8.14.

Table 8.14
Trial balance at the end of Year 2 for The Removals Company

Ledger account title		£	£
L1	Ownership interest		60,000
L2	Cash	62,000	
L3	Van at cost	60,000	
L4	Accumulated depreciation of van		18,000
L5	Sales		120,000
L6	Running costs	58,000	
L7	Depreciation	18,000	
Totals		198,000	198,000

Closing at the end of Year 2 and starting the ledger accounts for Year 3

At the end of the year the balances on asset and liability accounts are *carried forward* to the next year. The phrase 'carried forward' means that they are allowed to remain in the ledger account at the start of the new year. The balances on revenue and expense accounts are treated differently. After the trial balance has been prepared and checked, the amounts on each revenue account and expense account are *transferred to an income statement (profit and loss account)*. Transferring a balance requires an entry of the opposite type to the balance being transferred. A debit entry is made to transfer a credit balance. A credit entry is made to transfer a debit balance. Matching but opposite entries are made in the income statement (profit and loss account). This is called 'closing' the expense or revenue account.

L5 Sales

Date	Particulars	Page	Debit	Credit	Balance
Year 2			£	£	£
Jan.–Dec.	Cash	L2		120,000	(120,000)
Dec. 31	Transfer to profit and loss account	L8	120,000		nil

LEONA's comment: *The ledger account for sales shows a credit balance of £120,000 for the total transactions of the year. This is transferred to the income statement (profit and loss account) by making a debit entry of similar amount, so that the balance of the sales account is reduced to nil.*

L6 Running costs

Date	Particulars	Page	Debit	Credit	Balance
Year 2			£	£	£
Jan.–Dec.	Cash	L2	58,000		58,000
Dec. 31	Transfer to income statement (profit and loss account)	L8		58,000	nil

LEONA's comment: *The ledger account for running costs shows a debit balance of £58,000 for the total transactions of the year. This is transferred to the income statement (profit and loss account) by making a credit entry of similar amount, so that the balance of the running costs account is reduced to nil.*

L7 Depreciation of the year

Date	Particulars	Page	Debit	Credit	Balance
Year 2			£	£	£
Dec. 31	Depreciation of Year 2	L4	18,000		18,000
Dec. 31	Transfer to income statement (profit and loss account)	L8		18,000	nil

LEONA's comment: *The ledger account for depreciation expense shows a debit balance of £18,000 for the depreciation charge of the year. This is transferred to the income statement (profit and loss account) by making a credit entry of similar amount, so that the balance of the depreciation expense account of the year is reduced to nil.*

L8 Income statement (profit and loss account)

Date	Particulars	Page	Debit	Credit	Balance
Year 2			£	£	£
Dec. 31	Sales	L5		120,000	(120,000)
Dec. 31	Running costs	L6	58,000		(62,000)
Dec. 31	Depreciation of the year	L7	18,000		(44,000)

LEONA's comment: *The income statement (profit and loss account) in ledger form shows all items of revenue in the credit column and all items of expense in the debit column. The balance in the third column shows, at the end of the ledger account, the profit of £44,000 for the year. There is one final entry to be made, and that is to transfer the £44,000 balance of the income statement (profit and loss account) to the ownership interest account. That requires a debit entry in the income statement (profit and loss account) to remove the credit balance.*

L8 Income statement (profit and loss account)

Date	Particulars	Page	Debit	Credit	Balance
Year 2			£	£	£
Dec. 31	Sales	L5		120,000	(120,000)
Dec. 31	Running costs	L6	58,000		(62,000)
Dec. 31	Depreciation	L7	18,000		(44,000)
Dec. 31	Transfer to ownership interest	L1	44,000		nil

L1 Ownership interest

Date	Particulars	Page	Debit	Credit	Balance
Year 2			£	£	£
Jan. 1	Cash	L2		60,000	(60,000)
Dec. 31	Transfer from income statement (profit and loss account)	L8		44,000	(104,000)

LEONA's comment: *The transfer from the income statement (profit and loss account) is shown as a credit entry in the ledger account for the ownership interest. That credit entry matches the debit entry, removing the balance from the ledger account. As a check on the common sense of the credit entry, go back to the table at the start of this Supplement (Table 8.12), which shows that a credit entry records an increase in the ownership interest. In the ledger account the credit entry of £44,000 increases the ownership interest from £60,000 to £104,000.*

Subsequent years

The income statement (profit and loss account)s for Year 3 and Year 4 are identical to that for Year 2. The cash account flows on in a pattern similar to that of Year 2. These ledger accounts are therefore not repeated here for Years 3 and 4. Attention is concentrated on the asset at cost and the accumulated depreciation.

L3 Van at cost

Date	Particulars	Page	Debit	Credit	Balance
Year 2			£	£	£
Jan. 1	Cash	L2	60,000		60,000
Year 3	Balance	b/fwd			60,000
Year 4	Balance	b/fwd			60,000

LEONA's comment: *The asset continues in use from one year to the next and so the ledger account remains open with the balance of £60,000 remaining. At the start of each new year the balance on each asset account is brought forward (repeated) from the* *previous line to show clearly that this is the amount for the start of the new accounting year. Because this is merely a matter of convenience in tidying up at the start of the year, the abbreviation 'b/fwd' (for 'brought forward') is entered in the 'page' column to show that there are no debit or credit entries for transactions on this line.*

L4 Accumulated depreciation

Date	Particulars	Page	Debit	Credit	Balance
Year 2			£	£	£
Dec. 31	Depreciation of Year 2	L7		18,000	(18,000)
Year 3					
Dec. 31	Depreciation of Year 3	L7		18,000	(36,000)
Year 4					
Dec. 31	Depreciation of Year 4	L7		18,000	(54,000)

LEONA's comment: *The accumulated depreciation account is now showing more clearly what the word 'accumulated' means. Each year it is building in a further amount of £18,000 annual depreciation to build up the total shown in the 'balance' column. After three years the accumulated depreciation has built up to £54,000.*

L7 Depreciation of the year: Year 3

Date	Particulars	Page	Debit	Credit	Balance
Year 3			£	£	£
Dec. 31	Depreciation of Year 3	L4	18,000		18,000
Dec. 31	Transfer to income statement (profit and loss account)	L8		18,000	nil

L7 Depreciation of the year: Year 4

Date	Particulars	Page	Debit	Credit	Balance
Year 4			£	£	£
Dec. 31	Depreciation of Year 4	L4	18,000		18,000
Dec. 31	Transfer to income statement (profit and loss account)	L8		18,000	nil

LEONA's comment: *The depreciation of the year is an income statement (profit and loss account) item and so is transferred to the income statement (profit and loss account) each year in Years 3 and 4 in the manner explained earlier for Year 2.*

Disposal of the asset

At the end of Year 4 the asset is sold for a cash price of £6,000. To remove the asset requires entries in the 'Van at cost' account (L3), the 'Accumulated depreciation' account (L4) and the 'Cash' account (L2). The corresponding debit and credit entries are recorded in a 'Non-current (fixed) asset disposal' account (L9).

Table 8.15 shows the breakdown of the sale transaction into the removal of the asset at cost, the removal of the accumulated depreciation, and the collection of cash. The entry required to remove a balance on a ledger account is the opposite to the amount of the balance. So in the 'Van at cost' account (L3) a credit entry of £60,000 is required to remove a debit balance of £60,000. In the 'Accumulated depreciation' account (L4) a debit entry is required to remove a credit balance of £54,000. In the 'Cash' account (L2) there is a debit entry of £60,000 to show that the asset of cash has increased. In each case the 'Disposal' account (L9) collects the matching debit or credit.

Table 8.15
Analysis of debit and credit aspects of sale of a fixed asset

Date	Transaction or event	Amount	Dr	Cr
Year 4		£		
Dec. 31	Removal of asset at cost	60,000	Disposal	Van at cost
Dec. 31	Accumulated depreciation	54,000	Accumulated depreciation	Disposal
Dec. 31	Cash	6,000	Cash	Disposal

L3 Van at cost

Date	Particulars	Page	Debit	Credit	Balance
Year 2			£	£	£
Jan. 1	Cash	L2	60,000		60,000
Year 3	Balance	b/fwd			60,000
Year 4	Balance	b/fwd			60,000
Dec. 31	Disposal	L9		60,000	nil

L4 Accumulated depreciation

Date	Particulars	Page	Debit	Credit	Balance
Year 2			£	£	£
Dec. 31	Depreciation of Year 2	L7		18,000	(18,000)
Year 3					
Dec. 31	Depreciation of Year 3	L7		18,000	(36,000)
Year 4					
Dec. 31	Depreciation of Year 4	L7		18,000	(54,000)
Dec. 31	Disposal	L9	54,000		nil

L9 Non-current (fixed) asset disposal account

Date	Particulars	Page	Debit	Credit	Balance
Year 4			£	£	£
Dec. 31	Van at cost	L3	60,000		60,000
Dec. 31	Accumulated depreciation	L4		54,000	6,000
Dec. 31	Cash	L2		6,000	nil

LEONA's comment: *The disposal account is a very convenient way of bringing together all the information about the disposal of the van. The first two lines show the full cost and accumulated depreciation. The balance column, on the second line, shows that the difference between these two items is the net book value of £6,000. Collecting cash of £6,000 is seen to match exactly the net book value, which means that there is no depreciation adjustment on disposal.*

Sale for an amount greater than the net book value

In the main text of this chapter there is a discussion of the consequences of selling the van for £9,000 cash. There would be no problem in recording that in the bookkeeping system. Everything explained in the previous section would be unchanged except for the amount of the cash received. The Disposal account would now be recorded as:

L9 Non-current (fixed) asset disposal account

Date	Particulars	Page	Debit	Credit	Balance
Year 4			£	£	£
Dec. 31	Van at cost	L3	60,000		60,000
Dec. 31	Accumulated depreciation	L4		54,000	6,000
Dec. 31	Cash	L2		9,000	(3,000)
Dec. 31	Transfer to income state-ment (profit and loss account)	L8	3,000		nil

The income statement (profit and loss account) for Year 4 would be recorded as:

L8 Income statement (profit and loss account)

Date	Particulars	Page	Debit	Credit	Balance
Year 4			£	£	£
Dec. 31	Sales	L5		120,000	(120,000)
Dec. 31	Running costs	L6	58,000		(62,000)
Dec. 31	Depreciation of the year	L7	18,000		(44,000)
Dec. 31	Gain on disposal	L9		3,000	(47,000)

LEONA's comment: *This income statement (profit and loss account) in ledger form matches the income statement (profit and loss account) presented at Table 8.10 in the main text as a financial statement, although you will see that the latter is much more informative.*

Formula for calculating percentage rate for reducing-balance depreciation

The rate of depreciation to be applied under the reducing-balance method of depreciation may be calculated by the formula:

$$\text{rate} = (1 - {}^{n}|(R/C)) \times 100\%$$

where: n = the number of years of useful life
R = the estimated residual value
C = the cost of the asset.

For the example given in the main chapter:

N = 5 years
C = £1,000
R = £30 (The residual value must be of reasonable magnitude. To use an amount of nil for the residual value would result in a rate of 100%.)

$$\text{rate} = (1 - \sqrt[5]{(30/1,000)}) \times 100\%$$

To prove that the rate is 50% you will need a scientific calculator or a suitable computer package. You may know how to calculate a fifth root using logarithms. Otherwise, if you have a very basic calculator it may be easier to use trial-and-error methods.

S Test your understanding

S8.1   Prepare ledger accounts to report the transactions and events of questions C8.1 and C8.2.

S8.2   Write a short commentary on each ledger account prepared in S1, to enable a non-accountant to understand their purpose and content.

Chapter 9

Current assets

The fair value of cane roots and growing cane is determined using inputs that are unobservable, using the best information available in the circumstances for using the cane roots and the growing cane, and therefore fall into the level 3 fair value category.

Significant accounting policies: Inventories

Inventories are stated at the lower of cost and net realisable value. Cost includes raw materials, direct labour and expenses and an appropriate proportion of production and other overheads, calculated on a first-in first-out basis. Inventories for Primark are valued at the lower of cost and net realisable value using the retail method, calculated on the basis of selling price less appropriate trading margin. All Primark inventories are finished goods.

Note to the Balance sheet

15. Inventories	2014	2013
	£m	£m
Raw materials and consumables	334	348
Work in progress	23	29
Finished goods and goods held for resale	1,274	1,204
	1,631	1,581
Write down of inventories	(78)	(78)

Source: Associated British Foods plc Annual Report and Accounts 2014, pp. ii, 2, 38, 94, 113. http://www.abf.co.uk/documents/pdfs/2014/2014_abf_annual_report_and_accounts.pdf

Discussion points

1 What does the reader learn about inventory valuation from the accounting policy note?

2 How does the company value a current asset that is a growing crop?

Contents

Learning outcomes

After studying this chapter you should be able to:

- Define a current asset and apply the definition.
- Explain the operation of the working capital cycle.
- Explain the factors affecting recognition of inventories (stocks), receivables (debtors) and investments.
- Explain how the information presented in a company's statement of financial position (balance sheet) and notes, in relation to current assets, meets the needs of users.
- Explain the different approaches to measurement of inventories (stocks) and cost of goods sold.
- Analyse provisions for doubtful debts using a spreadsheet.
- Analyse prepayments using a spreadsheet.
- Explain the term 'revenue' and the application of principles of revenue recognition.

Additionally, for those who choose to study the supplement:

- Record receivables (debtors) and prepayments in ledger accounts.

9.1 Introduction

This chapter will continue the progress through the statement of financial position (balance sheet) which we began in Chapter 8. As in that chapter, the approach will be:

- What are the principles for defining and recognising these items?
- What are the information needs of users in respect of the particular items?
- What information is currently provided by companies to meet these needs?

- Does the information show the desirable qualitative characteristics of financial statements?
- What are the principles for measuring, and processes for recording, these items?

9.2 Definitions

Definitions were provided in Chapter 2. They are repeated here for convenience.

Definition An **asset** a present economic resource controlled by the entity as a result of past events. An **economic resource** is a right that has the potential to produce economic benefits.[1]

A **current asset** is an asset that satisfies any of the following criteria:

(a) it is expected to be realised in, or is intended for sale or consumption in, the entity's normal operating cycle;
(b) it is held primarily for the purpose of being traded;
(c) it is expected to be realised within twelve months after the reporting period;
(d) it is cash or a cash equivalent.[2]

The following list is a sample of the current assets found in most company statements of financial position (balance sheets):

- raw materials
- work in progress
- finished goods
- trade receivables (debtors)
- amounts owed by other companies in a group
- prepayments and accrued income
- investments held as current assets
- short-term bank deposits
- bank current account (also called 'cash at bank')
- cash in hand.

Activity 9.1 *Using the definition provided, explain why each item in the foregoing list may be classed as a current asset. Could a plot of land ever be treated as a current asset?*

The definition of a current asset refers to 'the entity's normal operating cycle'. The operating cycle experienced by many businesses lasts for 12 months, covering all the seasons of one year. One year is the reporting period most commonly used by most enterprises for reporting to external users of financial statements.

9.3 The working capital cycle

Working capital is the amount of long-term finance the business has to provide in order to keep **current assets** working for the business. Some short-term finance for current assets is provided by the suppliers who give credit by allowing time to pay, but that is not usually sufficient. Some short-term finance for current assets is provided by short-term bank loans but, in most cases, there still remains an excess of **current assets** over **current liabilities**.

The working capital cycle of a business is the sequence of transactions and events, involving current assets and current liabilities, through which the business makes a profit.

Figure 9.1 shows how the working capital cycle begins when suppliers allow the business to obtain goods on credit terms, but do not insist on immediate payment. While they are waiting for payment they are called **trade creditors**. The amounts owing to suppliers as creditors are called **trade payables** in the statement of financial position (balance sheet). The goods obtained by the business are used in production, held for resale or used in providing a service. While the goods acquired are held by the business they are called the **inventories (stocks)** of the business. Any products manufactured from these goods and held for resale are also part of the inventories (stocks) of the business. The resulting product or service is sold to customers who may pay immediately in cash, or may be allowed time to pay. If they are allowed time to pay they become **debtors** of the business. Debtors eventually pay and the business obtains cash. In the statement of financial position (balance sheet) the amount due from **trade debtors** is described as **trade receivables**. **Cash** is a general term used to cover money held in the bank, and money held in notes and coins on the business premises. Cash held in the bank will be in an account such as a current account which allows immediate access. Finally the cash may be used to pay the suppliers who, as creditors, have been waiting patiently for payment.

Inventories (stocks), receivables (debtors) and cash are all current assets of the business and will be dealt with in this chapter. Creditors who have supplied goods to the business are current liabilities and will be dealt with in the next chapter.

Working capital is calculated as **current assets** minus **current liabilities**. If the working capital is low, then the business has a close match between current assets and current liabilities but may risk not being able to pay its liabilities as they fall due. Not

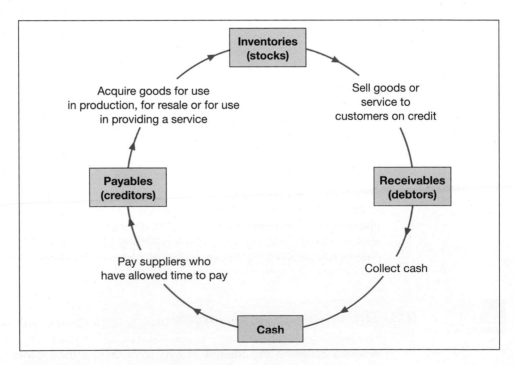

Figure 9.1
The working capital cycle for a manufacturing or service business

all the current assets are instantly available in cash. There may be some delay in selling the inventories (stocks) of unsold goods. An impatient supplier or bank manager may cause difficulties if cash is not available when payment of a liability is due. On the other hand, if current assets are very much greater than current liabilities, then the business has a large amount of finance tied up in the current assets when perhaps that finance would be better employed in the acquisition of more fixed assets to expand the profit-making capacity of the operations.

Definition

> **Working capital** is the amount which a business must provide to finance the current assets of a business, to the extent that these are not covered by current liabilities. It is calculated by deducting current liabilities from current assets.

9.4 Recognition and measurement

The recognition criteria and methods of measurement were set out in Chapter 2. There is no doubt that inventories (stocks), receivables (debtors), investments and cash are commonly recognised in a statement of financial position (balance sheet) but it is useful to be aware of the element of doubt which may be attached to the economic benefit which creates the asset and to the measurement. That awareness is essential to understanding the level of uncertainty which surrounds reported financial statements.

The rest of this section explains how the current assets are recognised. Measurement and recording are explained in section 9.7 onwards.

9.4.1 Inventories (stocks)

'Inventories' means lists of items. You might come across an inventory if you rent a flat and the owner has a list of the contents that is checked at the start and end of your tenancy. The pronunciation is *IN-ven-trees*, with stress on the first syllable 'IN' and not *INVENTOR-ees*, which sounds like a collection of inventors.

Definition

> **Inventories** are assets:
>
> (a) held for sale in the ordinary course of business;
> (b) in the process of production for sale; or
> (c) in the form of materials or supplies to be consumed in the production process or in the rendering of services.[3]

If a company is presenting its financial statements using the IASB's accounting system you will probably see the description 'inventories'. If the company is following UK company law and UK FRC standards then you will probably see the description 'stocks'. The remainder of this chapter explains the IASB's system for reporting inventories. The rules of UK law and standards are very similar. In business entities there are three main categories of inventories: raw materials, work in progress and finished goods. Consider these in reverse order.

Finished goods

The economic benefit expected from finished goods is that they will be sold to customers for a price which exceeds the cost of purchase or manufacture. That makes a profit which increases the ownership interest. However, until the sale is agreed with the customer, this expected benefit is uncertain and the concept of **prudence** (explained in Chapter 4) dictates that it is safer not to anticipate that the profit will arise. The value of the inventories of finished goods is therefore measured at the **cost** of purchase or manufacture. In most cases that is a valid measure because it is based on recorded costs and is not anticipating an uncertain selling price. Sometimes there may be a disappointment where goods are manufactured and then it is found there is a lack of demand. Where there is strong doubt about the expected selling price, such that it might be less than the cost of purchase or manufacture, the inventories (stock) of finished goods are valued at the net realisable value. This is defined as the estimated proceeds from sale of the items in question, less all costs to be incurred in marketing, selling and distributing these items.

The accounting policy note of most companies confirms this prudent approach. You will see in a later section of this chapter that Safe and Sure plc recognises inventories in its statement of financial position (balance sheet) at the lower of cost and net realisable value.

Work in progress

During the course of production the asset of finished goods is gradually being created. The expected benefit of that activity is gradually building up as the work moves towards completion. A business could wait until the asset is totally finished, before recognising the asset in the statement of financial position (balance sheet). That would satisfy the concept of **prudence**, supported by the characteristic of **faithful representation**, but would run into problems with the characteristic of **relevance**. Where work in progress is a substantial aspect of the operations of the business, users need to know how much work in progress there is, whether it is increasing or decreasing, and what risks are attached. The risks attached to work in progress are often greater than those attached to finished goods because there is the risk of non-completion to add to all the risks faced when the goods are completed and awaiting sale. There is a faithful measurement, in the cost of work completed at the date of the financial year-end, but careful checking is required by the managers of the business to ensure that this is a valid measure.

A particularly important type of **work in progress** is the construction contract (long-term contract) such as may be found in the engineering and building industries. A company building a bridge over three years will want to tell the shareholders about the progress being made in creating profit. Each year a portion of the total contract price will be reported as turnover and costs of the period will be matched against that turnover to calculate profit. The value of the work completed will be recognised as an asset in the statement of financial position (balance sheet), sometimes called work in progress. The reporting of profit on construction contracts (long-term contracts) is reviewed later in this chapter, in section 9.11.

Raw materials

The approach to recognition is the same as that for finished goods. Raw materials are expected to create a benefit by being used in the manufacture of goods for sale. On grounds of prudence the profit is not anticipated and the raw materials are measured at the lower of cost and net realisable value.

9.4.2 Receivables (debtors) and prepayments

Debtors are those persons who owe money to a business. Usually the largest amount shown under this heading relates to customers buying goods on credit. These are the **trade receivables (trade debtors)**. Additionally, the business may have lent money to another enterprise to help that enterprise in its activities. There may be loans to employees to cover removal and relocation expenses or advances on salaries. The business may be due to receive a refund of overpaid tax.

Trade receivables (debtors) meet the recognition criteria because there is a potential benefit when the customer pays. The profit on the sale of the goods is known because the customer has taken the goods or service and agreed the price. Trade receivables (debtors) are therefore measured at the selling price of the goods and the profit is recognised in the income statement (profit and loss account). There is a risk that the customer will not pay, but the view taken is that the risk of non-payment should be seen quite separately from the risk of not making a profit on a sale. The risk of non-payment is dealt with by reducing the reported value of the asset using an estimate for doubtful debts. That process is explained later in the chapter.

Prepayments are amounts of expenses paid in advance. Insurance premiums, rent of buildings, lease charges on a vehicle, road fund licences for the delivery vans and lorries are all examples of items which have to be paid for in advance. At the date of the financial year-end some part of the future benefit may remain. This is recognised as the prepayment. Take the example of an insurance premium of £240 paid on 1 October to cover a 12-month period. At the company's year-end of 31 December, three months' benefit has expired but nine months' benefit remains. The statement of financial position (balance sheet) therefore reports a prepayment of £180.

Definition	**Prepayment** An amount paid for in advance for an benefit to the business, such as insurance premiums or rent in advance. Initially recognised as an asset, then transferred to expense in the period when the benefit is enjoyed.

9.4.3 Investments

Investments held as current assets are usually highly marketable and readily convertible into cash. They have the potential to produce economic benefit and therefore meet the criteria for definition and recognition. As a general principle the measurement of current asset investments is at fair value. Using the market value is called **marking to market**. The change in fair value is reported in the income statement (profit and loss account).

9.4.4 Cash

Recognising cash is no problem either in the potential for benefit or in the measurement of the asset. The amount is known either by counting cash in hand or by looking at a statement from the bank which is holding the business bank account. The potential benefit lies in making use of the cash in future to buy fixed assets or to contribute to the working capital cycle so that the business earns a profit. In the meantime, cash which is surplus to immediate requirements should be deposited in such a way that it is earning interest. Where a company has substantial cash balances there should be indications in the income statement (profit and loss account) that investment income has been earned, to provide a benefit to the business.

Activity 9.2	*This section has covered in some detail the characteristics of various groups of current assets. Before reading the next section, write down what information you would expect to see, in respect of these groups of assets, in the statement of financial position (balance sheet) and notes to the accounts. Then read the section and consider similarities to, or differences from, the views given there.*

9.5 Users' needs for information

Investors have an interest in knowing that current assets are not overstated. If the assets are overstated the profit of the business will be overstated (see the explanation in Chapter 4, using the accounting equation). They will want to know particularly whether there has been allowance for inventories of goods which may not lead to sales and whether there has been allowance for customers who may not be able to pay the debts shown as due to the business. They may also want the reassurance that the auditors have established the existence of all the current assets, particularly ensuring that a very portable asset such as cash is where it ought to be in the ownership of the company.

The needs of users do not stop with the investors. The trade creditors who supply goods and services to the business are strongly reliant on the working capital cycle for their eventual payment. Employees look for their salaries and wages from the cash generated during the working capital cycle. They want to know that the cash will be there on the day it is required, rather than being tied up in inventories or receivables (debtors) awaiting release as cash. Tax collecting authorities, such as HMRC, have definite dates on which payments are required. All these persons have an interest in the working capital of the business and how it is managed. The concern of creditors and employees is primarily with the flow of cash and its availability on the day required. That information will not appear in the statement of financial position (balance sheet) but there will be some indications of flow in the statement of cash flows (outlined in Chapter 3).

9.6 Information provided in the financial statements

In Chapter 7 the statement of financial position (balance sheet) of Safe and Sure plc contained three lines relating to current assets:

	Notes	Year 7 £m	Year 6 £m
Current assets			
Inventories (stocks)	5	266	243
Amounts receivable (debtors)	6	1,469	1,347
Six-month deposits		20	–
Cash and cash equivalents		1,053	905
Total current assets		2,808	2,495

There is more information provided in the notes to the statement of financial position (balance sheet).

9.6.1 Details in notes

There are two relevant notes, of which note 5 deals with inventories and note 6 with receivables (debtors):

Note 5	Year 7 £m	Year 6 £m
Inventories (stocks)		
Raw materials	62	54
Work in progress	19	10
Finished products	185	179
	266	243

This company is a service company so it is not surprising that inventories do not figure prominently in the overall collection of current assets. It is perhaps more surprising that there are inventories of finished products, but reading the description of the business shows that there is a Products Division which manufactures special cleaning chemicals under the company name.

The note on receivables (debtors) shows that the main category is trade receivables (debtors) with information to help assess the risks of the asset:

Note 6	Year 7	Year 6
Amounts receivable (debtors)	£m	£m
Trade receivables (trade debtors)	1,333	1,218
Less: provision for impairment of receivables	(52)	(48)
Trade receivables, net	1,281	1,170
Other receivables (debtors)	109	98
Prepayments and accrued income	79	79
	1,469	1,347

The ageing of the Group's year end overdue receivables, against which no provision has been made, is as follows:

	Year 7	Year 6
	£m	£m
Not impaired		
Less than 3 months	194	121
3 to 6 months	3	3
Over 6 months	1	–
	198	124

The individually impaired receivables relate to customers in unexpectedly difficult circumstances. The overdue receivables against which no provision has been made relate to a number of customers for whom there is no recent history of default and no other indication that settlement will not be forthcoming.

The carrying amounts of the Group's receivables are denominated in the following currencies:

	Year 7	Year 6
	£m	£m
Sterling	808	794
US Dollar	336	291
Euro	272	255
Other	53	34
	1,469	1,374

Movements in the Group's provision for impairment of trade receivables are as follows:

	Year 7	Year 6
	£m	£m
At 1 January	48	49
(Released)/charged to income statement	3	(1)
Net write off of uncollectible receivables	1	–
At 31 December	52	48

Amounts charged to the income statement are included within administrative expenses. The other classes of receivables do not contain impaired assets.

There is no indication of the nature of 'other receivables (debtors)'. It could indicate employees who have received loans or advances of salaries. It could indicate a loan to a company which has trading links with the group but is not a full subsidiary. Prepayments are expenses paid in advance of gaining the benefit, as explained in the previous section of this chapter.

9.6.2 Accounting policy

It will be shown later in this chapter that the valuation of inventories is a matter of potential variation from one person to the next, so it is important to know that the company has followed an acceptable policy in its valuation of inventories. The accounting policy note of Safe and Sure provides that confirmation (see Exhibit 9.1).

Exhibit 9.1
Accounting policy note

> **Safe and Sure plc Accounting policy**
>
> Inventories (stocks and work in progress) are stated at the lower of cost and net realisable value, using the first in first out principle. Cost includes all direct expenditure and related overheads incurred in bringing the inventories to their present condition and location.

For the moment you will have to accept that this form of wording represents standard practice, but each phrase will be explained later in the chapter.

9.6.3 Strategic report

The strategic report of Safe and Sure comments as follows:

The group's businesses are structured to utilise as little fixed and working capital as is consistent with the profit and earnings growth objective in order to produce a high cash flow.

The focus on **working capital** is perhaps an indication of the importance seen in explaining how the company manages its current assets and current liabilities. It also shows that for this business the high cash flow is planned and is not an accident of events.

9.6.4 Analyst's view

DAVID WILSON *comments: This is a service business and so holds inventories of goods to be used in the service process. The note to the statement of financial position (balance sheet) does not actually say what the inventories are, so I asked when I made my visit. They tell me the raw materials are inventories of cleaning materials and chemicals for processes such as disinfecting. My main concern is to be assured that there is nothing in the inventories which could carry a risk of losing value through obsolescence or deterioration. There is not much problem of that with cleaning materials. The finished goods took me by surprise until I found out that there is a Products Division. It was actually the cleaning products that I knew best from years ago but I thought they had moved entirely into service contracts.*

In any event, inventories are not all that important for this company. The receivables (debtors) amount is much larger. I know they have a relatively low risk of bad debts because most customers pay in advance for their contracts.

When I started as an analyst I worked alongside someone who had 20 years' experience. He told me that he had always used what he called 'the 10% test' when looking at inventories (stocks) and receivables (debtors) in a statement of financial position (balance sheet). He worked out what effect a 10% error in the inventories or receivables would have on the profit before tax. In this case a 10% error in inventories would be £27m. The profit from operations is £1,952m. A difference of £27m on £1,952m is 1.4%. An error of 1.4% in profit would not have a significant impact on the view of most investors. So in this company inventories is not a matter which needs time taken for questions. On the other hand, a 10% error in receivables (debtors) would be £147m. That is 7.5% of profit from operations. So receivables (debtors) are worth more attention. The extended note explaining the areas of risk is useful. If this were a company I didn't know, I would ask about the quality of the asset and the type of customer who is given credit. In fact I do know the answer here. The finance director told me that when I met him. The receivables (debtors) are largely public sector bodies such as local authorities and hospitals who insist on paying after the work has been done to their satisfaction. There could be a risk of non-payment because of shoddy work but there is little risk of non-payment through default.

The final point to note in relation to current assets is that this company is a cash-generating business. I looked at the statement of cash flows for the past five years which shows that the group builds up cash balances, buys another company, and then generates even more cash. I suppose that can't go on for ever but there are no signs of problems at present.

LEONA: *I told you I would be looking for admissions of how much you rely on the auditor without knowing it. Your '10% test' is a very rough-and-ready example of the ratio analysis we carry out on a systematic basis as part of our analytical review of the financial statements. Maybe one day I'll tell you more about that. We have quite a long list of ratios which we calculate. We also look at interrelationships between ratios and relative changes in one compared with another.*

It is also an application of what we call 'materiality'. When we see an asset – in this case it is receivables (debtors) – where an error in estimation of the asset value could cause a serious impact on profit, we identify that as a matter for special attention. We would probably spend more time on receivables (debtors) than on inventories in our audit of this company but we would target the risk-related aspects of what is reported about each asset. For receivables (debtors) it is the risk of non-payment through either disputed debts or lack of funds. For inventories it is the risk of obsolescence or similar loss which is not covered by insurance.

Have you decided on how the company's information on current assets meets the list of desirable qualitative characteristics?

DAVID: *You're trying to get me to admit that I need the auditors. Reliability is in the auditors' hands as far as the numbers go, but I place a lot of reliance on my assessment of the qualities of senior management when I meet them. You can't audit that kind of feeling. It's all a matter of chemistry. Also, the main current asset is receivables (debtors) and I know they are reliable because the finance director told me what class of customer was involved. I didn't need the auditors for that. Relevance probably scores about eight out of ten because there aren't any complications here with unusual types of inventories. Faithful representation and neutrality are something I leave to the auditors for now but I'll be asking questions next year if the information in the financial statements turns out not to be neutral. Prudence, I know, is built into all aspects of accounting which uses historical cost measures. That sometimes works against relevance. Completeness is not a problem for current assets. The company is unlikely to leave anything out. They are more likely to include too much. I do expect the auditor to check that the assets are there. Comparability is a matter of presentation. This company has a five-year summary elsewhere in the annual report and gives the previous year's amounts in the financial statements. As for understandability, I like to think that I can see my way around figures for inventories, receivables (debtors) and cash. I usually get the answers I want when I phone the financial controller.*

LEONA: *But don't you see that by admitting that you have to ask more questions to help you understand the amounts, there must be some further explanations which the company could give in the annual report so that your understanding may be shared by others?*

DAVID: *My fund manager colleagues would say that only the professional investors have the expertise. Even if more information were reported by companies, only the professionals would know how to use it.*

9.7 Measurement and recording

Inventories (stocks) of raw materials, work in progress and finished goods are measured at the *lower* of **cost** and **net realisable value**.[4] Any profit that might arise cannot be known until the inventories are used or sold. It is therefore prudent to value at cost and not anticipate profit. Accounts receivable (debtors) are measured at selling price because the related profit is earned when the sale is made and not when the credit customer chooses to pay. The selling price is also the **fair value** of the receivable.

The next three sections look at issues of measurement and recording, in relation to inventories, receivables (debtors) and current asset investments, which are essential to an understanding of how much variability and uncertainty lies behind the apparent confidence of the numbers reported in financial statements.

9.8 Inventories (stocks) of raw materials and finished goods

The analysis of transactions involving inventories of raw materials, work in progress and finished goods has been explained in detail in Chapter 6 and will not be repeated here. This section examines the problems created by the general rule that inventories must be valued at the lower of cost and net realisable value. This rule is a consequence of the **prudence** concept, based on not anticipating a sale until the goods are delivered to the customer.

Net realisable value means the estimated selling price in the ordinary course of business less the estimated costs of completion and the estimated costs necessary to make the sale. For example, damaged inventories are sold at auction for £10,000. The auctioneer charges selling commission of 20% which is £2,000. The amount received by the seller is £8,000, called the net realisable value.

Definition	**Net realisable value** is the estimated selling price in the ordinary course of business less the estimated costs of completion and the estimated costs necessary to make the sale.[5]

This section covers first of all the accounting equation in relation to the rule. It then looks at the meaning of cost and the allocation of overhead costs. Various specific models to deal with changing input prices are then discussed and the section concludes with the rules to be applied in financial reporting.

9.8.1 Lower of cost and net realisable value

Consider the example of a container of coffee beans purchased by a coffee manufacturer at a cost of £1,000. The beans are held for three months up to the date of the financial year-end. During that time there is a fall in the world price of coffee beans and the container of coffee beans would sell for only £800 in the market.

When the asset is acquired, the impact on the accounting equation is an increase of £1,000 in the asset of inventories and a decrease of £1,000 in the asset of cash.

Assets ↑↓	–	Liabilities	=	Ownership interest
+ £1,000 inventories – £1,000 cash				

At the end of the year the asset is found to be worth £800 and the ownership interest is reduced because the asset has fallen in value. The asset is reduced by £200 and an expense of loss of value in inventories value is reported in the income statement (profit and loss account).

Assets ↓	–	Liabilities	=	Ownership interest ↓
– £200 inventories				**– £200 expense**

If a business fails to report a fall in the value of the asset of inventories, the profit of the period will be overstated.

Where there are separate categories of inventories the rule of 'lower of cost and net realisable value' must be applied to each category separately. Suppose, for example, there is an inventory (stock) of paper at a cost of £2,000 with a net realisable value of £2,300 and an inventory (stock) of pens with a cost of £1,800 and a net realisable value of £1,400. The lower amount must be taken in each case, giving a value of £3,400 for inventories (calculated as £2,000 plus £1,400).

9.8.2   Meaning of cost

The **cost** of inventories comprises all costs of purchase, costs of conversion and other costs incurred in bringing the inventories to their present location and condition.[6] This expenditure will include not only the cost of purchase but also costs of converting raw materials into finished goods or services.

Costs of purchase include the price charged by the supplier, plus transport and handling costs, plus import duties and less discounts and subsidies.[7] Costs of conversion include items readily identifiable with the product, such as labour, expenses and subcontractors' costs directly related to the product. They also include production overheads and any other overheads directly related to bringing the product or service to its present condition and location. **Production overheads** are items such as depreciation of machines, service costs, rental paid for a factory, wages paid to supervisory and support staff, costs of stores control and insurance of production facilities.

Example

Take the example of a business which purchases 10 wooden furniture units for conversion to a customer's specification for installation in a hotel. The units cost £200 each and the labour cost of converting them is £100 each. Production overheads for the period are fixed at £3,500. Two units remain unsold at the end of the period. These two units will be recorded in the statement of financial position (balance sheet) at £1,300, calculated as £650 each (materials cost of £200 plus labour cost of £100 plus a share of the production overheads at £350 per item).

That was easy because there were 10 identical units to take equal shares of the production overheads. But suppose they had all been different and required different amounts of labour? Would it have been fair to share the overheads equally? Probably not. The problems of sharing out production overhead costs create a chapter in themselves and are studied further as part of management accounting. You need to be aware, in reading published accounting information, that there is considerable scope for discretion to be exercised by management in the allocation of overheads between completed goods and goods held in inventories. The general risk of overstatement of assets applies here. If the asset is overstated by having too much production overhead allocated, the profit of the period is also overstated because it is not bearing the share of production overheads which it should.

9.8.3 Costs when input prices are changing

One very tiresome problem faced by the accounts department in its record keeping is that suppliers change their prices from time to time. Goods held in store may have arrived at different times and at different unit prices. How does the accounts department decide on the unit price to be charged to each job when all the materials look the same once they are taken into store?

In some cases it may be possible to label the materials as they arrive so that they can be identified with the appropriate unit price. That is a very time-consuming process and would only be used for high-value low-volume items of materials. In other cases a convenient method is needed which gives an answer that is useful and approximately close to the true price of the units used. Some possibilities are shown in Table 9.1 using three options – first in first out (FIFO), last in first out (LIFO) and average cost. In each case, Table 9.1 takes a very simple approach, not complicated by having inventory at the start of the period. In real life the calculations can be even more tricky.

Table 9.1
Pricing the issue of goods to production

There are three parts to this illustration. Part (a) contains a table setting out the data to be used in the calculation. Part (b) defines the three bases of calculation. Part (c) uses the data from part (a) to illustrate each of the three bases.

(a) Data

Date	Received	Unit price	Price paid	Issued to production
	Units	£	£	Units
1 June	100	20	2,000	–
20 June	50	22	1,100	–
24 June	–	–	–	60
28 June	–	–	–	70
Total	150		3,100	130

(b) Bases of calculation
First in first out (FIFO)
Assume that the goods which arrived first are issued first.

Last in first out (LIFO)
Assume that the goods which arrived last are issued first.

Average cost
Assume that all goods are issued at the average price of the inventories held.

(c) Calculations

Basis	Date	Quantity and unit price	Issued to production £	Held in inventories £	Total £
FIFO					
	24 June	60 units at £20	1,200		
	28 June	40 units at £20			
		30 units at £22	1,460		
	30 June	20 units at £22		440	
Total			2,660	440	3,100
LIFO					
	24 June	50 units at £22	1,300		
		10 units at £20			
	28 June	70 units at £20	1,400		
	30 June	20 units at £20		400	
Total			2,700	400	3,100
Average					
	24 June	60 units at *£20.67	1,240		
	28 June	70 units at *£20.67	1,447		
	30 June	20 units at *£20.67		413	
Total			2,687	413	3,100

Note: * Weighted average [(100 × 20) + (50 × 22)]/150 = £20.67.

9.8.4　Approximation when dates are not recorded

In business there may not be time to keep the detailed records shown in the calculations in Table 9.1. In such cases the sales volume is known in total but the dates of sales are not recorded. The calculation then uses the best approximation available, which usually means working through the costs from the oldest date, for FIFO, or the most recent date, for LIFO, without attempting to match the various batches bought and sold during the year.

9.8.5　Choice of FIFO, LIFO or average cost

Look at table (c) of Table 9.1 and compare it with table (a) of that table. You will see from table (a) that the total amount spent on materials during the month was £3,100. You will see from table (c) that the total of the cost of goods issued to production, plus the cost of unsold goods, is always £3,100 irrespective of which approach is taken. All that differs is the allocation between goods used in production and goods remaining unsold. Cost can never be gained or lost in total because of a particular allocation process, provided the process is used consistently over time. The FIFO approach suffers the disadvantage of matching outdated costs against current revenue. The LIFO approach improves on FIFO by matching the most recent costs against revenue, but at the expense of an inventory value which becomes increasingly out of date. The average cost lies between the two and becomes more intricate to recalculate as more items come into inventory. In practice, the choice for internal reporting in management accounting is a matter of finding the best method for the purpose.

There is an effect on profit of the year which may influence management choice. When prices are rising and inventories volumes are steady or increasing, FIFO gives a lower cost of sales and so a higher profit than LIFO. If there were no regulations, companies that wished to show high profits (perhaps to impress investors buying shares in the company) might prefer FIFO. Companies that wished to show lower profits (perhaps to reduce tax bills) might prefer LIFO.

The IASB standard IAS 2 prohibits the use of LIFO. In the UK the tax authorities will not accept LIFO valuation. In the USA the LIFO method of valuation is permitted. Investors need to read the accounting policy note in the financial statements to find which approach a company has used.

Activity 9.3	Look back to Table 9.1 and write your own table of data for goods received, unit price, price paid and goods issued to production. Create calculations of cost of goods sold, using the various models in Table 9.1 (FIFO, LIFO and average price). Check that the value of goods issued to production, plus the value of goods held in stock, will always add up to the same answer in total.

9.9 Receivables (debtors)

The measurement of receivables (debtors) requires attention to bad and doubtful debts. A debt is described as a **bad debt** when there is no further hope of the customer paying the amount owed. This might be due to the customer being declared bankrupt or else disappearing without trace. If the customer is known to be in difficulties or there is some dispute over the amount owed, the debt is described as a **doubtful debt**. The company still hopes to recover the cash owed but realistically has some doubt. Evidence of doubtful debts may be seen in slow payment, partial payments, the need for several reminders or even rumours in the business community. A company will usually analyse the age of its debts to help identify those which may be doubtful.

The asset of accounts receivable is reported in two parts. The first part is the full recorded value of accounts receivable and the second part is a deduction for the doubtful debts. This deduction has a range of different names including:

● provision for doubtful debts
● provision for doubtful receivables
● allowance for uncollectible accounts
● valuation allowance for doubtful debts.

In this book we use 'provision for doubtful debts' which is familiar in the UK.

Example

At the end of Year 1 the Garden Pond Company has a statement of financial position (balance sheet) comprising £2,000 receivables (debtors), £7,000 other assets and £9,000 ownership interest that consists of £1,800 ownership interest at the start of the period and £7,200 profit of the period. On the date of the financial year-end the manager of the company reviews the receivables (debtors) list and decides that debts amounting to £200 are doubtful because there are rumours of a customer not paying other suppliers in the trade. The statement of financial position (balance sheet) at the end of

Table 9.2

Spreadsheet to analyse the effect of provision for doubtful debts at the end of Year 1, using the accounting equation

Date	Transaction or event	Assets			Ownership interest	
Year 1		Receivables (debtors)	Provision for doubtful debts	Other assets	Ownership interest at start	Profit of the period
		£	£	£	£	£
Dec. 31	Statement of financial position (balance sheet) first draft	2,000		7,000	1,800	7,200
Dec. 31	Recognition of doubtful debts		(200)			(200)
Dec. 31	Revised statement of financial position (balance sheet)	2,000	(200)	7,000	1,800	7,000

Year 1 is amended to show that the asset is of lower value than was thought and the ownership interest has consequently diminished.

Table 9.2 shows the spreadsheet for analysis set out to reflect the accounting equation. The new column is the one headed **provision for doubtful debts**. This is included in the assets section because it tells the user more about the asset of receivables (debtors), although it is the negative part of the asset. It causes some confusion to those who meet it for the first time because anything called a provision is usually reported under the heading of liabilities. However, on grounds of usefulness to readers and relevance to the provision of information about the asset, the provision for doubtful debts has special treatment in being included as a negative aspect within the asset section of the statement of financial position (balance sheet).

It is quite a difficult matter for a company to be prudent in expressing doubt about a debtor while still pursuing the non-payer with a view to collection of the debt. To remove the debt from the record would be to admit defeat. Even to show a separate provision among the liability headings might lead other customers to think, 'Why not me also?' However, companies are expected to provide information about impairment of assets, as indicated in the case study of Safe and Sure.

The statement of financial position (balance sheet) after incorporating a provision for the doubtful debt would appear as in Table 9.3.

Table 9.3

Statement of financial position (balance sheet) of Garden Pond Company showing the presentation of information on doubtful debts

Garden Pond Company Statement of financial position (balance sheet) at 31 December Year 1	£	£
Other assets		7,000
Receivables (debtors)	2,000	
Less: provision for doubtful debts	(200)	
		1,800
		8,800
Ownership interest at the start of the year		1,800
Profit of the year		7,000
		8,800

There is no single method of calculating the provision for doubtful debts. Some companies consider separately the amount owed by each customer. To economise on time, most companies use previous experience to estimate a percentage of total receivables (debtors). A mixture of approaches could be used, with known problems being identified separately and a general percentage being applied to the rest.

9.9.1 Change in a provision

During Year 2 matters take an upward turn and in July the customer who was showing signs of financial distress manages to pay the amount of £200 owed. The effect on the accounting equation is that the asset of cash is increased and the asset of debtor is reduced by £200. The provision for doubtful debts is now no longer required and could be transferred back to the income statement (profit and loss account), but in practice it tends to be left for tidying up at the end of the year.

The business continues and at the end of Year 2 the receivables (debtors) amount to £2,500. A review of the list of receivables (debtors) causes considerable doubt regarding an amount of £350. It is decided to create a new provision of £350. The old provision of £200 related to last year's receivables (debtors) and is no longer required.

Table 9.4 shows the spreadsheet at the end of Year 2, before and after recording the new provision for doubtful debts. It is assumed that the other assets have grown to £10,000 and there is a profit of £3,500 before amending the provision for doubtful debts.

The income statement (profit and loss account) could show two separate entries, one being £200 increase in ownership interest and the other being £350 decrease in ownership interest. It is rather cumbersome in that form and most enterprises would report as an expense, in the income statement (profit and loss account), the single line:

Increase in provision for doubtful debts   £150

Table 9.4
Spreadsheet to analyse the effect of provision for doubtful debts at the end of Year 2, using the accounting equation

Date	Transaction or event	Assets			Ownership	
Year 2		Receivables (debtors)	Provision for doubtful debts	Other assets	Ownership interest at start	Profit of the period
		£	£	£	£	£
Dec. 31	Statement of financial position (balance sheet) first draft	2,500	(200)	10,000	8,800	3,500
Dec. 31	Elimination of provision no longer required		200			200
Dec. 31	Creation of new provision		(350)			(350)
Dec. 31	Revised statement of financial position (balance sheet)	2,500	(350)	10,000	8,800	3,350

9.10 Prepayments

Prepayments arise when an item of expense is paid in advance of the benefit being received. A common example is the payment of an insurance premium. The payment is made in advance for the year ahead and the benefit is gradually used up as the

Table 9.5

Spreadsheet recording prepayment of insurance at the financial year-end date

Date	Transaction or event	Assets		Ownership interest
Year 2		Cash £	Prepayment £	Expense £
Oct. 1	Payment of premium	(1,200)		(1,200)
Dec. 31	Identification of asset remaining as prepayment		900	900
	Total	(1,200)	900	(300)

year goes along. The statement of financial position (balance sheet) recognises the unexpired portion of the insurance premium as an asset, while the income statement (profit and loss account) reports the amount consumed during the period.

Example

On 1 October Year 1 a company paid £1,200 for one year's vehicle insurance. At the financial year-end date of 31 December there have been three months' benefit used up and there is a nine-month benefit yet to come. The transactions relating to insurance would be reported as in Table 9.5.

The effect of identifying the asset is to reduce the expense of the period from £1,200 to £300 and to hold the remaining £900 as a benefit for the next accounting period. In Year 2 the amount of £900 will be transferred from the prepayment column to the expense column, so that the decrease in the ownership interest is reported in the period in which it occurs.

9.11 Revenue recognition

The sale of goods and services creates **revenue** for the business. Sometimes that revenue is referred to as **sales** or **turnover**. The term revenue may also be applied to rents received from letting out property, or interest received on investments made. In the conceptual frameworks of various countries, different views are held of the exact meaning and extent of the word *revenue*. The IASB defines revenue in terms of equity (ownership interest).

Definition

Revenue is income arising in the course of an entity's ordinary activities. **Income** is defined as 'increases in assets or decreases in liabilities that result in increases in equity, other than those relating to contributions from holders of equity claims'.[8]

The main problem in recognition of revenue lies in the timing. Assets are recognised at a point in time but revenue is created over a period of time. What are the rules for deciding on the time period for which revenue should be reported? One suggestion has been that the **critical event** is the important factor.[9] When goods are produced or services are carried out, there is one part of the process which is critical to providing sufficient reassurance that the revenue has been earned by the efforts of the enterprise. For the sale of goods the point of delivery to the customer is the usual critical event which determines the date of revenue recognition. For a contract of service, the critical event is the performance of the service.

9.11.1 Contract revenue

Where the service extends over more than one time period, the revenue may be split over the time periods involved. That may happen in a civil engineering or a building contract. In each year of the contract a portion of the revenue will be matched against costs of the period so as to report a portion of profit.

Take the example of a two-year bridge-building contract. The contract price is £60m. Two-thirds of the work has been completed in Year 1 and it is expected that the remainder will be completed in Year 2. The costs incurred in Year 1 are £34m and the costs expected for Year 2 are £17m.

The income statement (profit and loss account) of the business for Year 1 will report, in respect of this contract, turnover of £40m less costs of £34m giving profit of £6m. This gives a fair representation of the profit earned by the activity of the year (as two-thirds of the total). An independent expert, in this case an engineer, would confirm that the work had been completed satisfactorily to date. The effect on the accounting equation would be:

Assets ↓↑	–	Liabilities	=	Ownership interest ↑
+ £40m − £34m				+ £6m

Reporting contract revenue of £40m in Year 1 will increase the ownership interest by £40m. A matching asset will be reported, representing the value of the contract at that stage. The value of £40m shown for the construction contract represents the aggregate amount of costs incurred plus recognised profits to date.

In the income statement (profit and loss account) the expenses of £34m are reported in the usual way and a profit of £6m results. All being well, the income statement (profit and loss account) of Year 2 will report the remaining £20m of revenue minus £17m of expenses, leaving a profit of £3m. Over the two years the total profit of £9m will be reported.

Users of accounting information need to pay particular attention to contract revenue in a business and ask some careful questions. Has prudence been exercised in deciding what portion of revenue to report? Is there a risk that the future costs will escalate and there will be an overall loss? They should look carefully at the provisions section of the statement of financial position (balance sheet) (see Chapter 11).

Where the customer has paid money in advance as an instalment towards the final contract price, the effect on the accounting equation is to increase the asset of cash and create a liability towards the customer. These amounts received in advance from customers may be described as 'progress billings', 'payments on account', or 'payments in advance'. There is a liability because the business has an obligation to repay the customer if the contract is not completed on time or on specification. Although it might be expected that the liability towards the customer would appear in the current liabilities section of the statement of financial position (balance sheet), that does not happen. The liability in respect of payments made in advance is deducted from the value of the contract and the resulting net figure is reported as *construction contracts* in the current assets section of the statement of financial position (balance sheet). That may mean that, at first glance at the statement of financial position (balance sheet), the reader does not realise the true size of the contract being undertaken for the customer. There is no guarantee that any better information will be found anywhere else in the financial statements, because turnover is aggregated for all activities. For the analyst as an expert user, construction contracts (long-term contracts) require a great deal of careful questioning if the underlying details are to be understood.

9.11.2   A continuing debate

There are problems in revenue recognition that have continued to be debated. Consider three examples. In the first, a film production company sells a programme to a television company which agrees to pay royalties every time the programme is broadcast. In the second, a farmer sells a cow to a neighbour in return for five sheep. In the third, a mobile phone company charges customers a start-up fee that is 24 times the monthly rental and service charge. For many years there was no specific accounting standard to cover any of these situations. One approach to each is to ask, 'Has the revenue been earned?' The companies would all answer, 'Yes, we have completed our side of the transaction.' So perhaps revenue should be recognised in all three cases. Another approach is to ask, 'Are there any risks related to recognising revenue?' The answer is, 'Yes – the programme may never be broadcast; we are not sure about the exchange values between cows and sheep; and the telephone company may not be able to provide the service for the long period implied by the high initial charge.' So perhaps the revenue should not be reported until the risks are diminished. Both views have been applied, with the result that there has been some lack of clarity and comparability as new types of business have emerged. It is always necessary to pay careful attention to the accounting policy on revenue recognition.

IFRS 15, effective from January 2017, establishes a comprehensive framework for determining when to recognise revenue and how much revenue to recognise. It focuses on reporting revenue when performance obligations have been carried out. The core principle in that framework is that a company should recognise revenue to depict the transfer of promised goods or services to the customer in an amount that reflects the consideration to which the company expects to be entitled in exchange for those goods or services. 'Consideration' is usually received in the form of cash or a promise of cash. The standard sets out five steps:

Step 1   Identify the contract(s) with the customer.

Step 2   Identify the performance obligations in the contract. Performance obligations are promises in a contract to transfer to a customer goods or services that are distinct.

Step 3   Determine the transaction price.

Step 4   Allocate the transaction price to each performance obligation within the contract, using the relative stand-alone selling prices of each distinct good or service.

Step 5   Recognise revenue when a performance obligation is satisfied.

9.12   Summary

- A **current asset** is an asset that satisfies any of the following criteria:
  - (a) it is expected to be realised in, or is intended for sale or consumption in, the entity's normal operating cycle;
  - (b) it is held primarily for the purpose of being traded;
  - (c) it is expected to be realised within 12 months after the date of the financial year-end;
  - (d) it is cash or a cash equivalent.

- **Working capital** is the amount which a business must provide to finance the current assets of a business, to the extent that these are not covered by current liabilities. It is calculated by deducting current liabilities from current assets.

- Inventories (stocks), receivables (debtors), investments and cash are commonly **recognised** in a balance sheet. If there is doubt attached to the economic benefit which creates the asset and to the measurement, then this is recognised by making a **provision** such as the provision for doubtful debts.
- Users need information about the working capital of the business to judge whether it is suitable to support the activities of the business. Information provided to help users includes: detailed notes of current assets and current liabilities; notes of accounting policy describing the valuation of current assets; and a discussion of working capital management in the strategic report.
- **Inventories** (stocks) are measured at the lower of cost and net realisable value.
- Receivables (debtors) are measured at the amount receivable on settlement less any provision for doubtful debts.
- **Prepayments** are amounts paid in advance for benefits expected. Prepayments are assets until the benefit is used up. The amount is then transferred from an asset to an expense.
- **Revenue** is income arising in the course of an entity's ordinary activities. **Income** is increases in assets or decreases in liabilities that result in increases in equity, other than those relating to contributions from equity participants.
- If revenues are earned over more than one time period (e.g. on long-term contracts) then the revenue is allocated across time periods in proportion to the amount of work completed.

QUESTIONS

The Questions section of each chapter has three types of question. 'Test your understanding' questions to help you review your reading are in the 'A' series of questions. You will find the answers to these by reading and thinking about the material in the book. 'Application' questions to test your ability to apply technical skills are in the 'B' series of questions. Questions requiring you to show skills in problem solving and evaluation are in the 'C' series of questions. A letter [S] indicates that there is a solution at the end of the book. Other solutions are provided in the Instructor's Manual, where there are further questions parallel to those set out here.

A   Test your understanding

A9.1   What is the definition of a current asset? (Section 9.2)

A9.2   What is the working capital cycle? (Section 9.3)

A9.3   What are the features of raw materials, work in progress and finished goods which justify their recognition in a balance sheet? (Section 9.4.1)

A9.4   What information do users need about current assets? (Section 9.5)

A9.5   What is meant by FIFO, LIFO and the average cost method of pricing issues of goods? (Section 9.8.3)

A9.6   How is a provision for doubtful debts decided upon? (Section 9.9)

A9.7   What is a prepayment? (Section 9.10)

A9.8   What is meant by 'revenue recognition'? (Section 9.11)

A9.9   Why are there problems with revenue recognition? (Section 9.11.2)

A9.10 [S] The Sycamore Company has inventories which include the following four items:

Description	Purchase cost	Selling price	Cost of selling
	£	£	£
Engine	6,500	8,250	350
Chassis	2,000	1,800	200
Frame	4,800	4,900	300

What amount should be reported as total inventory in respect of these three items?

A9.11 [S] On reviewing the company's financial statements, the company accountant discovers that items of year-end inventory of goods which cost £18,000 have been omitted from the record. What will be the effect on the income statement (profit and loss account) and the statement of financial position (balance sheet) when this omission is rectified?

A9.12 [S] On reviewing the financial statements, the company accountant discovers that an amount of £154,000 owed by a customer will be irrecoverable because the customer has fled the country. What will be the effect on the income statement (profit and loss account) and the statement of financial position (balance sheet) when this event is recognised?

B   Application

B9.1 [S]

During its first month of operations, a business made purchases and sales as shown in the table below:

Date	Number of units purchased	Unit cost	Number of units sold
Jan. 5	100	£1.00	
Jan. 10			50
Jan. 15	200	£1.10	
Jan. 17			150
Jan. 24	300	£1.15	
Jan. 30			200

All sales were made at £2 each.

Required

Calculate the profit for the month and the stock value held at the end of the month using:

(a) the FIFO approach to the issue of units for sale, where:
   (i) the calculation is carried out at the date of sale; and
   (ii) the calculation is carried out at the end of the month without regard for the date of sale; and
(b) the LIFO approach to the issue of units for sale, where:
   (i) the calculation is carried out at the date of sale; and
   (ii) the calculation is carried out at the end of the month without regard for the date of sale; and
(c) the average-cost approach to the issue of units for sale, making the calculation at the end of the month without regard for the date of sale.

B9.2 [S]

A company has a stock of goods consisting of four different groups of items. The cost and net realisable value of each group is shown in the table below.

Group of items	Cost	Net realisable value
	£	£
A	1,000	1,400
B	1,000	800
C	2,100	1,900
D	3,000	3,100

Required

Calculate the amount to be shown as the value of the company's stock.

B9.3

At the end of Year 3 the Bed Company has a statement of financial position (balance sheet) comprising £3,000 receivables (debtors), £8,000 other assets and £11,000 ownership interest, consisting of £2,000 ownership interest at the start of the period and £9,000 profit of the period. On the date of the financial year-end the manager of the company reviews the receivables (debtors) list and decides that debts amounting to £450 are doubtful because the customers have not replied to repeated requests for payment.

Required

(a) Prepare an accounting equation spreadsheet to show the effect of the provision. (See Table 9.2 for an illustration.)

(b) Show the statement of financial position (balance sheet) information. (See Table 9.3 for an illustration.)

B9.4

The Bed Company continues trading during Year 4. The statement of financial position (balance sheet) at the end of Year 4, in its first draft, showed receivables (debtors) as £4,850 and the provision for doubtful debts unchanged from Year 3 at £450. Enquiry showed that during Year 4 some of the receivables (debtors) at the end of Year 3 had been confirmed as bad. They amounted to £250 but nothing had yet been recorded. The management wish to make the provision £550 at the end of Year 4. Other assets amount to £12,000, ownership interest at the start of Year 4 is £10,550 and the profit is £5,750.

Required

Prepare an accounting equation spreadsheet to show the effect of the bad debt being recognised and of the decision to make a provision at the end of Year 4. (See Table 9.4 for an illustration.)

B9.5

On 1 December Year 1 a company paid £2,400 as an insurance premium to give accident cover for the 12 months ahead. The accounting year-end is 31 December.

Required

Prepare an accounting equation spreadsheet to show the effect of the prepayment in the year ended 31 December Year 1.

C   Problem solving and evaluation

C9.1

A fire destroyed a company's detailed stock records and much of the merchandise held in stock. The company accountant was able to discover that stock at the beginning of the period was £40,000, purchases up to the date of the fire were £250,000, and sales up to the date of the fire were £400,000. In past periods, the company has earned a gross profit of 35% of sales.

Required

Calculate the cost of the stock destroyed by the fire.

C9.2

It is the policy of Seaton Ltd to make provision for doubtful debts at a rate of 10% per annum on all debtor balances at the end of the year, after deducting any known bad debts at the same date. The following table sets out the total receivables (debtors) as shown by the accounting records and known bad debts to be deducted from that total. There is no provision at 31 December Year 0.

Year-end	Debtor balances	Known bad debts
	£	£
31 Dec. Year 1	30,000	2,000
31 Dec. Year 2	35,000	3,000
31 Dec. Year 3	32,000	1,500
31 Dec. Year 4	29,000	1,000

Required

(a) Calculate the total expense in the income statement (profit and loss account) in respect of bad and doubtful debts.

(b) Set out the statement of financial position (balance sheet) information in respect of receivables (debtors) and provision for doubtful debts at each year-end.

Activities for study groups

Turn to the annual report of a listed company which you have used for activities in previous chapters. Find every item of information about current assets. (Start with the financial statements and notes but look also at the strategic report, chief executive's review and other non-regulated information about the company.)

As a group, imagine you are the team of fund managers in a fund management company. You are holding a briefing meeting at which each person explains to the others some feature of the companies in which your fund invests. Today's subject is current assets. Each person should make a short presentation to the rest of the team covering:

1 The nature and significance of current assets in the company.

2 The effect on profit of a 10% error in estimation of any one of the major categories of current asset.

3 The company's comments, if any, on its present investment in working capital and its future intentions.

4 The risks which might attach to the inventories of the company.

5 The liquidity of the company.

6 The trends in current assets since last year (or over five years if a comparative table is provided).

7 The ratio of current assets to current liabilities.

Notes and references

1. IASB (2016), *Conceptual Framework*.
2. IASB (2016), IAS 1, para. 66.
3. IASB (2016), IAS 2 *Inventories*, para. 6.
4. IASB (2016), IAS 2 *Inventories*, para. 9.
5. IASB (2016), IAS 2 *Inventories*, para. 6.
6. IASB (2016), IAS 2 *Inventories*, para. 10.
7. IASB (2016), IAS 2 *Inventories*, para. 11.
8. IASB (2016), *Conceptual Framework*
9. J. H. Myers (1959), 'The critical event and recognition of net profit', *Accounting Review*, 34: 528–32; and ASB (1999), *Statement of Principles for Financial Reporting*, ch. 5, paras 5.33–5.36.

Bookkeeping entries for (a) bad and doubtful debts; and (b) prepayments

The debit and credit recording aspects of inventories of raw materials and finished goods were explained in the supplement to Chapter 6. That leaves, for this supplement, the recording of bad and doubtful debts as a new area where potential care is needed. Prepayments are also illustrated here.

Provision for doubtful debts

The following ledger accounts illustrate the recording of the transactions analysed in section 9.9. Look back to that section for the description and analysis of the transactions. The debit and credit analysis is shown in Table 9.6. So that you will not be confused by additional information, the ledger accounts presented here show only sufficient information to illustrate the recording of transactions relating to doubtful debts. Leona comments on the main features.

Table 9.6
Analysis of debit and credit aspect of each transaction and event

Date		Debit	Credit
Year 1			
End of year	Manager identifies doubtful debts £200	Profit and loss account £200	Provision for doubtful debts £200
Year 2			
July	Customer who was doubtful pays £200 in full	Cash £200	Receivables (debtors) £200
End of year	Manager identifies new provision required £350	Profit and loss account £350	Provision for doubtful debts £350
End of year	Former provision no longer required	Provision for doubtful debts £200	Profit and loss account £200

The ledger accounts required are as follows:

L1	Receivables (debtors)	L3	Cash
L2	Provision for doubtful debts	L4	Profit and loss account

Also required to complete the double entry, but not shown here as a ledger account, is ledger account L5 Ownership interest.

The full list of transactions for the year would be too cumbersome to deal with here, so dots are used to show that the ledger account requires more information for completeness.

L1 Receivables (debtors)

Date	Particulars	Page	Debit	Credit	Balance
Year 1			£	£	£
	. . .		. . .		. . .
Dec. 31	Balance at end of year				2,000
Year 2					
	. . .		. . .		. . .
July	Cash from customer	L3		200	. . .
	. . .		. . .		. . .
Dec. 31	Balance at end of year				2,500

LEONA: *The ledger account for receivables (debtors) has no entries relating to doubtful debts. That is important because although there may be doubts from the viewpoint of the business, the customer still has a duty to pay and should be encouraged by all the usual means. Keeping the full record of amounts due is an important part of ensuring that all assets of the business are looked after.*

L2 Provision for doubtful debts

Date	Particulars	Page	Debit	Credit	Balance
Year 1			£	£	£
Dec. 31	Profit and loss account – new provision	L4		200	(200)
Year 2					
Dec. 31	Profit and loss account – old provision	L4	200		nil
Dec. 31	Profit and loss account – new provision	L4		350	(350)

LEONA: *The provision for doubtful debts is a credit balance because it is the negative part of an asset. It keeps a separate record of doubt about the full value of the asset. A credit entry in the ledger account increases the amount of the provision and a debit entry decreases the amount of the provision.*

L3 Cash

Date	Particulars	Page	Debit	Credit	Balance
Year 2			£	£	£
	. . .		. . .		. . .
July	Cash from debtor	L1	200		
	. . .		. . .		. . .

LEONA: *Receiving cash from the doubtful customer looks like any other transaction receiving cash. It is important that the cash is collected and the debt is removed by receiving the full amount due.*

L4 Profit and loss account

Date	Particulars	Page	Debit	Credit	Balance
Year 1			£	£	£
	. . .		. . .		. . .
Dec. 31	Balance before provision for doubtful debts				(7,200)
Dec. 31	Provision for doubtful debts	L2	200		(7,000)
Dec. 31	Transfer to ownership interest	L5	7,000		nil
Year 2					
	. . .		. . .		. . .
Dec. 31	Balance before provision for doubtful debts				(3,500)
Dec. 31	Removal of provision no longer required	L2		200	(3,700)
Dec. 31	New provision for doubtful debts	L2	350		(3,350)
Dec. 31	Transfer to ownership interest	L5	3,350		nil

LEONA: *In Year 1 of this example the provision is established for the first time so there is one debit entry to establish an expense which decreases the profit (as a part of the ownership interest). In Year 2 of this example the old provision is removed and a new provision created. The overall effect is that the provision increases by £150. Some people would take a shortcut and make one entry of £150 to increase the provision from £200 to £350 but I am not keen on shortcuts. They sometimes lead to disaster. Separate entries make me think carefully about the effect of each.*

Recording a doubtful debt which turns bad

Suppose that in July of Year 2 it was found that the doubtful debt turned totally bad because the customer was declared bankrupt. The effect on the accounting equation is that the asset of debtor is removed. That would normally reduce the ownership interest but on this occasion the impact on ownership interest was anticipated at the end of Year 1 and so the provision for doubtful debts is now used to match the decrease in the asset. The analysis of the transaction would be:

Date	Transaction or event	Debit	Credit
Year 2			
July	Doubtful debt becomes bad	Provision for doubtful debts £200	Receivables (debtors) £200

The consequence of using the provision for doubtful debts is that there is no impact on the income statement (profit and loss account) of Year 2 of a bad debt which was known to be likely at the end of Year 1. However, when the provision for doubtful debts is reviewed at the end of Year 2 there is no reversal of the £200 because that has already been used during the year. The charge of £350 for Year 2 relates solely to the provision for doubt in respect of receivables (debtors) owing money at the end of Year 2.

Prepayments

The prepayment transaction analysed in the chapter was as follows. On 1 October of Year 1 a company paid £1,200 for one year's vehicle insurance. At the financial year-end date of 31 December there have been three months' benefit used up and there is a nine-month benefit yet to come. (See Table 9.7.)

Table 9.7
Analysis of prepayment of insurance, Year 1

Date	Transaction or event	Debit	Credit
Year 1			
Oct. 1	Payment of premium £1,200	Expense (insurance)	Cash
Dec. 31	Identification of asset remaining as a prepayment £900	Asset (prepayment)	Expense (insurance)

Ledger accounts required to record the prepayment are:

L6   Expense of insurance
L7   Prepayment

Not shown, but necessary for completion of the debit and credit record, are:

L3   Cash
L4   Profit and loss account

L6 Expense of insurance					
Date	Particulars	Page	Debit	Credit	Balance
Year 1			£	£	£
Oct. 31	Cash	L3	1,200		1,200
Dec. 31	Prepayment	L7		900	300
Dec. 31	Transfer to profit and loss account	L4		300	nil

LEONA: *Although it is known in October that there will be a balance remaining at the end of the year, it is usually regarded as more convenient to debit the entire payment as an expense of the period initially. The expense is reviewed at the end of the year and £900 is found to be an asset which benefits the future. It is transferred to the asset account for prepayments, leaving only the expense of £300 relating to this period, which is transferred to the income statement (profit and loss account).*

L7 Prepayment

Date	Particulars	Page	Debit	Credit	Balance
Year 1			£	£	£
Oct. 31	Insurance expense prepaid	L6	900		900

LEONA: *The prepayment account is an asset account and therefore the balance remains in the account until the benefit asset is used up. During Year 2 the benefit will disappear and the asset will become an expense. The bookkeeping treatment will be to credit the prepayment account and debit the insurance expense account.*

S Test your understanding

S9.1 Record the transactions of question B9.3 in ledger accounts for L1 Receivables (debtors), L2 Provision for doubtful debts, L3 Cash and L4 Profit and loss account.

S9.2 Record the transactions of question B9.4 in ledger accounts for L1 Receivables (debtors), L2 Provision for doubtful debts, L3 Cash and L4 Profit and loss account.

S9.3 Record the transactions of question B9.5 in ledger accounts for L6 Expense of insurance and L7 Prepayment.

Current liabilities

WHSmith plc: reporting current liabilities

WHSmith plc is one of the UK's leading retailers and is made up of two core businesses – Travel and High Street.

Extracts from Annual report and accounts

About us

WHSmith has a presence in a wide range of locations including airports, train stations, motorway service areas, hospitals and UK high streets, with a growing international business.

Alamy Images/Robert Convery

Principal risks and uncertainties (extract): Key suppliers and supply chain management

Risk/description

The Group has agreements with key suppliers in the UK, Europe and the Far East. The interruption or loss of supply of core category products from these suppliers to our stores may affect our ability to trade. Quality of supply issues may also impact the Group's reputation and impact our ability to trade.

Mitigation

The Group conducts risk assessments of all its key suppliers to identify alternatives and develop contingency plans in the event that any of these key suppliers fail. All suppliers have to comply with the conditions laid out in our Supplier Code of Conduct which covers areas such as production methods, employee working conditions and quality control. The Group has contractual and other arrangements with numerous third parties in support of its business activities. None of these arrangements are individually considered to be essential to the business of the Group.

Ethical trading and human rights

WHSmith is a member of the Ethical Trading Initiative, an alliance of companies, trade unions and NGOs that promote respect for workers' rights around the world.

We are committed to good labour standards and respecting the environment in our supply chain. Our Ethical Trading Code of Conduct and Human Rights Policy states our expectations of our suppliers.

The in-house supplier audit team based in our Far East sourcing office carries out a regular programme of supplier audits to monitor labour standards. They visit each new direct-source supplier factory to assess its performance, ensure that minimum standards are met, and, where necessary, agree an action plan to ensure that the factory is improving its performance. We provide support as suppliers make these improvements, and aim to ensure that all direct source suppliers and Asia-based suppliers of UK agents are audited at least every two years.

Against the background of our rigorous audit programme, we continue to engage with our key suppliers to support them as they seek to improve their performance. This engagement continues to focus on improving worker representation in factories. We are working with our largest 12 suppliers to help improve worker representation and thereby staff satisfaction and retention rates.

All of the participating factories now have an elected worker representative committee in place and WHSmith is working with the factories to ensure that the committees are structured properly to give workers the level of representation they seek. A copy of our Ethical Trading Code of Conduct and Human Rights Policy is available at www.whsmithplc.co.uk/corporate_responsibility/our_policies/.

Note to the balance sheet

Note 16. Trade and other payables – current

£m	2014	2013
Trade payables	95	99
Other tax and social security	24	27
Other creditors	62	56
Accruals and deferred income	49	50
	230	232

Trade and other payables principally comprise amounts outstanding for trade purchases and ongoing costs. The average credit period taken for trade purchases is 60 days (2013: 59 days). The directors consider that the carrying amount of trade and other payables approximates to their fair value.

Source: WHSmith plc Annual report and accounts 2014, pp. 1, 18, 20, 74. http://whsmithplc.co.uk/investors/company_reports

Discussion points

1 How does the narrative information add insight into the nature of the liability for trade payables?

2 How significant is the amount of trade payables in the current liabilities?

Contents

Learning outcomes

After studying this chapter you should be able to:

- Define a liability and explain the distinguishing feature of current liabilities.
- Explain the criteria for recognition of liabilities.
- Explain how the information presented in a company's statement of financial position (balance sheet) and notes, in relation to liabilities, meets the needs of users.
- Explain the features of current liabilities and the approach to measurement and recording.
- Explain the terms 'accruals' and 'matching concept' and show how they are applied to expenses of the period.
- Explain how liabilities for taxation arise in companies.

Additionally, for those who choose to study the supplement:

- Prepare the ledger accounts to record accruals.

10.1 Introduction

The theme running through this textbook is the accounting equation:

Assets	minus	**Liabilities**	equals	**Ownership interest**

It was explained in Chapter 2 that the ownership interest is the residual amount found by deducting all liabilities of the company from total assets. Chapters 8 and 9 have taken you through aspects of non-current and current assets which are particularly significant to users of financial statements. Chapters 10 and 11 complete the left-hand side of the equation by providing a similar overview of current liabilities and non-current liabilities.

This chapter follows the approach established in Chapters 8 and 9:

- What are the principles for defining and recognising these items?
- What are the information needs of users in respect of the particular items?
- What information is currently provided by companies to meet these needs?
- Does the information show the desirable qualitative characteristics of financial statements?
- What are the principles for measuring, and processes for recording, these items?

10.2 Definitions

The definition of a liability, as provided in Chapter 2, is repeated here:

Definitions

A **liability** is a present obligation of the entity to transfer an economic resource as a result of past events. An **economic resource** is a right that has the potential to produce economic benefits.[1]

A **current liability** is a liability which satisfies any of the following criteria:

(a) it is expected to be settled in the entity's normal operating cycle;
(b) it is held primarily for the purpose of being traded;
(c) it is due to be settled within twelve months after the reporting period.[2]

Supplement 7.1 to Chapter 7 sets out the information to be presented on the face of the statement of financial position (balance sheet) of companies using the IASB system in their financial statements. The only current liabilities listed there are item (j) trade and other payables, item (l) financial liabilities (where these are short-term loans) and (m) liabilities for current tax.

Supplement 7.2 to Chapter 7 sets out the information to be presented in the financial statements of companies that are using the UK Companies Act and UK FRC standards. There is one heading for current liabilities and a detailed list below. The list is as follows:

E Creditors: amounts falling due within one year
1 Debenture loans
2 Bank loans and overdrafts
3 Payments received on account
4 Trade creditors
5 Bills of exchange payable
6 Amounts owed to group undertakings
7 Amounts owed to undertakings in which the company has a participating interest
8 Other creditors including taxation and social security
9 Accruals and deferred income

Activity 10.1

Look back to Table 2.3, which analyses some common types of liability. Set up on a blank sheet a similar table with four columns and headings for: type of liability; obligation; transfer of economic benefits; and past transaction or event. Then close the book and write down any ten liabilities you have come across during your study. Fill in all the columns as a check that, at this stage, you really understand what creates a liability.

10.3 Recognition and measurement

The recognition criteria and methods of measurement were set out in Chapter 2. In practice, recognition problems related to liabilities centre on ensuring that none is omitted which ought to be included. This is in contrast to the case of assets where there is a need, in practice, to guard against over-enthusiastic inclusion of items which do not meet the recognition criteria. The rest of this section explains how the current liabilities are recognised. Measurement and recording are explained in section 10.6 onwards.

10.3.1 Risk of understatement of liabilities

The risk related to liabilities is therefore the risk of understatement. This is explained in Chapter 4 under the heading of prudence. The risk of understatement of liabilities is that it will result in overstatement of the ownership interest.

In recent years the standard-setting bodies have devoted quite strenuous efforts to discouraging companies from keeping liabilities (and related assets) off the statement of financial position (balance sheet). This problem is called **off-balance sheet finance** and will be explained in Chapter 14.

10.3.2 Non-recognition: contingent liabilities

There are some obligations of the company which fail the recognition guidance because there is significant uncertainty about the possible outcomes relating to an event. The uncertainty may be about the occurrence of the event or about the measurement of the consequences. These are called **contingent liabilities** because they are contingent upon (depend upon) some future event happening. Examples are:

- A company is involved in legal action where a customer is seeking damages for illness allegedly caused by the company's product. If the customer is successful, there will be more claims. The company does not believe that the customer will succeed.
- A parent company has given guarantees to a bank that it will meet the overdraft and loans of a subsidiary company if that company defaults on repayment. At the present time there is no reason to suppose that any default will take place.
- A company is under investigation by the Competition Commission for possible price-fixing within the industry in contravention of an order prohibiting restrictive practices. If there is found to be a restrictive practice, a penalty may be imposed.
- The company has acquired a subsidiary in Australia where the tax authorities have raised an action for tax due on a disputed transaction which occurred before the subsidiary was acquired. The action is being defended strenuously.

In each of these examples, the company is convinced that it will not have a liability at the end of the day, but the users of the financial statements may wish to have some indication of the upper bounds of the liability if the company's optimism proves unfounded. There may, however, be a problem for the company in publishing an estimate of the amount of the possible liability because it may be seen as admitting liability and furthermore may require disclosure of commercially sensitive confidential information.

Where a **contingent liability** is identified, the obligation is not recognised in the statement of financial position (balance sheet) but it may be important that users of the financial statements are aware of the problem. There will therefore be a note to the statement of financial position (balance sheet) reporting the circumstances of the contingent liability and sometimes giving an indication of the amount involved.

Because of the confidentiality aspect, companies tend to give little information about the financial effect of a contingent liability, but some will try to set the outer limits of the liability.

Definition

A **contingent liability** is either:

(a) a possible obligation that arises from past events and whose existence will be confirmed only by the occurrence of one or more uncertain future events not wholly within the control of the entity; or

(b) a present obligation that arises from past events but is not recognised because:

   (i) either it is not probable that a transfer of economic benefits will be required to settle the obligation;

   (ii) or the amount of the obligation cannot be measured with sufficient reliability.[3]

A company should disclose a brief description of the nature of the contingent liability and, where practicable:

(a) an estimate of its financial effect;

(b) an indication of the uncertainties relating to the amount or timing of any outflow; and

(c) the possibility of any reimbursement.[4]

Rules about measurement are given in detail in the accounting standard. The detail is not necessary for an introductory course.

10.3.3 Changing thoughts on contingencies

In 2005 the IASB issued a proposal to eliminate the term 'contingent liability' because if the item cannot be recognised in a statement of financial position (balance sheet) then it cannot be a true liability. The proposal of the IASB was that items carrying an unconditional obligation should be recognised as a liability and measured at the best estimate. Any uncertain event affecting the measurement of the obligation would be explained in a note. Items that do not carry an unconditional obligation are seen as business risks. Such business risks would be reported as a note to the financial statements because they may have a significant effect on the carrying amount of assets and liabilities in the near future. These changing thoughts on contingencies do not change the overall amount of information to be disclosed about contingencies but the method of disclosure may change. This development was not taken further because the financial crisis of 2007–08 brought other accounting problems to the fore. At some point the IASB will revisit contingent liabilities.

Activity 10.2

Consider the four examples of contingent liability given at the start of this section. Based on the definition, explain why each is a contingent liability.

10.4 Users' needs for information

There are two aspects of information in relation to liabilities. The first relates to the amount owed (sometimes called the **principal sum** or the **capital** amount) and the second relates to the cost of servicing the loan (usually the payment of **interest**).

In respect of current liabilities, other than a bank overdraft or bank loans repayable within the year, it is unlikely that interest will be payable, and so generally there will be no information about interest charges. The shareholders in the company will be concerned that there are adequate current assets to meet the current liabilities as they fall due. Those who supply goods and services will want to be reassured that payment will be made on the due date.

Owners of a company need to know how much the company owes to other parties because the owners are at the end of the queue when it comes to sharing out the assets of the company if it closes down. Many of those who supply goods and services are what is known as unsecured creditors, which means they come at the end of the list of creditors. They will also have an interest in the balance of long-term and current liabilities.

10.5 Information provided in the financial statements

The statement of financial position (balance sheet) of Safe and Sure plc, set out in Chapter 7, contains the following information in relation to current liabilities:

	Notes	Year 7 £m	Year 6 £m
Current liabilities			
Amounts payable (creditors)	7	(1,598)	(1,575)
Bank overdraft	8	(401)	(626)
		(1,999)	(2,201)

Notes to the statement of financial position (balance sheet) explain more about the statement of financial position (balance sheet) items. Note 7 lists the details of current liabilities.

Note 7 Current liabilities: amounts payable	Year 7 £m	Year 6 £m
Deferred consideration on acquisition	11	43
Trade payables (trade creditors)	236	204
Corporation tax	315	265
Other tax and social security payable	245	212
Other payables (creditors)	307	238
Accruals and deferred income	484	613
	1,598	1,575

Trade payables (trade creditors) comprise amounts outstanding for trade purchases. The average credit period taken for trade purchases is 27 days. Most suppliers charge no interest on the trade payables for the first 30 days from the date of the invoice. Thereafter, interest is charged on the outstanding balances at various interest rates. The Group has financial risk management policies in place to ensure that all payables are paid within the agreed credit terms.

The note describing payment policy provides reassurance about avoiding the risk of additional costs through late payment. The company is complying with the financial reporting standard IFRS 7 *Financial Instruments: Disclosures.* Its general objective is to provide qualitative and quantitative information about exposure to risks arising from financial instruments. Any financial liability is an example of a financial instrument. You will therefore see descriptions of risk relating to financial liabilities in annual reports. The detail of that standard is beyond the scope of a first-level text.

Note 8 gives information on bank overdrafts due on demand and confirms that the interest charges incurred on these loans are payable at commercial rates:

Note 8 Bank borrowings: current liabilities	Year 7	Year 6
	£m	£m
Bank overdrafts due on demand:	<u>401</u>	<u>626</u>

Interest on overdrafts is payable at normal commercial rates appropriate to the country where the borrowing is made.

The report of the finance director provides further insight into the currency spread of the bank borrowings:

Foreign currency: £352m of foreign currency bank borrowings have been incurred to fund overseas acquisition. The main borrowings were £268m in US dollars and £84m in Japanese yen. The borrowings are mainly from banks on a short-term basis, with a maturity of up to one year, and we have fixed the interest rate on $200m of the US dollar loans through to November, Year 7, at an overall cost of 4.46%.

All material foreign currency transactions are matched back into the currency of the group company undertaking the transaction.

David Wilson has already commented in Chapters 4 and 7 on some aspects of the liabilities in the financial statements of Safe and Sure plc. Here he is explaining to Leona, in the coffee bar at the health club, his views on current liabilities in particular.

DAVID: *Current liabilities are relatively similar in total to last year so there are no particular questions to ask there.*

Then I start to think about the limits of risk. There is £401m due for repayment to the bank within the year. Will the company have any problem finding this amount? With £1,050m in cash and cash equivalents, it seems unlikely that there could be a problem. The entire current liabilities are £1,999m, all of which could be met from the cash and cash equivalents and receivables (debtors).

There is another risk that £40m shown as owing to the banks may be the wrong measure of the liability if exchange rates move against the company. Whenever I see foreign borrowings I want to know more about the currency of borrowings. You know from your economics class the theory of interest rates and currency exchange rates. It backs up my rule of thumb that borrowing in currencies which are weak means paying high rates of interest. Borrowing in currencies which are strong will mean paying lower rates of interest but runs a greater risk of having to use up additional pounds sterling to repay the loan if the foreign currency strengthens more. Information about the currency mix of loans is something I can probably get from the company if I need it. In this case, the finance director's report is sufficiently informative for my purposes. In past years, before finance directors started providing explanations in the annual report, we were asking these questions at face-to-face meetings.

LEONA: *What you have described is similar in many respects to the analytical review carried out by the auditors. We do much more than merely check the bookkeeping entries and the paperwork. We are looking at whether the statement of financial position (balance sheet) makes sense and whether any items have changed without sufficient explanation.*

10.6 Measurement and recording

Current liabilities are measured at the amount originally received from the lender of finance or supplier of goods and services, plus any additional charges incurred such as rolled-up interest added to a loan. Chapter 2 explains that the fair value of a liability is the price that would be paid to transfer a liability in an orderly transaction between market participants at the measurement date. In the case of current liabilities the repayment period is short. Consequently, the **fair value** is measured as the amount due to be repaid to the lender, which is identical to the historical cost measurement.

From the accounting equation it may be seen that an increase in a liability must be related either to an increase in an asset or a decrease in the ownership interest. Usually any related decrease in the ownership interest will be reported in the statement of financial position (balance sheet) as an expense.

The most significant current liabilities for most companies are bank borrowing and trade creditors. Both of these are essential sources of finance for small companies and are an important aspect, if not essential, for larger companies.

Activity 10.3   *Write down the documentation you would expect to see as evidence of the money amount of the following liabilities:*

● *bank overdraft;*
● *amount owing to a trade supplier.*

Now read the next sections and find whether your answer matches the information in the text.

10.6.1   Bank overdraft finance

Banks provide short-term finance to companies in the form of an overdraft on a current account. The advantage of an overdraft is its flexibility. When the cash needs of the company increase with seasonal factors, the company can continue to write cheques and watch the overdraft increase. When the goods and services are sold and cash begins to flow in, the company should be able to watch the overdraft decrease again. The most obvious example of a business which operates in this pattern is farming. The farmer uses the overdraft to finance the acquisition of seed for arable farming, or feed through the winter for stock farming and to cover the period when the crops or animals are growing and maturing. The overdraft is reduced when the crops or the animals are sold.

The main disadvantage of an overdraft is that it is repayable on demand. The farmer whose crop fails because of bad weather knows the problem of being unable to repay the overdraft. Having overdraft financing increases the worries of those who manage the company. The other disadvantage is that the interest payable on overdrafts is variable. When interest rates increase, the cost of the overdraft increases. Furthermore, for small companies there are often complaints that the rate of interest charged is high compared with that available to larger companies. The banks answer that the rates charged reflect relative risk and it is their experience that small companies are more risky.

10.6.2   Trade payables (trade creditors)

It is a strong feature of many industries that one enterprise is willing to supply goods to another in advance of being paid. Most suppliers will state terms of payment (e.g. the invoice must be paid within 30 days) and some will offer a discount for prompt payment. In the UK it has not been traditional to charge interest on overdue accounts but this practice is growing as suppliers realise there is a high cost to themselves of not collecting cash in good time. A supplier who is waiting to be paid is called a **trade creditor**.

Trade creditors rarely have any security for payment of the amount due to them, so that if a customer fails to pay the supplier must wait in the queue with other suppliers and hope for a share of some distribution. They are described as **unsecured creditors**.

Some suppliers will include in the contract a condition that the goods remain the property of the supplier should the customer fail to pay. This is called retention of title (ROT) and will be noted in the statement of financial position (balance sheet) of a company which has bought goods on these terms. Retention of title may offer some protection to the unpaid supplier but requires very prompt action to recover identifiable goods in the event of difficulty.

Some suppliers send goods to a customer on a sale-or-return basis. If there are no conditions to prevent return then the goods will not appear as stock in the statement of financial position (balance sheet) of the customer and there will be no indication of a liability. This practice is particularly common in the motor industry where manufacturers send cars to showrooms for sale or return within a specified period of time. Omitting the inventories and the related potential liability is referred to as **off-balance sheet finance**, a topic explored further in Chapter 14.

Suppliers send **invoices** to the customer showing the amount due for payment. These invoices are used in the customer's accounts department as the source of information for liabilities. At the end of the month the suppliers send statements as a reminder of unpaid invoices. Statements are useful as additional evidence of liabilities to suppliers.

Measurement of trade creditors is relatively straightforward because the company will know how much it owes to short-term creditors. If it forgets the creditors, they will soon issue a reminder.

Recording requires some care because omission of any credit transaction will mean there is an understatement of a liability. In particular, the company has to take some care at the end of the year over what are called **cut-off procedures**. Take the example of raw materials provided by a supplier. The goods arrive at the company's store by delivery van but the invoice for their payment arrives a few days later by mail. The accounts department uses the supplier's invoice as the document which initiates the *recording* of the asset of stock and the liability to the supplier. In contrast, the event which *creates* the liability is the acceptance of the goods. (It is difficult for the accounts department to use the delivery note as a record of the liability because it shows the quantities but not the price of the goods delivered.) So, at the end of the accounting year the accounts department has to compare the most recent delivery notes signed by the storekeeper with the most recent invoices received from the supplier. If goods have been received by the company, the statement of financial position (balance sheet) must include the asset of stock and the related liability. Using a similar line of reasoning, if a supplier has sent an invoice ahead of delivery of the goods, it should not be recorded as a liability because there is no related asset.

The recording of purchases of goods for resale is shown in Chapter 6. In the illustration of the process for recording the transactions of M. Carter there is a purchase of goods from the supplier, R. Busby, on credit terms. Payment is made later in the month. The purchase of the goods creates the asset of stock and the liability to the supplier. Payment to the supplier reduces the asset of cash and eliminates the liability to the supplier. The liability is described as an 'account payable'.

10.7 Accruals and the matching concept

At the financial year-end date there will be obligations of the company to pay for goods or services which are not contained in the accounting records because no document has been received from the supplier of the goods or services. It is essential that all obligations are included at the financial year-end date because these obligations fall under the definition of liabilities even although the demand for payment has not been received. The process of including in the statement of financial position (balance sheet) all obligations at the end of the period is called the accrual of liabilities and is said to reflect the **accruals basis** or accruals concept (see Chapter 4).

Definition

> **Accrual accounting** depicts the effects of transactions and other events and circumstances on a reporting entity's economic resources and claims in the periods in which those effects occur, even if the resulting cash receipts and payments occur in a different period. This is important because information about a reporting entity's economic resources and claims and changes in its economic resources and claims during a period provides a better basis for assessing the entity's past and future performance than information solely about cash receipts and payments during that period.[5]

The argument contained in the previous paragraph is based on the definition of a liability, but some people prefer to arrive at the same conclusion using a different argument. They say that all expenses of the accounting period must be matched against the revenue earned in the period. If a benefit has been consumed, the effect must be recorded whether or not documentation has been received. This argument is referred to as the **matching concept**.

In the *Conceptual Framework,* the IASB explains that in the income statement there is a direct association between the costs incurred and the earning of specific items of income. This process is called the matching of costs with revenues. As an example, the expenses that make up the cost of goods sold are recognised at the same time as the revenue derived from the sale of the goods.[6]

The accruals concept and the matching concept are, for most practical purposes, different ways of arriving at the same conclusion. (There are exceptions but these are well beyond the scope of a first-level text.)

10.7.1 The distinction between the expense of the period and the cash paid

A company starts business on 1 January Year 1. It has a financial year-end of 31 December Year 1. During Year 1 it receives four accounts for electricity, all of which are paid ten days after receiving them. The dates of receiving and paying the accounts are as follows:

Date invoice received	Amount of invoice £	Date paid
31 Mar. Year 1	350	10 Apr. Year 1
30 June Year 1	180	10 July Year 1
30 Sept. Year 1	280	10 Oct. Year 1
31 Dec. Year 1	340	10 Jan. Year 2
	1,150	

The company has used electricity for the entire year and therefore should match against revenue the full cost of £1,150. Only three invoices have been paid during the year, the final invoice not being paid until the start of Year 2. That is important for cash flow but is not relevant for the measurement of profit. The transactions during the year would be recorded as shown in Table 10.1. The arrival of the electricity invoice causes a record to be made of the increase in the liability and the increase in the expense (decreasing the ownership interest). The payment of the amount due requires a separate record to be made of the decrease in the liability and the decrease in the asset of cash.

The payment made to the electricity company in January Year 2 is not recorded in Table 10.1 because it is not a transaction of Year 1. It will appear in a spreadsheet for January Year 2. The totals at the foot of the spreadsheet show that the transactions of Year 1 have caused the cash of the company to decrease by £810. There remains a liability of £340 to the electricity company at the end of Year 1. The profit and loss account for the year will show an expense of £1,150. The spreadsheet satisfies the accounting equation because there is a decrease in an asset, amounting to £810, and an increase in a liability amounting to £340. These together equal the decrease of £1,150 in the ownership interest:

Asset ↓	−	**Liability ↑**	=	**Ownership interest ↓**
− £810		+ £340		− £1,150

Table 10.1
Spreadsheet analysis of transactions relating to the expense of electricity consumed, Year 1

Date	Transactions with electricity company	Asset	Liability	Ownership interest: profit of the period
		Cash	Electricity company	Electricity expense
Year 1		£	£	£
Mar. 31	Invoice received £350		350	(350)
Apr. 10	Pay electricity company £350	(350)	(350)	
June 30	Invoice received £180		180	(180)
July 10	Pay electricity company £180	(180)	(180)	
Sept. 30	Invoice received £280		280	(280)
Oct. 10	Pay electricity caompany £280	(280)	(280)	
Dec. 31	Invoice received £340		340	(340)
	Totals	(810)	340	(1,150)

That one needs a little careful thought because several things are happening at once. You might prefer to think about it one stage at a time. You know from earlier examples in Chapters 2, 5 and 6 that a decrease in an asset causes a decrease in the ownership interest. You also know that an increase in a liability causes a decrease in the ownership interest. Put them together and they are both working in the same direction to decrease the ownership interest.

10.7.2 Accrual where no invoice has been received

Now consider what might happen if the final electricity invoice for the year has not been received on 31 December Year 1. If no invoice has been received then there will be no entry in the accounting records. That, however, would fail to acknowledge that the electricity has been consumed and the company knows there is an obligation to pay for that electricity. In terms of the matching concept, only nine months' invoices are available to match against revenue when there has been twelve months' usage. The answer is that the company must make an *estimate* of the accrual of the liability for electricity consumed. Estimates will seldom give the true answer but they can be made reasonably close if some care is taken. If the company keeps a note of electricity meter readings and knows the unit charge, it can calculate what the account would have been.

The entries in the spreadsheet at the end of the month are shown in Table 10.2. They will be the same numerically as those in the final line of Table 10.1 but the item shown at 31 December will be described as an accrual.

Table 10.2
Spreadsheet entry for accrual at the end of the month

Date	Transactions with electricity company	Asset	Liability	Ownership interest: profit of the period
		Cash	Electricity company	Electricity expense
Year 1		£	£	£
Dec. 31	Accrual for three months		340	(340)

10.7.3 The nature of estimates in accounting

Making an accrual for a known obligation, where no invoice has been received, requires estimates. In the example given here it was a relatively straightforward matter to take a meter reading and calculate the expected liability. There will be other examples where the existence and amount of an expense are both known with reasonable certainty. There will be some cases where the amount has to be estimated and the estimate is later found to be incorrect. That is a normal feature of accounting, although not all users of financial statements realise there is an element of uncertainty about the information provided. If a liability is unintentionally understated at the end of a period, the profit will be overstated. In the next accounting period, when the full obligation becomes known, the expense incurred will be higher than was anticipated and the profit of that period will be lower than it should ideally be. If the error in the estimate is found to be such that it would change the views of the main users of financial statements, a prior year adjustment may be made by recalculating the profits of previous years and reporting the effect, but that is a relatively rare occurrence.

Activity 10.4

Write down five types of transaction where you might expect to see an accrual of expense at the year-end. Against each transaction type write down the method you would use to estimate the amount of the accrued expense.

10.8 Liabilities for taxation

In the statement of financial position (balance sheet) of a company there are two main categories of liability related directly to the company. The first is the **corporation tax** payable, based on the taxable profits of the period, the second is **deferred taxation**. Each of these will be discussed here. You will also see in the current liabilities section of a statement of financial position (balance sheet) the words 'other tax and social security payable'. This refers to the amounts deducted from employees' salaries and wages by the company on behalf of HMRC and paid over at regular intervals. In respect of such amounts the company is acting as a tax collecting agent of HMRC.

10.8.1 Corporation tax

Companies pay corporation tax based on the taxable profit of the accounting period (usually one year). The taxable profit is calculated according to the rules of tax law. That in itself is a subject for an entire textbook but one basic principle is that the taxable profit is based on profit calculated according to commercially accepted accounting practices. So, apart from some specific points of difference, the accounting profit is usually quite close to the taxable profit. Assume that the corporation tax rate is 20% of the taxable profit. (The tax rate each year is set by the Chancellor of the Exchequer.) Analysts will evaluate the tax charge in the income statement (profit and loss account) as a percentage of taxable profit and start to ask questions when the answer is very different from 20%. The explanation could be that there are profits earned abroad where the tax rate is different, but it could also be that there has been some use of provisions or adjustments for accounting purposes which are not allowed for tax purposes. That will lead to more probing by the analysts to establish whether they share the doubts of the tax authorities.

Large companies must pay corporation tax by four quarterly instalments. A company with a year-end of 31 December Year 1 will pay on 14 July Year 1, 14 October Year 1, 14 January Year 2 and 14 April Year 2. The amount of tax due is estimated by making a forecast of the profit for the year. As the year progresses the forecast is revised and the tax calculation is also revised. This means that at the end of the accounting year there is a liability for half that year's tax bill. A 'large' company is any company that pays corporation tax at the full rate. Small companies, which have a special, lower, rate of corporation tax, pay their tax bill nine months after the end of the accounting period. The precise limits for defining 'large' and 'small' companies change with tax legislation each year. (You will be given the necessary information in any exercise that you are asked to attempt.) Suppose the taxable profit is £15m and the tax payable at 20% is £3m. During the year £1.5m is paid in total on the first two instalment dates. At the statement of financial position (balance sheet) date there will remain a liability of £1.5m to be paid in total on the final two instalment dates.

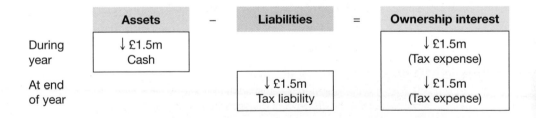

10.8.2 Deferred taxation liability

It was explained earlier in this section that the taxable profit is based on the accounting profit unless there are taxation rules which indicate otherwise. There are taxation rules which allow companies to defer the payment of some taxation on the full accounting profit. ('Deferring' means paying much later than the normal period of nine months.) The deferral period might be for a few months or it might be for a few years. The obligation to pay tax eventually cannot be escaped but the liability becomes long term. This is reflected, in terms of the accounting equation, by reporting the decrease in ownership claim in the profit and loss account but showing the deferred liability as a separate item under **non-current liabilities**.

10.9 Summary

- A **current liability** is a liability which satisfies any of the following criteria:

 (a) it is expected to be settled in the entity's normal operating cycle;
 (b) it is held primarily for the purpose of being traded;
 (c) it is due to be settled within 12 months after the financial year-end date.

- The risk of understatement of liabilities is that it will result in overstatement of the ownership interest.

- **Off-balance sheet finance** means keeping liabilities (and related assets) off the statement of financial position (balance sheet).

- There are some obligations of the company which fail the recognition test because there is significant uncertainty about future events that may cause benefits to flow from the company. These are reported as **contingent liabilities** in the notes to the financial statements.

- Users need to know about the existence of liabilities, the amount and timing of expected repayments and interest charges payable on loans.

- Under the **accruals** basis, the effects of transactions and other events are recognised when they occur (and not as cash or its equivalent is received or paid) and they are recorded in the accounting records and reported in the financial statements of the periods to which they relate.

- Liabilities for unpaid expenses are often called **accruals**.

- The **matching concept** is the idea that all expenses of the accounting period must be matched against the revenue earned in the period. If a benefit has been consumed, the effect must be recorded whether or not documentation has been received.

- Companies pay corporation tax. The arrangements vary depending on the size of the company but there will usually be a liability for unpaid corporation tax in the current liabilities section of the statement of financial position (balance sheet). Where government policy allows payment to be delayed for more than 12 months the liability is described as **deferred taxation**.

QUESTIONS

The Questions section of each chapter has three types of question. 'Test your understanding' questions to help you review your reading are in the 'A' series of questions. You will find the answers to these by reading and thinking about the material in the book. 'Application' questions to test your ability to apply technical skills are in the 'B' series of questions. Questions requiring you to show skills in problem solving and evaluation are in the 'C' series of questions. A letter [S] indicates that there is a solution at the end of the book. Other solutions are provided in the Instructor's Manual, where there are further questions parallel to those set out here.

A Test your understanding

A10.1 What is the definition of a liability? (Section 10.2)

A10.2 What is the distinction between a long-term liability and a current liability? (Section 10.2)

A10.3 What is the effect of understatement of liabilities? (Section 10.3.1)

A10.4 What is a contingent liability? (Section 10.3.2)

A10.5 What information do users of financial statements need to have concerning current liabilities of a company? (Section 10.4)

A10.6 How are the current liabilities for (a) bank overdraft and (b) trade creditors measured? (Section 10.6)

A10.7 What is meant by an accrual? How is it recorded? (Section 10.7)

A10.8 Explain what is meant by the matching concept. (Section 10.7)

A10.9 [S] On reviewing the financial statements, the company accountant discovers that a supplier's invoice for an amount of £10,000 has been omitted from the accounting records. The goods to which the invoice relates are held in the warehouse and are included in stock. What will be the effect on the profit and loss account and the statement of financial position (balance sheet) when this error is rectified?

A10.10 [S] On reviewing the financial statements, the company accountant discovers that a payment of £21,000 made to a supplier has been omitted from the cash book and other internal accounting records. What will be the effect on the profit and loss account and the statement of financial position (balance sheet) when this omission is rectified?

A10.11 [S] On reviewing the financial statements, the company accountant discovers that an invoice for the rent of £4,000 owed to its landlord has been recorded incorrectly as rent receivable of £4,000 in the company's accounting records. What will be the effect on the profit and loss account and the statement of financial position (balance sheet) when this error is rectified?

B Application

B10.1 [S]

White Ltd commenced trading on 1 July Year 3 and draws up its accounts for the year ended 30 June Year 4. During its first year of trading the company pays total telephone expenses of £3,500. The three-month bill paid in May Year 4 includes calls of £800 for the quarter up to 30 April Year 4 and advance rental of £660 to 31 July Year 4. The bill received in August Year 4 includes calls of £900 for the quarter up to 31 July Year 4 and advance rental of £660 to 31 October Year 4.

Required

Show calculations of the telephone expense to be recorded in the profit and loss account of White Ltd for its first year of trading.

B10.2 [S]

Plastics Ltd pays rent for a warehouse used for storage. The quarterly charge for security guard services is £800. The security firm sends an invoice on 31 March, 30 June, 30 September and 31 December. Plastics Ltd always pays the rent five days after the invoice is received. The security services have been used for some years. Plastics Ltd has an accounting year-end of 31 December.

Required

Prepare a spreadsheet to show how the transactions of one year in respect of security services are recorded.

B10.3 [S]

The accountant of Brown Ltd has calculated that the company should report in its profit and loss account a tax charge of £8,000 based on the taxable profit of the period. Of this amount,

£6,000 will be payable nine months after the accounting year-end but £2,000 may be deferred for payment in a period estimated at between three and five years after the accounting year-end. Using the accounting equation explain how this information will be reported in the financial statements of Brown Ltd.

C | Problem solving and evaluation

C10.1 [S]

The following file of papers was found in a cupboard of the general office of Green Ltd at the end of the accounting year. Explain how each would be treated in the financial statements and state the total amount to be reported as an accrued liability on the financial year-end date. The year-end is 31 December Year 1.

Item	Description	Amount £
1	Invoice dated 23 December for goods received 21 December.	260
2	Invoice dated 23 December for goods to be delivered on 3 January Year 2.	310
3	Foreman's note of electricity consumption for month of December – no invoice yet received from electricity supply company.	100
4	Letter from employee claiming overtime payment for work on 1 December and note from personnel office denying entitlement to payment.	58
5	Telephone bill dated 26 December showing calls for October to December.	290
6	Telephone bill dated 26 December showing rent due in advance for period January to March Year 2.	90
7	Note of payment due to cleaners for final week of December (to be paid in January under usual pattern of payment one week in arrears).	48
8	Invoice from supplier for promotional calendars received 1 December (only one-third have yet been sent to customers).	300
9	Letter dated 21 December Year 1 to customer promising a cheque to reimburse damage caused by faulty product – cheque to be sent on 4 January Year 2.	280
10	Letter dated 23 December promising donation to local charity – amount not yet paid.	60

Activities for study groups

Turn to the annual report of a listed company which you have used for activities in previous chapters. Find every item of information about current liabilities. (Start with the financial statements and notes but look also at the strategic report, chief executive's review and other non-regulated information about the company.)

Divide into two groups. One group should take on the role of the purchasing director and one should take on the role of a company which has been asked to supply goods or services to this company on credit terms.

- *Supplier group*: What questions would you ask to supplement what you have learned from the annual report?
- *Purchasing director*: What questions would you ask about the supplier? What might you learn about the supplier from the annual report of the supplier's company?

Notes and references

1. IASB (2016), *Conceptual Framework*.
2. IASB (2016), IAS 1, para. 69.
3. IASB (2016), IAS 37, *Provisions, Contingent Liabilities and Contingent Assets*, para. 10.
4. *Ibid.*, para. 86.
5. IASB (2016), *Conceptual Framework*.
6. IASB (2016), *Conceptual Framework*.

Bookkeeping entries for accruals

In the main part of the chapter the accruals for electricity were analysed. Now consider the debit and credit recording. The following transactions are to be recorded.

A company starts business on 1 January Year 1. It has a financial year-end of 31 December Year 1. During Year 1 it receives three accounts for electricity, all of which are paid ten days after receiving them. The dates of receiving and paying the accounts are as follows:

Amount of invoice £	Date invoice received	Date paid
350	31 Mar. Year 1	10 Apr. Year 1
180	30 June Year 1	10 July Year 1
280	30 Sept. Year 1	10 Oct. Year 1

At 31 December the final invoice for the year has not arrived because of delays in the mail but the amount due for payment is estimated at £340.

Activity 10.5

Before you read further, attempt to write down the debit and credit entries for: each of the three invoices received; the payments of those three invoices; and the estimated amount due for payment at the end of the year. You may find help in looking back to Tables 10.1 and 10.2.

Table 10.3 sets out the debit and credit aspect of each transaction and event. The amount of the liability to the supplier cannot be recorded until the invoice is received. The credit entry for the estimate of the amount owing to the supplier is therefore shown in a separate account called *accruals* which will be the basis for the amount shown in the statement of financial position (balance sheet) under that heading.

The ledger accounts required here are:

L1 Expense (electricity)
L2 Liability to supplier
L3 Accrual

Also required to complete the double entry, but not shown here as a ledger account, are:

L4 Cash
L5 Profit and loss account

Table 10.3
Analysis of debit and credit aspect of each transaction and event

Date	Transaction	Debit	Credit
Year 1			
Mar. 31	Receive invoice for electricity £350	Expense (electricity)	Liability to supplier
Apr. 10	Pay supplier £350	Liability to supplier	Cash
June 30	Receive invoice for electricity £180	Expense (electricity)	Liability to supplier
July 10	Pay supplier £180	Liability to supplier	Cash
Sept. 30	Receive invoice for electricity £280	Expense (electricity)	Liability to supplier
Oct. 10	Pay supplier £280	Liability to supplier	Cash
Dec. 31	Estimate amount owing to supplier £340	Expense (electricity)	Accruals

L1 Expense (electricity)

Date	Particulars	Page	Debit	Credit	Balance
Year 1			£	£	£
Mar. 31	Invoice from supplier	L2	350		350
June 30	Invoice from supplier	L2	180		530
Sept. 30	Invoice from supplier	L2	280		810
Dec. 31	Estimated accrual	L3	340		1,150
Dec. 31	Transfer to profit and loss account	L5		1,150	nil

LEONA: *The electricity account for the year shows a full 12 months' expense which is transferred to the profit and loss account at the end of the year.*

L2 Liability to supplier

Date	Particulars	Page	Debit	Credit	Balance
Year 1			£	£	£
Mar. 31	Invoice for electricity expense	L1		350	(350)
Apr. 10	Cash paid	L4	350		nil
June 30	Invoice for electricity expense	L1		180	(180)
July 10	Cash paid	L4	180		nil
Sept. 30	Invoice for electricity expense	L1		280	(280)
Oct. 10	Cash paid	L4	280		nil

LEONA: *The supplier's account is showing a nil liability because all invoices received have been paid. We know there is another invoice on the way but the bookkeeping system is quite strict about only making entries in the ledger when the documentary evidence is obtained. The document in this case is the supplier's invoice. Until it arrives the liability has to be recognised as an accrual rather than in the supplier's account.*

L3 Accrual

Date	Particulars	Page	Debit	Credit	Balance
Year 1			£	£	£
Dec. 31	Estimate of electricity expense	L1		340	(340)

LEONA: *The statement of financial position (balance sheet) will record a nil liability to the supplier but will show an accrual of £340 for electricity. When the supplier's invoice arrives in January of Year 2, the debit and credit entries will be:*

Date	Transaction	Debit	Credit
Year 2			
Jan. 4	Receive invoice for electricity £340	Accrual	Liability to supplier

In this way the liability remaining from Year 1 is recorded without affecting the expense account for Year 2. The credit balance on the accrual account at the end of Year 1 is eliminated by being matched against the debit entry at the start of Year 2.

S | Test your understanding

S10.1 Prepare bookkeeping records for the information in question B10.1.

S10.2 Prepare bookkeeping records for the information in question B10.2.

S10.3 Prepare bookkeeping records for the information in question B10.3.

S10.4 Prepare bookkeeping records for the information in question C10.1.

Chapter 11

Provisions and non-current (long-term) liabilities

Rio Tinto: reporting long-term liabilities

Extracts from Annual report

Introduction to Rio Tinto

Rio Tinto is a leading global mining group that focuses on finding, mining and processing the Earth's mineral resources. Our vision is to be a company that is admired and respected for delivering superior value, as the industry's most trusted partner.

Imagestate Media/John Foxx Collection

Critical accounting policies and estimates: (v) Close-down, restoration and environmental obligations

Provision is made for close-down, restoration and environmental costs when the obligation occurs, based on the net present value of estimated future costs with, where appropriate, probability weighting of the different remediation, closure or other activities required to achieve relinquishment. The ultimate cost of close-down and restoration is uncertain and management uses its judgment and experience to provide for these costs over the life of the operations. Cost estimates can vary in response to many factors including: changes to the relevant legal or local/national government ownership requirements or the Group's closure and environmental policies; review of remediation and relinquishment options; the emergence of new restoration techniques; the timing of the expenditures and the effects of inflation. Experience gained at other mine or production sites is also a significant consideration.

Cost estimates are updated throughout the life of the operation. The accuracy range for operations with a remaining life of ten to 40 years is +/−30 per cent. For operations with a remaining life of five to ten years, the accuracy range is +/−20 per cent. Five years prior to the estimated date of closure, operations must produce a full decommissioning plan with an accuracy range of +/−15 per cent.

The expected timing of expenditure included in cost estimates can also change, for example in response to changes to expectations relating to ore reserves and resources, production rates, operating licence or economic conditions. Expenditure may occur before and after closure and can continue for an extended period of time depending on the specific site requirements. Some expenditure can continue into perpetuity.

Cash flows must be discounted if this has a material effect. The selection of appropriate sources on which to base the calculation of the risk-free discount rate used for such obligations also requires judgment.

As a result of all of the above factors, there could be significant adjustments to the provision for close-down, restoration and environmental costs which would affect future financial results. Increases and decreases in environmental obligations are charged directly to the income statement. Increases and decreases in close-down obligations are capitalised for operating businesses. An increase in close-down and restoration provisions would increase the unwind of the discount and depreciation charges in the income statement in future years and increase the carrying value of property, plant and equipment potentially impacting any future impairment charges or reversals.

Notes to the financial statements

26 Provisions (including post retirement benefits) (extract)

(Figures in US$m)

At 31 December 2013	US$m
Pensions and post retirement healthcare	3,599
Other employee entitlements	941
Close down and restoration/environmental	8,582
Other	959
Total 2013	14,081
Restated Total 2012	16,981

Source: *Rio Tinto plc Annual report 2013,* pp. 1, 129–130, 154.
http://www.riotinto.com/annualreport2013/_pdfs/rio-tinto-2013-annual-report.pdf

Discussion points

1 Why is there a provision for close down and restoration when those events may take place many years into the future?

2 What are the significant uncertainties in estimating the amount of the provision?

Contents

Learning outcomes	After studying this chapter you should be able to:

After studying this chapter you should be able to:

- Define a non-current (long-term) liability.
- Explain the needs of users for information about non-current (long-term) liabilities.
- Explain the different types of non-current (long-term) loan finance which may be found in the statements of financial position (balance sheets) of major companies.
- Understand the purpose of provisions and explain how provisions are reported in financial statements.
- Understand the nature of deferred income and explain how it is reported in financial statements.
- Know the main types of loan finance and capital instruments used by companies and understand the principles of reporting information in the financial statements.

Additionally, for those who choose to study the supplement to this chapter:

- Prepare the ledger accounts to record provisions and deferred income.

11.1 Introduction

Supplement 7.1 to Chapter 7 sets out the information to be presented on the face of the statement of financial position (balance sheet) of companies using the IASB system in their financial statements. The non-current liabilities listed there are item (l) provisions, (m) financial liabilities (where these are loans due in more than one year's time) and (o) deferred tax liabilities.

Supplement 7.2 to Chapter 7 sets out the information to be presented in the financial statements of companies that are using the UK Companies Act and UK FRC standards. There is one heading for non-current liabilities, with a detailed list below, as follows:

H Creditors: amounts falling due after more than one year
1 Debenture loans
2 Bank loans and overdrafts
3 Payments received on account
4 Trade creditors
5 Bills of exchange payable
6 Amounts owed to group undertakings
7 Amounts owed to undertakings in which the company has a participating interest
8 Other creditors including taxation and social security
9 Accruals and deferred income

Comparing Supplements 7.1 and 7.2 it could appear that companies using the IASB system face fewer detailed rules. However, those companies still produce a great deal of detailed information in practice because the IASB has other standards that require more detail.

In this chapter we follow the pattern established in earlier chapters by asking:

- What are the principles for defining and recognising these items?
- What are the information needs of users in respect of the particular items?
- What information is currently provided by companies to meet these needs?
- Does the information show the desirable qualitative characteristics of financial statements?
- What are the principles for measuring, and processes for recording, these items?

This chapter looks first at provisions, then turns to non-current (long-term) liabilities and finally covers deferred income. General principles of definition and recognition of liabilities are dealt with in Chapter 10 and you should ensure you have read and understood that chapter before embarking on this one. For convenience the definitions from Chapter 2 are repeated here.

Definitions

A **liability** is a present obligation of the entity to transfer an economic resource as a result of past events. An **economic resource** is a right that has the potential to produce economic benefits.[1]

A **current liability** is a liability which satisfies any of the following criteria:

(a) it is expected to be settled in the entity's normal operating cycle;
(b) it is held primarily for the purpose of being traded;
(c) it is due to be settled within 12 months after the reporting period.[2]

A **non-current liability** is any liability that does not meet the definition of a current liability.[3] Non-current liabilities are also described as **long-term liabilities**.

11.2 Users' needs for information

There are two aspects of information needed in relation to liabilities. The first relates to the amount owed (sometimes called the **principal sum** or the **capital amount**) and the second relates to the cost of servicing the loan (usually the payment of **interest**).

Owners of a company need to know how much the company owes to other parties because the owners are at the end of the queue when it comes to sharing out the assets of the company if it closes down. Lenders to the company want to know how many other lenders will have a claim on assets if the company closes down and how much the total claim of lenders will be. They may want to take a **secured loan**, where the agreement with the company specifies particular assets which may be sold by the lender if the company defaults on payment.

Cash flow is important to a range of users. Interest payments are an expense to be reported in the income statement (profit and loss account), but paying interest is a drain on cash as well as affecting the ownership interest by a reduction in profit. Owners of the company want to know if there will be sufficient cash left to allow them a **dividend** (or **drawings** for partnerships and sole traders) after interest has been paid. Lenders want to be reassured that the company is generating sufficient cash flow and profit to cover the interest expense.

Both owners and lenders want to see the impact of borrowing on future cash flows. They need to know the scheduled dates of repayments of loans (sometimes referred to as the **maturity profile of debt**), the currency in which the loan must be repaid and the structure of interest rates (e.g. whether the loan period is starting with low rates of interest which are then stepped up in future years).

Finally, owners and lenders are interested in the **gearing** of the company. This means the ratio of loan capital to ownership interest in the statement of financial position (balance sheet) or the ratio of interest payments to net profit in the income statement (profit and loss account). Chapter 13 will provide more detail on the calculation and interpretation of gearing.

Activity 11.1

Imagine you are a shareholder in a company which is financed partly by long-term loans. Write down the information needed by users in the order of importance to you as a shareholder and explain your answer.

11.3 Information provided in the financial statements

The statement of financial position (balance sheet) of Safe and Sure plc, set out in Chapter 7, contains the following information in relation to non-current (long-term) liabilities:

	Notes	Year 7 £m	Year 6 £m
Non-current liabilities			
Amounts payable (creditors)	9	(27)	(26)
Bank and other borrowings	10	(2)	(6)
Provisions	11	(202)	(222)
Net assets		4,643	3,704

Notes to the statement of financial position (balance sheet) explain more about each item. Note 9 gives some indication of the type of creditors due after more than one year.

Note 9 Non-current liabilities: payables (creditors)

	Year 7 £m	Year 6 £m
Deferred consideration on acquisition	6	–
Other payables (creditors)	21	26
	27	26

Note 10 distinguishes secured and unsecured loans among the borrowings due after one year and also gives a schedule of repayment over the immediate and medium-term or longer-term future. For this company, bank borrowings all mature within five years. Note 10 also confirms that commercial rates of interest are payable.

Note 10 Non-current liabilities: bank and other borrowings

	Year 7 £m	Year 6 £m
Secured loans	–	3
Unsecured loans	2	3
	2	6
Loans are repayable by instalments:		
Between one and two years	1	2
Between two and five years	1	4
	2	6

Interest on long-term loans, which are denominated in a number of currencies, is payable at normal commercial rates appropriate to the country in which the borrowing is made. The last repayment falls due in Year 11.

Note 11 gives information on provisions for liabilities which will occur at a future date, as a result of past events or of definite plans made.

Note 11 Provisions

	Year 7 £m	Year 6 £m
Provisions for treating contaminated site:		
At 1 January	142	145
Utilised in the year	(22)	(3)
At 31 December	120	142
Provisions for restructuring costs:		
At 1 January	42	–
Created in year	10	43
Utilised in year	(10)	(1)
At 31 December	42	42
Provision for deferred tax:		
At 1 January	38	27
Transfer to income statement	5	12
Other movements	(3)	(1)
At 31 December	40	38
Total provision	202	222

Finally, note 33 sets out contingent liabilities. (Contingent liabilities are defined and explained in Chapter 10.) Two contingent items have the amount quantified. The impact of litigation (legal action) is not quantified. The company may think that to do so would be seen as an admission of legal liability.

Note 33 Contingent liabilities

The company has guaranteed bank and other borrowings of subsidiaries amounting to £30m (Year 6: £152m). The group has commitments, amounting to approximately £419m (Year 6: £285m), under forward exchange contracts entered into in the ordinary course of business.

Certain subsidiaries have given warranties for service work. These are explained in the statement on accounting policies. There are contingent liabilities in respect of litigation. None of the actions is expected to give rise to any material loss.

The accounting policy statement contains three items relevant to liabilities:

Accounting policies

Deferred tax
The provision for deferred tax recognises a future liability arising from past transactions and events. Tax legislation allows the company to defer settlement of the liability for several years.

Warranties
Some service work is carried out under warranty. The cost of claims under warranty is charged against the income statement (profit and loss account) of the year in which the claims are settled.

Deferred consideration
For acquisitions involving deferred consideration, estimated deferred payments are accrued in the statement of financial position (balance sheet). Interest due to vendors on deferred payments is charged to the income statement (profit and loss account) as it accrues.

In this extract the word 'charged' appears several times. In relation to interest or taxes, the use of the word **charge** describes the reduction in ownership interest reported in the income statement (profit and loss account) due to the cost of interest and tax payable.

Because the level of borrowing is low in this company, and therefore would not create any concern for investors or new lenders, the finance director has very little to say about it in his report. To some extent the chairman takes the initiative earlier in the annual report:

Finance

Once again, during Year 7 we had a strong operating cash flow, amounting to £1,967m (up from £1,635m in Year 6). This funded expenditure of £246m on acquisition of other companies and businesses (after allowing for £31m received from a disposal of a company) and the group still ended the year with an increase in its cash balances.

David Wilson has already commented in Chapters 4 and 7 on some aspects of the liabilities in the financial statements of Safe and Sure plc. Here he is explaining to Leona, in the coffee bar at the health club, his views on liabilities in particular.

DAVID: *Where do I start in explaining how I look at liabilities? Well, I always read the accounting policy notes before I look at any financial statements. This company provides three accounting policy notes relating to matters of liabilities. The policy on warranties is interesting because it confirms that the company does not record any expected liability on warranties. The first time I saw this in the annual report I was quite concerned about lack of prudence, but on my first visit to the company I was shown the warranty settlement file. There are very few claims under warranty because the company has lots of procedures which have to be followed by employees who carry out service work. Warranty claims are relatively unusual and unpredictable for this company so there is no previous pattern to justify setting up a liability in the form of a provision for future claims.*

The deferred consideration arises because this company has acquired another business and wants to look into all aspects of the newly acquired investment before making full payment.

Deferred tax provisions are common to many companies. They are an attempt to line up the accounting profit with the tax charge based on taxable profits, which are usually different. I don't understand the technical details but my test of importance is to look at the amount charged to the income statement (profit and loss account) for the year. It is less than 1% of the profit after tax, so I shan't be giving it much attention on this occasion.

Provisions for restructuring are my real headache. These are a measure of the costs expected when the company plans a restructuring such as changing the management structure with redefinition of the role of some employees and redundancy for others. It sounds reasonable to give warning of what all this will cost but the standard-setters have to be strict about the details because in the past the use of provisions has been linked to some creative accounting in the income statement (profit and loss account). Do you know anything about that?

LEONA: *Yes. On the one hand, you would like to know that a company is prudent in reporting in the income statement (profit and loss account) now the likely losses which will arise in future years because of a decision to reorganise. On the other hand, you would not like to think that a company has loaded the income statement with lots of bad news this year so that it can make next year look much better when the results are published. The accounting standard-setter has prevented companies from being excessively prudent. I could explain more but not at this time on a Friday night. What do you see in the statement of financial position (balance sheet) and the other information provided by the company?*

DAVID: *After reading and thinking about the items in the accounting policy notes I look to the breakdown between current liabilities and longer-term liabilities. I also look to the amount of long-term finance compared with the amount of the equity holders' funds. The borrowings in this company are relatively low in relation to equity-holders' funds, so there is not a high financial risk, but I still want to look for unexplained changes since the previous year. Again, there is nothing which springs to the eye.*

The contingent liability note is usually quite interesting. One of my senior colleagues says that you should start at the end of the annual report and read it backwards. Then you find the best parts first. The contingent liability note is always near the end. I would be asking lots of questions about the forward exchange contracts, if I had not already asked the financial controller. He confirmed in more detail what the finance director says rather briefly. The forward exchange contracts are used as part of prudent financial management to put a limit on any potential loss through adverse currency movements on transactions in different countries.

LEONA: *Much of what you say is reflected in what auditors carry out by way of analytical review. What we don't provide is a view to the future. What are your thoughts there?*

DAVID: *This is a cash-rich company and it has very little in the way of complicated financial structures. For a major company that is probably unusual, but it means I can concentrate on the operating aspects of the business and on whether it will continue to generate cash. It uses cash generated to buy other businesses and expand further, but I wonder what will happen when the scope for that expansion ceases. It is unlikely to be a problem in the near future because the company has a foothold in expanding markets in Asia. When that scope for expansion comes to an end the company may have to start borrowing to finance expansion rather than relying on internal cash flows.*

11.4 Provisions

Making a provision is an accounting process similar to that of making accrual for a known obligation.

Definition	A **provision** is a liability of uncertain timing or amount.[4]

The distinguishing feature of a provision often lies in the larger element of uncertainty which surrounds a provision. Such a provision will appear in the liabilities section of a statement of financial position (balance sheet). (This book has already considered in Chapter 8 the provision for depreciation and in Chapter 9 the provision for doubtful debts. These are examples of what is regarded as an adjustment to the reported value of an asset, rather than an adjustment for significant uncertainty. They are therefore reported as adjustments to the asset and do not appear in the liabilities section.) The following are examples of provisions which may be found in the liabilities sections of published accounts:

- losses on contracts
- obsolescence of stock
- costs related to closure of a division of the company
- costs of decommissioning an oil rig
- cost of landscaping a site at the end of the period of use
- warranties given for repair of goods.

Recording a **provision** is relatively straightforward. The ownership interest is reduced by an expense in the income statement (profit and loss account) and a liability is created under the name of the provision:

Assets – **Liabilities** ↑	equals	**Ownership interest ↓ (expense)**

When the provision is no longer required it is released to the income statement (profit and loss account) as an item of revenue which increases the ownership interest and the liability is reduced:

Assets – **Liabilities** ↓	equals	**Ownership interest ↑**

The provision may also be released to the income statement (profit and loss account) so as to match an expense which was anticipated when the provision was made. The effect on the accounting equation is an increase in the ownership interest – the same effect as results from regarding the release of the provision as an item of revenue.

Of the topics covered in this chapter, provisions give the greatest scope for international variation in accounting treatment. In countries where the accounting system and the tax system are linked, there may be specific rules about the level and nature of provisions allowed. In countries that have a strong culture of **conservatism** (strong **prudence**) the provisions may be used to understate profit. The problem with such an approach is that the unnecessary provision may then be released in a year when profits would otherwise be lower. This has the effect of 'smoothing out' the peaks and troughs of profit. The IASB believes that provisions should only be used under carefully defined conditions. This approach also applies in the USA.

The IASB has proposed[5] to change the description of provisions to become 'non-financial liabilities'. A Research project began in 2012. The IASB 'Work plan' web page will give updates. One suggestion is that any items satisfying the definition of a liability should be recognised unless they cannot be measured reliably. Any unconditional obligation would be recognised so there would no longer be a need to estimate the likelihood of the obligation being implemented. Uncertainty about the amount or timing of the economic benefits required to settle the non-financial liability would be recognised in the measurement of the liability.

Example of a provision

During the year ending 31 December Year 5, a company's sales of manufactured goods amounted to £1m. All goods carry a manufacturer's warranty to rectify any faults arising during the first 12 months of ownership. At the start of the year, based on previous experience, a provision of 2.5% of sales was made (estimating the sales to be £1m). During Year 5 repairs under warranty cost £14,000. There could be further repair costs incurred in Year 6 in respect of those items sold part-way through Year 5 whose warranty extends into Year 6.

Using the accounting equation, the effect of these events and transactions may be analysed. When the provision is established there is an increase in a liability and an expense to be charged to the income statement (profit and loss account):

Assets	–	Liabilities ↑	=	Ownership interest ↓ (expense)
		+ £25,000		– £25,000

As the repairs under warranty are carried out, they cause a decrease in the asset of cash and a decrease in the provision. They do not directly affect the income statement (profit and loss account) expense:

Assets ↓	–	Liabilities ↓	=	Ownership interest
– £14,000		– £14,000		

The overall effect is that the income statement (profit and loss account) will report an expense of £25,000 but the provision will only be used to the extent of £14,000, leaving £11,000 available to cover any further repairs in respect of Year 5 sales. The repairs, when paid for, decrease the asset of cash but are not seen as decreasing the ownership interest. They are seen as meeting a liability to the customer (rather like making a payment to meet a liability to a supplier). The creation of the provision establishes the full amount of the liability and the decrease in the ownership interest which is to be reported in the income statement (profit and loss account).

The spreadsheet for analysis is contained in Table 11.1.

Table 11.1
Spreadsheet for analysis of provision for warranty repairs

Date	Transaction or event	Asset	Liability	Ownership interest
		Cash	Provision	Profit and loss account
Year 5		£	£	£
Jan. 1	Provision for repairs		25,000	(25,000)
Jan.–Dec.	Repairs under warranty	(14,000)	(14,000)	
	Totals	(14,000)	11,000	(25,000)

Activity 11.2

Test your understanding of the previous section by analysing the following information and entering it in a spreadsheet to show analysis of the impact of the information on the accounting equation:

Jan. 1 Year 1   Make a provision for repairs, £50,000.
During Year 1   Spend £30,000 against the provision and carry the rest forward.
Jan. 1 Year 2   Make a further provision for repairs, £10,000.
During Year 2   Spend £25,000 against the provision and carry the rest forward.
Jan. 1 Year 3   Reduce the remaining provision to £3,000.

11.5 Deferred income

For companies located in areas of the country where there are particular problems of unemployment or a need to encourage redevelopment of the location, the government may award grants as a contribution to the operating costs of the company or to the cost of buying new fixed assets.

Consider the award of a government grant to a company, intended to help with the cost of training employees over the next three years. The asset of cash increases, but there is no corresponding effect on any other asset or liability. Consequently, the ownership interest is increased. The obvious label for this increase is **revenue**. However, the benefit of the grant will extend over three years and it would therefore seem appropriate to spread the revenue over three years to match the cost it is subsidising. The accounting device for producing this effect is to say that the cash received as an asset creates a liability called **deferred income**. This does not meet the definition of a liability stated at the start of this chapter because the practice of deferring income is dictated by the importance of **matching** revenues and costs in the income statement (profit and loss account). It is one of the cases where established custom and practice continues because it has been found to be useful although it does not fit neatly into the conceptual framework definitions.

Example

A company receives a grant of £30,000 towards the cost of employee retraining. The retraining programme will last for three years and the costs will be spread evenly over the three years.

The income statement (profit and loss account) will show revenue of £10,000 in each year. At the outset the deferred income will be recorded in the statement of

Table 11.2
Recording deferred income and transfer to profit or loss

Date	Transaction or event	Asset	Liability	Ownership interest
		Cash	Deferred income	Revenue
Year 1		£	£	£
Jan. 1	Receiving the grant	30,000	30,000	
Dec. 31	Transfer to profit and loss account of first year's revenue		(10,000)	10,000
Year 2				
Dec. 31	Transfer to profit and loss account of second year's revenue		(10,000)	10,000
Year 3				
Dec. 31	Transfer to profit and loss account of third year's revenue		(10,000)	10,000

financial position (balance sheet) as £30,000. By the end of Year 1 the deferred income will be reduced to £20,000. At the end of Year 2 the deferred income will be reduced to £10,000. At the end of Year 3 the deferred income is reduced to nil. The accounting records are shown in Table 11.2.

Where grants are received towards the acquisition of non-current assets there is a similar approach of spreading the grant over the period during which the company will benefit from use of the asset. Some companies show the revenue as a separate item in the income statement (profit and loss account) while others deduct it from the depreciation expense. This is a matter of presentation which makes no difference to the overall profit. The statement of financial position (balance sheet) treatment is more controversial. Some companies report separately the net book value of the asset and the deferred income. Others deduct the deferred income from the net book value of the asset. This does not affect the ownership interest but shows a lower amount in the fixed assets section of the statement of financial position (balance sheet). In consequence, the user who calculates profit as a percentage of non-current (fixed) assets or a percentage of total assets will obtain a higher answer where a company shows the lower amount for net assets. Most companies report the asset and deferred income separately, but some argue for the **net** approach which sets one against the other. (Both methods are permitted by the international accounting standard and by the UK national standard. There is a view that the net approach may not be complying with the Companies Act 2006 and so relatively few UK companies have taken the net approach.) The choice will be set out in the notes on accounting policies. This is a useful illustration of the importance of reading the note on accounting policies.

Activity 11.3

Consider a grant received as a contribution to staff retraining costs over the next three years. Write down three arguments in favour of reporting the entire grant in the income statement (profit and loss account) in the year it is received and write down three arguments in favour of spreading the grant across the period of retraining. Which set of arguments do you find more persuasive?

11.6 Non-current (long-term) liabilities

The statement of financial position (balance sheet) requires a separate heading for all liabilities payable after one year. Users of financial statements need information about when the liabilities will be due for repayment (the **maturity** pattern).

Users also need to know about the nature of the liability and any risks attaching to expected outflows of economic benefit from the liability. The risks lie in: the interest payable on the loan; the currency of the loan; and the eventual amount to be repaid to the lender. Interest payable may be at a fixed rate of interest or a variable rate of interest. The currency of borrowing is important when foreign exchange rates alter. Repayment amounts may equal the amount borrowed initially, in some cases. In other cases there may be a **premium** (an extra amount) payable in addition to the sum borrowed. There are some very complex accounting aspects to reporting non-current (long-term) liabilities, the technical aspects of which are well beyond the capacity of a first-level text, but they are all directed towards ensuring that liabilities are recorded in full and the matching concept is observed in relation to interest charges.

Users want to know about the risks of sacrificing particular assets if the loan is not repaid on the due date. A claim to a particular asset may be made by a creditor who has a loan **secured** on a particular asset or group of assets.

11.6.1 Measurement

Fair value measurement is the general principle applied to all long-term liabilities. Chapter 2 explains that **fair value** is the price that would be paid to transfer a liability in an orderly transaction between market participants at the measurement date. Some non-current liabilities, such as loan stock, are traded in stock markets and have fair values that can be measured in the market. Other non-current liabilities, such as a requirement to reinstate the site of open-cast mining, may not have an obvious market value. The fair value may then be based on discounting the expected liability using market rates of interest. The rest of section 11.6 gives some simplified examples, but the topic is complex and goes beyond the initial level of study.

11.6.2 Recording

This section concentrates on the terminology of non-current (long-term) liabilities and the general issues of recording and measurement that they raise. The basic feature of non-current (long-term) loan finance is that it is:

- provided by a lender for a period longer than one year;
- who expects payment of interest at an agreed rate at agreed points in time; and
- expects repayment of the loan on an agreed date or dates.

The names given to loan capital vary depending on the type of lender, the possibility that the loan will be bought and sold like ordinary shares, the currency in which the loan has been provided and the legal form of the documents creating the loan. Some of the names you will see are: loan stock, debentures, bonds, commercial paper, loan notes and bank facility.

- **Loan stock.** If a company shows loan stock in its statement of financial position (balance sheet) this usually indicates that the stock is available for purchase and sale, in a manner similar to the purchase and sale of shares in a company.

- **Debenture.** The legal meaning of the term **debenture** is a written acknowledgement of a debt. This means there will be a contract, in writing, between the company and the lender. The contract is called the debenture deed and is held by a trustee who is required to look after the needs of the lenders. If the company does not pay interest, or repay capital, on the due date, the trustee must take action to recover what is owed to the lenders. Debentures may be secured or unsecured, depending on what is stated in the debenture deed.
- **Bond.** The term **bond** has been in common use in the USA for some time as a name for loan capital. It is now found increasingly frequently in the statements of financial position (balance sheets) of UK companies, particularly when they are raising finance in the international capital markets where the US terminology is more familiar.
- **Commercial paper**, **loan notes** and **bank facility**. These are all names of short- to medium-term financing provided by banks or similar organisations. The interest payable is usually variable and the loans are unsecured.

This is only a sample of the main variations of names given to loan finance. It is not exhaustive because the name does not matter greatly for the purposes of accounting records and interpretation. The essential information needed for the users of accounting information is the answer to five questions:

1 How much was borrowed (the **principal sum**)?
2 How much has to be repaid (the capital sum plus any additional interest charge)?
3 When is repayment required?
4 What are the interest payments required?
5 Has the lender sought any security for repayment of the interest and the principal sum?

You will find detailed notes to the statement of financial position (balance sheet) setting out the interest costs and repayment conditions for loans reported as liabilities.

11.6.3 Secured and unsecured loans

- **Unsecured loan.** An **unsecured loan** is one where the lender has no first claim on any particular assets of the company and, in the event of default, must wait for payment alongside all the other unsecured creditors. If there is no wording to indicate that the loan is secured, then the reader of financial statements must assume it is unsecured.
- **Secured loan.** Where any loan is described as **secured**, it means that the lender has first claim to named assets of the company. Where a debenture or loan stock is secured, and the company defaults on payment, the trustee for the debenture will take possession of the asset and use it to make the necessary repayment. In the event of the company not being able to pay all the amounts it owes, secured lenders come before unsecured lenders in the queue for repayment.

Activity 11.4

A financial weekly magazine contains the following sentence:

Telecoms plc this week raised cash by selling $1m bonds with five-year and ten-year maturities.

Explain each part of the sentence.

11.6.4 Loan having a range of repayment dates

When a loan is made to a business, conditions will be negotiated regarding the amount and date of repayment. Some banks are willing to offer a range of repayment dates, say any time between 10 and 15 years hence, with the company being allowed to choose when it will repay. If the company needs the money and the interest rate is favourable, the company will borrow for the longest period allowed under the contract. If the company finds it no longer needs the money, or else the interest rate is burdensome, the company will repay at the earliest possible opportunity. For statement of financial position (balance sheet) purposes the preparer of accounts has to decide which date to use as a basis for classification.

The general principle is that if there is an obligation to transfer economic benefits, there will be a liability in the statement of financial position (balance sheet). Where there is a range of possible dates for repayment, the maturity date will be taken as the earliest date on which the lender can require repayment.[6]

11.6.5 Change in the nature of finance source

Some types of finance provided to a business may be arranged so as to allow a change in the nature of the source during the period of financing. As an example, consider the case of convertible loans.

A **convertible loan** is a source of finance which starts its life as a loan but, at some point in the future, may be converted to ordinary shares in the company (e.g. the lender is promised five shares per £100 of loan capital). At the date of conversion, the lender becomes a **shareholder**. This kind of financial arrangement is attractive to those providing finance because it provides the reassurance of loan finance and a payment of interest in the early years of a new development, with the option of switching to shares if the project is successful. If the project is not successful and the share price does not perform as expected, then the lender will not convert and will look for repayment of the loan on the due date. For the company there are some tax advantages in issuing loan finance. Also, the rate of interest required by investors in a convertible loan is usually lower than that required for a straight (non-convertible) loan because investors see potential additional rewards in the convertible loan.

While a convertible loan remains unconverted it is reported as a loan. Companies are not allowed to say, 'We are almost certain there will be a conversion', and report the convertible loan as share finance from the outset. However, there is an awareness that the eventual conversion will dilute the existing shareholders' claim on future profits and so the company will report the earnings per share before and after taking into account the effect of this dilution. Consequently, you will see 'fully diluted earnings per share' at the foot of the income statement (profit and loss account).

11.6.6 Interest payable on the loan

Companies and their banks may negotiate a variety of patterns for interest payment on loans. The pattern of interest payment might be based on a low percentage charge in earlier years and a higher percentage charge in later years, because the company expects that profits will be low initially but will rise later to cover the higher interest payments. For many years the income statement (profit and loss account) would have reported the interest charge based on the amount paid in each year, but now the standard-setters require the interest charge to be reported as it would be if a compound interest rate were applied over the life of the loan. This is described as the **effective interest rate**.[7]

Definition	The **effective interest rate** is the rate that exactly discounts estimated future cash payments or receipts through the expected life of the financial instrument.

The reasoning behind this approach is that, for purposes of reporting profit, the flexibility of negotiation of interest payment patterns makes comparability difficult to achieve. The banks will, however, ensure that they receive the overall compound interest they require and this gives a commercially relevant basis for comparability in the matching of interest charges against the profits of the period.

The general principle is that the amount shown as the expense of interest payable in the income statement (profit and loss account) should be based on the compound rate of interest applying over the entire period of the loan. This will not always be the same as the amount of interest paid in cash during the period. The spreading of interest charges over the period of the loan is an application of the accruals or matching concept. As an example, consider stepped bonds and deep discount bonds.

Stepped bonds

A **stepped bond** is a form of lending where the interest rate increases over the period of the loan. Take as an example a loan of £5m which carries a rate of interest of 8% per annum for the first three years, 10% per annum for the next three years and 13% per annum for the final four years. The cash payment for interest starts at £400,000 and by the tenth year has risen to £650,000. The overall payments may be shown to be equivalent to a compound rate of 10.06% per annum. Table 11.3 shows that the income statement (profit and loss account) charge of £503,000 would start higher than the cash amount, £400,000. By the final year the income statement (profit and loss account) charge of £517,000 would be lower than the cash amount, £650,000. The pattern followed on each line of Table 11.3 is to start with the amount owing, add interest at 10.06% and deduct the amount of the cash payment, leaving the amount owing at the end of the period which becomes the amount owing at the start of the next period. By the end of the ten years the amount owing is exactly £5,000,000, the amount required by the lender.

It may be seen from Table 11.3 that the expense charged in the income statement (income statement (profit and loss account)) has a smoother pattern than that of the cash payments. Over the life of the loan the total expense charged must equal the total of the cash payments. The accounting processes for recording these amounts are too complex for a first-level course. The important point to note is that all companies are required to use this approach in calculating the expense charged in calculating profit. The cash flow implications of interest payments may be quite different and it will be necessary to look to the cash flow statement for evidence of the cash flow effect.

Deep discount bonds

A **deep discount bond** is issued at a price lower than (at a 'discount' to) its repayment amount. The interest rate (**coupon**) paid during the life of the loan may be very low (a 'low coupon' bond) or there may be no interest paid at all during the period of the loan (a 'zero coupon' bond). As an example, consider a zero coupon bond issued at £28m with a redemption value of £41m in four years' time. The cash payments of interest are zero but the income statement (profit and loss account) would show an annual charge of 10% per annum (starting at £2.8m in Year 1 and rising to £3.73m by Year 4). If there were no pattern of annual interest the entire discount of £13m would be shown as an expense of Year 4, distorting the underlying pattern of trading profit. Table 11.4 shows the pattern of interest charges for the income statement (profit and loss account).

Table 11.3
Calculation of expense charged in income statement (profit and loss account) for interest based on compound interest calculation

Year	Loan at start	Expense charged	Cash payment record	
		Interest at 10.06%	Cash paid	Loan at end
	(a)	(b)	(c)	(a) + (b) – (c)
	£000s	£000s	£000s	£000s
1	5,000	503	400	5,103
2	5,103	513	400	5,216
3	5,216	525	400	5,341
4	5,341	537	500	5,378
5	5,378	541	500	5,419
6	5,419	545	500	5,464
7	5,464	550	650	5,364
8	5,364	540	650	5,254
9	5,254	529	650	5,133
10	5,133	517	650	5,000
Total		5,300	5,300	

Table 11.4
Schedule of interest charges for zero coupon bond

Year	Loan at start £m	Interest £m	Loan at end £m
1	28.00	2.80	30.80
2	30.80	3.08	33.88
3	33.88	3.39	37.27
4	37.27	3.73	41.00
Total		13.00	

In the statement of financial position (balance sheet) the amount recorded for the liability will start at £28m and rise to £41m as shown in the final column of Table 11.4, so that the liability at the end represents the total amount due.

Activity 11.5

A three-year loan of £100,000 will be repaid at the end of three years as £133,100. No interest is payable during the three-year period. The interest included in the loan repayment arrangement is equivalent to a compound annual charge of 10% per annum. Explain how this transaction would appear in the income statement (profit and loss account) and statement of financial position (balance sheet) over the three-year period.

11.6.7 Complex capital instruments

It is impossible to read the statement of financial position (balance sheet) of most major listed companies without realising rapidly that there is a bewildering array of capital instruments being used to raise money for business. The reasons are complex but lie in the need to provide conditions which are attractive to both borrower and lender when they may be based in different countries and may have different perspectives on interest rates and currency exchange rates. This section explains the term 'interest rate swaps', which are increasingly used by companies, and takes an illustration from a major company to indicate the variety of capital instruments (sources of finance) in use. Detailed descriptions and discussion are beyond the scope of this text but would be found in a finance manual.

Interest rate swaps

Suppose there are two companies, A and B. Both have identical amounts of loan finance. Company A is paying fixed rates of interest, but would prefer to be paying variable rates, while Company B is paying variable rates of interest, but would prefer to be paying fixed rates. The reasons could be related to patterns of cash flow from trading, cash flow from investments or beliefs about future directions of interest rates. Whatever the reason, it would seem quite acceptable for them to swap (exchange) so that A pays the variable interest on behalf of B and B pays the fixed interest on behalf of A. This type of arrangement has to be explained carefully because neither company can escape from the legal obligation on the loans taken out initially. The explanation will usually be found in a note to the accounts which gives information on the legal obligation and on the actual impact on the income statement (profit and loss account) of implementing the swap.

Capital instruments of a listed company

The following illustration is based upon the statement of financial position (balance sheet) of a major UK listed company:

Note on borrowings:		Year 2 £m	Year 1 £m
Unsecured borrowings:			
10½% euro-sterling bonds Year 17		1,000	1,000
Loan stocks			
13.625%	Year 16	250	250
5.675% – 9.3%	Year 3/Year 10	59	61
Zero coupon bonds Year 3		966	872
Variable rate multi-option bank facility		158	1,552
Bank loans, overdrafts, commercial paper, short- and medium-term notes		2,570	2,448

. . . the nominal value of the zero coupon bonds is £1,000m and the effective annual rate of interest is 10.85% . . .

Comment. The euro-sterling bonds and the loan stocks are reported at the amount due for repayment at the end of the loan period. The euro-sterling bonds are loans raised in the eurobond market, repayable in sterling. Those loans which have fixed rates of interest are indicated in the table by a fixed percentage rate. Zero coupon means a zero percentage rate of annual interest payable. That does not mean the company escapes interest payment altogether. The liability on the zero coupon bonds increases by 10.85% each year as indicated in the extract note at the foot of the table. It is presumably due for repayment part-way through Year 3 since the liability shown at the end of Year 2 is quite close to the £1,000m amount due (called the **nominal value** in the note). The remaining loans are variable rate and so the annual interest charge depends on current rates of interest. Professional investors might want to know more about the nature of the bank facility and also the breakdown of the various components of the figure £2,570m.

11.7 Summary

- A **non-current liability** is any liability that does not meet the definition of a current liability. Non-current liabilities are also described as **long-term liabilities**.

- Users need information about the **principal sum** repayable and the **interest** payable during the lifetime of a liability. They also need to know the dates on which significant payments will be required (called the **maturity profile of debt**).

- Detailed information about **non-current liabilities** is found in the notes to the financial statements.

- A **provision** is a liability of uncertain timing or amount. The amount of a provision is reported in the liabilities section of a statement of financial position (balance sheet). Changes in provisions are reported in the income statement (profit and loss account).

- **Deferred income** arises where a business receives a government grant or receives cash for goods or services before these are provided. The cash received is reported as an increase in cash and an increase in a liability to represent the obligation to satisfy the conditions of the grant or provide the goods or services. When the conditions are satisfied the liability is reduced and the ownership interest is increased by recording the revenue.

QUESTIONS

The Questions section of each chapter has three types of question. 'Test your understanding' questions to help you review your reading are in the 'A' series of questions. You will find the answers to these by reading and thinking about the material in the book. 'Application' questions to test your ability to apply technical skills are in the 'B' series of questions. Questions requiring you to show skills in problem solving and evaluation are in the 'C' series of questions. A letter [S] indicates that there is a solution at the end of the book. Other solutions are provided in the Instructor's Manual, where there are further questions parallel to those set out here.

A   Test your understanding

Skills outcomes

A11.1 Explain why a provision may be required. (Section 11.4)

A11.2 Give three examples of situations which may lead to provisions. (Section 11.4)

A11.3 Explain how deferred income is recorded. (Section 11.5)

A11.4 Is it justifiable to report deferred income under the category of liability? (Section 11.5)

A11.5 Explain what is meant by each of the following terms: (Section 11.6)

    (a) loan stock;
    (b) debenture;
    (c) bond;
    (d) maturity date; and
    (e) convertible loan stock.

A11.6 [S] On reviewing the financial statements, the company accountant discovers that a grant of £60,000 towards expenditure of the current year plus two further years has been reported entirely as revenue of the period. What will be the effect on the income statement (profit and loss account) and the statement of financial position (balance sheet) when this error is rectified?

A11.7 [S] On reviewing the financial statements, the company accountant discovers that there has been no provision made for urgent repairs to external doors and window frames, already identified as being of high priority on grounds of health and safety. The amount of £50,000 should be provided. What will be the effect on the income statement (profit and loss account) and the statement of financial position (balance sheet) when this error is rectified?

B Application

B11.1 [S]
The Washing Machine Repair Company gives a warranty of no-cost rectification of unsatisfactory repairs. It has revenue from repair contracts recorded as:

Year	Amount of revenue
	£
1	80,000
2	90,000

Based on previous experience the manager makes a provision of 10% of revenue each year for warranty costs. In respect of the work done during Years 1 and 2, repairs under warranty are carried out as follows:

Date of repair work	Amount in respect of Year 1 revenue	Amount in respect of Year 2 revenue	Total
Year	£	£	£
1	4,500		4,500
2	3,200	4,800	8,000
3		5,000	5,000

Required
(a) Show how this information would be recorded in the financial statements of the Washing Machine Repair Company.
(b) Explain how the financial statements would appear if the company made no provision for warranty costs but charged them to income statement (profit and loss account) when incurred.

B11.2 [S]
General Engineering Ltd receives a government grant for £60,000 towards employee training costs to be incurred evenly over the next three years. Explain how this transaction will be reported in the financial statements.

C Problem solving and evaluation

C11.1
Explain why each of the following is recognised as a provision in the statement of financial position (balance sheet) of a telecommunications company:

(a) On 15 December Year 2, the Group announced a major redundancy programme. Provision has been made at 31 December Year 2 for the associated costs. The provision is expected to be utilised within 12 months.
(b) Because of the redundancy programme, some properties have become vacant. Provision has been made for lease payments that cannot be avoided where subletting is not possible. The provision will be utilised within 15 months.
(c) There is a legal claim against a subsidiary in respect of alleged breach of contract. Provision has been made for this claim. It is expected that the provision will be utilised within 12 months.

C11.2
(Refer also to Chapter 10, section 10.3.2, on Contingent liabilities.)
Explain why each of the following is reported as a contingent liability but not recognised as a provision in the statement of financial position (balance sheet).

(a) Some leasehold properties which the group no longer requires have been sublet to third parties. If the third parties default, the group remains responsible for future rent payments. The maximum liability is £200,000.
(b) Group companies are defendants in the USA in a number of product liability cases related to tobacco products. In a number of these cases, the amounts of compensatory and punitive damages sought are significant.
(c) The Department of Trade and Industry has appointed Inspectors to investigate the company's flotation ten years ago. The directors have been advised that it is possible that circumstances surrounding the flotation may give rise to claims against the company. At this stage it is not possible to quantify either the probability of success of such claims or of the amounts involved.

Activities for study groups

Turn to the annual report of a listed company which you have used for activities in previous chapters. Find every item of information about liabilities. (Start with the financial statements and notes but look also at the strategic report, chief executive's review and other non-regulated information about the company.)

As a group, imagine you are the team of fund managers in a fund management company. You are holding a briefing meeting at which each person explains to the others some feature of the companies in which your fund invests. Today's subject is liabilities. Each person should make a short presentation to the rest of the team covering:

(a) The nature and significance of liabilities in the company.
(b) The effect on profit of a 10% error in estimation of any one of the major categories of liability.
(c) The company's comments, if any, on its future obligations.
(d) The risks which might attach to the liabilities of the company.
(e) The liquidity of the company.
(f) The trends in liabilities since last year (or over five years if a comparative table is provided).
(g) The ratio of current assets to current liabilities.

Notes and references

1. IASB (2016), *Conceptual Framework.*
2. IASB (2016), IAS 1, para. 69.
3. IASB (2016), IAS 1, para. 69.
4. IASB (2016), IAS 37, *Provisions, Contingent Liabilities and Contingent Assets,* para. 10.
5. IASB (2005), Exposure draft of proposed amendments to IAS 37 *Provisions, Contingent Liabilities and Contingent Assets,* para. 1.
6. IFRS 7 (2016), *Financial Instruments: Disclosures,* para. B11C.
7. IASB (2011), IAS 39 *Financial Instruments: Recognition and Measurement.* Definitions section.

Bookkeeping entries for provisions and deferred income

Provisions

In the main text of this chapter there is an example based on the recording of provision for repairs under warranty. The analysis of the transactions and events is set out in Table 11.1. The ledger account will appear as follows:

L3 Provision for warranty repairs					
Date	Particulars	Page	Debit	Credit	Balance
Year 5			£	£	£
Jan. 1	Provision in respect of Year 5	L2		25,000	(25,000)
Jan.–Dec.	Repairs carried out	L1	14,000		(11,000)

LEONA: *At the start of the year (or possibly in practice at the end of each month) the provision is recorded by debiting the profit and loss account (L2) and crediting the provision. When the repairs are carried out there is a credit entry in the cash account (L1) and a debit entry in the provision account. Nothing is recorded as an income statement (profit and loss account) expense at that time. The overall effect is that the income statement (profit and loss account) carries an expense of £25,000 and the provision account shows a potential liability of £11,000 to cover any further repairs arising from work done during Year 5 (since some of the goods sold will remain under warranty into Year 6).*

Deferred income

In the main text of this chapter there is an example based on the recording of deferred income arising under a grant. The analysis of the transactions and events is set out in Table 11.2. The ledger account will appear as follows:

L3 Deferred income (statement of financial position/balance sheet)					
Date	Particulars	Page	Debit	Credit	Balance
Year 1			£	£	£
Jan. 1	Grant received	L1		30,000	(30,000)
Dec. 31	Transfer to profit and loss account	L2	10,000		(20,000)
Year 2					
Dec. 31	Transfer to profit and loss account	L2	10,000		(10,000)
Year 3					
Dec. 31	Transfer to profit and loss account	L2	10,000		nil

LEONA: *The deferred income account is reported as a liability in the statement of financial position (balance sheet). It is established by a credit entry matched by a debit in the cash account (L1). Each year there is a transfer of one-third to the profit and loss account (L2) so that the revenue is spread evenly over the period.*

S   Test your understanding

S11.1 Prepare bookkeeping records for the information in question B11.1.

S11.2 Prepare bookkeeping records for the information in question B11.2.

Ownership interest

Mothercare: Rights issue of shares

Mothercare, the buggy-to-babywear retailer, has launched a £100m rights issue to pay down debt and close up to 75 UK stores to transform the property-heavy group into a "digitally led business".

The 9-for-10 rights issue will be issued at 125p per share, a discount of 34.2 per cent to Monday's closing price. It is fully underwritten by Numis, JPMorgan Cazenove and HSBC. It is expected to raise £95m net of expenses.

Profits from Mothercare's portfolio of international stores have been severely dented by the poorly performing UK retail business in recent years. Management said it aimed to improve its earnings performance by "reshaping and modernising the UK store portfolio" as well as investing in IT and ecommerce.

Mark Newton-Jones, chief executive, said the investment would return the lossmaking UK business to profitability within a "three-year horizon".

UK sales have suffered as competition from the supermarkets and low-cost clothing retailers such as Primark intensifies, and the group remains locked into fixed costs on the property leases of its UK stores.

On Tuesday, Mothercare said it would use the cash to pay down a £40m loan, exit between 50 and 75 high street stores and overhaul its website. It plans to open up to 20 new stores on retail parks in due course.

"Today, two-thirds of our stores are on high streets and one-third are on out-of-town retail parks," said Mr Newton-Jones. "We want to change that over the next four years to the polar opposite. You can't offer services such as fitting car seats when a customer's car is parked half a mile away from the store."

The digital investment in the business will include setting up a customer database that can personalise marketing and promotions.

"Once we know the due date, we know the development of that customer and the journey of that child," he added.

Stores will be modernised so digital features such as customer reviews and stock levels are also visible to in-store customers.

Following the rights issue, the retailer will have paid down all its net debt, but is set to agree a new £50m working capital facility.

 Source: Barrett, C (2014) Mothercare launches £100m rights issue, *Financial Times*, 23 Sept 2014
© The Financial Times Limited. All Rights Reserved.

Discussion points

1 Why has Mothercare made the rights issue?

2 What accounting information is provided in the article?

Contents

Learning outcomes

After reading this chapter you should be able to:

● Define ownership interest.

● Explain and demonstrate how the ownership interest is presented in company accounts.

● Understand the nature and purpose of the statement of changes in equity in the IASB system.

● Explain the needs of users for information about the ownership interest in a company.

● Read and interpret the information reported by companies in their annual reports, in respect of the ownership interest.

● Explain the accounting treatment of dividends.

● Understand the methods by which a company's shares may be issued when the company has a Stock Exchange listing.

● Show that you understand the impact of transactions and events on ownership interest in company accounts.

Additionally, for those who choose to study the supplement:

● Record end-of-period adjustments as debit and credit adjustments to a trial balance taken from the ledger accounts and produce figures for financial statements.

12.1 Introduction

The final element of the accounting equation has been reached. It was explained in Chapter 2 that the ownership interest is the residual amount found by deducting all liabilities of the entity from all of the entity's assets:

Assets	minus	**Liabilities**	equals	**Ownership interest**

The terminology was also explained in Chapter 2. The words equity and net assets both appear in the press and in commentaries in connection with the ownership interest. **Equity** is a word used to describe the ownership interest in the assets of the business after all liabilities are deducted. This is also referred to as the **net assets**, calculated as the assets minus the liabilities.

The structure which has been adopted for Chapters 8 to 12 is based on a series of questions:

● What are the principles for defining and recognising these items?
● What are the information needs of users in respect of the particular items?
● What information is currently provided by companies to meet these needs?
● Does the information show the desirable qualitative characteristics of financial statements?
● What are the principles for measuring, and processes for recording, these items?

Each of these questions will be addressed in turn.

12.2 Definition and recognition

The definition of **ownership interest** was presented in Chapter 2 as: 'the residual amount found by deducting all of the entity's liabilities from all of the entity's assets'.

Because the ownership interest is the residual item of the equation, it can only increase or decrease if something happens to an asset or to a liability. Recognition criteria are applied to assets and liabilities but there cannot be any additional recognition criteria applied to the ownership interest.

Events which change assets or liabilities include:

1 Making a profit (or loss) through the operations of the business – earning revenue and incurring expenses;
2 A contribution of cash by incoming shareholders purchasing new shares;
3 Holding an asset which increases or decreases in value;
4 Holding a liability which increases or decreases in value.

Each one of these events is important to the users of the financial statements and affects the claims of owners on the assets of the business. Since owners are the user group most interested in the ownership interest, this chapter will focus primarily on the information which is helpful to them. Item (1) of this list, reporting a profit or a loss in the income statement through the operations of the business, has been dealt with in some length in previous chapters. In this chapter we concentrate on item (2), the issue of new shares, and on items (3) and (4), the events which cause increases or decreases in assets and liabilities which are *not* reported in the income statement (profit and loss account). Items (3) and (4) are part of what is called other comprehensive income (where 'comprehensive' means 'including everything that creates income for the owners').

12.3 Presentation of ownership interest

Chapters 7 to 11 have concentrated primarily on the limited liability company. For any limited liability company the **income statement (profit and loss account)** is the primary financial statement which reports the revenues and expenses of the business that arise through operations.

The change in value of an asset or liability while it is *held* by the company gives more cause for debate. If the asset has increased in value while still being held by the company, then there may be an increase in the valuation for financial reporting purposes. That is not a **realised** gain and so cannot be reported in the income statement (profit and loss account). There is another primary financial statement which companies must use to report **unrealised** gains. For companies using the IASB system in their financial statements, the unrealised gains are reported in a **statement of other comprehensive income** (Supplement 7.3 Chapter 7). All changes in ownership interest, including contributions and withdrawals by owners, are reported in a **statement of changes in equity**.

Example of an unrealised gain

A business buys a building at a cost of £10m. One year later similar buildings are selling for £13m. The business does not intend to sell but would like to report the potential increase in the fair value of the asset. Because there is no sale, the £3m estimate of the increase in value is unrealised. It is not reported in the income statement (profit and loss account) but is reported in the statement of other comprehensive income.

The presentation of the ownership interest is therefore a potentially complex affair, using more than one financial statement. There is information about the current position of the ownership interest contained in the statement of financial position (balance sheet) and the related notes to the accounts. There is information about changes in the ownership interest in the income statement (profit and loss account) and the statement of other comprehensive income. The approach taken in this chapter is first of all to 'walk through' the early years of operating a limited liability company and the various types of ownership interest which arise.

12.3.1   Issue of shares at the date of incorporation

When the company first comes into existence it issues shares to the owners, who become **equity holders (shareholders)**. The date on which the company comes into existence is called the date of incorporation.

Each share has a *named value* which is called its **nominal value**. Sometimes it is referred to as the **par value**. This amount is written on the **share certificate** which is the document given to each owner as evidence of being a shareholder. Exhibit 12.1 shows the share certificate issued by a company which confirms that J. A. Smith is the owner of 100,000 ordinary shares of 25p nominal value each. This means that J. A. Smith has paid £25,000 to the company and that is the limit of this person's liability if the company fails.

All share certificates are recorded in the share register by the company secretary. The share certificate is a piece of paper which may be sold by the existing owner to another person who wishes to become a shareholder. The person who wishes to become a shareholder is often referred to as a **prospective investor**. That is not a legal term but is a useful way of indicating a person who has an interest in finding out more about the company, without having the legal rights of ownership. When the new owner has acquired the shares, the term 'investor' may continue to be used as a description which emphasises that this person now has a financial interest in knowing that the company is performing well.

The issue of 100,000 shares at a price of 25 pence each will collect £25,000 cash for the company. The effect on the accounting equation is that the asset of cash increases by £25,000 and the ownership interest is increased by £25,000.

Exhibit 12.1
Share certificate issued by a company

Certificate number 24516

Public Company plc

SHARE CERTIFICATE

This is to certify that

J. A. Smith

is the registered owner of 100,000 ordinary shares of 25 pence each.
Given under Seal of the Company the 15th day of August 20XX

Signed   *P McDowall*   *J Jones*

Company Secretary   *W Brown*

                                    Directors

Assets ↑	–	Liabilities	=	Ownership interest ↑
Increase in cash £25,000				Increase in nominal value of shares £25,000

For a company, the ownership interest created by the issue of new shares at their nominal value is recorded as **share capital**.

Activity 12.1

Look at the financial pages of a newspaper. Find the daily list of share prices. What information does the newspaper provide about shares in each company? Which of these items of information would you expect to find in the annual report of the company? Give reasons for your answer.

12.3.2 Buying and selling shares

The company itself has no concern about the purchase and sale of shares from one owner to another, other than having to record the new owner's name in the share register. The purchase and sale may take place by private arrangement or may take place in an established **stock market** (also called a **stock exchange**) if the company is a public limited company. If the shares are traded in an established stock market they are called listed shares because the daily prices are listed on screens for buyers and sellers to see. If there is high demand for the shares, their price will rise. If there is little demand, the price will fall. The market price on any day will depend on investors' expectations about the future of the company. Those expectations will be influenced by announcements from the company, including financial information but also covering a much wider range of company news. The expectations may also be influenced by information about the industry in which the company operates. One of the main purposes of a well-regulated stock exchange is to ensure that all investors have access to the same information at the same time so that no one has an advantage.

12.3.3 Issue of further shares after incorporation

As time goes by, the company may wish to raise new finance and to issue new shares. This could be intended to buy new non-current (fixed) assets, or even to provide cash so that the company may purchase the shares of another company and create a larger group.

Although the **nominal value** remains the same, the **market value** may be quite different.

Example

Suppose a company has shares of nominal value 25 pence but finds that its shares are selling in the market at 80 pence each. If the company issues 200,000 new shares it will collect £160,000 in cash. That is the important piece of information for the company because it can use the cash to buy new assets and expand the activities of the business. The asset of cash has increased by £160,000 and the ownership interest has increased by £160,000.

The accounting records are required by company law to show separately the nominal value of the shares and any extra amount over the nominal value. The nominal value is 25 pence and the total amount collected per share is 80 pence. So the extra amount collected is 55 pence. This extra amount is called a **premium** (the word means 'something extra'). So the £160,000 increase in the ownership interest is recorded as two separate items, namely the **nominal value** of £50,000 and the **share premium** of £110,000.

Assets ↑	–	Liabilities	=	**Ownership interest ↑**
Increase in cash £160,000				Increase in nominal value of shares £50,000 *and* increase in share premium £110,000

12.3.4 Retained earnings

Once the business is in operation it starts to make profits. The income statement (profit and loss account) shows the profit earned in a time period. This profit increases the ownership interest. The accumulation of past profits in the statement of financial position (balance sheet) is called **retained earnings**. The retained earnings represent the ownership interest in the net assets of the business. It is one type of **reserve**. At any point in time someone could ask the owner 'How much would you expect to receive if this business were to close down today?' The owner would look at the statement of financial position (balance sheet) and reply with the total of the **ownership interest**, shown by **equity share capital** plus all **reserves**.

You should be aware that the reserves are given different names in different countries. In some there is a legally defined reserve with a tax-deductible transfer to the reserve from the income statement (profit and loss account). It requires careful reading of the ownership interest section of the statement of financial position (balance sheet). An understanding of the changes in retained profits is helped by reading the **statement of comprehensive income**, explained in section 12.3.5.

12.3.5 Statement of comprehensive income

Look back to the accounting equation explained in Chapter 3. Section 3.4.1 describes ownership interest as:

> *Capital at the start of the year*
> *plus/minus*
> *Capital contributed or withdrawn*
> *plus*
> *Profit of the period*

That chapter gives the simplest possible definition of 'profit' as 'revenue minus expenses'. A broader definition of 'profit' would be to say 'any changes in assets and liabilities other than those caused by capital contributed or withdrawn'. Chapters 9 and 10 have shown that many changes in inventories, accounts receivable and accounts payable will lead to changes in revenue and expenses, reported in the income statement (profit and loss account). This section and section 12.3.6 of this chapter show that other factors may affect the values of assets and liabilities.

The IASB wants to encourage companies to report all changes in assets and liabilities, whatever the cause, in a **statement of comprehensive income**. The word 'comprehensive' means 'including everything'. However, many companies would like to retain the separate income statement as explained in Chapters 5 and 6. Consequently the IASB allows a two-part approach:

1 A separate income statement
2 A second statement beginning with profit or loss from the income statement and incorporating other components of comprehensive income.

This two-part approach is used by many. UK companies which report using IFRS. Details are in Supplement 7.3 to Chapter 7. It is used in this chapter to illustrate the comprehensive income approach. Two examples are provided in the following sections. The first is the revaluation of non-current assets and the second is the reporting of changes in exchange rates of foreign currency.

12.3.6 Revaluation of non-current (fixed) assets

Suppose a company buys a hotel costing £560,000. The hotel is run successfully for a period of three years and at the end of that period a professional valuer confirms that the hotel, if sold, would probably result in sale proceeds of £620,000 because of the change in property values and the reputation which the hotel has established. The directors of the company may wish to tell shareholders about this increased fair value of the company's non-current (fixed) asset.

There are two ways of informing shareholders in the financial statements. One is to continue to record the value at £560,000 (the historical cost) in the statement of financial position (balance sheet) but to include also a note to the financial statements explaining that the fair value has been confirmed as £620,000 by an expert. That information would allow the investor to think, 'That makes me feel better off by £60,000.'

This feeling of investor happiness is surrounded by a note of caution, because the gain in value is not **realised**. The asset has not in fact been sold in the market. It only needs a rumour of pollution on the local beach to depress the market value of all the hotels in the town. Some companies feel that this note of caution is conveyed by providing the information on the increase in value in the notes to the financial statements rather than the statement of financial position (balance sheet) itself.

Other companies take a bolder view and decide that, in the interests of providing information which is relevant to the needs of users, the company should apply the accounting equation on behalf of the readers of the financial statement. These companies then have a problem of deciding on the name to be given to describe this £60,000 increase in the ownership interest. It cannot be called revenue and included in the income statement (profit and loss account) because it has not been realised by the operations of the business. It represents a new ownership interest as a newly identified 'reserve' of wealth. The wealth lies in the asset, but the interest in that wealth is a claim which belongs to the owners. The increased wealth is caused by revaluation of the asset, and so the name chosen for this claim is **revaluation reserve**. In terms of the accounting equation there is an increase in the value of an asset and an increase in the ownership interest.

This section has explained the accounting processes for revaluing non-current (fixed) assets at fair value. You may see revaluation of non-current assets in some annual reports of UK companies. It is not compulsory but if companies choose to revalue then they must do so regularly as explained in Chapter 8. Revaluation of property, plant and equipment is permitted by the IASB but is not a requirement.

Example

A company, Office Owner Ltd, is formed on 1 January Year 1 by the issue of 4m ordinary shares of 25 pence nominal value each. The cash raised from the issue is used on 2 January to buy an office block which is rented to a customer for an annual rent of £50,000. The tenant carries all costs of repairs. The company's administration costs for the year are £10,000. At the end of the year the office block is valued by an expert at £1,015,000. On the last day of the year the company issues a further 2 million ordinary shares at a price of 40 pence each, to raise cash in Year 2 for expansion plans.

Activity 12.2

For the analysis of each transaction you should look back to the previous sections where each type of transaction is dealt with in detail. Write down the effect of each transaction on the accounting equation. Check your answer against Table 12.1. When you are satisfied that you understand Table 12.1 go to Table 12.2 where you will find the amounts entered in the spreadsheet.

Table 12.1
Office Owner Ltd – analysis of transactions for Year 1

Date	Transaction or event		Effect on assets	Effect on ownership interest
Year 1		£000s		
Jan. 1	Issue of shares at nominal value	1,000	Increase asset of cash	Increase share capital at nominal value
Jan. 2	Purchase of office block	1,000	Increase asset of property	Decrease asset of cash
Jan.–Dec.	Rent received	50	Increase asset of cash	Revenue of the period
Jan.–Dec.	Administration costs	10	Decrease asset of cash	Expense of the period
Dec. 31	Revaluation of asset	15	Increase asset of property	Increase ownership interest by revaluation
Dec. 31	Issue of further shares nominal value share premium	500 300	Increase asset of cash	Increase share capital at nominal value and increase share premium

Table 12.2
Office Owner Ltd – spreadsheet of transactions for Year 1

Date	Transaction or event	Cash	Office block	Share capital	Share premium	Income statement (profit and loss account)	Revaluation reserve
Year 1		£000s	£000s	£000s	£000s	£000s	£000s
Jan. 1	Issue of shares	1,000		1,000			
Jan. 2	Purchase of office block	(1,000)	1,000				
Jan.–Dec.	Rent received	50				50	
Jan.–Dec.	Administration costs	(10)				(10)	
Dec. 31	Revaluation of asset		15				15
Dec. 31	Issue of further shares	800		500	300		
		840	1,015	1,500	300	40	15

└——— 1,855 ———┘ └———————— 1,855 ————————┘

Entering the amounts in the spreadsheet of Table 12.2 shows, in the final line, that the accounting equation is satisfied and allows a statement of comprehensive income and a statement of financial position (balance sheet) to be prepared as in Table 12.3.

Table 12.3
Office Owner Ltd – income statement and statement of other comprehensive income at end of Year 1

Income statement for Year 1	
	£000s
Revenue: rent received	50
Administration costs	(10)
Profit for the year	40
Statement of other comprehensive income for Year 1	
Profit for the year	40
Revaluation of asset	15
Total comprehensive income for the year	55

Office Owner Ltd – statement of financial position (balance sheet) at end of Year 1

Office Owner Ltd Statement of financial position (balance sheet) at end of Year 1	
	£000s
Non-current (fixed) asset: Office block (at valuation)	1,015
Current asset: Cash	840
Net assets	1,855
Share capital	1,500
Share premium	300
Revaluation reserve	15
Retained earnings	40
	1,855

Activity 12.3

Suppose you note that a company has revalued its land and buildings as reported in the statement of financial position (balance sheet). What evidence would you expect to see as justification for the amount of the revaluation? What questions might you ask about the basis of revaluation?

12.3.7 Changes in exchange rates of foreign currency

All information in the financial statements of a UK company is shown in pounds (£) sterling. Where exchange rates alter, a company may lose or gain purely because of the exchange rate movement. That loss or gain must be reported.

The accounting process is called translation. Translation from one currency to another is particularly important when the financial statements of companies in a group are added together and so must all be restated in a common currency. The word 'translation' is used because the process is comparable to translating words from one language to another.

There are different methods of reporting depending on the type of transaction or event. Two different stories are considered here. The first is the purchase of an asset located in a foreign country. The second is the purchase, by a group of companies, of the share capital of a company in a foreign country.

Purchase of an asset

Take first of all the example of a UK company which buys a factory in Sweden. The factory is priced at Kr10,000,000. At the date of purchase of the factory the exchange rate is Kr10 = £0.70. The UK company has agreed to pay for the factory on the day of the transfer of legal title.

For accounting purposes the cost of the factory is recorded at the amount paid at the date of purchase, expressed in £s. This is calculated as:

$$\frac{0.70}{10} \times \text{Kr10,000,000} = £700,000$$

The effect of the transaction on the statement of financial position (balance sheet) of the UK company is:

That is the end of the story so far as the UK company is concerned. The exchange rate between the krona and the £ may fluctuate, and this may affect the company's view of the price for which the factory might eventually be sold, but that information will not appear in the financial statements of the UK company until such time as the factory is sold.

Purchase of shares in another company

Suppose now that a UK group of companies has decided to purchase the entire share capital of a Swedish company whose only asset is the same factory. The purchase price is Kr10,000,000. The Swedish company distributes its entire profit as dividend each year so that the only item remaining in its statement of financial position (balance sheet) is the factory at a cost of Kr10,000,000. (This is a very simplistic example but is sufficient to illustrate the exchange rate problem.)

At the date of purchase of the investment, the factory will be recorded in the group statement of financial position (balance sheet) at £700,000.

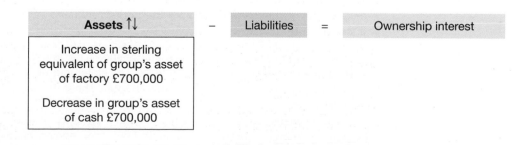

One year later the exchange rate has altered to Kr10 = £0.68. The factory is the only asset of the subsidiary. In the Swedish accounts it remains at Kr10,000,000 but, translated into £ sterling, this now represents only £680,000:

$$\frac{0.68}{10} \times Kr10,000,000 = £680,000$$

This represents a potential loss of £20,000 on the translated value of the asset at the start of the year. The loss is unrealised but as a matter of prudence the fall in the translated asset value should be reported. However, there have been strong feelings expressed by companies over many years that the unrealised loss should not affect the reported profit of the period. Consequently the relevant accounting standard[1] allows the effect on the ownership interest to be shown in the **statement of comprehensive income** as an increase or decrease for the period.

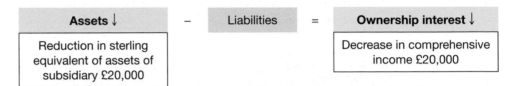

The reporting of the reduction in the asset value as a decrease in reserves is controversial because less attention is sometimes paid to reserves than is paid to the income statement (profit and loss account). This means that the impact on the ownership interest may pass unnoticed. The IASB is hoping that the use of the statement of comprehensive income will increase the transparency of such information.

This practice of translation is required by the accounting standard on the subject. In group accounting there is considerable complexity to the technical aspects of which exchange rate effects must pass through the income statement (profit and loss account) and which may pass through the reserves. The important message for the reader of the annual reports is to be alert to the possibility of exchange rate effects on the ownership interest being reported in reserves and to look carefully at the statement of comprehensive income.

12.4 Statement of changes in equity

In Chapter 7 it was noted that the IASB specifies four primary financial statements:[2]

1 a statement of financial position (balance sheet)
2 an income statement (showing the profit or loss for the period), as part of a larger statement of comprehensive income
3 a statement of changes in equity for the period, and
4 a statement of cash flows.

The statement of financial position (balance sheet), income statement and statement of cash flows were dealt with in Chapter 7. The statement of comprehensive income has been explained in section 12.3.5 of this chapter. The statement of changes in equity is now explained.

The IASB has decided that all 'owner' changes in equity should be presented in the statement of changes in equity, separately from 'non-owner' changes in equity. The detailed requirements are set out in IAS 1.

An 'owner' change occurs when share capital changes or dividends are paid. A 'non-owner' change results from an event in the business, reported either as income or as other comprehensive income. As explained in section 12.3.5, all non-owner changes in equity are required to be presented in one statement of comprehensive income or in two statements (a separate income statement and a statement of other comprehensive income).

Dividends are distributions to owners in their capacity as owners. Consequently dividends paid are reported in the statement of changes in equity. There will also be a separate note on the dividend per share paid during the year.

The statement of changes in equity includes the following information:

- total comprehensive income for the period, showing separately the total amounts attributable to owners of the parent and to non-controlling interests;
- for each component of equity, the effects of retrospective application or retrospective restatement recognised in accordance with IAS 8; and
- for each component of equity, a reconciliation between the carrying amount at the beginning and the end of the period, separately disclosing changes resulting from:

(i)   profit or loss;
(ii) other comprehensive income; and
(iii) transactions with owners in their capacity as owners, showing separately contributions by and distributions to owners.

The term 'components of equity' includes, for example, each class of contributed equity, the accumulated balance of each class of other comprehensive income and retained earnings.

12.5 Users' needs for information

The owners of a company, and potential investors in a company, are primarily interested in whether the business will make them better off or worse off. They also want to be reassured that the business has taken care of the resources entrusted to it (carrying out the function of **stewardship**). The first source of an increase in the ownership interest is the **profit** generated by the company. Professional investors will use the phrase **quality of earnings** to refer to the different components of profit. They tend to regard profits generated by the main operating activity as being of higher quality than windfall gains such as profits on the sale of non-current (fixed) assets which are not a regular feature of the company's activity.

Owners of a company expect to receive a reward for ownership. One form of reward is to watch the business grow and to know that in the future a sale of shares will give them a satisfactory gain over the period of ownership. That requires a long-term horizon. Some investors prefer to see the reward more frequently in the form of a dividend. They want to know that the ownership interest is adequate to support the dividend and yet leave sufficient assets in the business to generate further profits and dividends.

Creditors of a company know that they rank ahead of the shareholders in the event of the company being wound up, but they want to know that the company is generating sufficient wealth for the owners to provide a cushion against any adverse events. Therefore creditors will also be concerned with the ownership interest and how it is being maintained or is growing.

Employees, suppliers and customers similarly look for reassurance as to the strength of the business to continue into the future. The ownership interest is a convenient focus which summarises the overall impact of the state of assets and liabilities, although what employees are really interested in is the preservation of the earnings capacity of the business.

12.6 Information provided in the financial statements

In Chapter 7 the statement of financial position (balance sheet) of Safe and Sure plc was presented. The final section of that statement of financial position (balance sheet) presented information on the capital and reserves representing the claim of the shareholders on the assets.

		Year 7 £m	Year 6 £m
Capital and reserves			
Called-up share capital	12	196	195
Share premium account	13	85	55
Revaluation reserve	14	46	46
Retained earnings	15	4,316	3,408
Equity holders' funds		4,643	3,704

In the discussion contained in Chapter 7 it was emphasised that the most important feature of this information is that, in total, it represents the shareholders' legal claim. There is nothing to see, touch, count or hold. If the company were to cease trading at the date of the financial statements, sell all its assets for the statement of financial position (balance sheet) amount and pay off all liabilities, the shareholders would be left with £464.3m to take away. The shareholders have the residual claim, which means that if the assets were to be sold for more than the statement of financial position (balance sheet) amount, the shareholders would share the windfall gain. If the assets were sold for less than the statement of financial position (balance sheet) amount, the shareholders would share the loss.

The total ownership interest is a claim which is described by this company as 'equity holders' funds'. It is equal to the **net assets** of the company. The total claim is subdivided so as to explain how the various parts of the claim have arisen. This section now considers each part of the claim in turn.

12.6.1 Share capital

The information shown by the company at note 12 is as follows:

Note 12 Share capital

	Year 7 £m	Year 6 £m
Ordinary shares of 2 pence each		
Authorised: 10,500,000,000 shares (Year 6: 10,000,000,000)	210	200
Issued and fully paid: 9,781,474,870 shares	196	195

Certain senior executives hold options to subscribe for shares in the company at prices ranging from 33.40p to 244.33p under schemes approved by equity holders at various dates. Options on 34,795,070 shares were exercised during Year 7 and 669,700 options lapsed. The number of shares subject to options, the years in which they were granted, the option price and the years in which they can be exercised are:

Options granted	Exercisable	Option price (pence)	Numbers
	Year 8	33.40	137,500
All granted	Year 9	53.55	1,100,000
10 years	Year 10	75.42	5,425,000
before	Year 11	100.22	14,290,000
exercisable	Year 12	120.33	28,266,000
	Year 13/14	150.45	35,399,420
	Year 15	195.20	36,909,500
	Year 16	201.50	22,792,700
	Year 17	244.33	32,793,630
			177,113,750

Called up means that the company has called upon the shareholders who first bought the shares to make payment in full. When a new company is brought to the stock market for the first time, investors may be invited to buy the shares by paying an instalment now and the rest later. That was quite common in the 1980s when former nationalised industries, such as electricity and water companies, were being sold to the private sector. The **prospectus**, which is issued to invite the purchase of shares, specifies the dates on which the company would make a call for the rest of the share price due. After all the cash has been received by the company, the shares are described as **fully paid**.

Ordinary shareholders are entitled to vote at meetings, usually in proportion to the number of shares held. That means that the power of the individual shareholder depends on the number of shares held. For most large companies there are relatively small numbers of shareholders who control relatively large proportions of the share capital. A company which is part of a larger group of companies is required to report in the notes to the accounts the name and country of the ultimate parent company. Companies that are listed on the Stock Exchange are required to disclose in the directors' report the name of any shareholder interested in 3% or more of the company's issued share capital.

Before the directors of a company may issue new shares, they must be authorised to do so by the existing shareholders. The existing shareholders need to be aware that their claim will be diluted by the incoming shareholders. (If there are 50 shares owned equally by two persons, each controls 50% of the company. If 25 new shares are issued to a third person, then all three have 33.3% each, which dilutes the voting power of the first two persons.)

One of the controversial aspects of share capital in recent years has been the privilege of share options taken by directors and other employees (usually senior employees of the business but sometimes spreading to the wider employee range). A share option allows the person holding the option to buy shares in the company, at any future date up to a specified limit in time, at an agreed fixed price. The argument in favour of such an arrangement is that it gives senior management an incentive to make the company prosperous because they want the share price to increase above the price they have agreed to pay. The argument against it is that they have no very strong incentive because the worst that can happen to directors and other employees is that they decide not to take up the option when the share price has not performed well. Until 1995 there were also some personal tax advantages in taking options rather than a normal portion of salary, but since then, the tax rules have limited such benefits.

Major companies now disclose, in the directors' report, the options held by each of the directors.

The analyst's view

David and Leona are on the plane flying from London to Aberdeen for a week's holiday in the Cairngorms. David has brought the annual report of Safe and Sure plc as a precaution against inclement weather disturbing their plans for outdoor activities.

While they wait for lunch to be served, David turns to the annual report and finds it is quite helpful to have Leona alongside him.

DAVID: *At the present time nothing seems to excite more comment from the financial journalists than the salaries paid to the directors and the options they hold. I have to confess that it's something I look for in the annual report. Maybe I'm looking for my future earning potential! One of my more cynical colleagues says that directors can't lose on options. If the share price rises they make money, which we don't mind because our investment is rising in value. What happens if the share price falls? The directors take new options at the lower price and then wait for the market to rise again so that they make a profit! We can't do that for our investment.*

I always look at the note on share capital to see whether new shares have been issued during the year. It reminds me to find out the reason. In this case the increase is £0.1m and the reason is explained in the accounts as being due entirely to the issue of options.

12.6.2 Share premium

It was explained earlier in this chapter that when shares are issued by a company it may well be that the market price of the shares is greater than the nominal value. What really matters to the company is the amount of cash contributed by the new shareholders, but company law insists that the claim of these new shareholders is split into a nominal amount and a share premium (the amount received in excess of the nominal amount).

Note 13 Share premium account

	Year 7	Year 6
	£m	£m
At 1 January	55	36
Premium on shares issued during the year under the share option schemes	30	19
At 31 December	85	55

DAVID: *I look at the share premium account only as a check on the amount of cash raised by issuing shares during the year. If I add the £30m shown in this note to the £1m shown as an increase in nominal value, then I know that £31m was raised in total by the issue of shares. I can check that in the cash flow statement.*

12.6.3 Revaluation reserve

Earlier in the chapter the effect of revaluing assets was explained in terms of the accounting equation. It was also explained that the effects of foreign currency exchange rates may appear in reserves. The note to the accounts of Safe and Sure plc appears as follows:

Note 14 Revaluation reserve

	Year 7	Year 6
	£m	£m
At 1 January	46	46
At 31 December	46	46

DAVID: *I always look at the reserves note to see what is happening to the overall shareholders' claim. There is no change in the reserve during Year 6 or Year 7 so does that mean the company has not revalued the non-current assets in that period?*

LEONA: *The directors are required to review the valuations at each statement of financial position (balance sheet) date. So if there is no change in the revaluation reserve there must have been no change in the value of the assets involved.*

12.6.4 Statement of comprehensive income

Safe and Sure plc
Group statement of other comprehensive income

	Year 7	Year 6
	£m	£m
Profit for the period	1,148	946
Other comprehensive income:		
Exchange rate adjustments	55	(60)
Total comprehensive income for the year	1,203	886

LEONA: *Let me take you through the Statement of other comprehensive income. It brings together the items which cause an overall decrease or increase in the ownership interest. On the first line you can see the profit for the period which comes from the income statement. On the next line there are the exchange rate adjustments that relate to translation of investments held in other currencies. In Year 6 the exchange rates worked against the interests of equity holders but in Year 7 there was a favourable effect.*

12.6.5 Statement of changes in equity

Group statement of changes in equity for the year ended
31 December Year 7

	Share capital	Share premium	Revaluation reserve	Retained earnings (including exchange rate adjustments)	Total
	£m	£m	£m	£m	£m
Balance at 1 Jan Year 6	194	36	46	2,766	3,042
Total comprehensive income				886	886
Transactions with owners:					
Share capital issued	1	19			20
Less dividend	—	—	—	(244)	(244)
Balance at 1 Jan Year 7	195	55	46	3,408	3,704
Total comprehensive income				1,203	1,203
Transactions with owners:					
Share capital issued	1	30			31
Less dividend	—	—	—	(295)	(295)
Balance at 31 Dec Year 7	196	85	46	4,316	4,643

LEONA: *Now you really can start to tie things together. The statement of changes in equity shows changes during Year 7 in the lower part of the statement, with comparative figures for Year 6 in the upper part of the statement. Starting at the top of the table we see the amounts for the different components of equity at the start of Year 6. Share capital was issued, increasing the nominal value and the share premium reserve. The comprehensive income of the period increased the retained earnings. Dividends paid decreased the retained earnings. That takes us to the start of Year 7 with an overall total of £3,704m. On the next line we see that the new share capital issued is £31m which is a combination of the increase of £30m in share premium (Note 13) and the increase of £1m in nominal share capital (Note 12). That is really tricky to sort out from the Notes – it's very helpful to have the reconciliation give the information in one place. The comprehensive income is taken from the statement of comprehensive income and is shown as increasing retained earnings. The next line shows the dividend of £295m paid during Year 7. That dividend relates to the profits earned in Year 6. For the dividend recommended in respect of Year 7 we have to look at the Finance Director's review. Finally the statement shows all the separate components adding to the overall total of £4,643m.*

DAVID: *You have given me plenty to think about. I can see the drinks trolley on its way – what would you like?*

12.7 Dividends

Shareholders who invest in a company do so because they want the value of their shares to increase over time and return greater wealth when eventually sold. In the meantime the shareholders look for an income to spend each year. That comes to some of them by means of dividends.

Companies are not obliged to pay dividends and may decide not to do so if there is a shortage of cash or it is needed for other purposes. The directors make a recommendation to the shareholders in the annual general meeting. The shareholders may vote against taking the dividend but that happens only very rarely. Final dividend payments usually take place soon after the annual general meeting. Some companies also pay an interim dividend during the accounting year. Major UK companies have in past years ensured that a dividend was paid every year, however small, because it allowed the shares to be regarded as sufficiently 'safe' for investors such as trustees of charitable institutions.

When a company decides it wants to pay a dividend, there are two essential tests. The first is, 'Does the company have the cash resources to pay a dividend?' The second is, 'Has the company made sufficient profits, adding this year to previous years, to justify the dividend as being paid out of wealth created by the business?'

Even where the company has cash in the bank from which to pay the dividend, it must look forward and ensure that there are no other commitments in the near future which will also need cash. The company may decide to borrow short term to finance the dividend. In such a situation the company has to weigh the interest cost of borrowing against the risk of its shares being undervalued because of lack of interest from shareholders. These are all problems of cash management (more often called 'treasury management').

Company law imposes a different viewpoint. It takes the view that a company should not return to shareholders, during the life of the company, a part of the capital contributed by the shareholder body. Accordingly there is a requirement that dividends must be covered by accumulated reserves of past profit in excess of accumulated reserves of past losses. It is not required that the dividend is covered by the profit of the year. A company might choose to smooth things over by keeping the dividend reasonably constant even where profits are fluctuating.

The dividend declared by the company is usually expressed in pence per share. Shareholders receive dividend calculated by multiplying the dividend in pence per share by the number of shares held. For the company there is a reduction in the asset of cash and a reduction in the ownership claim. The management of the company may regard the dividend as an expense of the business but it is more properly regarded as a reduction in the claim which the owners have on the net assets as a whole. The reduction in the ownership interest is reported in the statement of changes in equity because it is a transaction with the owners.

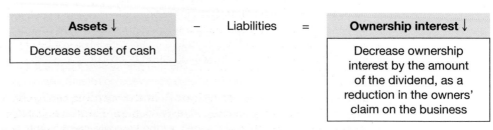

Assets ↓	–	Liabilities	=	Ownership interest ↓
Decrease asset of cash				Decrease ownership interest by the amount of the dividend, as a reduction in the owners' claim on the business

At the end of the accounting period the company will calculate profit and then declare a recommended dividend. The dividend is recommended by the directors to the shareholders. The shareholders, in the annual general meeting, may accept or decline but are not allowed to increase the amount. At the balance sheet date there is no legal liability because the shareholders' meeting has not been held. Therefore there is no information reported in the financial statements. The directors' report, which is required by company law, will contain a statement of the recommended dividend for the year. There will probably also be information in the chairman's statement or on a 'highlights' page.

12.8　Issue of further shares on the Stock Exchange

Once a company has a listing on the Stock Exchange it may decide to issue further shares. There are different methods by which this may be done, depending on the company's motive for the action. This section describes an offer for sale, a capitalisation issue and a rights issue.

12.8.1　Offer for sale

When a company seeks a listing of its shares for the first time, it must offer those shares to the public (using the services of a member firm of the Stock Exchange as a sponsor) and issue a **prospectus** setting out information about itself. Some of the information to be included in the prospectus is required by the Companies Act but this is expanded upon by the **Listing Rules**. The prospectus is a highly informative document, revealing far more about a company than would be found in the annual report. There is a requirement for an accountant's report which includes a three-year history of the financial statements. In particular, there must be a specific statement confirming the adequacy of working capital.

There may also be a forecast of the expected profits for the next accounting period. The reporting accountants will be asked to give an opinion on the forecast. Particularly interesting are the assumptions on which the forecast is based. The reporting accountants will confirm that the amounts in the forecast are consistent with the assumptions but the reader will have to decide how appropriate the assumptions themselves are.

Exhibit 12.2 contains an example of a statement of assumptions taken from a company prospectus.

Exhibit 12.2
Assumptions on which profit forecast is based

> The forecasts have been prepared on a basis consistent with the accounting policies normally accepted by the Group and on the following principal assumptions:
>
> (i)　there will be no changes in taxation or other legislation or government regulations or policies which will have a significant effect on the Group; and
> (ii)　the operations of the Group and its suppliers will not be significantly affected by weather conditions, industrial action or civil disturbances.

You may be surprised to learn that the wording in Exhibit 12.2 is extracted from the prospectus of a company retailing high-quality chocolates. You may be further surprised to learn that very similar wording appeared in the prospectus of a company offering dry cleaning services. There is no regulation which says that the statement of assumptions has to be helpful to the user of the annual report.

12.8.2 Capitalisation issue

After the shares have been listed for some time, the market value may have grown to the point where the shares are less marketable because the price of each is too large for convenient trading in small lots. The company may decide to increase the number of shares held by shareholders without making any change to the assets or liabilities of the company. One way of achieving this is to convert reserves into share capital. Take the simplified statement of financial position (balance sheet) in Table 12.4. The company decides to convert £1m of reserves into share capital. It writes to each shareholder saying, 'You will receive one new share for each share already held'. The statement of financial position (balance sheet) now becomes as shown in Table 12.5.

The shareholder now holds twice as many shares by number but is no better or worse off financially because the total value of the company has not changed. The shares will each be worth one-half of the market price of an old share at the moment of issue. This process is sometimes referred to as a bonus issue because the shareholders receive new share certificates, but in reality there is no bonus because no new wealth is created.

Table 12.4
Statement of financial position (balance sheet) of company prior to capitalisation

	£m
Assets	7
Liabilities	(4)
Net assets	3
Share capital, in shares of 25 pence each	1
Reserves	2
	3

Table 12.5
Statement of financial position (balance sheet) of company after capitalisation

	£m
Assets	7
Liabilities	(4)
Net assets	3
Share capital, in shares of 25 pence each	2
Reserves	1
	3

In terms of the accounting equation the effect on the statement of financial position (balance sheet) is:

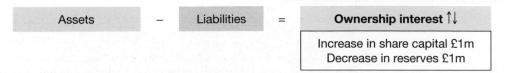

Assets	–	Liabilities	=	**Ownership interest** ↑↓
				Increase in share capital £1m
				Decrease in reserves £1m

12.8.3 Rights issue

Once a company has a market listing it may decide that it needs to raise further finance on the stock market. The first people it would ask are the existing shareholders, who have already shown their commitment to the company by owning shares in it. Furthermore, it is desirable to offer them first chance because if strangers buy the shares the interests of the existing shareholders may be diluted. Suppose the company in Table 12.4 wishes to raise £3m new finance. It will offer existing shareholders the right to pay for, say, 2 million new shares at 150 pence each. There are already 4 million shares of 25p nominal value in issue, so the letter to the shareholders will say: 'The company is offering you the right to buy 1 new share at a price of 150p for every 2 existing shares you hold.' Existing shareholders will be attracted by this offer provided the market price stays above 150 pence for existing shares. They may take up the rights themselves or sell the right to someone else. In either event, the company will receive £3m cash, the company will issue 2 million new shares at 150 pence each and the statement of financial position (balance sheet) will appear as in Table 12.6.

Table 12.6
Statement of financial position (balance sheet) after rights issue

	£m
Assets	7.0
New cash	3.0
	10.0
Liabilities	(4.0)
Net assets	6.0
Share capital, in shares of 25 pence each	1.5
Share premium	2.5
Reserves	2.0
	6.0

The issue price of 150 pence is split for accounting purposes into the nominal value of 25 pence and the premium of 125 pence. In terms of the accounting equation the effect of the rights issue on the statement of financial position (balance sheet) is:

Assets ↑	−	Liabilities	=	**Ownership interest** ↑
Increase in cash £3m				Increase in share capital £0.5m Increase in share premium £2.5m

12.8.4   Buying back shares that have been issued

Companies are permitted to buy back shares that have been issued. The Companies Act sets limits on the proportion of shares that may be bought back from existing shareholders and sets conditions on the availability of retained earnings to support the buy-back. Two possible reasons for buying back shares are (1) to return surplus cash to shareholders and reduce the shareholding base, and (2) to stabilise share prices in the short term where investors want to sell but for some reason there is a temporary lack of demand in the market.

When companies buy back their own shares they may either cancel the shares or hold them as 'treasury shares'. Shares held as 'treasury shares' will be shown as a deduction from share capital in the equity section of the statement of financial position (balance sheet) and the transaction will be reported in the Statement of changes in equity.

Activity 12.4   *Look in the financial section of a newspaper for the list of recent issues of new shares. Obtain the address of one company from a trade directory and write politely to ask for a copy of the prospectus. If you are sufficiently fortunate to obtain a copy of a prospectus, look at the accounting information and compare it with the amount and type of information published in the annual report. Why are they not the same?*

12.9 Summary

- **Ownership interest** is the residual amount found by deducting all of the entity's liabilities from all of the entity's assets.

- Unrealised gains are reported in a **statement of comprehensive income**.

- Each share has a named value when the company is formed. This is called its **nominal value**. It does not change unless the shareholders agree to split shares into smaller units.

- When the shares are sold on a stock market they have a **market value**. The market value of frequently traded shares changes daily with the forces of supply and demand.

- The difference between the nominal value and the market value is called the **share premium**. When the company issues further shares at market price the share premium is recorded separately from the nominal value.

- When non-current assets are revalued, the **unrealised** increase in value is added to the **revaluation reserve**.

- **Dividends** paid to shareholders reduce the ownership interest and are reported in the **statement of comprehensive income**. The effect on the accounting equation is reported when dividends are paid. Dividends proposed to be paid in future are described in the directors' report.

- When a company issues more shares after incorporation it may be through a capitalisation issue, an offer for sale or a rights issue. A **capitalisation issue** gives more shares to equity shareholders. It changes the relationship between share capital and reserves but brings no new resources into the business. An **offer for sale** increases the ownership interest and brings in new cash. A **rights issue** also increases the ownership interest and brings in new cash but it gives the existing shareholders the first choice of maintaining their proportionate interest in the company.

QUESTIONS

The Questions section of each chapter has three types of question. 'Test your understanding' questions to help you review your reading are in the 'A' series of questions. You will find the answers to these by reading and thinking about the material in the book. 'Application' questions to test your ability to apply technical skills are in the 'B' series of questions. Questions requiring you to show skills in problem solving and evaluation are in the 'C' series of questions. A letter [S] indicates that there is a solution at the end of the book. Other solutions are provided in the Instructor's Manual, where there are further questions parallel to those set out here.

A Test your understanding

A12.1 Why may it be said that the ownership interest is the residual item in the accounting equation? (Section 12.1)

A12.2 What is the definition of ownership interest? (Section 12.2)

A12.3 What is the effect on the accounting equation where new shares are issued for cash? (Section 12.3.1)

A12.4 Why does the company not record the buying and selling of shares in its statement of financial position (balance sheet)? (Section 12.3.3)

A12.5 What is a share premium? How is it recorded? (Section 12.3.4)

A12.6 How is the revaluation of a non-current (fixed) asset reported? (Section 12.3.5)

A12.7 Why may the revaluation of a non-current (fixed) asset not be reported in the profit and loss account? (Section 12.3.5)

A12.8 Where may the reader of the annual report find out about the effect of movements in foreign exchange rates? (Section 12.3.6)

A12.9 What is the purpose of the statement of total recognised income and expenses? (Section 12.6.4)

A12.10 What is the purpose of the reconciliation of movements in equity? (Section 12.6.5)

A12.11 How do the directors report their recommended dividend for the financial period, to be agreed at the shareholders' meeting? (Section 12.7)

A12.12 What is meant by:

(a) offer for sale; (Section 12.8.1)
(b) capitalisation issue; and (Section 12.8.2)
(c) rights issue? (Section 12.8.3)

Explain the effect of each of the above on the statement of financial position (balance sheet) of a company.

B Application

B12.1 [S]
Explain the effect on the accounting equation of each of the following transactions:

(a) At the start of Year 1, Bright Ltd issues 200,000 shares at nominal value 25 pence per share, receiving £50,000 in cash.
(b) At the end of Year 2, Bright Ltd issues a further 100,000 shares to an investor at an agreed price of 75 pence per share, receiving £75,000 in cash.
(c) At the end of Year 3 the directors of Bright Ltd obtain a market value of £90,000 for a company property which originally cost £70,000. They wish to record this in the statement of financial position (balance sheet).

B12.2 [S]
Explain the effect on the accounting equation of the following transactions and decisions regarding dividends:

(a) The company pays a dividend of £20,000 during the accounting period.
(b) The directors recommend a dividend of £30,000 at the end of the accounting year. It will be paid following shareholder approval at the Annual General Meeting, held two months after the accounting year-end.

B12.3 [S]
The following is a summarised statement of financial position (balance sheet) of Nithsdale Ltd.

	£000s
Cash	20
Other assets less liabilities	320
	340
Ordinary shares (400,000 of 25 pence each)	100
Share premium	40
Reserves of retained profit	200
	340

The company is considering three possible changes to its capital structure:

(a) issue for cash 50,000 additional ordinary shares at £1 per share, fully paid; or
(b) make a 1 for 4 capitalisation issue of ordinary shares; or
(c) make a 1 for 5 rights issue at £3 per share.

Show separately the impact of each change on the statement of financial position (balance sheet) of the company.

B12.4 [S]

Fragrance plc has owned a factory building for many years. The building is recorded in the statement of financial position (balance sheet) at £250,000, being historical cost of £300,000 less accumulated depreciation of £50,000. The recent report of a professional valuer indicated that the property is valued at £380,000 on an open market basis for its existing use. Explain the effect this information will have on the reported financial statements.

B12.5 [S]

Suppose the factory building in question B12.4 was valued by the professional expert at £240,000. What effect would this information have on the reported financial statements?

C Problem solving and evaluation

This question reviews your understanding of Chapters 8–12 and the effect of transactions on ownership interest.

C12.1

Set out below is a summary of the accounting records of Titan Ltd at 31 December Year 1:

	£000s	£000s
Assets		
Land and buildings	200	
Plant and machinery	550	
Investment in shares	150	
Stock	250	
Trade receivables (debtors)	180	
Cash	150	
Liabilities		
Trade payables (creditors)		365
Debenture loan 10% nominal rate of interest		250
Ownership interest		
Share capital		600
Retained earnings at 1 Jan. Year 1		125
Revenue		
Sales		1,815
Cost of goods sold	1,505	
Expenses		
Overhead expenses	145	
Debenture interest paid	25	
Totals	3,155	3,155

The summary of the accounting records includes all transactions which have been entered in the ledger accounts up to 31 December, but investigation reveals further adjustments which relate to the accounting period up to, and including, that date.

The adjustments required relate to the following matters:

(i) No depreciation has been charged for the year in respect of buildings, plant and machinery. The depreciation of the building has been calculated as £2,000 per annum and the depreciation of plant and machinery for the year has been calculated as £55,000.

(ii) The company is aware that electricity consumption during the months of November and December, Year 1, amounted to around £5,000 in total, but no electricity bill has yet been received.

(iii) Overhead expenses include insurance premiums of £36,000 which were paid at the start of December, Year 1, in respect of the 12-month period ahead.

(iv) The stock amount is as shown in the accounting records of items moving into and out of stock during the year. On 31 December a check of the physical stock was made. It was discovered that raw materials recorded as having a value of £3,000 were, in fact, unusable. It was also found that an employee had misappropriated stock worth £5,000.

(v) The company proposes to pay a dividend of £30,000.

(vi) The corporation tax payable in respect of the profits of the year is estimated at £45,000, due for payment on 30 September, Year 2.

Required

(a) Explain how each of the items (i) to (vi) will affect the ownership interest.

(b) Calculate the amount of the ownership interest after taking into account items (i) to (vi).

(*Hint:* first calculate the profit of the year.)

Activities for study groups

Turn to the annual report of a listed company which you have used for activities in earlier chapters. Find every item which relates to the ownership interest (including any discussion in the non-regulated part of the annual report).

As a group, imagine you are shareholders in this company. You are holding a meeting of the shareholders' action group calling for clarity of information about your total interest in the business. Make lists of the good points and weak points in the quality of information available to you and then arrange the weak points in descending order of importance. Then draft an action plan for improved communication with shareholders which you would propose sending to the company.

Notes and references

1. IASB (2016), IAS 21, *The Effects of Changes in Foreign Exchange Rates*, International Accounting Standards Board.

2. IASB (2016), IAS 1, *Presentation of Financial Statements*, para. 10.

A spreadsheet for adjustment to a trial balance at the end of the accounting period

End-of-period adjustments and the ownership interest

If you look back to Chapter 6 you will see that it finished with a trial balance and a promise that the trial balance would be used later as the starting point for preparation of financial statements. The moment has now arrived where the trial balance is used as a starting point for making end-of-period adjustments to show the change in the ownership interest during the period.

The accruals concept (or the parallel argument of matching in the income statement [profit and loss account]) requires all items relevant to the period to be included in the financial statements of the period. Most items will be included because they will have been recorded in the ledger and hence in the financial statements. However, there will be some items of information, emerging from enquiry at the end of the period, which have not yet resulted in a transaction but which are undoubtedly based on events relevant to the period.

The enquiry will take a routine form of:

- estimating the depreciation of non-current (fixed) assets where this has not already been recorded;
- examining non-current (fixed) assets for signs of obsolescence beyond the amount allowed for in the depreciation charge;
- counting the inventory (stock) of raw materials, work in progress and finished goods, for comparison with the accounting record;
- evaluating the doubtful debts;
- checking files for any purchase invoices received but not yet recorded;
- checking files for any sales invoices for goods sent out but not yet recorded;
- considering whether any resource has been consumed, or service received, for which a supplier has not yet sent an invoice.

Returning to the trial balance contained in Table 6.15 of Chapter 6, it may be noted that the depreciation for the month has been charged, there are no trade receivables (debtors) and therefore no concerns about doubtful debts, and it would appear from the list of transactions for the month that all sales and purchases have been recorded carefully. Suppose, however, that when M. Carter checks the inventory (stock) of goods at the end of the month it is found that the roof has been leaking and rainwater has damaged goods worth £500. Furthermore, the business uses gas to heat a water boiler and it is estimated that consumption for the month amounts to £80.

These items of information are called *end-of-period adjustments*. Both events could, and would, be recorded in the ledger accounts by the business. If you were presented with this information as a class exercise, or you were the auditor taking the trial balance and adjusting it for this further information, you would use a spreadsheet which set out the trial balance and then provided further columns for the end-of-period adjustments. The spreadsheet for this example is set out in Table 12.7 but before looking at that you should read through the next section which explains the recording of end-of-period adjustments. In this case a one-month period is covered and so the adjustments are referred to as month-end adjustments.

Analysis of the month-end adjustments

Before any entries may be made in the adjustments columns of the spreadsheet, the effect of each adjustment on the accounting equation must be considered so that the debit and credit entries may be identified.

(a) At the end of the month it is found that the roof has been leaking and rainwater has damaged goods worth £500

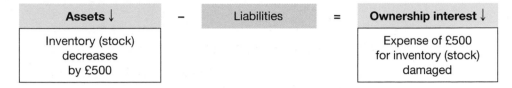

Assets ↓	–	Liabilities	=	Ownership interest ↓
Inventory (stock) decreases by £500				Expense of £500 for inventory (stock) damaged

The loss of inventory (stock) causes the ownership interest to decrease and is recorded as a debit entry in the expense of cost of goods sold. The decrease in the inventory (stock) is recorded as a credit entry in the ledger account.

Dr	Cost of goods sold	£500	
Cr	Inventory (stock) of goods		£500

(b) The business uses gas to heat a water boiler and it is estimated that consumption for the month amounts to £80

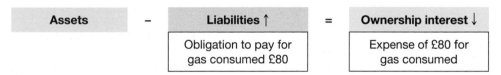

Assets	–	Liabilities ↑	=	Ownership interest ↓
		Obligation to pay for gas consumed £80		Expense of £80 for gas consumed

The event of consuming the gas causes the ownership interest to decrease and is recorded as a debit entry in an expense account for gas consumed. The obligation to pay for the gas at a future time is recorded as a credit entry in the ledger account for accruals.

Dr Expense of gas	£80	
Cr Accruals		£80

The spreadsheet

Table 12.7 contains, in the left-hand pair of debit and credit columns, the trial balance of Table 6.15 from Chapter 6. The next pair of columns contains the debit and credit entries necessary for the end-of-period adjustments. The third pair of columns shows the resulting amounts on each line of income statement (profit and loss account) items. The final pair of columns shows the resulting amounts on each line of statement of financial position (balance sheet) items. The entire spreadsheet could be thought of as a series of ledger accounts stretched across the page, with one line for each ledger account.

The debit and credit entries identified by the foregoing analysis are shown in the adjustments columns of the spreadsheet with identifying letters in brackets alongside. Where no suitably named line exists, a new line may be inserted. The use of a new line is shown here for accruals and the expense of gas. If the exercise is being carried out using a computer spreadsheet package, the insertion of an extra line is not a problem. For a handwritten exercise it may be necessary to leave spaces at possible insertion points.

Once all adjustments have been entered, each of the adjusted amounts can be carried across to one of the final four columns, depending on whether the item belongs to the income statement (profit and loss account) or the statement of financial position

Table 12.7
Trial balance of M. Carter at the end of May, before month-end adjustments

Ledger account title	Trial balance Dr £	Trial balance Cr £	Adjustments Dr £	Adjustments Cr £	Income (profit) statement Expense £	Income (profit) statement Revenue £	Statement of financial position A £	Statement of financial position L + OI £
L3 Buildings	30,000						30,000	
L4 Equipment	5,750						5,750	
L5 Inventory (stock) of goods	8,000			500 (a)			7,500	
L11 R. Welsby	nil							
L1 Cash	6,400						6,400	
Accruals				80 (b)				80
L6 R. Busby		nil						
L2 Ownership interest		49,000						49,000
Subtotal	50,150	49,000					49,650	49,080
Difference: profit of the month								570
L10 Sales		7,000				7,000		
L9 Cost of goods sold	3,500		500 (a)		4,000			
L7 Electricity	100				100			
Gas			80 (b)		80			
L8 Wages	2,000				2,000			
L12 Depreciation	250				250			
Subtotal	5,850	7,000	580	580	6,430	7,000		
Difference: profit of the month					570			
Total of each column	56,000	56,000	580	580	7,000	7,000	49,650	49,650

(balance sheet). Each pair of columns is added and the difference between the totals in the income statement (profit and loss account) columns should equal the difference between the totals in the statement of financial position (balance sheet) columns. If that is not the case, it means that an error has taken place at some point in the spreadsheet and must be found.

Revised statement of profit

The statement of profit before adjustments is shown in section 6.6.2 of Chapter 6 and the statement of financial position (balance sheet) is in section 6.6.3. From the final four columns of the spreadsheet in Table 12.7, these could now be restated as follows:

<table>
<tr><td colspan="3" align="center">**M. Carter, Wholesaler**
Income statement (profit and loss account) (adjusted)
for the month of May Year XX</td></tr>
<tr><td></td><td align="right">£</td><td align="right">£</td></tr>
<tr><td>Revenue (sales)</td><td></td><td align="right">7,000</td></tr>
<tr><td>Cost of goods sold</td><td></td><td align="right">(4,000)</td></tr>
<tr><td>Gross profit</td><td></td><td align="right">3,000</td></tr>
<tr><td>*Other expenses*</td><td></td><td></td></tr>
<tr><td>Wages</td><td align="right">(2,000)</td><td></td></tr>
<tr><td>Electricity</td><td align="right">(100)</td><td></td></tr>
<tr><td>Gas</td><td align="right">(80)</td><td></td></tr>
<tr><td>Depreciation</td><td align="right">(250)</td><td></td></tr>
<tr><td></td><td></td><td align="right">(2,430)</td></tr>
<tr><td>Net profit</td><td></td><td align="right">570</td></tr>
</table>

Statement of financial position (balance sheet)

<table>
<tr><td colspan="2" align="center">**M. Carter, Wholesaler**
Statement of financial position (balance sheet) (adjusted) at 31 May Year XX</td></tr>
<tr><td>***Non-current (fixed) assets***</td><td align="right">£</td></tr>
<tr><td>Buildings</td><td align="right">30,000</td></tr>
<tr><td>Equipment</td><td align="right">6,000</td></tr>
<tr><td></td><td align="right">36,000</td></tr>
<tr><td>Depreciation</td><td align="right">(250)</td></tr>
<tr><td>*Total non-current (fixed) assets*</td><td align="right">35,750</td></tr>
<tr><td>**Current assets**</td><td></td></tr>
<tr><td>Inventory (stock)</td><td align="right">7,500</td></tr>
<tr><td>Cash at bank</td><td align="right">6,400</td></tr>
<tr><td>*Total current assets*</td><td align="right">13,900</td></tr>
<tr><td>*Total assets*</td><td align="right">49,650</td></tr>
<tr><td>Accruals</td><td align="right">(80)</td></tr>
<tr><td>Net assets</td><td align="right">49,570</td></tr>
<tr><td>**Ownership interest**</td><td></td></tr>
<tr><td>Capital at start</td><td align="right">50,000</td></tr>
<tr><td>Add profit</td><td align="right">570</td></tr>
<tr><td>Less drawings</td><td align="right">(1,000)</td></tr>
<tr><td>**Total ownership interest**</td><td align="right">49,570</td></tr>
</table>

This completes the study of double-entry bookkeeping in this book. You are now in a position to be able to carry out the following tasks in relation to the business of a sole trader:

- record transactions in ledger accounts
- prepare a trial balance
- make end-of-period adjustments to the trial balance
- prepare an income statement (profit and loss account) and statement of financial position (balance sheet).

S   Test your understanding

S12.1   (a)   Using the information provided in question C12.1, prepare a spreadsheet containing a trial balance, adjustment and resulting figures for income statement (profit and loss account) and statement of financial position (balance sheet) items. (Table 12.7 provides a pattern to follow.)

       (b)   Present the income statement (profit and loss account) for the year and the statement of financial position (balance sheet) at the end of the year in an informative and useful manner.

Part 4

Analysis and issues in reporting

Chapter 13

Ratio analysis

REAL WORLD CASE

Operating profit margins

The following extracts show the different ways in which companies report their operating profit margins (operating profit as a percentage of sales). This ratio is an indicator of the performance of the business, or segments of the business. It provides useful information for investors, but may also help competitors.

Alamy Images/Gary Moseley

National Express

Measuring our progress

Metric: Margin %

[Bar chart showing Margin % with y-axis from 0 to 15 (intervals of 3). Categories on x-axis, each with '13' and '14' bars:]
- Spain: 13 ≈ 14.5, 14 ≈ 14
- North America: 13 ≈ 10.5, 14 ≈ 9.5
- UK Bus: 13 ≈ 11.5, 14 ≈ 12
- UK Coach: 13 ≈ 11.5, 14 ≈ 10
- Rail: 13 ≈ 7, 14 ≈ 6.5

KPI definition
Operating margin is the ratio of normalised operating profit to revenue.

Comment
Margin gains driven by strong performance in UK Coach and UK Bus.

Source: *National Express plc, Annual Report and Accounts, 2014*, p. 15. http://nexgroup.blob.core.windows.net/media/2293/ar2014-full.pdf

Stagecoach Group

Overview of financial results

Operating profit by division is summarised below:

OPERATING PROFIT – YEAR TO 30 APRIL	2014		2013 (restated)	
	£m	% margin	£m	% margin
Continuing Group operations				
UK Bus (regional operations)	147.4	14.6%	143.2	14.8%
UK Bus (London)	23.9	9.8%	19.0	8.2%
North America	23.7	5.5%	13.4	3.3%
UK Rail	34.3	2.7%	41.2	3.4%
Group overheads	(13.9)		(15.7)	
Restructuring costs	(0.9)		(1.7)	
	214.5		199.4	

Source: *Stagecoach Group Annual Report and Financial Statements 2014*, p. 14. http://www.stagecoach.com/investors/financial-analysis/reports/2014.aspx

Next plc

NEXT Retail operating margin movement	2014	2013
Net operating margin last year	15.1%	14.8%
Increase in achieved gross margin	+1.3%	+0.6%
Decrease/increase in store payroll	+0.1%	−0.1%
Increase in store occupancy	−0.7%	−0.4%
Increase/decrease in other costs	−0.2%	+0.2%
Net operating margin this year	**15.6%**	**15.1%**

Gross margin is the difference between the cost of stock and the initial selling price; achieved gross margin is after markdown and stock related costs. Net operating margin is profit after deducting markdowns and all direct and indirect trading costs. All are expressed as a percentage of achieved VAT exclusive sales.

Source: *Next plc Annual Report and Accounts January 2014*, p. 19. http://www.nextplc.co.uk/~/media/Files/N/Next-PLC/pdfs/reports-and-results/2014/Next%20AR2014%20web.pdf

Morrisons plc

Results

In the year, total turnover of £17.7bn was down 2% (2012/13: £18.1bn). When compared to prior year the underlying operating margin of 4.9% fell by 40bps. This increased to 50bps after adjusting for the impact of a lower proportion of fuel sales in the mix this year.

Source: *Wm Morrisons Supermarkets plc Annual Report and Financial Statements 2013/14*, p. 5. http://www.morrisons-corporate.com/Documents/Corporate2014/Morrisons_AnnualReport13-14_Complete.pdf

Discussion points

1 What does the reader learn about operating performance in each company?

2 What further information would you need to help you evaluate the relative success in performance?

Contents

Learning outcomes

After reading this chapter you should be able to:

- Define, calculate and interpret ratios that help analyse and understand (a) performance for investors, (b) management performance, (c) liquidity and working capital and (d) gearing.
- Explain investors' views of the balance of risk and return, and the risks of investing in a geared company when profits are fluctuating.
- Explain how the pyramid of ratios helps integrate interpretation.
- Describe the uses and limitations of ratio analysis.
- Carry out a practical exercise of calculating and interpreting ratios.

13.1 Introduction

Ratios are widely used as a tool in the interpretation of financial statements. The ratios selected and the use of the resulting information depend on the needs of the person using the information. What investors really want to do is choose the best moment to sell shares when the share price is at its highest. To choose that best moment, the investors will monitor the company's performance. Bankers lending to the company will also monitor performance, and look for indicators of solvency and ability to repay interest and capital.

Many users will rely on others to monitor ratios on their behalf. Employees will look to their advisers, perhaps union officials, to monitor performance. Small private investors with limited resources will rely heavily on articles in the financial sections of newspapers. Professional fund managers will look to their own research resources and may also make use of the analysts' reports prepared by the brokers who act for the fund managers in buying and selling shares. Each broker's analyst seeks as much information as possible about a company so that he or she can sell information which is of better quality than that of any other broker's analyst. There is fierce competition to be a highly rated analyst because that brings business to the broking firm and high rewards for the analyst.

In monitoring performance the expert analysts and fund managers will use ratios rather than absolute amounts. A figure of £100m for sales (revenue) means nothing in isolation. The reader who knows that last year's sales (revenue) amounted to £90m sees immediately an increase of 11.1%. The reader who knows that fixed (non-current) assets remained constant at £75m knows that the fixed (non-current) assets this year have earned their value in sales (revenue) 1.33 times (100/75 = 1.33) whereas last year they earned their value in sales (revenue) 1.2 times (90/75 = 1.2). Ratios show changes in relationships of figures which start to create a story and start to generate questions. They do not provide answers.

The fund managers and analysts all have their own systems for calculating ratios and some keep these a carefully guarded secret so that each may hopefully see an important clue before the next person does so. That means there is no standard system of ratio analysis. There are, however, several which are used frequently. A selection of these will be used here as a basic framework for analysis. As you start to read more about company accounts you will find other ratios used but you should discover that those are largely refinements of the structure presented here.

13.2 A note on terminology

Ratio analysis is not a standardised exercise. It is often taught in finance courses and management accounting courses as well as in financial accounting courses. Businesses use ratios to describe their own performance. There is a tendency towards creating ratios that suit the purpose and towards using descriptions that are personal choices of the presenter. This chapter gives commonly used names for ratios (such as 'gross profit percentage') and links these to the terminology of the IASB system of accounting by using additional descriptions in brackets. For example, the title 'gross profit percentage' is used as a name for a ratio and it is defined as follows:

$$\frac{\text{Gross profit}}{\text{Sales (revenue)}} \times 100\%$$

In the denominator of this ratio the word 'sales' describes the activity that creates gross profit; the additional word (revenue) in brackets reminds you that the information will be found in financial statements under 'revenue'. Similarly 'fixed assets (non-current assets)' uses the commonly established words 'fixed assets' with the addition of (non-current assets) in brackets to remind you of where the information will be found in the statement of financial position (balance sheet).

13.3 Systematic approach to ratio analysis

A systematic approach to ratio analysis seeks to establish a broad picture first of all, and then break that broad picture down until there are thumbnail sketches of interesting areas. Four key headings commonly encountered in ratio analysis are:

1 *Investor ratios.* Ratios in this category provide some measure of how the price of a share in the stock market compares to key indicators of the performance of the company.

2 *Analysis of management performance.* Ratios in this category indicate how well the company is being run in terms of using assets to generate sales (revenue) and how effective it is in controlling costs and producing profit based on goods and services sold.

3 *Liquidity and current assets.* The management of cash and current assets and the preservation of an adequate, but not excessive, level of liquidity is an essential feature of business survival especially in difficult economic circumstances.

4 *Gearing (referred to in American texts as 'leverage').* Gearing is a measure of the extent to which there is financial risk indicated in the statement of financial position (balance sheet) and in the income statement (profit and loss account) (see section 13.4 on risk and return). Financial risk means the risk associated with having to pay interest and having an obligation to repay a loan.

In the following sections key ratios for each of these aspects of a systematic analysis are specified by the name of the ratio and the definition in words. Below each definition there is a brief discussion of the meaning and interpretation of the ratio.

13.3.1   Investor ratios

Investors who buy shares in a company want to be able to compare the benefit from the investment with the amount they have paid, or intend to pay, for their shares. There are two measures of benefit to the investors. One is the profit of the period (usually given the name **earnings** when referring to the profit available for equity holders (ordinary shareholders)). The other is the **dividend** which is an amount of cash that is paid to the shareholders. Profit indicates wealth created by the business. That wealth may be accumulated in the business or else paid out in the form of dividend. Four ratios are presented with a comment on each.

Earnings per share	$\dfrac{\text{Profit after tax for ordinary equity holders}}{\text{Number of issued ordinary shares}}$

Comment. **Earnings per share** is the most frequently quoted measure of company performance and progress. The percentage change from year to year should be monitored for the trend. Criticisms are that this strong focus on annual earnings may cause 'short-termism' among investors and among company managers. The IASB would like to turn the attention of preparers and users of accounts away from reliance on earnings per share as a single performance measure, but the earnings per share remains a strong feature of comments on company results.

You may also see 'fully diluted earnings per share'. This is explained in section 11.6.4.

Price–earnings ratio	$\dfrac{\text{Share price}}{\text{Earnings per share}}$

Comment. The **price–earnings ratio** (often abbreviated to 'p/e ratio') compares the amount invested in one share with the earnings per share. It may be interpreted as the number of years for which the currently reported profit is represented by the current share price. The p/e ratio reflects the market's confidence in future prospects of the company. The higher the ratio, the longer is the period for which the market believes the current level of earnings may be sustained.

In order to gain some feeling for the relative magnitude of the p/e ratio of any individual company, it should be compared with the average p/e ratio for the industry, given daily in the *Financial Times*. The p/e ratio is quite commonly used as a key item of input information in investment decisions or recommendations.

Dividend per share	$$\frac{\text{Dividend of the period}}{\text{Number of issued ordinary shares}}$$

Comment. The **dividend** per share is one of the key measures announced by the company at the end of the financial year (and sometimes as an interim dividend during the year as well). Shareholders immediately know how much to expect in total dividend, depending on the number of shares held. The figure of dividend per share is the cash amount paid by the company. It may or may not be subject to tax in the hands of the recipient, depending on whether or not the recipient is a taxpayer.

The dividend of the period is equal to any interim dividend paid plus the final recommended dividend (see section 12.7). To find the recommended dividend you will have to look beyond the financial statements. The directors' report will contain a note on the recommended dividend which is to be paid to shareholders following their agreement at the annual general meeting. There may also be a description of the recommended dividend in the chairman's statement, or a highlights statement, or the strategic report.

Dividend cover (payout ratio)	$$\frac{\text{Earnings per share}}{\text{Dividend per share}}$$
Also calculated as	$$\frac{\text{Profit after tax for ordinary equity holders}}{\text{Total dividend for ordinary equity holders}}$$

Comment. Companies need cash to enable them to pay dividends. For most companies the profits of the business must generate that cash, so the dividend decision could be regarded as a two-stage question. The first part is, 'Have we made sufficient profits?' and the second stage is, 'Has that profit generated cash which is not needed for reinvestment in fixed or current assets?' The **dividend cover** helps in answering the first of these questions. It shows the number of times the dividend has been covered by the profits (earnings) of this year. It could be said that the higher the dividend cover, the 'safer' is the dividend. On the other hand, it could be argued that a high dividend cover means that the company is keeping new wealth to itself, perhaps to be used in buying new assets, rather than dividing it among the shareholders.

The dividend policy of the company is a major decision for the board of directors. Many companies like to keep to a 'target' dividend cover with only minor fluctuations from one year to the next. The evidence from finance research is that company managers have two targets, one being the stability of the dividend cover but the other being a desire to see the dividend per share increase, or at least remain stationary, rather than decrease. Dividends are thought to carry a signal to the market of the strength and stability of the company.

Dividend yield	$$\frac{\text{Dividend per share}}{\text{Share price}} \times 100\%$$

Comment. The **dividend yield** is a very simple ratio comparing dividend per share with the current market price of a share. It indicates the relationship between what the investor can expect to receive from the shares and the amount which is invested in the shares. Many investors need income from investments and the dividend yield is an important factor in their decision to invest in, or remain in, a company. It has to be noted that dividends are not the only benefit from share ownership. Section 13.4 on risk and return presents a formula for return (yield) which takes into account the growth in share price as well as the dividend paid. Investors buy shares in expectation of an increase in the share price. The directors of many companies would take the view that the dividend yield should be adequate to provide an investment income, but it is the wealth arising from retained profits that is used for investment in new assets which in turn generate growth in future profits.

13.3.2 Analysis of management performance

Management of a business is primarily a function requiring **stewardship**, meaning careful use of resources for the benefit of the owners. There are two central questions to test this use of resources:

1 How well did the management make use of the investment in assets to create sales (revenue)?
2 How carefully did the management control costs so as to maximise the profit derived from the sales (revenue)?

Return on shareholders' equity	$\dfrac{\text{Profit after tax for ordinary equity holders}}{\text{Share capital} + \text{Reserves}} \times 100\%$

Comment. A key measure of success, from the viewpoint of shareholders, is the success of the company in using the funds provided by shareholders to generate profit. That profit will provide new wealth to cover their **dividend** and to finance future expansion of the business. The **return on shareholders' equity** is therefore a measure of company performance from the shareholders' perspective. It is essential in this calculation to use the profit for ordinary equity holders, which is the profit after interest charges and after tax. The formula uses the phrase **equity** holders which will probably be the wording that you see in the financial statements. It has the same meaning as ordinary shareholders.

Return on capital employed	$\dfrac{\text{Operating profit (before interest and tax)}}{\text{Total assets} - \text{Current liabilities}} \times 100\%$

or

Return on capital employed	$\dfrac{\text{Operating profit (before interest and tax)}}{\text{Ordinary share capital} + \text{reserves} + \text{long-term loans}} \times 100\%$

Comment. **Return on capital employed** (ROCE) is a broader measure than return on shareholders' equity. ROCE measures the performance of a company as a whole in using all sources of long-term finance. Profit before interest and tax is used in the numerator as a measure of operating results. It is sometime called 'earnings before interest and tax' and is abbreviated to EBIT. Return on capital employed is often seen as a measure of management efficiency. The denominator can be written in two ways, as shown in the alternative formulae. Think about the accounting equation and rearrange it to read:

Total assets – current liabilities = Ordinary share capital plus reserves plus long-term loans

The ratio is a measure of how well the long-term finance is being used to generate operating profits.

Return on total assets	$\dfrac{\text{Operating profit (before interest and tax)}}{\text{Total assets}} \times 100\%$

Comment. Calculating the **return on total assets** is another variation on measuring how well the assets of the business are used to generate operating profit before deducting interest and tax.

Operating profit as % of sales (revenue)	$\dfrac{\text{Operating profit (before interest and tax)}}{\text{Sales (revenue)}} \times 100\%$

Comment. The ratio of operating profit as a percentage of sales (revenue) is also referred to as the **operating margin**. The aim of many successful business managers is to make the margin as high as possible. The margin reflects the degree of competitiveness in the market, the economic situation, the ability to differentiate products and the ability to control expenses. At the end of this section it is shown that companies are not obliged to seek high **margins**. Some cannot, because of strong competitive factors. Yet they still make a satisfactory return on capital employed by making efficient use of the equipment held as fixed (non-current) assets.

Gross profit percentage	$\dfrac{\text{Gross profit}}{\text{Sales (revenue)}} \times 100\%$

Comment. The gross profit as a percentage of sales (revenue) is also referred to as the **gross margin**. It has been seen in earlier chapters that the gross profit is equal to sales (revenue) minus all cost of sales. That gross profit may be compared with sales (revenue) as shown above. The gross profit percentage concentrates on costs of making goods and services ready for sale. Small changes in this ratio can be highly significant. There tends to be a view that there is a 'normal' value for the industry or for the product that may be used as a benchmark against which to measure a company's performance.

Because it is such a sensitive measure, many companies try to keep secret from their competitors and customers the detailed breakdown of gross profit for each product line or area of activity. Companies do not want to give competitors any clues on how much to undercut prices and do not want to give customers a chance to complain about excessive profits.

Total assets usage	$\dfrac{\text{Sales (revenue)}}{\text{Total assets}}$

Comment. **Total assets usage** indicates how well a company has used its fixed and current assets to generate sales (revenue). Such a ratio is probably most useful as an indication of trends over a period of years. There is no particular value which is too high or too low but a sudden change would prompt the observer to ask questions.

Fixed assets (non-current assets) usage	$\dfrac{\text{Sales (revenue)}}{\text{Fixed assets (non-current assets)}}$

Comment. **Fixed assets usage** is a similar measure of usage, but one which concentrates on the productive capacity as measured by non-current (fixed) assets, indicates how successful the company is in generating sales (revenue) from fixed assets (non-current assets). The ratio may be interpreted as showing how many £s of sales (revenue) have been generated by each £ of fixed assets. The ratio is usually based on the amount of property, plant and equipment.

13.3.3 Liquidity and working capital

Liquidity is a word which refers to the availability of cash in the near future after taking account of immediate financial commitments. Cash in the near future will be available from bank deposits, cash released by sale of stocks and cash collected from customers. Immediate financial commitments are shown in current liabilities. The first ratio of liquidity is therefore a simple comparison of current assets with current liabilities.

Current ratio	Current assets:Current liabilities

Comment. If the current assets amount to £20m and the current liabilities amount to £10m the company is said, in words, to have 'a current ratio of 2 to 1'. Some commentators abbreviate this by saying 'the current ratio is 2'. Mathematically that is incorrect wording but the listener is expected to know that the words 'to 1' have been omitted from the end of the sentence.

The current ratio indicates the extent to which short-term assets are available to meet short-term liabilities. A current ratio of 2:1 is regarded, broadly speaking, as being a reasonable order of magnitude. As with other ratios, there is no 'best' answer for any particular company and it is the trend in this ratio which is more important. If the ratio is worsening over time, and especially if it falls to less than 1:1, the observer would look closely at the cash flow. A company can survive provided it can meet its obligations as they fall due. Some companies therefore operate on a very tight current ratio because they are able to plan the timing of inflows and outflows of cash quite precisely.

Companies which generate cash on a daily basis, such as retail stores, can therefore operate on a lower current ratio. Manufacturing businesses which have to hold substantial stocks would operate on a higher current ratio.

Acid test	Current assets minus inventories (stock):Current liabilities

Comment. In a crisis, where short-term creditors are demanding payment, the possibility of selling stocks (inventories) to raise cash may be unrealistic. The **acid test** takes a closer look at the liquid assets of the current ratio, omitting the stocks (inventories). For many companies this ratio is less than 1:1 because it is unlikely that all creditors will require payment at the same time. As with the current ratio, an understanding of the acid test has to be supported by an understanding of the pattern of cash flows. Analysts in particular will often ask companies about the peak borrowing requirements of the year and the timing of that peak in relation to cash inflows.

Stock holding period (inventories holding period)	$\dfrac{\text{Average inventories (stock) held}}{\text{Cost of sales (revenue)}} \times 365$

Comment. The **stock holding period** (inventories holding period) measures the average period during which stocks (inventories) of goods are held before being sold or used in the operations of the business. It is usually expressed in days, which is why the figure of 365 appears in the formula. If months are preferred, then the figure 12 should be substituted for the figure 365. One point of view is that the shorter the period, the better. An opposite point of view is that too short a period may create a greater risk of finding that the business is short of a stock item.

In calculating the stock holding period it is preferable to use the average of the stock (inventories) held at the start of the year and the stock (inventories) held at the end of the year. Some analysts use only the year-end figure if the start-of-year figure is not available. Whatever variation is used, it is important to be consistent from one time period to the next.

Customers (trade debtors collection period)	$\dfrac{\text{Trade receivables (trade debtors)}}{\text{Credit sales (revenue)}} \times 365$

Comment. The **customers'** (trade debtors') **collection period** measures the average period of credit allowed to credit customers. An increase in this measure would indicate that a company is building up cash flow problems, although an attempt to decrease the period of credit allowed might deter customers and cause them to seek a competitor who gives a longer period of credit. It is important to be aware of the normal credit period for the industry. Some companies offer discount for prompt payment. Any offer of discount should weigh the cost of the discount against the benefit of earlier receipt of cash from customers. When you are looking for information in the annual report of companies using the IASB system you will probably have to start on the face of the statement of financial position (balance sheet) with the heading 'trade and other receivables' and then read the corresponding Note to the statement of financial position (balance sheet) to find the amount of trade receivables. If you are looking at the statement of financial position (balance sheet) of a company that does not use the IASB system you will have to find the Note to the statement of financial position (balance sheet) that gives detailed information about trade debtors.

Suppliers (trade creditors) payment period	$\dfrac{\text{Trade payables (trade creditors)}}{\text{Credit purchases}} \times 365$

Comment. The **suppliers'** (trade creditors') **payment period** measures the average period of credit taken from suppliers of goods and services. An increase in this measure could indicate that the supplier has allowed a longer period to pay. It could also indicate that the company is taking longer to pay, perhaps because of cash flow problems. If payment is delayed then the company may lose discounts available for prompt payments. A reputation for being a slow payer could make it more difficult to obtain supplies in future. Some large companies have gained a reputation for delaying payment to smaller suppliers. There was a requirement in company law for company directors to make a statement of policy in relation to creditor payment. It has been removed in favour of a broader policy to encourage a culture of responsible payment.

Companies do not usually report **purchases** directly, so the figure must be calculated as follows:

$$\text{Purchases} = \text{Cost of goods sold} + \text{Closing stock} - \text{Opening stock}$$

Analysts often use **cost of goods sold** rather than calculate purchases, arguing that stock levels are broadly similar at corresponding period-ends.

Working capital cycle	Stock (inventories) holding period PLUS Customers (trade debtors) collection period MINUS Suppliers (trade creditors) payment period

Comment. You saw in Chapter 9 (Figure 9.1) the **working capital cycle** whereby stocks (inventories) are purchased on credit, then sold to customers who eventually pay cash. The cash is used to pay suppliers and the cycle starts again. We can now put some timings into the diagram. The working capital represents the long-term finance needed to cover current assets that are not matched by current liabilities. The longer the total of the stock holding period and customer collection period, compared to the suppliers payment period, the greater the need for working capital to be financed long term.

13.3.4 Gearing

The term **gearing** is used to describe the mix of loan finance and equity finance in a company. It is more properly called **financial gearing** and in American texts is called **leverage**. There are two main approaches to measuring gearing. The first looks at the statement of financial position (balance sheet) and the second looks at the income statement (profit and loss account).

Debt/equity ratio	$\dfrac{\text{Long-term liabilities plus Preference share capital*}}{\text{Equity share capital} + \text{reserves}} \times 100\%$

* Where preference share capital is in existence.

Comment. From the statement of financial position (balance sheet) perspective the **gearing** measure considers the relative proportions of long-term (non-current) loans and equity in the long-term financing of the business. The precise meaning of long-term liabilities will vary from one company to the next. It is intended to cover the loans taken out with the aim of making them a permanent part of the company's financing policy. As they come due for repayment, they are replaced by further long-term finance. The starting point is the loans (but not the provisions) contained in the section headed *non-current liabilities.* However, the accounting rules require separate reporting of loans due for repayment within one year, reported as current liabilities. It is necessary to look in the *current liabilities* for bank loans that are becoming due for repayment. In some companies the bank overdraft is a semi-permanent feature and so is included in this ratio calculation.

Preference share capital is included in the numerator because it has the characteristics of debt finance even although it is not classed as debt in company law. The preference shareholders have the first right to dividend, before the ordinary shareholders receive any dividend. This is why they are called 'preference' shares. The amount of the dividend is usually fixed as a percentage of nominal value of shares. The amount repaid to preference shareholders on maturity is the amount of the share capital only. They do not normally take a share of accumulated profits.

Some companies say 'we have interest-bearing obligations such as bank overdrafts, long-term liabilities and preference shares but we also have cash and cash equivalents that are earning interest. We prefer to deduct the assets from the liabilities to calculate the **net debt**'. An alternative form of gearing ratio is therefore defined by calculating net debt as all interest-bearing liabilities minus cash and cash equivalents.

Debt/equity ratio	$\dfrac{\text{Net debt}}{\text{Equity share capital} + \text{reserves}} \times 100$

Different industries have different average levels, depending on the types of assets held and the stability or otherwise of the stream of profits. A low gearing percentage indicates a low exposure to financial risk because it means that there will be little difficulty in paying loan interest and repaying the loans as they fall due. A high gearing percentage indicates a high exposure to financial risk because it means that there are interest charges to be met and a requirement to repay the loans on the due date.

Interest cover	$\dfrac{\text{Operating profit (before interest and tax)}}{\text{Interest}}$

Comment. The importance of being able to meet interest payments on borrowed funds is emphasised by measuring gearing in terms of the income statement (profit and loss account). If the profit generated before interest and tax is sufficient to give high cover for the interest charges, then it is unlikely that the company is over-committing itself in its borrowing. If the interest cover is falling or is low, then there may be increasing cause for concern.

Activity 13.1	*Write down the name of each ratio given in this section. Close the book and test your knowledge by writing down the formula for each ratio. Then write one sentence for each ratio which explains its purpose. Be sure that you know each ratio and understand its purpose before you proceed with the rest of the chapter.*

13.4 Investors' views on risk and return

Uncertainty about the future means that all investments contain an element of risk. For investors who are averse to risk, there is a fear of income falling below an acceptable level and a fear of losing the capital invested in the company. Given a choice between two investments offering the same expected return, risk-averse investors will choose the least risky investment.

13.4.1 Return

The word **return** has many meanings but for an investor the basic question is, 'What have I gained from owning these shares?' One simple formula which answers that question is:

$$\frac{(\textit{Market price of share today} - \textit{Price paid for share}) + \textit{Dividends received}}{\textit{Price paid for share}} \times 100\%$$

Investors in a company which is in a low-risk industry may be willing to accept a low rate of return. Investors in a company which is in a high-risk industry will be seeking a higher rate of return to compensate for the additional risk they take.

Research has shown that share prices react very rapidly to any item of information which is sufficiently important to affect investors' decisions. This phenomenon is sometimes referred to as the **efficient markets hypothesis**, which is a statement that share prices react immediately to make allowance for each new item of information made available. The annual results of a listed company are announced through the Stock Exchange approximately two months after the accounting year-end. The annual report then goes to the printers and is distributed to shareholders about three months after the related year-end.

When investors evaluate share price by calculating return, they take the most up-to-date price available.

13.4.2 Risk

There are two main types of risk: operating risk and financial risk.

Operating risk exists where there are factors which could cause sales (revenue) to fluctuate or cause costs to increase. Companies are particularly vulnerable to operating risk when they have a relatively high level of fixed operating costs. These fixed costs are incurred independently of the level of activity. If sales (revenue) fall, or the direct costs of sales increase, the fixed costs become a greater burden on profit.

Financial risk exists where the company has loan finance, especially long-term loan finance where the company cannot relinquish its commitment. Loan finance carries an obligation to pay interest charges and these create a problem similar to the fixed costs problem. If the sales (revenue) are strong and the direct costs of sales are well under control, then interest charges will not be a problem. If sales (revenue) fall, or the direct costs of sales rise, then a company may find that it does not have the cash resources to meet the interest payments as they fall due. Repaying the loan could become an even greater worry.

Both operating risk and financial risk are important to the company's shareholders because they have the residual claim on assets after all liabilities are met. If the company's assets are growing then these risks will not pose a problem but if the business becomes slack then the combination of high fixed operating costs and high interest charges could be disastrous. As a rule of thumb, investors look for low financial risk in companies which have high operating risk and, conversely, will tolerate a higher level of financial risk where there is relatively low operating risk.

The terms **operating gearing** and **financial gearing** are frequently used to describe the extent of operating risk and financial risk. (Financial gearing has been explained in the previous section.) In terms of the income statement (profit and loss account) they are defined as follows:

Operating gearing	$\dfrac{\text{Profit before fixed operating costs}}{\text{Fixed operating costs}}$

Financial gearing	$\dfrac{\text{Profit before interest charges}}{\text{Interest charges}}$

In analysis of published accounting information, it is not possible to estimate the operating gearing because detailed information on fixed costs is not provided. Thus the term **gearing** is applied only in measuring financial gearing. Despite the lack of published information, professional investors will be aware of the importance of operating gearing and will try to understand as much as possible about the cost structure of the company and of the industry. The next section illustrates the benefits to shareholders of having gearing present when operating profits are rising and the risks when operating profits are falling.

13.4.3 Impact of gearing when profits are fluctuating

In a situation of fluctuating profits the presence of a fixed charge, such as an interest payment, will cause the profit for ordinary shareholders to fluctuate by a greater percentage. Table 13.1 sets out data to illustrate this fluctuation. Company X has no gearing but company Y has loan finance in its capital structure.

Table 13.2 uses the data to ask 'what happens to earnings per share if there is an increase or a decrease in operating profit?'

The conclusion to be drawn from Table 13.2, panels (a) and (b), is that a 20% increase or decrease in operating profit causes a corresponding 20% increase or decrease in profit for ordinary shareholders in the ungeared company but a 40% increase or decrease in profit for ordinary shareholders in the geared company. It would appear preferable to be a shareholder in a geared company when profits are rising but to be a shareholder in an ungeared company when profits are falling.

13.5 Pyramid of ratios

The various ratios which contribute to the analysis of management performance may be thought of as forming a pyramid, as in Figure 13.1.

Table 13.1
Data to illustrate the effect of gearing on profits for ordinary shareholders

	X plc £m	Y plc £m
Summary statement of financial position (balance sheet)		
Total assets minus current liabilities	1,000	1,000
Ordinary shares (£1 nominal value per share)	1,000	500
Loan stock (10% per annum)	–	500
	1,000	1,000
Expected level of profit		
Operating profit	100	100
Interest	–	(50)
Net profit for ordinary shareholders (A)	100	50

Table 13.2
Fluctuations in profit

(a) Effect of 20% decrease in operating profit		
Operating profit	80	80
Interest		(50)
Net profit for ordinary shareholders (B)	80	30
Percentage decrease of (B) on (A)	20%	40%
(b) Effect of 20% increase in operating profit		
Operating profit	120	120
Interest	–	(50)
Net profit for ordinary shareholders (C)	120	70
Percentage increase of (C) on (A)	20%	40%

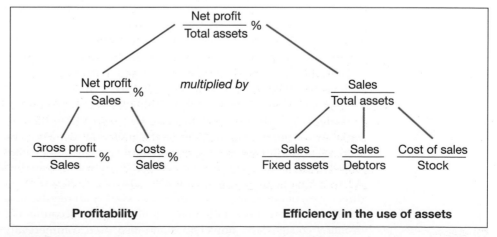

Figure 13.1
Pyramid of ratios for analysis of management performance

At the apex is the **return on capital employed** (measuring capital employed here as total assets). As the pyramid spreads out there are more detailed explanations of how the pyramid is built up. Net profit as a percentage of total assets has two components. One is the net profit as a percentage of sales (revenue) and the other is sales (revenue) as a multiple of total assets. Multiply these two together and you return to the net profit as a percentage of total assets. This relationship indicates that there could be two quite different types of business, both of which may be highly successful. One business trades on low margins, charging prices which look highly competitive, and succeeds by having a high level of sales (revenue) so that the assets are being used very effectively. The other business trades on high margins and sells goods or services less frequently. You could contrast the discount furniture store on the outskirts of town, where the car park is always full and the prices are unbeatable, with the old-world charm of the retail furnisher in the town centre whose prices look high but which attracts customers preferring extra service and attention. Both businesses are able to earn sufficient return on total assets to satisfy the owners.

The pyramid then spreads out into two areas: profitability and efficiency in the use of assets. The relationships here are additive – each component explains a little of the profitability of sales (revenue) or the efficiency in the use of assets. The pyramid is a useful tool of detective work to trace the cause of a change in return on capital employed.

13.6 Use and limitations of ratio analysis

The important feature of ratios is that they indicate trends and deviations from expected patterns. Ratios taken in isolation for a single company or a single period of time are of limited usefulness. The first requirement is to find a benchmark against which to compare ratios calculated for one period only.

13.6.1 Evaluating ratios by comparison

The comparison could be made with any or all of:

- the company's prior expectations of the outcome
- external observers' prior expectations of the outcome
- ratios based on previous years' figures for this company
- ratios calculated from this year's figures for other companies
- ratios calculated from previous years' figures for other companies
- industry averages published by commercial organisations.

The company's prior expectations are set out in a budget which is usually kept confidential. It is therefore unlikely that the user of the financial statements will have access to such a high-quality source of comparison. External observers may also have prior expectations. Professional analysts make forecasts of profits to help them or their clients in making investment decisions. The forecasts may be sent to clients of professional advisers, by way of investment advice bulletins. There are directories which publish such forecasts.

In the absence of information based on expectations, the user of the annual report may have to rely on the past as a possible predictor of the future, or on comparisons with other companies and industry norms. Professional investment advisers will collect data from annual reports and calculate ratios in their preferred manner. Advisory services will process the information and sell the results in the form of directories, online search facilities or CD-ROM with regular updates. One of the most widely used sources of ratio analysis of company accounts is Datastream, available in many colleges and universities and also used commercially. Organisations such as Reuters publish regular analyses of company information but usually charge a commercial fee. Newspapers and weekly journals such as the *Financial Times* and the *Investors Chronicle* are yet another source of information which will include ratios.

It could be argued that companies should themselves publish the norms against which their own particular results may be compared, but most would claim that their business is unique and no comparisons would be entirely valid.

13.6.2   Limitations

No two companies are exactly alike in the nature of their operations. Comparisons must make allowances for differences in the types of business or the relative weighting of different types of business. Many companies operate in more than one industry so that comparison with industry norms has to be treated with care.

Accounting numbers are used in ratio analysis and it has been a theme of the preceding chapters that accounting numbers may be affected by different accounting policies. The most common causes of variation due to accounting policy differences lie in depreciation and stock valuation, both of which are highly subjective.

Ratios are primarily a starting point from which to identify further questions to ask about the present position and future directions of the operations and the financing of a company. They do not provide answers in themselves.

13.7   Worked example of ratio analysis

In the following worked example, information is provided about a company buying and selling television and video equipment. Data are given for the current year in the first pair of columns and there are comparative figures for the previous year in the second pair of columns. Ratios are calculated for the two years as an indication of trends. Tentative comments are provided as to the possible interpretation of the resulting figures.

13.7.1   Financial statements to be analysed

Peter (Television) plc
Income statement (profit and loss account)
for the year ended 31 December Year 2

	Year 2		Year 1	
	£m	£m	£m	£m
Revenue		720		600
Cost of sales		(432)		(348)
Gross profit		288		252
Distribution costs	(72)		(54)	
Administrative expenses	(87)		(81)	
		(159)		(135)
Operating profit		129		117
Interest payable		(24)		(24)
Profit before taxation		105		93
Taxation		(42)		(37)
Profit for the period for ordinary equity holders		63		56

Extract from directors' report

The directors propose a dividend of 6.0 pence per share in respect of Year 2 (Year 1: 5.0 pence), amounting to £30m in total (Year 1: £25m).

Statement of changes in equity (summarised)

	£m
Share capital and reserves at the end of year 1	842
Less dividend paid in respect of year 1	(25)
Add profit for year 2	63
Share capital and reserves at the end of year 2	880

**Statement of financial position (balance sheet)
as at 31 December Year 2**

	Year 2 £m	Year 1 £m
Non-current (fixed) assets:		
Land and buildings	600	615
Plant and equipment	555	503
Total non-current assets	1,155	1,118
Current assets:		
Inventories (stock)	115	82
Trade receivables (debtors)	89	61
Prepayments	10	9
Bank	6	46
Total current assets	220	198
Total assets	1,375	1,316
Current liabilities		
Trade payables (creditors)	(45)	(30)
Taxation	(21)	(19)
Accruals	(29)	(25)
Total current liabilities	(95)	(74)
6% debentures	(400)	(400)
Total liabilities	(495)	(474)
Net assets	880	842
Ordinary shares of £1 each	500	500
Retained earnings	380	342
Share capital and reserves	880	842

13.7.2 Share price information

When investors evaluate share price, they take the most up-to-date price available. However, for the exercise of comparing financial ratios it is useful to take the share prices immediately after the preliminary announcement at the end of February or beginning of March, representing the market's opinion when the accounting information has not become too much out of date.

Market price at 1 March Year 2   202 pence
Market price at 1 March Year 3   277 pence

13.7.3 Presenting the ratio calculations

Because there are so many variations on the methods of calculating ratios in accounting, it is extremely important to practise a useful and informative layout. That must include, at a minimum:

● the name of each ratio
● the formula in words
● the workings to show how the formula has been applied
● the value of the ratio
● a narrative comment.

Tables 13.3 to 13.6 present this information in a set of ratio calculations for Peter (Television) plc, each exhibit covering one of the main headings explained earlier. The calculations are given first for the more recent year, Year 2, followed by the comparative figures for Year 1. A commentary is provided for each table.

Table 13.3
Investor ratios

Ratio	Definition in words	Year 2		Year 1	
		Workings	Result	Workings	Result
Earnings per share	$\dfrac{\text{Profit after tax for ordinary equity holders}}{\text{Number of issued ordinary shares}}$	$\dfrac{63}{500}$	12.6p	$\dfrac{56}{500}$	11.2p
Price earnings ratio	$\dfrac{\text{Share price}}{\text{Earnings per share}}$	$\dfrac{277}{12.6}$	22	$\dfrac{202}{11.2}$	18
Dividend per share	$\dfrac{\text{Dividend of the period}}{\text{Number of issued ordinary shares}}$	$\dfrac{30}{500}$	6.0p	$\dfrac{25}{500}$	5.0p
Dividend cover (payout ratio)	$\dfrac{\text{Earnings per share}}{\text{Dividend per share}}$	$\dfrac{12.6}{6.0}$	2.1 times	$\dfrac{11.2}{5.0}$	2.24 times
Dividend yield	$\dfrac{\text{Dividend per share}}{\text{Share price}} \times 100$	$\dfrac{6.0}{277} \times 100\%$	2.17%	$\dfrac{5.0}{202} \times 100\%$	2.48%

Comment. Earnings per share increased over the period, indicating an improved profit performance for shareholders. The price earnings ratio rose, indicating greater confidence in the stock market about the sustainability of this new level of profit. The dividend cover has fallen marginally, but is still more than twice covered. This marginal decrease in dividend cover is caused by increasing the dividend per share from 5 pence to 6 pence. The dividend yield has fallen, despite the increased dividend per share, because the market price has risen. The fall in yield may not be significant if it reflects a general trend in the market where, possibly, all shares have risen in price over the year. To say anything more about these ratios requires comparative figures for the industry and for the market as a whole. Both types of data would be found in the *Financial Times*.

Table 13.4
Analysis of management performance

Ratio	Definition in words	Year 2 Workings	Year 2 Result	Year 1 Workings	Year 1 Result
Return on shareholders' equity	$\dfrac{\text{Profit after tax for ordinary equity holders}}{\text{Share capital} + \text{Reserves}} \times 100\%$	$\dfrac{63}{880} \times 100\%$	7.2%	$\dfrac{56}{842} \times 100\%$	6.7%
Return on capital employed	$\dfrac{\text{Operating profit (before interest and tax)}}{\text{(Total assets} - \text{Current liabilities)}} \times 100\%$	$\dfrac{129}{1,280} \times 100\%$	10.1%	$\dfrac{117}{1,242} \times 100\%$	9.4%
Operating profit on sales (revenue)	$\dfrac{\text{Operating profit (before interest and tax)}}{\text{Sales (revenue)}} \times 100\%$	$\dfrac{129}{720} \times 100\%$	17.9%	$\dfrac{117}{600} \times 100\%$	19.5%
Gross profit percentage	$\dfrac{\text{Gross profit}}{\text{Sales (revenue)}} \times 100\%$	$\dfrac{288}{720} \times 100\%$	40%	$\dfrac{252}{600} \times 100\%$	42%
Total assets usage	$\dfrac{\text{Sales (revenue)}}{\text{Total assets}}$	$\dfrac{720}{(1,155 + 220)}$	0.52 times	$\dfrac{600}{(1,118 + 198)}$	0.46 times
Fixed assets (non-current assets) usage	$\dfrac{\text{Sales (revenue)}}{\text{Fixed assets (non-current assets)}}$	$\dfrac{720}{1,155}$	0.62 times	$\dfrac{600}{1,118}$	0.54 times

Comment. The return on shareholders' equity and the return on capital employed both show an improvement on the previous year. This is due to an improvement in the use of assets (total assets and fixed assets) which more than offsets a fall in the operating profit as a percentage of sales (revenue). The gross profit percentage fell by a similar amount, which suggests that the price charged for goods and services is not keeping pace with increases in costs. The company should look carefully at either increasing prices or attempting to control costs of goods sold more effectively.

Table 13.5
Liquidity and working capital

Ratio	Definition in words	Year 2		Year 1	
		Workings	Result	Workings	Result
Current ratio	Current assets:Current liabilities	220:95	2.3:1	198:74	2.7:1
Acid test	(Current assets – inventories):Current liabilities	(220 – 115):95	1.11:1	(198 – 82):74	1.11:1
Stock holding period (inventories holding period)	$\dfrac{\text{Average inventories (stock) held}}{\text{Cost of sales}} \times 365$	$\dfrac{(115 + 82)/2}{432} \times 365$	83.2 days	$\dfrac{(*82 + 82)/2}{348} \times 365$	86 days
Customers (trade debtors) collection period	$\dfrac{\text{Trade receivables (trade debtors)}}{\text{Credit sales (revenue)}} \times 365$	$\dfrac{89}{720} \times 365$	45.1 days	$\dfrac{61}{600} \times 365$	37.1 days
Suppliers (trade creditors) payment period	$\dfrac{\text{Trade payables (trade creditors)}}{\text{Credit purchases}} \times 365$	$\dfrac{45}{432 + 115 - 82} \times 365$	35.3 days	$\dfrac{30}{348 + 82 - *82} \times 365$	31.5 days

Note: *Assuming the opening inventories are the same as the closing inventories.

Comment. The current ratio has fallen over the period while the acid test ratio remains constant. The ratios appear relatively high and are probably still within acceptable ranges (although this needs to be confirmed by comparison with industry norms). One cause of the relatively high current ratio at the start and end of the period appears to be in the combination of stock holding period and customers collection period compared to the suppliers payment period. The period of credit taken by customers has increased and this should be investigated as a matter of urgency. There is a marginal decrease in the stock holding period but it remains relatively long, compared to the creditors payment period. The acid test remains similar because there is an increase in the number of customer days for payment and a similar increase in the number of supplier days for payment.

Table 13.6
Gearing (leverage)

Ratio	Definition in words	Year 2		Year 1	
		Workings	Result	Workings	Result
Debt/equity ratio	$\dfrac{\text{Long-term liabilities plus Preference share capital}}{\text{Equity share capital + reserves}} \times 100\%$	$\dfrac{400}{880} \times 100\%$	45.5%	$\dfrac{400}{842} \times 100\%$	47.5%
Interest cover	$\dfrac{\text{Operating profit (before interest and tax)}}{\text{Interest}} \times 100\%$	$\dfrac{129}{24}$	5.38 times	$\dfrac{117}{24}$	4.88 times

Comment. Gearing in the statement of financial position (balance sheet) has remained almost constant and the interest cover has increased marginally. The relative stability of the position indicates that there is probably no cause for concern but the ratios should be compared with those for similar companies in the industry.

Use the ratios explained in section 13.6 to carry out a full analysis of the Year 2 column of the accounts of Peter (Television) plc. Prepare your analysis before you read Tables 13.3 to 13.6. When you have finished, compare your analysis with the ratios calculated. Where your answers differ, be sure that you understand whether it is due to an arithmetic error or a more fundamental point. Keep a note of your score of the number of items calculated correctly.

Then go back to Year 1 and repeat the exercise. Hopefully your score of correct items will have increased.

13.8 Linking ratios to the statement of cash flows

In Chapter 7 the statement of cash flows of a company was illustrated and discussed. Any ratio analysis which seeks to interpret liquidity, management performance or financial structure should be related to the information provided by the statement of cash flows. Ratios give a measure of position at a particular point in time while the statement of cash flows gives some understanding of the movements in cash and cash-related items.

The operating cash flow will be explained by a note showing the movements in working capital and these may usefully be linked to changes in the rate of movement of stock or the period of credit allowed to customers and taken from suppliers. The ratio will give the change in terms of number of days, while the statement of cash flows will indicate the overall impact on liquid resources.

If the efficiency in the use of fixed assets appears to have fallen, it may be that new assets were acquired during the year which, at the statement of financial position (balance sheet) date, were not fully effective in generating sales. That acquisition will appear in the statement of cash flows. If the gearing has changed, the impact on cash flow will be revealed in the statement of cash flows.

Activity 13.3 *Read again the sections of Chapters 3, 4 and 7 on statements of cash flows. What is the purpose of the statement of cash flows? What are the main headings? Which ratios may be used in conjunction with the statement of cash flows to help understand the financial position of the company?*

13.8.1 Explanation of a statement of cash flows

The statement of cash flows in Table 13.7 is calculated from the statements of financial position (balance sheets) and income statement (profit and loss account) of Peter (Television) plc (see section 13.6). It is presented using headings similar to those of Safe and Sure in Chapter 7. The headings are taken from the international accounting standard IAS 7.

In Chapters 3, 5 and 6 you saw simple statements of cash flows prepared using the information entered in the cash column of a spreadsheet. Those were examples of what is called the **direct method** of preparing a statement of cash flows because the figures came directly from the cash column of the transaction spreadsheet. The statement of cash flows in Table 13.7 is said to be prepared using the **indirect method** because it takes an indirect route of starting with an accruals-based profit figure and then making adjustments to arrive at the cash figure. Consider each line in turn.

One purpose of the statement of cash flows is to answer the question, 'Why do we have a cash problem despite making an operating profit?' We saw in Table 3.7 of Chapter 3 that profit and cash flow can be different because the cash generated in making a profit is spent in various ways. The statement of cash flows emphasises ways in which cash has come into, or moved out of, the company. So we start with profit before taxation of £129m.

Table 13.7
Statement of cash flows

Peter (Television) plc
Statement of cash flows
for the year ended 31 December Year 2

Notes: assume depreciation charge for year is £50m.
  No non-current (fixed) assets were sold.

The words and figures printed in italics are not normally shown in published statements of cash flows – they are to help you with interpretation.

	£m	£m
Cash flows from operating activities		
Profit before taxation		129
Adjustment for items not involving a flow of cash:		
Depreciation		50
		179
Increase in inventories (stocks) *(115 – 82)*	33	
Increase in trade receivables (debtors) *(89 – 61)*	28	
Increase in prepayments *(10 – 9)*	1	
Reduction in cash due to increases in current assets	62	
Increase in trade payables (creditors) *(45 – 30)*	(15)	
Increase in accruals *(29 – 25)*	(4)	
Increase in cash due to increases in liabilities	(19)	
Reduction in cash due to working capital changes		(43)
Cash generated from operations		136
Interest paid		(24)
Taxes paid *(42 + 19 – 21)*		(40)
Net cash inflow from operating activities		72
Cash flows from investing activities		
Capital expenditure *(1,155 – 1,118 + 50)*		(87)
		(15)
Cash flows from financing activities		
Equity dividends paid (dividend proposed at end of Year 1)		(25)
Decrease in cash		(40)
Check in statement of financial position (balance sheet)		
Decrease in bank (46 – 6) = 40		

Depreciation is an expense in the income statement (profit and loss account) which represents cost being shared across accounting periods. There is no cash flow and so there should be no deduction for this item. To correct the position, depreciation of £50m is 'added back' as an adjustment to the accounting profit.

Next we consider how changes in working capital have affected cash flow. Looking first at current assets, we find that the inventories (stocks) have increased from £82m to £115m. Allowing inventories (stocks) to increase has reduced the cash available for other purposes. Trade receivables (debtors) have increased from £61 to £89. This means the cash is flowing less fast and so cash is reducing. Prepayments have increased from £9m to £10m. This is also using up cash. In total the increases in current assets have used up £62m of the cash generated in making profit.

Looking next at current liabilities, we see that trade payables (creditors) have increased from £30m to £45m. If payables (creditors) are increasing, it means they are not being paid. This helps cash flow by not spending it. Accruals have increased by £4m, again helping cash flow by not making a payment. It is not a good idea to help cash flow indefinitely by not paying creditors, but where stocks and debtors are expanding to use up cash flow, it is helpful if current liabilities are expanding in a similar way to hold back cash flow.

Interest paid is taken from the income statement (profit and loss account) as £24m. There is no liability for unpaid interest at either the start or end of the period so the amount in the income statement (profit and loss account) must equal the amount paid.

The taxation payment involves more calculation. Cash has been required to meet the liability of £19m remaining in the Year 1 statement of financial position (balance sheet), and also to pay half of the tax expense of Year 2, which is £21m. The calculation is: tax expense of the year as shown in the income statement (profit and loss account), minus liability at the end of the year in the statement of financial position (balance sheet), plus liability at the start of the year in the statement of financial position (balance sheet).

Capital expenditure is calculated by comparing the book values at the beginning and end of the year and adjusting for changes during the year. We are told there were no sales of fixed assets so any increase must represent an addition. The balance started at £1,118m, fell by £50m for depreciation, increased by the unknown figure for additions, and finished at £1,155m. The missing figure is calculated as £87m.

The dividend paid during Year 2 was the dividend proposed at the end of Year 1. If you look back to section 13.7.1, you will see the dividend paid as an entry in the 'reconciliation of movements on equity'.

Finally the right-hand column of the statement of cash flows is added and produces a figure of £40m which is then checked against the statement of financial position (balance sheet) figures. This shows that cash has fallen from £46m to £6m and so the calculation is confirmed as being correct.

13.8.2 Analyst's commentary

Here is the comment made by one analyst in a briefing note to clients.

> Despite making a profit before taxation of £129m, the cash balances of the company have decreased by £40m during the year.
>
> The cash generated by operating profit is calculated by adding back depreciation of £50m because this is an accounting expense which does not involve an outflow of cash. The resulting cash flow of £179m was eroded by allowing current assets to increase by more than the increase in current liabilities. This suggests that we should ask questions about the rate of usage of inventories (stocks) and the period of credit allowed to credit customers (debtors). Our analysis [see section 13.7] shows that the inventories (stocks) holding period reduced marginally from 86 to 83 days, which is not unexpected in the industry. The period of credit taken from suppliers increased by 4 days but the customers collection period increased by 8 days. Our attention should focus on the control of credit customers to look for any weaknesses of credit control and a potential risk of bad debts.
>
> After paying interest charges and taxation the company was still in cash surplus at £72m but swung into cash deficit through capital expenditure of £87m. Taking in the dividend payment of £25m the positive cash flow of £72m changed to a negative cash flow of £40m.
>
> We take the view that in the short run it is reasonable to run down cash balances in this way. The company probably had excessive liquidity at the end of Year 1. However, if there is to be a further major investment in non-current assets we would want to see long-term finance being raised, either through a share issue or through a new long-term loan.

13.8.3 EBITDA

EBITDA stands for earnings before interest, taxation, depreciation and amortisation. It is increasingly used by analysts as an approximate measure of cash flow because it removes the non-cash expenses of depreciation and amortisation from profit. Instead of a price–earnings multiple based on earnings per share, the analyst will relate share price to EBITDA. The reason appears to be a desire to get away from the subjectivity of accruals-based profit and closer to cash flow as something objectively measured.

13.8.4　Free cash flow

'Free cash flow' is a phrase that you may encounter in company reports, particularly in the narrative discussions by the chief executive and the finance director. It is a term that is used differently by different people and so you have to read it in the setting where it is used. A common theme is to say, 'We have calculated our operating cash flow and allowed for investment in working capital and we have deducted the amount of cash invested in capital expenditure.' How much cash does that leave free to pay dividends or to invest in new ideas for expansion?

Following this theme, the calculation of free cash flows generally starts with the net cash flow generated from operations (operating cash flow after tax) and then deducts the capital expenditure of the period. This leaves an amount of 'free' cash (in the sense of 'freely available' for future planning). The free cash is available to pay dividends to shareholders and to pay for further investment to expand the business. Directors have to decide their priorities and allocate the cash accordingly. If the free cash flow is a negative figure then the company will need to borrow to pay dividends or finance expansion.

13.9　Combining ratios for interpretation

Researchers have asked 'Can we find ways of combining ratios to predict types of management behaviour in companies?' There have been many answers published as academic research papers. This section explains two answers that have developed from academic research into commercial applications. The Z-score is used to predict the risk of bankruptcy. The M-score is used to predict overstatement of earnings.

13.9.1　Z-score

An American academic, Edward Altman, published in 1968 the results of statistical analysis of a large set of failed companies to establish a formula that could predict the likelihood of a company failing through becoming bankrupt.[1] This statistical analysis applied a combination of accounting ratios. Altman called the result a 'z-score'. A UK-based academic, Richard Taffler, developed a similar analysis for UK companies, publishing the results in 1983. The Altman and Taffler z-score calculations are frequently applied in practice by analysts, such as credit analysts working in banks, to assess the risk of an investment or a loan.

Taffler's model for analysing fully listed industrial firms is:

$$Z = 3.20 + 12.18^*x_1 + 2.50^*x_2 - 10.68^*x_3 + 0.029^*x_4$$

x_1 = profit before tax/current liabilities (measures profitability)
x_2 = current assets/total liabilities (measures working capital position)
x_3 = current liabilities/total assets (measures financial risk)
x_4 = no-credit interval (measures liquidity).

[No-credit interval = (quick assets − current liabilities)/daily operating expenses. Daily operating expenses = (sales − pre-tax profit − depreciation)/365]

Firms with a computed z-score less than 0 are at risk of failure (in the 'at risk' region); those with z-score greater than 0 are financially solvent.

13.9.2　M-score

Messod Beneish, an academic based in the USA, published in 1999 a statistical analysis to be used in detecting overstatement of earnings.[2] He used a combination of financial ratios which he called an 'M-score'. He pointed out that such analysis should be used with caution in screening companies, to consider whether any distortions in the financial statement numbers result from earnings manipulation or have another root. For example the distortions could be the result of a material acquisition during the period examined, a material shift in the company's value maximising strategy, or a significant change in the company's economic environment. The formula does not detect understatement of earnings.

The formula has been applied by Stockopedia, a stock-screening website. A discussion of this approach is provided in the Real World Case at the end of this section.

The M score is based on a combination of the following eight different indices:

1 **DSRI = Days' Sales in Receivables Index**. This measures the ratio of days' sales in receivables versus prior year as an indicator of revenue inflation.
2 **GMI = Gross Margin Index**. This is measured as the ratio of gross margin versus prior year. A firm with poorer prospects is more likely to manipulate earnings.
3 **AQI = Asset Quality Index**. Asset quality is measured as the ratio of non-current assets other than plant, property and equipment to total assets, versus prior year.
4 **SGI = Sales Growth Index**. This measures the ratio of sales versus prior year. While sales growth is not itself a measure of manipulation, the evidence suggests that growth companies are likely to find themselves under pressure to manipulate in order to keep up appearances.
5 **DEPI = Depreciation Index**. This is measured as the ratio of the rate of depreciation versus prior year. A slower rate of depreciation may mean that the firm is revising useful asset life assumptions upwards, or adopting a new method that is income friendly.
6 **SGAI = Sales, General and Administrative expenses Index**. This measures the ratio of SGA expenses to the prior year. This is used on the assumption that analysts would interpret a disproportionate increase in sales as a negative signal about firms' future prospects.
7 **LVGI = Leverage Index**. This measures the ratio of total debt to total assets versus prior year. It is intended to capture debt covenants incentives for earnings manipulation.
8 **TATA – Total Accruals to Total Assets**. This assesses the extent to which managers make discretionary accounting choices to alter earnings. Total accruals are calculated as the change in working capital accounts other than cash less depreciation.

The eight variables are then weighted together according to the following formula:

$$M = -4.84 + 0.92*DSRI + 0.528*GMI + 0.404*AQI + 0.892*SGI + 0.115*DEPI - 0.172*SGAI + 4.679*TATA - 0.327*LVGI$$

Beneish found that companies with a composite score greater than −1.78 had a higher probability of manipulating their earnings favourably.

REAL WORLD CASE

'M-Score' flags dubious company earnings

Shareholders seeking an early warning of when to sell up, and traders aiming to profit from falling prices, can now use an online indicator to spot companies with potentially unreliable earnings.

Stockopedia, the stock-screening website, has calculated the 'M-Score' for the 2,300 UK companies in its database, which aims to identify those that may have, in some way, 'manipulated' their earnings per share figures.

In early April, according to Stockopedia chief executive Edward Page-Croft, this M-Score correctly predicted problems at SuperGroup – the clothing company that was later forced to issue a profit warning, claiming 'arithmetic errors' in its most recent profit forecast. SuperGroup shares fell 38 per cent on the day.

Page-Croft says: 'We'd been discussing SuperGroup's appearance on our high-risk list just earlier in the week . . . the M-Score for SuperGroup was −1.19, well above the −1.78 threshold for high risk. It was showing the following risk factors: receivables increasing strongly as a proportion of sales, excessive sales growth and high accruals as a proportion of assets.'

More than a decade earlier, students at Cornell University had demonstrated the value of the M-Score, by using it to identify Enron as an 'earnings manipulator', before the company's collapse in 2001 – something equity analysts failed to do.

M-Scores were first devised in the late 1990s by Professor Messod Beneish of Indiana University, using a mathematical model of eight financial ratios that can help to detect signs of 'earnings manipulation' – which is not illegal. These signs include extending customer credit terms and reporting high sales growth.

Stockopedia believes M-Scores can now be used as a way of screening the market for shares to 'short-sell' – by borrowing stock, selling it and buying it back cheaper, or by simply trading derivatives on the stock.

When Beneish tested this strategy over the period 1993–2003, it generated a hedged return of nearly 14 per cent per annum.

However, Page-Croft says an M-Score should only be used as a starting point. 'You can't be sure without forensic accounting whether a company has genuinely been fiddling their numbers but, as an indicator to do further research, it's pretty useful,' he argues.

Professional investors suggest company accounts still need close scrutiny.

'When a company is having problems it normally first appears on the company's balance sheet before reaching the profit and loss figures,' says Richard Brown, investment specialist at Henderson Global Investors. 'For this reason, we spend a great deal of time looking at the debt level of a company. We also look for more subtle indicators, such as inventory levels or accounts receivable. An increase in either may suggest that a company is finding it difficult to reach its sales targets and are having to offer clients better terms.'

Nicolas Ziegelasch, analyst at broker Killik & Co, says stockpickers also need to check for: the capitalisation of expenses, to see if expenses from the current year are being shifted into the future; the use of 'accrual accounting or reserves' to smooth out earnings; the revaluation of assets or liabilities after an acquisition to release earnings; the classification of large expenses as 'one-off items'; and the recording of sales revenues in different financial years.

How and when revenue is recognised is 'the key manipulation', says James Butterfill, equity strategist at Coutts. 'Booking all in one year would make earnings very large for that year and consequently distort valuations,' he warns.

Ziegelasch recommends studying cash flow. 'Look at the ratio of operating earnings to operating cash flows,' he says. 'Often a company making profits but not generating any cash is a warning sign of manipulation.'

Discussion points

1 How should an investor interpret any given M-score?
2 Should companies be expected to report the M-score in their annual reports?

13.10 Summary

The main areas of ratio analysis explained in this chapter are:

- investor ratios (summarised in Table 13.3)
- analysis of management performance (summarised in Table 13.4)
- liquidity and working capital (summarised in Table 13.5)
- gearing (summarised in Table 13.6).

Section 13.8 explains how the interpretation of ratios may be linked to an understanding of cash flows. Section 13.9 explains how ratios may be combined to detect financial distress or overstatement of earnings.

It is essential to treat ratio analysis with great caution and to understand the basis of calculation and the nature of the data used. For that reason the illustrations have been set out in detail using a layout that allows you to demonstrate your knowledge of the formula, your ability to collect data for calculation, and the result of that calculation which can then be interpreted. In this chapter all the information has been made available to you as and when you required it. In Chapter 14 we move on to consider published financial statements where more exploration may be required to find the most useful information.

The general principles explained in this chapter can be applied to the annual report of any profit-seeking business. The precise formulae may require adaptation to suit particular national characteristics. However, international comparison requires great caution. Accounting policies and practices are not yet harmonised entirely. If the underlying data are not comparable then neither are the ratios.

The key is to ask first, 'What value do we expect for this ratio?' Then calculate the ratio and seek an interpretation of the similarity or difference.

QUESTIONS

The Questions section of each chapter has three types of question. 'Test your understanding' questions to help you review your reading are in the 'A' series of questions. You will find the answers to these by reading and thinking about the material in the book. 'Application' questions to test your ability to apply technical skills are in the 'B' series of questions. Questions requiring you to show skills in problem solving and evaluation are in the 'C' series of questions. A letter [S] indicates that there is a solution at the end of the book. Other solutions are provided in the Instructor's Manual, where there are further questions parallel to those set out here.

A   Test your understanding

A13.1   Which ratios provide information on performance for investors? (Section 13.3.1)

A13.2   Which ratios provide information on management performance? (Section 13.3.2)

A13.3   Which ratios provide information on liquidity and working capital? (Section 13.3.3)

A13.4   Which ratios provide information on gearing? (Section 13.3.4)

A13.5   What is the view of investors on risk and return? (Section 13.4)

A13.6   Why is financial gearing riskier for a company which has fluctuating profits? (Section 13.4.3)

A13.7   Explain the use of the pyramid of ratios in analysis of performance. (Section 13.5)

A13.8   What are the limitations of ratio analysis? (Section 13.6)

B Application

B13.1 [S]

The following financial statements relate to Hope plc:

Income statement (profit and loss account)
for the year ended 30 June Year 4

	£000s
Revenue	6,200
Cost of sales	(2,750)
Gross profit	3,450
Administration and selling expenses	(2,194)
Operating profit	1,256
Debenture interest	(84)
Profit before taxation	1,172
Taxation	(480)
Profit for equity holder	692

The directors have recommended a dividend of 36.7 pence per share in respect of Year 4, to be paid following approval at the next annual general meeting.

Statement of financial position (balance sheet)
as at 30 June Year 4

	£000s
Non-current (fixed assets) net of depreciation	1,750
Current assets:	
Inventory	620
Trade receivables (debtors)	1,540
Cash	200
Total current assets	2,360
Total assets	4,110
Current liabilities:	
Trade payables (creditors)	(300)
Other creditors and accruals	(940)
Total current liabilities	(1,240)
Non-current liabilities	
6% debentures	(1,400)
Total liabilities	(2,640)
Net assets	1,470
Share capital and reserves	
Issued share capital:	
900,000 ordinary shares of 50p nominal value	450
Retained earnings	1,020
	1,470

Required

(a) Calculate ratios which measure:
  (i) liquidity and the use of working capital;
  (ii) management performance; and
  (iii) gearing.
(b) Explain how each ratio would help in understanding the financial position and results of the company.
(c) The market price is currently 1,100 pence per share. Calculate ratios which are useful to investors.

B13.2

The following financial statements relate to Charity plc:

Income statement (profit and loss account)
for year ended 30 September Year 4

	£000s
Revenue	2,480
Cost of sales	(1,100)
Gross profit	1,380
Administration and selling expenses	(678)
Operating profit	702
Debenture interest	(31)
Profit before taxation	671
Taxation	(154)
Profit for equity holders	517

Note: The directors have recommended a dividend of 11.4 pence per share in total in respect of Year 4, to be paid following approval at the next annual general meeting.

Statement of financial position (balance sheet)
as at 30 September Year 4

	£000s
Non-current assets, net of depreciation	785
Current assets:	
Inventories (stocks)	341
Trade receivables (debtors)	801
Cash	110
Total current assets	1,252
Total assets	2,037
Current liabilities	
Trade payables (creditors)	(90)
Other payable and accruals	(654)
Total current liabilities	(744)
Net current assets	508
Non-current liabilities	
7% debentures	(440)
Total liabilities	(1,184)
Net assets	853
Share capital and reserves	
Issued share capital	
(1,360,000 ordinary shares of 25p nominal value)	340
Retained earnings	513
	853

Required

(a) Calculate ratios which measure:
   (i) liquidity and the use of working capital;
   (ii) management performance; and
   (iii) gearing.
(b) Explain how each ratio would help in understanding the financial position and results of the company.
(c) The market price of one share is 800 pence. Calculate ratios which will be of interest to investors.

C   Problem solving and evaluation

C13.1

Carry out a ratio analysis of Safe and Sure plc, using the financial statements set out in Appendix I (at the end of this book) and applying the method of analysis set out in section 13.6. Making a comparison of Year 7 with Year 6, write a short commentary on each ratio separately and then summarise the overall themes emerging from the ratios. Assume a share price of 260 pence is applicable at 31 December Year 7 and a share price of 210 pence is applicable at 31 December Year 6.

Notes and references

1. Agarwal, V. and Taffler, R. J. (2007), Twenty-five years of the Taffler z-score model: Does it really have predictive ability? *Accounting and Business Research*, 37(4): 285–300.
2. Beneish, Messod D. (1999), The Detection of Earnings Manipulation, *Financial Analysts Journal*, 55(5): 24–36.

Chapter 14

Reporting corporate performance

Associated British Foods: reporting business strategy

Extracts from Annual Report and Accounts

Business structure

Our businesses are organised so that they are close to the markets and customers that they serve.

They are managed as five business segments that bring together common industry expertise, operational capability and market intelligence. Operational decisions are made locally because, in our experience, they are most

successful when made by the people who have the best understanding of their markets and who have to implement them. The corporate centre aims to provide a framework in which our business leaders have the freedom and decision-making authority to pursue opportunities with entrepreneurial flair. The centre is small and uses short lines of communication to ensure prompt, incisive and unambiguous decision-making. It seeks to ensure that business activities are appropriately monitored and supported.

Strategy

The corporate centre agrees strategy and budgets with the businesses and monitors their performance closely.

The group balance sheet is managed to ensure long-term financial stability, regardless of the state of capital markets, and capital funding is made available to all of our businesses where returns meet or exceed clearly defined criteria. The centre provides selected services where the scale of its operations enables a more cost-effective or efficient delivery, where expertise that might not be available at a business level can be retained by the group, or where the provision of such services would otherwise distract business executives. Such services include investor relations, pensions, insurance, tax and treasury management, where specialist expertise is brought together in one place for the benefit of the group as a whole. The centre also co-ordinates selected value-added capabilities to support the businesses in their local markets such as talent management and development, procurement, and the sharing of best practice in, for example, health and safety or engineering risk management. We operate to high ethical standards as an organisation and expect the same of our employees. We encourage an open and honest culture in all our dealings and ensure that our core values are fully implemented throughout the group.

Source: *Associated British Foods plc, Annual Report and Accounts 2014*, p. 9. http://www.abf.co.uk/documents/pdfs/2014/2014_abf_annual_report_and_accounts.pdf

Discussion points

1 How does an understanding of the business structure and strategy help the user of financial statements to interpret the financial health of the company?

2 Which items of non-accounting information in the extracts are most relevant to the potential usefulness of accounting information in the financial statements?

Contents

Learning outcomes

After reading this chapter you should be able to:

● Explain the importance of the operating and financial review as a component of the annual report of a company.

● Describe and explain other useful information in the annual report that is relevant to analysis of corporate performance.

● Relate the interpretation of ratios to the information in a statement of cash flows.

● Explain how segmental information is useful to the analysis of corporate performance.

14.1 Introduction

You have learned from Chapter 13 the basic techniques of ratio analysis that may help you to interpret the performance of a company relative to other companies or other periods of time. You have also learned how the ratios may be linked to the statement of cash flows to interpret the factors affecting cash flow. It might be helpful to users of annual reports if companies themselves would carry out some analysis and interpretation of this type. There was a time when it was felt that the role of the company should stop at the presentation of the financial statements. Today, however, there is an expectation that companies will recognise the need to give more information to users, such as an objective discussion. The title of the discussion that is included in the annual report is the **strategic report**. Companies may choose to provide other guidance such as highlights statements and trends of data. Most large companies report group accounts which, as explained in Chapter 7, are quite complex. Because of this complexity, analysts like to receive segmental information that breaks the total information into key areas of activity of the business. Some companies have sought to avoid disclosing all their activities in group accounts by use of 'off-balance sheet finance'. Because this omission may distort the view of performance, the standard-setters have tried to restrict the use of off-balance sheet finance and encourage full reporting of group activities.

Beyond the responsibility for financial performance, the managers of companies have a responsibility and accountability to society in terms of their social and environmental activities. They are expected to demonstrate accountability by reporting on social and environmental activity in the annual report. The managers are also expected to follow best practice in the way they operate their business and in their relations with shareholders. Compliance with good practice in corporate governance must also be explained in the annual report.

Finally this chapter gives a taste of four areas of debate that extend beyond a first-level course in accounting but which help the student to be aware that studying accounting should include a questioning and thoughtful approach to what is being learned. These four areas of debate are: the meaning of 'true and fair'; the nature of value; risk reporting and the relevance of the stakeholder model.

14.2 Strategy and performance

UK quoted companies, and all large or medium-sized unquoted companies, are required by company law to prepare a narrative strategic report as part of their annual report. This requirement has applied since 2013.[1] There is also a long-standing requirement for all companies to produce a report by the board of directors, giving information required by company law.

14.2.1 Development of narrative reporting in the UK

The Operating and Financial Review (OFR) was created in 1993 by the UK Accounting Standards Board (ASB) to provide shareholders with narrative information on a company's performance and prospects. From 1993 to 2005 the provision of an OFR in an annual report was voluntary. The ASB hoped that giving companies wide discretion would encourage the development of best practice in reporting rather than a slavish adherence to rules which might result in a lacklustre document. Most larger quoted companies published an OFR in the annual report.

In 2004, the European Commission issued its Modernisation Directive requiring all member states to incorporate a business review in the legislation governing annual reports. Initially the UK government intended to meet this requirement by making the OFR mandatory by law, because it felt that the OFR could cover all the requirements of the business review and achieve other useful purposes in communicating with shareholders. Very briefly, in 2005, the OFR became mandatory but, by the start of 2006, the legislation was repealed because the government decided that a mandatory OFR would be adding unnecessarily to the regulatory burden facing UK companies (referred to as 'gold plating' the regulation). Instead, the Companies Act 2006 introduced a requirement for a business review. There were many similarities between the OFR and the business review, but it emerged that most companies preferred to use the 'business review' description.

The Coalition Government formed in 2010 promised a review of narrative reporting to find whether there would be support for reinstating a mandatory OFR. In 2011, the Government issued a consultation document which proposed the alternative idea of a strategic report to succeed the business review. The Government's stated objectives at the outset of its review of narrative reporting were to drive up the quality of narrative reporting to the standard of the best, including on social and environmental issues, to empower shareholders and to achieve coherence without increasing the regulatory burden on business. Following the Government's response in 2012 the legislation for a strategic report emerged in 2013 from this consultation process.[2]

14.2.2   Strategic report in the UK

The Companies Act 2006 sets out the legal requirements for the strategic report. The Financial Reporting Council (FRC) provides guidance[3] intended to encourage preparers to consider how the strategic report fits within the annual report as a whole, with a view to improving the overall quality of financial reporting.

The *Guidance on the Strategic Report* is a best practice statement and is persuasive rather than mandatory. It encourages entities to 'tell their story'. The Guidance states that the purpose of the strategic report is:

(a) to provide insight into the entity's business model and its main strategy and objectives;

(b) to describe the principal risks the entity faces and how they might affect its future prospects; and

(c) to provide an analysis of the entity's past performance.

The business model is defined as 'the basis on which the company generates or preserves value over the longer term'.

The strategic report should be fair, balanced and understandable. It should address the positive and negative aspects of the development, performance, position and future prospects of the entity openly and without bias. The directors should seek to ensure that shareholders are not misled as a result of the presentation of, or emphasis given to, information in the strategic report, or by the omission of material information from it.

There are three main elements of content, each with more detailed requirements:

1 *Strategic management* – how the entity intends to generate and preserve value:
   - strategy and objectives;
   - business model.
2 *Business environment* – the internal and external environment in which the entity operates:
   - trends and factors;
   - principal risks and uncertainties;
   - environmental, employee, social, community and human rights matters.
3 *Business performance* – how the entity has developed and performed and its position at the year-end:
   - analysis of performance and position;
   - key performance indicators (KPIs);
   - employee gender diversity.

Companies may choose to include other material in the strategic report. In practice they are using 'Strategic Report' as a major heading that includes the chairman's statement and the chief executive officer's report on strategy and performance.

14.2.3   Key performance indicators (KPIs)[4]

The FRC's *Guidance on the Strategic Report* explains how to report **key performance indicators (KPIs)**. It defines KPIs as quantitative measures used by directors to assess progress against objectives or strategy, track principal risks, or otherwise monitor the development, performance or position of the business.

The KPIs used in the analysis should be those that the directors judge to be most effective in assessing progress against objectives or strategy, monitoring principal risks, or are otherwise utilised to measure the development, performance or position of the entity. The analysis in the strategic report should include financial and non-financial KPIs.

The entity should provide information that enables shareholders to understand each KPI used in the strategic report. For example, the following information should be identified and explained where relevant:

(a) its definition and calculation method;
(b) its purpose;
(c) the source of underlying data;
(d) any significant assumptions made; and
(e) any changes in the calculation method used compared to previous financial years, including significant changes in the underlying accounting policies adopted in the financial statements which might affect the KPI.

Examples of KPIs are:

● Return on capital employed (see Chapter 13).
● Market share – the revenue of the entity as a percentage of the industry total (e.g. a market leader demonstrating dominant position).
● Average revenue per customer (e.g. in a pay-per-view television service).
● Sales per square foot of selling space (e.g. a chain of retail stores).
● Employee costs per £ of sales (any labour-intensive business).
● Environmental spillage (e.g. in a business using toxic chemicals).

The following extract from the annual report of Safe and Sure plc shows how Key Performance Indicators are reported.

Safe and Sure plc: Key Performance Indicators
The Board reviews the following indicators:
Non Financial Performance Indicators

	Year 6	Year 7
CO_2 emissions[i]	119	108
Water consumption[ii]	13	12
Colleague engagement	70%	70%
Colleague enablement	68%	68%
Sales colleague retention	64%	64%
Service colleague retention	74%	76%
Customer satisfaction[iii]	n/a	19%
State of Service	98%	97%
Number of Lost Time Accidents[iv]	1.53	1.72

(i)   Total CO_2 emissions in tonnes per £m turnover reported on a total company basis.
(ii) Water consumed – litres per kilogramme of textiles processed in continental European plants.
(iii) Customer satisfaction score, represents the net balance of those customers promoting our service compared with those neutral or not promoting.
(iv) LTA equals accidents per 100,000 hours worked.

14.2.4 Directors' and auditors' responsibilities for the strategic report[5]

The directors of the company are responsible for the preparation of the strategic report. The auditors read the strategic report, along with other narrative sections of the annual report, to satisfy themselves that there are no inconsistencies between the information in the narrative report and that in the financial statements. If they find an inconsistency they will discuss it with the directors and attempt to resolve the problem. When the previous requirement for a business review was being introduced the government wanted a stronger form of audit that would review the process by which the business review was prepared, but this stronger form of audit was resisted by both auditors and directors. Commentators felt that too strong a burden would be placed on auditors and directors if subsequent events did not correspond to expectations raised by the business review.

14.2.5 Directors' report in the UK[6]

The regulation for the directors' report under the Companies Act 2006 was updated in 2013 alongside the regulation for the strategic report. Some of the disclosures have a social or political interest. Some overlap with the information in the strategic report. The fullest disclosure requirements apply to quoted companies. Some exemptions apply for small companies but all produce a directors' report of some type.

The main categories of disclosure in the directors' report are:

- matters of a general nature including political donations and expenditure;
- the acquisition by a company of its own shares or a charge on them;
- the employment, training and advancement of disabled persons;
- the involvement of employees in the affairs, policy and performance of the company;
- certain disclosures required by publicly traded companies; and
- disclosures in relation to greenhouse gas emissions.

Examples of disclosures are:

- names of directors who held office during the year;
- the principal activities of the company (and subsidiaries) during the year;
- the amount of any dividend, if any, recommended by the directors;
- political contributions;
- important post-balance sheet events for the company (and subsidiaries);
- mention of any likely future developments for the company (and subsidiaries);
- details of research and development by the company (and subsidiaries);
- where the average number of employees exceeds 250 during the year, the company's policy on employing and continuing to employ disabled people and on their training, career development and promotion; and a statement of employee involvement, including details of communication, procedures for consulting employees and arrangements to encourage involvement in the company's performance, such as an employee share scheme.

Many of the items in the foregoing list have been required for many years and the list has grown in a piecemeal way depending on current political interests. The most recent new disclosure covers greenhouse gases and applies to quoted companies. The report must state the annual quantity of emissions in tonnes of carbon dioxide equivalent from activities for which that company is responsible including

(a) the combustion of fuel; and

(b) the operation of any facility.

The report must state the annual quantity of emissions in tonnes of carbon dioxide equivalent resulting from the purchase of electricity, heat, steam or cooling by the company for its own use. Methodologies used for calculations must be stated.

These disclosures apply only to the extent that it is practical for the company to obtain the information in question; but where it is not practical for the company to obtain some or all of that information, the report must state what information is not included and why.

The directors' report must state at least one ratio which expresses the quoted company's annual emissions in relation to a quantifiable factor associated with the company's activities. Comparative figures are required for quantitative data.

IASB management commentary[7]

The IASB has published guidance on a Management Commentary that may be included in annual reports. The guidance is called a Practice Statement and is not a mandatory standard. It provides the following definition:

> *A management commentary is a narrative report that relates to financial statements that have been prepared in accordance with IFRSs. Management commentary provides users with historical explanations of the amounts presented in the financial statements, specifically the entity's financial position, financial performance and cash flows. It also provides commentary on an entity's prospects and other information not presented in the financial statements. Management commentary also serves as a basis for understanding management's objectives and its strategies for achieving those objectives.*

The guidance explains that a management commentary should provide users of financial statements (existing and potential investors, lenders and other creditors) with integrated information providing a context for the related financial statements, including the entity's resources and the claims against the entity and its resources, and the transactions and other events that change them.

Management commentary should be consistent with the following principles:

- provide management's view of the entity's performance, position and progress (including forward looking information);
- supplement and complement information presented in the financial statements (and possess the qualitative characteristics described in the *Conceptual Framework for Financial Reporting*).

In presentation, a management commentary should be clear and straightforward and be presented with a focus on the most important information in a manner intended to address the principles described in the Practice Statement, specifically:

- being consistent with its related financial statements;
- avoiding duplicating disclosures made in the notes to the financial statements where practicable;
- avoiding generic and immaterial disclosures.

Companies based in Europe do not at present follow this guidance on a non-mandatory Management Commentary because national laws, under a directive of the European Commission, all require a management report or equivalent that covers similar ground.

USA

In the USA there is a requirement for a report called the Management's Discussion and Analysis (MD&A). This is required by the Securities and Exchange Commission (SEC) from all companies listed on one of the US stock exchanges (mainly the New York Stock Exchange or the NASDAQ over-the-counter market). The SEC has detailed regulations setting out the content of the MD&A. If you are studying or researching a US-listed company you may find the company's MD&A in its annual report or you may find it in the company's report to the SEC (called a 'form 10-K'). The company's web page for 'investors' is often the best place to search. Some UK companies have their shares listed on the New York Stock Exchange or NASDAQ. These companies also prepare an MD&A for the SEC but it is within a report called a 'form 20-F'. You will probably find this on the web page for 'investors' if you are studying or researching a UK company that has a listing in both London and New York.

14.2.8   International Integrated Reporting Council

The International Integrated Reporting Council (IIRC) was formed in August 2010 with the aim of creating a globally accepted framework for reporting value creation over time. It aimed to provide guidance to businesses on writing an integrated report. It defined an integrated report as a concise communication about how an organisation's strategy, governance, performance and prospects, in the context of its external environment, lead to the creation of value in the short, medium and long term. The IIRC is a global coalition of regulators, investors, companies, standard setters, the accounting profession, academics and non-governmental organisations (NGOs). It began in the UK with the support of the Prince of Wales but has now expanded internationally and operates through a not-for-profit company.

The *International Integrated Reporting <IR> Framework* was released in December 2013, following extensive consultation and testing by businesses and investors in all regions of the world, including the 140 businesses and investors from 26 countries that participate in the IIRC Pilot Programme. The purpose of the Framework is to establish Guiding Principles and Content Elements that govern the overall content of an integrated report, and to explain the fundamental concepts that underpin them.

The focus of the guidance is on reporting how an organisation creates value. It states that an integrated report includes eight Content Elements:

1 *Organisational overview and external environment:* What does the organisation do and what are the circumstances under which it operates?
2 *Governance:* How does the organisation's governance structure support its ability to create value in the short, medium and long term?
3 *Business model:* What is the organisation's business model?
4 *Risks and opportunities:* What are the specific risks and opportunities that affect the organisation's ability to create value over the short, medium and long term, and how is the organisation dealing with them?
5 *Strategy and resource allocation:* Where does the organisation want to go and how does it intend to get there?
6 *Performance:* To what extent has the organisation achieved its strategic objectives for the period and what are its outcomes in terms of effects on the capitals?
7 *Outlook:* What challenges and uncertainties is the organisation likely to encounter in pursuing its strategy, and what are the potential implications for its business model and future performance?
8 *Basis of presentation:* How does the organisation determine what matters to include in the integrated report and how are such matters quantified or evaluated?

You will see that many of these ideas overlap with the strategic report that is required by company law for quoted and many unquoted companies in the UK. The novel idea of the <IR> Framework is to build reporting around what the IIRC calls 'the capitals'. The capitals are stocks of value that are increased, decreased or transformed through the activities and outputs of the organisation. They are categorised in the <IR> Framework as financial, manufactured, intellectual, human, social and relationship, and natural capital. The IIRC hopes that building on these 'capitals' will improve the quality of information available to providers of financial capital to enable a more efficient and productive allocation of all types of capital.

Activity 14.1   *Read through the sections on the strategic report again. How much of the information suggested for the strategic report is extracted directly from the financial statements? How much of the information suggested for the strategic report provides additional understanding which is not available from the financial statements?*

14.3 Other guidance in analysis

In Figure 7.1, there is a list of narrative reports that may be found in the annual report. The first main heading there is the strategic report, explained in Section 14.2.2. Under that heading is the Chairman's statement, which usually appears at the start of the annual report, as a short narrative lasting no more than a page and often preceded by a Highlights statement of key financial measures. The Chairman sets out key features as an introduction to the detail that follows in later pages. The second main heading listed there is Corporate Governance, which includes the Directors' report, explained in Section 14.2.5. There will be an historical summary that allow trends to be seen over several years, with some companies giving five-year trends and others giving ten-year trends. Reporting on corporate social responsibility is explained in section 14.6. In this section we will consider how companies provide information on current and historical trends in ratios to aid interpretation.

14.3.1 Highlights statement

Safe and Sure plc presents Highlights of Year 7 as follows:

		Year 7 £m	Increase %	Year 6 £m
Revenue	United Kingdom	3,234	31.1	2,467
	Europe	1,643	7.0	1,535
	North America	1,045	30.5	801
	Asia Pacific and Africa	1,224	12.3	1,090
	Total revenue	7,146	21.3	5,893
Profit	United Kingdom	974	28.8	697
	Europe	453	12.4	403
	North America	170	22.3	139
	Asia Pacific and Africa	355	17.9	301
	Net interest income	23		30
	Profit before tax	1,975	25.8	1,570
Earnings	Earnings per share	11.74p	20.9	971p
Dividends paid (pence per share)		3.02p	20.8	2.50p

The Highlights statement shows what the company regards as important information for investors as the primary users of the annual report. Turnover is a measure of the size of operations, with growth of turnover being an indicator of expansion. Profit is the reward for shareholders, with growth again being an important indicator. Segment figures are provided for both turnover and profit. This company has a target profit growth of 20% per annum and so is emphasising that it has more than met the target. Earnings per share and dividend per share are the key indicators from which investors can calculate yields based on the current market price. There is no regulation of highlights statements and so other companies may give different information. Together with the Chairman's statement, the Highlights present the key messages of the annual report.

14.3.2 Historical summaries and trend analysis

Listed companies usually provide a historical summary of the financial statements of previous years. The historical summary for Safe and Sure may be found in Appendix I. The analyst may use this table to establish trends of:

- year-on-year growth of turnover and operating profit
- growth rates adjusted for annual inflation
- key ratios.

The company provides its own selection of ratios for key performance indicators. It is not always clear which formula has been used. Analysts may prefer to carry out their own calculations.

In general the companies leave the ratios for others to calculate and interpret. They will comment on a ratio where they know the expert users will ask further probing questions.

In the strategic report of Safe and Sure plc the chief executive officer states:

The pleasing return on our tangible net assets (42.4% per annum before tax on average net assets) reflects the high value of the intangible assets of the Safe and Sure brand and of businesses built up over the years. Such value is not reported in the statement of financial position (balance sheet).

Is it possible to check on the calculation? It has used pre-tax profit which is £1,770m (£1,975m from continuing minus £205m from discontinued operations) and the average of the tangible net assets. The respective figures for Year 7 and Year 6 are £4,643m and £3,704m. The average net assets figure is therefore £4,174m. The calculation of the ratio is:

$$\frac{1,770}{4,174} \times 100\% = 42.4\%$$

which confirms the figure given in the report. (It should be noted that confirming ratios reported in annual reports is not always so straightforward, although it ought to be.) We need other evidence before we can agree that 42.4% is a 'pleasing' return.

In the next section, David aims to explain his approach to using ratios to pinpoint target areas for probing by way of questions to the company, while Leona explains how ratios are useful to the auditor.

14.3.3 The analyst and the auditor

DAVID: *We subscribe to the major online database sources of information about companies, so I don't very often sit down to calculate ratios. I'm more interested in the interpretation. There are a few key ratios that I look at for major clues as to strange goings-on and then I scan a more detailed ratio report for unusual changes. We can program in an instruction to set a warning flag against any ratio which has altered by more than a specified range since the previous figures, or over a given period of time.*

What do I look to first? Gross margins on turnover and net margins on turnover, with as much segmental detail as I can find. Segmental information is an area where often we do have to carry out our own analysis using our skills, experience and specialist sources of information. Not many databases break down the company's results by segment. Then I'll check the tax charge as a percentage of the taxable profit. It should be around 20% if the company's accounts have been accepted for tax purposes, but if there are items which the tax authorities don't allow, then the percentage will be different. I'm always interested in what appears in the income statement (profit and loss account) but is not accepted by the tax rules. Depreciation is a notoriously variable figure and is difficult to spot because the accounting rules say that a change in depreciation rate or useful asset life is not a change in policy. Companies have to draw attention to a change in policy and explain the impact. Depreciation escapes that rule. So I calculate the depreciation charge as a percentage of total asset value. If that percentage changes then I start asking questions.

Common-size statements are very useful. That means turning all items in the financial statements to percentages with the total assets represented by 100% in the statement of financial position (balance sheet) and the turnover represented by 100% in the income statement (profit and loss account). It is also useful to have percentage changes from one year to the next. That is all relatively easy when you are using spreadsheets.

Over a period of time I monitor the variability of a ratio for a particular company. I calculate this as:

$$\frac{\text{Maximum value} - \text{Minimum value}}{\text{Mean value of ratio}}$$

Again I am looking for unusual movements outside an expected range.

LEONA: *The auditors don't rely on anyone else's calculations. We carry out our own ratio analysis as part of our analytical review. For commercial, manufacturing and service companies we monitor a standard list of ratios which is:*

- *acid test ratio*
- *current ratio*
- *customers collection period*
- *inventories (stocks) holding period*
- *gearing*
- *interest cover*
- *return on capital employed*
- *return on total assets*
- *gross profit margin.*

We are looking at these with a focus on the particular concerns of the auditor. Possible liquidity crises or working capital shortages could raise a question as to whether the company is a going concern. Customer collection period provides a clue to whether the doubtful debt provision is adequate. Inventories holding period may indicate a need for provision for slow-moving inventories. Gearing and interest cover are further indicators of financial stability or otherwise in relation to the going concern issue. Return on capital employed and on total assets may show inefficient use of assets and perhaps point to assets which have no future benefit. Gross margins may cause us to ask questions about incorrect records of sales or stocks if the margins are different from the norms.

For listed companies we also look at the dividend cover and the Altman Z-score. The Z-score is a model developed for use in predicting insolvency. You need to read a finance textbook to get the details, but basically it is a combined score based on a list of key variables all pointing to potential insolvency problems. We have to be able to say that the business is a going concern, so that kind of information is important to us.

DAVID: *That's OK for the current year. What about trends?*

LEONA: *Yes, trends are an important part of our review. We try to use a predictive approach and estimate the current year's figure from the previous data rather than merely compare this year with last. Taking a predictive approach encourages us to challenge fluctuations and to seek persuasive explanations. We use all the familiar forms of trend analysis – graphical representation, moving averages and simple regression analysis.*

DAVID: *How much reliance do you place on these analytical procedures?*

LEONA: *It can range from conclusive reliance to no reliance at all. It depends very much on the nature of the assertions being tested, the plausibility and predictability of the relationships involved, and the extent to which data is available and reliable.*

DAVID: *Maybe I have underestimated auditors in the past. None of the activities you describe is really apparent from the audit report. Perhaps you undersell your work.*

LEONA: *I probably have to admit that our work stops when we have gained sufficient assurance to write the audit report. We don't give information to the reader – that is not the function of the audit.*

DAVID: *You and I need to spend more time together on this question of analysis in depth. Analysts with insight command top ratings and that's what I'm looking for. And I think the benefit would not all be one-way – I can help you with broader awareness of the strategies used by management in giving the markets the messages they want to convey.*

LEONA: *Sounds fine to me.*

14.4 Segmental information

In sections 7.7 and 7.8, you read about the group structure used by many companies, and saw the method of construction of consolidated financial statements. Safe and Sure presents consolidated financial statements, which are discussed in section 7.4. The process of consolidation of financial information in group accounts is intended to be an improvement on sending the parent company shareholders a bundle of the separate financial statements of each member of the group. It lets them see, in one set of financial statements, the full picture of the group. On the negative side, the process of aggregation causes a loss of information about the various different activities of the group. In order to balance the benefits of aggregation with the need for detail, accounting provides additional information about the various segments of the group on a year-by-year basis.

14.4.1 Users' needs for information

Consolidated financial statements are a very convenient means of bringing together a large volume of data, but they suffer a major defect in losing much of the rich detail available from seeing each constituent company separately. It is particularly important for users of financial statements to know how the results of various activities compare, where the group of companies is involved in more than one product line and more than one type of market.

Segmental reporting has developed as a means of supplementing the consolidated financial statements by providing more insight into the activities of the group. In particular it reports information about the different types of products and services that an entity produces and the different geographical areas in which it operates.

The accounting standard which deals with segmental reporting[8] requires the entity to disclose information to enable users of its financial statements to evaluate the nature and financial effects of the business activities in which it engages and the economic environments in which it operates. To achieve this objective the managers start by identifying the operating segments from which it earns revenues and incurs expenses. These operating segments will be regularly reviewed by the entity's 'chief operating decision maker'. The information provided about each segment will correspond to that provided to the chief operating decision maker. In this way the standard seeks to help the user of financial statements view the business in the way it is seen by its managers.

The entity must disclose some general information about how the reportable segments have been identified and the types of products and services from which each reportable segment derives its revenues. It must also report a measure of profit or loss and total assets for each reportable segment and a measure of liabilities for each segment if that information is regularly provided to the chief operating officer.

The entity must also disclose specific accounting information as set out in the following list, if these items are reported to the chief operating decision maker:

(a) revenues from external customers
(b) revenues from transactions with other operating segments of the same entity
(c) interest revenue

(d) interest expense

(e) depreciation and amortisation

(f) material items of income and expense

(g) the entity's interest in the profit or loss of associates and joint ventures

(h) income tax expense or income

(i) material non-cash items other than depreciation and amortisation.

When the accounting standard containing these requirements took effect, commentators who were concerned felt that it gave too much discretion to the company management and could even be damaging to the quality of corporate governance. The IASB supported the standard by referring to research showing that when a similar standard was introduced in the US no detrimental effects were observed.

Research[9] has shown that under IFRS 8 the number of segments has increased and the extent of the segmental note disclosure has increased. Interviews with users of reports have welcomed the management-based approach but have expressed some concern that the flexibility of the standard could allow managerial manipulation of disclosures. There is not always consistency between the narrative sections of the annual report and the IFRS 8 segmental note disclosure.

14.4.2 Information provided in the financial statements

The group statement of financial position (balance sheet) and income statement (profit and loss account) of Safe and Sure plc are presented in full in Chapter 7 and have been explored in more detail in subsequent chapters. Consequently you are already familiar with much of the information about the assets and liabilities of the group.

Parent company

Some companies publish the statement of financial position (balance sheet) of the parent company alongside or near to the group statement of financial position (balance sheet). This is a requirement for groups that continue to report under UK rules, but is not compulsory for group accounts prepared under the IASB system. In most cases the parent company statement of financial position (balance sheet) confirms that the parent is primarily a holding company whose main asset is the investment in its subsidiaries. It owns some of the group's land and buildings and a small portion of the vehicle fleet. Its current assets consist mainly of amounts owed by subsidiaries and dividends due from subsidiaries. Its current liabilities consist mainly of amounts owed to subsidiaries and dividends payable to its own shareholders. The parent company has some long-term liabilities for money borrowed to purchase subsidiaries. Most of the cash used for purchase of new subsidiaries is provided by the new wealth generated by the group as a whole.

Group

Information about the Safe and Sure group is very much more interesting than information about the parent company alone. That is why the preceding chapters have used the group information about Safe and Sure to explain the treatment of assets, liabilities and ownership interest. There are a few particular items of interest in respect of acquisitions of new subsidiaries and the use of the goodwill reserve. There is also some interesting information about the various segments of the business which contribute to the overall picture. This section summarises those particular features of the annual report.

14.4.3 Identifying segments

The IASB system requires the operating segments reported by an entity to be the organisational units for which information is reported regularly to the chief operating decision maker. The chief operating decision maker is likely to be the chief executive, working with the board of directors to use the information for evaluating past performance and making decisions about future allocation of resources. So the intention is that the segment reporting reflects the information that management is using in running the business.

14.4.4 Segmental information in Safe and Sure

As an illustration of the type of segmental information available, the note to the income statement (profit and loss account) of Safe and Sure plc is set out in Note 16 to the financial statements. It is one of the lengthiest notes provided by the company.

Note 16 Operating segments

For the purposes of reporting to the chief operating decision maker, the group is currently organised into two operating divisions, (1) disposal and recycling, (2) security and cleaning. Disposal and recycling includes all aspects of collection and safe disposal of industrial and commercial waste products. Security and cleaning is undertaken by renewable annual contract, predominantly for hospitals, other healthcare premises and local government organisations.

The group's disposal and recycling operation in North America was discontinued with effect from 30 April Year 7.

Business sector analysis

	Disposal and recycling		Security and cleaning		Total	
	Year 7	Year 6	Year 7	Year 6	Year 7	Year 6
	£m	£m	£m	£m	£m	£m
REVENUES (all from external customers)						
Continuing	5,089	4,550	2,057	1,343	7,146	5,893
Discontinued	200	110			200	110
Total revenues	5,289	4,660	2,057	1,343	7,346	6,003
Operating profit (loss) by service						
Continuing	1,766	1,396	186	144	1,952	1,540
Discontinued	(205)	(100)			(205)	(100)
Total operating profit					1,747	1,440
Interest receivable (net)					23	30
Profit before tax					1,770	1,470
Taxation					(622)	(524)
Profit for the period					1,148	946

All costs of head office operations are allocated to divisions on an activity costing basis. The company does not allocate interest receivable or taxation paid to reportable segments.

Depreciation and amortisation included in the income statement are as follows:

	Disposal and recycling		Security and cleaning		Total	
	Year 7	Year 6	Year 7	Year 6	Year 7	Year 6
	£m	£m	£m	£m	£m	£m
Depreciation	302	251	30	39	332	290
Impairment of goodwill	16	–	–	–	16	–

The segment assets and liabilities at the end of Years 7 and 6, with capital expenditure for each year are as follows:

	Disposal and recycling		Security and cleaning		Unallocated		Total	
	Year 7	Year 6	Year 7	Year 6	Year 7	Year 6	Year 7	Year 6
	£m	£m	£m	£m	£m	£m	£m	£m
Total assets	4,985	3,709	687	1,327	1,201	1,123	6,873	6,159
Total liabilities	1,317	1,479	613	855	300	121	2,230	2,455
Capital expenditure	500	450	102	25	–	–	602	475

Information about geographical areas

The group's two business segments operate in four main geographical areas, even though they are managed on a worldwide basis. In the following analysis, revenue is based on the country in which the order is received. It would not be materially different if based on the country in which the customer is located. Non-current assets are allocated based on where the assets are located.

	Revenues from external customers		Non-current assets	
	Year 7	Year 6	Year 7	Year 6
	£m	£m	£m	£m
CONTINUING				
United Kingdom	3,234	2,467	1,742	1,487
Continental Europe	1,643	1,535	903	930
North America	1,045	801	859	492
Asia Pacific & Africa	1,224	1,090	561	750
	7,146	5,893	4,065	3,659
DISCONTINUED				
North America	200	110	–	5
Total	7,346	6,003	4,065	3,664

The information contained in Note 16 relates to a service business, so it might be expected that the non-current assets would be relatively low compared to the turnover and operating profit. Professional analysts would be particularly interested in the relationships and trends underlying these figures.

David and Leona have returned from their holiday and are again working on Leona's flat. In the middle of a less than successful attempt to fit a carpet, David pauses for coffee and explains how he looked at the segmental information presented by the company.

DAVID: *The first thing I did here was to feed all these tables of segmental information into our spreadsheet package. I asked for two printouts initially. The first calculated the sales (revenue) as a multiple of net assets and the operating profit as a percentage of sales, using continuing activities in each case because the assets remaining at the end of the period do not include the assets of the discontinued activity. [The results are shown in Table 14.1, panel (a).] The second printout shows the sales to non-current assets for each geographical area. [The results are shown in Table 14.1, panel (b).] From this the relative strengths and weaknesses within the organisation begin to emerge. The percentage changes (Table 14.2) also show some interesting differences. I need to ask why the total assets for security and cleaning have reduced so much when there was no disposal in this segment. Perhaps the assets were transferred into disposal and recycling to replace those that were discontinued.*

Table 14.1
Analysis

(a) Analysis of business segment revenues and operating profit (based on continuing activities)

	Revenues as a multiple of total assets		Operating profit as a % of sales	
	Year 7	*Year 6*	*Year 7*	*Year 6*
			%	%
Segment				
Disposal and recycling	1.02	*1.23*	34.7	*30.7*
Security and cleaning	2.99	*1.01*	9.0	*10.7*

(b) Analysis of geographical segment sales compared to non-current assets

	Sales as a multiple of non-current assets	
	Year 7	*Year 6*
Geographical analysis		
United Kingdom	1.86	*1.66*
Continental Europe	1.82	*1.65*
North America	1.22	*1.63*
Asia Pacific and Africa	1.76	*1.61*

Table 14.2
Percentage changes on previous year

	Disposal and recycling	Security and cleaning	Total
	Year 7	*Year 7*	*Year 7*
	% on Year 6	% on Year 6	% on Year 6
Sales (revenue)	+11.8	+53.0	+21.3
Operating profit	+26.5	+29.2	+25.0
Total assets	+34.4	negative	+11.6

Then I turned to the front of the annual report. The importance of segmental information becomes apparent as soon as you start to read the chairman's statement and it continues through the business reviews, presented on a segmental basis with some helpful illustrations to reinforce the message. The chief executive's review continues the segmental theme strongly and gives further information to augment the basic tables which I have already analysed. That attention to detail in their reports is a reflection of the thorough questioning which these people receive from the fund managers and analysts who follow the company closely. I know one analyst who would put Sherlock Holmes in the shade. She collects the accounts of each individual UK company in the group, and as many overseas subsidiary companies as she can get hold of. She puts them all together like a jigsaw and then starts to ask intensive questions based on what she has and what she can deduce about the missing pieces. Seasoned finance directors wilt visibly under her interrogation!

LEONA: *Segmental reporting is an area where you and your analyst friends probably put more pressures on the companies than we can as auditors. That's a good example of market forces at work, but it does assume that the information you prise out of the company is made available more widely. Companies make use of the strategic report to answer the questions which they know the investors ask on a regular basis.*

14.5 Off-balance sheet finance

One major problem for UK accounting emerged in the 1980s in a period of business expansion. To finance expansion, companies were borrowing and therefore increasing their gearing ratios. Some companies looked for ways of avoiding disclosing in the statement of financial position (balance sheet) the full extent of the commitment on borrowed funds. Omitting the item from the statement of financial position (balance sheet) could not remove the commercial obligation but it could reduce the questions arising from those who would read the financial statements.

The accounting question is: How do you remove, or fail to include, a liability so that no one will notice? The answer, as with all accounting questions, starts in the accounting equation. To keep the equation in balance, any removal of a liability must be matched by removal of an asset of equal amount.

Many ingenious schemes emerged, but one of the least complex is the sale and leaseback of land and buildings.

14.5.1 Sale and leaseback of property

Consider the following scenario. A company has the following statement of financial position (balance sheet):

	£m
Land and buildings	20
Other assets, *less* current liabilities	15
	35
Less long-term loan	(20)
Net assets	15
Share capital	15

The company sells the land and buildings for £20m and repays the loan. The statement of financial position (balance sheet) now appears to contain no gearing:

	£m
Other assets, *less* current liabilities	15
Share capital	15

However, enquiry behind the scenes reveals a complex arrangement. The land and buildings were sold to a consortium of finance companies, but on the same day a lease was signed that allowed the company to continue occupying the property at a rental payment which would vary according to current rates of interest and would be calculated as a percentage of the £20m cash received. In five years' time the company would have the option to repurchase the land and buildings at £20m and the consortium of finance companies would have the option to force the company to repurchase at £20m. These options would mean that if the price rose over the next five years the company would wish to buy at £20m. If the price fell over the next five years the consortium would insist on repurchase.

Now ask yourself, where do the benefits and risks of this contract lie? The benefits of a rise in value and the risks of a decrease in value remain with the company, as they would if the company had remained the owner. The company will pay a rental which looks very much like an interest payment on a loan of £20m. If the company fails to meet its obligations, then the consortium will claim the asset. The commercial effect of this transaction is that of a loan based on the security of the asset of land and buildings.

14.5.2   UK response

In the absence of a standard to back up the argument, auditors felt unable to argue against the directors of companies who moved assets and liabilities off the statement of financial position (balance sheet). After some years of consultation and discussion with interested parties, the UK standard-setter decided that such transactions did not change the commercial substance of the transaction and it is the commercial substance which matters. A standard was introduced to require a transaction of this type to be reported on the statement of financial position (balance sheet)[10] in the form of an asset and matching liability. Not all countries shared this view because it involved making a judgement on the balance of risks and rewards. Making judgements leaves the company and the auditors open to challenge and so it could be argued that specific rules are preferable to general principles. In particular the US had a more rules-based approach to defining recognition on and off the statement of financial position (balance sheet).

14.5.3   Special purpose entities

The problems associated with off-balance sheet finance received a high public profile at the end of 2001, running into 2002, with the failure of a large US company called Enron. Because of the size of the company and the political impact of its failure, hearings were called by the US Congress at which witnesses gave evidence on accounting practices, among other matters. One of the accounting issues discussed was the question of 'off-balance sheet finance'. The Chief Accountant of the Securities and Exchange Commission described to the House of Representatives how money could be borrowed at advantageous rates of interest using a 'special purpose entity' which was not consolidated with the rest of the group accounts. Provided the assets of the special purpose entity retained sufficient value, the lender would be content with the arrangement. If the assets fell in value then the lender would look to the parent company for reimbursement. Shareholders in the parent would be unaware of the extent of such borrowing until the lenders demanded repayment. At the time of the failure of Enron the US standard-setting body (the Financial Accounting Standards Board) was still in the process of providing guidance on consolidation of such special purpose entities. The International Accounting Standards Board had no standard that directly addressed such entities.

Subsequently the US regulators and the IASB strengthened their rules relating to special purpose entities, to bring more of these entities into group financial statements.

Despite these efforts at improvement, the use of special purpose entities, to take transactions off the balance sheet, became a concern again during the financial crisis of 2007–08. Some of the problems experienced in the banking sector had remained out of sight in off-balance sheet arrangements. The leading world economies, through the G20, asked the standard setters to address the continuing problems associated with off-balance sheet finance. The IASB responded in 2011 with three new accounting standards, covering consolidated financial statements, joint arrangements and disclosures of interests in other entities. The IASB claimed these changes would provide a check on off-balance sheet activities and would give investors a much clearer picture of the nature and extent of a company's involvement with other entities. The detail is beyond the scope of a first-level textbook but this outline shows why annual reports are becoming ever more lengthy and detailed.

Activity 14.2

Off-balance sheet finance is one example of information which would never come to the attention of the users of financial statements but for the concern of some auditors. Make a list of other types of information which may be evident to the auditors but which are unlikely to be conveyed to the readers. Consider this list in the light of the requirement that financial statements must show a true and fair view. To what extent is the reader of financial statements reliant on the directors and the auditors?

14.6 Corporate social responsibility

Corporate social responsibility means that entities report to stakeholders on the ways in which social and environmental concerns are integrated with their business operations.

Definition

Corporate social responsibility means that companies integrate social and environmental concerns in their business operations and in their interactions with stakeholders.

Companies disclose in their annual reports more information than is represented only in financial statements. Depending on social attitudes or pressures, companies may voluntarily disclose additional information intended to confirm the company's sense of social responsibility. In some instances, the provisions of law eventually catch up with the values of society and disclosures become mandatory. Section 14.2.2 explains that in the UK the strategic report includes information about environmental, employee, social, community and human rights matters.

Investors are increasingly asking questions about the corporate social responsibility of the companies in which they invest. Many investors want to be reassured that the businesses in which they have a stake adopt ethical business practices towards employees, the community and the environment. You will see increasing numbers of what are described as 'ethical investment funds' which make careful enquiry before buying shares. Some ethical investors feel that they are best placed to influence a company if they become shareholders; others feel that they should not become shareholders until the company has a sound policy.

14.6.1 Types of disclosure

The strategic report should include information about:

(a) environmental matters (including the impact of the business of the entity on the environment);
(b) the entity's employees; and
(c) social, community and human rights issues.

The information should include a description of any relevant policies in respect of those matters and the effectiveness of those policies. For guidance on human rights issues, the FRC points directors to the *UN Guiding Principles on Human Rights.*

Examples of corporate social disclosure on mandatory topics include: information about pensions for employees, employees' share option schemes, policy regarding employment of disabled persons and consultation with employees. Social disclosure on a voluntary basis includes: information about employee matters, health and safety, community work, energy and the environment.

In terms of relative volume, the amount of information disclosed about employee-related matters exceeds other types of social and environmental disclosures, but the area where there is the fastest growth in interest is that of environmental issues. Many leading companies now have an 'environment' section in the annual report and some go even further in producing a separate environmental report.

Below are extracts from the 'environment' section of the report of the directors of Safe and Sure plc, the company used for illustration throughout this text.

Safe and Sure is committed to the provision of services and products which improve the quality of life, both for our customers and the community, using working practices designed to protect the environment.

Heightened awareness of environmental issues and increased legislation provide a focal point for developing greener techniques and solutions to problems, both in our more traditional businesses and also in offering opportunities to develop new businesses.

Antibacterial deep cleaning of premises, in particular high-risk areas such as washrooms, drains and food production and preparation areas, has been developed to meet increased legislation and concern as to health and food safety.

It is the responsibility of the company and all its employees to ensure that all services and products are procured, produced, packaged and delivered, and waste materials ultimately disposed of, in ways which are appropriate from an environmental viewpoint. It is the responsibility of our employees to carry out their work in a manner that will not cause damage to the environment.

14.6.2   Need for measurement

Environmental obligations create liabilities that must be recognised and measured. For example, an oil rig in the North Sea will eventually have to be removed. The accounting standard on liabilities and provisions describes the case of an entity which operates an offshore oilfield where its licensing agreement requires it to remove the oil rig at the end of production and restore the seabed. Ninety per cent of the eventual costs relate to the removal of the oil rig and restoration of damage caused by building it, and ten per cent arise through the extraction of oil. At the end of the most recent accounting period, the rig has been constructed but no oil has been extracted. There is a liability because there is a present obligation (the agreement to remove the rig) as a result of a past event (the contract of the licensing agreement). A transfer of economic resources will take place when the rig is removed. A provision is recognised for the best estimate of the ninety per cent of costs that relate to removal of the rig and putting right the damage. The remaining ten per cent of costs will be recognised as a liability when the oil is extracted.

14.6.3   The Global Reporting Initiative

The Global Reporting Initiative (GRI) is a venture that was started through a link between the United Nations Environmental Programme and a US body called the Coalition for Environmentally Responsible Economies. It has developed into a global institution that sets out a reporting framework, called the GRI Guidelines, for sustainability reporting. Companies are increasingly referring to the GRI Guidelines in designing parts of their annual report. The recommendations include reporting on vision and strategy, the profile of the organisation, the governance structure and management system and performance indicators. These indicators should cover economic, environmental and social performance. This combination is sometimes referred to in the press as 'the triple bottom line'. The reason for this description is that for many years the earnings for equity holders has been described as 'the bottom line' (of the income statement): extending to three performance measures leads to a triple bottom line.

14.6.4 Climate change accounting

International agreements on supporting sustainable development have consequences for accounting. One example is seen in the Kyoto Protocol, an agreement resulting from a conference held in Kyoto, Japan in 1997 as an amendment to the United Nations Framework Convention on Climate Change. The Kyoto Protocol set out measures for dealing with problems of climate change by reducing greenhouse gas emissions. Some countries were more reluctant than others to ratify the agreement (confirm that they will make it operational) although gradually more countries have agreed. All member states of the EU have ratified the Protocol.

The Kyoto agreement has made slow progress. In 2011, the United Nations Climate Change Conference was held in Durban, South Africa. It agreed to a legally binding deal covering all countries, to be prepared by 2015 and take effect in 2020. At subsequent conferences, some of the main countries have not participated and there appears to have been a lack of political will to combat climate change.

The Kyoto agreement requires action to be taken to reduce carbon-based emissions (particularly carbon dioxide) over a defined timescale. Countries are given limits of emissions of greenhouse gases. The countries then set limits on companies in specified industries.

One interesting feature of the Kyoto agreement is that companies are given 'allowances to emit'. The allowance, in the form of a licence, is capable of being transferred from one company to another. The entity that buys a licence to emit acquires an asset. This in turn creates new assets and liabilities for individual companies. The liabilities are easier to see: companies which do not reduce emissions will face penalties. However, there are also opportunities to take actions that prevent emissions and extract value from the new carbon market. If these actions meet the definition and recognition criteria, they are regarded as assets. The European Union Greenhouse Gas Emissions Trading Scheme began in January 2005. It establishes a market in carbon dioxide gas emissions for companies in specified industry sectors.

There is no international accounting standard dealing directly with accounting for the environment and sustainable development but there are interested groups working on the accounting issues in various countries.

A survey of accounting practices[11] observed in annual reports found that many companies report the asset of emissions allowances as an intangible asset measured at cost. If the allowances are granted by the government then the cost to the company is zero. Only when allowances are purchased does a cost appear. Fair value is an alternative method of measurement but is rarely used. The obligation to deliver up allowances to match emissions of the period is generally reported at the cost of the allowances granted, which is zero. In a cost-based system the obligation only has a measured value if there are excess emissions requiring the company to purchase additional allowances. Fair value could be used as an alternative but is rarely found.

Activity 14.3 *Write down the accounting equation: Assets minus Liabilities equals Ownership interest. Suppose you are the accountant for an oil company and you have been asked to record the full liability for dismantling an oil rig in 20 years' time. How would you make the accounting equation balance?*

14.7 Corporate governance

The term **corporate governance** is used to describe the way in which companies are directed and controlled. In Chapter 1 the idea of stewards and their agents was put forward briefly as a model of the relationship between shareholders and the directors of a company. It could be argued that these two groups could be left together to work out their fate, but a series of well-publicised corporate failures and financial scandals of the 1980s raised concern that such a system does not always work and the public interest may suffer as a result.

There has therefore been considerable interest in intervening to improve the quality of corporate governance. The issue has been high on the agenda in several of the English-speaking countries and the ideas have strong international interest although perhaps translated into different words and phrases.

14.7.1   The UK Corporate Governance Code

In the UK, the government has taken some action through legislation but has largely followed the traditional route of encouraging the self-regulatory approach. The self-regulatory approach is outlined in section 4.5.4 in Chapter 4. The origin of this self-regulatory approach was the 1992 report of what is usually referred to as the Cadbury Committee.[12]

The Cadbury Committee was set up by the Financial Reporting Council, the London Stock Exchange and the **accountancy profession**. It was asked to report on a range of issues concerned with the way directors run their companies and auditors monitor those companies, considering also the links between directors, auditors and shareholders. The recommendations of the Cadbury Committee were wide-ranging but included proposed improvements in financial reporting such as:

- more detail in the interim reports
- clearer information about directors' remuneration
- effective use of the operating and financial review
- the effectiveness of the internal control procedures used by the business
- reassurance that the business is a going concern
- a statement of the responsibilities of directors.

Although the report was issued in 1992 it took some time for further working parties to agree on the manner of reporting on internal controls and the going concern confirmation. By the end of 1995 these were in place and 1996 saw the start of a review of the first three years of implementing the Cadbury Report.

The review was chaired by Sir Ronald Hampel, so that the report which eventually appeared in 1998 was called 'The Hampel Report'.[13] It took as its starting point the view that good corporate governance was not merely a matter of complying with a number of hard and fast rules. There was seen to be a need for broad principles. It was important to take account of the diversity of circumstances and experience among companies, and within the same company over time. On this basis Hampel suggested that the true safeguard for good corporate governance lay in the application of informed and independent judgement by experienced and qualified individuals – executive and non-executive directors, shareholders and auditors. Relatively little was said about financial reporting, beyond the assertion that the board of directors should present a balanced and understandable assessment of the company's position and prospects.

Following the Hampel Report, the Stock Exchange issued a Combined Code for listed companies containing recommendations on directors; directors' remuneration; relations with shareholders; and accountability and audit. The accountability section emphasised the responsibilities of directors in respect of financial reporting. They should present a balanced and understandable assessment of the company's position and prospects. In particular they should explain their responsibilities and they should also report that the business is a going concern.

The Combined Code was subsequently taken into the responsibility of the Financial Reporting Council. It is now called the UK Corporate Governance Code. Companies must report on how they have applied the code in their annual report and accounts.

The information provided by companies in their annual reports is based on the principle of 'comply or explain', first set out in the Cadbury Report. The **Listing Rules** of the Financial Conduct Authority require that companies should report whether they have followed the recommendations of the Code. If they have not done so, they should explain the reason. Companies with a Premium Listing (see section 4.5.5) must provide a 'comply or explain' statement in the annual report explaining how the company has applied the UK Corporate Governance Code.

Most companies have a separate 'Corporate Governance' section in their annual report. This section tends to grow longer each year as more headings are added. The detailed nature of most Corporate Governance sections suggests that companies are moving closer to a practice of 'comply *and* explain' rather than the principle of 'comply *or* explain'. The following typical list of headings is extracted from the Corporate Governance section of an annual report:

- Introduction
- Putting governance into practice
- The Board
- Non-executive Directors
- Board Committees
- Board meetings
- Attendance at meetings
- Induction, development and support
- Election of directors
- Board performance evaluation
- Relations with shareholders
- Internal control
- Performance reporting and information
- Review of effectiveness of internal control.

14.7.2 Directors' remuneration

There is a continuing interest in the subject of directors' remuneration, partly because it provides opportunities for newspaper headlines. Typically the interest of financial journalists focuses on the salary of the highest paid director and the amount that person is gaining through share option schemes. These schemes allow directors to obtain each year the option to buy shares at an agreed price. If the share price rises subsequently the directors exercise the option, buy the share at the agreed price and may sell immediately at a profit. Some companies offer such options to some or all of their employees by way of encouraging loyalty to the company and supplementing cash salaries. There are constant questions about whether remuneration is justified by meeting performance targets.

In response to well-publicised concerns about the need to disclose and control the level of directors' remuneration, a study group chaired by Sir Richard Greenbury (1995) produced a code of best practice on disclosure and remuneration policy.[14] These recommendations are now incorporated partly in the Companies Act 2006 and partly in the Corporate Governance Code. A typical annual report of a listed company contains several pages on the remuneration policy and the payments to directors. There is a particular focus on how performance targets are set and monitored.

Activity 14.4

Obtain the annual report of a listed company. Turn to the report on corporate governance. What does the company say about corporate governance and about compliance with the Corporate Governance Code? What do the auditors say about the report on corporate governance? What is disclosed about the remuneration committee? What information is given elsewhere in the annual report, relating to directors' remuneration?

14.8 Meaning of 'fair presentation' and 'true and fair view'

The IASB system of accounting requires financial statements to *present fairly* the financial position, financial performance and cash flows of an entity.[15] In virtually all circumstances a fair presentation is achieved by compliance with the applicable IFRSs.[16] Entities cannot use notes or explanatory material to compensate for inappropriate accounting policies – the choice of policies must in itself achieve a fair presentation.[17] In the extremely rare circumstances where management considers that compliance with a requirement of an IFRS would conflict with the objective of a fair presentation, the entity will depart from the requirement and explain the reasons and consequences.[18]

The Companies Act 2006 requires that financial statements of companies should show *a true and fair view*.[19] In most situations a company will achieve a true and fair view by following the requirements of company law and UK accounting standards. In the rare circumstances where management considers that compliance with a requirement of law and standards would conflict with the true and fair view, the entity will depart from that requirement and explain the reasons and consequences.

14.8.1 Equivalence of meaning

The question arises as to whether 'fair presentation' and 'a true and fair view' have different meanings. The Financial Reporting Council (FRC)[20] has obtained legal opinion that 'fair presentation' and 'true and fair view' are not different requirements. They are different ways of expressing the same concept. The FRC has also pointed out that the IASB Framework equates 'true and fair view' and 'fair presentation' in asserting that the application of the principal qualitative characteristics and of appropriate accounting standards normally results in financial statements that convey what is generally understood as a true and fair view or a fair presentation of information.[21]

The remainder of this section discusses the meaning of 'true and fair view' because it has a longer history of debate and development in the UK. The phrase 'true and fair' was taken into European Directives when the UK joined as a member state but it has never found an exact equivalent in the underlying meaning. For example the French wording 'image fidèle' is closer to 'a faithful picture'.

The UK has traditionally taken the position that it may be necessary for individual companies to take action which contravenes legal rules, in the interest of presenting 'a true and fair view'. In other countries, including the US, the position taken is generally that the law prevails and any questions about fair presentation should be analysed within the legal framework. The US wording is 'faithful representation'.

14.8.2 Meaning of a true and fair view

The UK Companies Act provides no definition of the meaning of 'a true and fair view'. Consequently from time to time those who set accounting standards have sought the opinion of expert legal advisers. The lawyers have put forward the view that the requirement for a true and fair view is a dynamic concept which changes its nature as the general values of society change. Although the words stay the same, the meaning of the words changes because the opinions of society in general change.

What does that mean in practice? The lawyers have provided an example.[22] The Bill of Rights 1688 prohibited 'cruel and unusual punishments'. The dictionary definition of 'cruel' has changed little since that time but a judge today would characterise as 'cruel' some punishments which a judge of 1688 would not have regarded as cruel.

The meaning of the word remains the same but the facts to which it is applied have changed. Based on reasoning of that type, the lawyers have argued that the words 'true and fair' may carry the same dictionary meaning from one time to another but the accounting principles and practice contributing to a true and fair view will change as circumstances change.

One very important issue is the question of whether society, and the public interest, would expect the application of accounting standards to be necessary as evidence of intent to apply a true and fair view. The FRC has given the following guidance, based on legal opinion:

> *Accounting standards are arrived at after extensive consultation and after full due process. Further reviews are performed to ensure that IFRS meet the criteria for endorsement by the European Commission to ensure they would give a true and fair view.*
>
> *These processes should result in accounting standards that, in the vast majority of cases, are complied with when presenting a true and fair view. The statement in IAS 1 that departures from the standards should only be necessary in extremely rare circumstances should be understood in the context of the consultation and other due processes that preceded the issue of the standards. It does not release directors from their legal obligation to only approve particular accounts if they are satisfied that they give a true and fair view and directors should not rely on it to avoid making appropriate judgements.*[23]

Although departure from an accounting standard may become necessary in the interests of presenting a true and fair view, it is likely that a solution to a problem will be found within the accounting standards. The FRC continues to emphasise the importance of professional judgement:

> *Whilst there has been a gradual shift over time to more detailed accounting standards, the preparation of financial statements cannot be reduced to a mechanistic following of the relevant accounting standards. Objective professional judgement must be applied to ensure that financial statements give a true and fair view.*[24]

14.8.3 Who is responsible for the true and fair view?

Under company law, it is the directors who are responsible for ensuring that the accounts are prepared in such a way as to show a true and fair view. The auditors state whether, in their opinion, the accounts show a true and fair view. If you turn back to Chapter 4 you will see an example of the statement of directors' responsibilities which now appears in many company reports and also a copy of the auditors' report. Both contain the phrase 'a true and fair view' and emphasise the different types of responsibility held by directors and auditors.

14.8.4 How specific is the 'true and fair' concept?

You should have gained an understanding, from various chapters of this book, that there is more than one accounting treatment for many transactions and events. It is a great puzzle to many people that companies could produce different accounting statements for one particular period of time, each of which would show a true and fair view. The answer lies in one very small word. The requirement of law is for 'a true and fair view' but not for 'the true and fair view'. Thus the directors do not have to find 'the very best true and fair view', which may surprise some users of financial statements. It also becomes very difficult for auditors to enter into dispute with directors where there are two acceptable alternatives, either of which could result in a true and fair view. To be successful in contradicting the directors, the auditors need to show that a particular practice does *not* show a true and fair view. If they can successfully argue that opinion then the company has the choice of revising the proposed treatment or facing a *qualified* audit opinion. Here is an example of a qualified audit opinion where the auditor and directors were in disagreement:

Qualified audit opinion
We found that the company has made no provision for doubtful debts, despite circumstances which indicate that such a provision is necessary.
In our opinion the accounts do not give a true and fair view . . .

It is therefore essential, in reading the annual report, to read the auditors' report at an early stage in order to be aware of any problems with the financial statements. It is also essential to realise that the meaning of 'true and fair' is highly subjective and changes over a period of time.

Activity 14.5   *Looking back through Chapters 8 to 12, identify matters of accounting practice where more than one accounting policy is permitted. If you were an auditor, how would you decide whether one or other of the permitted choices gave a true and fair view?*

14.9 Measurement of value

Chapter 2, section 2.2.3, defines **historical cost** and **fair value**. When you read the 'Accounting policies' section of the annual report of a UK quoted company you are likely to see the following wording:

These financial statements have been prepared under the historical cost convention, as modified by the revaluation of certain financial assets and liabilities (including derivative instruments) at fair value through profit or loss.

In the annual reports of UK companies there is a general adherence to historical cost, but some financial assets and liabilities are recorded at fair value and the change in value is reported in the income statement. Where non-current assets are recorded at fair value, the change in value is reported in the statement of comprehensive income.

The International Financial Reporting Standard IFRS 9, which applies to all financial assets and financial liabilities, requires fair value to be used. In some cases where it is difficult to find a fair value, the standard provides equivalent alternatives.

The International Accounting Standard IAS 16, which applies to non-current property, plant and equipment, permits entities to choose either the cost model or the revaluation model. Under the cost model, property, plant and equipment are carried at cost less accumulated depreciation. Under the revaluation model, an item of property, plant and equipment may be carried at a revalued amount. The revalued amount is fair value less accumulated depreciation. Revaluations must be made regularly so that the carrying amount remains close to fair value at the date of the financial statements.

Throughout the majority of this financial accounting text the value of assets and liabilities has been measured at historical cost. That means the price paid, or the liability agreed, when the transaction was first undertaken. In times when prices are changing, that information about the cost at the date of the transaction will become less relevant to the needs of users (although it may be seen as a faithful measure). The IASB *Conceptual Framework* says relatively little about measurement,[25] perhaps because of the difficulties of obtaining international agreement. A useful overview is provided by the ICAEW.[26]

14.9.1 Stages of recognition and measurement

At the moment when the transaction takes place, the historical cost is also the current value, where current value is regarded as the value of the item at the accounting date. This is identified as the point of initial recognition. If an asset or a liability is involved, then there will be various points at which it may be appropriate to remeasure the amount at which the asset or liability is recorded. This is referred to as subsequent remeasurement. Finally there may come a point at which the asset or liability should be removed from the financial statements. This is referred to as derecognition.

The criteria to be applied in deciding on initial **recognition** have been explained in Chapter 2. **Derecognition** reverses the criteria so that an asset or a liability should cease to be recognised if the entity loses control of an asset or no longer has an obligation for a previously recognised liability.[27]

14.9.2 Limitations of historical cost accounting

Throughout this text you have studied historical cost accounting where the acquisition of assets is recorded at the amount paid at the time of acquisition. The academic literature is bursting at the seams with criticisms of historical cost accounting, but the practice has proved hard to change. There were brief practical attempts in the UK to apply a different approach for a period from the mid-1970s to the mid-1980s but the rate of inflation then became less of a problem and interest waned.

Critics of historical cost accounting have said that in the statement of financial position (balance sheet) there is the addition of items bought at different times and with £s of different purchasing power. That is not a satisfactory procedure. In the income statement (profit and loss account) the costs are matched against revenue without regard for the fact that goods were bought and expenses paid for at an earlier point in time. Sales are therefore matched against outdated costs. The tax system takes the accounting profit as its starting point and therefore the tax payable is dictated by outdated accounting figures.

Supporters of historical cost accounting point to its reliability and objectivity because the monetary amount of the transaction is known. Verifiability is straightforward because documentation exists. The preference for historical cost values remains strong; if companies do decide to revalue non-current assets then the companies keep the current values up to date in each year's statement of financial position (balance sheet).[28]

14.9.3 Subsequent remeasurement

Subsequent remeasurement poses more problems and is one of the more controversial aspects of setting accounting standards. Each standard sets relevant conditions, with a general principle that there should be a change in the amount at which an asset or liability is recorded if there is sufficient evidence that: (a) the amount has changed and (b) the new amount can be measured with sufficient reliability.[29] In times of inflation (when prices generally are increasing), the idea of remeasurement becomes particularly important. Even when inflation is not a major problem, there may be one particular asset whose value increases through scarcity of supply or decreases through lack of demand.

That leads into an extremely controversial question: 'How do you measure value?' Methods of valuation are listed in the IASB *Conceptual Framework*,[30] but without any firm preferences being expressed.

14.9.4   Entry price and exit price

Taking non-current assets and inventories as the main examples to begin with, it could be said that there are two different categories of measures of value. There is a price which the organisation will have to pay to acquire the asset and there is a price at which the organisation will be able to sell the asset to someone else. If you have ever tried buying and selling second-hand goods you will know that the buying price and the selling price are often quite different. The student who tries to sell an outdated laptop through an advertisement on the college noticeboard knows that any enquirer will try to push the price downwards. The student attempting to enquire about a similar item of equipment knows that the seller will try to keep the price high. Somehow the price for which you are able to sell your second-hand possessions invariably appears to be lower than the price someone else is asking for their unwanted belongings.

The price paid by a business to acquire an asset is called in accounting the **entry price** and the price at which the business would be able to sell the asset is called the **exit price**. Academic authors will argue long and hard on both sides of the case and if you pursue the study of accounting further you will meet that academic debate. In the real world a decision has to be made. In the UK, that decision was made by the standard-setting body at the beginning of the 1980s, when SSAP 16 required companies to use the entry price approach and to measure the value of non-current assets and inventories at the cost of replacement at the date of the financial statements. That approach was used to provide additional information in annual reports of the UK for the first half of the 1980s, but gradually the enthusiasm of companies waned and by the late 1980s they had reverted to their traditional practice of using primarily historical cost for most aspects of measurement.

14.9.5   Current values[31]

In a current value system, changes in value are recorded as they occur. This idea, if accepted, puts quite a large hole in the concept of **realisation**, which is at the heart of traditional accounting practice. It has been the practice to record changes in ownership interest only when the change in an asset or liability is realised, in the form either of cash or of other assets the ultimate realisation of which can be assessed with reasonable certainty. That practice finds continuing support in the Companies Act 2006 which states that the income statement (profit and loss account) reported under the Act may report only those profits which are realised (although this requirement does not apply to companies reporting under full IFRS).

Chapter 12 has explained how some gains and losses on revaluation may be reported in Other Comprehensive Income. There is an unanswered question of how to measure current value.

The argument favoured by some commentators in the UK, is the one which leads to a measurement system based on **value to the business**. Those who support this idea start by asking: What is the worst that can happen to a person, or business, which owns a non-current asset or item of inventory? The answer is that they may be deprived of the item, perhaps by theft, fire, obsolescence or similar cause. The next question is: What would the owners need in order to be returned to the position they enjoyed previously? The answer, in most cases, is that they need to be provided with the cost of replacement of a similar item so that they may continue with the activity of the business. In a few rare cases, where the owners may have decided to sell rather than continue using the asset, the selling price is the measure of deprival.

From this analysis it is argued that the value to the business of a non-current asset or an item of inventory is usually the **replacement cost** at the accounting date. The replacement cost is that of a similar item in a similar state. Such a replacement cost might be found in a catalogue of prices of used equipment or it could be estimated by starting with the cost of a new item and applying an appropriate proportion of depreciation.

14.9.6 Fair value

The IASB standards have moved towards a fair value approach to valuation rather than a 'value to the business' approach. Several of the standards in the IASB system permit or require the use of **fair value**, which to based on exit price. The definition has been provided in Chapter 2 and applied in subsequent chapters, where relevant.

Definition

Fair value is the price that would be received to sell an asset or paid to transfer a liability in an orderly transaction between market participants at the measurement date.[32]

The definition of fair value has been agreed between the IASB and the US standard-setter, the FASB (Financial Accounting Standards Board). Ideally the price should be found from an active market, in which transactions for the asset or liability take place with sufficient frequency and volume to provide pricing information on an ongoing basis. If the company operates in more than one market, then the price should be taken from the market that maximises the amount that would be received to sell the asset or minimises the amount that would be paid to transfer the liability, after taking into account transaction costs and transport costs.

In some cases there is no active market for an asset or a liability. The accounting standard then sets out a sequence of attempts (a 'hierarchy') to be followed in deciding on fair value. Companies must explain how they have applied this hierarchy. For property, plant and equipment[33] a company might use depreciated replacement cost where market-based evidence is not available. For biological assets a range of suggestions is given, such as market price of similar assets or discounted present value of future cash flows.[34]

Activity 14.6

Look at the items you possess. These might include a house or a flat or a car, but equally well they could be a bicycle and some modest items of furniture. Whatever their nature, write down on a piece of paper a figure in £s which answers the question: What is the value of these possessions? Now think about how you arrived at that figure. Did you use the original cost because that was the amount you paid to acquire them? Did you use replacement cost because that is the amount you would have to pay to replace them? Did you use selling price because that is the amount you could collect in cash for conversion to other uses? Did you have some other method? What was the reason for the method you chose? Would you obtain the same answer using all the methods listed for this activity? Which answer is the most relevant for your information needs? Would other students answer these questions as you have done?

14.10 Risk reporting

One of the major causes of increasing disclosure in annual reports is the need to explain the risks that the business faces. For UK company reporting there are several sources of requirements for risk reporting in the notes to the accounts and in the narrative sections of the annual report. Many companies provide additional voluntary information about risks because they are aware of its importance to investors and other users of the annual report.

The strategic report requires companies to provide information on description of the principal risks and uncertainties facing the company. It is for companies to decide how to implement this requirement. The Financial Reporting Council has provided guidance on how to report principal risks and uncertainties, including the following:

● The risks and uncertainties included in the strategic report will generally be matters that the directors regularly monitor and discuss because they are likely to occur or are large in magnitude.

● Principal risks may be financial or non-financial and may result from strategic decisions, operations, organisation or behaviour, or from external factors over which the board may have little or no direct control. Risks include threats to solvency and liquidity.

● The directors should explain how principal risks and uncertainties are managed or mitigated, so that shareholders can assess the impact on the future prospects of the entity.

● Significant changes in principal risks should be highlighted and explained.

● A risk or uncertainty may be unique to the entity, a matter that is relevant to the market in which it operates, or something that applies to the business environment more generally. Where the risk or uncertainty is more generic, the description should make clear how it might affect the entity specifically.

This guidance is intended to encourage companies to provide meaningful and understandable information.

Researchers have found that risk information is important for analysts, professional and private investors. While the annual report is an important source of risk information for the private investor, the professional investors say they prefer one-to-one meetings with companies to explore risk information. There is a feeling that most of the information disclosed in the annual report is already known to the well informed professional investor before the report is published, because these investors keep in contact with the company on a regular basis. It seems that the information published is of greatest potential use to the private investor or to persons less closely familiar with the company.

14.11 Developing issues: how valid is the stakeholder model?

This book takes as its starting point the IASB's *Conceptual Framework*, and has constantly returned to that *Conceptual Framework* for explanation or discussion of the accounting practices explained in various chapters. The *Conceptual Framework* is, in its turn, built on a model which sees the objective of accounting as serving the needs of a wide range of users. Those users are sometimes referred to as **stakeholders** and the *Conceptual Framework* is regarded as an example of a stakeholder model of the process of regulating accounting.

There are, however, those who would argue that the stakeholder model is the wrong place to start and therefore the significant problems of accounting will not be solved using a statement of principles of this type. At the basic level of understanding existing accounting practice, which is the limit of this book, the validity of one model versus another may not be a critical issue, but you should be aware that there are views that more complex accounting problems may not be solved using a stakeholder approach.

Those who argue against the 'user needs' approach suggest that accounting regulation is a much more complex process of social interaction. Standard-setters producing accounting rules in a self-regulatory environment need to be sure of a consensus of opinion supporting the proposed rules. They will therefore seek out a range of opinions and will undoubtedly be subjected to lobbying (letters of comment and personal contact) by persons or organisations seeking to put forward a particular viewpoint. Indeed, part of the standard-setting process involves issuing an exposure draft for comment before a financial reporting standard is issued, although there is no way of knowing what lobbying occurs behind the scenes.

The process of standard-setting may therefore be regarded as one of negotiating and balancing various interests. There has been research after the event, both in the UK and in other countries, which has shown that the standard-setting bodies were influenced by one or more powerful forces. One particularly clear example may be seen in the development of an accounting standard to tighten up practices in reporting expenditure on research and development.[35] There is a significant amount of academic literature on factors influencing the process of setting accounting standards.

Those who have identified these 'political' pressures would suggest that the accounting standard-setting process should openly admit that there are influential factors such as: the relative balance of power among those who prepare and those who use accounting information; relative dependency of some on others; the balance of individual liberty against collective need; and the ideology observed in particular systems of social relations. (Ideology means that a group in society may hold strong beliefs which make it genuinely unable to appreciate different positions taken by others.)

Thus claims that the standard-setting process is neutral in its impact on the economy or on society may be unrealistic. This book does not seek to impose any particular view on its readers. It has used the *Conceptual Framework* as a consistent basis for explaining current practice, but it leaves to the reader the task of taking forward the knowledge of external financial reporting and the understanding of what influences the future development of external financial reporting.

14.12 Summary

- The **strategic report** provides a balanced and comprehensive analysis of the business, its year-end position, the trends in performance during the year and factors likely to affect future position and performance. It is a requirement for quoted UK companies.

- A **highlights statement** in the annual report shows what the company regards as important information for investors as the primary users of the annual report. A table of five-year trends is also useful in evaluating the position and performance of the business.

- **Segmental reporting** has developed as a means of supplementing the consolidated financial statements by providing more insight into the activities of the group. In particular it reports information about the different types of products and services that an entity produces and the different geographical areas in which it operates.

- **Off-balance sheet finance** describes the situation where an asset and a liability are omitted from the financial statements of an entity. Over the years, standard setters have tightened their rules on cases where control and benefits remain with the reporting entity.

- **Corporate social responsibility** means that companies integrate social and environmental concerns in their business operations and in their interactions with stakeholders. Many companies include social and environmental disclosures in their annual reports. The Global Reporting Initiative provides a framework for such disclosures.

- Carbon trading, arising from the Kyoto Protocol, provides a new form of asset in the licence to emit carbon dioxide and a new form of liability in the obligation to reduce emissions.

- The term **corporate governance** is used to describe the way in which companies are directed and controlled. Listed companies in the UK are required to follow the Corporate Governance Code. In the annual report the directors must either confirm compliance with the Code or explain reasons for non-compliance.

- Directors' remuneration is one aspect of corporate governance that receives a great deal of attention. There are rules and guidance on the disclosure of remuneration (pay) policy and the amount due to each director. The information is usually contained in the Directors' Remuneration Report.

- The IASB system of accounting requires financial statements to **present fairly** the financial position, financial performance and cash flows of an entity. The Companies Act 2006 requires that financial statements of companies should show a **true and fair view**. The Financial Reporting Council has given an opinion that the two phrases are broadly equivalent.

- There is a continuing debate on the methods of measuring assets and liabilities. **Faithful representation** points towards current values.

- **Entry price** values are values that measure the cost of buying, acquiring or replacing an asset or liability. **Exit price** values represent the sale, disposal or other form of realisation of an asset.

- **Fair value** is the price that would be received to sell an asset or paid to transfer a liability in an orderly transaction between market participants at the measurement date.

- Finally, it should be noted that this entire book on financial accounting has been built on a **stakeholder** model of user needs which itself is the basis of the IASB's *Conceptual Framework*. That idea meets general acceptance in the accounting profession from those who set accounting standards, but you need to be aware that further study of the academic literature will encourage you to question the user needs model.

Further reading

The following reference materials are all available free of charge on the relevant websites:

Abraham, S., Marston, C. and Darby, P. (2012), *Risk Reporting: Clarity, relevance and location.* The Institute of Chartered Accountants of Scotland.

Climate Disclosure Standards Board (2010), *Disclosure Framework.*

Crawford, L., Extance, H., Helliar, C. and Power, D. (2012), *Operating Segments: The usefulness of IFRS 8.* The Institute of Chartered Accountants of Scotland.

Financial Reporting Council (October 2010), *The UK Approach to Corporate Governance.*

Financial Reporting Council (July 2011), *True and Fair.*

Financial Reporting Review Panel Press notice FRRP PN 130 (Feb 2011), *The Financial Reporting Review Panel highlights challenges in the reporting of principal risks and uncertainties.*

ICAEW (2010), *Measurement in Financial Reporting.* The Institute of Chartered Accountants in England and Wales.

Lovell, H., Sales de Aguiar, T., Bebbington, J. and Larrinaga-Gonzalez, C. (2010), *Accounting for Carbon.* Association of Chartered Certified Accountants.

QUESTIONS

The Questions section of each chapter has three types of question. 'Test your understanding' questions to help you review your reading are in the 'A' series of questions. You will find the answers to these by reading and thinking about the material in the book. 'Application' questions to test your ability to apply technical skills are in the 'B' series of questions. Questions requiring you to show skills in problem solving and evaluation are in the 'C' series of questions. A letter [S] indicates that there is a solution at the end of the book. Other solutions are provided in the Instructor's Manual, where there are further questions parallel to those set out here.

A   Test your understanding

A14.1   What is the purpose of the strategic report? (Section 14.2.2)

A14.2   Why is there no prescribed format for the strategic report? (Section 14.2.2)

A14.3   What are the aims of the FRC for the strategic report? (Section 14.2.2)

A14.4   What are the main contents of the strategic report? (Section 14.2.2)

A14.5   What are key performance indicators (KPIs)? (Section 14.2.3)

A14.6   What are the particular requirements that must be reported in a strategic report? (Section 14.2.2)

A14.7   What are the responsibilities of the directors and auditors in relation to the strategic report? (Section 14.2.4)

A14.8   What is the purpose of a highlights statement? (Section 14.3.1)

A14.9   How does a five-year summary of historical results help investors? (Section 14.3.2)

A14.10   How does segmental information help the users of financial statements? (Section 14.4.1)

A14.11   Which items are reported on a segmental basis? (Section 14.4.1)

A14.12   How are segments identified? (Section 14.4.3)

A14.13   Why is off-balance sheet finance a problem in accounting? (Section 14.5)

A14.14   What principles were recommended by the UK standard-setter for determining whether assets and liabilities should be reported on the statement of financial position (balance sheet)? (Section 14.5.2)

A14.15   What is a special purpose entity? (Section 14.5.3)

A14.16   What is corporate social responsibility? (Section 14.6)

A14.17   What is the Global Reporting Initiative? (Section 14.6.3)

A14.18   What accounting issues arise in relation to carbon trading? (Section 14.6.4)

A14.19   What is meant by corporate governance? (Section 14.7)

A14.20   What is the UK Corporate Governance Code? (Section 14.7.1)

A14.21   How does financial reporting help to improve corporate governance? (Section 14.7)

A14.22   Why has it been found impossible to write a definitive guide on the meaning of 'a true and fair view'? (Section 14.8)

A14.23   What are the limitations of historical cost accounting? (Section 14.9.2)

A14.24   Why is it desirable to remeasure assets and liabilities subsequent to acquisition? (Section 14.9.3)

A14.25   Explain what is meant by entry price and exit price. (Section 14.9.4)

A14.26   Explain what is meant by fair value. (Section 14.9.6)

A14.27   Should accounting standards focus primarily on the needs of users? (Section 14.10)

B   Application

B14.1
Suggest, with reasons, three KPIs for each of the following types of business, and explain why it is unlikely that two businesses will choose identical KPIs.

(a) a private hospital
(b) a car repair garage
(c) a clothing manufacturer.

C   Problem solving and evaluation

C14.1 [S]
Carry out a trend analysis on Safe and Sure plc, using the historical summary set out in Appendix I. Write a short report on the key features emerging from the trends.

Activities for study groups

Case 14.1

Turn to the annual report of a listed company which you have used for activities throughout the previous chapters. Split the group to take two different roles: one half of the group should take the role of the finance director and the other half should take the role of the broker's analyst writing a report on the company.

Look through the annual report for any ratio calculations performed by the company and check these from the data in the financial statements, so far as you are able. Prepare your own calculations of ratios for analysis of all aspects of performance. Find the current share price from a current newspaper.

Once the data preparation is complete, the finance director subgroup should prepare a short report to a meeting with the analysts. The analysts should then respond with questions arising from the ratio analysis. The finance directors should seek to present answers to the questions using the annual report. Finally write a short report (250 words) on problems encountered in calculating and interpreting financial ratios.

Case 14.2

Turn to the annual report of a listed company which you have used for activities in previous chapters. Is this a group? How do you know? Where is the list of subsidiary companies?

If you do not have a group report, obtain another annual report which is for a group of companies (nearly all large listed companies operate in group form). As a group, imagine that you are a team of analysts seeking to break down the component segments of the group for analytical purposes. How much information can you find about the segments? What are the problems of defining segments in this group? If you can obtain the annual report for the previous year, compare the definitions of segments. Are they consistent from one year to the next?

Based on your analysis, prepare a short essay (250 words): 'The usefulness of segmental information in the analysis of group performance'.

Case 14.3

Divide the group into sections to take on four different roles: a private shareholder in a company; a financial journalist; a finance director of a company; and a broker's analyst providing an advisory service to clients.

In each section develop your opinion on the subject. Taking the user needs perspective will solve all the problems of accounting.

Arrange a meeting to present all four opinions and then discuss the extent to which the International Accounting Standards Board will be able to obtain the co-operation of all parties in solving accounting problems.

Notes and references

1. The Companies Act 2006 (Strategic Report and Directors' Report) Regulations 2013.
2. *The future of narrative reporting: a further consulation* (2011); https://www.gov.uk/government/consultations/the-future-of-narrative-reporting-a-further-consultation); *The Future of Narrative Reporting – the government response* (2012) (https://www.gov.uk/government/uploads/system/uploads/attachment_data/file/136489/12-588-future-of-narrative-reporting-government-response.pdf
3. FRC (2014), *Guidance on the Strategic Report,* June 2014, Financial Reporting Council.
4. ASB (2006), RS 1 paras 75–7.
5. FRC (2014), *Audit and Assurance Bulletin,* April 2014.
6. See (1) above
7. www.ifrs.org.
8. IASB (2012), IFRS 8 *Operating Segments,* International Accounting Standards Board.
9. Crawford et al. (2012), *Operating Segments: The usefulness of IFRS 8.*
10. ASB (1994), Financial Reporting Standard (FRS 5), *Reporting the Substance of Transactions,* Accounting Standards Board.
11. Lovell et al. (2010), *Accounting for Carbon.*
12. The Committee on the Financial Aspects of Corporate Governance (1992) *The Financial Aspects of Corporate Governance* (The Cadbury Report), December. (The Committee Chairman was Sir Adrian Cadbury.)
13. *The Committee on Corporate Governance Final Report* (1998), Gee Publishing Ltd. (The Committee chairman was Sir Ronnie Hampel.)
14. *Report of a Study Group on Directors' Remuneration* (1995) (The Greenbury Report), Gee Publishing Ltd.
15. IASB (2016), IAS 1 *Presentation of financial statements,* para. 15.
16. IASB (2016), IAS 1 para. 15.
17. IASB (2016), IAS 1 para. 18.
18. IASB (2016), IAS 1 paras 19 and 20.
19. The Companies Act 2006, section 393.
20. FRC (2014), *True and Fair.* Financial Reporting Council website, www.frc.org.uk, June 2014.
21. IASB (2016), *Conceptual Framework.*
22. Hoffman, L. and Arden, M. H. (1983), 'Legal opinion on "true and fair"', *Accountancy,* November, pp. 154–6.
23. FRC (2014), *True and Fair,* 1–4
24. *Ibid.,* page 1.
25. IASB *Conceptual Framework* (2010), paras 4.54–4.56.
26. ICAEW (2006), *Measurement in Financial Reporting.*
27. Explained in various IFRS such as IFRS 9 *Financial Instruments.*
28. IASB (2016), IAS 16 *Property, Plant and Equipment,* para. 31; FRC (2013), FRS 102, para. 176.
29. E.g. IAS 16 *Property, Plant and Equipment,* para. 31.
30. IASB (2016) *Conceptual Framework.*
31. ICAEW (2006), *Measurement in Financial Reporting.* The Institute of Chartered Accountants in England and Wales.
32. IASB (2016), IFRS 13 *Fair Value Measurement.*
33. IASB (2014), IFRS 13, paras 72–75.
34. IASB (2016), IAS 41 *Agriculture,* paras 13–25.
35. Hope, T. and Gray, R. (1982), 'Power and policy making: the development of an R&D standard', *Journal of Business Finance and Accounting,* 9(4): 531–58.

Chapter 15

Reporting cash flows

ITV: no news, good news?

Five years ago ITV, the UK broadcaster, was the lead in a tragic story of large debts and little profits, with a market capitalisation below £3bn. Since 2010, when Adam Crozier became chief executive, ITV has benefited from a rewrite. Boy meets company, company cuts costs, market loves boy, high ratings all round. The shares now trade at 15 times estimated forward earnings and the market cap is more than £8bn. However, previews for next year look dicey.

ITV has plenty of cash flow, comfortably exceeding its capital spending and dividends combined last year. That free cash flow has enabled the company to cut debt. In 2009 operating earnings barely covered interest payments; last year the coverage reached more than 12 times. Yes, the UK economy has dramatically improved, lifting advertising spend. But still, good show.

And all that has not gone unnoticed. Liberty Global, the US-listed cable company with European ambitions, has bought a six per cent stake in the company from BSkyB.

What ITV does with this cash flow is the latest twist. Berenberg notes that ITV's audience share, for all its channels, has fallen to five-year lows. To counter this trend, ITV has bought stakes in production companies to make shows such as Pawn Stars (a reality show about pawnbrokers).

But the best hope for continued profit growth comes from the prospect that ITV could begin charging for the shows it now gives to BSkyB and Virgin for free under its UK public obligation. Credit Suisse thinks that fees for retransmission could add nearly a fifth to its market value. But do not count on a quick resolution. Discussion on this issue could go on for a long time.

Mr Crozier has built a reputation at ITV (and Royal Mail before) as a cost cutter, not a growth visionary. Spending to create content sounds colourful but is risky. Viewers are fickle. Shareholders prefer things in black and white.

Source: Lex team, *Financial Times*, 8 October 2014. http://www.ft.com/cms/s/3/64144f84-4e2a-11e4-bfda-0144feab7de .html\#axzz3G6ZBpeuK

Discussion points

1 What does the article say about the importance of cash flow to the company?

2 How does the article contrast cash flow and profit as measures of success?

Contents

Learning outcomes

After reading this chapter you should be able to:

- Explain why statements of cash flows are regarded as providing useful information.
- Explain the meaning of cash and cash equivalents.
- Explain the direct and the indirect forms of presentation of a statement of cash flows.
- Prepare a statement of cash flows using the direct and the indirect method.

15.1 Introduction

The statement of cash flows is one of the primary financial statements. It provides information that can not be seen in the balance sheet and income statement (profit and loss account) alone. Users of financial statements want to know about changes in financial position. This involves providing information about an entity's ability to generate cash flows and the entity's use of those cash flows.

Chapter 3 gives a very simple introduction to the statement of cash flows. In particular it shows why cash flow and profit differ because of the different timings of cash flow and profits. Chapter 9 indicates the working capital cycle through which inventories are acquired from suppliers on credit and sold to customers on credit. The cash eventually received from customers is used to pay suppliers and the cycle starts again. Chapter 13 illustrates a statement of cash flows prepared from the statements of financial position and income statement of the illustrative company used in that chapter. The case study of Safe and Sure plc runs throughout several chapters with outline discussion of the statement of cash flows in Chapter 4.

This chapter provides a more thorough explanation of a statement of cash flows as presented in the IASB system. It explains in sections 15.2 and 15.3 the nature of the two choices – the 'direct' and the 'indirect' methods. Section 15.4 explains the nature and purpose of each line item of a statement of cash flows prepared using the indirect system. Section 15.5 explains the nature and purpose of each line item of a statement of cash flows prepared using the direct system. Section 15.6 presents a worked example for those who wish to practise preparation of a statement of cash flows based on the IASB system.[1]

15.2 Cash and cash equivalents

The IASB system[2] presents a statement of cash flows that explains changes in **cash** and **cash equivalents**.

Definitions

Cash comprises cash on hand and demand deposits.

Cash equivalents are short-term, highly liquid investments that are readily convertible to known amounts of cash and which are subject to an insignificant risk of changes in value.[3]

Cash is relatively easy to understand – it is cash that is immediately available. Cash equivalents are investments that are held to meet short-term commitments. To qualify as a cash equivalent the investment must be readily convertible to a known amount of cash and there must be an insignificant risk of changes in value. An investment qualifies as a cash equivalent only when it has a short maturity of, say, three months or less from the date of acquisition.[4]

Bank borrowings are generally considered to be financing activities. However, bank overdrafts that are repayable on demand are part of the cash management of a business. The bank balance fluctuates from a positive balance to an overdrawn balance at different times of the year.[5]

15.3 The direct method and the indirect method

There are two approaches to presenting the cash flows arising from operations. The direct method presents cash inflows from customers and cash outflows to suppliers and employees, taken from the entity's accounting records of cash receipts and payments. The indirect method starts with the operating profit and makes a series of adjustments to convert profit to cash. The data in Table 15.1 and Table 15.2 are used to illustrate each method.

Table 15.1
Income statement (profit and loss account), Year 2

	£m
Revenue	100
Cost of sales: materials	(40)
Wages	(20)
Depreciation	(10)
Operating profit	30

Table 15.2
Statements of financial position (balance sheets), end of Years 1 and 2

	Year 2 £m	Year 1 £m
Non-current assets	90	100
Current assets		
Inventory (stock) of materials	55	40
Trade receivables (debtors)	12	15
Cash	35	10
Total current assets	102	65
Total assets	192	165
Current liabilities		
Trade payables (creditors)	(11)	(14)
Non-current liabilities		
Long-term loans	(100)	(100)
Total liabilities	(111)	(114)
Net assets	81	51
Ownership interest	81	51

15.3.1 Direct method

The direct method reports the cash inflows from customers and cash outflows to suppliers, employees and other aspects of operations. This information is contained in the cash book or in the cash receipts and cash payments records used as input to the bookkeeping records in the general ledger. The direct method calculation is presented in Table 15.3. It is followed by a comment on each line in the calculation.

Table 15.3
Direct method

Operating cash flow, Year 1	
	£m
Cash received from customers	103
Cash paid to suppliers	(58)
Wages paid	(20)
Operating cash flow	25

General comment. In the direct method the cash flows are taken from the cash records. The cash records have to be analysed into categories suitable for the statement of cash flows. In Chapters 5 and 6 you have seen spreadsheets in which the cash record is the 'cash at bank' column. That column was used as the basis for the simple statement of cash flows on the direct method illustrated in those chapters (see sections 5.5.1 and 6.6.1). This chapter does not provide the detail of the cash records of receipts and payments but the following comments explain how the cash figures can be confirmed from the information in the balance sheet and the income statement (profit and loss account).

Cash received from customers. The cash inflows from customers may be confirmed by starting with the revenue earned in the period. Some of the revenue has been earned from selling to customers on credit. The amounts receivable from customers (debtors) at the start of the period will have been collected in cash during the period. The amounts shown as receivable from customers (debtors) at the end of the period are the revenue not yet collected in cash. This analysis is presented in the following calculation:

	£m
Revenue of the period	100
Add receivables at the start of the period	15
Less receivables at the end of the period	(12)
Cash received from customers	103

Cash paid to suppliers. The cash outflows to suppliers may be confirmed by starting with the materials purchased in the period. Some of the purchases have been obtained from suppliers on credit. The amounts payable to suppliers (creditors) at the start of the period will have been paid in cash during the period. The amounts shown as payable to suppliers (creditors) at the end of the period are the payments not yet made.

The next question is – how to confirm the figure for purchases?

The purchases of materials are needed to supply the goods sold and to provide an inventory at the end of the period. If there is an inventory (stock) at the start of the period this reduces the need to make purchases. This analysis is presented in the following calculation:

	£m
Cost of materials sold in the period	40
Add inventory at the end of the period	55
Less inventory at the start of the period	(40)
Purchases of materials	55

Then the payment to suppliers is calculated.

	£m
Purchases of the period	55
Add payables at the start of the period	14
Less payables at the end of the period	(11)
Cash paid to suppliers	58

Wages paid. Usually the wages are paid as soon as the work is done so the amount shown for wages in the income statement (profit and loss account) is the same as the cash payment. To confirm the wages payment, if any amount of wages remains unpaid at the start or end of the period then the wages cost must be adjusted for these unpaid amounts in a manner similar to the calculation of cash paid to suppliers.

15.3.2 Indirect method

The indirect method starts with the operating profit and makes adjustments to arrive at cash flow from operations. The indirect method calculation is presented in Table 15.4. It is followed by an explanation of each line in the calculation.

Table 15.4
Indirect method

Operating cash flow, Year 1	
	£m
Operating profit	30
Add back depreciation	10
	40
(Increase) in inventory	(15)
Decrease in receivables	3
(Decrease) in payables	(3)
Operating cash flow	25

Operating profit. This figure is taken from the income statement in Table 15.1.

Add back depreciation. **Depreciation** is an accounting expense that does not involve any flow of cash. It is an **allocation** of the cost of the non-current (fixed) asset. So if we are looking for the cash generated by making profits, this depreciation needs to be excluded. It was deducted as an expense to calculate profit, so now it is added back to exclude it.

(Increase) in inventory. When a business acquires inventory it uses up cash. The cash is recovered when the inventory is sold. The greater the build-up of inventory, the greater the amount of cash that the business is waiting to recover. So an increase in inventory uses cash. A decrease in inventory releases cash and so is a source of cash.

Decrease in receivables. When a business sells goods or services to customers on credit it has to wait to collect the cash. The greater the increase in receivables (debtors) the greater is the amount of cash that the business is waiting to collect. So an increase in receivables has the effect of decreasing cash flow. A decrease in receivables releases cash and so is a source of cash.

(Decrease) in payables. When a business buys goods or services from suppliers on credit it delays payment of the cash. The greater the increase in payables (creditors) the greater is the amount of cash payment that the business is delaying. So an increase in payables has the effect of increasing cash flow by postponing payments. A decrease in payables means that suppliers are being paid sooner and so is equivalent to a use of cash.

Change in cash in the statement of financial position. Finally it is important to check that the cash flow matches the change in cash in the statement of financial position. Looking at the statements of financial position in Table 15.2 you will see that the cash has increased from £10m to £35m which equals the positive cash flow of £25m calculated by both the direct and the indirect method.

15.3.3 Which to choose – direct or indirect?

When students are asked at this point whether they prefer the direct or the indirect method they usually choose the direct method because it looks less cumbersome. In practice almost all companies choose the indirect method because it can be prepared from the opening and closing statements of financial position and the income statement (profit and loss account). Some supporters also argue that it is useful to highlight the effect of working capital on cash flows.

The direct method needs more work to identify all the operating flows from the cash records. Bookkeeping records, as illustrated in the supplements to previous chapters in this book, are based on ledger accounts which include non-cash items. The sales ledger account, for example, combines cash sales and credit sales. All expense accounts combine expenses paid in cash and expenses obtained on credit. In practice the direct method creates additional work in analysing the accounting records, because there are many aspects to operating cash flow. Supporters of cash flow reporting advocate the direct method because it gives a clearer picture of cash flows. It also provides information on details of cash flows that is not available under the indirect method.

The standard-setters recognise that there are valid arguments for and against each method and so continue to permit both. The IASB 'encourages' entities to report cash flow from operating activities using the direct method,[6] but this encouragement appears to have been ineffective in many cases.

15.4 Preparing a statement of cash flows: the indirect method

Most companies prepare their statement of cash flows using the **indirect method**. This means they start with the reported operating profit and then make adjustments to work back to the cash amounts that are incorporated in profit and in working capital. This section explains the indirect method. A format for a statement of cash flows is presented in Table 15.5. Line numbers have been added at the left-hand side. Each line is explained in the section following Table 15.5.

Line 1 Cash flows from operating activities

This line indicates the start of the first major section of the statement of cash flows, showing how cash flows are generated from the operations of the business.

Line 2 Profit before taxation

The indirect method always starts with the operating profit *before* deducting interest and taxation, taken from the income statement (profit and loss account). This is because interest is seen as a separate payment to reward lenders and taxation is seen as a separate outflow of cash to government which needs to be emphasised. If the operating profit includes any investment income or interest received this must

Table 15.5
Format for statement of cash flows, indirect method

Line		£m	£m
1	**Cash flows from operating activities**		
2	Profit before taxation		xx
3	Adjustment for items not involving a flow of cash:		
4	Depreciation, amortisation, gain or loss on disposal of non-current assets etc.		<u>xx</u>
5	*Adjusted profit*		xx
6	(Increase)/decrease in inventories	xx	
7	(Increase)/decrease in trade receivables	xx	
8	(Increase)/decrease in prepayments	<u>xx</u>	
9	Increase/*(decrease)* in cash due to (increases)/decreases in current assets	<u>xx</u>	
10	Increase/(decrease) in trade payables	xx	
11	Increase/(decrease) in accruals	<u>xx</u>	
12	Increase/(decrease) in cash due to increases/(decreases) in liabilities	<u>xx</u>	
13	Increase/(decrease) in cash due to working capital changes		<u>xx</u>
14	Cash generated from operations		xx
15	Interest paid		(xx)
16	Taxes paid		<u>(xx)</u>
17	*Net cash inflow from operating activities*		xx
18	**Cash flows from investing activities**		
19	Purchase of non-current assets	xx	
20	Proceeds from sale of non-current assets	xx	
21	Interest received	xx	
22	Dividends received	<u>xx</u>	
23	*Net cash used in investing activities*		xx
24	**Cash flows from financing activities**		
25	Proceeds from issue of share capital	xx	
26	Proceeds from long-term borrowing	xx	
27	Dividends paid	<u>xx</u>	
28	*Net cash used in financing activities*		xx
29	Increase/(decrease) in cash and cash equivalents		xx
30	**Cash and cash equivalents at the start of the period**		xx
31	**Cash and cash equivalents at the end of the period**		xx

also be removed because it is reported in the separate section for investing activities (see lines 21 and 22). So the following checklist should be used to ensure the correct starting point:

	£m
Operating profit before taxes	xx
Is there any interest expense included in this figure? If so add it back to arrive at:	xx
Operating profit before deducting interest payable and taxes	xx
Is there any interest received/receivable or any dividends received in this figure? If so deduct it to arrive at:	(xx)
Operating profit before deducting interest payable and taxes and before including interest receivable and dividends received.	xx

Line 3 Adjustment for items not involving a flow of cash

The finance director now looks at the profit figure and asks, 'Are there any items in here that do not involve a flow of cash? If so we want to remove these so that we can get closer to cash.' Most income statements (profit and loss accounts) contain depreciation and amortisation, which have no effect on cash. Other items to look out for are changes in provisions, unrealised gains and losses on foreign currency translation.

Line 4 Adding back depreciation, amortisation, gain or loss on disposal etc

So the depreciation and amortisation are 'added back' to remove them from the profit figure. This usually causes some problems for readers of a statement of cash flows. If it worries you, just ask yourself – how did the depreciation get in there in the first place? The answer is that it was deducted as an expense, so if we add it back we exclude the expense. Other items that could come under this heading of 'not involving a flow of cash' are changes in provisions charged through income statement and gains or losses calculated on disposal of a non-current (fixed) asset. The following table summarises the action to be taken in the statement of cash flows:

Item in calculation	Reason
Add back any **expenses** that do not involve a flow of cash (e.g. depreciation, amortisation, loss on disposal of non-current assets).	These expenses reduced the profit but they do not involve any flow of cash and so must be excluded by adding back.
Deduct any **revenue** that does not involve a flow of cash (e.g. gain on disposal of non-current assets).	These revenues increased the profit but they do not involve any flow of cash and so must be excluded by deducting.

Line 5 Adjusted profit

In some presentations of the statement of cash flows this line is not shown separately, but it is a useful subtotal to remind yourself that you have now removed all non-cash items and you are ready to think about how working capital changes affect cash flow from operations.

Line 6 (Increase)/decrease in inventories (stocks)

When a business buys inventories of raw materials or produces work in progress and finished goods, it uses up cash. The cash is only recovered when the inventories are sold. While the inventories are increasing the cash invested in them is increasing and there is a negative impact on cash flow.

The following table summarises the action to be taken in the statement of cash flows:

Item in calculation	Reason
Deduct increase in inventories	Allowing inventories to increase takes up more cash in paying for them, or prevents cash being obtained through sale.
Add decrease in inventories	Allowing inventories to decrease reduces the cash needed to pay for them, or allows cash to be obtained through sale.

Line 7 (Increase)/decrease in trade receivables (debtors)

When a business sells goods and services on credit to customers, these customers are given some time to pay. They become debtors of the business until they pay cash. Selling goods and services on credit encourages customers to buy from the business but it delays the flow of cash to the business. The longer the period of credit taken by customers, the longer the delay. The danger of allowing the period of credit to increase is that the customer may become increasingly reluctant to pay. Chapter 13 explains how to estimate the average period of credit taken by credit customers.

The following table summarises the action to be taken in the statement of cash flows:

Item in calculation	Reason
Deduct increase in receivables	Allowing amounts of receivables to increase means that cash is not being collected from credit customers.
Add decrease in receivables	Allowing amounts of receivables to decrease means that cash is being collected faster from credit customers.

Line 8 (Increase)/decrease in prepayments

When a business makes payments for expenses in advance of enjoying the benefit of the payment, there is an outflow of cash. Examples are rent in advance or insurance premiums in advance (see Chapter 9 for the accounting treatment of prepayments). If the business is making more prepayments, there is a greater outflow of cash. If the business reduces its prepayments the cash flow position improves.

The following table summarises the action to be taken in the statement of cash flows:

Item in calculation	Reason
Deduct increase in prepayments	If prepayments increase then more cash is being used to make payments in advance.
Add decrease in prepayments	If prepayments decrease then less cash is being used to make payments in advance.

Line 9 Increase/(decrease) in cash due to (increases)/decreases in current assets

This line adds all the increases in current assets and deducts all the decreases in current assets. If the current assets have increased in total then the cash flow has decreased. If the current assets have decreased in total then the cash flow has increased. It is good practice to delete the alternative words here that do not apply to the particular circumstances of the company. Some published statements of cash flows leave all the words in the statement but this can be very confusing to readers.

Line 10 Increase/(decrease) in trade payables (creditors)

When a business buys goods or services on credit, the supplier often allows a period of credit. This helps the cash flow of the business in the gap between buying inputs and selling outputs of goods or services. The longer the period of credit taken from the supplier, the better the effect on cash flow. The danger of delaying payment beyond an agreed date is that the supplier may refuse to supply more goods or services and may even begin legal action for recovery of amounts owing. Chapter 13 explains how to calculate the average period of credit taken from suppliers.

The following table summarises the action to be taken in the statement of cash flows:

Item in calculation	Reason
Deduct decrease in payables	Allowing amounts of payables to decrease means that more cash is being paid to suppliers and other creditors.
Add increase in payables	Allowing amounts of payables to increase means that less cash is being paid to suppliers and other creditors.

Line 11 Increase/(decrease) in accruals

Accruals is the general description for unpaid expenses. If a business delays paying expenses there is a benefit for cash flow. If the accruals increase then there is a greater benefit for cash flow. The danger of delaying payment beyond an agreed date is that the supplier may refuse to supply more goods or services and may even begin legal action for recovery of amounts owing.

The following table summarises the action to be taken in the statement of cash flows:

Item in calculation	Reason
Deduct decrease in accruals	Allowing amounts of unpaid expenses (accruals) to decrease means that more cash is being paid to settle these obligations.
Add increase in accruals	Allowing amounts of unpaid expenses (accruals) to increase means that less cash is being paid to settle these obligations.

Line 12 Increase/(decrease) in cash due to increases/(decreases) in liabilities

This line adds all the increases in current liabilities and deducts all the decreases in current liabilities. If the current liabilities have increased in total then the cash flow has benefited – less cash has been paid to settle current liabilities. If the current liabilities have decreased in total then the cash flow has suffered – more cash has been paid to settle liabilities. It is good practice to delete the alternative words here that do not apply to the particular circumstances of the company. Some published statements of cash flows leave all the words in the statement but this can be very confusing to readers.

Line 13 Increase/(decrease) in cash due to working capital changes

This line shows the result of comparing the change in current assets with the change in current liabilities. There are several combinations of increases and decreases in current assets and liabilities so the easiest way to think about the outcome is to ask 'what has happened to working capital (current assets less current liabilities) overall?'

If the working capital has *increased*, then cash flow has *decreased*.
If the working capital has *decreased*, then cash flow has *increased*.

Line 14 Cash generated from operations

This is a subtotal combining the cash flow effect of the adjusted profit and the cash flow effect of the changes in working capital.

Line 15 Interest paid

Interest must be paid on loans. If it is not paid on time the lender will take action to demand payment of the interest and might even demand immediate repayment of the loan in full, depending on the conditions of the loan agreement. The interest expense in the income statement represents the interest cost of the accounting period but if the payment dates fall outside the accounting period there may be an accrual of unpaid interest in the statement of financial position. A calculation is required to arrive at the amount of cash paid during the accounting period.

Item in calculation	Reason
Interest expense in income statement	We are starting with the expense in the income statement, to adjust it to a cash figure.
minus liability at end of period	This is the part of the expense that has not yet been paid in cash.
plus liability at start of period	During this period the liability at the start of the period has been paid.
equals cash paid to lenders	

Line 16 Taxes paid

There is a corporation tax expense in the income statement (profit and loss account). The due dates for payment depend on the size of the company, as explained in Chapter 10. Any unpaid taxation at the start or end of the period will appear as a liability in the statement of financial position. A calculation is required to arrive at the amount of tax paid in the accounting period.

Item in calculation	Reason
Taxation expense in income statement	We are starting with the expense in the income statement, to adjust it to a cash figure.
minus liability at end of period	This is the part of the expense that has not yet been paid in cash.
plus liability at start of period	During this period the liability at the start of the period has been paid.
equals cash paid to tax authorities	

Line 17 Net cash inflow from operating activities

This is a subtotal that indicates the end of the first major section of the statement of cash flows.

Line 18 Cash flows from investing activities

This line starts the second major section of the statement of cash flows showing how cash has been used for making new investment in non-current assets and also released from sales of existing investment in non-current assets.

Line 19 Purchase of non-current assets

In many cases the amount spent on non-current assets will be known from the accounting records. However, if you are preparing a statement of cash flows using only the statement of financial position and income statement plus some notes, you may find that you need to calculate the amount spent on non-current assets. The following table summarises the calculation of changes in non-current assets which includes the cash payment. It assumes that all assets of one type are recorded together as one category (e.g. vehicles, plant and machinery).

Item in calculation	Reason
Original cost of non-current assets in a specified category at start of period	Begin with the amount of the assets at the start of the period.
plus cash paid for additions	**Cash is spent during the period on additions to the assets.**
minus disposals at original cost	Assets are removed – see later calculation of gain or loss on disposal.
equals Non-current assets at end of period	The result is the amount of the assets at the end of the period.

Line 20 Proceeds from sale of non-current assets

This line reports the cash received from sale or disposal of non-current assets. It is important to use the cash received from the disposal of the asset and not the gain or loss on disposal recorded in the income statement (profit and loss account). Look back to Chapter 8 and you will see that the gain or loss on disposal arises only when the cash received is different from the book value. If the depreciation had been calculated with perfect foresight then the net book value would be equal to the cash received and there would be no gain or loss. A gain or loss on disposal is the result of estimating depreciation at the start of the asset's life when the proceeds on disposal have to be estimated.

The following table summarises the calculation relating to the sale or disposal of non-current assets which includes the cash received.

Item in calculation	Comment
Original cost of non-current asset at start of period	This item of information is shown as 'disposal' in the 'cost' section of the schedule of non-current assets.
minus accumulated depreciation of non-current asset at start of period	This item of information is shown as 'disposal' in the 'accumulated depreciation' section of the schedule of non-current assets.
minus **cash received on disposal**	**This is the amount of cash received for the asset sold.**
equals gain or loss on disposal	The gain or loss on disposal is reported in the income statement.

Line 21 Interest received

Interest received is a reward for investment and so it is regarded as part of the cash flows relating to investing activities. Look back to the calculations in the workings for line 2 and you will see the item:

> Is there any interest received/receivable or any dividends received in this figure? If so deduct it.

The interest receivable is removed in calculating operating profit at line 2 so that interest received can be inserted at line 21. The following table summarises the action to be taken in the statement of cash flows:

Item in calculation	Reason
Interest receivable in the income statement	We are starting with the revenue reported in the income statement, to adjust it to a cash figure.
minus asset at end of period	This is the part of the revenue that has not yet been received in cash.
plus asset at start of period	During this period the asset at the start of the period has been received.
equals interest received in cash	

Line 22 Dividends received

The dividends received relate to equity investments held by the company. The calculation is very similar to that for interest received.

Item in calculation	Reason
Dividend receivable in the income statement	We are starting with the revenue reported in the income statement, to adjust it to a cash figure.
minus asset at end of period	This is the part of the revenue that has not yet been received in cash.
plus asset at start of period	During this period the asset at the start of the period has been received.
equals dividend received in cash	

Line 23 Net cash used in investing activities

This subtotal indicates the end of the second major section of the statement of cash flows. It will usually be a negative figure showing that the business is expanding through more investment in non-current assets. Less commonly, a business may be selling off existing investments to raise cash for future plans. Having the separate subtotal draws attention to the magnitude and direction of investing activities.

Line 24 Cash flows from financing activities

This line starts the third and final major section of the statement of cash flows showing how cash has been raised from financing activities. This usually means issuing new share capital and raising or repaying long-term loans.

Line 25 Proceeds from issue of share capital

Chapter 12 explains the process of issuing share capital, both when the business starts and when it looks for more finance some time later. In many cases the shares are issued at market price, which is higher than nominal value. The difference is called a share premium. The total cash raised is measured in terms of the market price but company law requires separate reporting of the change in nominal value and the changes in the share premium. The calculation required is as follows:

Item in calculation	Reason
Increase in nominal value of share capital *Increase* in share *plus* premium reserve *equals* cash received from issue of shares	The amount of cash raised by issuing shares at market price is the nominal value plus the share premium.

Line 26 Proceeds from long-term borrowings

The proceeds from long-term borrowings can be seen from the change in the statement of financial position figures for long-term borrowings, after allowing for any long-term borrowings that have changed category to short term in the accounting period.

Item in calculation	Reason
Long-term borrowing in balance sheet at the start of the period	We are starting with amount reported in the balance sheet at the start of the accounting period.
minus long-term reclassified as short-term during the period	This is the part of loan that is reclassified but remains in the balance sheet.
plus new loans taken up in cash	Cash received.
minus loans repaid	Cash paid out.
equals long-term borrowing in balance sheet sheet at the end of the period	The amount reported in the balance at the end of the accounting period.

Line 27 Dividends paid

The dividend paid during the period may be a combination of the dividend paid in respect of the previous year's profit plus an interim dividend for the current year.

Chapter 12 explains in more detail the accounting procedures for reporting dividends. The amount of dividend paid will appear in the statement of changes in equity.

Line 28 Net cash used in financing activities

This subtotal indicates the end of the third section of the statement of cash flows.

Line 29 Increase/(decrease) in cash and cash equivalents

This line is the arithmetic total of the three separate sections as reported in lines 17 + 23 + 28.

Lines 30 and 31 Cash and cash equivalents at the start and end of the period

This is the moment of truth where you find out whether you have made errors on the way through the statement of cash flows. Lines 30 and 31 are taken from the statement of financial position. If your statement of cash flows is correct then line 29 plus line 30 will equal line 31. The following table is used to record the information extracted from the statement of financial position.

	Start of period	End of period
Cash on hand and balances with banks	xx	xx
Short-term investments	xx	xx
Cash and cash equivalents	xx	xx

15.5 Preparing a statement of cash flows: the direct method

Line 1 Cash flows from operating activities

This line indicates the start of the first major section of the statement of cash flows, showing how cash flows are generated from the operations of the business.

Line 2 Cash receipts from customers

This line reports the total cash received from customers in the period. Some customers may have paid immediate cash for goods and services. Others may have taken credit and paid later.

Line 3 Cash paid to suppliers

This line reports the total cash paid to suppliers in the period. The business may have paid immediate cash for some goods and services. In other cases the suppliers may have allowed a period of credit to be paid later.

Line 4 Cash paid to employees

This line reports the total cash paid to employees in the period. Usually the employees are paid promptly each week or each month and so the cash payments are closely related to the wages expense.

Lines 14 to 31 have the same meaning as described for these lines in Section 15.4.

The alternative *direct method* is shown in Table 15.6 and explained as follows.

Table 15.6
Format for statement of cash flows, direct method

Line		£m	£m
1	**Cash flows from operating activities**		
2	Cash receipts from customers		xx
3	Cash paid to suppliers		xx
4	Cash paid to employees		xx
5–13	*(Lines not used)*		
14	Cash generated from operations		xx
15	Interest paid		(xx)
16	Taxes paid		(xx)
17	*Net cash inflow from operating activities*		xx
18	**Cash flows from investing activities**		
19	Purchase of non-current assets	xx	
20	Proceeds from sale of non-current assets	xx	
21	Interest received	xx	
22	Dividends received	xx	
23	*Net cash used in investing activities*		xx
24	**Cash flows from financing activities**		
25	Proceeds from issue of share capital	xx	
26	Proceeds from long-term borrowing	xx	
27	Dividends paid	xx	
28	*Net cash used in financing activities*		xx
29	Increase/(decrease) in cash and cash equivalents		xx
30	**Cash and cash equivalents at the start of the period**		xx
31	**Cash and cash equivalents at the end of the period**		xx

15.6 Interpretation of cash flow information

The cash flow information is useful in itself in showing trends in the company's cash resources. Some businesses operate on cycles lasting several years where the cash position moves from negative to positive. The industry position is often a useful starting point for understanding company cash flows. If the industry is cyclical and all companies in the sector have negative cash flow then we might expect any company in the sector to show the same trends. Equally, any company in the sector should be showing signs of improvement as the cycle moves upwards.

For the indirect method, which reports the cash flow effects of working capital, it may be useful to link the increases or decreases in working capital items to the number of days in the working capital cycle. The calculation of the working capital cycle appears in Chapter 13. For example, if there is an increase in cash invested in inventory there are two possible causes: one is a lengthening of the inventory holding period and the other is an increase in sales volume causing more inventory to be held. The inventory holding period helps to narrow down the possible cause. If the trade receivables increase there are two possible causes. One is that customers are taking longer to pay and the other is that credit sales are increasing. The period of credit given to customers helps to narrow down the cause here.

The amount of cash invested in capital expenditure is an important sign of the continuing development of the business. Ratios are used by analysts in comparing capital expenditure to depreciation and comparing capital expenditure to the existing asset base.

15.7 Illustration

The following information is used to illustrate the indirect method and then compare the direct method of preparing and presenting a statement of cash flows.

Income statement Year 2

	£m
Revenue	246
Cost of sales	(110)
Gross profit	136
Investment income – interest received	4
Gain on disposal of equipment	5
Depreciation	(30)
Administrative and selling expenses	(10)
Operating profit before interest	105
Interest expense	(15)
Profit after deducting interest	90
Taxation	(30)
Profit after tax	60

Statements of financial position (balance sheets) at 31 December

	Year 2 £m	Year 1 £m
Non-current assets		
Property, plant and equipment at cost	150	100
Accumulated depreciation	(60)	(40)
	90	60
Investments	100	100
Total non-current assets	190	160
Current assets		
Inventory (stock)	20	15
Trade receivables (debtors)	18	16
Cash and cash equivalents	32	5
Total current assets	70	36
Total assets	260	196
Current liabilities		
Trade payables (creditors)	(14)	(13)
Interest payable	(6)	(7)
Taxes payable	(8)	(7)
Total current liabilities	(28)	(27)
Non-current liabilities		
Long-term loans	(20)	(15)
Total liabilities	(48)	(42)
Net assets	212	154
Capital and reserves		
Share capital	140	130
Share premium	20	18
Retained earnings	52	6
	212	154

Further information

1 The dividend paid during Year 2 was £14m. The retained earnings increased by £60m profit of the period and decreased by the amount of the dividend £14m.
2 During Year 2 the company acquired property, plant and equipment costing £80m.
3 During Year 2 the company sold property, plant and equipment that had an original cost of £30m and accumulated depreciation of £10m. The proceeds of sale were £25m.

15.7.1 Indirect method

A statement of cash flows using the indirect method is presented in Table 15.7.

Table 15.7
Statement of cash flows using the indirect method

Notes		£m	£m
	Cash flows from operating activities		
1	Profit before taxation		101
	Adjustment for items not involving a flow of cash:		
2	Depreciation	30	
3	Gain on disposal of equipment	(5)	
			25
	Adjusted profit		126
4	(Increase) in inventories	(5)	
5	(Increase) in trade receivables	(2)	
6	Increase in trade payables	1	
	Increase/(decrease) in cash due to working capital changes		(6)
	Cash generated from operations		120
7	Interest paid		(16)
8	Taxes paid		(29)
	Net cash inflow from operating activities		75
	Cash flows from investing activities		
9	Purchase of non-current assets	(80)	
10	Proceeds from sale of non-current assets	25	
11	Interest received	4	
	Net cash used in investing activities		(51)
	Cash flows from financing activities		
12	Proceeds from issue of share capital	12	
13	Proceeds from long-term borrowing	5	
14	Dividends paid	(14)	
	Net cash used in financing activities		3
	Increase/(decrease) in cash and cash equivalents		27
15	**Cash and cash equivalents at the start of the period**		5
15	**Cash and cash equivalents at the end of the period**		32

Working note 1

	£m
Operating profit before taxes	90
Is there any interest expense included in this figure? If so add it back to arrive at:	15
Operating profit before deducting interest payable and taxes	105
Is there any interest received/receivable or any dividends received in this figure? If so deduct it to arrive at:	(4)
Operating profit before deducting interest payable and taxes and before including interest receivable and dividends received.	101

Working note 2

The depreciation is seen in the income statement (profit and loss account). It is added back to exclude the effect of a non-cash item.

Working note 3

The gain on disposal is seen in the income statement (profit and loss account). It is added back to exclude the effect of a non-cash item.

Working note 4

There is an increase in inventory seen by comparing the statements of financial position at the end of Year 1 and Year 2. This decreases the cash flow.

Working note 5

There is an increase in trade receivables (debtors) seen by comparing the statements of financial position at the end of Year 1 and Year 2. This decreases the cash flow.

Working note 6

There is an increase in trade payables (creditors) seen by comparing the statements of financial position at the end of Year 1 and Year 2. This has a positive effect on the cash flow by increasing the amount unpaid.

Working note 7

Interest paid is calculated from the income statement expense £15m plus the unpaid interest at the start of the year £7m minus the unpaid interest at the end of the year, £6m.

Working note 8

Taxes paid are calculated from the income statement charge £30m plus the unpaid liability at the start of the year £7m minus the unpaid liability at the end of the year £8m.

Working note 9

The purchase cost of non-current assets is given in the further information. It can be checked by taking the cost at the start of the year £100m, adding £80m and deducting the £30m cost of the disposal to leave £150m as shown in the statement of financial position at the end of the year.

Working note 10

The proceeds of sale £25m are given in the further information. This can be checked by taking the net book value of the asset sold (£30m − £10m = £20m) and adding the gain on disposal, the £5m shown in the income statement.

Working note 11

The interest received is taken from the income statement. There is no interest receivable shown in the statement of financial position so the income statement figure must be the same as the cash figure.

Working note 12

The proceeds from the share issue are the total of the increase in share capital £10m plus the increase in share premium £2m.

Working note 13

The proceeds from long-term borrowings are the increase in long-term loans calculated by comparing the opening and closing statements of financial position.

Working note 14

The dividend paid is given in the further information. It can be checked by taking the retained earnings at the start of the period, £6m, add the profit of the period, £60m, and deduct dividend £14m to arrive at the retained earnings at the end of the period, £52m.

Working note 15

The cash and cash equivalents at the start and end of the period are taken from the statement of financial position.

15.7.2 Direct method

A statement of cash flows presented by the direct method is presented in Table 15.8.

Table 15.8
Statement of cash flows using the direct method

Notes		£m	£m
	Cash flows from operating activities		
1	Cash receipts from customers		244
2	Cash paid to suppliers and employees		(114)
3	Cash paid for administrative and selling expenses		(10)
	Cash generated from operations		120
4	Interest paid		(16)
5	Taxes paid		(29)
	Net cash inflow from operating activities		75
	Cash flows from investing activities		
6	Purchase of non-current assets	(80)	
7	Proceeds from sale of non-current assets	25	
8	Interest received	4	
	Net cash used in investing activities		(51)
	Cash flows from financing activities		
9	Proceeds from issue of share capital	12	
10	Proceeds from long-term borrowing	5	
11	Dividends paid	(14)	
	Net cash used in financing activities		3
	Increase/(decrease) in cash and cash equivalents		27
12	**Cash and cash equivalents at the start of the period**		5
12	**Cash and cash equivalents at the end of the period**		32

In practice the cash receipts from customers and cash payments to suppliers and employees are taken from the records of cash received and paid, which requires analysis of the cash records. In this relatively straightforward situation the figures may be confirmed from the information in the statement of financial position and income statement.

Working note 1

The cash receipts from customers may be confirmed from revenue £246m, plus receivables at the start of the period £16m, minus receivables at the end of the period £18m, equals £244m.

Working note 2

There are two stages to the confirmation of cash paid to suppliers. First the purchases are calculated from cost of sales £110m plus inventory at the end £20m minus inventory at the start £15m = £115m. Next the payment to suppliers is confirmed from purchases: £115m plus liability at the start £13m minus liability at the end £14m = £114m. It is assumed that the wages are all paid when the work is done so there is no accrual.

Working note 3

The administrative and selling expenses are seen in the income statement. There is no accrual indicated in the statement of financial position and so the cash figure equals the expense figure.

Working notes 4 to 12

See working notes 7 to 15 for the indirect method.

15.7.3   Comment on statement of cash flows

The cash flow from operating activities amounted to £75m. The purchase of non-current (fixed) assets cost £80m but this was offset by £25m proceeds of sale of non-current assets no longer required and was also helped by the £4m interest received from investments. The net outflow from investments was £51m. This left £24m of cash flow available to increase cash resources but £14m was required for dividend payments. The remaining £10m was added to the proceeds of a share issue, £12m and an increase in long-term loans, £5m, giving an overall cash inflow of £27m.

15.8   Summary

- The statement of cash flows provides information about changes in financial position that adds to the understanding of the business obtainable from the statement of financial position and income statement (profit and loss account).
- It explains changes in cash and cash equivalents arising from operating activities, investing activities and financing activities.
- **Cash** comprises cash on hand and demand deposits.
- **Cash equivalents** are short-term, highly liquid investments that are readily convertible to known amounts of cash and which are subject to an insignificant risk of changes in value.
- The **indirect method** and the **direct method** are alternative approaches to calculating the cash flow arising from operating activities.
- The **indirect method** starts with the profit from operations, eliminates non-cash expenses such as depreciation, and adds on or deducts the effects of changes in working capital to arrive at the cash flow arising from operating activities.
- The **direct method** takes each item of operating cash flow separately from the cash records to arrive at the cash flow arising from operating activities.
- The cash flow is useful in analysis when combined with ratio analysis that shows relationships of liquidity, working capital management, rates of investment in non-current assets and financial gearing.

Further reading

The following standard is too detailed for a first-level course, but the definitions section may be helpful and the Appendices give illustrations of statements of cash flows.

IASB (2012), IAS 7, *Statement of Cash Flows*, International Accounting Standards Board.

QUESTIONS

The Questions section of each chapter has three types of question. 'Test your understanding' questions to help you review your reading are in the 'A' series of questions. You will find the answers to these by reading and thinking about the material in the book. 'Application' questions to test your ability to apply technical skills are in the 'B' series of questions. Questions requiring you to show skills in problem solving and evaluation are in the 'C' series of questions. A letter [S] indicates that there is a solution at the end of the book. Other solutions are provided in the Instructor's Manual, where there are further questions parallel to those set out here.

A   Test your understanding

A15.1   What is the definition of 'cash'? (Section 15.2)

A15.2   What is the definition of 'cash equivalent'? (Section 15.2)

A15.3   What is meant by the 'direct method' of calculating operating cash flow? (Section 15.3.1)

A15.4   What is meant by the 'indirect method' of calculating operating cash flow? (Section 15.3.2)

A15.5   Why is depreciation 'added back' to operating profit in the indirect method of calculating operating cash flow? (Section 15.3.2)

A15.6   What is the effect on cash flow of an increase in inventory levels? (Section 15.3.2)

A15.7   What is the effect on cash flow of an increase in trade receivables (debtors)? (Section 15.3.2)

A15.8   What is the effect on cash flow of an increase in trade payables (creditors)? (Section 15.3.2)

A15.9   What are the relative benefits of the direct method compared to the indirect method? (Section 15.3.3)

A15.10 What are the three main sections of a statement of cash flows? (Section 15.4)

A15.11 What kinds of items in an income statement do not involve a flow of cash? (Section 15.4)

A15.12 What happens to cash flow when working capital increases? (Section 15.4)

A15.13 How is taxation paid calculated from the taxation payable and the taxation liability at the start and end of the period? (Section 15.4)

A15.14 How is the cash paid for additions to fixed assets if we know the opening and closing balances and there are no disposals? (Section 15.4)

A15.15 Explain how the proceeds of sale of a non-current asset differ from the net book value. (Section 15.4)

A15.16 Explain how the cash proceeds of a share issue are calculated from knowledge of the share capital and the share premium reserve. (Section 15.4)

A15.17 Explain how cash received from customers is calculated if we know the sales of the period and the receivables (debtors) at the start and end of the period. (Section 15.5)

A15.18 Explain how the purchases of goods or materials is calculated if we know the cost of goods sold and the inventory (stock) at the start and end of the period. (Section 15.5)

A15.19 Explain how the cash paid to suppliers is calculated if we know the purchases and the payables (creditors) at the start and end of the period. (Section 15.5)

B   Application

B15.1 [S]
Sales on credit during Year 2 amount to £120m. The trade receivables (debtors) at the start of Year 2 were £8. The trade receivables (debtors) at the end of Year 2 were £10. What is the amount of cash received from customers during Year 2?

B15.2 [S]
Purchases on credit during Year 3 amount to £20m. The trade payables (creditors) at the start of Year 3 were £6m. The trade payables (creditors) at the end of Year 3 were £4m. What is the amount of cash paid to suppliers during Year 3?

B15.3 [S]

The equipment at cost account at the start of Year 2 records a total of £34m. The equipment at cost account at the end of Year 2 records a total of £37m. An asset of original cost £5m was sold during the period. What was the amount spent on acquisition of equipment?

B15.4

A vehicle costing £20m and having accumulated depreciation of £12m was sold for £5m. How will this information be reported in the statement of cash flows?

B15.5

The share capital account increased by £40m during Year 4. The share premium reserve increased by £20m. What amount of cash was raised by the issue of shares?

B15.6

The corporation tax charge in the income statement (profit and loss account) for Year 2 was £30m. The tax liability in the statement of financial position at the start of Year 2 was £6m. The tax liability in the statement of financial position at the end of Year 2 was £10m. What was the amount of cash paid in taxation during Year 2?

B15.7

D Ltd has an operating profit of £12m, which includes a depreciation charge of £1m. During the year the trading stock has increased by £4m, trade debtors have increased by £3m and trade creditors have increased by £5m. Prepare a statement of cash flow from operations.

B15.8

E Ltd has an operating profit of £16m, which includes a depreciation charge of £2m. During the year the trading stock has increased by £1m, trade debtors have decreased by £3m and trade creditors have decreased by £2m. Prepare a statement of cash flow from operations.

C   Problem solving and evaluation

C15.1 [S]

The directors of Fruit Sales plc produced the following income statement (profit and loss account) for Year 2 and balance sheet at the end of Year 2.

Income statement for Year 2

	£m
Revenue	320
Cost of sales	(143)
Gross profit	177
Investment income – interest received	5
Gain on disposal of equipment	7
Depreciation	(39)
Administrative and selling expenses	(13)
Operating profit before interest	137
Interest expense	(20)
Profit after deducting interest	117
Taxation	(35)
Profit after tax	82

Statements of financial position (balance sheets) at 31 December

	Year 2 £m	Year 1 £m
Non-current assets		
Vehicles at cost	195	130
Accumulated depreciation	(79)	(52)
	116	78
Investments	100	80
Total non-current assets	216	158
Current assets		
Inventory (stock)	26	20
Trade receivables (debtors)	23	21
Cash and cash equivalents	43	6
Total current assets	92	47
Total assets	308	205
Current liabilities		
Trade payables (creditors)	(18)	(13)
Interest payable	(8)	(7)
Taxes payable	(10)	(7)
Total current liabilities	(36)	(27)
Non-current liabilities		
Long-term loans	(26)	(18)
Total liabilities	(62)	(45)
Net assets	246	160
Capital and reserves		
Share capital	152	120
Share premium	26	23
Retained earnings	68	17
	246	160

Further information

1 The dividend paid during Year 2 was £31m. The retained earnings increased by £82m profit of the period and decreased by the amount of the dividend £31m.
2 During Year 2 the company acquired vehicles costing £90m.
3 During Year 2 the company sold vehicles that had an original cost of £25m and accumulated depreciation of £12m. The proceeds of sale were £20m.
4 Cost of sales consists entirely of purchases of fruit on credit from suppliers. Wages are included in administrative and selling expenses and are paid when incurred.

Required

1 Prepare a statement of cash flows using (a) the direct method and (b) the indirect method of calculating operating cash flow.
2 Write a comment on the cash flow of the period.

C15.2
Consider the following:

	£m
Revenue	320
Cost of sales	(143)
Gross profit	177
Investment income – interest received	5
Loss on disposal of equipment	(8)
Depreciation	(39)
Administrative and selling expenses	(13)
Operating profit before interest	122
Interest expense	(6)
Profit after deducting interest	116
Taxation	(39)
Profit after tax	77

Statements of financial position (balance sheets) at 31 December

	Year 2	Year 1
	£m	£m
Property, plant and equipment at cost	225	150
Accumulated depreciation	(90)	(60)
	135	90
Investment	70	100
Total non-current assets	205	190
Inventory (stock)	30	22
Trade receivables (debtors)	27	24
Cash and cash equivalents	48	8
Total current assets	105	54
Total assets	310	244
Trade payables (creditors)	(21)	(20)
Interest payable	(9)	(11)
Taxes payable	(12)	(9)
Total current liabilities	(42)	(40)
Long-term loans	(20)	(15)
Total liabilities	(62)	(55)
Net assets	248	189
Share capital	144	140
Share premium	26	23
Retained earnings	78	26
	248	189

Further information

1 The dividend paid during Year 2 was £25m. The retained earnings increased by £77m profit of the period and decreased by the amount of the dividend, £25m.
2 During Year 2 the company acquired property, plant and equipment costing £94m.
3 During Year 2 the company sold for scrap property, plant and equipment that had an original cost of £19m and accumulated depreciation of £9m. The proceeds of disposal were £2m.
4 Investments were sold during the year for cash proceeds of £30m. There were no purchases of investments.

Required

1 Prepare a statement of cash flows using (a) the direct method and (b) the indirect method of calculating operating cash flow.
2 Write a comment on the cash flow of the period.

Notes and references

1. Statements of cash flows in published financial statements are often prepared for a group as a whole. The details of group statements of cash flows are too complex for a first-level text, but in general appearance they are similar to those for individual companies.
2. IASB (2016), IAS 7 *Statement of Cash Flows.*
3. IAS 7 para. 6.
4. IAS 7 para. 7.
5. IAS 7 para. 8.
6. IAS 7 para. 19.

MANAGEMENT ACCOUNTING

Part 5

Setting the scene and defining the basic tools of management accounting

Functions of management accounting

This case study shows a typical case in which management accounting can be helpful. Read the case study now but only attempt the discussion points after you have finished reading the chapter.

Chartered Institute of Management Accountants (CIMA)

This case study describes the role of management accountant, in extracts taken from the website of the CIMA, which is the world's largest professional body of management accountants.

Shutterstock.com/Konstantin Chagin

What is management accounting?

Management accounting combines accounting, finance and management with the leading edge techniques needed to drive successful businesses.

Chartered management accountants:

- Advise managers about the financial implications of projects.
- Explain the financial consequences of business decisions.
- Formulate business strategy.
- Monitor spending and financial control.
- Conduct internal business audits.
- Explain the impact of the competitive landscape.
- Bring a high level of professionalism and integrity to business.

The management accounting skillset

Our members are qualified to work across an organisation, not just in finance. In addition to strong accounting fundamentals, CIMA teaches strategic business and management skills:

- Analysis – they analyse information using it to make business decisions.
- Strategy – they formulate business strategy to create wealth and shareholder value.
- Risk – they identify and manage risk.
- Planning – they apply accounting techniques to plan and budget.
- Communication – they determine what information management needs and explain the numbers to non-financial managers.

Ethical code

CIMA members and students are required to comply with the CIMA code of ethics and to adopt the fundamental principles to their working lives. CIMA members are at the heart of business as its conscience, adding judgment, independence and objectivity to their professional qualification.

Source: CIMA Global website, October 2014. http://www.cimaglobal.com/About-us/What-is-management-accounting/

Discussion points

1 Imagine you are working as a management accountant in a company that is planning a project to build a suspension bridge across a river mouth. What kind of work might you contribute to the project?

2 Imagine you are working as a management accountant in a company which is not making sufficient profits because its working methods are outdated and the labour force needs retraining. How might you contribute to improving the profitability of the company?

Contents

<table>
<tr><td>

Learning outcomes

</td><td>

After studying this chapter you should be able to:

● Explain how the definition of 'accounting' represents the subject of management accounting.

● Explain the needs of internal users of accounting information.

● Describe the management functions of planning, decision making and control and show how these are related within a business activity.

● Describe the roles of management accounting in directing attention, keeping the score and solving problems.

● Analyse simple cases where management accounting may contribute to making judgements and decisions.

● Understand that the terminology of management accounting is less well defined than that of financial accounting, so that you will need to be flexible in interpreting the use of words.

</td></tr>
</table>

16.1 Introduction

In Financial accounting, section 1.1, we defined accounting:

Definition   **Accounting** is the process of identifying, measuring and communicating financial information about an entity to permit informed judgements and decisions by users of the information.[1]

The process of identifying, measuring and communicating financial information has been explained and illustrated in Parts 1 to 5, Financial accounting, by reference to communicating with users external to the entity. However, many would argue that the foremost users of accounting information about an organisation must be those who manage it on a day-to-day basis. This group is referred to in broad terms as **management**, which is a collective term for all those persons who have responsibilities for making judgements and decisions within an organisation. Because they have close involvement with the business, they have access to a wide range of information (much of which may be confidential within the organisation) and will seek those aspects of the information which are most relevant to their particular judgements and decisions. Because this group of users is so broad, and because of the vast amount of information potentially available, a specialist branch of accounting has developed, called **management accounting**, to serve the particular needs of management.

Activity 16.1   *Imagine that you are in charge of a cycle hire business in a holiday resort. You have 50 cycles available for hire. Some customers hire cycles for one day; others take them for up to one week. Write down any three decisions that you might make as a manager, where accounting information would be helpful in making the decision.*

16.1.1 Applying the definition

Consider the following three scenarios which are typical of comments in the 'management' section of the financial press. As you read each scenario, think about how it relates to the definition of 'accounting' given at the start of this section. Then read the comment following the scenario and compare it with your thinking.

Scenario 16.1

'In the 12 months to June 30, net profits dropped from £280m to £42m, depressed by hefty investments, increased paper costs and poor advertising spending . . . The chief executive has explained the company's plans for improving its margins to the average level for the industry. The directors are also committed to getting the assets to work creatively together.' (*Report on a magazine publishing company*)

Scenario 16.1 indicates decision making related to **profit margins** and the effective use of assets. The profit margins will be improved either by improving **sales**, or by controlling **costs**, or through a mixture of both. **Assets** will be used more effectively if they create more profit or higher sales. Achieving these targets requires a range of managerial skills covering sales, production and asset management. Identifying the relevant **costs** and **revenues**, measuring the achievement of targets and communicating the outcomes within the organisation are all functions of management accounting. The chief executive will need to form a judgement on whether the decisions taken are likely to satisfy investors and maintain their confidence in the management team.

Scenario 16.2

Salespersons at a car manufacturer's dealership noticed business was slow in April. They reacted by encouraging customers to take more time in deciding whether to buy a car. What was the reason? They were paid a monthly bonus where sales exceeded a specified target. They could see that the April sales would not reach the target and so encouraged customers to wait until May, to increase the likely volume of May sales. In a brewing company the sales manager set a low sales target, in the hope of exceeding it easily. This caused the company to reduce production, so that when demand for beer rose to a higher level because of good weather, the company could not provide adequate supplies. (*Journalist's comment on how unrealistic targets can distort achievement of company objectives.*)

Scenario 16.2 shows that at some point in the past a decision was taken to create employee incentives by setting quantifiable targets. Unfortunately this has led to a narrow focus on measuring the achievement of the targets. There was a problem in allowing the employees too much freedom to influence either the setting of the target or the achievement of the target, and no judgement about the best interests of the company. A further decision is now required to balance the motivation of the employees against the best interests of the company. Communication is an important feature of getting the decision right.

Scenario 16.3

'Engineers are challenging the assumption that companies are run by number-crunchers . . . The hidden skill of engineers is their ability to be analytical and numerate. As someone who has to evaluate and sit on the boards of information technology and software development companies, I have the ability to understand the basics of their business.' (*Managing director of a venture capital company, qualified engineer.*)

The term 'number-cruncher' tends to be used as a somewhat uncomplimentary description of an accounting specialist. The engineer quoted in Scenario 16.3 has related to the measurement aspect of accounting and has identified the need to make judgements ('evaluate') using analytical skills. However, this quotation has made no mention either of communication or of decision making. There is an increasing expectation that the management accountants in an organisation will work with the engineers or other technical specialists, that they will try to understand the nature of the business and will ensure that the judgements are communicated to the experts so that cost-effective decisions can be made.

16.1.2 Matching the approach to the judgements or decisions

Management accounting methods have developed in a variety of ways depending on the judgements or decisions required. This is sometimes described in terms of a **contingency theory** of management accounting. The management accounting approach is conditioned by (is contingent upon) the situation. Management accounting methods have been developed within particular industries. In the UK economy approximately 75% of output is provided by service industry with only 25% of output being provided by manufacturing industry. However, management accounting began to develop in the twentieth century at a time when manufacturing industry dominated. As the service sector has grown, management accounting has developed to meet its particular needs. What remains of the manufacturing sector has moved from being labour intensive to being capital intensive. In some parts of the world, manufacturing remains labour intensive. The agricultural sector may be stronger. All these differences lead to different judgements and decisions, and hence different approaches to identifying, measuring and communicating accounting data. The following chapters will explain management accounting techniques that have been developed to meet particular needs in making judgements and decisions.

16.1.3 Strategic management accounting

The traditional approach to management accounting has been to regard internal decision makers as inward looking. This has led to developing techniques for identifying, measuring and communicating costs where only internal comparisons have been thought relevant. Those techniques remain useful in some cases and are sufficiently widely used to justify studying them in an introductory course. However, the later years of the twentieth century brought an increasing awareness that company managers must be outward looking. They must form a strategy for their business that has regard to what competitors are achieving. This requires management accounting to identify, measure and communicate data on the company relative to data for other similar companies. Managers must consider competitive forces such as the threat of new entrants, substitute products or services, rivalry within the industry and the relative bargaining strength of suppliers and customers. Managers must also consider how their organisation adds value in creating its product. There is a flow of business activity from research and development through production, marketing, distribution and after-sales support. This chain of activities creates costs which must be compared with the value added by the organisation. The term **strategic management accounting** applies to the identification, measurement and communication of cost data in all these situations where the organisation is being judged against the performance of competitors.

16.2 Meeting the needs of internal users

Although the definition of accounting remains appropriate for internal reporting purposes, its application will be different because internal users need to form judgements and make decisions that are different from those of external users. External users form judgements on the overall performance of the entity and make decisions about their relationship with it. Their decisions are of the type: 'Shall I invest money in this business?', 'Shall I continue to be an investor in this business?', 'Shall I supply goods to this business?', 'Shall I continue to supply goods to this business?', 'Shall I become a customer of this business?', 'Shall I continue to be a customer of this business?'

The internal users make different types of judgements and different types of decisions. They may have to judge the performance of the various products of the organisation as compared with those of competitors. They may have to judge the performance of different divisions within the organisation. Their decisions are of the type: 'Shall I invest in manufacturing more soap powder, or do I switch resources into toothpaste?', 'Shall I continue offering a television repair service as support for my sales of televisions?', 'Is it cost-effective to have three separate locations at which my tenants can pay their rent?', 'Will this investment in a new factory pay for itself over the next ten years?' There is great variety in the judgements and decisions made by those who manage the business. Their needs are so wide ranging that management accounting has developed as a separate discipline, within the overall 'accounting' umbrella, in order to serve the particular needs of management.

The use of accounting as a tool which will assist in the management of a business raises two significant questions:

1 What types of informed judgements are made by management and about management?
2 What types of decisions are made by management?

It is presumed that many of those reading this text for the first time may not have a great deal of experience of the types of judgements and decisions made in business. This chapter therefore devotes space to four case study illustrations of management situations where management accounting will have a contribution to make. The case studies are uncomplicated so that the management accounting applications are intuitively obvious. After each case study outline there is a comment on the management accounting aspects. You will then meet Fiona McTaggart, a management accounting consultant, who explains how she sees the management accountant's contribution to the management issues raised in each of the four case studies.

Before exploring the case studies, this chapter sets out, in section 16.3, some basic categories of management functions and then outlines, in section 16.4, the role of management accounting in helping to meet the information needs of those management functions.

16.3 Management functions

This section describes three management functions: planning, decision making and control.

To be effective, each of these functions requires the application by management of communication and motivation skills. To ensure that the entity's operations are effective, those who work in the entity must be persuaded to identify with its objectives. Managers require the skills to motivate those for whom they are responsible, creating a sense of teamwork. The communication process is a vital part of creating a sense of teamwork and ensuring that all the players understand the role they play in achieving targets. They must also be motivated to want to achieve the targets. Management accounting has a particularly important role in that process of communication and motivation.

16.3.1 Planning

Planning is a very general term which covers longer-term strategic planning and shorter-term operational planning. These two types of planning differ in the timescale that they cover. **Strategic planning** involves preparing, evaluating and selecting *strategies* to achieve objectives of a long-term plan of action. **Operational planning** relates to the detailed plans by which those working within an organisation are expected to meet the short-term objectives of their working group.

Strategic planning is based on objectives set by those who manage the entity at a senior level. If the entity is a legal entity such as a limited liability company or a public sector corporation, objectives will be set for the corporate entity which will require high-level **corporate strategic planning**. Within the company or corporation there will be major divisions of activities into key business areas, each with their own objectives requiring **business strategic planning**.

The corporate entity may contain many different businesses and those who manage the corporate entity as a whole must manage the entire collection of businesses. They must decide which businesses to develop in the corporate interest, which to support when in temporary difficulties, and which to dispose of as no longer contributing to the corporate well-being. Business strategic planning focuses on each of the separate businesses which have to consider not only their position within the corporate group of businesses but also their position within the industry or sector to which the business belongs.

Shorter-term operational planning is also referred to as **functional strategic planning**. It concentrates on the actions of specific functions within the business. Although these functions may have a longer-term existence they must also plan their activity in shorter-term periods so that achievement of targets may be monitored regularly.

At a practical level, managers find that they have to plan ahead in making major decisions on such things as **sales, production** and **capital expenditure**. Such planning is required for the immediate future and for the longer term. Businesses will typically make a detailed plan for the year ahead and a broader plan for a two- to five-year period. Plans for sales require decisions on which products to sell, which markets to target and what price to charge. Plans for production require decisions on the mix of resources, including labour, the source of raw materials or component parts, the level of stock of raw materials and finished goods to hold and the most effective use of productive capacity. Plans for capital expenditure require a longer-term perspective, taking into account the expected life of the capital equipment acquired. As well as investing in **fixed assets**, the business will need **working capital** as a base for a new project. Decisions will be required on the level of working capital which is appropriate. If the enterprise is to move ahead, plans must lead to decisions.

16.3.2 Decision making

Decision making is central to the management of an enterprise. The manager of a profit-making business has to decide on the manner of implementation of the objectives of the business, at least one of which may well relate to allocating resources so as to maximise profit. A non-profit-making enterprise (such as a department of central or local government) will be making decisions on resource allocation so as to be economic, efficient and effective in its use of finance. All organisations, whether in the private sector or the public sector, take decisions which have financial implications. Decisions will be about resources, which may be people, products, services or long-term and short-term investment. Decisions will also be about activities, including whether and how to undertake them. Most decisions will at some stage involve consideration of financial matters, particularly cost. Decisions may also have an impact on the working conditions and employment prospects of employees of the organisation, so that cost considerations may, in making a final decision, be weighed against social issues. Where the owners are different persons from the manager (e.g. shareholders of a company as separate persons from the directors), the managers may face a decision where there is a potential conflict between their own interests and those of the owners. In such a situation cost considerations may be evaluated in the wider context of the responsibility of the managers to act in the best interests of the owners.

16.3.3   Control

Once a decision has been taken on any aspect of business activity, management must be in a position to **control** the activity and to have a view on whether the outcome is in accordance with the initial plans and with the objectives derived from those plans. This might involve identifying areas in the business where managers are in a position to control and account for costs and, in some cases, profit. To implement the control process, individual managers will require timely, relevant and accurate information about the part of the business for which they are responsible. Measurement, including cost measurement, is therefore an important ingredient in carrying out the control function.

To carry out the control function, a management control system is needed. A useful definition of a management control system is the following:

Definition

> A **management control system** is a system involving organisational information-seeking and gathering, accountability and feedback designed to ensure that the enterprise adapts to changes in its substantive environment and that the work behaviour of its employees is measured by reference to a set of operational sub-goals (which conform with overall objectives) so that the discrepancy between the two can be reconciled and corrected for.[2]

This definition points to some of the aspects of control which will be encountered in later chapters. It acknowledges the process of seeking and gathering information but emphasises the importance of adaptation and meeting operational goals. Later chapters will refer to feedback processes and also to techniques for measuring differences between actual performance and sub-goals set for that performance.

The information provided to individual management is an essential part of the communication process within a business. For effective communication, there must be an organisational structure which reflects the responsibility and authority of management. Communication must cascade down through this organisational structure and the manner of communication must have regard for the motivation of those who are part of the control process. For control to be effective there must also be a reverse form of communication upwards so that management learn of the concerns of their staff. Motivation, expectations and personal relationships are all matters to be considered and to be harnessed effectively by the process of control.

Activity 16.2   *Think of an organised activity in which you participate at college or at home. To what extent does this activity involve planning, decision making and control? Who carries out the planning? Who makes the decision? Who exercises control?*

16.3.4   An organisation chart

Figure 16.1 presents a simple organisation chart showing various types of relationships in a manufacturing company. It illustrates line relationships within the overall finance function of the business, showing separately the management accounting and financial accounting functions. In most medium to large companies, the management accounting function will be a separate area of activity within the finance function. The term 'management accountant' is used here as a general term, but a brief perusal of the 'situations vacant' pages of any newspaper or professional magazine advertising accountancy posts would indicate the range of titles available and the versatility expected (see Case 16.1 at the end of the chapter). Two other functions have been shown in the chart as 'project accountant' and 'systems accountant'. Such specialists

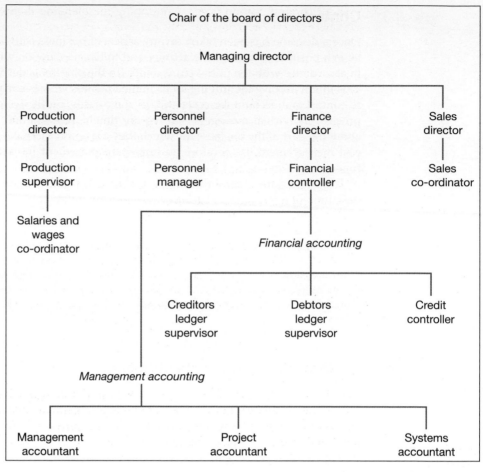

Figure 16.1

Part of an organisation chart for a manufacturing company, illustrating line relationships within the overall finance function of the business

have specific roles in the internal accounting process within the enterprise which are relevant, although not exclusive, to the management accounting function.

The organisation chart shows individual people, each with a different job to do. Each person has a specialisation indicated by the job title, but he or she also has responsibilities to others higher in the structure and with authority over others lower in the structure. In the interests of the business as a whole, individuals must communicate up and down the line relationships and also across the horizontal relationships.

Taking one line relationship as an example, the finance director must make plans for the year ahead which are communicated to the financial controller. The financial controller must consult the systems accountant to ensure that the accounting systems are in place to record and communicate these plans within the organisation. The financial controller must also consult the project accountant to ensure that there is an evaluation of any capital investment aspects of the finance director's plans. The management accountant will prepare accounting statements showing how the plans will be implemented. The financial controller will bring together the details supplied by each person, summarising and evaluating the main factors so that the results may be relayed to the finance director.

Horizontal relationships can be more difficult when communications channels are being planned, because there are so many potential combinations. It is a responsibility of management to decide which horizontal relationships have the greatest communication needs. Continuing the planning theme, the finance director will be expected to communicate the financial plan to the other members of the board of directors, who in turn will want to see that it fits the board's overall strategy and that it is compatible with the capacity of their particular areas of activity in the business. The financial plan will depend on the projected level of sales and will reflect strategy in production and personnel management. The plan will therefore need to be communicated to the sales co-ordinator, the production supervisor and the personnel manager. The sales co-ordinator, production supervisor and personnel manager will in turn provide feedback to the financial controller. The detailed analysis of the plans for the period, and the expected impact of those plans, will be evaluated by the management accountant, project accountant and systems accountant. They will report back to the financial controller who in turn will channel information to the finance director and the rest of the board of directors.

Activity 16.3	*Think again about the organised activity which you identified in Activity 16.2. Prepare an organisation chart to include all the persons involved in the activity. Draw green lines with arrows to show the direction of communication. Draw red lines with arrows to show the direction of responsibility. What does the pattern of red and green lines tell you about communication and co-ordination in the organisation? What is the mechanism for motivation? Does it use the communication network?*

16.3.5 Illustration of the interrelationships

The three management functions of **planning**, **decision making** and **control** are all interrelated in the overall purpose of making judgements and decisions. Figure 16.2 shows how a company owning a chain of shops supplying motorcycle spares might go about the business of planning to open a new shop in the suburbs of a city. The shop will sell motorcycle spares and will also provide advice on basic repair work which motor cyclists can safely undertake themselves.

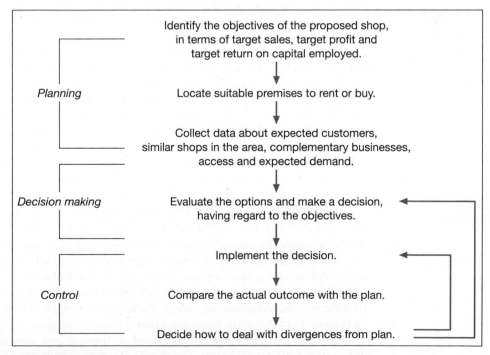

Figure 16.2
Managing a decision on the location of a new business

The shop's objectives will be concerned with achieving target sales and profit, and with making an adequate return on the capital invested in establishing the shop. Because of the desire to offer an advice service as well as selling spare parts, there will be non-financial objectives expressed in terms of customer satisfaction. These non-financial objectives will have indirect financial implications because satisfied customers will lead to increased sales and increased profits. The location of the shop, other types of shop close by, hours and days of opening and approach to stock control are all factors which are considered in the planning process. The choice of shop premises will depend upon the rent to be paid, any costs associated with the property, such as refurbishment and repairs, access for delivery and collection and security. If the shop is to trade successfully there will need to be parking facilities, good access by road and preferably public transport back-up for those who need spare parts but whose motorcycles are too much in need of repair to be used as transport to the shop. Location requires careful consideration. Is it preferable to have the shop in a neighbourhood where a high proportion of residents own motorcycles or to locate it on a main road along which they travel to work? Evaluation for decision-making purposes will require information about planned costs and revenues, although non-cost factors may also influence the decision.

Knowing the objectives and planning to meet those objectives will result in a decision, but the decision to start up the shop is not the end of the story. There has to be a continuing judgement as to whether the shop is successful and, eventually, there may be another decision on expanding or contracting the shop's activity. The continuing exercise of judgement will require a management accounting information outcome of the judgement. Any future decision to expand or contract will similarly include a requirement for information on planned costs and revenues.

Planning, decision making and control are shown on the diagram in Figure 16.2 as separate parts of the total activity. Communication is shown by arrows from one stage to the next. Motivation is not easily shown on a diagram, so there is no attempt to do so, but it remains an important part of the communication process. The greater the number of communication trails built into the process, the more effective will be the understanding and motivation of those who carry out the work of the business at various levels of management. Ideally, the diagram would be criss-crossed with communication trails so that all participants are well informed.

Activity 16.4

Imagine that you want to set up a business as a travel agent booking low-cost holidays with the emphasis on good value. List two activities that you might carry out in each of the stages of planning, decision making and control.

16.4 Role of management accounting

In the previous illustration of planning where to open a new shop, there is work for the management accountant: first, in directing attention to accounting information which is relevant to making plans and taking the decision; second, in keeping the score for making judgements on the effectiveness of decisions; and third, in helping to solve problems which arise when the results of decision making do not work out as expected. So there are three roles that management accounting could play in this exercise that will be found to be general features of any decision-making situation encountered by management. These are: directing attention, keeping the score and solving problems.

16.4.1　Directing attention

Directing attention is a matter of being able to answer questions such as 'Who should take action?' or 'Whose responsibility is this loss?' or 'Who is to be congratulated on this favourable result?' Managers are busy people. They do not always have time to consider every detail of cost information about the operation or process they control. They look to the management accountant to direct their attention to the exceptional points of interest, be these good or bad. One way of carrying out that function is to highlight those costs which have departed from expectations – provided everyone understands at the outset what the expectations are. Words such as *fairness* and *timeliness* are almost bound to be involved in attention-directing processes.

Managers are also sensitive people. They do not like being blamed unjustly for something they see as being beyond their control. So the management accounting information has to be presented in such a way as to relate to the level of responsibility and degree of authority held by the manager concerned. On the other side of the coin, managers enjoy being praised for achievements and may welcome management accounting information which helps them to demonstrate their accountability for the resources entrusted to them.

In any organisation emphasising strategic management, it will be part of the role of management accounting to direct the attention of management towards information about competitors. Competitive forces include: the threat posed by new entrants to the industry, the emergence of substitute products or services, the relative strength of suppliers and customers in controlling prices and conditions in the industry and the intensity of rivalry within the industry. Such information is often well known on an anecdotal basis. The management accountant may be required to collect and present information in a useful and focused manner.

The role of management accounting in directing attention will therefore depend on how managers wish their attention to be directed. A business which retains an inward-looking approach to management will expect management accounting to direct attention inwards. A business which is thinking strategically about its position in the market for goods and services will expect management accounting to include an outward-looking perspective.

Strategic management accounting has been defined as:

Definition	The provision and analysis of financial information on the firm's product markets and competitors' costs and cost structures and the monitoring of the enterprise's strategies and those of its competitors in these markets over a number of periods.[3]

The practical effects of the different types of management accounting approaches are summarised in Table 16.1.

16.4.2　Keeping the score

Keeping the score is very much a case of being able to answer the questions 'How much?' or 'How many?' at any point in time. It requires careful record keeping and a constant monitoring of accounting records against physical quantities and measures of work done. The emphasis is on *completeness* but also on *fairness*. Questions such as 'How much?' may involve sharing, or allocating, costs. Accounting is concerned with allocations of various types, all concerned with aspects of *matching*. That could require matching costs to a time period, matching costs to an item of output, or matching costs against revenue for the period. For this matching process to be effective, information must be complete and the basis of allocation must be fair.

Table 16.1

Contrasting an inward and outward focus of management

Possible limitations of an inward focus for management	Benefits of an outward focus for management
A risk of placing too much emphasis on evaluating past actions.	Management accounting includes a prospective element evaluating the potential outcomes of various strategies.
A risk of focusing on the business entity alone.	Management accounting sets information about the business entity in the context of other businesses in the sector.
A tendency to focus on a single reporting period.	Management accounting sets the results of one period in a longer-term analysis.
Directing attention towards separate single issues of decision making.	Management accounting directs attention towards sequences and patterns in decision making.
Directing attention to the outcome of the manufacturing or service activity of the particular organisation.	Management accounting directs attention to the competition for the manufacturing or service activity.
A tendency to concentrate on existing activities.	Management accounting is also expected to look to prospective activities.
Risk of not considering linkages within the organisation or potential for effective linkages beyond.	Management accounting is expected to direct attention to effective linkages which will improve competitive position.

For the business which has a strong emphasis on strategic management, score keeping will include being able to answer questions such as 'How much of the market share?' or 'How many compared to our competitors?' Questions of fairness of allocation within the business may be important but it may be even more important to understand the performance of the business in relation to others. Such questions will be answered by both financial and non-financial measures.

16.4.3 Solving problems

Solving problems involves a different type of question. It might be 'Why did that plan go well?' or 'Why did that action fail?' or 'Which of these three choices is the best to take?' In solving problems of this type, *relevance* is an important issue. People who have taken a decision are often reluctant to admit that it has not turned out as expected and may continue making worse mistakes unless someone points out that past events are of little or no relevance to decisions on future action. Where choices are concerned, those choices will involve people, each of whom may have different motives for preferring one choice above others. Management accounting information may have a role in providing an objective base for understanding the problem to be solved, even where at the end of the day a decision is based on non-accounting factors.

Some problems resemble making a jigsaw, or perhaps deciding which piece of the jigsaw has gone missing. Other problems are like solving crosswords where the answers must interlock but some of the clues have been obliterated. In solving any problem of that type, logical reasoning is essential. No one can memorise the answer to every conceivable question which might arise. You will find that management accounting tests your powers of logical reasoning in that every problem you encounter will never entirely resemble the previous one.

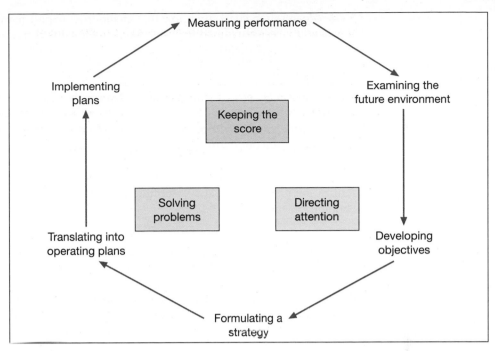

Figure 16.3
Stages in the cycle of profit planning and control

Figure 16.3 illustrates a combination of the management accounting functions of directing attention, keeping the score and solving problems. It shows the cycle of profit planning and control, starting with the measurement of existing performance, which is an example of the score-keeping aspects of management accounting. From the measurement of existing performance the cycle moves through an examination of the future environment of the business, where techniques of economic analysis would be used. In developing objectives, the management accountant would provide accounting information on targets to be achieved. Formulating a strategy is a management task but the management accountant is then expected to provide detailed budgets which translate that strategy into operating plans. When the plans are implemented the management accountant must be ready to measure the results and compare these with the outcome expected when the operating plans were set. From there the cycle is repeated.

Activity 16.5	*Look back to your list from Activity 16.4 for planning, decision making and control in setting up a travel agency business. Make another list of ways in which management accounting will help in directing attention, keeping the score and solving problems.*

16.5 Judgements and decisions: case study illustrations

You are now presented with four cases in which there is a need for decisions and for judgements. After each case study there is a brief analysis of the decisions and judgements which will arise in each.

These four cases indicate areas where management accounting could serve as a tool to provide information which is relevant to decision making and to the formation of judgement at all levels within an organisation. Hopefully, you will have recognised some situations in each case where accounting information will be of help.

The organisation chart in Figure 16.1 includes an expert management accountant. It has already been explained that most medium to large companies include specialist management accountants on their staff. However, from time to time a consultant may be called in to give a wider and more frank appraisal than might be feasible for a paid employee. In this and subsequent chapters you will meet Fiona McTaggart, a freelance management accountant, who is prepared to offer advice on a variety of case study situations. In practice, the management accountant within the organisation might provide similar advice, but this text uses the management consultant so that her comments are not unduly constrained by existing limitations within the business.

Fiona explains what she could offer from her management accounting experience in each of these four case study situations. Read her explanations and in each case identify the places where she is hinting at directing attention, keeping the score or solving problems.

Activity 16.6

Read the text of the case study (set out in the box at the beginning of each case) and then make a note of the way in which you think management accounting may help each person. Compare your answer with the discussion which follows each case.

16.5.1 Case study: Jon Okike

Jon Okike has taken early retirement at the age of 50 in order to develop his hobby of model shipbuilding into a full-time business. He has several models already assembled and has advertised in the model builders' weekly journal. Interested enquiries are starting to come in and he realises that he does not know what price to charge for the models.

Analysis of decisions and judgements

Jon Okike needs to make a decision about pricing policy. That will involve many factors such as looking at what competitors are charging, having regard to the type of customer he expects to attract, and making sure that the price covers the cost of making and selling the models. After he has decided on a pricing policy he will need to measure its success by making judgements on the level of **sales** achieved and on the **profitability** of the product in relation to the capital he has invested in the business.

FIONA: *Jon Okike needs to know the cost of the models he is making. That sounds easy – he has a note of the money he has spent on materials for the models and he has detailed plans which tell him exactly how much material is used for each one. But that's not the end of the story. Jon puts a tremendous amount of time into the model building. He says it is all enjoyment to him, so he doesn't treat that time as a cost, but I have to persuade him that making the models represents a lost opportunity to do something else. The cost of his time could be measured in terms of that lost opportunity.*

Then there are his tools. He has a workshop at the end of the garage and it's stacked high with tools. They don't last for ever and the cost of depreciation should be spread over the models produced using those tools. He needs heat to keep the workshop warm, power for the electric tools and packing material for the models sent in response to a postal enquiry. He has paid for an advertisement in the model builders' magazine and there is stationery, as well as postage and telephone calls, to consider.

Costs never seem to end once you start to add them up. It can all be a bit depressing, but it is much more depressing to sell something and then find out later that you've made a loss. I could help Jon work out his costs and make sure the price he charges will leave a profit so that he builds up his investment in the business.

Making the decision on selling price would not be the end of my involvement. I would continue to measure costs each month and compare these with sales. I would give Jon reports on profit and cash flow and warnings if working capital was starting to build up. If he gives credit he'll need to keep an eye on the level of debtors, and there will always be a stock, either of raw materials or of finished goods or of both. Trade creditors will fund some of the stock but working capital mismanagement has been the downfall of many a business which tried to expand too fast.

I will also need to keep Jon down to earth in ensuring that what has until now been a hobby can become a successful business. I will direct his attention to professional business reports for this kind of specialist service. I will encourage him to subscribe to information services and I will incorporate such information in my reports to Jon so that he can take a realistic view of his performance compared with what might be expected in the general business of special craft work.

In advising Jon Okike, Fiona McTaggart will direct attention to the costs which are relevant to the pricing decision, she will keep the score by calculating profits once the business is in production and will help solve problems by monitoring the working capital position.

16.5.2   Case study: Sara Lee

> Sara Lee has been operating a small hairdressing business for several months. She would like to expand by employing an assistant and by purchasing new dryers and washing equipment. She cannot decide whether the investment would be justified.

Analysis of decisions and judgements

Sara Lee will be taking a longer-term view in making a decision about investing in new equipment. That equipment must generate cash flows over its expected life. Sara's decision to invest will take into account the number of customers she expects, the prices she is able to charge them, and the cost of paying the proposed assistant, projected ahead for several years. It will also take into account the percentage **return** expected on the capital invested in the equipment.

If she decides to invest, she will need to monitor the success of that investment by making judgements on the profitability of the product in relation to the capital she has invested in it, and on whether the **return on the investment** is adequate in the light of having expanded the business.

 FIONA: *Sara Lee needs help in taking a longer-term perspective. To assess the profitability of the new equipment and the assistant, I'll first of all need Sara to tell me how many customers she can realistically expect and what she will be able to charge them. I'll need those estimates over the life of the equipment, which will probably be around five years.*

Once I have the estimates of cash inflows from customers over the five years, I can set against that the cash outflows in terms of payments for all the costs of providing the service, including the wages of the intended assistant. Then I will apply to those cash flows a factor which makes an allowance for uncertainty in the future and also takes account of the rate of interest Sara could earn if she invested her money in financial markets rather than hairdryers. I'll then compare the expected cash flows with the initial cost of acquiring the equipment, to see whether it's a good idea. Of course, if Sara gets the cash flow estimates wrong, then the answer won't mean very much, but that's not my problem.

If Sara makes the decision to invest, I'll be needed after that to monitor the success of the project. I can measure the cash flows after the event and give an indication of how well they met expectations. I can compare the cost of the assistant with the revenue generated by the extra work available.

Problems might arise if there is a change of fashion and everyone decides they prefer short straight hair. That could cause chaos in the hairdressing industry and might make some of the washing equipment surplus to requirements. There is a great temptation in such situations to hang on to the past because of the cash which was sunk into it. That's often the wrong thing to do because it brings disaster ever closer. It may be better to cut off the activity altogether and limit the losses. I can give a dispassionate view based on cost rather than sentiment and emotion.

Fiona McTaggart will provide information which is relevant to the investment decision by drawing attention to the cost in comparison with the expected cash inflows. She will keep the score on the cash inflows and outflows once the project is established and she will help in problem solving by evaluating the losses arising if an unsuccessful project continues in operation.

16.5.3 Case study: Central Ltd

Central Ltd is a small business manufacturing and assembling plastic components for use in car manufacture. It has been drawn to the attention of the financial controller that one of the plastic components could be purchased elsewhere at a price less than the cost of manufacture. What action should the production director take?

Analysis of decisions and judgements

The production director of Central Ltd needs to decide whether to continue manufacturing the component within the business or to cease production and buy the component elsewhere. To make that decision requires a knowledge of the full cost of manufacture and reassurance that the cost has been calculated correctly. It also depends on the relative aims and objectives of the financial controller and the production director, who may be in conflict and who may be putting their own point of view at the expense of the overall good of the business. Costs of ceasing manufacture will also need to be taken into account. Beyond the accounting costs there are human costs and business risks. Is there alternative employment for the staff released from this internal production? Will there be redundancy costs? Is it safe to rely on this outside supplier? What are the risks to Central Ltd if supplies dry up?

Whatever decision is taken, there will be a subsequent need for judgement in monitoring the effectiveness of the decision and its impact on profitability. In the decision and in the subsequent judgements of the effectiveness of that decision, there will be a need for communication and interaction between the financial controller and the production director.

FIONA: *Central Ltd is an example of the football game situation where sometimes the players in a team forget that they are on the same side. I saw a game last week when the home team won on the away team's own goals. The same thing could happen for Central. When people have a defined role in an organisation they can be too closely involved in their own work to see the bigger picture. The financial controller sees the costs of manufacturing and assembling the parts and has identified a cost saving based on a simple comparison. It's hard for the production director to fight the logic of that argument but I can see he's worried.*

What I can do is turn his worries into cost arguments which should be considered alongside the direct make-or-buy comparison. The costs may not be capable of such precise calculation but I'll give estimates of the risk to the business and the sensitivity of the situation. I'll give particular attention to the quality issues and to the risk of disruption of supply. It's more than likely that the financial controller and the production director will still not agree even when they have the information, so I'll present my information in a way which the board of directors can relate to the overall objectives and strategy of the company. Whatever decision is taken, I'll establish a monthly reporting system, to be operated by the financial controller, which will give the earliest possible warning of whether the decision remains in the best interests of the company.

That is the traditional management accounting role which I am happy to provide. However, I will also indicate, in conversation with the financial controller and the production director, that it would be important to discover first of all what their competitors are doing about this problem. The competitors will not answer the question directly but potential suppliers of the components may be willing to indicate that there is a similar demand emerging elsewhere. If the problem here is that production costs are too high in relation to the rest of the industry then perhaps the board of directors has to focus on cost reduction rather than external purchase. If the price is lower externally, someone somewhere has apparently found a better approach to cost control.

Fiona McTaggart will provide information directly relevant to the make-or-buy decision. She will help in problem solving by setting out the information in such a way that others in the organisation can be satisfied that a decision will be in the best interests of the company as a whole. Finally, she will establish a score-keeping system which continues to monitor the effectiveness of the decision taken.

16.5.4   Case study: Anita Khan

Anita Khan is a hospital manager having responsibility for ensuring that the cost of treatment is recovered in full by invoicing the patient or the appropriate organisation which is financing the patient care. Pricing policy is dictated at a more senior level.

Analysis of decisions and judgements

Anita Khan has no direct decision-making responsibility but the information she collates and the records she keeps, in relation to identifying costs and charging these costs to patients, will be used in the decision-making process at a more senior level. It will also be used as a tool of judgement on the effectiveness of the hospital's cost control and charging policy for the various treatments and services provided. In this case the criteria for the judgement may be rather different in that there may be less emphasis on **profitability** and more on the quality of service in relation to the cost of providing that service.

FIONA: *Anita Khan doesn't have direct decision-making responsibility. She is a smaller cog in a large machine. However, the efficiency with which she carries out her job will have a direct impact on the performance of the hospital and will have an impact on future decision making at a more senior level. Charging out to patients the cost of their care is a difficult matter and requires very careful record keeping. Patients who are ill don't question their treatment at the time, but when they are convalescing they have lots of time to look through the bill, especially if the medical insurance company is asking questions. Some patients may be paid for through the health service but at the end of the line there is a fundholder who wants to ensure that the funds are used to best advantage.*

The cost of, say, major surgery can be the least difficult to work out because the time in theatre will be known, the staff on duty will be listed and their salary costs can be apportioned over the time taken. But when the patient is back on the ward recovering, there have to be records kept of the type of nursing care, the specialist equipment and supplies, food costs and the hotel-type services associated with providing a bed. Then there have to be charges to cover the overhead costs of heating, maintaining and cleaning the buildings.

Anita Khan needs an effective recording system which is accurate in terms of care for each patient but is not so cumbersome to apply that the nurses' time is entirely taken up with clerical recording. Many costs can be applied to patient care on a predetermined charge-out rate based on previous experience. A computerised cost recording system, with a carefully thought out coding system for each cost, is essential. Of the four cases I have considered here, this will be the most time-consuming to set up, but it will give satisfaction all round when it is working and seen to be fair to patients in terms of individual charge-out costs as well as giving the hospital reassurance that all costs are being recovered.

The cost-recording system will provide information for the decision-making process in relation to future pricing policy and also for the more difficult decisions as to which specialised medical functions at the hospital are cost-effective and which functions do not fully cover costs. There are bound to be problems within the hospital if decisions are needed on expanding or cutting back. Everyone hates the accountant at those times, but at least I can design a system which provides an objective starting point even though non-financial factors are eventually the determining factor.

Fiona McTaggart is describing here the score-keeping aspects of management accounting. That score keeping will be used as information for the decision-making process and may also have a problem-solving aspect if disputes arise where medical decisions have a cost impact.

16.5.5 Comment

These case study discussions have given some insight into how the management accountant has a role to play in contributing to the management of an organisation. Three general themes have been explored, namely **keeping the score**, **directing attention** and **solving problems**. The case studies have shown that within each of these three themes there are many different approaches to be taken, depending on the circumstances. By way of illustration of the scope of management accounting activity, Fiona McTaggart has the following list of special studies she has undertaken, as an adviser on management accounting, where problem-solving skills have been required:

- product cost comparisons
- evaluation of product profitability
- alternative choices of resource usage
- asset management
- labour relations
- capital investment
- investigation on behalf of customer for contract pricing purposes
- directing attention to the activities of competitors.

All of these, and other problem situations, will be encountered in subsequent chapters. This chapter ends with a warning that there will be some new terminology to learn and a summary of the role of the management accountant.

16.6 The language of management accounting

Management accounting is not a difficult subject but to understand it requires a logical mind. To be successful, methods of management accounting must reflect a reasoned approach to a judgement on a situation problem and a logical basis for making decisions. If reason and logic are strong, then it should not be difficult to understand the approach.

Unfortunately, as with most specialist subjects, management accounting has grown a language of its own, which is helpful to those who work closely with the subject but can sometimes cause problems at the outset for newcomers. This chapter has avoided using specialist terminology, relying on intuitive ideas. However, progress in understanding management accounting will be limited without the use of that terminology, so subsequent chapters will introduce the technical terms, each of which will be explained. End-of-chapter questions will help you to test your understanding of new terminology before you move on to each new chapter.

One important difference from financial accounting is that there is no official regulatory process governing management accounting. This is very different from the framework of company law, accounting standards and other regulatory processes which are found throughout financial reporting to external users. Consequently there is relative freedom in management accounting to tailor the accounting process to the management function. That does not mean that management accounting is any less rigorous professionally than other forms of accounting reporting. In the UK there is a professional body, the Chartered Institute of Management Accountants (CIMA), which provides guidance to its members on good practice in management accounting. That guidance includes a wide range of publications ranging from definitions of terminology to reports on newly emerging techniques. Similar professional bodies having a management accounting specialism exist in other countries.

16.7 Summary

You have seen from the discussion in section 16.1.3 and the case studies that management accounting should direct attention towards strategic issues of surviving and prospering in a competitive environment. The remaining chapters of this book will introduce the various techniques that have been developed in management accounting for keeping the score, directing attention and solving problems. The traditional techniques are described, with current thinking and developments explained and contrasted as relevant.

Key themes in this chapter are:

- Management accounting is concerned with reporting accounting information within a business, for management use only.
- Management takes its widest meaning in describing all those persons (managers) responsible for the day-to-day running of a business.
- The managers of a business carry out functions of **planning**, **decision making** and **control**.
- Management accounting supports these management functions by **directing attention**, **keeping the score** and **solving problems**.
- The **contingency theory** of management accounting explains how management accounting methods have developed in a variety of ways depending on the judgements or decisions required.
- **Strategic management accounting** pays particular attention to the provision and analysis of financial information on the firm's product markets and competitors' costs and cost structures, and the monitoring of the enterprise's strategies and those of its competitors in these markets over a number of periods.

Further reading

CIMA (2005), *Official Terminology*, CIMA Publishing and Elsevier.

QUESTIONS

The Questions section of each chapter has three types of question. 'Test your understanding' questions to help you review your reading are in the 'A' series of questions. You will find the answers to these by reading and thinking about the material in the book. 'Application' questions to test your ability to apply technical skills are in the 'B' series of questions. Questions requiring you to show skills in problem solving and evaluation are in the 'C' series of questions. A letter [S] indicates that there is a solution at the end of the book. Other solutions are provided in the Instructor's Manual, where there are further questions parallel to those set out here.

A Test your understanding

A16.1 Define 'management accounting'. (Section 16.1)

A16.2 Explain why management decisions will normally require more than a management accounting input. (Section 16.1.1)

A16.3 What is meant by a 'contingency theory' of management accounting? (Section 16.1.2)

A16.4 Why is management accounting required to take on an outward-looking role of contributing to business strategy by identifying, measuring and communicating financial information about a wider business community? (Section 16.1.3)

A16.5 Explain the needs of internal users for management accounting information. (Section 16.2)

A16.6 Explain, giving a suitable example in each case, what is meant by the management functions of:

(a) planning; (Section 16.3.1)
(b) decision making; (Section 16.3.2) and
(c) control. (Section 16.3.3)

A16.7 Explain, giving a suitable example in each case, how management accounting may serve the purposes of:

(a) directing attention; (Section 16.4.1)
(b) keeping the score; (Section 16.4.2) and
(c) solving problems. (Section 16.4.3)

A16.8 Describe, and explain each stage of, the cycle of profit planning and control. (Section 16.4.3)

A16.9 In the chapter there are four case studies where Fiona McTaggart explains what she is able to offer in four situations, using her management accounting experience. Her advice is primarily inward-looking and based on the traditional approaches to planning, control and decision making. Add two sentences to each of Fiona's explanations in order to present a more strategic awareness of the activities of competitors. (Section 16.5)

A16.10 Suggest reasons for the lack of an agreed set of standard words in the language of management accounting. (Section 16.6)

B Application

B16.1
(a) Imagine you are the finance director of a company which is planning to open a new supermarket chain. Prepare a chart similar to that shown in Figure 16.2 which sets out key aspects of the planning, decision making and control.

(b) Give two examples of financial objectives and two examples of non-financial objectives which you might expect of the sales manager of the new supermarket chain.

(c) Explain how management accounting skills would be required in providing product costs comparisons when the supermarket chain becomes operational.

B16.2

A record company is planning to launch an Internet music service. Subscribers who pay £15 per month will be allowed to download 100 songs per month to a personal computer. If the subscription lapses, access to the music will be lost. The quality of the file transfer is guaranteed to be high. Legal advice has been obtained to confirm that the arrangement is within copyright regulations. Royalties will be paid to recording artists based on the number of times that a song is requested.

(a) Identify the judgements and decisions to be made here.

(b) Explain how management accounting may help in directing attention, keeping the score or solving problems.

B16.3

A group of doctors operates a joint surgery. They are planning to provide a private clinic where minor surgery can be performed on a day basis (no overnight facilities will be offered). The project will require investment in a new building and operating theatre. Three theatre nurses will be required and three healthcare assistants will be employed. Admissions will be dealt with by the existing medical secretaries. The fees charged will cover costs plus a profit percentage based on cost.

(a) Identify the judgements and decisions to be made here.

(b) Explain how management accounting may help in directing attention, keeping the score or solving problems.

B16.4

A recently retired police officer has received a lump sum award and a pension. She has a hobby of making soft toys which have for some years been sold to friends and colleagues at a price to cover the cost of materials. She now wishes to turn this into a commercial venture and to sell them through a children's clothing shop which has agreed to provide shelf space for the sale of 20 toys per month. She is not concerned initially about making a high profit and will be satisfied with covering costs. The shop will take a fee of 5% of the sale price of each toy sold.

(a) Identify the judgements and decisions to be made here.

(b) Explain how management accounting may help in directing attention, keeping the score or solving problems.

C | Problem solving and evaluation

C16.1

You have been invited to write a proposal for the development of a new production line to process dog food. The production of dog food will take up space previously devoted to cat food. Write 250 words (approximately) explaining how management accounting would be used to justify any decision by the production manager to replace cat food with dog food in the production process.

C16.2

Chris and Alison Weston have been manufacturing and selling children's toys from a workshop attached to their house. Alison has carried out the manufacturing activity and Chris has provided the marketing and financial support. The scale of customers' orders has reached a point where they must make a decision about renting a production unit on a nearby trading estate and employing two assistants. One assistant would be required to help make the toys and the other would carry out routine record keeping, allowing Chris to spend more time on marketing. Write 250 words (approximately) explaining (a) the main judgements and decisions which will arise; and (b) the kind of advice that could be offered by a management accounting expert.

C16.3

Set out below is a selection of advertisements for posts in management accounting. Read the text of the advertisement and relate the specified requirements to the three management accounting roles set out in this chapter, namely:

(a) directing attention;
(b) keeping the score; and
(c) solving problems.

PLANNING AND REPORTING CONTROLLER

Reporting to the group finance director, your key task will be to drive a step change in all areas of corporate reporting and planning and provide analytical impetus to the development of business strategy.

Responsibilities will include:

● ownership and control of the quality of reporting and forecasting throughout the business;
● managing the group's quarterly strategic business unit review, forecasting and annual planning cycles;
● managing the day-to-day treasury processes including cash-flow forecasting;
● supporting the finance director in all corporate activities including financing, acquisitions, presentations and ad hoc projects as required.

This is a high-profile role which interfaces directly with directors, shareholders, advisers, banks, head office functions and divisions.

The ideal candidate will be an ambitious graduate qualified accountant with a minimum of four years' post-qualified experience. First-class communication skills and good systems knowledge will complement your proven technical expertise.

HEAD OF MANAGEMENT INFORMATION

Reporting to the financial director, you will be responsible for:

● developing and automating the production of management accounts and contract cash reporting;
● implementing and managing a robust process for all contract valuations;
● managing all aspects of budgeting, forecasting and group reporting;
● developing relationships with operational teams to improve controls and increase commercial awareness;
● full review of financial processes and implementation of new systems and controls.

The successful candidate will be commercially minded and profit-motivated with the ability to manage a strong team.

MANAGEMENT ACCOUNTANT

This is a major support services organisation, supplying services and products to government agencies and commercial businesses worldwide. Working closely with the commercial teams, you will provide them with full financial support at every stage of the contract life cycle. Main responsibilities include:

● assisting with the compilation of new bids and tenders;
● ongoing contract monitoring including budgeting and forecasting;
● development of key performance indicators for the business;
● production of monthly management accounts, analysis and commentary.

You will need to have excellent business acumen and highly developed communication skills.

MANAGEMENT ACCOUNTANT
(Charitable organisation)

This is a leading charity providing safe, secure and affordable housing for young people and working with homeless young people to provide safe shelter. Reporting to the head of finance, the role involves working closely with various departments identifying areas of concern and solutions.

Key responsibilities include:

1 Reviewing of trial balance and generation and review of management accounts; identifying and resolving any issues and offering a business support function.
2 Attending committee meetings to present the accounts to the trustees.
3 Identifying trends in the management accounts and advising management as to recommendations.
4 Development of budgets and forecasts.
5 Investigating and improving financial performance in the operations of the residential centres.

This role would suit an individual who is looking to shape the continuing development of the work of the charity.

HEAD OF MANAGEMENT ACCOUNTS
(The finance office of a university)

You will be responsible for the setting, monitoring, control and reporting on budgets and the regular production of management accounts. In addition, you will ensure the provision of a comprehensive payroll service and be responsible for arranging and accounting for capital finance.

PRINCIPAL MANAGEMENT ACCOUNTANT
(Public sector organisation)

This is one of the most successful police forces in the country. With 2,000 employees and an annual budget of over £80 million, it is essential that the organisation has appropriate and well-maintained financial management and information systems to support the demands of modern policing.

We now require a dynamic team leader to ensure the continued development of these systems and to provide a comprehensive financial advice/support service to senior managers.

The successful candidate will be closely involved in the production of medium-term financial plans, annual budgets, financial information systems upgrades as well as the training and development of non-technical staff on financial management.

You will be self-reliant and able to work to tight deadlines whilst maintaining high standards, be capable of clearly communicating financial concepts in a persuasive and effective manner and have a suitable professional qualification with three years' experience in financial management.

Activities for study groups

Case 16.1

Form a study group of four to six persons who are to act out the role of the finance director and related staff on the accounting team of a company planning to open a new supermarket chain at an out-of-town location. Give a ten-minute presentation to the rest of the class explaining the major issues you will be expected to deal with in making a contribution to the decision and the subsequent monitoring of that decision.

Case 16.2

Form a study group of four to six persons who are to negotiate the development of a new production line to process canned peas. The canned peas will replace an existing product, canned carrots. Half of the team will argue on behalf of the canned peas while the other half will argue on behalf of the canned carrots. Give a ten-minute presentation to the class (five minutes for each half of the team) explaining how management accounting information will help you to justify the decision you propose and to monitor the implementation of the decision.

Notes and references

1. AAA (1966), *A Statement of Basic Accounting Theory*, American Accounting Association, Evanston, Illinois, p. 1.
2. Lowe, E. A. (1971), 'On the idea of a management control system', *Journal of Management Studies*, 8(1): 1–12.
3. Bromwich, M. (1990), 'The case for strategic management accounting: the role of accounting information for strategy in competitive markets', *Accounting, Organizations and Society*, 15(1/2): 27–46.

Chapter 17

Classification of costs

This case study shows a typical case in which management accounting can be helpful. Read the case study now but only attempt the discussion points after you have finished reading the chapter.

Corbis

UK haulage costs

This case study describes an annual survey of haulage costs for grain in the UK, transporting grain from the farm to the processing unit.

Average grain haulage costs in 2014 down 1.2%, but costs for longer journeys increase.

Last updated: 9 May 2014

Results from AHDB/HGCA's UK Grain Haulage Survey 2014 show a 1.2 per cent decline in average journey costs, compared with last year's survey.

The average journey in 2014 cost £8.43/t, compared with £8.53/t in 2013. However, when a journey exceeded 80 miles the cost of transport increased year on year. The cost of a journey of 90 miles or more was the highest since at least 2004.

The survey of 227 journeys across the UK revealed varying changes in costs, depending on distance and region.

In 2014, a journey of 10 miles was £0.59/t lower (–12.0%) than in 2013, whereas a journey of 150 miles was £0.59/t higher (+4.4%).

Regional trends

- Scotland: highest journey costs for distances of 80 miles plus, however lower costs for 150-mile journeys compared with 2013
- Midlands: lower costs for 50 to 150-mile journeys compared with 2013 (there is no comparable 2013 data for 10 to 40-mile journeys)
- Eastern England: the only region to report year-on-year higher haulage costs for 10 to 150-mile journey

The average retail diesel price from July 2013 until end-April 2014 was 138.52 pence per litre, two per cent lower than during the same time period in 2012/13. The strengthening of the pound sterling against the US dollar is a key factor behind the decline in price.

AHDB/HGCA Senior Analyst, Amandeep Kaur Purewal, said: 'From this survey we can see that fuel costs are not the only factor affecting grain haulage rates. Higher costs for longer distances may be due to empty, or lower than capacity, back-loads. Lower production in 2013/14 may have meant that the wheat crop travelled over longer distances in the UK. The north of the country has experienced more of a deficit than usual, so more grain has had to travel from the south-east.'

Source: http://www.hgca.com/press/2014/may/09/grain-haulage-survey.aspx

United Kingdom Haulage Costs

£ per tonne

Distance (miles)	2004	2005	2006	2007	2008	2009	2010	2012	2013	2014	% Change 2013/2014
10	4.05	4.29	4.09	4.18	4.83	4.24	4.54	4.28	4.92	4.33	−12.0
20	4.52	4.77	4.57	4.69	5.35	4.81	5.03	4.90	5.54	5.03	−9.2
30	5.00	5.26	5.05	5.20	5.87	5.38	5.52	5.51	6.15	5.73	−6.8
40	5.47	5.74	5.53	5.72	6.40	5.95	6.01	6.13	6.76	6.42	−5.0
50	5.94	6.23	6.02	6.23	6.92	6.52	6.50	6.75	7.38	7.12	−3.5
60	6.42	6.71	6.50	6.74	7.45	7.09	6.98	7.36	7.99	7.82	−2.1
70	6.89	7.20	6.98	7.25	7.97	7.67	7.47	7.98	8.60	8.52	−0.9
80	7.36	7.68	7.46	7.76	8.49	8.24	7.96	8.59	9.22	9.22	0.0
90	7.84	8.17	7.94	8.27	9.02	8.81	8.45	9.21	9.83	9.91	+0.8
100	8.31	8.65	8.43	8.78	9.54	9.38	8.94	9.83	10.44	10.61	+1.6
125	9.50	9.87	9.63	10.06	10.85	10.81	10.16	11.37	11.97	12.36	+3.3
150	10.68	11.08	10.84	11.34	12.16	12.23	11.39	12.91	13.51	14.10	+4.4

Source: HGCA Haulage Survey. http://www.hgca.com/markets/survey-results.aspx

HGCA is a division of the Agriculture and Horticulture Development Board (AHDB), a statutory levy board, funded by farmers, growers and others in the supply chain and managed independently of both commercial industry and of Government. Its purpose is to make agriculture and horticulture industries more competitive and sustainable through factual, evidence-based advice, information and activity.

Discussion points

1 Explain how the article makes a distinction between variable costs and fixed costs.

2 What other costs, in addition to those mentioned, would you expect to see included in the estimate of annual haulage costs?

Learning outcomes

After reading this chapter you should be able to:

- Define 'cost'.
- Explain the need for cost classification.
- Define 'activity' and 'output'.
- Explain and distinguish fixed costs and variable costs.
- Explain and distinguish direct costs and indirect costs.
- Explain and distinguish product costs and period costs.
- Explain how cost classification can be developed to be relevant to the circumstances of planning, decision making and control.
- Explain and devise a cost coding system.
- Explain how costs may be selected and reported for the type of activity required (cost unit, cost centre, profit centre or investment centre).

17.1 Definition of a cost

The cost of an item of input or output may be analysed in terms of two measurements:

1 a physical quantity measurement multiplied by
2 a price measurement.

Where a production process uses 100 kg of material which has a price of £5 per kg, the cost is £500. Where a production process uses 200 hours of labour time at a rate of £4 per hour, the cost is £800. That may appear to be a statement of the obvious, but the breaking down of cost into physical quantity and price is frequently essential for the application of management accounting methods where the physical flow of inputs and outputs may sometimes be recorded separately from the unit price. The analysis of the separate elements of quantity and price will be dealt with in more detail in Chapter 22.

17.2 The need for cost classification

Cost classification systems in practice are as varied as the businesses they serve. In Chapter 16 the functions of management are described as planning, decision making and control. For purposes of classification it is convenient to take planning and control as a combined function because the classifications required by each are similar. For decision making, particular care has to be taken to use classifications of cost which are relevant to the decision under consideration.

This chapter will first explain three *traditional* types of cost classification:

1 **variable costs** and **fixed costs** (section 17.4);
2 **direct costs** and **indirect costs** (section 17.5); and
3 **product costs** and **period costs** (section 17.6).

Each of these cost classifications will then be related to the **management** functions of **planning**, **decision making** and **control** (section 17.7). It is important to emphasise here that the three types of cost classification are *different* ways of looking at costs. Any particular item of cost could have more than one of these classifications attached to it, depending on the purpose of the classifications being used.

Finally, the chapter will explain the importance of correct coding of costs in a computer-based system (section 17.8), and will show how costs are selected and reported according to the unit of the business for which information is required (section 17.9).

17.3 The meaning of 'activity' and 'output'

The word **activity** will be used in this book as a general description to cover any physical operation that takes place in an enterprise. In a business providing bus transport for schoolchildren the activities will include driving the bus, cleaning the bus, making telephone calls to check routes and times, and ensuring that the administrative requirements, such as insurance and licences, are in place. In a local government department providing assistance to elderly persons, the activities will include sending out home helps, paying the home helps, telephoning the clients to arrange visits, and checking that spending is within the budget allowed. In a manufacturing business providing floor cleaning machines the activities will include ordering parts, assembling parts, delivering the finished products to shops for sale, taking in returns for repair under warranty, paying employees, and checking on the quality of the goods produced. These are all activities and they all cause costs to be incurred. The idea of activities causing costs ('driving costs') is central to much of the classification of costs and the collection of costs relating to a specific activity. You will find later that the phrase **activity-based costing** (ABC) has been created to recognise that management accounting is most effective when it links costs to the activities of the business.

Activities have to be measured. For the soap manufacturer the measure of activity is the number of cartons of washing powder sold. For the retail store it could be the number of items of clothing sold, or it could be the value of clothing sold. Selling a large number of small-value items causes higher staffing costs than does selling a small number of high-value items. For the road haulage business the measure of activity could be the hours worked by drivers or the number of miles driven. Hours worked takes no account of whether the drivers are on the road or waiting at the depot. Miles driven are a better measure of productive activity but do not distinguish full loads from empty trucks. Fuel costs are higher for a full load than for an empty truck. Activity might be measured using a combined unit of kilogram-miles.

Throughout the following chapters the word **activity** will be used and measures of activity will be described. You will be expected to show your analytical skills in thinking about the meaning of the word and the relevance of the measure of activity to cost classification and cost behaviour.

Output is a particular kind of activity. It is the product or service provided by the enterprise or by one of its internal sections. The output of a soap manufacturer is washing powder; the output of a retail store is the clothing that it sells; the output of a service engineer might be the repair of washing machines; the output of a garden centre is pot plants grown from seed; the output of a road haulage business is the loads delivered by its drivers; the output of a refuse disposal company is the service of emptying household dustbins; the output of an airline is the passenger loads carried; the output of a school is the successful education of its pupils.

Activity 17.1	*(This is another use of the word 'activity' where you are asked to pause and think actively about what you have read.) Think about any activity that you carry out during a week (e.g. travel to college, eating meals, washing clothes). How would you measure the volume of that activity in a week? How might the cost of the activity be affected by the volume of activity? For example, could you share some travel costs; would one large meal cost more or less than two small meals; would one large wash cost more or less than two small washes?*

17.4 Variable costs and fixed costs

Costs behave in different ways as the level of activity changes. Some costs increase in direct proportion to the increased level of activity. These are called variable costs. Some costs do not vary, whatever the level of activity. These are called **fixed costs**. Some show elements of both features. These are called **semi-variable costs**. Fixed costs that increase in steps are called **step costs**.

17.4.1 Variable costs

Definition	A **variable cost** is one which varies directly with changes in the level of activity, over a defined period of time.

Examples of **variable costs** are:

● materials used to manufacture a unit of output or to provide a type of service
● labour costs of manufacturing a unit of output or providing a type of service
● commission paid to a salesperson
● fuel used by a haulage company.

Table 17.1 shows the costs of clay used by a pottery company for various levels of output of clay vases for garden ornaments. The clay required for each vase costs £10.

Table 17.1
Costs of clay related to activity levels

Output (number of vases)	100	200	300
Total cost (£s)	£1,000	£2,000	£3,000

The **total cost** increases by £10 for every vase produced, and is described as *variable*. The **unit cost** is £10 per vase and is *constant*. Sometimes students find it a little confusing at this point to decide whether they should be thinking about the total cost or the unit cost. It may help you to think of yourself as the owner of the business manufacturing the vases. If you were the owner, you would be most interested in the total cost because that shows how much finance you will need in order to carry on production. You will only recover the cost of buying the clay when you sell the finished goods to the customers. Until then you need finance to buy the clay. The more you produce, the more finance you will need. If you approach the bank manager to help you finance the business you will be asked 'How much do you need?', a question which is answered by reference to total cost.

Figure 17.1 shows, in the form of a graph, the information contained in Table 17.1. It plots activity level (number of vases produced) on the horizontal axis and total cost on the vertical axis. The graph reinforces the idea that the total cost is a variable cost. It shows a straight line moving upwards to the right. The fact that the line is straight, rather than curving, means that the total cost increases in direct proportion to the increase in activity (that is, total cost increases by £10 for every unit of output).

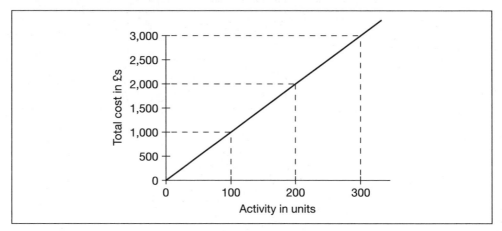

Figure 17.1
Graph of variable cost measured as activity increases

17.4.2   Fixed costs

Definition

A **fixed cost** is one which is not affected by changes in the level of activity, over a defined period of time.

A **fixed cost** is by definition unchanged over a period of time, but it may vary in the longer term. Rent, for example, might be fixed for a period of one year, but reviewed at the end of every year with the possibility of an increase being imposed by the landlord. Other examples of fixed costs are:

- rent of buildings
- salary paid to a supervisor
- advertising in the trade journals
- business rates paid to the local authority
- depreciation of machinery calculated on the straight-line basis.

Continuing our illustration based on a pottery company, Table 17.2 sets out the cost to the pottery company of renting a building in which to house its kiln and other production facilities. The total cost remains *fixed* at £3,000 irrespective of how many vases are produced. The unit cost is *decreasing* as output increases, as shown in Table 17.3, because the fixed cost is spread over more vases. Here again, it is more important usually to think about total cost because unless the pottery can pay its rent it cannot continue in business. This type of cost is therefore described as a fixed cost. The cost of rent is shown in graphical form in Figure 17.2.

Table 17.2
Costs of rental related to activity levels

Output (number of vases)	100	200	300
Total cost (£s)	£3,000	£3,000	£3,000

Table 17.3
Unit cost of the pottery rental

Output (number of vases)	Unit cost (£)
100	30
200	15
300	10

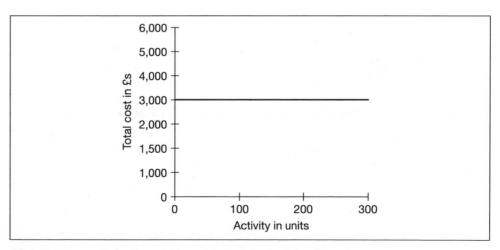

Figure 17.2
Illustration of fixed cost

17.4.3   Semi-variable costs

Definition   A **semi-variable cost** is one which is partly fixed and partly varies with changes in the level of activity, over a defined period of time.

Examples of **semi-variable cost** are:

- office salaries where there is a core of long-term secretarial staff plus employment of temporary staff when activity levels rise;
- maintenance charges where there is a fixed basic charge per year plus a variable element depending on the number of call-outs per year.

Table 17.4 sets out the costs incurred by a telephone sales company which pays a fixed rental of £2,000 per month and a call charge of £1 per telephone sale call. This total cost has a mixed behaviour, which may be described as semi-variable. It has a fixed component of £2,000 and a variable component of £1 per telephone sale.

Table 17.4
Telephone rental costs

Activity (number of calls)	100	200	300
Cost (£s)	2,100	2,200	2,300

The graph of this semi-variable cost is shown in Figure 17.3. The fixed cost is shown by the point where the line of the graph meets the vertical axis. The variable component is shown by the slope of the graph. The slope of the graph shows the total cost increasing by £1 for every extra unit of activity. The fixed component of £2,000 is shown as the point where the line of the graph meets the vertical axis.

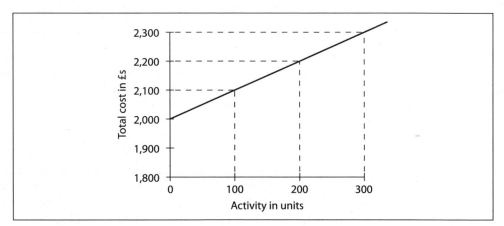

Figure 17.3
Illustration of semi-variable cost

Examples of semi-variable cost are:

- office salaries where there is a core of long-term secretarial staff plus employment of temporary staff when activity levels rise;
- maintenance charges where there is a fixed basic charge per year plus a variable element depending on the number of call-outs per year.

17.4.4 Step costs

A fixed cost that increases in steps is called a **step cost**. The cost is fixed over a specified level of activity but then increases as a further amount of fixed cost is incurred. One example is the cost of renting storage space. The rent is unchanged while the output can be fitted into one store but as soon as a second store has to be rented the total rental cost increases. Another example is the cost of paying a supervisor of a team of employees. Suppose one supervisor can manage up to 20 employees. Cost of supervision will be fixed for the level of activity from 1 to 20 employees. Beyond that level a second supervisor will be needed, causing a sudden increase in fixed cost.

Figure 17.4 shows a step cost of rent increasing annually over five years. The rental starts at £1,000 and increases by £100 each year.

The graph in Figure 17.4 is different from those shown earlier in the chapter because the horizontal axis measures time rather than activity. However, it is also possible to estimate the activity levels expected over the five-year period. Whatever the expected activity level, the relationship between total cost and activity level will be more complex than the simple fixed, variable and semi-variable relationships already shown. For the purposes of the rest of this book all the costs you meet will be simplified as fixed, variable or semi-variable, within a defined period of time.

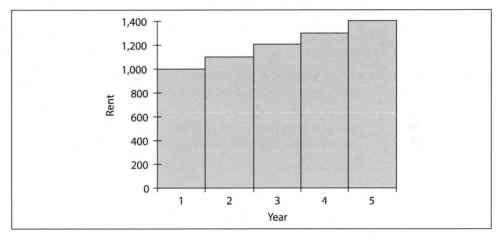

Figure 17.4
Step cost for five-year period, with annual increase

17.4.5 Importance of the time period chosen

The extent to which a cost varies with activity depends on the period of time chosen. In manufacturing picnic tables, the cost of the plastic frame and the table top are variable costs, as is the labour cost of assembly. The annual rent of the warehouse where the tables are assembled is a **fixed cost** for the year, but will increase in steps (a **step cost**) over a period of several years if there is a rent review each year.

Activity 17.2

At this point, be sure that you are comfortable with the idea of variable costs, fixed costs and semi-variable costs. These will appear frequently in later chapters and it is important to understand them. If you are not familiar with graphs, go back through the section and try to draw the graph from the data presented. If you are familiar with graphs, make up some cost patterns and plot these on graph paper to confirm that you can link the graphic presentation to the pattern of numbers.

17.5 Direct costs and indirect costs

The costs of a business activity can also be classified as direct and indirect costs. **Direct costs** are those which are directly related to a particular object (such as a product which has been manufactured) or a particular service (such as a repair job completed) or a particular location (such as a department within the organisation). **Indirect costs** are those which cannot be directly related to a particular object or service or location and therefore have to be apportioned on a basis which is as fair as can be devised.

The first question you should ask, whenever you see the words 'direct' or 'indirect' is 'Direct or indirect in which respect?' This will remind you that the words have no meaning in isolation. An item which is a direct cost for a department could be an indirect cost for the units of output produced by the department. Take the example of electricity consumed in a department. If the department has a meter, then the amount of electricity used may be identified directly with the department. However, if all items produced within the department share the benefit of the electricity supply, then the cost will need to be shared among them as an indirect cost so far as products are concerned.

Definitions

The definition of **direct** and **indirect costs** depends on the purpose for which the cost will be used.

Direct costs are directly traceable to an identifiable unit, such as a product or service or department of the business, for which costs are to be determined.

Indirect costs are spread over a number of identifiable units of the business, such as products or services or departments, for which costs are to be determined. Indirect costs are also called **overhead costs.**

Overhead costs are the costs which cannot be identified directly with products or services.

Fiona McTaggart gives an example of how she would distinguish direct costs and indirect costs in a particular situation.

FIONA: *I was working recently with a publishing firm about to bring out a new children's magazine series based on a popular cartoon programme. The publisher had already incurred market research costs in respect of the new magazine series and it looked like a good idea.*

The magazine is to be produced in a department where there are already ten other magazines in production. Writers work freelance and are paid fees on a piecework basis for each item they write. Graphic artists are employed full-time in the department, producing designs and drawings for all the magazines. Once the magazine production is completed, it is sent for external printing at another company which charges on the basis of volume of output. I was asked to help design a monthly cost analysis statement for the new magazine.

I pointed out that some costs were easy to identify because they were directly traceable to the product. Working back from the end of the story, the external printer's charge would be a direct cost of the new magazine because it is directly related to that specific output. The work of the freelance writers is also a direct cost of the new magazine because it is easy to make a list of fees paid to them in respect of particular work on the new magazine.

The work of the graphic artists is an indirect cost so far as the product is concerned, because their time is spread over all magazines produced. They do not keep detailed records of every design they produce. Many designs can be used in more than one magazine title. I suggested that a fair basis of allocation would be to share their cost across all magazines in proportion to the number of illustrated pages in each. That turned out to be a bad idea because some illustrated pages may contain full-size pictures while others may contain a quarter-page design, so it was eventually decided to apply a factor to each page depending on whether it was fully illustrated or partly illustrated.

Although the graphic artists are an indirect cost so far as the product is concerned, they are a direct cost for the department, because they don't work in any other department. I suggested that the full cost of the new magazine would only be known when it was also carrying its share of the direct costs and indirect costs of the department as a whole. Direct costs for the department could include heat and light, maintenance of the operating equipment, machine depreciation and supervisor's salary, while indirect costs could include a share of administration costs and a share of rent and business rates. It is not easy to ensure that all costs are included for purposes of planning and control.

In her explanation, Fiona has repeatedly used the words 'direct' and 'indirect', but at the start of the explanation she is referring to the direct and indirect costs of the new magazine while at the end she is referring to the direct and indirect costs of the whole department. The departmental costs, taken together, are all indirect costs so far as the *products* of the department are concerned.

Activity 17.3	*Think of some activity observed in your everyday life where costs are involved. (It could, for example, be travelling on a bus, watching the sales assistant in a shop, or asking the television repair service to call.) Write down five costs which might be incurred in that activity. How would you decide which costs are direct and which are indirect?*

17.6 Product costs and period costs

Another way of looking at the cost of a unit of output of a business is to distinguish product costs and period costs. **Product costs** are those which are identified with goods or services intended for sale to customers. These costs belong to the products and stay with them until they are sold. If goods remain unsold, or work in progress remains incomplete, then the product costs stay with the unsold goods or work in progress under the heading of inventory (stock). **Period costs** are those costs which are treated as expenses of the period and are not carried as part of the inventory (stock) value.

Definitions	**Product costs** are those costs associated with goods or services purchased, or produced, for sale to customers. **Period costs** are those costs which are treated as expenses in the period in which they are incurred. Product costs include direct *and* indirect costs of production. Table 17.5 sets out a statement of product cost that includes direct and indirect costs. The total of direct costs is described as the **prime cost**.

Table 17.5 uses the words **production overhead** to describe the total of the indirect costs of production. Examples are:

- depreciation of machinery
- insurance of the factory premises
- rental of warehouse storage space for raw material.

There are many other types of overhead costs which you will encounter in your progress through later chapters. They all consist of indirect costs, with the type of cost determining the particular name given to the overhead cost.

Table 17.5
Statement of product cost

	£	£
Direct materials		xxx
Direct labour		xxx
Other direct costs		xxx
Prime cost		xxx
Indirect materials	xxx	
Indirect labour	xxx	
Other indirect costs	xxx	
Production overhead cost		xxx
Total product cost		xxx

Definitions

Prime cost is the total of direct materials, direct labour and other direct costs.

Production overhead cost comprises indirect material, indirect labour and other indirect costs of production.

Example of product costs and period costs in a service business

A financial adviser provides each client with three hours' consultation prior to arranging a pension plan. The cost of the adviser's time is estimated at £500 per hour. Advertising costs £2,000 per month. The client is charged £2,100 commission on completion of the three-hour sequence of consultation. During one week the financial adviser provides 20 hours of consultation. The statement of costs would be:

		£
Product cost	Labour: 20 hours at £500 per hour	10,000
Period cost	Advertising	2,000

Suppose that the consultations are complete for six clients (18 hours) but unfinished for one client, who has been provided with only two hours' consultation by the end of the week. The incomplete consultation is described as work in progress. There was no work in progress at the start of the week. The calculation of profit would be:

		£	£
Product cost	Sales (commission) 6 clients at £2,100 each		12,600
	Labour: 20 hours at £500 per hour	10,000	
	Less work in progress 2 hours at £500 per hour	(1,000)	
	Product cost of goods sold		(9,000)
Period cost	Advertising	2,000	(2,000)
	Operating profit		1,600

Example of product costs and period costs in a manufacturing business

A toy manufacturer produces hand-crafted rocking horses. During one week six rocking horses are completed. The direct materials costs of wood and leather materials amount to £180 per completed horse. The indirect materials cost of glue and paint amount to £20 per completed horse. The direct labour cost for craft working is £150 per completed horse. The indirect labour cost of handling within the production department is £50 per completed horse. Advertising amounted to £1,200 per week.

Five completed rocking horses are sold for £1,000 each. There were none in inventory (stock) at the start of the week. The statements of costs would be:

		£
Product cost	Direct materials, wood and leather, 6 @ £180	1,080
	Indirect materials, glue and paint, 6 @ £20	120
	Direct labour: craft work, 6 @ £150	900
	Indirect labour: handling 6 @ £50	300
Period cost	Advertising	1,200

The calculation of profit would be:

		£	£
Product cost	Sales: 5 completed rocking horses		5,000
	Direct materials, wood and leather, 6 @ £180	1,080	
	Indirect materials, glue and paint, 6 @ £20	120	
	Direct labour: craft work, 6 @ £150	900	
	Indirect labour: handling 6 @ £50	300	
		2,400	
	Less unsold inventory (stock), 1 × (180 + 20 + 150 + 50)	(400)	
	Product cost of 5 horses sold		(2,000)
Period cost	Advertising		(1,200)
	Operating profit		1,800

In each of these examples the **product cost** of completed services and of goods sold is matched against sales **revenue** of the week. The **product cost** of **work in progress** and of unsold goods is carried in the inventory (stock) valuation to be matched against sales **revenue** of a future week. The **period costs** are all matched against sales **revenue** of the week.

In a service organisation, all costs incurred up to the point of completion of the service are regarded as **product costs**. Any costs incurred beyond the act of service, such as advertising the service or collecting cash from customers, would be a **period cost**.

In a manufacturing organisation, all manufacturing costs are regarded as **product costs**. This will include the direct and indirect costs of manufacturing. Chapter 19 will explain the methods of calculating the indirect manufacturing costs for each product item. Costs incurred beyond the completion of manufacture, such as the costs of administration and selling, are **period costs**. The valuation of unsold inventory (stock) is based on the **product** cost.

17.7   Cost classification for planning, decision making and control

Sections 17.4, 17.5 and 17.6 have described fixed and variable costs, direct and indirect costs and product and period costs. Each of these may have a role to play in planning, decision making and control. The idea of contingency, explained in Chapter 16, is important here; the classification is chosen to suit the intended use.

17.7.1   Planning

Planning involves looking forward and asking questions of the 'what if . . . ?' type. Table 17.6 gives examples of planning questions and sets out the cost classifications that may be appropriate to each.

Table 17.6
Cost classification for planning purposes

Planning question	*Cost* classification
1 What is the cost impact of a change in levels of production over a period of time?	**Fixed** and **variable** costs. Fixed costs will not be affected by production levels; variable costs will alter proportionately.
2 What is the cost effect of planning to expand operations by opening a new outlet in a separate location?	**Direct** and **indirect** costs, in relation to the location. The direct costs will include the rental and running costs of the chosen location; indirect costs will be that location's share of the general running costs of the business.
3 What is the cost impact of remaining open for longer hours to improve on existing client services?	**Fixed** and **variable** costs. The new service will incur variable costs. Will it cause any step increase in fixed costs?

17.7.2 Decision making

Decision making involves asking questions of the type 'Should we do ... ?' Table 17.7 gives examples of decision-making questions and sets out the cost classifications that may be appropriate to each.

For decision-making purposes, the key word is 'relevance'. The costs used in the decision-making process must only be those which are relevant to the decision. In this respect, the classification into variable and fixed costs is particularly important. That is because, in the short term, little can be done by a business in relation to **fixed costs**, so that the need for a decision may focus attention on the **variable costs**. Fiona McTaggart explains how she would use such a classification to present information for decision making.

Table 17.7
Cost classification for decision-making purposes

Decision-making question	*Cost classification*
1 Should the company produce components in this country or produce them overseas?	**Fixed** and **variable** costs. The variable costs of production should be compared for each country. Fixed costs are not relevant to the decision if they are incurred regardless of the location. Fixed costs are relevant if they can be avoided by changing location.
2 Should the company continue to provide a service when demand is falling?	**Fixed** and **variable** costs. The price paid by customers must at least cover the variable costs. In the longer term there must be sufficient revenue to cover variable and fixed costs.

FIONA: *The Garden Decor Company is thinking of making two garden ornaments, gnomes and herons. The variable cost of making a gnome would be £24 and the variable cost of making a heron would be £14. Market research indicates that garden ornaments of similar types are selling in the shops for around £20 each. Output up to the level of 20,000 garden ornaments, in any combination of output of each, would lead to fixed rental and insurance costs of £6,000.*

My recommendation would be that the company should not even contemplate the garden gnomes because the expected selling price of £20 will not cover the variable cost of £24 per unit. The company will make a loss as it produces each item. The selling price of the herons would cover their variable cost and make a contribution of £6 each (£20 minus £14) to the fixed cost. If they can sell 1,000 herons or more, the £6 contribution from each will cover the £6,000 additional fixed costs and any further herons sold will give a profit clear of fixed costs.

Fiona has used the word 'contribution' in this discussion. You can probably guess its meaning from the context in which it is used, but you will meet the word again as a technical term in Chapter 20.

17.7.3   Control

Control involves looking back and asking questions of the 'how and why . . . ?' type. Table 17.8 gives examples of **control** questions and sets out the cost classifications that may be appropriate to each.

Table 17.8
Cost classification for control purposes

Control question	Cost classification
1 How closely do the costs of each product match the targets set?	**Direct** and **indirect** costs in relation to the product. If the direct costs do not match the targets set then questions must be asked about the product itself. If the indirect costs do not match the targets then questions must be asked about the control of those costs and the method of apportioning (sharing) them across the products.
2 How closely do the costs of a service department match the budget set for the department?	**Direct** and **indirect** costs related to the department. The direct costs are closely under the control of the departmental manager, who should explain any deviations. The indirect costs are shared across several departments and so questions may be asked about the basis of apportioning (sharing) those costs.
3 Is the value of the inventory (stock) of unsold goods stated correctly?	**Product** costs and **period** costs. The unsold inventory (stock) should be carrying its share of the product costs.

Activity 17.4

Imagine you are the manager of a department store in the centre of town. Write down one planning question, one decision-making question and one control question that you might ask and suggest a cost classification that would provide management accounting information relevant to the question.

17.7.4   Cost classification to meet changing circumstances

Chapter 16 noted the contingency approach to management accounting which emphasises that management accounting should be flexible to meet changing circumstances of planning, decision making and control. Some of the changes of recent years, to which management accounting practices have been adapted, are:

- The need to identify more closely the costs incurred in a business with the activities which drive those costs.
- The introduction of new technologies in which labour costs have diminished in relation to the cost of operating flexible computer-based operating systems.
- The reduction in inventory (stock) of raw materials and finished goods as the business has linked up with suppliers and customers to ensure that items are delivered just at the time when they are needed.
- The emphasis on managing the quality of output and the cost of achieving that quality.
- Comparing the cost structures of the business with those of others in the industry.

These have led particular businesses to develop management accounting practices which suit their particular needs. Observers of those new practices, particularly academic writers, have identified new patterns of management accounting to which they have given titles such as:

- activity-based costing
- just-in-time purchasing
- cost of quality
- benchmarking costs.

These approaches reflect dissatisfaction with the traditional approach in particular instances, but they do not indicate that the traditional approach has entirely failed. Consequently it remains necessary to study the traditional approach while having regard to continuing developments.

17.8 Cost coding

We will now look in more detail at an approach to cost recording that allows classification systems to be applied accurately and speedily.

Most costing systems are computerised. In a computerised system every cost item is given a **cost code** number which allows the cost to be traced through the computerised system. The coding is critical to effective use of the cost information. Computers allow selective retrieval of information quickly, but only if the coding is correctly designed to suit the needs of the organisation.

A cost code must be unique to the cost which it identifies. The code should be as short as possible and it is preferable to have a code structure which creates consistent images in the mind of the user. The code may be entirely numerical or may have a mixture of letters and numbers (an *alphanumeric* code).

Definition A **cost code** is a system of letters and numbers designed to give a series of unique labels which help in classification and analysis of cost information.

The design of the coding system and the assignment of code numbers should be carried out centrally so that the system is consistent throughout the organisation. The code system may have built into it the structure of the organisation, so that the code starts by specifying a major unit of the organisation and gradually narrows down to a particular cost in a particular location. Here is Fiona McTaggart to explain a cost coding system she has recently designed.

FIONA: *This company, producing and selling books, has 15 different departments. Within each department there are up to six cost centres. There are three different types of book – reference, academic and leisure. The list of costs to be coded contains 350 items, down to detail such as bindings purchased for special strength in reference works.*

The coding is based on a six-digit alphanumeric code. The department is represented by the first digit of the code, taking one of the letters A to Z (except that the company decided not to use letters I and O because of the confusion with numerical digits). Each cost centre has a letter code, which appears in the second position. (Again the letters I and O are not used.) The next digit is the letter R, A or L depending on whether the book is reference, academic or leisure. The last three digits are numbers taken from a cost code list which covers all 350 items but which could in principle expand up to 999 items in total. Within those three digits, there is further grouping of costs by code – for example, 100 to 199 are reserved for fixed asset items; 200 to 399 are various types of material cost; 400 to 599 are various types of labour cost; 600 to 899 are a whole range of production overhead costs; and 900 to 999 are administration and selling costs.

So, under code number HCA246, it would be possible to find the cost of paper used in printing an academic textbook on the new printing machine. Working backwards through the code, item 246 is paper, letter A is an academic book, letter C denotes the new printing machine (which is itself a cost centre) and letter H indicates the printing department.

Activity 17.5

Create a six-digit coding system which would allow you to classify all the items of expenditure you make in a year. (You will need to write down the items of expenditure first of all and then look for patterns which could be represented in a code.) To test your code, ask a friend to write down three transactions, converting them to code. Then use your knowledge of the code to tell your friend what the three transactions were.

17.9 Cost selection and reporting

Once the costs have been coded, a computerised accounting system can be programmed to retrieve the costs in a systematic manner for reporting purposes. The code structure must include alphanumeric characters that cover each of the purposes for which cost is required.

The code structure outlined by Fiona McTaggart above would allow classification of cost by reference to items of output and would allow classification of cost by reference to a cost centre. A **cost centre** is only one of the units into which an organisation is subdivided for cost collection purposes. Two others are a **profit centre** and an **investment centre**. The chapter ends with definitions of the following terms that will be encountered in subsequent chapters in relation to cost selection and reporting: cost centre, profit centre and investment centre.

17.9.1 Cost centre

A **cost centre** is a unit of the organisation in respect of which a manager is responsible for costs under their control. A cost centre could be a location (e.g. a department) or a function (e.g. the manufacture of a product), or it could even be a production machine or group of similar machines. One essential feature of a cost centre is that it must be a homogeneous unit carrying out a single form of activity. A second essential feature is that it must correspond to an identifiable managerial responsibility.

Identification of a cost centre with managerial responsibility leads to a further type of cost classification, namely **controllable** and **non-controllable** costs. Costs allocated to a cost centre should be classified according to whether they are controllable or non-controllable by the manager of that cost centre.

Definitions

A **cost centre** is a unit of the organisation in respect of which a manager is responsible for costs under their control.

A **controllable cost** is one which is capable of being managed by the person responsible for the cost centre, profit centre or investment centre to which the cost is reported.

17.9.2 Profit centre

A **profit centre** is a unit of the organisation in respect of which a manager is responsible for revenue as well as costs. In practice an operating division would be a profit centre if it produced output whose selling price could be determined in some manner. The selling price could be based on an internal transfer between departments at an agreed price. It would not necessarily require a sale to a third party outside the business entity.

A profit centre is similar to a cost centre in that it must relate to an area of managerial responsibility, although the activity may be less homogeneous than that of a cost centre. The profit centre, though, is likely to contain more than one cost centre.

Definition

A **profit centre** is a unit of the organisation in respect of which a manager is responsible for revenue as well as costs.

17.9.3 Investment centre

An **investment centre** is a unit of the organisation in respect of which a manager is responsible for **capital investment** decisions as well as **revenue** and **costs**. These decisions could be related to such matters as purchase and disposal of equipment or acquisition of premises. The investment centre will be undertaking business activity in such a way that it will probably carry out an operation which is significant to the overall profit-earning capacity of the organisation. As is the case with a profit centre, the investment centre must relate to an area of managerial responsibility, but the activities of the investment centre need not be homogeneous. There will probably be a number of cost centres and profit centres within the investment centre.

Definition

An **investment centre** is a unit of the organisation in respect of which a manager is responsible for capital investment decisions as well as revenue and costs.

17.10 Summary

Key themes in this chapter are:

- Costs may be classified using one or more of the following pairs of definitions:
  - **fixed/variable cost**
  - **direct/indirect cost**
  - **product/period cost**.
- The choice of cost classification should be matched to the management function of planning, decision making or **control**.

- **Cost coding** is essential to make the cost classification system operational in a computer-based recording system.

- Cost classification must be relevant to the responsibility level for which the costs are reported, which may be a **cost centre**, or a **profit centre**, or an **investment centre**.

The chapter has set out the basic terminology of cost classification to be used throughout the book. In later chapters you will meet more detailed classifications such as controllable/non-controllable and avoidable/unavoidable.

Further reading

The following references go well beyond a first-level course but they are noted so that you may delve more deeply into any of the cost aspects outlined in this chapter. You should, however, be aware that there is no standard terminology in the field of management accounting, so every author will have a slightly different form of wording to define a given concept.

CIMA (2005), *Official Terminology*, CIMA Publishing and Elsevier.

Smith, J. A. (editor) (2007), *The Handbook of Management Accounting*, fourth edition, CIMA Publishing and Elsevier.

QUESTIONS

The Questions section of each chapter has three types of question. 'Test your understanding' questions to help you review your reading are in the 'A' series of questions. You will find the answers to these by reading and thinking about the material in the book. 'Application' questions to test your ability to apply technical skills are in the 'B' series of questions. Questions requiring you to show skills in problem solving and evaluation are in the 'C' series of questions. A letter [S] indicates that there is a solution at the end of the book. Other instructions are provided in the Instructor's Manual, where there are further questions parallel to those set out here.

A   Test your understanding

A17.1   Explain what is meant by 'cost'. (Section 17.1)

A17.2   Explain the meaning of 'activity' and 'output'. (Section 17.3)

A17.3   For each of the following cost classification terms, give a definition and give one example of how the definition applies in practice to a person providing car repairs from a rented garage:

(a) variable cost; (Section 17.4.1)
(b) fixed cost; (Section 17.4.2)
(c) semi-variable cost; (Section 17.4.3)
(d) step cost; (Section 17.4.4)
(e) direct cost; (Section 17.5)
(f) indirect cost; (Section 17.5)
(g) product cost; (Section 17.6) and
(h) period cost. (Section 17.6)

A17.4   Explain how each of the following cost items could be classified under more than one of the headings given in question A17.3:

(a) raw materials to be used in production;
(b) subcontracted labour in a special contract; and
(c) rent of a warehouse for one year to allow temporary expansion of output.

A17.5 Classify each of the following as being primarily a fixed cost or a variable cost, and, if necessary, explain why you think such a classification would be difficult without more information being provided (Section 17.4):

(a) direct materials;
(b) factory insurance;
(c) production manager's salary;
(d) advertising of the product;
(e) direct labour;
(f) indirect labour;
(g) depreciation of machinery;
(h) lubricants for machines;
(i) payment of a licence fee for the right to exclusive manufacture; and
(j) canteen manager's salary.

A17.6 What are the component costs of the total cost of production? (Section 17.5)

A17.7 State the cost headings which are combined to give each of the following: (Section 17.6)

(a) prime cost;
(b) production overhead cost;
(c) total product cost.

A17.8 Explain how cost classification must be matched to the purpose of planning, decision making or control. (Section 17.7)

A17.9 How does cost classification vary to meet particular circumstances? (Section 17.7.4)

A17.10 Explain the importance of an unambiguous system of cost coding. (Section 17.8)

A17.11 What are:

(a) a cost centre; (Section 17.9.1)
(b) a profit centre; (Section 17.9.2) and
(c) an investment centre? (Section 17.9.3)

B Application

B17.1
Give an example of a management planning question for which it would be useful to classify costs as fixed and variable.

B17.2
Give an example of a management planning question for which it would be useful to classify costs as direct and indirect.

B17.3
Give an example of a management control question for which it would be useful to classify costs as direct and indirect.

B17.4
Give an example of a management control question for which it would be useful to classify costs as period and product costs.

B17.5 [S]
(a) Identify the cost behaviour in each of the following tables as:
  (i) fixed cost; or
  (ii) variable cost; or
  (iii) semi-variable cost.
(b) Draw a graph for each table to illustrate the cost behaviour.

Cost X

Output (units)	100	200	300	400	500
Total cost (£)	600	600	600	600	600
Unit cost (£)	6.00	3.00	2.00	1.50	1.20

Cost Y

Output (units)	100	200	300	400	500
Total cost (£)	300	600	900	1,200	1,500
Unit cost (£)	3.00	3.00	3.00	3.00	3.00

Cost Z

Output (units)	100	200	300	400	500
Total cost (£)	660	720	780	840	900
Unit cost (£)	6.60	3.60	2.60	2.10	1.80

B17.6 [S]

Oven Pies Ltd plans to buy a delivery van to distribute pies from the bakery to various neighbourhood shops. It will use the van for three years. The expected costs are as follows:

	£
New van	15,000
Trade-in price after 3 years	600
Service costs (every 6 months)	450
Spare parts, per 10,000 miles	360
Four new tyres, every 15,000 miles	1,200
Vehicle licence and insurance, per year	800
Fuel, per litre*	0.70

* Fuel consumption is 1 litre every five miles.

(a) Prepare a table of costs for mileages of 5,000, 10,000, 15,000, 20,000 and 30,000 miles per annum, distinguishing variable costs from fixed costs.
(b) Draw a graph showing variable cost, fixed cost and total cost.
(c) Calculate the average cost per mile at each of the mileages set out in (a).
(d) Write a short commentary on the behaviour of costs as annual mileage increases.

B17.7 [S]

During the month of May, 4,000 metal towel rails were produced and 3,500 were sold. There had been none in store at the start of the month. There was no inventory (stock) of raw materials at either the start or end of the period. Costs incurred during May in respect of towel rails were as follows:

	£
Metal piping	12,000
Wages to welders and painters	9,000
Supplies for welding	1,400
Advertising campaign	2,000
Production manager's salary	1,800
Accounts department computer costs for dealing with production records	1,200

(a) Classify the list of costs set out above, into product costs and period costs.
(b) Explain how you would value inventory (stock) held at the end of the month.

C   Problem solving and evaluation

C17.1
Supermarket checkout operators are paid a weekly wage plus overtime at an hourly rate. One operator has recently resigned from work. The supermarket manager has been asked whether the direct costs of the supermarket operation could be maintained within the annual target by not filling the vacancy created. What should be the reply?

C17.2
Tots Ltd manufactures babies' play suits for sale to retail stores. All play suits are of the same design. There are two departments: the cutting department and the machining department. You are asked to classify the costs listed below under the headings:

(a) Direct costs for the cutting department.
(b) Direct costs for the machining department.
(c) Indirect costs for the cutting department.
(d) Indirect costs for the machining department.
(e) Direct costs for the play suits.
(f) Indirect costs for the play suits.

List of costs
(i)   towelling materials purchased for making the play suits;
(ii)   reels of cotton purchased for machining;
(iii)   pop-fasteners for insertion in the play suits;
(iv)   wages paid to employees in the cutting department;
(v)   wages paid to employees in the machining department;
(vi)   salaries paid to the production supervisors;
(vii)   oil for machines in the machining department;
(viii) rent paid for factory building;
(ix)   depreciation of cutting equipment;
(x)   depreciation of machines for sewing suits;
(xi)   cost of providing canteen facilities for all staff.

Activities for study groups

Case 17.1

You are the management team in a business which makes self-assembly kitchen units and sells them to large do-it-yourself stores. One person should take on the role of the financial controller but the rest of the team may take any managerial roles they choose. Each manager will have responsibility for a cost centre. The group should decide, at the outset, on the name and purpose of each cost centre.

In stage 1 of the team exercise, each manager should write down the name of the cost centre and a list of the costs for which the manager expects to have responsibility. A copy of the cost centre name and the list of costs should be supplied to each member of the team.

In stage 2, each manager should separately write down his or her requirements from a company-wide cost coding system, yet to be designed, which has been specified in outline as having six alphanumeric characters. Each manager should also make a note of any costs which are shared with another manager or managers.

While the managers are carrying out the second stage, the financial controller should prepare a cost coding system which would meet the needs as specified on the lists of costs provided by each manager from stage 1.

In stage 3, the group should come together for a management meeting at which the financial controller will provide his or her cost coding system and each manager will respond with his or her ideas. If possible, a mutually agreed solution should be found but, at the very least, the group should identify the areas where further negotiation will be required. Finally, the group should make a five-minute presentation to the class describing the negotiations on the coding system and commenting on the practical problems of such negotiation.

Case 17.2

The group is the management team of a supermarket chain operating ten shops in out-of-town locations. Each member of the group should choose a management role, one of which must be the financial controller. Work together to prepare a proposal for establishing one profit centre, together with three cost centres within the profit centre for which each manager will be responsible, writing a definition of the responsibilities of each profit centre and cost centre.

Then work together further to produce a list of costs for each cost centre, in a table as follows:

Type of cost	Fixed/variable cost	Direct/indirect for the cost centre	Product/period cost

Set out *one* question relating to planning, *one* question relating to control and *one* question relating to decision making. Explain how the table of cost classification will help answer each of these questions.

Chapter 18

Product costs: materials, labour and overheads

This case study shows a typical case in which management accounting can be helpful. Read the case study now but only attempt the discussion points after you have finished reading the chapter

Seabrook Crisps

This case study illustrates how the costs of a product are viewed by a company's management and how strategy is planned in relation to the activity of a competitor.

Alamy Images/studiomode

Cost control and risk awareness see Bradford's Seabrook Crisps stage turnaround

BOSSES at Bradford-based snacks firm Seabrook Crisps are hailing the success of a turnaround programme which saw it bounce back into profit last year.

They are anticipating further growth in a highly competitive marketplace through targeted marketing of the Seabrook brand and a series of new product launches.

Latest accounts at Companies House show that the family-owned business converted a £430,000 loss in 2012 into a pre-tax profit of £1.64 million in the 12 months to March 30, with turnover rising to £24.5 million from £22.8 million.

Seabrook said profitability continued to increase as the year progressed and as cost savings extended into every aspect of its operations. The company said that, in spite of significant cost increases affecting the majority of its material costs, it managed to remain profitable month on month throughout the year.

In its strategic report, Seabrook states: 'The business has been through a turnaround and the positive results are now fully evident.'

'The creation of a sustainable, scalable business, appropriately structured for growth, represented the first phase of the turnaround but the development of the brand will enable additional growth and create a further step change in profitability.'

'The board are aware of the continued tough trading environment but are confident that the business is well placed to meet these challenges, positive movement within our core markets and a conservative approach to managing the risk in this area means we have cost certainty throughout 2014/15.'

'This conservative approach to risk, a higher grip on operational and administrative costs, significant momentum within our core products and three new launches in 2014/15, should culminate in an exciting and prosperous year ahead for the business.'

Seabrook said it would build on the platform created in the past year to further leverage what is already a 'successful, well established and loved brand.'

In June the Lord Mayor of Bradford Cllr Mike Gibbons officially launched a new £300,000 production facility at the Duncombe Street factory which employs around 150 people.

New lines being introduced include straight cut crisps, the UK's first lattice crisps and a sticks snack.

It was the first phase of an investment programme to help increase Seabrook's turnover to £35 million over the next two years. Jonathan Bye, chief executive, said Seabrook had the ambition to become the number one challenger to the dominant brand, Walkers.

He said: 'It's a David and Goliath situation and we could never match Walkers in size but we do have the advantage of being able to make decisions and act quickly to meet market demand and have a flexible approach.'

'If we can grow turnover to £35 million in next two years it not only secures 150 jobs, it gives us an opportunity to create additional work opportunities locally.'

Source: *Bradford Telegraph and Argus*, 25 September 2014. http://www.thetelegraphandargus.co.uk/business_news/11495745 .Cost_control_and_risk_awareness_see_Bradford_s_Seabrook_Crisps_stage_turnaround/

Discussion points

1 Where are the product costs of materials, labour and overheads mentioned in the article?

2 What additional costs are likely to be incurred in meeting the company's targeted growth of turnover in the next two years?

Contents

Learning outcomes

After reading this chapter you should be able to:

- State the main components of total product cost.
- Explain the process of controlling and recording costs of materials.
- Explain the process of controlling and recording costs of labour.
- Explain the traditional approach to allocating and apportioning production overheads to products.
- Explain how cost drivers may be used to allocate overhead costs in activity-based costing.
- Contrast the traditional and activity-based methods of dealing with overhead costs.

18.1 Introduction

Some businesses manufacture goods, while others perform a service. Whatever the nature of the business, all will at some stage use materials, they will employ labour and they will incur overhead costs (the name given to other costs which are necessary to the operation of the manufacturing or service process).

In this chapter we outline traditional procedures for recording the costs of materials, labour and production overheads and indicate some of the problems which are encountered. Many of these procedures remain a cornerstone of present-day management accounting but others, particularly those related to overhead costs, have caused management accountants to look for new procedures.

A statement of the cost of a unit of output provides a useful starting point for this chapter in setting out a list of items to be explained in more detail (see Exhibit 18.1).

This chapter explains how costs are recorded and traced to products. Products may be goods or services. Direct costs are directly traceable to the relevant products. Indirect costs (overheads) must be shared across more than one product. Figure 18.1 summarises the way in which costs are traced to products. It relates to a cost centre where the output consists of three different products (goods or services). Materials and labour are part of the **product cost** (where products may be goods or services). The direct materials and direct labour are part of the **prime cost**. The indirect materials and indirect labour are part of the **production overhead costs**.

Definition

Prime cost is the cost of direct materials, direct labour and other direct costs of production.

Exhibit 18.1
Statement of cost of a production item

	£	£
Direct materials		xxx
Direct labour		xxx
Other direct costs		xxx
Prime cost		xxx
Indirect materials	xxx	
Indirect labour	xxx	
Other indirect costs	xxx	
Production overhead cost		xxx
Total product cost		xxx

The **direct costs** in Figure 18.1 consist of direct materials, direct labour and any other costs that are directly identifiable with a product. We know how much material is needed for the product, we know how much labour time is worked on the product and we know about any other costs related only to that product. So the arrows flowing downwards in Figure 18.1 show the direct costs of each product flowing directly to that product.

Some materials, some labour and some other costs are classified as **indirect** because they are spread across a range of products. These have to be shared in some way across the products. Figure 18.1 shows the overhead costs being **apportioned** ('shared') across products. One debate in management accounting focuses on how to carry out that process of **apportionment**. This chapter presents two approaches in that debate.

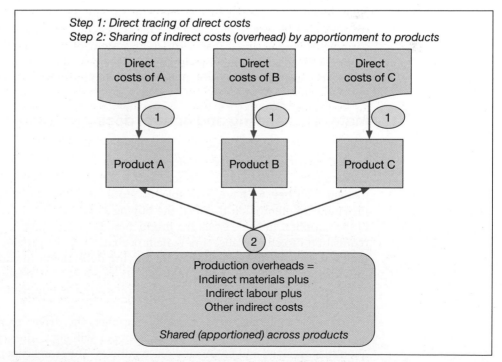

Figure 18.1
Tracing costs of products A, B and C in a single cost centre

Sections 18.2 and 18.3 of this chapter describe methods for recording and controlling the costs of materials and labour. The nature of the materials and labour, and the type of output of the enterprise, will lead to classification of **direct** and **indirect costs** of materials and labour.

Section 18.4 brings together all the indirect costs of production and groups them under the heading **production overhead cost**. It describes the process of ensuring that overhead costs reach the products, using the **traditional** approach. Section 18.5 sets out an alternative to section 18.4 by sharing out the production overhead costs using an **activity-based costing** (ABC) approach. Section 18.6 compares the traditional and the ABC approaches.

Activity 18.1	Look at some item in the room where you are sitting as you read this chapter (perhaps a table or a desk or a window). What words would you use to describe the cost of producing that item (e.g. wood, plastic, work in assembly, running costs of workshop)? How would you start to measure the cost of producing that item? Write down your thoughts now, and then look back after you have finished this chapter. That will help you consider what you have learned from the chapter.

18.2 Accounting for materials costs

Figure 18.2 shows the sequence of activities which control the ordering, delivery and safekeeping of materials, together with the subsequent payment to suppliers. Information which is useful for accounting purposes will be collected from the documentation that is created during these procedures.

It is not difficult to see that with so many procedures involved there needs to be careful control over materials moving into, and out of, store. Each stage in the process requires a document as evidence that the transaction or process has been completed correctly. Every business has a different system of documentation which suits its particular needs. The following description is typical of the documents encountered in materials handling and control. Italics are used to indicate each document.

18.2.1 Materials handling and control documentation

When the storekeeper notes that the inventory (stock) has fallen to the minimum level, triggering a reorder requirement, a *purchase requisition* will be sent to the buying department. The buying department will have a list of items which the production manager wishes to have available in store and the quantity to be reordered. Provided the item is on that list, the buying department will send a *purchase order* to the supplier. In some cases the production manager may have issued a purchase requisition directly because a new item of materials, not previously held in store, is required. It is the responsibility of the buying department to choose a supplier who provides reliable service and a high-quality product at a competitive price. A copy of the purchase order will be sent to the storekeeper as notification that the materials have been ordered.

When the materials arrive from the supplier, the driver of the delivery vehicle will bring a *delivery note* which the storekeeper will sign, after checking against the quantities received and noting any discrepancies. The storekeeper will then prepare a *materials received note,* sending one copy to the buying department and another to the accounts department. Soon after the materials arrive, the accounts department will

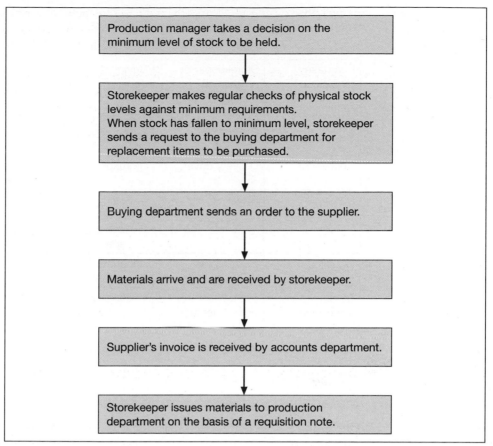

Figure 18.2
Materials control procedures

receive the *supplier's invoice,* showing the quantities of the materials supplied and the price charged for them. The accounts department will check the quantities against the materials received note and will check the invoice price against an agreed price list provided by the buying department. If all is correct, the accounts department will pay the supplier.

Finally, the materials will be needed by the various production departments. To release the materials from store, the production departments will produce a *stores requisition* which the storekeeper will check and will then pass on to the accounts department for use in keeping the management accounting records.

Exhibit 18.2 provides a summary of the various documents, their origin, destination and use for recording purposes. The two essential pieces of information for determining the cost of materials used in production are the price per unit and the quantity of materials issued. These are highlighted in **bold** in Exhibit 18.2. As you will see, the price and quantity are taken from different documents, the supplier's price being taken from the invoice while the quantity of materials used is taken from the stores requisition.

The documents listed in Exhibit 18.2 are referred to as *primary sources* because they form the first evidence that a transaction or event has taken place. From these primary sources the accounting records are created. Clearly, the accuracy of the accounting records is heavily dependent on careful and accurate processing of the primary documents.

Exhibit 18.2
Documentation in materials control procedures

Document	Origin	Destination	Use
Purchase requisition	Storekeeper or production manager	Buying department	Authority for purchase of materials from supplier
Purchase order	Buying department	1 Supplier 2 Storekeeper	Authority to supply materials Indication that materials will arrive
Delivery note	Delivery driver	Storekeeper	Check on quantity received, in good state
Materials received note	Storekeeper	1 Buying department 2 Accounts department	Confirmation that buying process is complete Evidence of quantities for checking against invoice
Supplier's invoice	Supplier	Accounts department	Shows quantities received and unit price
Stores requisition	Production departments	1 Storekeeper 2 Accounts department	Authority to release materials from store Record of quantities used in production

18.2.2 Materials costs when input prices are changing

One problem faced by the accounts department is that suppliers change their prices from time to time. Materials held in store may have arrived at different times and at different unit prices. How does the accounts department decide on the unit price to be charged to each job when all the materials look the same once they are taken into store? The usual procedure is to assume, for pricing purposes, that the first materials to arrive in store are the first ones to leave. This is usually abbreviated to FIFO (first in first out).

Some businesses prefer to use the average cost of all items in inventory (stock) as the basis for pricing issues. For management purposes the best method for the purpose should be applied. Management accounting escapes the constraints of statute law, accounting standards and tax law which restrict practice in financial accounting. (Section 9.8.3 of Chapter 9 shows a detailed example of pricing the issue of materials when input prices are changing.)

18.2.3 Costs of wastage and scrap

The term **waste** is applied to any materials that have no value, whatever the reason. If some waste material can be sold for disposal, usually at a very low price in relation to its original cost, then it is called **scrap**.

In the ideal situation, all materials received into stores are issued to production. Real life is not always like that, because stores may disappear before they have a chance to be used in the production process. The disappearance may be caused by deterioration or damage in store, the materials may become obsolete or unsuitable for use in production or they may be stolen. Sometimes materials may appear to have gone missing when in reality it is the accounting records which are incorrect because a stores requisition note has been lost or an item has been allocated to the wrong product-cost record, or perhaps there is a calculation error on a stores list. It is always worthwhile to check the accuracy of the accounting records before assuming that materials have disappeared.

For the management accountant the loss of materials creates another cost problem. The cost must be charged somewhere in the system but it cannot appear as a direct cost because the materials never reached the production department. The cost of wastage therefore has to be noted as a separate indirect materials cost, to be spread over the cost of all products. If any cash can be recovered by selling as scrap some obsolete or damaged materials, then the proceeds of sale may be recorded as reducing the overall cost of wastage.

18.2.4   Cost classification and materials costs

The cost classification system is required to show whether costs are **direct** or **indirect** and whether they are **fixed** or **variable**.

How are direct and indirect materials costs distinguished?

The earlier description of materials costing procedures has shown how multiplying unit price by the quantity of materials used will give a measure of cost, although there may need to be a choice of unit price to be applied (see section 18.2.2). Materials issued to production are usually made available on the basis of a stores requisition, so there should be no problem in identifying direct materials costs for the job in question.

Some materials costs may be spread over a range of products and activities, each of which must take a share. The case of wastage before the materials are issued to production has already been discussed. Other examples would include transportation costs and all the costs of receiving, issuing and handling stores (such as the storekeeper's wages). It is preferable to record materials costs as direct costs, identified with the job, wherever possible. On the other hand, the cost of spending time on keeping records must be weighed against more productive uses of that time.

How are fixed and variable materials costs distinguished?

Most materials costs will be **variable** costs, irrespective of whether they are direct or indirect so far as the job is concerned. If output is not being achieved, then materials will not be used and will be held in store for use in a future period.

To be a **fixed cost**, the materials would have to be required for use in a period irrespective of whether or not production takes place. That is an unlikely situation in most business operations.

Activity 18.2

You have been employed as a storekeeper at a superstore selling vehicle accessories. Write down the main procedures you would carry out to ensure that:

- *the materials in store are held securely;*
- *the accounting records of inventory (stock) are accurate; and*
- *the materials are issued only to authorised persons.*

18.3 Accounting for labour costs

The cost of any resource used in a business is the product of the amount of resource used and the price per unit of the resource. For the resource of labour, the amount of resource is usually measured in terms of hours worked and the price is usually expressed as a rate paid per hour.

18.3.1 Types of pay scheme

The first problem which the management accountant meets in dealing with labour costs is that different employees are on different pay schemes. Some employees receive a monthly salary, paid at the end of the month worked. They are expected to work whatever number of hours is necessary to complete the tasks assigned to them. This type of remuneration is most commonly found in the case of administrative staff where the emphasis is on undertaking tasks which are necessary to the overall duties and responsibilities of the post. Other employees receive a basic salary per week, or per month, which is augmented by extra payments depending on output levels or targets achieved. This type of pay scheme has a 'loyalty' element in the basic salary together with a reward for effort in the output-related extra payments. Other employees may be paid an hourly rate based on actual hours worked, receiving no payment where no hours are worked. Finally, there may be some employees paid on a piecework basis, receiving a fixed amount for every item produced, regardless of time taken. To add to the problem, there may be labour costs of the business which are not paid to the employee in the form of wages or salary. These would include the provision of a car, free medical insurance, clothing allowances, rent allowances, relocation and disruption payments, inducements to join the company and lump sum payments on leaving the company. There are also the employer's labour costs, such as employer's contributions to National Insurance, which are part of the total labour cost as far as the business is concerned.

18.3.2 Determining the labour cost in an item of output

The differences outlined in section 18.3.1 all add to the problems of the management accountant in converting the variety of schemes to a uniform basis for costing purposes. Usually, calculating a rate per hour is sufficient to provide such a uniform basis, provided the number of hours worked is known. The cost of labour used on any job may then be determined by multiplying the hourly cost by the number of hours worked.

18.3.3 Cost classification and labour costs

The classification system is concerned with whether costs are **direct** or **indirect** and whether they are **fixed** or **variable**.

How are direct and indirect labour costs distinguished?

Multiplying unit cost by the number of hours worked is fine provided there is a time record and provided that time can be allocated exclusively to one product at a time. In some businesses it might be feasible to keep track of specialist labour time spent on each product. This part of the labour cost is regarded as the direct cost.

Some labour costs may never be allocated directly to a specific job because they are spread over a range of jobs and activities, each of which must take a share (e.g. supervisor's salary, cleaner's wages, or non-productive time when skilled employees are not able to work because equipment needs attention). This part of the labour cost is called indirect cost. Indirect labour costs also include holiday pay, bonus payments and overtime pay. That gives the management accountant a further problem in deciding on a fair basis of apportionment of indirect labour costs. Apportionment of indirect costs will be dealt with in section 18.5 on production overhead costs.

How are fixed and variable labour costs distinguished?

One quite difficult question with labour costs is to decide whether they are **fixed** or **variable** costs. If the employee is on a contract which provides a fixed basic salary, then the total salary is a fixed cost for the organisation. The employee will then spend time on producing output and that amount of time will vary depending on the level of output. Thus the *direct* labour cost attributable to that employee will be a **variable** cost, depending on level of output. The remaining time, when the employee is not producing output, will be classed as an *indirect* cost of non-productive labour.

18.3.4 Recording labour costs

The system for recording labour costs must be capable of dealing with the payroll aspects (keeping track of how much is paid to each employee) and with the cost allocation aspect of tracing those payroll costs, together with other labour costs, to the products of the business. That in turn requires a careful recording of the total time worked by the employees each week, analysed into the time spent on each product and the amount of non-productive time.

Direct labour costs will be calculated using hours worked and the hourly rate for each employee. The hours worked will be collected from employee time sheets which show the time spent on each product unit. Hourly rates for each employee will be available from personnel records, based on the cost of employing that particular person.

In practice, it is likely that costing records will be kept by computer, with employees entering data online.

Activity 18.3	*You are employed in the personnel department of a large organisation. Explain how the records kept by the personnel department would be useful to the accounting department in preparing the monthly payroll.*

18.4 Production overheads: traditional approach

Production overhead was defined in Chapter 17 as comprising **indirect materials**, **indirect labour** and other **indirect costs** of production. Indirect materials and indirect labour have been explained earlier in this chapter. Other indirect costs will include any item which relates to production and which is not a materials cost or a labour cost. The type of **indirect cost** will depend on the nature of the business and, in particular, on whether it is a manufacturing business or a service business. Examples are:

● In a manufacturing business: repair of machinery; rent of factory buildings; and safety procedures.
● In a service business: cost of transport to jobs; replacement of tools; and protective clothing.

Whatever their nature, all the production overhead costs have to be **absorbed** into the products.

Normally the management accountant has to devise a scheme of **allocation** and **apportionment**. There are some essential features for any successful scheme. It must be:

● fair to all parties involved in the process of allocation and apportionment;
● representative of the benefit each party gains from the shared cost;
● relatively quick to apply so that provision of information is not delayed;
● understandable by all concerned.

This chapter will use arithmetically simple models for illustrative purposes, although the mechanism for apportionment does not have to be arithmetically simple provided a computer can be used.

The process to be described here has three stages:

1 **allocating** and **apportioning** indirect costs to cost centres;
2 **apportioning** service department costs over production cost centres;
3 **absorbing** costs into products.

Definitions

Allocate means to assign a whole item of cost, or of revenue, to a single cost unit, centre, account or time period.

Apportion means to spread costs over two or more cost units, centres, accounts or time periods. (It is referred to by some books as 'indirect allocation'.)

Absorb means to attach overhead costs to products or services.

Allocation, apportionment and absorption in job costing

- Direct materials are **allocated** to products.
- Direct labour costs are **allocated** to products.
- Indirect materials costs and indirect labour costs are **allocated** and **apportioned** to cost centres.
- Total indirect costs of service cost centres are **apportioned** over production cost centres.
- Total overhead costs of production cost centres are absorbed into products.[1]

Figure 18.3 provides a diagram to show the three stages in the flow of indirect costs. The calculations are explained in detail in section 18.4.4.

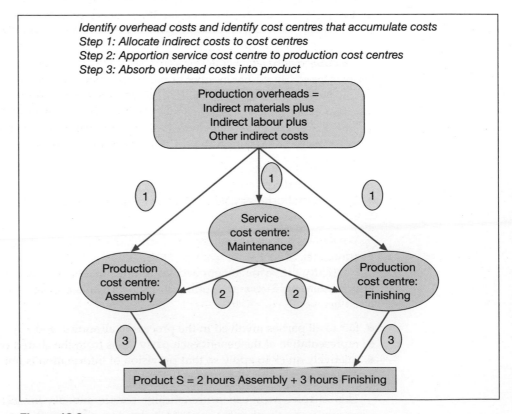

Figure 18.3
Traditional approach to the flow of overhead costs

18.4.1   Allocating and apportioning indirect costs to cost centres

There are two main types of cost centre in any business, namely service cost centres and production cost centres. The **production cost centres** are those directly involved in the production activity. The **service cost centres** are not directly involved in the production activity but provide essential backup. To sustain long-term profitability, the products of the business must sell at a price which makes a profit after covering the costs of the service cost centres as well as those of the production cost centres.

The management accountant will first of all divide the overhead costs into two categories: those which may be **allocated** as a whole to each cost centre, and those which have to be **apportioned** (or shared) over a number of cost centres according to how the cost centres benefit from the cost incurred. Exhibit 18.3 sets out some common methods of **apportionment** where costs are regarded as **indirect** so far as each cost centre is concerned.

Exhibit 18.3
Examples of methods of apportionment of costs over cost centres

Cost item	Method of apportionment over cost centres
Rent of building	Floor area of each cost centre
Lighting	Floor area of each cost centre
Power for machines	Number of machines in each cost centre
Production supervisor's salary	Number of employees in each cost centre
Canteen costs	Number of employees in each cost centre
Depreciation and insurance of machinery	Value of machinery in each cost centre

If the records were sufficiently detailed, then most of the costs in Exhibit 18.3 could be turned into items of cost which could be allocated as a whole to each cost centre, avoiding the need for apportionment. Electricity meters could be installed in each cost centre to measure directly the cost of heating and lighting. Employees could be given tickets for the canteen which could be collected and recorded for each cost centre. The production supervisor could keep a diary of time spent in each cost centre. Depreciation could be calculated for each machine. The insurance company could be asked to quote a separate premium for each machine. However, all these procedures would in themselves create a new cost of administration which the business might decide was too high a price to pay for a marginal improvement in the accuracy of allocation of costs.

18.4.2   Apportioning service department costs over production cost centres

As explained earlier, **service cost centres** exist to support production but do not make a direct contribution to the product. Once the costs of the organisation have been channelled into the various cost centres, they must be apportioned from service cost centres over production cost centres. The essential features remain the same, namely that the method chosen must be:

- fair to all parties involved in the process of apportionment;
- representative of the benefit each party gains from the shared cost;
- relatively quick to apply so that provision of information is not delayed;
- understandable by all concerned.

Exhibit 18.4 sets out the titles of some service cost centres and gives examples of some methods by which their costs could be apportioned over production cost centres.

Exhibit 18.4

Examples of methods of apportioning total costs of service cost centres across production cost centres

Service cost centre	Method of apportionment over production cost centres
Maintenance department	Number of machines in each cost centre
Employees' restaurant and coffee bar	Number of employees in each cost centre
Stores department	Total value of stores requisitions from each cost centre
Finished goods quality inspection	Value of goods produced by each cost centre
Safety inspectors	Number of employees in each cost centre

18.4.3 Absorbing overhead costs into products

You have now reached the final stage of the process where all the overhead costs are collected in the **production cost centres**, ready to be **absorbed** into products. The essential features, as before, are that the method must be:

- fair to all parties involved in the process of absorption;
- representative of the benefit each party gains from the shared cost;
- relatively quick to apply so that provision of information is not delayed;
- understandable by all concerned.

To absorb a fair share of overhead into each product, the method must make use of the best measure of work done on a product. The best measure is usually labour hours or machine hours, depending on whether the production process is labour intensive or machinery intensive.

Direct labour hours are frequently used because overhead cost is incurred when people are working. The longer they work, the more overhead is incurred.

Sometimes direct labour hours are not the best measure of work performed. In a machinery-intensive environment, machine hours may be preferred to labour hours as a basis for absorbing overhead.

There are occasions when the direct labour hours worked on a job are not known because they are not recorded. In such circumstances a cost per £ of direct labour could be applied. This is acceptable but has a disadvantage in that a change in the labour rate could affect the amount of labour cost and hence the allocation of overhead.

Where all products are identical, a cost per unit would be sufficient. However, in a job-costing system such identical products are unlikely.

In summary, four possible methods of absorbing overhead costs into products are:

1 cost per direct labour hour;
2 cost per machine hour;
3 cost per £ of labour cost;
4 cost per unit.

18.4.4 Illustration

This section provides an illustration of the **allocation** and **apportionment** of overhead costs and shows how the overhead cost is absorbed into products. Kitchen Units Company assembles and finishes kitchen units to customers' orders. Assembly involves creating the basic units, while Finishing involves adding the laminated surfaces and interior fittings as specified by the customer. The machinery and tools required for the work are kept in working order by a Maintenance department. The Assembly and Finishing departments are *production departments* because they both do work on the product. The Maintenance department is a *service department* because it helps the work of the production departments but does not deal directly with the product. The illustration shows how the overhead costs of one month are **allocated** and **apportioned**, and then **absorbs** the costs into Product S, a kitchen unit which spends two hours in Assembly and three hours in Finishing. It follows the sequence of Figure 18.3, earlier.

A calculation of an overhead cost rate might be set out as in Exhibit 18.5, which shows a statement of overhead cost rate for an organisation having two production cost centres, the Assembly Department and the Finishing Department, and one service cost centre, the Maintenance Department. In Exhibit 18.5, the indirect costs incurred by the business are set out in Table 18.1. These costs relate to some or all of the three departments and must be shared among them on a fair basis. Table 18.2 sets out information about each department which will be helpful in this fair sharing. The remaining tables of Exhibit 18.5 show the sharing process, step by step.

Exhibit 18.5
Illustration of the calculation of an overhead cost rate

Table 18.1 sets out the indirect costs incurred by the business on behalf of all departments taken together. The costs must be apportioned (shared) over the departments because there is insufficient information to permit allocation of costs as a whole. Table 18.2 sets out relevant information about each department which will be used in the process of determining an overhead cost rate.

Table 18.1
Indirect costs incurred by the business

Cost item	Total cost this month
	£
Indirect materials	36,000
Indirect labour	40,000
Rent	1,000
Insurance	1,600
Depreciation	2,000
Total	80,600

Table 18.2
Information about each department

	Assembly	Finishing	Maintenance
Direct materials used for production	£400,000	£500,000	not applicable
Number of employees	10	25	5
Floor area	100 sq m	200 sq m	100 sq m
Value of machinery	£30,000	£50,000	£20,000
Number of direct labour hours worked on production	55,000	64,000	not applicable

Exhibit 18.5 continued

There are four steps in calculating the overhead cost to be allocated to each product.

Step 1: Apportioning costs over departments, using a suitable method for each cost

In Table 18.3, each of the cost items contained in Table 18.1 is shared across the three departments on an appropriate basis chosen from Table 18.2.

Table 18.3
Apportioning (sharing) cost items over the three departments

	Total	Assembly	Finishing	Maintenance
	£	£	£	£
Indirect materials*	36,000	16,000	20,000	nil
Indirect labour†	40,000	10,000	25,000	5,000
Rent‡	1,000	250	500	250
Insurance§	1,600	480	800	320
Depreciation¶	2,000	600	1,000	400
Total	80,600	27,330	47,300	5,970

Notes

* The cost of indirect materials is likely to be dependent on direct materials so the proportions applied in sharing out the indirect materials costs are 4:5. The direct materials are used only in Assembly and Finishing, so the indirect materials will relate only to these two departments.

† The cost of indirect labour is likely to be dependent on the total number of employees working in the organisation, so the proportions applied in sharing out the indirect labour costs are 10:25:5.

‡ Rent costs may be shared out on the basis of floor space occupied by each department, in the proportions 1:2:1.

§,¶ Insurance and depreciation may both be shared out by reference to the value of the machinery used in each department, in the proportions 3:5:2.

Step 2: Apportioning service department costs to production departments on the basis of value of machines in each department

The maintenance department provides service in proportion to the machinery used in each department, so it is appropriate to share out the maintenance costs on the basis of value of machinery in Assembly and in Finishing, in the proportions 30,000:50,000:

$$\frac{30,000}{80,000} \times 5,970 = 2,239$$

$$\frac{50,000}{80,000} \times 5,970 = 3,731$$

Table 18.4
Apportioning (sharing) of maintenance costs between Assembly and Finishing

	Total	Assembly	Finishing	Maintenance
	£	£	£	£
Total cost per dept (from Table 18.3)	80,600	27,330	47,300	5,970
Transfer maintenance costs to Assembly and Finishing		2,239	3,731	(5,970)
Total per department	80,600	29,569	51,031	nil

Step 3: Absorbing total overhead costs of each production department into units produced during the period

Dividing the total cost of each department by the number of direct labour hours, we obtain the following overhead cost rates:

> Assembly: £29,569/55,000 hours = 53.76 pence per direct labour hour
> Finishing: £51,031/64,000 hours = 79.74 pence per direct labour hour

Step 4: Finding the overhead costs of any product

Now the overhead cost rate may be used to determine how much overhead cost should be absorbed by (charged to) each product. The answer will depend on the number of direct labour hours required in each production department, for any product. Take as an example product S, which spends two hours in the Assembly department and three hours in the Finishing department. The overhead cost allocated to product S is calculated as follows:

Table 18.5
Example of absorbing overhead cost into Product S

Department	Calculation	£
Assembly	53.76 pence × 2 hours	1.075
Finishing	79.74 pence × 3 hours	2.392
Total overhead cost		3.467

That's all there is to it. The process of allocation, apportionment and absorption of production overheads takes time because every cost has to be traced through to the product, but it is systematic in that all costs eventually find their way through to a product.

Activity 18.4

Return to the start of Exhibit 18.5 and try to work the example for yourself. It is very important for later chapters that you understand the purpose of Exhibit 18.5 and the method of calculation used. There are some features of the tables in Exhibit 18.5 which are worth noting for future reference. First, it is important to keep totals for each column of figures and a total of all the column totals in order to ensure that there are no arithmetic errors that result in costs appearing from nowhere or disappearing to oblivion. Second, it is important to show working notes at all times because there are so many variations of possible method that the person who reads your calculations will need the working notes to understand the method chosen.

18.4.5   Predetermined overhead cost rates

This chapter has explained methods by which *actual* overhead cost for a period may be absorbed into jobs. However, the calculation of overhead cost rates based on the actual overhead costs incurred during the period means that job cost calculations have to be postponed until the end of the period, because the overhead cost cannot be obtained before that time. This creates practical problems where timely information on job costs is essential if it is to be used for estimating the value of work in progress or calculating monthly profit. As a result of this demand for information before the actual costs are known, many businesses will use **predetermined overhead cost rates**, estimated before the start of a reporting period. This rate will then be applied to all output of the period. At the end of the period, when the actual overhead is known, there will be an adjustment to bring the estimated overhead cost into line with the actual overhead cost.

Estimating the predetermined overhead rate

How does a manager make the estimate of the predetermined overhead cost rate? It could be based on the known overhead costs of previous periods. It could be a 'best guess' of what will happen in the forecast period. The predetermined overhead cost rate is then applied to the output of the period. This is also described as **overhead cost recovery** because the cost will be 'recovered' when the output is completed and sold.

Estimates abound in accounting and part of the reporting process involves explaining why the actual out-turn did, or did not, match up to the estimate. Chapter 23 will introduce the techniques of standard costing and variance analysis, which provide a formal means of analysing and investigating differences between estimated and actual amounts. Provided the estimation process is carried out with care, the benefits of using predetermined overhead costs, in terms of having information early rather than late, by far outweigh the possible negative aspects of having to explain differences between estimated and actual overhead costs charged to products.

Exhibit 18.6 gives the information necessary to calculate a **predetermined overhead cost rate**. The steps of the calculation are then described.

Exhibit 18.6
Calculating a predetermined fixed overhead cost rate

Estimated direct labour hours for normal activity	10,000 hours
Estimated fixed overhead cost in total	£50,000
Predetermined overhead cost rate	£5 per direct labour hour

Step 1

The accounting period is one month. Before the start of the month, the manager estimates that there will be 10,000 labour hours worked, under normal activity conditions, and that fixed overhead of £50,000 will be incurred.

Step 2

The manager calculates the predetermined fixed overhead cost rate as £5 per labour hour (= £50,000/10,000).

Step 3

Throughout the reporting period, as work is done, the manager applies £5 of fixed overhead for every labour hour of each item of output from the business. If exactly 10,000 hours of work are carried out then each item of output will carry its fair share of the overhead. The process of **overhead cost recovery** is complete.

18.4.6 Under-recovery and over-recovery of overheads

The calculations of overhead cost recovery are not always as neat and tidy as in section 18.4.5. This section explains how under-recovery and over-recovery can occur.

Under-recovered overhead: underestimating hours worked

Supposing things do not work out as planned in section 18.4.5. The manager finds out at the end of the month that only 8,000 hours were actually worked. In Step 3, fixed overhead of £5 will be charged to jobs for each hour worked, so £40,000 will be charged in total. We can also say that there is **recovery** of £40,000. At the end of the month the manager confirms that the cash book shows the **actual overhead cost** incurred is £50,000, corresponding exactly to the estimated amount. The manager has a total fixed overhead cost of £40,000 **recovered** (charged to jobs) but an actual cost of £50,000 as an expense for the financial profit and loss account. The fixed overhead cost recorded on the job records is said to be **under-recovered**. In the management accounting profit and loss account the fixed overhead element of the cost of goods sold is recorded at £40,000 using the predetermined rate, and a separate cost of £10,000 is recorded as **under-recovered fixed overhead**, so that the total fixed overhead expense of the month equals £50,000.

Under-recovered overhead: underestimating overhead cost

Suppose that the actual hours worked do match the expected hours, so that in Step 3 there is **recovery** of the full amount of £50,000 (based on 10,000 hours at £5 per hour). However, when the manager checks the cash book, it shows that the actual overhead cost of the month is £55,000 due to an unforeseen rise in fixed service charges. The fixed overhead cost recorded on the job records is again said to be **under-recovered**. In the management accounting profit and loss account the fixed overhead element of the cost of goods sold is recorded at £50,000 using the predetermined rate, and a separate cost of £5,000 is recorded as **under-recovered fixed overhead**, so that the total fixed overhead expense of the month equals £55,000.

Definition

> **Under-recovered fixed overhead** occurs when the overhead cost recovered (applied), using a predetermined overhead cost rate, is less than the actual overhead cost of the period. This may be because the actual hours worked are less than the estimate made in advance, or it may be because the actual overhead cost incurred is greater than the estimate of the overhead cost.

Over-recovered overhead: underestimating hours worked

Now suppose an alternative picture. The manager finds out at the end of the month that 11,000 hours were actually worked. In Step 3, fixed overhead of £5 will be charged to jobs for each hour worked, so £55,000 will be charged in total. We can also say that there is **recovery** of £55,000. At the end of the month the manager also confirms that the cash book shows the actual overhead cost incurred is £50,000, corresponding exactly to the estimated amount. The manager has a total fixed overhead cost of £55,000 recovered (charged to jobs) but an actual cost of £50,000 as an expense for the financial profit and loss account. The fixed overhead cost recorded on the job records is said to be **over-recovered**. In the management accounting profit and loss account the fixed overhead element of the cost of goods sold is recorded at £55,000 using the predetermined rate, and a separate reduction in cost of £5,000 is recorded as **over-recovered fixed overhead**, so that the total fixed overhead expense of the month equals £50,000.

Over-recovered overhead: overestimating overhead cost

Suppose that the actual hours worked do match the expected hours, so that in Step 3 there is **recovery** of the full amount of £50,000 (based on 10,000 hours at £5 per hour). However, when the manager checks the cash book, it shows that the actual overhead cost of the month is £48,000 due to an unexpected rebate of charges for heating. The fixed overhead cost recorded on the job records is again said to be **over-recovered**. In the management accounting profit and loss account the fixed overhead element of the cost of goods sold is recorded at £50,000 using the predetermined rate, and a separate reduction in cost of £2,000 is recorded as **over-recovered fixed overhead**, so that the total fixed overhead expense of the month equals £48,000.

Definition

> **Over-recovered fixed overhead** occurs when the overhead recovered (applied), using a predetermined overhead cost rate, is greater than the actual overhead cost of the period. This may be because the actual hours worked are greater than the estimate made in advance, or it may be because the actual overhead cost incurred is less than the estimate of the overhead cost.

Effect on profit

If there is **over-recovered fixed overhead** then too much cost is charged in the management accounts, when compared to the actual cost incurred. The management accounting profit will be too low. To restore the profit to the actual level achieved, the over-recovery must be deducted from the cost charged.

If there is **under-recovered fixed overhead** then too little cost is charged in the management accounts, when compared to the actual cost incurred. The management accounting profit will be too high. To restore the profit to the actual level achieved, the under-recovery must be added to the cost charged.

18.4.7 More questions about overhead cost rates

Overhead cost is one of those topics which make you want to ask a new question every time you have an answer to the previous question. Here are some of the questions which might have occurred to you in thinking about overhead cost rates:

- Is it necessary to have an overhead cost rate for each cost centre or could there be one rate to cover all production?
- How is it possible to calculate an overhead cost rate per direct labour hour for fixed overhead costs, when these do not vary with direct labour hours?
- What is the best way of ensuring that the process of allocation, apportionment and absorption of costs most closely represents the behaviour of those costs?

The answers to all these questions will be found in thinking about the four conditions for determining a suitable overhead cost rate:

1 fair to all parties involved in the process;
2 representative of the benefit each party gains from the shared cost;
3 relatively quick to apply so that provision of information is not delayed;
4 understandable by all concerned.

The answers are therefore as follows.

Is it necessary to have an overhead cost rate for each cost centre or could there be one rate to cover all production?

If there is a wide product range and products spend different amounts of time in different cost centres, it would be undesirable to have one rate to cover all production because that single rate would average out the time spent in the different departments. Thus it is said that 'blanket overhead cost rates' or 'plant-wide rates' should be avoided where possible, or used with great caution. The overhead cost rate to use will be one which can be used with confidence that it meets the four conditions stated earlier.

How is it possible to calculate an overhead cost rate per direct labour hour for fixed overhead costs when, by definition, fixed costs do not vary with direct labour hours?

This question is more difficult to answer and the best starting point is a reminder that accounting is often based on estimates. The fixed overhead costs will have to be absorbed into products eventually. However, this can only be achieved accurately after production is completed. Job cost estimation cannot always wait that long. Therefore, a predetermined fixed overhead cost rate is applied to each job on the basis of some measure of work done, such as direct labour hours. If the estimating process is accurate, the estimated hours to be worked will equal the actual hours worked and there will be no problem. If the actual hours are greater than, or less than, the estimate, then there will be a difference, referred to as overapplied or underapplied fixed overhead. Exhibit 18.6 has set out an illustration of underapplied fixed overhead.

What is the best way of ensuring that the process of absorbing costs into products most closely represents the behaviour of those costs?

This question has aroused considerable excitement in management accounting circles in recent years, as some thinking people realised that too much time had been spent in reading books and theorising. Researchers had omitted to find out whether the actual practice of management accounting was so bad after all. They therefore went out to look, and found that some practical management accountants were having some very good ideas but that those ideas were not finding their way into books.

As a result of those investigations, many articles and books have been written on the importance of *cost drivers*, which are the events that are significant determinants of the cost of an activity. If an oil company has an offshore platform where the supervisor is constantly calling up the helicopter for unplanned visits ashore, the total transport cost for the oil company will rise. The helicopter flight is the cost driver and the platform supervisor needs to be aware that the flight cost is part of the cost of running the platform. If a stores department is receiving frequent deliveries of small quantities, the cost driver for the stores department is the number of deliveries. Cost drivers are not an earth-shattering discovery in themselves, but they have been built into a description of activity-based costing (ABC) which you will find in section 18.5. Activity-based costing has led many companies to re-examine their approach to allocating overhead costs to products, based on finding a method which most closely models the factors driving the cost.

18.5 Activity-based costing (ABC) for production overheads

ABC is a relatively new approach to assigning overhead costs to products. The proponents of the subject claim that ABC provides product cost information which is useful for decision making. The claims of ABC will be explored in this chapter by outlining the principles and then examining a case study.

Definition

> **Activity-based costing** (ABC) traces **overhead costs** to products by focusing on the **activities** that drive costs (cause costs to occur).

There are five stages to establishing an activity-based costing system. These are:

1 Identify the major activities which take place in an organisation.
2 Identify the factors which most closely influence the cost of an activity. These factors are called the **cost drivers** and are a direct indication of how the activity demands cost.
3 Create a cost pool for each activity and trace costs to cost pools.
4 Calculate a **cost driver rate** as the total costs in a **cost pool** divided by the number of times that the **activity** occurs.
5 **Allocate costs** to products using the demand for each **activity**.

See Figure 18.4 which shows the costs flowing through cost pools to the product.

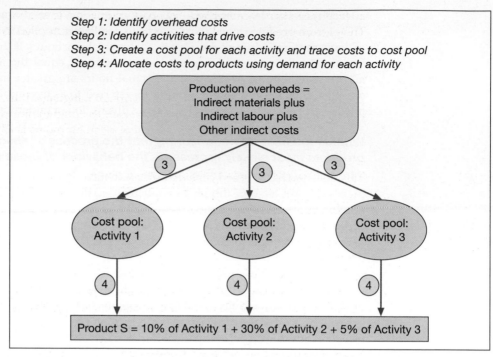

Figure 18.4
Activity-based approach to the flow of overhead costs

18.5.1 Reasons for the development of ABC[2]

In the 1980s Professors Cooper and Kaplan in the USA found the focus on activities and cost drivers in some large US manufacturing businesses which had become dissatisfied with the traditional approach to overhead costing. Cooper and Kaplan wrote up their observations as case studies at Harvard University and then published papers on their findings. The cause of change was that business organisations were changing their nature at the time, with an increase in indirect costs related to changes in processes, new ways of dealing with customers and new investment in more sophisticated operating systems. There was a swing from variable to fixed overhead costs. Labour resources were replaced to some extent by automation. It became apparent that production volumes were no longer the main drivers of overhead costs. Organisations were looking for a costing system that would be more realistic in tracking the consumption of resources that gives rise to cost.

18.5.2 Nature of an activity

An **activity**, in its broadest sense, is something which happens in the business. An activity could be using materials to make a physical product or using labour to carry out a service operation. In ABC language, that would be an example of a **unit activity**, which is performed each time a product is produced. Other activities are performed to enable output of products but are not so closely dependent on how many units are produced. These are called **product-sustaining activities**. Examples would be product design, product testing and marketing. Some activities are classified as **batch-related activities** which are fixed for a given batch of products. This would include costs of the buying department, costs of moving stores from the warehouse to the factory floor, and costs of planning a production schedule. Where there are expenses such as rent or insurance which are not driven by making products, they are designated as **facility-sustaining activities** and no attempt is made to allocate these to products. They are charged as a total cost against all products after the separate profit margins on each product are determined.

Example 1

A language college teaches English as a Foreign Language. It has two departments: E (European mother tongue) and A (Asian mother tongue). Information about each is shown in Exhibit 18.7. The overhead cost of cleaning rooms is £32,000 per year.

Exhibit 18.7
Information for Example 1: departments E and A

Department	E	A
Number of teaching staff	12	18
Annual teaching labour cost	£600,000	£1,000,000
Number of rooms	18	16

The traditional method of allocating cleaning overhead cost to departments has been to apply a rate of 2% of the labour cost of teaching. This is shown in Exhibit 18.8.

Exhibit 18.8
Traditional treatment of cleaning overhead

	E	A
Overhead cost rate	2% of labour cost	2% of labour cost
Apportionment of cost £32,000	£12,000	£20,000

The head tutor of Department A feels this is unfair because it has fewer classrooms than Department E and so requires less cleaning effort.

Assume that cleaning cost may be regarded as a cost pool and show how activity-based costing can be applied where the number of classrooms is the cost driver for cleaning.

The apportionment of cost by the activity-based method is shown in Exhibit 18.9.

Exhibit 18.9
Activity-based costing for cleaning overhead

	E	A
Cost pool: Cleaning, £32,000		
Cost driver: Fraction of classroom usage	18/34	16/34
Apportionment of cost £32,000	£16,940	£15,060

Comment. The head of Department A will be happier with the use of **activity-based costing** because it reflects the lower usage of cleaning driven by fewer classrooms. On the other hand, it may be that this is not the best **cost driver**. For instance, suppose that the head of Department E responds by pointing out that their classrooms are kept tidy and are therefore easier to clean. The debate over **cost drivers** might take some time to resolve.

Example 2

In the office of a firm of solicitors and estate agents there are **overhead costs** incurred relating to the cost of office support for the staff preparing legal documentation. There are two departments preparing legal documentation. Department A has dealt with 15 property transactions having an average value of £100,000 each, while Department B has dealt with 5 property transactions having an average value of £1m each.

The total amount of the office overhead costs for the period is £100,000. The traditional approach to overhead cost has been to apportion the amount of £100,000 in proportion to the number of property deals dealt with by each department. They are now asking for an activity-based approach to costing, where the cost driver is the value of transactions in each department, because high-value transactions involve more work.

The traditional approach (see Exhibit 18.10) gives the same unit cost regardless of size of transaction.

Exhibit 18.10
Traditional treatment of cleaning overhead

	A	B
Cost pool: Office overhead, £100,000		
Cost driver: Number of transactions	15/20	5/20
Apportionment of cost £100,000	£75,000	£25,000
Cost per transaction	£5,000	£5,000

Comment. The **activity-based** approach (see Exhibit 18.11) puts much more of the **overhead cost** on to Department B because that one is driving more of the overheads. When the cost per transaction is calculated, the activity-based approach, based on value, loads the cost towards the high-value transaction and so produces a relatively higher cost per unit for these transactions.

Exhibit 18.11
Activity-based costing for office overhead

	A	B
Overhead cost rate	1,500/6,500	5,000/6,500
Apportionment of cost £100,000	100,000 × 1.5/6.5	100,000 × 5/6.5
	= £23,000	= £77,000
Cost per transaction	£1,530	£15,400

18.5.3 Role of the management accountant

Activity-based costing allows the attention-directing functions of the management accountant to come to the fore. The management accountant takes a key role in understanding the operation of the business and translating into cost terms the **activities** as perceived by those who carry them out.

Because **activity-based costing** requires a very thorough analysis of how products drive the costs of various activities, it is not feasible to work through a full illustration here. Instead, one activity, that of purchasing materials for use in a hotel restaurant, will be explored by case study in some detail. Hopefully, that will give you a flavour of the complexity and fascination of ABC and encourage you to read further.

18.5.4 Case study: Glen Lyon Hotel

The Glen Lyon Hotel has two main product lines, with quite different characteristics. In the restaurant, meals are provided on a daily basis to the chef's high standards of perfection. In the conference suite, banquets are arranged for special functions such as weddings. There is a restaurant manager, responsible for restaurant meals, and a functions manager, responsible for banquets. The hotel seeks to offer competitive prices subject to meeting all costs and earning an adequate profit.

The hotel has a purchasing department which purchases the food required by the hotel restaurant and all supplies required for special functions, including crockery and cutlery. The purchasing officer is concerned that the restaurant manager insists on buying food in relatively small quantities, because the chef is very particular about monitoring the continued high quality of supplies. The functions manager also creates problems for the purchasing department because she insists on buying crockery and cutlery in bulk, to save cost, which requires time being taken by the purchasing officer to negotiate the best terms with the supplier. Even the suppliers can create a great deal of work because they are constantly changing their prices and this has to be recorded on the computer system of the purchasing department. The purchasing officer would like to show that these activities are all costly because they drive the amount of work undertaken by the purchasing department.

Fiona McTaggart was called in to help, and she now explains how she went about the task of applying activity-based costing in relation to the activities of the purchasing department.

FIONA: *First of all I asked for a list of all the costs incurred by the department in a year (see Exhibit 18.12).*

Exhibit 18.12
List of costs incurred by resources used in the purchasing department

Resource cost	£
Salary of purchasing officer	15,000
Wages of data processing clerk	9,000
Telephone calls	3,000
Total costs to be allocated	27,000

Identifying the cost drivers

Then I sat down with the purchasing officer for a long meeting during which we talked about how the purchasing process worked. From those discussions I found that a number of activities were driving the work of purchasing and I listed all those (see Exhibit 18.13).

Exhibit 18.13
List of activities in the purchasing department

- Agreeing terms with supplier
- Processing an order
- Updating the price lists
- Updating the supplier records
- Processing queries about invoices.

I explained to the purchasing officer that, although the purchasing department was an identifiable unit of the organisation for staff management purposes, it would no longer be treated as a cost centre under activity-based costing. The purchasing process would be regarded as a set of activities consuming 'resources' such as salaries, wages and telephone calls. Each activity would collect a 'pool' of cost as the resources were used up. The pool of costs would be passed on to those other departments drawing on the services of the purchasing department and from those departments the costs would find their way into products.

Creating the cost pools

The next stage was to decide how much of each resource cost was attributable to the activity driving that cost. This part was quite tricky because the purchasing officer only had a 'feel' for the relative impact in some cases. Take as an example the processing of an order. When the restaurant manager asks for food to be ordered, the purchasing officer first has to phone the supplier to check availability and likely delivery time. Then she checks that someone will be available to open the cold store when the delivery arrives. She is then able to fax the order to the supplier who will phone back to confirm that the goods are available and that delivery will be as requested. Once the goods arrive, the purchasing officer has to check that the delivery note agrees with what was ordered. That whole process takes about 20 minutes for each order.

We carried on talking and I was able to identify, for each resource cost, some measure of how the activity was being driven. The starting point was salaries. We estimated that the purchasing officer spent the equivalent of two days per week agreeing terms with suppliers. The remaining three days were divided equally over the other activities listed. The data processing clerk spent three days per week in processing orders, half a day each week on updating price lists and updating suppliers' records, and one day per week on checking and processing questions from the accounts department about invoices received for payment. The final cost heading was telephone calls. The destination and duration of each call is logged by the telephone system so we took a sample of one week's calls and decided that 60% of telephone calls were routine calls to place an order, 20% were dealing with queries over price changes and the remainder were spread equally over agreeing terms, updating the supplier records and dealing with invoice queries. Following these discussions I sketched a diagram of the ABC approach (see Figure 18.5) and then drew up a table showing how each cost item could be allocated to the various activities so that a cost pool is created for each activity (see Exhibit 18.14).

Demand for each activity

The next stage was to determine how many times each activity driver was put into action. This involved measuring the volume of each activity, as a measure of the demand for that activity. Agreeing terms with the supplier is not easy to quantify, but we were aware that there are discussions with each supplier at some time during the year, so we took the number of suppliers as the measure of volume driving that activity. It was relatively easy to establish the number of orders processed at the request of the restaurant manager.

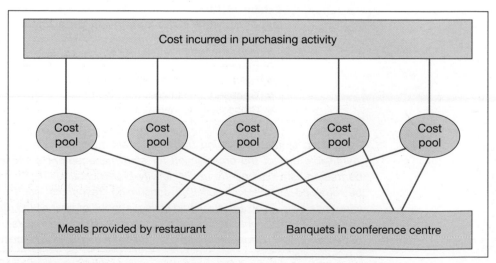

Figure 18.5
Sketch of the ABC approach applied to the activity of purchasing

Exhibit 18.14
Creating a cost pool: allocation of resource costs to activities

Resource	Resource cost	Activity cost pools				
		Agreeing terms with supplier	Processing an order	Updating the price list	Updating the supplier records	Process-ing invoice queries
	£	£	£	£	£	£
Salary	15,000	6,000	2,250	2,250	2,250	2,250
Wages	9,000		5,400	900	900	1,800
Telephone	3,000	200	1,800	600	200	200
	27,000	6,200	9,450	3,750	3,350	4,250

The price list has to be updated every time the supplier changes the price of any items, and they all change at least twice per month, so we decided that the number of items on the order list was a reasonable measure. Updating supplier records involves changing minor details for existing suppliers but takes more time to record a new supplier. So we used the number of new suppliers as the measure of the volume of that activity. Processing invoice queries depends on the number of such queries.

Cost driver rates

My final accounting statement was a calculation of the cost per activity unit for each activity (see Exhibit 18.15). This was determined by dividing the cost in the pool by the measure of how that activity was being driven by products.

Using the calculation of cost per activity unit for each activity I was able to explain the benefits of activity-based costing. The purchasing department is providing a service to the rest of the organisation, but at a cost. That cost could be made more visible using activity-based costing because the factors driving the cost could be quantified in their effect. Looking at Exhibit 18.15, it is not difficult to see that the most significant cost drivers are the activities of agreeing terms with suppliers and of updating the suppliers' records. Each new supplier causes a further £159.166 (£103.333 + £ 55.833) to be incurred at an early stage. The restaurant manager needs to be aware that placing large numbers of low-volume orders causes cost to be incurred on each order. The total cost incurred could be reduced

Exhibit 18.15
Calculation of cost per activity unit for each activity

		Activity cost pools				
		Agreeing terms with supplier	Processing an order	Updating the price list	Updating the supplier records	Processing invoice queries
Cost per Exhibit 18.14		£6,200	£9,450	£3,750	£3,350	£4,250
Activity driver		Number of suppliers	Number of orders	Number of items listed	Number of suppliers updated	Number of queries
Activity volume		60	1,600	7,000	60	150
Cost per activity unit		£103.333	£5.906	£0.536	£55.833	£28.333

by moving to a lower number of orders, each being of higher volume. (Someone would need to check that that did not create larger new costs in storage of the goods.) The next most costly activity, in terms of cost per unit, is that of answering queries about invoices. The accounts department should be made aware that each enquiry costs £28.333.

I also looked back to the old way of allocating the cost of the purchasing department (see Exhibit 18.16). Before activity-based costing was considered, the organisation charged the purchasing costs to products as a percentage of the value of materials ordered. Looking back to Exhibit 18.14, the total purchasing department costs are shown as £27,000. The purchasing department handles goods to the value of £800,000 in a year. The purchasing department costs were therefore charged to products at 3.375% of cost.

Exhibit 18.16
Previous methods of allocation, based on percentage of value of items requested

	Restaurant manager	Functions manager	Accounts department
	£	£	£
Goods purchased through purchasing department	300,000	500,000	–
3.375% of goods purchased	10,125	16,875	nil

Note: Allocation base equals 3.375% of goods purchased.

Why was this not the best approach? The answer is that there were two main product lines, having quite different characteristics. One was restaurant meals provided on a routine basis and the other was special banquets for functions such as weddings. My further enquiries revealed that the high-price purchases required for special functions caused relatively few problems in agreeing terms with suppliers and relatively few queries arose over the invoices. Where problems of negotiation and invoicing did arise was in the low-price, high-volume ingredients used routinely in the dining room meals. The information on cost per unit of each activity allowed a much more precise allocation of cost, although I was now in for even more work in tracing the costs from the various activity pools through to the products.

Tracing costs through to products

To trace costs through to products I obtained estimates of the quantity of each activity demanded by the restaurant manager and the function manager (see Exhibit 18.17) and multiplied each quantity by the cost per activity unit calculated in Exhibit 18.15. The result is shown in Exhibit 18.18.

Compare this with the cost allocation under the traditional system which is shown in Exhibit 18.16.

Exhibit 18.17
Quantity of activity demanded by each function

Activity	Demanded by restaurant manager	Demanded by functions manager
Agreeing terms with supplier	10 new suppliers	50 new suppliers
Processing an order	1,200 orders	400 orders
Updating the price list	4,000 items	3,000 items
Updating the supplier records	10 new suppliers	50 new suppliers
Processing invoice queries	All 150 demanded by accounts department	

Exhibit 18.18

Allocation of purchasing cost to restaurant manager, functions manager and accounts department

Activity	Restaurant manager	Functions manager	Accounts department	Total
	£	£	£	£
Agreeing terms with supplier	1,033	5,167		6,200
Processing an order	7,088	2,362		9,450
Updating the price list	2,143	1,607		3,750
Updating the supplier records	558	2,792		3,350
Processing invoice queries			4,250	4,250
Total cost allocated	10,822	11,928	4,250	27,000

My conclusions were that the accounts department had previously been unaware of the costs it was causing the purchasing manager whenever an invoice query was raised. Using activity-based costing would allow the allocation of cost to the accounts department each time a question was raised. Some care might need to be taken to examine the size and significance of the invoice query in relation to the cost allocation. It would not be a good idea for the accounts department to allow a £50,000 error to go unchecked because they feared a charge of £28.33. The implementation of activity-based costing might need to be accompanied by the use of performance measures which show how the benefits of an activity exceed the costs incurred.

The functions manager would incur less overhead cost under the activity-based system than under the previous approach. The recorded cost of functions would therefore decrease. As I explained earlier, the high-priced purchases of food for special functions cause relatively few problems in processing a smaller number of orders. The functions manager seems to have a relatively high number of new suppliers. Cost could be controlled further if fewer suppliers were used for functions. Less purchasing effort would be required.

The restaurant manager experiences little difference in cost under either approach. To improve overhead costs there would need to be a quantum leap in practice, such as reducing the order frequency to the stage where one less person was employed in the purchasing department, or else where a part-time employee could do the work presently undertaken full-time. Merely reducing the order frequency would not be enough if the purchasing staff are still present full-time and the same cost is being spread over a lower volume of activity. Although there is little impact, these figures give the restaurant manager food for thought.

Product costs

In the full application of ABC, the costs would be taken into the final product cost. I have not done that here because the purchasing department's costs are only one small corner of the total business. Activity-based costing creates a lot of work, but a well-coded computerised accounting system can handle that. I spent the best part of one day dealing only with the analysis of the purchasing department costs, so it would take a few weeks of consultancy to cover the entire range of activities which contribute to the cost of the products. My consultancy fees would be another overhead to be allocated, but I believe the hotel would find the effort well worth it in terms of more effective management over a period of years.

Activity 18.5

Imagine you are the owner of a business which rents ice-cream stalls from the local council. You employ people to run each stall. Write down a list of the costs you would expect to incur. Write another list of the drivers of cost. How could activity-based costing help you understand and control the costs of your business?

18.6 Comparing the traditional approach and ABC

18.6.1 Contrasting treatments

Allocating direct costs to products is not a problem. The particular need for activity-based costing lies in the area of absorbing overhead costs into products. The traditional approach to absorbing overhead costs to products was explained in section 18.4. In that section it was shown that, traditionally, costs are first allocated and apportioned to cost centres and then absorbed into products which pass through those cost centres. Activity-based costing follows a different approach to channelling costs towards products. Exhibit 18.19 sets out the contrasting treatments.

Exhibit 18.19
Contrasting activity-based costing and traditional overhead cost allocation

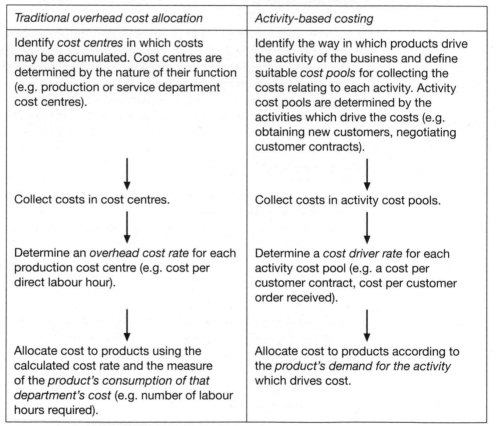

Traditional overhead cost allocation	Activity-based costing
Identify *cost centres* in which costs may be accumulated. Cost centres are determined by the nature of their function (e.g. production or service department cost centres).	Identify the way in which products drive the activity of the business and define suitable *cost pools* for collecting the costs relating to each activity. Activity cost pools are determined by the activities which drive the costs (e.g. obtaining new customers, negotiating customer contracts).
Collect costs in cost centres.	Collect costs in activity cost pools.
Determine an *overhead cost rate* for each production cost centre (e.g. cost per direct labour hour).	Determine a *cost driver rate* for each activity cost pool (e.g. a cost per customer contract, cost per customer order received).
Allocate cost to products using the calculated cost rate and the measure of the *product's consumption of that department's cost* (e.g. number of labour hours required).	Allocate cost to products according to the *product's demand for the activity* which drives cost.

18.6.2 Benefits claimed for activity-based costing

Activity-based costing appeared first in the academic literature during the late 1980s. It had reached the professional accountancy journals by the early 1990s and by that time was already being used (or tested) by companies with progressive attitudes. The main benefits claimed are that it provides product cost information which, although it includes an allocation of overheads, is nevertheless useful for decision-making purposes. It is useful because the overhead costs are allocated to the products in a way that reflects the factor driving the cost. If a product cost is thought to be too high, then it can be controlled by controlling the factors driving the most significant elements of its cost. Attention is directed towards problem areas. Activity-based costing is seen as a valuable management tool because it collects and reports on the significant activities of the business. It is also attractive for service-based organisations which have found the traditional, manufacturing-based costing methods not suited to the different nature of the service sector.

You may ask at this point, 'If activity-based costing is the best approach, why has it not replaced the traditional approach to overhead cost apportionment?' The answer to that question is, first, that the technique is still relatively rare in practical application, despite the amount written about it. Second, no allocating mechanism can produce accurate results unless the cost item which is being processed is of high reliability and its behaviour is well understood. The successful application of activity-based costing depends on a thorough understanding of basic principles of cost behaviour and the ability to record and process costs accurately.

Activity-based costing will not solve all problems of forward planning. The analytical method relies on historical data and therefore shares with many other aspects of accounting the disadvantage of being a backward-looking measure which must be used with caution in forward-looking decisions.

Finally, activity-based costing requires detailed accounting records and a well-structured cost-coding system so that costs are allocated correctly to cost pools and from there to products. There may need to be a considerable investment in discovering and installing the best information system for the job.

18.7 Summary

Key themes in this chapter are:

- Total product cost is defined as consisting of direct materials, direct labour and production overhead cost.
- **Prime cost** is the cost of direct materials, direct labour and other direct costs of production.
- The purchasing, storage and use of materials are controlled by documentation and processes that are designed to safeguard the assets and ensure the accuracy of recording systems.
- FIFO (first in first out) and LIFO (last in first out) are methods of pricing the issue of goods from inventory, and the valuation of inventory, in times when prices are changing.
- Accounting for materials is explained, highlighting the importance of documentation, the distinction between **direct** and **indirect** costs of materials and between **fixed** and **variable** costs of materials.
- The costs of **waste** and **scrap** are **indirect** costs that form part of the total **production cost**. Any cash received for scrap should be deducted from the cost of buying the materials.
- Labour costs are recorded and controlled in a way that ensures employees are paid correctly for work done and labour costs of activities are recorded accurately.
- Accounting for labour costs is explained, highlighting the distinction between **direct** and **indirect** labour costs and between **fixed** and **variable** costs of labour.
- **Total product cost** is defined as consisting of direct materials, direct labour and production overhead cost.
- **Production overhead costs** comprise indirect materials, indirect labour and other indirect costs of production.

- **Allocation** of indirect costs to cost centres means that the entire cost item is identified with one cost centre.
- **Apportionment** of indirect costs across cost centres means that the cost item is shared across those cost centres on some basis which is a fair representation of how the cost item is used by each cost centre.
- **Absorption** is the process by which overhead costs are absorbed into units of output, or 'jobs'.
- The processes of **apportionment** and **absorption** are said to be *arbitrary* (meaning 'a matter of choice rather than of strict rules'). To ensure that the best result is obtained, the scheme of apportionment and absorption must be:
  - fair to all parties involved in the process
  - representative of the benefit each party gains from the shared cost
  - relatively quick to apply so that the provision of information is not delayed; and understandable by all concerned.
- The sequence of **allocate**, **apportion** and **absorb** is called the **traditional** approach to product costing.
- **activity-based costing** (ABC) traces **overhead costs** to products by focusing on the **activities** that **drive** costs (cause costs to occur).
- **activity-based costing** provides a method of spreading overhead costs by asking: what drives each cost?
- **Costs** are collected in **cost pools** and then spread over products based on cost per unit of activity for the **activity** in question.
- **Costs** are then allocated to products on the basis of a cost per unit of activity.
- **Cost drivers** have taken on an increasingly important role in apportioning indirect costs to cost centres.
- Contemporary management accounting practice focuses on the accountant becoming part of the operational team so as to ensure that the job costs derived are understood and reflect the factors that drive the costs to be incurred.

Further reading

Bjørnenak, T. and Mitchell, F. (2002), 'The development of activity-based costing journal literature, 1987–2000', *The European Accounting Review*, 11(3): 281–508.

Innes, J. and Mitchell, F. (1995), 'Activity-based costing', in Ashton, D., Hopper, T. and Scapens, R. (eds), *Issues in Management Accounting*, Prentice Hall, Chapter 6.

Soin, K., Seal, W. and Cullen, J. (2002), 'ABC and organizational change: an institutional perspective', *Management Accounting Research*, 13: 249–71.

QUESTIONS

The Questions section of each chapter has three types of question. 'Test your understanding' questions to help you review your reading are in the 'A' series of questions. You will find the answers to these by reading and thinking about the material in the book. 'Application' questions to test your ability to apply technical skills are in the 'B' series of questions. Questions requiring you to show skills in problem solving and evaluation are in the 'C' series of questions. A letter [S] indicates that there is a solution at the end of the book. Other solutions are provided in the Instructor's Manual, where there are further questions parallel to those set out here.

A   Test your understanding

A18.1   What are the main items in a statement of the cost of production of an item of output? (Section 18.1)

A18.2   How may a system of materials-control procedures ensure accurate accounting information for job-costing purposes? (Section 18.2.1)

A18.3   Which source documents should be used to create the accounting record for direct materials costs? (Section 18.2.1)

A18.4   What is meant by the term 'FIFO', when used in deciding on the cost price of goods issued to production? (Section 18.2.2)

A18.5   What are the problems of accounting for wastage and scrap? (Section 18.2.3)

A18.6   Is direct labour cost a fixed cost or a variable cost? Explain your answer. (Section 18.3)

A18.7   Give three examples of production overheads in: (Section 18.4)

     (a) a manufacturing business; and
     (b) a service business.

A18.8   For each of your answers to the previous question, say whether the cost is a fixed cost or a variable cost. (Section 18.4)

A18.9   What are the important features of any successful scheme of allocating, apportioning and absorbing indirect costs to products? (Section 18.4.2)

A18.10   For each of the following overhead costs, suggest one method of apportioning cost to cost centres: (Section 18.4.2)

     (a) employees' holiday pay;
     (b) agency fee for nurse at first-aid centre;
     (c) depreciation of floor-polishing machines used in all production areas;
     (d) production manager's salary;
     (e) lighting;
     (f) power for desktop workstations in a financial services business;
     (g) cost of servicing the elevator;
     (h) fee paid to professional consultant for advice on fire regulation procedures.

A18.11   Explain how each of the following service department costs could be apportioned over production centres: (Section 18.4.2)

     (a) Cleaning of machines in a food-processing business.
     (b) Vehicle maintenance for a fleet of vans used by service engineers.
     (c) Canteen services for a company operating a large bus fleet.
     (d) Quality control department of an engineering business.
     (e) Planning department of a bridge-building company.
     (f) Research department of a chemical company.

A18.12   State the principles to be applied in absorbing costs into products. (Section 18.4.3)

A18.13   Using your answer to question A18.12, compare the relative merits of calculating overhead costs per unit of products using each of the following methods: (Section 18.4.3)

     (a) Cost per direct labour hour.
     (b) Cost per unit of output.
     (c) Cost per direct machine hour.
     (d) Cost per £ of direct labour.

A18.14   What are the benefits and what are the possible problems of using overhead cost rates estimated in advance of the actual costs being recorded? (Section 18.4.5)

A18.15   How does under-recovery of production overhead arise? (Section 18.4.6)

B Application

B18.1 [S]

A factory manufactures garden huts. The production process is classified into two production departments, Assembly and Joinery. There is one service department, the canteen. The relevant forecast information for the year ahead is as follows:

Indirect costs for all three departments in total:

	Total
	£
Indirect labour	90,000
Indirect material	81,000
Heating and lighting	25,000
Rent and rates	30,000
Depreciation	56,000
Supervision	45,000
Power	36,000
Total	363,000

The following information is available about each department:

	Total	Assembly	Joinery	Canteen
	£	£	£	£
Floor space (sq. metres)	50,000	20,000	24,000	6,000
Book value of machinery (£)	560,000	300,000	240,000	20,000
Number of employees	150	80	60	10
Kilowatt hours of power	18,000	9,000	8,000	1,000
Direct materials (£)		100,000	50,000	
Direct labour (£)		50,000	42,000	
Maintenance hours		8,000	6,000	
Labour hours		12,640	8,400	

The canteen is used by both production cost centres.

Required

1 Apportion production overhead costs over the Assembly, Joinery and Canteen departments using a suitable method for each department.
2 Apportion service department costs over production departments.
3 For each production department, calculate an overhead cost rate, based on labour hours, which may be used to absorb production overhead cost into jobs.
4 Find the overhead cost of a job which spends three labour hours in the Assembly department and four labour hours in the Joinery department.

B18.2 [S]

A company manufactures golf bags. Golf bags have the following manufacturing costs:

	£ per bag
Labour (5 hours at £5.00/hour)	25
Materials	40
Variable production overheads	10

In addition, the company has monthly fixed production overhead costs of £100,000.
5,000 golf bags are manufactured every month.

Required

Prepare a statement of total product cost for a batch of 5,000 golf bags which shows prime cost and production overhead cost as subtotals.

B18.3 [S]

Budgeted information relating to two departments of Rydons Tables Ltd for the next period is as follows:

Department	Production overhead £	Direct material cost £	Direct labour cost £	Direct labour hours	Machine hours
1	270,000	67,500	13,500	2,700	45,000
2	18,000	36,000	100,000	25,000	300

Individual direct labour employees within each department earn differing rates of pay according to their skills, grade and experience.

Required

(a) Rydons Tables intends to use a production overhead cost rate of £6 per machine hour for absorbing production overhead cost into jobs, based on the budget. Write a short note to the managers of the business commenting on this proposal.

(b) During the past year, Rydons Tables has been using a production overhead cost rate of £5.60 per machine hour. During the year overheads of £275,000 were incurred and 48,000 machine hours worked. Were overheads under-absorbed or over-absorbed, and by how much?

C   Problem solving and evaluation

C18.1

In a general engineering works the following routine has been followed for several years to arrive at an estimate of the price for a contract.

The process of estimating is started by referring to a job cost card for some previous similar job and evaluating the actual material and direct labour hours used on that job at current prices and rates.

Production overheads are calculated and applied as a percentage of direct wages. The percentage is derived from figures appearing in the accounts of the previous year, using the total production overhead cost divided by the total direct wages cost.

One-third is added to the total production overhead cost to cover administrative charges and profit.

You have been asked to draft a short report to management outlining, with reasons, the changes which you consider desirable in order to improve the process of estimating a price for a contract.

C18.2

You have been asked for advice by the owner of a small business who has previously estimated overhead costs as a percentage of direct labour cost. This method has produced quite reasonable results because the products have all been of similar sales value and have required similar labour inputs. The business has now changed and will in future concentrate on two products. Product X is a high-volume item of relatively low sales value and requires relatively little labour input per item. It is largely produced by automatic processes. Product Y is a low-volume item of relatively high sales value and requires considerably more labour input by specially skilled workers. It is largely produced by manual craft processes.

What advice would you give to the owner of the business about allocation of overhead costs comprising:

● the owner's salary for administrative work;
● rent paid on the production facilities; and
● depreciation of production machinery?

Compare the effect of having one overhead recovery rate for all three costs in aggregate, and the effect of identifying the factors which 'drive' each cost in relation to the production process.

Activities for study groups

Case 18.1

As a group you are the senior teaching staff of a school where each subject department is regarded as a cost centre. The direct costs of each cost centre are teachers' salaries, books and worksheets for pupils. The overhead costs of the school administration are charged to each cost centre as a fixed percentage of teachers' salaries in the cost centre. The languages department argues that this is unfair to them as they have a higher ratio of teachers to pupils due to the need for developing spoken language skills. The art department objects to the percentage charge because it includes accommodation costs without recognising that they are housed in portacabins where the roof leaks. The maths department says that they should not have to share the costs of expensive technical equipment when all they need for effective teaching is a piece of chalk. One member of staff has read about 'cost drivers' and the teachers have decided that they would like to meet the school accountant to put forward some ideas about using cost drivers. So far they have made a list of the main overhead costs as:

- heating and lighting
- head teacher, deputy heads and office staff salaries
- cleaning
- maintenance
- library
- computing services for staff
- computing labs for pupils
- insurance of buildings and contents.

Allocate among your group the roles of staff in the languages, art and maths departments. Discuss cost drivers for each of the overhead costs listed and attempt to arrive at an agreement on cost drivers to be presented to the school accountant. What are the problems of agreeing the drivers? What are the benefits?

Case 18.2

Two bus companies are competing for passengers on the most popular routes in a major city. The long-established company has strong customer loyalty, provides weekend and evening services as well as frequent daytime services and covers the cost of unprofitable routes from the profits on popular routes. The incoming company has larger resources from which to support a price war and can be selective in running only at peak times on the most popular routes. There are fears that if the incomer wins the bus war, the quality of service provision will diminish in the evenings and at weekends and on unprofitable routes.

As a group allocate the roles of: (a) passenger representatives, (b) the financial controller's department of the long-established company, (c) members of the city council's transport committee, (d) representatives of the police force. In the separate roles discuss the areas where cost savings might be achieved by the long-established company to make it competitive on price. Then come together and negotiate a support package for the company which focuses on improving the financial performance of the company.

Notes and references

1. CIMA (2005), *Official Terminology*, CIMA Publishing and Elsevier.
2. Innes, J. and Mitchell, F. (1995), 'Activity based costing', in Ashton, D., Hopper, T. and Scapens, R. W. (eds), *Issues in Management Accounting*, Prentice Hall, Chapter 6.

Part 6

Job costs and stock valuation

Chapter 19

Job costing

Shutterstock.com/kentoh

Cake Boss

How much should I charge for my cakes?

I have read that a good way to price cakes is to charge for the cost of ingredients times 2 (or 3).

We firmly believe that the 'ingredients times 2 or 3' method of pricing is arbitrary and not rooted in any kind of business theory. In our experience, this method results in **grossly underpricing** your product. The cost of the cake lies not in the ingredients, but in the labor invested.

How do I know what people will pay for a cake in my community?

Call other custom bakeries in your area and ask them how much they charge per slice for wedding, party and sheet cakes. Set your prices close to theirs, or maybe *slightly* lower if you are still building your skill level. Do NOT undercut them – this is a disservice to them, and to other decorators in your community.

To price your cakes, there are four elements to be aware of:

1. Ingredients and supplies

To know how much to charge, you **must** understand how much you are spending. It takes a time investment to calculate your ingredient costs, but it is vital to understanding what a cake costs you to make. Don't forget the cost of the boards, boxes, foil, and dowels.

2. Time

When you start thinking about it, the time you spend on a cake is so much more than just the time spent decorating. There is time spent consulting with the customer, planning a custom design, shopping, baking, cooling, making fillings, frostings, fondant, and sometimes custom work like fondant or gumpaste toppers or figurines. You deserve to be compensated a fair hourly rate for the time you spend on a cake. Don't forget cleanup time! We've all seen what our kitchens look like after a big cake!

3. Overhead

When you bake a cake, you use your oven, your utilities, your pans, your mixer, your dishwasher, and soap. These things all required an initial investment by you, and a nominal fee for their use should be added to the cost of the cake.

4. Delivery

Your customer lives two hours away and wants the cake delivered? Then you must certainly be compensated for your time, your gas, wear and tear on your vehicle, and any tolls that are incurred on the trip. The current federal reimbursement rate for mileage is 56.5 cents per mile, so this is a good place to start. Remember to charge for the entire round-trip!

Source: Cake Boss. http://www.cakeboss.com/Cake-Stuff/Articles/How-Much-Should-I-Charge

Discussion points

1 Why is a job-costing approach suitable for estimating the cost of baking specialist cakes to meet customers' orders?
2 What advice is given on (i) adding a multiple to the cost of ingredients; and (ii) evaluating competition?

Contents

Learning outcomes	After reading this chapter you should be able to:

After reading this chapter you should be able to:

- Explain the contents of a job-cost record.
- Prepare a job-cost record showing direct material, direct labour, other direct costs and production overhead.
- Analyse transactions involved in job costing, using the accounting equation.
- Compare profit using absorption costing with profit using marginal costing.
- Explain how activity-based costing may be useful in calculating the cost of a job.

19.1 Introduction

In Chapter 18 direct materials, direct labour and production overheads were explained. This chapter brings together the elements of a **job-costing system** and explains the procedures for analysing them to calculate the cost of a job undertaken during a period of time. In a job-costing system there will be a job-cost record for each job, showing the costs incurred on that job. A job-cost record is illustrated in Table 19.1. The transactions of the period are analysed and recorded using the accounting equation.

A job-costing system for recording the cost of output is appropriate to a business which provides specialised products or makes items to order, so that each customer's

Table 19.1
Illustration of a job-cost record

JOB-COST RECORD JOB NO..........		Customer reference .... Product description		Product code	
DATE	CODE	DETAILS	QUANTITY	£	p
		Direct materials:			
		Type A	kg		
		Type B	kg		
		Type C	litres		
		Direct labour:			
		Employee A	hrs		
		Employee B	hrs		
		Employee C	hrs		
		Other direct costs			
		PRIME COST X			
		Indirect materials			
		Indirect labour			
		Other indirect costs			
		TOTAL PRODUCTION OVERHEAD Y			
		TOTAL PRODUCT COST X + Y			

requirements constitute a separate job of work. Job costing is appropriate in manufacturing industries such as shipbuilding, bridge building, construction, property development and craft industries. Job costing would also be used in costing the provision of services by professional persons such as lawyers, doctors, architects and accountants. It could also be used for repair contracts, or specialist service contracts.

Definition	A **job-costing system** is a system of cost accumulation where there is an identifiable activity for which costs may be collected. The activity is usually specified in terms of a job of work or a group of tasks contributing to a stage in the production or service process.

The **job-cost record** shows the costs of materials, labour and overhead incurred on a particular job. The accounts department knows from the stores requisition the quantity of materials issued to production and knows from the invoice the price per unit charged by the supplier. This allows the cost of **direct materials** to be recorded as the materials are used. Each job will have a job number and that number will be entered on all stores requisitions so that the materials can be traced to the job-cost record.

Direct labour costs will be calculated using hours worked and the hourly rate for each employee. The hours worked will be collected from employee time sheets which show each job under its own job number. Hourly rates for the employee will be available from personnel records.

Other **direct costs** will be charged to jobs by entering on the expense invoice the appropriate job number. The invoices will be used as the primary source from which information is transferred to the job-cost record.

Production overhead costs will be shared among the jobs to which they relate, as explained in Chapter 18.

Activity 19.1	*You have been employed as the management accountant at a car repair garage. Write down a list of the types of costs you would expect to find on a job-cost record for a car service and repair. (You don't need to put any money amounts into the list.)*

Table 19.1 shows sufficient details of direct materials, direct labour and other direct costs to give the **prime cost of production**. Addition of indirect costs (production overhead) gives the **total product cost** of a job.

Definitions	**Prime cost of production** is equal to the total of direct materials, direct labour and other direct costs.
	Production overhead cost comprises indirect materials, indirect labour and other indirect costs of production.
	Total product cost comprises prime cost plus production overhead cost.

19.2 Job-cost records: an illustration

Job costing is illustrated in the example of Specialprint, a company which prints novelty stationery to be sold in a chain of retail stores. The company has only one customer for this novelty stationery. Table 19.2 contains relevant information for the month of June in respect of three separate jobs, 601, 602 and 603. Symbols are attached to each transaction so that the information may be traced through the job-cost records.

Table 19.2
Specialprint: transactions for the month of June

Date	Symbol	Transaction
1 June	✧	Bought 60 rolls of paper on credit from supplier, invoiced price being £180,000. The rolls of paper acquired consisted of two different grades. 40 rolls were of medium-grade paper at a total cost of £100,000 and 20 rolls were of high grade at a total cost of £80,000.
1 June	♣	Bought inks, glues and dyes at a cost of £25,000 paid in cash. The inks cost £9,000 while the glue cost £12,000 and the dyes £4,000.
2 June	⊗	Returned to supplier one roll of paper damaged in transit, cost £2,500. The roll of paper returned was of medium grade.
3 June	†	Rolls of paper issued to printing department, cost £120,000. 20 high-grade rolls were issued, together with 16 medium-grade rolls. There were three separate jobs: references 601, 602 and 603. The high-grade rolls were all for job 601 (notepaper); 12 medium-grade rolls were for job 602 (envelopes) and the remaining 4 medium-grade rolls were for job 603 (menu cards).
4 June	ø	Issued half of inks, glues and dyes to printing department, £12,500. Exactly half of each item of inks, glue and dyes was issued, for use across all three jobs.
14 June	ψ	Paid printing employees' wages £8,000. Wages were paid to 10 printing employees, each earning the same amount.
14 June	λ	Paid maintenance wages £250. Maintenance wages were paid to one part-time maintenance officer.
16 June	‡	Paid rent, rates and electricity in respect of printing, £14,000 in cash. Payment for rent was £8,000, rates £4,000 and electricity £2,000.
28 June	ϖ	Paid printing employees' wages £8,000. Wages were paid to the same 10 employees as on 14 June.
28 June	φ	Paid maintenance wages £250. Maintenance wages were paid to the same maintenance officer as on 14 June.
30 June	♥	Employee records show that: 5 printing employees worked all month on job 601; 3 printing employees worked on job 602; and 2 printing employees worked on job 603.
30 June	ξ	It is company policy to absorb production overheads in proportion to labour costs of each job.
30 June	#	Transferred printed stationery to finished goods stock at a total amount of £160,000, in respect of jobs 601 and 602, which were completed, together with the major part of job 603. There remained some unfinished work in progress on one section of job 603, valued at £3,000. Separate finished goods records are maintained for notepaper, envelopes and menu cards.
30 June	≈	Sold stationery to customer on credit, cost of goods sold being £152,000. The customer took delivery of all notepaper and all envelopes, but took only £7,600 of menu cards, leaving the rest to await completion of the further items still in progress.

19.2.1 Information for the job-cost record

The **job-cost record** requires information on direct materials, direct labour and production overhead. This information must be selected from the list of transactions for the month of June. Care must be taken to extract only that information which is relevant to each job.

From Table 19.2 note the transactions which you think are directly relevant to the cost of jobs 601, 602 and 603. Then read the rest of this section and compare your answer with the text. (Use Table 19.1 to remind yourself of the information needed for a job cost record.)

Direct material

Materials are purchased on 1 June and taken into store but that is of no relevance to determining the cost of a job. For job cost purposes what matters is the issue of paper on 3 June. That is entered on each of the job-cost records using the detail given for the event on 3 June.

Direct labour

Employees are paid during the month and there are records (time sheets) of the jobs on which they work. It is only at the end of the month that the employee records are checked to find where the work was carried out. At that point the relevant direct labour costs are entered on each job-cost record.

Production overhead

Production overhead comprises indirect materials (ink, glue and dyes), indirect labour (maintenance wages), rent, rates and electricity.

		£
Indirect materials	ø	12,500
Indirect labour	λ φ	500
Rent	‡	8,000
Rates	‡	4,000
Electricity	‡	2,000
Total production overhead	ξ	27,000

An **overhead cost rate** is required to determine how much production overhead should be absorbed into each job. We are told in Table 19.2 that it is company policy to absorb production overheads in proportion to the direct labour costs of each job. The total direct labour cost for the period is £16,000 and so the overhead cost rate must be calculated as:

$$\text{overhead cost rate } (in \text{ £ per £ of direct labour}) = \frac{27,000}{16,000}$$

$$= £1.6875 \text{ per £}$$

This rate is then applied to the amounts of direct labour cost already charged to each job (which was £8,000 for job 601, £4,800 for job 602 and £3,200 for job 603). The resulting amounts are recorded in the relevant job records.

Job number	Calculation	Production overhead
		£
Job 601	8,000 × £1.6875	13,500 ζ
Job 602	4,800 × £1.6875	8,100 ζ
Job 603	3,200 × £1.6875	5,400 ζ
		27,000 ζ

19.2.2 Presentation of the job-cost records

The job-cost records are set out in Table 19.3. Jobs 601 and 602 are finished in the period and this is shown on the job-cost record by a transfer to finished goods of the full cost of the job. Job 603 has a problem with unfinished work in progress but the rest of that job is completed and transferred to finished goods. That information is recorded on the job-cost record card as shown in Table 19.3.

The total work in progress record is useful as a check on the separate job costs and is also useful for accounting purposes in providing a total record of work in progress at any point in time. It is created by using the totals of the direct materials issued to production, the total direct labour used on jobs and the total production overhead incurred during the month. Table 19.4 shows the total work in progress record.

Table 19.3
Job-cost records for jobs 601, 602 and 603

	Job-cost record: Job 601	
3 June	Direct materials	80,000 †
30 June	Direct labour	8,000 ♥
	Prime cost	88,000
30 June	Production overhead:	13,500 ξ
	Total production cost	101,500
	To finished goods	(101,500)
	Work in progress	nil
	Job-cost record: Job 602	
3 June	Direct materials	30,000 †
30 June	Direct labour	4,800 ♥
	Prime cost	34,800
30 June	Production overhead:	8,100 ξ
	Total production cost	42,900
	Finished goods	(42,900)
	Work in progress	nil
	Job-cost record: Job 603	
3 June	Direct materials	10,000 †
30 June	Direct labour	3,200 ♥
	Prime cost	13,200
30 June	Production overhead:	5,400 ξ
	Total production cost	18,600
	Finished goods	(15,600)
1 July	Work in progress	3,000

Table 19.4
Record of total work in progress for month of June

	Total work in progress	
3 June	Direct materials	120,000 †
30 June	Direct labour	16,000 ♥
30 June	Production overhead	27,000 ξ
		163,000
30 June	Finished goods	(160,000)
1 July	Work in progress	3,000

19.3 Job costing: applying the accounting equation to transactions

The job-cost record cards used only a part of the information contained in Table 19.2. All the transactions must be recorded for purposes of preparing financial statements, using the accounting equation as shown in Chapter 3. This section analyses the transactions of Table 19.2 using the accounting equation and concludes with a spreadsheet record of the transactions for the month. The symbols contained in Table 19.2 are used throughout to help follow the cost trail.

In management accounting there is strong emphasis on the flow of costs. This flow starts when materials, labour and other resources are either acquired on credit terms or paid for immediately in cash (line A in Figure 19.1). The management accounting records trace these credit transactions and cash payments through to separate records for materials, labour, production overhead and the administration and selling costs (line B). The separate records are then considered in more detail.

The materials record includes both direct and indirect materials. When the direct materials are issued for use in production, a stores requisition note is produced and this is the basis for transferring that amount of direct materials cost from the materials record to the work in progress record (line C). When the indirect materials are issued for use in production a further stores requisition note is produced. This is the basis for transferring that amount of indirect materials cost from the materials record to the production overhead record.

The labour cost (line B) record will include both direct and indirect labour. Direct labour hours are recorded on a time sheet and calculation of the cost of these hours is the basis for transferring that amount of direct labour cost from the labour cost record to the work in progress record. Calculation of indirect labour cost is the basis for transferring that amount of indirect labour cost from the labour cost record to the production overhead record.

Some items of indirect cost, not involving either materials or labour, will be transferred from the bank payment record (such as payment of rent, electricity or gas). At the end of the accounting period, probably each month, all the production overhead of the period is transferred to the work in progress record.

Finally on line B there is the record of administration and selling costs. These are not part of the cost of work in progress because they are not costs of production. At the end of the accounting period the total of these costs is transferred to the work in progress record.

When the work in progress (line C) is completed there is a transfer of cost to the record for finished goods stock (line D). When the finished goods are sold there is a transfer of the cost of those items to the profit and loss account as cost of goods sold.

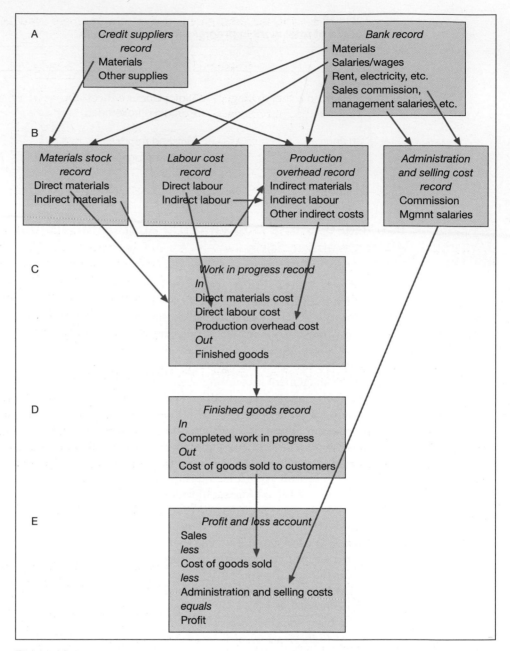

Figure 19.1
Flow of costs in a management accounting information system

The profit and loss account (line E) brings together the sales, cost of goods sold and administration and selling costs in a calculation of profit.

✧♣⊗ 19.3.1 Acquisition of inventory: direct and indirect materials

In purchasing the rolls of paper, the business acquires an asset. In taking credit from the supplier it incurs a liability. (✧)

Asset ↑ – **Liability** ↑ = Ownership interest

In purchasing the inks, glue and dyes, the business acquires a further asset. In paying cash, the asset of cash is diminished. (♣)

> **Asset** ↑↓ – Liability = Ownership interest

Returning the damaged roll of paper reduces the asset of materials stock and reduces the liability to the trade creditor. (⊗)

> **Asset** ↓ – **Liability** ↓ = Ownership interest

† 19.3.2 Converting raw materials into work in progress: direct materials

When the rolls of paper are issued from the stores to the printing department, they become a part of the work in progress of that department. Since this work in progress is expected to bring a benefit to the enterprise in the form of cash flows from sales when it is eventually finished and sold, it meets the definition of an asset. There is an increase in the asset of work in progress and a decrease in the stock of materials. (†)

> **Asset** ↑↓ – Liability = Ownership interest

ø 19.3.3 Issuing indirect materials to production

Inks, glue and dyes are indirect materials. The indirect cost is part of the production overhead cost, to be accumulated with other indirect costs and later added to work in progress as a global amount for production overhead. In this case, only half of the indirect materials have been issued (£12,500), the rest remaining in stock. There is a decrease in the asset of materials stock and an increase in the asset of work in progress. (ø)

> **Asset** ↑↓ – Liability = Ownership interest

ψλϖφ 19.3.4 Labour costs

There are two amounts of direct labour costs paid during the period in respect of the printing employees (ψϖ); and two amounts of indirect wages in respect of maintenance (λφ).

In practice, it will only be after analysis of the labour records for the period that an accurate subdivision into direct and indirect costs may be made. Although it is assumed here that all wages of printing employees are direct costs, it could be that enforced idle time through equipment failure would create an indirect cost. Taking the simplified illustration, the direct wages paid become a part of the prime cost of work in progress while the indirect wages paid become part of the production overhead cost within work in progress.

For the purposes of this illustration it is assumed that the manager of the business knows that all printing employees' wages are direct costs (♥) and so may be recorded immediately as direct costs of work in progress. The asset of cash decreases and the asset of work in progress increases.

> **Asset** ↑↓ – Liability = Ownership interest

It is further assumed that the manager of the business knows that all indirect labour costs will become production overheads (x) and hence added to the value of work in progress.

$$\boxed{\text{Asset} \uparrow\downarrow - \text{Liability} = \text{Ownership interest}}$$

‡ξ 19.3.5 Production overhead costs

Rent, rates and electricity costs (‡) paid from cash in respect of printing are production overhead costs (ξ). For management accounting purposes they are regarded as part of the cost of the asset of work in progress (‡ ξ).

$$\boxed{\text{Asset} \uparrow\downarrow - \text{Liability} = \text{Ownership interest}}$$

For financial reporting purposes the overhead costs paid are regarded immediately as reducing the ownership claim because they are part of the expense of production overhead. Figure 19.1 shows that in both financial reporting and management accounting the production overhead costs eventually emerge as a component of the expense of cost of goods sold.

19.3.6 Transferring work in progress to finished goods

When the asset of work in progress is completed, it changes into another asset, the stock of finished goods. In the accounting records the asset is removed from work in progress and enjoys a new description as the asset of finished goods. (#)

$$\boxed{\text{Asset} \uparrow\downarrow - \text{Liability} = \text{Ownership interest}}$$

≈ 19.3.7 Sale of goods

When a sale is made to a customer, that part of the asset of finished goods stock is transformed into the expense of cost of goods sold. Any finished goods remaining unsold continue to be reported as an asset. (≈)

$$\boxed{\text{Asset} \downarrow - \text{Liability} = \textbf{Ownership interest} \downarrow \textbf{(expenses)}}$$

19.3.8 Spreadsheet analysis

The transactions are brought together in spreadsheet form in Table 19.5 using a form similar to that found in Chapters 5 and 6 of *Financial Accounting*. The entries on each line correspond to the detailed analyses provided in this section. The totals at the foot of each column represent the amounts of the various assets, liabilities and ownership interest resulting from the transactions of the month. Cash has decreased overall by £55,500. The asset of stock of materials (paper, inks, glues and dyes) has increased by £70,000 and the asset of work in progress has increased by £3,000. The asset of finished goods has increased by £8,000. The liability to the creditor stands at £177,500. Overall the transactions of the month, as recorded here, have decreased the ownership interest by £152,000, the amount which is recorded as the cost of goods sold.

	£
Overall increase in assets	25,500
Overall increase in liabilities	177,500
Difference	(152,000)
Decrease in ownership interest	(152,000)

Table 19.5
Spreadsheet to show analysis of transactions for the month of June, using the accounting equation

Date	Transaction	Symbol	Assets				Liability	Ownership interest
			Cash	Stock of materials	Work in progress	Finished goods	Creditor	Cost of goods sold
			£	£	£	£	£	£
June 1	Bought 60 rolls of paper on credit from supplier, invoiced price being £180,000.	✧		180,000			180,000	
June 1	Bought inks, glue and dyes, cost £25,000 paid in cash.	♣	(25,000)	25,000				
June 2	Returned to supplier one roll, damaged in transit, £2,500.	⊗		(2,500)			(2,500)	
June 3	Rolls of paper issued to printing department, cost £120,000.	†		(120,000)	120,000			
June 4	Issued half of inks, glues and dyes to printing department, £12,500.	ø		(12,500)	12,500			
June 14	Paid printing employees' wages £8,000.	ψ	(8,000)		8,000			
June 14	Paid maintenance wages £250.	λ	(250)		250			
June 16	Paid rent, rates and electricity in respect of printing, £14,000, in cash.	‡	(14,000)		14,000			
June 28	Paid printing employees' wages £8,000.	ϖ	(8,000)		8,000			
June 28	Paid maintenance wages £250.	φ	(250)		250			
June 30	Transferred printed stationery to finished goods stock, valued at cost of £160,000.	#			(160,000)	160,000		
June 30	Sold stationery to customer on credit, cost of goods sold being £152,000.	≈				(152,000)		(152,000)
	Totals		(55,500)	70,000	3,000	8,000	177,500	(152,000)

19.4 Absorption costing and marginal costing

The problems of **apportioning** fixed production overheads were explained in detail in Chapter 18. Because of the **apportionment** problems, there are situations in management accounting where it is preferable to avoid the problem by allocating only **variable costs** to products. **Fixed costs** are regarded as costs of the period rather than costs of the product. The question to be addressed in this section is how the choice between **absorption costing** (which means absorbing all costs into products) and **marginal costing** (which means taking in only the variable costs of production) may be dependent on the purpose to which management accounting is being applied.

Definitions

In **absorption costing** (full costing), all production costs are absorbed into products and the unsold stock is measured at total cost of production.

In **marginal costing** (variable costing), only variable costs of production are allocated to products and the unsold stock is measured at variable cost of production. Fixed production costs are treated as a cost of the period in which they are incurred.

19.4.1 A note on terminology

Some authors refer to 'marginal costing' while others refer to 'variable costing'. The strict interpretation of 'marginal cost' in economics is the additional cost of one more unit of output. From the economists' viewpoint that extra cost could include a stepped increase in fixed cost if capacity has to be expanded to produce one more item or a new employee is required. For this section we assume that the range of **activity** is narrow so that a marginal change in cost involves variable costs only.

19.4.2 Illustration of absorption and marginal costing

Take the example of a business planning its operations for five trading periods. Data regarding budgeted selling price, budgeted variable cost per unit and fixed production overheads are given in Table 19.6, together with budgeted volumes of production and sales over the next five periods of production. The question to be answered is, 'How much profit is expected for each of the five trading periods?'

Table 19.6
Data for illustration of absorption versus marginal costing

	£
Selling price per unit	20
Variable cost per unit	9
Fixed costs for each period	500

	Period 1 units	Period 2 units	Period 3 units	Period 4 units	Period 5 units
Produced	230	270	260	240	250
Sold	200	210	260	280	300
Held in stock at end of period	30	90	90	50	nil

Under absorption costing the first task is to decide how the fixed costs for each period should be allocated to products. Where production volume is varying in the manner shown in Table 19.6, a common practice is to base the predetermined overhead cost rate on the normal level of activity. In this case, it might be reasonable to take a normal level of activity as the average production level, which is 250 units per period. The predetermined fixed overhead cost rate is therefore £2 per unit.

19.4.3 Absorption costing

Under absorption costing the opening and closing stock is valued at total cost of £11 per unit, comprising variable cost per unit of £9 and fixed cost per unit of £2. Table 19.7 illustrates the absorption costing approach.

Activity 19.3

Go back to the data of Table 19.6. Cover up the answer in Table 19.7 and then attempt to write out the profit calculation under absorption costing. Add a note of narrative explanation to each line as a means of helping understanding by yourself and others. Make sure that you understand the absorption costing approach fully.

Table 19.7
Profit per period under absorption costing

	Period 1 £	Period 2 £	Period 3 £	Period 4 £	Period 5 £	Total £
Opening stock	nil	330	990	990	550	nil
Cost of production:						
Variable cost	2,070	2,430	2,340	2,160	2,250	11,250
Fixed cost	500	500	500	500	500	2,500
Closing stock	(330)	(990)	(990)	(550)	nil	nil
Cost of goods sold	2,240	2,270	2,840	3,100	3,300	13,750
Sales	4,000	4,200	5,200	5,600	6,000	25,000
Gross profit	1,760	1,930	2,360	2,500	2,700	11,250

19.4.4 Marginal costing

Using marginal costing, the stock of unsold output at the end of each period would be valued at the variable cost of £9 per unit. The fixed cost would be regarded as a cost of the period, without allocation to products. Table 19.8 illustrates the marginal costing approach.

Table 19.8
Profit per period under marginal costing

	Period 1 £	Period 2 £	Period 3 £	Period 4 £	Period 5 £	Total £
Opening stock	nil	270	810	810	450	nil
Cost of production	2,070	2,430	2,340	2,160	2,250	11,250
Closing stock	(270)	(810)	(810)	(450)	nil	nil
Cost of goods sold	1,800	1,890	2,340	2,520	2,700	11,250
Fixed costs of period	500	500	500	500	500	2,500
Total costs	2,300	2,390	2,840	3,020	3,200	13,750
Sales	4,000	4,200	5,200	5,600	6,000	25,000
Gross profit	1,700	1,810	2,360	2,580	2,800	11,250

Look back at the data of Table 19.6. Before turning to the answer in Table 19.8 attempt to write out the profit calculation under marginal costing. Add a note of narrative explanation to each line as a means of helping understanding by yourself and others.

19.4.5 Comparison of profit under each approach

Table 19.9 compares the profit calculated under each approach. The first point to note from Table 19.9 is that over the total period of time, where total production equals total sales, there is no difference in total profit. The difference between absorption costing and marginal costing is purely a result of timing of the matching of fixed overhead with products.

Table 19.9
Comparison of profit, using absorption costing and marginal costing

	Period 1 £	Period 2 £	Period 3 £	Period 4 £	Period 5 £	Total £
Absorption costing	1,760	1,930	2,360	2,500	2,700	11,250
Variable costing	1,700	1,810	2,360	2,580	2,800	11,250
Difference	+ 60	+ 120	0	– 80	– 100	0

Before reading the rest of this section, write a brief commentary on the most significant features of Table 19.9.

The second point to note is that the differences between the two profit calculations are based entirely on the *change* in volume of stock during the period, multiplied by the fixed overhead cost rate of £2 per unit. During period 1, stock increases by 30 units over the period and, as a consequence, profit under absorption costing is £60 higher than under marginal costing. During period 2, stock increases by 60 units over the period and, as a consequence, profit under absorption costing is £120 higher. During period 3 stock levels remain constant and therefore both approaches give the same answer. During period 4, stock levels decrease by 40 units so that profit under absorption costing is £80 lower. During period 5, stock levels decrease by 50 units and therefore profit under absorption costing is £100 lower.

The third point to note is that the overall effect of the positive and negative differences over the business life is zero, provided the allocation process is applied consistently. Different allocation processes will cause costs to fall in different time periods, but they cannot create or destroy costs in the total.

Finally, the effect of the change in stock levels may be understood using Table 19.9. Making a general statement from this specific example, it appears safe to say that when stock levels are increasing, profit under absorption costing is higher than it is under marginal costing. That is because a portion of the fixed production cost incurred in the period is carried forward to the next period as part of the closing stock valuation.

Generalising further from the analysis, it may be said that when stock levels are decreasing, profit under absorption costing is lower than it is under marginal costing. That is because fixed costs incurred in earlier periods are brought to the current period as part of the opening stock, to be sold during the period.

When stock levels are constant, both approaches give the same answer.

19.4.6 Why is it necessary to understand the difference?

In Chapter 16 it was shown that management accounting has three major roles in **directing attention, keeping the score** and **solving problems**. The particular role which applies in any situation will depend upon the management function which is being served. That management function could relate to the formation of a judgement or to making a decision about a course of action. In Chapter 17 it was shown that the classification of costs is very much dependent on which of the three management accounting roles is the dominant one in any specific situation and on the type of management function.

Where the management function relates to **planning** and **control**, the management accountant is carrying out a score-keeping function and it is usually necessary to account for fixed overhead costs of production as a part of the **product cost**. That means absorption costing is the appropriate approach. In this situation there is a strong overlap with financial accounting and with external reporting to stakeholders in a business. If the stakeholders are company shareholders, then the external reporting will be regulated by company law and accounting standards that require fixed costs of production to be treated as product costs and provide guidance on the allocation process. Where the stakeholders are the electorate, in the case of a public sector body, or partners in a business partnership, the rules may be more flexible, but in many cases they conventionally follow the practice recommended for companies.

19.4.7 Arguments in favour of absorption costing

The arguments put forward in favour of absorption costing are:

1 Since all production costs are incurred with a view to creating a product for sale, all costs should attach to products until they are sold.
2 In the longer term, fixed overhead costs must be recovered through sales if the business is to survive. Setting the stock value by reference to full costs encourages a pricing policy which covers full cost.
3 If fixed production costs are treated as period costs (as happens in marginal costing) and there is a low level of sales activity in a period, then a relatively low profit or a loss will be reported. If there is a high level of sales activity, there will be a relatively high profit. Absorption costing creates a smoothing of these fluctuations by carrying the fixed costs forward until the goods are sold.

19.4.8 Arguments in favour of marginal costing

Where the management accounting role is primarily that of directing attention and the management function is primarily one of decision making, it may be dangerous to regard fixed production costs as product costs. The attractions of using marginal costing in such a situation are as follows:

1 In the short term, relevant costs are required for decision making and fixed overheads are largely non-relevant because they cannot be avoided. They are best seen as a committed cost of the period.
2 Profit calculation is not dependent on changes in stock levels. The illustration in Tables 19.7 to 19.9 shows the practical effect of disentangling fixed costs from stock values.
3 There is no risk of carrying forward in stock an element of fixed production overhead cost which may not be recovered through sales.

4 Allocating all production costs to products and then applying full-cost pricing may result in loss of sales which would have made a contribution to fixed production costs and profit.

5 Where sales volumes are declining but output is sustained, marginal costing provides the profit warning more rapidly than does absorption costing in a situation where attention needs to be drawn urgently to the profit implications.

Activity 19.6	Now that you understand the difference between marginal costing and absorption costing, write a short evaluation of the two approaches.

19.5 Moving forward

Fiona McTaggart has participated in a number of consultancy projects where the traditional job costing approach has been modified to reflect changing circumstances. Here she talks about three of them.

FIONA: *I recall learning job costing at college and thinking that there must be more to life than this. Since then I have found much more excitement in management accounting but I still have to return to some of the basic principles – seeking where possible to identify costs with products and making sensible allocations where such identification is not possible.*

One of my clients is a production engineering business. I was working with the plant controller, a qualified engineer with a good head for figures. The controller was looking for a new management system which escaped from the traditional role of a financial system. What was wanted was management in terms of the activities of the unit but with one eye on the consequences in dollars. The controller wanted the production and engineering personnel to feel that they were in ownership of the management system. So I found myself working in a team which drew on several specialisms, including engineering and human resource management. We had to ask the financial accounting department, very politely, to keep away while we developed our ideas because they kept quoting financial accounting guidelines which were cramping our style. At the end of the day we did work out the cost of a job undertaken by the business, but it was a cost which the engineers understood and could relate to.

Another client is a telecommunications division of a major conglomerate. Their problem was again related to engineers but with a different slant. The engineers were not sufficiently aware of how their choice of operating methods could significantly alter total costs. Traditional overhead costs were too blunt an instrument so we identified the actions which drove costs and effectively turned indirect costs into direct costs. Every time an engineer initiated a process, there was a cost reported. They soon began to concentrate on cost-effective solutions. The end result was to identify the cost of a job but the engineers knew how their choices had affected that cost.

My third client is a major hospital. In the area of health care, relations between medical specialists and the accountants are always somewhat strained and have to be dealt with carefully. The project in this case was to measure the cost of a treatment which involved balancing length of stay, costs and patient welfare. There is a widely held belief that the accountants merely calculate the cost of one overnight stay and then suggest reducing overnight stays for all patients. In reality we worked closely with the clinical specialists so that an element of mutual respect was built up. We helped them to understand our approach to determining the cost of a 'job' (not really the best term for treating a patient – the experts prefer a 'treatment protocol'). The treatment protocol is the standard method for treating a specific condition. That method is developed by the medical experts. The actual treatment does not necessarily follow the standard – if the patient needs extra care then it is given. However, knowing the cost of the standard protocol allows comparative evaluation of the actual treatment. Management accountants develop the cost systems which are used as information by the case managers. The relationship is a partnership – the accountants don't dictate the medical treatment but it remains necessary for the medical experts to know what each treatment of each patient has cost.

The common feature of all these cases which I have described is that the management accounting system produced a report which included a cost for each 'job'. However, it was by no means a mechanical process carried out in isolation. It involved the management accountant becoming part of the operational team. The days of a separate management accounting department in some remote part of an administrative office are gone. The management accountant has to be alongside those who are delivering the product.

19.6 Summary

This chapter has drawn on the information and definitions contained in Chapters 4 and 5 to show the method of preparing job cost statements. Job costing will be found in service businesses as well as in manufacturing. The essential condition is that there is an identifiable job (item of output) for which costs may be collected with a view to determining the cost of the job. The chapter has also explained the differences between absorption costing and marginal costing.

Key themes in this chapter are:

- A **job-costing system** is a system of cost accumulation where there is an identifiable activity for which costs may be collected. The activity is usually specified in terms of a job of work or a group of tasks contributing to a stage in the production or service process.

- A **job-cost record** shows the costs of materials, labour and overhead incurred on a particular job.

- The **prime cost** of production is equal to the total of direct materials, direct labour and other direct costs.

- The **production overhead cost** comprises indirect materials, indirect labour and other indirect costs of production.

- The **total product cost** comprises prime cost plus production overhead cost.

- In **absorption costing** (*full costing*), all production costs are absorbed into products. The unsold inventory is measured at total cost of production. Fixed production overhead costs are treated as a product cost.

- In **marginal costing** (*variable costing*), only variable costs of production are allocated to products. The unsold inventory is measured at variable cost of production. Fixed production overhead costs are treated as a period cost of the period in which they are incurred.

- Profit under absorption costing differs from profit under marginal costing when inventory levels are *changing*. If total production equals total sales there is no difference in total profit.

- When inventory levels are *falling*, profit under **absorption costing** is *lower* than profit under **marginal costing**. The difference is equal to the *decrease in inventory levels* multiplied by the *fixed overhead cost rate*.

- When inventory levels are *rising,* profit under **absorption costing** is *higher* than profit under **marginal costing**. The difference is equal to the *increase in inventory levels* multiplied by the *fixed overhead cost rate.*

- **Absorption costing** is usually required for inventory valuation in financial accounting standards or other regulations. Those using such financial statements need to be aware that reported profit can be affected by the change in the volume of inventory over the period.

- **Marginal costing** may be more useful for **decision making** because it treats fixed production overhead costs as a cost of the period. Reported profit is not affected by the changes in inventory held.

QUESTIONS

The Questions section of each chapter has three types of question. 'Test your understanding' questions to help you review your reading are in the 'A' series of questions. You will find the answers to these by reading and thinking about the material in the book. 'Application' questions to test your ability to apply technical skills are in the 'B' series of questions. Questions requiring you to show skills in problem solving and evaluation are in the 'C' series of questions. A letter [S] indicates that there is a solution at the end of the book. Other solutions are provided in the Instructor's Manual, where there are further questions parallel to those set out here.

A   Test your understanding

A19.1 Define prime cost, production overhead cost and total product cost. (Section 19.1)

A19.2 List the items you would expect to find in a job cost record. (Section 19.2)

A19.3 What is the effect on the accounting equation of purchasing direct and indirect materials? (Section 19.3.1)

A19.4 How does the accounting equation represent the conversion of raw materials into work in progress? (Section 19.3.2)

A19.5 How does the accounting equation represent the issue of indirect materials to production? (Section 19.3.3)

A19.6 How does the accounting equation represent the transfer of labour costs to work in progress? (Section 19.3.4)

A19.7 How does the accounting equation represent the transfer of production overhead costs to work in progress? (Section 19.3.5)

A19.8 How does the accounting equation represent the transfer of work in progress to finished goods? (Section 19.3.6)

A19.9 How does the accounting equation represent the sale of goods? (Section 19.3.7)

A19.10 [S] Explain how each of the following transactions is dealt with in a job-costing system:

(a) The production department orders 16 components from store at a cost of £3 each, to be used on job 59.

(b) An employee (A. Jones) receives a weekly wage of £600. In week 29 this employee's time has been spent two-thirds on job 61 and one-third on job 62.

(c) On 16 June, job 94 is finished at a total cost of £3,500. The job consisted of printing brochures for a supermarket advertising campaign.

A19.11 Define absorption costing. (Section 19.4)

A19.12 Define marginal costing. (Section 19.4)

A19.13 Explain why absorption costing and marginal costing may lead to different measures of profit in a period. (Sections 19.4.3 and 19.4.4)

A19.14 Set out the arguments in favour of absorption costing. (Section 19.4.7)

A19.15 Set out the arguments in favour of marginal costing. (Section 19.4.8)

B Application

B19.1 [S]
The following transactions relate to a dairy, converting milk to cheese, for the month of May:

1 May	Bought 600 drums of milk from supplier, invoiced price being £90,000.
1 May	Bought cartons, cost £6,000 paid in cash.
2 May	Returned to supplier one drum damaged in transit, £150.
3 May	500 drums of milk issued to cheesemaking department, cost £75,000.
4 May	Issued two-thirds of cartons to cheesemaking department, £4,000.
14 May	Paid cheesemakers' wages, £3,000.
14 May	Paid wages for cleaning and hygiene, £600.
16 May	Paid rent, rates and electricity in respect of dairy, £8,000, in cash.
28 May	Paid cheesemakers' wages, £3,000.
28 May	Paid wages for cleaning and hygiene, £600.
30 May	Transferred all production of cheese in cartons to finished goods stock. No work in progress at end of month.

Required
Prepare a calculation of the cost of production transferred to finished goods at the end of May.

B19.2 [S]
Restoration Ltd buys basic furniture units and creates period layouts in clients' homes. The following transactions relate to jobs 801, 802 and 803 in the month of May. Prepare job cost records for each job.

1 May	✧	Bought 70 furniture units on credit from supplier, invoiced price being £204,000. The furniture units acquired consisted of two different grades. 50 units were of standard size at a total cost of £140,000 and 20 units were of king size at a total cost of £64,000.
1 May	♣	Bought stain, varnish and paint at a cost of £30,000 paid in cash. The stain cost £12,000 while the varnish cost £14,000 and the paint £4,000.
2 May	⊗	Returned to supplier one furniture unit damaged in transit, £2,800. The furniture unit returned was of standard size.
3 May	†	Furniture units issued to Finishing department. 40 standard-size units were issued, together with 14 king-size units. There were three separate jobs: references 801, 802 and 803. The standard-size units were all for job 801 (Riverside Hotel); 10 king-size units were for job 802 (Mountain Lodge); and the remaining 4 king-size units were for job 803 (Hydeaway House).
4 May	ø	Issued stain, varnish and paint to Finishing department, £22,500.
14 May	ψ	Paid Finishing department employees' wages £10,000. Wages were paid to 8 printing employees, each earning the same amount.
14 May	λ	Paid security wages £350. Security wages were paid to one part-time security officer.

16 May	‡	Paid rent, rates and electricity in respect of Finishing department, £18,000 in cash. Payment for rent was £9,000, rates £5,000 and electricity £4,000.
28 May	ϖ	Paid Finishing department employees' wages £10,000. Wages were paid to the same 8 employees as on 14 May.
28 May	φ	Paid security wages £350. Security wages were paid to the same security officer as on 14 May.
30 May	♥	Employee records show that: 4 Finishing department employees worked all month on job 801; 2 Finishing department employees worked on job 802; and 2 Finishing department employees worked on job 803.
30 May	ξ	It is company policy to allocate production overheads in proportion to labour costs of each job.
30 May	#	Transferred all finished goods to finished goods stock. There remained no unfinished work in progress.
30 May	≈	Riverside Hotel and Mountain Lodge took delivery of their goods. Hydeaway House will take delivery on 10 June.

B19.3

Resistor Ltd manufactures electrical units. All units are identical. The following information relates to June and July Year 5.

(a) Budgeted costs and selling prices were:

	June £	July £
Variable manufacturing cost per unit	2.00	2.20
Total fixed manufacturing costs (based on budgeted output of 25,000 units per month)	40,000	44,000
Total fixed marketing cost (based on budgeted sales of 25,000 units per month)	14,000	15,400
Selling price per unit	5.00	5.50

(b) Actual production and sales recorded were:

	Units	Units
Production	24,000	24,000
Sales	21,000	26,500

(c) There was no stock of finished goods at the start of June Year 5. There was no wastage or loss of finished goods during either June or July Year 5.

(d) Actual costs incurred corresponded to those budgeted for each month.

Required

Calculate the relative effects on the monthly operating profits of applying the undernoted techniques:

1 absorption costing;
2 marginal costing.

C   Problem solving and evaluation

C19.1 [S]

Frames Ltd produces wooden window frames to order for the building industry. The size of frame depends on the specification in the contract. For the purposes of providing job cost estimates the size of frame is ignored and the job cost estimate is based on the type of frame produced, being either single-glazing or double-glazing.

The standard specification is as follows:

	Single-glazing £	Double-glazing £
Direct materials per unit	90.00	130.00
Direct labour per unit		
6.5 hours at £5.00 per hour	32.50	
8.0 hours at £5.00 per hour		40.00
Variable production overhead charged at £6 per hour	39.00	48.00

Fixed overhead is estimated at £160,000 per month for single-glazing and £100,000 per month for double-glazing. Estimated production per month for single-glazing is 4,000 units and for double-glazing is 2,000 units per month.

Required

Prepare a job cost estimate for a customer who intends to order 500 single-glazing and 200 double-glazing units.

C19.2 [S]

Insulation Ltd has been established to manufacture insulation material for use in houses. At present, one machine is installed for production of insulation material. A further similar machine can be purchased if required.

The first customer is willing to place orders in three different sizes at the following selling prices:

Order size	Selling price per package £
430 packages per day	25.20
880 packages per day	25.00
1,350 packages per day	24.80

The customer will enter into an initial contract of 30 days' duration and will uplift completed packages on a daily basis from the premises of Insulation Ltd.

The following assumptions have been made in respect of Insulation Ltd:

(a) In view of the competitive market the selling prices are not negotiable.
(b) Direct materials will cost £23.75 per package irrespective of the order size.
(c) The output of one machine will be 350 packages per shift.
(d) A maximum of three shifts will be available on a machine within one day. The depreciation charge for a machine will be £100 per day, irrespective of the number of shifts worked.
(e) Labour costs to operate a machine will be £100 for the first shift, £120 for the second shift and £160 for the third shift of the day. If labour is required for a shift, then the full shift must be paid for regardless of the number of packages produced.
(f) The total cost of supervising the employees for each of the first two shifts in any day will be £20 per machine. The supervision cost of the third shift will be £40 per machine.
(g) Other fixed overhead costs will be £280 per day if one machine is used. Buying and using an additional machine would result in a further £100 of fixed costs per day.
(h) Production and sales volume will be equal regardless of order size.
(i) The company does not expect to obtain other work during the term of the initial contract.

Required

Prepare a report for the production director of Insulation Ltd giving:

1 For each order size, details of the overall profitability per day and net profit per package.
2 An explanation of the differing amounts of profit per package.

Activities for study groups

Case 19.1

As a group, you are planning to establish a partnership supplying examination advice and tuition to school pupils in their homes. Each course of lessons will be regarded as a single 'job'. Courses may vary in length and in target ability level, depending on the requirements of the pupil to be tutored. Divide the group to take on three different roles. One role is that of a tutor who is also a member of the partnership, sharing equally the profits of the business. The second role is that of the accountancy adviser to the partnership. The third role is that of a parent making enquiries about the price charged and the justification for that price.

Each member of the group should take on one of the three roles and separately make a note of:

(a) The expected costs of a job (in terms of types of cost).
(b) How you would justify the costs (if supplying the service).
(c) How you would question the costs (if receiving the service).

Then all members of the group should come together, compare answers, and finally prepare a joint report on the problems of job costing in a service business.

Case 19.2

As a group you are planning a garden renovation service to take advantage of the current popularity of television programmes dealing with garden design. Within the group, allocate the following roles:

● design skills
● labouring and building skills
● business planning skills
● marketing skills.

As a team discuss the approach you would take to estimating the cost of a job for quoting to an intending customer. Discuss also the proposal in a gardening advice magazine that those starting out in a new business should seek only to recover variable costs until the reputation is established. Report back to the rest of the class on:

● the costs to be recorded;
● the extent to which team members agree or disagree on costs to be included;
● your views on the suggestion that only variable costs should be recovered initially.

Part 7

Decision making

20 Break-even analysis and short-term decision making

Chapter 20

Break-even analysis and short-term decision making

Gemfields eyes Colombian emerald venture

Gemfields hopes to buy a Colombian emerald venture to expand its stable of mines producing precious stones.

Ian Harebottle, chief executive, said a deal in Colombia – one of the world's main emerald producers – was a next goal for Gemfields, after it bought into a Sri Lankan sapphire venture this month. "We are hopeful of something in Colombia within the next financial year – we would be disappointed if not," Mr Harebottle said.

Aim-quoted Gemfields, which mines in Africa, swung to a pre-tax profit of $36m from a loss in 2013 of $20m. More auctions of its Zambian emeralds helped to lift annual group revenues from $48m to $160m, while earnings per share were 2 cents, compared with a 5 cents loss previously.

The miner also held its first auction of rubies from its mine in Mozambique, which raised $33.5m – covering the cost of Gemfields' spending so far at the Montepuez mine, the group said.

Gemfields is trying to establish a more regular and globalised way to supply and sell precious stones, believing that will help to create a more robust market with higher prices, similar to the world diamond market.

Mr Harebottle also said he was optimistic that Fabergé would reach a break-even point within the next year, after Gemfields bought the luxury brand in 2013 to support its marketing.

Fabergé "appears to be turning the corner with the company indicating higher volumes and improving margins", analysts at Investec said.

Output of Zambian emeralds and beryl should rise to between 25m and 30m carats this year, compared with 20m ct in the year to the end of June. Ruby output should rise from 6.5m ct to 8m, Gemfields said.

Gemfields shares rose 5.6 per cent to 51.75p.

Source: James Wilson, *Financial Times*, 22 September 2014. http://www.ft.com/cms/s/0/6977e036-4249-11e4-a9f4-00144feabdc0.html\#ixzz3GCVPUa8X

Discussion points

1 What does the chief executive mean when he says that he is optimistic that the company will reach a break-even point within the next year?

2 How will the expectation of higher volumes and improving margins help reach or exceed the break-even point?

Contents

After reading this chapter you should be able to:

- Explain how the accountant's view of cost behaviour differs from that of the economist.
- Define and calculate contribution and break-even point, and prepare a break-even chart and a profit–volume chart.
- Use break-even analysis to explore the effect of changing unit selling price, unit variable cost or fixed cost.
- Explain the limitations of break-even analysis.
- Explain applications of cost–volume–profit analysis.
- Show how calculation of contribution can be applied in short-term decision making.
- Explain how pricing decisions may be related to cost considerations.

20.1 Introduction

In Chapter 16 the role of management accounting was explained in terms of **directing attention**, **keeping the score** and **solving problems**. This chapter turns to the problem-solving aspect of the management accountant's work and in particular to the use of management accounting information to help with decisions in the short term (where the short term is typically a period of weeks or months, extending to 12 months at the most, in which some costs are fixed and others are variable, depending on the level of activity). Chapter 23 explains the use of management accounting in making decisions about the longer term.

Activity 20.1

The classification of costs was explained at length in Chapter 17. If you have any doubts about that chapter, go back and work through it again. It is essential that Chapter 17 is understood before this chapter is attempted.

This chapter will first explain how **costs** and **revenues** behave in the short term as the volume of activity increases. This is called **cost–volume–profit analysis**. It makes use of graphs which will help you follow the analysis of costs, revenues and profits. The chapter explains the calculation of **contribution** and shows how it is used to identify the **break-even point** of neither profit nor loss.

The chapter will then show how the distinction between **variable cost** and **fixed cost** may be used in short-term decision making in situations of special orders, abandonment of a product line and the existence of limiting factors. They are set out as case studies so that you will see that each problem, while using the same principles of cost–volume–profit analysis, requires some adaptability in using the analysis in the specific circumstances.

Pricing decisions will often require management accounting information about how the price charged for a product or service matches up to the cost of that product or service. Note, however, that the price which consumers are willing to pay may be decided by economic forces rather than by the costs incurred. You will see in this chapter the main approaches to pricing and the role of costs in those approaches.

20.2 Cost behaviour: fixed and variable costs

Chapter 17 explained that cost classification systems are as varied as the businesses they serve. Types of cost classification system were identified in that chapter by reference to questions which needed answers. Chapter 17 also provided definitions of variable cost and fixed cost, while Figures 17.1, 17.2 and 17.3 showed different types of cost behaviour as activity increased.

Definitions

A **variable cost** is one which varies directly with changes in the level of activity, over a defined period of time.

A **fixed cost** is one which is not affected by changes in the level of activity, over a defined period of time.

This chapter now moves on from that starting point outlined in Chapter 17 to ask more questions about the relationships between cost, volume of output and profit.

There are two ways of viewing the behaviour of cost in relation to **activity** level. One is referred to as *the economist's view* and the other is referred to as *the accountant's view*. Each is discussed here, and the use of the accountant's view is then justified as a reasonable short-term approximation.

20.2.1 The economist's view

Figure 20.1 shows total cost related to activity level over a wide range of activity within a business. Starting at zero activity, there is a total cost of £200,000 shown representing the fixed cost of the operations, including items such as rent of premises, business rates, administration salaries and any similar costs incurred to allow operations to commence. Initially, the slope of the graph rises relatively steeply because high levels of costs are incurred as activity begins. Then the slope becomes less steep as the business begins to enjoy the economies of scale, sharing fixed costs over a wider range of activity so that the marginal cost of producing an extra item becomes progressively less. At the extreme right-hand side of the graph the slope begins to rise more steeply again as further fixed costs are incurred. Perhaps high rental has to be paid for new premises at this point to allow expansion, or labour resources become more scarce and higher labour rates have to be paid to employ staff.

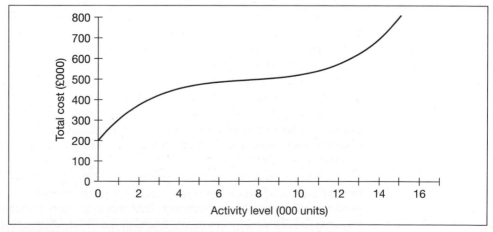

Figure 20.1
Total cost varying with activity

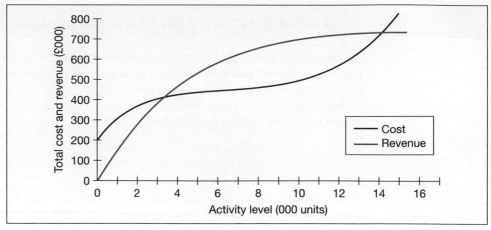

Figure 20.2
Revenue and costs: the economist's view

To calculate profit, a business must compare its cost with its revenue. The economist's portrayal of revenue is superimposed on the cost line in Figure 20.2. The total revenue starts at zero when there is zero activity. It rises rapidly when supply begins and customers are willing to pay relatively high prices for the goods. Then, as supply increases, the marginal selling price of each item decreases progressively as it becomes more difficult to sell larger volumes of output. Where the total revenue line is below the total cost line the business is making a loss, and where the total revenue line is above the total cost line the business is making a profit. The business represented by the graph in Figure 20.2 shows losses at the left-hand and right-hand sides of the diagram and a profit in the centre. Successful businesses aim to stay in the profit-making region.

20.2.2 The accountant's view

The economist's view of costs covers a very wide range of output. In any particular period, especially in the short term, the actual range of output will be relatively narrow. Looking at Figure 20.2 the lines close to the break-even point are close to being straight lines over a narrow range either side. Accounting assumes that at any point in time this relatively narrow range is available in practice and so the cost and revenue curves are approximately straight lines.

The data in Table 20.1 is used in this section to illustrate the accountant's view of how costs change with levels of activity.

Table 20.1
Table of data showing variable and fixed costs

Activity level	0 units	100 units	200 units	300 units
	£	£	£	£
Variable cost	0	10	20	30
Fixed cost	20	20	20	20
Total cost	20	30	40	50

The graph in Figure 20.2 represents activity level changes which could take some time to achieve as the business grows. The accountant takes a much shorter time perspective and looks at a relatively limited range of activity that might be achieved within that time period. In those circumstances, it may be reasonable to use straight-line graphs rather than curves, although great care is needed before assuming it is safe to use straight lines.

Using the data of Table 20.1, a graph of variable cost is shown in Figure 20.3 and a graph of fixed cost is shown in Figure 20.4.

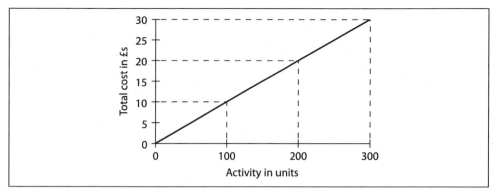

Figure 20.3
Variable cost

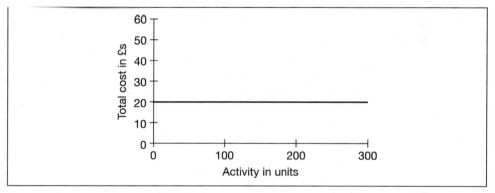

Figure 20.4
Fixed cost

In Figure 20.5, these two graphs are added together to give a graph of total cost. The total cost starts at £20 and increases by £10 for every 100 units of activity. The total cost line meets the vertical axis at the fixed cost amount of £20. The slope of the total cost line gives a picture of how fast the variable costs are rising as activity level increases.

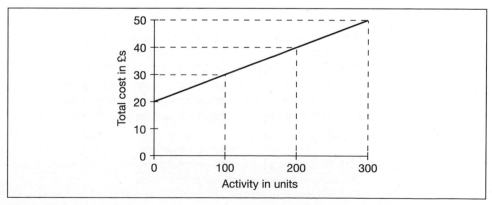

Figure 20.5
Total cost

The profit of the business is measured by comparing costs with revenues. Here again, the accountant takes the view that it may be reasonable, over a short timescale and relatively limited range of activity, to use a straight line. In Figure 20.6, a sales line is added based on a selling price of 30 pence per unit, so that total sales are £30 for 100 units, £60 for 200 units and £90 for 300 units.

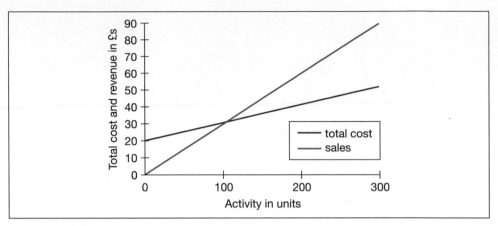

Figure 20.6
Total cost and total sales

The sales line is below the cost line at the left-hand side of the graph, crossing the cost line when the activity is 100 units. This shows that for activity levels below 100 units the business will make a loss. At 100 units of activity the business makes neither profit nor loss. This is called the **break-even point**. Beyond 100 units of activity the business makes a profit and the amount of profit is measured by the vertical difference between the sales and cost lines.

Definition	The **break-even point** is that point of activity (measured as sales volume) where total sales and total cost are equal, so that there is neither profit nor loss.

The graph shown in Figure 20.6 is more commonly called a **break-even chart**. It shows the activity level at which total costs equal total sales and at which the business makes neither a profit nor a loss. It also shows what happens to costs and revenues on either side of this break-even point. If activity falls below the break-even level, then the amount of loss will be measured by the vertical distance between the cost and sales line.

If activity rises above the break-even level then the amount of profit will be measured by the vertical distance between the sales and cost line. If the business is operating at an activity level higher than the break-even point, the distance between these two points is called the **margin of safety**. The margin of safety indicates how much activity has to fall from its present level before profit becomes zero.

Definition	The **margin of safety** is the difference between the break-even sales and the normal level of sales (measured in units or in £s of sales).

Figure 20.7 summarises the various features of a break-even chart. The use of a chart of this type to depict the behaviour of costs and sales over a range of activity in the short term has been found extremely helpful in presenting management accounting information to non-financial managers who are involved in making decisions which have financial consequences.

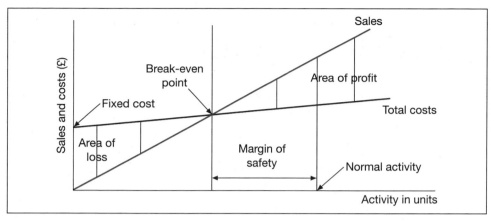

Figure 20.7
The features of a break-even chart

20.2.3 Cost–volume–profit analysis

Cost–volume–profit analysis is based on the idea that in the short run it is possible to survive in business providing sales revenue covers variable cost. The contribution from a product is the amount by which its selling price exceeds its variable cost. The excess of selling price over variable cost makes a contribution to covering fixed costs and then making a profit. In the short run it may be worth continuing in business if the selling price is greater than variable cost, so that there is a contribution to fixed costs, even where some part of the fixed costs is not covered. In the long term it is essential to earn sufficient sales revenue to cover *all* costs.

Definition | **Contribution per unit** is the selling price per unit minus the variable cost per unit. It measures the contribution made by each item of output to the fixed costs and profit of the organisation.

20.3 Break-even analysis

Break-even analysis is a technique of management accounting which is based on calculating the break-even point and analysing the consequences of changes in various factors calculating the break-even point. The idea of **contribution** is central to break-even analysis in evaluating the effects of various short-term decisions.

This section explains ways of finding the break-even point. It uses the information in Exhibit 20.1 to compare different approaches.

Exhibit 20.1
Illustration: market trader

A market trader rents a stall at a fixed price of £200 for a day and sells souvenirs. These cost the trader 50 pence each to buy and have a selling price of 90 pence each. How many souvenirs must be sold to break even?

Activity 20.2

Hopefully, you will find the case study so easy to solve that you will already have computed the answer. If so, then analyse how you arrived at the answer before you read the next paragraphs and compare your method with the descriptions given there. It is always better to work out a method for yourself, if it is a good one, than to try remembering something from a book.

20.3.1 Calculating the break-even point

Calculating contribution

The **contribution** from a product is the amount by which its selling price exceeds its variable cost. The idea of contribution is central to break-even analysis in evaluating the effects of various decisions.

Once the **contribution per unit** is known it can be compared with the **fixed costs**. The business does not begin to make a profit until the fixed costs are covered, so the formula is applied as:

Break-even point	equals	$\dfrac{\text{Fixed costs}}{\text{Contribution per unit}}$

Taking the data from the illustration in Exhibit 20.1, the contribution is 40 pence per souvenir (selling price 90 pence minus variable cost 50 pence) and the fixed costs are £200:

$$\text{Break-even point} = \frac{200}{0.40} = 500 \text{ units}$$

Algebraic method

The equation for the break-even point is:

Sales	equals	Fixed costs + Variable costs

If the number of souvenirs sold at the break-even point is n, then the total sales revenue is $0.9n$ and the total variable cost is $0.5n$:

$$0.9n = 200 + 0.5n$$
$$0.4n = 200$$

Solving the equation, $n = 500$ souvenirs need to be sold to break even.

20.3.2 Break-even chart

The general appearance of a break-even chart has already been shown in Figure 20.7. To plot the graph some points on each line are necessary. Because they are all straight lines only two points are needed, together with a ruler and pencil to join them. Points on a graph may be defined by specifying two co-ordinates in the form (x, y). A point defined as (10, 100) means that it lies at the intersection of a line up from 10 on the horizontal (x) axis and a line across from 100 on the vertical (y) axis. In Figure 20.8, two points are plotted, namely, (10, 100) and (30, 300). These may then be joined by a straight line.

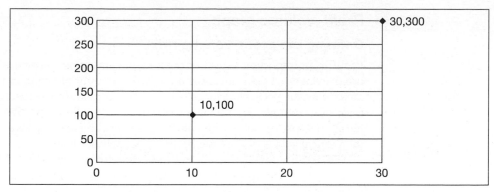

Figure 20.8
Plotting points for a graph

The graph needs to cover an activity scale wide enough to show both sides of the break-even point, so it is a useful idea to work round the break-even point by choosing one point which is loss making and one point which is profit making. The point of zero activity will usually be loss making because there is nil revenue but there are fixed costs. So the start of the sales line can be plotted at (0, 0) and the start of the cost line at (0, £200). For a position of profit, the sales and total cost must be calculated for a higher activity level, which in this case might be 900 souvenirs:

Sales of 900 souvenirs at 90 pence each = £810

The sales line will therefore join the points (0, £0) and (900, £810):

		£
Variable cost of 900 souvenirs at 50 pence each	=	450
Fixed cost	=	200
Total cost		650

The total cost line joins (0, £200) and (900, £650). Figure 20.9 shows the break-even chart with a break-even point at 500 units sold. Gridlines are added to show the points plotted.

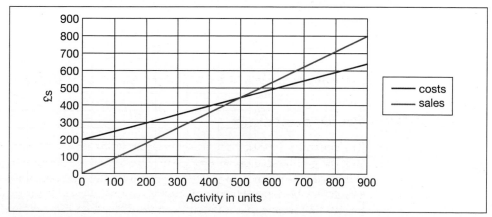

Figure 20.9
Break-even chart

20.3.3 Profit–volume graph

Defining the profit–volume ratio

Profit is an important aspect of most management accounting reports. However, the break-even chart does not show directly the amount of profit. It has to be estimated by measuring the vertical distance between the sales and total cost lines. There is another form of graph used in management accounting called a **profit–volume chart**. On the horizontal axis is plotted the volume, measured by activity level in £s of sales, and on the vertical axis is plotted the profit at that activity level.

The activity level is measured in £s of sales in order that the slope of the graph matches the **profit/volume ratio**, a slightly confusing name for the ratio which calculates contribution as a percentage of sales value:

Profit/volume ratio	equals	$\dfrac{\text{Contribution per unit}}{\text{Selling price per unit}} \times 100$

Figure 20.10 sets out a diagram showing the main features of a profit–volume chart.

Illustration of a profit–volume chart

Taking the data used in preparing Figure 20.8, the preparation of a profit–volume graph requires only the profit line to be drawn. When sales are zero, there will be a loss equal to the fixed cost, which gives the first point to plot at (£0, −£200). When 900 units are sold the sales are £810 and the profit is £160, giving the second point to plot at (£810, £160). The result is shown in Figure 20.11. The gridlines are included to

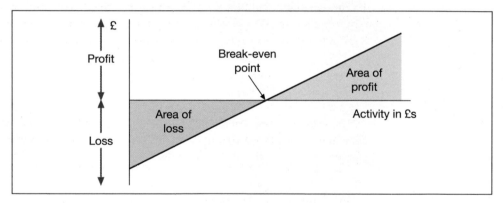

Figure 20.10
Profit–volume chart

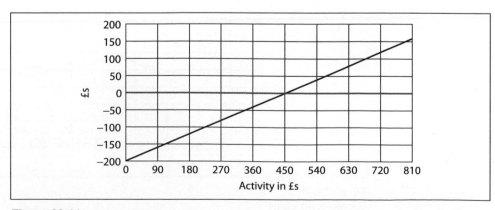

Figure 20.11
Profit–volume chart using data from the 'market trader' case study

show where the profit line has been plotted. The break-even point of zero profit or loss is at a sales level of £450. The graph rises by £40 of profit for every £90 increase in sales activity, giving a slope of 44.4%.

The profit/volume ratio is calculated by formula as:

$$\frac{\text{Contribution per unit}}{\text{Sales price per unit}} = \frac{40 \text{ pence}}{90 \text{ pence}} = 44.4\%$$

20.4 Using break-even analysis

Break-even analysis is a very useful tool. It may be used to answer questions of the following type:

- What level of sales is necessary to cover **fixed costs** and make a specified profit?
- What is the effect of **contribution per unit** beyond the break-even point?
- What happens to the **break-even point** when the selling price of one unit changes?
- What happens to the **break-even point** when the variable cost per unit changes?
- What happens to the **break-even point** when the fixed costs change?

Each of these questions is now dealt with in this section by an illustration and an explanation following the illustration.

20.4.1 Covering fixed costs and making a profit

To find the level of sales necessary to cover fixed costs and make a specified profit requires a knowledge of selling price per unit, variable cost per unit and the fixed costs together with the desired profit. These are set out in the data table.

Data	
Selling price per unit	80 pence
Variable cost per unit	30 pence
Fixed cost	£300
Desired level of profit	£400

The contribution per unit is 50 pence (80 pence – 30 pence). To find the break-even point, the fixed costs of £300 are divided by the contribution per unit to obtain a break-even point of 600 units.

To meet fixed costs of £300 and desired profit of £400 requires the contribution to cover £700 in all. This is achieved by selling 1,400 units.

$$\text{Volume of sales required} = \frac{700}{0.5} = 1,400 \text{ units}$$

Activity 20.3   *Check that 1,400 units at a contribution of 50 pence each gives a total contribution of £700. It is always a useful precaution to check the arithmetic of a calculation as a safeguard against carelessness.*

20.4.2 Beyond the break-even point

Beyond the break-even point the fixed costs are covered and the sales of further units are making a contribution to profit. The higher the contribution per unit, the greater the profit from any particular level of activity. The data table sets out some information on selling prices, variable costs and fixed costs of two products.

> *Data*
> A dry-cleaning shop takes two types of clothing. Jackets cost £6 to clean and the customer is charged £9 per garment. Coats cost £10 to clean and the customer is charged £12 per garment. The monthly fixed costs are £600 for each type of garment (representing the rental costs of two different types of machine). The shop expects to clean 500 jackets and 500 coats each month.

Activity 20.4

Before reading the analysis following Figure 20.11, calculate the contribution made by each product, work out the break-even point of each, and then explore the effect on the break-even point of:

(a) changes in the price charged to customers;
(b) changes in the variable costs; and
(c) changes in the fixed costs.

If you have access to a spreadsheet package this is the kind of problem for which spreadsheets are highly suitable.

The calculations set out in Table 20.2 show that, although both products have the same fixed costs, the jackets have a lower break-even point because they make a higher contribution per unit. Beyond the break-even point they continue to contribute more per unit. The profits at any given level of activity are therefore higher for jackets.

Table 20.2
Calculation of break-even point and of sales beyond the break-even point

	Jackets	Coats
	£	£
Selling price	9	12
Variable cost	6	10
Contribution per item	3	2
Fixed costs	£600	£600
Break-even point	200 units	300 units
Profit for sales of 500 units	£900	£400

20.4.3 Margin of safety

The **margin of safety** has been defined as the difference between the **break-even sales** and the normal level of sales, measured in units or in dollars of sales. In the case of the dry-cleaning shop, the margin of safety for jackets is 300 jackets (500 − 200) when 500 jackets are cleaned each month. The margin of safety for coats is 200 coats (500 − 300) when 500 coats are cleaned each month. The margin of safety is interpreted by saying that cleaning of jackets may fall by 300 per month before the break-even point is reached but cleaning of coats will reach the break-even point after a reduction of only 200 in coats cleaned. Cleaning coats is therefore riskier than cleaning jackets, if expected output is compared to break-even volume.

20.4.4   Change in selling price

If the selling price per unit increases and costs remain constant, then the contribution per unit will increase and the break-even volume will be lower. Take as an example the dry-cleaning business of the previous illustration. If the selling price of cleaning a coat rises to £15, then the contribution per unit will rise to £5. That will require cleaning only 120 coats to break even. The risk of raising the price is that customers may move elsewhere, so that while it may not be difficult to exceed the break-even point at a selling price of £12 it may be extremely difficult at a selling price of £15.

20.4.5   Change in variable cost

The effect of a change in variable cost is very similar to the effect of a change in selling price. If the variable cost per unit increases, then the contribution per unit will decrease, with the result that more items will have to be sold in order to reach the break-even point. If it is possible to reduce variable costs, then the contribution per unit will increase. The enterprise will reach the break-even point at a lower level of activity and will then be earning profits at a faster rate.

20.4.6   Change in fixed costs

If **fixed costs** increase, then more units have to be sold in order to reach the break-even point. Where the fixed costs of an operation are relatively high, there is a perception of greater risk because a cutback in activity for any reason is more likely to lead to a loss. Where an organisation has relatively low fixed costs, there may be less concern about margins of safety because the break-even point is correspondingly lower.

20.5   Limitations of break-even analysis

Break-even analysis is a useful tool for problem solving and decision making, but some of the limitations should be noted:

1 The break-even analysis assumes that cost and revenue behaviour patterns are known and that the change in activity levels can be represented by a straight line.
2 It may not always be feasible to split costs neatly into variable and fixed categories. Some costs show mixed behaviour.
3 The break-even analysis assumes that fixed costs remain constant over the volume range under consideration. If that is not the case, then the graph of total costs will have a step in it where the fixed costs are expected to increase.
4 Break-even analysis, as described so far in this book, assumes input and output volumes are the same, so that there is no build-up of stocks and work in progress.
5 Break-even charts and simple analyses can only deal with one product at a time.
6 It is assumed that cost behaviour depends entirely on volume.

These limitations may be overcome by modifying the break-even analysis. However, that would involve considerably more computation work and is beyond the scope of this book.

20.6 Applications of cost–volume–profit analysis

Break-even analysis is a particular example of the more general technique of cost–volume–profit analysis. This analysis emphasises the relationship between sales revenue, costs and profit in the short term. In this context the short term is a period of time over which some costs are fixed, whatever the level of output within a range limited by the existing capacity of the business. In the longer term, all costs become variable because the capacity of a business can be altered by acquiring new premises, hiring more employees or investing in more equipment.

Definition	**Cost–volume–profit analysis** evaluates the effects of forecast changes in sales, variable costs and fixed costs, to assist in decision making.

In using **cost–volume–profit analysis**, management accounting is meeting the needs of **directing attention** and **solving problems**. In the short term, decisions have to be made within the existing constraints of the capacity of the business and the aim of that decision making will be to maximise short-term profit. Typical decision-making situations requiring cost–volume–profit analysis would be:

● accepting a special order to use up spare capacity
● abandoning a line of business
● the existence of a limiting factor
● carrying out an activity in-house rather than buying in a service under contract.

Each of these situations is now considered in turn.

Activity 20.5	*Those who comment on the applications of cost–volume–profit analysis always emphasise that it is a short-run decision-making tool. Write a 200-word note explaining this view.*

20.6.1 Special order to use up spare capacity

In the short term, a business must ensure that the revenue from each item of activity at least covers variable costs and makes a contribution to fixed costs. Once the fixed costs are covered by contribution, the greater the level of activity, the higher the profit. When the business reaches full capacity there will be a new element of fixed cost to consider should the business decide to increase its capacity. If there is no increase in capacity, then the business should concentrate on those activities producing the highest contribution per unit or per item.

But supposing the business is *not* operating at full capacity. Should it lower its sales price in an attempt to increase the volume of activity? The question may arise in the form of a request from a customer for a special price for a particular order. (Customers may well know that the business is not operating at full capacity and may therefore try to use their bargaining power to force a lower sales price.) Should the business accept the special order? Cost–volume–profit analysis gives the answer that the special order is acceptable provided the sales price per item covers the variable costs per item and provided there is no alternative use for the spare capacity which could result in a higher contribution per item.

20.6.2 Abandonment of a line of business

The management of a business may be concerned because one line of business appears not to be covering all its costs. This situation may arise particularly where costs are being used for score-keeping purposes and all fixed costs have been allocated to products. As was shown in Chapter 18, the allocation of fixed costs to products is a process which is somewhat arbitrary in nature, and is not relevant to decision making because the fixed costs are incurred irrespective of whether any business activity takes place.

When a line of business comes under scrutiny as to its profitability, cost–volume–profit analysis shows that in the short term it is worth continuing with the line if it makes a contribution to fixed costs. If the line of business is abandoned and nothing better takes its place, then that contribution is lost but the fixed costs run on regardless.

20.6.3 Existence of a limiting factor

In the short term, it may be that one of the inputs to a business activity is restricted in its availability. There may be a shortage of raw materials or a limited supply of skilled labour. There may be a delivery delay on machinery or a planning restriction which prevents the extension of a building on the business premises. There may then be a need to choose from a range of possible activities so as to maximise short-term profit. The item which is restricted in availability is called the **limiting factor**.

Cost–volume–profit analysis shows that maximisation of profit will occur if the activity is chosen which gives the highest **contribution per unit of limiting factor**.

20.6.4 In-house activity versus bought-in contract

For a manufacturing business, there may be a decision between making a component in-house as compared with buying the item ready-made. For a service business there may be a decision between employing staff in-house and using the services of an agency which supplies staff as and when required. Cost–volume–profit analysis shows that the decision should be based on comparison of variable costs per unit, relating this to the difference in fixed costs between the options.

20.7 Cases in short-term decision making

Cost–volume–profit analysis is particularly well suited to management needs in short-term decision making. Fiona McTaggart now discusses four cases she has come across where cost–volume–profit analysis has been relevant. The first relates to a decision about taking on a special order to fill a gap where the business was not running at full capacity. The second relates to a potential abandonment of a line of business, the third deals with a limiting factor causing scarcity of an input to the production process, and the fourth relates to buying in services.

20.7.1 Decisions on special orders

FIONA: *My first story is about a car hire business in a holiday resort which was experiencing a temporary fall in activity in the run-up to the start of the tourist season. Their normal charge was £3.00 per mile, to cover all costs including the driver's wages. A telephone installation company offered a three-month contract to run engineers between two towns on a return journey of 100 miles, at a fixed price of £180 per journey. The car hire company asked my advice about accepting this offer of £1.80 per mile.*

I asked the company what the drivers and cars would be doing each day if the contract was not taken up and the answer was that they would not be doing anything other than waiting at the depot and cleaning their cars. My advice was that, on that basis, the contract would be worth undertaking if it covered the variable costs of each journey and made a contribution to fixed costs and profit.

We sat down to look at the fixed costs and produced the statement shown in Table 20.3. Quite deliberately I did not write any amounts against the separate items of fixed costs because I wanted to emphasise that these are the unavoidable element which will arise whether or not the contract is taken up.

Table 20.3
Analysis of variable and fixed costs of car hire firm

Variable costs:	
Petrol	£1.20 per litre
Fuel consumption	6 miles per litre
Tyre costs	£1,600 per set of four tyres
Tyre replacement	every 20,000 miles
Fixed costs:	£84,000
These covered:	
Driver's wages	
Insurance	
Licence fee for airport waiting	
Licence fee to town council	
Depreciation of vehicle	
Annual testing	
Radio control membership	
Average annual mileage per car:	40,000 miles

From the data provided, I calculated the variable cost per mile as 20 pence for petrol and 8 pence for tyres, giving 28 pence in all. The normal charge of £3.00 per mile is intended to cover this 28 pence per mile plus the fixed cost per mile, amounting to £2.10 per mile using the average annual mileage per car. That total cost of £2.38 per mile leaves a profit of 62 pence per mile or £24,800 per annum if the average mileage is achieved.

It is clear that to cover all costs the charge of £3.00 is probably about right, but if the drivers and cars are otherwise unoccupied, extra journeys on the special contract contribute £1.52 per mile (£1.80 – £0.28) to fixed costs and profit. I advised them to take up the contract on two conditions:

1 they must be as sure as they could be that there will not be an upturn in business during the hire period which would mean they were turning down the possibility of carrying passengers who would pay £3.00 per mile; and

2 if the journeys involve extra payments to drivers for overtime or late-night work, those extra payments should be regarded as part of the variable cost of the contract and the costings recalculated on that basis.

They took my advice and carried out the contract. It fitted perfectly into the quiet period of business and the company realised later that the contract had made a useful contribution to profit at a time when drivers and cars would otherwise have been inactive.

In Fiona's example, the company made use of the idea that, in the short term, any contract is worth taking on if it covers variable costs and makes some contribution to fixed costs and profit. Care needs to be taken that the special order does not create a precedent for future work, particularly if existing customers find that special treatment is being given which appears to undercut the price they are paying. The company may find it difficult in future to return to the price which covers all costs. In the long term, the company must charge a price which covers fixed costs as well as variable costs if it is to survive.

Fiona's second illustration relates to a decision on abandoning a line of activity.

20.7.2 Abandonment decisions

FIONA: *A private tuition college was providing two types of secretarial training course. The first was teaching word processing and the second was teaching office skills. The college had produced the profit and loss statement shown in Table 20.4.*

Table 20.4
Information for abandonment decision

	Word processing £000s	Office skills £000s	Total £000s
Tuition fee income	485	500	985
Variable costs	200	330	530
Fixed overhead	120	220	340
Total costs	320	550	870
Profit/(loss)	165	(50)	115

On the basis of this profit and loss statement the owners of the business were on the point of cancelling all further courses in office skills. I asked them how they had decided on the allocation of fixed overheads and they explained that these comprised primarily administrative staff costs and permanent teaching staff, plus items such as rent and business rates as well as depreciation of word processors and of the equipment used in the cabin which had been set up to simulate the most up-to-date office conditions. The cabin itself was depreciated over 20 years. Fixed overhead which could be allocated directly to the relevant courses, such as depreciation of equipment, was allocated in its entirety to the relevant course type. This approach was also used for teaching costs where these were specific to one course type. Fixed overhead which could apply to each type of course, such as administrative staff salaries, was spread in proportion to the number of courses given.

I pointed out to the owners that their profit and loss statement would be more informative if it were set out in the format shown in Table 20.5.

Table 20.5
Revised data for abandonment decision

	Word processing £000s	Office skills £000s	Total £000s
Tuition fee income	485	500	985
Variable costs	200	330	530
Contribution	285	170	455
Fixed overhead			340
Profit			115

From Table 20.5 it is relatively straightforward to see that the office skills programme is making a contribution of £170,000 to fixed costs and profit, after covering its own variable costs. If the programme were not offered, then the business would have only the contribution of £285,000 from word processing which would not cover the fixed overhead of £340,000. Far from abandoning the office skills programme, it was essential to retain it. The allocation of fixed overheads was, for short-term analysis purposes, irrelevant. The cabin and office equipment had already been purchased and would continue to depreciate whether used or not. If put up for sale, these assets would have a negligible value. Administrative and permanent staff were also in place and could not instantly be disengaged.

I advised them that while it was preferable in the short term to keep both programmes running, there were some questions they should ask themselves for longer-term planning:

1 To what extent do clients take up the word processing courses because the office skills course may be studied at the same time and in the same place?

2 How much fixed cost could be avoided in the longer term if either course ceased to exist?

3 Would it be a more effective use of resources to concentrate only on one type of course so that the fixed costs are restricted to one type of equipment and perhaps relatively fewer administrative staff?

The answers might lead to reorganisation towards one type of course only. On the other hand, it might be found that the two programmes are so interrelated that each needs the other and the fixed costs are effectively essential to both, whatever the accounting allocation process.

Fiona's third story concerns a business where there was a restriction in the amount of a factor of input to the production process.

20.7.3 Existence of limiting factors

FIONA: *A kitchen equipment service company had come across a problem of a shortage of trained engineers in a district because new oil exploration activity had attracted the best staff by making offers of high salaries.*

On a short-term basis the company felt it could not continue to service washing machines, dishwashers and built-in ovens in that area and would prefer to concentrate on the most profitable use of its labour resource. Table 20.6 shows the most recent annual data available, based on the situation before the employee shortage crisis arose. However, the total labour force now available was estimated in cost terms at £40,000 in total.

Table 20.6
Data for limiting factor problem

	Washing machines £000s	Dishwashers £000s	Built-in ovens £000s
Sales	80	120	180
Direct materials	10	20	18
Direct labour	30	30	60
Variable overhead	10	30	30
Total variable cost	50	80	108
Contribution	30	40	72

I advised them that, in these circumstances, the limiting factor of labour should be used so as to maximise the contribution from every £ of labour used. First, I calculated the contribution per £ of scarce resource for each of the three types of service contract (see Table 20.7).

Table 20.7
Calculation of contribution per £ of limiting factor

	Washing machines £000s	Dishwashers £000s	Built-in ovens £000s
Contribution	30	40	72
Direct labour	30	30	60
Contribution per £ of labour	£1.00	£1.33	£1.20

The highest contribution per £ of labour is therefore provided by dishwashers, followed by built-in ovens. So I explained that it would be best to use the scarce labour resource first of all to service dishwashers. At the existing level of sales that would take up £30,000 worth of labour, leaving the balance of £10,000 worth of labour to service built-in ovens on a restricted basis. If more dishwasher work became available, that would be the preferred choice for profit generation.

This would be a short-term solution, but in the longer term it would be essential to consider whether the market could stand higher charges for servicing equipment, which would allow higher wage rates to be paid and thus permit all three types of work to continue.

Fiona has used in this example a particular case of a general principle that where limiting factors apply, profit is made as high as possible where the greatest contribution is obtained each time the scarce resource is used.

20.7.4 Make or buy

The management of a manufacturing business may have to decide whether to make a component in-house or buy the item ready-made.

Fiona McTaggart explains the problem:

FIONA: *A car manufacturer has a problem regarding one quite small component used on a production line. The component may be purchased from an external supplier at £100 per item. It is currently being manufactured in-house at a cost of £110 per item, comprising fixed cost £30 per item and variable cost £80 per item. Annual output is currently 50,000 components and the trend of output is expected to be rising.*

The external price looks attractive at first glance but, before I can advise the car manufacturer, I need to know more about the fixed cost. It is currently £1,500,000 per annum (£30 times 50,000 components). If the company can avoid the fixed cost by purchasing from the outside supplier, then I will compare the additional variable cost of £20 (£100 – £80) with the saving of £1,500,000. The company breaks even at 75,000 components (calculated as fixed cost saving of £1,500,000 divided by additional variable cost of £20). If demand is less than 75,000 then it is more cost-effective to buy from the external supplier. If demand is more than 75,000 then it is more cost-effective to manufacture in-house (provided fixed costs do not change at a higher level of output).

If the fixed cost of £1,500,000 cannot be avoided (perhaps it represents rent and property costs which would be incurred even if there were no production), then there is no advantage in buying from the external supplier. The relevant comparison in such a situation is between the variable cost of £80 and the external price of £100.

I would also advise the company that non-financial matters such as quality control and reliability of supply should be taken into consideration when deciding on external purchase rather than internal production.

20.7.5 In-house activity compared to bought-in services

In her final example, Fiona describes a situation where a company was considering buying in services rather than employing its own staff. Cost–volume–profit analysis implies that the decision should be based on the costs saved by not undertaking the activity in-house (the variable costs and any fixed costs that are avoidable) together with the costs incurred in buying the product or service from an external supplier (price multiplied by quantity purchased).

FIONA: *A company had been employing its own legal department, comprising a qualified solicitor and two assistants. The solicitor was about to retire and the company had to decide whether to advertise for a replacement or to use a commercial law service as and when required. There would be no redundancy costs in respect of the two assistants because the younger one could be redeployed to a vacancy elsewhere in the organisation and the other would continue to be required as the internal contact with the commercial law service.*

I showed the management that, because the commercial law service would charge on an hourly basis, the costs to be compared were the variable costs per hour charged by the commercial service and the fixed costs per annum of the in-house solicitor's salary. We compared the hourly charge rate of £400 with the solicitor's salary of £60,000 and the assistant's salary of £36,000 and worked out that the break-even point would be 240 hours of the commercial law service each year. If more than 240 hours are requested next year, it would be worth continuing the in-house service.

20.7.6 Relevant costs

Throughout the examples above Fiona McTaggart has made use of the distinction between **fixed** and **variable costs**. She has also distinguished **relevant** from non-relevant costs. Generally the fixed costs have not been relevant to decision making but the variable costs have been relevant. Some fixed costs are relevant where they may be avoided by a specific course of action but others are not relevant because they may not be avoided.

Definition   **Relevant costs** are those future costs which will be affected by a decision to be taken. Non-relevant costs will not be affected by the decision.

20.8 Pricing decisions

One of the most important decisions taken by a business is that of pricing its product. If the price is too high, there will be no demand. If the price is too low, the organisation will be making a lower profit than could be achieved.

20.8.1 Economic factors affecting pricing

The method of arriving at a price depends on economic factors. If the business has a monopoly position (where one supplier has control of the market), it will be able to dictate its own price. However, the higher the price, the greater the attraction to incomers to break down the monopoly powers in seeking to share the benefits enjoyed by the monopolist.

Where the business is a market leader, it may be able to set its price by reference to covering its full costs and making a satisfactory profit. If there are only a few large sellers, each with a significant share of the market, the situation is described as an oligopoly. These few large sellers may compete with each other on price or they may prefer to set their prices at a level which covers all costs and to keep the price reasonably constant while competing on non-price factors such as quality of the product.

In a perfectly competitive market, no one supplier is in a position to dictate prices. Economic theory shows that the optimal price will be achieved where marginal cost equals marginal revenue. In other words, the additional cost of producing one more item of output equals the additional revenue obtained by selling that item. While the additional revenue exceeds the additional cost, the economist argues that it is worth producing more. When the additional revenue is less than the additional cost, production will not take place in the perfectly competitive market.

Pricing policy therefore depends primarily on the circumstances of the business. In many situations there is strong competition and the organisation must accept the market price and try to maximise its profit by controlling cost. In that situation, the most efficient organisation will achieve the highest profit as a percentage of sales. Sometimes the organisation may be faced with pressure from customers to reduce selling price. The decision to do so will require an evaluation of the lower price against costs. In other cases, the organisation may have some ability to control price and therefore has to decide on a price related to what the market will bear and related to covering its costs.

There are therefore some situations in which a cost-based pricing formula may be appropriate. These are now considered.

20.8.2   Full cost pricing

Full cost pricing is also called **cost-plus pricing**. The manager who is setting the price for goods or services calculates the total cost per unit of output and adds a percentage to that cost called the **percentage mark-up on cost**.

Calculation of total cost requires allocation of **overhead costs**. It was shown in Chapter 18 that there is more than one method of allocating production overhead costs. The same variety of method may be found in allocation of non-production overhead. Different organisations will have different ideas on which costs they want to cover in a cost-based pricing approach. What really matters is that the organisation understands its cost structure and ensures that all overhead costs are covered in some way by revenue in the longer term.

When the company is a price taker and is asked to take a lower price, or not to raise its existing price, then cost-plus pricing is still important, but it is also important for the organisation to ensure that it makes a decision using **relevant costs**. If the pricing decision is based on a short-term perspective, then the organisation may decide to accept any price provided that the additional revenue covers the variable costs. That is the accountant's version of the economist's rule that marginal cost should equal marginal revenue. In management accounting terms, the item should make a **contribution** to fixed costs but does not necessarily need to cover all fixed costs. In the longer term, the business must cover all costs, whether fixed or variable, but it is possible that some fixed costs may be avoidable. If, for example, a reduced price is forced upon the business, it may accept this in the short term but also take a long-term decision to cut back on permanent staff and rental of premises. Such a decision may be unpleasant to take, in terms of human consequences for staff, but may allow the business to survive in a harsher economic situation.

20.8.3   Mark-up percentages

The full cost approach to pricing requires a percentage to be added to cost. Where does this percentage come from? The answer is that it depends very much on the type of business and the type of product. Where the market is competitive, mark-up percentages will be low and the organisation relies for its success on a high volume of sales activity. This may be seen in the operation of supermarkets, which charge lower prices than the small shops and therefore have lower margins on the items sold, but customers take away their purchases by the car load rather than in small parcels. In the case of supermarket chains there is another aspect to pricing in that they themselves buy from suppliers. The supermarkets may use the strength of their position to dictate price terms to the suppliers, so that the margins are not as low as they would seem from the prices charged to the customers.

In some industries, or for some products, there appears to be a 'normal' mark-up which all companies apply fairly closely. This 'normal' mark-up may be so characteristic that it is used by the auditor as a check on how reasonable the gross profit amount appears and is also used by the tax authorities as a check on whether all sales and profit are being declared for taxation purposes.

For those businesses which are in a position to apply cost-plus pricing, it may encourage stability in the pricing structure because other businesses in the same industry may be in a position to predict the behaviour of competitors. Companies in an industry will know the mix of variable and fixed costs in the industry and will therefore have a good idea of how competitors' profits will be affected by a change of price.

20.8.4 Limitations of full cost pricing

Full cost pricing, if used without sufficient care, may not take into account the demand for the product. A business may charge a profit margin of 20% on sales when market research could have shown that the potential customers would have accepted up to 25% as a profit margin and still bought the goods or services.

Apportionment of fixed costs is an arbitrary process, with more than one approach being available. The profit estimated using the cost-plus basis will depend on the apportionment of fixed costs. If the price is distorted by the costing process, an optimal level of sales may not be achieved.

There may be a lack of benefit to customers where businesses are able to set prices on a cost-plus basis and, as a consequence, a group of companies works together to 'agree' a price. Such a situation is described in economics as a 'cartel', and in some situations a government will legislate against price fixing by cartels because it creates a monopoly position in a situation which appears at first sight to be competitive.

20.8.5 Marginal cost pricing

Chapter 9 showed that, in the short term, a business may decide to accept a price that is lower than full cost providing the price offered is greater than the variable cost, so that there is a **contribution** to fixed overhead costs. This reflects the economist's position that a business will continue to sell providing the marginal revenue exceeds the marginal cost. It is therefore called *marginal cost pricing*. The most likely situation is that a customer, knowing that the business has spare capacity, will offer a contract at a reduced price to take up some of the spare capacity. The manager will accept the offer provided there is a contribution to fixed costs and profits and providing no additional fixed costs are incurred because of the extra contract.

Activity 20.6	*Write down two products or services where the pricing might be based on cost plus a percentage to cover profits. Write down two products or services where the prices are determined in a highly competitive market. Write a short explanation (200 words) for an employee newsletter in a soap manufacturing business explaining why your product price is always a few pence higher in the shops than that of other leading brands.*

20.9 Summary

Key themes in this chapter are:

- The accountant's view of cost behaviour differs from that of the economist. The accountant assumes that total cost and total revenue vary on a straight-line basis as the volume of output and sales increases. The economist sees total cost varying in a non-linear manner due to economies of scale and sees total revenue gradually levelling off as customers reach the point where they do not wish to buy more of the item.

- **Contribution** is defined as sales minus variable cost. Contribution per unit is compared with fixed overhead cost to calculate break-even point. A break-even chart and a profit–volume chart are useful ways of showing how contribution and profit change as the volume of output and sales increases.

- **Break-even analysis** can be used to explore the effect of changing unit selling price, unit variable cost or fixed cost.

- **Break-even analysis** has limitations because it is only suitable *for short-term decision making* and can only focus on one product at a time.

- A **break-even chart** is a graph that shows sales and costs over a range of activity, including the activity level at which total costs equal total sales and at which the business makes neither a profit nor a loss.

- **Cost–volume–profit analysis** means comparing sales revenue with variable cost and fixed cost to calculate profit or loss over a range of activity, to help with short-term decision making.

- A **profit–volume chart** is a graph on which the horizontal axis shows the volume, measured by activity level in £s of sales, and the vertical axis shows the profit at that activity level.

- The **profit/volume ratio** is calculated as contribution as a percentage of sales value:

- The calculation of **contribution** can be applied in the short-term for decisions such as:

  - *Decisions on* special orders (Does a lower price leave a positive contribution?)

  - *Abandonment decisions* (Is the product or service making a positive contribution?)

  - *Limiting factors* (Which product or service gives the highest contribution per unit of limiting factor?)

  - *Make or buy* (How does the price of the external product or service compare with the internal variable cost and the fixed overheads that will be saved?)

- Pricing decisions may be related to cost if the market accepts **full cost pricing** (e.g. with a professional business where customers or clients seek out the personal service).

- Pricing decisions may be related to **marginal cost** if there is heavy competition and manufacturers take whatever price they can get in the market.

QUESTIONS

The Questions section of each chapter has three types of question. 'Test your understanding' questions to help you review your reading are in the 'A' series of questions. You will find the answers to these by reading and thinking about the material in the book. 'Application' questions to test your ability to apply technical skills are in the 'B' series of questions. Questions requiring you to show skills in problem solving and evaluation are in the 'C' series of questions. A letter [S] indicates that there is a solution at the end of the book. Other solutions are provided in the Instructor's Manual, where there are further questions parallel to those set out here.

A   Test your understanding

A20.1   Define 'variable cost' and 'fixed cost'. (Section 20.1)

A20.2   Contrast the economist's view of costs and revenues with that taken in management accounting. (Section 20.2)

A20.3   Explain the algebraic method for determining the break-even point. (Section 20.3.1)

A20.4   Explain the formula method for determining the break-even point. (Section 20.3.1)

A20.5   Sketch, and explain the main features of, a break-even chart. (Section 20.3.2)

A20.6   Sketch, and explain the main features of, a profit–volume chart. (Section 20.3.3)

A20.7   What happens to the break-even point when the sales price per unit falls? (Section 20.4.4)

A20.8   What happens to the break-even point when the variable cost per unit falls? (Section 20.4.5)

A20.9   What happens to the break-even point when fixed overheads increase? (Section 20.4.6)

A20.10   State the limitations of break-even analysis. (Section 20.5)

A20.11   Give three examples of applications of cost–volume–profit analysis. (Section 20.6)

A20.12   Explain how cost–volume–profit analysis may help in:

(a) decisions on special orders; (Section 20.6.1)
(b) abandonment decisions; (Section 20.6.2)
(c) situations of limiting factors; and (Section 20.6.3)
(d) a decision on buying in services. (Section 20.6.4)

A20.13   Explain how economic factors usually dictate prices of goods and services. (Section 20.8.1)

A20.14   Explain the situations where full cost pricing may be appropriate. (Section 20.8.2)

A20.15   What are the limitations of full cost pricing? (Section 20.8.4)

A20.16   Explain the situations where marginal cost pricing may be appropriate. (Section 20.8.5)

B   Application

B20.1 [S]
Fixed costs are £5,000. Variable cost per unit is £3 and the unit selling price is £5.50. What is the break-even volume of sales?

B20.2 [S]
Plot a break-even chart based on the following data and label the features of interest on the chart:

Number of units	Fixed cost £	Variable cost £	Total cost £	Sales £
10	200	100	300	150
20	200	200	400	300
30	200	300	500	450
40	200	400	600	600
50	200	500	700	750

B20.3 [S]

Montrose Glass Products Ltd manufactures three ranges of high-quality paperweights – Basic, Standard and Deluxe. Its accountant has prepared a draft budget for Year 7:

	Basic £000s	Standard £000s	Deluxe £000s	Total £000s
Revenue	45	35	40	120
Material	15	10	10	35
Labour	20	15	5	40
Variable overhead	5	12	5	22
Fixed overhead	9	5	6	20
	49	42	26	117
Profit/(loss)	(4)	(7)	14	3

Fixed overheads are allocated to each product line on the basis of direct labour hours.

The directors are concerned about the viability of the company and are currently considering the cessation of both Basic and Standard ranges, since both are apparently making losses.

Required

(a) If the directors close down only the manufacture of Basic paperweights, what is the effect on total profit?

(b) If the directors close down only the manufacture of Standard paperweights, what is the effect on total profit?

(c) What is the best decision with regard to keeping profit as high as possible?

B20.4 [S]

Chris Gibson Kitchenware Limited sells kitchen appliances to department stores. Product costs are ascertained using an absorption costing system from which the following statement has been prepared in respect of the business's three product lines:

	Dishwashers £000s	Fridges £000s	Ovens £000s	Total £000s
Sales	180	330	270	780
Less total costs	(200)	(250)	(220)	(670)
Profit/(loss)	(20)	80	50	110

It has been estimated that costs are 60% variable and 40% fixed.

Required

(a) Restate the table distinguishing variable and fixed costs.

(b) Advise whether dishwashers should be dropped from the product range in order to improve profitability.

B20.5 [S]

Capital Tours Limited sells weekend tours of London for £200 per person. Last month 1,000 tours were sold and costs were £180,000 (representing a total cost per tour of £180). These costs included £60,000 which were fixed costs.

A local college wishing to send 200 students on an educational trip has offered Capital Tours £140 per tour.

Required

(a) Explain with reasons whether Capital Tours should accept the offer.

(b) Explain the danger, in the long run, of Capital Tours using prices based on variable (marginal) costing.

C Problem solving and evaluation

C20.1 [S]

Dairyproducts Ltd has recently developed sales of cream in aerosol dispensers which are sold alongside the company's traditional products of cartons of cream and packets of cheese. The company is now considering the sale of cream cheese in aerosol dispensers.

It is company policy that any new product must be capable of generating sufficient profit to cover all costs, including estimated initial marketing and advertising expenditure of £1,000,000.

Current weekly production, with unit costs and selling prices, is as follows:

	Units of output	Variable cost (£)	Fixed cost (£)	Selling price (£)
Cartons of cream	400,000	0.45	0.15	0.75
Aerosol cans of cream	96,000	0.50	0.25	1.05
Packets of cheese	280,000	1.00	0.20	1.30

Sales volume is equal to production volume. A 50-week trading year is assumed. Rates of absorption of fixed costs are based on current levels of output.

In order to produce cream cheese in aerosol dispensers, the aerosol machine would require modification at a cost of £400,000 which is to be recovered through sales within one year. Additional annual fixed costs of £500,000 would be incurred in manufacturing the new product. Variable cost of production would be 50 pence per can. Initial research has estimated demand as follows:

Price per can (£)	Maximum weekly demand (cans)
1.50	60,000
1.40	80,000
1.15	100,000

There is adequate capacity on the aerosol machine, but the factory is operating near capacity in other areas. The new product would have to be produced by reducing production elsewhere and two alternatives have been identified:

(a) reduce production of cream cartons by 20% per annum; or
(b) reduce production of packet cheese by 25% per annum.

The directors consider that the new product must cover any loss of profit caused by this reduction in volume. They are also aware that market research has shown growing customer dissatisfaction because of wastage with cream sold in cartons.

Required

Prepare a memorandum to the board of directors of Dairyproducts Ltd showing the outcome of the alternative courses of action open to the company and make a recommendation on the most profitable.

C20.2

A company is able to sell four products and is planning its production mix for the next period. Estimated costs, sales and production data are as follows:

Product	L £	M £	N £	O £
Selling price per unit	60	90	120	108
Less Variable costs				
Labour (at £6 per hour)	18	12	42	30
Material (at £3 per kg)	18	54	30	36
= Contribution per unit	24	24	48	42
Resources per unit				
Labour (hours)	3	2	7	5
Material (kg)	6	18	10	12
Maximum demand (units)	5,000	5,000	5,000	5,000

Required

(a) Based on the foregoing information, show the most profitable production mix under each of the following mutually exclusive assumptions:
 (i) if labour hours are limited to 50,000 in a period; or
 (ii) if material is limited to 110,000 kg in a period.

(b) Write a short explanation, suitable for sending to the production director, explaining your recommendation in each case.

Activities for study groups

Case 20.1

Leisure Furniture Ltd produces furniture for hotels and public houses using specific designs prepared by firms of interior design consultants. Business is brisk and the market is highly competitive with a number of rival companies tendering for work. The company's pricing policy, based on marginal costing (variable costing) techniques, is generating high sales.

The main activity of Home Furniture Ltd is the production of a limited range of standard lounge suites for household use. The company also offers a service constructing furniture to customers' designs. This work is undertaken to utilise any spare capacity. The main customers of the company are the major chains of furniture retailers. Due to recession, consumer spending on household durables has decreased recently and, as a result, the company is experiencing a significant reduction in orders for its standard lounge suites. The market is unlikely to improve within the next year. The company's pricing policy is to add a percentage mark-up to total cost.

Required

Explain why different pricing policies may be appropriate in different circumstances, illustrating your answer by reference to Leisure Furniture Ltd and Home Furniture Ltd.

Case 20.2

In groups of three, take the role of finance director, production director and sales director in a company manufacturing pressure die castings, gravity die castings and sand castings. The three types of casting are manufactured in different locations but each is no more than 20 miles from either of the other locations. All castings are brought to central premises for finishing treatment. The costs of materials are around 56% of final sales price and the costs of labour are around 30% of sales price.

The finance director has been asked to explain to the production director and the sales director the effect of measuring profit using variable costing rather than absorption costing. It is important to keep separate the profit on each of the three product types. The finance director should provide a short explanation and the production director and sales director should ask questions about anything which is unclear or omitted from the explanation. After the discussion is completed (say, 30 minutes in all) the group should make a presentation to the class outlining the nature of their discussion and the conclusion reached as to how profit for each product should be measured.

Case 20.3

Your company manufactures furniture units to customers' specifications. In groups of three, take the role of sales director, production director and finance director. You have met to decide on the price to be charged for each contract. The sales director aims to maximise revenue, the finance director seeks to maximise profit and the production director wishes to continue operating at full capacity. Discuss the approach you will take to deciding the company's pricing policy for the year ahead. Present to the rest of the class the arguments you will present to the entire board of directors.

Part 8

Planning and control

Preparing a budget

This case study shows a typical case in which management accounting can be helpful. Read the case study now but only attempt the discussion points after you have finished reading the chapter

123RF.com

Lancashire Fire and Rescue Service

Revenue Budget 2014/15–2017/18

Information

In line with the Authority's objective to deliver affordable, value for money services the Authority's Budget Strategy remains one of:

- Maintaining future council tax increases at reasonable levels, reducing if possible
- Continuing to deliver efficiencies in line with targets
- Continuing to invest in improvements in service delivery
- Continuing to invest in improving facilities
- Setting a robust budget
- Maintaining an adequate level of reserves.

Budget requirement

In order to determine the future budget requirement, the Authority has used the approved 2013/14 budget as a starting point, and has uplifted this for inflation and other known changes and pressures, to arrive at a draft budgetary requirement, prior to utilising any reserves, as set out below:

	2014/15 £m	2015/16 £m	2016/17 £m	2017/18 £m
Preceding Years Draft Budget Requirement	59.8	58.1	55.9	56.4
Removal of drawdown from reserves in previous years	0.6	–	–	–
Inflation	0.7	0.8	1.3	1.4
Other Pay Pressures	(0.1)	0.9	0.6	0.2
Committed Variations	1.7	(1.2)	0.1	0.1
Efficiency Savings	(1.7)	–	–	–
Target £10m Efficiency Savings	(2.9)	(2.7)	(1.5)	(0.1)
Draft Budget Requirement	58.1	55.9	56.4	58.0
Additional staff costs	0.3	0.7	0.8	–
Budget Requirement	58.4	56.6	57.2	58.0
Budget (Decrease)/Increase	(2.4%)	(3.1%)	1.1%	1.4%

Removal of 2013/14 drawdown from reserves

Included within the 2013/14 was the drawdown of £0.6m of reserves in order to freeze council tax. This was a one-off measure to balance the position and as such needs to be added back into the start position to provide a true reflection of budgeted costs in 2013/14.

Inflation

The following amounts have been added to the budget in respect of inflationary pressures, in line with current estimates:

	2014/15 £m	2015/16 £m	2016/17 £m	2017/18 £m
A 1% pay award in 2014/15 and 2015/16 and 2.5% pay award thereafter	0.4	0.4	1.0	1.1
Non-pay inflation of 2.5% each year	0.3	0.4	0.3	0.3
	0.7	0.8	1.3	1.4

Note – a 1% change in the pay award equates to £0.4m per annum.
Source: Lancashire Fire and Rescue Service Budget Booklet – Capital Programme and Revenue Budget 2014/15.
http://www.lancsfirerescue.org.uk/financial-summary/

Discussion points

1 What is your view on the method of projecting future budgets by adding an uplift for inflation to the approved budget of a previous year?

2 What types of cost would you expect to find in the detailed budget in order to achieve the stated Budget Strategy?

Contents

Learning outcomes

After reading this chapter you should be able to:

- Explain the purpose and nature of a budgetary system.
- Describe the administration of the budgetary process.
- Explain the benefits of budgeting.
- Understand the problems of budgeting.
- Explain how budgets are used in public service organisations.
- Prepare the separate budgets that lead to a master budget.
- Prepare budgets for periods shorter than 12 months.

21.1 Introduction

This chapter considers the purpose and nature of the budgetary system and explains the method of preparation of budgets, with particular emphasis on the planning process. No two businesses will have an identical approach to budget preparation. Some involve all employees in the process while others deliver the budget as handed down from senior management with little or no consultation. A practical example is explained in detail to show the preparation of a master budget. Calculations are also shown for quarterly budgets.

21.2 Purpose and nature of a budget system

The purpose of a budget system is to serve the needs of management in respect of the judgements and decisions it is required to make and to provide a basis for the management functions of planning and control, described in Chapter 16. That chapter also refers to the importance of communication and motivation as an aspect of management to which management accounting should contribute.

This chapter considers the purpose and nature of the budgetary process and explains the method of preparation of budgets, with particular emphasis on the planning process. The use of budgets for control is touched upon in this chapter but elaborated in more detail in Chapter 22. No two businesses will have an identical approach to budget preparation. Some involve all employees in the process, while others deliver the budget from senior management with little or no consultation. This chapter discusses systems where there is a relatively high degree of participation and negotiation in setting budgets. It should be recognised that in some businesses the senior managers will take decisions without such extensive consultation. A discussion of the relative merits of consultation are well beyond the scope of this book but in learning about the budgetary process it may help the student to think about the ways in which each person having responsibility for administering a budget might also have a part to play in its construction.

In Figure 21.1 (later) there is an illustration of the interrelationships of these management functions in respect of the process by which a business such as a chain of shops supplying motorcycles might go about planning to open a new shop in the suburbs of a city. Where this type of planning is taking place, management accounting assists through a budget system by providing quantification of each stage of the planning process. That example of the motorcycle shop illustrates a simple type of long-range planning situation but a more complex example would show the way in which the long-range planning leads on to successively more detailed developments, finishing with a collection of short-term operational budgets covering a period such as a year, six months or perhaps no more than one month ahead.

21.2.1 Long-range planning

In **long-range planning**, the senior managers of a business will begin by specifying a mission statement which sets out in the broadest terms their vision of the future direction of the organisation. Based on this mission statement the senior managers will then prepare a list of objectives which will specify the intended future growth and development of the business. For example, a company might state its mission and its long-range corporate objectives, for a five-year period ahead, in the terms shown in Exhibit 21.1.

The corporate objectives shown in Exhibit 21.1 relate to the business as a whole. They will then be taken down to another level of detail to create objectives for each division of the business. Within divisions, they will be translated into departmental objectives.

21.2.2 Strategy

Having a mission statement and corporate objectives is an essential first step, but the organisation must then decide exactly how it will achieve those objectives.

Exhibit 21.1
Company's mission statement and long-range corporate objectives

> *Mission*
> The company intends to maintain its position as the market leader in the electrical repair industry, having regard to providing investors with an adequate rate of growth of their investment in the business.
>
> Corporate objectives
> - The company intends to increase the value of the investment by its shareholders at a minimum rate of 4% per annum, in real terms.
> - The company intends to remain in the electrical goods repair business and to concentrate on this as the core business.
> - The company will provide service in the customer's home and at its main repair centres.
> - The company will continue to maintain its geographical focus on the high-earning suburban areas around the three largest cities.
> - The company seeks to enlarge its market share in those geographical areas to 20% of the total market.
> - The company has a profit objective of 30% gross profit on turnover.

The term **strategy** is used to describe the courses of action to be taken in achieving the objectives set.

Developing the strategy will involve senior management from the various functions such as marketing, customer service, production, personnel and finance. These functions are separate but must work together in the interests of the company as a whole. Each functional manager has to understand how the plans made by that function will affect other functions and the company as a whole. This requires communication and co-ordination with the assistance of a management accountant.

For the purposes of quantifying the strategy of the business, management accounting has developed specialist techniques under the global heading of **budgetary planning and control**. The rest of this chapter explains the processes involved.

21.2.3 Budgets

Definition

> A **budget** is a detailed plan which sets out, in money terms, the plans for income and expenditure in respect of a future period of time. It is prepared in advance of that time period and is based on the agreed objectives for that period of time, together with the strategy planned to achieve those objectives.

Each separate function of the organisation will have its own budget. Figure 21.1 shows a typical scheme of budget structure within an organisation. It shows how the organisation moves from setting objectives, through the strategy stage and into the preparation of budgets. The long-term objectives are set first. It is important to note at that stage any key assumptions which might have a critical effect on future implementation of those objectives. The implementation of those long-term objectives is then formed into a strategy which results in some intermediate objectives for the short term. Again it is important to note any key assumptions which might later cause the organisation to question the objectives. In many businesses the critical factor determining all other budgets is the sales forecast. The business exists primarily to make sales and hence generate profit, so each separate function will be working towards that major target. Each function of the business then prepares its own budget as a statement of its operational plan for achieving the targets that have been set.

In practice these budgets would be prepared at the same time with a great deal of interaction among the managers of the various functions. That is difficult to show in

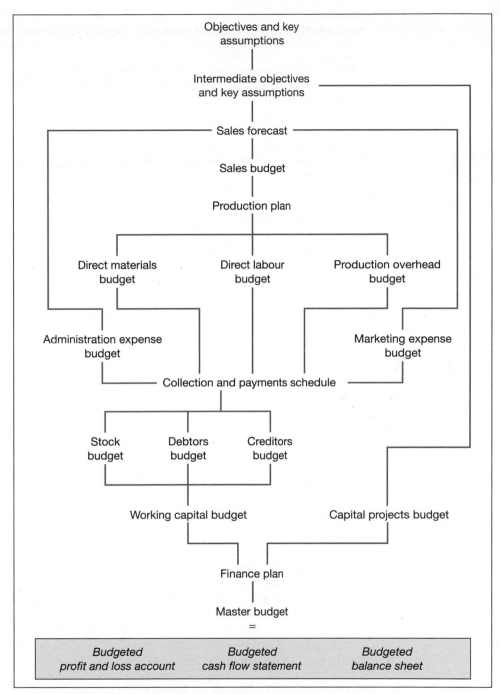

Figure 21.1
Budget planning and relationships

a diagram. Figure 21.1 shows only the main budget relationships, moving from the sales forecast to the **production plan** and the resulting **working capital** needs (stock, debtors and trade creditors) and capital investment in fixed assets. The various detailed budgets are brought together within a finance plan and then formed into conventional accounting statements such as budgeted profit and loss account, cash flow statement and balance sheet. This package is sometimes referred to as the **master budget**. The process leading to the preparation of the master budget, as outlined in Figure 21.1, will be used in the next section of this chapter as a basis for explaining the administration of the budgeting process.

Activity 21.1   *Imagine you are the managing director of a large company about to embark on budget preparation for the following year. How would you manage the various people you would need to meet in order to make operational the budget relationships shown in Figure 21.1? Would you meet them all together or have separate meetings? Would you take sole charge or would you establish teams? Write down your thoughts on this before you read the next section and then check it against your ideas.*

21.3   Administration of the budgetary process

The budgetary process has to be administered effectively in terms of initial planning, final approval and subsequent monitoring of implementation. A budget committee is usually formed to manage each stage of the budgetary process. The accounting staff will have a close involvement. The budget preparation procedures will need to be set out in a manual which is available to all participants. A continuing cycle evolves in which initial budgets are prepared, negotiations take place with line managers, the initial budgets are revised, the final budget is accepted and, later on, there is a review of actual and budgeted performance. The cycle then starts over again.

21.3.1   The budget committee

To implement the strategy decisions, a **budget committee** will be formed, comprising the senior managers who are responsible for designing the strategy. The budget committee receives the initial budgets from each functional manager. If the initial budget is based on unrealistic targets, then the functional manager will be asked to modify the budget within the organisation's overall targets. There is a motivational aspect of budget preparation, so it is important that the functional manager understands the need for revising the budget within the organisation's **strategy**. Budget negotiation can be quite a delicate process.

Fiona McTaggart describes her experiences of the initial budget formation in a conglomerate company having a stock exchange listing:

 FIONA: *There are four divisions whose activities are quite dissimilar but the linking theme is their ability to generate cash for the group which, in turn, is translated into dividends for the shareholders and capital investment for the divisions. The budget committee is formed from the board of directors of the holding company. Budget negotiations start each year when each divisional manager sets targets in six critical areas: capital expenditure, turnover, gross and net profit margins, cash flow and working capital requirements.*

The budget committee knows over the years that the transport division manager is always too enthusiastic for capital expenditure and has to be persuaded to be more cautious in replacing and expanding the fleet.

The musical instrument division is on a steady-state pattern without much growth, but is regarded as a steady source of cash flow, so is not encouraged to be more ambitious.

The knitwear division has some problems associated with fashion goods and tends to be too conservative in its planning. A measure of risk-taking is encouraged and almost every year that division has to be asked to revise its initial turnover targets upwards.

The fourth division is stationery supplies and their problem is profit targets in a competitive sector. Little can be done about gross profit, but there is plenty of scope for cost efficiencies to improve the contribution of net profit to cash flow.

21.3.2   The accounting department

The staff of the accounting department do not initiate the preparation of budgets but will be assisting in the practical aspects of budget preparation. They should have the knowledge and experience to provide advice to line managers on the preparation of budgets. The accounting department will have the computer facilities to prepare and co-ordinate the budget preparation process.

21.3.3 Sequence of the budgetary process

Figure 21.1 shows the relationships among the various budgets but does not portray the time sequence of the budgeting process. The principal stages of this sequence are:

1 communicate the details of objectives and strategy to those responsible for preparation of budgets;
2 communicate the details of budget preparation procedures to those responsible for preparation of budgets;
3 determine the limiting factor which restricts overall budget flexibility and forms the focus of the budget cascade;
4 prepare an initial set of budgets;
5 negotiate budgets with line managers;
6 co-ordinate and review budgets;
7 accept budgets in final form;
8 carry out ongoing review of budgets as they are implemented.

Communicate objectives and strategy

The long-range plan should be contained in a **strategy** document which is circulated within the organisation at intervals throughout the year. Regular circulation, with invitations to comment and a visible process of revision to accommodate changing circumstances, means that those responsible for the preparation of budgets have the fullest understanding of the basis for the budget process. The strategy document should contain clear narrative descriptions of the objectives of the organisation, supplemented by quantified illustrations of the impact on the organisation as a whole and on major divisions. The objectives may initially be expressed in non-financial terms such as production or sales targets by volume, or workforce targets by quantity and quality. Ultimately, all these non-financial targets will have a financial implication.

Communicate procedures

For communication of budget preparation procedures within the organisation there must be a **budget manual**. This will set out the timetable for budget preparation, formats to be used, circulation lists for drafts and arbitration procedures where conflicts begin to show themselves.

Determine the limiting factor

For many organisations, sales are the limiting factor. There is no point in producing goods and services which do not sell. There may be occasions when the demand is not a problem but the supply of materials or labour resources is restricted. (Such restrictions on production factors should be temporary in a competitive market because materials will eventually be found at a higher price, while labour will move from one geographical area to another or will train to develop new skills within the area.) Whatever the limiting factor, it must determine the starting point of the budgeting process. For this chapter it will be assumed that sales are the limiting factor. That assumption is the basis of the chart of budget relationships shown in Figure 21.1 where the cascade flows down from the top to the foot of the page.

Preparing an initial set of budgets

The **sales budget** is a representation of the volume of sales planned for the budget period, multiplied by the expected selling price of each item. For most organisations, sales volume is the major unknown item because it depends on customers whose choices may be difficult to predict. In practice an organisation will carry out some form of market research, ranging from very sophisticated market research surveys to some simple but effective techniques such as contacting past customers and asking them about their intentions for the period ahead. Sales representatives will, as part of their work, form continuous estimates of demand in their region of responsibility. Past performance in sales may usefully be analysed to identify trends which may be an indicator of future success in sales.

From the sales plan flow the **operational budgets**. Figure 21.1 shows the subsequent pattern of budget development once the sales budget has been determined. The **production plan**, setting out quantities of resource inputs required, leads into operational budgets for direct labour, direct materials and manufacturing overhead which combine resource quantities with expected price per unit. At the same time budgets for administration and marketing are being prepared based on quantities and prices of resources needed for production and sales.

That information provides the basis for a profit and loss account matching sales and expenses. A cash flow estimate is also required based upon working capital needs and fixed asset needs. **Working capital** depends on the mix of stock, debtors and creditors planned to support the sales and production levels expected. Fixed asset needs derive from the capital projects budgeted as a result of the objectives of the organisation.

This all feeds into a finance plan from which the **master budget** emerges containing the budgeted profit and loss account, the budgeted cash flow statement and the budgeted balance sheet.

Negotiate budgets with line managers

The success of the budgetary process is widely held to depend on the extent to which all participants are involved in the budget preparation process. The budgets will be initiated in each of the departments or areas responsible but each budget may have an impact on other line managers. There may be a problem of restricted resources which requires all budgets to be cut back from initial expectations. There may be a programme of expansion which has not been taken sufficiently into account by those preparing the budgets. Whatever the particular circumstances, a negotiation stage will be required which will usually involve the budget committee in discussions with various line managers. At the very least this will be a communications exercise so that each participant understands the overall position. More often it will be an opportunity for fine-tuning the plans so that the benefit to the organisation as a whole is maximised.

Although Figure 21.1 is presented as a downward-flowing cascade because of the increasing level of detail involved, it does not adequately represent the negotiation processes involved. Figure 21.2 is a different way of showing the budgetary process outlined in Figure 21.1. It emphasises people rather than the documentation resulting from the process, and also shows the combination of what is sometimes described as the 'bottom-up' preparation of budgets with the 'top-down' approval by senior management. In Figure 21.2, the black and pink lines show some of the interactions which might take place in the negotiation stage, distinguishing negotiations among the line managers (black lines) and negotiations between the line managers and the budget committee (pink lines). Quite deliberately, the lines are shown without directional arrows because the negotiation process is two-way. Even then a two-dimensional diagram cannot do justice to the time span and the sequence of negotiations over a relatively short space of time.

Co-ordinate and review budgets

Participants in each separate negotiation will reach a point where they are satisfied with the discussion, or else they understand where and why their opinions differ.

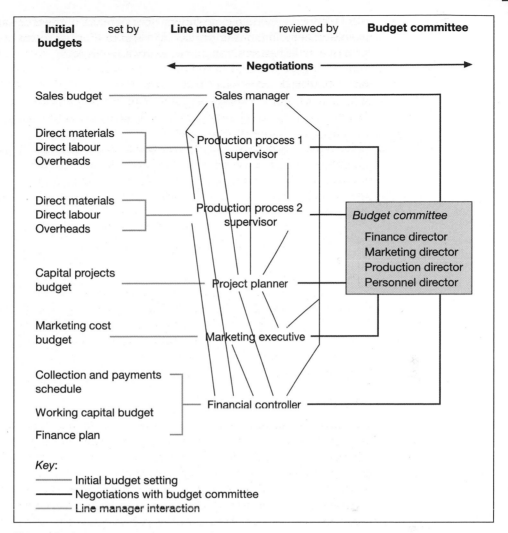

Figure 21.2
The negotiating aspects of budget planning

However, the budget committee has an obligation to serve the interests of the organisation as a whole. The separate budgets resulting from the negotiation process are brought together in a meeting of the budget committee. At this meeting the separate budgets are co-ordinated. If the sales manager has budgeted for a 10% expansion in the volume of sales in the coming year, while the production director has budgeted for steady-state levels of production, then this co-ordination exercise will show a potential reduction in stock levels. This may be acceptable in the circumstances, but the risks of inadequate stock levels must be added to the planning considerations. If the production director has budgeted for a change in employee grade which will increase the wages cost but the finance director has planned for a 'freeze' on payroll costs, the co-ordination exercise may result in one or the other budget giving way.

Co-ordination will involve examining all the separate budgets in terms of how well they serve the objectives and strategy defined at the outset. Review could take a variety of forms. The budget committee might review the budgets for reasonableness by comparing them with the budgets for the previous year and the outcome of that year. The review might concentrate on the effective use of cash. It might link the budget requests to indicators of performance. For example, there might be a view that departments that have performed well should receive even greater budgets to support this high performance. On the other hand, there might be a view that a department that has failed to perform to expectations needs greater budgets to support a catching-up exercise. Co-ordination and review may lead to a further round of negotiation in order to arrive at the best position for the entity as a whole.

Accept the budgets in final form

At the end of the negotiation period it will be necessary for the budget committee to approve and accept a definitive set of budgets which will set out the organisation's plan for the period ahead. It is possible that, as a result of the negotiation stage, some managers will feel more satisfied than others. A good system of budget setting will by this stage have ensured that all managers, whether disappointed or not, understand the reasoning and understand what is expected in their area of responsibility.

Ongoing review

The budget process is not an end in itself. It is a formal process of planning which guides subsequent action. Monitoring that subsequent action against the budget plan is therefore an essential follow-up to the budget process. An organisation might decide that monthly monitoring of progress against budget is adequate for control purposes and for contributing to future planning.

Within the control function, monthly monitoring of the actual outcome against the budget will allow corrective action to be taken at the earliest opportunity, although care is required in this respect. It could be that conditions have changed since the budget was set and the actual outcome is a better representation than the budget. In such a case it might even be appropriate to revise the budget in line with the changed conditions.

Budgeting is a continuous process which requires adaptation of existing budgets where a need for change is indicated, and the consideration of performance against past budgets when the next round of budget preparation begins. The budget committee is therefore active the whole year around.

Activity 21.2	Write down five ways in which budgets appear to benefit an organisation. Then read the next section. How does your list compare with the text? Have you identified benefits additional to those described? Have you used different words to describe a benefit which is in the text?

21.4 The benefits of budgeting

The budgetary process contributes to effective management in the following areas: planning, control, communication and co-ordination and performance evaluation. Each of these areas is now considered in turn.

21.4.1 Planning

The preparation of budgets forces management to carry out a formal planning exercise which identifies every part of the organisation and brings the separate parts together on a quantified basis. Major planning decisions are made as part of the long-term planning process, and these are then refined into progressively greater detail as management turn them into short-term operational plans. A formal planning process encourages all parts of the organisation to contribute on a regular basis to the formation of the overall plan and to identify potential difficulties at an early stage. Here is Fiona McTaggart to describe the budget planning process in a major multinational company.

FIONA: *I once participated in the planning process within a major international oil company. The financial year ran from January to December. The company's head office was in Brussels, with operational centres around the world. I was working in one of the UK operational centres, seeing the process from part-way along the chain. A company strategy group, comprising the senior management from head office and the operational centres, would form a rolling five-year statement of objectives. Having a rolling plan means that the company always looks to the next five years, but each January the rolling plan is reviewed, the current year is deleted and the fifth year ahead is added.*

The effect is that the rolling five-year plan is updated every January in respect of the five-year period starting the following January. That means the company has 12 months in which to prepare its operational budgets for the one year starting in the following January. Preparation of the five-year plan is described as Stage A. Each operational centre around the world then has two months to come back to head office with the results of its one-year budgeting, described as Stage B.

Stage B involves each operational centre specifying how the implementation of the five-year plan will be carried out for one year ahead within the operational centre, bringing out a master budget of quarterly cash flows and profit. At that stage they don't produce the detailed operational budgets within the operational centre, but each centre will have consulted with its various managers as to the way in which their departmental objectives for one year ahead will mesh with the five-year plan from head office and from the operational centre.

Stage C lasts one month and allows some fine-tuning of the five-year plan, by the head office, in the light of the reaction from the operational centres. That takes matters up to the end of June, and after that point there is little further opportunity for change in the five-year plan, or in the one-year targets of each operational centre, short of a major change in circumstances in the company or in the industry.

Stage D lasts four months and involves detailed budget planning within each operational centre. That will be an iterative process, where each manager of an operational unit produces a draft budget covering a 12-month period, the draft budgets are collected together, an overall view is taken and the draft budgets go back to the managers for revision.

Everything is tidied up by the end of October and then there are two months left to put the documentation together so that budgets are ready for implementation from the start of the next year in January.

Meanwhile, the senior managers in Brussels will have started, in October, their deliberations with a view to revising the rolling five-year plan in the following January. Then the whole process starts over again!

21.4.2 Control

Once the budget is in place, implementation of the organisation's plans takes place and the actual outcome may be compared against the budget. Some revenues and costs will behave according to expectations, but some will not. Attention needs to be given to the items which are not meeting expectations. Having a budget as a basis for comparison allows management to identify the exceptions which require attention. Identifying such matters at an early stage allows corrective action to be taken to remedy the problem.

Differences between the actual outcomes and budget expectations may signal the need for urgent action by the managers or the need for revisions to the budget. If the budget differences arise from factors under the control of the line managers, then urgent action may be required to rectify the causes of those differences. However, if the budget differences are the result of unforeseen or uncontrollable factors, then the need is for modification of the budget.

Here is Fiona to continue her story.

FIONA: *I've told you how the oil company produces its budgets for the year ahead. From January of each year the actual out-turn of the operations has to be compared against the* budget. That is where the problems really start, because the oil industry is at the high end of the uncertainty spectrum. The price of oil is controlled in world markets and influenced by world events well beyond the power of any company. A threat of war in some far-away country which borders on the main shipping lanes will send the price of oil up but threaten supplies for individual production companies seeking to take advantage of the price rise. Recession in developed countries will lower the demand and hence lower the price, so that companies have oil in the ground but may as well leave it there if demand has disappeared. These major changes occur on a short-term basis and may cause the short-term plans to require urgent change.

It would not be feasible to return to the five-year plan every month because of a crisis, so the operational centres have to adapt to change. A few years ago, the operational centres did nothing to amend the budgets after they had been finalised. The consequence was that the budgets grew increasingly irrelevant to reality as the year progressed. As a result, the operational managers largely ignored the budgets and set their own unofficial targets in operational terms without having regard to the precise financial implications.

Senior management realised that this bypassing of the management accounting budgets was linked to a lack of awareness of cost control, vital to a business which has little control over its selling prices. So a quarterly revision process was devised whereby the operational centre is allowed to revise the budgets to keep them relevant to changing circumstances. This may lead to a deviation from the five-year plan set at the start of the year, but the view is that the increased relevance to operational practice is more important than the deviation from the plan. Of course, information about the revision is fed back to head office as input to the next round of five-year planning.

It seems to be working, and the managers at the operational level, such as platform supervisors and supply service managers, now use their quarterly budgets as a basis for explaining how they control costs for which they are responsible. There is also a benefit to the five-year planning exercise because indications of change are fed in during the year and the long-term exercise itself is becoming smoother.

21.4.3 Communication and co-ordination

In Chapter 16 there is an organisation chart (Figure 16.1) which shows line relationships and horizontal relationships where effective communications are essential. Lines of communication ensure that all parts of the organisation are kept fully informed of the plans and of the policies and constraints within which those plans are formed.

Fiona continues with her experiences in an oil company.

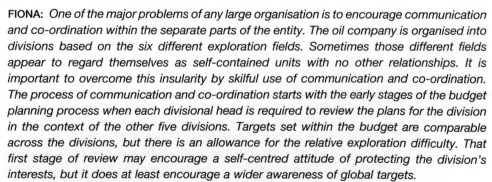

FIONA: One of the major problems of any large organisation is to encourage communication and co-ordination within the separate parts of the entity. The oil company is organised into divisions based on the six different exploration fields. Sometimes those different fields appear to regard themselves as self-contained units with no other relationships. It is important to overcome this insularity by skilful use of communication and co-ordination. The process of communication and co-ordination starts with the early stages of the budget planning process when each divisional head is required to review the plans for the division in the context of the other five divisions. Targets set within the budget are comparable across the divisions, but there is an allowance for the relative exploration difficulty. That first stage of review may encourage a self-centred attitude of protecting the division's interests, but it does at least encourage a wider awareness of global targets.

The communication process continues when detailed budget plans are prepared. Divisional heads attend monthly meetings when the budget planning team sets out the main features of the budgets. That allows one-to-one communication and creates an awareness of the possibilities of mutual savings by co-ordination. As one small example, a helicopter might be leaving the airport to take supplies out to a rig. The return trip could usefully be turned into a full payload by calling at a rig on a nearby field on the way back. That requires some co-ordination but could halve the overall flight cost for each field.

The control stage encourages further awareness of the need for co-ordination when the actual costs are compared with the budget. Each divisional head receives an exception report showing costs which are running over budget, and there is a system of marking cost headings where co-ordination could reduce overall costs. A commentary section attached to the exception report gives the divisional head guidance as to where co-ordination might usefully be applied.

21.4.4 Basis for performance evaluation

Performance evaluation within organisations must sooner or later be taken to the stage of detail which requires evaluation of the performance of individuals working within the organisation. In some situations there will be a monetary reward for high performance standards, in terms of bonus payments and possibly promotion. There may be penalties for underperforming, the most drastic of which is to be dismissed from the post. Apart from the organisation's needs to evaluate the performance of those working within the organisation, there is also an individual's need for self-assessment. Whatever the type of performance evaluation of the individual or group of individuals, targets must be set in advance which are known to, and understood by, all participants. The budgetary process forms a systematic basis for setting performance targets in financial terms.

The financial targets may then have to be translated into non-financial targets (such as number of items produced per week, or frequency of corrective work, or number of administrative tasks undertaken) because the person concerned will identify more readily with the non-financial performance measure. The subject of non-financial performance measures is explored further in Chapter 23.

Activity 21.3

Write down five ways in which budgeting may cause problems for an organisation. Then read the next section and compare your list with the text. Have you found additional problems? Are the problems you have identified more serious or less serious than those described in the text?

21.5 Behavioural aspects of budgeting

So far this chapter has presented what is largely conventional wisdom as to the desirability of, and a systematic approach to, the setting of budgets. In real life, things are not always so simple. We now move on to look at two potential problems, namely the behavioural aspects of budgeting and the limitations of line item budgets.

The earlier description of the technical process of setting a budget emphasised the need for involvement at all stages of the process. In an ideal world that would produce the best solution, but the world is not ideal and not everyone can be allowed to do exactly as they would wish at the first instance. So potential conflicts arise and those involved in the budgetary process need to be aware of the behavioural aspects in order to maximise the good points and minimise the problems.

The behavioural aspects may conveniently be summarised as relating to motivation, participation, feedback, group effects, budget slack and the politics of the organisation. In each of these areas there has been research into the effects, sometimes with inconclusive results. This chapter does not seek to give detailed reference to the research work, but rather to bring out some of the findings as points to consider in relation to the technical process.

21.5.1 Motivation

It was suggested earlier in this chapter that budgets should help in performance evaluation because they provide formal targets against which to measure performance. If the targets are set with care, there should be motivation for the individual to achieve those targets. The question then arises as to what type of targets should be set. Relatively easy targets will be achieved by all, but they will know the targets were easy and will not feel fully motivated by that level of evaluation of performance. If the targets are moderately difficult there will be a stronger motivation for some individuals to achieve those targets, with a sense of personal satisfaction in doing so. Others will fail and will become despondent. They may decide not to put any further effort in because the targets are too difficult.

The literature on goal setting suggests that it is important that the budget targets are accepted by the individuals involved. In that context, budget targets should be at the 'difficult' end of the range, by way of creating a challenge, but should be seen as being attainable. If budget targets are unrealistic there may be a negative reaction where the individual does not even attempt a reasonable level of performance. Communication between levels in the organisation is also important, so that the individual knows that achievement of targets is reported at a higher level and recognised in some form. Within all these considerations of positive factors of motivation, there may be personality problems which invalidate approaches which would otherwise be successful.

21.5.2 Participation

A full understanding of the behavioural aspects of the budgetary process requires an understanding of psychology. Research into behavioural aspects of budgeting has therefore included psychological studies of the individuals participating in the budgetary process. It is argued that individuals have needs for a sense of belonging, a sense of self-esteem and a sense of personal fulfilment. These needs do not necessarily have to be provided through remunerated employment or self-employment. They could be achieved through charitable work or dedication to a particular way of life. To the extent that people do spend a considerable part of their lives in paid employment, these needs may most readily be satisfied by that work.

Participation is one way of meeting those needs, and therefore participation in the budgetary process is a significant aspect of meeting human needs. Those individuals who participate in the budgetary process will gain a sense of ownership of the process, or belonging to the process. They will experience an increase in self-esteem through having a defined role in the process and will achieve a sense of personal fulfilment through successful implementation of the budget plans.

21.5.3 Feedback

Feedback on actual performance, as compared with the budget, is an essential part of the control process which follows from the setting of the budgets. Feedback is only effective if it is provided in a short time frame. Good news is preferred to bad news; individuals may thus concentrate on the positive feedback and hope that the negative feedback will disappear. The information on negative feedback may have to be presented in a constructive manner if it is to result in action. For example, 'Sales this month were 10% down' may be seen as a negative aspect about which little can be done after the event, but a statement such as 'Next month's sales effort must take account of the cause of last month's 10% decrease' requires positive action in identifying and seeking to remedy the cause of the decrease.

Feedback must relate closely to the responsibility level of the individual if it is to encourage remedial action. There may be a personality problem here, as elsewhere, if individuals see the feedback as criticism of their work. That adverse reaction to criticism could be a function of age or insecurity. Negative aspects of feedback may need a different form of communication from that needed for positive aspects.

21.5.4 Group effects

The impact of the budgetary process on a group of persons may be quite different from the impact on the individual within the group. Participation by individuals will lead to greater group interaction, which will be a good thing if the individuals value their membership of the group and see the goals of the group as being collective targets that they all regard as desirable. Such a group will show cohesion, which will be increased by participation in the budget process.

Where a group does not have such cohesion, or the majority pressure is towards lower targets, the performance of the individual may be reduced by participation within the group. It may therefore be important for senior management, wishing to make effective use of the budgetary process, to have careful regard for the composition of groups within the organisation.

21.5.5 Budget slack

Where budgets are used to measure performance, the managers who set those budgets may be tempted to build in some element of spare resources that allows a lapse from actual high levels of performance without deviating from budget targets. The element of spare resources could involve overestimating the time required for any particular task, or using the highest price of input materials available in the price list, or asking for more equipment than is strictly necessary. Quite apart from such deliberate creation of slack there could also be unintentional errors such as planning activity for 52 weeks in the year when the premises are only open for 50 weeks.

The use of such bias at a lower level of budget preparation may be countered by a correspondingly strict attitude at a higher level to compensate for the built-in slack. That could be unfortunate for the lower-level manager who does not build in slack but is penalised along with the rest. The answer to this problem is that the process of budget setting should be specific as to input information so that built-in slack is identified at the earliest possible stage. Flexibility in budgeting is also important to ensure that where slack does become evident it is dealt with by budget revision.

21.5.6 Politics of the organisation

Irrespective of the type of entity, it is almost inevitable that there will be a political aspect to its management structure. The word 'politics' here refers to the power struggle within the organisation. It might be a power struggle in which labour unions seek to impose their will on management. It might be a power struggle within the board of directors or between divisions of the enterprise. Whatever its nature, such a power struggle is evidenced in the budget process where various units of the enterprise are engaged in rivalry over the formulation of the budget. Thus the budgetary process may be more important as a manifestation of the political struggle than as an item of financial planning.

There may be two aspects to budgeting: the public image of resource allocation, and the private image of resolving conflict. For the purposes of this book we will concentrate on the technicalities of providing information for resource allocation, but the other potential aspects should not be ignored entirely. They form a significant element of more advanced study in management accounting.

21.6 Approaches to budgeting

This section contrasts input-based and output-based budget systems.

21.6.1 Input-based budget systems

The budgetary process described in this chapter has focused on the separate items which contribute to the overall budget. There will be a line for each item, such as direct materials, direct labour, various kinds of production overhead, various kinds of administration and selling and distribution costs. That type of budget is called a **line item budget**. The line item budget concentrates on the inputs to the process.

As an example, in the National Health Service the hospital services and support facilities are provided by NHS Trusts, each covering a geographical area. The Trusts must plan their budgets with regard for the objectives set by the government. As an example, Exhibit 21.2 sets out the financial objectives for one Trust.

Exhibit 21.2
Financial objectives for an NHS Trust

> 1 Taking one financial year with another, to ensure that a balance is maintained between income available to the Trust and expenditure properly chargeable against that income.
> 2 To achieve a surplus before interest of 6% on average net assets.

The budget shown in Table 21.1 fails by £2m to meet the required surplus. Since there is another target of maintaining a balance taking one year with another, we would now ask whether the previous year also fell below the required standard. If the trend was towards continuing a deficit there would be some concern.

Table 21.1
Budget for next year

Sources of income	£m
For patient services	
Health Board	144
Other Boards	16
Education and training grants	23
Total income from activities	183
Operating expenses	
Clinical services	120
Hotel services	6
Other support services	22
Transport and travel	2
Depreciation and amortisation	20
Research and development	4
	174
Budgeted surplus	9
Required surplus to meet 6% target	11

21.6.2 Output-based budget systems

It would be equally valid to approach the budgetary process from a totally different direction and concentrate on **outputs** from the process. An output-based approach could be taken by any organisation, but the greatest extent of its practical application has been observed in the non-profit-making organisations, where their activity output is the most important focus of their work.

An output-based approach to budgeting requires starting with an estimate of the quantity and quality of service to be provided. For the non-profit-making organisation the service output takes the place of sales for the profit-seeking organisation. Having defined the desired output the organisation then budgets to determine what will be required to achieve that output. If the organisation is a charity, it will then set about fund-raising. If it is central or local government, it will levy taxes. If the charitable funds available, or the tax revenues to be generated, do not meet all the requirements, then the output activities may be curtailed.

Such an output-based approach focuses on programmes of action. Various budgeting techniques have been suggested for dealing with output-based budgets. Two such techniques are planning, programming budgeting systems (PPBS) and zero-base budgeting (ZBB).

Planning, programming budgeting systems

Planning, programming budgeting systems (PPBS) is an approach that seeks to separate the policy planning aspects of budgeting from the short-term financial planning process. From the overall objectives, the organisation moves on to identify the programmes which will achieve those objectives. The costs and benefits of each programme are then identified so that the programmes may be given relative priorities. Subjective judgement is required to select the most suitable programmes for implementation and the resources required are then allocated to those programmes.

The techniques of PPBS were advocated with enthusiasm in the USA for government budgeting in the 1970s, but by the 1980s had disappeared from favour. The reason was that although the system sounds ideal, it is very difficult to administer because government departments are not organised by outcomes; they are organised on an input basis. In the late 1990s the state of Florida began new attempts to use programme budgets, with a focus on performance. As an example, the Department of Children and Family Services proposed programmes around specific groups such as persons with mental health problems. The agency then focused on achievement targets such as improving mental health, rather than on input targets such as providing specific hours of consultation. It was difficult to plan budgets forward on a programme basis because of the lack of adequately robust unit cost information. The budgets were mainly used as quantified confirmation that targets had remained within funding limits.

A programme to integrate into the community patients who have suffered mental illness may be taken as an example of PPBS. Such a programme will require the establishment of houses where the former patients may enjoy a degree of independence but will have access to help should it be required. That will involve a social welfare aspect and will increase the burden on the budget of the social services. The hospitals will have fewer long-stay mental patients and so will be able to close psychiatric wards. The health service will regard the corresponding funding as being released for other health service purposes such as acute medical care. Thus a programme which might be seen as having a positive social outcome may not result in a mutually amicable budgetary process where the two input departments are not under any constraint to work in harmony on achieving the overall objective.

The fact that PPBS has not worked effectively in a government budgeting context may be due more to the organisation of government departments than to any intrinsic weakness in the concept. If the organisation's objectives are set in terms of programmes, then the organisational structure needs to reflect those programmes or it risks being ineffective if employees relate more closely to their input function than to the defined outputs.

Zero-based budgeting

Zero-base budgeting (ZBB) was devised as a reaction to the traditional incremental approach to budgeting. That traditional approach favoured starting with the previous year's expenditure budget, adding a percentage to cover inflation and making adjustment for any unusual factors or incremental changes. The success of the incremental approach depended critically on the suitability of the previous year's figures. Any errors in estimation would continue indefinitely.

Zero-base budgeting requires a completely clean sheet of paper every year. Each part of the organisation has to justify over again the budget it requires. Some thought-provoking questions may need to be answered, such as:

- What is the need for this activity?
- How much of it is needed?
- Is there a more cost-effective way of carrying it out?
- What is the optimal cost?

The approach is particularly useful for the output-driven approach to budgeting because it forces questions to be asked about the programmes planned and the cost–benefit aspects of the plans. On the negative side, it is a time-consuming activity and is perhaps most usefully applied on a selective basis where the questioning approach is most useful. Some activities of an organisation carry an element of discretion and it is worthwhile reappraising them on occasions. Others form an essential core, so that it might be less appropriate to take a zero-based approach.

Activity 21.4	*Write down your personal budget for (a) the week ahead, and (b) the month ahead. Show money coming in and money going out. How difficult is it to prepare a budget? What problems did you encounter? To what extent is uncertainty about the future a problem? In the example which follows there is no uncertainty – it assumes the future may be forecast precisely. Work through the example and then consider how much such an exercise would be affected by uncertainty in the real world.*

21.7 Practical example – development of a budget

This practical example is based on the operational budgeting in the company called DressSense Partnership. There are two working partners who have built up, over ten years, a small but successful business which makes a range of ladies' dresses sold through boutiques and selected regional department stores. The image of an exclusive label is maintained by not selling through national department stores. The example sets out the mission statement and objectives of the company. It then sets out the budget details for Year 5, as agreed by line managers after negotiations in the later months of Year 4, together with the balance sheet expected at 31 December Year 4 as a starting point to the budget preparation for Year 5.

To help the reader follow the trail through the practical example, each table of information has a reference of the type (**T 1**) at the top left-hand corner. This reference is used in later tables to give a cross-reference to the source of data used in calculation. It is always good practice, in working practical examples, to give plenty of crossreferencing and to show full workings so that the reader can follow the sequence.

21.7.1 Mission statement and objectives

BestGear Partnership

Mission statement

The company intends to maintain its position in a niche market in supplying fashionable designer dresses at affordable prices for the discerning buyer. The relatively small scale of the operation will be maintained as part of the attraction of the product.

The two working partners, who together own the business, are committed to maintaining a close relationship with customers and staff so that quality of service remains uppermost at all times.

Objectives
- The company intends to recruit high-quality staff.
- The company will continue its no-quibble money-back-within-30-days policy.
- The company has a target gross profit of at least 35% on total sales.

21.7.2 Budget details for Year 5 as agreed by line managers after negotiations

The information presented in Tables T 1 to T 5 has been agreed by the line managers as a basis for preparation of the master budget and its component parts for Year 5.

Sales and production volumes and direct costs

(T 1)

	Evening	Smart casual	Holiday wear
Unit sales for year	900	1,200	1,500
	£	£	£
Unit selling price	510	210	150
Unit variable cost:			
Direct material	100	80	70
Direct labour	80	70	65

Direct labour costs are based on an average cost of £16,000 per person per year.

Other costs

(T 2)

Production heat and light	£7,000 for the year
Production business rates	£5,000 for the year
Partners' salaries	£60,000 for the year
Rent of premises	£10,000 for the year
Office staff salaries	£56,250 for the year
Marketing and distribution	20% of sales

Working capital targets

(T 3)

Debtors at end of year	One-and-a-half months' sales.
Trade creditors for material	One month's purchases.
Stock of raw materials	Enough for 80% of next month's production.
Stock of finished goods	No stock held, as goods are made to order and delivered to the customer when completed.

Sales and purchases are planned to be spread evenly over the year.

Capital budget plans

(T 4)

> Purchase one new cutting and sewing machine at £80,000, at the start of the year.
> Depreciate all machinery for full year at 15% per annum on a straight-line basis.

Balance sheet at 31 December Year 4

(T 5)

	£	£
Equipment at cost		100,000
Accumulated depreciation		30,000
Net book value		70,000
Stock of raw materials:		
For 56 evening @ £100 each	5,600	
For 85 smart casual @ £80 each	6,800	
For 80 holiday wear @ £70 each	5,600	
Trade debtors	83,000	
Cash	3,000	
	104,000	
Trade creditors	23,000	
Net current assets		81,000
Total assets *less* current liabilities		151,000
Partners' ownership interest		151,000

21.7.3 Preparation of individual budgets

From the information presented in Tables T 1 to T 5 the various detailed budgets are prepared as shown in Tables T 6 to T 18. These lead to the master budget set out in Tables T 19 to T 21.

Sales budget: sales and debtors

The sales budget sets out the volume of sales expected for each product, multiplied by the expected selling price, to obtain the total sales by value expected for each product. The total sales for the year ahead may then be calculated, shown in bold print in the sales budget.

(T 6)

Sales budget	Ref.	Evening	Smart casual	Holiday wear	Total for year
Unit sales for year	T 1	900	1,200	1,500	
		£	£	£	£
Unit selling price	T 1	510	210	150	
Total sales		459,000	252,000	225,000	**936,000**

The year-end debtors are calculated as one-and-a-half months' sales (one-eighth of the total year's sales if these are spread evenly throughout the year).

(T 7)

Debtors' budget	Ref.	Evening	Smart casual	Holiday wear	Total for year
		£	£	£	£
Total sales	T 6	459,000	252,000	225,000	936,000
		divide by 8	divide by 8	divide by 8	
Debtors at year-end		57,375	31,500	28,125	**117,000**

Production plan

The production plan starts with the volume of output, calculated by taking the planned sales volume and adjusting this for planned levels of opening and closing stock of finished goods. If it is planned to have a level of closing stock, then this will require additional production. To the extent that there exists stock at the start of the period, that will reduce the need for current production. From T 3 it may be noted that the business plans to have no amounts of opening or closing stock because all units are made to specific order. That is a simplification introduced to keep the length of this exercise reasonable, but it is somewhat unusual because most businesses will hold stock of finished goods ready for unexpected demand. As a reminder that stock plans should be taken into account, the production plans in T 8 are shown with lines for opening and closing stock of finished goods.

(T 8)

Production plan in units	Ref.	Evening	Smart casual	Holiday wear
Planned sales volume	T 1	900	1,200	1,500
add: Planned closing stock of finished goods	T 3	–	–	–
less: Opening stock of finished goods	T 3	–	–	–
Planned unit production for year		900	1,200	1,500

Direct materials budget: purchases, stock and trade creditors

Once the production plan has been decided, the costs of the various inputs to production may be calculated. Direct materials must be purchased to satisfy the production plans, but the purchases budget must also take into account the need to hold stock of raw materials. After the purchases budget has been quantified in terms of cost, the impact on trade creditors may also be established.

The purchases budget (calculated in T 9) is based on the units of raw material required for production in the period, making allowance for the opening and closing stock of raw materials. The plan is to hold sufficient stock at the end of the period to meet 80% of the following month's production (see T 3). The number of units to be purchased will equal the number of units expected to be used in the period, plus the planned stock of raw materials at the end of the period minus the planned stock of raw materials at the start of the period (calculated in T 9).

(T 9)

Purchases budget in units	Ref.	Evening	Smart casual	Holiday wear
Production volume	T 8	900	1,200	1,500
add: Raw materials stock planned for end of period	T 3	60 (80% of 900/12)	80 (80% of 1,200/12)	100 (80% of 1,500/12)
less: Raw materials stock held at start of period	T 5	56	85	80
Purchases of raw materials planned		904	1,195	1,520

(T 10)

Purchases budget in £s	Ref.	Evening	Smart casual	Holiday wear	Total for year
Volume of purchases (units)	T 9	904	1,195	1,520	
		£	£	£	£
Cost per unit	T 1	100	80	70	
Total purchase cost		90,400	95,600	106,400	**292,400**

Trade creditors are calculated as one month's purchases (see T 3), a relatively uncomplicated procedure in this instance because the purchases remain constant from month to month. The purchases made during December will be paid for after the end of the accounting period.

(T 11)

One month's purchases 292,400/12	**£24,367**

The direct materials to be included in the cost of goods sold must also be calculated at this point, for use in the budgeted profit and loss statement. The direct materials to be included in the cost of goods sold are based on the materials used in production of the period (which in this example is all sold during the period).

(T 12)

Direct materials cost of goods sold	Ref.	Evening	Smart casual	Holiday wear	Total for year
Production (units)	T 8	900	1,200	1,500	
		£	£	£	£
Materials cost per unit	T 1	100	80	70	
Total cost of goods to be sold		90,000	96,000	105,000	**291,000**

Direct labour budget

The direct labour budget takes the volume of production in units and multiplies that by the expected labour cost per unit to give a labour cost for each separate item of product and a total for the year, shown in bold print.

(T 13)

Direct labour budget	Ref.	Evening	Smart casual	Holiday wear	Total for year
Production (units)	T 8	900	1,200	1,500	
		£	£	£	£
Labour cost per unit	T 1	80	70	65	
Total cost		72,000	84,000	97,500	**253,500**

It is also useful to check on the total resource requirement which corresponds to this total labour cost, since it takes time to plan increases or decreases in labour resources. The average direct labour cost was given in T 1 as £16,000 per person per year. The following calculation assumes that the employees can work equally efficiently on any of the three product lines.

(T 14)

> *Resource requirement:*
> Based on an average cost of £16,000 per person per year, the total labour cost of £253,500 would require 15.8 employees. All are part-time workers.

Production overhead budget

Production overheads include all those overhead items which relate to the production activity. In this example it includes heat and light, business rates and depreciation. Depreciation is calculated at a rate of 15% on the total cost of equipment held during the year (£100,000 at the start, as shown in T 5, plus an additional £80,000 noted in T 4).

(T 15)

Production overhead budget	Ref.	£
Heat and light	T 2	7,000
Business rates	T 2	5,000
Depreciation	T 4	27,000
Total		**39,000**

Total production cost budget

Total production cost comprises the cost of direct materials, direct labour and production overhead.

(T 16)

Production cost budget	Ref.	£
Direct materials	T 12	291,000
Direct labour	T 13	253,500
Production overhead	T 15	39,000
Total		**583,500**

Administration expense budget

The administration expense budget includes the partners' salaries because they are working partners and their labour cost represents a management cost of the operations. The fact that the managerial role is carried out by the partners, who are also the owners of the business, is not relevant to the purposes of management accounting. What is important is to record a realistic cost of managing the business. Other administration costs in this example are rent of premises and the salaries of office staff (as shown in T 2).

(T 17)

Administration budget	Ref.	£
Partners' salaries (drawn monthly in cash)	T 2	60,000
Rent of premises	T 2	10,000
Office staff	T 2	56,250
Total		**126,250**

Marketing expense budget

The marketing expense budget relates to all aspects of the costs of advertising and selling the product. The information in T 2 specifies a marketing cost which is dependent on sales, being estimated as 20% of sales value.

(T 18)

Marketing expense budget	Ref.	£
20% of £936,000	T 2 & T 6	**187,200**

21.7.4 Master budget

The master budget has three components: the budgeted profit and loss account for the year, the budgeted cash flow statement and the budgeted balance sheet. These are now set out using the foregoing separate budgets. Where the derivation of figures in the master budget should be evident from the earlier budgets, no explanation is given, but where further calculations have been performed these are shown as working notes.

Budgeted profit and loss account

(T 19) Budgeted profit and loss account for the year ended 31 December Year 5

	Ref.	Evening £	Smart casual £	Holiday wear £	Total for year £
Total sales	T 6	459,000	252,000	225,000	**936,000**
Materials cost	T 12	90,000	96,000	105,000	**291,000**
Labour cost	T 13	72,000	84,000	97,500	**253,500**
Total variable cost		162,000	180,000	202,500	**544,500**
Contribution		297,000	72,000	22,500	**391,500**
% on sales		64.7%	28.6%	10.0%	37.7%
Production overhead	T 15				**39,000**
Gross profit					**352,500**
Administration cost	T 17				**126,250**
Marketing cost	T 18				**187,200**
Net profit					**39,050**

Budgeted cash flow statement

Where expenses are paid for as soon as they are incurred, the cash outflow equals the expense as shown in the budgeted profit and loss account. In the case of cash collected from customers, debtors at the start and end of the period must be taken into the calculation. In the case of cash paid to suppliers the creditors at the start and end of the period must be taken into account. The cash flow statement contains references to working notes which follow the statement and set out the necessary detail.

(T 20) Budgeted cash flow statement for the year ended 31 December Year 5

	Note	£	£
Cash to be collected from customers	1		902,000
Cash to be paid to suppliers	2	291,033	
Direct labour	3	253,500	
Heat and light	3	7,000	
Business rates	3	5,000	
Partners' salaries	3	60,000	
Rent of premises	3	10,000	
Office staff costs	3	56,250	
Marketing costs	3	187,200	
			869,983
Net cash inflow from operations			32,017
New equipment to be purchased			80,000
Net cash outflow			(47,983)
Cash balance at beginning			3,000
Cash balance at end			(44,983)

Note 1: Cash to be collected from customers	Ref.	£
Sales during the period	T 6	936,000
less: Credit sales which remain as debtors at the end of the year	T 7	117,000
		819,000
add: Cash collected from debtors at the start of the year	T 5	83,000
Cash to be collected from customers		902,000

Note 2: Cash to be paid to suppliers	Ref.	£
Purchases during the period	T 10	292,400
less: Credit purchases which remain as creditors at the end of the year	T 11	24,367
		268,033
add: Cash paid to creditors at the start of the year	T 5	23,000
Cash to be paid to suppliers		291,033

Note 3: Other cash payments
It has been assumed, for the convenience of this illustration, that all other expense items are paid for as they are incurred. In reality, this would be unlikely and there would be further calculations of the type shown in Note 2, making allowance for creditors at the start and end of the period.

Budgeted balance sheet

(T 21) Budgeted balance sheet at 31 December Year 5

	Note	£	£
Equipment at cost	1		180,000
Accumulated depreciation	2		57,000
Net book value			123,000
Stock of raw materials	3	19,400	
Trade debtors (T 7)		117,000	
		136,400	
Bank borrowing (T 20)		44,983	
Trade creditors (T 11)		24,367	
		69,350	
Net current assets			67,050
Total assets less current liabilities			190,050
Partners' ownership interest	4		190,050

Note 1

		£
Equipment at cost = £100,000 + £80,000	=	180,000

Note 2

Accumulated depreciation = £30,000 + £27,000	=	57,000

Note 3

Stock of raw materials:

For 60 evening @ £100 each	6,000
For 80 smart casual @ £80 each	6,400
For 100 holiday wear @ £70 each	7,000
	19,400

Note 4

Partners' ownership interest = £151,000 + £39,050	=	190,050

21.7.5 Interpretation of the practical example

Fiona McTaggart has reviewed the budget illustrated here and now offers some comments.

FIONA: This illustration shows how much detail has to go into even the simplest of budgeting exercises. Comparing the budget with the statement of objectives, I was a little surprised to find no provision in the budgeted profit and loss account in relation to the money-back promise. If I were involved in this exercise I would include a provision based on past experience of the level of returns. That wouldn't affect the cash flow of course because provisions are accounting allocations with no cash flow implications.

The target gross profit percentage will be achieved overall (gross profit shown in the master budget is 41.8% of total sales) but is heavily dependent on the high margin on evening wear. I hope there is plenty of market research to back up those sales projections. The overall net profit budgeted is 4.2% of total sales, which means there is little scope for error before the budgeted profit turns to a budgeted loss.

The budgeted cash flow statement shows an overall surplus on operations of the year, turning to a cash deficit when the effect of buying the new equipment is brought into the calculation, but that does not tell the whole story. The £80,000 cash outlay for the new equipment is needed at the start of the year whereas the cash inflows will be spread over the year, so the company will need to borrow early in the year to pay for the equipment. There will have to be a monthly statement of cash flows to show the bank how the cash will flow out and in over the year as a whole. The borrowing could perhaps be short-term borrowing in view of the overall surplus, but there are other potential cash flows which are not dealt with here. The partners are working partners and are taking salaries in cash but they may also need to draw out more cash to pay their tax bills.

It is interesting to compare these management accounts with the way in which external reporting for financial purposes might appear. The textbooks always suggest that partners' salaries are an appropriation of profit for financial reporting purposes and should appear as such in the partners' capital accounts with a matching entry for drawings.

That's all far too elaborate for management accounting purposes. What matters here is that these are working partners and if they did not do the work, someone else would have to. Provided the salary is a reasonable representation of a reward for the work done, it is far more sensible to show the expense in the profit and loss account.

21.8 Shorter budget periods

The illustration in section 21.7 is based on a 12-month period for relative ease of illustration. Management accounting information is demanded more frequently than this in reality. The following example of Newtrend shows the budget preparation on a quarterly basis. Most businesses budget monthly, with some producing figures more frequently than that.

21.8.1 Worked example: data

Newtrend Ltd is a new business which has been formed to buy standard radio units and modify them to the specific needs of customers.

The business will acquire fixed assets costing £200,000 and a stock of 1,000 standard radio units on the first day of business. The fixed assets are expected to have a five-year life with no residual value at the end of that time.

Sales are forecast as follows:

	Year 1				Year 2
	Quarter 1	Quarter 2	Quarter 3	Quarter 4	Quarter 1
Modified radio units	8,100	8,400	8,700	7,800	8,100

The selling price of each unit will be £90.
The cost of production of each unit is specified as follows:

	£
Cost of standard unit purchased	30
Direct labour	33
Fixed overhead	12
	75

The fixed overhead per unit includes an allocation of depreciation. The annual depreciation is calculated on a straight-line basis and is allocated on the basis of a cost per unit to be produced during the year.

Suppliers of standard radio units will allow one month's credit. Customers are expected to take two months' credit.

Wages will be paid as they are incurred in production. Fixed overhead costs will be paid as they are incurred.

The stock of finished goods at the end of each quarter will be sufficient to satisfy 20% of the planned sales of the following quarter. The stock of standard radio units will be held constant at 1,000 units.

It may be assumed that the year is divided into quarters of equal length and that sales, production and purchases are spread evenly throughout any quarter.

Required

Produce, for each quarter of the first year of trading:

(a) the sales budget;
(b) the production budget; and
(c) the cash budget.

21.8.2 Quarterly budgets

This section sets out a solution in the form of quarterly budgets. Note that in cases of this type there will often be more than one way of interpreting the information given. That is not a problem provided the total column is used to check for arithmetic consistency.

Sales budget

Selling price £90 per unit:

	Year 1				Total
	Quarter 1	Quarter 2	Quarter 3	Quarter 4	
Modified radio units	8,100	8,400	8,700	7,800	33,000
	£	£	£	£	£
Sales	729,000	756,000	783,000	702,000	2,970,000

Production budget for each quarter

By units, production must meet the sales of this quarter and 20% of the planned sales of the next quarter:

	Year 1				Total
	Quarter 1	Quarter 2	Quarter 3	Quarter 4	
Modified radio units	8,100	8,400	8,700	7,800	33,000
For sales of quarter	8,100	8,400	8,700	7,800	33,000
Add 20% of next quarter sales	1,680	1,740	1,560	1,620	1,620
	9,780	10,140	10,260	9,420	
Less stock of previous quarter	–	1,680	1,740	1,560	
Production required	9,780	8,460	8,520	7,860	34,620

Converting from units of production to costs of production

	Year 1				Total
	Quarter 1	Quarter 2	Quarter 3	Quarter 4	
Units to be produced	9,780	8,460	8,520	7,860	34,620
	£	£	£	£	£
Direct materials	293,400	253,800	255,600	235,800	1,038,600
Direct labour	322,740	279,180	281,160	259,380	1,142,460
Fixed overhead*	117,360	101,520	102,240	94,320	415,440
	733,500	634,500	639,000	589,500	2,596,500
*Includes depreciation of	11,300	9,776	9,844	9,080	40,000

Note that fixed overhead includes depreciation of £40,000 per annum, allocated on the basis of a cost per unit produced. Total production is 34,620 units so depreciation is £1.155 per unit.

Cash budget for each quarter

	Year 1				Total
	Quarter 1	Quarter 2	Quarter 3	Quarter 4	
	£	£	£	£	
Cash from customers					
⅓ current quarter	243,000	252,000	261,000	234,000	
⅔ previous quarter	–	486,000	504,000	522,000	
Total cash received	243,000	738,000	765,000	756,000	2,502,000
Purchase of fixed assets	200,000				200,000
Payment to suppliers**	225,600	267,000	255,000	242,400	990,000
Wages	322,740	279,180	281,160	259,380	1,142,460
Fixed overhead (excl. depn.)	106,060	91,744	92,396	85,240	375,440
Total cash payments	854,400	637,924	628,556	587,020	2,707,900
Receipts less payments	(611,400)	100,076	136,444	168,980	(205,900)

**Schedule of payments to suppliers.

	Quarter 1	Quarter 2	Quarter 3	Quarter 4	
	£	£	£	£	
Direct materials purchased	293,400	253,800	255,600	235,800	
Payment for initial stock	30,000				
Two months' purchases	195,600	169,200	170,400	157,200	
One month from previous qtr	–	97,800	84,600	85,200	
Total payment	225,600	267,000	255,000	242,400	990,000

There are three months in each quarter so some care is required in working out what amounts are paid to suppliers in each quarter. The schedule of payments to suppliers shows, in quarter 1, the payment for initial stock of 1,000 units (which occurs at the beginning of month 2). It also shows in quarter 1 the payment for purchases that took place in the first two months of that quarter. The purchases of the final month of quarter 1 are paid for in quarter 2, along with the purchases of the first two months of that quarter. Stock remains constant at 1,000 units and so the pattern of payments continues to the end of the year where there is a trade creditor for the one month's unpaid purchases of quarter 4. Figure 21.3 shows the pattern of purchases and payment.

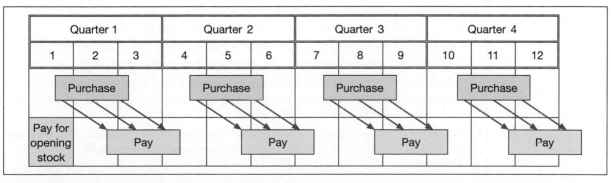

Figure 21.3
Purchases and payment where suppliers allow one month's credit

21.8.3 Comment on cash budget

A cash budget is the type of statement which would be required by someone being asked to lend money to the business. The start-up situation requires cash but there is a positive cash flow from operations. The lender would want to add to the cash budget a schedule of loan repayments and interest payments to see whether the operational cash flows could meet the financing needs of the business.

21.9 Summary

In this chapter you met the definition of a budget as a detailed plan that sets out, in money terms, the plans for income and expenditure in respect of a future period of time. It is prepared in advance of that time period and is based on the agreed objectives for that period of time, together with the strategy planned to achieve those objectives.

The short-term budgetary process plays its part in **long-range planning**. The administration of the budgeting process has been described and the benefits of budgeting have been put forward in terms of planning and control. The chapter has developed in detail a practical example of the preparation of a master budget.

Key themes in this chapter are:

- A **budgetary system** serves the needs of management in making judgements and decisions, exercising planning and control and achieving effective communication and motivation.

- **Long-range planning** begins with a vision statement setting out a vision for the future direction of the organisation. From this vision the long-range objectives are set covering a period of perhaps three to five years.

- A **strategy** describes the courses of action to be taken in achieving the long-range objectives. The different functions of the organisation will work together in developing the strategy.

- **Budgetary planning and control** provides a method of quantifying the strategy of the business.

- A **budget** is a detailed plan which sets out, in money terms, the plans for income and expenditure in respect of a future period of time. It is prepared in advance of that time period and is based on the agreed objectives for that period of time, together with the strategy planned to achieve those objectives.

- Administration of a budget requires a **budget committee** which will design the strategy, co-ordinate the inputs and communicate the objectives and strategy.

- Budget preparation usually starts with the **sales budget** because sales are the critical factor. From this the **operational budgets** are formed, leading to a finance plan and then the **master budget**, which consists of a budgeted profit and loss account, a budgeted balance sheet and a budgeted cash flow statement.

- Budgets may be **participative** through a bottom-up process, or **imposed** through a top-down process. A negotiated budget is based on a mixture of both approaches.

- Co-ordination and review by the budget committee may lead to a further round of negotiation in order to arrive at the best position for the entity as a whole, before final acceptance by the budget committee.

- The benefits of budgeting are seen in planning, control, communication and co-ordination. They also provide a basis for **performance evaluation**.

- The behavioural aspects have been outlined here as an introduction to a major area of study which will be encountered in subsequent study of the subject.

- The detailed case study in the chapter shows the sequence of preparation of all budgets leading to the **master budget**.

QUESTIONS

The Questions section of each chapter has three types of question. 'Test your understanding' questions to help you review your reading are in the 'A' series of questions. You will find the answers to these by reading and thinking about the material in the book. 'Application' questions to test your ability to apply technical skills are in the 'B' series of questions. Questions requiring you to show skills in problem solving and evaluation are in the 'C' series of questions. A letter [S] indicates that there is a solution at the end of the book. Other solutions are provided in the Instructor's Manual, where there are further questions parallel to those set out here.

A · Test your understanding

A21.1 Explain the purpose of long-range planning. (Section 21.2.1)

A21.2 Explain the purpose of setting a strategy. (Section 21.2.2)

A21.3 Define the term 'budget'. (Section 21.2.3)

A21.4 What is the role of the budget committee? (Section 21.3.1)

A21.5 What is the role of the accounting department? (Section 21.3.2)

A21.6 What is the sequence of the budgetary process? (Section 21.3.3)

A21.7 How does budgeting help the management function of planning? (Section 21.4.1)

A21.8 How does budgeting help the management function of control? (Section 21.4.2)

A21.9 How does budgeting help the management function of communication and co-ordination? (Section 21.4.3)

A21.10 What are the behavioural aspects of budgeting which may give rise to problems? (Section 21.5.1)

A21.11 How may these behavioural problems be avoided or minimised? (Section 21.5.1)

A21.12 What are the limitations of line item budgets? (Section 21.6.1)

A21.13 Explain the nature and purpose of planning, programming budgeting systems (PPBS). (Section 21.6.2)

A21.14 Explain the nature and purpose of zero-base budgeting (ZBB). (Section 21.6.2)

A21.15 [S] A company has 1,000 units of finished goods held in store at the start of the month. It produces a further 4,000 units during the month and sells 4,200. How many units are in store at the end of the month?

A21.16 [S] The sales budget for the BeeSee Company for the first six months of the year is:

	£
January	12,000
February	13,000
March	14,000
April	13,500
May	12,600
June	11,100

There are no debtors at the start of January. One month's credit is allowed to customers. What is the budgeted cash received in each month?

A21.17 [S] Trade creditors at the start of January are £12,500. They are all paid during January. During the month, goods costing £18,000 are purchased, and at the end of January there is an amount of £13,600 owing to trade creditors. State the amount of cash paid to trade creditors during January.

A21.18 [S] The cost of indirect materials in any month is 40% variable (varying with direct labour hours) and 60% fixed. The total cost of indirect materials during the month of March was budgeted at £500. During the month of April it is expected that the direct labour hours will be 20% higher than during March. What should be budgeted for the cost of indirect materials in April?

B Application

B21.1 [S]

The Garden Ornament Company manufactures two types of garden ornament: a duck and a heron. The information presented in Tables T 1 to T 5 has been prepared, as a result of discussions by line managers, for the purposes of preparing a master budget for Year 6.

Sales and production volumes and direct costs
(T 1)

	Ducks	Herons
Unit sales for the year	8,000	15,000
	£	£
Unit selling price	30	45
Unit variable cost:		
Direct material	14	16
Direct labour	12	13

Direct labour costs are based on an average cost of £15,000 per person per year.

Other costs
(T 2)

Production heat and light	£8,000 for the year
Production fixed overheads	£4,000 for the year
Partners' salaries	£55,000 for the year
Rent of premises	£11,000 for the year
Office staff salaries	£48,450 for the year
Marketing and distribution	18% of sales

Working capital targets
(T 3)

Debtors at end of year	Half of one month's sales.
Trade creditors for materials	One month's purchases.
Stock of raw materials	Enough for 60% of next month's production.
Stock of finished goods	No stock held, as goods are made to order and delivered to the customer on completion.

Sales and purchases are planned to be spread evenly over the year.

Capital budget plans
(T 4)

Purchase one new moulding machine at £70,000, at the start of the year. Depreciate all machinery for a full year at 20% per annum on a straight-line basis.

**Balance sheet at 31 December Year 5
(T 5)**

	£	£
Equipment at cost		190,000
Accumulated depreciation		(40,000)
Net book value		150,000
Stock of raw materials:		
For 400 ducks @ £14 each	5,600	
For 750 herons @ £16 each	12,000	
Trade debtors	32,000	
Cash	2,500	
	52,100	
Trade creditors	(30,000)	
		22,100
		172,100
Partners' capital		172,100

Required

Prepare a master budget and all supporting budgets.

B21.2 [S]

Tools Ltd is a new business which has been formed to buy standard machine tool units and adapt them to the specific needs of customers.

The business will acquire fixed assets costing £100,000 and a stock of 500 standard tool units on the first day of business. The fixed assets are expected to have a five-year life with no residual value at the end of that time.

Sales are forecast as follows:

	Year 1				Year 2
	Quarter 1	Quarter 2	Quarter 3	Quarter 4	Quarter 1
Modified tool units	4,050	4,200	4,350	3,900	4,050

The selling price of each unit will be £90.

The cost of production of each unit is specified as follows:

	£
Cost of standard unit purchased	24
Direct labour	30
Fixed overhead	10
	64

The fixed overhead per unit includes an allocation of depreciation. The annual depreciation is calculated on a straight-line basis and is allocated on the basis of a cost per unit to be produced during the year.

Suppliers of standard tool units will allow one month's credit. Customers are expected to take two months' credit.

Wages will be paid as they are incurred in production. Fixed overhead costs will be paid as they are incurred.

The stock of finished goods at the end of each quarter will be sufficient to satisfy 10% of the planned sales of the following quarter. The stock of standard tool units will be held constant at 500 units.

It may be assumed that the year is divided into quarters of equal length and that sales, production and purchases are spread evenly throughout any quarter.

Required

Produce, for each quarter of the first year of trading:

(a) the sales budget;

(b) the production budget; and

(c) the cash budget.

B21.3 [S]

Bright Papers Ltd has established a new subsidiary company to produce extra-large rolls of wall covering. Management forecasts for the first four years of trading are as follows:

	Year 1	Year 2	Year 3	Year 4
Sales (in units)	800,000	950,000	1,200,000	1,500,000
Production (in units)	850,000	1,000,000	1,300,000	1,600,000
	£	£	£	£
Selling price per unit	10.20	10.56	11.04	12.00
Costs per unit:				
Direct materials	2.04	2.28	2.64	3.00
Direct labour	0.60	0.75	0.90	0.90
Variable overhead	0.40	0.50	0.60	0.60
Fixed overhead	£5,000,000	£5,100,000	£5,200,000	£5,300,000
Average credit period given to customers	1 month	1 month	1.5 months	2 months
Average credit period taken from suppliers of materials	2 months	1.5 months	1.5 months	1 month

Further information

(a) Estimates for the average credit period given and taken are based on balances at the end of each year.

(b) Costs other than direct materials are to be paid for in the month they are incurred.

(c) The company will adopt the FIFO assumption in relation to cost of goods sold.

(d) No increases in production capacity will be required during the first four years of business.

(e) Fixed overhead costs include depreciation of £1,500,000 per annum.

(f) No stock of direct materials will be held. The supplier will deliver goods daily, as required. No work in progress will exist at the end of any year.

Required

Prepare annual cash budgets for the new subsidiary for each of the first four years of trading.

C Problem solving and evaluation

C21.1 [S]

The following budgeted accounting statements were submitted to the board of directors of Alpha Ltd on 1 October Year 4:

Budgeted profit and loss account for the year to 30 September Year 5

	£	£
Sales		15,600,000
Cost of sales		(10,452,000)
Gross profit		5,148,000
Fixed overheads:		
Selling and advertising	(1,500,000)	
General administration	(1,094,500)	
		(2,594,500)
Operating profit		2,553,500
Interest payable on medium-term loan	(135,000)	
Royalties payable on sales	(780,000)	
		(915,000)
Net profit		1,638,500

**Budgeted balance sheet at 30 September Year 5,
with comparative figures at 1 October Year 4**

	30 September Year 5 £	1 October Year 4 £
Fixed assets at cost	2,300,000	1,800,000
less: Accumulated depreciation	(585,000)	(450,000)
	1,715,000	1,350,000
Trading stock	3,200,000	4,000,000
Trade debtors	2,600,000	2,200,000
Cash in bank	1,854,750	–
Total assets	9,369,750	7,550,000
Share capital	4,400,000	4,400,000
Retained earnings	3,313,500	1,675,000
	7,713,500	6,075,000
Medium-term loan	1,000,000	1,000,000
Trade creditors	656,250	475,000
	9,369,750	7,550,000

At 31 March Year 5 the following information was available in respect of the first six months of the trading year:

(a) Sales were 20% below the budgeted level, assuming an even spread of sales throughout the year.

(b) The gross profit percentage was two percentage points below the budgeted percentage.

(c) Actual advertising expenditure of £100,000 was 50% below the budgeted amount. All other selling expenses were in line with the budget.

(d) General administration costs were 10% below the budgeted level.

(e) Trading stock at 31 March was £200,000 higher than the budgeted level. It was assumed in the budget that stock would decrease at a uniform rate throughout the year.

(f) Trade debtors at 31 March were equivalent to two months' actual sales, assuming sales were spread evenly throughout the six months.

(g) Trade creditors at 31 March were equivalent to one month's actual cost of goods sold, assuming costs were spread evenly throughout the six months.

(h) On 1 January Year 5 the rate of interest charged on the medium-term loan was increased to 16% per annum.

The budget for the second six months was revised to take account of the following predictions:

(a) Revenue during the second six months would continue at the level achieved during the first six months.

(b) Cost control measures would be implemented to restore the gross profit percentage to the budgeted level.

(c) Advertising, selling and general administration costs would be maintained at the levels achieved in the first six months.

(d) Trading stocks would be reduced to the level originally budgeted at 30 September.

(e) Trade debtors would be reduced to the equivalent of one month's sales.

(f) Trade creditors would be maintained at the equivalent of one month's cost of goods sold.

(g) Interest on the medium-term loan would remain at 16% per annum.

The directors of the company wish to know what change in the cash in bank will arise when the revised budget for the second six months is compared with the consequences of continuing the pattern in the first six months.

Taxation has been ignored.

Required

1 Prepare an accounting statement for the six months to 31 March Year 5 comparing the actual results with the original budget.

2 Prepare a revised budget for the second six months and compare this with the actual results which would have been achieved if the pattern of the first six months had continued.

C21.2

Holyrood Products Ltd makes cassette recorders. The management accountant has produced the following summary of the company's trading in the year ended 30 June Year 3:

	£	£
Sales: 30,000 recorders		375,000
add: Increase in finished goods stock		16,000
		391,000
Deduct:		
Direct materials	128,000	
Direct labour	96,000	
Works and administration overhead	50,000	
Selling overhead	20,000	
		294,000
Trading profit		97,000

The following additional information is available:

(a) Works and administration overhead was 64% variable and 36% fixed, the latter including £2,500 for depreciation of plant surplus to current requirements.
(b) Selling overhead was 75% variable and 25% fixed.
(c) For management accounting purposes, finished goods stock is valued at variable cost excluding selling overhead.
(d) There was an increase of 2,000 units in finished goods stock over the year.

The production manager has made the following estimates for the year to 30 June Year 4 which show that:

(a) The excess plant will be utilised for the production of a radio and a watch in quantities of 5,000 and 10,000 respectively. The variable costs are:

	Radio	Watch
	£	£
Direct materials	15,000	10,000
Direct labour	10,000	25,000
Works and administration overhead	2,500	15,000
Selling overhead	4,500	2,250

(b) Finished goods stock of cassette recorders will remain unchanged and stocks of radios and watches will be built up to 10% of production.
(c) Production of cassette recorders will be at the same level as that achieved in the year to 30 June Year 3.
(d) Fixed overhead is as follows:

	Cassette recorder	Radio	Watch
		£	£
Works and administration	No change	8,000*	13,500*
Selling	60% increase	2,250	6,750

* *Note:* excluding depreciation.

(e) Materials costs for cassette recorders will be increased by £1 per unit. Other variable costs will be held at the level attained in the year ended 30 June Year 3.

The marketing director has advised that each product should be priced so as to achieve a 25% profit on total cost.

Required

Prepare a statement of budgeted profit for the year ended 30 June Year 4.

Activities for study groups

Case 21.1

Today's task is to review the first stage of budget preparation in a major hospital dealing with a wide range of medical conditions, including accident and emergency services. (There are indications within the case study of how to allocate the time on the presumption that one hour is available in total, but the times may be adjusted proportionately for a different overall length.)

Before the activity starts obtain and look through the annual report and accounts of a hospital trust and a regional health authority, looking for discussion of the budgetary process and the way in which budgets are presented in the annual report.

Half of the group should form the budget committee, deciding among themselves the role of each individual within the hospital but having regard to the need to keep a balance between medical services, medical support staff and administration. The other half of the group should take the role of specialty team leaders presenting their budgets ('specialty' being the term used to describe one particular specialist aspect of hospital treatment, e.g. children's specialisms [paediatrics], women's conditions [obstetrics and gynaecology], or dealing with older persons [geriatrics]).

Initially the group should work together for 20 minutes to write a mission statement and set of corporate objectives. The budget committee should then hold a separate meeting lasting 10 minutes to decide: (a) what questions they will ask of the specialty team leaders when they present their budget plans, and (b) where the sources of conflict are most likely to be found. In the meantime each specialty team leader should set out a brief statement of objectives for that specialty team and a note of the main line items which would appear in the budget, indicating where conflict with other teams within the hospital is most likely to arise as a result of the budgeting process.

The budget committee should then interview each specialty manager (5 minutes each), with the other specialty managers attending as observers. After all interviews have been held, the budget committee should prepare a brief report dealing with the effectiveness and limitations of the budgetary process as experienced in the exercise. The specialty managers should work together to produce a report on their perceptions of the effectiveness and limitations of the budgetary process (15 minutes).

Case 21.2

As a group you are planning to launch a monthly student newsletter on the university's website. The roles to be allocated are: editor, reporters, webmaster, university accountant, student association representatives. Work together as a team to prepare a list of budget headings for the year ahead and suggest how you would gain access to realistic figures for inclusion in the budget. Include in your budget plan a note of the key risks and uncertainties.

Chapter 22

Standard costs

Summary of Industry Standards	
Prime Cost > Full-service–65% or less of total sales > Table-service–60% or less of total sales	**Payroll Cost** > Full-service–30% to 35% of total sales > Limited-service–25% to 30% of total sales
Food Cost > Generally–28% to 32% of total food sales	**Management Salaries** > 10% or less of total sales
Alcoholic Beverage Costs > Liquor–18% to 20% of liquor sales > Bar consumables–4% to 5% of liquor sales > Bottled beer–24% to 28% of bottled beer sales > Draft beer–15% to 18% of draft beer sales > Wine–35% to 45% of wine sale	**Hourly Employee Gross Payroll** > Full-service–18% to 20% of total sales > Limited-service–15% to 18% of total sales **Employee Benefits** > 5% to 6% of total sales > 20% to 23% of gross payroll
Nonalcoholic Beverage Costs > Soft drinks (post-mix)–10% to 15% of soft drink sales > Regular coffee–15% to 20% of regular coffee sales > Specialty coffee–12% to 18% of specialty coffee sales > Iced tea–5% to 10% of iced tea sales	**Sales Per Square Foot** > Losing Money Full-service–$150 or less Limited-service–$200 or less > Break-even Full-service–$150 to $250 Limited-service–$200 to $300 > Moderate Profit Full-service–$250 to $350 Limited-service–$300 to $400 > High Profit Full-service–More than $350 Limited-service–More than $400
Paper Cost > Full-service–1% to 2% of total sales > Limited-service–3% to 4% of total sales	**Rent and Occupancy** > Rent–6% or less of total sales > occupancy–10% or less of total sales

Information provided by RestaurantOwner.com. For more information go to www.RestaurantOwner.com

Source: Restaurant Benchmarks: How does your restaurant compare to the industry standard? Baker Tilly Virchow Krause, LLP, 2014. http://www.bakertilly.com/uploads/restaurant-benchmarking.pdf

Discussion points

1 Why is there a range given, rather than a single figure, for each of the industry standards?

2 The standards provided are based on the experience of US restaurants. What differences might arise in other countries?

Contents

Learning outcomes

After reading this chapter you should be able to:

- Define the terms 'standard cost' and 'variance'.
- Explain the purpose of using standard costs.
- Describe the problems of choosing the level of output for standards.
- Explain how the control process uses standard costs and variances.
- Define and calculate direct materials cost variance and its components.
- Define and calculate direct labour cost variance and its components.
- Define and calculate variable overhead cost variance and its components.
- Define and calculate fixed overhead expenditure variance.

- Combine calculation of all variances in a case study.
- Explain how variances may be investigated.
- Explain the application of flexible budgets in variance analysis.
- Use flexible budgeting to calculate variances in a case study.
- Discuss the usefulness of variance analysis.
- Understand the broader views that exist regarding variance analysis.

22.1 Introduction

Chapter 21 explained the budgetary process and illustrated in detail a method of preparing budgets for planning purposes. The use of budgets for control purposes was explained in that chapter in terms of comparing the actual outcome with the expected results as shown by the budget.

When actual costs are compared with budgeted costs, the comparison is of the total cost for the line item under consideration (e.g. cost of various types of materials, cost of various categories of labour or cost of a range of categories of overheads). Where there is a significant difference between the budget and the actual outcome, that difference may be investigated. (It has to be remembered, however, that the investigation will itself have a cost and that cost may be minimised by first trying to narrow down the causes of the difference.)

To analyse the difference between what was expected and what actually happened, it is useful to make comparisons in terms of cost per unit rather than total cost of a line item in the budget. Such costs per unit may be estimated in advance and used as a standard against which to compare the actual costs incurred. The cost per unit, measured in advance of the operations to be undertaken, is called a **standard cost**.

Definition **Standard cost** is the planned unit cost of the products, components or services produced in a period.[1]

Once the standard cost has been decided, the actual cost may be compared with the standard. If it equals the standard then the actual outcome has matched expectations. If the actual cost is greater than, or less than, the standard cost allowed, then there will be a variance to be investigated. This chapter explains how the standard costs may be determined and how the variances may be quantified.

Definition **A variance** is the difference between a planned, budgeted or standard cost and the actual cost incurred.[2]

22.2 Purpose of using standard costs

It has already been shown (in Chapter 17) that calculation of the cost of an item of input or output may be analysed in terms of two measurements:

1 a physical quantity measurement multiplied by
2 a price measurement.

Actual costs are measured after the event by reference to the quantity of the resource used and its price. When the actual cost is measured there is no doubt as to the quantity and price.

Standard costs are measured in advance of the period of time to which they relate, so that estimation is necessary. This requires estimation of physical inputs and outputs, and monetary estimates of prices of inputs and outputs. In order to determine useful standards it is necessary first of all to consider the purpose for which the standards will be used. The purpose could cover any or all of the following:

1 to provide product costs for stock valuation;
2 to increase control within a budgeting system;
3 to gauge performance of a business unit by use of variance analysis;
4 to integrate costs in the planning and pricing structure of a business;
5 to reduce record-keeping costs when transactions take place at different prices.

This chapter will concentrate on items 2, 3 and 4 of the foregoing list, showing how variance analysis may be used for purposes of control, performance evaluation and planning. First, the standard cost is explained. The control process is then outlined by means of a flow diagram. Most of the chapter deals with the calculation and interpretation of variances in the cost of direct materials, direct labour and production overhead. That provides information to management for use in making judgements and carrying out performance evaluations. The final section discusses the usefulness of variance analysis based on standard costing in planning the efficient operation of the business.

22.3 The level of output to be used in setting standards

Calculation of the standard cost requires a view to be taken on the most appropriate physical measurement to incorporate in the cost calculation. Three approaches are instanced here. The first uses a basic level of output, the second looks to an ideal level of output and the third uses a currently attainable level of output.

The **basic standard** is one which never changes and consequently remains a permanent basis for comparison. This gives a base line against which to make long-term comparisons. It has the disadvantage of becoming increasingly unrealistic as circumstances change.

The **ideal standard** is one which applies in dream conditions where nothing ever goes wrong. It represents the cost incurred under the most efficient operating conditions. It is an almost unattainable target towards which an organisation may constantly aim, but it may also cause a lowering of morale in the organisation if staff can never reach the target.

Currently attainable standards lie between these two extremes, defined as standards which should normally equal expectations under 'normally efficient operating conditions'. They may represent quite stiff targets to reach, but they are not beyond possibility. Currently attainable standards are the most frequently used because they give a fair base for comparisons, they set a standard which ought to be achieved and they give staff a sense of achievement when the attainable target is reached. Thus they contribute to all the management functions of planning and control which were explained in Chapter 16.

Setting standards also relates to performance. A standard may be set by estimating in advance the expected performance of a work unit. This sometimes is called an *ex ante* standard (where *ex ante* means 'before the event takes place'). Alternatively a standard may be set by observing performance and estimating what is realistically attainable. Because this method learns from the past performance it is sometimes called an *ex post* standard (where *ex post* means 'after the event has taken place').

Although the standard cost may be quantified as a single figure, it may in practice represent a whole range of possible figures because it is an estimate from a range of possible outcomes. This chapter will apply a single-figure standard in illustrative case studies, without questioning further the basis on which the standard was created.

Activity 22.1

These first three sections of the chapter have explained the meaning of a standard and the various different approaches to the creation of a standard. Read the sections again and satisfy yourself that you are aware of the differences. That awareness will help you in thinking about the interpretation of variances.

We now turn to an explanation of how standards are used in the control process.

22.4 The control process

Figure 22.1 shows the process of calculating and using standard costs for control purposes. The calculation of standards involves asking technical specialists, who are probably not management accountants, to specify the standard inputs of resources.

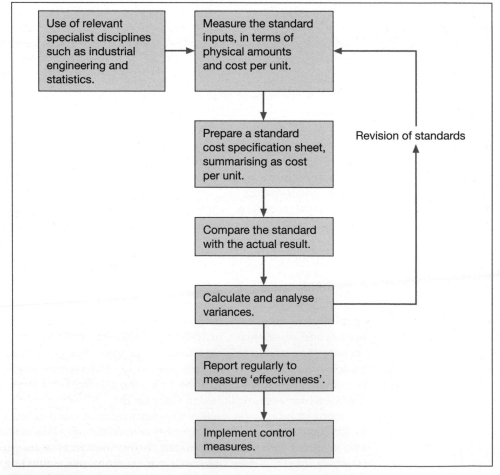

Figure 22.1
Use of standards in the control process

The management accountant takes this information and prepares a standard cost specification, usually converting that to a cost per unit of input or output. Actual costs are then measured and compared with the standard. Variances which emerge are quantified, analysed and reported. This may lead to control actions in relation to eliminating variances. It may also lead to revision of the standard costs if they are no longer relevant.

The presence of a standard cost provides a benchmark against which to evaluate the actual cost. The technical term for this process is **variance analysis**. Cost variances may be described as **adverse** or **favourable**, depending on how the standard and the actual costs compare. If the actual cost is greater than the standard expected, then the variance is said to be 'adverse'. If the actual cost is less than the standard expected, then the variance is said to be 'favourable'. The existence of either type of variance could lead to investigation of the cause. The component costs must be investigated separately so that they may be separately analysed and interpreted. We now move on to give more detail on the process of calculating and analysing variances for direct materials cost and direct labour cost.

Definitions	**An adverse variance** arises when the actual cost is greater than the standard cost.
	A favourable variance arises when the actual cost is less than the standard cost.

Activity 22.2	*Suggest three situations in which a business organisation might decide to revise standards, as indicated in Figure 22.1, following calculation and analysis of variances. Is revision equally likely for adverse and for favourable variances? Make sure that you know the definitions of adverse and favourable variances. They will appear frequently in the following sections.*

22.5 Direct materials cost variance

Take as a starting point one of the ingredients of prime cost: direct materials. If the actual cost differs from the standard cost, then the cause may lie in the materials usage, or in the price of the materials, or in a mixture of both. An adverse cost variance could indicate that the price paid was higher than expected when the standard was set, or it could indicate that the amount of materials used was greater than that expected.

In diagrammatic form:

Direct materials cost variance	
equals	
Direct materials price variance	Direct materials usage variance

Table 22.1 sets out in words the calculation of variances. Alongside there are abbreviated symbols for readers who are comfortable with an algebraic representation.

At this point in learning about variance analysis, some students will ask: 'Why are the formulae in this form? I can see other combinations of symbols which could break the cost variance down into two components.' The answer is that there are other

Table 22.1
Calculation and formulae for direct materials variances

Variance	Calculation	Formula
Total cost variance	Standard cost of materials (SC) minus actual cost of materials (AC)	SC − AC
	This may be shown in more detail as:	
	Standard cost (SC) = standard price per unit (SP) multiplied by standard quantity allowed (SQ)	SC = (SP × SQ)
	minus	minus
	Actual cost (AC) = actual price per unit (AP) multiplied by actual quantity used (AQ)	AC = (AP × AQ)
Direct material price variance	Actual quantity used (AQ), multiplied by the difference between the standard price per unit (SP) and the actual price per unit (AP)	AQ (SP − AP)
Direct material usage variance	Standard price per unit of materials (SP) multiplied by the difference between the standard quantity (SQ) allowed and the actual quantity used (AQ)	SP (SQ − AQ)

combinations but one of the aims of management accounting is to present relevant information. In the form given in the exhibit, these variances produce relevant information.

To understand the relevance of the variances, it may help to think of the standard cost as a rectangle whose area is measured by multiplying the standard price of materials by the standard quantity of materials used (Figure 22.2).

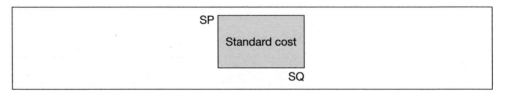

Figure 22.2
Representing standard cost as a rectangular area

Now imagine that the actual cost is greater than standard cost so that a rectangle representing actual cost will fit around the outside of the standard cost rectangle. Figure 22.3 shows the two rectangles together. The total cost variance is represented by the shaded area in the shape of an 'inverted L' to the top and right-hand side of the diagram. The top part of the blue shaded area represents variance caused by actual price being greater than standard price. The right-hand side represents variance caused by the actual quantity used being greater than the standard quantity allowed. In terms of management responsibility, the price variance will be in the hands of the purchasing department, while the usage variance will be in the hands of the production department. But who should be held accountable for the top right-hand corner where a question mark appears? This is a mixture of price variation and usage variation. The production manager will disclaim any responsibility for the price aspect and the buying department will say it has no control over quantity.

Management accounting is full of hard decisions and as far as possible tries to be fair. For the top right-hand corner of the diagram, that is almost impossible; however, there is a view that usage is within the organisation's control to a greater extent

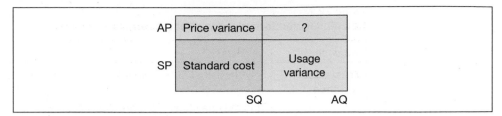

Figure 22.3
Representing actual cost and standard cost as two areas superimposed

than the price of inputs taken from an external supplier. Management accounting therefore takes the view that the production manager's responsibility for usage should be limited in order to leave out the area containing the question mark. By default, therefore, that area at the top right-hand corner is allowed to fall entirely into the price variance.

Activity 22.3   *Read this section again to ensure that you understand fully the method of calculating direct materials cost variance. Compare the formulae in Table 22.2 and the diagram in Figure 22.3. If there is any step which you do not understand, seek help at this stage from your tutor or a fellow student.*

22.6 Direct labour cost variance

The starting point in analysis of direct labour cost variances resembles closely that used for direct materials, except that the price variance changes its name to labour rate variance and the usage variance changes to labour efficiency variance.

Direct labour cost variance

equals

Direct labour rate variance	Direct labour efficiency variance

The formulae for calculating direct labour variances are similar to those used for direct materials. They are shown in Table 22.2.

At this point you meet a new idea, that of the **standard hour**. A standard hour is defined as the amount of work achievable, at standard efficiency levels, in one hour.[3] Suppose that a study has been carried out of work patterns at standard efficiency. It has been estimated that one employee can assemble 10 computer boxes in one hour. That defines the standard hour for that particular work. If 100 computer boxes are produced then the standard hours allowed are 10 hours. If the employee takes 11 hours to produce the 100 boxes, that is more than the standard allowed. Investigation will be required to find the cause. It could be the case that the employee worked too slowly. On the other hand, it could be the case that the employee worked at normal efficiency but the components supplied were not of the usual specification and there were difficulties with the assembly process.

Definition   **A standard hour** is defined as the amount of work achievable, at standard efficiency levels, in one hour.[4]

Table 22.2
Calculation and formulae for direct labour variances

Variance	Calculation	Formula
Total cost variance	Standard cost of labour (SC) minus actual cost of labour (AC)	SC − AC
	This may be shown in more detail as:	
	Standard cost (SC) = standard labour rate (SR) multiplied by standard hours allowed (SH)	SC = (SR × SH)
	minus	minus
	Actual cost (AC) = actual labour rate (AR) multiplied by actual hours worked (AH)	AC = (AR × AH)
Direct labour rate variance	Actual hours worked (AH), multiplied by the difference between the standard labour rate (SR) and the actual labour rate (AR)	AH (SR − AR)
Direct labour efficiency variance	Standard labour rate (SR) multiplied by the difference between the standard hours allowed (SH) and the actual hours worked (AH)	SR (SH − AH)

If you try to draw a diagram for direct labour variances, superimposing the actual cost on the standard cost as shown for direct materials in Figure 22.3, you will find that the area labelled with a question mark in Figure 22.3 has all been allocated to the rate variance. It is argued in management accounting that the organisation is more likely to have control over efficiency than it has over labour rate, which may well be determined by the labour market in general. The efficiency variance should therefore not include any element of variation in labour rate, and the top right-hand corner of the diagram is all taken into the rate variance.

Activity 22.4	Read this section again to make sure that you understand fully the formulae in Table 22.2. Try to produce a diagram for direct labour similar to that drawn in Figure 22.3 for direct materials. Note down the similarities and the differences between the formulae for direct materials variances and the formulae for direct labour variances.

22.7 Variable overhead cost variance

It was explained in Chapter 17 that the most effective method of calculating an overhead cost rate is to calculate the overhead cost per direct labour hour. This is because labour working usually causes most of the overhead costs to be incurred (unless the business is highly machine-intensive). It will be assumed throughout this chapter that a standard cost of variable overheads can be expressed as a cost per direct labour hour. As well as being the preferred choice from Chapter 17, it also makes the calculation of variable overhead variances look very similar to the calculation of direct labour variances.

Variable overhead cost variance	
equals	
Variable overhead rate variance	Variable overhead efficiency variance

The variances are expressed in words and formulae in Table 22.3.

Activity 22.5

Read this section again and make sure that you understand fully the formulae for calculating variable overhead cost variances. Compare these formulae with those used for direct labour cost variances. What are the points of similarity? What are the points of difference? Can you see consistent patterns in the variances for direct materials costs, direct labour costs and variable overhead costs?

Table 22.3
Calculations and formulae for variable overhead variances

Variance	Calculation	Formula
Total cost variance	Standard cost of variable overhead (SC) minus actual cost of variable overhead (AC)	SC − AC
	This may be shown in more detail as:	
	Standard cost (SC) = standard variable overhead rate (SR) multiplied by standard hours allowed (SH)	SC = (SR × SH)
	minus	minus
	Actual cost (AC) = actual variable overhead rate (AR) multiplied by actual hours worked (AH)	AC = (AR × AH)
Variable overhead rate variance	Actual hours worked (AH), multiplied by the difference between the standard variable overhead cost rate (SR) and the actual variable overhead cost rate (AR)	AH (SR − AR)
Variable overhead efficiency variance	Standard variable overhead cost rate (SR) multiplied by the difference between the standard hours allowed (SH) and the actual hours worked (AH)	SR (SH − AH)

22.8 Fixed overhead expenditure variance

Although a fixed overhead cost per unit may be calculated for purposes of valuing stock, it leads to all manner of problems because, by definition, fixed overhead costs do not vary with volume. For the purposes of control, it is more important to know whether the total amount of actual expenditure equals or exceeds the budgeted amount. Thus no attempt will be made here to deal with fixed overhead cost variances on the basis of a standard cost per unit. The variance which is most important is the *fixed overhead expenditure variance*, found by subtracting the actual fixed overhead incurred from the amount of fixed overhead budgeted (see Exhibit 22.1). If the actual fixed overhead is greater than the budget, there is an adverse variance. If the actual fixed overhead is less than the budget, there is a favourable variance.

Exhibit 22.1
Calculation and formula for fixed overhead variance

Fixed overhead expenditure variance	=	Budgeted fixed overhead (BFO) minus actual fixed overhead (AFO)

Activity 22.6 | *As a final check, go back to the start of the chapter and satisfy yourself that you understand everything presented up to this point. The rest of the chapter introduces no new technical material but it applies the formulae to a full example.*

22.9 Case study: Allerdale Ltd

The chapter now moves into a case study as a means of providing an illustration of the calculation and interpretation of variances. Allerdale Ltd uses a manufacturing process which involves fastening laminated surfaces on to workbenches. The material for the laminated plastic surface is purchased in large sheets and cut to size at the start of the process. The sheets of laminated plastic represent the direct materials cost of the process. Employees work on cutting and fastening the laminated surfaces and trimming them to fit. This work is classed as direct labour cost. Overhead costs are incurred in using indirect materials such as glues and staples, indirect labour such as cleaners for the production area, and the costs of heating, lighting and maintaining the factory premises. The overheads are partly variable (such as the indirect materials and power) and partly fixed (such as insurance, rent and business rates).

The variances in respect of direct materials, direct labour, variable overhead and fixed overhead are now explained in turn, using data provided by the accounting records.

22.9.1 Direct materials variances

Data for direct materials

The standard amount of laminated material allowed is two square metres per workbench. The standard price of the material is £0.90 per square metre. During the month of June, 200 workbenches were laminated. The amount of material used was 430 square metres and the price paid was £0.95 per square metre.

Calculations of direct materials variances are shown in Exhibits 22.2 and 22.3, using the formulae set out in Table 22.1.

Exhibit 22.2
Calculation of direct materials total variance

The standard allowance is 2 square metres each for 200 workbenches, which is 400 square metres standard quantity (SQ) in total. Standard price per unit (SP) is £0.90 per square metre. Actual quantity used (AQ) is 430 square metres and actual price per unit (AP) is £0.95 per square metre.

$$
\begin{aligned}
\text{Total cost variance} &= \text{standard cost minus actual cost (SC} - \text{AC)} \\
&= (\text{SP} \times \text{SQ}) \text{ minus } (\text{AP} \times \text{AQ}) \\
&= (£0.90 \times 400 \text{ sq metres}) \text{ minus } (£0.95 \times 430 \text{ sq metres}) \\
&= £360 \text{ minus } £408.50 \\
&= £48.50 \text{ adverse variance}
\end{aligned}
$$

In Exhibit 22.2, the variance is **adverse** because the actual cost is greater than the standard cost set for the direct materials to be used. The total variance may be subdivided into direct materials price and usage variances, using the formulae from Table 22.1 to give the analysis shown in Exhibit 22.3. The data for this calculation have already been set out in words and in symbols at the start of Exhibit 22.2. The same symbols and figures are used in Exhibit 22.3.

Exhibit 22.3
Calculation of direct materials price and usage variances

Price variance	Usage variance
= AQ (SP – AP)	= SP (SQ – AQ)
= 430 sq metres (£0.90 – £0.95)	= £0.90 (400 – 430)
= £21.50 adverse variance	= £27.00 adverse variance

You will see that the actual price per unit of materials is 95 pence, which is greater than the 90 pence per unit set as a standard cost. The price variance of £21.50 is therefore adverse. The actual amount of direct materials used is 430 square metres, which is greater than the 400 square metres set as a standard. The usage variance is therefore also adverse. The two variances, added together, equal the total adverse variance of £48.50 calculated in Exhibit 22.2. We now know that the overall variance is caused by both price and usage effects but that the usage problem is the greater of the two.

22.9.2   Adverse or favourable variances?

If you have followed these calculations yourself you will have obtained negative signs in each calculation. The negative sign corresponds to an adverse variance because in each case the actual outcome is worse than the predetermined standard. However, it is risky to rely on plus and minus signs, because it is easy to make careless errors in calculations and to turn the formula round accidentally. It is always safer to look at each calculation on a common-sense basis. The total cost variance will be adverse where the actual outcome is worse than the standard cost allowed. The price variance will be adverse where the actual unit price is greater than the standard price allowed. The usage variance will be adverse where the actual quantity used is greater than the standard quantity allowed.

22.9.3   What caused the variance?

It is often impossible to be definite about the cause of a particular variance, but suggestions may be made as a basis for further investigation. A variance in the *price* of materials indicates that the actual price paid per unit differs from that expected when the standard was set. That could be because the price has changed, in which case the standard should be revised. The variance could be due to purchasing a more expensive quality of material, in which case there will need to be an investigation as to whether this was due to the production department requesting a higher quality than that permitted when the standard was set, or whether it was a procedural error in the buying department. Perhaps the higher quality was found to be necessary because the previous quality of materials was causing too much labour time to be wasted on substandard products. Variances may interact, which means it is important to look at the cost control picture as a whole.

A variance in the *usage* of materials may be an indication that lack of quality in the materials is causing too much wastage. It may be that employees have not received sufficient training in the best way of using the material. Perhaps a new machine has been installed which operates much faster to meet expanding demand levels but has a naturally higher wastage rate.

Once the calculation of two variances has been mastered, the mathematically minded student soon realises that the subdivisions could be taken further. The usage variance may be split into a yield variance, comparing what goes in with what comes out of the process, and a mix variance, looking at the effect of having a different mix of input materials than was planned when the standard was set. That level of detailed analysis will not be taken further here, but you should be aware that there is a world of detail, to explore at another time, in relation to variance analysis.

Some of the foregoing causes of variance may lead to remedial action. Others may lead to a decision that it is in the interests of the organisation to accept the difference and revise the standard accordingly. Fiona McTaggart gives her views.

FIONA: *I see my job as reporting the variances accurately and in good time. The decisions on how to use those variances are for those who manage the operations of the business. If they tell me that a variance has become an accepted part of the operation, I will discuss with them whether the new data should be incorporated in a revised standard, or whether there is a continuing control aspect of identifying that variance to ensure that it stays within acceptable limits.*

The case study now continues to illustrate the calculation of direct labour cost variances.

22.9.4 Direct labour variances

> *Data for direct labour*
> Allerdale Ltd has set a standard labour rate of £4 per direct labour hour. Actual hours worked in June were 9,820 at an actual cost of £37,316. The standard allowance of direct labour hours, for the output achieved, was 10,000 hours.

Calculations of variances are shown in Exhibits 22.4 and 22.5, using the formulae set out in Table 22.2. In Exhibit 22.4, the variance is favourable because the actual cost is less than the standard cost set for the direct labour to be used. The total variance may be subdivided into direct labour rate and efficiency variances, using the formulae from Table 22.2, to give the analysis shown in Exhibit 22.5. The symbols and the relevant figures needed for these variances are set out at the start of Exhibit 22.4.

The actual rate of pay per hour is less than the standard rate and the rate variance is therefore favourable. The actual hours worked are less than the standard hours allowed which means that the efficiency variance is also favourable. The total favourable variance of £2,684 has, therefore, two components of which the rate variance of £1,964 is the more important.

Exhibit 22.4
Calculation of direct labour total variance

> The standard allowance of direct labour time is 10,000 standard hours (SH). The standard labour rate set (SR) is £4 per hour. Actual hours worked (AH) are stated to be 9,820. The actual labour rate (AR) is not stated but can be calculated by dividing the actual cost (AC) of £37,316 by the actual hours of 9,820, to give £3.80 per hour.
>
> Total cost variance = standard cost minus actual cost (SC – AC)
> = (SR × SH) minus (AR × AH)
> = (£4 × 10,000) minus (£3.80 × 9,820)
> = £40,000 minus £37,316
> = £2,684 favourable variance

Exhibit 22.5
Calculation of direct labour rate and efficiency variances

Rate variance	Efficiency variance
= AH (SR – AR)	= SR (SH – AH)
= 9,820 hours (£4.00 – £3.80)	= £4.00 (10,000 – 9,820)
= £1,964 favourable variance	= £720 favourable variance

22.9.5 What caused the variance?

With direct labour, as with direct materials, it is easier to apply conjecture than to find sure and certain explanations. A favourable variance in the *labour rate* is an indication that the actual wage rate per employee was lower than that which was expected when the standard was set. That could be due to an anticipated pay increase having failed to materialise. Alternatively, it could suggest that the mix of employees is different from that intended when the standard was set, so that the average wage paid is lower than planned. A variance in labour efficiency means that fewer hours were worked than were expected when the standard was set. This could be due to a new training scheme, or less than the expected amount of enforced idle time when machinery is not operating. Perhaps better-quality material was purchased, giving a higher purchase price, but this caused less wastage and allowed employees to work more efficiently in producing the finished goods.

As with direct materials, there is no particular reason to stop with analysing only two variances. A change in the mix of employees could be a cause for variance within the overall efficiency variance. The number of subdivisions depends only on the ingenuity of those devising the variance analysis. This book will, however, be content with analysing only two causes of direct labour cost variance.

Fiona McTaggart has discovered that often there are interlocking effects in variances on direct materials and direct labour. She was recently in discussion with the plant manager:

FIONA: *It is the management accountant's job to produce the variance report and it is the plant manager's job to interpret the result, but naturally I am always interested in the explanation. Last month we had a favourable variance on direct materials price but unexpected adverse variances on direct materials usage and direct labour efficiency. On investigation, it was found that the buying department had seen a special offer on metal sheeting which dramatically cut the unit cost of material, so they bought six months' supply. What they didn't know was that the machinery on the factory floor can't deal with that particular type of metal sheeting because it slips intermittently in the rollers. The result was far more wastage of materials than expected, labour time lost through having to process materials twice, and some very irate operatives who lost bonuses because so much time was wasted. The problem was so bad that after one month the remaining unused material was sold for scrap and the correct specification was purchased. It was a very expensive lesson in the need for interdepartmental communication.*

22.9.6 Variable overhead cost variance

> *Data for variable overhead*
> Allerdale Ltd has set a standard variable overhead cost rate of £2 per direct labour hour. Actual hours worked in June were 9,820 and the actual variable overhead cost incurred was £22,586. The standard allowance of direct labour hours, for the output achieved, was 10,000 hours.

Calculations of variances are set out in Exhibits 22.6 and 22.7, using the formulae set out in Table 22.3. The standard allowance of direct labour time is 10,000 standard hours (SH). The standard variable overhead cost rate set is £2 per direct labour hour. The actual variable overhead cost rate (AR) is not stated but can be calculated by dividing the actual cost (AC) of £22,586 by the actual direct labour hours of 9,820, to give £2.30 per direct labour hour.

The symbols and the relevant figures needed in order to calculate the variable overhead rate and efficiency variances are set out at the start of Exhibit 22.6. The actual variable overhead cost rate of £2.30 per direct labour hour is greater than the

Exhibit 22.6
Calculation of variable overhead cost variance

$$
\begin{aligned}
\text{Total cost variance} &= \text{standard cost minus actual cost (SC} - \text{AC)} \\
&= (\text{SR} \times \text{SH}) \text{ minus } (\text{AR} \times \text{AH}) \\
&= (£2 \times 10{,}000) \text{ minus } (£2.30 \times 9{,}820) \\
&= £20{,}000 \text{ minus } £22{,}586 \\
&= £2{,}586 \text{ adverse variance}
\end{aligned}
$$

Exhibit 22.7
Calculation of variable overhead rate and efficiency variances

Rate variance	Efficiency variance
= AH (SR − AR)	= SR (SH − AH)
= 9,820 hours (£2.00 − £2.30)	= £2.00 (10,000 − 9,820)
= £2,946 adverse variance	= £360 favourable variance

standard rate of £2 and there is an adverse variance of £2,946. This is offset to some extent by a favourable efficiency variance due to the actual hours worked being less than the standard allowed, but this gives a favourable variance of only £360 so that the combination of the two explains the overall adverse variance of £2,586.

22.9.7 What caused the variance?

The adverse rate variance means that some item of variable overhead has cost more than expected. There is not sufficient detail available here for an answer to emerge but in practice the management accountant would now look at the unit cost of each item, such as glues, staples, paint, cleaning costs and any other variable cost items, to find which had risen above the standard set. The favourable efficiency variance is directly due to labour hours being less than expected when the standard was set. The explanation will be the same as that given for the favourable efficiency variance on direct labour.

22.9.8 Fixed overhead expenditure variance

Data for fixed overhead
Allerdale Ltd budgeted fixed overhead expenditure at £10,000 for the month of June. The actual amount of fixed overhead expenditure was £11,000.

The most important question to answer here is, 'Why did we spend more than expected?' This is quantified in the fixed overhead expenditure variance, calculated as budgeted fixed overhead minus actual fixed overhead. In this example, the result is an adverse variance of £1,000. Causes could include an increase in the cost of fixed overhead or an extra category of fixed overhead, neither of which was expected when the budget was set.

Activity 22.7

Copy out the data for the case study, then close the book and test yourself by producing the calculations and analyses. That exercise will establish your confidence in knowing the technical material of the chapter.

22.10 Investigating variances

Once the variances have been calculated, those who manage the business have to decide which variances should be investigated. Should every adverse variance be investigated? Such an investigation takes time and so itself involves a further cost in searching for a cause. Is it worth incurring this further cost to find out what happened to the costs under investigation? Such an investigation might unearth some unwelcome facts about the world beyond accounting. It has been suggested that the accountant feels 'safe' in a separate accountant's world. Perhaps no one, other than the management accountant, believes in the system in any event. These radical thoughts have been expressed in various parts of the academic literature. One extreme conclusion which might be drawn is that it is safer to avoid any type of investigation.

It is fairly obvious that a reasonable answer lies between the two extremes of investigating everything and investigating nothing. Nevertheless, it may be useful to think about the extreme cases in order to justify the middle ground. Many who take a traditional approach prefer to use judgement in deciding which variance to investigate. Such persons would run their eye down the variance report, item by item, using their knowledge and experience to identify variances for further investigation. That approach is called 'intuition' and is fine for the experienced manager but risky when applied by a trainee manager or someone not familiar with the operational factors behind the variances. It is also difficult to write a computer program for the intuitive approach. If the accounting information is being processed by computer, it is often convenient to let the computer do the work of highlighting the variances for investigation. So some systematic approach is needed.

This may be achieved by setting a *filter rule* which filters out the unimportant but draws attention to the matters regarded as significant. This might be, 'Investigate all variances which are more than 10% of the total standard cost of this cost centre'. It might be, 'Investigate all variances which are more than £10,000 in amount each month'. Establishing filters is a matter of experience and judgement in order to ensure that no significant difference by amount is overlooked.

Using filters may not always be the perfect approach. The choice of what is important may vary depending on the nature of the variance or the nature of the cost item. Using the filter does not take into account the costs and benefits of variance investigation. It does not incorporate the past history of performance in that item, where inefficiencies are persisting through lack of remedial action. The item may be one where the variance has suddenly worsened dramatically but still falls within the filter limits. (For example, where a cost item has habitually shown a variance within 2% of standard cost but then suddenly increases to 15%, that could be highly significant even though the predetermined filter is set at 20%.)

The selection of variances for investigation is therefore very much dependent on circumstances and on the person making the selection. Fiona McTaggart gives her description of the management accountant's role in deciding on which variances to investigate.

FIONA: *In my work I keep in close contact with each of the production supervisors. We have informal meetings once each month to look at the specifications for the standards. They give me their views on the type and level of variance which they regard as significant to their part of the business. From that list I create a set of filters which I apply to the monthly report on how actual costs measure up against standards. I also add some filters based on company policy as to what is material to the overall production operations. My choice of filters has regard to existing pricing policy and a need for management of working capital. These filters produce a variance exception report. The production supervisors are expected to make a comment to the production director on the action to be taken in*

respect of the variances highlighted by the filter process. Every six months I meet with the production director to review the effectiveness of the filters being applied.

We now move on to consider the practical problems of calculating variances when the level of output is different from that expected at the time the budget was set.

22.11 Flexible budgets and variance analysis

One of the most commonly occurring problems in variance analysis is deciding which benchmark to use as a basis for comparison. When the standard costs are set at the beginning of a reporting period, they will be presented in the form of a budget based on activity levels expected at that point. Suppose activity levels subsequently fall because of a downturn in demand? Is it preferable to base the variance analysis on the standard set for the original level of output, or to introduce some flexibility and compare actual outcome with the standard expected for the new lower level of activity? Putting the question in that form leads to an almost inescapable conclusion that flexibility is required, but it is surprising how that obvious need for flexibility may be overlooked when a table of figures appears on a page. A case study is now used to show the application of a flexible budget.

22.12 Case study: Brackendale Ltd

Case study description

When the standards for the year ahead were set, it was expected that monthly output of units manufactured would be 10,000 units. By the time July was reached, output had fallen to 8,000 units per month because of a fall in market share of sales. Table 22.4 reports the original budget and the actual outcome for the month of July.

The original budget is based on a standard direct material cost of £4 per kg of raw material, a standard direct labour cost of £10 per hour and a standard variable cost rate of £6 per direct labour hour. Each unit of output requires 0.5 kg of raw materials and 6 minutes of labour time. The actual cost of direct materials was found to be £4.40 per kg, the actual cost of direct labour was found to be £11 per hour and the actual variable overhead cost rate was £5.60 per direct labour hour. 3,800 kg of materials were used and the actual labour hours worked were 1,000.

Data relevant to the month of July are set out in Table 22.4, as follows:

Table 22.4
Original budget and actual costs for July

	Original budget	Actual for July
Units manufactured	10,000	8,000
	£	£
Direct material	20,000	16,720
Direct labour	10,000	11,000
Variable overhead	6,000	5,600
Fixed overhead	7,000	7,500
Total product costs	43,000	40,820

Fiona McTaggart now talks through the problem.

FIONA: *It is quite tempting to compare these two columns of figures directly and call the difference the cost variance. But that would be totally misleading because the budget is based on 10,000 units of output and the actual output was down to 8,000 units. Direct materials, direct labour and variable overhead are all variable costs which depend on the level of output. The first step I would take is to introduce a new column headed 'flexible budget' which shows the expected cost of all variable costs if the standard costs per unit are applied to the new output level. Then I would prepare a data analysis sheet so that I am clear in my own mind what the materials and labour quantities are for the new output level. From there, I would analyse the direct materials cost variance into a price variance and a usage variance based on the new output level. Similarly I would analyse both direct labour cost and variable overhead cost variance into rate variance and efficiency variance based on the new output level. Fixed overhead would be analysed in terms of an expenditure variance only. Finally I would write a brief report setting out some guide to the figures so that the production supervisor can give some thought to possible causes.*

Fiona's working notes are now set out in detail. Italics are used in each table to show where she has calculated a new figure using the data already provided. You should follow her workings through the tables and check that you understand how the figures in italics have been calculated.

22.12.1 Summary statement of variances

The summary statement of variances (see Table 22.5) takes the information for original budget and actual costs contained in the case study description. The flexible budget is created by taking 8/10ths of the original budget costs (because the units manufactured are 8/10ths of the volume originally budgeted). The variances are then calculated by deducting the actual costs from the flexible budget figures. Italics are used to show the flexible budget figures which have been calculated as 8/10ths of the original budget. The only exception is fixed overhead cost, where it would not be expected that the cost was variable. Accordingly there is no flexibility with regard to fixed overhead.

Table 22.5
Calculation of variances using a flexible budget: summary statement of variances

	Original budget (1)	Flexible budget (2)	Actual for July (3)	Variance (2) – (3)
Units manufactured	10,000	8,000	8,000	
	£	£	£	£
Direct materials	20,000	*16,000*	16,720	720 (A)
Direct labour	10,000	*8,000*	11,000	3,000 (A)
Variable overhead	6,000	*4,800*	5,600	800 (A)
Fixed overhead	7,000	*7,000*	7,500	500 (A)
Total product costs	43,000	*35,800*	40,820	5,020 (A)

22.12.2 Data analysis sheet

The data analysis sheet (see Table 22.6) uses the information contained in the case study description or in Table 22.4 and fills in the gaps by calculation. Italics show the calculated figures in Table 22.6, and the workings are at the foot of Tables (a) and (b). Note that fixed overheads are not flexible and are therefore excluded from Tables (a) and (b). The output level for the period is 8,000 units.

Table 22.6
Calculation of variances using a flexible budget: data analysis sheet

(a) Analysis of standard cost

Item	Standard cost of item	Standard amount of item per unit of output	Standard quantity for output level 8,000 units[1]	Standard cost for output level 8,000 units[2]
	£			£
Direct material	4.00 per kg	0.5 kg	4,000 kg	16,000
Direct labour	10.00 per hour	6 mins	800 hours	8,000
Variable overhead	6.00 per dlh[3]	6 mins dlh	800 dlh	4,800

Notes: 1 [8,000 × 0.5 kg = 4,000 kg] and [8,000 × 6 mins = 800 hours].
2 [4,000 kg × £4 = £16,000]; [800 hours × £10 = £8,000]; [800 hours × £6 = £4,800].
3 dlh = direct labour hours.

(b) Analysis of actual cost

Item	Actual cost of item	Actual amount of item per unit of output	Actual quantity for output level 8,000 units	Actual cost for output level 8,000 units
	£			£
Direct material	4.40 per kg	0.475 kg	3,800 kg	16,720
Direct labour	11.00 per hour	7.5 mins	1,000 hours	11,000
Variable overhead	5.60 per dlh	7.5 mins	1,000 hours	5,600

Note: 1 [3,800 kg/8,000 = 0.475 kg] and [1,000 hours/8,000 = 7.5 mins].

22.12.3 Direct materials variance

Total cost variance = standard cost minus actual cost (all based on the new output level)
= £16,000 minus £16,720
= £720 adverse variance

The variance is adverse because the actual cost is greater than the standard allowed by the flexible budget for the output of 8,000 units.

Price variance	Usage variance
= AQ (SP − AP)	= SP (SQ − AQ)
= 3,800 kg (£4.00 − £4.40)	= £4.00 (4,000 − 3,800)
= £1,520 adverse variance	= £800 favourable variance

The price variance is adverse because the actual price per kg is greater than the standard price per kg. The usage variance is favourable because the actual quantity used, 3,800 kg, is less than the standard allowed, 4,000 kg, for the actual level of output.

22.12.4   Direct labour variance

> Total cost variance = standard cost minus actual cost
> = £8,000 minus £11,000
> = £3,000 adverse variance

The variance is adverse because the actual cost is greater than the standard allowed by the flexible budget for the output of 8,000 units.

Rate variance	Efficiency variance
= AH (SR − AR)	= SR (SH − AH)
= 1,000 hours (£10.00 − £11.00)	= £10.00 (800 − 1,000)
= £1,000 adverse variance	= £2,000 adverse variance

The direct labour rate variance is adverse because the actual rate is higher than the standard rate per hour. The direct labour efficiency variance is adverse because the actual hours worked (1,000) were greater than the standard allowed (800) for the output achieved.

22.12.5   Variable overhead variance

> Total cost variance = standard cost minus actual cost
> = £4,800 minus £5,600
> = £800 adverse variance

The variance is adverse because the actual cost is greater than the standard allowed by the flexible budget for the output of 8,000 units.

Rate variance	Efficiency variance
= AH (SR − AR)	= SR (SH − AH)
= 1,000 hours (£6.00 − £5.60)	= £6.00 (800 − 1,000)
= £400 favourable variance	= £1,200 adverse variance

The variable overhead rate variance is favourable because the actual rate is less than the standard rate per hour. The variable overhead efficiency variance is adverse because the actual hours worked (1,000) were greater than the standard allowed (800) for the output achieved.

22.12.6   Fixed overhead variance

The fixed overhead expenditure variance is equal to the budgeted fixed overhead minus the actual fixed overhead. That has already been shown to be £500 adverse due to overspending compared with the budget.

22.12.7   Variance report

From the foregoing calculations a variance report may be prepared. This brings to the attention of the production manager the main items highlighted by the process of variance analysis, as shown in Exhibit 22.8.

Exhibit 22.8
Brackendale Ltd: variance report

BRACKENDALE LTD
Variance report

To: Production manager
From: Management accountant
Subject: **Variance report for July**

During the month of July there were 8,000 units manufactured, as compared with 10,000 expected when the budget was set. Allowing flexibility for the lower level of output, there was nevertheless an adverse variance of £5,020 for the month, of which £720 related to direct material, £3,000 related to direct labour, £800 related to variable overhead and £500 related to fixed overhead.

The most serious of these is clearly the direct labour variance, where adverse changes in labour rate contributed £1,000 and less efficient working contributed £2,000 to the total £3,000. The direct materials cost variance of £720 looks worse when decomposed into an adverse price variance of £1,520 offset partially by a favourable usage variance of £800. The variable overhead cost variance of £800 adverse also looks worse when decomposed into an adverse efficiency variance of £1,200, partly offset by a favourable rate variance of £400. Overspending on fixed overheads was £500 for the month.

While the investigation of these problems is a matter for yourself, I might venture to suggest that from past experience we have noticed that a favourable materials usage variance may arise when employees are instructed to work more carefully and, as a consequence, take longer time, which leads to an adverse labour efficiency variance. If that is the case, then the more careful working has had an overall negative effect because the £800 favourable materials usage variance must be compared with the £2,000 adverse labour efficiency variance and the £1,200 adverse variable overhead efficiency variance.

The variance in materials price is almost certainly due to the recent increase in the price of goods supplied. That is not a matter we can control from within the company and the standard cost will be revised next month.

The variance in labour rate is due partly to a recent pay award not included in the original budget, but it is also due to employees being paid at overtime rates because of the extra time spent on working more carefully with materials. There may need to be a major review of how this part of the business is operating, with a view to minimising total variance rather than taking items piecemeal.

Although the variable overhead rate variance is favourable, the categories of variable overhead will be reviewed to see whether any of the standard costs are out of date. Overspending on fixed overhead was due to a change in the depreciation rate of equipment due to revised asset lives. The budget will be revised at the half-yearly review which is coming up next month.

Activity 22.8

Copy out the data for the foregoing case study, close the book and attempt the variance analysis yourself. This will test your understanding of the technical material. Make a note of any problems or difficulties and consult your tutor about these.

22.13 Is variance analysis, based on standard costs, a useful exercise?

Academic opinion is divided on the usefulness of variance analysis. Solomons[5] has claimed that standard costing probably represents the greatest advance in accounting since the development of bookkeeping. There is another view that perhaps this historical leap forward has given standard costing more importance than it deserves. In this chapter the standard has been portrayed as a single figure, but it is actually an estimate based on the best expectations of the future conditions envisaged in the organisation. If the organisation has a stable technology and works within safely attainable levels of productivity, then there is relatively little likelihood of finding that the expected cost is far away from the true cost. But if the organisation is much riskier in the nature of its operations, perhaps using a less stable technology and working at the upper limits of productivity, then the expected standard cost may be an average measure of a wide range of possible outcomes.

Anthony and Govindarajan[6] questioned whether any scientific enquiry into variance analysis is in reality carried out and have questioned further whether such enquiry is worth doing in any event. They identified, in practice, a strong intuitive approach to variance analysis.

It may be that accountants tend to overemphasise their own importance. The causes and control of variances lie with those managing and operating the technical aspects of the business. Management accountants only present the information which, if in a relevant and useful form, may help in identifying cause and establishing better control. Setting standards is first and foremost an industrial engineering problem. It might be safer to leave the variance analysis to the engineers and forget about the cost aspects.

Chapter 16 instanced the management functions of planning and control, and the importance of communication and motivation. Well-planned variance reports, based on up-to-date and realistic standards, will provide information for the planning process, encourage control and communicate the effects of operational actions on the costs of the organisation. Motivation will be enhanced if the variance report is seen to be specific to the information needs of each level of management and if the standard costs are seen to be a fair measure of expected achievement. Motivation could be reduced by a badly designed or carelessly implemented variance report.

Chapter 16 listed three management accounting functions of directing attention, keeping the score and solving problems. Standard costs contribute to all three, when used in conjunction with variance analysis. The variance report, by using predetermined filters, may direct attention to areas of significance. The preparation of the report, on a regular basis, is a vital part of the score-keeping operation. Analysis of the variances, to which the management accountant will make a contribution in deciding on the level of detail, will be a problem-solving exercise requiring logical and systematic analysis of the problem represented by the accounting figures.

22.14 A broader view of applications of variance analysis

At the start of the chapter a list was set out of five ways in which standard costs may be used by an organisation:

1 to provide product costs for stock valuation;
2 to increase control within a budgeting system;
3 to gauge performance of a business unit by use of variance analysis;
4 to integrate costs in the planning and pricing structure of a business;
5 to reduce record-keeping costs when transactions take place at different prices.

Are these purposes useful? Is it worthwhile to make the effort of developing standard costs? Some brief answers are now provided.

● The objective of providing product costs for purposes such as stock valuation falls within the general heading of 'What should it cost?', a question which in turn leads to more questions about the effective use of resources. It is as important to ask questions about the cost of goods not sold as it is to look at the variance in cost of the goods which have been sold. If stock is valued at actual cost, it will carry with it a share of the problems which led to a cost variance and will burden the next reporting period with those problems. If the stock is valued at standard cost, all variances in price are dealt with in the period when they arose.

- A budgeting system may be based on actual costs, but it will have greater usefulness if it is based on standard costs as a measure of the predetermined targets for a period. A budget relates to an activity or operation as a whole, while a standard cost is a cost per unit which gives a very precise focus to the budgetary planning process. Budgets do not necessarily need to be based on standard cost, but the standard costs bring additional benefits in allowing the organisation to examine more precisely how the budget compares with the actual outcome.

- Performance is gauged by comparing actual costs with standard costs and analysing the differences. The resulting variance may indicate where, in the control of the organisation, future action is required. Performance may be related to responsibility so that the management accounting information is matched to the management aims of the organisation.

- Planning and pricing are aspects of long-term decision making which require a strategic outlook on business problems. Pricing will usually be a forward-looking activity based on estimated costs and out-turns. Standard costs provide a benchmark against which to plan pricing and, in retrospect, to evaluate the success of a pricing policy in terms of recovering costs incurred.

- If all costs are recorded on a standard basis, then the variations in quantity may be separated analytically from the variations in price. In practice the price variations are isolated as soon as the goods are purchased. Thereafter, the progress of costs, in moving through to finished goods and to output in the form of sales, is all monitored at standard cost so that the emphasis is on quantity and variations in quantity. That reflects the control process in that, once the goods have been purchased, or services paid for, there is no further opportunity to take action over price. Success in cost control thereafter depends entirely on control of usage, which is in the hands of those controlling and carrying out operations.

22.15 Summary

In this chapter we have shown how control through the use of standard costs per unit leads to a more specific analysis than is available where control is through the use of budgets. Budgets give only the total cost of each line item. Standard costing allows decomposition into cost per unit and quantity of units.

Variances have been defined and illustrated for:

- direct materials (total cost variance, analysed into price and usage variances)
- direct labour (total cost variance, analysed into rate and efficiency variances)
- variable overhead (total cost variance, analysed into rate and efficiency variances)
- fixed overhead (expenditure variance only).

Flexible budgeting has also been explained, showing that where the level of output is different from that expected when the budget was prepared, the standard costs should be used to prepare a new flexible budget for the new level of output. All variable costs should be recalculated to reflect the change in output. Fixed overhead costs are independent of activity level and therefore have no flexibility.

The chapter has also given some flavour of the debate on the importance and usefulness of standard costs. They are widely used but, to be effective, must be chosen with care to meet the needs of the business and of the management purposes of planning and control.

QUESTIONS

The Questions section of each chapter has three types of question. 'Test your understanding' questions to help you review your reading are in the 'A' series of questions. You will find the answers to these by reading and thinking about the material in the book. 'Application' questions to test your ability to apply technical skills are in the 'B' series of questions. Questions requiring you to show skills in problem solving and evaluation are in the 'C' series of questions. A letter [S] indicates that there is a solution at the end of the book. Other solutions are provided in the Instructor's Manual, where there are further questions parallel to those set out here.

A   Test your understanding

A22.1 What is a standard cost? (Section 22.1)

A22.2 Why are standard costs useful? (Section 22.2)

A22.3 How are standard costs related to levels of output? (Section 22.3)

A22.4 How are standard costs used in the control process? (Section 22.4)

A22.5 How are direct materials price and usage variances calculated? (Section 22.5)

A22.6 Give three possible causes of an adverse direct materials price variance. (Section 22.5)

A22.7 Give three possible causes of a favourable direct materials usage variance. (Section 22.5)

A22.8 How are direct labour rate and efficiency variances calculated? (Section 22.6)

A22.9 Give three possible causes of a favourable direct labour rate variance. (Section 22.6)

A22.10 Give three possible causes of an adverse direct labour efficiency variance. (Section 22.6)

A22.11 Explain how you would identify which variances to investigate. (Section 22.10)

A22.12 Explain the importance of using a flexible budget with variance analysis. (Section 22.11)

A22.13 Give three reasons for regarding variance reports as a useful tool of management. (Section 22.13)

A22.14 [S] It was budgeted that to produce 20,000 concrete building blocks in one month would require 100,000 kg of material. In the month of May, only 16,000 blocks were produced, using 80,080 kg of material. The standard cost of materials is £3 per kg. What is the materials usage variance?

A22.15 [S] The standard cost of direct labour in the month of August is £36,000. There is a direct labour rate variance of £6,000 adverse and a direct labour efficiency variance of £2,500 favourable. What is the actual cost of direct labour in the month?

A22.16 [S] Fixed overhead for the month of October has been budgeted at £16,000 with an expectation of 8,000 units of production. The actual fixed overhead cost is £17,500 and the actual production is 7,000 units. What is the variance?

B Application

B22.1 [S]

The monthly budget of Plastics Ltd, manufacturers of specialist containers, was prepared on the following specification:

Production and sales	30,000 units
Selling price	£70 per unit
Direct materials input	5 kg per unit at a cost of £1.20 per kg
Direct labour input	2 hours per unit at a rate of £4 per hour
Variable overhead	£2 per direct labour hour
Fixed overhead	£90,000 per month

The following actual results were recorded for the month of May Year 8:

Stock of finished goods at start of month	8,000 units
Sales	40,000 units
Production	42,800 units
Stock of finished goods at end of month	10,800 units

Actual costs incurred were:

	£
Direct material	267,220 (213,776 kg at £1.25 per kg)
Direct labour	356,577
Variable overhead	165,243
Fixed overhead	95,000

Further information

(a) Throughout May the price paid for direct materials was £1.25 per kg. Direct material is used as soon as it arrives on site. No stocks of materials were held at the start or end of May.
(b) The labour rate paid throughout the month was £4.10 per hour.
(c) The selling price of finished goods was £70 per unit throughout the month.
(d) Stocks of finished goods are valued at standard cost of production.

Required

(a) Calculate the budgeted profit for May Year 8, based on the actual sales volume achieved.
(b) Calculate the cost variances for the month of May.
(c) Explain how cost variances may be used to identify responsibility for cost control within the company.

B22.2 [S]

The upholstery department of a furniture manufacturing business prepared the following statement of standard costs at the start of the calendar year:

Standard cost per unit

	£
Direct material	250
Direct labour	150
Fixed manufacturing overhead	100
	500

In preparing the statement, it was budgeted that 100 units would be completed each month.

During the month of May the following results were reported:

	£
Direct materials cost	31,200
Direct labour cost	16,800
Fixed manufacturing overhead	9,600
	57,600

The actual level of production achieved in May was 120 units.

The budget for direct materials was based on an allowance of 10 kg materials per unit produced. The budgeted cost of materials was £25 per kg. Actual materials used during May amounted to 1,300 kg.

The budget for direct labour was based on an allowance of 15 hours per unit, at a labour rate of £10 per hour. At the start of May, an agreed incentive scheme increased the labour rate to £12 per hour. All employees receive the same rate of pay.

Stocks of finished goods are valued at full standard cost of manufacture.

Required
(a) Prepare an accounting statement reconciling the budgeted costs for the month of May with the actual costs incurred, including in your answer relevant cost variances.
(b) Suggest possible causes for the variances you have calculated.

B22.3 [S]
Carrypack Ltd manufactures and sells plastic cases for portable computers. Production each month equals sales orders received.

The following monthly budget was prepared at the start of Year 6, to apply throughout the year:

	Units	£	£
Sales (@ £50 per unit):	12,000		600,000
Production:	12,000		
Production costs:			
Direct materials		132,000	
Direct labour		108,000	
Variable overheads		72,000	
Fixed overheads		48,000	
			360,000
Budgeted profit			240,000

Further information
(a) Budgeted direct materials used per month were set at 26,400 kg.
(b) Budgeted direct labour hours per month were set at 36,000 hours.

The following actual report was produced for the month of April Year 6:

	Units	£	£
Sales (@ £50 per unit):	12,300		615,000
Production:	12,300		
Production costs:			
Direct materials		136,220	
Direct labour		129,200	
Variable overheads		72,200	
Fixed overheads		49,400	
			387,020
Actual profit			227,980

Further information
(a) Actual direct materials used during April were 27,800 kg.
(b) Actual direct labour hours worked during April were 38,000 hours.

Required
(a) Prepare an explanation, using variances, of the difference between the budgeted profit and the actual profit for the month of April.
(b) Comment on possible causes for the variances you have calculated.

B22.4
DEF Products Ltd manufactures and assembles one type of furniture unit. The following information is available for the year ended 31 August Year 7.

The budgeted costs and the actual costs incurred during the year were as follows:

Cost	Budgeted production overhead cost £000s	Actual production overhead cost £000s	Nature of cost
Supervision	100	85	Fixed
Machine power	30	22	Varies with machine hours
Heat and light	30	27	Varies with direct labour hours
Rates and insurance	220	203	Fixed
Lubricants	60	45	Varies with machine hours
Indirect materials	50	38	Varies with units of output
Machine depreciation	180	180	Fixed
Maintenance and repairs	80	60	Varies with machine hours
	750	660	

The budgeted and actual activity for the year was as follows:

	Machine hours	Direct labour hours	Units of output
Budget	255,000	500,000	100,000
Actual	180,000	440,000	80,000

At the end of the year, the production director made the following report to his colleagues on the board of directors: 'We budgeted for £750,000 overhead cost based on 500,000 direct labour hours. We incurred £660,000 actual cost but only worked 440,000 hours. This appears to me to be a satisfactory proportionate reduction in costs and there are consequently no adverse variances from budget to be explained.'

The other directors felt this comment ignored the distinction between fixed overhead cost and variable overhead cost. They were also concerned that the production director referred only to the fall in direct labour hours worked, when it was known that some overheads depended on the number of machine hours worked. They asked for a more detailed analysis of the expected level of overhead costs in relation to the activity levels achieved.

Required
Prepare a memorandum to the production director:
(a) proposing, with reasons, a suitable method for calculating overhead cost rates;
(b) setting out a variance analysis which distinguishes fixed overheads from variable overheads.

C   Problem solving and evaluation

C22.1 [S]
The following report has been prepared for the production department of Cabinets Ltd in respect of the month of May Year 4:

	Actual costs or quantities recorded	Variance £
Direct materials price	£2.80 per kg	2,240 favourable
Direct materials usage	11,200 kg	4,800 adverse
Direct labour rate	£9 per hour	5,600 adverse
Direct labour efficiency	3.5 hours per unit	6,400 adverse
Fixed overhead expenditure	£39,000	3,000 adverse

The department manufactures storage cabinets. When the budget was prepared, it was expected that 1,800 units would be produced in the month but, due to a machine breakdown, only 1,600 units were produced.

Required

(a) Reconstruct the original budget, giving as much information as may be derived from the data presented above.

(b) Provide an interpretation of the performance of the production department during the month of May Year 4.

C22.2 [S]

Fixit Ltd is a manufacturing company which produces a fixed budget for planning purposes. Set out below is the fixed monthly budget of production costs, together with the actual results observed for the month of July Year 7.

	Budget	Actual
Units produced	5,000	5,500
	£	£
Costs:		
Direct materials	20,000	22,764
Direct labour	60,000	75,900
Variable production overhead	14,000	14,950
Fixed production overhead	10,000	9,000
Depreciation	4,000	4,000

In preparing the fixed budget, the following standards were adopted:

Direct material	10 kg of materials per unit produced.
Direct labour	2 hours per unit produced.
Variable production overhead	A cost rate per direct labour hour was calculated.
Fixed production overhead	A cost rate per unit was calculated.
Depreciation	Straight-line method is used for all assets.

The following additional information is available concerning the actual output:

(a) the actual usage of materials in July was 54,200 kg; and

(b) the nationally agreed wage rate increased to £6.60 per hour at the start of July.

Required

(a) Prepare a flexible budget in respect of Fixit Ltd for the month of July Year 7.

(b) Analyse and comment on cost variances.

C22.3 [S]

Concrete Products Ltd manufactures heavy paving slabs for sale to local authorities and garden paving slabs for domestic use.

The board of directors meets early in each month to review the company's performance during the previous month. In advance of each meeting, the directors are presented with a computer printout summarising the activity of the previous month. The computer printout in respect of the month of December Year 8 is set out below:

	Heavy paving		Garden paving	
	Actual tonnes	Budget tonnes	Actual tonnes	Budget tonnes
Sales volume	29,000	27,500	10,500	8,500
Production volume	29,000	27,500	10,500	8,500
	£000s	£000s	£000s	£000s
Revenue	720	690	430	300
Variable cost of sales	280	270	170	127
Contribution	440	420	260	173

Further information

(a) The actual fixed costs incurred during the month equalled the budgeted fixed costs of £310,000.

(b) Stocks are valued at standard cost.

You have recently been appointed a director of Concrete Products Ltd. At an earlier meeting with the finance director you received an explanation of the basis for the company's monthly budget and you are satisfied that the budget has been prepared on a realistic basis.

Required

(a) Prepare, from the information contained in the computer printout, your analysis and comments on the company's performance during the month of December Year 8, as background for the board meeting.

(b) List, with reasons, three questions you would ask at the meeting in order to give you a fuller understanding of the company's performance during the month.

C22.4 [S]

Nu-Line Ltd purchases manufactured machine tools for conversion to specialist use. The converted tools are sold to the textile industry. The following information relates to the month of July Year 3.

	Budget (units)	Actual (units)
Purchases of machine tools	180	180
Completed production	180	140
Sales	130	150
Stock of finished goods at 1 July Year 3	15	15
Stock of finished goods at 31 July Year 3	65	5

There was no stock of purchased machine tools or work in progress at either the start or the end of the month.

Finished goods are valued at full standard cost of production. The standard cost of one completed production unit is:

	£
Purchased machine tool	600
Direct labour	300
Fixed production overhead	200
Variable production overhead	100
	1,200

The fixed production overhead per unit was determined by reference to the budgeted volume of production per month.

A standard selling price of £2,000 per completed unit was specified in the budget and was achieved in practice.

Actual costs incurred during the month were as follows:

	£
Invoiced price of machine tools purchased	86,800
Direct wages paid	47,500
Fixed production overhead	35,000
Variable production overhead	13,000

Required

(a) Prepare a statement of the budgeted profit and the actual profit for the month of July.

(b) Using variances, reconcile the budgeted profit with the actual profit.

Activities for study groups

Case 22.1

You are the Student Union management committee representative in charge of student transport affairs. Members have proposed that the Union should operate a campus bus service to operate between the campus and the nearby shopping precinct (5 miles distant and 15 minutes by bus). Prepare a five-minute presentation to the rest of the management committee explaining how you would use standard costing to plan and control the activities of the proposed bus service.

Case 22.2

You are the Student Union management committee representative in charge of academic affairs. Members have proposed that the Union should publish a study guide for sale to incoming students. It is expected that 2,000 new students will register at the start of the academic year. Prepare a five-minute presentation to the rest of the management committee explaining how you would use standard costing to plan and control the publication of the study guide.

Notes and references

1. CIMA (2005), *Official Terminology*, CIMA Publishing and Elsevier.
2. *Ibid.*
3. *Ibid.*
4. *Ibid.*
5. Solomons, D. (1978), 'Flexible budgets and the analysis of overhead variances', in H. R. Antony, P. A. Firmin and H. D. Grove (eds), *Issues in Cost and Managerial Accounting: A Discipline in Transition*, Houghton Mifflin, Boston.
6. Anthony, R. and Govindarajan, V. (1997), *Managerial Control Systems*, 9th edn, McGraw-Hill, New York.

Chapter 23

Performance evaluation and feedback reporting

REAL WORLD CASE

This case study shows how a mixture of financial and non-financial performance measures are reported.

Natural England
About us

Our general purpose is 'to ensure that the natural environment is conserved, enhanced and managed for the benefit of present and future generations, thereby contributing to sustainable development.'

Our 2013/14 Performance

Our performance across the 19 KPIs in our Corporate Plan Update shows that one was assessed as 'Red'; one was assessed as 'Amber Red'; five were 'Amber Green'; and twelve were 'Green'. Therefore, 90 per cent of the KPIs in our Corporate Plan Update are either 'Green' or 'Amber Green' at the end of Quarter Four.

Alamy Images/Arterra Picture Library

Year-End KPI Performance Summary Scorecard

A healthy well-functioning natural environment	2013/14 Performance	Sustainable use of the natural environment	2013/14 Performance
Large scale conservation initiatives	AMBER GREEN	**Support farm businesses & lane managers**	GREEN
Protected sites	RED	Water Framework Directive	AMBER GREEN
Priority habitats	GREEN	**Our regulation supports growth**	GREEN
Priority species	GREEN	**Sustainable development solutions**	GREEN
Diversity and character of England's landscape	GREEN	Our regulatory casework	GREEN
Protecting wildlife and landscapes through designation	AMBER GREEN		

People are inspired to value and conserve the natural environment	2013/14 Performance
Our National Nature Reserves	GREEN
National Trails	AMBER GREEN
Delivering coastal access	GREEN

A secure environmental future	2013/14 Performance
Our evidence base	AMBER RED
Our evidence standard	AMBER GREEN

Excellent Public Body	2013/14 Performance
Staff knowledge and expertise	GREEN
Excellent customer Service	AMBER GREEN
Managing our budget	GREEN

Note: Our Top Six Key Performance Indicators we report monthly to Defra are headed in bold in the above table.

Detail of 'Protected sites'

Maintain and Improve the condition of protected sites (Top 6 KPI reported to Defra Supervisory Board)

Metrics:

1. 37 per cent of terrestrial SSSIs in favourable condition
2. 52 per cent of NNRs in favourable condition
3. 53 per cent of marine protected features in favourable or recovering condition
4. 47 per cent of terrestrial protected sites with conservation objectives
5. 20 per cent of marine protected areas with conservation objectives and associated advice

2013/14 Performance	RED

This KPI is 'Red' at year-end as we have only fully achieved one of our five metrics.

As part of our in-year performance review of this target, we considered the delivery of our key underpinning work – Conservation Objectives, Favourable Condition Tables (FCTs) and Marine Conservation Objective and associated advice packages. This resulted in a rebalancing of resources – with an increased focus on quality, to ensure that we invest in the evidence base we need to secure SSSI favourable condition in the longer term.

We agreed that to achieve this, staff development was a critical investment which we could not delay in pursuit of securing this year's target outputs. Our revised programme on the two metrics below was supported by the Secretary of State and Defra officials during the discussion of our performance at our November Ministerial Performance Review.

From an April baseline of 29 per cent, our predicted delivery of Conservation Objectives and FCTs was revised down in October 2013 in agreement with Defra to 43.9 per cent from our 47 per cent target to enable us to address quality control issues. At year-end we had delivered 41.2 per cent, slightly below this revised year-end target.

Our target for setting conservation objectives for marine sites was revised down from 20 to 3 per cent of sites in October 2013. We achieved this revised target, prioritising our delivery within the Liverpool City Deal area. This enabled us to ensure robust guidance was in place for the longer term delivery of objectives and advice for the remaining Marine Protected Areas.

We also fell slightly short of our year-end targets on the following two metrics.

51.72 per cent of National Nature Reserves are in favourable condition, slightly below our year-end target of 52 per cent. Gains during the year have been spread across the country.

52.9 per cent of marine protected areas are in favourable or recovering condition, following our completion of the planned site surveys and condition assessments of Marine Special Areas of Conservation and SSSIs. This is slightly below our year-end target of 53 per cent.

However, we successfully maintained 37.55 per cent of terrestrial Sites of Special Scientific Interest (SSSIs) in favourable condition above our target of 37 per cent for the year as a whole.

Detail of 'Managing our budget'

We manage our money effectively and efficiently

Metrics:

1. Our actual expenditure is 100 per cent of our planned/budget expenditure
2. We deliver £18 million of efficiencies and service changes this financial year as set out in our Spending Review 2010 settlement. This would represent £35 million of cumulative efficiencies

2013/14 Performance	GREEN

At year-end, our financial performance reported to Defra shows we have a £0.5 million or 0.3 per cent under-spend, against a full year forecast of £184.5 million.

After allowing for capital expenditure, the underlying position on our revenue forecast is a £0.1 million or 0.1 per cent under-spend which is within our agreed budget tolerance. Our financial performance will now undergo our annual external audit review.

We have delivered the £18 million of efficiency savings arising from our 2013/14 financial settlement.

Source: Natural England Annual Report and Accounts 1 April 2013 to 31 March 2014, pp. 4, 67–70,80. https://www.gov.uk/government/uploads/system/uploads/attachment_data/file/326495/ne-annual-report-accounts-2013-2014-print-ready.pdf. Contains public sector information licensed under the Open Government Licence (OGL) v3.0.http://www.nationalarchives.gov.uk/doc/open-government-licence.

Discussion points

1 What is the mix of financial and non-financial performance measures used by Natural England in its report of performance?

2 How effectively do the reported performance measures relate to the stated general purpose?

Contents

Learning outcomes

After studying this chapter you should be able to:

- Distinguish feedforward control from feedback control.
- Explain the main features of performance reports.
- Explain how performance evaluation is carried out.
- Explain the use of benchmarking in performance evaluation.
- Explain and give examples of non-financial performance indicators.
- Explain the nature and use of the balanced scorecard.
- Understand how management may set standards of performance and reward achievement of standards.

23.1 Introduction

This management accounting text has been based throughout on the view that those who manage a business have a need and a desire to make informed judgements and decisions. In a continuing cycle of management action, there will be a judgement, from which a decision will be formed, followed by evaluation of that decision and a new judgement based on that evaluation. The stage at which the decision is evaluated requires management accounting to exercise its score-keeping function by devising quantitative measures of performance. It also calls on management accounting to direct attention to those areas most urgently requiring a judgement and a further decision. Management functions have been described in Chapter 16 in terms of **planning**, **decision making** and **control**.

Planning is sometimes referred to as **feedforward control**. This means making predictions of outputs expected at some future time and then quantifying those predictions, in management accounting terms. The budgetary process (Chapter 21) and setting standards (Chapter 22) are examples of management accounting approaches which have a feedforward (or planning) aspect. Feedforward control systems are very effective, if carried out well, because they anticipate problems rather than wait for them to happen.

Chapter 22 also dealt with variance analysis as a technique for control in comparing the actual outcome with the standard expected. This is sometimes referred to as **feedback control**. This is useful for looking back at what went wrong (or what went well) and for taking corrective action to ensure that a problem does not continue.

In this chapter we consider feedback control in more depth, which involves comparing outputs achieved against outputs desired and taking corrective action if necessary. To provide this type of control it is essential to identify the responsibility for the costs and for taking whatever action is required. The term **responsibility centre** is used to identify the unit to which a feedback report is to be made. A responsibility centre could be a **cost centre** where the individual manager has responsibility only for costs, a **profit centre** where the individual manager has responsibility for costs and revenues, or an **investment centre** where the individual manager has responsibility for costs, revenues and investment in assets. (Cost centre, profit centre and investment centre are defined in Chapter 17.)

Definitions

> **Feedforward control** means making predictions of outputs expected at some future time and then quantifying those predictions, in management accounting terms.
>
> **Feedback control** involves comparing outputs achieved against outputs desired and taking corrective action if necessary.
>
> **A responsibility centre** is an area of responsibility which is controlled by an individual. It might be a cost centre, a profit centre or an investment centre.

In any control process, feedforward or feedback, there are three essential elements:

1 there must be objectives which state the aim or purpose of the control;
2 there must be a model which can be used to predict an expected outcome;
3 there must be power to act in order to take corrective action.

In addition, for feedback control there must be the ability to measure the actual outcome on the same basis as the predicted outcome.

For a feedback control system to be effective, the following basic principles should be observed:

● the benefits from the system should exceed the costs of implementing it;
● the performance criteria being measured should be reported promptly so that rapid action may be taken;
● reports should be as simple as possible and readily understood;
● reports should highlight the significant factors requiring management attention;
● the reporting framework should be integrated with the organisational structure so that responsibility is identified correctly.

The operation of feedback control will be explored in this chapter in relation to short-term decision making. (Feedback on long-term decision making will be covered in section 24.8.2.) First, in this chapter we discuss the nature of the report to be written for performance measurement purposes.

23.2 Preparing performance reports

There are three basic questions in relation to report preparation:

1 To whom should the report be addressed?
2 What should be reported?
3 How frequently should the report be presented?

23.2.1 To whom should the report be addressed?

In the context of the management of responsibility centres, the report should be addressed to the manager in charge of the responsibility centre. That could be a cost centre, a profit centre or an investment centre. If the report is to have meaning for the manager concerned, it must include only those costs which may be controlled by the manager of the responsibility centre.

The level of detail in the report will be influenced by the managerial position of the person to whom it is addressed. Reports to senior management will be condensed so that those managers can see the broader picture. They will of course also have access to the more detailed reports, should they so wish.

23.2.2   What should be reported?

The report should be designed to identify clearly those items that are controlled by the manager of the particular responsibility centre. If the responsibility centre controls the price and quantity of an item, then both should be reported and the combined effect quantified. If the responsibility centre controls quantity but not the price of an item, then the report should be designed to emphasise the quantity aspects of transactions in the reporting period.

It could be that, despite a lack of direct responsibility, it would be helpful for the manager of the responsibility centre to be aware of all the costs incurred as a result of the activity of the centre. If that information is felt to be useful, then it could be included in the report, but subheadings would be required to make clear the distinction between controllable and non-controllable costs.

The design of the report is extremely important because the manager of the cost centre, profit centre or investment centre will not use the report effectively if it does not provide useful information in a helpful manner. Managers should be consulted on design of reports, and there should be trial periods of experimentation with a new design of report before it comes into routine use. Graphs, bar charts and pie diagrams may be ways of communicating more effectively than through tables of figures alone.

23.2.3   How frequently should the report be presented?

The frequency of reporting should be related to management's information needs. There may be a need for information on a daily basis. Computers provide on-screen access to information so that the traditional concept of a reporting period, with a printed report at the end of each period, may no longer be appropriate in all circumstances. There is, however, a danger in reporting all items too frequently. Reports have to be read and acted upon, and reporting which occurs too frequently could result in too much time being spent on the review activities.

The question of frequency of reporting is perhaps best answered in terms of the frequency of the cycle of review and corrective action. If daily action is required in an operation, then daily provision of information about the activity will allow corrective action at the earliest possible opportunity. If a monthly review cycle is more appropriate, then the reporting system should be designed to provide monthly summaries. It is vitally important that, whatever the frequency chosen, the reports are produced in a timely manner.

If a computer is in use to record costs and quantities, then the program should be such that the reports required are generated as part of the process so that there is no delay in transferring information for reporting purposes.

Activity 23.1	*Look back to the variance report on Brackendale presented in Chapter 22, p. 646. Comment on the good and weak points of that report, in the light of the first two sections of this chapter, and suggest ways in which the report could be improved.*

23.3 Performance evaluation

Performance evaluation requires the management accountant to carry out the following process:

- decide on what to measure
- plan how to report
- consider the behavioural aspects.

23.3.1 What to measure

In looking at what to measure, we will draw on the material of previous chapters, selecting aspects of management accounting which lead to a measure of performance. Because each management accounting technique serves a different purpose, the decision on what to measure will also depend on the intended purpose and will be discussed in the context of specific applications.

23.3.2 How to report

In planning how to report, the general principles applied will be those of responsibility and the separation of **controllable** and **non-controllable** costs. All costs are controllable at some level of management but they may not be controllable at a lower level. Breaking down cost into the separate elements of quantity and price, the extent of control may vary for each element. There will be those in the organisation who have authority to acquire resources, thus controlling quantity and price. There will be others whose job it is to make use of the resources acquired, in which case they will control only the quantity element of cost. There will be others again whose job is to find the best price for resources. They will control only the price element of cost.

It is important to distinguish controllable from non-controllable costs when seeking to establish responsibility for costs. Frequently, the responsibility will be shared, and it is important that the sharing is correctly identified.

Definitions

A **controllable cost** is a cost which is capable of being regulated by a manager within a defined boundary of responsibility.

A **non-controllable cost** is one which is not capable of being regulated by a manager within a defined boundary of responsibility, although it may be a cost incurred so that the responsibility may be exercised.

Performance reporting is partly concerned with planning and control, so the idea of controllable and non-controllable costs is important. However, it is also applied in decision making, and further classifications into relevant/non-relevant and avoidable/unavoidable costs may therefore also be used within the same report.

When a decision is taken there is usually more than one option available. Avoidable costs are those costs that may be saved by not taking a particular option. Unavoidable costs will not be saved by such an action.

Definitions

An **avoidable cost** is one which may be eliminated by not taking a particular option.

An **unavoidable cost** will not be eliminated by taking a particular action.

23.3.3   Behavioural aspects

Performance evaluation has behavioural aspects because measurement of performance has a direct impact on the organisation's perceptions of how its staff are performing and on the individual staff member's perception of their relative performance. As a general guide, favourable reactions to performance reporting are likely to be maximised if staff are made aware in advance of how the performance measures will be calculated and how the responsibility for costs will be allocated. If the individual has control over quantities and prices, then that person should be regarded as having control over, and responsibility for, that item. If the individual has control over quantities but not prices, then it may be appropriate to report the cost to that individual but only regard responsibility as extending to the quantity aspects. If the individual has no control over quantity or price, then no responsibility for the cost of that item can be identified, although there may be a separate question of whether that item should be reported to the individual in order to heighten awareness of the impact of non-controllable costs.

Activity 23.2	*You are the team leader for a group of social workers who specialise in dealing with the needs of elderly persons in their homes. You have been told by your line manager that your team's budgeted spending limit will be exceeded by the end of the year if you continue with the present level of activity. The major items of cost are: team members' salaries, travel to clients' homes for visits and a charge from the local authority for the provision of office facilities. Salaries have increased because of a national pay award not allowed for in the budget. Travel costs have increased over budget because of fuel price increases. The local authority has kept the charge for office facilities within the budget. Your line manager has some discretion to make savings under one expense heading to match overspending under another. How will your team explain its performance in the end-of-year report?*

Chapter 22 concentrated on the technical aspects of cost control by way of variance analysis. There also needs to be a concern with the human implications of variance analysis. It may be that the variance analysis approach is seen as a means of managerial review of subordinates, in which favourable variances receive praise and adverse variances are seen as a cause for corrective action to be taken. That approach may have undesirable consequences for a number of reasons:

1 Employees may reject standards because they were not adequately consulted in setting them.
2 Those under review may divert their efforts into minimising the adverse variances rather than making positive steps towards overall performance improvement.
3 Negative feedback may reduce motivation, leading to reduced effort and lower performance levels.

Those who are concerned at these negative aspects of traditional variance analysis have suggested that there may be a need for accounting systems which are less evaluative in approach. The emphasis should perhaps move to learning and improvement rather than stressing personal responsibility, accountability and past achievement. Later in this chapter there are some ideas about performance measurement using non-financial measures which may be more relevant than financial measures at the individual manager level. First, however, a case study is used to illustrate the traditional variance analysis approach to performance evaluation and control.

Activity 23.3	You are the financial manager of a school where some teaching departments are spending more than their budget allowance on materials and others are being frugal and spending less. It is six months into the financial year and you would like to give a warning to the overspenders, but also find out why there are underspenders. Suggest two ways of dealing with this problem, of which one way would probably create friction between yourself and the teachers, while the other would encourage the teachers to work with you in controlling the overall budget for the school.

23.3.4 Case study: evaluating and reporting performance

Fiona McTaggart now explains a situation where she prepared performance reports using flexible budgets and also shows how the performance report appeared in each case.

 FIONA: *My client was in a manufacturing business which produced hand-crafted cane furniture. I was asked to devise a monthly performance reporting system which would provide performance measurement of the manufacturing activity. Three levels of reporting were required. The managing director required a brief summary of any matter requiring executive action but did not want all the details each month. The furniture supervisor needed a much more specific analysis of the performance of the activity as a whole and the relative performance of each employee. There was also a proposal to give each employee a personal performance statement that showed some indication of the average performance of the activity as a whole, without giving individuals access to information which was best kept personal to each employee.*

The budget was set at the start of the year based on average monthly output of 300 chairs and 80 tables. In practice the actual monthly output varied around this average. I recommended a three-column form of report which would show the original budget for one month's output, the flexible budget showing the costs expected for the actual level of output achieved and the actual costs incurred.

I made a list of all the costs incurred in making cane furniture. The main direct costs were materials and skilled labour. Although the employees were employed on full-time contracts, it was useful to identify separately the time they spent in productive activity making the furniture, which I classed as a direct cost, and the time they spent in non-productive activity, which I classed as an indirect cost.

I then listed all the indirect costs and subdivided them according to various levels of responsibility. Each employee was responsible for a portion of indirect materials used in fastening the cane together and was also responsible for a portion of equipment maintenance and depreciation. This indirect cost was allocated in proportion to the output produced. It might sound rather hard that the employee's responsibility for cost increased as the output increased, but it was decided in discussion that staff needed to be aware of the costs incurred when productive output takes place. Individual employees would not be regarded as being responsible for unproductive time unless they directly caused it as a result of their individual actions.

The furniture supervisor was responsible for control of the total costs allocated to the individual operative staff, plus the cost of non-productive time (to the extent that this was in the control of the supervisor), and the overhead costs of heating and lighting the workshop area.

The managing director had ultimate responsibility for all costs, including the cost of administration, providing adequate working conditions, the employer's share of employment costs and any non-productive work due to causes beyond the control of the furniture supervisor.

Table 23.1 shows how the performance report was designed. There were three separate parts to the report. The first was for individual members of staff. The second was for the furniture supervisor, who also had access to the individual staff reports, and the third was for the managing director, who had access to the more detailed reports if these were required.

Each report set out the variances from flexible budget for each element of cost. At the foot of the report was a section for highlighting matters for attention and a space below for the person receiving the report to write a comment. In the case of individual employees, a comment was expected on any action planned in response to matters noted. This action plan would be discussed and agreed with the supervisor. In the case of the report to the supervisor, the comment was expected to show the action planned for the production activity as a whole, or for individual employees where there was a particular problem. In

Table 23.1

Monthly performance report: (a) employee report; (b) supervisor's report; (c) managing director's report

Part A: Employee report			Name.............. *Employee X*	
Date of statement	....			
	Budget	Flexible budget	Actual	Variance
Output: target/actual	100 chairs 20 tables	110 chairs 18 tables	110 chairs 18 tables	
Direct materials	...	...	...	...
Direct labour	...	...	...	...
Controllable indirect costs	...	...	...	...
Indirect materials	...	...	...	...
Total controllable costs for employee X	...	...	...	...
Cumulative controllable costs for year to date	...	...	...	...
Maintenance	...	...	...	...
Depreciation	...	...	...	...
Total for employee X	...	...	...	...
Cumulative for year to date	...	...	...	...
Matters for attention				
Action planned				

Table 23.1 continued

Part B: Supervisor's report	Name..			
Date of statement	....			
	Budget	Flexible budget	Actual	Variance
Output: target/actual	300 chairs 80 tables	320 chairs 76 tables	320 chairs 76 tables	
From Part A Controllable costs for each employee				
Costs of employee X	...	...	...	...
Costs of employee Y	...	...	...	...
Costs of employee Z	...	...	...	...
Total controllable costs				
Overheads				
Controllable indirect costs	...	...	...	...
Non-productive time	...	...	...	...
Heating & lighting	...	...	...	...
Matters for attention Action planned				
In practice this report would also include cumulative totals for the year to date, as shown on Part A, but they are omitted here so that the main features are more readily seen.				

the case of the report to the managing director, the comment was expected to confirm discussions with the supervisor but also to note any action on indirect costs regarded as the managing director's responsibility.

We had a trial run of this reporting format for three months, to iron out any wrinkles, and during that time there were some difficulties in getting the overhead responsibility allocation right. Everyone denies responsibility for indirect costs but, at the end of the day, they have to be incurred and are an unavoidable consequence of business activity. It was eventually agreed that the direct cost allocation would remain, but that, for employees and the supervisor, the emphasis would be on responsibility for the volume aspects of the allocation, with any external price increases being regarded as non-controllable or else a matter for discussion with the purchasing section.

Fiona's description has concentrated very much on the two questions regarding what to measure and how to report. Since she is describing the early stages of designing and implementing a new system, there is no information on the behavioural aspects of how the reporting system operated in practice. There is a description of the trial run and the extent to which the views of participants were taken into account in the design of the final report. The case study would need to be followed up after a period of, say, three months of operation, to find out how effectively the new system was achieving satisfactory control.

Table 23.1 continued

Part C: Managing director's report		Subject: Cane furniture production		
Date of statement	....			
	Budget	Flexible budget	Actual	Variance
Output: target/actual	300 chairs 80 tables	320 chairs 76 tables	320 chairs 76 tables	
From Part B				
Total employee controllable costs	...	...	...	...
Total indirect costs for which supervisor is responsible	...	...	...	...
Other overheads				
Administration	...	...	...	...
Employment costs	...	...	...	...
Abnormal non-productive time	...	...	...	...
Total				
Matters for attention				
Action discussed with supervisor				
In practice this report would also include cumulative totals for the year to date, as shown on Part A, but they are omitted here so that the main features are more readily seen.				

Activity 23.4   *Read the case study again and identify the points at which Fiona McTaggart's actions match the principles of reporting set out in this chapter.*

23.4 Benchmarking

Benchmarking is the name given to the process of measuring the organisation's operations, products and services against those of competitors recognised as market leaders, in order to establish targets which will provide a competitive advantage.

The stages of benchmarking are:

1 Decide what area of activity to benchmark (e.g. customer services, business processes in particular departments, quality of employees, standard of training).
2 Select a competitor who is reputedly the best in the area of activity to be benchmarked. Major companies in one country may target an international

competitor rather than a domestic company. In some benchmarking situations the competitor may agree to an exchange of information because both parties believe they can benefit from the exchange.

3 Decide on the appropriate measurements to be used in defining performance levels.

4 Determine the competitor's strengths and compare these with the company's own record.

5 Use the information collected as the basis for an action plan. To be effective, this action plan must involve all grades of employee working in the area of activity.

The management accountant has a role throughout this process because the emphasis is on improving profit and measuring performance. The management accounting role starts with directing attention, by producing the performance measures and showing the relationship with profit improvement. It moves into problem solving as the information on comparative performance measures is collected and has to be transformed into an action plan for the organisation. It then takes on the score-keeping aspect as the achievement of total quality is monitored.

23.5 Non-financial performance measures

Within an organisation, people are employed to carry out specific activities. The only aspect of their work over which they have direct control may well be the volume and the quality of tasks they undertake. Applying revenues and costs to these activities may be important for the organisation as a whole, but will have little meaning for the individual employee who does not sell the goods or services directly and does not purchase the input materials.

To ensure that the motivation of employees is consistent with the profit objectives of the organisation, it may be necessary to use non-financial performance measures to indicate what is required to achieve the overall financial targets. Using non-financial performance measures does not mean that the financial performance measures may be disregarded. They are ways of translating financial targets and measures into something that is more readily identifiable by a particular employee or group of employees.

The non-financial performance measures should cover both quantity and quality.

23.5.1 Quantity measures

It is necessary to convert the accounting numbers to some measure of quantity which relates more closely to individual members of an organisation. If the employees are involved in the entire productive process, then the financial target may be converted to units of product per period. That approach may be more difficult when a service activity is involved or a group of employees is involved in only part of a production process.

As an illustration of the problems of performance measurement in a service business, take an example of a school where activities are subdivided by subject area. The primary measure of activity will be the number of pupils taught, but the individual departments will have no control over that number. If teaching staff are appointed on permanent contracts, so that salary costs are largely fixed costs, then the cost per student will vary depending on the number of students taught in any period. A performance measure of cost per student may be attractive to the management accountant but will have little impact on the staff of the history department whose main aim is to ensure that their pupils achieve high grades in the end-of-year examinations. For them, examination success rates are the prime performance measure and they will be concerned to ensure that fluctuations in pupil numbers do not affect that success rate. A performance report on the history department would therefore emphasise first of all the non-financial performance, in terms of examination success, but would then additionally report the cost implications so that the consequences of achieving a high, or a low, success rate could be linked to the cost of that activity.

23.5.2 Quality measures

The ultimate measure of quality is customer satisfaction. Companies will invest time and effort in measuring customer satisfaction, perhaps by questionnaire survey or possibly by telephone interview. Indirect measures of customer satisfaction may be found in complaints records, frequency of repairs under warranty and level of goods being returned as unwanted.

Another important aspect of quality is the process undertaken by the organisation. This is so important that an external agency (often the auditors) may be employed to provide independent certification of the quality of the process and the controls within the process.

Finally, quality is measured also in terms of the inputs to the process, where inputs may be materials, labour and capital equipment. Quality of inputs may be controlled directly by imposing standards on suppliers, or may be monitored by reviewing the rate of return of unsatisfactory goods, the non-productive time incurred because of faulty equipment, or the reliability of delivery dates and quantities.

Some examples of non-financial performance measures are:

1 in respect of demand for products:
   (a) number of enquiries per advertisement placed; and
   (b) percentage of customers who remember the advertisement;
2 in respect of delivering the products:
   (a) error-free deliveries as a percentage of total deliveries;
   (b) number of complaints as a percentage of units sold; and
   (c) time between receiving customer order and supplying the goods or service.

An electricity supply company provided the following information about non-financial performance over a one-year period:

Restore supply in three hours	Target	80%
	Performance	**83.8%**
Restore supply in 24 hours	Target	99%
	Performance	**99.9%**
Moving a meter inside 15 working days	Target	95%
	Performance	**96.7%**
Reply to telephone calls within 10 seconds	Target	90%
	Performance	**91.1%**

Activity 23.5 *Write out five non-financial performance measures which could be reported by an organisation which delivers parcels to the general public and to businesses.*

23.6 The Balanced Scorecard

Section 23.5 has illustrated some of the non-financial measures of performance that may be used alongside the financial measures. There is a danger of creating increasingly long lists of performance measures with no way of balancing the perspectives resulting from these different aspects of performance. Kaplan and Norton (2001) put forward an idea which they called *the Balanced Scorecard* as a way of linking performance measures. It focuses on the key goals of the organisation and the measurement of performance in achieving those goals.

They suggested that performance measurement can be viewed by asking four questions:

- How do our customers see us? (Customer perspective)
- How do our shareholders see us? (Financial perspective)
- How do we see ourselves? (Internal business perspective)
- Can we learn and grow to improve and create value? (Learning and growth perspective)

For each of these four questions the organisation should set major goals and define performance measures which demonstrate that the goals are being achieved. It might be reasonable to set three or four goals in each case. This would lead to a scorecard that would fit on a single sheet of paper. There is no specific form for the scorecard (Figure 23.1 shows an example). Here we see the management strategy being applied to set the goals for each section of the scorecard, and the performance measures being used to give feedback to management on how well the goals have been achieved.

Fiona now gives an example of work she has carried out to create a balanced scorecard system in a service business.

FIONA: *I have recently worked on designing a Balanced Scorecard for a company which owns a chain of hotels in major towns and cities around the country and wanted to evaluate the relative performance of the separate hotels. The hotels are designed to a standard model of 'no-frills' value for money and comfort, with secure parking for cars. Customers are likely to stay for one or two nights, either as business customers looking*

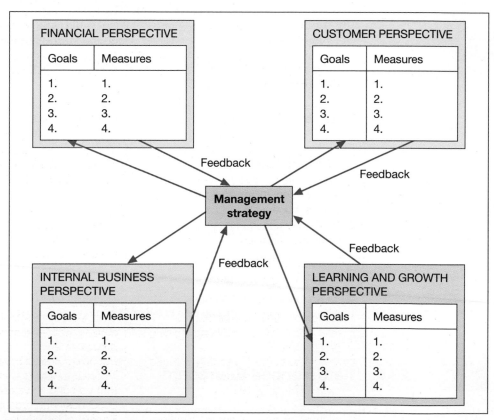

Figure 23.1
Creating a Balanced Scorecard

for convenience and reasonable pricing, or as families and tourists on short-stay visits. As this was the first attempt at creating a scorecard we used only three goals for each aspect of the balanced scorecard. It was important to involve all staff in setting up the scorecard so we established focus groups in each city or town to give their input to the goals and measurements. Each focus group included an operations manager, catering and cleaning staff and a regular customer. The result is set out in Table 23.2.

Table 23.2
Creating a Balanced Scorecard for a hotel chain

Financial perspective	
Goal	*Measure*
1 To reduce unfilled room rate by 3% over the previous year, by offering discount for a third-day stay.	Marginal revenue from additional room occupancy, compared with marginal costs of creating that occupancy, with estimate of revenue lost on third-day discount.
2 To control fixed overhead costs within 3% overall increase on previous year.	Cost records – monthly update of fixed overhead actual cost against target.
3 To control variable costs per room per night at 50% of room charge.	Cost records – monthly report on variable room costs compared to room rents received.

Customer perspective	
Goal	*Measure*
1 To increase market share by 5% over 12 months.	Market share surveys published in trade journals, plus reports commissioned from benchmarking organisations.
2 That 50% of customers return for a second visit.	Customer satisfaction questionnaire left in bedroom plus follow-up telephone enquiry.
3 That 90% of customers express general satisfaction with the service, especially cleanliness and staff courtesy.	Customer satisfaction questionnaire left in bedroom plus follow-up telephone enquiry.

Internal business perspective	
Goal	*Measure*
1 To improve customer satisfaction by improving checkout times.	Number of checkouts completed between 7a.m. and 9a.m. each day.
2 To improve the cycle of laundry delivery and return from 4 days to 3 days, on average.	Records of laundry despatch and return.
3 To identify and implement one innovative practice.	Staff suggestion box – list of staff suggestions and note of actions taken to review and implement each.

Learning and growth perspective	
Goal	*Measure*
1 To achieve 60% participation of relevant staff in a vocational training programme.	Staff records of attendance and achievement in vocational training programme.
2 To empower staff in setting personal goals that are consistent with organisational goals.	Record of annual appraisal reviews where appraising manager confirms that personal development plans are consistent with organisational goals.
3 To improve internal communication process by weekly bulletin to staff.	Record of bulletin issues and staff feedback on relevance and usefulness.

Kaplan and Norton soon realised that the Balanced Scorecard was more than a performance report. It was a useful tool in the system of strategic management. They set out five principles for a strategy-focused organisation:

1 Translate the strategy into operational terms.
2 Align the organisation to the strategy.
3 Make strategy everyone's everyday job.
4 Make strategy a continual process.
5 Mobilise leadership for change.

This makes the Balanced Scorecard a tool of forward planning for change, as well as being a retrospective view of past performance. An important aspect of using the Balanced Scorecard is the involvement of employees in all stages of setting the scorecard and monitoring the outcome. It is flexible so that the Balanced Scorecard can be designed to be relevant to the organisation and its operations or procedures.

Activity 23.6	*Imagine that you are planning to start a business operating a taxi service. Write a balanced scorecard containing two goals and two measurements of achieving the goals for each of the four sections of the Balanced Scorecard (Customer perspective, Financial perspective, Internal business perspective and Learning and growth perspective).*

23.7 Management use of performance measurement

This chapter has concentrated largely on how the management accountant may provide measures of performance. For such measures to have relevance in a managerial context, they should satisfy three criteria:

1 There should be well-defined performance measures which represent a range of performance from bad to good.
2 There should be defined standards of performance which indicate what is good and what is not good.
3 There should be rewards attached to successful attainment of targets and penalties attached to non-attainment of targets.

This section describes a case study bringing together the use of benchmarking and performance standards to achieve the objectives and strategy of the organisation.

23.7.1 Performance measures

Fiona McTaggart describes a recent experience in establishing performance measures through benchmarking:

FIONA: *I have recently completed a project advising a parcel delivery business on establishing a performance measurement system for distribution depots spread across the country. The business has a series of warehouse depots at locations convenient to major towns. Parcels are carried by lorry from one depot to another so that the delivery targets are met with careful attention to cost control. The non-financial performance measure which most concerns customers is meeting targets. Other companies in competition with this company are also performance conscious and will publicise their performance in meeting delivery targets. The financial performance measure which most concerns management is cost containment in a competitive business. Depot managers find they are expected to have regard to customer delivery targets and cost control.*
My first task in advising the company was to contact a benchmarking expert in order to find out as much as possible about the competition. The expert had plenty of information

on non-financial targets, including surveys undertaken by consumer organisations. The expert also had a broad outline of the cost structure of the leading operator in the field, which regards itself as a very well-controlled business.

Fiona emphasises here the importance of a **strategic management** approach, looking beyond the organisation, and of understanding the effective limits on targets where there is an established leader in the field. In the next section she explains how the targets were set at a level which would be acceptable to depot managers while meeting customers' expectations.

23.7.2 Standards of performance

Standards may be set by an inward-looking process which builds on the management perception of the performance required to achieve desired goals. Demonstrating that such targets are achievable may require reference to the performance of previous time periods and of similar units elsewhere in the organisation. The competitive position of the organisation requires that standards are set by reference to performance in other organisations. That may be relatively difficult or relatively easy to obtain, depending on the relative secrecy or openness of the sector.

Fiona McTaggart continues her description:

FIONA: *After collecting all the information available, senior management decided they wanted depot managers to concentrate on: (a) performance as a profit centre; (b) delivery targets; and (c) sales and customer care. The system is now in place.*

Performance as a profit centre requires targets for sales and costs. Each depot had initial targets set by reference to average performance over the past three years. The national reporting of target achievement is achieved by concentrating on percentages above and below target.

Delivery targets are reported according to the depot which last handled a parcel before it reached the customer. However, where a delivery target is not met, it is permissible for the depot manager to produce a summary of documentation showing where a previous depot in the chain caused a delay. These summaries are reviewed by head office and a supplementary report prepared showing bottleneck situations.

Customer care is monitored by customer feedback questionnaires. These are sent out by head office and collected there. The questions concentrate on delivery target time, condition of parcel, attitude of company personnel and perceived value for money. Depot summary reports are prepared.

Weekly reports are provided for depot managers which summarise the performance of the specific depot and show rankings against other depots. A narrative commentary by the managing director makes specific mention of the highest and lowest performers and explains how well the company is performing in relation to competitors.

Fiona has indicated that a mixture of financial and non-financial performance measures is used to create a part of the balanced scorecard. In the next section she comments on the rewards and penalties.

23.7.3 Rewards and penalties

If there are no rewards and no penalties it may be difficult to motivate employees in relation to performance targets. One view is that self-satisfaction in personal attainment is sufficient reward. Equally it could be argued that personal shame in not achieving a target would be sufficient penalty. However, more may be required.

Rewards and penalties are often difficult to administer because they involve human relations. The input of the individual must be seen in the context of the contribution of a team. Achieving a goal of the organisation may require team effort where it is difficult to identify the relative contributions of each member of the team. That may be overcome in relation to rewards by ensuring that no team member is deprived of a reward. Application of penalties, however, is more difficult because employment law generally seeks to protect employees against unjust treatment.

Rewards and penalties are linked to motivation. It has been suggested by experts in the theory of motivation that there are different needs at different levels of employment. Initially the employee is seeking the basic satisfaction of food and shelter which a paid job provides. A secure job provides safety in the longer term. Working in an organisation with clear goals provides the security of membership of a group. Developing personal potential in meeting performance targets leads to rewards of respect and praise. Taking a lead in meeting the goals of the organisation is evidence of realising one's potential. Studies of motivation have at various times emphasised achievement, recognition, challenge and promotion as aspects of rewards which motivate. Fairness (equity) is also seen as important, as is meeting expectations.

Fiona McTaggart completes her description of performance measurement in a transport company:

FIONA: *As I have already mentioned, the managing director writes a weekly letter to all depot managers noting in particular the best and worst performers. That gives a sense of achievement to some managers and perhaps shames others into moving up from the bottom of the league tables. There is also a real reward of an all-expenses-paid weekend break holiday for the best-performing manager over the year. The difficulty with league-table-type performance is that someone necessarily has to be bottom of the league, so while this system is motivating in a competitive sense, it has some negative aspects in that the performance measures are relative to other depots rather than relative to achievable targets. I have pointed out to the managing director that there may be some demotivating aspects to this system but he is very keen on competition and survival of the fittest.*

Fiona has indicated that using performance targets for motivation is not an easy matter and depends very much on the personalities involved.

23.8 Summary

Key themes in this chapter are:

- **Feedforward control** means making predictions of outputs expected at some future time and then quantifying those predictions, in management accounting terms.

- **Feedback control** involves comparing outputs achieved against outputs desired and taking corrective action if necessary.

- A **responsibility centre** is an area of responsibility which is controlled by an individual. It might be a cost centre, a profit centre or an investment centre.

- The key questions to ask in designing a performance report are: to whom should the report be addressed? What should be reported? How frequently should the report be presented?

- The key stages in **performance evaluation** are: decide on what to measure; plan how to report; and consider the behavioural aspects.

- It is important to distinguish **controllable** from **non-controllable** costs when seeking to establish responsibility for costs.

- **Benchmarking** is the name given to the process of measuring the organisation's operations, products and services against those of competitors recognised as market leaders, in order to establish targets which will provide a competitive advantage.

- **Non-financial performance measures** should cover both quantity and quality of performance. The measures should be related to the procedures under consideration.
- A **balanced scorecard** has four perspectives (customer perspective; financial perspective; internal business perspective; and learning and growth perspective).

Further reading

CIMA (2008), *Performance Measurement*. Topic gateway series No. 9.

Kaplan, R. S. and Norton, D. P. (2001), 'Transforming the balanced scorecard from performance measurement to strategic management: Part I', *Accounting Horizons*, 15(1): 87–104.

Kaplan, R. S. and Norton, D. P. (2001), 'Transforming the balanced scorecard from performance measurement to strategic management: Part II', *Accounting Horizons*, 15(2): 147–60.

Simons, R. (2000), *Performance Measurement and Control Systems for Implementing Strategy*, Prentice Hall.

QUESTIONS

The Questions section of each chapter has three types of question. 'Test your understanding' questions to help you review your reading are in the 'A' series of questions. You will find the answers to these by reading and thinking about the material in the book. 'Application' questions to test your ability to apply technical skills are in the 'B' series of questions. Questions requiring you to show skills in problem solving and evaluation are in the 'C' series of questions. A letter [S] indicates that there is a solution at the end of the book. Other solutions are provided in the Instructor's Manual, where there are further questions parallel to those set out here.

A   Test your understanding

A23.1 Define 'feedback control'. (Section 23.1)

A23.2 Define 'feedforward control'. (Section 23.1)

A23.3 Define 'responsibility centre'. (Section 23.1)

A23.4 What are the three basic questions to be asked in relation to report preparation? (Section 23.2)

A23.5 How does an organisation decide on the frequency of internal reporting? (Section 23.2.3)

A23.6 What is required of the management accountant in carrying out performance evaluation? (Section 23.3)

A23.7 Define a 'controllable cost'. (Section 23.3.2)

A23.8 Define a 'non-controllable cost'. (Section 23.3.2)

A23.9 Define an 'avoidable cost'. (Section 23.3.2)

A23.10 Define an 'unavoidable cost'. (Section 23.3.2)

A23.11 What are the behavioural aspects of performance evaluation? (Section 23.3.3)

A23.12 Explain what is meant by 'benchmarking'. (Section 23.4)

A23.13 Explain the meaning of 'non-financial performance measures'. (Section 23.5)

A23.14 Give two examples of quantitative non-financial performance measures. (Section 23.5.1)

A23.15 Give two examples of qualitative non-financial performance measures. (Section 23.5.2)

A23.16 What are the four main aspects of a Balanced Scorecard? (Section 23.6)

A23.17 Give one example of a goal and one example of a matching measurement, for each of the four main aspects of a Balanced Scorecard. (Section 23.6)

A23.18 What are the benefits and problems of linking rewards and penalties to a performance measurement system in an organisation? (Section 23.7.3)

B Application

B23.1
Suggest six non-financial performance measures for a company which offers contract gardening services to companies which have landscaped sites surrounding their offices. Give reasons for your choice.

B23.2
Suggest three financial and three non-financial performance measures for a business which provides training in the workplace for updating wordprocessing and computing skills. Each training course lasts two weeks and there is a standard fee charged per trainee.

B23.3
Design a balanced scorecard for a restaurant business which owns three restaurants in the same town. Include three goals and three measurements of performance for each of the four aspects of the balanced scorecard, and write a short note justifying your choices.

C Problem solving and evaluation

C23.1 [S]
Standard pine benches are assembled and packed in the bench assembly department of Furniture Manufacture Ltd. The department is treated as a cost centre. Control reports prepared every month consist of a statement comparing actual costs incurred in the department with the level of costs which was budgeted at the start of the month.

For the month of June Year 6 the following control report was produced, and received favourable comment from the directors of the company.

Bench Assembly Department

Control Report for June Year 6

	Budgeted cost			Actual cost	Variance	
	Fixed £	Variable £	Total £	£	£	
Direct labour	–	36,000	36,000	30,000	6,000	(F)
Indirect labour	6,000	8,000	14,000	14,000	–	
Indirect materials	–	4,000	4,000	3,500	500	(F)
Power	3,000	12,000	15,000	9,000	6,000	(F)
Maintenance materials	–	5,000	5,000	3,000	2,000	(F)
Maintenance labour	5,000	4,000	9,000	15,000	6,000	(A)
Depreciation	85,000	–	85,000	75,000	10,000	(F)
Production overhead	–	20,000	20,000	15,000	5,000	(F)

Note: (F) = favourable; (A) = adverse.

Due to a power failure, the level of production achieved was only 75% of that expected when the budget was prepared. No adjustment has been made to the original budget because the departmental manager claims that the power failure which caused the loss of production was beyond his control.

Required

Prepare a memorandum to the directors of the company:

1 Explaining the weaknesses in the existing form of control report.
2 Presenting the control report in such a way as to give a more meaningful analysis of the costs.
3 Assessing the performance of the Bench Assembly Department during the month.

C23.2 [S]

Dairies Ltd operates a milk processing and delivery business. The retail distribution of milk is controlled by a regional head office which has overall responsibility for five geographical distribution areas. Each area is run by an area manager who has responsibility for ten depots. At each depot there is a depot manager in charge of 20 drivers and their milk floats. Milk is bottled at a central processing plant and sent to depots by lorry.

All information regarding the operation of each depot and each area office is sent to the divisional head office accounting department. This department produces weekly reports to be sent to each depot manager, each area manager and the manager of the distribution division.

A pyramidal system of reporting is in operation whereby each manager receives an appropriate weekly report containing the financial information on the operations for which he is responsible.

Required

1 Explain what is meant by responsibility accounting.
2 List, giving reasons, the information which should be contained in the weekly reports to each of the three levels of manager specified.

C23.3

You are the management accountant at the head office of a company which owns retail shoe shops throughout the country. The shops are grouped into areas, each having an area manager. Goods for sale are bought through a central purchasing scheme administered by head office. Shop managers have discretion to vary sales prices subject to the approval of the area manager. It is the responsibility of shop managers to record on a wastage sheet any shoes which are discarded because of damage in the shop. Shop managers have total control over the number of staff they employ and the mix of permanent and casual staff, subject to interview in the presence of the area manager. Shop managers also arrange for cleaning of the premises and are responsible for heat and light and other overhead costs.

The head office accounting system has produced the following information with regard to the Southern area:

	Shop A £	Shop B £	Shop C £	Area target %
Turnover	450,000	480,000	420,000	100
Costs:				
Cost of goods sold	355,000	356,000	278,000	69
Wastage	5,000	4,000	2,000	
	360,000	360,000	280,000	
Salaries and wages:				
Branch manager	15,000	16,000	16,000	
Bonus for manager	1,000	1,500	1,500	
Permanent assistants	9,000	7,000	7,000	
Bonus for assistants	450	480	420	
Casual workers	3,000	4,000	5,000	
	28,450	28,980	29,920	6
Heat, light, cleaning and other overheads	7,600	8,500	8,200	2

	Shop A £	Shop B £	Shop C £	Area target %
Operating profit before Area office recharges	53,950	82,520	101,880	
Area office recharges	3,000	3,000	3,000	—
	50,950	79,520	98,880	22

Further information

(a) The Southern area has an overall operating profit target of 20% of sales. The area office has a target allowance of 2% of sales to cover its expenses other than those recharged to shops.

(b) Details of area office expenses are:

	£
Area manager's salary	18,000
Area manager's bonus	3,000
Other office expenses	2,400
	23,400
Area office recharges	(9,000)
	14,400

(c) It is the policy of the company to disclose sufficient information to motivate and inform the appropriate level of management or staff, but to avoid reporting excessive detail, particularly where such detail would unnecessarily disclose information about wages or salaries of individual employees.

Required

Prepare three separate reports including comments on and interpretation of the quantitative performance data as follows:

1 To the area manager on the overall performance of the area and the relative performance of each shop within the area.
2 To the manager of shop A on the performance of that shop relative to the rest of the area and to the area target.
3 To the employees of shop B showing them how their shop performed relative to the rest of the area.

Activities for study groups

Case 23.1

Lightwave Radio Ltd produces a range of products at its assembly plant. Due to recent rapid expansion the company's system of management control is now inadequate. The board has established a working party drawn from all disciplines of management to develop the structure for a new computer-based management control and reporting system.

As chief accountant, you represent the finance department on the working party and believe that the management reporting system should be based on the division of the production process into a series of cost centres.

Required

(a) Explain the essential features of a cost centre.
(b) Identify the main features you would expect to find in a cost control report prepared for use at individual cost centre level.
(c) List three objections or questions which you might anticipate receiving from other members of the working party, and explain how you would answer each.

Case 23.2

You are the managing director of Combine Ltd, a company engaged in the manufacture and sale of refrigerators and freezers. The board of directors has agreed to reorganise the company into two divisions – the domestic refrigerator division and the industrial freezer division. At the next board meeting the measures to be used to monitor management performance are to be discussed.

Prepare a five-minute presentation to your fellow directors which explains:

- the key factors to be considered in the design of financial performance measures for the divisional managers; and
- the use of non-accounting measures for appraising short-term divisional management performance.

Suggest three examples of non-accounting measures which could be used to monitor sales performance in the company.

Case 23.3

Obtain the annual report of a large listed company. Look throughout the report for mention of non-financial performance indicators. Having read the report, prepare a list of non-financial performance indicators which you think would be useful to readers in understanding more about the company. For each indicator suggested, you should give a reason. The aim should be to have a table of indicators covering no more than one side of A4 paper in printed form.

Part 9

Capital investment appraisal and business strategy

Chapter 24

Capital investment appraisal

This case study shows a typical case in which management accounting can be helpful. Read the case study now but only attempt the discussion points after you have finished reading the chapter.

Drax power station

Drax power station in Yorkshire is in the process of being converted from coal-fired to being powered by biomass. The following extracts give the company's description of the investment, followed by an article from the Financial Times.

Shutterstock.com/TTstudio

Capital expenditure

Fixed asset additions were £286 million in the year ended 31 December 2013, compared to £224 million in 2012. This includes £228 million on our biomass transformation project (2012: £180 million).

At the Drax Power Station site we completed the commissioning of the new receipt, storage and distribution systems for our first converted unit by the end of 2013, and we expect to have largely completed the on-site investment required to support three converted units by the end of 2014. These systems will provide us with the ability to unload rail wagons efficiently, store up to around 300 thousand tonnes of biomass on-site and deliver it direct to the combustion system.

Our investment in upstream supply chain infrastructure continues, with the construction of our two pellet plants in Mississippi and Louisiana and our port development at Baton Rouge (also Louisiana) having started in the Summer. All three projects remain on schedule and on budget. We are targeting the first half of 2015 for commercial operations to begin reaching full capacity within six months.

We expect to spend £650–£700 million in total on progressively converting three generating units to biomass together with the supporting infrastructure and systems required, completing the two US pellet plants and port facility and ensuring compliance with the requirements of the Industrial Emissions Directive ('IED').

Extensive research has been undertaken over the past few years to determine the optimal solution for IED compliance. As described in the Chief Executive's statement, a lead solution has been identified and initial trials towards this will commence in 2014. The estimated capital cost is £75 million to £100 million over four years.

In addition, as described in the Chief Executive's statement, we have now developed technical solutions to deliver output of 630MW in a biomass unit, with efficiency only 0.5% lower than that of a coal unit. We estimate that capital investment of approximately £90 million (over three years) is required to secure these performance improvements. Beyond this, we are evaluating further investments in the supply chain, (including options for additional pelleting facilities in the US) and the conversion of a fourth unit to biomass.

Source: Drax Group plc Annual report and accounts 2013, p. 42. http://www.drax.com/media/32649/drax_ar13_final.pdf

Drax biomass conversion a first for Osborne infrastructure scheme

A coal-fired power station in Yorkshire will partially be converted to run on biomass with the help of the chancellor's "guarantee" scheme for infrastructure.

The deal marks the first such use of the scheme, launched by George Osborne last summer with the promise of helping up to £40bn worth of projects to get the go-ahead.

Drax has used a £75m Treasury guarantee to secure the private funding to convert its plant.

The UK guarantees are designed to use the government's balance sheet to have transport, energy and waste projects built without outlay by taxpayers.

Ministers have said that companies have been in discussions over 50 projects worth some £50bn.

However, the Drax site is the first to be signed off. Progress is slower on other schemes, including the westward extension of London Underground's Northern line towards Battersea. That project, which involves Transport for London, is awaiting a final sign-off.

Other schemes understood to be in the pipeline include the Mersey Gateway, a six-lane toll bridge. The guarantee could also be applied to the Thames "super sewer", a tunnel under the river in London.

Mr Osborne said the Drax agreement was proof that the Treasury could use its fiscal "credibility" to support investment in the economy.

But, in private, many members of the coalition are frustrated at the slow progress of its infrastructure plans. One example, an attempt to shoehorn £20bn of pension fund money into a new "infrastructure platform", has fallen far short of expectations.

 Source: Pickard, J. (2013), *Financial Times, 24 April 2013.* http://www.ft.com/cms/s/0/26526d1c-acf4-11e2-b27f-00144feabdc0.html?siteedition=uk\#axzz3G82tUShy © The Financial Times Limited. All Rights Reserved.

Discussion points

1 What questions would you ask in appraising the investment in the project to replace coal with biomass as the new fuel for the power station?

2 How do the two accounts differ in the way they describe the motivation for the investment?

Learning outcomes	After reading this chapter you should be able to:

- Explain the purpose of capital investment appraisal and the role of the management accountant.
- Explain the payback method and calculate the payback period.
- Explain and calculate the accounting rate of return.
- Explain and calculate the net present value of a project.
- Explain and calculate the internal rate of return of a project.
- Explain how capital investment appraisal is used to choose from mutually exclusive projects.
- Explain which methods of capital investment appraisal are encountered in business practice.
- Explain the control processes applied to investment projects.
- Explain how advanced manufacturing technologies lead to a demand for new ways of evaluating investment projects.

24.1 Purpose of capital investment appraisal

The word 'capital' can have more than one meaning in accounting. In financial reporting in particular it is used to denote the finance provided to the business by owners and long-term lenders. Economists use the term 'capital' to refer to the fixed assets and working capital of a business which are purchased with the money provided by the owners and lenders. This chapter uses the term 'capital' in a manner similar to that used by the economists.

When the managers of a business make plans for the long term they have to decide whether, and how much, to invest in **fixed assets** and **working capital** to maintain or increase the productive capacity of the business. They will usually be faced with choices of projects available, each requiring a different type of investment, and only a limited amount of finance available. They have to ask themselves a number of questions, including:

1 How many of the proposed projects are worth undertaking?
2 How much finance, in total, should we commit to new projects?
3 Where should the finance be obtained?
4 After the event, was the investment in the proposed project successful?

These questions cross an academic spectrum of study which begins in management accounting and ends in finance. The first and fourth of these questions are normally dealt with in management accounting books, while the second and third form the focus of finance books. Some books in either discipline will attempt to deal with all the questions. This chapter focuses on the first and fourth questions. It explains techniques that can be applied to evaluate (appraise) an investment project in order to decide whether it is worthwhile to start the project.

Definition | **Capital investment appraisal** is a process of management accounting which assists management decision making by providing information on the investment in a project and the benefits to be obtained from that project, and by monitoring the performance of the project subsequent to its implementation.

24.1.1 The role of the management accountant in capital investment appraisal

The management accountant's role was set out in Chapter 16 as **directing attention**, **keeping the score** and **solving problems**. In **capital investment appraisal** it is the role of **directing attention** which is important. Information about proposed capital projects must be presented in a way which will direct management's attention towards the significant information for decision-making purposes. There will most probably be problems to solve in terms of gathering and presenting the information. After the project is implemented there will be a score-keeping aspect in terms of comparing the actual outcome with the plans and expectations.

This chapter concentrates on the techniques of presenting information so as to direct attention to the significant aspects of the capital project for decision-making purposes. It concludes with an explanation of the retrospective evaluation of a project by a post-completion audit.

24.1.2 The assumptions adopted

This chapter makes an assumption that all future cash inflows and outflows of a long-term project may be predicted with certainty. It also assumes that there are no taxes and there is no inflation to cause prices to increase over the life of the project. For some of the calculations in the chapter there is an assumption that all cash flows take place on the final day of an accounting period. Making assumptions of this type may seem a rather unrealistic starting point, but it is necessary to do so in order to analyse the principles of capital investment appraisal without having too many real-world complications crowding in.

24.1.3 Making a decision on a capital investment

Chapter 16 contains a specification of the processes of **planning** and **control** which are necessary for a systematic approach to making an investment decision in locating a new retail outlet. In general terms, that process is as shown in Figure 24.1.

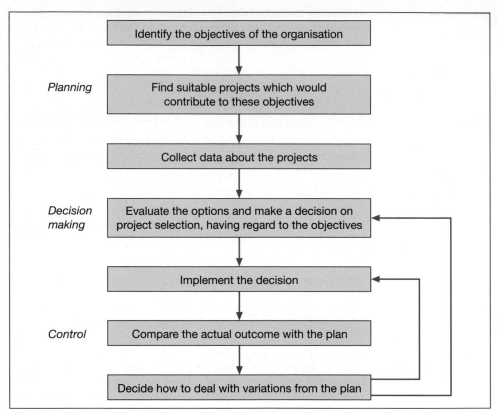

Figure 24.1
Planning and control for a capital investment decision

To be successful the business must first of all discover projects which have the potential for success. All the management accounting in the world will not create a successful project. The successful entrepreneur is the person who has the flair and imagination to identify projects and to see how they might successfully operate. The role of management accounting, through the **capital investment appraisal** process, is to ensure that the excitement of creating new investment opportunities does not cause management to lose sight of the need to meet the organisation's objectives.

24.1.4 Selecting acceptable projects

Suppose there has been a meeting of the board of directors of a company at which the managing director has said: 'We want to ensure that any cash we invest in a project comes back as soon as possible in the form of cash flows which give us a profit overall and provide the cash to reinvest in the next project.'

A second director has replied by saying: 'It's fine for you to talk about cash flows but the outside world judges our success by our profit record. I would like to see us choosing projects which maximise the return on assets invested in the project.'

A third member of the board has joined in with: 'I agree with the cash flow perspective but I want to be sure that, at the minimum, we cover the interest charges we have to pay on the money we borrow to finance the project. Ideally, there should be cash flows generated which exceed the cost of borrowing, so that we have surplus funds to use for investment in further projects or for increasing dividends to our shareholders.'

Reading carefully what each has said, it is apparent that there are similarities and differences in the targets they would like to set. They are all looking to cash flows from the project, but the first director is emphasising the speed of collecting cash flows, while the second director wants to convert cash flows to profit by deducting depreciation, and the third director is more concerned about the amount of cash flows in total and whether they provide a surplus after covering all costs.

Management accounting can provide information for **capital investment appraisal** purposes which would satisfy the criteria set by any one of the three directors, but there would remain the question as to which of the three directors is using the best approach so far as the business is concerned. Four methods of capital investment appraisal will now be explained. These are: the **payback** method, the **accounting rate of return**, the **net present value** method and the **internal rate of return** method. Each management accounting technique will be described in turn and the advantages and disadvantages of each will be discussed.

Activity 24.1

Decide now which of the three directors you think has the most desirable approach and why you think that way. Then monitor the development of your views as you read the chapter.

24.2 Payback method

24.2.1 Method of calculation

The first director wanted cash invested in a project to come back as quickly as possible in the form of cash flows. To test whether this objective has been met by a capital project, the payback method of project appraisal is used. It provides a calculation of the length of time required for the stream of cash inflows from a project to equal the original cash outlay. The most desirable project, under the payback method, is the one which pays back the cash outlay in the shortest time. Data are set out in Exhibit 24.1 which will be used to illustrate all the capital investment appraisal methods explained in this chapter. An illustration of the payback calculation is provided in Table 24.1, and from this table of calculations it may be seen that project A offers the *shortest* **payback period**. Thus if the most important measure of success in investment is the recovery of the cash investment, then Project A is the preferred choice. Project C is next in rank and Project B is the least attractive.

Definition

The payback method of project appraisal calculates the length of time required for the stream of cash inflows from a project to equal the original cash outlay.

The **payback period** is the length of time required for a stream of net cash inflows from a project to equal the original cash outlay.

Exhibit 24.1
Data for illustration of methods of capital investment appraisal

Data
A haulage company has three potential projects planned. Each will require investment in two refrigerated vehicles at a total cost of £120,000. Each vehicle has a three-year life. The three projects are:

A Lease the vehicles to a meat-processing factory which will take the risks of finding loads to transport and will bear all driver costs for a three-year period. Expected net cash inflows, after deducting all expected cash outflows, are £60,000 per annum.

B Enter into a fixed-price contract for three years to carry frozen foods from processing plants in the UK to markets in continental Europe, returning with empty vehicles. This will require employing drivers on permanent contracts. Expected cash inflows, after deducting all expected cash outflows, are £45,000 per annum.

C Employ a contracts manager to find loads for outward and return journeys but avoid any contract for longer than a six-month period so as to have the freedom to take up opportunities as they arise. Drivers will be hired on short-term contracts of three months. Expected cash inflows, after deducting all expected cash outflows, are £40,000 in Year 1, £70,000 in Year 2 and £80,000 in Year 3.

Table 24.1
Calculations for payback method

Cash flows	Project A	Project B	Project C
	£	£	£
Outlay	120,000	120,000	120,000
Cash inflows, after deducting all outflows of the year			
Year 1	60,000	45,000	40,000
Year 2	60,000	45,000	70,000
Year 3	60,000	45,000	80,000
Payback period	2 years	2.67 years	2.125 years
(expressed in years and months)	2 yrs 0 mths	2 yrs 8 mths	2 yrs 1.5 mths
Workings	$60 + 60 = 120$	$45 + 45 + \frac{30}{45}$	$40 + 70 + \frac{10}{80}$

24.2.2 Impact of uncertainty in real life

This calculation assumes certainty about the cash flows predicted for each project. Hopefully, as you were reading the conditions of the three different contracts set out in Exhibit 24.1, you had some thoughts about the relative commercial risk of each project and the risks attached to the cash flows. In this chapter we do not make allowance for the relative risks of each project, because we make an assumption of certainty of predicted cash flows but, in real life, Project C would be regarded commercially as the high-risk option, while projects A and B provide greater certainty through having contracts in place for the three-year period. Of these two, project B looks the less attractive but leaves opportunities for casual earnings if loads can be found for the return journey.

24.2.3 Usefulness and limitations of the payback approach

The **payback** method of **capital investment appraisal** is widely used in practice, possibly because it is relatively painless in its arithmetic. Furthermore, there is a reflection of commercial realism in concentrating on projects which give early returns of cash flow. That may be important to organisations which face cash flow constraints. It may also be seen as a cautious approach to take where product markets are uncertain and it is difficult to predict the longer-term cash flows expected from a product.

One major limitation of using the payback method of capital investment appraisal as described here is that it ignores the fact that investing funds in a long-term project has a cost in terms of the interest charges on borrowed funds (or interest forgone when money is tied up in fixed assets). Economists refer to this interest cost as the **time value of money**. This is the name given to the idea that £1 invested today will grow with interest rates over time (e.g. £1 become £1.10 in one year's time at a rate of 10%).

Definition

> The **time value of money** is the name given to the idea that £1 invested today will grow with interest rates over time (e.g. £1 become £1.10 in one year's time at a rate of 10%).

The cash flows earned from a project should repay the capital sum invested, but they should also be sufficient to provide a reward to investors which equals the interest cost of capital.

A second major limitation is that, in concentrating on the speed of recovery of cash flows, the method ignores any cash flows arising after the payback date. A project which would make a long-term contribution to the overall cash flows of the business could be sacrificed for short-term benefits in a project with a limited time horizon.

Activity 24.2

Check that you understand fully the calculation of the payback period and its interpretation. Write a 200-word note on the meaning and usefulness of the payback period as a means of evaluating the suitability of a project.

24.3 Accounting rate of return

24.3.1 Method of calculation

The **accounting rate of return** differs from the payback method in using accounting profits rather than cash flows. As you will by now have realised, the calculation of profits includes depreciation, which is an accounting allocation but has no cash flow effect. The attraction of using profit in a method of capital investment appraisal is that it links long-term decision making to profit as the conventional measure of success in business.

Definition

> The **accounting rate of return** is calculated by taking the average annual profits expected from a project as a percentage of the capital invested.
>
> **Average annual profit** is calculated as average annual cash flow minus annual depreciation.

Some books recommend as denominator the initial amount of capital invested while others suggest the use of the average capital invested. Calculation of the average involves making some arbitrary assumptions about the way capital is used up over the project. A simple pattern is to assume it is used up evenly. Suppose a project requires £1,000 invested at the start, there will be nothing left at the end and the capital is used up equally each year. Then the average investment is £500 (which is the average of £1,000 at the start and £nil at the end). This book will use the initial investment for illustrative purposes, but you should be aware that different definitions will be used in practice and it is important to know how any return on capital has been defined.

The data in Exhibit 24.1 may be used to illustrate the accounting rate of return as a method of **capital investment appraisal**. A straight-line method of depreciation is applied, assuming a zero residual value, so that depreciation of £40,000 per annum (calculated as £120,000/3) is deducted from cash flows. The resulting profits and accounting rate of return are shown in Table 24.2.

Table 24.2 shows that Project C has the highest rate of return, Project A is next in rank and Project B has the lowest rate of return. The accounting rate of return gives a ranking of the three projects different from that given by the payback method. Project B remains the least attractive but the positions of Projects A and C are reversed. That is because C creates more cash flow in total but the cash flows of A arise earlier than those of C.

Table 24.2
Calculations for the accounting rate of return

Cash flows	Project A	Project B	Project C
	£	£	£
Outlay (a)	120,000	120,000	120,000
Profits, after deducting depreciation from cash flows			
Year 1	20,000	5,000	Nil
Year 2	20,000	5,000	30,000
Year 3	20,000	5,000	40,000
Average annual profit (b)	20,000	5,000	23,000
Accounting rate of return (b × 100/a)	16.7%	4.2%	19.2%

24.3.2 Usefulness and limitations of accounting rate of return

The accounting rate of return is regarded as a useful measure of the likely success of a project because it is based on the familiar accounting measure of profit. It is also regarded as useful because it takes into the calculation all the profits expected over the project life (in contrast to the payback method which ignores all cash flows beyond the payback date).

A major defect of the accounting rate of return is that it ignores the **time value of money**. It makes no distinction between two projects of the same average profit, one of which gives most of its profits at an early stage and the other of which gives most of its profits at a later stage.

A less serious defect, but nevertheless a limitation, is that the accounting rate of return depends on profit which, in turn, includes a subjective accounting estimate of depreciation. That may not matter too much in an example of the type illustrated in Table 24.2, where average profits are used and straight-line depreciation is applied across all projects, but there could be situations where different depreciation policies could distort a decision based on the accounting rate of return.

Activity 24.3   *Before proceeding further, make sure that you understand fully the calculation and usefulness of the accounting rate of return. Write a 200-word note on the limitations of relying on the accounting rate of return when evaluating a project.*

24.4 Net present value method

The **net present value** (NPV) method of **capital investment appraisal** is a technique which seeks to remedy some of the defects of **payback** and the **accounting rate of return**. In particular it takes into account all cash flows over the life of the project and makes allowance for the time value of money. Before the net present value method can be explained further, it is necessary to make a short digression into the **time value of money**.

24.4.1 Time value of money

If £100 is invested at 10% per annum, then it will grow to £110 by the end of the year. If the £100 is spent on an item of business machinery, then the interest is lost. So the act of investing leads to a lost opportunity of earning investment. The idea of applying calculations of the time value of money is a way of recognising the reward needed from a project to compensate for the lost opportunity.

Suppose now that you have been given a written promise of £100 to be received in one year's time. Interest rates are 10%. You do not want to wait one year to receive cash and would like the money now. What is the price for which you could sell that promise? Most students see the answer as £90.91 intuitively, but they do not all see immediately how they arrived at that answer. (It might be useful for you to think out your own approach before you read the next few paragraphs. It is much easier to work something out for yourself than to try remembering formulae which you will forget in a crisis.)

The intuitive answer is that £90.91 is the amount which, invested now at 10%, would grow to £100 in one year's time. Provided the promise is a good one, there would be no problem in selling the £100 promise for £90.91 now. Both the buyer and the seller would be equally satisfied that the price reflected the time value of money.

Now make it a little harder. Suppose the promise of £100 was for payment in *two* years' time. What is the price for which you could sell that promise now? The answer is £82.64 because that would grow at 10% to £90.91 at the end of one year and to £100 at the end of two years.

The calculation of the value of the promise today can be conveniently represented in mathematical notation as follows:

Definition   The **present value** of a sum of £1 receivable at the end of n years when the rate of interest is r% per annum equals:

$$\frac{1}{(1 + r)^n}$$

where r represents the annual rate of interest, expressed in decimal form, and n represents the time period when the cash flow will be received.

The process of calculating present value is called **discounting**. The interest rate used is called the **discount rate**.

Using this calculation to illustrate the two calculations already carried out intuitively, the present value of a sum of £100, due one year hence, when the discount rate (interest rate) is 10%, is calculated as:

$$\frac{£100}{(1 + 0.1)^1} = £90.91$$

The **present value** of a sum of £100, due two years' hence, when the interest rate is 10%, is calculated as:

$$\frac{£100}{(1 + 0.1)^2} = £82.64$$

The calculation using this formula is no problem if a financial calculator or a spreadsheet package is available, but can be tedious if resources are limited to a basic pocket calculator. In such circumstances, some people prefer to use tables of discount factors which give the present value of £1 for every possible rate of interest and every possible time period ahead. A full table of discount factors is set out in the supplement at the end of this chapter.

In this supplement, the column for the discount rate of 10% has the following discount factors:

At end of period	Present value of £1
1	0.909
2	0.826
3	0.751

Using the tables, for the discount rate of 10%, it may be calculated that the present value of £100 receivable at the end of Year 1 is £100 × 0.909 = £90.90, while the present value of £100 receivable at the end of Year 2 is £100 × 0.826 = £82.60. (There is a difference in the second place of decimals when this answer is compared with the result of using the formula. The difference is due to rounding in the discount tables.)

Now that you are familiar with the calculation of the present value of a promised future cash flow, the explanation of the net present value method of capital investment appraisal may be given.

Activity 24.4
Use your calculator to check the discount factors for the present value of £1 at the end of one year, two years and three years for a discount rate of 10%. Write a parallel table for 8% and 12%. Show that the discount factor decreases as the discount rate increases.

24.4.2 The net present value decision rule

The **net present value** (NPV) method of **capital investment appraisal** is based on the view that a project will be regarded as successful if the present value of all expected cash inflows is greater than, or equal to, the capital invested at the outset. It is called *net present value* because, in calculation, the capital invested is deducted from the present value of the future cash flows. (Use of the word 'net' always means that one item is being deducted from another.) If the present value of the expected cash flows is greater than the capital invested, then the net present value will be positive. If the present value of the expected cash flows is less than the capital invested, then the net present value will be negative. A positive net present value indicates that the project should be accepted, while a negative net present value indicates that it should be rejected.

The NPV decision rule is as follows:

1 Where the net present value of the project is *positive,* accept the project.
2 Where the net present value of the project is *negative,* reject the project.
3 Where the net present value of the project is zero, the project is acceptable in meeting the cost of capital but gives no surplus to its owners.

If an organisation seeks to maximise the wealth of its owners, then it should accept any project which has a positive net present value. If finance markets are working efficiently, funds will always be available to finance projects which meet or exceed their cost of capital.

24.4.3   The cost of capital

The rate of interest used in the calculation of net present value is called the **discount rate**. It is based on the cost to the business of raising new finance. This is called the **cost of capital**. If the project is to be financed only by borrowing from banks then the cost of capital is the rate of interest that a bank would charge for a new loan. If the project is to be financed only by issuing new share capital then the cost of capital is the dividend yield required by investors. If the project is to be financed by cash that has been saved within the business, then the shareholders have allowed this saving rather than take dividend, so the cost of capital is the opportunity cost reflected in the dividend yield.

When the business finances projects by a mixture of sources of finance, the cost of capital is a mixture of the related costs. It is calculated by a weighted average of the interest rate on loans and the dividend yield on share capital. The weights used are based on the relative amounts of loan finance and equity finance used by the company. If you study corporate finance you will learn more about estimating the weighted average cost of capital. For any exercise in this book you will be informed of the discount rate to be used.

24.4.4   Residual value

At the end of a project's life there may be cash flows that can be collected from sale of equipment or recovery of cash invested in inventories and debtors. Any cash flows from residual value should be included in the projected cash flows and discounted from the end of the project.

24.4.5   Illustration

The illustration in Table 24.3 sets out the data for Project A taken from Exhibit 24.1. Table 24.4 sets out the net present value calculation, assuming a discount rate of 10%. Based on the **net present value** rule Project A will be accepted as it gives a positive net present value.

Table 24.3
Data for net present value illustration

Cash flows	Project A
	£
Outlay	120,000
Cash inflows, after deducting all outflows of the year:	
Year 1	60,000
Year 2	60,000
Year 3	60,000

Table 24.4
Calculation of net present value: project A

Using the formula approach the net present value is calculated as:

$$\frac{£60,000}{(1.10)} + \frac{£60,000}{(1.10)^2} + \frac{£60,000}{(1.10)^3} - £120,220$$
$$= £54,550 + £49,590 + £45,080 - £120,000 = £29,220$$

Using the discount tables the net present value is calculated as:

End of year	Cash flow	Discount factor	Present value
	£		£
1	60,000	0.909	54,540
2	60,000	0.826	49,560
3	60,000	0.751	45,060
Present value of cash flows			149,160
Less initial outlay			(120,000)
Net present value			29,160

Rounding errors

The answer obtained from the discount tables (£29,160) differs marginally from that obtained from the formula (£29,220), because the discount factors are rounded to three decimal places. In many cases, such differences are marginal to the overall calculation and you should not worry about them. If, in any particular case, the rounding errors are likely to have an impact, then the formula should be used rather than the tables of discount factors. In real life it is questionable whether any decision should be based on fine-tuning of rounding errors. The conclusion should be clear from the overall magnitudes being calculated and should not be dependent on differences of very small magnitude.

Activity 24.5

If you have access to a spreadsheet package, find out whether it has a net present value (NPV) function. If so, use the data in Table 24.3 to satisfy yourself that the spreadsheet produces answers similar to those derived here.

Cash flow patterns assumed by the net present value calculation

It is worth pausing to analyse the cash flow patterns which are assumed by the net present value calculation. This analysis helps in understanding when it is safe to use the net present value approach to capital investment appraisal and when it should be applied with caution.

Assume the investor who has provided the capital of £120,000 requires 10% interest at the end of each year, to be paid out of the cash flows. Assume that any surplus cash flows are retained in the business and reinvested at 10%. The accumulation of cash generated by the project is shown in Table 24.5. The cash balance at the end of Year 3 is £159,000, out of which the original capital of £120,000 is repaid, leaving an actual surplus of £39,000. That surplus arising at the end of Year 3 has a present value of £29,000 (£39,000 × 0.751) which is the answer derived earlier by the net present value calculation (allowing for rounding differences).

Table 24.5
Accumulation of cash during a project

Year	Balance of cash at start of year		Interest earned on balance invested		Cash flow		Interest paid		Balance of cash at end of year
	(1) £000s	+	(2) £000s	+	(3) £000s	−	(4) £000s	=	(1 + 2 + 3 − 4) £000s
1	nil	+	−	+	60	−	12	=	48
2	48	+	5	+	60	−	12	=	101
3	101	+	10	+	60	−	12	=	159

Table 24.5 is provided here to illustrate one of the assumptions of the net present value calculation which requires some thought. It assumes that surplus cash generated during the project can be invested at the cost of capital. Whether or not that is the case for a particular project is more an issue for study in the area of finance, but in real life it is rare that the interest earned on deposited funds is as high as that paid on borrowings. What is possible in many situations is that the surplus cash is used to start further projects in the business and those new projects are also successful in creating positive net present values of cash flows at the organisation's cost of capital.

Projects B and C

Now consider Projects B and C. The net present value of each project is calculated in Tables 24.6 and 24.7.

Project C has the highest net present value, followed by Project A. Both would be acceptable because both have a positive net present value. Project B would be rejected because it gives a negative net present value.

Table 24.6
Calculation of net present value: project B

Using the discount tables the net present value is calculated as follows:

End of year	Cash flow £	Discount factor	Present value £
1	45,000	0.909	40,905
2	45,000	0.826	37,170
3	45,000	0.751	33,795
			111,870
Less initial outlay			(120,000)
Net present value			(8,130)

Table 24.7
Calculation of net present value: project C

Using the discount tables the net present value is calculated as follows:

End of year	Cash flow £	Discount factor	Present value £
1	40,000	0.909	36,360
2	70,000	0.826	57,820
3	80,000	0.751	60,080
			154,260
Less initial outlay			(120,000)
Net present value			34,260

In real life, obtaining finance may be difficult because of temporary imbalance in the capital markets or because the supply of capital within the organisation is constrained. If the organisation is in the public sector it may be subject to a cash limit of capital expenditure. If it is in the private sector and is a subsidiary or a division within a group, it may be restricted by the group's plans for total fund-raising by the group. Such practical problems are sometimes referred to as *capital rationing* and will lead to organisations devising decision rules for ranking projects. These ranking decisions will not be explored in detail here but it is important to note that any project which is rejected, when it has a positive net present value, will be a loss to the potential wealth of the owners of the business.

24.5 Internal rate of return

Net present value is only one method in capital investment appraisal which takes into account the time value of money. The decision rule is based on the absolute amount of the net present value of the surplus generated by the project. There is some evidence from research into the practical use of capital investment appraisal techniques that decision makers feel more comfortable with a percentage rather than an absolute amount. (The reason is not so clear but could be linked to the historical reliance on the accounting rate of return as a percentage.)

The **internal rate of return** (IRR) is another method in capital investment appraisal which uses the time value of money but results in an answer expressed in percentage form. It is a discount rate which leads to a net present value of zero, where the present value of the cash inflows exactly equals the cash outflows.

Definition

The **internal rate of return** (IRR) is the discount rate at which the present value of the cash flows generated by the project is equal to the present value of the capital invested, so that the net present value of the project is zero.

24.5.1 Method of calculation

The calculation of the internal rate of return involves a process of repeated guessing at the **discount rate** until the present value of the cash flows generated is equal to the capital investment. That guessing may be carried out by computer, asking the computer to try values of the discount factor in the formula. Most spreadsheet computer packages have the facility to perform a calculation of internal rate of return once the initial investment and cash flows have been entered on the spreadsheet.

$$\text{Initial investment} = \frac{C_1}{(1 + d)} + \frac{C_2}{(1 + d)^2} + \frac{C_3}{(1 + d)^3} + \cdots + \frac{C_n}{(1 + d)^n}$$

That process of repeated guessing is extremely time-consuming if a computer is not used. Even where a computer is used, it needs to be provided with a first guess which is reasonably close. For a manual process of estimation it may be easier to use discount tables, with an aim of arriving at a reasonably close answer, rather than worrying too much about figures beyond the decimal point.

Take, as an illustration, the data on Project A of Exhibit 24.1, repeated in Table 24.3. The starting point for calculating IRR is to find two values of NPV using discount rates lying either side of the IRR. Table 24.8 sets out two such calculations. A first guess of 20% produces a net present value which is positive. The aim is to find the discount rate which gives a zero net present value, so the first guess must have been too low and a higher discount rate of 24% is used for the second guess.

Table 24.8
Calculation of net present value at 20% and at 24%

	Cash flows £	Discount rate 20%	£	Discount rate 24%	£
End of Year 1	60,000	0.833	49,980	0.806	48,360
End of Year 2	60,000	0.694	41,640	0.650	39,000
End of Year 3	60,000	0.579	34,740	0.524	31,440
			126,360		118,800
Outlay			(120,000)		(120,000)
Net present value			6,360		(1,200)

The second guess was a fortunate one because the net present value changed from being positive at 20% to being negative at 24%. That means that the net present value of zero must be found at a discount rate between these two rates. If the second guess had failed to give a negative net present value, a further guess would have been required.

The actual discount rate which gives a zero net present value may now be found by assuming a linear interval between 20% and 24%. (The interval is not exactly linear but may be taken as approximately so over a narrow difference in rates.)

The difference between the two net present values is £6,360 − (−£1,200), that is £7,560. The difference between the two discount rates is 4% and therefore, using simple proportion calculations, the net present value of zero lies at:

$$20\% + \left(\frac{6,360}{7,540} \times 4\right) = 23.365\%$$

Figure 24.2 sets out the linear relationship which is assumed in the calculation. The process of estimation shown there is called *interpolation*. In words, the formula used in this calculation is:

$$\frac{\text{Lower of the pair}}{\text{of discount rates}} + \left(\frac{\text{NPV at lower rate}}{\text{Difference between the NPVs}} \times \text{Difference in rates}\right)$$

The internal rate of return answer, as produced by a computer package, is 23.375%. The use of a simple proportion calculation appears to provide a good approximation.

Activity 24.6

If you have access to a computer spreadsheet package which has an internal rate of return function, test the data used in the chapter. It will ask you for a first guess and will then proceed to repeat the calculation of IRR until it arrives at a net present value of zero.

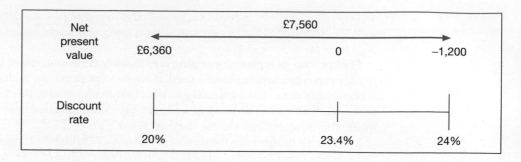

Figure 24.2
Locating the internal rate of return between two discount rates of known net present value

It is also possible to plot a graph of net present value against discount rate, as shown in Figure 24.3. The internal rate of return is the discount rate at which the graph crosses the horizontal line representing zero net present value. That point is designated with a letter P in the graph and is shown to be around 23.4% by a vertical dotted line from P to the horizontal axis.

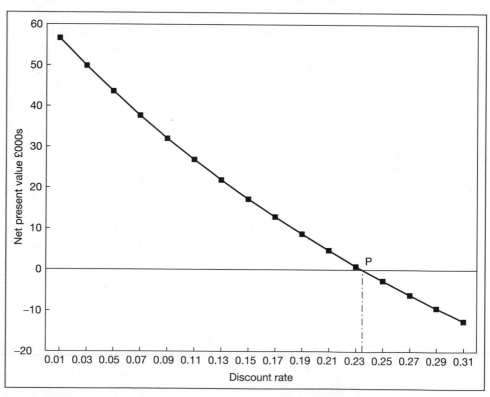

Figure 24.3
Graph of net present value against discount rate showing internal rate of return

24.5.2 The internal rate of return decision rule

The decision rule is that a project is acceptable where the **internal rate of return** is greater than the cost of capital. Under those conditions the net present value of the project will be positive. A project is not acceptable where the internal rate of return is less than the cost of capital. Under those conditions the net present value of the project will be negative.

1 Where the IRR of the project is greater than the cost of capital, accept the project.
2 Where the IRR of the project is less than the cost of capital, reject the project.
3 Where the IRR of the project equals the cost of capital, the project is acceptable in meeting the required rate of return of those investing in the business but gives no surplus to its owners.

When the net present value and the internal rate of return criteria are applied to an isolated project, they will lead to the same accept/reject decision because they both use the discounting method of calculation applied to the same cash flows. For an isolated project the use of either technique is a matter of personal preference. Where a choice of competing projects has to be made, the practice may be more complicated. The techniques available for dealing with that problem are beyond the scope of this book, but the next section outlines the nature of the problem.

24.6 Mutually exclusive projects

An organisation may need to make a choice between two projects which are **mutually exclusive** (perhaps because there is only sufficient demand in the market for the output of one of the projects, or because there is a limited physical capacity which will not allow both). Some care is then required in using the net present value and the internal rate of return as decision criteria. In many cases they give the same answer on relative ranking, but occasionally they may give different answers, as shown in the following case example.

24.6.1 Case study: whisky distillery

A distillery is planning to invest in a new still. There are two plans, one of which involves continuing to produce the traditional mix of output blends and the second of which involves experimentation with new blends. The second plan will produce lower cash flows in the earlier years of the life of the still, but it is planned that these cash flows will overtake the traditional pattern within a short space of time. Only one plan may be implemented. The project is to be appraised on the basis of cash flows over three years. The cash flows expected are shown in Table 24.9. The cost of capital is 12% per annum. At this discount rate the net present values are shown in the second table of Table 24.9. The internal rates of return are also shown in that table.

Table 24.9
Cash flows, NPV and IRR for two mutually exclusive projects

Project	Initial investment	Cash flows		
		Year 1	Year 2	Year 3
	£	£	£	£
A	120,000	96,000	48,000	12,000
B	120,000	12,000	60,000	108,000

Project	NPV at 12%	IRR
	£	
A	12,521	20.2%
B	15,419	17.6%

It may be seen from Table 24.9 that, looking at the net present value at the cost of capital, project B appears the more attractive with the higher net present value. Looking at the internal rate of return, project A appears most attractive. Both are acceptable because they give a positive net present value and the ideal answer would be to find the resources to undertake both projects. In this example, the two are mutually exclusive (which means that taking on one project excludes the possibility of the other).

If the business has the aim of maximising net present value, then one further decision rule may be helpful, based on the **profitability index**.

Definition

> The **profitability index** is the present value of cash flows (discounted at the cost of capital) divided by the present value of the investment intended to produce those cash flows.

The project with the highest profitability index will give the highest net present value for the amount of investment funding available. Taking the data in Table 24.9, the profitability index calculations are:

$$\text{Project A: Profitability index} = \frac{132,521}{120,000} = 1.10$$

$$\text{Project B: Profitability index} = \frac{135,419}{120,000} = 1.13$$

This confirms that, of the two, project B is preferable at a cost of capital of 12%. Where the investment in both projects is of the same amount, as in this case, the profitability index confirms what is already obvious, but where there are competing projects of differing initial investment, it is a useful device for ranking projects to maximise net present value.

24.6.2 Sensitivity to changes in the discount rate

To understand the apparently different conclusions from the NPV and IRR approaches, it is helpful to plot a graph of the net present value of each project against a range of discount rates. The graph is shown in Figure 24.4.

From Figure 24.4, it will be seen that, for both projects, the net present value decreases as the discount rate increases but that the net present value of project B decreases more rapidly. Starting at the left-hand side of the graph, the net present value of project B is higher than that of project A at all discount rates above the point, M, at which they intersect (around 14.2%). In particular project B has a higher net present value than project A at the cost of capital 12% (point N on the graph). For discount rates above 14.2%, the net present value of project B is always higher than that of project A. The internal rate of return of each project is the discount rate at which they cross the line of zero net present value (i.e. at point P for project B and point Q for project A).

How does this help the decision maker? If it is absolutely certain that the cost of capital will remain at 12% throughout the life of the project, then the net present value method correctly leads to a choice of project B in preference to project A. On the other hand, 12% is quite close to the point of intersection at 14.2%, where project A takes over. If there is a chance that the cost of capital will in reality be higher than the 12% expected, then it might be safer to choose project A. The line of the graph for project A is less steep and this project is said to be less sensitive to changes in the discount rate. There is therefore no clear-cut answer to the problem and the final decision will be based on an assessment of sensitivity. Looking at Figure 24.4, the different ranking by net present value and by internal rate of return was a useful clue to the need to consider the relative sensitivities as shown in the graph.

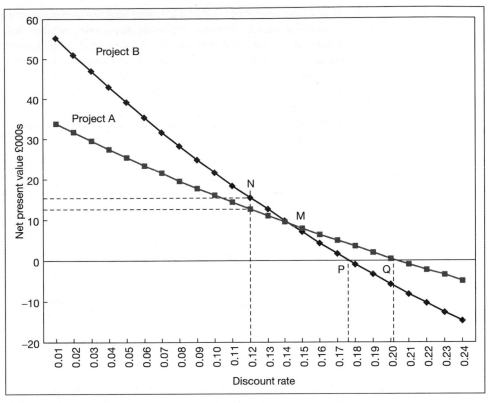

Figure 24.4
Net present value of competing projects using a range of discount rates

24.7 Which methods are used in practice?

This chapter has now explained the capital investment appraisal techniques of payback, accounting rate of return, net present value and internal rate of return. The benefits and limitations of each have been discussed in the respective sections. It could be argued that the proof of the value of each technique lies in the extent to which it is used in practice. There exists a considerable volume of survey research seeking an answer to the question of which methods are most commonly used in practice. The conclusions from each project are not totally unanimous because they depend on the time period covered by the research, the nature of the sample chosen, the country in which the questions are asked and the questions asked. There are themes which may be discerned in the research results, the first of which is that the payback method appears to be the most frequently used technique in the UK but discounted cash flow methods are found more commonly in the USA. It is also found that organisations will use more than one method of capital investment appraisal. Where discounting methods are used, internal rate of return appears more popular than net present value.

Research investigations are able to collect information of this type. Once the patterns are known, it is interesting to speculate on the motives behind these patterns of choice. Perhaps the payback method is most frequently used because there are many small businesses undertaking lots of small projects. It might not matter that discounting methods are used less frequently provided they are used on the larger projects in larger organisations. This issue has also been tested in research and it has been shown that larger companies do make relatively more use of discounting techniques. Perhaps the payback method, in many cases, shows so clearly that a project is acceptable that it would be a waste of time to carry out lengthy discounting calculations to arrive at the same conclusion. Perhaps those using payback realise that, in some instances, its emphasis on early cash flows is not so different from that of the net present value approach in situations where the later cash flows are relatively low.

24.8 Control of investment projects: authorisation and review

The capital investment projects of an organisation represent major commitments of resources. It would be a mistake to be over-enthusiastic about decision-making techniques without also considering how management accounting may help in the subsequent implementation of the project.

The organisation should have in place a procedure by which new project suggestions are investigated and evaluated using the techniques described in this chapter, or suitable alternatives. There should then be a decision-making group, perhaps called the capital investment appraisal committee or the management review committee, which makes decisions on the projects to be selected. Once the decision has been made and the capital investment appraisal committee has authorised the project to proceed, the management accountant is again needed in implementing a system for reviewing and controlling the project.

The two important aspects of control and review are:

1 controlling the amount of the expenditure needed to make the project operational;
2 post-completion audit of cash inflows and outflows.

24.8.1 Controlling capital expenditure

The specification of the project will have included an estimate of the initial outlay required and the timing of that outlay. For simplification, the illustrations used in this chapter assumed a single amount being paid out at the start of the project, but in real life the capital expenditure will be spread over a period of time on an agreed schedule. If the capital expenditure involves constructing a building, there will be a contract for the building work which sets out the dates for completion of each stage and the amount of cash to be paid at that point. The payment will only be made when an expert (such as the architect supervising the project) has confirmed that the work has been carried out according to the specification. If a contract has been drawn up with care, it will contain safeguards to ensure that the work is completed on time and within the original cost estimates. There may be a penalty clause, so that a part of the cash payment may be withheld if the contract is not performed as promised.

Activity 24.7

Write a list of key points to be made in a recommendation to the board of directors on the implementation of an expenditure control process for capital investment plans.

24.8.2 Post-completion audit

A **post-completion audit** involves a review of the actual results of a project in order to compare these with the expectations contained in the project proposals. It is called an audit because it requires a more flexible approach than would be found in management accounting evaluations of short-term plans (as covered in Chapter 20). The post-completion audit might require a view of the wider implications of the project rather than concentrating too much on annual cash flows item by item. A project might take a different turn from that envisaged at the outset and a longer-term view would be required of the likely outcome of that different turn. In real life, uncertainty is a factor which cannot easily be built into the project plans and the audit may have to take account of factors which could not have been foreseen at the outset.

There could be dangers in such an audit process if managers of projects see themselves as being held to blame for a subsequent failure to meet expectations. They might be motivated to put forward only those projects which they saw as safe but unadventurous. The review process has to be flexible to allow for the unknown but also to discourage unrealistic or over-enthusiastic plans.

24.9 Advanced manufacturing technologies

Advanced manufacturing technologies (AMTs) have been developed by engineers as a means of competing more effectively. To compete, organisations need to manufacture innovative products of high quality at low cost. The product life-cycle may be short, demand may be changing more rapidly, and international competition creates a further element of uncertainty. As with any business activity, these changes represent new approaches to the management of the business, and management accounting must keep pace with the change in management approach.

24.9.1 Types of new technology

Engineers have produced new technology of four main types:

1 design innovations;
2 planning and control techniques;
3 execution; and
4 overarching technologies.

Each of these new technologies is considered in turn.

The *design innovations* have covered computer-aided design (CAD), computer-aided engineering (CAE), computer-aided process planning (CAPP) and design for manufacture and assembly. CAD uses computers to evaluate various designs of the product, while CAE includes design but also encompasses evaluation and testing so that the initial design becomes a working product. CAPP uses computers to plan the detailed processes required to manufacture the design proposed. Finally, the computer can also be used to design a system which makes the manufacture and assembly process meet the demand for the output.

Planning and control techniques have covered materials requirements planning (MRP), manufacturing resource planning (MRP II) and statistical process control (SPC). MRP involves matching stock levels to the production process and controlling incoming customer orders to match the availability of materials. MRP II applies similar controls to all resources used in the manufacturing process. They both use computers to break down a customer's order into various stages which can be matched against resource availability. SPC uses statistical analysis to identify the most likely causes of bottlenecks in the manufacturing process, which can then be corrected before a crisis arises.

Execution means converting raw materials and components into finished goods. The technologies have included robotics, automated guided vehicles (AGVs), flexible manufacturing systems (FMS) and automated storage and retrieval systems (ASRS). These titles are self-descriptive of the activities involved.

The *overarching technologies* are those which take a total perspective of the organisation. They include total quality management (TQM), just-in-time (JIT), focused factory and computer-integrated manufacturing (CIM). TQM and JIT are described in Chapter 25.

24.9.2 Capital investment appraisal of AMT projects

The conventional methods of investment appraisal have been presented as payback, accounting rate of return, net present value and internal rate of return. These techniques have considerable benefit for many situations where a fixed investment is made and the outcome may be projected forward. However, they are not capable of taking into account the flexibility which management may have in some situations. As flexible technology takes over from fixed inflexible capital equipment, there are options facing the business manager which must be considered in project evaluation.

In particular there are options to make modifications to projects or add on new aspects. Abandonment may be less difficult where technology is flexible. Companies may feel that they can afford to wait and learn before investing. A project can be scaled down if there are changes in demand for a product. These options make project development quite exciting but they also offer a challenge to the management accountant in making sure the options are evaluated.

Fiona McTaggart describes an example of capital investment in an AMT situation:

FIONA: *One case I encountered was that of a flexible manufacturing system being used to machine metal into engineering components. There was hardly a person in sight on the production line. Computer-controlled machines were each performing one part of the treatment of the metal. Cutting tools were making metal shapes, transport systems were moving components around and then, depending on where the shapes were delivered, there were more machines to turn, mill, polish and shape. The whole process was controlled by a host computer and was sufficiently flexible that if the transport system was revised then the activities performed on the metal changed as well.*

The company adapted its investment appraisal methods by involving the engineers and the management accountants as a team. Essentially they evaluated reduced labour costs, increased effectiveness in utilisation of machines, cost saving through just-in-time control of materials and the reduction in indirect costs. Discounted cash flows were included in order to take account of the longer term but the emphasis was more strongly on the short term and the flexibility for change if conditions changed.

The debate on the role of capital investment appraisal techniques in relation to advanced manufacturing technologies is a useful example of the wider point that management accounting must continually be changing to adapt to changed circumstances. A book can present basic ideas, but those ideas will only work effectively in a practical situation if moulded to meet the needs of the situation.

24.10 Summary

Key themes in this chapter are:

- **Capital investment appraisal** is the application of a set of methods of quantitative analysis which give guidance to managers in making decisions as to how best to invest long-term funds. Four methods of quantitative analysis are explained in the chapter.

- The **payback period** is the length of time required for a stream of net cash inflows from a project to equal the original cash outlay.

- The **accounting rate of return** is calculated by taking the average annual profits expected from a project as a percentage of the capital invested.

- The process of calculating present value is called **discounting**. The interest rate used is called the **discount rate**. The net present value method of investment appraisal and the internal rate of return method are both based on discounting.

- The **net present value** of a project is equal to the present value of the cash inflows minus the present value of the cash outflows, all discounted at the cost of capital. The decision rules are:

  1 Where the net present value of the project is *positive*, accept the project.
  2 Where the net present value of the project is *negative*, reject the project.
  3 Where the net present value of the project is zero, the project is acceptable in meeting the cost of capital but gives no surplus to its owners.

- The **internal rate of return** (IRR) is the discount rate at which the present value of the cash flows generated by the project is equal to the present value of the capital invested, so that the net present value of the project is zero. The decision rules are:

  1 Where the IRR of the project is greater than the cost of capital, accept the project.
  2 Where the IRR of the project is less than the cost of capital, reject the project.
  3 Where the IRR of the project equals the cost of capital, the project is acceptable in meeting the required rate of return of those investing in the business but gives no surplus to its owners.

- **Mutually exclusive** projects are found wherever a choice is needed because of limited resources of capital, labour, materials, or any other constraint.

- The **profitability index** may be used to rank projects in situations of capital rationing or mutually exclusive projects.

- Effective **capital investment appraisal** requires control procedures to be in place for establishing the suitability of a project and for post-completion audit to evaluate the success of the project.

- **Advanced manufacturing technologies** have led to a demand for new ways of evaluating investment projects because new projects may require continuous investment of resources rather than a single outlay at the outset.

Further reading

Brounen, D., de Jong, A. and Koedijk, K. (2004), 'Corporate finance in Europe: confronting theory with practice', *Financial Management,* 33(4): 71–101.

QUESTIONS

The Questions section of each chapter has three types of question. 'Test your understanding' questions to help you review your reading are in the 'A' series of questions. You will find the answers to these by reading and thinking about the material in the book. 'Application' questions to test your ability to apply technical skills are in the 'B' series of questions. Questions requiring you to show skills in problem solving and evaluation are in the 'C' series of questions. A letter [S] indicates that there is a solution at the end of the book. Other solutions are provided in the Instructor's Manual, where there are further questions parallel to those set out here.

A   Test your understanding

A24.1   What is the purpose of capital investment appraisal? (Section 24.1.1)

A24.2   What is meant by the assumption of certainty of cash flows? (Section 24.1.2)

A24.3   What are the main steps in making a decision about a capital investment? (Section 24.1.3)

A24.4 What is the payback method of evaluating a project? (Section 24.2)

A24.5 What are the advantages and limitations of the payback method? (Section 24.2.3)

A24.6 What is the accounting rate of return? (Section 24.3)

A24.7 What are the advantages and limitations of the accounting rate of return as a technique for use in capital investment appraisal? (Section 24.3.2)

A24.8 What is meant by the time value of money? (Section 24.4.1)

A24.9 What is meant by the present value of a cash flow? (Section 24.4.1)

A24.10 What is meant by the term 'discounting'? (Section 24.4.1)

A24.11 Define net present value and explain how it is calculated. (Section 24.4.2)

A24.12 State the net present value decision rule to be used in capital investment appraisal. (Section 24.4.2)

A24.13 Define internal rate of return and explain how it is calculated. (Section 24.5.1)

A24.14 State the internal rate of return decision rule to be used in capital investment appraisal. (Section 24.5.2)

A24.15 Explain the problems which may arise in choosing between mutually exclusive projects. (Section 24.6)

A24.16 Explain the processes necessary for authorisation and review of capital projects. (Section 24.8)

A24.17 Explain what is meant by advanced manufacturing technologies. (Section 24.9)

A24.18 Explain why present value techniques may not be suitable for project evaluation where a business uses advanced manufacturing technologies. (Section 24.9.2)

A24.19 [S] Calculate the present value of £100 receivable at the end of (a) one year, (b) two years and (c) three years, using a discount rate of 8% per annum.

A24.20 [S] Calculate the present value of £100 receivable at the end of five years using a discount rate of (a) 4%, (b) 6% and (c) 8% per annum.

B Application

B24.1 [S]
Projects Ltd intends to acquire a new machine costing £50,000 which is expected to have a life of five years, with a scrap value of £10,000 at the end of that time.

Cash flows arising from operation of the machine are expected to arise on the last day of each year as follows:

End of year	£
1	10,000
2	15,000
3	20,000
4	25,000
5	25,000

Calculate the payback period, the accounting rate of return and the net present value, explaining the meaning of each answer you produce. (Assume a discount rate of 10% per annum.)

B24.2 [S]

In a calculation of the internal rate of return of a project it is found that the net present value is +£122m at 22% discount rate and −£58m at 24% discount rate. What is the internal rate of return?

B24.3 [S]

XYZ Ltd is considering purchasing a new machine, and the relevant facts concerning two possible choices are as follows:

	Machine A	Machine B
Capital expenditure required	£65,000	£60,000
Estimated life in years	4	4
Residual value	nil	nil
Cash flow after taxation each year	£25,000	£24,000

The company's cost of capital is 10%.

Required

Calculate, for each machine, the payback period, the net present value and the profitability index. State, with reasons, which machine you would recommend.

B24.4 [S]

Marsh Limited has investigated the possibility of investing in a new machine. The following data have been extracted from the report relating to the project:

● Cost of machine on 1 January Year 6: £500,000.
● Estimated scrap value at end of Year 5: Nil.

Year	Net cash flows £000
1	50
2	200
3	225
4	225
5	100

The company's cost of capital is 8%.

Required

Evaluate the acceptability of the project using the net present value method of investment appraisal.

B24.5

In a calculation of the internal rate of return of a project it is found that the net present value is +£60m at 24% discount rate and −£20m at 26% discount rate. What is the Internal Rate of Return?

C   Problem solving and evaluation

C24.1 [S]

Offshore Services Ltd is an oil-related company providing specialist firefighting and rescue services to oil rigs. The board of directors is considering a number of investment projects to improve the cash flow situation in the face of strong competition from international companies in the same field.

The proposed projects are:

Project	Description
ALPHA	Commission an additional firefighting vessel.
BRAVO	Replace two existing standby boats.
CHARLIE	Establish a new survival training course for the staff of client companies.
DELTA	Install latest communications equipment on all vessels.

Each project is expected to produce a reduction in cash outflows over the next five years. The outlays and cash benefits are set out below:

	End of year	ALPHA £000s	BRAVO £000s	CHARLIE £000s	DELTA £000s
Outlay	–	(600)	(300)	(120)	(210)
Cash flow benefits:					
	1	435	–	48	81
	2	435	–	48	81
	3	–	219	48	81
	4	–	219	48	81
	5	–	219	48	81
Internal rate of return		28.8%	22.0%	28.6%	26.8%

Any project may be postponed indefinitely. Investment capital is limited to £1,000,000. The board wishes to maximise net present value of projects undertaken and requires a return of 10% per annum.

Required

Prepare a report to the board of directors containing:

1 calculations of net present value for each project, and
2 a reasoned recommendation on maximisation of net present value within the £1,000,000 investment limit.

C24.2 [S]

The directors of Advanced plc are currently considering an investment in new production machinery to replace existing machinery. The new machinery would produce goods more efficiently, leading to increased sales volume. The investment required will be £1,150,000 payable at the start of the project. The alternative course of action would be to continue using the existing machinery for a further five years, at the end of which time it would have to be replaced.

The following forecasts of sales and production volumes have been made:

Sales (in units)

Year	Using existing machinery	Using new machinery
1	400,000	560,000
2	450,000	630,000
3	500,000	700,000
4	600,000	840,000
5	750,000	1,050,000

Production (in units)

Year	Using existing machinery	Using new machinery
1	420,000	564,000
2	435,000	637,000
3	505,000	695,000
4	610,000	840,000
5	730,000	1,044,000

Further information

(a) The new machinery will reduce production costs from their present level of £7.50 per unit to £6.20 per unit. These production costs exclude depreciation.
(b) The increased sales volume will be achieved by reducing unit selling prices from their present level of £10.00 per unit to £8.50 per unit.
(c) The new machinery will have a scrap value of £150,000 after five years.
(d) The existing machinery will have a scrap value of £30,000 at the start of Year 1. Its scrap value will be £20,000 at the end of Year 5.
(e) The cost of capital to the company, in money terms, is presently 12% per annum.

Required

1 Prepare a report to the directors of Advanced plc on the proposed investment decision.
2 List any further matters which the directors should consider before making their decision.

C24.3

The board of directors of Kirkside Glassware Ltd is considering the following proposed investment projects:

Project	Nature
A	Establishment of a staff training scheme
B	Major improvements to the electrical system
C	Installation of a computer
D	Development of a new product
E	Purchase of a warehouse space, presently leased

It is estimated that each product will provide benefits in terms of reduced cash outflows, measured over the coming five years. The outlays and cash flow benefits, net of taxation, are set out below:

	End of year	Project A £	Project B £	Project C £	Project D £	Project E £
Outlay	–	(40,000)	(70,000)	(180,000)	(100,000)	(200,000)
Cash flow benefits:						
	1	16,000	27,000	66,000	–	145,000
	2	16,000	27,000	66,000	–	145,000
	3	16,000	27,000	66,000	73,000	–
	4	16,000	27,000	66,000	73,000	–
	5	16,000	27,000	66,000	73,000	–
Internal rate of return		28.65%	26.82%	24.32%	22.05%	28.79%

Each project has two separate phases of equal cost and providing equal cash flow benefits. The board is willing to consider adopting the first phase of any project without the second, if this appears necessary. Any project or phase not undertaken immediately may be postponed indefinitely. Capital available for investment is limited to £300,000. The board aims, as far as possible, to maximise the net present value of projects undertaken.

The company requires a return of 10% per annum based on the net cash flows of any project.

Required

Prepare a report to the board of directors:

1 setting out a decision rule which could be applied in ranking the investment projects, and
2 listing other factors which the board of directors might wish to consider when selecting projects for implementation.

Activities for study groups

Case 24.1

Using a suitable computer spreadsheet package, set up a spreadsheet which will calculate net present values and internal rates of return for projects having cash flows for a ten-year period. Test the spreadsheet with sample data and then write a brief instruction sheet. Save the spreadsheet to a disk and exchange disks and instruction sheets with another group in the class.

Case 24.2

Now write an evaluation of the spreadsheet you have received from another group. Consider the following:

(a) Does it deal with all possible types of cash flows (e.g. a negative flow at some point)?
(b) Does it provide a recommendation on accept/reject (e.g. using a conditional function)?
(c) Does it allow for relatively easy variation of the discount rate?
(d) Does the instruction sheet explain how to produce graphs of net present value plotted against discount rate?

List any other features of the spreadsheet which you would use in evaluating its effectiveness and user-friendliness.

Table of discount factors

Number of years	1%	2%	3%	4%	5%	6%	7%	8%	9%	10%	11%	12%	13%	14%	15%
1	0.990	0.980	0.971	0.962	0.952	0.943	0.935	0.926	0.917	0.909	0.901	0.893	0.885	0.877	0.870
2	0.980	0.961	0.943	0.925	0.907	0.890	0.873	0.857	0.842	0.826	0.812	0.797	0.783	0.769	0.756
3	0.971	0.942	0.915	0.889	0.864	0.840	0.816	0.794	0.772	0.751	0.731	0.712	0.693	0.675	0.658
4	0.961	0.924	0.888	0.855	0.823	0.792	0.763	0.735	0.708	0.683	0.659	0.636	0.613	0.592	0.572
5	0.951	0.906	0.863	0.822	0.784	0.747	0.713	0.681	0.650	0.621	0.593	0.567	0.543	0.519	0.497
6	0.942	0.888	0.837	0.790	0.746	0.705	0.666	0.630	0.596	0.564	0.535	0.507	0.480	0.456	0.432
7	0.933	0.871	0.813	0.760	0.711	0.665	0.623	0.583	0.547	0.513	0.482	0.452	0.425	0.400	0.376
8	0.923	0.853	0.789	0.731	0.677	0.627	0.582	0.540	0.502	0.467	0.434	0.404	0.376	0.351	0.327
9	0.914	0.837	0.766	0.703	0.645	0.592	0.544	0.500	0.460	0.424	0.391	0.361	0.333	0.308	0.284
10	0.905	0.820	0.744	0.676	0.614	0.558	0.508	0.463	0.422	0.386	0.352	0.322	0.295	0.270	0.247
11	0.896	0.804	0.722	0.650	0.585	0.527	0.475	0.429	0.388	0.350	0.317	0.287	0.261	0.237	0.215
12	0.887	0.788	0.701	0.625	0.557	0.497	0.444	0.397	0.356	0.319	0.286	0.257	0.231	0.208	0.187
13	0.879	0.773	0.681	0.601	0.530	0.469	0.415	0.368	0.326	0.290	0.258	0.229	0.204	0.182	0.163
14	0.870	0.758	0.661	0.577	0.505	0.442	0.388	0.340	0.299	0.263	0.232	0.205	0.181	0.160	0.141
15	0.861	0.743	0.642	0.555	0.481	0.417	0.362	0.315	0.275	0.239	0.209	0.183	0.160	0.140	0.123
16	0.853	0.728	0.623	0.534	0.458	0.394	0.339	0.292	0.252	0.218	0.188	0.163	0.141	0.123	0.107
17	0.844	0.714	0.605	0.513	0.436	0.371	0.317	0.270	0.231	0.198	0.170	0.146	0.125	0.108	0.093
18	0.836	0.700	0.587	0.494	0.416	0.350	0.296	0.250	0.212	0.180	0.153	0.130	0.111	0.095	0.081
19	0.828	0.686	0.570	0.475	0.396	0.331	0.277	0.232	0.194	0.164	0.138	0.116	0.098	0.083	0.070
20	0.820	0.673	0.554	0.456	0.377	0.312	0.258	0.215	0.178	0.149	0.124	0.104	0.087	0.073	0.061
21	0.811	0.660	0.538	0.439	0.359	0.294	0.242	0.199	0.164	0.135	0.112	0.093	0.077	0.064	0.053
22	0.803	0.647	0.522	0.422	0.342	0.278	0.226	0.184	0.150	0.123	0.101	0.083	0.068	0.056	0.046
23	0.795	0.634	0.507	0.406	0.326	0.262	0.211	0.170	0.138	0.112	0.091	0.074	0.060	0.049	0.040
24	0.788	0.622	0.492	0.390	0.310	0.247	0.197	0.158	0.126	0.102	0.082	0.066	0.053	0.043	0.035
25	0.780	0.610	0.478	0.375	0.295	0.233	0.184	0.146	0.116	0.092	0.074	0.059	0.047	0.038	0.030
26	0.772	0.598	0.464	0.361	0.281	0.220	0.172	0.135	0.106	0.084	0.066	0.053	0.042	0.033	0.026
27	0.764	0.586	0.450	0.347	0.268	0.207	0.161	0.125	0.098	0.076	0.060	0.047	0.037	0.029	0.023
28	0.757	0.574	0.437	0.333	0.255	0.196	0.150	0.116	0.090	0.069	0.054	0.042	0.033	0.026	0.020
29	0.749	0.563	0.424	0.321	0.243	0.185	0.141	0.107	0.082	0.063	0.048	0.037	0.029	0.022	0.017
30	0.742	0.552	0.412	0.308	0.231	0.174	0.131	0.099	0.075	0.057	0.044	0.033	0.026	0.020	0.015

Note: Present value of £1 to be received after n years when the rate of interest is r% per annum equals $1/(1 + r)^n$.

Number of years	16%	17%	18%	19%	20%	21%	22%	23%	24%	25%	26%	27%	28%	29%	30%
1	0.862	0.855	0.847	0.840	0.833	0.826	0.820	0.813	0.806	0.800	0.794	0.787	0.781	0.775	0.769
2	0.743	0.731	0.718	0.706	0.694	0.683	0.672	0.661	0.650	0.640	0.630	0.620	0.610	0.601	0.592
3	0.641	0.624	0.609	0.593	0.579	0.564	0.551	0.537	0.524	0.512	0.500	0.488	0.477	0.466	0.455
4	0.552	0.534	0.516	0.499	0.482	0.467	0.451	0.437	0.423	0.410	0.397	0.384	0.373	0.361	0.350
5	0.476	0.456	0.437	0.419	0.402	0.386	0.370	0.355	0.341	0.328	0.315	0.303	0.291	0.280	0.269
6	0.410	0.390	0.370	0.352	0.335	0.319	0.303	0.289	0.275	0.262	0.250	0.238	0.227	0.217	0.207
7	0.354	0.333	0.314	0.296	0.279	0.263	0.249	0.235	0.222	0.210	0.198	0.188	0.178	0.168	0.159
8	0.305	0.285	0.266	0.249	0.233	0.218	0.204	0.191	0.179	0.168	0.157	0.148	0.139	0.130	0.123
9	0.263	0.243	0.225	0.209	0.194	0.180	0.167	0.155	0.144	0.134	0.125	0.116	0.108	0.101	0.094
10	0.227	0.208	0.191	0.176	0.162	0.149	0.137	0.126	0.116	0.107	0.099	0.092	0.085	0.078	0.073
11	0.195	0.178	0.162	0.148	0.135	0.123	0.112	0.103	0.094	0.086	0.079	0.072	0.066	0.061	0.056
12	0.168	0.152	0.137	0.124	0.112	0.102	0.092	0.083	0.076	0.069	0.062	0.057	0.052	0.047	0.043
13	0.145	0.130	0.116	0.104	0.093	0.084	0.075	0.068	0.061	0.055	0.050	0.045	0.040	0.037	0.033
14	0.125	0.111	0.099	0.088	0.078	0.069	0.062	0.055	0.049	0.044	0.039	0.035	0.032	0.028	0.025
15	0.108	0.095	0.084	0.074	0.065	0.057	0.051	0.045	0.040	0.035	0.031	0.028	0.025	0.022	0.020
16	0.093	0.081	0.071	0.062	0.054	0.047	0.042	0.036	0.032	0.028	0.025	0.022	0.019	0.017	0.015
17	0.080	0.069	0.060	0.052	0.045	0.039	0.034	0.030	0.026	0.023	0.020	0.017	0.015	0.013	0.012
18	0.069	0.059	0.051	0.044	0.038	0.032	0.028	0.024	0.021	0.018	0.016	0.014	0.012	0.010	0.009
19	0.060	0.051	0.043	0.037	0.031	0.027	0.023	0.020	0.017	0.014	0.012	0.011	0.009	0.008	0.007
20	0.051	0.043	0.037	0.031	0.026	0.022	0.019	0.016	0.014	0.012	0.010	0.008	0.007	0.006	0.005
21	0.044	0.037	0.031	0.026	0.022	0.018	0.015	0.013	0.011	0.009	0.008	0.007	0.006	0.005	0.004
22	0.038	0.032	0.026	0.022	0.018	0.015	0.013	0.011	0.009	0.007	0.006	0.005	0.004	0.004	0.003
23	0.033	0.027	0.022	0.018	0.015	0.012	0.010	0.009	0.007	0.006	0.005	0.004	0.003	0.003	0.002
24	0.028	0.023	0.019	0.015	0.013	0.010	0.008	0.007	0.006	0.005	0.004	0.003	0.003	0.002	0.002
25	0.024	0.020	0.016	0.013	0.010	0.009	0.007	0.006	0.005	0.004	0.003	0.003	0.002	0.002	0.001
26	0.021	0.017	0.014	0.011	0.009	0.007	0.006	0.005	0.004	0.003	0.002	0.002	0.002	0.001	0.001
27	0.018	0.014	0.011	0.009	0.007	0.006	0.005	0.004	0.003	0.002	0.002	0.002	0.001	0.001	0.001
28	0.016	0.012	0.010	0.008	0.006	0.005	0.004	0.003	0.002	0.002	0.002	0.001	0.001	0.001	0.001
29	0.014	0.010	0.008	0.006	0.005	0.004	0.003	0.002	0.002	0.002	0.001	0.001	0.001	0.001	0.000
30	0.012	0.009	0.007	0.005	0.004	0.003	0.003	0.002	0.002	0.001	0.001	0.001	0.001	0.000	0.000

Business strategy and management accounting

This case study shows a typical case in which management accounting can be helpful. Read the case study now but only attempt the discussion points after you have finished reading the chapter.

Bombardier Transportation

In September 2014 Bombardier Transportation presented its largest portfolio of mobility solutions to date at InnoTrans, the world's biggest rail industry fair. The following extracts are taken from the company's website.

Courtesy of Bombardier Transportation Ltd

About us

Bombardier is the world's only manufacturer of both planes and trains. Our vast offering of products includes trains, rail equipment and control solutions for all market segments, as well as category-defining business jets and commercial aircraft.

Solutions for the future of public transportation

Rail technology leader Bombardier Transportation presents its largest portfolio of mobility solutions to date at InnoTrans, the world's biggest rail industry fair. From September 23 to 28, visitors to the show can witness Bombardier's holistic approach to interconnected mobility that is shaping the future of seamless public transportation across the globe.

Under the motto 'The Evolution of Mobility', Bombardier presents the rail industry's leading solutions to tomorrow's mobility challenges. These solutions are based on proven platforms that can be tailored to suit the individual needs of each customer perfectly.

'The Evolution of Mobility' is not just about innovation and technology, but also partnership and collaboration,' said Lutz Bertling, President and Chief Operating Officer of Bombardier Transportation. 'No two cities are the same, which means transport solutions are not one-size-fits-all. With our innovative products and worldwide experience, we offer our customers the most competitive Total Cost of Ownership approach. We build and maintain efficient mobility solutions that lower overall lifecycle costs by responding to the unique needs of each of our customers.'

At InnoTrans, Bombardier presents its products and technologies based on three pillars that define current and future mobility challenges: capacity, efficiency and urban flow.

Efficiency: smart solutions for reducing total lifecycle costs

On display at InnoTrans will be the *BOMBARDIER TRAXX* F140 AC electric locomotive with the Last Mile feature that delivers seamless logistics to an increasingly competitive market. Able to run on both electric and non-electric tracks, the *TRAXX* F140 AC electric locomotive eliminates the need for transition stopping. Plus, the Last Mile technology includes an efficient diesel engine that enables the locomotive to run entirely on battery power over short distances – completely emission free. Also on display will be the *TRAXX* P160 DE Multi-Engine diesel locomotive. With its innovative four-diesel engine concept that controls each engine's output separately, the *TRAXX* Multi-Engine diesel locomotive is not only more eco-friendly and quieter, but also markedly reduces fuel consumption, emissions and lifecycle costs when compared to diesel locomotives with similar performance.

Source: The Evolution of Mobility: Bombardier Transportation Presents Solutions for the Future of Public Transportation at InnoTrans 2014 (Bombardier) Berlin Transportation, Press Release, http://uk.bombardier.com/en/media/newsList/details.bombardier-transportation 20140917theevolutionofmobilitybombardie.bombardiercom.html?

Discussion points

1 How does Bombardier propose to reduce total lifecycle costs for its customers?

2 How might management accounting help evaluate the other two challenges of capacity and urban flow?

Contents

Learning outcomes

After studying this chapter you should be able to:

- Define 'business strategy'.
- Explain how strategic management accounting is a feature of business strategy.
- Explain just-in-time management.
- Explain value chain analysis and the role of management accounting.
- Explain total quality management and the cost of quality.
- Explain business process re-engineering.
- Explain e-business and e-commerce and outline ways in which management accounting may help in developing business strategies that use e-business methods in general and e-commerce in particular.

25.1 Introduction

In this chapter we take the theme of business strategy and the role of management accounting. A strategy may be defined as 'an integrated set of actions aimed at securing a sustainable competitive advantage'.[1]

Using this definition a strategy is something more than a long-term plan. It is a statement of how the business intends to reach some preferred state in the future by changing its competitive position to meet changing circumstances.

This chapter explains and illustrates some of the approaches that have been proposed to developing business strategy, where management accounting has a contributory role to play. You have already encountered activity-based costing (Chapter 18), benchmarking (Chapter 23), the balanced scorecard (Chapter 23) and investment appraisal for advanced manufacturing technologies (Chapter 24), all of which are techniques developed to support strategic change. They have become an established part of the management accountant's contribution to ensuring that a business stays vigilant to competitive forces.

25.2 Strategic management accounting

The successful management of a business depends on having a successful business strategy. It has been argued that if the business strategy gives the organisation its competitive edge, then the management accounting should reflect that strategy as closely as possible. The traditional emphasis on costs and revenues may not achieve this aim. What really matters is the influence of the external environment.

Strategy usually includes planning to achieve a better performance than competitors. It is argued that management accounting should show the extent to which the organisation is beating its competitors. Market share, market prospects and the impact of product mix would all be useful information to include in a management accounting report as factors contributing to sales, profits and cash flows.

Another way of looking at the influence of the external environment is to consider competitive advantage in costs. If the business has an influential position as a purchaser of goods and services, then its strategy may include an aggressive policy of negotiating contracts for those goods and services. The **just-in-time** strategy of ordering goods from suppliers to arrive exactly when they are needed may put strains on the suppliers and force up their costs, increasing the price of the goods. The concept of a **value chain** has been proposed to describe how the corporate strategy affects the entire chain of value-creating activities. Strategic management accounting might show that £1 saved at one point in the chain has been offset by an extra £2 incurred at another stage.

Advocates of **strategic management accounting** seek to provide financial and other related information on competitors' costs and cost structures so that the company's strategies may be monitored against those of its competitors over a period of time. Furthermore there is a need for new forms of internal analysis and accounting processes that will help management devise better strategies. There is strong support for this general direction of strategic management accounting but less agreement on how it may be achieved.

It is not necessary to abandon all that has been learned in the earlier chapters of this book. Advocates of strategic management accounting would relate the accounting technique to the strategic aims of the business. Take the example of two companies, one of which is aiming to achieve cost leadership (carrying out activities in a more cost-effective manner than competitors) while the other is focusing on product differentiation (persuading customers that there is a unique aspect of the company's products). The use of standard costing in assessing performance is very important to the cost leadership company but relatively unimportant to the product differentiation company. Analysis of marketing costs may not be so important in a cost leadership setting but is absolutely essential to the product differentiation situation.

You have already seen the **Balanced Scorecard** approach which requires an organisation to translate its vision and strategy into four perspectives: financial focus, customer focus, internal business processes and learning and growth. Companies are encouraged to develop performance indicators under each of these headings which provide a complete view of the company's performance.

Fiona McTaggart describes her experience of a situation where a strategic approach helped a business to achieve improved performance.

FIONA: *One of my clients was a telephone utility company. It was in a competitive market where the customer base was growing fast. Costs had been reduced to the limit and competition focused on delivering a good quality of service to the customer.*

The first action taken by management was to change the attitude of employees, moving away from an organisation based on functions and towards an organisation based on process. As an example, the sales ledger department was disbanded. Some of the staff joined a customer enquiry unit which allowed one point of contact for matters ranging from sales orders through repairs to accounts enquiries. Others moved to the information technology unit which concentrated on providing information within the organisation. This move recognised internal 'customers' as well as external customers.

The next move was to invest in a training programme to encourage customer focus. Staff joining the customer enquiry unit were all trained in customer focus but were also made aware of the way in which their activities drive the costs of the organisation. Their training included a course provided by benchmarking experts who had information about the standards achieved by leading competitors. The company was quite surprised to find how much other companies will share through benchmarking.

You might be thinking that this does not sound much like management accounting but the focus on activities driving costs led to a rearrangement of management accounting information to use cost drivers and activity-based costing. That approach was used to evaluate type of customer, geographical area of sales and types of product promotion.

The result was continued growth in sales and profit for the company and an expansion in employment opportunities for staff.

25.3 The just-in-time approach

Just-in-time manufacturing is a methodical approach to reducing machine set-up times, accepting only perfect incoming resources, allowing no deviation from standards and matching output exactly to the demands of the customer. Every activity occurs exactly at the time needed for effective execution, and the activity always happens exactly as planned. It reduces stockholding costs, minimises idle time for production resources and creates a demand-driven business.

Fiona McTaggart describes her experience of a just-in-time management system.

FIONA: *I recently participated in a pilot project involving a leading company manufacturing car engines. There were two shifts planned, one using manual labour and one entirely operated by robots. A just-in-time (JIT) philosophy applied throughout. Each item required for the manufacture of an engine was planned to arrive on the production line at exactly the right time. Delivery from suppliers was similarly timed with care. The computer recording*

system was designed so that the arrival of the component was recorded and barcoding allowed the cost to be recorded at the same time. There was no need to wait for an invoice to arrive before the cost of the component could be ascertained. Reports on direct costs could therefore be generated simultaneously with reports on physical activity. Dealing with overhead costs was more difficult, but a system was proposed where overhead costs were applied to activities using an activity-based approach and a focus on machine hours as the main measure of use of an activity.

The JIT approach emphasises elimination of waste. The management accounting report for the two shifts had a waste exception report section which allowed rapid identification of departure from accepted waste levels on each shift. Linking the accounting records to the physical activity meant that each shift could be identified separately.

The pilot project was receiving a cautious welcome from the technical managers. They had regarded traditional management accounting as an unavoidable nuisance but they could see that the pilot scheme was bringing the accounting information closer to their perspective of the operation.

25.4 Value chain analysis

The idea of the **value chain** was popularised by Porter (1998) as a way of describing and analysing the sequence of activities that bring a product or service from its initial stage of production to the final stage of delivery to the customer.

In a competitive environment the business manager should ask: 'What is our competitive advantage; what do we do well?' That requires questions about competition – where are the threats? There could be new entrants seeking to join the sector; there could be substitute products or services. There may be strong rivalry within the industry or there may be little interest in competing. Suppliers may have a strong bargaining position; customers may have a strong bargaining position. The manager considers the kind of competition that exists and then plans to deal with that position. Perhaps this business can reduce costs below those of competitors; perhaps it can find a way of differentiating its product to make it attractive to consumers. Porter took the view that a business should choose either a cost focus or a differentiation focus, rather than try to do too much at the same time.

The value chain for any business is a description of the key processes, starting with inputs. Take the example of a plant nursery which grows plants from seedlings and sells them to customers in a garden centre. The managers have identified the competitive advantage as their reputation for growing plants that are hardy to the climate of this region. The value chain is shown in Exhibit 25.1.

Exhibit 25.1
Value chain for nursery and garden centre

Seed selection → Growing seedlings →
Transfer to retail outlet → Advice desk → Sale to customer

Each stage of the value chain adds value for the business. It is focused on product differentiation. The price may be marginally higher than the prices that would be charged by national chains selling plants as part of home improvement stores, but the customer is less likely to find the plant has wilted and died within weeks of planting. Advice is given to any enquirers coming into the garden centre, and the advice is based on local knowledge.

Fiona McTaggart has been advising the business on the steps required for value chain analysis. She explains here how she worked with management.

FIONA: *First we identified the value chain and assigned costs and assets to each stage. Seed selection involves labour cost and storage for seeds taken from the nursery's own plants. The nursery also buys in new varieties to strengthen the existing strains. Growing seedlings involves further labour cost, greenhouse maintenance, security and plant care materials. There is also a wastage rate to be built in. Transfer to the retail outlet involves transport costs and a risk of loss through inadequate handling. The advice desk is a heavy labour cost specific to this business. The retail sales outlet carries costs similar to those of any retail operation.*

Next we considered the cost drivers of each value activity and the interaction of cost drivers. Then we considered the value chains of competitors who can undercut the business on price but compete less well on product durability. We worked out the relative costs and looked at ways for this business to cut its costs. For example, transferring plants to the garden centre on a just-in-time basis would reduce wastage but requires customer surveys to know when the peaks of demand will arise. We were able to identify some areas for cost control that would enable the business to remain competitive on price without eroding the product differentiation. The managers are pleased that they have this approach to focusing on how they add value at each stage of the chain.

25.5 Total quality management and cost of quality

The success of Japanese companies in the later 20th century has caused intense interest in Japanese styles of management. One aspect of Japanese management is the approach of 'get it right first time'. In this spirit, *total quality management* (TQM) has the customer as its focal point.

Quality is defined as fully satisfying agreed customer requirements at the lowest internal price. TQM is therefore a management function which could be added to those explained in Chapter 16. It straddles the traditional management functions of planning and control. The use of the TQM approach is seen as the key to improving profitability because there is a cost associated with failing to meet quality standards in products and services. Such costs could arise through loss of customers, claims for refunds in respect of defective supplies, and the work of putting right mistakes. If costs can be controlled through TQM, then profits will increase.

Those who are enthusiastic for TQM believe that it is possible to obtain defect-free work first time on a consistent basis. That may be an idealistic target but to have such a target encourages a culture where prevention of error is a key feature of the operations.

This activity of improving quality to improve profits will itself cause cost to be incurred. The term **cost of quality** is a collective name for all costs incurred in achieving a quality product or service.

Cost of quality may be defined by the 'prevention–appraisal–failure' model.

Prevention costs are the costs of designing, implementing and maintaining the TQM system. They include: quality planning, quality assurance, training and determining specifications for incoming materials, for processes carried out in the operations of the business and for finished products.

Appraisal costs are the costs of evaluating suppliers and obtaining an evaluation by customers. They include checking incoming materials and supplies, inspecting equipment and collecting information from customers on satisfaction with goods and services.

Failure costs are of two main types: *internal failure costs* are the costs incurred when it is found, before delivery to customers, that the work does not reach the desired specification; *external failure costs* are the costs incurred when poor-quality work is discovered after the supply to the customer has taken place. Examples of internal failure costs are: waste, scrap, rectification, re-inspection of rectified work and analysis of the causes of failure. External failure costs include: repairs, warranty claims, complaints, returns, product liability litigation and loss of customer goodwill.

The traditional picture of quality control is that in the absence of quality control, failures occur which create failure costs. Detection of failure relies on checking after the failure has occurred. The checking process involves further checking costs. With quality controls in place, as prevention work is undertaken, the costs of failure should begin to fall. At the outset, the prevention costs will be additional to the costs of checking for failures, but as confidence grows, and the frequency of failure decreases, the need for checking should diminish. The quality exercise will be successful in cost terms if there is a reduction in total cost over the three headings of prevention, appraisal and failure costs.

TQM ideas are widely practised and there are many non-financial performance measures being used in business organisations. Measuring the cost of quality is a relatively undeveloped area although a few businesses have a well-developed approach. The management accountant as score-keeper is ideally placed to record and monitor cost of quality, but many of the initiatives emerging are in special units within an organisation which are separate from the 'traditional' management accounting functions. Management accountants may need to be proactive in seeking out new ways of applying their generic skills.

25.6　Business process re-engineering

Business process re-engineering involves a dramatic redesign of business processes, organisation structures and use of technology to achieve breakthroughs in business competitiveness. The benefits claimed are that operations can be streamlined, and consequently costs can be cut, while creating process excellence in all key aspects of the organisation.

The phrase 'breaking the china' has been used by those who describe the technique. They are looking for a quantum leap into being a world leader. They draw the analogy of passing a treasured set of family china from one generation to the next. One day the entire collection falls to the floor in pieces. Putting it together again produces a totally different pattern in the china. In a similar way, if the whole business process is broken up and then restructured with the aim of being a world leader, an entirely new policy will emerge.

The advocates of business process re-engineering explain that, while concentrating on innovations such as TQM and JIT, businesses were retaining the traditional ways of working in functional groups. Quality teams were given the task of creating new ways of working within their specific areas or functions. In contrast, business process re-engineering concentrates on the process rather than the function.

Take an example of a company manufacturing engines for heavy goods vehicles. The castings provided by the supplier did not align exactly with the machine which carried them to the assembly line. This had always been accepted as a function of the business operation despite the fact that it caused a pause in production at regular intervals to allow maintenance work necessitated by wear and tear. As a re-engineering of the business process, the supplier was asked to manufacture the castings to a different specification which would align with the machine. This allowed the process to speed up by 30% on previous activity levels and quickly recovered the extra costs charged by the supplier due to the redesign of the castings.

Take as a second example the processing of customer orders. In the traditional approach a sales representative visited the customer and took an order. The sales representative initiated the order documentation, giving it an order number and setting up a file on the computer. The product manager received the order, checked that the resources were available for implementation and rewrote the order so that the customer's description of what was required could be specified in terms of the operations carried out by the business. The customer's credit rating was checked by the credit controller. This process all took a considerable amount of time because it was not well co-ordinated and there were gaps of time between the stages. As a re-engineering move, the business process was shortened by giving the sales representative a portable computer and a modem to be taken out on visits to clients. This allowed credit rating to be checked online even while the job specification was being discussed with the customer. The computer also included a data sheet on which the sales representative could enter the customer's order in such a way as to match the specification required by the production department. The information passed directly to the manufacturing premises by way of the modem and the confirmed specification was returned by fax to the customer. The entire operation of specifying and confirming the order could be completed within one hour, while the sales representative was still on hand at the customer's premises.

The advocates of business process re-engineering emphasise three goals: customer satisfaction, market domination and increased profitability. To win the claim to be a world leader requires success in all three. The business therefore has to identify the core business processes which drive it and to think in terms of process enhancement. Identifying the core business process and 'reading the market' helps the company to find a 'break point' where a change in the business process can cause a significant positive reaction in the market and take the company into a leadership position.

For some business, re-engineering may be too drastic, especially when new products are being introduced. Continuous quality improvement may be a more achievable target, where analysis of strengths and weaknesses is used to identify short-term achievable improvements on an incremental basis.

25.7 E-business and e-commerce

This section gives a very brief summary of some aspects of e-business and shows how management accounting has a role to play in e-business. You can learn more about e-business by using the 'Further reading' listed at the end of the chapter.

Electronic business, usually described as **e-business**, uses technology to automate and to change existing business practices. It affects product development, marketing, sales and the ways in which goods and services are delivered to customers.

Electronic commerce, usually described as **e-commerce**, is one part of e-business. It relates to all transactions between the company and its customers or suppliers, where electronic media are involved. The customer may wish to inspect a catalogue advertising products. The supplier may wish to draw the company's attention to changes in prices or products. The acts of buying and selling may take place electronically. E-commerce involves aspects of sharing business information about products and services, together with carrying out business transactions.

The theme throughout this book has been that management accounting has a role in:

- planning
- decision making
- control.

Now we consider each aspect of the role of management accounting in e-business and e-commerce.

25.7.1 Planning

The first question that might be asked is: 'Should we start an e-business venture?' The entrepreneur may have a vision of a new product or a new market but for any business the key accounting-related questions are: 'Can we make a profit?' and 'Will there be adequate cash flow?'

Revenue and cash inflow

There are examples of e-commerce where businesses sell existing products or services over the Internet rather than through shops and offices or by postal mail. From the management accounting point of view there are new challenges in ensuring that the recording of revenue matches the delivery of goods and services. New control procedures must be devised, with particular attention to the security of electronic data and cash transmission. The accounting records for revenue earned and cash received will be broadly similar to those used in any business. Cash flow may speed up if customers make electronic payment ahead of delivery. Revenue may be lost if the Internet-based system is difficult to use, or is not available throughout the day.

Greater challenges arise for management accounting where new forms of revenue are earned by a company through the nature of e-business. These may be described generally as 'digital services'. Examples include:

- selling banner advertising space on the company's website;
- earning commission on sales of goods by other business that have a hyperlink from the company's website;
- fees charged for allowing another business to have a 'shop-front' on the company's website.

These create accounting problems where two businesses 'swap' advertising space. 'I will let you advertise on my website if you will let me advertise on yours.' No cash changes hands but each business is gaining a benefit. This is called 'barter', a system of trading which starts in the school playground and extends around the world in places where cash is not readily available. Clearly there is no cash flow. Should each business estimate 'revenue' earned from the sale of advertising? There are costs of creating the advertisements so it seems a reasonable idea to estimate a figure for revenue. However, there is no transaction for the sale of advertising and it is far from clear that the advertiser would actually pay a fee if asked. If that is the case then the estimated value of revenue is zero. There are no easy answers on how to record the value gained from barter transactions.

Costs and cash outflow

For the business selling products and services electronically there remain the costs of producing the product or service. Beyond that, the e-business approach may reduce some costs and increase or create others. The costs that involve cash outflows may be subdivided into (a) set-up costs and (b) operating costs. The role of management accounting in planning is to estimate these costs for comparison with expected revenues.

Set-up costs include the costs of hardware and software, including internal networks and external links to suppliers and customers. The set-up costs also include the costs of managing the introduction of the project, developing and testing software, transferring data from the conventional business records to the new electronic system and training staff in using the new technology.

Operating costs include all staff costs relating to operating the new system, plus maintenance costs for the electronic system.

Cost savings may be set against these new operating costs. The business may be able to reduce the costs of staffing branch outlets, or having more staff time available to deal with problematic incoming telephone enquiries because the routine enquiries are dealt with through the website.

25.7.2 Decision making

Chapter 24 has explained various approaches to decision making related to long-term investments. Payback, accounting rate of return, discounted cash flow and internal rate of return have been explained and the calculations illustrated. At the end of that chapter the problems of appraising advanced manufacturing technologies were discussed. They require a different approach to investment appraisal and decision making. E-business offers similar challenges to management accounting for investment appraisal.

Typical questions that might be asked in an e-business decision are:

- Should we make the proposed investment in hardware, software and staff training for information systems to support e-commerce?
- Which of our existing business operations will give the highest return if converted to e-commerce methods?

The difficult task for the management accountant is to identify the incremental cash flows. The questions to be asked are: how much additional revenue can be generated by this new way of working? How much additional cost will be incurred after taking into consideration any planned cost saving? The uncertainties relating to e-business and e-commerce are such that discounted cash flow techniques may be of limited relevance. Payback focuses on how quickly the original outlay can be recovered through cash flows generated.

25.7.3 Control

Management accounting helps managers in their control activities through comparing actual costs and revenues with budgeted estimates and through quantifying and highlighting variances. The management accountant is also involved in systems design and the processing controls necessary to protect the assets and the accuracy of accounting records. Non-financial performance measures are a significant element of controlling the e-business activity.

The business receiving cash from e-commerce transactions must have adequate security measures in place. Secure connections are necessary to set up secure links between supplier and customer. Encryption (a coded message) is used for information that is being transferred and for the records held at either end of the link. The customer must be given confidence in the security controls of the supplier. The supplier must be sure that the customer has a good reputation and that the transaction will be honoured.

Data migration is one important aspect of moving to e-commerce where the management accountant may have a particularly useful role. Data migration means transferring data from the existing system to the new system. Sometimes this activity is called populating the database. Whatever it is called, the activity requires careful control and testing to ensure that no data are lost or corrupted in the process.

Indicators of success that evaluate the relative effectiveness of an e-business activity must include a mixture of financial and non-financial measures (sometimes called *metrics*). Two questions to be asked about effectiveness might be:

1 Is the marketing effective?
2 Is the business outcome effective?

Effective marketing requires attracting the attention of the potential customer. *Visitor activity* on the site can be measured by *hits* or by *site visits*. A 'hit' is recorded every time a piece of information is downloaded, so one visit to the site might result in several hits. Intending customers may be asked to register an email address or to give information about themselves. This is all part of the marketing information that will be analysed by the organisation to reflect activity.

Effective business outcomes are assessed using accounting information on revenues and costs. The business might set a target proportion of revenues to be achieved by Internet selling. The management accountant will report on achievement of the target. Analysts often enquire about marketing costs because these are effectively an investment for the future. The ratio of marketing costs to revenues for Internet business might be compared with the ratio for conventional business.

Non-financial indicators of effective business outcomes might include customer satisfaction surveys, delivery response times, complaints received or frequency of errors in delivery and invoicing.

25.7.4 Advising small businesses

Fiona has found that her work advising small and medium-sized enterprises (SMEs) is requiring her to develop an expertise in e-business and e-commerce.

FIONA: *I read a survey recently which found that most British SMEs prefer to maintain their own website and run their own e-business. That means they have to cover the cost of designing the website and they pay an in-house webperson to maintain it, involving a salary and other costs of employment. More than 80% of UK businesses have a website. Some 500,000 companies are trading online but many more companies, including most of the 1.9m SMEs, use the Internet as a shop window. Many UK companies are saying that the Internet has transformed sales and marketing, delivery, operations and processing.*

However, it seems to me as a management accountant, that cost planning and control do not appear to rank highly in the decision to move to e-business activity. There is perhaps too strong a focus on revenue and lack of attention to costs and cash flow. As a result we have seen the failure of some 'dot.com' businesses where the cash resources have become exhausted. Another survey that I came across found there was little emphasis on budgets or management in the development of e-commerce strategies.

Is e-commerce suited to all SMEs? A decision to move to e-commerce must be related to the overall business strategy and the sales strategy. The business should ask itself:

- Will e-commerce contribute to the competitive advantage of the business?
- Will it add value?
- Will the benefits outweigh the costs?

Take the example of a family business which has built its reputation for selling specialist hand tools to tradespersons and do-it-yourself enthusiasts. It has shops in several large towns but its reputation extends beyond those towns and customers will travel considerable distances to buy specialist tools. The business would be well placed to enter into e-commerce selling because its name is well known, its reputation is established in the retail outlets, which will continue to operate, and the Internet can widen the market through direct customer order and delivery to the door.

Take another example of an antiquarian bookseller who buys and sells rare books. Again the bookseller has an established reputation in trade journals and has been using catalogue-based mail order sales for some years. The business would be well placed to enter into e-commerce by adding a website reference to existing advertising material. It may also improve the bookseller's ability to find sources of rare books well beyond the local sources traditionally used. Furthermore, since competitors have already established e-commerce outlets, the bookseller may lose market share if it does not move to Internet buying and selling.

25.8 Summary

You might ask, having read this chapter, why it is necessary to pay any attention to the previous nine chapters. The answer is that the ideas described in this chapter are exciting and forward-looking but they are being used primarily by a selection of the market leaders and the innovators. There is a vast range of businesses which are still using traditional management accounting techniques. That will necessitate an understanding of the traditional approach for some time yet, in a spirit of evolution rather than revolution. So while you should read and think about the new ideas, you will also find it necessary to understand and apply the aspects of management accounting which have been taught traditionally. If you have a strong command of the approach to management accounting set out in the chapters of this book, then you will have the basis on which to build an understanding of the present practice in most business organisations. You will also be in a position to move on to an in-depth study of developments in management accounting in both the academic and the practical spheres.

Further reading

Chaffey, D. (2011), *E-Business and E-Commerce Management*, Pearson.

Porter, M. E. (1998), *Competitive Advantage: Creating and Sustaining Superior Performance*, Simon & Schuster.

QUESTIONS

The Questions section of each chapter has three types of question. 'Test your understanding' questions to help you review your reading are in the 'A' series of questions. You will find the answers to these by reading and thinking about the material in the book. 'Application' questions to test your ability to apply technical skills are in the 'B' series of questions. Questions requiring you to show skills in problem solving and evaluation are in the 'C' series of questions. There are no solutions at the end of the book because the questions on sections B and C are open-ended for you to think about from reading the material in this chapter.

A   Test your understanding

A25.1   Define 'business strategy'. (Section 25.2)

A25.2   How does strategic management accounting make use of information about competitors? (Section 25.2)

A25.3   How does just-in-time management reduce costs of control of an inventory of raw materials? (Section 25.3)

A25.4   What is meant by a cost-reduction approach to value chain analysis? How does it differ from product differentiation? (Section 25.4)

A25.5   What is the management philosophy represented by total quality management? (Section 25.5)

A25.6   What are the main components of the cost of quality? (Section 25.5)

A25.7   What is the stated purpose of business process re-engineering? (Section 25.6)

A25.8   What are the three goals of business process re-engineering? (Section 25.6)

A25.9   What is e-business? (Section 25.7)

A25.10 What is e-commerce? (Section 25.7)

A25.11 How can management accounting contribute to planning, decision making and control in e-business and e-commerce? (Section 25.7)

B   Application

B25.1

The directors of Craigielaw plc have decided that specialist paints for use on buses and lorries should become the focus of a new e-business strategy. 'All we have at present is a call centre where our customers phone in orders', said the sales manager. 'Our two main competitors are improving their business-to-business activities by linking to Internet providers. Our strengths lie in customer loyalty and the reputation of our product for quality.'

Explain how value chain analysis can be combined with the development of an e-business strategy (300 words).

B25.2

A company manufacturing specialised medical equipment and supplies is currently having a debate internally about developing an e-business strategy. The sales manager wants to develop an e-commerce website. The managing director thinks that electronic methods are not necessary; what really matters is intensive marketing and offering good technical support for the products.

Explain how the management accountant could provide useful information to help this debate come to a conclusion (300 words).

B25.3

Explain how a low-cost airline can use strategic management accounting in developing a business strategy for competing with the traditional airlines (300 words).

C   Problem solving and evaluation

C25.1

A company is reviewing its total quality management programme, which does not appear to be making the progress expected. Problems have been identified in:

- fear of exposing weaknesses in the organisation;
- lack of commitment from senior executives;
- seeing it as someone else's problem.

How could the management accountant help in addressing these problems (300 words)?

C25.2

How could planning of business strategy be useful to a public sector organisation such as a public library service? Does the idea of competition have any meaning? How can the management accountant help in planning a business strategy for a public library service (300 words)?

Activities for study groups

Case 25.1

A company selling life insurance policies is planning to implement the balanced scorecard approach. The board of directors is aware that it should consider four aspects of vision and goals:

- financial perspective
- customer perspective
- internal business processes
- innovation and learning.

Prepare a short introduction for a meeting of administrative staff which is intended to ask them to suggest items for inclusion under these four headings. Make your own list of three items for each heading so that you can help the discussion if it needs some prompting.

Case 25.2

A manufacturer of toothpaste has estimated the price at which the product will sell, making use of market surveys and consumer analysis. A profit margin has been set. Finally a target cost has been established by subtracting the target cost from the estimated selling price. The plant manager and the research and development unit have been asked to design the product in such a way that it can be produced within the target cost.

A rival manufacturer of toothpaste takes a different approach. Here the selling price is again estimated from market surveys and consumer analysis and a profit margin is set. However, the product design is then accepted on the recommendation of the research and development unit and the plant manager then focuses on a programme of continuous improvement which will keep costs within acceptable limits.

Is there a role for management accounting in either of these situations?

Case 25.3

Search the management feature pages of a business newspaper such as the *Financial Times* for a period of one month. Find articles about management which have a management accounting angle. Select one of the articles and write a response setting out the ways in which management accounting will contribute to the management purposes described in the article.

Note and reference

1. Wilson, R. M. S. (1995), 'Strategic management accounting', in Ashton, D., Hopper, T. and Scapens, R. W. (eds), *Issues in Management Accounting*, Prentice Hall, Chapter 8.

Coventry University London

Financial accounting terms defined

The definition of one word or phrase may depend on understanding another word or phrase defined elsewhere in the reference list. Words in **bold** indicate that such a definition is available.

account payable An amount due for payment to a supplier of goods or services, also described as a **trade creditor**.

account receivable an amount due from a customer, also described as a **trade debtor**.

accountancy firm A business partnership (or possibly a limited company) in which the partners are qualified accountants. The firm undertakes work for clients in respect of audit, accounts preparation, tax and similar activities.

accountancy profession The collective body of persons qualified in accounting, and working in accounting-related areas. Usually they are members of a professional body, membership of which is attained by passing examinations.

accounting The process of identifying, measuring and communicating financial information about an entity to permit informed judgements and decisions by users of the information.

accounting equation The relationship between assets, liabilities and ownership interest.

accounting period Time period for which financial statements are prepared (e.g. month, quarter, year).

accounting policies Accounting methods which have been judged by business enterprises to be most appropriate to their circumstances and adopted by them for the purpose of preparing their financial statements.

accounting standards Definitive statements of best practice issued by a body having suitable authority.

Accounting Standards Board The authority in the UK which issued definitive statements of best accounting practice until 2012.

accruals basis The effects of transactions and other events are recognised when they occur (and not as cash or its equivalent is received or paid) and they are recorded in the accounting records and reported in the financial statements of the periods to which they relate (see also **matching**).

accumulated depreciation Total **depreciation** of a **non-current (fixed) asset**, deducted from original cost to give **net book value**.

acid test The ratio of liquid assets to current liabilities.

acquiree Company that becomes controlled by another.

acquirer Company that obtains control of another.

acquisition An acquisition takes place where one company – the **acquirer** – acquires control of another – the **acquiree** – usually through purchase of shares.

acquisition method Production of **consolidated financial statements** for an **acquisition**.

administrative expenses Costs of managing and running a business.

agency A relationship between a principal and an agent. In the case of a limited liability company, the shareholder is the principal and the director is the agent.

agency theory A theoretical model, developed by academics, to explain how the relationship between a principal and an agent may have economic consequences.

aggregate depreciation See **accumulated depreciation**.

allocate To assign a whole item of cost, or of revenue, to a simple cost centre, account or time period.

allocated, allocation See **allocate**.

amortisation Process similar to **depreciation**, usually applied to intangible fixed assets.

annual report A document produced each year by limited liability companies containing the accounting information required by law. Larger companies also provide information and pictures of the activities of the company.

articles of association Document setting out the relative rights of shareholders in a limited liability company.

articulation The term 'articulation' is used to refer to the impact of transactions on the balance sheet and profit and loss account through application of the accounting equation.

asset A present economic resource controlled by the entity as a result of past events. An economic resource is a right that has the potential to produce economic benefits.

associated company One company exercises significant influence over another, falling short of complete control.

audit An audit is the independent examination of, and expression of opinion on, financial statements of an entity.

audit manager An employee of an accountancy firm, usually holding an accountancy qualification, given a significant level of responsibility in carrying out an audit assignment and responsible to the partner in charge of the audit.

bad debt It is known that a credit customer (**debtor**) is unable to pay the amount due.

balance sheet A statement of the financial position of an entity showing assets, liabilities and ownership interest. Under the **IASB system** the preferred title is **statement of financial position**.

bank facility An arrangement with a bank to borrow money as required up to an agreed limit.

bond The name sometimes given to loan finance (more commonly in the USA).

broker (stockbroker) Member of a stock exchange who arranges purchase and sale of shares and may also provide an information service giving buy/sell/hold recommendations.

broker's report Bulletin written by a stockbroking firm for circulation to its clients, providing analysis and guidance on companies as potential investments.

business combination A transaction in which one company acquires control of another.

business cycle Period (usually 12 months) during which the peaks and troughs of activity of a business form a pattern which is repeated on a regular basis.

business entity A business which exists independently of its owners.

called up (share capital) The company has called upon the shareholders who first bought the shares, to make their payment in full.

capital An amount of finance provided to enable a business to acquire assets and sustain its operations.

capital expenditure Spending on **non-current** (fixed) assets of a business.

capitalisation issue Issue of shares to existing shareholders in proportion to shares already held.

Raises no new finance but changes the mix of share capital and reserves.

cash Cash on hand (such as money held in a cash box or a safe) and deposits in a bank that may be withdrawn on demand.

cash equivalents Short-term, highly liquid investments that are readily convertible to known amounts of cash and which are subject to an insignificant risk of changes in value.

cash flow projections Statements of cash expected to flow into the business and cash expected to flow out over a particular period.

chairman The person who chairs the meetings of the board of directors of a company (preferably not the chief executive).

charge In relation to interest or taxes, describes the reduction in ownership interest reported in the income statement (profit and loss account) due to the cost of interest and tax payable.

chief executive The director in charge of the day-to-day running of a company.

close season Period during which those who are 'insiders' to a listed company should not buy or sell shares.

commercial paper A method of borrowing money from commercial institutions such as banks.

Companies Act The Companies Act 2006. Legislation to control the activities of limited liability companies.

comparability Qualitative characteristic expected in financial statements, comparable within company and between companies.

completeness Qualitative characteristic expected in financial statements.

conceptual framework A statement of principles providing generally accepted guidance for the development of new reporting practices and for challenging and evaluating the existing practices.

conservatism See **prudence**. Sometimes used with a stronger meaning of understating assets and overstating liabilities.

consistency The measurement and display of similar transactions and other events is carried out in a consistent way throughout an entity within each accounting period and from one period to the next, and also in a consistent way by different entities.

consolidated financial statements Present financial information about the group as a single reporting entity.

consolidation Consolidation is a process that aggregates the total assets, liabilities and results of the parent and its subsidiaries (the group) in the **consolidated financial statements**.

contingent liabilities Obligations that are not recognised in the balance sheet because they depend upon some future event happening.

control The power to govern the financial and operating policies of an entity so as to obtain benefits from its activities.

convertible loan Loan finance for a business that is later converted into **share capital**.

corporate governance The system by which companies are directed and controlled. Boards of directors are responsible for the governance of their companies.

corporate recovery department Part of an accountancy firm which specialises in assisting companies to recover from financial problems.

corporate social responsibility Companies integrate social and environmental concerns in their business operations and in their interactions with stakeholders.

corporation tax Tax payable by companies, based on the taxable profits of the period.

cost of a non-current asset is the cost of making it ready for use, cost of finished goods is cost of bringing them to the present condition and location.

cost of goods sold Materials, labour and other costs directly related to the goods or services provided.

cost of sales See **cost of goods sold**.

coupon Rate of interest payable on a loan.

credit (bookkeeping system) Entries in the credit column of a ledger account represent increases in liabilities, increases in ownership interest, revenue, or decreases in assets.

credit (terms of business) The supplier agrees to allow the customer to make payment some time after the delivery of the goods or services. Typical trade credit periods range from 30 to 60 days but each agreement is different.

credit note A document sent to a customer of a business cancelling the customer's debt to the business, usually because the customer has returned defective goods or has received inadequate service.

credit purchase A business **entity** takes delivery of goods or services and is allowed to make payment at a later date.

credit sale A business **entity** sells goods or services and allows the customer to make payment at a later date.

creditor A person or organisation to whom money is owed by the entity.

critical event The point in the business cycle at which **revenue** may be recognised.

current asset An asset that is expected to be converted into cash within the trading cycle.

current liability A liability which satisfies any of the following criteria: (a) it is expected to be settled in the entity's normal operating cycle; (b) it is held primarily for the purpose of being traded; (c) it is due to be settled within 12 months after the balance sheet date.

current value A method of valuing assets and liabilities which takes account of changing prices, as an alternative to historical cost.

customers' collection period Average number of days credit taken by customers.

cut-off procedures Procedures applied to the accounting records at the end of an accounting period to ensure that all transactions for the period are recorded and any transactions not relevant to the period are excluded.

debenture A written acknowledgement of a debt – a name used for loan financing taken up by a company.

debtor A person or organisation that owes money to the entity.

deep discount bond A loan issued at a relatively low price compared to its nominal value.

default Failure to meet obligations as they fall due for payment.

deferred asset An asset whose benefit is delayed beyond the period expected for a current asset, but which does not meet the definition of a fixed asset.

deferred income Revenue, such as a government grant, is received in advance of performing the related activity. The deferred income is held in the balance sheet as a type of liability until performance is achieved and is then released to the income statement.

deferred taxation The obligation to pay tax is deferred (postponed) under tax law beyond the normal date of payment.

depreciable amount Cost of a **non-current (fixed) asset** minus **residual value**.

depreciation The systematic allocation of the **depreciable amount** of an asset over its useful life. The depreciable amount is cost less **residual value**.

derecognition The act of removing an item from the financial statements because the item no longer satisfies the criteria for **recognition**.

difference on consolidation Difference between **fair value** of the payment for a **subsidiary** and the **fair value** of **net assets** acquired, more commonly called **goodwill**.

direct method (of operating cash flow) Presents cash inflows and cash outflows.

Directive A document issued by the European Union requiring all member states to adapt their national law to be consistent with the Directive.

director(s) Person(s) appointed by shareholders of a limited liability company to manage the affairs of the company.

disclosed, disclosure An item which is reported in the notes to the accounts is said to be disclosed but not **recognised**.

discount received A supplier of goods or services allows a business to deduct an amount called a discount, for prompt payment of an invoiced amount. The discount is often expressed a percentage of the invoiced amount.

dividend Amount paid to a shareholder, usually in the form of cash, as a reward for investment in the company. The amount of dividend paid is proportionate to the number of shares held.

dividend cover Earnings per share divided by dividend per share.

dividend yield Dividend per share divided by current market price.

doubtful debts Amounts due from credit customers where there is concern that the customer may be unable to pay.

drawings Cash taken for personal use, in **sole trader** or **partnership** business, treated as a reduction of **ownership interest**.

earnings for ordinary shareholders Profit after deducting interest charges and taxation and after deducting preference dividends (but before deducting extraordinary items).

earnings per share calculated as **earnings for ordinary shareholders** divided by the number of shares which have been issued by the company.

economic resource A right that is capable of producing economic benefits.

effective interest rate The rate that exactly discounts estimated future cash payments or receipts through the expected life of the financial instrument.

efficient markets hypothesis Share prices in a stock market react immediately to the announcement of new information.

endorsed International financial reporting standards approved for use in member states of the European Union through a formal process of **endorsement**.

endorsement See **endorsed**.

enterprise A business activity or a commercial project.

entity, entities Something that exists independently, such as a business which exists independently of the owner.

entry price The value of entering into acquisition of an asset or liability, usually **replacement cost**.

equities analyst A person who investigates and writes reports on ordinary share investments in companies (usually for the benefit of investors in shares).

equity A description applied to the **ordinary share** capital of an entity.

equity accounting Reports in the **balance sheet** the parent or group's share of the investment in the **share capital** and **reserves** of an **associated company**.

equity holders Those who own ordinary shares in the **entity**.

equity interest See **ownership interest**.

equity portfolio A collection of **equity shares**.

equity shares/share capital Shares in a company which participate in sharing dividends and in sharing any surplus on winding up, after all liabilities have been met.

eurobond market A market in which bonds are issued in the capital market of one country to a non-resident borrower from another country.

exit price See **exit value**.

exit value A method of valuing assets and liabilities based on selling prices, as an alternative to **historical cost**.

expense Decreases in assets or increases in liabilities that result in decreases in equity, other than those relating to distributions to holders of equity claims.

external reporting Reporting financial information to those users with a valid claim to receive it, but who are not allowed access to the day-to-day records of the business.

external users (of financial statements) Users of financial statements who have a valid interest but are not permitted access to the day-to-day records of the company.

fair value The price that would be received to sell an asset or paid to transfer a liability in an orderly transaction between market participants at the measurement date.

faithful representation Financial information must faithfully represent the economic events reported.

financial accounting A term usually applied to *external reporting* by a business where that reporting is presented in financial terms.

financial adaptability The ability of the company to respond to unexpected needs or opportunities.

financial gearing Ratio of loan finance to equity capital and reserves.

financial information Information which may be reported in money terms.

Financial Reporting Standard Title of an accounting standard issued by the UK Financial Reporting Council as a definitive statement of best practice (issued from 1990 onwards – predecessor documents are Statements of Standard Accounting Practice).

financial risk Exists where a company has loan finance, especially long-term loan finance where the company cannot relinquish its commitment. The risk relates to being unable to meet payments of interest or repayment of capital as they fall due.

financial statements Documents presenting accounting information which is expected to have a useful purpose.

financial viability The ability to survive on an ongoing basis.

financing activities Activities that result in changes in the size and composition of the contributed equity and borrowings of the entity.

fixed asset An asset that is held by an enterprise for use in the production or supply of goods or services, for rental to others, or for administrative purposes on a continuing basis in the reporting entity's activities.

fixed assets See **non-current assets**.

fixed assets usage Revenue divided by **net book value** of **fixed assets**.

fixed capital Finance provided to support the acquisition of fixed assets.

fixed cost One which is not affected by changes in the level of output over a defined period of time.

floating charge Security taken by lender which floats over all the assets and crystallises over particular assets if the security is required.

forecast estimate of future performance and position based on stated assumptions and usually including a quantified amount.

format A list of items which may appear in a financial statement, setting out the order in which they are to appear.

forward exchange contract An agreement to buy foreign currency at a fixed future date and at an agreed price.

fully paid Shares on which the amount of share capital has been paid in full to the company.

fund manager A person who manages a collection (portfolio) of investments, usually for an insurance company, a pension fund business or a professional fund management business which invests money on behalf of clients.

gearing (financial) The ratio of debt capital to ownership claim.

general purpose financial statements Documents containing accounting information which would be expected to be of interest to a wide range of user groups. For a limited liability company there would be: a balance sheet, a profit and loss account, a statement of recognised gains and losses and a cash flow statement.

going concern basis The assumption that the business will continue operating into the foreseeable future.

goodwill An asset measured as the excess of the cost of a business combination over the fair value of the net assets acquired.

gross Before making deductions.

gross margin Sales minus cost of sales before deducting administration and selling expenses (another name for **gross profit**). Usually applied when discussing a particular line of activity.

gross margin ratio Gross profit as a percentage of sales.

gross profit Sales minus cost of sales before deducting administration and selling expenses (see also **gross margin**).

group Economic **entity** formed by **parent** and one or more **subsidiaries**.

highlights statement A page at the start of the annual report setting out key measures of performance during the reporting period.

historical cost Method of valuing assets and liabilities based on their original cost without adjustment for changing prices.

HM Revenue and Customs (HMRC) The UK government's tax-gathering organisation (previously called the Inland Revenue).

IAS International Accounting Standard, issued by the IASB's predecessor body.

IASB International Accounting Standards Board, an independent body that sets accounting standards accepted as a basis for accounting in many countries, including all Member States of the European Union.

IASB system The accounting standards and guidance issued by the **IASB**.

IFRS International Financial Reporting Standard, issued by the **IASB**.

impairment A reduction in the carrying value of an **asset**, beyond the expected **depreciation**, which must be reflected by reducing the amount recorded in the **balance sheet**.

impairment review Testing assets for evidence of any **impairment**.

impairment test Test that the business can expect to recover the carrying value of the intangible asset, through either using it or selling.

improvement A change in, or addition to, a **non-current (fixed) asset** that extends its useful life or increases the expected future benefit. Contrast with repair which restores the existing useful life or existing expected future benefit.

income statement Financial statement presenting revenues, expenses, and profit. Also called **profit and loss account**.

incorporation, date of The date on which a company comes into existence.

indirect method (of operating cash flow) Calculates operating cash flow by adjusting operating profit for non-cash items and for changes in working capital.

insider information Information gained by someone inside, or close to, a listed company which could confer a financial advantage if used to buy or sell shares. It is illegal for a person who is in possession of inside information to buy or sell shares on the basis of that information.

institutional investor An organisation whose business includes regular investment in shares of companies, examples being an insurance company, a pension fund, a charity, an investment trust, a unit trust, a merchant bank.

intangible Without shape or form, cannot be touched.

interest (on loans) The percentage return on **capital** required by the lender (usually expressed as a percentage per annum).

interim reports Financial statements issued in the period between annual reports, usually half-yearly or quarterly.

internal reporting Reporting financial information to those users inside a business, at various levels of management, at a level of detail appropriate to the recipient.

inventory Stocks of goods held for manufacture or for resale.

investing activities The acquisition and disposal of long-term assets and other investments not included in cash equivalents.

investors Persons or organisations which have provided money to a business in exchange for a share of ownership.

invoices When a sale is made on credit terms the invoice is the document sent to the customer showing the quantities sold and the amount due to be paid.

joint and several liability (in a partnership) The partnership liabilities are shared jointly but each person is responsible for the whole of the partnership.

key performance indicators (KPIs) Quantified measures of factors that help to measure the performance of the business effectively.

leasing Acquiring the use of an **asset** through a rental agreement.

legal form Representing a transaction to reflect its legal status, which might not be the same as its economic form.

leverage Alternative term for **gearing**, commonly used in the USA.

liability A present obligation of the entity to transfer an economic resource as a result of past events. An economic resource is a right that has the potential to produce economic benefits.

limited liability A phrase used to indicate that those having liability in respect of some amount due may be able to invoke some agreed limit on that liability.

limited liability company Company where the liability of the owners is limited to the amount of capital they have agreed to contribute.

liquidity The extent to which a business has access to cash or items which can readily be exchanged for cash.

listed company A company whose shares are listed by the Stock Exchange as being available for buying and selling under the rules and safeguards of the Exchange.

listing requirements Rules imposed by the Stock Exchange on companies whose shares are listed for buying and selling.

Listing Rules Issued by the UK Listing Authority of the Financial Services Authority to regulate companies listed on the UK Stock Exchange. Includes rules on accounting information in annual reports.

loan covenants Agreement made by the company with a lender of long-term finance, protecting the loan by imposing conditions on the company, usually to restrict further borrowing.

loan notes A method of borrowing from commercial institutions such as banks.

loan stock Loan finance traded on a stock exchange.

long-term finance, long-term liabilities Money lent to a business for a fixed period, giving that business a commitment to pay interest for the period specified and to repay the loan at the end of the period. Also called **non-current liabilities** information in the financial statements should show the commercial substance of the situation.

management Collective term for those persons responsible for the day-to-day running of a business.

management accounting Reporting accounting information within a business, for management use only.

market value (of a share) The price for which a share could be transferred between a willing buyer and a willing seller.

marking to market Valuing a marketable **asset** at its current market price.

margin Profit, seen as the 'margin' between revenue and expense.

matching Expenses are matched against revenues in the period they are incurred (see also **accruals basis**).

material See **materiality**.

materiality Information is **material** if its omission or misstatement could influence the economic decisions of users taken on the basis of the financial statements.

maturity The date on which a liability is due for repayment.

maturity profile of debt The timing of loan repayments by a company in the future.

memorandum (for a company) Document setting out main objects of the company and its powers to act.

merger Two organisations agree to work together in a situation where neither can be regarded as having acquired the other.

minority interest see **non-controlling interest**.

net After making deductions.

net assets Assets minus **liabilities** (equals **ownership interest**).

net book value Cost of **non-current (fixed) asset** minus **accumulated depreciation**.

net debt Borrowings minus cash balances.

net profit Sales minus cost of sales minus all administrative and selling costs.

net realisable value The proceeds of selling an item, less the costs of selling.

neutral Qualitative characteristic of freedom from bias.

nominal value (of a share) The amount stated on the face of a share certificate as the named value of the share when issued.

non-controlling interest The proportion of the equity interest in subsidiaries held by shareholders outside the group, previously called minority interest.

non-current assets Any asset that does not meet the definition of a current asset. Also described as **fixed assets**.

non-current liabilities Any liability that does not meet the definition of a **current liability**. Also described as **long-term liabilities**.

notes to the accounts Information in financial statements that gives more detail about items in the **financial statements**.

off-balance sheet finance An arrangement to keep matching assets and liabilities away from the entity's balance sheet.

offer for sale A company makes a general offer of its shares to the public.

operating activities The principal revenue-producing activities of the entity and other activities that are not investing or financing activities.

operating gearing The ratio of fixed operating costs to variable operating costs.

operating margin Operating profit as a percentage of sales.

operating risk Exists where there are factors, such as a high level of fixed operating costs, which would cause profits to fluctuate through changes in operating conditions.

ordinary shares Shares in a company which entitle the holder to a share of the dividend declared and a share in net assets on closing down the business.

ownership interest The residual amount found by deducting all of the entity's liabilities from all of the entity's assets. (Also called **equity interest**.)

par value See **nominal value**.

parent company Company which controls one or more subsidiaries in a group.

partnership Two or more persons in business together with the aim of making a profit.

partnership deed A document setting out the agreement of the partners on how the partnership is to be conducted (including the arrangements for sharing profits and losses).

partnership law Legislation which governs the conduct of a partnership and which should be used where no partnership deed has been written.

portfolio (of investment) A collection of investments.

portfolio of shares A collection of shares held by an investor.

preference shares Shares in a company which give the holder a preference (although not an automatic right) to receive a dividend before any ordinary share dividend is declared.

preliminary announcement An informal description of the first announcement by a listed company of its profit for the most recent accounting period. Precedes the publication of the full annual report. The regulated announcement is made to the entire stock market so that all investors receive information at the same time.

premium An amount paid in addition, or extra.

prepaid expense An expense paid in advance of the benefit being received, e.g. rentals paid in advance.

prepayment An amount paid for in advance for an benefit to the business, such as insurance premiums or rent in advance. Initially recognised as an asset, then transferred to expense in the period when the benefit is enjoyed. (Also called a **prepaid expense**.)

present fairly A condition of the **IASB system**, equivalent to **true and fair view** in the UK system.

price–earnings ratio Market price of a share divided by earnings per share.

price-sensitive information Information which, if known to the market, would affect the price of a share.

primary financial statements The balance sheet, profit and loss account, statement of total recognised gains and losses and cash flow statement.

principal (sum) The agreed amount of a loan, on which interest will be charged during the period of the loan.

private limited company (Ltd) A company which has **limited liability** but is not permitted to offer its shares to the public.

production overhead costs Costs of production that are spread across all output, rather than being identified with specific goods or services.

profit Calculated as revenue minus expenses.

profit and loss account Financial statement presenting revenues, expenses, and profit. Also called **income statement**.

prospective investor An investor who is considering whether to invest in a company.

prospectus Financial statements and supporting detailed descriptions published when a company is offering shares for sale to the public.

provision A liability of uncertain timing or amount.

provision for doubtful debts An estimate of the risk of not collecting full payment from credit customers, reported as a deduction from **trade receivables (debtors)** in the **balance sheet**.

prudence A degree of caution in the exercise of the judgements needed in making the estimates required under conditions of uncertainty, such that gains and assets are not overstated and losses and liabilities are not understated.

public limited company (plc) A company which has **limited liability** and offers its shares to the public.

purchase method Method of producing consolidated financial statements (see **acquisition method**).

purchases Total of goods and services bought in a period.

qualified audit opinion An audit opinion to the effect that: the accounts do *not* show a true and fair view; or the accounts show a true and fair view *except for* particular matters.

quality of earnings Opinion of investors on reliability of earnings (profit) as a basis for their forecasts.

quoted company Defined in section 385 of the Companies Act 2006 as a company that has been included in the official list in accordance with the provisions of Part VI of the Financial Services and Markets Act 2000, or is officially listed in an EEA state, or is admitted to dealing on either the New York Stock Exchange or the exchange known as Nasdaq.

realised profit, realisation A profit arising from revenue which has been earned by the entity and for which there is a reasonable prospect of cash being collected in the near future.

recognised An item is recognised when it is included by means of words and amount within the main financial statements of an entity.

recognition See **recognised**.

Registrar of Companies An official authorised by the government to maintain a record of all annual reports and other documents issued by a company.

relevance Qualitative characteristic of influencing the economic decisions of users.

replacement cost A measure of **current value** which estimates the cost of replacing an asset or liability at the date of the balance sheet. Justified by reference to **value to the business**.

reserves The claim which owners have on the *assets* of a company because the company has created new wealth for them over the period since it began.

residual value The estimated amount that an entity would currently obtain from disposal of the asset, after deducting the estimated cost of disposal, if the asset were already of the age and in the condition expected at the end of its useful life.

retained earnings Accumulated past profits, not distributed in dividends, available to finance investment in assets.

retained profit Profit of the period remaining after **dividend** has been deducted.

return The yield or reward from an investment.

return on capital employed (ROCE) Operating profit before deducting interest and taxation, divided by share capital reserves plus long-term loans.

return on shareholders' equity Profit for shareholders divided by share capital plus reserves.

return on total assets Operating profit before deducting interest and taxation, divided by total assets.

return (in relation to investment) The reward earned for investing money in a business. Return may appear in the form of regular cash payments (dividends) to the investor, or in a growth in the value of the amount invested.

revaluation reserve The claim which owners have on the **assets** of the business because the balance sheet records a market value for an asset that is greater than its historical cost.

revenue Income arising in the course of an entity's ordinary activities.

rights issue A company gives its existing shareholders the right to buy more shares in proportion to those already held.

risk (in relation to investment) Factors that may cause the profit or cash flows of the business to fluctuate.

sales See **revenue, turnover**.

sales invoice Document sent to customers recording a sale on credit and requesting payment.

secured loan Loan where the lender has taken a special claim on particular assets or revenues of the company.

segmental reporting Reporting revenue, profit, cash flow assets, liabilities for each geographical and business segment within a business, identifying segments by the way the organisation is managed.

share capital Name given to the total amount of cash which the shareholders have contributed to the company.

share certificate A document providing evidence of share ownership.

share premium The claim which owners have on the assets of a company because shares have been purchased from the company at a price greater than the nominal value.

shareholders Owners of a **limited liability company**.

shareholders' funds Name given to total of **share capital** and **reserves** in a company balance sheet.

shares The amount of share capital held by any shareholder is measured in terms of a number of shares in the total capital of the company.

short-term finance Money lent to a business for a short period of time, usually repayable on demand and also repayable at the choice of the business if surplus to requirements.

sole trader An individual owning and operating a business alone.

specific purpose financial statements Documents containing accounting information which is prepared for a particular purpose and is not normally available to a wider audience.

stakeholders A general term devised to indicate all those who might have a legitimate interest in receiving financial information about a business because they have a 'stake' in it.

statement of cash flows Provides information about changes in financial position.

statement of changes in equity A financial statement reporting all items causing changes to the ownership interest during the financial period, under the **IASB system**.

statement of comprehensive income Provides information on all gains and losses causing a change in **ownership interest** during a period, other than contributions and withdrawals made by the owners.

statement of financial position Provides information on assets, liabilities and equity at a specified reporting date. It is the preferred title under the **IASB system** for the document that is also called a **balance sheet**.

statement of principles A document issued in 1999 by the Accounting Standards Board in the United Kingdom setting out key principles to be applied in the process of setting accounting standards.

stepped bond Loan finance that starts with a relatively low rate of interest which then increases in steps.

stewardship Taking care of resources owned by another person and using those resources to the benefit of that person.

stock A word with two different meanings. It may be used to describe an **inventory** of goods held for resale or for use in business. It may also be used to describe **shares** in the ownership of a company. The meaning will usually be obvious from the way in which the word is used.

stock exchange (also called **stock market**). An organisation which has the authority to set rules for persons buying and selling shares. The term 'stock' is used loosely with a meaning similar to that of 'shares'.

stock holding period Average number of days for which inventory (stock) is held before use or sale.

stock market See **stock exchange**.

strategic report Section of the **annual report** which provides the entity's business model, strategy, development, performance, position and future prospect.

subsidiary company Company in a group which is controlled by another (the parent company). (*See* Chapter 7 for full definition.) Sometimes called subsidiary undertaking.

substance (economic) Information in the financial statements should show the economic or commercial substance of the situation.

subtotal Totals of similar items grouped together within a financial statement.

suppliers' payment period Average number of days credit taken from suppliers.

tangible fixed assets A **fixed asset** (also called a **non-current asset**) which has a physical existence.

timeliness Qualitative characteristic that potentially conflicts with **relevance**.

total assets usage Sales divided by total assets.

trade creditors Persons who supply goods or services to a business in the normal course of trade and allow a period of credit before payment must be made.

trade debtors Persons who buy goods or services from a business in the normal course of trade and are allowed a period of credit before payment is due.

trade payables Amounts due to suppliers (**trade creditors**), also called **accounts payable**.

trade receivables Amounts due from customers (**trade debtors**), also called **accounts receivable**.

treasury shares Shares which a company has repurchased from its own shareholders and is holding with the intention of reselling the shares in the future.

true and fair view Requirement of UK company law for UK companies.

turnover The sales of a business or other form of revenue from operations of the business.

understandability Qualitative characteristic of financial statements, understandable by users.

unlisted (company) Limited liability company whose shares are not **listed** on any stock exchange.

unrealised Gains and losses representing changes in values of assets and liabilities that are not **realised** through sale or use.

unsecured creditors Those who have no claim against particular assets when a company is wound up, but must take their turn for any share of what remains.

unsecured loan Loan in respect of which the lender has taken no special claim against any assets.

value to the business An idea used in deciding on a measure of **current value**.

variance The difference between a planned, budgeted or standard cost and the actual cost incurred. An adverse variance arises when the actual cost is greater than the standard cost. A favourable variance arises when the actual cost is less than the standard cost.

working capital Finance provided to support the short-term assets of the business (stocks and debtors) to the extent that these are not financed by short-term creditors. It is calculated as current assets minus current liabilities.

working capital cycle Total of stock holding period plus customers collection period minus suppliers payment period.

work in progress Cost of partly completed goods or services, intended for completion and recorded as an asset.

written down value See **net book value**.

Management accounting terms defined

The definition of one word or phrase may depend on understanding another word or phrase defined elsewhere in the reference list. Words in **bold** indicate that such a definition is available.

ABC See **activity-based costing**.

AMTs See **advanced manufacturing technologies**.

absorb, absorbed See **absorption**.

absorption The process by which overhead costs are absorbed into units of output, or 'jobs'.

absorption costing All production costs are absorbed into products and the unsold inventory is valued at total cost of production.

accounting The process of identifying, measuring and communicating financial information about an entity to permit informed judgements and decisions by users of the information.

accounting rate of return Calculated by taking the average annual profits expected from a project as a percentage of the capital invested.

accrual See **accrued expense**.

accrued expense (accrued liability) An expense which remains unpaid at the accounting date and is therefore recognised as a liability.

activity any physical operation that takes place in an enterprise. For **ABC** see also **unit activity, product-sustaining activities, batch-related activities** and **cost drivers**.

activity-based costing (ABC) traces **overhead costs** to products by focusing on the **activities** that drive costs (cause costs to occur).

activity cost pool See **cost pool**.

actual overhead cost Overhead cost of the period, arising either through cash spending or through trade credit.

advanced manufacturing technologies New methods developed by engineers in order to compete more effectively.

adverse variance This arises when the actual cost is greater than the standard cost.

allocate To assign a whole item of cost, or of revenue, to a simple cost centre, account or time period.

allocated, allocation See **allocate**.

annual report A document produced each year by limited liability companies containing the accounting information required by law. Larger companies also provide information and pictures of the activities of the company.

apportion To spread cost over two or more cost units, centres, accounts or time periods on some basis which is a fair representation of how the cost item is used by each cost centre.

apportioned, apportionment See **apportion**.

asset A present economic resource controlled by the entity as a result of past events. An economic resource is a right that has the potential to produce economic benefits.

average annual profit Calculated as average annual cash flow minus annual depreciation.

avoidable cost One which may be eliminated by taking a particular action.

balanced scorecard Links performance measures for key goals in customer perspective, financial perspective, internal business perspective and learning and growth perspective.

balance sheet A statement of the financial position of an entity showing assets, liabilities and ownership claim.

basic standard A **standard cost** that remains a permanent basis for comparison.

batch-related activities (in **ABC**) Product-sustaining **activities** that are fixed for a given batch of products.

benchmarking is the process of measuring the organisation's operations, products and services against those of competitors recognised as market leaders, in order to establish targets which will provide a competitive advantage.

bottom-up budget Initiated by inviting those who will implement the budget to participate in the process of setting the budget. Also called a **participative budget**.

break-even analysis A technique of management accounting which is based on calculating the break-even point and analysing the consequences of changes in various factors calculating the break-even point.

break-even chart Graph that shows sales and costs over a range of activity, including the activity level at which total costs equal total sales and at which the business makes neither a profit nor a loss.

break-even point That point of activity (measured as sales volume) where total sales and total costs are equal, so that there is neither profit nor loss.

break-even sales See **break-even point**.

budget A detailed plan which sets out, in money terms, the plans for income and expenditure in respect of a future period of time. It is prepared in advance of that time period and is based on the agreed objectives for that period of time, together with the strategy planned to achieve those objectives.

budget committee A group of people brought together to manage each stage of the budgetary process.

budget manual A document setting out procedures and instructions including the timetable for **budget** preparation, formats to be used, circulation lists for drafts, and arbitration procedures where conflicts begin to show themselves.

budgetary planning and control Specialist techniques to quantify the strategy of the enterprise.

budgetary system Serves the needs of management in making judgements and decisions, exercising planning and control and achieving effective communication and motivation.

budgeted fixed overhead cost rate Fixed overhead cost rate per unit set in advance. See **predetermined overhead cost rate**.

business strategic planning Involves preparing, evaluating and selecting **strategy** to achieve objectives of a long-term plan of action within a defined business activity.

capital budgeting A process of management accounting which assists management decision making by providing information on the investment in a project and the benefits to be obtained from that project, and by monitoring the performance of the project subsequent to its implementation.

capital expenditure Spending on resources which bring a long-term benefit to an organisation, in generating cash flows or providing other benefits relating to the purpose of the organisation.

capital investment See **capital expenditure**.

capital investment appraisal The application of a set of methods of quantitative analysis which give guidance to managers in making decisions as to how best to invest long-term funds.

capital rationing There is not sufficient finance (capital) available to support all the projects proposed in an organisation.

cash flow projections Statements of cash expected to flow into the business and cash expected to flow out over a particular period.

cash flows Calculated as profit before deducting depreciation and amortisation.

contingency theory An explanation that management accounting methods have developed in a variety of ways depending on the judgements or decisions required.

contribution Sales minus variable cost.

contribution per unit The sales price minus the variable cost per unit. It measures the contribution made by each item of output to fixed costs and profit.

contribution per unit of limiting factor Used in ranking, choosing the highest value of this ratio to make the most profitable use of restricted resources.

control The power to govern the financial and operating policies of an entity so as to obtain benefits from its activities. One of three functions of management that are supported by management accounting. See also **decision making** and **planning**.

controllable cost A cost which is capable of being regulated by a manager within a defined boundary of responsibility.

controlling See **control**.

corporate strategic planning Involves preparing, evaluating and selecting strategies to achieve objectives of a long-term plan of action for the corporate **entity** as a whole.

cost centre A unit of the organisation in respect of which a manager is responsible for costs under her or his control.

cost code A system of letters and numbers designed to give a series of unique labels which help in classification and analysis of cost information.

cost coding Codes used for recording costs in an accounting system.

cost driver rate Total costs in a **cost pool** divided by the number of times that the **activity** occurs.

cost drivers The factors that most closely influence the cost of an activity.

cost of capital The cost to the business of raising new finance.

cost of quality All costs incurred in achieving a quality product or service.

cost-plus pricing Setting a price based on full cost of production plus desired profit. Also called **full cost pricing**.

cost pool The costs collected that relate to each **activity**.

cost(s) An amount of expenditure on a defined activity. The word 'cost' needs other words added to it, to give it a specific meaning.

cost–volume–profit analysis Emphasises the relationship between sales revenue, costs and profit in the short term.

creditors Persons or organisations that are owed money by the **entity**.

current asset An asset that is expected to be converted into cash within the trading cycle.

current liability A liability that is expected to be repaid within a short period of time, usually within one year.

currently attainable standard A **standard cost** based on expectations under normally efficient operating conditions.

debtors Persons or organisations who owe money to the **entity**.

decision making One of three functions of management which are supported by management accounting. See also **planning** and **control**.

depreciable amount The cost of an asset, or another amount such as replacement cost substituted for cost, less its **residual value**.

depreciation The systematic allocation of the depreciable amount of an asset over its useful life.

direct cost Cost that is directly traceable to an identifiable unit, such as a product or service or department of the business, for which costs are to be determined.

direct labour Direct cost of labour.

direct materials Direct cost of materials.

directing attention One of three functions of management accounting to support management actions of **planning, decision making** and **control**. See also **keeping the score** and **solving problems**.

discount rate Most suitable rate of interest to be applied in calculating **present value**. Could be based on one particular type of finance but more usually is the cost of mixed sources.

discounting The process of calculating **present value** of projected cash flows.

division A part of the organisation where the manager has responsibility for generating revenues, controlling costs and producing a satisfactory return on capital invested in the division.

e-business Electronic business: the use of technology to automate business practices.

e-commerce Electronic commerce: the use of electronic media for transactions between the company and its customers or suppliers; one aspect of **e-business**.

entity An identifiable organisation for which accounting information is needed (e.g. limited liability company, public sector body). Also a legal/economic unit which exists independently of its owners.

facility-sustaining activity (in ABC**) Activity** that is not driven by making products.

favourable variance This arises when the actual cost is less than the standard cost.

feedback control Involves comparing outputs achieved against outputs desired and taking corrective action if necessary.

feedforward control Means making predictions of outputs expected at some future time and then quantifying those predictions, in management accounting terms.

financial accounting A term usually applied to external reporting by a business where that reporting is presented in financial terms.

financial statements Documents containing accounting information presented to meet the needs of users.

fixed asset An asset that is held by an enterprise for use in the production or supply of goods or services, for rental to others, or for administrative purposes on a continuing basis in the reporting entity's activities.

fixed cost One which is not affected by changes in the level of output over a defined period of time.

flexible budget A **budget** that is designed to change when the volume of activity changes, to achieve comparability.

full cost of production Direct cost plus indirect cost of production. Also calculated as **prime cost** plus **production overhead cost**.

full cost pricing See **cost-plus pricing**.

functional strategic planning Also called **operational planning**. The detailed plans by which those working within an organisation are expected to meet the short-term objectives of their working group, based on the functions that are carried out by the group.

gross Before making deductions.

ideal standard A standard cost set under the most efficient operating conditions.

impairment An asset is impaired when the business cannot expect to recover the carrying value of the intangible asset (as shown in the balance sheet), either through using it or through selling it.

imposed budget See **top-down budget**.

incremental analysis means analysing the changes in costs and revenues caused by a change in **activity**.

incremental budget Prepared by adding a percentage to the **budget** of the previous year, usually to represent the effects of inflation.

incremental costs The additional costs that arise from an activity of the organisation. To justify incurring incremental costs it is necessary to show they are exceeded by **incremental revenue**.

incremental revenue The additional revenue that arises from an **activity** of the organisation. To justify accepting incremental revenue it is necessary to show it exceeds **incremental costs**.

indirect cost Cost that is spread over a number of identifiable units of the business, such as products or services or departments, for which costs are to be determined.

indirect labour Labour costs that cannot be allocated directly to an identifiable unit for which costs are to be determined.

indirect materials Materials costs that cannot be allocated directly to an identifiable unit for which costs are to be determined.

integrated system Accounting records that serve the needs of both financial accounting and management accounting.

internal rate of return The discount rate at which the present value of the cash flows generated by the product is equal to the present value of the capital invested, so that the net present value of the project is zero.

internal reporting Reporting financial information to those users inside a business, at various levels of management, at a level of detail appropriate to the recipient.

inventory, cost of holding The costs related to storing inventory until it is sold.

inventory, cost of ordering The administrative costs related to buying and receiving materials.

investment centre A unit of the organisation in respect of which a manager is responsible for capital investment decisions as well as revenue and costs.

invoice A document sent by a supplier to a customer showing the quantity and price of goods or services supplied.

job cost The cost of a product or service provided to a customer, consisting of **direct** and **indirect** costs of production. See also **product cost**.

job-cost record Shows the costs of materials, labour and overhead incurred on a particular job.

job-costing system A system of cost accumulation where there is an identifiable **activity** for which costs may be collected. The **activity** is usually specified in terms of a job of work or a group of tasks contributing to a stage in the production or service process.

just-in-time purchasing is a system of contracts with suppliers to deliver goods as closely as possible to the time when they are required for operations. Just-in-time theory can be applied to manufacturing, management systems, etc.

keeping the score One of three functions of management accounting to support management actions of **planning**, **decision making** and **control**. See also **directing attention** and **solving problems**.

limiting factor An item which is temporarily restricted in availability.

line item budget Each line in the budget relates to a function in the organisation.

liquidity The extent to which a business has access to cash or items which can readily be exchanged for cash.

long-range planning Begins with a vision statement setting out a vision for the future direction of the organisation. From this vision the long-range objectives are set covering a period of perhaps three to five years.

management Collective term for those persons responsible for the day-to-day running of a business.

management accounting Reporting accounting information within a business, for **management** use only.

management control system A system of organisational information-seeking and gathering, accountability and feedback designed to ensure that the enterprise adapts to changes in its substantive environment and that the work behaviour of its employees is measured by reference to a set of operational sub-goals so that the discrepancy between the two can be reconciled and corrected for.

margin Frequently used as a short description of **profit**, particularly in the financial press. May be expressed as a percentage of **sales** or percentage of **revenue**.

margin of safety The difference between the **break-even sales** and the normal level of sales (measured in units or in £s of sales).

marginal costing See **variable costing**.

master budget Combination of budgeted profit and loss account, cash flow statement and balance sheet, created from detailed budgets brought together within a finance plan.

mutually exclusive Investment projects that are competing for scarce resources, where choosing one eliminates another.

net After making deductions.

net present value The net present value (of a project) is equal to the present value of the cash inflows minus the present value of the cash outflows, all discounted at the cost of capital.

non-controllable cost One which is not capable of being regulated by a manager within a defined boundary of responsibility, although it may be a cost incurred so that the responsibility may be exercised.

non-financial performance measures Measurement of performance using targets that are not available in the financial reporting system.

normal level of activity Estimated by management, taking into account the budgeted level of activity in recent periods, the activity achieved in recent periods, and the expected output from normal working conditions.

operational budgets Budgets representing the quantification of **operational planning**, including materials and labour budgets.

operational planning The detailed plans by which those working within an organisation are expected to meet the short-term objectives of their working group. See also **functional strategic planning**.

opportunity cost A measure of the benefit sacrificed when one course of action is chosen in preference to another. The measure of sacrifice is related to the best rejected course of action.

output The product or service provided by the enterprise or one of its operating units.

overhead cost Cost that cannot be identified directly with products or services. See also **indirect costs**.

overhead cost rate Overhead cost divided by a measure of activity such as production to give a cost per unit of activity.

overhead cost recovery **Absorbing** overhead cost into a unit of product so that the overhead cost will eventually be **recovered** in the sale of the product.

over-recovered fixed overhead cost The overhead **recovered** (applied) using a **predetermined overhead cost rate** is greater than the actual overhead cost of the period.

ownership interest The residual amount found by deducting all of the entity's liabilities from all of the entity's assets.

participative budget See **bottom-up budget**.

payback period The length of time required for a stream of cash inflows from a project to equal the original cash outlay.

percentage mark-up on cost adds a percentage to the total cost to calculate a selling price.

performance evaluation Requires the management accountant to decide on what to measure, plan how to report and consider the behavioural aspects.

period costs Costs that are treated as expenses in the period in which they are incurred.

planning Involves setting objectives, then establishing, evaluating and selecting strategy, tactics and actions required to achieve those objectives. One of three functions of management which are supported by management accounting. See also **control** and **decision making**.

planning programming budget system (PPBS) An output-based approach to **budgets** that focuses on programmes of action in the enterprise.

post-completion audit A review of the actual results of a project in order to compare these with the expectations contained in the project proposals.

predetermined overhead cost rate Estimated before the start of a reporting period.

prepayments Expenses paid in advance, such as rent or insurance, where a future benefit remains at the accounting date.

present value A sum of £1 receivable at the end of n years when the rate of interest is $r\%$ per annum equals $\dfrac{1}{(1 + r)^n}$ where r represents the annual rate of interest, expressed in decimal form, and n represents the time period when the cash flow will be received.

primary records Provide the first evidence that a transaction or event has taken place.

prime cost of production Equal to the total of direct materials, direct labour and other **direct costs**.

product cost Cost associated with goods or services purchased, or produced, for sale to customers. See also **job cost**.

product differentiation The business may be able to charge a higher price (a premium) for the reputation or quality of its product.

product life cycle The sequence of development of a product from initial development through maturity of sales to eventual decline in sales.

product-sustaining activities (in ABC) Activities that are performed to enable output of products but are not closely dependent on how many units are produced.

production Creating output in a business process, by using materials, labour and other resources available within the business.

production cost centre Cost centre that produces output of goods or services.

production overhead (cost) Comprises **indirect materials**, **indirect labour** and other **indirect costs** of production.

production plan Sets out quantities of resource inputs required, for use in **operational budgets**.

products See **output**.

profit The increase in the ownership interest in an entity over a specified period of time, due to the activities of the entity. The word 'profit' needs other words added to it, to give it a specific meaning.

profit centre A unit of the organisation in respect of which a manager is responsible for **revenue** as well as **costs**.

profit margin Profit as a percentage of **sales**.

profitability The ability to generate profit, based on a comparative measure e.g. profit as a percentage of sales; profit per month; profit related to capital investment.

profitability index The **present value** of cash flows (discounted at the **cost of capital**) divided by the present value of the investment intended to produce those cash flows.

profit–volume chart A graph showing on the horizontal axis the volume, measured by activity level in £s of sales, and on the vertical axis the profit at that activity level.

profit/volume ratio **Contribution** as a percentage of **sales** value.

recovered, recovery Costs are recovered by charging a selling price that covers **costs** and makes a **profit**.

relevant costs Those future costs which will be affected by a decision to be taken. Non-relevant costs will not be affected by the decision.

relevant revenues Those future revenues which will be affected by a decision to be taken. Non-relevant revenues will not be affected by the decision.

re-order level The point at which the buying department places its order for replacement materials.

reporting period The period in respect of which the accounting information is prepared. In management accounting the period may be as frequent as the management chooses – weekly, monthly, quarterly and annual reporting are all used.

residual value The estimated amount that an entity would currently obtain from disposal of an **asset**, after deducting the estimated costs of disposal, if the asset were already of the age and condition expected at the end of its useful life.

responsibility centre An area of responsibility which is controlled by an individual. It might be a cost centre, a profit centre or an investment centre.

retention of title A supplier provides goods to a customer but retains ownership (title) the right to claim the goods if they are not paid for.

return (in relation to investment) The reward earned for investing money in a business. Return may appear in the form of regular cash payments (dividends) to the investor, or in a growth in the value of the amount invested.

revenue Income arising in the course of an entity's ordinary activities.

sales Delivering goods or services to a customer, either for cash or on credit terms.

sales budget Budget of sales volumes and prices for a future period.

scrap Unwanted material sold for disposal, usually at a very low price in relation to its original cost.

semi-variable cost One which is partly fixed and partly varies with changes in the level of **activity**, over a defined period of time.

sensitivity analysis Asks 'what . . . if' questions such as 'What will be the change in profit if the selling price decreases by 1%?' or 'What will be the change in profit if the cost increases by 1%?'

service cost centre **Cost centre** that provides services to other **cost centres** within the organisation.

short-term finance Money lent to a business for a short period of time, usually repayable on demand and also repayable at the choice of the business if surplus to requirements.

single period capital rationing Capital rationing in one period only during the life of a project (usually in the first period).

solving problems One of three functions of management accounting to support management actions of **planning**, **decision making** and **control**. See also **directing attention** and **keeping the score**.

standard cost Target cost which should be attained under specified operating conditions. Expressed in cost per unit.

standard hour The amount of work achievable, at standard efficiency levels, in one hour.

statement (from supplier) A document sent by a supplier to a customer at the end of each month summarising all **invoices** awaiting payment by the customer.

step cost A fixed cost which increases in steps over a period of several years.

strategic management accounting The provision and analysis of financial information on the firm's product markets and competitors' costs and cost structures and the monitoring of the enterprise's strategies and those of its competitors in these markets over a number of periods.

strategic planning Involves preparing, evaluating and selecting *strategies* to achieve objectives of a long-term plan of action.

strategy A plan setting out the actions and resources needed to achieve a stated objective of the long-term plan.

sunk cost Cost that has been incurred or committed prior to a decision point. It is not relevant to subsequent decisions.

time value of money The name given to the idea that £1 invested today will grow with interest rates over time (e.g. £1 become £1.10 in one year's time at a rate of 10%).

top-down budget Set by management without inviting those who will implement the budget to participate in the process of setting the budget. Also called an **imposed budget**.

total cost Calculated as **variable cost** plus **fixed cost**; or **direct cost** plus **indirect cost**; or **product cost** plus **period cost**.

total product cost Comprises **prime cost** plus **production overhead cost**.

trade creditors Persons (suppliers) who supply goods or services to a business in the normal course of trade and allow a period of credit before payment must be made.

trade debtors Persons (customers) who buy goods or services from a business in the normal course of trade and take a period of credit before paying what they owe.

traditional approach to overhead costs. **Allocate** and **apportion** to cost centres and then **absorb** into products which pass through those **cost centres**.

transfer price The price charged between two divisions of an organisation in transferring goods and services between each other.

turnover The **sales** of a business or other form of **revenue** from operations of the business.

unavoidable cost A cost that is *not* eliminated by taking a particular action.

under-recovered fixed overhead cost The overhead **recovered** (applied) using a **predetermined overhead cost rate** is less than the actual overhead cost of the period.

unit activity (in ABC) An **activity** that is performed each time a product is produced.

unit cost The **cost** of one unit of **output**.

value chain A way of describing and analysing the sequence of activities that bring on product/service from initial stage of production to final stage of delivery.

variable cost One which varies directly with changes in the level of **output**, over a defined period of time.

variable costing Only **variable costs** of production are absorbed into products and the unsold inventory is valued at variable cost of production. **Fixed costs** of production are treated as a cost of the period in which they are incurred.

variance The difference between a planned, **budgeted** or **standard cost** and the actual cost incurred. An adverse variance arises when the actual cost is greater than the standard cost. A favourable variance arises when the actual cost is less than the standard cost.

variance analysis Quantitative breakdown of cost **variance** into main causes, e.g. price and usage.

waste Any materials that have no value.

working capital Finance provided to support the short-term **assets** of the business (inventory and **debtors**) to the extent that these are not financed by short term creditors. It is calculated as **current assets** minus **current liabilities**.

work in progress A product or service that is partly completed.

zero-based budget (ZBB) Budget preparation starts with a blank sheet of paper and justifies every item entered.

Information extracted from annual report of Safe and Sure Group plc, used throughout Financial Accounting

Safe and Sure Group plc
Group statement of financial position (balance sheet)
at 31 December

	Notes	Year 7 £m	Year 6 £m
Non-current assets			
Property, plant and equipment	1	1,375	1,219
Intangible assets	2	2,603	2,376
Investments	3	28	20
Taxation recoverable	4	59	49
Total non-current assets		4,065	3,664
Current assets			
Inventories (stocks)	5	266	243
Amounts receivable (debtors)	6	1,469	1,347
Six-month deposits		20	–
Cash and cash equivalents		1,053	905
Total current assets		2,808	2,495
Total assets		6,873	6,159
Current liabilities			
Amounts payable (creditors)	7	(1,598)	(1,575)
Bank overdraft	8	(401)	(626)
Total current liabilities		(1,999)	(2,201)
Non-current liabilities			
Amounts payable (creditors)	9	(27)	(26)
Bank and other borrowings	10	(2)	(6)
Provisions	11	(202)	(222)
Total non-current liabilities		(231)	(254)
Total liabilities		(2,230)	(2,455)
Net assets		4,643	3,704
Capital and reserves			
Called-up share capital	12	196	195
Share premium account	13	85	55
Revaluation reserve	14	46	46
Retained earnings	15	4,316	3,408
Equity holders' funds		4,643	3,704

Safe and Sure Group plc
Group income statement (profit and loss account)
for the year ended 31 December Year 7

	Notes	Year 7 £m	Year 6 £m
Continuing operations			
Revenue	16	7,146	5,893
Cost of sales	16	(4,910)	(4,063)
Gross profit		2,236	1,830
Distribution costs		(22)	(25)
Administrative expenses	17	(262)	(265)
Profit from operations		1,952	1,540
Interest receivable (net)	18	23	30
Profit before tax	19	1,975	1,570
Tax	20	(622)	(524)
Profit for the period from continuing operations		1,353	1,046
Discontinued operations			
Loss for the period from discontinued operations	21	(205)	(100)
Profit for the period attributable to equity holders		1,148	946

Safe and Sure plc
Group statement of other comprehensive income
for the year ended 31 December Year 7

	Year 7 £m	Year 6 £m
Profit for the period	1,148	946
Other comprehensive income:		
Exchange rate adjustments	55	(60)
Total comprehensive income for the year	1,203	886
Earnings per share (Note 22)	11.74	9.71

Safe and Sure plc
Group statement of changes in equity for the year ended 31 December Year 7

	Share capital	Share premium	Revaluation reserve	Retained earnings (including exchange rate adjustments)	Total
	£m	£m	£m	£m	£m
Balance at 1 Jan Year 6	194	36	46	2,766	3,042
Total comprehensive income				886	886
Transactions with owners:					
Share capital issued	1	19			20
Less dividend	—	—	—	(244)	(244)
Balance at 1 Jan Year 7	195	55	46	3,408	3,704
Total comprehensive income				1,203	1,203
Transactions with owners:					
Share capital issued	1	30			31
Less dividend	—	—	—	(295)	(295)
Balance at 31 Dec Year 7	196	85	46	4,316	4,643

Safe and Sure Group plc
Group statement of cash flows for the year ended 31 December Year 7

	Notes	Year 7 £m	Year 6 £m
Cash flows from operating activities			
Cash generated from operations	23	1,967	1,635
Interest paid		(31)	(24)
UK corporation tax paid		(201)	(183)
Overseas tax paid		(305)	(265)
Net cash from operating activities		**1,430**	**1,163**
Cash flows from investing activities			
Purchase of property, plant and equipment		(600)	(475)
Sale of property, plant and equipment		120	101
Purchase of companies and businesses		(277)	(901)
Sale of a company		31	–
Movement in short-term deposits		(307)	363
Interest received		50	59
Net cash used in investing activities		**(983)**	**(853)**
Cash flows from financing activities			
Issue of ordinary share capital		31	20
Dividends paid to equity holders		(295)	(244)
Net loan movement (excluding overdraft)		162	(240)
Net cash used in financing activities		**(102)**	**(464)**
Net increase/(decrease) in cash and cash equivalents*		**345**	**(154)**
Cash and cash equivalents at the beginning of the year		279	453
Exchange adjustments		28	(20)
Cash and cash equivalents at the end of the year	28	652	279

*Cash on demand and deposits of maturity less than 3 months, net of overdrafts.

Accounting policies (extracts)

Intangible non-current (fixed) assets

Purchased goodwill is calculated as the difference between the fair value of the consideration paid for an acquired entity and the aggregate of the fair values of that entity's identifiable assets and liabilities. An impairment review has been undertaken at the balance sheet date.

Freehold and leasehold property

Freehold and leasehold land and buildings are stated either at cost (Security and Cleaning) or at their revalued amounts less depreciation (Disposal and Recycling). Full revaluations are made at five-year intervals with interim valuations in the intervening years, the most recent full revaluation being in Year 5.

Provision for depreciation of freehold land and buildings is made at the annual rate of 1% of cost or the revalued amounts. Leasehold land and buildings are amortised in equal annual instalments over the periods of the leases subject to a minimum annual provision of 1% of cost or the revalued amounts. When properties are sold the difference between sales proceeds and net book value is dealt with in the income statement (profit and loss account).

Plant and equipment

Plant and equipment are stated at cost less depreciation. Provision for depreciation is made mainly in equal annual instalments over the estimated useful lives of the assets as follows:

4 to 5 years   vehicles
5 to 10 years   plant, machinery and equipment

Inventories (stocks and work in progress)

Inventories (stocks and work in progress) are stated at the lower of cost and net realisable value, using the first in first out principle. Cost includes all direct expenditure and related overheads incurred in bringing the inventories to their present condition and location.

Deferred tax

The provision for deferred tax recognises a future liability arising from past transactions and events. Tax legislation allows the company to defer settlement of the liability for several years.

Warranties

Some service work is carried out under warranty. The cost of claims under warranty is charged against the profit and loss account of the year in which the claims are settled.

Deferred consideration

For acquisitions involving deferred consideration, estimated deferred payments are accrued in the balance sheet. Interest due to vendors on deferred payments is charged to the profit and loss account as it accrues.

Notes to accounts

Note 1 Property, plant and equipment

	Land and buildings £m	Plant and equipment £m	Vehicles £m	Total £m
Cost or valuation				
At 1 January Year 7	283	964	1,048	2,295
Additions at cost	39	185	378	602
On acquisitions	3	10	7	20
Disposals	(6)	(31)	(247)	(284)
At 31 December Year 7	319	1,128	1,186	2,633
Aggregate depreciation				
At 1 January Year 7	22	588	466	1,076
Depreciation for the year	5	135	192	332
On acquisitions	1	7	6	14
Disposals	(2)	(28)	(134)	(164)
At 31 December Year 7	26	702	530	1,258
Net book value at 31 December Year 7	293	426	656	1,375
Net book value at 31 December Year 6	261	376	582	1,219

Analysis of land and buildings at cost or valuation

	Year 7 £m	Year 6 £m
At cost	104	71
At valuation	215	212
	319	283

The group's freehold and long-term leasehold properties in the Disposal and Recycling division were revalued during Year 5 by independent valuers. Valuations were made on the basis of the market value for existing use. The book values of the properties were adjusted to the revaluations and the resultant net surplus was credited to the revaluation reserve.

Analysis of net book value of land and buildings

	Year 7 £m	Year 6 £m
Freehold	245	210
Leasehold:		
Over 50 years unexpired	21	24
Under 50 years unexpired	27	27
	293	261

If the revalued assets were stated on the historical cost basis the amounts would be:

	Year 7 £m	Year 6 £m
Land and buildings at cost	157	145
Aggregate depreciation	(22)	(19)
	135	126

Note 2 Intangible non-current assets

	Year 7 £m	Year 6 £m
Goodwill at 1 January	2,376	1,391
Additions in year	243	985
Reduction in year	(16)	–
Goodwill at 31 December	2,603	2,376

The reduction of £16m results from the annual impairment review.

Note 3

Relates to investments in subsidiary companies and is not reproduced here.

Note 4

Explains the nature of taxation recoverable after more than 12 months from the balance sheet date. The detail is not reproduced here.

Note 5 Inventories (stocks)

	Year 7 £m	Year 6 £m
Raw materials	62	54
Work in progress	19	10
Finished products	185	179
	266	243

The value of inventories of finished products is stated after impairment of £6m (Year 6 – £4m), due to obsolescence.

Note 6 Amounts receivable (debtors)

	Year 7 £m	Year 6 £m
Trade receivables (trade debtors)	1,333	1,218
Less: provision for impairment of receivables	(52)	(48)
Trade receivables, net	1,281	1,170
Other receivables (debtors)	109	98
Prepayments and accrued income	79	79
	1,469	1,347

The ageing of the Group's year-end overdue receivables, against which no provision has been made, is as follows:

	Year 7 £m	Year 6 £m
Not impaired		
Less than 3 months	194	121
3 to 6 months	3	3
Over 6 months	1	–
	198	124

The individually impaired receivables relate to customers in unexpectedly difficult circumstances. The overdue receivables against which no provision has been made relate to a number of customers for whom there is no recent history of default and no other indication that settlement will not be forthcoming.

The carrying amounts of the Group's receivables are denominated in the following currencies:

	Year 7 £m	Year 6 £m
Sterling	808	794
US Dollar	336	291
Euro	272	255
Other	53	34
	1,469	1,374

Movements in the Group's provision for impairment of trade receivables are as follows:

	Year 7 £m	Year 6 £m
At 1 January	48	49
(Released)/charged to income statement	3	(1)
Net write off of uncollectible receivables	1	–
At 31 December	52	48

Amounts charged to the income statement are included within administrative expenses. The other classes of receivables do not contain impaired assets.

Note 7 Current liabilities: amounts payable

	Year 7	Year 6
	£m	£m
Deferred consideration on acquisition	11	43
Trade payables (trade creditors)	236	204
Corporation tax	315	265
Other tax and social security payable	245	212
Other payables (creditors)	307	238
Accruals and deferred income	484	613
	1,598	1,575

Trade payables (trade creditors) comprise amounts outstanding for trade purchases. The average credit period taken for trade purchases is 27 days. Most suppliers charge no interest on the trade payables for the first 30 days from the date of the invoice. Thereafter, interest is charged on the outstanding balances at various interest rates. The Group has financial risk management policies in place to ensure that all payables are paid within the agreed credit terms.

Note 8 Bank borrowings: current liabilities

	Year 7	Year 6
	£m	£m
Bank overdrafts due on demand:	401	626

Interest on overdrafts is payable at normal commercial rates appropriate to the country where the borrowing is made.

Note 9 Non-current liabilities: payables (creditors)

	Year 7	Year 6
	£m	£m
Deferred consideration on acquisition	6	–
Other payables (creditors)	21	26
	27	26

Note 10 Non-current liabilities: bank and other borrowings

	Year 7	Year 6
	£m	£m
Secured loans	–	3
Unsecured loans	2	3
	2	6
Loans are repayable by instalments:		
Between one and two years	1	2
Between two and five years	1	4
	2	6

Interest on long-term loans, which are denominated in a number of currencies, is payable at normal commercial rates appropriate to the country in which the borrowing is made. The last repayment falls due in Year 11.

Note 11 Provisions

	Year 7 £m	Year 6 £m
Provisions for treating contaminated site:		
At 1 January	142	145
Utilised in the year	(22)	(3)
At 31 December	120	142
Provisions for restructuring costs:		
At 1 January	42	–
Created in year	10	43
Utilised in year	(10)	(1)
At 31 December	42	42
Provision for deferred tax:		
At 1 January	38	27
Transfer to income statement	5	12
Other movements	(3)	(1)
At 31 December	40	38
Total provision	202	222

Note 12 Share capital

	Year 7 £m	Year 6 £m
Ordinary shares of 2 pence each		
Authorised: 10,500,000,000 shares		
(Year 6: 10,000,000,000)	210	200
Issued and fully paid: 9,781,474,870 shares	196	195

Certain senior executives hold options to subscribe for shares in the company at prices ranging from 33.40p to 244.33p under schemes approved by equity holders at various dates. Options on 34,795,070 shares were exercised during Year 7 and 669,700 options lapsed. The number of shares subject to options, the years in which they were purchased and the years in which they will expire are:

Options granted	Exercisable	Option price (pence)	Numbers
	Year 8	33.40	137,500
All granted 10	Year 9	53.55	1,100,000
years before	Year 10	75.42	5,425,000
exercisable	Year 11	100.22	14,290,000
	Year 12	120.33	28,266,000
	Year 13/14	150.45	35,399,420
	Year 15	195.20	36,909,500
	Year 16	201.50	22,792,700
	Year 17	244.33	32,793,630
			177,113,750

Note 13 Share premium account

	Year 7 £m	Year 6 £m
At 1 January	55	36
Premium on shares issued during the year under the share option schemes	30	19
At 31 December	85	55

Note 14 Revaluation reserve

	Year 7 £m	Year 6 £m
At 1 January	46	46
At 31 December	46	46

Note 15 Retained earnings

	Year 7 £m	Year 6 £m
At 1 January	3,408	2,766
Exchange adjustments	55	(60)
Profit for the year	1,148	946
Dividend paid	(295)	(244)
At 31 December	4,316	3,408

Note 16 Operating segments

For the purposes of reporting to the chief operating decision maker, the group is currently organised into two operating divisions: (1) disposal and recycling, (2) security and cleaning. Disposal and recycling includes all aspects of collection and safe disposal of industrial and commercial waste products. Security and cleaning is undertaken by renewable annual contract, predominantly for hospitals, other healthcare premises and local government organisations.

The group's disposal and recycling operation in North America was discontinued with effect from 30 April Year 7.

Business sector analysis

	Disposal and recycling		Security and cleaning		Total	
	Year 7 £m	Year 6 £m	Year 7 £m	Year 6 £m	Year 7 £m	Year 6 £m
REVENUES (all from external customers)						
Continuing	5,089	4,550	2,057	1,343	7,146	5,893
Discontinued	200	110			200	110
Total revenues	5,289	4,660	2,057	1,343	7,346	6,003
Operating profit (loss) by service						
Continuing	1,766	1,396	186	144	1,952	1,540
Discontinued	(205)	(100)			(205)	(100)
Total operating profit					1,747	1,440
Interest receivable (net)					23	30
Profit before tax					1,770	1,470
Taxation					(622)	(524)
Profit for the period					1,148	946

All costs of head office operations are allocated to divisions on an activity costing basis. The company does not allocate interest receivable or taxation paid to reportable segments.

Depreciation and amortisation included in the income statement are as follows:

	Disposal and recycling		Security and cleaning		Total	
	Year 7 £m	Year 6 £m	Year 7 £m	Year 6 £m	Year 7 £m	Year 6 £m
Depreciation	302	251	30	39	332	290
Impairment of goodwill	16	–	–	–	16	–

The segment assets and liabilities at the end of Years 7 and 6 are as follows:

	Disposal and recycling		Security and cleaning		Unallocated		Total	
	Year 7 £m	Year 6 £m	Year 7 £m	Year 6 £m	Year 7 £m	Year 6 £m	Year 7 £m	Year 6 £m
Total assets	4,985	3,709	687	1,327	1,201	1,123	6,873	6,159
Total liabilities	1,317	1,479	613	855	300	121	2,230	2,455
Expenditure	500	450	102	25	–	–	602	475

Information about geographical areas

The group's two business segments operate in four main geographical areas, even though they are managed on a worldwide basis. In the following analysis, revenue is based on the country in which the order is received. It would not be materially different if based on the country in which the customer is located. Non-current assets are allocated based on where the assets are located.

	Revenues from external customers		Non-current assets	
	Year 7 £m	Year 6 £m	Year 7 £m	Year 6 £m
CONTINUING				
United Kingdom	3,234	2,467	1,742	1,487
Continental Europe	1,643	1,535	903	930
North America	1,045	801	859	492
Asia Pacific & Africa	1,224	1,090	561	750
	7,146	5,893	4,065	3,659
DISCONTINUED				
North America	200	110	–	5
Total	7,346	6,003	4,065	3,664

Notes 17–20

Contain supporting details for the profit and loss account and are not reproduced here.

Note 21 Discontinued operations

On 31 March Year 7, the Group entered into a sale agreement to dispose of Carers Inc., its recycling business in North America. The purpose of the disposal was to prevent further loss-making activity. The disposal was completed on 30 April Year 7, on which date control of Carers Inc. passed to the acquirer.

The results of the discontinued operations which have been included in the consolidated income statement, were as follows:

	Year 7 £m	Year 6 £m
Revenue	200	110
Expenses	(405)	(210)
Loss attributable to discontinued operations	(205)	(100)

Note 22

Contains supporting details for earnings per share and is not reproduced here.

Note 23 Cash flow from operating activities

Reconciliation of operating profit to net cash flow from operating activities

	Year 7 £m	Year 6 £m
Profit before tax from continuing operations	1,952	1,540
Loss from discontinued operations	(205)	(100)
Profit from operations	1,747	1,440
Depreciation charge	332	301
Increase in inventories (stocks)*	(19)	(11)
Increase in trade receivables (debtors)*	(74)	(53)
Decrease in trade payables (creditors)*	(04)	(36)
Net cash inflow from continuing activities	1,982	1,641
Cash outflow in respect of discontinued item	(15)	(6)
Net cash inflow from operating activities	1,967	1,635

Note: It is not possible to reconcile these figures with the balance sheet information in the Statement of Financial Position because of the effect of acquisitions during the year.

Note 24 Information on acquisitions (extract)

The group purchased 20 companies and businesses during the year for a total consideration of £25m. The adjustments required to the balance sheet figures of companies and businesses acquired, in order to present the net assets at fair value, are shown below:

	£m
Net assets of subsidiaries acquired, as shown in their balance sheets	41
Adjustments made by directors of Safe and Sure plc	(34)
Fair value of net assets acquired (**a**)	07
Cash paid for subsidiaries (**b**)	250
Goodwill (**b** – **a**)	243

From the dates of acquisition to 31 December Year 7, the acquisitions contributed £135m to revenue, £27m to profit before interest and £22m to profit after interest.

If the acquisitions had been completed on the first day of the financial year, they would have contributed £300m to group revenues for the year and £5m to group profit attributable to equity holders of the parent.

Notes 25–27

Contain supporting detail for the cash flow statement and are not reproduced here.

Note 28 Cash and cash equivalents

Reconciliation of cash flow for the year to the balance sheet items

	Year 7 £m	Year 6 £m
Balance sheet items		
Cash and cash equivalents	1,053	905
Bank overdraft	(401)	(626)
Net	652	279

Notes 29–32

Contain various other items of information required by company law and are not reproduced here.

Note 33 Contingent liabilities

The company has guaranteed bank and other borrowings of subsidiaries amounting to £30m (Year 6: £152m). The group has commitments, amounting to approximately £419m (Year 6: £285m), under forward exchange contracts entered into in the ordinary course of business.

Certain subsidiaries have given warranties for service work. These are explained in the statement on accounting policies. There are contingent liabilities in respect of litigation. None of the actions is expected to give rise to any material loss.

Note 34

Contains commitments for capital expenditure and is not reproduced here.

Five-year summary
(Continuing and discontinued operations combined)

	Year 3	Year 4	Year 5	Year 6	Year 7
	£m	£m	£m	£m	£m
Group revenue	3,091	3,890	4,741	6,003	7,346
Group profit before tax	744	904	1,145	1,470	1,770
Tax	(272)	(339)	(443)	(524)	(622)
Group profit after tax	472	565	702	946	1,148
Earnings per share	4.88p	6.23p	8.02p	9.71p	11.74p
Dividends per share	1.32p	1.69p	2.17p	2.50p	3.02p
	£m	£m	£m	£m	£m
Share capital	194	194	194	195	196
Reserves	1,608	1,953	2,848	3,509	4,447
Total equity	1,802	2,147	3,042	3,704	4,643

Strategic report
The following are extracts from the company's strategic report.

Our business
We operate our business through two business divisions: Disposal and Recycling; Security and Cleaning.

Disposal and Recycling includes all aspects of collection and safe disposal of industrial and commercial waste products. During Year 7 all our operational landfill sites gained certification to the international environment management standard. Organic waste deposited in landfill sites degrades naturally and gives off a gas rich in methane which has to be controlled for environmental reasons. However, landfill sites can also be a cheap, clean and highly efficient source of renewable energy. Through strategic long-term contracts, we are generating 64 MW of electricity each year from landfill waste to energy schemes. New waste transfer and recycling centres in Germany and France were added to the Group's network during Year 7.

Security and Cleaning is undertaken by renewable annual contract, predominantly for hospitals, other healthcare premises and local government organisations. During Year 7, we acquired a security company in the UK and some smaller operations in Switzerland and Spain. Improved margins in contract cleaning reflected continued demands for improved hygiene standards and our introduction of new techniques to meet this need.

Strategy
Our ultimate objective is to achieve for our equity holders a high rate of growth in earnings and dividends per share each year. Our strategies are to provide customers with the highest standards of service and to maintain quality of service as we enter new fields. We also operate a prudent financial policy of managing our businesses to generate a strong operating cash flow.

Group results
Group revenue from continuing operations in Year 7 increased by 21.3% to £7,146m, while continuing profits before tax increased by 25.8% to £1,975m. Earnings per share increased by 20.9% to 11.74 pence. These results show the benefits of our geographic diversification across the major economies of the world. We have achieved excellent growth in the UK, together with continued good growth in North America. Growth in Europe continued to be constrained by depressed economies, while excellent results in Australia were held back by disappointing growth in South East Asia. Segmental results are set out in detail in Note 16 to the financial statements. In Disposal and Recycling, revenue improved by 13.4% and profits improved by 20.4%. Revenue in Security and Cleaning improved by 53.2% and profits improved by 29.2%.

Profits

Operating profits, including the effect of discontinued operations, rose to £1,747m in Year 7, up from £1,440m in Year 6. Interest income fell £7m to £23m in Year 7, as a result of the cash spent on acquisitions towards the end of Year 6. At constant average Year 6 exchange rates, the Year 7 profit before tax, including the effect of discontinued operations, would have been £6m higher at £1,776m, an increase of 20.8% over the reported Year 6 figures.

Cash flow

The Group's businesses are structured to utilise as little fixed and working capital as is consistent with the profit and earnings growth objective in order to produce a high cash flow. The impact of working capital on cash flow was held to an increase in Year 7 of £97m (Year 6: £100m). A net cash flow of £1,967m was generated from operating activities. That was boosted by other amounts of cash from interest received. After paying interest and tax, the Group had £1,430m remaining. Fixed assets required £480m after allowing for the proceeds of selling some of our vehicle fleet in the routine replacement programme. That left £950m from which £246m was required to pay for acquisitions. The remaining £704m covered dividends of £295m leaving £409m. We received £50m interest on investments and £31m in ordinary share capital to give a net inflow of liquid funds in the year of £490m. Out of that amount, short-term deposits have increased by £145m, leaving an increase in cash of £345m.

Foreign currency

We borrowed £352m of foreign currency bank borrowings to fund overseas acquisitions. The main borrowings were £268m in US dollars and £84m in yen (to fund our Japanese associate investment). The borrowings are mainly from banks on a short-term basis with a maturity of up to one year. We have fixed the interest rate on $200m of the US dollar loans through to November Year 8 at an overall cost of 4.5%.

All material foreign currency transactions are matched back into the currency of the Group company undertaking the transaction. It is not the Group's current practice to hedge the translation of overseas profits or assets back into sterling, although overseas acquisitions may be financed by foreign currency borrowings.

Capital expenditure

The major items of capital expenditure are vehicles, equipment used on customers' premises and office equipment, particularly computers. Disposals during the year were mainly of vehicles being replaced on a rolling programme.

Taxation

The overall Group taxation charge comprises tax at 30% on UK profits and an average rate of 38% on overseas profits, reflecting the underlying rates in the various countries in which the Group operates.

Key performance indicators

The Board reviews the following indicators:

Financial Performance Indicators

[Not included in extract]

Non Financial Performance Indicators

	Year 6	Year 7
CO_2 emissions[i]	119	108
Water consumption[ii]	13	12
Colleague engagement	70%	70%
Colleague enablement	68%	68%
Sales colleague retention	64%	64%
Service colleague retention	74%	76%
Customer satisfaction[iii]	n/a	19%
State of service	98%	97%
Number of lost time accidents[iv]	1.53	1.72

(i) Total CO_2 emissions in tonnes per £m turnover reported on a total company basis.

(ii) Water consumed – litres per kilogramme of textiles processed in continental European plants.

(iii) Customer satisfaction score, represents the net balance of those customers promoting our service compared with those neutral or not promoting.

(iv) LTA equals accidents per 100,000 hours worked.

Future development and performance

Once again, in Year 7 Safe and Sure met its declared objective of increasing its pre-tax profits and earnings per share by at least 20% per annum. The board expects a return to much better growth in Europe and a substantially improved performance in the USA to underpin good Group growth for the year.

Principal risks and uncertainties

The group operates through a wide range of activities across many countries. The principal risks and uncertainties identified by the directors relate to the market conditions in which we operate and to management's capability to deliver the large number of change programmes and recovery strategies currently underway across the businesses.

The principal risks we face may be summarised as: (1) a weakening of the economies in which we operate; and (2) the number, scope, complexity and interdependencies of many initiatives – risk of management stretch and overlapping priorities.

We outline below the principal risks we have identified and the actions we take to mitigate these risks.

Description of risk	Management action
Operating costs In the Disposal and Recycling Division across France, Belgium and Germany we have experienced rising wages and increasing employment costs such as taxes. Such costs are determined by the governments of those countries and not under our own control.	Actions to mitigate these risks include passing on price increases to customers to counter cost inflation and pricing contracts appropriately to remain competitive.
State of the economy The group is exposed to the economic environments in more than 20 countries across the world. Whilst the UK represents a large proportion of the group's businesses our international diversification means that our economic and geopolitical risks are spread widely. Current unrest in two African countries has caused us to suspend security and cleaning contracts.	Divisional managers monitor economic activity in their respective geographical areas. In relation to areas of unrest, we take advice from the Foreign and Commonwealth Office, having particular regard to the safety of personnel and long-term security of contracts.
Market demand and competition In France, Belgium and the Netherlands we experienced competitive pricing pressure in the Disposal and Recycling Division. This resulted in a number of contract losses earlier in the year and also affected the division's ability to win new contracts.	In those circumstances where our competitors are engaging in aggressive price discounting and where we believe that to offer similar prices would compromise service levels, our only mitigating course of action is to ensure that contract losses do not directly result from poor customer care, service or relationships. Further mitigating actions include improving the competitiveness of the business through significant restructuring programmes in Belgium and France and through extensive cost-savings programmes across all businesses.
Regulation The Disposal and Recycling Division is vulnerable to increased costs due to changing national regulations regarding hazardous waste and safe disposal in the countries where we operate.	We monitor national initiatives on regulation of disposal and recycling in the countries where we operate. Anticipated increased costs are built into contract negotiations. We also include flexible clauses in contracts to reflect the impact of regulatory change.

Description of risk	Management action
Currency and interest rates The group is exposed to market risk primarily related to foreign exchange and interest rate risk. The group's objective is to reduce, where it is deemed appropriate to do so, fluctuations in earnings and cash flows associated with changes in interest rates, foreign currency rates and the exposure of certain net investments in foreign subsidiaries.	Management actively monitors these exposures and the group enters into currency and interest rate swaps, forward rate agreements and forward foreign exchange contracts to manage the volatility relating to these. The majority of sales and purchases are local, limiting transaction risk. The policy is therefore to accept the risk, except where significant acquisitions or disposals are to be undertaken, where the transaction may be hedged to give certainty of pricing.
People The company's current management team is implementing a five-year recovery plan based on operational excellence which itself is built around five key strategies, namely: to deliver outstanding customer service, to develop capability, to drive operational excellence, to operate at lowest cost and to generate profitable growth. The principal risk for the group is that management has the capacity and capability to deliver the key strategies.	Within each of the five key strategies there are a large number of improvement initiatives which individually are managed through a proper risk control process. The Nominations Committee scrutinises all appointments to senior management posts, The Remuneration Committee sets strict targets for performance rewards.

Directors' report (extract)

The directors recommend a final dividend of 3.54 pence per ordinary share to be paid to shareholders on the register on 31 March Year 8. The proposed dividend for Year 8 of 3.02 pence per share was paid on 31 March Year 7. There is no interim dividend in either Year 6 or Year 7.

Solutions to numerical and technical questions in Financial Accounting

Note that solutions are provided only for numerical and technical material since other matters are covered either in the book or in the further reading indicated.

Chapter 1 has no solutions given in this Appendix because there are no numerical questions.

Chapter 2

Application **B2.1**

Classify each of the items in the following list as: asset; liability; neither an asset nor a liability:

Cash at bank	Asset
Loan from the bank	Liability
Letter from the bank promising an overdraft facility at any time in the next three months	Neither
Trade debtor (a customer who has promised to pay later)	Asset
Trade debtor (a customer who has promised to pay later but has apparently disappeared without leaving a forwarding address)	Neither
Supplier of goods who has not yet received payment from the business	Liability
Inventory (stock) of finished goods (fashion clothing stored ahead of the spring sales)	Asset
Inventory (stock) of finished goods (fashion clothing left over after the spring sales)	Neither, unless value remains
Investment in shares of another company where the share price is rising	Asset
Investment in shares of another company where the share price is falling	Asset while there is still some benefit expected
Lender of five-year loan to the business	Liability
Customer to whom the business has offered a 12-month warranty to repair goods free of charge	Liability
A motor vehicle owned by the business	Asset
A motor vehicle rented by the business for one year	Neither
An office building owned by the business	Asset
An office building rented by the business on a 99-year lease, with 60 years' lease period remaining	Asset, but may not be shown

B2.2

Yes to all, except the rented building where risks and benefits are mainly for the owners, not the users.

B2.3

A letter from the owner of the business, addressed to the bank manager, promising to guarantee the bank overdraft of the business.	There is no past event. The guarantee will only be called upon in future if the business cannot repay the loan.
A list of the customers of the business.	Has benefit for the future but no event, also not measurable with reliability.
An order received from a customer.	Future benefit expected but insufficient evidence that it will be obtained.
The benefit of employing a development engineer with a high level of 'know-how' specifically relevant to the business.	Future benefit exists but not measurable with sufficient reliability.
Money spent on an advertising campaign to boost sales.	Future benefit exists but not measurable with sufficient reliability.
Structural repairs to a building.	Repairs put right the problems of the past – do not create future benefits.

Chapter 3

Application **B3.1**

Sunshine Wholesale Traders
Statement of financial position (balance sheet) at 30 June Year 2

	£
Non-current (fixed) assets	
Fleet of delivery vehicles	35,880
Furniture and fittings	18,800
Total fixed assets	54,680
Current assets	
Receivables (debtors)	34,000
Bank deposit	19,000
Total current assets	53,000
Total assets	107,680
Current liabilities	
Trade payables (trade creditors)	(8,300)
Net assets	99,380
Ownership interest at the start of the year	56,000
Profit of the year	43,380
Ownership interest at end of year	99,380

Note that ownership interest at the start of the year is entered as the missing item.

Sunshine Wholesale Traders
Income statement (profit and loss account) for the year ended 30 June Year 2

	£	£
Revenues		
Sales		294,500
Expenses		
Cost of goods sold		(188,520)
Gross profit		105,980
Wages and salaries	(46,000)	
Transport costs	(14,200)	
Administration costs	(1,300)	
Depreciation	(1,100)	
Total expenses		(62,600)
Net profit of the year		43,380

B3.2

Statement of financial position (balance sheet) at . . .

	£
Non-current (fixed) assets	
Land and buildings	95,000
Vehicles	8,000
Total non-current assets	103,000
Current assets	
Inventory (stock) of goods for resale	35,000
Cash at bank	9,000
Total current assets	44,000
Total assets	147,000
Current liabilities	
Trade payables (trade creditors)	(43,000)
Wages due	(2,000)
	(45,000)
Liabilities due after one year	(20,000)
Total liabilities	65,000
Net assets	82,000
Ownership interest	82,000

(a) Decrease liability to employees £2,000, decrease asset of cash £2,000.
(b) Decrease ownership interest by £8,750, decrease asset of inventory (stock) by £8,750.
(c) Increase asset of inventory (stock) £5,000, increase liability of trade creditors £5,000.

Test your understanding S3.1
(a) Debit liability to employees £2,000, credit asset of cash £2,000.
(b) Debit ownership interest £8,750, credit asset of inventory (stock) £8,750.
(c) Debit asset of inventory (stock) £5,000, credit liability of trade creditors £5,000.

Chapter 4

Application B4.1
This requires a narrative answer based on sections 4.5.1, 4.5.3 and 4.5.5.

B4.2
This requires a narrative answer based on section 4.3. The more difficult aspect of this question is explaining how each convention affects current accounting practice. One example of each would be:

- *Going concern:* In historical cost accounting the fixed assets of an enterprise are recorded in the statement of financial position (balance sheet) at the historical cost, after deducting depreciation, rather than at estimated selling price, because the enterprise is a going concern and it is expected that the fixed assets will be held for long-term use.

- *Accruals:* The expense of electricity consumed during a period includes all units of electricity used, irrespective of whether an invoice has been paid.
- *Consistency:* It would be inconsistent, in a statement of financial position (balance sheet), to measure inventory (trading stock) at selling price at one point of time and at cost at another point of time.
- *Prudence:* It is prudent to measure inventory (stock of goods) at cost, rather than at selling price, because to value at selling price would anticipate a sale which may not take place.

B4.3

This is an essay which shows the student's understanding of the issues in the chapter and the ability to think about them in the context of a variety of users' needs. It requires the student to link the information in Chapter 4 with the ideas set out in section 1.5.

Chapter 5

Test your understanding

A5.1

Transaction	Asset	Liability	Ownership interest
(a) Owner puts cash into the business	Increase[†]		Increase
(b) Buy a vehicle for cash	Increase and decrease[†]		
(c) Receive a bill for electricity consumed		Increase	Decrease*
(d) Purchase stationery for office use, paying cash	Increase and decrease[†]		
(e) Pay the electricity bill in cash	Decrease[†]	Decrease	
(f) Pay rental for a computer, used for customer records	Decrease[†]		Decrease*
(g) Buy spare parts for cash, to use in repairs	Increase and decrease[†]		
(h) Buy spare parts on credit terms	Increase	Increase	
(i) Pay garage service bills for van, using cash	Decrease[†]		Decrease*
(j) Fill van with petrol, using credit account at local garage, to be paid at the start of next month		Increase	Decrease*
(k) Carry out repairs for cash	Increase[†]		Increase*
(l) Carry out repairs on credit terms	Increase		Increase*
(m) Pay wages to an employee	Decrease[†]		Decrease*
(n) Owner takes cash for personal use	Decrease[†]		Decrease

A5.2

Symbol * shows items which will have an effect on an income statement (profit and loss account).

A5.3

Symbol [†] shows items which will have an effect on a statement of cash flows.

A5.4

All items other than those asterisked will have a direct effect on a statement of financial position (balance sheet). The asterisked items will collectively change the accumulated profit which will increase the ownership interest reported in the statement of financial position (balance sheet).

A5.5

Transactions analysed to show the two aspects of the transaction:

		£		
Apr. 1	60,000	Increase asset of cash	Increase ownership interest
Apr. 1	800	Decrease asset of cash	Decrease ownership interest (expense)
Apr. 2	35,000	Increase asset of equipment	Decrease asset of cash
Apr. 3	5,000	Increase asset of supplies	Increase liability to trade creditor
Apr. 4	1,200	Increase asset of cash	Increase ownership interest (revenue)
Apr. 15	700	Decrease asset of cash	Decrease ownership interest (expense)
Apr. 20	500	Decrease asset of cash	Decrease ownership interest (voluntary)
Apr. 21	2,400	Increase asset of cash	Increase ownership interest (revenue)
Apr. 29	700	Decrease asset of cash	Decrease ownership interest (expense)
Apr. 29	1,900	Increase asset of debtor	Increase ownership interest (revenue)
Apr. 30	80	Decrease asset of cash	Decrease ownership interest (expense)
Apr. 30	*1,500	Decrease asset of supplies	Decrease ownership interest (expense)

* Inventory (stock) acquired £5,000, less amount remaining £3,500 = £1,500 asset used in period.

Application B5.1

		Cash and bank	Other assets	Liabilities	Capital contributed or withdrawn	Revenue	Expenses
		£	£	£	£	£	£
April 1	Jane Gate commenced her dental practice on April 1 by depositing £60,000 in a business bank account.	60,000			60,000		
April 1	Rent for a surgery was paid, £800, for the month of April.	(800)					800
April 2	Dental equipment was purchased for £35,000, paying in cash.	(35,000)	35,000				
April 3	Dental supplies were purchased for £5,000, taking 30 days' credit from a supplier.		5,000	5,000			
April 4	Fees of £1,200 were collected in cash from patients and paid into the bank account.	1,200				1,200	
April 15	Dental assistant was paid wages for two weeks, £700.	(700)					700
April 20	Jane Gate withdrew £500 cash for personal use.	(500)			(500)		
April 21	Fees of £2,400 were collected in cash from patients and paid into the bank.	2,400				2,400	
April 29	Dental assistant was paid wages for two weeks, £700.	(700)					700
April 29	Invoices were sent to patients who are allowed 20 days' credit, for work done during April amounting to £1,900.		1,900			1,900	
April 30	Telephone bill for April was paid, £80.	(80)					80
April 30	Dental supplies unused were counted and found to be worth £3,500, measured at cost price (i.e. inventory [stock] decreased by £1,500).		(1,500)				1,500
	Totals	25,820	40,400	5,000	59,500	5,500	3,780

Accounting equation:

Cash	plus	other assets	less	liabilities		
25,820	+	40,400	–	5,000	=	61,220
Capital contributed or withdrawn	plus	revenue	less	expenses		
59,500	+	5,500	–	3,780	=	61,220

B5.2

Dental Practice of Jane Gate
Statement of cash flows for the month of April Year XX

	£
Operating activities	
Inflow from fees	3,600
Outflow: rent paid	(800)
wages	(1,400)
telephone	(80)
Net inflow from operations	1,320
Investing activities	
Payment for equipment	(35,000)
Net outflow for investing activities	(35,000)
Financing activities	
Capital contributed by owner	60,000
Capital withdrawn as drawings	(500)
Net inflow from financing activities	59,500
Increase in cash at bank over period	25,820

Dental Practice of Jane Gate
Income statement (profit and loss account) for the month of April Year XX

	£	£
Fees charged		5,500
Dental supplies used	1,500	
Wages	1,400	
Rent	800	
Telephone	80	
		3,780
Profit		1,720

Dental Practice of Jane Gate
Statement of financial position (balance sheet) at 30 April Year XX

	£
Non-current (fixed) assets	
Dental equipment at cost	35,000
Current assets	
Dental supplies	3,500
Receivables (debtors)	1,900
Cash at bank	25,820
Total current assets	31,220
Total assets	66,220
Current liabilities	
Trade payables (trade creditors)	(5,000)
Net assets	61,220
Capital at start	60,000
Add profit	1,720
Less drawings	(500)
Total ownership interest	61,220

Chapter 6

A6.1

(a) Profit is only reported when there is a sale. The number of items sold is 60. Each one gives a profit of £5 so the total profit is £300.

(b) When the 200 items are purchased there is an increase of £4,000 in the asset of inventory (stock) of spare parts and a decrease of £4,000 in the asset of cash. When the 60 items are sold for £1,500 there is an increase in the asset of cash and an increase in the ownership interest reported as revenue. The 60 items cost £1,200 to purchase and so at the date of sale there is a reduction in the asset of inventory (stock) amounting to £1,200 and a decrease in the ownership interest due to the expense of cost of goods sold £1,200.

A6.2

(a) Transactions summarised by spreadsheet

	Cash	Inventory (stock)	Revenue	Expense
	£	£	£	£
Purchase 200 items @ £20 each	(4,000)	4,000		
Sell 60 items @ £25	1,500		1,500	
Cost of goods sold 60 @ £20		(1,200)		1,200
Totals	(2,500)	2,800	1,500	1,200

(b) Inventory (stock) increases by £2,800 while cash decreases by £2,500, overall increase in assets amounting to £300. Ownership interest increases by £300 when expenses of £1,200 are set against revenue of £1,500.

A6.3

(a) Calculation of profit on sale:

	£
Sale of 50 trays for £8 each	400
Cost of 50 trays at £5.50 each	275
Profit on sale	125

(b) Analysis of transactions using the accounting equation

	£		
June 1	300	Increase asset of inventory (stock) of raw materials.	Decrease asset of cash.
June 3	210	Decrease asset of inventory (stock) of raw materials.	Increase asset of work in progress.
June 5	175	Decrease asset of cash.	Increase asset of work in progress.
June 6	385	Increase asset of finished goods.	Decrease asset of work in progress.
June 11	275	Decrease ownership interest: expense of cost of goods sold.	Decrease asset of finished goods.
June 14	400	Increase asset of cash.	Increase ownership interest: revenue.

A6.4

Date	Amount £		
Apr. 1	60,000	Increase asset of cash.	Increase ownership interest.
Apr. 2	20,000	Increase asset of buildings.	Decrease asset of cash.
Apr. 4	12,000	Increase asset of equipment.	Decrease asset of cash.
Apr. 6	8,500	Increase asset of inventory (stock).	Decrease asset of cash.
Apr. 7	7,000	Increase asset of inventory (stock).	Increase liability to supplier.
Apr. 11	7,000	Decrease liability to supplier.	Decrease asset of cash.
Apr. 14	400	Decrease ownership claim (expense).	Decrease asset of cash.
Apr. 17	5,500	Decrease ownership claim (expense).	Decrease asset of inventory (stock).
Apr. 17	6,000	Increase asset of cash.	Increase ownership claim (revenue).
Apr. 17	4,200	Increase asset of debtor.	Increase ownership claim (revenue).
Apr. 24	4,200	Increase asset of cash.	Decrease asset of debtor.
Apr. 28	2,700	Decrease ownership claim (voluntary withdrawal).	Decrease asset of cash.
Apr. 30	2,800	Decrease ownership claim (expense).	Decrease asset of cash.
Apr. 30	550	Decrease ownership claim (expense of depreciation).	Decrease asset of equipment.

Application B6.1 (a)

		Cash at bank	Non-current assets and debtors	Inventory (stock) of goods	Trade payables	Capital contributed or withdrawn	Revenue	Expenses
		£	£	£	£	£	£	£
Apr. 1	The owner pays cash into a bank account for the business.	60,000				60,000		
Apr. 2	The business acquires buildings for cash.	(20,000)	20,000					
Apr. 4	The business acquires equipment for cash.	(12,000)	12,000					
Apr. 6	The business purchases an inventory (stock) of goods for cash.	(8,500)		8,500				
Apr. 7	The business purchases goods on credit from R. Green and receives an invoice.			7,000	7,000			
Apr. 11	The business pays R. Green in cash for the goods it acquired on credit.	(7,000)			(7,000)			
Apr. 14	The business pays a gas bill in cash.	(400)						400
Apr. 17	Some of the goods purchased for resale (items costing £5,500) are removed from the store because sales have been agreed with customers for this date.			(5,500)				5,500
Apr. 17	The business sells goods for cash.	6,000					6,000	
Apr. 17	The business sells goods on credit to P. Weatherall and sends an invoice.		4,200				4,200	
Apr. 24	P. Weatherall pays in cash for the goods obtained on credit.	4,200	(4,200)					
Apr. 28	The owner draws cash from the business for personal use.	(2,700)				(2,700)		
Apr. 30	The business pays wages to employees, in cash.	(2,800)						2,800
Apr. 30	The business discovers that its equipment has fallen in value over the month.		(550)					550
	Totals	16,800	31,450	10,000	nil	57,300	10,200	9,250

(b) Accounting equation:

Assets	–	Liabilities	=	Ownership interest
16,800 + 31,450 + 10,000		nil	=	57,300 + 10,200 – 9,250
58,250				58,250

B6.2

Peter Gold, furniture supplier
Statement of cash flows for the month of April Year XX

	£
Operating activities	
Cash from customers	10,200
Outflow: payment for goods	(8,500)
payment to supplier (R. Green)	(7,000)
Wages	(2,800)
Gas	(400)
Net outflow from operations	(8,500)
Investing activities	
Payment for buildings	(20,000)
Payment for equipment	(12,000)
Net outflow for investing activities	(32,000)
Financing activities	
Capital contributed by owner	60,000
Capital withdrawn as drawings	(2,700)
Net inflow from financing activities	57,300
Increase in cash at bank over period	16,800

Peter Gold, furniture supplier
Income statement (profit and loss account) for the month of April Year XX

	£	£
Revenue		10,200
Cost of goods sold		(5,500)
Gross profit		4,700
Other expenses		
Wages	(2,800)	
Gas	(400)	
Depreciation	(550)	
		(3,750)
Net profit		950

Peter Gold, furniture supplier
Statement of financial position (balance sheet) at 30 April Year XX

	£
Non-current (fixed) assets	
Buildings	20,000
Equipment	12,000
	32,000
Depreciation	(550)
Depreciated cost of fixed assets	31,450
Current assets	
Inventory (stocks)	10,000
Cash at bank	16,800
	26,800
Net assets	58,250
Capital at start	60,000
Add profit	950
Less drawings	(2,700)
Total ownership interest	58,250

Chapter 7

Application B7.1 to B7.4

The questions at the end of Chapter 7 provide opportunities for writing about accounting information. An outline for an answer could be developed from the chapter and it could be illustrated by using annual reports obtained from companies or their websites.

To write a short essay for question B7.1 or question B7.3 the IASB *Conceptual Framework* would be very helpful.

Problem solving and evaluation

Question C7.1 requires you to show that you have thought about all the material in the first seven chapters of the book. A reader of your essay might expect to find some or all of the following questions addressed:

(a) This is a listed company and so shares are bought and sold through the stock market. Does your answer show that you have thought about this active market process?

(b) In giving advice on principles have you made use of the IASB *Conceptual Framework*?

(c) Have you given examples of the kind of information which would be relevant to the *Conceptual Framework*? Furthermore, have you carried out some research on company annual reports so that you can provide first-hand examples or illustrations?

Chapter 8

Test your understanding A8.14

Judgement on value, amount and economic benefit.

Application B8.1

(a) The amount of £8,000 has been reported as an asset. Since this is a repair it must be removed from the assets. Removing an asset causes a decrease in the ownership interest through an additional expense of £8,000 in the income statement (profit and loss account).

Problem solving and evaluation

C8.1 The Biscuit Manufacturing Company

(a) Depreciation calculated on a straight-line basis: $\dfrac{22,000 - 2,000}{4} = £5,000$ per annum

	Transaction or event	Machine at cost	Accumulated depreciation of van	Cash	Capital contributed or withdrawn	Profit = revenue minus expenses
			Assets		*Ownership interest*	
Year 1		£	£	£	£	£
1 Jan.	Owner contributes cash			22,000	22,000	
1 Jan.	Purchase biscuit machine	22,000		(22,000)		
All year	Collected cash from customers			40,000		40,000
All year	Paid for wages, other costs			(17,000)		(17,000)
31 Dec.	Calculate annual depreciation		(5,000)			(5,000)
	Totals	22,000	(5,000)	23,000	22,000	18,000

		Assets			Ownership interest		
	Transaction or event	Machine at cost	Accumulated depreciation of machine	Cash	Ownership interest at start of year	Capital contributed or withdrawn	Profit = revenue minus expenses
Year 2		£	£	£	£	£	£
1 Jan.	Amounts brought forward at start of year	22,000	(5,000)	23,000	40,000		
All year	Collected cash from customers			40,000			40,000
All year	Paid for wages, fuel, etc.			(17,000)			(17,000)
31 Dec.	Calculate annual depreciation		(5,000)				(5,000)
	Totals	22,000	(10,000)	46,000	40,000		18,000

		Assets			Ownership interest		
	Transaction or event	Machine at cost	Accumulated depreciation of machine	Cash	Ownership interest at start of year	Capital contributed or withdrawn	Profit = revenue minus expenses
Year 3		£	£	£	£	£	£
1 Jan.	Amounts brought forward at start of year	22,000	(10,000)	46,000	58,000		
All year	Collected cash from customers			40,000			40,000
All year	Paid for wages, fuel, etc.			(17,000)			(17,000)
31 Dec.	Calculate annual depreciation		(5,000)				(5,000)
	Totals	22,000	(15,000)	69,000	58,000		18,000

		Assets			Ownership interest		
	Transaction or event	Machine at cost	Accumulated depreciation of machine	Cash	Ownership interest at start of year	Capital contributed or withdrawn	Profit = revenue minus expenses
Year 4		£	£	£	£	£	£
1 Jan.	Amounts brought forward at start of year	22,000	(15,000)	69,000	76,000		
All year	Collected cash from customers			40,000			40,000
All year	Paid for wages, fuel, etc.			(17,000)			(17,000)
31 Dec.	Calculate annual depreciation		(5,000)				(5,000)
	Totals	22,000	(20,000)	92,000	76,000		18,000

(b)

Biscuit Manufacturing Company
Statement of financial position (balance sheet) at 31 December Year 3

	£
Non-current (fixed) assets	
Machine at cost	22,000
Accumulated depreciation	(15,000)
Net book value	7,000
Current assets	
Cash	69,000
Total assets	76,000
Ownership interest	
Ownership interest at the start of the year	58,000
Profit of the year	18,000
	76,000

Biscuit Manufacturing Company
Income statement (profit and loss account) for the year ended
31 December Year 3

	£	£
Revenue		
Sale of biscuits		40,000
Expenses		
Wages, ingredients and running costs	(17,000)	
Depreciation	(5,000)	
		(22,000)
Net profit		18,000

C8.2

(a)

		Assets			Ownership interest		
	Transaction or event	Machine at cost	Accumulated depreciation of machine	Cash	Ownership interest at start of year	Capital contributed or withdrawn	Profit = revenue minus expenses
Year 4		£	£	£	£	£	£
1 Jan.	Amounts brought forward at start of year	22,000	(15,000)	69,000	76,000		
All year	Collected cash from customers			40,000			40,000
All year	Paid for wages, fuel, etc.			(17,000)			(17,000)
31 Dec.	Calculate annual depreciation		(5,000)				(5,000)
31 Dec.	Machine disposal	(22,000)	20,000	3,000			1,000
	Totals	nil	nil	95,000	76,000		19,000

Note that at the end of Year 4 the net book value is £2,000 (cost £22,000 less accumulated depreciation £20,000). The cash received £3,000 is therefore £1,000 more than expected. The amount of £1,000 is recorded as an increase in the ownership interest.

(b)

Biscuit Manufacturing Company
Statement of financial position (balance sheet) at 31 December Year 4

	£
Non-current (fixed) assets	
Machine at cost	nil
Current assets	
Cash	95,000
Total assets	95,000
Ownership interest	
Ownership interest at the start of the year	76,000
Profit of the year	19,000
	95,000

Biscuit Manufacturing Company
Income statement (profit and loss account) for the year ended
31 December Year 4

	£	£
Revenue		
Sale of biscuits		40,000
Expenses		
Wages, ingredients and running costs	(17,000)	
Depreciation less gain on disposal	(4,000)	
		(21,000)
Net profit		19,000

(c) There is apparently a gain on disposal because the cash collected is greater than the net book value of the asset. In reality, all that has happened is that the estimate of depreciation over the asset life is, with the benefit of hindsight, a marginally incorrect estimate. Perfect foresight at the outset would have used £3,000 as a residual value, rather than £2,000, in calculating the annual depreciation charge. However, it is known that accounting involves estimates so it would be inappropriate in most cases to attempt to rewrite the income statements (profit and loss accounts) of the past. Accordingly all of the 'gain' is reported in Year 4, as a deduction from annual depreciation.

C8.3 Souvenir Company

(a) Straight-line depreciation

Machine cost £16,000, estimated residual value £1,000, so depreciate the difference, £15,000, over five-year life to give annual depreciation of £3,000.

End of Year	Depreciation of the year (b)	Total depreciation (c)	Net book value of the asset (£16,000 – (c))
	£	£	£
1	3,000	3,000	13,000
2	3,000	6,000	10,000
3	3,000	9,000	7,000
4	3,000	12,000	4,000
5	3,000	15,000	1,000

(b) Guess a rate which is at least twice the percentage applied on a straight-line basis (i.e. in this case guess 20% × 2 = 40%).
Calculation of reducing balance depreciation (as in Table 8.2):

Year	Net book value at start of year (a)	Annual depreciation (b) = 40% of (a)	Net book value at end of year (a – b)
	£	£	£
1	16,000	6,400	9,600
2	9,600	3,840	5,760
3	5,760	2,304	3,456
4	3,456	1,382	2,074
5	2,074	830	1,244

(The residual value at the end of Year 5 should ideally be £1,000, so a first estimate which arrives at £1,244 is quite reasonable.)

(c) The net book value at the end of Year 5 is £1,000 and therefore disposal at £2,500 gives an apparent gain of £1,500 which is best described as caused by over-depreciation of earlier years. The effect on the accounting equation is that the asset of machine decreases by £1,000 while the asset of cash increases by £2,500 so that overall the ownership interest increases by £1,500.

(d) The net book value at the end of Year 5 is £1,000 and therefore disposal at nil scrap value gives an apparent loss of £1,000 which is best described as caused by underdepreciation of earlier years. The effect on the accounting equation is that the asset of machine decreases by £1,000 with no increase in any other asset so that overall the ownership interest decreases by £1,000.

Chapter 9

Test your understanding

A9.10

Use lower of cost and net realisable value on each category separately:

Description	Basis	Inventory value £
Engine	Cost	6,500
Chassis	Net realisable value	1,600
Frame	Net realisable value	4,600

A9.11

The recorded inventory (stock) will increase by £18,000 and the ownership interest will increase by £18,000 (reported as a reduction in the cost of goods sold).

A9.12

The asset of debtor (trade receivable) will be reduced by £154,000 and the ownership interest will decrease by £154,000 (reported as an expense of cost of bad debts).

Application

B9.1

(a) The FIFO approach to the issue of units for sale, where:

(i) the calculation is carried out at the date of sale; and

(ii) the calculation is carried out at the end of the month without regard for the date of sale.

Date	Number of units purchased	Unit cost	Number of units sold	Cost of goods sold (i) £	Cost of goods sold (ii) £	Inventory (stock) (i)	Inventory (stock) (ii)
Jan. 5	100	£1.00					
Jan. 10			50	50			
Jan. 15	200	£1.10					
Jan. 17			150	50			
				110			
Jan. 24	300	£1.15					
Jan. 30			200	110	100		
				115	220		
					115		
	600		400	435	435	230	230

	£
Sales 400 × £2	800
Cost of goods sold	435
Profit	365

Inventory (stock) = 200 × £1.15 = £230

(b) The LIFO approach to the issue of units for sale, where:
   (i) the calculation is carried out at the date of sale; and
   (ii) the calculation is carried out at the end of the month without regard for the date of sale; and

Date	Number of units purchased	Unit cost	Number of units sold	Cost of goods sold (i) £	Cost of goods sold (ii) £	Inventory (stock) (i)	Inventory (stock) (ii)
Jan. 5	100	£1.00					
Jan. 10			50	50		50	
Jan. 15	200	£1.10					
Jan. 17			150	165		55	
Jan. 24	300	£1.15					
Jan. 30			200	230	345	115	100
					110		110
	600		400	345	455	220	210

either (i):

	£
Sales 400 × £2	800
Cost of goods sold	345
Profit	455

Inventory (stock) = (50 × £1.00) + (50 × £1.10) + (100 × £1.15)
= 50 + 55 + 115 = 220

or (ii):

	£
Sales 400 × £2	800
Cost of goods sold	455
Profit	345

Inventory (stock) = (100 × £1) + (100 × £1.10)
= 100 + 110 = £210

Note that in all cases the Cost of goods sold plus the unsold Inventory (stock) = £665.

(c) The average-cost approach to the issue of units for sale, making the calculation at the end of the month without regard for the date of sale.

Date	Number of units purchased	Unit cost	£
Jan. 5	100	£1.00	100
Jan. 10			
Jan. 15	200	£1.10	220
Jan. 17			
Jan. 24	300	£1.15	345
Jan. 30			
	600		665

Average cost = £665/600 = £1.108

	£
Sales 400 × £2	800
Cost of goods sold 400 × £1.108	443
Profit	357

Inventory (stock) 200 × £1.108 = £222

B9.2

Group of items	Basis	Inventory (stock) value £
A	Cost	1,000
B	Net realisable value	800
C	Net realisable value	1,900
D	Cost	3,000
Total inventory (stock)		6,700

Chapter 10

A10.9

The liability to the supplier will increase and the ownership interest will decrease (recorded as an increase in the cost of goods sold).

A10.10

The recorded asset of cash will decrease and the recorded liability to the supplier will decrease.

A10.11

First the original incorrect entry must be reversed. When the entry was made, it was treated as an increase in the ownership interest and an increase in the asset of debtor. This error must be reversed by decreasing the ownership interest and decreasing the asset of debtor.

Then the correct entry must be made which is a decrease in the ownership interest and an increase in a liability to the landlord.

B10.1

The aim of the calculation is to show the cost of telephone used during the year.

	£
Cash paid	3,500
Less rental in advance for July, one-third of £660	(220)
Add calls for May and June, two-thirds of £900	600
Expense of the period	3,880

The rental paid in advance will be shown as a prepayment of £220 in the statement of financial position (balance sheet) and the calls made during May and June will be shown as an accrual of £600 in the statement of financial position (balance sheet).

B10.2

		Asset	Liability	Ownership interest profit of the period
Date	Transactions with security company	Cash	Security company	Security expense
Year 1		£	£	£
Mar. 31	Invoice received £800		800	(800)
Apr. 5	Security company paid £800	(800)	(800)	
June 30	Invoice received £800		800	(800)
July 5	Security company paid £800	(800)	(800)	
Sept. 30	Invoice received £800		800	(800)
Oct. 5	Security company paid £800	(800)	(800)	
Dec. 31	Invoice received £800		800	(800)
	Totals	(2,400)	800	(3,200)

B10.3

The tax charge reduces the ownership interest and is shown as an expense of £8,000 in the income statement (profit and loss account). The accounting equation remains in balance because there is a matching liability of £8,000 recorded. However, the liability is split as £6,000 current liability and £2,000 deferred liability to reflect different patterns of payment of the overall liability.

Problem solving and evaluation C10.1

The year-end is 31 December Year 1.

Item	Description	Amount £		
1	Invoice dated 23 December for goods received 21 December.	260	Increase asset of inventory (stock).	Increase liability to supplier.
2	Invoice dated 23 December for goods to be delivered on 3 January Year 2.	310	Nothing recorded – this will be an asset and a liability of the following year.	
3	Foreman's note of electricity consumption for month of December – no invoice yet received from electricity supply company.	100	Decrease ownership interest (expense of electricity).	Increase liability to electricity supplier.
4	Letter from employee claiming overtime payment for work on 1 December and note from personnel office denying entitlement to payment.	58	Nothing recorded in the financial statements because it is not yet clear that there is an obligation (might be a contingent liability note).	
5	Telephone bill dated 26 December showing calls for October to December.	290	Decrease ownership interest (expense of telephone calls).	Increase liability to phone company.
6	Telephone bill dated 26 December showing rent due in advance for period January to March Year 2.	90	Nothing recorded – this will be an expense of the following year.	
7	Note of payment due to cleaners for final week of December (to be paid on 3 January under usual pattern of payment one week in arrears).	48	Usually nothing recorded if payment in arrears is normal, since the corresponding payment from January Year 1 will be included in the year's expense.	
8	Invoice from supplier for promotional calendars received 1 December (only one-third have yet been sent to customers).	300	Decrease ownership interest £300 (expense of calendars).	Increase liability to calendar supplier £300.
			Increase inventory (stock) of calendars by £200.	Reduce expense by £200.
9	Letter dated 21 December Year 1 to customer promising a cheque to reimburse damage caused by faulty product – cheque to be sent on 4 January Year 2.	280	Decrease ownership interest (expense of damage).	Increase liability to customer.
10	Letter dated 23 December promising donation to local charity – amount not yet paid.	60	Decrease ownership interest (expense of donation).	Increase liability to charity.

Chapter 11

Test your understanding A11.6

Reduce revenue by £40,000 (two-thirds of £60,000) and increase statement of financial position (balance sheet) deferred income by £40,000. Effect on income statement (profit and loss account) is to reduce reported profit. Reason is application of the matching concept. The £40,000 deferred income will be transferred to income statement (profit and loss account) over the next two years.

A11.7

Increase expense of provision for repairs by £50,000 (reporting as an expense in the income statement (profit and loss account)) and create a liability under the 'provisions' heading. Effect on income statement (profit and loss account) is to reduce reported profit.

Application **B11.1**

The income statement (profit and loss account) would show an expense of £8,000 provision in Year 1 and an expense of £9,000 provision in Year 2. The actual amount of expenditure as shown in the question would be set against the provision in the statement of financial position (balance sheet).

Date of repair	Income statement expense	Statement of financial position (balance sheet) provision in total before expense charged	Actual expense matched against provision	Provision remaining in statement of financial position (balance sheet)
Year	£	£	£	£
1	8,000	8,000	4,500	3,500
2	9,000	12,500	8,000	4,500
3	*500	4,500	*4,500	nil

* The actual cost in Year 3 is £5,000 but there is only £4,500 provision remaining, so the extra £500 must be charged to income statement (profit and loss account) as an unexpected expense.

Note that the total amount charged to income statement (profit and loss account) is £17,500 and the total amount paid out for repair work is also £17,500. The accounting entries in the income statement (profit and loss account) are an attempt to spread the expense on the basis of matching with revenue, but the total must be the same over the three-year period, whatever matching approach is taken.

Date of repair	Income statement expense using provision approach	Income statement expense using actual repair amount paid
	£	£
1	8,000	4,500
2	9,000	8,000
3	*500	5,000
Total	17,500	17,500

B11.2

The grant will initially be recorded as an increase in the asset of cash and an increase in the statement of financial position (balance sheet) liability item headed 'deferred income'. The deferred income is transferred from the liability to revenue over three years (so that the ownership interest increases evenly over the three-year period).

Chapter 12

Application **B12.1**

(a) Increase the asset of cash by £50,000. Increase the ownership interest by the nominal value of shares, £50,000.
(b) Increase the asset of cash by £75,000. Increase the ownership interest by (i) nominal value of shares £25,000 and (ii) share premium £50,000.
(c) Increase asset of property by £20,000. Increase ownership interest by revaluation reserve £20,000.

B12.2

(a) Decrease asset of cash by £20,000. Decrease ownership interest by £20,000 as a reduction in the owners' claim on the business.
(b) Record a note in the directors' report. There is no liability at the date of the financial statements.

B12.3 Nithsdale Ltd

		(a)	(b)	(c)
	£000s	£000s	£000s	£000s
Cash	20	70.0	20	260
Other assets less liabilities	320	320.0	320	320
	340	390.0	340	580
Ordinary shares (400,000 of 25 pence each)	100	112.5	125	120
Share premium	40	77.5	40	260
Reserves of retained profit	200	200.0	175	200
	340	390.0	340	580

B12.4

If the directors decide that they wish to incorporate the revaluation in the statement of financial position (balance sheet), then the asset will be reported at £380,000. The difference between the previous recorded book value £250,000 and the new value £380,000 is £130,000. This is an increase in the ownership interest and will be reported as a revaluation reserve as part of the total ownership interest.

B12.5

In this case the value has decreased by £10,000. This is a reduction in the value of the asset and a decrease in the ownership claim. On grounds of prudence the loss should be reported in the income statement (profit and loss account) immediately and the recorded book value of the asset should be reduced.

Chapter 13

Application **B13.1**

(a) Hope plc

(i) Liquidity

		Hope plc	
Ratio	Definition in words	Workings	Result
Current ratio	Current assets:Current liabilities	2,360:1,240	1.90:1
Acid test	(Current assets − Inventory (stock)): Current liabilities	(2,360 − 620):1,240	1.40:1
Inventory (stock) holding period*	$\dfrac{\text{Average inventory held}}{\text{Cost of sales}} \times 365$	$\dfrac{620}{2,750} \times 365$	82.3 days
Customers' collection period	$\dfrac{\text{Trade receivables (debtors)}}{\text{Credit sales}} \times 365$	$\dfrac{1,540}{6,200} \times 365$	90.7 days
Suppliers' payment period[†]	$\dfrac{\text{Trade payables (creditors)}}{\text{Credit purchases}} \times 365$	$\dfrac{300}{2,750} \times 365$	39.8 days

* Assuming the opening inventory (stock) is the same as the closing inventory (stock).
[†] Assuming purchases = cost of goods sold.

(a) 50,000 × 25p = £12,500; 50,000 × £0.75 = £37,500.
(b) Transfer £25,000 from reserves to share capital.
(c) 80,000 × £3 = £240,000; 80,000 × 25p = £20,000; 80,000 × £2.75 = £220,000.

(ii) Analysis of management performance

Ratio	Definition in words	Hope plc	
		Workings	Result
Return on shareholders' equity	$\dfrac{\text{Profit after tax}}{\text{Share capital} + \text{Reserves}} \times 100\%$	$\dfrac{692}{1,470} \times 100$	47.1%
Return on capital employed	$\dfrac{\text{Profit before interest and tax}}{\text{Total assets} - \text{Current liabilities}} \times 100\%$	$\dfrac{1,256}{2,870} \times 100$	43.8%
Net profit on sales	$\dfrac{\text{Profit before interest and taxes}}{\text{Sales}} \times 100$	$\dfrac{1,256}{6,200} \times 100$	20.3%
Gross profit percentage	$\dfrac{\text{Gross profit}}{\text{Sales}} \times 100$	$\dfrac{3,450}{6,200} \times 100\%$	55.6%
Total assets usage	$\dfrac{\text{Sales}}{\text{Total assets}}$	$\dfrac{6,200}{1,750 + 2,360}$	1.5 times
Fixed assets usage	$\dfrac{\text{Sales}}{\text{Non-current (fixed) assets}}$	$\dfrac{6,200}{1,750}$	3.5 times

(iii) Gearing (leverage)

Ratio	Definition in words	Hope plc	
		Workings	Result
Debt/equity ratio	$\dfrac{\text{Debt} + \text{Preference share capital}}{\text{Ordinary share capital reserves}} + 100\%$	$\dfrac{1,400}{1,470} + 100$	95.2%
Interest cover	$\dfrac{\text{Profit before interest and tax}}{\text{Interest}}$	$\dfrac{1,256}{84}$	15.0 times

(c) Investor ratios

Ratio	Definition in words	Hope plc	
		Workings	Result
Earnings per share	$\dfrac{\text{Profit after for ordinary shareholders}}{\text{Number of ordinary shares}}$	$\dfrac{692}{900}$	76.9 pence
Price/earnings ratio	$\dfrac{\text{Share price}}{\text{Earnings per share}}$	$\dfrac{1,100}{76.9}$	14
Dividend cover (payout ratio)	$\dfrac{\text{Earning per share}}{\text{Dividend per share}}$	$\dfrac{76.9}{36.7}$	2.1 times
Dividend yield	$\dfrac{\text{Dividend per share}}{\text{Share price}} \times 100\%$	$\dfrac{36.7}{1,100} \times 100\%$	3.34%

Chapter 14

Problem solving and evaluation

C14.1 Trend analysis: Safe and Sure

	Year 3	Year 4	Year 5	Year 6	Year 7
Group revenue	3,091	3,890	4,741	6,003	7,346
Group profit before tax	744	904	1,145	1,470	1,770
Tax	(272)	(339)	(443)	(524)	(622)
Group profit after tax	472	565	702	946	1,148
Earnings per share	4.88	6.23	8.02	9.71	11.74
Dividends per share	1.32	1.69	2.17	2.50	3.02
Share capital	194	194	194	195	196
Reserves	1,608	1,953	2,654	3,509	4,447
Total equity	1,802	2,147	2,848	3,704	4,643
Ratios					
Pre-tax profit to sales	24.1%	23.2%	24.2%	24.5%	24.1%
Tax charge as % of pre-tax profit	36.6%	37.5%	38.7%	35.6%	35.1%
Dividend cover	3.70	3.70	3.70	3.88	3.89
Growth in revenue	n/a	25.9%	21.9%	26.6%	22.4%
Growth in eps	n/a	27.7%	28.7%	21.1%	20.9%
Growth in dividend per share	n/a	28.0%	28.4%	15.2%	20.8%
Return on shareholders' equity	26.2%	26.3%	24.7%	25.5%	25.3%

Commentary. The company has exceeded its annual earnings growth target of 20% in each year for which calculations can be made. The dividend cover is relatively high, indicating a policy of retaining new wealth to finance expansion. In Year 6 the dividend cover increased because the dividend growth decreased. In Year 7 the cover remains higher and the dividend growth improved. With the expansion the company has maintained its rate of return on shareholders' equity. The company is likely to be attractive to investors if future prospects are similar to the historical trend.

Chapter 15

Application

B15.1
£120m + £8m − £10m = £118m

B15.2
£20m + £6m − £4m = £22m

B15.3
£34m − £5m + ? = £37m Missing number is £8m acquisition.

Problem solving C15.1
and evaluation Fruit Sales plc – indirect method

Notes		£m	£m
	Cash flows from operating activities		
1	Profit before taxation		132
	Adjustment for items not involving a flow of cash:		
	Depreciation	39	
	Gain on disposal of equipment	(7)	
			32
	Adjusted profit		164
	(Increase) in inventories	(6)	
	(Increase) in trade receivables	(2)	
	Increase in trade payables	5	
	Increase/(decrease) in cash due to working capital changes		(3)
	Cash generated from operations		161
2	Interest paid		(19)
3	Taxes paid		(32)
	Net cash inflow from operating activities		110
	Cash flows from investing activities		
4	Purchase of vehicles	(90)	
5	Proceeds from sale of vehicles	20	
6	Investments acquired	(20)	
	Interest received	5	
	Net cash used in investing activities		(85)
	Cash flows from financing activities		
7	Proceeds from issue of share capital	35	
8	Proceeds from long-term borrowing	8	
	Dividends paid	(31)	
	Net cash raised from financing activities		12
	Increase/(decrease) in cash and cash equivalents		37
9	**Cash and cash equivalents at the start of the period**		6
9	**Cash and cash equivalents at the end of the period**		43

Working note 1

	£m
Operating profit before taxes	117
Is there any interest expense included in this figure? If so add it back to arrive at:	20
Operating profit before deducting interest payable and taxes	137
Is there any interest received/receivable or any dividends received in this figure?	
If so deduct it to arrive at:	(5)
Operating profit before deducting interest payable and taxes and before including interest receivable and dividends received.	132

Working note 2
Interest paid = expense £20m plus liability at the start £7m minus liability at the end £8m.

Working note 3
Taxes paid = tax charge of the period £35m plus liability at the start £7m minus liability at the end £10m.

Working note 4

The vehicles at cost start with a balance of £130m. Additions are £90m and disposals cost £25m originally, leaving a balance of £195m.

Vehicles at cost – ledger account

	Debit	Credit	Balance
	£m	£m	£m
Balance at start	130		130
Additions	90		220
Disposals		25	195

Working note 5

The accumulated depreciation starts with a balance of £52m. This increases by the expense of the period £39m and decreases by the accumulated depreciation of the vehicles sold £12m, leaving a balance of £79m. The net book value of the vehicles sold was £13m (£25m – £12m). Deduct this from the proceeds of sale £20m to calculate the gain on disposal of £7m shown in the income statement.

Vehicles accumulated depreciation – ledger account

	Debit	Credit	Balance
	£m	£m	£m
Balance at start		52	(52)
Depreciation expense for the period		39	(91)
Accumulated depreciation on vehicles sold	12		(79)

Vehicles disposal – ledger account

	Debit	Credit	Balance
	£m	£m	£m
Asset at cost	25		25
Accumulated depreciation		12	13
Proceeds of sale		20	(7)
Transfer to income statement, gain on disposal	7		nil

Working note 6

The statement of financial position (balance sheet) investments increase by £20m. Assume no sales.

Working note 7

Increase in share capital £32m plus increase in share premium £3m.

Working note 8

Increase in borrowings £8m. Assume no repayments.

Fruit sales plc – direct method

Notes		£m	£m
	Cash flows from operating activities		
1	Cash receipts from customers		318
2	Cash paid to suppliers and employees		(144)
	Cash paid for administrative and selling expenses		(13)
	Cash generated from operations		161
	Interest paid		(19)
	Taxes paid		(32)
	Net cash inflow from operating activities		110
	Cash flows from investing activities		
	Purchase of vehicles	(90)	
	Proceeds from sale of vehicles	20	
	Investments acquired	(20)	
	Interest received	5	
	Net cash used in investing activities		(85)
	Cash flows from financing activities		
	Proceeds from issue of share capital	35	
	Proceeds from long-term borrowing	8	
	Dividends paid	(31)	
	Net cash used in financing activities		12
	Increase/(decrease) in cash and cash equivalents		37
	Cash and cash equivalents at the start of the period		6
	Cash and cash equivalents at the end of the period		43

Working note 1

Revenue in income statement £320m plus receivables at start of period £21m minus receivables at the end of the period £23m.

Accounts receivable – ledger account

	Debit	Credit	Balance
	£m	£m	£m
Balance at start	21		21
Revenue – sales	320		341
Cash received		318	23

Working note 2

Purchases = cost of goods sold £143m plus inventory at the end £26m less inventory at the start £20m = £149m.

Purchases – ledger account

	Debit	Credit	Balance
	£m	£m	£m
Balance of inventory at start	20		(20)
Purchases of supplies	149		(169)
Cash paid		144	26

Payment to suppliers = £149m plus payables at the start £13m less payables at the end £18m.

Accounts payable – suppliers

	Debit	Credit	Balance
	£m	£m	£m
Balance of payables at start		13	(13)
Purchases		149	(162)
Cash paid	144		(18)

Appendix III

Solutions to numerical and technical questions in Management Accounting

Note that solutions are provided only for numerical and technical material since other matters are covered either in the book or in the further reading indicated.

Chapters 16 and 25 have no solutions given in this Appendix because there are no numerical questions.

Chapter 17

Application **B17.5**

(a) Cost X is a fixed cost because *total* cost does not vary with output.

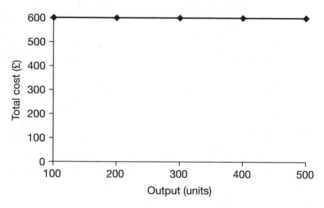

(b) Cost Y is a variable cost because total cost varies in direct proportion to output and is zero when output is zero.

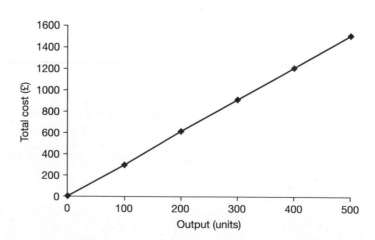

(c) Cost Z is a semi-variable cost because total cost varies in direct proportion to output but has a value of £600 when output is zero (seen by extending the graph until it meets the vertical axis). The fixed cost is £600.

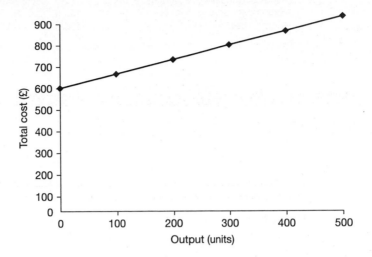

B17.6

(a) The table of costs for one year based on variable mileage within the year is as follows:

Mileage per annum	5,000	10,000	15,000	20,000	30,000
	£	£	£	£	£
Variable costs					
Spare parts	180	360	540	720	1,080
Fuel	700	1,400	2,100	2,800	4,200
Tyres	400	800	1,200	1,600	2,400
Total variable cost	1,280	2,560	3,840	5,120	7,680
Fixed costs					
Service costs per year	900	900	900	900	900
Insurance	800	800	800	800	800
Depreciation	4,800	4,800	4,800	4,800	4,800
Total fixed cost	6,500	6,500	6,500	6,500	6,500

(b) Note that in drawing the graph it is necessary to insert a point for 25,000 miles (although no calculation is required because the straight line is formed from the data already calculated).

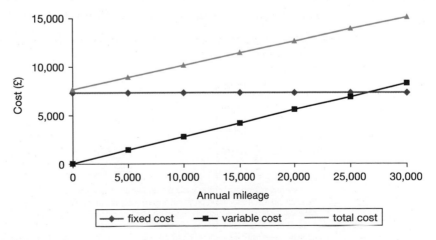

(c) Average cost per mile

Mileage per annum	5,000	10,000	15,000	20,000	30,000
Variable cost per mile (pence)	25.6	25.6	25.6	25.6	25.6
Fixed cost per mile (pence)	130.0	65.0	43.3	32.5	21.7
Average cost per mile (pence)	155.6	90.6	68.9	58.1	47.3

(d) All total costs follow a straight line. Total fixed costs do not depend on mileage. Total variable costs increase directly with mileage. Total fixed plus variable costs start at £6,500 for zero miles and increase in direct proportion to mileage. The average cost per mile for each year falls as the annual mileage increases. Note that for tyres a proportionate cost has been calculated where the mileage is not exactly 15,000 miles. Note also that depreciation has been included as a fixed cost because it does not depend on mileage covered.

B17.7

		£
Metal piping	Product	12,000
Wages to welders and painters	Product	9,000
Supplies for welding	Product	1,400
Advertising campaign	Period	2,000
Production manager's salary	Period	1,800
Accounts department computer costs for dealing with production records	Period	1,200

The costs incurred during May relate to 4,000 towel rails, so allocate costs on this basis. Product costs are £22,400 in total, or £5.60 per towel rail. There are 500 towel rails remaining in stock at the end of the month which would have a value of £(500 × 5.60) = £2,800.

Most business would use a value higher than £5.60 to take some of the period costs into account (e.g. a proportion of the production manager's salary). However, this is a matter of judgement where others would charge all period costs in the profit and loss account.

Chapter 18

Application **B18.1**

Step 1: Allocate costs to departments using a suitable method for each department.

	Total £	Assembly £	Joinery £	Canteen £
Indirect labour[1]	90,000	48,000	36,000	6,000
Indirect material[2]	81,000	54,000	27,000	–
Heating and lighting[3]	25,000	10,000	12,000	3,000
Rent and rates[4]	30,000	12,000	14,400	3,600
Depreciation[5]	56,000	30,000	24,000	2,000
Supervision[6]	45,000	24,000	18,000	3,000
Power[7]	36,000	18,000	16,000	2,000
	363,000	196,000	147,400	19,600

Notes
1 Allocate indirect labour on the basis of number of employees 80:60:10.
2 Allocate indirect materials in proportion to direct materials 100:50.
3 Allocate heating and lighting in proportion to floor space 20:24:6.
4 Allocate rent and rates in proportion to floor space 20:24:6.
5 Allocate depreciation by reference to the value of machinery used in each department 300:240:20.
6 Allocate supervision on the basis of number of employees 80:60:10.
7 Allocate power on the basis of kilowatt hours 9:8:1.

Step 2: Allocate service department costs to production departments.

	Total £	Assembly £	Joinery £	Canteen £
From previous table	363,000	196,000	147,400	19,600
Allocate canteen to assembly and joinery 80:60		11,200	8,400	(19,600)
	363,000	207,200	155,800	

Step 3: Allocate total overhead costs of each production department to units produced during the period.

Divide the total cost of each department by the number of direct labour hours.

Assembly: £207,200/12,640 = £16.39 per direct labour hour
Joinery: £155,800/8,400 = £18.55 per direct labour hour

Step 4: Find the overhead cost of a specific job.

		£
Assembly	£16.39 × 3 hours	49.17
Joinery	£18.55 × 4 hours	74.20
Total overhead cost		123.37

B18.2

Statement of cost of production of 5,000 golf bags:

	£	£
Direct materials 5,000 × £40	200,000	
Direct labour 5,000 × £25	125,000	
Prime cost		325,000
Variable production overhead 5,000 × £10	50,000	
Fixed production overhead	100,000	
Production overhead cost		150,000
Total product cost		475,000

B18.3

(a) The use of a machine hour rate is appropriate for Department 1, which is heavily dependent on machine hours, but not for Department 2, which is more dependent on labour hours. The production overhead should be allocated according to the factor which most closely causes it to be incurred. In Department 1 this is likely to be machine hours but in Department 2 it is more likely to be labour hours.

(b) Applying a rate of £5.60 to 48,000 machine hours, the overhead absorbed was £268,800. This was less than the amount of overhead incurred, £275,000, and so it is said that overheads are underabsorbed by £6,200. The use of estimated overhead absorption rates, based on budget, is necessary for an estimation of cost before the true costs are known. However, the full actual costs have to be accounted for at the end of the period and so a further £6,200 must be charged to the profit and loss account in addition to the costs charged as jobs proceeded.

Chapter 19

Test your understanding

A19.10

(a) 16 components are charged to the job card and used as part of the value of work in progress.
(b) The amount of £600 is added to work in progress, split as shown between the two jobs mentioned.
(c) The job card is closed and the record is transferred to finished goods stock.

Application B19.1

Direct costs	
Materials used:	£
500 drums of milk	75,000
Cartons	4,000
Cheesemakers' wages	6,000
Prime cost	85,000
Overhead costs	
Cleaning and hygiene	1,200
Rent, rates, electricity	8,000
Cost of production	94,200

B19.2

Job cost record: Job 801		
3 May	Direct materials	112,000 †
30 May	Direct labour	10,000 ♥
	Prime cost	122,000
30 May	Production overhead:	20,600
	Total production cost	*142,600*
	To finished goods	(142,600)
	Work in progress	*nil*

Job cost record: Job 802		
3 May	Direct materials	32,000 †
30 May	Direct labour	5,000 ♥
	Prime cost	37,000
30 May	Production overhead:	10,300
	Total production cost	*47,300*
	Finished goods	(47,300)
	Work in progress	*nil*

Job cost record: Job 803		
3 June	Direct materials	12,800 †
30 June	Direct labour	5,000 ♥
	Prime cost	17,800
30 June	Production overhead:	10,300
	Total production cost	*28,100*
	Finished goods	28,100
1 May	*Work in progress*	*nil*

Note on production overheads:

	£
Rent, rates and electricity	18,000 †
Stain, varnish, etc.	22,500 ♣
Security	700 ɸ
	41,200

Labour cost is £20,000 in total so production overhead is £2.06 per £ of labour.

Problem solving and evaluation

C19.1 Frames Ltd

Job cost estimate for 500 single- and 200 double-glazed units:

	Single	Double	Total
Quantity	500	200	
	£	£	£
Direct material[1]	45,000	26,000	71,000
Direct labour[2]	16,250	8,000	24,250
Prime cost	61,250	34,000	95,250
Variable production overhead[3]	19,500	9,600	29,100
Fixed production overhead[4]	20,000	10,000	30,000
Total cost of production	100,750	53,600	154,350

Notes

1   Direct material: single 500 × £90 = £45,000; double 200 × £130 = £26,000.
2   Direct labour: single 500 × £32.50 = £16,250; double 200 × £40 = £8,000.
3   Variable production overhead: single 500 × £39 = £19,500; double 200 × £48 = £9,600.
4   Fixed overhead rates: single 160/4 = £40 per unit; double 100/2 = £50 per unit; applied to 500 units single = £20,000 and to 200 units double = £10,000.

C19.2

430 packages (needs 2 shifts): profit for 1 day

	£	£
Selling price 430 packages at £25.20		10,836
Cost of direct materials 430 at £23.75	10,213	
Cost of labour (£100 + £120)	220	
Supervision £40	40	
Other fixed overheads £280	280	
Depreciation £100	100	
		10,853
Net loss		(17)

880 packages (needs 3 shifts): profit for 1 day

	£	£
Selling price 880 packages at £25.00		22,000
Cost of direct materials 880 at £23.75	20,900	
Cost of labour (£100 + £120 + £160)	380	
Supervision £40 + £40	80	
Other fixed overheads £280	280	
Depreciation £100	100	
		21,740
Net profit		260
Net profit per package		£0.30

1,350 packages (needs 3.8 shifts): profit for 1 day

	£	£
Selling price 1,350 packages at £24.80		33,480
Cost of direct materials 1,350 at £23.75	32,063	
Cost of labour (£100 + £120 + £160 + £100)	480	
Supervision £40 + £40 + £20	100	
Other fixed overheads £280 + £100	380	
Depreciation £100 + £100	200	33,223
Net profit		257
Net profit per package		£0.19

Explanation. The 880-package option is the preferred one because it gives the benefit of a higher volume of profit without increasing the fixed costs. The 1,350-package option takes up more fixed costs and so reduces unit profit.

Chapter 20

Application

B20.1

Contribution is £5.50 − 3.00 = £2.50.
Break-even point equals fixed cost/contribution = 5,000/2.50 = 2,000 units.

B20.2

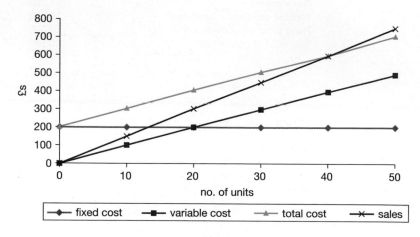

B20.3 Montrose Glass Products Ltd

(a) If Basic closes down there is a lost contribution of [£45 − £(15 + 20 + 5)] = £5. Fixed costs are carried in any event.

(b) If Standard closes down, the variable cost of £37 is saved, compared with revenue of £35. The company will gain £2,000 from closing down the Standard line.

(c) The best advice is to close down Standard but not Basic.

B20.4 Chris Gibson Kitchenware Ltd

(a)

	Dishwashers £000s	Fridges £000s	Ovens £000s	Total £000s
Sales	180	330	270	780
Variable costs	(120)	(150)	(132)	(402)
Contribution	60	180	138	378
Fixed cost				(268)
Total profit				110

(b) Dishwashers should not be dropped, because they make a contribution to fixed cost and profit. If production ceased the contribution of £60,000 would be lost but the fixed overheads would continue at £268,000. Overall the profit would reduce to £50,000. It may be that in the longer term an element of fixed cost can be identified as related to dishwashers alone. If this element were to exceed £60,000 it might be reasonable to discontinue production of dishwashers and discontinue the fixed cost.

B20.5 Capital Tours Ltd

(a) Total costs are £180,000 of which £60,000 are fixed costs. Variable cost is therefore £120,000 over 1,000 tours, or £120 per tour.
Selling price = £200 per person, contribution = £80 per person.
At new offer price of £140 per tour, contribution = £20 per person and so is acceptable in the short term.

(b) The offer is acceptable provided it does not displace any tours for which £200 would be paid. Also there must be no risk of offending existing customers who have already paid £200. If the new lower price became common knowledge, the price might be driven down so that the break-even point would increase and more tours would have to be sold to achieve the same total profit.

Problem solving and evaluation

C20.1 Dairyproducts Ltd

	Cartons of cream	Aerosol cans of cream	Packets of cheese	Total
Units of output	400,000	96,000	280,000	
	£	£	£	£
Selling price	0.75	1.05	1.30	
Variable cost	0.45	0.50	1.00	
Contribution per unit	0.30	0.55	0.30	
Total contribution	120,000	52,800	84,000	256,800
Fixed cost	60,000	24,000	56,000	140,000
Net profit of current prodn, per week				116,800
Annual profit				5,840,000

Range of demand for aerosol cream cheese

		£	£	£
Volume		60,000	80,000	100,000
		£	£	£
Sales price		1.50	1.40	1.15
Variable cost		0.50	0.50	0.50
Contribution per unit		1.00	0.90	0.65
Total contribution per week		60,000	72,000	65,000
Annual for 50 weeks			3,600,000	
Less:				
Additional advertising			(1,000,000)	
Modification cost			(400,000)	
Additional fixed cost			(500,000)	
Net benefit			1,700,000	

Reducing production of cream cartons by 20% per annum will lose £120,000 × 50 × 20%, i.e. £1,200,000.

Reducing production of packet cheese by 25% per annum will lose £84,000 × 50 × 25%, i.e. £1,050,000.

The net benefit of the new product is therefore greater than the loss on either of the options withdrawn.

The recommendation is to reduce packet cheese and replace with aerosol cream cheese. The only possible warning here is that there is only £150,000 of difference between withdrawing cream cartons and withdrawing packet cheese. If the growing customer dissatisfaction with cream in cartons is serious, the longer-term view might prevail over the short-term recommendation.

Chapter 21

Test your understanding

A21.15

1,000 + 4,000 − 4,200 = 800 units in store

A21.16

	Jan	Feb	Mar	Apr	May	June
	£	£	£	£	£	£
Sales	12,000	13,000	14,000	13,500	12,600	11,100
Cash received – budget	Nil	12,000	13,000	14,000	13,500	12,600

A21.17

	£
Goods purchased during January	18,000
Owing to creditors at end of January	13,600
Cash paid for January purchases	4,400
Payment for amounts owed at start	12,500
Total paid	16,900

A21.18

Cost of indirect materials in March £500, split £200 variable and £300 fixed.

During April direct labour hours will be 20% higher and it is known that variable indirect material is proportionate to direct labour hours, so increase variable cost by 20% from £200 to £240. Fixed cost remains constant so total budget is £540.

Application

B21.1 Garden Ornament Company

From the information presented in Tables T 1 to T 5 the various detailed budgets are prepared as shown In Tables T 6 to T 18. These lead to the master budget set out in Tables T 19 to T 21.

Sales budget: sales and debtors

The sales budget sets out the volume of sales expected for each product, multiplied by the expected selling price, to obtain the total sales by value expected for each product. The total sales for the year ahead may then be calculated, shown in bold print in the sales budget.

(T 6)

Sales budget	Ref.	Ducks	Herons	Total for year
Unit sales for year	T 1	8,000	15,000	
Unit selling price	T 1	£30	£45	
Total sales		£240,000	£675,000	**£915,000**

The year-end debtors are calculated as half of one month's sales (one-twenty-fourth of the total year's sales if these are spread evenly throughout the year).

(T 7)

Debtors' budget	Ref.	Ducks	Herons	Total for year
Total sales	T 6	£240,000	£675,000	£915,000
		divide by 24	divide by 24	
Debtors at year-end		£10,000	£28,125	**£38,125**

Production plan
(T 8)

Production plan in units	Ref.	Ducks	Herons
Planned sales volume	T 1	8,000	15,000
Add planned closing stock of finished goods	T 3	–	–
Less opening stock of finished goods	T 3	–	–
Planned unit production for year		8,000	15,000

Direct materials budget: purchases, stock and trade creditors

Once the production plan is decided, the costs of the various inputs to production may be calculated. Direct materials must be purchased to satisfy the production plans, but the purchases budget must also take into account the need to hold stock of raw materials. After the purchases budget has been quantified in terms of cost, the impact on trade creditors may also be established.

The *purchases budget* is based on the units required for production in the period, making allowance for the opening and closing stock of raw materials. The plan is to hold sufficient stock at the end of the period to meet 60% of the following month's production (see T 3). The number of units to be purchased will equal the planned production for the period, plus the planned stock of raw materials at the end of the period (shown in the opening balance sheet at T 5), minus the planned stock of raw materials at the end of the period (calculated in T 8).

(T 9)

Purchases budget in units	Ref.	Ducks	Herons
Production volume	T 8	8,000	15,000
Add raw materials stock planned for end of period	T 3	400 60% of (8,000/12)	750 60% of (15,000/12)
Less raw materials stock held at start of period	T 5	400	750
Purchases of raw materials planned		8,000	15,000

(T 10)

Purchases budget in £s	Ref.	Ducks	Herons	Total for year
Volume of purchases	T 9	8,000	15,000	
		£	£	£
Cost per unit	T 1	14	16	
Total purchase cost		112,000	240,000	**352,000**

Trade creditors are calculated as one month's purchases, a relatively uncomplicated procedure in this instance because the purchases remain constant from month to month.

(T 11)

One month's purchases 352,000/12	**£29,333**

The direct materials cost of goods sold must also be calculated at this point, for use in the budgeted profit and loss account. The direct materials cost of goods sold is based on the materials used in production of the period (which in this example is all sold during the period).

(T 12)

Direct materials cost of goods sold	Ref.	Ducks	Herons	Total for year
Production in units	T 8	8,000	15,000	
		£	£	
Materials cost per unit	T 1	14	16	
Total cost of goods to be sold		£112,000	£240,000	**£352,000**

Direct labour budget

The direct labour budget takes the volume of production in units and multiplies that by the expanded labour cost per unit to give a labour cost for each separate item of product and a total for the year, shown in bold print.

(T 13)

Direct labour budget	Ref.	Ducks	Herons	Total for year
Production in units	T 8	8,000	15,000	
		£	£	£
Labour cost per unit	T 1	12	13	
Total cost		96,000	195,000	**291,000**

It is also useful to check on the total resource requirement which corresponds to this total labour cost, since it takes time to plan increases or decreases in labour resources. The average direct labour cost was given in (T 1) as £15,000 per person per year. The following calculation assumes that the employees can work equally efficiently on any of the three product lines.

(T 14)

Resource requirement:
Based on an average cost of £15,000 per person per year, the total labour cost of £291,000 would require 19.4 full-time equivalent persons.

Production overhead budget

Production overheads include all those overhead items which relate to the production activity. In this example it includes heat and light, business rates and depreciation. Depreciation is calculated at a rate of 20% on the total cost of equipment held during the year (£190,000 at the start, as shown in (T 5), plus an additional £70,000 noted in (T 4) (£260,000 × 20% = £52,000).

(T 15)

Production overhead budget	Ref.	£
Heat and light	T 2	8,000
Production fixed overheads	T 2	4,000
Depreciation	T 4	52,000
Total		**64,000**

Total production cost budget

Total production cost budget comprises the cost of direct materials, direct labour and production overhead.

(T 16)

Production cost budget	Ref.	£
Direct materials	T 12	352,000
Direct labour	T 13	291,000
Production overhead	T 15	64,000
Total		**707,000**

Administration expense budget
(T 17)

Administration budget	Ref.	£
Partners' salaries (taken in cash)	T 2	55,000
Rent of premises	T 2	11,000
Office staff	T 2	48,450
Total		**114,450**

Marketing expense budget

The marketing expense budget relates to all aspects of the costs of advertising and selling the product. The information in (T 2) specifies a marketing cost which is dependent on sales, being estimated as 18% of sales value.

(T 18)

Marketing expense budget	Ref.	£
18% of £915,000	T 2 & T 6	**164,700**

Master budget

The master budget has three components: the budgeted profit and loss account for the year, the budgeted cash flow statement and the budgeted balance sheet. These are now set out using the foregoing separate budgets. Where the derivation of figures in the master budget should be evident from the earlier budgets, no explanation is given, but where further calculations have been performed these are shown as working notes.

Budgeted profit and loss account
(T 19)

Budgeted profit and loss account for the year ended 31 December Year 5

	Ref.	Ducks £	Herons £	Total for year £
Total sales	T 6	240,000	675,000	915,000
Material cost	T 12	112,000	240,000	352,000
Labour cost	T 13	96,000	195,000	291,000
Total variable cost		208,000	435,000	643,000
Contribution		32,000	240,000	272,000
% on sales		13.3%	35.6%	
Production overhead	T 15			64,000
Gross profit				**208,000**
Administration cost	T 17			(114,450)
Marketing cost	T 18			(164,700)
Net loss				**(71,150)**

Budgeted cash flow statement

Where expenses are paid for as soon as they are incurred, the cash outflow equals the expense as shown in the budgeted profit and loss account. In the case of cash collected from customers, debtors at the start and end of the period must be taken into the calculation. In the case of cash paid to suppliers the creditors at the start and end of the period must be taken into account. The cash flow statement contains references to working notes which follow the statement and set out the necessary detail.

(T 20)

Budgeted cash flow statement for the year ended 31 December Year 5

	Note	£	£
Cash to be collected from customers	1		908,875
Cash to be paid to suppliers	2	352,667	
Direct labour	3	291,000	
Heat and light	3	8,000	
Production fixed overheads	3	4,000	
Partners' salaries	3	55,000	
Rent of premises	3	11,000	
Office staff costs	3	48,450	
Marketing costs	3	164,700	
			934,817
Net cash inflow from operations			25,942
New equipment to be purchased			70,000
Net cash outflow			(95,942)
Cash balance at start of year	T 5		2,500
Cash balance at end of year			(93,442)

Working notes for budgeted cash flow statement

Note 1: Cash to be collected from customers:

	Ref.	£
Sales during the period	T 6	915,000
Less credit sales which remain as debtors at the end of the year	T 7	38,125
		876,875
Add cash collected from debtors at the start of the year	T 5	32,000
Cash to be collected from customers		908,875

Note 2: Cash to be paid to suppliers:

	Ref.	£
Purchases during the period	T 10	352,000
Less credit purchases which remain as creditors at the end of the year	T 11	29,333
		322,667
Add cash paid to creditors at the start of the year	T 5	30,000
Cash to be paid to suppliers		352,667

Note 3: Other cash payments

It has been assumed, for the convenience of this illustration, that all other expense items are paid for as they are incurred. In reality this would be unlikely and there would be further calculations of the type shown in Note 2, making allowance for creditors at the start and end of the period.

Budgeted balance sheet
(T 21)

Budgeted balance sheet at 31 December Year 5

	£	£
Equipment at cost (Note 1)		260,000
Accumulated depreciation (Note 2)		(92,000)
Net book value		168,000
Stock of raw materials (Note 3)	17,600	
Trade debtors (T 7)	38,125	
	55,725	
Bank borrowing (T 20)	(93,442)	
Trade creditors (T 11)	(29,333)	
	(122,775)	
Net current liabilities		(67,050)
Total assets less current liabilities		100,950
Partners' capital (Note 4)		100,950

Working notes for budgeted balance sheet

Note 1

Equipment at cost = £190,000 + £70,000	=	£260,000

Note 2

Accumulated depreciation = £40,000 + £52,000	=	£92,000

Note 3

Stock of raw material

For 400 ducks @ £14 each	5,600
For 750 herons @ £16 each	12,000
	17,600

Note 4

Partners' capital = £172,100 + (£71,150)	=	£100,950

Comment. Not a promising picture of where the business is likely to be heading but this amount of detail will help identify where action needs to be taken to improve profit and cash flow.

B21.2 Tools Ltd

Note that in questions of this type there will often be more than one way of interpreting the information given. That is not a problem provided the total column is used to check for arithmetic consistency.

Sales budget

Selling price £90 per unit

	Year 1				Total
	Quarter 1	*Quarter 2*	*Quarter 3*	*Quarter 4*	
Modified tool units	4,050	4,200	4,350	3,900	16,500
	£	£	£	£	£
Sales	364,500	378,000	391,500	351,000	1,485,000

Production budget for each quarter

By units, production must meet the sales of this quarter and 100% of planned sales of the next quarter:

	Year 1				Total
	Quarter 1	*Quarter 2*	*Quarter 3*	*Quarter 4*	
Modified tool units	4,050	4,200	4,350	3,900	16,500
For sales of quarter	4,050	4,200	4,350	3,900	
Add 10% of next qtr sales	420	435	390	405	405
	4,470	4,635	4,740	4,305	
Less stock of previous qtr	–	420	435	390	
Production required	4,470	4,215	4,305	3,915	16,905

Converting from units of production to costs of production

	Year 1				Total
	Quarter 1	Quarter 2	Quarter 3	Quarter 4	
Units to be produced	4,470	4,215	4,305	3,915	16,905
	£	£	£	£	£
Direct materials	107,280	101,160	103,320	93,960	405,720
Direct labour	134,100	126,450	129,150	117,450	507,150
Fixed overhead*	44,700	42,150	43,050	39,150	169,050
	286,080	269,760	275,520	250,560	1,081,920
* Includes depreciation of	5,288	4,987	5,093	4,632	20,000

(Note that fixed overhead includes depreciation of £20,000 per annum, allocated on the basis of a cost per unit produced. Total production is 16,905 units so depreciation is £1.183 per unit.)

Cash budget for each quarter

	Year 1				Total
	Quarter 1	Quarter 2	Quarter 3	Quarter 4	
	£	£	£	£	£
Cash from customers					
⅓ current quarter	121,500	126,000	130,500	117,000	
⅔ previous quarter	–	243,000	252,000	261,000	
Total cash received	121,500	369,000	382,500	378,000	1,251,000
Purchase of fixed assets	100,000				100,000
Payment to suppliers*	83,520	103,200	102,600	97,080	386,400
Wages	134,100	126,450	129,150	117,450	507,150
Fixed overhead (excl depn)	39,412	37,163	37,957	34,518	149,050
Total cash payments	357,032	266,813	269,707	249,048	1,142,600
Receipts less payments	(235,532)	102,187	112,793	128,952	(108,400)

* Schedule of payments to suppliers on one month's credit.

The initial stock of 500 units will be paid for at the start of month 2 together with one-third of the units required for month 1's production. Thereafter the payment is always on a one-third basis because the 500 units of stock remains constant.

	Quarter 1	Quarter 2	Quarter 3	Quarter 4	Total
	£	£	£	£	£
Direct materials purchased	107,280	101,160	103,320	93,960	405,720
Payment for initial stock	12,000				12,000
Two months' purchases	71,520	67,440	68,880	62,640	
One month from previous qtr	–	35,760	33,720	34,440	31,320
Total payment	83,520	103,200	102,600	97,080	386,400

Comment on cash flow statement

This is the type of statement which would be required by someone being asked to lend money to the business. The start-up situation requires cash but there is a positive cash flow from operations. The lender would want to add to the cash flow statement a schedule of loan repayments and interest payments to see whether the operational cash flows could meet the financing needs of the business.

B21.3 Bright Papers Ltd
Cash from customers
(£000s)

Sales budget	Year 1	Year 2	Year 3	Year 4
Unit sales for year	800	950	1,200	1,500
Unit selling price	£10.20	£10.56	£11.04	£12.00
Total sales	£8,160	£10,032	£13,248	£18,000

The year-end debtors are calculated on the basis that the sales are spread evenly throughout the year.

(£000s)

Debtors' budget	Year 1	Year 2	Year 3	Year 4
Total sales	£8,160	£10,032	£13,248	£18,000
Months/12	1/12	1/12	1.5/12	2/12
Debtors at year-end	£680	£836	£1,656	£3,000

Cash received from customers is equal to the year's sales plus debtors at the start of the year less debtors at the end of the year.

(£000s)

Cash received budget	Year 1	Year 2	Year 3	Year 4
Total sales	£8,160	£10,032	£13,248	£18,000
Debtors at start	–	£680	£836	£1,656
Debtors at year-end	£(680)	£(836)	£(1,656)	£(3,000)
Cash received	£7,480	£9,876	£12,428	£16,656

Cash paid to suppliers

The purchases budget is based on the units required for production in the period (if necessary making allowance for the opening and closing stock of raw materials).

(£000s)

Purchases budget in units	Year 1	Year 2	Year 3	Year 4
Production volume	850	1,000	1,300	1,600
Add raw materials stock planned for end of period	nil	nil	nil	nil
Less raw materials stock held at start of period	nil	nil	nil	nil
Purchases of raw materials planned	850	1,000	1,300	1,600

(£000s)

Purchases budget	Year 1	Year 2	Year 3	Year 4
Volume of purchases	850	1,000	1,300	1,600
Cost per unit	£2.04	£2.28	£2.64	£3.00
Total purchase cost	£1,734	£2,280	£3,432	£4,800

Trade creditors allow different credit periods in different years.

(£000s)

Creditors' budget	Year 1	Year 2	Year 3	Year 4
Total purchases	£1,734	£2,280	£3,432	£4,800
Months/12	2/12	1.5/12	1.5/12	1/12
Creditors at year-end	£289	£285	£429	£400

(£000s)

Cash paid to suppliers	Year 1	Year 2	Year 3	Year 4
Total purchase cost	£1,734	£2,280	£3,432	£4,800
Add creditors at start	–	£289	£285	£429
Less creditors at end	(£289)	(£285)	(£429)	(£400)
Cash paid	£1,445	£2,284	£3,288	£4,829

Payments to employees for wages – direct labour budget

The direct labour budget takes the volume of production in units and multiplies that by the expected labour cost per unit to give a labour cost for each separate item of product and a total for the year, shown in bold print.

(£000s)

Direct labour budget	Year 1	Year 2	Year 3	Year 4
Production in units	850	1,000	1,300	1,600
Labour cost per unit	£0.60	£0.75	£0.90	£0.90
Total cost	£510	£750	£1,170	£1,440

Payment for overheads – production overhead budget

Total production overhead comprises variable and fixed overhead. The variable overhead is calculated using the variable overhead cost per unit multiplied by the number of units produced. The fixed overhead is fixed for each year and is not affected by volume of activity in the period.

(£000s)

Production overhead budget	Year 1	Year 2	Year 3	Year 4
Production in units	850	1,000	1,300	1,600
Variable overhead cost per unit	£0.40	£0.50	£0.60	£0.60
Total variable overhead cost	£340	£500	£780	£960
Fixed overhead*	£5,000	£5,100	£5,200	£5,300
Total prodn overhead	£5,340	£5,600	£5,980	£6,260

* For cash flows deduct £1,500 each year.

Cash budgets for each of the four years

	Year 1	Year 2	Year 3	Year 4
	£	£	£	£
Cash from customers	7,480	9,876	12,428	16,656
Cash paid to suppliers	1,445	2,284	3,288	4,829
Wages paid	510	750	1,170	1,440
Variable overhead	340	500	780	960
Fixed overhead*	3,500	3,600	3,700	3,800
Total paid	5,795	7,134	8,938	11,029
Net cash flow	1,685	2,742	3,490	5,627

* Excluding depreciation because that does not involve a cash flow.

Problem solving and evaluation

C21.1 Alpha Ltd

Budgeted profit and loss account

	Original for half-year to 31 March £	Actual for half-year to 31 March £	Note
Sales	7,800,000	6,240,000	Down 20%
Cost of sales	(5,226,000)	(4,305,600)	
Gross profit (original budget at 33%)	2,574,000	1,934,400	31%
Fixed overheads:			
Selling and advertising	(750,000)	(650,000)	Advtg-50%
General administration	(547,250)	(492,525)	
Operating profit	1,276,750	791,875	
Interest payable on medium-term loan	(67,500)	(73,750)	
Royalties payable on sales	(390,000)	(312,000)	
Net profit	819,250	406,125	

(Note the impact of the increase in stock levels has been ignored in this and the next statement because it is a temporary fluctuation which is put right by the end of the year.)

	Actual for half-year to 31 March £	Revised budget for half-year to 30 Sept £
Sales	6,240,000	6,240,000
Cost of sales	(4,305,600)	(4,180,800)
Gross profit (original budget at 33%)	1,934,400	2,059,200
Fixed overheads:		
Selling and advertising	(650,000)	(650,000)
General administration	(492,525)	(492,525)
Operating profit	791,875	916,675
Interest payable on medium-term loan	(73,750)	(80,000)
Royalties payable on sales	(312,000)	(312,000)
Net profit	406,125	524,675

The question asks only for the results at 31 March and the revised budget thereafter but the information may be used to reply to the question asked by the directors in relation to the cash flow impact. You may find this more difficult but it is something which you can at least think out in general terms. First of all the measures taken to restore the gross profit must have an impact. Then the directors are controlling the level of stock so that it is not using up resources in the form of cash. Reducing the period of credit given to trade debtors will improve cash flow (basing the calculation on the lower level of actual sales achieved and expected). Finally the cost of goods sold has been controlled better in the second half. This will reduce the amount owing to creditors, even though the period of credit remains unchanged.

Statement of cash flow:
improvement through measures taken in second half

	£	£
Additional profit generated through measures taken		118,550
Reduction in stock level	200,000	
Reduction in debtors from two months to one month 6,240,000/6	1,040,000	
One month's creditors based on cost of goods sold:		
saving (4,305,600 − 4,180,800)/12	10,400	
		1,250,400
Improvement in cash flow due to measures taken at half-year		1,368,950

It may be seen that the most effective improvement in cash flow can be obtained by paying attention to collection of debts, but other measures also have a beneficial effect.

Chapter 22

Test your understanding

A22.14

20,000 blocks require 100,000 kg of material so standard usage is 5 kg per block.
16,000 blocks should use 80,000 kg but actual usage is 80,080 kg. Adverse usage variance is 80 kg at standard cost of £3 per kg, i.e. adverse variance £240.

A22.15

Total variance is £6,000 adverse less £2,500 favourable = £3,500 adverse. So actual costs were £3,500 higher than standard cost, i.e. £39,500.

A22.16

Fixed overhead expenditure variance is £1,500 adverse.

Application **B22.1 Plastics Ltd**

	Budget for May	Actual for May	Variance
Production in units	42,800	42,800	
	£	£	£
Direct material	256,800	267,220	(10,420) (A)
Direct labour	342,400	356,577	(14,177) (A)
Variable overhead	171,200	165,243	5,957 (F)
Fixed overhead	90,000	95,000	(5,000) (A)
Total production cost	860,400	884,040	(23,640) (A)
Less stock at standard cost,			
2,800 units at £21	58,800	58,800	
Cost of goods sold	801,600	825,240	
Sales 40,000 × £70	2,800,000	2,800,000	
Net profit	1,998,400	1,974,760	(23,640) (A)
Note on standard cost			
Budgeted cost per unit	£		
Direct material 5 kg × £1.20	6		
Direct labour 2 hours × £4	8		
Variable overhead 2 hours × £2	4		
Fixed overhead £90,000/30,000	3		
	21		

Analysis of variances

Direct materials (total variance £10,420 adverse):

Price variance = AQ (SP − AP)	Usage variance = SP (SQ − AQ)
= 213,776 kg (£1.20 − £1.25)	= £1.20 (214,000 − 213,776)
= £10,688 adverse variance	= £268 favourable variance

Direct labour (total variance £14,177 adverse):

Rate variance = AH (SR − AR)	Efficiency variance = SR (SH − AH)
= 86,970 hours (£4.00 − £4.10)	= £4.00 (85,600 − 86,970)
= £8,697 adverse variance	= £5,480 adverse variance

Variable overhead (total variance £5,957 favourable):

Rate variance = AH (SR − AR)	Efficiency variance = SR (SH − AH)
= 86,970 hours (£2.00 − £1.90)	= £2.00 (85,600 − 86,970)
= £8,697 favourable variance	= £2,740 adverse variance

Fixed overhead expenditure variance is £5,000 adverse, indicating overspending.

One possible interpretation of the variance analysis is that less wastage of material occurred through buying higher-quality material at a higher unit price. Labour was paid more than expected, which may have been due to an unexpected pay award, but nevertheless worked less efficiently than expected. The inefficient working has a consequence also on the efficiency of using variable overheads although this was more than offset by a lower than expected rate of variable overhead cost.

B22.2 Budgeted and actual costs for the month of May

	Budget	Actual	Variance	
	£	£	£	
Actual level of output (units)	120	120		
Direct materials	30,000	31,200	(1,200)	(A)
Direct labour	18,000	16,800	1,200	(F)
Fixed manufacturing overhead	12,000	9,600	2,400	(F)
Total costs of production	60,000	57,600	2,400	(F)

Analysis of variances

Direct materials (total variance £1,200 adverse):

Price variance = AQ (SP − AP) = 1,300 kg (£25 − £24) = £1,300 favourable variance	Usage variance = SP (SQ − AQ) = £25 (1,200 − 1,300) = £2,500 adverse variance

Direct labour (total variance £1,200 favourable):

Rate variance = AH (SR − AR) = 1,400 hours (£12 − £10) = £2,800 adverse variance	Efficiency variance = SR (SH − AH) = £10 (1,800 − 1,400) = £4,000 favourable variance

Fixed overhead variance is an expenditure variance reflecting less spent than expected.

One possible explanation here is that the company tried to save money by buying cheaper material but this had the wrong effect because it increased wastage and hence usage was greater. The rate variance indicates that the incentive payment was successful: it had a cost which was more than offset by greater efficiency.

B22.3 Carrypack Ltd – month of April Year 6

	Flexible budget 12,300 units	Actual 12,300 units	Variance	
	£	£	£	
Sales: 12,300 units @ £50 each	615,000	615,000	nil	
Production: 12,300 units				
	£	£	£	
Direct materials	135,300	136,220	920	(A)
Direct labour	110,700	129,200	18,500	(A)
Variable overheads	73,800	72,200	1,600	(F)
Fixed overhead	48,000	49,400	1,400	(A)
Total cost	367,800	387,020	19,220	(A)
Actual profit	247,200	227,980	19,220	(A)

Direct materials (total variance £920 adverse):

Price variance = AQ (SP − AP) = 27,800 kg (£5.00 − £4.90) = £2,780 favourable variance	Usage variance = SP (SQ − AQ) = £5 (*27,060 − 27,800) = £3,700 adverse variance

* 26,400 kg is standard for 12,000 units so proportionately 27,060 kg is standard for 12,300 units.

Direct labour (total variance £18,500 adverse):

Rate variance = AH (SR − AR) = 38,000 hours (£3.00 − £3.40) = £15,200 adverse variance	Efficiency variance = SR (SH − AH) = £3.00 (36,900 − 38,000) = £3,300 adverse variance

Variable overhead (total variance £1,600 favourable):

Rate variance = AH (SR − AR) = 38,000 hours (£2.00 − £1.90) = £3,800 favourable variance	Efficiency variance = SR (SH − AH) = £2.00 (36,900 − 38,000) = £2,200 adverse variance

Fixed overhead expenditure variance is £1,400 adverse, indicating overspending.

Comment. Direct materials needs investigating for controllability of the usage variance and whether low-price goods have been purchased with a consequence of more wastage. Direct labour is the variance of most concern because of its magnitude. If the labour rate has changed then the budget should be revised so that the non-controllable variance of £15,200 is not reported. The inefficiency of labour working is matched by inefficiency in use of variable overhead and the cause of the unexpected extra hours should be investigated.

Problem solving and evaluation

C22.1 Cabinets Ltd
Reconstructed budget for May Year 4

Production units budgeted	1,800
	£
Direct materials £3.00 × (9,600 × 1,800/1,600)	32,400
Direct labour £8.00 × (4,800 × 1,800/1,600)	43,200
Fixed overhead	36,000
Total budgeted cost	111,600

In the following tables, the figures in italics are the items which have been calculated from a knowledge of the other items in the table.

Direct materials (total variance £2,560 adverse):

Price variance = AQ (SP − AP) = 11,200 kg (*£3.00* − £2.80) = £2,240 favourable variance	Usage variance = SP (SQ − AQ) = £3.00 (*9,600* − 11,200) = £4,800 adverse variance

Direct labour (total variance £12,000 adverse):

Rate variance = AH (SR − AR) = 5,600 hours (*£8.00* − £9.00) = £5,600 adverse variance	Efficiency variance = SR (SH − AH) = £8.00 (*4,800* − 5,600) = £6,400 adverse variance

Fixed overhead expenditure variance is £3,000 adverse, indicating the budget was £36,000.

One possible interpretation is that cheaper material was bought but resulted in more wastage, the adverse effect on usage exceeding the price saving. The labour rate increased, possibly due to an agreed wage rise, but the efficiency worsened, perhaps because of the cheaper material. The adverse fixed overhead expenditure indicates overspending which is not related to volume effects.

C22.2 Fixit Ltd

	Flexible budget	Actual	Variance	
Production in units	5,500	5,500		
	£	£	£	
Direct materials	22,000	22,764	(764)	*(A)*
Direct labour	66,000	75,900	(9,900)	*(A)*
Variable production overhead	15,400	14,950	450	*(F)*
Fixed production overhead	10,000	9,000	1,000	*(F)*
Depreciation	4,000	4,000	–	
	117,400	126,614	(9,214)	*(A)*

Analysis of variances

Direct materials (total variance £764 adverse):

Price variance = AQ (SP − AP) = 54,200 kg (£0.40 − £0.42) = £1,084 adverse variance	Usage variance = SP (SQ − AQ) = £0.40 (55,000 − 54,200) = £320 favourable variance

Direct labour (total variance £9,900 adverse):

Rate variance = AH (SR − AR) = 11,500 hours (£6.00 − £6.60) = £6,900 adverse variance	Efficiency variance = SR (SH − AH) = £6.00 (11,000 − 11,500) = £3,000 adverse variance

Variable overhead (total variance £450 favourable):

Rate variance = AH (SR − AR) = 11,500 hours (£1.40 − £1.30) = £1,150 favourable variance	Efficiency variance = SR (SH − AH) = £1.40 (11,000 − 11,500) = £700 adverse variance

Fixed overhead expenditure variance is £1,000 favourable, indicating underspending.

Comment. More expensive material may have produced better quality and caused some offsetting in less material wastage. However, efficiency of working was lower than expected, affecting both labour and variable overhead costs. The variable overhead rate was lower than expected, suggesting some saving on the cost of overheads, but the labour rate was higher than expected, suggesting an unexpected pay award.

C22.3 Concrete Products Ltd
Heavy paving

	Actual tonnes	Budget tonnes	Flexible budget tonnes	Variance	
Sales volume	29,000	27,500	29,000		
Production volume	29,000	27,500	29,000		
	£000s	£000s	£000s	£000s	
Revenue	720	690	727	(7)	(A)
Variable cost of sales	280	270	285	5	(F)
Contribution	440	420	442	(2)	(A)

Garden paving

	Actual tonnes	Budget tonnes	Flexible budget tonnes	Variance	
Sales volume	10,500	8,500	10,500		
Production volume	10,500	8,500	10,500		
	£000s	£000s	£000s	£000s	
Revenue	430	300	370	60	(F)
Variable cost of sales	170	127	157	13	(A)
Contribution	260	173	213	47	(F)

Comment. The comparison between budget and actual must be made on the basis of a flexible budget which allows for the revised levels of production and sales. In both cases the activity has been greater than was expected when the budget was set. Making comparison with a flexible budget shows that heavy paving made a contribution which was £2,000 less than expected while garden paving made a contribution which was £47,000 greater than expected.

Questions to ask

1 Has there been a change in the sales price of these items? If so the budget should be revised to take account of the new price, and the variance for the period would be £8,000 adverse.

2 Has there been a change in the cost of direct materials? If so the budget should be revised to avoid giving the impression of an adverse variance of £8,000. The usefulness of variance analysis lies in identifying controllable variances, not in relating to outdated budgets.

3 On the presumption that there has been no change in the labour rate, is the supervisory team working effectively? One explanation of the adverse cost variance could be inefficient working in the production department.

C22.4 Nu-Line Ltd

Calculation of cost of production

	Flexible budget	Actual	Variance	
Units of production	140	140		
	£	£	£	
Cost of machine tools (for 140)	84,000	*67,510	16,490	(F)
Direct labour	42,000	47,500	(5,500)	(A)
Variable production overhead	14,000	13,000	1,000	(F)
	140,000	128,010	11,990	(F)
Fixed production overhead	†36,000	35,000	1,000	(F)
Total production cost	176,000	163,010	12,990	(F)
Add opening stock, 15 at £1,200	18,000	18,000		
Less stock, 5 items at £1,200 each	(6,000)	(6,000)		
Cost of goods sold	188,000	175,010	12,990	(F)
Sales 150 at £2,000 each	300,000	300,000		
	112,000	124,990	12,990	(F)

* Actual cost of £86,800 related to 180 units, but only 140 were used, so cost of 140 is taken proportionately as £67,510.

† Fixed production overhead of £200 per unit multiplied by budgeted production at 180 units because the fixed overhead budget is not flexible with volume of activity.

Calculation of units of inventory

	Original budget	Actual
Stock of finished goods at start of year	15	15
Production	180	140
Sales	(130)	(150)
Stock of finished goods at end of year	65	5

Comment. The original sales level expected was 130 units. Additional profit has been created by selling 150 units but beyond that there is a favourable variance of £12,990. This is primarily due to the cost of purchased machine tools being less than expected (£482 rather than £600 each). The direct labour variance was adverse but we are not provided with sufficient information to break this down into rate and efficiency variances. A similar limitation on analysis applies to the favourable variance on variable production overhead. The fixed production overhead shows a marginal saving on budget.

Chapter 23

Problem solving and evaluation

C23.1 Furniture Manufacture Ltd

A control report should emphasise the costs which are controllable within the organisation and which are most closely the responsibility of the manager concerned.

Although the power failure was beyond the control of the departmental manager, the company needs to know the cost of that failure. If there was a power failure then there can have been no productive work from direct labour and it is likely that indirect labour, indirect materials and indirect production overhead would not have been incurred during that time. The fixed overheads will have been incurred irrespective but the variable maintenance costs may not have been incurred where there was no activity to maintain. So the budgeted cost should be recalculated at 75% of the expected cost and compared with actual. This may give a better comparison with the actual cost.

	Budgeted cost				Actual cost	Variance	
	Fixed	Original variable	Revised variable	Total		(F) = favourable (A) = adverse	
	£	£	£	£	£	£	
Direct labour	–	36,000	27,000	27,000	30,000	3,000	(A)
Indirect labour	6,000	8,000	6,000	12,000	14,000	2,000	(A)
Indirect materials	–	4,000	3,000	3,000	3,500	500	(A)
Power	3,000	12,000	9,000	12,000	9,000	3,000	(F)
Maintenance materials	–	5,000	3,750	3,750	3,000	750	(F)
Maintenance labour	5,000	4,000	3,000	8,000	15,000	7,000	(A)
Depreciation	85,000	–	–	85,000	75,000	10,000	(F)
Production overhead	–	20,000	15,000	15,000	15,000	–	

The revised table suggests that the bench assembly department manager should not be quite so complacent as was indicated from the earlier table. The labour costs appear to be higher than would be expected for a power failure period, unless the explanation is that they have been paid overtime rates to catch up on the work. Questions also need to be asked about the maintenance labour. It may be that the explanation is that additional maintenance was undertaken during the enforced idleness, although this explanation depends on being able to undertake maintenance without an electricity supply.

C23.2
(a) For explanation of responsibility accounting see the chapter.
(b) Manager of distribution depot needs:
- area totals for demand (5 columns)
- area totals for running costs of floats
- area totals for drivers' wages and managers' salaries
- area totals for cash collection and note on areas of slow payment problems, with action taken
- copy of area returns as back up if required
- exception report from each area manager highlighting problem areas and action taken
- ratios identifying relationships of key variables.

Area manager needs:
- depot totals for demand (10 columns)
- depot totals for running costs of floats
- depot totals for drivers' wages and managers' salaries
- depot totals for cash collected and note on dealing with slow payers
- copy of depot returns as back up if required
- ratios identifying relationships of key variables.

Depot manager needs:
- delivery demand analysed by driver
- running costs of float analysed by driver
- drivers' wages for each employee
- cash collection analysed by driver
- ratios relating input to output.

Chapter 24

Test your understanding

A24.19
(a) £92.60; (b) £85.70; (c) £79.40.

A24.20
(a) £82.20; (b) £74.70; (c) £68.10.

Application **B24.1 Projects Ltd**

Payback period

The cumulative cash flows are:

End of year	£
1	10,000
2	25,000
3	45,000
4	70,000

The payback of £50,000 occurs one-fifth of the way into Year 4, i.e. payback is 3.2 years.

Accounting rate of return

Total profit over 5 years is £95,000 less depreciation of £40,000, i.e. £55,000.
Average profit is therefore £11,000 per annum.
Accounting rate of return is 11,000/50,000 = 22%.

Net present value

(Using assumed discount rate of 10%.)

Using the formula approach the net present value is calculated as:

$$\frac{10,000}{(1.10)} + \frac{15,000}{(1.10)^2} + \frac{20,000}{(1.10)^3} + \frac{25,000}{(1.10)^4} + \frac{*35,000}{(1.10)^5} - 50,000$$

$$= 9,090 + 12,397 + 15,026 + 17,075 + 21,732 - 50,000$$
$$= 75,320 - 50,000$$
$$= 25,320$$

* Cash flow forecast for Year 5 plus scrap value expected at end.

Using the discount tables the net present value is calculated as:

End of Year	Cash flow £	Discount factor	Present value £
1	10,000	0.909	9,090
2	15,000	0.826	12,390
3	20,000	0.751	15,020
4	25,000	0.683	17,075
5	35,000	0.621	21,735
			75,310
Less initial outlay			(50,000)
Net present value			25,310

Difference from formula-based answer is due to rounding.

B24.2

Difference = 122 + 58 = 180.
IRR = 22 + 2 (122/180) = 23.36%.

B24.3

	Machine A	Machine B
Capital expenditure required	£65,000	£60,000
Estimated life in years	4	4
Residual value	Nil	Nil
Cash flow after taxation each year	£25,000	£24,000
Payback	2 + 15/25 = 2.6 years	2 + 12/60 = 2.2 years
NPV	79,225 − 65,000 = 14,225	76,056 − 60,000 = 16,056
Profitability index	79,225/65,000 = 1.22	76,056/60,000 = 1.26

On payback Machine A is preferable; on NPV and profitability index Machine B is preferable but in all cases the answers are close so that other non-financial factors may also need to be considered.

B24.4

Year	Net cash flows £000	Discount factor at 8% £000	Present value £000
1	50	.926	45.1
2	200	.857	171.4
3	225	.794	178.7
4	225	.735	165.4
5	100	.681	681.0
			1,241.6
	Cost		−500.0
	NPV		741.6

Problem solving and evaluation

C24.1 Offshore Services Ltd

	Yr	ALPHA £000s	ALPHA Disct	BRAVO £000s	BRAVO Disct	CHARLIE £000s	CHARLIE Disct	DELTA £000s	DELTA Disct
Outlay	–	(600)	(600)	(300)	(300)	(120)	(120)	(210)	(210)
Cash flow benefits:									
	1	435	395	–		48	44	81	74
	2	435	359	–		48	40	81	67
	3	–		219	164	48	36	81	61
	4	–		219	150	48	33	81	55
	5	–		219	136	48	30	81	50
Total PV			754		450		183		307
NPV			154		150		63		97
Total PV/outlay			1.26		1.50		1.53		1.46
Internal rate of return			28.8%		22.0%		28.6%		26.8%

All the projects are acceptable because they all have a positive net present value but the maximisation of net present value from an investment of £1m requires selection of the projects which give the highest net present value per £ of investment. This is most conveniently estimated by comparing the total present value with the outlay (sometimes referred to as the *profitability index*). The order of preference is therefore:

Bravo, Charlie, Delta, Alpha.

The highest net present value within a £1m limit would be £309,000 obtained from Bravo, Charlie and Delta. If the additional funding can be borrowed then Alpha is also desirable.

C24.2 Advanced plc
This question requires evaluation of the investment of £1,150,000 as compared with continuing on the existing basis with no investment.

	Year 1 £000s	Year 2 £000s	Year 3 £000s	Year 4 £000s	Year 5 £000s
Existing sales volume at £10 each	4,000	4,500	5,000	6,000	7,500
Proposed sales volume at £8.50	4,760	5,355	5,950	7,140	8,925
Incremental cash flow from sales	760	855	950	1,140	1,425
Existing production outflow at £7.50	3,150	3,263	3,788	4,575	5,475
New production outflow at £6.20	3,497	3,949	4,309	5,208	6,473
Incremental cash outflow on production	347	686	521	633	998
Excess inflow over outflow	413	169	429	507	427
Incremental scrap value					130
	413	169	429	507	557
Discount factors at 12%	0.893	0.797	0.712	0.636	0.567
Present value	369	135	305	322	316

Total present value = 1,447,000.

Investment required is £1,150,000 and there is 'lost' scrap value of £30,000, giving a total outlay of £1,180,000.

So compare present value of £1,447,000 with outlay of £1,180,000. Net present value is positive therefore investment is acceptable.

Other matters – is demand sustainable, are production costs controllable at lower level, is scrap value forecast realistic?

Index